Cyclopedia of LITERARY CHARACTERS

Revised Edition

Volume Two

Demian–Jonah's Gourd Vine

edited by
A. J. Sobczak

original editions edited by
Frank N. Magill

associate editor
Janet Alice Long

SALEM PRESS, INC.
Pasadena, California   Englewood Cliffs, New Jersey

Editor in Chief: Dawn P. Dawson
Managing Editor: Chris Moose
Project Editor: A. J. Sobczak
Acquisitions Editor: Mark Rehn
Research Supervisor: Jeffry Jensen
Research: Jun Ohnuki
Production Editor: Janet Alice Long
Layout: William Zimmerman

The Revised Edition includes *Cyclopedia of Literary Characters*, 1963 (first edition); *Cyclopedia of Literary Characters II*, 1990; and material new to this edition.

∞ The paper used in these volumes conforms to the American National Standard for Permanence of Paper for Printed Library Materials, Z39.48-1984.

Library of Congress Cataloging-in-Publication Data

Cyclopedia of literary characters / edited by A. J. Sobczak ; associate editor, Janet Alice Long. — Rev. ed.
p. cm.
"This comprehensive revised edition of Cyclopedia of literary characters combines all the titles from the original Cyclopedia of literary characters and from Cyclopedia of literary characters II . . . adds character descriptions from titles included in Masterplots (revised second edition, 1996) and the Masterplots II sets covering African American literature (1994), women's literature (1995), and American fiction (supplement, 1994) . . . 3,300 titles [in all]."—Publisher's note.
Includes index
1. Literature—Stories, plots, etc. 2. Literature—Dictionaries. 3. Characters and characteristics in literature. I. Sobczak, A. J. II. Long, Janet Alice.
PN44.M3 1998
809'.927—dc21
ISBN 0-89356-438-9 (set) 97-45813
ISBN 0-89356-440-0 (vol. 2) CIP

SECOND PRINTING
PRINTED IN THE UNITED STATES OF AMERICA

CONTENTS

KEY TO PRONUNCIATION

As an aid to users of the *Cyclopedia of Literary Characters, Revised Edition*, guides to pronunciation have been provided for particularly difficult character names. These guides are rendered in an easy-to-use phonetic manner. Stressed syllables are indicated by small capital letters. Letters of the English language, particularly vowels, are pronounced in different ways depending on the context. Below are letters and combinations of letters used in the phonetic guides to represent various sounds, along with examples of words in which those sounds appear.

Symbols	Pronounced As In
a	answer, laugh, sample, that
ah	father, hospital
aw	awful, caught
ay	blaze, fade, waiter, weigh
ch	beach, chimp
ee	believe, cedar, leader, liter
eh	bed, head, said
ew	boot, lose
g	beg, disguise, get
i	buy, height, lie, surprise
ih	bitter, pill
j	digit, edge, jet
k	cat, kitten, hex
[n]	bon (French "silent" n)
o	cotton, hot
oh	below, coat, note, wholesome
oo	good, look
ow	couch, how
oy	boy, coin
rr (rolled r)	guerrilla (Spanish pronunciation)
s	cellar, save, scent
sh	champagne, issue, shop
uh	about, butter, enough, other
ur	birth, disturb, earth, letter
y	useful, young
z	business, zest
zh	seizure, vision

Cyclopedia
of
LITERARY CHARACTERS

DEMIAN: The Story of Emil Sinclair's Youth
(Demian: Die Geschichte von Emil Sinclairs Jugend)

Author: Hermann Hesse (1877-1962)
First published: 1919
Genre: Novel
Locale: Germany, Austria, and Switzerland
Time: 1905-1915
Plot: Bildungsroman

Emil Sinclair, the protagonist and author-narrator, who looks back on his youth. At the beginning of the story, he is about ten years old; he is about eighteen at its close. He is the son of well-to-do parents. From a sheltered and bright childhood world, Sinclair is first plunged into a world that he had hitherto regarded as separate from his, the world of the lower classes, surrounded by darkness and mystery. He had bragged about having stolen apples to impress an older fellow student, Franz Kromer; Kromer blackmails and otherwise harasses him. When Sinclair meets Max Demian, another older student, his life changes once again, as Demian protects him and forces Kromer to leave Sinclair alone. Sinclair's growing pains, trials, and tribulations are accompanied by Demian's role as a mentor and friend. They recognize each other by the "mark of Cain" on their foreheads, which, though invisible, is the sign of a nonconformist, of one who believes in the human race as one that is yet to come. Demian gradually leads Sinclair to this visionary insight, which draws a line between himself and the "masses" who are driven by a herdlike instinct. Sinclair's path toward acceptance of what fate has in store for him is one of self-exploration, including the freedom to become what he is. He later encounters Demian again and, for the first time, meets Eva, Demian's mother. When Sinclair sees Demian for the last time, Demian has been mortally wounded in battle. After Demian's death, Sinclair's introspection reveals that his and Demian's images have merged into one.

Max Demian, an older student and Sinclair's friend and mentor. He is a born leader and intellectual. His friendship with the younger Sinclair is based on a kinship of spirit and mind. He introduces Sinclair to a world of inner freedom and natural courage. Sinclair sends him a drawing of a bird (a sparrow hawk) as it breaks out of its shell, represented by a globe. Demian displays the picture prominently in his mother's house. Demian is a lieutenant in the army and one of the first to go to the front. There, having been mortally wounded, he comes to be in the same field hospital as Sinclair. He declares Sinclair independent of his leadership, as Sinclair will find that he has by now internalized Demian's own image and potential.

Pistorius, an organist and former theology student, Sinclair's other mentor. He is stocky and short, with a face that is both "stern around the forehead and eyes and soft around the mouth." Pistorius becomes Sinclair's mentor in the town where Sinclair is attending boarding school. Pistorius, interested in myths and cults and their celebration, introduces Sinclair to the Abraxas myth.

Frau Eva, Demian's mother. She is tall, beautiful, and dignified. She tells Sinclair to call her Frau Eva, a privilege granted to her closest friends. Her head and face suggest both male and female qualities. She is the object of Sinclair's worldly and spiritual dreams and fantasies. Her world is one of love, fairy tales, and dreams. She is the driving force behind the group around Demian that seeks the spiritual rebirth of humankind.

Franz Kromer, a thirteen-year-old boy in Sinclair's hometown. He is robust and strong, the son of a tailor. He attends public elementary school and is, on occasion, associated with the children of the Latin School. He is given to cruelty, exploiting the inexperience of some of the sheltered younger boys of the upper-middle class of the town. Thus, he comes into contact with Sinclair and blackmails him by threatening to expose him for something about which Sinclair has merely boasted. After Demian's intervention, Kromer comes to fear Sinclair and avoids any further contact with him.

Knauer (NOW-uhr), a slight, slender, eighteen-year-old. He is Sinclair's classmate in the boarding school and seeks his advice and friendship. He is sexually abstinent and seeks the counsel of Sinclair, who is himself sexually inexperienced. He finally attempts to commit suicide but is stopped by Sinclair.

—*Arthur Tilo Alt*

DEMOCRACY

Author: Joan Didion (1934-)
First published: 1984
Genre: Novel
Locale: Hawaii and Southeast Asia
Time: 1952-1975
Plot: Political

Inez Christian Victor, an attractive member of an entrenched, wealthy Hawaiian family that lacks warmth and closeness. At the age of twenty, in 1955, she weds Harry Victor, who in 1969 becomes a U.S. senator and is later considered to be presidential material. Politics, she decides, costs her her memory and privacy. Consequently, she looks for intimacy in an intermittent affair with Jack Lovett, who, however, as an international adventurer is rarely available. After his death, she decides to assist refugees in Kuala Lumpur, with whom she can identify emotionally.

Paul Christian, a ruthless aristocrat whose business interests often take him away from Hawaii. Obsessed with protecting his wealth and power, he not only drives away his wife and his daughter Inez but, in 1975, also kills his other daughter, Janet, for making land deals with Japanese American entrepreneur Wendell Omura. He is placed in a state asylum.

Carol Christian, a California model who, in 1934, marries Paul Christian. Naïvely expecting to be embraced by the people of privilege in Hawaii, instead she remains an outsider. Out of loneliness, she often keeps her young children at home with her. Still uncomfortable in a society that ignores her, she finally abandons the islands and starts a career, booking celebrities for radio interviews in San Francisco. After Janet's wedding, word comes of Carol's death in a plane crash near Reno, Nevada.

Janet "Nezzie" Christian Ziegler, Carol's younger daughter. Disturbed by her mother's absence, she looks for stability in real estate. She marries Dick Ziegler, who once made a modest fortune in Hong Kong, but undercuts his business with the complicity of Omura and her uncle Dwight. She is shot to death by her father for frustrating his dynastic plans.

Harry Victor, who succeeds so well as a liberal in the Justice Department that he becomes a senator and in 1972 is spoken of as a possible presidential candidate. In the process of becoming a public figure, his sense of personal identity and his performance as husband and father suffer. He loses his family but becomes special envoy to the Common Market.

Adlai Victor, Inez's directionless son. He is responsible for an accident that costs a fifteen-year-old girl one eye and a kidney. Sometimes he claims to be attending an "alternative" Boston college as if he were a liberal, but finally he joins the establishment as a clerk for a federal judge.

Jessica Victor, Adlai's twin sister and a heroin addict. At the age of eighteen, she goes to Vietnam even as the war there is worsening. She has to be rescued as an "escorted orphan," just before the general evacuation.

Billy Dillon, a public relations front man and arranger of photo opportunities for Harry Victor. He considers Inez's interest in refugees to be too controversial and makes her a consultant on embassy paintings. He tries to prevent Paul Christian from having to stand trial, endeavoring to cover up the business connections and racism behind the murders of Wendell Omura and Janet.

Jack Lovett, a handsome adventurer, twice divorced. His mysterious occupation as an international consultant seems connected with CIA control of weapons and fuel. He sees war as a commercial enterprise and claims to be devoid of ethics and emotion, except for his love for Inez ever since they met in Honolulu in 1952. At Inez's request, he brings Jessica safely out of Vietnam. In Jakarta, finally together with Inez, he drowns accidentally in the shallow end of a hotel swimming pool.

Joan Didion, who knew Inez when they both worked at *Vogue* magazine in 1960. While teaching at the University of California, Berkeley, in 1975, she reads of Janet's murder, then is summoned by Inez to hear her chronicle of family tragedies in the hope of extracting some meaning from all that has happened. She serves primarily as a listener and sympathetic but limited witness who allows Inez to reveal whatever she wants to and can about her life among powerful landholders and politicians.

— Leonard Casper

THE DEMON: An Eastern Tale
(Demon)

Author: Mikhail Lermontov (1814-1841)
First published: 1841
Genre: Poetry

Locale: Unidentified
Time: Indeterminate
Plot: Mythic

The Demon, an unnamed demoniac power whose identity is a matter of some controversy, as Russian has no articles (hence, he may be either "the" or "a" demon, though commentators tend to agree that he is a specific demon). Like Lucifer or Satan, he has been expelled from heaven. His role apparently is to lead humans into evil and death, but unlike John Milton's Satan, he longs for the lost paradise and has the capacity to fall in love with a mortal (Satan perceives Eve's beauty and is filled with envy, but he has no romantic interest in her). Unlike Johann Wolfgang von Goethe's Mephistopheles, the Demon is bored with the prospect of an eternity spent in deluding puny human beings. Although he is indifferent to the beauties of nature, he proves susceptible for some reason to the beauty of Tamara, and despite his coldness and his vicious will to destroy, he is somewhat sympathetic. Some commentators insist that Lermontov identifies himself with the Demon, so that his loneliness and alienation combined with his desire for beauty and love cause him to appeal to the reader even as he appeals, fatally, to Tamara. In his seduction of Tamara, the Demon shows himself to be a master of rhetoric.

Tamara, a beautiful Caucasian princess with bright, shining eyes. She is the only daughter of a famous bandit chief, Prince Goudal, a minor character in the poem. Her mother appears to have died. As she prepares for her wedding, she shows herself to be a graceful dancer, and she is described as "freedom's joyous, willful pet." She has misgivings about her new life, and when her intended is killed, her sorrow seems minimal. The Demon's distant "voice" appeals to her quite swiftly, and she is moved by his "unearthly" good looks. Nevertheless, she does perceive that her lover is demoniac, and she has herself committed to a convent in order to avoid his almost vampiric attraction. Passionate by nature, she is unable to resist the Demon's love, and when he confronts her guardian angel, the Demon is able to insist that she already has sinned in her heart and belongs to him. She succumbs to temptation not simply because he flatters her and offers her pleasure and power but also because she accepts the sincerity of his love for her, sympathizes with his forlorn condition, and believes his oath, in which he swears that he desires reconciliation with God. She is saved because she has been "severely tried" and because she "yearned for earthly love but lost it."

The guardian angel, a generic figure. The angel makes only a feeble effort to defend Tamara against the Demon when he comes to the convent to seduce her, presumably because she has indeed "sinned," as the Demon claims. At the end, however, the angel disdainfully repudiates the Demon's claims to Tamara's soul and indicates that the Demon once again has been sentenced to damnation.

Prince Goudal, Tamara's devoted father and a Caucasian robber chief. He is a conventionally religious man who grants his daughter's wish to enter a convent, even though he would presumably prefer to marry her to another suitor after her intended is killed. Grief-stricken at Tamara's death, he erects a church high in the mountains and eventually is buried there.

The young bridegroom, Tamara's betrothed, who appears briefly in the poem as he rides toward his wedding in such haste that, tempted by the Demon with thoughts of his beloved, he passes up the local custom of praying at a roadside shrine. When he impulsively pursues an Ossetian bandit, he is shot.

The aged guardian, who serves the convent as a night watchman. He appears very briefly in the poem so that the impact of Tamara's mysterious death will be recorded at what one might call the subconscious level.

— *Ron McFarland*

THE DEMONS
(Die Dämonen: Nach der Chronik des Sektionsrates Geyrenhoff)

Author: Heimito von Doderer (1896-1966)
First published: 1956
Genre: Novel
Locale: Vienna and its environs
Time: 1926-1927 and 1955
Plot: Historical

Councillor Georg von Geyrenhoff (GAY-ohrg GI-rehn-hohf), a retired civil servant who assumes the roles of narrator, editor, and chronicler of the story of "Our Crowd" and other people during 1926-1927 in Vienna. He revises and edits the story again in 1955, when he feels he can be more objective. He requests others to aid him in writing about events that he cannot personally witness, accepts unsolicited manuscripts for inclusion in edited form, and directs a team of assistants who are unaware that they are spies, reporters, and collaborators for him. His major concern in 1955 is to examine the events of twenty-eight years before, including the burning of the Palace of Justice in 1927 by an angry mob of demonstrating workers. Geyrenhoff sees this event as leading to the takeover of Austria by the Nazis and its destruction in World War II.

Kajetan von Schlaggenberg (KAY-yeh-tahn fon SCHLAHG-gehn-behrg), a professional writer, major collaborator on the chronicle, and modern ideologue. Kajetan is enraged by the popular notion that the ideal of feminine beauty is the extremely thin woman. He develops "Kajetan's Theory of the Necessity of Fat Females to the Sex Life of the Superior Man Today." Geyrenhoff extensively censors this "Chronique Scandaleuse" of fat women because he considers it one of the foolish and dangerous ideologies that imperil society. Kajetan is the greatest provider of information on the second life of the people from all segments of society in Vienna. In 1927, he ends his flirtations with ideologies and becomes a serious novelist.

Anna Kapsreiter (KAPS-ri-tehr), an elderly widow and author of "Kap's Night Book." This book is a diary of thirteen dreams that Anna has during the early months of 1927. Geyrenhoff includes them in the chronicle without editing because they disclose an unusual perspicacity of the times. She actually predicts the future, although no one knows that until 1955.

Ruodlieb von der Vlantsch (REWOHD-leeb fon dehr vlayntsh), the author of a manuscript about sorceresses. Like Kajetan's "Chronique Scandaleuse," Geyrenhoff includes this story to offer another example of an absurd and ominous ideology.

René von Strangeler (reh-NAY fon STAN-geh-lehr), a brilliant young historian. He secures his professional future when Jan Herzka, the owner of the Ruodlieb von der Vlantsch manuscript and a medieval castle, engages René to read and interpret the manuscript and to direct the modernization of the castle. Professor Bullogg, a medievalist at Harvard, visits René in Vienna in June, 1927, and guides him in the preparation of a critical edition of the manuscript. With all this good fortune in his professional life, he is able to marry Grete Siebenschein, his fiancée of long standing.

Financial Counselor Levielle (leh-VEEL), the villain. As longtime adviser to the Ruthmayr family, Levielle tries to embezzle the substantial inheritance that the late Captain Ruthmayr had designated for his illegitimate daughter, Charlotte von Schlaggenberg. Geyrenhoff enlists the help of a group of boys to recover the will. This act leads to Levielle's discovery, and the charlatan is forced to flee to Paris.

Charlotte von Schlaggenberg (shahr-LOHT-teh), often called **Quapp**, Kajetan's sister. Charlotte wants to become a virtuoso violinist but realizes that even with hard work she will not be successful because she lacks the necessary musical gift. She is frequently seen in "Our Crowd" in the company of Imre von Gyurkicz. Although there are moments of great passion, the tempestuous relationship soon ends. When she inherits a significant sum of money, she settles down and marries Géza von Orkay.

Leonhard Kakabsa (LAY-ohn-hahrt kah-KAHB-zah), a self-educated young factory worker. One day, quite by accident, Leonhard finds a Latin grammar book and starts to learn Latin. Although he has no thought of changing his lifestyle, he notices that he has attained a considerable degree of linguistic freedom that his fellow workers do not possess. He meets Mary K. only a short while after beginning his self-help educational program. Through Mary K., Leonhard is introduced to Prince Alfons Croix, who not only offers to pay for his further education but also hires him as a librarian for his distinguished and vast private library. At the same time, Leonhard falls in love with Mary K., and they plan to marry as soon as he is established professionally.

Mary K., a widow who lost a leg in a streetcar accident. Everyone is astonished at the way Mary K. has recovered from the trauma of her accident. She is now a beautiful and poised woman. Although there is a considerable age difference between Mary K. and Leonhard, their rare and exquisite love for each other will lead to a perfect marriage.

Friederike Ruthmayr (free-deh-REE-keh REWT-mi-ehr), a wealthy widow. The most elegant social events take place at the Palais Ruthmayr during the 1926-1927 social season. There is one unexplainable flaw in this otherwise perfectly respectable person: The story is told by reliable sources that "Our Crowd," while on one of their wild nighttime carouses, stopped at the Palais Ruthmayr, and Friederike joined them by drinking cognac right out of the bottle. She and Geyrenhoff marry, but Friederike dies during the war.

Grete Siebenschein (GREH-teh ZEE-behn-shin), René von Strangeler's fiancée and Mary K.'s upstairs neighbor. As the daughter of a typical middle-class family, Grete experiences the usual problems in persuading her parents to approve of René as a suitable husband.

Imre von Gyurkicz (IHM-reh fon GYUHR-kits), a painter and newspaper cartoonist. A Hungarian and member of "Our Crowd," Imre has created a questionable genealogy for himself that he uses to enhance his social position. Politically very active, he is killed during the riots of 1927.

Géza von Orkay (GAY-tsah fon OHR-ki), Geyrenhoff's cousin. Géza is an important diplomat at the Hungarian embassy in Vienna. Through Geyrenhoff, he meets Charlotte von Schlaggenberg, whom he marries prior to his transfer to a more important post in Basel. The last meeting of "Our Crowd" takes place at the railway station when they gather to say farewell to the newlyweds.

— *Thomas H. Falk*

THE DEPTFORD TRILOGY

Author: Robertson Davies (1913-1995)
First published: 1983
Genre: Novels
Locale: Canada and Switzerland
Time: 1908 to the 1970's
Plot: Psychological realism

Fifth Business, 1970

Dunstan Ramsay, a fussy bachelor whose memoirs elucidate the meaning of his life and that of his boyhood friends, Boy Staunton and Paul Dempster. Although on the surface he is simply an elderly schoolteacher, what is important is his inner life, which is preoccupied with religion, magic, and myth. He is "fifth business" of the title; this theatrical term indicates an actor whose secondary role serves a crucial function in the plot. Dunstan's role in the life of Boy Staunton is a spiritual one, and although his stern Presbyterian upbringing tends to make him petty and withholding, he becomes a kind of saint. He occasions poetic justice in the life of Boy Staunton and is perpetually in search of the transcendent meaning of things. His spiritual destination is suggested by his name change from its original Dunstable to the saint's name of Dunstan and by his writing of books of saints' lives. Eventually, it becomes clear to him that his life has been shaped by a boyhood incident in which Boy attacks him with a piece of granite hidden in a snowball but instead hits Paul's mother, Mary. As the keeper of the conscience of Boy Staunton as well as the keeper of the offending piece of pink granite, Dunstan realizes the guilt he carries and the connection he forms with Mary Dempster as the most important aspects of his long and busy life. As he distances himself from his puritanical roots in small-town Canadian life, Dunstan develops a mystical side to his personality, joining Paul, now the great magician Magnus Eisengrim, as "permanent guest" at the castle of the grotesque theatrical impresario and occult priestess, Liesl Vitzlipützli.

Boy Staunton, originally named Percy. His nickname affirms an ideal based on energetic virility. It is Boy who throws the stone-filled snowball at Dunstan, hitting Mary Dempster instead. He assumes no guilt for his incident and instead becomes a successful, politically influential businessman with a reputation as a sexual athlete.

Mary Dempster, Paul Dempster's mother. Though addled by the snowball thrown by Boy, she is forgiving and lives by her inner lights, making her a possible saint.

The Manticore, 1972

David Staunton, the son of Boy Staunton. A successful criminal lawyer, he undergoes a midlife crisis after the death of his father. Unmarried, alcoholic, warped by an overly legalistic mind, and haunted by his relationship with his father, he travels to Switzerland for Jungian therapy. He learns that he is like a mythical beast called the Manticore, a monster who is only partially human. His one-sided emphasis on masculinity and cold reason has estranged him from the world of women and feeling, as well as making him unconscious of the dark side of his own personality. David comes to appreciate the women in his life and understands that his father had blocked both his spirituality and his capacity for intimacy. Like Paul and Dunstan, he engages significantly with Liesl Vitzlipützli, who initiates him into his own mystical and poetic unconscious.

Boy Staunton, who neglects his ailing, lonely wife and has a disturbing effect on his son David. His crimes and evasions catch up to him when, his emotional life withered, he commits suicide. With the assistance of both Paul and Dunstan, retribution is achieved when the stone that hurt Mary Dempster is mysteriously placed in Boy's mouth at his death.

World of Wonders, 1975

Paul Dempster, alias **Magnus Eisengrim**, the son of Mary Dempster. Her dementia, combined with a harsh religious upbringing, forces Paul, at the age of ten, to join a traveling circus in which he becomes the sexual servant of a seedy magician. Descending into a criminal underworld, Paul survives by his wits and eventually joins a theatrical troupe whose romantic values of love and imagination transform him from a tough little criminal into a great artist. After experimenting with a series of alter egos, Paul emerges as Magnus Eisengrim, the world's greatest magician and illusionist. The imagery of greatness (Magnus) and wolfishness (Eisengrim) suggests the intimidating power of his final identity. His early years of suffering and hardship have led to a life rich in experience and feeling, and he becomes the close companion of the wise sorceress, Liesl Vitzlipützli.

Liesl Vitzlipützli, a grotesque mistress of a mansion called Sorgenfrei (carefree). She is a theatrical impresario, sage, and figure of charismatic female power. Her name derives from a minor devil from Johann Wolfgang von Goethe's *Faust* (1790-1833), and she presides as a priestess of a strange magical world beneath the modern one.

— *Margaret Boe Birns*

THE DEPUTY
(Der Stellvertreter)

Author: Rolf Hochhuth (1931-)
First published: 1963
Genre: Drama
Locale: Berlin, Rome, and the Auschwitz-Berkenau extermination camp in Poland
Time: August, 1942-November, 1944
Plot: Historical

Father Riccardo Fontana, an idealistic young Jesuit priest who opposes the Catholic church's concordat with Adolf Hitler and who tries unsuccessfully to persuade the pope to speak out against the Nazi atrocities against the Jews. Joining a group destined for Auschwitz, he becomes, in effect, the pope's representative, or "deputy," accepting for himself the morally correct role he believes the pope has abdicated.

Kurt Gerstein, an officer in the SS and member of the Protestant Confessing church. Gerstein is a devout Christian who attempts to destroy the Nazi system from within. As an SS officer, he has evidence that the Jews are being gassed in the concentration camps and, knowing the Nazis' fear of the moral authority of the church, believes that intervention by the pope could stop the persecution.

Pope Pius XII, **Eugenio Pacelli** (ew-JEH-nee-oh pah-CHEHL-lee), who is portrayed with grand gestures and aristocratic coolness. He is a symbol of the church as an institution. He does not protest the arrest of the Jews except in empty, diplomatic language and wishes the church to be an impartial mediator for Adolf Hitler and Franklin Delano Roosevelt. The symbolic washing of hands reinforces his refusal to speak out against the mass killings.

The Doctor, an inhuman figure with a charming, likable manner. He sorts the Auschwitz prisoners into the ones who will work and the ones who will die immediately. His role is that of absolute evil, confronting Riccardo with doubts about the existence of God.

Count Fontana, a high-ranking lay adviser to the pope. As Riccardo's father, he makes the personal confrontation between his son and the pope possible. He is valuable to the Vatican as a financier and business manager and shows himself to be a man of kindness and feeling who well understands the dynamics and politics of the Vatican.

Cesare Orsenigo (cheh-ZAH-reh ohr-SEH-nee-goh), the apostolic nuncio in Berlin and Riccardo's superior. The nuncio is sixty-nine years old and a man of great self-discipline with a candid and tolerant expression. His role is to articulate the position of the church—that Western civilization must be protected from Russian communism, even if that means dealing with Hitler.

Baron von Rutta, a distinguished aristocrat and member of the Reichs Armaments Cartel. This character, along with Müller-Saale of the Krupp works, articulates the position of the German industrialists, whose main concern is using the Jews as forced labor to make profits.

The Abbot, the father general of a religious order. He wants the pope to speak out for the Jews but is committed to his vow of obedience if the pope does not do so. A man of conscience, the Abbot has saved hundreds of lives by protecting individuals who are attempting to escape.

The Cardinal, a suave, somewhat ruthless diplomat in the service of the pope. A man with remarkable intelligence who rose out of poverty, he considers himself a realist in supporting the church position that Hitler can be used to block communism.

Professor August Hirt, a Strassburg University anatomist who attempts to prove Nazi racial theories by examining the skulls of concentration camp victims.

Helga, a waitress and later a secretary. She is a young, attractive blonde who enjoys flirting but is oblivious to politics and the evil around her. She falls under the spell of the Doctor and accompanies him to Auschwitz, where she becomes his mistress.

Air Force Lieutenant von Rutta, the baron's son, a young man of about twenty years who has just won the Knight's Cross. An innocent and likable person, he is a brave soldier and shy with women.

Jacobson, a Jew whom Gerstein hides and then attempts to smuggle out of Germany.

Adolf Eichmann, a colorless bureaucrat who efficiently plans the transport of Jews to the camps.

Lieutenant Colonel Dr. Fritsche, a doctor of jurisprudence who allocates inmates to the industrial plants near Auschwitz.

Carlotta, a converted Catholic whose Italian fiancé has died in battle. She is considered a full-blooded Jewess and is sent to Auschwitz.

Dr. Lothar Luccani (lew-CHAH-nee),
Julia,
Luccani, Sr.,
a boy of nine,
a girl of five, and
Pippa (the baby), a part-Jewish family living within view of the papal palace. Luccani, Sr., is a Catholic, and the family has made arrangements to hide in a monastery when the SS comes to arrest them.

Signora Simonetta (see-moh-NEHT-tah), a neighbor of the Luccanis who takes care of the baby when the family members are taken prisoner.

— *Susan L. Piepke*

DESCENT INTO HELL

Author: Charles Williams (1886-1945)
First published: 1937
Genre: Novel
Locale: Battle Hill, a residential area near London
Time: June and July, sometime during the 1930's
Plot: Moral

Pauline Anstruther, the twenty-six-year-old orphaned heroine of the novel. She is consigned to care for her grandmother Anstruther and might have drowned in self-pity were it not for the terrifying, unpredictable appearances of her twin, a *Doppelgänger*. Fear, not self-pity, rules Pauline's life until she learns to exchange fear for love. Decent and good-hearted, Pauline is intellectually immature, but as she joins the cast, as choral leader, of Peter Stanhope's play, she intelligently interprets its clues about a design for human salvation. Once Pauline masters Stanhope's doctrine of "substituted love" and allows him to bear her burden of fear while she in turn bears others' burdens, not only are the sources of fear overcome but she also becomes aware of her role in a cosmic plan. Pauline's integration of active understanding with passions and will that is otherwise predisposed to goodness opens the way for her vision of the City of God, giving joy and assurance that her decision finally to "go to the City" will lead to her life's perfection.

Peter Stanhope, the author of the poetic drama in which the villagers are involved. He is extraordinarily wise, benevolent, and talented. In his character, the supernatural and angelic potential of humankind intersects with the human and natural to create a whimsical yet fulfilled Christian hero. Having created the play, he good-naturedly allows the villagers to interpret it according to their own visions of reality and art. His name, Peter, means "rock." Stanhope, which evokes "long-standing hope," signals his allegorical connection to enduring faith as the essential Christian virtue. He exhibits a third cardinal virtue, charity, when he carries Pauline's burden of fear long enough to allow her to deal with the *Doppelgänger* phenomenon and to teach her the practice of substituted love. The most theological of the characters, Stanhope is this novel's Christ figure.

Lawrence Wentworth, in his early fifties, is a bachelor-scholar of military history. He has been protected by luck and a certain kind of tactical intelligence from the pitfalls of his vanity. He finds himself in need of reassurance about his sexual attractiveness and the rightness of his scholarly opinions. His "descent into hell," a barely perceptible spiritual journey and the subject of his strange, recurring dream, is defined by his petty and unjust hatred of his scholarly rival Aston Moffat and his pathetic lust for a woman (Adela Hunt, he supposes) who will serve his vain illusions of self-importance. He is a false and miscreant lover, betraying both Adela Hunt and himself as lover and finally as scholar. His descent begins with self-indulgence, progresses through egotistical obsessions, and ends in teeth-gnashing loathing of himself and others, a final madness, and suicide.

Margaret Anstruther, Pauline's elderly grandmother. She looks forward joyfully to the exchange of life for death. Fulfilled and saintly, Margaret sustains a working life devoted to prayers for the salvation of others. She is sweet-tempered, endlessly patient, and inevitably courteous, even to the evil Lily, who tries foolishly to manipulate her. Margaret is the most clear-headed, confident, and realistic of the female characters. Through her mediation and spiritual direction, Pauline acts to save the suicide-ghost who haunts the housing development in the suburbs where the novel is set.

Adela Hunt, the leading lady of Stanhope's play. She is desired by Lawrence Wentworth and Hugh Prescott. Vain and self-centered, with an excessive sexual egoism, she is an unworthy object for her admirers. As her name implies, she is a predatory idol. Hugh's recognition of this is key to his salvation; Wentworth's lack of acknowledgment leads him to choose damnation.

Hugh Prescott, a suitor to Adela. Hugh is the leading man in Stanhope's play, and in the novel he is the object of Wentworth's jealousy. In his habit of seeing life clearly, he functions as a foil to Wentworth.

Lily Sammile, a supernatural but evil character. She appears as a neighbor of Mrs. Anstruther but is a mere phenomenon, actually a minor and ineffective disciple of Satan. Her role is allegorical, as False Love, as her name implies. Lilith is William's stock representative of illusory love, and Sammile is probably an allusion to a demon Samael, similarly named in the occult tradition of the Zohar. Lily cannot fool the enlightened Christian characters in the novel, only narcissists such as Adela.

— *Diane Brotemarkle*

DESIGN FOR LIVING

Author: Noël Coward (1899-1973)
First published: 1933
Genre: Drama
Locale: Paris, London, and New York City
Time: The 1930's
Plot: Comedy

Gilda, who is about thirty years old. She is Ernest's wife and the mistress of both Otto and Leo. Gilda is attracted to Otto, an unsuccessful painter, and lives with him in his Paris studio, hoping to further his career. Although Gilda does not wish to marry, claiming that marriage provides nothing she wants, she is humiliated by the way in which feminine impulses sway her life. When Leo returns from New York as a successful playwright, Gilda deserts Otto and goes to live with Leo in London. After eighteen months with Leo, however, Gilda is still unhappy. She distrusts (and perhaps envies) Leo's continuing success and dislikes the social life it entails. She also thinks that success has affected the quality of Leo's work, a criticism he resents. While he is away, Otto reappears, and Gilda sleeps with him. After leaving Otto and marrying Ernest,

Gilda not only has tired of fulfilling her desire for artistic success via men but also has come to believe that she deluded herself into thinking she contributed anything to her lovers' creative lives.

Leo, a playwright, Gilda's lover and a friend of Otto and Ernest. Leo is offended that Gilda first chose Otto, and his taking Gilda away has an element of revenge in it. He enjoys his success and refuses to believe that starving in a garret is a prerequisite for producing effective art. When Gilda leaves, however, he is shattered and turns to Otto. They depend on each other for consolation and then travel together and reclaim Gilda together.

Otto, a painter, Gilda's lover and a friend of Leo and Ernest. Otto is furious that Leo and Gilda have betrayed him but, after being apart from them, he realizes that he misses his friends too much to bear a grudge. He, like Leo, suffers from Gilda's departure and consoles himself by going on a cruise with Leo. He forms part of the *ménage à trois* when all three return to Paris at the end of the play.

Ernest, an art dealer, Gilda's husband and a friend of Otto and Leo. Apparently he is American. Early in the play, he brings news of Leo's success and scolds Gilda for the untidiness of her emotional life. Later, he listens to her complaints about feeling superfluous and informs her that he has bought a penthouse in New York City and is intending to settle down. Gilda leaves with him, and they are subsequently married. Ernest is resentful when Gilda later leaves him to return to her lovers, either because she needs them to need her or because all of them fail to resist their impulses. Ernest is made to look foolish when he tries to retain his wife, and all three artists are laughing at him as the curtain goes down.

— *Jocelyn Creigh Cass*

DESIRE UNDER THE ELMS

Author: Eugene O'Neill (1888-1953)
First published: 1925
Genre: Drama
Locale: A farmhouse in New England
Time: 1850
Plot: Tragedy

Ephraim Cabot, a greedy, harsh, old New England widower. He has taken over his second wife's farm and worked her to death. He has brutalized his three sons, working them like animals on the farm until they hate him bitterly. At the age of seventy-six, he marries thirty-five-year-old Abbie Putnam, a deed intended to cheat his sons of their inheritance. The two older sons have left the farm, but Eben, the youngest, remains. Abbie, whom Eben hates, cleverly seduces him, and he fathers a child that Ephraim, duped by flattery, believes is his own. Taunted by his father, Eben threatens to kill Abbie for tricking him. By this time, she has fallen in love with Eben. As her way of proving this love, she murders the baby. When Abbie is about to be arrested, Eben realizes that he now loves her, and he insists on accepting part of the blame for her crime. As the sheriff takes them away, Ephraim is left alone to contemplate his empty victory over his sons.

Eben Cabot, Ephraim's son by his second wife. He hates Ephraim for the way the self-righteous old hypocrite treated his mother. Believing that the farm is really his, Eben buys out the potential claim of his brothers by giving each three hundred dollars from a hoard of gold his mother had hidden. He bitterly resents the arrival of a young stepmother, and he continues to hate her even after she seduces him and he fathers her child. Her final act of love toward him changes his hatred of her to love, and he willingly goes away with her to share her punishment.

Abbie Putnam, Ephraim's third wife, less than half his age. She marries him to get a home. Her appearance heightens the hostility that exists between Ephraim and Eben. Abbie seduces Eben to get a child who will be Ephraim's heir and who will deprive Eben of his expected inheritance. Although Eben tells her that he hates her, Abbie has fallen in love with him. To prove this love, she smothers the baby she has tricked him into fathering. Shocked by this crime, Eben goes for the sheriff, but when he begins to realize that he really loves Abbie, he tells the sheriff that he is an accomplice in the crime and is taken away with her.

Simeon and

Peter Cabot, Ephraim's sons and Eben's half brothers. Hating their father and wanting desperately to join the gold rush to California, they accept Eben's offer of three hundred dollars each and renounce all claims to the farm.

DESSA ROSE

Author: Sherley Anne Williams (1944-)
First published: 1986
Genre: Novel
Locale: Marengo County, Alabama
Time: 1847-1848
Plot: Historical realism

Dessa Rose, an African American woman who experiences both gender and racial inequality. As a slave, she knows not only marginality but also extreme violence, danger, and cruelty. She is a strong person, determined not to surrender her life or her child's life to slavery's victimization. She leads a slave rebellion. As the story develops, Dessa enters an intimate relationship with another fugitive slave, Harker. She escapes to freedom in the West with Harker, her son, and their friends.

Ruth Elizabeth Carson (also known as **Miz Rufel** and **Rufel**), a white woman who harbors and provides strategic aid to runaway slaves. She becomes an ally and friend for Dessa Rose, her baby, and Dessa's fellow escaped slaves. When she becomes involved in a sexual relationship with Nathan, one of those slaves, Dessa so disapproves of their union that she refers to Miz Rufel as "Miz Ruint."

Adam Nehemiah, a white man who wishes to record the story of Dessa Rose's rebellion on the Wilson coffle, to be included as a case in his next book on slave management and slave uprisings. He is ambitious, and he hopes that this new book, coupled with the success of his first book, will help him to establish a place in planter society. He is ill-equipped, however, for a match of wits with Dessa Rose. After she escapes from prison, he obsessively tracks her.

Nathan and

Harker, two of the slaves who participate in the slave-coffle rebellion that nearly costs them their lives. While in hiding with Dessa Rose, these characters plan a brilliant deception that, with the assistance of Rufel, allows them to generate income by selling themselves back into slavery repeatedly, only to elude their prospective owners.

Kaine, Dessa's lover and the father of her child, who is brutally and senselessly murdered before the events in the novel. Through memories and flashbacks, readers learn of him as a strong man, a tender partner to Dessa, and an ongoing inspiration to her struggle to resist slavery and escape its injustices.

— *Linda S. Watts*

DESTINY BAY

Author: Donn Byrne (Brian Oswald Donn-Byrne, 1889-1928)
First published: 1928
Genre: Novel
Locale: Ireland
Time: Early twentieth century
Plot: Regional

Kerry MacFarlane, the narrator, the heir to Destiny Bay.

Jenepher MacFarlane, Kerry's blind but beautiful aunt. She has a deep perception of human goodness. She is Sir Valentine's sister.

Sir Valentine MacFarlane, Kerry's redheaded, red-bearded uncle, the lord of Destiny Bay. He is courtly and hospitable. Loving people, he does all he can to help them.

The Duke of la Mentera, a Spanish nobleman. A relatively poor man, he comes to Destiny Bay in search of a treasure chest lost from the Spanish Armada by an ancestor.

Don Anthony (Ann-Dolly), the duke of la Mentera's supposed grandson, who turns out to be a beautiful girl, known then as Ann-Dolly. She falls in love with and marries Jenico Hamilton.

James Carabine, Sir Valentine's faithful valet. A great prizefighter, he fell on evil ways in New York City. He was rescued from drunkenness and failure by Sir Valentine, who went to America to bring him back to Ireland.

Jenico Hamilton, Kerry's cousin, who lives near Destiny Bay. He marries Ann-Dolly.

Patrick Herne, Jenepher's husband. He looks like Digory Pascoe, Jenepher's dead fiancé, who, though killed in a fight, is kept alive for Jenepher for twelve years by Sir Valentine through letters written as though from Digory to Jenepher. Sir Valentine brings Patrick home as Digory. He and Jenepher fall in love and are married, after Jenepher learns he is not truly her supposed first fiancé.

The Fair Maid of Wu, a Chinese girl whom Cosimo MacFarlane saw three times and came to love.

Cosimo MacFarlane, Sir Valentine's brother. He is a great, happy, joyous man. A heavy drinker who reforms, he works to reform other drunkards and ends up as the bishop of Borneo.

Anselo Loveridge, Cosimo's friend, a gipsy rescued from the hangman's noose by Cosimo. He finds the Fair Maid of Wu for his benefactor.

DEVIL IN A BLUE DRESS

Author: Walter Mosley (1952-   )
First published: 1990
Genre: Novel
Locale: Los Angeles, California
Time: The late 1940's
Plot: Detective and mystery

Ezekial "Easy" Rawlins (ee-ZEE-kee-uhl), a factory worker turned detective. He is originally from Houston, Texas, but moved to California in search of a wartime factory job and to escape the influence of his friend Raymond Alexander. He has no family connections and is largely self-educated. Fired from his job in an aircraft factory after an incident with his foreman involving race, Easy is drawn into a moneymaking scheme by a friend. He is attempting to live the American Dream; he has managed to buy a home and now must take on unfamiliar work in order to pay his mortgage. He is haunted by his combat experiences in Europe and is increasingly uncomfortable with the violent situation into which he is drawn. Eventually, Rawlins discovers that detective work provides him with an independence and self-confidence that he had not experienced previously.

Daphne Monet (moh-NAY), a companion to rich businessmen and crime figures; she is the devil in a blue dress of the title. Her real name is **Ruby Hanks**, and her mother is African American. As Daphne Monet, she passes as white. She leaves Lake Charles, Louisiana, and the identity of Ruby Hanks to escape the memory of an incestuous relationship with her father. She has so perfected her escape from the past that she is described as a chameleon. She is able to assume different racial identities and even radically different personalities.

Raymond "Mouse" Alexander, Rawlins' friend and partner from Houston. He appears in Los Angeles, having been notified that Rawlins needs his help. Little is known about Mouse's past, other than that he killed his stepfather to acquire inheritance money that he had been denied. Mouse is violent and unpredictable but values loyalty and friendship.

Dewitt Albright, a lawyer turned "criminal handyman." Like Mouse, he is violent and unpredictable. He seems to have no morals or scruples. He hires Rawlins to help him find Daphne Monet.

— *James C. Hall*

THE DEVIL IN TEXAS
(El diablo en Texas)

Author: Aristeo Brito (1942-)
First published: 1976
Genre: Novel
Locale: The Texas-Mexico border towns of Presidio and Ojinaga and the surrounding area
Time: The 1850's to the 1970's
Plot: Historical realism

Ben Lynch, or **Don Benito** (beh-NEE-toh), an Anglo-American landowner who represents everything undesirable. He acquires his land in a legal but unethical agreement with Tía Paz, who was in no shape mentally to resist his overtures. In order to secure his position among the Mexican American population, he marries Francisco's sister. The story of his vengeance against anyone who opposes him reveals the extent to which he will go in his exploitation and manipulation of the minority population. By virtue of his Anglo-American heritage, he is able to find support from law enforcement agencies. His character personifies everything evil.

Francisco Uranga (ew-RAHN-gah), also called **Don Pancho** (PAHN-choh), a pathetic figure whose life as a journalist and a lawyer is spent trying to correct the injustices he sees perpetrated upon the Chicano population. Francisco speaks for himself, his family, and the Mexican American population in general. It is through his acts of resistance, which are reinforced by his sons and their sons, that the reader sees a panorama of abuse that extends over several generations and clearly is suggestive of similar abuses in other communities with the same racial mix. What Francisco's character lacks in depth, it makes up for in intensity. His persistent dedication to exposing abuse and cruelty along the Texas border, despite the alienation he experiences on both sides of the river, helps to establish him as a sympathetic character whose determination to right wrongs merits respect.

Jesús (heh-SEWS) and

Reyes (RREH-yehs), Francisco's sons, who continue the resistance effort in their own manner. Jesús is killed by Lynch's men because he refuses to stop transporting Mexican workers across the border. Reyes becomes a part of a renegade band of Mexican Americans who sabotage Lynch at every opportunity by organizing resistance to the Texas Rangers.

José Uranga (hoh-SEH), who as a fetus "speaks" from Marcela's womb. He returns to Presidio when his father is dying in 1970. His character represents the typical Chicano youth (perhaps inspired by the author's own experiences) who escapes from an oppressive environment and experiences some success in the dominant Anglo-American culture, only to realize as a mature adult the strong ties he still feels for Chicano culture.

Marcela Uranga (mahr-SEH-lah), the mother of José Uranga. Like many Mexican American wives, she is trapped in a society that often deprives her of physical and emotional support. When her husband escapes to Mexico, she is left to deal with deprivation and physical discomfort. Upon attending a mass, she sees an apparition of the Devil winking at her with a mocking grin. The emotional trauma she experiences pushes her to the edge of insanity.

Chente (CHEHN-teh), Marcela's uncle, who dies an untimely death that is brought about by extreme working conditions, reinforcing the prevalence of exploitation across all aspects of Mexican American life. His conversations with Vicke, Marcela's mother, are poignant reminders of the hopelessness and helplessness of the Mexican laborer.

The Devil, the most powerful character in the story. He takes many forms, both real and symbolic. He is the snake coiled around the cross that stands high on the mountain overlooking the river; the river and later the bridge that control the destiny of the Mexican Americans; Ben Lynch, who has more power in Texas than God himself; the goat-footed stranger who appears at a party; the tall cowboy who winks at Marcela in church; the train conductor; and the Green Devil who operates the capitalistic agrarian system. In fact, the Devil is anything and everything evil and oppressive and symbolizes the blatant insensitivity and evil intention of the Anglo-American population along the border with Mexico.

THE DEVIL TO PAY IN THE BACKLANDS
(Grande Sertão: Veredas)

Author: João Guimarães Rosa (1908-1967)
First published: 1956
Genre: Novel
Locale: The Brazilian backlands
Time: The late nineteenth and early twentieth centuries
Plot: Psychological realism

Riobaldo (ree-oh-BAHL-doh), the narrator and protagonist. His life takes a major turn when, at the age of fourteen, he meets Diadorim, a girl who passes for a boy and who belongs to a family heavily involved in politically oriented armed movements in the backlands. After the death of his mother, he goes to live with his godfather, who teaches him the ways of the *jagunço* or gunman. He then enters the *jagunço* life. In his travels, Riobaldo again meets Diadorim and joins her band. With her support and the strength he acquires from a supposed encounter with the devil, he wins the leadership of the band and achieves victory over Heremógenes, the murderer of Diadorim's father, Joca Ramiro. As a wealthy old farmer, Riobaldo tells the story that is the novel as a way of discovering if he, in fact, sold his soul to the devil.

Diadorim (dee-ah-DOHR-eem), the daughter of Joca Ramiro. She lives her life as a man. She befriends Riobaldo and later becomes his faithful companion. After the murder of her father at the hands of Heremógenes, she becomes obsessed with taking revenge. Riobaldo's rise to leadership is the vehicle by which she is given the opportunity to realize her goal. During the last battle, she meets Heremógenes in hand-to-hand combat. Both die in a bloody scene. After her death, Riobaldo discovers that she is a woman.

Zé Bebelo (seh beh-BEH-loh), an outsider who seeks to bring law and order to the backlands. He also wants to become an elected official after his days as a *jagunço* leader. He fails in both of his attempts to achieve dominance. In the first, he is defeated by Joca Ramiro, and in the second, he is deposed by Riobaldo. He makes a third appearance at the end of the novel as a cattle buyer and entrepreneur.

Heremógenes (ehr-eh-MOH-hehn-ehs), the leader of a band under Joca Ramiro. He is there when Zé Bebelo is defeated and speaks against him at the trial. He becomes disgruntled when Joca Ramiro allows Zé Bebelo to go free. Heremógenes later murders Joca Ramiro. Many of the characters believe that his success as a leader comes from having made a pact with the devil. His physical appearance lends credence to that notion. His death leaves the lingering question of whether the devil really exists and whether he can have dominion over a person.

Madeiro Vaz (mah-DAY-roh vahs), a strong and committed leader with an impeccable reputation. The followers of Joca Ramiro rally to him after the death of Joca Ramiro. His commitment is so absolute that he burned his possessions before he departed to become a leader.

Joca Ramiro (HOH-kah rra-MEE-roh), the leader of the *jagunço* bands in the backlands. He is revered even during his life. His death sets the stage for the climax of the story.

THE DEVIL UPON TWO STICKS
(Le Diable boiteux)

Author: Alain-René Lesage (1688-1747)
First published: 1707
Genre: Novel
Locale: Madrid
Time: Early eighteenth century
Plot: Picaresque

Don Cleophas Leandro Perez Zambullo (KLEH-oh-fahs leh-AHN-droh PEH-rehs sahm-BEW-yoh), a student. At the home of his inamorata, Donna Thomasa, he finds himself worsted in a fight with hired ruffians. He flees to the rooftops and enters a garret, where he finds the demon Asmodeus and frees him from a bottle in which he is imprisoned. In return for this favor, the demon takes Don Cleophas on a flight over Madrid, during which he gives the student glimpses into the varied life of the city. He provides explanations of the sights they see, wreaks vengeance for Don Cleophas on the treacherous Donna Thomasa, rescues the beautiful Donna Seraphina from imminent death, and bequeathes her to the young man as a bride.

Asmodeus (ahs-moh-DEH-uhs), the Devil on Two Sticks, the friend of hapless lovers. Imprisoned in a bottle by a magician, he is freed from his captivity by Don Cleophas Leandro Perez Zambullo, whom he takes on a flying trip over Madrid.

Donna Thomasa (toh-MAH-sah), Don Cleophas' treacherous inamorata.

Donna Seraphina (seh-rah-FEE-nah), a beautiful lady rescued from a fire by Asmodeus disguised as Don Cleophas Leandro Perez Zambullo, whom she later marries.

Don Pedro de Escolano (PEH-droh deh ehs-koh-LAH-noh), Donna Seraphina's father.

The Count de Belflor (BEHL-flohr), a court gallant,

Leonora de Cespedes (leh-oh-NOHR-ah deh SEHS-peh-dehs), loved by the Count de Belflor,

Marcella (mahr-SEH-yah), Leonora de Cespedes' treacherous duenna,

Don Luis de Cespedes (lew-EES), Leonora's father,

Don Pedro, Leonora's brother, in love with Donna Eugenia, and

Donna Eugenia (eh-ew-HEH-nee-ah), the Count de Belflor's sister, characters in a story told to Don Cleophas Leandro Perez Zambullo by Asmodeus as they watch a wedding festival through a window.

Don Juan de Zarata (hwahn deh sahr-AH-tah) and

Don Fabricio de Mendoza (fah-BREE-see-oh deh mehn-DOH-sah), devoted friends in love with Donna Theodora de Cifuentes,

Don Alvaro Ponza (AHL-vah-roh POHN-sah), the rejected suitor of Donna Theodora de Cifuentes,

Donna Theodora de Cifuentes (teh-oh-DOH-rah deh sih-FWEHN-tehs), a beautiful widow in love with Don Juan de Zarata, and

The Dey of Algiers, characters in a story of true friendship and love told by Asmodeus.

THE DEVILS

Author: John Whiting (1917-1963)
First published: 1961
Genre: Drama
Locale: France
Time: 1623-1634
Plot: Tragedy

Urbain Grandier (ur-BAYN grahn-DYAY), the vicar of St. Peter's Church in Loudun, France. Grandier is a brilliant, proud, and sensuous man who is obviously superior, intellectually and emotionally, to most of his parishioners, yet he is a persistently religious person as well. He struggles with his libertine impulses and passionate appreciation of physical beauty, which threaten to deify flesh over spirit. He makes powerful enemies in a deliberate attempt to bring about his own destruction, to test his capacity for suffering and as a way of doing penance to God for his rebellious spirit. Women are drawn to him, a fact of which he often takes advantage but that ultimately destroys him. When he is accused of witchcraft, he receives the excruciating trial he sought, enduring torture and painful death with a fortitude and grace equal to his former arrogance and sensuality.

Sewerman, a workman with whom Grandier often converses in the street. He is a foil for Grandier's philosophic meditations on the nature of humanity, casting doubt on Grandier's aspirations and comparing human beings to walking sewer systems. His is a materialistic and skeptical but honest voice that Grandier respects.

Sister Jeanne of the Angels (zhahn), the prioress of St. Ursula's Convent, the ultimate weapon for Grandier's destruction, though one he did not choose. He never meets the pathetic, hunchbacked mother superior, except to decline an invitation to be her father confessor. She has observed him longingly, however, from the grating of her barren room. His crime against her is the culmination of a more pervasive one to which she is particularly vulnerable—part of the cultural crime of keeping beauty and tender passion forever beyond her reach. She joins her special agony to the ugliness and ferocity of the rest of the world to blot out his careless affront to mediocrity and inferiority. Her claim that he possessed her sexually as a devil has elements of both hysteria and deliberate role-playing.

Mannoury (mah-new-REE), a surgeon, and

Adam, a chemist, who demonstrate the malice, envy, and small-mindedness of some middle-class persons who resent Grandier, as well as the gross sadism that permeates the examination of the nuns at Loudun for evidence of demoniac possession. Grandier is contemptuous of their pretensions to knowledge and importance.

Phillipe Trincant (fee-LEEP trahn-KAN), a young girl, the daughter of the public prosecutor. Grandier marries her in a secret ceremony, an action that he explains to the Sewerman as an attempt to find a way to salvation through commitment to another person. When Phillipe becomes pregnant, however, Grandier recommends to her father that he marry her off to an old man.

Louis Trincant (lwee), the public prosecutor, an enemy of Grandier because of his treatment of Phillipe.

Cardinal Richelieu (reesh-LYOO), a far more formidable enemy. Grandier opposes Richelieu's project of tearing down the fortifications of Loudun as part of a campaign to reduce local sovereignty and unify France with a strong central government. This political motivation for the government's part in Grandier's conviction is further enhanced by an old insult Richelieu suffered at the hands of the insolent Grandier before Richelieu became virtually the ruler of France.

De la Rochepozay (rohsh-poh-ZAY), the bishop of Poitiers, an ascetic who despises the senses and condemns all self-assertion.

Jean D'Armagnac (zhahn dahr-mah-NYAHK), the governor of Loudun, who, like Grandier, would like to preserve the independence of the city.

Prince Henri de Condé (an-REE deh kohn-DAY), a decadent nobleman described as an "exquisite and handsome sodomite." He comes, leaning on painted boys, to observe the nuns pretending demoniac possession. He is nobody's fool and devises a clever test that reveals their fraud. He tells the commissioner to destroy Grandier for his opposition and his strength, not on such flimsy grounds as demoniac possession, of which he is innocent.

Sister Claire,

Sister Gabrielle, and

Sister Louise, who join Sister Jeanne in an obscene display of possession for the delectation of a prurient audience of townspeople.

The Demons, imaginary beings who obtain an almost existential reality as the projection of pain, malice, and lust in an atmosphere of hysteria. They speak through the women, and their laughter is heard in other volatile situations. Their "reality" is balanced by Grandier's transcendent religious experience, after which he says he has "created God."

— *Katherine Snipes*

THE DEVIL'S ELIXIRS: From the Posthumous Papers of Brother Medardus, a Capuchin Friar
(Die Elixiere des Teufels: Nachgelassene Papiere des Bruders Medardus, eines Kapuziners)

Author: E. T. A. Hoffmann (1776-1822)
First published: 1815-1816
Genre: Novel
Locale: Germany and Italy
Time: The eighteenth century
Plot: Fantasy

Medardus (meh-DAHR-dews), a monk. He is put in charge of the relics of his order, which include among them an elixir reputed to cause any who drink it to belong to the devil; if two people should taste the potion, they would be as one in thought and desire while secretly wishing to destroy each other. Medardus drinks of the elixir and is then confronted with all the devices of the powers of darkness, which weave about him a web of falsehoods, murders, mistaken identities, and madness until he recovers and is purged of his guilt. He is then asked by Father Spiridion, the monastery librarian, to put his life story in writing.

Count Victorin, Medardus' brother, who has also drunk of the devil's elixir. Unknown to each other as brothers, the two resemble each other and have the same desires. In one guise or another, each tries continually to destroy the other.

Aurelia (ah-ew-REH-lee-ah), a young noblewoman loved by Medardus but claimed by Victorin as his intended bride. She is killed by Victorin as she is taking her vows as a nun.

Hermogen (EHR-moh-jehn), Aurelia's brother, killed by Medardus.

Baron von F——, the father of Aurelia and Hermogen.

Euphemia (ew-FEH-mee-ah), Baron von F——'s sinister wife, engaged in an affair with Victorin.

Pietro Belcampo (pee-EH-troh behl-KAHM-poh), a hairdresser and Medardus' benefactor.

Francesco (frahn-CHEHS-koh), a painter revealed as Medardus' father.

Leonardus (leh-oh-NAHR-dews), a prior and Medardus' spiritual adviser, from whom he receives forgiveness for his crimes.

Reinhold, an old man at Baron von F——'s castle.

Prince von Rosenthurm, at whose castle Medardus learns that Francesco is his father.

The duke of Neuenburg, the prince's brother, murdered on his wedding night.

Father Spiridion (spee-REE-dee-ohn), the librarian of the Capuchin monastery at Konigswald.

DEVOTION
(Die Widmung)

Author: Botho Strauss (1944-)
First published: 1977
Genre: Novel

Locale: West Berlin
Time: Summer, 1976
Plot: Psychological realism

Richard Schroubek (SHREW-behk), a thirty-one-year-old bookseller by trade, recently abandoned by his girlfriend, Hannah Beyl. For Richard, who calls separation the most terrifying and shattering of all types of personal catastrophe, Hannah's departure means the destruction of all prior connection to and identification with society. Without actually quitting or calling in sick, he simply stops working and sells an inherited Max Beckmann etching as a means of financially supporting his state of misery. He establishes a postal checking account, forgoing interest for the sake of solitude (he can withdraw money through the mail), and retreats to his apartment. Richard's isolation is interrupted initially only by Frau N., the cleaning woman, and then by Fritz, another man rejected by Hannah. Gradually, the protagonist develops bad habits such as not bathing, not changing clothes regularly, and not cleaning. The general dirtiness and disorderliness of the apartment are greatly intensified by the mishaps to which the protagonist becomes prone.

Hannah Beyl (bil), the twenty-five-year-old girlfriend who suddenly and without explanation abandons Richard. Later, she spends three days with Fritz, only to leave him just as suddenly. Twice, Hannah seemingly attempts to re-establish contact with Richard. It is obvious from her appearance at an eventual meeting with Richard that she has suffered since leaving him. Her eyes are red and her face ashen; she has lost weight; she is drunk, dirty, and unkempt; and she seems to be involved in some questionable financial dealings. Hannah remains indifferent and unresponsive toward Richard, unwilling to engage herself in the dialogue he so desperately desires.

Fritz, a school porter. Fat, in his mid-twenties, and very nervous, Fritz enjoyed a brief affair with Hannah. Apparently deeply disturbed by her sudden disappearance, Fritz pushes his way into Richard's apartment and attempts to enter her study; however, Richard, who regards Fritz's misery and suffering as superficial in comparison to his own, blockades himself in Hannah's former room. He leaves when Hannah calls to arrange a meeting; she calls back later to cancel, but Richard already has left and Fritz answers the phone. Fritz arranges to meet Hannah and is still in her company just prior to Richard's arrival.

Frau N., the house cleaner. The same age as and originally hired by Hannah, Frau N. stops coming to clean the apartment when Richard can no longer pay her. Richard misses her normality, her loquaciousness, and her constant references to Hannah.

— *Linda C. DeMeritt*

THE DEVOTION OF THE CROSS
(La devoción de la cruz)

Author: Pedro Calderón de la Barca (1600-1681)
First published: 1634
Genre: Drama

Locale: Siena, Italy
Time: The seventeenth century
Plot: Tragedy

Eusebio (ay-ew-SAY-byoh), one of two infants abandoned by a wayside cross. Surviving several disasters in which the sign of the cross is miraculously manifested, he feels himself ennobled by his devotion to the cross and worthy of Julia, whom he loves. After he kills her brother, Lisardo, in a duel, she orders him out of her life. He turns bandit and spares only victims who mention the cross. During ensuing adventures, he learns his identity; that of his father, Curcio; and that of his brother and sister, Lisardo and Julia. Fatally wounded, he wins redemption because of his devotion to the cross.

Julia (HEW-lyah), who is loved by Eusebio. Later, by the sign of the cross on her breast, she is revealed as Eusebio's sister, the other infant abandoned at the wayside cross.

Lisardo (lee-SAHR-doh), Julia's brother, killed in a duel by Eusebio and later revealed to be Eusebio's brother.

Curcio (KEWR-thyoh), the father of Eusebio, Julia, and Lisardo. A baseless suspicion of his wife's unfaithfulness causes him to abandon the twins, Eusebio and Julia, by a wayside cross. When he fatally wounds Eusebio in a fight, his son's identity is established by the cross on his body.

Father Alberto (ahl-BAYR-toh), a priest whose life is saved by the bandit Eusebio. In thankfulness for being spared, he hears the outlaw's last confession.

Gil (heel) and

Menga (MEHN-gah), peasant witnesses to the duel between Eusebio and Lisardo.

THE DHARMA BUMS

Author: Jack Kerouac (1922-1969)
First published: 1958
Genre: Novel
Locale: California, North Carolina, and the Washington Cascades
Time: 1955-1956
Plot: Autobiographical

Raymond (Ray) Smith, the first-person narrator, a wanderer based on the author. Ray is an intellectual who has turned from the Catholicism of his youth to Buddhism in his search for the ultimate truth of existence. He is disgusted with the shallowness and hypocrisy of American civilization in the 1950's. In fact, his major problem is that he cannot live or get along in the world as it is and must retreat periodically from it. He is able to practice meditation successfully on mountaintops, in forests, and in deserts, but when he comes back to civilization, he feels that he is back in "hell" again. Gradually, through his meditation and conversations with friends, especially Japhy Ryder, his spiritual mentor, he comes to realize the Buddhist wisdom of the emptiness and consequent unity of all things and determines to try and live successfully within the dust and commotion of the city.

Japhy Ryder, an outdoorsman, Buddhist, scholar, and poet who becomes Smith's friend and mentor. He is based on Gary Snyder. Like Ray, Japhy recognizes the crass materialism and hypocrisy of American life in the 1950's, but he is able to cope successfully with it and live in the real world. Unlike Ray, who must meditate with his eyes closed, he can meditate with his eyes open and can meditate in a crowded bar as well as on a mountaintop. Japhy participates fully in life and tries to introduce Ray to various aspects of living in the world. He introduces Ray to his many friends and takes him along on two mountain-climbing trips, on which he teaches Ray about his own philosophy. Japhy leaves for Japan on a study scholarship but first arranges for Ray to spend the summer alone on a mountaintop as a fire lookout. He hopes Ray will attain enlightenment while on that job.

Alvah Goldbook, a poet and a friend of Ray, with whom he shares a cottage in Berkeley. Although he agrees with Raymond's and Japhy's pessimistic views of American society, he is not as much of a believer in Buddhism as they are. He serves as a more prosaic, down-to-earth counter to Ray's occasional excesses of esoteric Buddhist philosophy about the nonreality of all things. Alvah is far too busy enjoying life and finding beauty where he might to worry about the reality or nonreality of material objects. His idea is not to be concerned with the ultimate meaning of existence and just take life as it comes.

Cody Pomeray, an old friend of Smith, based on Neal Cassady. Cody is the most important character other than the autobiographical narrator in most of the author's fiction. He functions as a combination lost-brother figure and idolized friend. In this novel, Cody has a peripheral role, appearing briefly as a reminder to Ray that bad things are happening constantly and people need to be enlightened. Cody's girlfriend commits suicide and gives Ray cause to reflect on the unhappiness he sees around him.

Sean Monahan, an old friend of Japhy. Sean is the primary example in the book of what it would be like to have the enlightenment of Japhy and live a normal married life. Sean, the only married friend of Japhy and Ray, lives with his wife and two children in a rustic cottage in Marin County. He not only practices Buddhist meditation and reads sutras but also goes off during the day to work as a carpenter. His wife stays at home, walking around barefooted, baking bread, cooking simple but delicious meals, and being a mother to two children. His house is the gathering place for those interested in Buddhism or alternative lifestyles.

— *James V. Muhleman*

DIANA OF THE CROSSWAYS

Author: George Meredith (1828-1909)
First published: 1885
Genre: Novel
Locale: England
Time: The nineteenth century
Plot: Psychological realism

Diana Merion Warwick, a witty, charming, and beautiful woman. She is a person who makes mistakes because she does not believe that the conventional thing is always the right thing. She learns from her experiences, however, and becomes a wiser woman. She marries Augustus Warwick primarily as a matter of convenience. When she becomes friendly with the elderly Lord Dannisburgh, her husband accuses her of infidelity. She is found not guilty of this charge by a court, but she refuses to return to her husband. She becomes a novelist, but her initial success does not last, and she finds herself reduced to poverty. In these circumstances, she sells some information told to her by Sir Percy Dacier, who is in love with her, thus betraying his confidence. She finally consents to become the wife of a man who has loved her for many years. Diana makes many enemies, but she is also the sort of woman who is loved and admired by many men.

Augustus Warwick, the politician whom Diana marries when she is a young woman. He is calculating and ambitious and is completely incapable of understanding his wife's innocence of the demands of conventionality. He tries to force Diana to return to him, but she will not. He is finally struck down and killed by a cab in the street.

Sir Percy Dacier, a young politician who falls in love with Diana after she has refused to return to her husband. He spends a great deal of time following her about and, in a moment of indiscretion, tells her a very important political secret. Diana sends him away. Needing money desperately, she sells his information to a newspaper. Feeling betrayed, he turns from her and marries an heiress.

Thomas Redworth, a brilliant member of Parliament who falls in love with Diana. He announces his love too late, after she is engaged to Warwick. He is steadfast, however, and, when Diana is forced to sell her family home and all of her belongings, he buys them, expecting that some day she will consent to become his wife. His loyalty is rewarded when Diana marries him.

Lady Emma Dunstane, a friend of Diana who introduces her to Redworth. She remains faithful to Diana through all of her troubles and unpopularity.

Lord Dannisburgh, the older man with whom Diana is friendly and with whom she appears, rather indiscreetly, while her husband is away on a government mission. He is Sir Percy Dacier's uncle. When he dies, he leaves Diana a sum of money in his will.

Sullivan Smith, a hot-tempered Irishman who challenges Redworth to a duel because he objects to Redworth's attentions to Diana. He proposes to Diana, but she refuses him.

THE DIARY OF A COUNTRY PRIEST
(Journal d'un curé de campagne)

Author: Georges Bernanos (1888-1948)
First published: 1936
Genre: Novel
Locale: France
Time: The 1920's
Plot: Psychological realism

A Priest, the thirty-year-old cleric of Ambricourt Parish, in France, who strives to be frank with himself. Lonely and sympathetic, a child of poverty, he tries to help his people materially as well as spiritually. He believes the rich have a duty to the poor. His efforts to help his people undermine his health and bring scorn upon him. He fails again and again; only in death does he find peace, believing in God.

Dr. Maxence Delbende (mahk-SAHNS dehl-BAHND), a thwarted, bitter man. He helps frustrate the priest's efforts to aid the parish materially. When disappointed at not receiving an expected legacy, he commits suicide.

The Curé de Torcy (tohr-SEE), the priest's superior and ideal. He thwarts the priest's efforts to raise living standards and ridicules the priest for his spiritual and worldly failures.

Seraphita Dumouchel (say-rah-fee-TAH dew-mew-shehl), a sensual girl in the priest's catechism class. She thrusts unsavory attentions on the priest and spreads the word that he is addicted to drink.

The Count, a local aristocrat. He carries on an affair with the family governess and embitters his family by a series of infidelities over the years.

Mlle Chantal (shahn-TAHL), daughter of the Count and Countess. Upset and filled with hatred, she threatens to kill either herself or the governess with whom her father is having an affair.

The Countess, a woman of atheistic tendencies. With the priest's help, she dies in spiritual peace, though she is consumed by physical agony.

Mlle Louise, the governess who is the count's mistress.

M. Dufrety (dew-fruh-TEE), the priest's seminary friend. He is with the priest at his death.

Dr. Laville (leh-VEEL), a drug addict. He bluntly tells the priest he is dying of stomach cancer. The priest was supposed to go to another doctor, but he consults the wrong physician.

DIARY OF A MAD OLD MAN
(Fūten rōjin nikki)

Author: Jun'ichirō Tanizaki (1886-1965)
First published: 1961-1962
Genre: Novel
Locale: Tokyo and Kyoto, Japan
Time: Early 1960's
Plot: Psychological realism

Tokusuke Utsugi, the seventy-seven-year-old patriarch of a well-to-do Tokyo family. Impotent, toothless, plump, and continually pained by neuralgia, backaches, and circulation problems, Utsugi is attended at home by a full-time nurse. Long fascinated by visions of his own death and funeral, he journeys to Kyoto to select a fitting burial place. He is increasingly preoccupied with masochistic fantasies involving his daughter-in-law, Satsuko. For her small and grudging favors, he pays with ever more expensive gifts. Even after a series of debilitating seizures in the winter, Utsugi looks forward to spring, the construction of a swimming pool, and walks in the garden with Satsuko.

Satsuko Utsugi, a beautiful former chorus girl. She has been married to Utsugi's son for ten years, and they occupy the second floor of Utsugi's Tokyo house. Although she is the mother of a six-year-old son, Satsuko devotes her days to shopping, classical flower arranging, films, boxing matches, and an adulterous affair with Utsugi's nephew, Haruhisa. Motivated by greed or by emotional generosity, she offers her father-in-law kisses for gifts such as a car, a designer scarf, a purse, and a cat's-eye ring. She is regarded by her sisters-in-law as spiteful, sarcastic, lying, cold, and manipulative and is disregarded by her husband.

Jokichi Utsugi, the only son of Tokusuke. A successful thirty-six-year-old businessman away from home a considerable amount of the time, he is seemingly little interested in his wife and family.

Itsuko, Utsugi's widowed daughter. She lives in the Nanzenji district with her two grown sons, Kikutaro and Keijiro, and has never gotten along well with her father.

Kugako, Utsugi's daughter. When the eldest of her three children wishes to marry, Kugako asks her father for a short-term loan of twenty thousand yen. He refuses her. Not long afterward, Satsuko extracts three million yen from him as the price of a kissing session. Family resentment of Satsuko escalates.

Nurse Sasaki, Utsugi's live-in attendant. She sleeps in the bed next to him all but one or two nights a month. She tends to his incessant pains and administers his medications.

— *Virginia Crane*

DIARY OF THE WAR OF THE PIG
(Diario de la guerra del cerdo)

Author: Adolfo Bioy Casares (1914-)
First published: 1969
Genre: Novel
Locale: Buenos Aires, Argentina
Time: Near future
Plot: Social satire

Don Isidro Vidal (ee-SEE-droh vee-DAHL), an elderly widower, the novel's protagonist. Small and slightly built, he has a sharp fox's nose and a mustache. He is obsessively proud of his new set of false teeth. Don Isidro is the leader of a social group of elderly men, the "pigs" referred to in the novel's title, who are under attack and are being murdered by a group of young men. He is a compassionate individual who has faith in the fundamental brotherhood of humanity.

Isidorito Vidal (ee-see-dohr-EE-toh), Don Isidro's son. His meager earnings support both his father and himself. When the gang of youths begins to terrorize the town, Isidorito tries to placate both sides. He participates in the group's activities but sometimes warns the old men when they are targeted as victims. He is murdered by the group when he tries to save his father's life; they consider Isidorito a traitor.

Nélida (NEH-lee-dah), the young woman who falls in love with Don Isidro. She is engaged to a young man but breaks the engagement to be with Don Isidro, to whom she is increasingly drawn, as he is to her. When he fears for his life and attempts to hide from the youth group, she shelters him in her apartment.

Arturo Farrall (ahr-TEW-roh fah-RRAHL), the leader of the gang of youths, the "Young Turks," whose death squads terrorize and murder the town's elderly citizens. The reasons he gives for the "war on the pigs" is that the population is growing too large and that the elderly are becoming a burden on society.

Néstor Labarthe (NEHS-tohr lah-BAHR-teh), an elderly friend of Don Isidro. He is the first of Vidal's group who is murdered. He is thrown over the stands and trampled at a soccer match. His brutal murder, in the presence and possibly with the consent of his own son, causes a serious split in the Young Turks between those who attempt to avoid danger by conforming and those who try to rebel against the terrorism of this youth-oriented society.

Leandro Rey (leh-AHN-droh ray), a Spanish-born elderly friend of Don Isidro. He is nicknamed "The Thinker" by the group of aging men. Unlike the others in the group, he is not retired: He works as a baker. He is described as cold, self-centered, tightfisted, and a formidable adversary in business or at the card table. He is also a terrible glutton.

James (Jimmy) Newman, a member of the group of elderly men. He is also called the "M. C." because of his quick mind and lively manner. Of Irish descent, he is tall and ruddy cheeked, and he has a plump face. He always speaks in deadly earnest. He is kidnapped by the youth gang for a time and allegedly turns informer to obtain his release.

Dante Révora (DAHN-teh REH-voh-rah), a member of Don Isidro's group who tries desperately to look young by dyeing his hair. He has a reputation for being an educated man. He is terrified for his life and thinks that he can escape death by attempting to look younger than he is.

Lucio Arévalo (LEW-see-oh ah-REH-vah-loh), another member of Don Isidro's group, formerly a newspaperman. He is described as being extremely ugly. Usually ill-shaved, he has cigarette-stained hands and flecks of dandruff on his poncho. He is the picture of an asthmatic, ailing old man. Don Isidro considers it strange that no member of their group has ever set foot in Arévalo's house. Because of his longtime affair with a teenage girl, he ends up in the hospital, kicked and beaten by a gang of youths.

— *Genevieve Slomski*

A DIFFERENT DRUMMER

Author: William Melvin Kelley (1937-)
First published: 1962
Genre: Novel
Locale: The Deep South
Time: 1931-1961
Plot: Impressionistic realism

Tucker Caliban, the "different drummer" who, by destroying his farm and departing with his family, precipitates the exodus of the black population from the fictitious southern state in which the story is set. The land previously belonged to the Willsons, the white clan that Tucker's family had served even after emancipation. Tucker buys the land from David Willson, saying, "You tried to free us once, but we didn't go and now we got to free ourselves." Physically small, with a large head and wearing wire-rimmed glasses, Tucker often appears inscrutable to the other characters. His actions demonstrate an almost instinctive self-reliance. He refuses, for example, to support the National Society for Colored Affairs because he denies that anyone else can achieve his rights for him.

Bethra, Tucker's wife, a tall, slim, and beautiful woman. Poised and intelligent, she had been working as the Willsons' maid to earn money to finish college. Her college plans are dropped, however, when she falls almost girlishly in love with Tucker, and they marry. More educated than her husband,

Bethra is at first embarrassed by his rejection of her friends' civil rights causes, and she leaves him. She returns, however, in a week, having come to see the truth of his commitment to independent action. Dymphna Willson, who made Bethra her confidant, acknowledges that the black woman has taught her much about life.

Mister Harper, the town philosopher. A retired army officer, he went to West Point but, being too young for the Civil War and too old for World War II, never put into practice his military training. His son, however, was killed in World War II. Thereafter, feeling "knocked down by life," he stayed in a wheelchair. From his porch, he dispenses analyses of the world's chaotic events to townspeople who daily gather around. For example, he offers the "genetic" explanation for the exodus of the black people, telling the story of the near-mythic, prodigiously powerful, and elusive African who was Tucker's ancestor. He leaves his wheelchair for the first time in thirty years to watch Tucker Caliban destroy his farm.

Harry Leland, a sharecropper. He admonishes his son for using the word "nigger"; in contrast with others in the town, he recognizes the need for adapting to change and for getting along with all kinds of people. Having been a sergeant in the Korean War, he theorizes that the black people are conducting a "strategic withdrawal," a prudent action for which he admires them.

Harold Leland, called **Mister Leland**, Harry Leland's son, an active eight-year-old with sandy hair. He has considered Tucker a friend ever since Tucker bought him some peanuts he had been eyeing in the store window; the reason Tucker gave for the gift was the way in which Harry Leland was rearing Mister Leland. The night Bennett T. Bradshaw is lynched on Tucker's property, Mister Leland hears laughing and singing coming from the spot; he thinks that a party is going on to celebrate Tucker's return and plans to go out there the next morning to see his friend again.

David Willson, a descendant of Dewey Willson, who is called the General and is a former Confederate war hero and state governor. David is considered by the townspeople to be a usurper of the family name. While at college, he became active in left-wing issues and struck up a friendship with Bennett T. Bradshaw, a black intellectual and fellow student. The two roomed together and shared a concern for the wasted potential of their respective peoples. Returning to the South after graduation, David finds work as a journalist for a local newspaper. He is fired, however, once he is exposed as the author of articles espousing a radical stance on racial issues, written under a pen name for a communist magazine in New York City. Anxious that he is not finding work, and with a child on the way, he returns to the Willson home to take up the family business, one that he despises: collecting rent from sharecroppers on Willson land. Feeling himself to be a coward for not living up to his ideals, he retreats emotionally from his wife and children. He experiences a renewal, however, when he agrees to sell Tucker the land by which Tucker means to free himself.

Camille Willson, David's wife. She met him at a party hosted by bohemian friends, and their courtship included going with him on assignments for the newspaper. She continues to have faith in him even as he keeps from her his pseudonymous articles and afterward, when he gets fired. She offers to move with him to New York City, but he misjudges her sincerity. In the Willson home, she feels like a stranger and despairs at the loss of intimacy in her marriage.

Dewey Willson III, David's college-age son. He has a recurring nightmare in which the General entrusts him with the bleeding head he tears from his own body. On his tenth birthday, Dewey got a new bike and begged Tucker, then thirteen, to teach him to ride. Tucker was later punished because they were late for dinner, the older boy having relented to Dewey's plea that they "try once more." Dewey feels guilty about this injustice but never said anything to Tucker about it. He is with Bennett when the lynching mob drags the black man away, and although he tries to save him, he cannot.

Dymphna Willson, David's teenage daughter. Somewhat selfish and a self-professed schemer, her initial consideration in being friends with Bethra was that Bethra, being black, would not compete with her for boyfriends. By the time Bethra leaves the Willson household, she has taught the younger girl that "the most you can do for people you love is leave them alone"—a wisdom that helps Dymphna come to terms with her parents' relationship.

Bennett T. Bradshaw, David's black college roommate, who had to drop out before graduating to support his family. Active in the Civil Rights movement, he places David's articles in leftist magazines in New York City. Later, David reads in a national magazine that Bennett has been fired from the National Society for Colored Affairs because of alleged communist affiliations and has founded the Resurrected Church of the Black Jesus Christ of America, Inc., a black supremacist group. Bennett appears in town in a chauffeur-driven limousine, investigating Tucker's departure and the ensuing exodus of blacks. He is resentful at becoming obsolete as a leader, given the impact of Tucker's independent action. At the novel's climax, he is beaten, humiliated, and taken away to Tucker's farm to be lynched.

—Amy Adelstein

DIGBY GRAND

Author: George J. Whyte-Melville (1821-1878)
First published: 1853
Genre: Novel
Locale: England, Scotland, and Canada
Time: Early nineteenth century
Plot: Picaresque

Digby Grand, a spirited young Englishman, perfectly willing to follow his father's wish that he be a man of fashion. Leaving Eton, he is commissioned as an ensign in a regiment of infantry. After being stationed first in Scotland and then in Canada, Digby finds that his father has purchased him a lieutenancy in the most social brigade in the service, the Life Guards, stationed in London. Digby is popular in the best society, but he goes heavily into debt. He falls in love with a penniless girl whom his father forbids him to marry. Prevented by creditors from leaving England to go to India as a general's aide, he sells everything he owns, including his commission and, upon his father's death, his estate. Left only his title, he is taken into business by a friend who has become a wine merchant. Business prospers, and Digby, settling down at last, makes plans to marry his old sweetheart.

Sir Peregrine Grand, of Haverley Hall, Digby's father, who wants his son to be a man of great social position and to marry a wealthy heiress.

Tom Spencer, Digby's boyhood chum. Studying for holy orders at Oxford, Tom co-signs moneylenders' notes for Digby. As a result, he is later arrested and consequently cannot finish his degree at Oxford. He then becomes a successful wine merchant and takes Digby into the business with him.

Flora Belmont, the fortuneless daughter of a retired colonel. Digby falls in love with her, but his father opposes the marriage. Well off at last and ready to settle down, Digby finds her still single, and they make plans to marry.

Coralie de Rivolte, a famous dancer with whom Digby has an affair.

Colonel Cartouch, Digby's commanding officer, who likes him and who intervenes to prevent the teenaged ensign from marrying the young French-Canadian girl with whom he has an affair in Canada. Later, prosecuting a man forging checks in his name, Colonel Cartouch finds out that the forger is married to Coralie de Rivolte and that Coralie is his own daughter.

Shadrach, a moneylender who lends Digby money at high interest. To satisfy him and other creditors, Digby gives up everything he owns.

Captain Levanter, one of Digby's fellow officers. He introduces Digby to Shadrach.

General Sir Benjamin Burgonet, who likes Digby and makes it possible for him to secure his original commission. He later makes Digby his aide, but Digby is prevented from leaving for India by his creditors.

Lady Burgonet, a woman in her thirties who, while Digby is stationed in Scotland, almost succeeds in tricking him into marriage. Instead, she becomes the wife of the regimental drum major. When he is preparing to go with the general to India, Digby is aghast to find that the woman is now Lady Burgonet.

Dubbs, the regimental drum major, Lady Burgonet's husband before her marriage to General Burgonet.

St. Heliers, a young peer with whom Digby is friendly in London.

Mrs. Mantrap, a woman who basks in the attentions of young men. She is one of Digby's London friends.

Zoe, a French-Canadian girl with whom Digby has an affair in Canada.

THE DINING ROOM

Author: A. R. Gurney (1930-)
First published: 1982
Genre: Drama
Locale: A dining room, somewhere in the northeastern United States
Time: Approximately 1930-1980
Plot: Comedy

The Dining Room Table, the focal point in the formal dining room. It serves not only as the basic prop but also as the inanimate main character for the play's eighteen vignettes analyzing "white Anglo-Saxon Protestant" (WASP) life in America in the twentieth century. The table is large, elegant, and deeply burnished, with armed chairs at either end, two armless chairs along each side, and several matching chairs against the walls of the room. The table sits on an elegant hardwood floor covered with a fine oriental rug. Into this archetypal dining room come almost sixty characters, their attitudes toward the table and the dining room helping to define the history of WASP America.

Father, the authoritarian head of an affluent 1930's family. He is conceited, priggish, and sexist. He believes that government programs in the 1930's are ruining the country by encouraging people not to work. At breakfast with his young son and daughter, Father reads the newspaper, gently chastises the maid, and instructs his children on fine points of grammar, table manners, and the proper way to address one's mother. For him, the dining room is a central arena for exercising a highly ritualistic approach to life.

Architect, a professional consultant from the 1970's who presents a remodeling plan to his client, a psychiatrist who has just bought the house. Efficient, businesslike, and decisive, the Architect does not see elegance in the dining room, only vast space that can be manipulated for more efficient use. Having grown up in a home with a formal dining room, the Architect is familiar with what the room stands for, but as a child he hated its formality.

Aunt Harriet, a woman near the age of sixty who is unaware that her nephew, Tony, an Amherst College student, is interviewing her for an anthropology project on the eating habits of the vanishing WASP culture of the northeastern United States. Steeped in the propriety and traditions of upper-middle-class elegance, Aunt Harriet is proud of the table setting she is displaying for Tony, who takes photographs for documentation. She comments on the delicacy and value of the crystal, silver, linen, and china, relating each item to the genealogy of the family, and then demonstrates the proper use of the finger bowls.

Jim, a father in his late sixties, emotionally distant from his thirty-year-old daughter Meg, who has separated from her husband. Jim ushers Meg into the dining room because it is a good place to talk, but then he tries to avoid Meg's request to live with them.

Ruth, a hostess preparing the table for an elegant dinner party. Refined, sensitive, generous, and precise, Ruth describes her recurrent dream of a perfect dinner party in the formal dining room of the past, before her grandmother's silver was stolen, before the movers broke the china, and before the finger bowls were misplaced.

Peggy, a mother setting the table for a children's birthday party. She is strict in her discipline with the raucous children. Peggy is having an extramarital affair with Ted, the father of one of the children.

Grandfather, the family patriarch, eighty years old. Businesslike and thorough in his cross-examination, he receives his fourteen-year-old grandson in the dining room and gives him money for the boy's education.

Paul, a former stockbroker, now a carpenter, in his middle thirties. He carefully examines the dining room table for the owner of the house and recommends repairs.

Sarah, a teenage girl in the 1970's. In the dining room, she and her girlfriend sneak vodka and gin from the liquor cabinet and prepare to meet their boyfriends to smoke marijuana.

— *Terry Nienhuis*

DINNER AT THE HOMESICK RESTAURANT

Author: Anne Tyler (1941-)
First published: 1982
Genre: Novel
Locale: Baltimore, Maryland
Time: 1924-1980
Plot: Family

Pearl Cody Tull, who is eighty-six years old, small, fair-haired, gray-eyed, and indomitable. Her insight into herself and her relationships with her long-absent husband and her three children sharpens and becomes focused as her eyesight fades to blindness. Never able to nurture close relationships, Pearl instead allowed her grim determination and high expectations to drive her husband away; as a single mother, her occasional murderous rages almost obscured her powerful love of and concern for her children. Despite an abiding sense of grievance, Pearl always longs to have the children's confidence and trust, but, especially as adults, they remain at arm's length. Their feelings for her range from near hatred through tolerance to baffled love. Pearl's only oblique acknowledgment of her approaching death is her recognition of her own shortcomings. Perception comes as she lies dying, listening for clues from her own youthful diaries read aloud by Ezra, her mind drifting through the events of her life.

Beck Tull, a salesman, Pearl's husband and the father of their three children. The young Beck, black-haired, boldly blue-eyed, and flashily handsome, rescues Pearl from spinsterhood in a whirlwind courtship and marriage. In 1944, disappointed in his career and overwhelmed by the burden of Pearl's unspoken but fierce disappointment in him, he abandons the family, afterward maintaining a link with Pearl through the increasingly rare notes and checks he sends. Because Pearl never openly acknowledges his desertion, Beck hovers on the edge of the family's consciousness for thirty-five years until he appears (at Ezra's invitation) at Pearl's funeral. Now elderly, and still dapper if slightly sleazy, Beck is ready for reconciliation and recognition as the Tull patriarch, but his commitment lasts only through the day of the funeral, to the end of the one Tull family dinner ever to lurch to completion at the Homesick Restaurant.

Cody Tull, Pearl's eldest child, who is tall, dark-haired, and handsome. His youthful rebellious behavior and adult success as a time-study expert mask a deep-seated lack of self-confidence. The focus of his resentment is his brother Ezra, who manages to attract female admiration even though he is graceless and passive. Cody, curdled by his grievances, exacts revenge first by ensnaring and marrying Ezra's fiancée, Ruth, and last by castigating the newly returned and conciliatory Beck. In the first flush of his successful career, Cody buys a farm, dreaming of an idyllic domestic life; his hopes soured, he eventually abandons the farm, leaving Pearl and Ezra to try and shore it up against disintegration, just as they try to maintain the crumbling family.

Ezra Tull, Pearl's second son and middle child. With his pale eyes, shock of fair hair, and wide, shapeless body, Ezra appears soft; his mildness in childhood becomes a passivity in adulthood that is his main flaw but also his saving grace. Ezra simply allows life to happen to him, accepting with unthinking loyalty his mother's angry love, his mentor Mrs. Scarlatti's generosity, and even his catastrophic loss to Cody of Ruth, the only woman ever to rouse him to passion. In his revealingly named Homesick Restaurant, however, Ezra comes alive, crafting dishes to tempt his clients, pouring out his oddly maternal humanity into sturdy soups and comforting, lovingly prepared meals. Time and again, marking the milestones in the lives of his fractious family, Ezra attempts to unite and reconcile the Tulls at meals in the Homesick Restaurant's forgiving atmosphere, but he is doomed to failure. Ezra's constancy stands always in contrast to his family's restless volatility.

Jenny Tull, Pearl's third child and only daughter; she is dark-haired, dark-eyed, and intense. Jenny's thin, angular body matures into a beauty that she expends carelessly. Her becoming a pediatrician seems the natural fulfillment of her intellectual self-discipline; however, as the child most vulnerable to Pearl's alternating devotion and volcanic rages, she also displays a curious ambivalence. Sensitive like Cody, she mostly keeps her emotional distance. Also warmly accepting like Ezra, in her third marriage she tumbles contentedly into domestic muddle with her new husband, her daughter Becky, and six stepchildren, all of whose problems she treats with laughing offhandedness that masks her compassion and gratitude for people who really need her.

Ruth Spivey Tull, first Ezra's fiancée but finally Cody's wife. An unschooled, rural tomboy, Ruth is a superb country cook who meets the Tulls when she is employed as a chef at the Homesick Restaurant. Tiny, freckled, and carrot-haired, with pebbly, pale-blue eyes, young Ruth has a brisk, scrappy manner that captivates Ezra and fascinates Cody. Once overwhelmed by and married to Cody, however, Ruth subsides awkwardly into middle-class domesticity, her energy smothered by Cody's moody silences and her little body pathetically lost in unsuitable feminine clothing. As Pearl once followed Beck, Ruth follows Cody to a succession of strange towns and houses, never again able to express her scornful, independent spirit. Her sole satisfaction comes from mothering Luke, their serious, lonely son.

— *Jill Rollins*

THE DINNER PARTY
(Le Dîner en Ville)

Author: Claude Mauriac (1914-)
First published: 1959
Genre: Novel

Locale: An apartment in Paris, France
Time: The 1950's
Plot: Experimental

Bertrand Carnéjoux, the forty-five-year-old host of the dinner party and husband of Martine Carnéjoux. He is the editor in chief of *Ring*, a newspaper, and author of the book *Sober Pleasures*, an experimental novel. He has been having affairs with Marie-Ange Vasgne, Armande, the chambermaid, and his secretary, Colette. Throughout the dinner, he reminisces about Marie-Plum, the only woman he ever loved. He once slept with Lucienne Osborn, almost twenty years ago, but he does not recognize her until near the end of the party. He obsesses about his own death, giving the pair of jeweled cufflinks he would be buried in to Jérôme Aygulf. Bertrand is jealous of the dance Martine had with Gilles Bellecroix and fears there may be an attraction between them.

Martine Carnéjoux, nicknamed **Pilou**, the hostess of the dinner party and wife of Bertrand. She is twenty-five years old and has two children, Jean-Paul, age four, and Rachel, age two, who form the emotional nucleus of her life. Shortly before the party, she had a nose job. She knows about her husband's numerous affairs, but despite this, she has been faithful to him throughout their ten-year marriage. She had a memorable dance with Gilles Bellecroix the previous January and is sexually attracted to him.

Marie-Ange Vasgne, a twenty-three-year-old French Canadian model. A country girl from Quebec, she was raped by a redheaded man when she was fourteen years old. This rape altered the course of her life. She became a prostitute, using men to advance her career. Eventually, she moved to France and became a magazine model. She comes to the dinner party hoping to seduce John Osborn so that he will give her a part in a movie he is directing. He does not show up. Throughout the dinner, she fantasizes about sleeping with all the men there, especially the wealthy Roland Soulaires. By the end of the party, she decides to go home with Jérôme Aygulf, another redhead. She imagines marrying him and settling down.

Gilles Bellecroix, a failed novelist but successful screenwriter. He is forty-nine years old and has been happily married for ten years to Bénédicte, who is twenty years younger. Devoted to Bénédicte and their three-year-old son, Nicolas, he has never been unfaithful. He dislikes writing screenplays and wants to go back to writing novels. Throughout the dinner party, he thinks about sleeping with Martine Carnéjoux. In the 1930's, Eugénie Prieur was his lover.

Jérôme Aygulf, a third-year law student and childhood friend of Martine Carnéjoux's younger sister. He is a twenty-year-old leftist who dislikes the bourgeois atmosphere of the dinner party. He loves Martine, but she does not love him. He was invited to this dinner solely because another guest could not attend. He resides with his grandparents and feels hypocritical because he lives off their money. Toward the end of the dinner, his latent homosexuality manifests itself in his unspoken attraction for Bertrand Carnéjoux.

Roland Soulaires, the president and director of the Loubski mines. He is forty-three years old, fat, bald, wealthy, and unmarried. Throughout his life, he has suffered from bouts of impotence and tends to fear women because of this. During the dinner, he is preoccupied with stock prices and discusses literature and history with Eugénie Prieur. Recently, Marie-Louise temporarily "cured" his impotency, and he fantasizes about sleeping with Marie-Ange Vasgne.

Eugénie "Gigi" Prieur, a sixty-five-year old, once beautiful, famous fixture at all the best society parties. Throughout the dinner, she debates French history and literature with Roland Soulaires. In 1919, she became pregnant by the author Jean-Jacques Limher; she had an abortion, which has haunted her ever since. She feels estranged from her only child, Marie-Therese. She and Gilles Bellecroix were lovers in the 1930's.

Lucienne Osborn, the wife of the American director John Osborn. A forty-one-year-old, nearsighted Capricorn, she constantly watches her horoscope. She is concerned about her looks and obsesses about her suntan and her dachshund, Zig, whom she left at home. She does not love her eighty-year-old husband, who is having an affair with Ivy Luck. She looks forward to her husband's death and is sleeping with Léon-Pierre, the only man to sexually satisfy her. Almost twenty years ago, Bertrand Carnéjoux was her lover.

— Scott Blackwell

DIRTY LINEN and NEW-FOUND-LAND

Author: Tom Stoppard (Tomas Straussler, 1937-)
First published: 1976
Genre: Drama

Locale: London, England
Time: The 1970's
Plot: Farce

Dirty Linen, 1976

Maddie Gotobed, the new secretary to the Select Committee of Members of Parliament, which meets in an overspill meeting room in Big Ben. Voluptuous and inexperienced, she evidently has been involved in affairs with all the male members of Parliament (MPs) on the Select Committee, which has been commissioned to investigate sexual misbehavior in the House of Commons. Each member, as he arrives, slips her a pair of lace panties, evidently left at their last rendezvous, so that by the end of the play she has collected a drawer full of "knickers." Maddie is nobody's fool, however, and by the end of the play it is she who dictates her own text for the committee's resolution: that MPs have as much right to private life as any other citizens and that as long as they break no laws, their privacy should not be broken to indulge public curiosity.

Cocklebury-Smythe, the first of the MPs on this committee. He longs to move into the House of Lords. Like his fellow committee members, he urges Maddie to put out of her mind the various restaurants at which they have met.

McTeazle, the second of the nearly interchangeable MPs. He pulls Maddie's panties from his briefcase at the end of a long, huffy speech explaining recent press allegations of bad behavior among MPs. He, too, urges Maddie to forget the locales of their meetings, some of them the same places she has met Cocklebury-Smythe.

Chamberlain, another of the lecherous MPs on the committee. Although he has a wife and family in Dorking, he still writes Maddie a note instructing her to forget more restaurants.

Withenshaw, the chairman of the committee. He is from Lancaster, as his speech sometimes betrays. He may be the author of the original draft of the resolution, a cliché-ridden document that says nothing and that is rapidly being revised in several directions by the committee members.

French, the stickler for detail on the committee. He is the member who moves to scrap Withenshaw's resolution in favor of Maddie's.

New-Found-Land, 1976

Arthur, a junior Home Office official. He and Bernard are making a preliminary review of an American's application for British citizenship. His attempt to tell Bernard about the United States becomes a heroic monologue in which he catalogs every cliché about American life as he surveys the American landscape from Long Island to California.

Bernard, a very senior (and very deaf) Home Office official. He tells Arthur a long story about how he once won a five-pound note from Lloyd George, but he sleeps through Arthur's monologue.

— *Ann Davison Garbett*

DISAPPEARING ACTS

Author: Terry McMillan (1951-   )
First published: 1989
Genre: Novel
Locale: Brooklyn, New York
Time: 1982
Plot: Domestic realism

Zora Banks, the protagonist and one of the narrators, an independent teacher and talented singer who describes herself as a strong, smart, sexy, and good-hearted black woman. She has had experience with the destabilizing effects of heterosexual love and is wary of inviting another man into her life, but when she meets Franklin, she again sees an opportunity for happiness in a monogamous relationship. She enters into a romance defined by conflict, in which her autonomy is jeopardized continually by Franklin's dominance. She becomes pregnant and gives birth to a son at Franklin's urging, only to face escalating emotional and physical abuse. To a certain extent, she reclaims her independence and makes plans to return to her father's home in Ohio with her baby, but when Franklin shows up again, she is clearly attracted and, hence, vulnerable to him even as the novel concludes. Zora is a developed character, rounded and complex. She faces the very real dilemma of wanting a loving marriage and family while not being sure of how much she must or should give up of her own autonomy and self-respect in order to secure that illusive ideal.

Franklin Swift, the other narrator, a handsome, intelligent, married high school dropout who works sporadically as a construction worker and drinks heavily. He has goals of getting a college education and owning his own business. Often out of work because of racial discrimination, he feels helpless because he can not contribute money to the life he shares with Zora. He wants her to have their baby, perhaps because it will bolster his faltering sense of masculinity, which is being destroyed in the workplace. Deprived of all socially acceptable ways to feel "in charge" of himself and his family, Franklin resorts to physical strength, the only kind of power he still has, rapes Zora, and wrecks her apartment before leaving her. He returns months later, clearly faring better. Although their sexual passion is reignited, he states bluntly that he is not back to stay. It is difficult to sympathize with Franklin, even with an understanding of the cultural conditions that have made him such a bitter man. He falls too completely into a villainous role. Zora's enduring attraction to him becomes frustratingly inexplicable, though not unrealistic.

Jeremiah, Zora and Franklin's son. Zora must take complete responsibility for the baby even though she had been hesitant about having it.

Portia, an outspoken member of Zora's close network of girlfriends. She also becomes pregnant by a married man, Arthur. Unlike Franklin, Arthur gets a divorce in order to marry Portia. Zora's girlfriends are an important support group for Zora, and her loyalty to them is a constant source of jealous irritation for Franklin.

— *Janet Mason Ellerby*

THE DISCIPLE
(Le Disciple)

Author: Paul Bourget (1852-1935)
First published: 1889
Genre: Novel
Locale: Paris and Riom
Time: Late nineteenth century
Plot: Psychological realism

Adrien Sixte (ah-DRYEHN seekst), a brilliant philosopher, teacher, and writer who develops a deterministic theory that each effect comes from a cause, and that if all causes are known, results can be predicted accurately in all forms of human activity. The strict regularity of his life is interrupted by Robert's arrest, and his reading of Robert's confessional manuscript makes him feel morally responsible for Robert's acts. Again, at Robert's funeral, Adrien feels a moral guilt in the death of his disciple.

Robert Greslou (grehs-LEW), his disciple, a precocious student of philosophy who tests his master's theory by seducing Charlotte after providing causes that produce the result he wishes to achieve. Pretending to enter a suicide pact, he spends a night with her, then repudiates the pact and leaves. Arrested on suspicion of murder, he is willing to die to keep Charlotte's suicide a secret, but he is acquitted after André's testimony. As they reach the street after the trial, André shoots Robert in the head.

M. de Jussat (zhew-SAH), a hypochondriac and a boorish nobleman.

Charlotte, his beautiful young daughter who, suffering from discovery of Robert's duplicity, drinks strychnine after writing a suicide note to André.

André, her older brother, an army officer fond of hunting and riding. Influenced by Adrien to free Robert from the murder charge, he then avenges his sister's seduction and death.

Lucien (lew-SYAHN), Charlotte's younger brother, a fat, simple boy of thirteen who is tutored by Robert.

THE DISPOSSESSED: An Ambiguous Utopia

Author: Ursula K. Le Guin (1929-   )
First published: 1974
Genre: Novel
Locale: The planet Urras and its moon Anarres
Time: Distant future
Plot: Science fiction

Shevek, a physicist who studies time. Tall, lean, and long-haired, Shevek is a citizen of Anarres, a world populated seven generations earlier by the followers of Odo, a woman who developed and organized a syndicalist anarchist movement. Shevek, as a genius in a society that has become increasingly conformist to a collective will, has difficulty pursuing and publishing his work, a General Temporal Theory that promises to open possibilities for faster-than-light communication and travel. Against the objections of his society, he travels to the sister planet of Urras, from which the Odonians emigrated, hoping to find there the freedom to present his discoveries. On Urras, however, major discoveries become military secrets to be used to acquire and hold national power. He finally evades the restrictions of both planets by broadcasting his discovery to all the known worlds, making possible instantaneous communication between distant planets. He is nearing the age of forty when he returns to Anarres.

Takver, a fish geneticist. She is tall, dark, intelligent, and not very pretty. Marriage does not exist on Anarres, but she becomes Shevek's permanent sexual partner. Although their work and the social needs of Anarres often separate them, they have children and support each other in their careers. She encourages him to compromise with the conservative scientific establishment to have his works published off-planet. Later, she helps him form a group to support the sharing of knowledge with other worlds.

Vea, a wealthy and attractive socialite on Urras. In private visits with her, Shevek learns to understand the spiritual inner workings of Urras society, especially with regard to the relations between the sexes and the psychological and social effects of the private accumulation of power and wealth.

Rulag, an engineer. Although Shevek rarely sees her, Rulag is his mother. When he proposes opening communication with and then traveling to Urras, from which Odonians have separated themselves as if from a source of infection, she becomes the leader of his political opposition.

Sabul, a physicist. He dominates the practice of physics on Anarres, even though it is supposed to be controlled by a syndicate of all physicists. Playing on fear of "infection" by anti-Odonian thought, he achieves power and status by regulating scientific communication between Anarres and Urras. When Shevek produces a major treatise on time, he must publish it off-world under his and Sabul's names.

Dr. Atro, a Urras physicist. The aged Atro, the founder of modern physics, recognizes the importance of Shevek's work and invites him to Urras. Shevek finds him to be a genial old genius but caught up in nationalist, propertarian, and sexist attitudes that restrict the freedom of his thought.

Efor, Shevek's servant in his Urras quarters. By observing Efor, Shevek learns about attitudes of the working classes. Efor eventually provides the contacts that put Shevek in touch with revolutionary forces on Urras and that take him to the Earth embassy from which he broadcasts his theory.

— *Terry Heller*

DISTANT RELATIONS
(Una familia lejana)

Author: Carlos Fuentes (1928-   )
First published: 1980
Genre: Novel
Locale: Paris, Mexico, and the Caribbean
Time: Early 1980's
Plot: Occult

The Comte de Branly, a wealthy French aristocrat whose primary interest is foreign travel. At the age of eighty-three, this highly intelligent, cultured man is emaciated and nearly bald but still retains a rigid military bearing. Most of this complex novel of parallel lives and reincarnations concerns the Comte's surrealistic adventure in a strange mansion outside Paris where he is confined as the result of an auto accident. Because of his advanced age, however, it is probable that much of what he believes to have occurred was in fact hallucinations. Although he is the viewpoint character, he is the passive victim of circumstances throughout the novel.

The narrator, a Latin American author who has taken France as his adopted country. Only at the end is it revealed that this character is **Carlos Fuentes** himself. Characteristically, Fuentes has chosen a complex manner of telling his tale: The narrator supposedly is writing out an account of incidents described to him by his friend Branly, and parts of what Branly tells him were narrated to the Comte himself by others. By this device, the author is able to maintain a distance from the events described and is therefore not committed to vouching for them. This complex method of developing the story creates a multidimensional, hallucinatory effect. Readers are forced to make their own interpretations and thus become involved as active participants in the events.

The Mexican Victor Heredia, (heh-reh-DEE-ah)a twelve-year-old upper-class Mexican student. This handsome and aristocratic youth has been badly spoiled by a doting father. Victor displays outbursts of a violent temper, beating domestic servants when they displease him and, in one crucial instance, deliberately slamming the door of Branly's Citroën on the chauffeur's hand. When Branly tries to drive the car himself, he runs into a tree and is confined to bed as an involuntary guest of the French Victor Heredia. The young Mexican Victor Heredia is the catalyst of most of what happens in the novel.

The French Victor Heredia, a wealthy businessman with social pretensions who proves to be vulgar and sadistic, in striking contrast to the truly aristocratic Branly. The French Victor Heredia is old but has a youngish face, suggesting an immortal nature like that of a vampire. The young Mexican Victor Heredia, who frequently travels with his father, plays a game of looking in foreign telephone directories to see if anyone is listed with the same name as himself or his father. If he finds such persons, he telephones them and tries to strike up an acquaintance. In this manner, he drags his host, the Comte de Branly, into their strange encounter with the satanic French Victor Heredia, who takes advantage of the fact that the Comte is confined to bed under his roof to play cruel psychological tricks on him. In the meantime, an unwholesome relationship develops between the Mexican Victor Heredia and André Heredia.

André Heredia, the son of the French Victor Heredia, a boy about the same age as young Victor. Like his father, André is cruel and overbearing, the product of inferior breeding. At one point, Branly catches the French boy sodomizing the Mexican boy in the backseat of the wrecked Citroën. After this unnatural copulation, the two boys somehow merge into a single new supernatural individual, evidently symbolizing a merging of French and Latin American cultures. The Mexican Victor Heredia disappears for the rest of the story. The reader is left to wonder whether this truly occurred or is attributable to Branly's senility, the trauma of the auto accident, or his host's mistreatment.

Hugo Heredia, a Mexican archaeologist, father of the Mexican Victor Heredia. This dignified scholar's decision to visit France with his son leads to all the shocking events that occur. Hugo is absent throughout most of the story, leaving his son in the care of the Comte de Branly. When his son vanishes, however, having merged identities with André Heredia, the father reacts in a strange manner that makes the reader believe he was in enforced collusion with the French Victor Heredia and anticipated what was going to happen.

— *Bill Delaney*

THE DIVINE COMEDY
(La divina commedia)

Author: Dante Alighieri (1265-1321)
First transcribed: c. 1320
Genre: Poetry

Locale: Hell, Purgatory, and Paradise
Time: The Friday before Easter, 1300
Plot: Allegory

Dante (DAHN-tay), the exile Florentine poet, who is halted in his path of error through the grace of the Virgin, Saint Lucy, and Beatrice, and is redeemed by his journey through Hell, Purgatory, and Paradise. He learns to submerge his instinctive pity for some sinners in his recognition of the justice of God, and he frees himself of the faults of wrath and misdirected love by participating in the penance for these sins in Purgatory. He is then ready to grow in understanding and love as he moves with Beatrice nearer to the presence of God.

Beatrice (beh-ah-TREE-cheh), his beloved, who is transformed into an angel, one of Mary's handmaids. Through her intercession, her compassion, and her teaching, Dante's passion is transmuted into divine love, which brings him to a state of indescribable blessedness.

Virgil, Dante's master, the great Roman poet who guides him through Hell and Purgatory. The most favored of the noble pagans who dwell in Limbo without hope of heavenly bliss, he represents the highest achievements of human reason and classical learning.

Saint Lucy, Dante's patron saint. She sends him aid and conveys him through a part of Purgatory.

Charon (KAY-ron), traditionally the ferryman of damned souls.

Minos (mee-nohs), the monstrous judge who dooms sinners to their allotted torments.

Paolo (pah-OH-loh) and

Francesca (frahn-CHEH-skah), devoted lovers, murdered by Paolo's brother, who was Francesca's husband. Together even in hell, they arouse Dante's pity with their tale of growing affection.

Ciacco (CHEE-ahk-koh), a Florentine damned for gluttony, who prophesies the civil disputes that engulfed his native city after his death.

Plutus, the bloated, clucking creature who guards the entrance of the fourth circle of Hell.

Phlegyas (FLEHJ-ee-as), the boatman of the wrathful.

Filippo Argenti (fee-LEEP-poh ahr-JEHN-tee), another Florentine noble, damned to welter in mud for his uncontrollable temper.

Megaera (MEHG-ah-rah),

Alecto (ah-LEHK-toh), and

Tisiphone (tih-SIF-oh-nee), the Furies, tower warders of the City of Dis.

Farinata Degli Uberti (fah-ree-NAH-tah deh-ylee ew-BEHR-tee), the leader of the Ghibelline party of Florence, condemned to rest in an indestructible sepulchre for his heresy. He remains concerned primarily for the fate of his city.

Cavalcante (kah-vahl-KAHN-tay), a Guelph leader, the father of Dante's friend Guido. He rises from his tomb to ask about his son.

Nessus (NEHS-uhs),

Chiron (KI-ron), and

Pholus (FOH-luhs), the courteous archer centaurs who guard the river of boiling blood that holds the violent against men.

Piero Delle Vigne (pee-EH-roh dehl-leh VEEN-nay), the loyal adviser to Emperor Frederick, imprisoned, with others who committed suicide, in a thornbush.

Capaneus (kah-PAH-neh-ews), a proud, blasphemous tyrant, one of the Seven against Thebes.

Brunetto Latini (brew-NEHT-toh lah-TEE-nee), Dante's old teacher, whom the poet treats with great respect; he laments the sin of sodomy that placed him deep in Hell.

Guido Guerra (GWEE-doh gew-EHR-rah),

Tegghiaio Aldobrandi (teeg-GEE-ah-ee-oh ahl-doh-BRAHN-dee),

Jacopo Rusticucci (YAHK-oh-poh rews-tee-KEW-chee), and

Guglielmo Borsiere (gew-glee-EHL-moh bohr-SEE-ehr-ay), Florentine citizens who gave in to unnatural lust.

Geryon (JEE-ree-on), a beast with a human face and a scorpion's tail, symbolic of fraud.

Venedico Caccianemico (veh-neh-DEE-koh kah-CHEE-ah-neh-MEE-koh), a Bolognese pander.

Jason, a classical hero, damned as a seducer.

Alessio Interminei (ah-LEHS-syoh een-tehr-mee-neh-ee), a flatterer.

Nicholas III, one of the popes, damned to burn in a rocky cave for using the resources of the church for worldly advancement.

Amphiaraus (ahm-fee-AHR-ah-ews),

Tiresias (tee-reh-SEE-ahs),

Aruns (AH-rewnz),

Manto,

Eurypylus (ew-RIHP-ih-luhs),

Michael Scot, and

Guido Bonatti (boh-NAHT-tee), astrologers and diviners whose grotesquely twisted shapes reflect their distortion of divine counsel.

Malacoda (mah-lah-KOH-dah), the chief of the devils who torment corrupt political officials.

Ciampolo (chee-ahm-POH-loh), one of his charges, who converses with Dante and Virgil while he plans to outwit the devils.

Catalano (kah-tah-LAH-noh) and

Loderingo (loh-deh-REEN-goh), jovial Bolognese friars who wear the gilded leaden mantles decreed eternally for hypocrites.

Caiphas (KAH-ee-fahs), the high priest who had Christ condemned. He lies naked in the path of the heavily laden hypocrites.

Vanni Fucci (VAHN-nee FEW-chee), a bestial, wrathful thief, the damned spirit most arrogant against God.

Agnello,

Francisco,

Cianfa (CHEE-ahn-fah),

Buoso (bew-OH-soh), and

Puccio (pew-CHEE-oh), malicious thieves and oppressors who are metamorphosed from men to serpents, then from serpents to men, before the eyes of the poet.

Ulysses (y-lihs-ees) and

Diomed (DEE-oh-mehd), Greek heroes transformed into tongues of flame as types of the evil counselor. Ulysses retains the splendid passion for knowledge that led him beyond the limits set for men.

Guido de Montefeltro, another of the evil counselors, who became involved in the fraud and sacrilege of Pope Boniface.

Mahomet,

Piero da Medicina (pee-EH-roh dah meh-dee-CHEE-nah), and

Bertran de Born, sowers of schism and discord whose bodies are cleft and mutilated.

Capocchio (kah-POH-chee-oh) and

Griffolino (gree-foh-LEE-noh), alchemists afflicted with leprosy.

Gianni Schicchi (jee-AHN-nee shee-chee) and

Myrrha, sinners who disguised themselves because of lust and greed, fittingly transformed into swine.

Master Adam, a counterfeiter.

Sinon and

Potiphar's wife, damned for malicious lying and treachery.

Nimrod,

Antaeus (AN-taeh-ews), and

Briareus (BRI-ahr-eh-ews), giants who rebelled against God.

Camincion de' Pazzi (kah-meen-CHEE-ohn deh PAHZ-zee),

Count Ugolino (ew-goh-LEE-noh),

Fra Alberigo (ahl-behr-EE-goh),

Judas Iscariot (JEW-dahs ees-KAH-ree-oht),

Brutus, and

Cassius (KAHS-see-uhs), traitors to family, country, and their masters. They dwell forever in ice, hard and cold as their own hearts.

Cato (KAH-toh), the aged Roman sage who was, for the Middle Ages, a symbol of pagan virtue. He meets Dante and Virgil at the base of Mount Purgatory and sends them on their way upward.

Casella (kah-SEHL-lah), a Florentine composer who charms his hearers with a song as they enter Purgatory.

Manfred, a Ghibelline leader,

Belacqua (beh-LAHK-wah),

La Pia (PEE-ah),

Cassero (kahs-SEH-roh), and

Buonconte da Montefeltro (BWON-kon-teh dah mohn-teh-FELH-troh), souls who must wait many years at the foot of

Mount Purgatory because they delayed their repentance until the time of their death.

Sordello, the Mantuan poet, who reverently greets Virgil and accompanies him and his companion for part of their journey.

Nino Visconti and

Conrad Malaspina (mah-lah-SPEE-nah), men too preoccupied with their political life to repent early.

Omberto Aldobrandesco (ohm-BEHR-toh ahl-doh-brahn-DEHS-koh),

Oderisi (oh-deh-REE-see), and

Provenzan Salvani (sahl-VAH-nee), sinners who walk twisted and bent over in penance for their pride in ancestry, artistry, and power.

Sapia (sah-PEE-ah), one of the envious, a woman who rejoiced at the defeat of her townspeople.

Guido del Duca (DEW-kah), another doing penance for envy. He laments the dissensions tearing apart the Italian states.

Marco Lombardo, Dante's companion through the smoky way trodden by the wrathful.

Pope Adrian, one of those being purged of avarice.

Hugh Capet (ka-PAY), the founder of the French ruling dynasty, which he castigates for its crimes and brutality. He atones for his own ambition and greed.

Statius (STA-tih-uhs), the author of *The Thebaid*. One of Virgil's disciples, he has just completed his penance for prodigality. He tells Dante and Virgil of the liberation of the truly repentant soul.

Forese Donati (foh-RAY-seh doh-NAH-tee), Dante's friend, and

Bonagiunta (boh-nah-gee-EWN-tah), Florentines guilty of gluttony.

Guido Guinicelli (gwee-nee-CHEHL-lee) and

Arnaut (ahr-NOH), love poets who submit to the flames that purify them of lust.

Matilda, a heavenly lady who meets Dante in the earthly paradise at the top of Mount Purgatory and takes him to Beatrice.

Piccarda (peek-KAHR-dah), a Florentine nun, a fragile, almost transparent spirit who dwells in the moon's sphere, the outermost circle of heaven, since her faith wavered, making her incapable of receiving greater bliss than this.

Justinian, the great Roman emperor and lawgiver, one of the champions of the Christian faith.

Charles Martel, the heir to Charles II, king of Naples, whose early death precipitated strife and injustice.

Cunizza (kew-NEEZ-zah), Sordello's mistress, the sister of an Italian tyrant.

Falco, a troubadour who was, after his conversion, made a bishop.

Rahab, the harlot who aided Joshua to enter Jerusalem, another of the many whose human passions were transformed into love of God.

Thomas Aquinas (ah-KWI-nahs), the Scholastic philosopher. He tells Dante of Saint Francis when he comes to the sphere of the sun, the home of those who have reached heaven through their knowledge of God.

Saint Bonaventura, his companion, who praises Saint Dominic.

Cacciagiuda (kah-CHEE-ah-jee-EW-dah), Dante's great-great-grandfather, placed in the sphere of Mars as a warrior for the church.

Peter Damian (DAY-mee-ahn), a hermit, an inhabitant of the sphere of Saturn, the place allotted to spirits blessed for their temperance and contemplative life.

Saint Peter,

Saint James, and

Saint John, representatives of the virtues of faith, hope, and love. The three great disciples examine the poet to ensure his understanding of these three qualities.

Adam, the prototype of fallen man, who is, through Christ, given the greatest redemption; he is the companion of the three apostles and sits enthroned at the left hand of the Virgin.

Saint Bernard, Dante's guide during the last stage of his journey, when he comes before the throne of the queen of Heaven.

THE DIVINE FIRE

Author: May Sinclair (1863-1946)
First published: 1904
Genre: Novel
Locale: England
Time: The 1890's
Plot: Psychological

Savage Keith Rickman, a young unknown poet, a genius, who for all his warring personality traits is always honorable. Disillusioned over dishonorable dealings between his bookseller father and a financier, and kept from success by the indecisiveness of a literary editor, he spends years slaving and starving himself to redeem what he considers a debt of honor. At last his genius is acknowledged, and success enables him to go to the woman for whom he has loved and slaved.

Horace Jewdwine, the literary editor who believes he has discovered a genius but who fears to jeopardize his reputation by proclaiming it. He encourages Rickman privately, but fails him in every important matter and finally loses the credit for his "discovery."

Lucia Harden, a baronet's daughter, Jewdwine's cousin and Rickman's inspiration. Rickman's aim in life is to redeem and to return to Lucia her father's library, of which his own father cheated her and then lost to an unscrupulous financier. When she finally receives Rickman's gift, Lucia is ill and unable to walk. However, realizing that her malady is only heartbreak, she recovers.

Mr. Pilkington, an unethical financier. He holds the Harden library mortgage and enjoys the spectacle of the young genius' apparently doomed struggle to redeem it.

Flossie Walker, a conventional young woman and Rickman's fellow boarder. Her goal is a house in the suburbs, and with this in mind she traps Rickman into a proposal of marriage. Yet she refuses to wait the years necessary for the paying off of his "debt of honor"; to his relief, she marries another.

THE DIVINERS

Author: Margaret Laurence (1926-1987)
First published: 1974
Genre: Novel
Locale: Manawaka, Toronto, and Vancouver, Canada
Time: 1930 to the 1970's
Plot: Bildungsroman

Morag Gunn, the protagonist, a forty-seven-year-old novelist writing the novel containing her story. As she looks back over her life, she believes that her artistic talent always was evident. After her parents died of poliomyelitis, she was reared by Christie Logan in a poor part of town where Métis (half-breeds), like her first lover, Jules, also lived. She grew up listening to Christie haranguing about the muck of life in the past and present. Christie thought he was creating pride and identity in Morag by telling her stories about her family, the Gunns, coming from Scotland to Manitoba. Morag also wrote her own stories, which she later reworked to create stories of family history for her daughter, Pique. Writing for local, college, and Vancouver newspapers enlarges Morag's sensitivities about the Métis, the Gersons, and others. Her passion leads to an out-of-wedlock pregnancy, however, just as her spirit of independence leads her to leave her husband.

Jules "Skinner" Tonnerre, Morag's first lover. While Morag was still in her teens, Jules seduced her in his father's shack. He told Morag tales of the Métis view of encounters with Scottish emigrants, such as his grandfather who fought with Riel at Batoche and lost.

Pique Gunn Tonnerre, Morag and Jules's daughter. In a London school, she does not experience prejudice like she does as a teenager in the high school in the small Ontario town of McConnell's Landing. She stands up to her boyfriend, Dan, who expects her to work as a cashier while he spends their money to raise horses. With her father's and her own songs, she sets off again for Manawaka and Galloping Mountain, alone this time, to find her own identity from her roots. Some peace comes from her decisions and actions to express the views she embodies.

Brooke Skelton, Morag's husband, a professor of English in Winnipeg. He woos her in her senior year to satisfy his sexual needs and enhance his professional career: After they move to Toronto, he becomes chairman of the department. He has difficulty expressing his feelings. Reared in India by an omah who was dismissed when found in his bed, he grew up stoic like his British mother and father. His obsession with controlling Morag leads to her departure.

Dan McRaith, a Scottish painter in his mid-forties who becomes Morag's lover after they meet in a bookshop in London. Each inspires the artistic endeavors of the other. Morag visits Scotland, where his wife and seven children live in Crombruach, near Culloden. Once in Scotland, Morag realizes that the physical place is not as real or as important as what Christie had built in her heart with tales of Piper Gunn and his people coming from there. Dan and Morag correspond for years.

Christie Logan, a garbage collector ("scavenger") in Manawaka and Morag's foster father. Although his appearance and lack of education alienate Morag, eventually she realizes that he inspired her with stories of Piper Gunn leading Highlanders in Scotland and Canada and with tales of World War I. Always ranting, he divines the character of townspeople according to their garbage. He advises her to get out of Manawaka and go to college, using the money from the sale of her parents' farm. He is pleased when she returns to Prin's deathbed and, later, his.

Prin Logan, Christie's lethargic, fat wife and kind foster mother to Morag. Prin (short for "Princess") dresses Morag in clothes from the Nuisance Grounds until Morag, working at Ludlow's in her teens, learns to dress smartly.

Royland, a diviner of water at McConnell's Landing. Previously a preacher, he abused his wife, who ran away and drowned herself. His gift of divining water finally leaves him.

— *Greta McCormick Coger*

DO WITH ME WHAT YOU WILL

Author: Joyce Carol Oates (1938-   )
First published: 1973
Genre: Novel
Locale: Primarily Detroit, Michigan
Time: The 1960's and 1970's
Plot: Social realism

Elena Ross Howe, the protagonist. Abused as a child by a neglectful father and an uncaring mother, Elena becomes passive, pliant, and malleable to the wills of others. She is an undefined, shadowy figure without her own identity until, at the end of the novel, she is strengthened by redemptive love. Elena is beautiful, blond, and statuesque, but she uses her beauty to mask the nothingness behind it. Elena occasionally narrates the novel as fragments of her thoughts or projected conversations slip into the story.

Jack Morrissey, Elena's lover. Jack is an attorney who is more intrigued by the power and the media attention he can garner from the profession of law than he is in serving justice. Although married to Rachel, he becomes enamored of Elena, maintains a long-term affair with her, and serves as the vehicle for her emancipation.

Marvin Howe, Elena's husband. A high-powered attorney with implied underworld connections, Marvin is the catalyst for much of the action in the story. When Jack is a child, Marvin defends his father against a murder charge and initiates Jack's interest in the law. He also "rescues" Elena from her materialistic mother, but in the process he imprisons her. He is interested in acquisition and ownership of things and people.

Ardis Howe/Marya Sharp, Elena's mother. Ardis is self-serving, controlling, vain, and manipulative. She is a shape-shifter, changing her name and her physical appearance several times throughout the novel. Once she has placed Elena into Marvin Howe's wealthy, successful hands, she ignores her daughter and pretends she does not exist.

Leo Ross, Elena's father. A peripheral figure, Leo is featured at the outset of the story when, crushed by his divorce from Ardis, he kidnaps Elena and forces her to go across country with him in the name of "love." During their flight, he forces Elena to hide out, dye her hair black, and go without food, traumatizing the child in the process. Leo disappears until the end of the novel, when he is shown homeless, embittered, and still potentially dangerous.

Meredith (Mered) Dawe, Elena's spiritual guide. A lecturer on passive resistance and universal love, Mered becomes a spiritual guide for Elena, giving her impetus to define herself and break free. He is also a pivotal figure for Jack, indirectly showing him the imperfections of the law.

Rachel Morrissey, Jack's wife. A political and human rights activist, Rachel is the only character in the work who is purely unselfish; consequently, she is rejected and abandoned by her husband.

— *Joyce Duncan*

DOCTOR COPERNICUS

Author: John Banville (1945-   )
First published: 1976
Genre: Novel

Locale: Ermland, Prussia, and Italy
Time: 1473-1543
Plot: Historical

Nicolas Koppernigk (KOH-pehr-nihk), known as **Copernicus** (kuh-PUHR-nih-kuhs), the central character, son of a provincial merchant in the Ermland province of late medieval Prussia. He becomes a canon, a scholar, and an astronomer, ultimately revolutionizing the central concepts of astronomy and cosmology. After losing his mother at an early age and his father before he is ten years old, Nicolas is reared by his Uncle Lucas, a bishop, who has him educated in the church for the ecclesiastical life. Phenomenally quick at his studies, Nicolas is less adept socially, as he is shy, retiring, retreating before bullies, and uncomfortable with the physical. Perhaps because of his nature, he gives himself easily to the intellectual world, particularly to geography and astronomy, the mathematical triumphs of the period. He develops a fierce allegiance to truth as mathematically demonstrated. Because of this mathematical orientation, he begins to formulate the principles of a scientific method; recognizing that this will threaten philosophical and theological orthodoxy, however, he temporizes. His entire life is a struggle between the abstract to which he is drawn and the concrete that is forced on him. Thus, he repeatedly discovers that what life offers is not what he wants. The church offers security and membership in an elite class; the university offers academic prestige and membership in another elite class. During his episode in Italy, his fellow intellectuals offer love, both in fellowship and physically. Each appeals to different aspects of his personality. Each also requires, however, both accepting the status quo and abandoning his eccentric theories, that is, his unorthodox pursuit of the truth. This conflict leads him to delay publication of his masterwork, *De revolutionibus*, until he is on his deathbed.

Andreas Koppernigk, Nicolas' older brother, a playboy and a sensualist. As frivolous as Nicolas is single-minded and serious, Andreas addresses himself solely to the sport of living. As a boy at school, he constantly torments and teases his master; later, at the university and after, he pursues only pleasure. As a result, he suffers the physical consequences of such a course in that period of primitive medicine: His body deteriorates rapidly. His suicidal lack of self-control and restraint is his chief characteristic and leads him to paradoxical extremes. For example, he is at times the chief advocate and exponent of Nicolas' radical ideas; at others, he embarrasses, drains, and burdens Nicolas by demanding money for support (and further extravagance). He is the indulgent counterpart to the asceticism of Nicolas, and the two share a common fatalism. Andreas becomes one of the early victims of the syphilis epidemic of the late fourteenth and early fifteenth centuries and literally rots to death.

George Joachim von Lauchen (yo-AH-khihm fon LOW-khehn), called **Rheticus**, a Lutheran neo-Ptolemaic astronomer and assistant to Nicolas. A flamboyant publicist rather than a true scientist, Rheticus attempts to pressure Nicolas into publishing his book; however, his motives are hardly above reproach. His real object is to make his own reputation out of refuting the Copernican theory once it is published. He also contributes to the public discredit of Nicolas by seducing one of the boy-wards of the chapter. Because he resides for a time in Nicolas' house, however, he is able to challenge the accusation that Nicolas' housekeeper actually is his mistress. Rheticus does publish two preliminary summaries of the Copernican theories.

Lucas Waczelrodt (VAK-tsehl-roht), the bishop of Ermland, Nicolas' maternal uncle. After the early death of Nicolas' parents, Bishop Waczelrodt adopts and educates Nicolas and Andreas. He arranges for both to become canons of his chapter, or minor clergy assigned to his cathedral, and he sends both to the university in Cracow and later to represent the chapter in Rome. Eventually, he appoints Nicolas as court physician at Heilsberg. Externally a blunt, abrupt, unsympathetic man concerned only with his administrative image, the bishop does care for and protect his wards, though he is quite ready to have Andreas killed when he becomes an embarrassment by his excesses.

Tiedeman Giese (TEE-deh-mahn GEE-seh), a fellow canon with Nicolas, later his visitator, or supervisor, and successor to Waczelrodt as bishop. A friend and admirer of Nicolas, Giese attempts to shelter him from the attacks of those who find his theories blasphemous and dangerous and are willing to seize on any pretext to humiliate and silence him.

Johannes Flachsbinder (FLAKS-bihn-dehr), called **Danticus**, the bishop of Kulm (at Löbau), Nicolas' nominal superior in his later years. Concerned like most ecclesiastics with appearances of propriety, he is rigid about cases of apparent scandal. Thus, he keeps putting pressure on Giese and Nicolas to remove any traces of impropriety from their jurisdictions.

He seems to be doing little more than using the administrative tactic of keeping on the pressure.

Girolamo Fracastoro (jee-roh-LAH-moh frah-kah-STOH-roh), a poet and member of the group of avant-garde intellectuals and revolutionary thinkers in Ferrara. Languorous, charming, and arrogant, Girolamo fascinates the young Nicolas and attempts to entice him into the intellectual elite. When Nicolas learns that Girolamo actually is wealthy and that his support of new ideas is a glamorous pose, he loses faith in intellectuals.

Anna Schillings, Nicolas' cousin and eventually his housekeeper. Abandoned by her husband and left with two children during the military upheavals of the time, she throws herself on Nicolas' mercy as her final resort. He gives in, reluctantly, and for the remaining years of his life she lives with him as his housekeeper, providing a source for the rumors that were used to discredit him.

Domenico Maria de Novara (doh-MEHN-ee-koh mah-REE-ah deh noh-VAH-rah), an astronomer, advocate of the new learning of the Renaissance, Neoplatonist mystic, and leader of the intellectual elite. Nicolas is at first dazzled by the apparent depth of his learning and his devotion to revolutionary causes but then discovers that both are closer to rhetorical and verbal manipulation than to rational analysis and demonstration.

— *James L. Livingston*

DOCTOR FAUSTUS: The Life of the German Composer Adrian Leverkühn as Told by a Friend
(Doktor Faustus: Das Leben des deutschen Tonsetzers Adrian Leverkühn, erzäht erzählt von einem Freunde)

Author: Thomas Mann (1875-1955)
First published: 1947
Genre: Novel
Locale: Germany
Time: 1885-1945
Plot: Philosophical

Adrian Leverkühn (LEH-vehr-kewn), or **Adri**, a gifted musical composer who is convinced that he has entered into a twenty-four-year compact with Satan in which he has pledged his soul for an extended period of creativity. Like his Faustian predecessor in legend, he masters various academic goals while studying at Kaiseraschern, Halle, and Leipzig. At first he intends to become a student of theology, but while at Halle he deserts this field as arid and unchallenging. As a composer, he is influenced greatly by the technique of Arnold Schönberg. His most significant works are "Apocalypsis cum figuris" and the monumental "The Lamentation of Dr. Faustus," for both of which he feels he has received unearthly inspiration at the expense of his salvation. Affable and spirited in his early years, he becomes literally and emotionally darker and more reclusive as his obsession intensifies. At the conclusion of the twenty-four years, in which time he has become internationally respected for his genius, he calls his friends to him and in anguish describes the imminent payment he must make of his soul. As he strikes the opening chords of "The Lamentation of Dr. Faustus," he suddenly collapses over the keyboard, a victim of a paralytic stroke from which he never recovers in either mind or body. The novel, narrated by Leverkühn's warmest and most sympathetic friend, Serenus Zeitblom, is presented as the biography of this afflicted genius.

Serenus Zeitblom (zeh-REH-news TSIT-blohm), or **Seren**, a doctor of philosophy, the narrator of the novel. A retired professor of classical languages, sixty years of age at the time he is writing, he describes the creative life and the hideous transformation of Leverkühn, whom he has known since childhood and with whom he studied at Halle and Leipzig. Through Zeitblom, Mann creates a double chronology that achieves a rich, symbolic pattern. While the professor describes the life and death of his friend in a symbolic form that shows evil meeting its inevitable reward in chaos and destruction, he constantly refers to the current global struggle motivated by Adolf Hitler and his fanatic dreams for the German Fatherland. The description of Leverkühn's destruction (1930) prefigures the collapse of the perverted Nazi power (1945); hence, the symbolic motif is present in both an individual and national pattern.

Wendell Kretschmar (VEHN-dehl KREHT-shmahr), a cathedral organist who is Leverkühn's first music teacher. A short, bullet-headed man with a clipped mustache, he is prone to stuttering. He gains over his student an uncanny power, which he exercises throughout his life. He directs Leverkühn for several years and introduces him to new concepts of scale and harmony. Largely responsible for Leverkühn's decision to devote his life to music rather than to theology, Kretschmar is Mann's symbolic Mephistopheles.

Rüdiger Schildknapp (REW-dih-gehr SHIHLD-knap), a frequent companion of Leverkühn, an author who is forced by necessity to perform the hack work of translation. Having inherited his father's anguish of unfulfilled ambition, he is a parasitic admirer of Leverkühn's creative genius.

Rudolf Schwerdtfeger (SHVEHRT-feh-gehr), a gifted young violinist, a member of the Zapfenstosser Orchestra. He persuades Leverkühn to compose a violin sonata for him.

Sammael (SAM-mah-ehl), the name that Satan assumes when he visits Leverkühn and discusses the terms of the twenty-four-year agreement. He also is known as or **Dicis et non Facis**.

Nepomuk (NEH-poh-muhk), also called **Nepo** (NEH-poh) and **Echo**, Leverkühn's young nephew, who brings new joy and hope into his uncle's life as the contract nears its fulfillment. When the young man is fatally stricken with meningitis, Leverkühn is convinced that Satan is ruthlessly destroying his last hope and joy.

Inez Rodde Institoris (ih-NEHZ ROH-deh ihn-stih-TOH-rihs), a woman who, although married, can find satisfaction only in an adulterous relationship with Rudolf Schwerdtfeger. When he tires of her love, she shoots him.

Clarissa Rodde, an aspiring actress who commits suicide rather than face the truth concerning her lack of talent.

Jonathan Leverkühn (LAY-vur-kewn) and

Elsbeth Leverkühn, Adrian's parents living in Kaiseraschern. Jonathan, an apothecary by trade, possesses a passion to investigate the mysteries of nature, even at the expense of negating various religious beliefs of his society.

Max Scheigestill (SHI-geh-shtihl) and

Else Scheigestill, the owners of the home in which Leverkühn lives in Pfeiffering during much of his adult life.

Ehrenfried Kumpf (AY-rehn-freed kewmpf) and

Eberhard Schleppfus (AY-behr-hahrt SHLEHP-fews), professors of theology, Leverkühn's teachers at the University of Halle.

Marie Godeau (goh-DOH), a beautiful woman loved by Leverkühn. Hesitant to woo her forthrightly, he entrusts the courtship to his friend, Schwerdtfeger. The violinist falls in love with her, however, and woos her for himself.

Madame de Tolna, a wealthy Hungarian widow, Leverkühn's benefactress.

Jeanette Scheurl (shoyrl), a novelist, a friend of Leverkühn.

Esmerelda, the prostitute from whom Leverkühn contracts a venereal infection.

DOCTOR FAUSTUS

Author: Christopher Marlowe (1564-1593)
First published: 1604
Genre: Drama
Locale: Germany
Time: The sixteenth century
Plot: Tragedy

Faustus (FOWS-tuhs), a learned scholar and theologian. Ambitious for boundless knowledge, he abandons the accepted professions for black magic and sells his soul for knowledge and power. Although haunted by remorse, he is unrepentant. After he gains power, his character deteriorates, and he adds cruelty to cowardice in asking tortures for an old man who tries to save his soul. He shows a final flash of nobility in sending his friends away before the expected arrival of the devils, and he delivers a poignant soliloquy while awaiting his death and damnation.

Mephistophilis (mehf-ih-STOF-ih-lihs), a tormented devil aware of the horror of being an outcast from the sight of God. He speaks frankly to Faustus before the signing of the bond; after that, he is not concerned with fair play, being sometimes tricky and sometimes savage. At the appointed time, he carries Faustus off to Hell.

Lucifer (LEW-sih-fur), the commander of the fallen spirits. Eager for human souls to join him in misery, he puts forth great efforts to keep Faustus from escaping by repentance.

Belzebub (BEHL-zee-buhb), the third evil spirit of the perverted trinity.

An Old Man, a godly elder concerned with saving Faustus' soul. Rejected by Faustus and made the physical prey of devils, he escapes them and rises to God by means of his great faith.

Alexander the Great,

Alexander's paramour, and

Helen of Troy, spirits raised by Mephistophilis and Faustus. The beauty of Helen, "the face that launched a thousand ships," further entangles Faustus in evil and confirms his damnation.

Valdes (VAHL-days) and

Cornelius, learned magicians to whom Faustus turns for counsel when he decides to engage in black magic.

Wagner, the comical and impudent servant of Faustus. He follows his master in conjuring and furnishes a ridiculous contrast to the tragic Faustus.

Three Scholars, friends of Faustus for whom he produces the apparition of Helen and to whom he makes his confession just before his death.

The Pope, a victim of Faustus' playful trickery.

The Cardinal of Lorrain, an attendant to the pope.

Charles V, the emperor of Germany. Faustus and Mephistophilis entertain him with magical tricks.

A Knight, a scornful skeptic whom Faustus abuses and infuriates by making stag horns grow on his head. He is restored to his normal state at the request of the emperor.

The Duke of Vanholt and

the Duchess of Vanholt, patrons of Faustus whom he gratefully entertains.

The Good Angel and

the Evil Angel, who contend for Faustus' soul, each urging him to choose his way of life.

Robin, an ostler, and

Ralph, a servingman, comical characters who find Faustus' books and raise Mephistophilis, to their great terror.

A Vintner, the victim of Robin's and Ralph's pranks.

A Horse Courser, a trader deceived and abused by Faustus.

A Clown, the gullible victim of Wagner's conjuring.

Baliol and

Belcher, evil spirits raised by Wagner to terrify the Clown.

Pride,

Covetousness,

Wrath,

Envy,

Gluttony,

Sloth, and

Lechery, the Seven Deadly Sins, who appear in a pageant for Faustus.

The Chorus, who serves as prologue, commentator, and epilogue to the play.

THE DOCTOR IN SPITE OF HIMSELF
(Le Médecin malgré lui)

Author: Molière (Jean-Baptiste Poquelin, 1622-1673)
First published: 1666
Genre: Drama
Locale: Paris, France
Time: The seventeenth century
Plot: Farce

Sganarelle (zgah-nah-REHL), a wood gatherer whose wife accuses him of drunkenness, gambling, and lechery. Although he admits that she is a good wife, he intends to be the boss of the household. Because he believes that beatings increase affection, he whips her. When he is mistaken for a doctor, through his wife's trickery to have him beaten in turn, he displays—though he has had no education beyond the lowest class in school—wit, quick thinking, and convincing inventiveness by his use of garbled Latin, jumbled anatomical terms, and quotations from Cicero and Hippocrates. Learning that his patient suffers dumbness only because of thwarted love, he prescribes a remedy known to make parrots talk, bread soaked in wine. He displays avarice when he gets what money he can from Géronte to cure his daughter, from Léandre to enable him to see Lucinde, and from Perrin to help his mother. At the happy ending to this farce, Sganarelle forgives his wife the beatings he has received, but he reminds her that she must hereafter show greater respect for him, for he is now a doctor and not a wood gatherer.

Martine (mahr-TEEN), Sganarelle's wife, who nags her husband about his drinking and gambling, and for selling their household possessions for these purposes. She seeks revenge for his frequent beatings by claiming that Sganarelle is an eccentric doctor who amuses himself by cutting wood and who must be beaten before he will admit to being a physician. After her husband has successfully cured his patient, she overtakes him just as he is about to be hanged for helping in an elopement. She decides to witness the hanging to give him courage. When he is not hanged after all, she demands thanks for making him a doctor.

Géronte (zhay-ROHNT), the father of a daughter who feigns loss of speech because he objects to her marriage to anyone other than the wealthy man he has chosen. A great quoter of maxims, he is deceived by Sganarelle's garbled Latin and anatomical jargon. When he learns that his daughter's lover has inherited his uncle's wealth, he finds virtue in the young man and gives the couple his blessing.

Lucinde (lew-SAHND), Géronte's daughter, who stubbornly refuses to marry any of her father's selected suitors and feigns illness and loss of speech. Her clever pretense allows her to elope with Léandre.

Léandre (lay-AHNDR), Lucinde's lover. Disguised as an apothecary working with the physician, he is able to elope with Lucinde. He soon returns to ask Géronte's permission for their marriage, a request readily granted when he tells of his inheritance from his uncle.

Valère (vah-LEHR), Géronte's simple, credulous servant, who tries to reason with Sganarelle before beating him as a means of making the wood gatherer admit that he is a doctor.

Lucas (lew-KAH), another servant to Géronte, the foster father of Valère and husband of Géronte's nurse. He is an ill-tempered man who jealously prevents Sganarelle from embracing and fondling his wife, Jacqueline.

Jacqueline (zhahk-LEEN), Lucas' wife and nurse to Lucinde. She is a sensible, realistic woman who sees that Lucinde is feigning an illness that love will cure.

M. Robert (roh-BEHR), Sganarelle's neighbor, a busybody who objects to wife-beating. He is forced to admit his meddling to avoid a similar drubbing.

Thibaut (tee-BOH), a peasant who, hearing of Sganarelle's fame as a physician, comes to the wood gatherer. Trying to tell about his wife's illness, he talks in garbled medical terms.

Perrin (pehr-RAHN), Thibaut's son.

DOCTOR PASCAL
(Le Docteur Pascal)

Author: Émile Zola (1840-1902)
First published: 1893
Genre: Novel

Locale: The south of France
Time: Late nineteenth century
Plot: Naturalism

Pascal Rougon (pahs-KAHL rew-GOHN), a dedicated and selfless doctor interested in heredity. Using experimental methods, he is, to his mother's dismay, using the members of his family as the field for his investigations. Feeling betrayed by the family's efforts to destroy his files, Dr. Pascal fails in health. He is temporarily restored by a love affair with Clotilde but later suffers a heart attack and dies, after which the records of his research are destroyed.

Clotilde (kloh-TEELD), Pascal Rougon's niece. Living in quiet happiness with Dr. Pascal and Martine, a growing religious conviction causes her to try to persuade Pascal to destroy his files on heredity. Urged by Dr. Ramond to marry him, she realizes that Pascal is the one she loves, and she becomes his mistress. She bears his child after his death.

Félicité Rougon (fay-lee-see-TAY), Dr. Pascal's mother. Ashamed because her son is not the kind of successful physician she wishes him to be, and terrified lest his papers on heredity fall into the hands of strangers, she continually seeks ways to destroy his files. She succeeds in this design immediately after Dr. Pascal's death.

Martine (mahr-TEEN), Dr. Pascal's devoted housekeeper.

Dr. Ramond (reh-MOH[N]), Dr. Pascal's friend and Clotilde's suitor.

Maxime (mahk-SEEM), Clotilde's dissolute brother.

DOCTOR THORNE

Author: Anthony Trollope (1815-1882)
First published: 1858
Genre: Novel

Locale: Barsetshire, England
Time: Mid-nineteenth century
Plot: Domestic realism

Dr. Thomas Thorne, the benevolent physician of Greshamsbury in East Barsetshire. He had adopted Mary, the illegitimate child of his brother and Mary Scatcherd, a village girl, after his brother was killed by Roger Scatcherd, Mary's brother. Dr. Thorne conceals Mary's identity until after she has inherited Roger Scatcherd's fortune. A humane man, Dr. Thorne is friendly with both the Scatcherds and with the aristocratic Greshams of Greshamsbury Park.

Mary Thorne, the niece of Dr. Thorne, unaware, until the end of the novel, of her illegitimate origin. She was brought up with the young Greshams at Greshamsbury Park and is in love with Frank Gresham, the heir. Although banished from Greshamsbury Park because Frank must marry money, Mary remains true to Frank. When she learns of her origin and her inheritance, she is able to marry Frank.

Frank Gresham, the young heir to Greshamsbury Park. Although his mother constantly insists on his need to marry a wealthy heiress, Frank never wavers in his devotion to Mary. Sent to win wealthy Miss Dunstable, Frank cannot overcome his innate honesty, despite family pressure.

Francis Newbold Gresham, the father of Frank and squire of Greshamsbury. He has dissipated his family fortune in an unsuccessful attempt to regain his father's seat in Parliament. He has also sired ten children and watched his land gradually sold in order to pay his bills. Although kindly, he recognizes that his son must marry money in order to rebuild the family's holdings.

Lady Arabella De Courcy Gresham, wife of Squire Gresham and mother of Frank. A proud member of the De Courcy clan, she is ambitious for her son and eager to assert her lineage. She insists that Frank marry money and banishes Mary Thorne from her house.

Sir Roger Scatcherd, the poor stonemason who served six months in jail for killing Dr. Thorne's brother after he betrayed Mary Scatcherd. Through intelligence and industry, he becomes a wealthy railroad manufacturer. He is elected to Parliament but later is unseated when an election fraud of which he is innocent is uncovered. Always fond of alcohol, he then drinks himself to death. His will leaves all his property to his son, and, in the event of his son's death, to his sister's child.

Lady Scatcherd, Sir Roger's loyal and patient wife. She is a good friend to Dr. Thorne and was once wet nurse to young Frank Gresham.

Louis Philippe Scatcherd, Sir Roger's only son, a drunkard. He is in love with Mary Thorne; rejected, he drinks himself to death. His early death brings the family fortune to Mary Thorne.

Countess Rosina De Courcy, sister-in-law of Lady Arabella, equally ambitious both politically and socially. She invites young Frank to Courcy Castle to give him his chance at an heiress.

Earl De Courcy, the owner of Courcy Castle and one of the principal Whig aristocrats of Barsetshire. He is completely overshadowed by his wife.

Lord Porlock, the oldest son and heir to Courcy Castle.

The Honourable George De Courcy, the second son, neither honorable nor wise.

The Honourable John De Courcy, the third son, a spendthrift.

Martha Dunstable, the wealthy heiress to a patent medicine fortune, accustomed to refusing importunate young men. Frank Gresham is expected to win her at Courcy Castle, and she is rather charmed by his naïve inability to be dishonest (she is ten years older than he). They become good friends, and she gives him advice about Mary Thorne. The Honourable George proposes to her but is not accepted.

Augusta Gresham, the dutiful eldest daughter of the squire of Greshamsbury, jilted by her fiancée, Mr. Moffat.

Mr. Moffat, a local member of Parliament, defeated by Sir Roger Scatcherd. He jilts Augusta Gresham when he realizes that the Greshams have less money than he has assumed.

Beatrice Gresham, the second daughter of the squire of Greshamsbury and particular friend of Mary Thorne, later married to the Reverend Caleb Oriel.

The Reverend Caleb Oriel, the young rector of Greshamsbury, an adherent of High Church doctrine.

Patience Oriel, his sister, a close friend to Mary Thorne.

Lady Amelia De Courcy, eldest daughter of the De Courcys. She maintains rigorous standards of propriety and social caste.

Mortimer Gazebee, a hardworking and opportunistic young attorney of no family. He proposes to Augusta Gresham, who, on the advice of her cousin, Lady Amelia, rejects him. He later marries Lady Amelia.

Dr. Fillgrave, the Barchester physician who sometimes attends Sir Roger Scatcherd.

Harry Baker, a friend of Frank Gresham.

Mr. Nearthewinde, a Parliamentary agent.

Mr. Closerstil, another Parliamentary agent.

Mr. Romer, a barrister who manages Sir Roger Scratcherd's campaign for Parliament.

Mrs. Proudie, the aggressive wife of the Bishop of Barchester.

Mr. Reddypalm, a publican interested in politics.

The Duke of Omnium, owner of Gatherum Castle and the leading Whig aristocrat in the vicinity.

Fothergill, the duke's agent.

Miss Gushing, a young lady in love with the Reverend Caleb Oriel; she later marries Mr. Rantaway.

Jonah (Joe), a brutal servant to Louis Philippe Scatcherd.

Mr. Bideawhile, a London attorney.

Lady Rosina De Courcy,

Lady Margaretta De Courcy, and

Lady Alexandrina De Courcy, younger daughters of the De Courcys.

DOCTOR ZHIVAGO
(Doktor Zhivago)

Author: Boris Pasternak (1890-1960)
First published: 1957
Genre: Novel

Locale: Moscow, the Eastern Front, and Siberia
Time: 1903-1943
Plot: Social realism

Yuri Andreievich Zhivago (YEW-ree ahn-DREH-yeh-vihch zhih-VAH-goh), the protagonist. When Zhivago's mother dies at the beginning of the novel, he becomes practically an orphan because his father, a wealthy man ruined by alcohol, already has abandoned his family. Yuri Zhivago is then reared by a maternal uncle, Nikolai Vedeniapin, a liberal journalist and intellectual who is the first character to express something like Christian idealism. Later, in his school years, Yuri lives in the home of Alexander Gromeko, a chemistry professor with a wealthy, good-hearted, physically frail wife and daughter. These associations are important in the formation of Yuri Zhivago's character and interests. The influence of his uncle impels him toward poetry, and the influence of Gromeko toward medicine. Zhivago is dark and not particularly handsome. He possesses intelligence that shows in his features. He is passive and idealistic, sustained through the chaos of Russia in the 1920's by the women, stronger than himself, who love him. He is more convincing as a poet and idealist than as a doctor.

Antonina (Tonia) Alexandrovna Gromeko (ahn-TOH-nih-nah ah-lehk-SAHN-drov-nah groh-MEH-koh), the daughter of Alexander and Anno Gromeko. Yuri Zhivago meets her when he is a schoolboy living in the Gromeko home. Relations change as Yuri and Tonia mature, and Tonia becomes Zhivago's wife. Tonia has all the good qualities one might expect in the daughter of civilized, educated people. She is a composed, polished young woman who is nevertheless capable of strong emotion, endurance, and resourcefulness. She remains loyal to Zhivago even after the circumstances of revolutionary Russia part them for good.

Larisa (Lara) Feodrovna Guishar (lah-RIH-sah FYOH-doh-rov-nah GI-shahr), Yuri Zhivago's great love and the leading female character in the novel. Her parents came to Russia from Western Europe (France and Belgium), but Lara is thoroughly Russianized and might be thought of as the author's ideal Russian woman. She is quite beautiful and susceptible to passion, which compromises her when she is little more than a girl. Like Zhivago, she makes a good and sensible marriage, hers to Pavel Antipov (Pasha), but is then permanently separated from her husband by World War I and the revolution that follows. Zhivago is a doctor during the war, and Lara is a nurse who works with him. They are later reunited in Yuriatin, east of the Ural mountains, where Zhivago has fled with his family during the revolution. When both Lara and Zhivago find themselves alone through forced separations, they turn to each other and form the liaison that becomes the novel's principal love story. After they are finally separated, again by circumstances, Lara bears Yuri's child.

Victor Ippolitovich Komarovsky (ee-poh-LIH-toh-vihch koh-mah-ROV-skee), a complicated man who seduces Lara while she is a teenager and he is the lover of Lara's mother. Late in the novel, it is hinted that he encourages a separation between Lara and Tanya, her daughter by Zhivago. He is a capable man, not devoid of feeling for Lara and concerned, in his way, with saving her from harm. A lawyer in czarist Russia, he is able to manage various difficulties after the revolution.

Pavel (Pasha) Pavlovich Antipov (PAH-vyehl PAH-vloh-vihch ahn-TIH-pov), the husband of Lara, whom he admires intensely in his student days. He becomes a teacher. He is extremely bright and is idealistic about revolution and the establishment of a new order. He enters World War I and becomes involved with the Bolsheviks after the revolution begins. In his revolutionary activities, he is single-minded and ruthless; he is known as Strelnikov (the shooter). Antipov is strong, but he commits suicide.

Marina Shchapov (mah-REE-nah SHCHAH-pov), the daughter of the former porter at the Gromekos' house. After Zhivago is separated from Lara and drifts back to Moscow, he enters a common-law marriage with Marina. She is devoted to him and sustains him as he fails both in health and in purpose. She is badly shaken by Zhivago's death.

Evgraf Andreievich Zhivago (YEHV-graf), Yuri Zhivago's half brother. He is a principled man who accommodates himself to the realities of Bolshevik power, rises to military eminence, and smoothes the way for Yuri more than once.

— John Higby

DODSWORTH

Author: Sinclair Lewis (1885-1951)
First published: 1929
Genre: Novel
Locale: The United States and Europe
Time: The 1920's
Plot: Social realism

Sam Dodsworth, a wealthy automobile manufacturer from Zenith. Retired from business, with ample money and leisure, he takes his wife Fran on what is planned as a long trip to Europe. He is eager to see the places he has read so much about, but he finds it difficult to adjust to European life and impossible to please his wife, whose restlessness and social climbing, as well as her endless criticism of him, get more and more on his nerves. No sooner does he begin to enjoy one country than she wants to move on to another. She begins to consider herself a European and constantly reminds him that he is an uncultivated American businessman who cannot appreciate what he sees. The climax comes in Germany, when she announces that she wants a divorce so that she can marry Count von Obersdorf, an impecunious Austrian nobleman. Sam leaves her in Berlin to arrange for the divorce. In Paris, he is so lonely that he drifts into a brief affair with Fernande Azerede. Tiring of this affair, he goes to Venice and there meets a Mrs. Cortright, an attractive widow whom he had met casually before. They become interested in each other and are considering marriage when Fran writes that Obersdorf has declined to marry her. Out of a sense of duty, Sam returns to his temporarily penitent wife, but on the voyage to America he realizes that he can no longer endure her continual criticism. He finally breaks with her, to return to Italy and Mrs. Cortright, with whom he can find happiness. He is a portrait of the American trying desperately to understand the older culture of Europe, which he both admires and dislikes.

Frances (Fran) Dodsworth, Sam's wife, the daughter of a rich brewer. She is spoiled, selfish, and superficial, and she is constantly critical of her husband, whose good qualities she can never see. She demands attention and yet is insulted when the attention becomes serious. Thus she encourages Major Lockert, then is furious when he makes love to her. In Germany, she meets the aristocratic Count von Obersdorf, whom she wants to marry. Sam agrees to a divorce, but Fran finds that Obersdorf's mother considers her "déclassée," and the count is eager to escape from the marriage. She appeals to Sam to forgive her, but during the trip home she resumes her nagging criticisms, thus driving him away forever. She is last seen in New York, a lonely and pathetic figure. She is Lewis' bitter portrait of the American woman.

Brent Dodsworth, their son, a student at Yale University and a future go-getter.

Emily Dodsworth, their daughter. Married, she no longer needs her father.

Edith Cortright, the widow of an Englishman. She is sincere and dependable, the exact opposite of Fran. She and Sam plan to marry.

Major Clyde Lockert, an Englishman whom the Dodsworths meet on shipboard and who introduces them to English social life. Attentive to Fran, he infuriates her by making love to her.

Count Kurt von Obersdorf, an impoverished Austrian, head of one of the greatest families in Europe. Fran wants to divorce Sam to marry Obersdorf, but the count ends the affair when his mother objects to the marriage.

Renée de Pénable (reh-NAY deh pay-NAHBL), a mysterious international character who lives on rich Americans. She completely fools Fran.

Fernande Azerede (fehr-NAHND ah-zeh-REHD), a Parisian wanton with whom Sam has a brief affair.

Tub Pearson, Sam's best friend, a typical Babbitt.

Matey Pearson, his wife. Crude but warm-hearted and intelligent, she sees through Fran perfectly.

Ross Ireland, a journalist, whose function is to speak the author's scathing comments on America.

Lord Herndon and

Lady Herndon, Lockert's cousins in London, who give a dinner party at which Fran revels in snobbery while Sam feels completely out of place.

Hurd, London manager of Sam's former company, who educates him concerning the pleasures of living abroad.

Arnold Israel, a Jewish playboy with whom Fran has an affair.

The Biedners, Fran's cousins in Berlin, through whom she meets Count von Obersdorf.

THE DOG BENEATH THE SKIN: Or, Where Is Francis?

Authors: W. H. Auden (1907-1973) and Christopher Isherwood (1904-1986)
First published: 1935
Genre: Drama
Locale: Mythologized Europe
Time: Mid-1930's
Plot: Social satire

Alan Norman, an honest and sincere young villager. Chosen by lot in an annual ceremony, he is promised a portion of the estate and the hand of the daughter of the deceased master of the lands of the English village of Pressan Ambo if he can, unlike the others who have tried, successfully complete the quest to find the missing son and heir, Sir Francis Crewe. Alan's simple acceptance of his task and his sustaining dream of marrying Iris, Sir Francis' sister, make him an unquestioning Everyman who will be transformed by his travels in postwar Europe from the prototypical unquestioning good citizen to one who learns something of the treachery and dishonesty of governments, whether national or local. As a hero, he is distinguished by his steadiness and single-mindedness of purpose, not so much acting as being acted upon.

Sir Francis Crewe, a baronet, the missing heir who is literally the dog beneath the skin, for in his disillusionment with the modern world after the end of the war, he hides in a costume of a dog's skin and sees the world from the ground up. He attaches himself to Alan Norman after years of learning what the Pressan Ambo villagers are like; hidden as he is by his role as a dog, people speak freely in front of him. He makes the journey with Alan to the Continent, where he experiences at first hand the politics of the village enlarged in national terms of fascism, mind control, and corrupt capitalism. Near the end of the quest, after their return to England, he reveals himself to Alan and advises him not to buy into the rewards offered by the village, detailing the perfidiousness of the villagers until one of them stabs him in response. The ways in which the village powers cover up his death confirm everything about which he has warned Alan.

Miss Iris Crewe, of Honeypot Hall, the fair lady who, as Sir Francis Crewe's sister, is the prize promised to the successful quester in this mock epic. She is a creature of her time and place and not capable of being faithful to her vow. Self-centered, spoiled, and shallow, she, like many of the characters, is without depth and roundness.

The Vicar of Pressan Ambo, a member of the power structure of the village. He uses religion as an instrument for conformity and control of the masses and willingly enters into the conspiracy at the end of the play, lying to maintain the "reputation" of the village and preserve the status quo.

The General, who, like the vicar, is an oppressor. He is a representative of fascism, of the military mind that controls through force, under the guise of nationalism and patriotism. His vision of the world is the advance of the British Empire at whatever cost. Now retired, he rules his home and his wife like a brigade, with a hand of iron. He involves himself in the concealment of the death of Sir Francis Crewe in the end by pretending that the heir was never found.

Journalists, British reporters for *The Evening Moon* and *The Thunderbolt*. They follow Alan on his quest because they sense a good story. Worldly-wise, they provide foils to Alan's simplicity and provide a source of commentary on the frightening political tendencies of the postwar world. Ultimately, however, they are perhaps more culpable than other characters, because in spite of their knowledge and perspective, they preserve the status quo by choosing to report what their readers already want to read.

— Donna Gerstenberger

DOG SOLDIERS

Author: Robert Stone (1937-)
First published: 1974
Genre: Novel

Locale: South Vietnam and California
Time: Early 1970's
Plot: Social morality

John Converse, a journalist covering the Vietnam War. Timid and paranoid, Converse once aspired to be a serious writer, but now he squanders his talent by writing for Elmer Bender's sensationalist tabloid *Nightbeat*. He plots to smuggle three kilograms of pure heroin from Vietnam to the United States with the help of his friend Ray Hicks; however, Converse loses control of the action he starts. When he returns to California, he discovers that both Hicks and Marge have disappeared, taking the smuggled heroin with them. Converse is tortured by two hoodlums who work for the corrupt lawman Antheil, and he is forced to pursue his wife and friend to retrieve the heroin. In the end, Converse abandons the heroin to the brutal lawmen and escapes with Marge.

Ray Hicks, a merchant marine, drug smuggler, and self-taught mystic. A believer in the philosophies of Friedrich Nietzsche and Zen, Hicks takes risks and is indifferent to the possible consequences of those risks, as when he smuggles the heroin to the United States. When his meeting with Converse's wife, Marge, is interrupted by Antheil's brutal agents, Hicks and Marge flee for their own safety, taking the heroin with them. Later, Hicks attempts to sell the drugs to Eddie Peace, a sleazy Hollywood pusher, but the plan backfires. In a second attempt to get rid of the heroin, Hicks takes Marge to see his old guru, Dieter, who lives near the Mexican border; later, he is shot in a gunfight with Antheil and his henchmen. Hicks dies during his trek through the desert flatlands to rendezvous with Converse and Marge.

Marge, Converse's wife and Bender's daughter, a drug addict. While her husband is in Vietnam, Marge works at a pornographic movie theater to support herself and their daughter. She is addicted to dilaudid. Confused and unsure about her husband's plan to smuggle in the heroin, she reluctantly agrees to take charge of the heroin from Hicks. After she and Hicks flee from Antheil's men and her supply of dilaudid runs out, she becomes addicted to the heroin. Marge eventually finds herself torn between her feelings for Converse and for Hicks.

Elmer Bender, Marge's father, a former Communist, owner and editor of the tabloid *Nightbeat*. Bender, who served during the Spanish Civil War as a member of the Lincoln Brigade, now publishes sensationalist news stories. Like many of the other characters, he is a man whose former ideals are now lost as a result of the confusion of the times. He sends Marge and Converse's daughter to friends in Canada, fearing for the girl's safety. He becomes angry at Converse for smuggling the heroin into the United States and for endangering the lives of his daughter and granddaughter.

Dieter, Hicks's former guru. Living in an encampment on a mountain near the Mexican border, Dieter laments the end of a former, more idealistic time. A believer in spiritual innocence, Dieter tries to persuade Hicks to give up the heroin and join him in the mountain encampment. He also tries to persuade Marge that her addiction to the heroin will only kill her. Although Dieter consumes hallucinogenic mushrooms, he regards heroin as a filthy drug.

Antheil, a corrupt lawman. As he directs the hunt for the smuggled heroin, Antheil employs sadistic methods to torture Converse. Tracking down the heroin as well as Hicks and Marge becomes an obsession for Antheil, and he will go as far as killing all three to get it.

— Dale Davis

DOG YEARS
(Hundejahre)

Author: Günter Grass (1927-)
First published: 1963
Genre: Novel

Locale: Danzig and West Germany
Time: Mid-1920's to late 1940's
Plot: Social realism

Walter Matern (VAHL-tehr MAH-tehrn), the stocky son of a miller. Walter, known as the "grinder" for constantly grinding his teeth, is the protector, friend, and blood brother to Eddi Amsel. Their lives, along with the changes in Germany, are traced from their boyhood in the mid-1920's through the early post-World War II period. Walter is expelled from the Young Prussia Athletic Club for distributing Communist leaflets, and his career as an aspiring actor is cut short by his excessive drinking. He joins the brown-shirted Nazi Sturm Abteilung (SA) on the urging of Amsel, who wants a source of uniforms for scarecrows. Walter, however, eventually reports Amsel for making animated SA dummies. In times of exasperation or anger, Walter reviles his friend as "sheeny." He and his fellow thugs beat Amsel, and Walter personally knocks out all of Amsel's teeth. Walter is later kicked out of the SA and joins the army to escape punishment for his political opinions. He commands an antiaircraft unit in which Harry Liebenau serves, but eventually he is condemned to a penal battalion for anti-Nazi statements. Released from an English prison camp as an anti-Fascist, he eventually becomes a radio star because of the dynamism of his voice. Subjected to a brutal and accusatory review of his life on a live radio program directed by Harry, Walter in disgust decides to leave the capitalistic West. In Berlin, however, he meets Amsel, whom he does not at first recognize, and is taken on a tour of his fantastic scarecrow production center.

Eddi Amsel, a short and corpulent boy with reddish-blond hair and an ample supply of freckles. Amsel, from a village near Danzig, has a marvelous voice, is a talented artist, and has an especially creative talent for making scarecrows. The son of a wealthy Jewish merchant and a German peasant, he inherits their money, much of which he invests in Switzerland. After the beating by the SA, Amsel is transformed as he lies in the snow: As it melts, his corpulence shrinks away. Thin and toothless, he leaves for Berlin, where he purchases gold replacements for his lost teeth. After the arrest of Jenny Brunies' stepfather, Amsel, now known as Hermann Haseloff, returns to Danzig and takes his beloved Jenny back to Berlin, where she becomes the star of his ballet company. After the war, going by the name Goldmouth, he becomes a rich speculator and businessman. As Brauxel or Brauchsel, he purchases a mine, which is transformed into a production center for elaborate scarecrows, which embody the mechanical and spiritless character of West German society.

Anton Matern, Walter's father, the miller, whose right ear was flattened as a result of carrying sacks of flour on his shoulder. The ear, deaf to ordinary sounds, is capable of hearing predictions of the future from mealworms in flour sacks. As a refugee in West Germany after World War II, he works for Goldmouth. The miller keeps him informed of future financial trends, and he hires out the miller's services as a financial adviser to a wide clientele of important German industrial and financial figures.

Harry Liebenau (LEE-beh-now), a historian and writer of radio plays. Though younger than Amsel and Matern, he knows them and is hired by Brauxel to write the memories of his childhood in Danzig. Liebenau does this in the form of love letters to his cousin, Tulla Pokriefke, whose family lived in the building owned by his father, a carpenter.

Jenny Brunies (BREW-neez), a foundling originally named **Estersweh**. After she was deserted by a gypsy, Bidandengero, she was adopted by the bachelor Oswald Brunies, who gave her the name Jenny. She was grotesquely fat but musically talented. She studied piano with Herr Felsner-Imbs, who had moved into the Liebenau building, and took ballet lessons. Encased in a snowman by Tulla, Jenny shrinks with the melting of the snowman and is transformed into a cold and detached but thin and graceful person. Although she later professes to love Harry, she is devoid of emotional intensity. As Jenny Angustri, she becomes a noted ballerina in Haseloff's company, but she loses her toes in an Allied bombing raid. She then becomes the proprietor of a small bar financed by Goldmouth.

Dr. Oswald Brunies, the boys' amiable middle-aged teacher. Brunies' round face is creased with wrinkles caused by his frequent laughter and continuous grinning. He collects rocks and is addicted to cough drops that he concocted himself. An opponent of Adolf Hitler, he refuses to fly the Nazi flag from his apartment. When he eats vitamin pills intended for his students, he is sent to a concentration camp, where he dies.

Ursula "Tulla" Pokriefke (TEWL-lah pohk-REEF-keh), Harry's sexually active cousin, baptized Ursula but called Tulla for Thula, a Koshnavian water nymph. Tulla is a thin, pale bundle of motion and energy. Her nostrils are the biggest feature on her face, but in her frequent bouts of anger she rolls her small and deep-set eyes until only bloodshot white is visible. The odor of bone glue, brought home by her father, who mixes it in Liebenau's carpenter shop, clings to everything she touches. Tulla has a cruel streak and enjoys tormenting other people, including Harry, whose love for her is not reciprocated.

Inge Sawatzki (SVAHTS-kee), the wife of Jochen Sawatzki, Walter Matern's SA group leader, who had Matern expelled for stealing SA funds. After the war, Matern wanders around Germany avenging himself against people who had wronged him by sleeping with their wives or daughters. Jochen Sawatzki welcomes him into his house and allows Inge, who falls in love with Matern, to become his mistress. Matern fathers Inge's daughter, Walli.

Senta,
Harras, and
Prinz, the dogs. Pawel, who worked for the miller, Matern, had brought a dog named Perkun with him from Lithuania. He claims that Perkun had been sired by a half-wolf. Perkun sires the miller's dog Senta, who whelps Harras. The Danzig carpenter, Friedrich Liebenau, buys Harras, who sires Prinz. Amsel is fascinated with Harras and paints his portrait, but Walter, who regards the pitch-black dog as a symbol of evil, poisons it. Prinz, an exact likeness of Harras, is given to Hitler and becomes his favorite dog. Prinz, however, deserts Hitler on the Führer's birthday during the Battle of Berlin. The dog heads west and eventually finds Walter in an English prison camp. Prinz attaches himself to the released Walter, who renames him Pluto.

— *Bernard A. Cook*

DOGEATERS

Author: Jessica Tarahata Hagedorn (1949-)
First published: 1990
Genre: Novel
Locale: Manila, the Philippines
Time: 1956-1961
Plot: Social realism

Rio Gonzaga (RREE-oh gohn-SAH-gah), a first-person narrator. She recalls, from an unspecified time in the future, events of her childhood from the ages of ten to fifteen.

Joey Sands, another first-person narrator, named for the Las Vegas casino. Joey is effectively orphaned in early childhood when his mother, a beautiful prostitute named Zenaida, drowns herself. Joey has no idea who his father is, other than that he was a black American soldier. A small-time pimp and drug pusher, Uncle, pays for the mother's funeral expenses and takes Joey into his shack in the slum district of Tondo.

Uncle teaches Joey to steal at the age of seven and arranges for Joey to have sex with a prostitute at the age of ten. Grown up, Joey works as a disc jockey at CocoRico, a club owned by Andres Alacran, a relative of the wealthy and influential businessman Severo Alacran. At the club, Joey meets prosperous foreigners, with whom he has homosexual affairs and from whom he sometimes steals drugs and money.

General Nicasio Ledesma (nee-KAH-see-oh leh-DEHS-mah), the army chief who runs torture camps for subversives. His wife, Leonor, has devoted herself to a sacrificial life of praying on the cold cement floor of her tiny bedroom, fasting on water, and on "good days" doing charity work for the Sisters of Mercy orphanage. The general does not seem to mind, perhaps because he keeps a mistress, film actress Lolita Luna, who is always out of money and usually high on drugs.

Senator Domingo Avila (doh-MEEN-goh a-VEE-lah), the opposition party leader and father of Daisy Consuelo Avila. Senator Avila is assassinated.

Daisy Consuelo Avila (kohn-SWEH-loh), the daughter of Senator Domingo Avila. After winning a national beauty pageant, Daisy promptly becomes a recluse suffering from protracted crying spells. Finally, Daisy consents to an interview with Cora Camacho, host of the television show *Girl Talk*. Daisy denounces the pageant and shortly thereafter marries an Englishman, Malcolm Webb. The marriage founders, and Malcolm returns to England. Reputed to have fled to the mountains with her guerrilla lover, she is captured by General Ledesma and tortured and raped by all of Ledesma's men except Pepe Carreon.

Romeo (Orlando) Rosales (rho-MEH-oh roh-SAHL-ehs), a waiter at the exclusive Monte Vista Golf and Country Club. He is shot by the police and then charged with the murder of Senator Avila. He is at the assassination scene, the SPORTEX department store, to break up with his girlfriend, Trinidad Gamboa, who works there as a clerk.

Pepe Carreon (PEH-peh kah-rreh-OHN), an ambitious man with a bad complexion who elopes with Baby Alacran, daughter of the wealthy Severo and Isabel Alacran. His army career is marked by rapid advancement to the position of aide to General Ledesma.

— *L. M. Grow*

THE DOLLMAKER

Author: Harriette Arnow (1908-1986)
First published: 1954
Genre: Novel
Locale: Appalachian Kentucky and Detroit, Michigan
Time: Late autumn, 1944-late autumn, 1945
Plot: Social realism

Gertie Nevels, the dollmaker, a wood-carver and a strong, resilient woman from the mountains of Kentucky. Gertie stashes any extra money she has in the hem of her coat, and with these savings she dreams of buying a farm. When her husband, Clovis, finds work in Detroit and sends for the family, she tries to buy a farm, but the purchase is prevented by her mother, who believes that Gertie's place is with her husband. Her mountain nature is at odds with the city, but her resourcefulness helps pay the bills when Clovis is laid off and later, after Clovis is forced to hide from the police after killing a man in a labor dispute. With Clovis' help, she mass-produces wooden toys and other wood carvings, which her children hawk on the street. When her daughter Cassie is killed by a train, Gertie uses her savings to bury the child. Her final surrender occurs when a large order for wooden toys arrives. Unable to buy wood, she splits the large block of cherry wood brought from Kentucky on which she had been carving a bust of Christ.

Clovis Nevels, Gertie's husband, possibly as gifted with machines as Gertie is with wood. Clovis, although well intentioned, does not provide well for his family. His unhappiness with the mountain life leads him to Detroit, where he finds work, then sends for his family. Through his extravagance, the family goes deeply into debt, and when he is laid off, the burden of providing for the family shifts to Gertie's shoulders. During a labor dispute, Clovis is beaten by a thug, whom he later kills. Because he is forced to hide from the police and therefore is unable to find work, his ability to provide for the family is further damaged.

Clytie Nevels, their fourteen-year-old daughter, who quickly adapts to Detroit. In doing so, she helps Gertie adjust to the city. Along with her brother Enoch, she sells her mother's carvings on the street, thus ensuring the family's survival.

Enoch Nevels, the Nevelses' nine-year-old son, who, along with Clytie, adjusts to the city environment.

Reuben Nevels, the Nevelses' twelve-year-old son, who is not able to adjust to Detroit. He runs away from home and goes back to Kentucky to live with his grandparents.

Cassie Nevels, the Nevelses' five-year-old daughter. The dreamer of the family, she retreats from the horrors of city schools into her own world, inhabited by a make-believe friend, Callie Lou. Her make-believe leads her to the train yard, where she is run over by a train and bleeds to death.

Amos Nevels, the Nevelses' three-year-old son. When he cannot breathe because of diphtheria, Gertie performs an emergency tracheotomy with her whittling knife and a cane branch, saving his life.

Granma Kendrick, Gertie's mother, a hypochondriac. A deeply religious woman, she constantly whines about the burdens of her life. She gives Gertie the money from Henley's insurance policy but spends it all herself when Gertie tries to use it to buy a farm.

Henley Kendrick, Gertie's brother, who is killed in the war.

Victor, a generous Polish American neighbor who helps the Nevelses adjust to their new life in Detroit.

Max, Victor's young wife, who leaves him for another man.

Sophronie, another congenial Detroit neighbor and a fellow Southerner. She is forced to leave her children to work the graveyard shift in the factory.

Whit, Sophronie's husband, also from the South.

Joe, an immigrant from Sicily who sells vegetables and gives Gertie much-needed credit.

Joe's nephew, an illegal immigrant from Sicily who attacks Clovis during a labor fight. He is later hunted down and killed by Clovis with Gertie's whittling knife.

Mr. Daly, an insufferable Detroit neighbor.

Mrs. Daly, the mother of ten children. A patient, frazzled woman who suffers miserably at the hands of her husband.

— *Geraldine L. Hutchins*

A DOLL'S HOUSE
(Et dukkehjem)

Author: Henrik Ibsen (1828-1906)
First published: 1879
Genre: Drama
Locale: Norway
Time: The nineteenth century
Plot: Social realism

Nora, the "doll-wife" of Torvald Helmer. Seeking always to charm her husband, Nora is his "singing lark," his pretty "little squirrel," and his "little spendthrift." She seems to be a spendthrift because secretly she is paying off a debt she incurred to finance a year in Italy for the sake of Torvald's health. To get the money, she had forged her dying father's name to a bond at the bank. Krogstad, a bookkeeper at the bank where Torvald has recently been appointed manager, is aware that the bond was signed after the death of Nora's father. He puts pressure on Nora to persuade Torvald to promote him. Frightened, Nora agrees to help him. When her friend Christine Linde, a widow and formerly Krogstad's sweetheart, also asks for help, Nora easily persuades Torvald to give Christine an appointment at the bank. The position, unfortunately, is Krogstad's. Torvald, finding Krogstad's presumption unbearable, plans to discharge him. While Christine helps Nora prepare a costume for a fancy dress ball in which she will dance the tarantella, Krogstad writes a letter, following his dismissal, telling Torvald of Nora's forgery. Nora desperately keeps Torvald from the mailbox until after the dance. She decides to kill herself so that all will know that she alone is guilty and not Torvald. After the dance, Torvald reads the letter and tells Nora in anger that she is a criminal and can no longer be his wife, although she may continue to live in his house to keep up appearances. When Krogstad, softened by Christine's promise to marry him and care for his motherless children, returns the bond, Torvald destroys it and is willing to take back his little singing bird. Nora, realizing the shallow basis of his love for her as a "doll-wife," leaves Torvald to find her own personality away from him. She leaves him with the faint hope that their marriage might be resumed if it could be a "real wedlock."

Torvald Helmer, the newly promoted manager of a bank. Concerned with business, he is unaware that his wife, Nora, whom he regards as a plaything, is capable of making serious decisions. When he discovers her forgery, he is horrified and convinced that he will be blamed as the instigator, and he plans to try to appease Krogstad to forestall his own disgrace. As soon as the bond is returned, Torvald becomes himself again, wants his pet reinstated, and is eager to forget the whole affair. He is baffled when Nora says that she no longer loves him and is leaving him. At the end, he has a sudden hope that what Nora has called "the most wonderful thing of all" might really happen, the "real wedlock" she wanted, but Nora has gone.

Nils Krogstad, a bookkeeper at the bank, dissatisfied with his appointment and with life in general. At first, Krogstad appears as a sinister blackmailer threatening Nora with disaster if she does not help him achieve a promotion at the bank. Later, when he finds the love of Christine Linde, whose loss had embittered him in the first place, he becomes a changed man and returns the bond.

Christine Linde, a widow and Nora's schoolfriend. When Mrs. Linde first appears, she is quite worn and desperate for work. She had married for money that she needed to support her mother and two young brothers. Now husband and mother are dead, and the brothers are grown. In the end, when she and Krogstad have decided to marry, she is happy because she will have someone for whom to care. She decides that Nora cannot continue to deceive Torvald and that Krogstad should not retrieve his letter. Presumably, Krogstad will retain his position at the bank.

Dr. Rank, a family friend who is in love with Nora. Suffering bodily for his father's sins, Dr. Rank is marked by death. Nora starts to ask Dr. Rank to help her pay off the debt, but after he reveals his love for her, she will not ask this favor of him. He tells Nora that he is soon to die and that when death has begun, he will send her his card with a black cross on it. The card appears in the mailbox with Krogstad's letter. Dr. Rank serves no purpose in the play except to show Nora's fidelity to Torvald when she refuses Rank's offer of help after she knows that he loves her.

DOMBEY AND SON

Author: Charles Dickens (1812-1870)
First published: 1846-1848
Genre: Novel
Locale: England
Time: Early nineteenth century
Plot: Social realism

Paul Dombey, a London merchant, referred to as **Mr. Dombey** throughout the novel. Twenty successful years in the firm of Dombey and Son have brought wealth to the stern and pompous Mr. Dombey. Ten years of marriage finally bring a son and happiness (despite his wife's death) to the unemotional, dignified, glossy businessman, for the son will occupy his rightful place in the firm. Jealous and possessive, Mr. Dombey resents his son's affection for Florence, the older Dombey daughter. Later he sends Walter Gay, a young clerk attentive to the daughter, on an extended trip to the West Indies, and he loses his second wife because he approaches personal relationships as if they were business transactions in his office. Through reversals in both personal and business affairs, Mr. Dombey senses that his shortcomings lie in what he has always considered his strength: a belief in his indomitability. This realization results in a modicum of happiness for him as he accepts his daughter's love after spurning her all her life.

Paul Dombey, his son and heir, who is the essence of Dombey's life. Before the child was born, Mr. Dombey had yearned for a son; during Paul's life, he is jealous of his attentions to others, over-solicitous for his health, and unrealistic in treating the child as his longed-for business partner. After Paul's death at the age of six, Mr. Dombey in his disillusionment considers the death a personal injustice to himself. Paul, a weak, precocious child, is uncommonly preoccupied with death, an interest that seems, in the Dickensian manner, to portend his early demise.

Florence Dombey, six years older than Paul. Until she is grown, Florence bears the brunt of her father's unreasonable animosity. Courageous and compassionate, she withstands her father's affronts and ill-temper. Of strong faith, she does not despair at failures or rebuffs. Devoted and appreciative of love, she is a good wife to Walter Gay. Ultimately, Florence's altruism comes full circle when she has a son, Paul, who aids in her father's realization of his daughter's longstanding love.

Walter Gay, her childhood friend and later her husband. The model of good upbringing and training, he is instrumental in her safety and well-being. The last instance of his protectorship is as her husband and father of their children, when the Gays return to London to save Dombey from self-destruction and to give him renewed interest in life when he sees his grandchildren in the light in which he should have viewed his own daughter and son.

Mrs. Fanny Dombey, Mr. Dombey's first wife, the mother of Florence and Paul.

Mrs. Edith Granger, Dombey's second wife and his female counterpart in stubbornness and pride. Thwarted in her role as wife, she strikes back by pretending to elope with James Carker, Dombey's head clerk. Her wounded pride continues through the years; she finally declares her innocence of an affair with Carker, but she refuses to see Dombey to ask his forgiveness.

James Carker, Dombey's trusted head clerk and manager, whose villainy brings about his employer's professional and personal ruin. Deserted by Mrs. Dombey in the hour of their elopement, he is killed by a train while trying to avoid a meeting with Dombey.

Solomon Gills, a maker of nautical instruments and Walter Gay's uncle. With his loyal friend and partner, Captain Cuttle, he produces instruments that make his name a byword in safe navigation.

Edward Cuttle, an old sailor generally known as **Captain Cuttle** or **Captain Ned**. Adding much to the story with his salty mariner jargon, he becomes Florence Dombey's protector when she is rejected by her father.

Miss Lucretia Tox, a friend of Dombey's sister, who finds the wet nurse for the infant Paul. In her attentions to the child, she obviously has designs on Dombey, her devotion to him being sustained in a platonic manner throughout his life.

Major Joseph Bagstock, a retired army officer, a neighbor and an admirer of Miss Tox. The typically proud old officer is introduced to point up the transition in Miss Tox's affections. It is he who introduces Mr. Dombey to Edith Granger.

Mrs. Polly Toodle, the wet nurse, renamed Richards, a more respectable appellation for the atmosphere of the Dombey house. Summarily dismissed for negligence after Florence strays and suffers a traumatic experience with a derelict woman, Mrs. Toodle remains in the story in connection with Miss Tox and lesser characters.

Mr. Toodle, Polly Toodle's husband, a stoker and engine-driver.

Robin Toodle, their son, also called **Biler** and **Rob the Grinder**. Mr. Dombey secures him a place in the establishment of "The Honorable Grinders," but he meets with so much ridicule and abuse that he runs away. Later, he acts as a spy for James Carker; still later, he enters the employ of Miss Tox in his attempt to regain respectability.

Dr. Blimber, the owner of a select private school attended by Paul Dombey.

Mrs. Blimber, his wife, a silly, stupid woman.

Cornelia Blimber, their daughter, a bluestocking and a lover of dead languages.

John Carker, James Carker's brother and an under-clerk in the employ of Dombey and Son. Years before, he had stolen money from the firm, but because he had been led astray by bad companions, he had not been discharged. He repays this trust by years of faithful service. Dismissed after his brother's elopement with Mrs. Dombey, he inherits his brother's fortune and is able to live quietly but comfortably. After Mr. Dombey goes bankrupt, he turns the interest of his fortune over to his former employer and pretends that he is repaying an old, forgotten debt.

Harriet Carker, the sister of James and John Carker. She marries Mr. Morfin.

Mr. Morfin, the cheerful head clerk at Dombey and Son. He befriends John Carker and marries his sister Harriet.

Susan Nipper, Florence Dombey's maid and companion. Discharged after she reproves Mr. Dombey for his treatment of his daughter, she marries Mr. Toots.

Mr. P. Toots, a pupil at Doctor Blimber's school for young gentlemen. Rich and eccentric, he spends much of his time writing letters to himself and signing them with the names of famous personages, and his most commonplace remarks are filled with biblical and literary allusions. He falls in love with Florence Dombey, but when she discourages his attentions, he marries Susan Nipper instead and fathers a large brood of children.

Captain Jack Bunsby, Captain Cuttle's close friend. Innocently unaware of the wiles of women, he marries Mrs. MacStinger, his landlady.

Mrs. MacStinger, a domineering, designing widow, as quick with her hand as with her tongue. She marries Captain Bunsby.

Alexander,
Charles (Chowley), and
Juliana, Mrs. MacStinger's children by her first marriage.

Mrs. Pipchin, an ill-favored widow with whom Paul and Florence Dombey are sent to board at Brighton, later Mr. Dombey's housekeeper.

Berinthia, also called **Berry**, Mrs. Pipchin's unmarried niece and servant.

Alice Brown, also called **Alice Marwood**, James Carker's former mistress, transported for felony. She returns, filled with hate and defiance, to England.

Mrs. Brown, her mother.

Mrs. Louisa Chick, Mr. Dombey's sister, a good-natured but smug woman.

John Chick, her husband, who constantly hums or whistles tunes.

Mr. Feeder, an assistant at Doctor Blimber's school and later his son-in-law.

The Reverend Alfred Feeder, his brother.

The Hon. Mrs. Skewton, also called **Cleopatra**, an aged beauty and Edith Dombey's mother, who puts her daughter up for the highest bidder in the marriage market. She dies soon after her daughter's marriage to Mr. Dombey.

Lord Feenix, Mrs. Skewton's superannuated nephew, a man about town.

The Game Chicken, a professional prize fighter and Mr. Toot's boxing instructor.

The Reverend Melchisedech Howler, a ranting clergyman who predicts the end of the world.

Sir Barnet Skettles, a time-serving, self-seeking member of the House of Commons.

Lady Skettles, his wife.

Barnet Skettles, a pupil at Doctor Blimber's school.

Tozer and

Briggs, Paul Dombey's roommates at Doctor Blimber's school.

Anne, a housemaid,

Thomas Towlinson, a footman, and

Mary Daws, a kitchen maid, servants in the Dombey household.

Mr. Clark, a clerk, and

Mr. Perch, a messenger, employees of Dombey and Son.

Mrs. Perch, the messenger's wife, usually in an interesting condition.

Dr. Parker Peps, the attending physician at the birth of Paul Dombey because of his reputation as an obstetrician.

Dr. Pilkins, Mr. Dombey's family doctor.

DOMINIQUE

Author: Eugène Fromentin (1820-1876)
First published: 1862
Genre: Novel
Locale: France
Time: The nineteenth century
Plot: Psychological

Dominique de Bray (doh-mee-NEEK deh breh), a gentleman who tells the narrator the story of his life up to his early retirement to a quiet, happy life with his wife and children. Attracted to Madeleine de Nièvres during his schooldays, his love for her, after she marries another, fills his life with conflicts between the emotions and the disciplines of the mind. Finally realizing the mediocrity of his talents as a writer and the hopelessness of his and Madeleine's love, he retires to the Château des Trembles to become the unpretentious and beloved friend of all in the community.

Olivier d'Orsel (oh-lee-VYAY dohr-SEHL), Dominique's friend. A wealthy, luxury-loving man of engaging manner, he comes to hate the world and himself and suddenly retires from social life. Hearing of Olivier's attempted suicide, Dominique is led to tell the narrator the story of his own life.

Augustin (oh-gew-STA[N]), Dominique's practical, disciplined tutor. He attempts to help his pupil solve his emotional problems by encouraging him in the pursuits of the mind.

Madeleine de Nièvres (mahd-LEHN deh NYEH-vruh), beloved of Dominique. A married woman, her love for Dominique brings her the conflicts of a troubled conscience that causes her to send her lover away.

Monsieur de Nièvres, the husband of Madeleine.

Madame Ceyssac (seh-SAHK), Dominique's aunt.

Julie (zhew-LEE), Madeleine de Nièvres' sister, in love with Olivier d'Orsel.

DON CARLOS, INFANTE OF SPAIN
(Don Carlos, Infant von Spanien)

Author: Friedrich Schiller (1759-1805)
First published: 1787
Genre: Drama
Locale: Spain
Time: The sixteenth century
Plot: Historical

Don Carlos, the sensitive, twenty-three-year-old heir to the throne of Spain. His life is a constant battle with his father, with neither holding any love for the other. Resenting his father's second marriage—Don Carlos had been in love with the bride, Elizabeth de Valois—the prince wants to leave Madrid. He hopes to free himself of the constant reminder of his continuing love for his father's wife and, as heir to the throne, establish his stature as an emissary to Flanders. Despite the unstinting efforts of his close friend for Don Carlos' happiness, Carlos' implied lot is commitment by his father to a monastery.

Philip the Second, the king of Spain. An austere monarch lacking in compassion, he knows no love either as the loved or as the lover. In only one instance is he forgiving, toward an admiral who lost a fleet in rough seas. The king's goodness, much acclaimed by his court, is motivated more by self-gain than by altruism. Jealous and insecure, Philip is easily duped by any talebearer. He blames the church for not protecting him by warning him of forces working against him. He is rebuked, in turn, for not asking the help of the church. Philip's character is quickly reflected in the question put to him: "When you whine for sympathy, is not the world your equal?"

The marquis de Posa, the friend of Don Carlos, who calls him Roderigo. Posa swore lifelong allegiance to Don Carlos for his defense of Posa in a childhood mishap. A hero in every sense of the word, Posa shows military prowess, is beneficent in his role as confidant to the major personages, is studious, and is forthright with and unmoved by those who seek to injure their fellow men. His marked influence reaches its height when he secures Philip's approval to move about the court at will. This permission follows Posa's fervent, unselfish plea to Philip for better conditions for humankind. Posa, it is learned after his death, is a peripatetic member of a monastic group, roaming to spread his philosophy of brotherly love.

The duke of Alva, the trusted agent of Philip, working to alienate the king against Don Carlos. His duplicity is abetted by other members of the court, a group resenting the king's ready acceptance of Posa.

Elizabeth de Valois (vahl-WAH), the queen of Spain, Philip's second wife. The queen's love for Don Carlos intensifies her hatred for the king and motivates her to contemplate intrigue to further Don Carlos' ambition for the throne. Immediately before her death of grief, the love she and Carlos have for each other is purified of selfish passion as he goes forth to fight, in Posa's memory, for oppressed humankind.

The princess de Eboli (EH-bohl-ee), an attendant on the queen, whose letters to Don Carlos are mistaken for the queen's writing. The princess' affair with Philip makes her a likely accomplice to aid Alva in his conspiracy against Don Carlos. Her treacheries are abhorred by Posa, who, as confidant to Philip, would banish her from the court.

The Grand Inquisitor of Spain, the blind cardinal who identifies Posa as a member of a religious order. Rebuked for his indifference to the church, Philip delivers Don Carlos to the Inquisitor to serve in place of murdered Posa.

Domingo, the confessor to the king. He works with Alva in his plots. Because of Don Carlos' religious beliefs, Domingo deplores the thought of Carlos becoming king.

Count Lerma, the colonel of the royal bodyguard. Lerma's chief role is talebearer to Don Carlos. Much of the news he brings is half reports that distort facts and bring anguish to Don Carlos.

The marchioness de Mondecar (MOHN-deh-kahr), an attendant to the queen. Sacrificing herself to the queen's happiness, she is dismissed by Philip when she reports that it was she, not the queen, in the garden with Don Carlos.

Don Raimond de Taxis (RRI-mohnd deh TAH-hee), the postmaster general, who reveals Posa's letters in which Posa pictures himself as the queen's lover, in order to vindicate Don Carlos and allow him to escape from Spain. The letters lead to Posa's murder.

Don Louis Mercado (mehr-KAH-doh), physician to the queen. The accomplice of Don Carlos in arranging the final meeting between the prince and the queen, Mercado prepares the monkish disguise that allows Don Carlos to pass into the queen's chambers.

The duke of Medina Sidonia (meh-DEE-nah see-DOHN-nee-ah), the admiral of the king's fleet. His negligence is forgiven, making the king appear humane in the eyes of the court.

THE DON FLOWS HOME TO THE SEA
(Tikhii Don)

Author: Mikhail Sholokhov (1905-1984)
First published: 1928-1940
Genre: Novel

Locale: Russia
Time: 1918-1920
Plot: Historical

Gregor Melekhov (GREH-gohr MEH-leh-khohv), a soldier in the White Army fighting the Reds. He returns home to his wife, but when he discovers that the Red government of his village intends to arrest him, he escapes. He joins a Cossack rebellion against the Reds and becomes a ruthless fighter after his brother is killed in cold blood. He has a reputation for not keeping live prisoners. He comes home on furlough and takes up his affair with Aksinia, his former mistress. Finally, tired of fighting, Gregor throws away his arms and returns to his house and his son.

Piotra Melekhov (PYOH-trah), Gregor's elder brother, also a soldier in the White Army. Once saved through his friendship with Fomin, a Red commander, he is eventually killed by Koshevoi. He has none of Gregor's ambivalence of mind and is decidedly anti-Red.

Aksinia Astakhova (ak-SEE-nyah as-TA-khoh-vah), Gregor's mistress, who, scorning her husband, Stepan Astakhov, tries to escape with Gregor to the south. She falls ill of typhus and has to be left behind. She is killed by a Red patrol. She was once the mistress of a rich Cossack officer, Eugene Listnitsky, but she was cast aside after Eugene married Olga, the widow of a fellow officer.

Natalia Melekhova (nah-TAH-lyah meh-leh-KHOH-vah), Gregor's wife, who becomes cold toward him when she finds that he has taken up with his former mistress. She refuses to bear him another child and tries to have an abortion, but it is clumsily done, and she bleeds to death.

Mikhail Koshevoi (mih-hah-IHL ko-shee-VOY), a Communist sympathizer who is put in charge of the government in Gregor's village, Tatarsk, in which job he is assisted by a professional Red named Stockman. After becoming a full-fledged Communist, he kills Piotra outright. Koshevoi's family disappears, and his father's house is destroyed; he then takes great joy in firing at the wealthy landowners' houses in revenge. After he becomes commissar of Tatarsk, he brazenly marries Dunia, the sister of Gregor and Piotra.

Daria Melekhova (DAHR-yah), Piotra's wife, who kills the man she thinks is responsible for her husband's death. She soon recovers from her grief and begins to have various affairs. She catches syphilis and drowns herself.

DON GOYO

Author: Demetrio Aguilera Malta (1909-1981)
First published: 1933
Genre: Novel

Locale: Islands off the coast of Ecuador
Time: Indeterminate
Plot: Realism

Don Goyo Quimi (GOY-oh KEE-mee), the first inhabitant of the islands and founder of the town of Cerrito de Morrenos. He is a 150-year-old patriarch who commands the respect and obedience of all the *cholos* (part-Indians). Although he has heard unfavorable reports about the conduct of white men, he recruits *cholos* to help Don Carlos. When he sees that the *cholos* are being exploited, he convinces them to abandon Don Carlos to work for themselves again. The oldest mangrove tree warns him that white men have come to corrupt and rob the *cholos*. Don Goyo gives the *cholos* the message of the mangrove tree and tells them to stop harvesting mangrove trees. By cutting down mangrove trees, the *cholos* are cutting themselves down because they are made of mangrove. After the *cholos* indicate that they are going to resume cutting down mangrove trees anyway, Don Goyo disappears, then dies with the oldest mangrove tree. The *cholos* find him tangled in its fallen branches.

Cusumbo (kew-SEWM-boh), a young highlander who comes to the islands to escape prosecution for murdering his boss and his wife when he had caught them making love. As a highlander, he had worked for the landowner by cultivating rice, fishing, and caring for dairy cattle. After he comes to the islands, he fishes for a livelihood until he falls in love with Gertru, who insists that she will marry only a mangrove cutter. He becomes a mangrove cutter to please her and to make enough money to marry her. When he becomes infected with a venereal disease, he is cured by Don Goyo after hospital treatment is unsuccessful. He asks Gertru to marry him after they both witness an apparition of a triumphant Don Goyo after his death.

Gertrudis (Gertru) Quimi (hehr-TREW-dees), the sensible daughter of Don Goyo and his second wife, Doña Andrea. She resists Cusumbo's amorous advances at first because she wants a commitment from him. She accepts Cusumbo's marriage proposal after her father's death.

Don Carlos, a tall, blond, blue-eyed white man who settled on the islands with his family. He claims to want to improve life on the islands for everyone and solicits Don Goyo's help in securing the cooperation of the *cholos*. After providing some initial prosperity, Don Carlos begins to cheat the workers, and they fall into debt. Before Don Goyo's death, he plots the seizure of Don Goyo's island, trying to find out if Don Goyo has papers to substantiate his claim on the land.

Don Leitón (lay-TOHN), a mangrove cutter who leads the opposition to Don Goyo's sanction against mangrove tree cutting. After the cutters unsuccessfully try to earn a living fishing for a few days, he speaks up for the others and asks Don Goyo for permission to return to mangrove tree cutting.

— Evelyn Toft

DON JUAN

Author: George Gordon, Lord Byron (1788-1824)
First published: 1819-1826
Genre: Drama

Locale: Spain, Turkey, Russia, and England
Time: Late eighteenth century
Plot: Satire

Don Juan (JEW-awn), the young son of Donna Inez and Don Jose, a hidalgo of Seville. He is a handsome, mischief-making boy whose education, after his father's death, is carefully supervised by his mother, who insists that he read only classics expurgated in the text but with all the obscenities collected in an appendix. He is allowed to associate only with old or ugly women. At the age of sixteen, he learns the art of love from Donna Julia, a young matron. The ensuing scandal causes Donna Inez to send her son to Cadiz, and from there to take ship for a trip abroad. The vessel on which he is a passenger sinks after a storm. He experiences a romantic interlude with the daughter of a Greek pirate and slave trader. He is sold to the Turks and takes part in the siege of Ismail, a Turkish fort on the Danube River. He becomes the favorite of Empress Catherine of Russia, and he is sent on a diplomatic mission to England, where he becomes a critical observer of English society.

Donna Inez (I-nehz), Don Juan's mother, a domineering and short-sighted woman who first tries to protect her son from the facts of life but later rejoices in his good fortune and advancement when he becomes the favorite of Empress Catherine of Russia.

Don Jose (hoh-SEH), Don Juan's father, a gallant man often unfaithful to his wife, with whom he quarrels constantly. He dies while his son is still a small boy.

Donna Julia, Don Juan's first love, a woman of twenty-three married to the fifty-year-old Don Alfonso. She is forced to enter a convent after her irate husband discovers his wife and her young lover in her bedchamber. In a long letter, written on the eve of Don Juan's departure from Spain, she professes her undying love for him.

Don Alfonso, the cuckold husband who discovers Don Juan hiding in a closet in his wife's bedroom.

Haidée (HI-dee), the second love of Don Juan. A tall, lovely child of nature and passion, she finds him unconscious on the seashore following the sinking of the ship on which he had sailed from Spain. Filled with love and sympathy, she hides and protects him. This idyllic island romance ends when Lambro, her pirate father, returns from one of his expeditions and finds the two sleeping together after a great feast that Lambro has watched from a distance. Don Juan, wounded in a scuffle with Lambro's men, is bound and put aboard one of the pirate's ships. Shortly afterward, Haidée dies, lamenting her vanished lover, and his child dies with her.

Lambro (LAM-broh), Haidée's father, "the mildest-manner'd man that ever scuttled ship or cut a throat." Returning from one of his piratical expeditions, he surprises the young lovers and sends Don Juan, wounded in a fight with Lambro's men, away on a slave ship. Later, he regrets his hasty action when he watches his only child die of illness and grief.

Gulbeyaz (GEWL-beh-yaz), the sultana of Turkey. Having seen Don Juan in the slave market where he is offered for sale, along with an Italian opera troupe sold into captivity by their disgusted impresario, she orders one of the palace eunuchs to buy the young man. She has him taken to the palace and dressed in women's clothes. Even though she brings her strongest weapon, her tears, to bear, she is unable to make Don Juan her lover.

The sultan of Turkey, the father of fifty daughters and four dozen sons. Seeing the disguised Don Juan in his wife's apartments, he orders the supposed female slave to be taken to the palace harem.

Baba, the African eunuch who buys Don Juan at the sultana's command. He later flees with Don Juan and John Johnson from Constantinople.

Lolah,

Katinka, and

Dudu, three girls in the sultan's harem. Dudu, lovely and languishing, has the disguised Don Juan for her bed fellow. Late in the night, she awakes screaming after a dream in which she reached for a golden apple and was stung by a bee. The next morning, jealous Gulbeyaz orders Dudu and Don Juan executed, but they escape in the company of Johnson and Baba.

John Johnson, a worldly Englishman fighting with the Russians in the war against the Turks. Captured, he is bought in the slave market along with Don Juan. The two escape and make their way to the Turkish lines before Ismail. Johnson is recognized by General Suwarrow, who welcomes him and Don Juan as allies in the attack on Ismail.

Leila, a ten-year-old Muslim girl whose life Don Juan saves during the capture of Ismail. He becomes her protector.

General Suwarrow, the leader of the Russian forces at the siege and taking of Ismail.

Catherine, the empress of Russia, to whose court Don Juan is sent with news of the Turkish victory at Ismail. Voluptuous and rapacious in love, she receives the young man with great favor and he becomes her favorite. After he becomes ill, she reluctantly decides to send him on a diplomatic mission to England.

Lord Henry Amundeville, an English politician and the owner of Norman Abbey. Don Juan meets the nobleman in London, and the two become friends.

Lady Adeline Amundeville, his wife, who also becomes Don Juan's friend and mentor. She advises him to marry because she is afraid that he will become seriously involved with the notorious duchess of Fitz-Fulke. During a house party at Norman Abbey, she sings a song telling of the Black Friar, a ghost often seen wandering the halls of the abbey.

The duchess of Fitz-Fulke, a woman of fashion notorious for her amorous intrigues. She pursues Don Juan after his arrival in England and finally, disguised as the ghostly Black Friar of Norman Abbey, succeeds in making him her lover.

Miss Aurora Raby, a young Englishwoman with whom Don Juan contemplates matrimony. She seems completely unimpressed by his attentions, and he is piqued by her lack of interest.

Pedrillo (peh-DRIHL-oh), Don Juan's tutor. When the ship on which he and his master sail from Cadiz sinks after a storm, they are among those set adrift in a longboat. When the food runs out, the unlucky pedagogue is eaten by his famished companions. Although Don Juan considers the man an ass, he is unable to eat the hapless fellow.

Zoe (ZOH-ee), Haidée's maid.

Lady Pinchbeck, a woman of fashion who, after Don Juan's arrival in London, takes Leila under her protection.

DON JUAN
(Dom Juan: Ou, Le Festin de Pierre)

Author: Molière (Jean-Baptiste Poquelin, 1622-1673)
First published: 1682
Genre: Drama
Locale: Sicily
Time: The seventeenth century
Plot: Social satire

Don Juan (hwahn), a philanderer and scoundrel. A seducer of women of whom he soon tires, a neglecter of debts, and a dishonorer of friends, Don Juan is called on to repent. He replies by becoming a greater hypocrite than ever, continuing his evil ways until he finally offends heaven itself and is destroyed.

Sganarelle (sgah-nah-REHL), Don Juan's valet, who hates his master's evil acts but remains loyal to him because of fear.

Elvire (ehl-VEHR), Don Juan's betrayed wife. Finally free of her passion for her husband, she agrees to return to the convent from which he had abducted her. She begs him to reform and escape the wrath of heaven.

Don Carlos and

Don Alonse (ah-LONS), Elvire's brothers, who seek vengeance on Don Juan for his betrayal of their sister.

The Statue of the Commander, part of the tomb of one of Don Juan's victims. Don Juan and Sganarelle ask the statue to dine with them. It accepts, thus causing Don Juan to pretend conversion and repentance. The statue reappears, threatening a terrible death for the really unrepentant sinner.

Don Louis (lwee), Don Juan's distressed father.

Monsieur Dimanche (dee-MAHNSH), Don Juan's creditor, hypocritically put off by his debtor.

Charlotte and

Mathurine (mah-tew-REEN), country girls each deceived by Don Juan into thinking she is his only love.

Pierrot (pyeh-ROH), a country lad.

DON JUAN TENORIO

Author: José Zorrilla (1817-1893)
First published: 1844
Genre: Drama
Locale: Seville, Spain
Time: c. 1545
Plot: Comedy

Don Juan Tenorio (hwahn teh-NOH-ree-oh), a wild young gallant whose life is so devoted to vice that he wagers his friend Mejia that he can perform more evil deeds than Mejia in a year's time. Don Juan wins the wager but in doing so he ravishes his fiancée, Inés, kills her father, ravishes Mejia's fiancée, and kills Mejia. Inés dies of grief. Don Juan's saddened father establishes a cemetery containing statues of his son's victims. Years later, when Don Juan visits the cemetery, Inés' statue pleads with him to repent. He hesitates, but her love is so strong that she saves him just as he is about to be dragged off to Hell.

Marcos Ciutti (see-EW-tee), Don Juan's villainous servant. He bribes Ana's duenna to admit his master, and Brigida to carry a note to Inés.

Inés de Ulloa (ee-NEHS deh ew-YOH-ah), a novice in a convent whom Don Juan hopes to marry. Her appearance to Don Juan after her death persuades him to repent, so that at the end she can save him from Hell's eternal fire.

Don Luis Mejia (lew-EES meh-HEE-ah), a gallant of Seville, engaged to Ana and killed seeking revenge for her wrongs from Don Juan.

Don Gonzalo de Ulloa (gohn-ZAH-loh), *comendador* (knight commander) of Calatrava. His attempt to rescue Inés results in his death.

Don Diego Tenorio (dee-EH-goh), who visits a Seville inn to check on his son's bad reputation. He later establishes a cemetery containing statues of Don Juan's victims.

Ana de Pantoja (pahn-TOH-hah), the fiancée of Mejia.

Brigida (BRE-hee-dah), the duenna of Inés.

Two officers, who witness the discussion of the wager and five years later explain to Don Juan the significance of the cemetery. He invites them and the statue of the *comendador* to come to dinner.

DON QUIXOTE DE LA MANCHA
(El ingenioso hidalgo don Quixote de la Mancha)

Author: Miguel de Cervantes (1547-1616)
First published: Part 1, 1605; part 2, 1615
Genre: Novel
Locale: Spain
Time: Late sixteenth century
Plot: Mock-heroic

Don Quixote (kee-HOH-teh), possibly a gentle but impoverished man named Alonso Quijano (or perhaps Quixana) of Argamasilla, in the Spanish province of La Mancha. Driven mad by reading many romances of chivalry, he determines to deck himself out in rusty armor and a cardboard helmet and to become a knight-errant. Under the name of "Don Quixote" he will roam the world, righting wrongs. His squire calls him "The Knight of the Sorrowful Countenance." He has moments of lucidity, especially at the end of the novel when a victorious enemy forces him to give up his questing. He returns home, repents of his folly, and dies.

Sancho Panza (SAHN-choh PAHN-sah), a paunchy rustic at first described as "long-legged." He is persuaded by promises of governorship of an island to become squire and attendant of the knight. He is the best drawn of the 669 characters in this 461,000-word novel. He does get his island, but he abdicates upon news of the approach of a hostile army.

Rocinante (rroh-see-NAHN-teh), the nag that carries Don Quixote on his journeying. His companion is Dapple, the donkey of Sancho Panza.

Aldonza Lorenzo (ahl-DOHN-sah loh-REHN-zoh), a sweaty peasant girl of Toboso, whom Don Quixote idealizes under the name of **Dulcinea del Toboso**; he chooses her to be his queen of love and beauty, the inspiration of his knightly questing.

Antonia Quixana (kee-HAH-nah), Don Quixote's niece, who by the terms of his dying will can marry only a man who is not given to reading books of chivalry.

Teresa Cascajo (teh-REH-sah kahs-KAH-hoh), also called **Juana Gutierrez** (HWAH-nah gew-tee-EH-rrehs), the wife of Sancho Panza.

An innkeeper, the fat master of a roadside inn that Don Quixote mistakes for a fortress. He dubs Don Quixote a knight.

Andrés (ahn-DREHS), an unpaid servant, temporarily saved from a beating in Don Quixote's first attempt at righting wrongs.

Pedro Pérez (PEH-droh PEH-rehs), the curate who burns the knight's library of chivalric romances in an attempt to cure him of his madness.

Master Nicolás (nee-koh-LAHS), the village barber, who assists in burning the books. Dressed in women's clothes, he impersonates Dulcinea in an effort to persuade Don Quixote to leave the Sierra Morena.

Cardenio (kahr-DEH-nee-oh), who meets Don Quixote in the Sierra Morena and tells his sad story.

Dorotea (doh-roh-TEH-ah), another ill-starred wanderer with a melancholic tale. She pretends to be a damsel in distress in order to persuade the knight to go home.

Ginés de Pasamonte (hee-NEHS deh pah-sah-MOHN-teh), a criminal condemned to the galleys. Don Quixote rescues him and a dozen more from the chain gang, only to be stoned by them.

Two friars, acting as escort for a noble lady in a coach. The knight believes they are abducting her and attacks the retinue; they beat up Sancho Panza.

Roque Guinart (rroh-keh gee-NAHRT), a man driven to banditry by bad luck. He captures Don Quixote and Sancho. Refusing to be persuaded by them to turn knight-errant, he sends his prisoners to a neighboring bandit and recommends them as entertaining persons.

Master Pedro, the owner of a divining ape and a puppet show whose characters the knight mistakes for real people. He tries to rescue the leading lady.

A barber, whose shaving basin Don Quixote mistakes for Mambrino's golden helmet.

A carter, taking caged lions from the governor of Oran to King Philip. In outfacing one of them, Don Quixote achieves his only successful adventure in the novel.

A duke and his duchess, who invite Don Quixote and Sancho Panza to their palace and play jokes on them, such as a supposed ride through space on a magic wooden horse, Clavijero. They make Sancho governor of an island, a village owned by the Duke.

Samson Carrasco (kah-RRAHS-koh), a neighbor who disguises himself as the Knight of the Mirrors and the Knight of the White Moon. He eventually overcomes Don Quixote and sentences him to abandon knight-errantry and return home. There Don Quixote dies after denouncing knight-errantry as nonsense, never realizing that he himself has been a true knight and a gallant gentleman.

DON SEGUNDO SOMBRA: Shadows on the Pampas

Author: Ricardo Güiraldes (1886-1927)
First published: 1926
Genre: Novel
Locale: Argentina
Time: Late nineteenth century
Plot: Regional

Don Segundo Sombra (seh-GEWN-doh SOHM-brah), an elderly Argentine gaucho who for five years allows Fabio to accompany him in his wanderings and instructs him in the life and the culture of the pampas. He then persuades Fabio to accept the responsibility of the ranch he has inherited and stays with him until he gets established.

Fabio (FAH-bee-oh), a waif who turns to Sombra for understanding, and in many adventures with him learns courage and self-reliance.

Two aunts, who rear Fabio without interest or affection.

Don Fabio Cáceres (KAH-seh-rehs), Fabio's father, who ignores him as a child but later wills him a ranch and a fortune.

Pedro Barrales (PEH-droh bah-RRAH-lehs), a one-time gaucho companion who brings Fabio news of his inheritance.

Don Leandro Galvan (leh-AHN-droh gahl-VAHN), a rancher and later Fabio's guardian.

Paula, a fickle country girl over whom Fabio duels with a rancher's son.

DOÑA BÁRBARA

Author: Rómulo Gallegos (1884-1969)
First published: 1929
Genre: Novel
Locale: Arauca Valley, Venezuela
Time: Early twentieth century
Plot: Regional

Doña Bárbara (BAHR-bahr-ah), a beautiful but unscrupulous mestiza, once wronged by a white man and now taking her revenge on all men. She is superstitious and given to witchcraft. For a time she was the mistress of Lorenzo Barquero, heir to half the Altamira ranch, and by him had a daughter, Marisela. Then she ran him off his land and took possession. With the help of her cowboys, she is acquiring the rest of the ranch by moving the boundary fences and stealing the cattle. She has won over the local authorities. Unfortunately, she falls in love with Santos Luzardo, heir to the other half of the estate. When she goes soft, her followers desert her. Finally she rides to Altamira to shoot her daughter, whom she considers her rival, only to soften at the sight of Santos' display of affection for Marisela. She draws up papers leaving the Barquero land to Marisela and restoring what she has been stealing, then rides off, never to be heard of again.

Dr. Santos Luzardo (SAHN-tohs lew-SAHR-doh), a descendant of owners of the other half of the ranch. Taken to Caracas as a child, he studies law, then returns to his ancestral property in the wildest section of the Arauca River basin of Venezuela in order to get the land ready for sale. Seeing its deterioration under irresponsible overseers, he determines to restore the ranch to productivity. To end the long feud between the Luzardos and the Barqueros, he brings the dying Lorenzo Barquero and his daughter Marisela from their swamp cabin to live at the Altamira ranch house. From his knowledge of law, he is able to force the magistrate to call for a round-up to separate the cattle. He also sends some of his cowboys to collect heron feathers, from whose sale he will get money to repair his fences. They are murdered and the feathers stolen. When the local magistrate does nothing, Santos decides to follow the law of the jungle and match violence with violence. Hunting the feathers, on a tip from Bárbara, he finds the Wizard, her most trusted henchman, and leaves him dead.

Lorenzo Barquero (loh-REHN-soh bahr-KEH-roh), the weak-willed heir to half the Altamira ranch. Doña Bárbara becomes his mistress and gives him a daughter, Marisela. Tiring of him, Bárbara drives him off his land and begins to take over the ranch.

Marisela (mahr-ee-SEH-lah), a young girl, beautiful under her dirt, the daughter of Lorenzo Barquero. Her mother Bárbara abandons her, and her father sells her to William Danger for five bottles of whiskey. But Santos determines to civilize her. She falls so deeply in love with him that she is willing to challenge her mother's witchcraft in order to get him for herself. Finally they marry, and the two halves of the estate are reunited.

Señora Luzardo, the mother of Santos, whose life has been tragic. Not only has she seen the constant feuding between the two branches of the family, but her husband killed her oldest son in a quarrel and in remorse starved himself to death. She takes Santos back to the civilization of Caracas to study, but she cannot keep him there.

William Danger, a North American squatter who enjoys demoralizing Lorenzo Barquero by giving him liquor. He is compelled by Santos to build fences, since his herd is too small to run wild.

Antonio Sandoval (SAHN-doh-vahl), a cowboy faithful to Santos who helps him rebuild the ranch.

Balbino Paiba (bahl-BEE-noh PI-bah), the Luzardo overseer, whose love for Doña Bárbara makes him unfaithful to his employers. To make money, he steals feathers and kills Santos' cowboys. He is killed at Bárbara's orders when she tires of him and prefers Santos Luzardo.

Carmelito López (kahr-mehl-EE-toh LOH-pehs), one of Santos' cowboys, killed by Balbino.

Pajarote (pah-hah-ROH-teh), a cowboy who helps Santos.

Ambrosio (ahm-BROH-see-oh), a one-eyed cowboy musician.

Melquíades Gamarra (mehl-KEE-ah-dehs gah-mah-rrah), called **The Wizard**, Bárbara's trigger man.

Juan Primito (hwahn pree-MEE-toh), a demented cowboy who feeds the birds of ill omen and prophesies evil.

Ño Pernalete (nyoh PEHR-nah-leh-teh), the local magistrate, partial at first to Doña Bárbara, but compelled by Santos to administer justice.

Mujiquita (mew-hee-KEE-tah), the clerk of the court.

DONA FLOR AND HER TWO HUSBANDS: A Moral and Amorous Tale
(Dona Flor e Seus Dois Maridos)

Author: Jorge Amado (1912-   )
First published: 1966
Genre: Novel
Locale: Salvador, in the state of Bahia, Brazil
Time: The 1960's
Plot: Social morality

Dona Flor dos Guimarães (gee-mah-RAYNSH), a cook of genius. Flor's Cooking School of Savor and Art attracts pupils from all over the state of Bahia, Brazil, and ensures her a measure of dignity and independence. Thirtyish, easygoing, plump, coppery-skinned, and graceful, Flor is very feminine and at the peak of her charms when her husband of seven years, Vadinho, dies, leaving her chilled and lonely in her grief, with no outlet for her sensuality and *joie de vivre*. She also is beset by marriage-making friends, a gigolo on the make, and her overbearing mother. Her instinct for calm, order, and propriety, however, is satisfied by her second husband. At the end of the novel, her life is complete when Vadinho is called back from death by the power of her desire to fulfill the other, hidden side of her double nature.

Waldomiro Guimarães, usually called **Vadinho**, Dona Flor's first husband, a gambler and profligate. The bastard scion of an important family, Vadinho lives a life that is a series of picaresque adventures. Good for nothing except making love and friends, he initially courts Flor in a cynical attempt at defloration but ends with as much tenderness as nature has granted him to give. He is a bad husband—unfaithful (even with Flor's pupils) and spendthrift (once even hitting her to get his hands on her savings)—but a wonderful lover: His peremptory bedroom demands allow her to let go of her modesty. With the proceeds of his wildest gambling spree, he buys her a fabulous necklace of turquoise and showers the bed with banknotes. He drops dead dancing the samba during Carnival at the age of thirty-one, burned out by reckless living. He returns from the shades at Flor's call, materializing naked in the bedroom she now shares with his "colleague," her second husband. He is visible only to Flor but enjoys fixing the gambling tables so that his friends strike it rich on his lucky number, seventeen.

Dr. Teodoro Madureira, Flor's second husband, part owner and druggist-in-charge of the Scientific Pharmacy and an enthusiastic member of the Amateur Orchestra of the Sons of Orpheus. Gentlemanly and upright, he is an outstanding member of the community whose watchword is order: Wednesday and Saturday are duly designated as days to make love once Flor has accepted his completely correct written proposal. A romantic and (too) respectful lover, he tenderly cherishes his wife, providing for her financial and physical welfare and, at one memorable concert, also performing on his bassoon a solo "Lullaby to Floripedes."

Dona Norma de Ze Sampaio, the neighborhood guardian angel, the wife of a hypochondriac shoe-store owner. She helps Flor marry, establish her school, and survive her widowhood.

Dona Gisa, an ingenuous teacher who is stuffed with book learning and incapable of even comfortable lies. Born a *gringa* in America but now a Brazilian citizen (her Portuguese accent is execrable), Dona Gisa keeps up a ten-cent psychologist's commentary on the events of Flor's life.

Dona Rozilda, Flor's mother, a malicious harridan with a tongue like a knife, unable to control her spasmodic outbursts of hate, particularly for Vadinho, who initially tricked her into thinking him a model suitor. Her daughter's widowhood offers her an opportunity to get Flor back under her thumb, and Flor's second marriage offers the means of basking in the social success she has bitterly craved.

Dionisia, a mulatto model and whore, a votary of the god Oxossi. Beautiful and a powerful worker of magic, she helps Flor conjure Vadinho back from the shades.

— Joss Lutz Marsh

DOÑA PERFECTA

Author: Benito Pérez Galdós (1843-1920)
First published: 1876
Genre: Novel
Locale: Orbajosa, Spain
Time: Late nineteenth century
Plot: Social morality

Doña Perfecta Polentinos (DOHN-yah pehr-FEHK-tah poh-lehn-TEE-nohs), a wealthy and intensely religious woman who lives in the provincial town of Orbajosa, Spain. She represents the old order of provincial Spanish life: reactionary traditionalism, country (versus city) values, regional (versus central) government control, and, above all, neo-Catholicism characterized by religious intolerance and often profound hypocrisy. Her religious convictions—indeed, her whole way of life—are challenged when her nephew and ideological foil Pepe Rey appears on the scene from Madrid. He offends local sensibilities at every turn and, worst of all, proposes marriage to Doña Perfecta's daughter, Rosario, a prospect that Doña Perfecta simply cannot abide. Seeking to protect her way of life, as well as her family's reputation, Doña Perfecta engages in a battle of wills with Pepe, whom she sees as a symbol of evil. She will stop at nothing to oppose him. In the end, as Pepe attempts to elope with Rosario, Doña Perfecta gives the order to have him killed. The rest of her days are spent in intense religious activity as a form of self-punishment and martyrdom. Given her behavior, Doña Perfecta's name is, to say the least, ironic.

José "Pepe" Rey (hoh-SEH PEH-peh rreh), a young, handsome, well-traveled, impeccably educated, and outspoken engineer from Madrid who symbolizes a modern, progressive, free-thinking Spain. He is therefore Doña Perfecta's exact ideological opposite. Worse yet, he is quite blunt, even tactless, in the expression of his unwelcome opinions, particularly those concerning the church. Although the novel focuses on the issue of social morality, it also reads in many ways like a Greek tragedy because of Pepe's fatal flaw of not being wise enough to express his opinions less often and more moderately. Arriving in Orbajosa at the request of his father, a celebrated lawyer in Madrid, he soon clashes with Doña Perfecta's world and finds himself opposed at virtually every turn and at various levels, from his attempts to do surveying work in the region (through the loss of government contracts), to his pursuit of Rosario's hand in marriage (the final roadblock to which is his murder). He is clearly out of his element and unwanted. He successfully connects with Rosario, however, and makes plans to elope with her, against her mother's wishes. Any possible positive symbolism regarding the union of the old order and the new that might be read into a marriage between Pepe and Doña Perfecta's daughter, however, is dashed emphatically when Doña Perfecta has Pepe killed.

Rosario (rroh-SAHR-ee-oh), Doña Perfecta's daughter, who is dominated by her mother and torn between her love for Pepe and her obligation to her mother. Near the end of the novel, she agrees to elope with Pepe. Rosario goes insane as a result of Pepe's murder, a lamentable fate for the one character who represents a ray of light in an otherwise dismal environment and situation.

Don Inocencio (dohn ee-noh-SEHN-see-oh), a local canon who successfully incites Pepe with incessant sarcasm and who is in many ways Doña Perfecta's partner in crime, or at least her chief adviser regarding her outspoken nephew and how she should handle him. Although Don Inocencio clearly holds the same values as Doña Perfecta, his opposition to Pepe goes beyond simple ideology: He wants his great-nephew Jacinto, not Pepe, to marry Rosario, a fact that leads the priest to work to end all talk of marriage between the cousins. As in the case of Doña Perfecta, Don Inocencio's name is ironic.

María Remedios (mah-REE-ah reh-MEH-dee-ohs), Don Inocencio's niece and housekeeper, who wants her son Jacinto to marry Rosario. She too plots against Pepe at every opportunity.

Jacinto (hah-SEEN-toh), María Remedios' son, a lawyer, who wishes to marry Rosario and who opposes Pepe for other reasons.

Caballuco (kah-bah-YEW-koh), a regional guerrilla fighter against the central government. He, like so many in the novel, hates all outsiders. He kills Pepe on Doña Perfecta's orders.

— Keith H. Brower

DONALD DUK

Author: Frank Chin (1940-   )
First published: 1991
Genre: Novel
Locale: The Chinatown area of San Francisco, California
Time: The 1980's
Plot: *Bildungsroman*

Donald Duk, a twelve-year-old schoolboy in a well-to-do Chinese family. He is suffering from an identity crisis. He is ashamed of his Chinese ancestry, his father's occupation as a restaurant owner, and his name, resembling that of a cartoon character. His father, King Duk, treats him affectionately and humorously, recognizing his desire to give up everything Chinese to be fully American. His father suggests that he must have taken a little white boy home from the hospital. Like his mother and sisters, Donald is fascinated by old Hollywood films and fancies himself as the Chinese Fred Astaire. He takes up tap dancing. In the days leading up to the Chinese New Year, Donald is inspired by a character in Chinese folklore, Kwan Kung. Donald's uncle, whose name is the same as Donald's, tells Donald that one of his ancestors was a bloodthirsty warrior and that Donald's grandfather, who was one of the first of his family to come to America, had worked laying track for the transcontinental railway. He shows Donald a photograph of the Golden Spike Ceremony, during which the tracks from the east and the west were joined. That night, Donald dreams that he is in the midst of a camp of Chinese railroad workers, watching one of them brandish a battle-ax weighing more than one hundred pounds. Describing it as formerly the weapon of Kwan Kung, he throws it to his twelve-year-old son, who catches it and throws it back. Then the swordsman exhorts the workers to outdo the Irish on the eastern section of track by laying ten miles in a single day. This dream recurs. In a later version, Donald tells Fred Astaire that the Chinese are passive and without the spirit of competition. He then finds himself in a railroad camp where Kwan Kung is foreman and participates in a Chinese lion dance, celebrating the laying of ten miles of track in a day. In another dream, he is given a chance to sign his name in Chinese characters on the last railroad tie to be put in place, but he hesitates, as though ashamed. The next day, he goes to the library to research the history of the railroad. He finds the names of eight Irish workers who were present at the Golden Spike Ceremony but no mention of the Chinese who had broken the record. After a further dream in which the railroad officials destroy the tie bearing the names of the Chinese workers and prevent the Chinese from attending the ceremony, Donald deliberately picks a fight with his best friend, a white schoolmate. He admits that he is now afraid to dream because everything he dreams is or was true. Now he hates all white people. When he returns to his private school, he corrects his history teacher, Mr. Meanwright, for describing the Chinese as passive and noncompetitive.

King Duk, Donald's father, who combines, in his restaurant menu, items from the major cuisines of the world; he accepts the American multicultural society in which he lives. For years, he has been building a collection of model military airplanes. He plans to set them afire, after launching, as part of the Chinese New Year celebration. Having played the role of Kwan Kung in a Chinese opera, he tells Donald that whoever has that part takes on the traits and personality of the character, acquiring an invincible source of power. Despite this display of ethnic pride, King does not condemn American history books for failing to honor the contribution of the Chinese in building American railroads. He attributes this omission to the Confucian doctrine of "the mandate of heaven." King plays the part of Kwan Kung in a performance by a visiting opera troupe led by Donald's uncle. After the performance, he goes to the roof of his apartment house, launches his model airplanes, and sets them afire when aloft. The burning planes symbolize the rise and fall of kingdoms, King's confidence in the Chinese way of life, and his adjustment to the pluralistic society in which he lives.

Uncle Donald Duk, who at his own expense brings his opera company to perform for the New Year as a tribute to King Duk. He buys jackets for all the boys at Donald's private school and supervises the distribution of fifty-pound gift sacks of rice, one for every apartment on the side of the block where Donald lives.

—A. Owen Aldridge

DÔRA, DORALINA

Author: Rachel de Queiroz (1910-)
First published: 1975
Genre: Novel
Locale: Brazil
Time: The 1930's to the 1940's
Plot: Psychological realism

Maria das Dores, called **Dôra** or **Doralina**, the narrator and central character, who recounts her life from her late teenage years through her marriage, her career as an actress traveling around Brazil, her years in Rio de Janeiro, and her return to the Northeastern ranch where she was reared. Her ambivalent relationship with her mother is not resolved until the end, when she takes her mother's place as the head of the Soledade ranch. Dôra's resentment of her mother leads to early acts of defiance: She shelters and protects a wounded bandit, Raimundo Delmiro, when she is fourteen years old and at twenty-two marries a young surveyor, Laurindo Quirino, who courts both Dôra and her mother. Twenty-six years old when Laurindo dies, she leaves the ranch and lives for a time in the nearby city of Fortaleza, then joins an itinerant company of actors, using the stage name of Nely Sorel. The company tours Brazil and, as it travels toward Rio, Dôra meets a handsome ship captain and falls in love. She and the Captain settle in Rio, living there for a number of years. When he dies of typhoid, she seeks refuge at Soledade and busies herself putting the long-neglected ranch back into good running order.

Senhora, Dôra's mother, widowed when Dôra was young. She presides over the Soledade ranch and the people who live there. Dôra feels that her mother is cold and uncommunicative, that she never really shares her life or her power with her daughter but instead considers her to be a competitor and rival. Only when her mother dies does Dôra feel that she can go home again to Soledade and make a life for herself there.

Laurindo Quirino (kih-REE-new), a distant relative of Senhora's family, an agricultural engineer and a surveyor who covets the Soledade ranch and becomes Dôra's husband and Senhora's lover. He dies young in a mysterious shooting accident for which Delmiro may be responsible.

Asmodeu Lucas (azh-meh-DAY-ew), called **the Captain**, the great love of Dôra's life. Originally a river pilot from Pirapora, Minas, Lucas is captain of the ship *J. J. Seabra* when Dôra meets him. When he loses that job because he is caught smuggling diamonds, Lucas moves in with Dôra in Rio, becomes involved in a new smuggling enterprise, and also works as a police academy shooting instructor. He and Dôra live together in Rio for many years, until he dies of typhoid.

Raimundo Delmiro, a bandit pursued by the police when he first appears at Soledade. He lives out his life on an isolated corner of the ranch. It is Dôra who gives him medical aid, and she is the only one to whom he confides the story of his life. She allows him to recuperate on the ranch and then gives him a patch of land on which to live. Grateful and loyal only to Dôra, Delmiro is with her when she discovers Laurindo's liaison with her mother. He is almost surely responsible for Laurindo's subsequent death in a shooting accident. He continues to live a hermitlike existence on the ranch and dies shortly before Dôra's return to Soledade.

Carleto Brandini, a man of great charm and generosity, impresario of the theatrical company he persuades Dôra to join in Fortaleza. In addition to organizing the company and its performances, he writes or adapts the plays and musicals it performs and sings the lead roles. He and his wife, Estrela, become Dôra's best friends. Dôra lives with them for a time in Rio before she and the Captain move into their own house.

Estrela Vésper Brandini, the leading actress of the theatrical company, wife of its impresario, and a kind, generous friend to Dôra through their many years of close association. She invites Dôra (and later the Captain as well) to stay at their house in Rio and is a supportive friend during their many difficulties.

Francisca Xavier (Xavinha) Miranda, a distant relative of Senhora's family, a faithful housekeeper and seamstress at Soledade who serves first Senhora and later Dôra. It is Xavinha who writes to Dôra during her years away from Soledade.

— *Mary G. Berg*

THE DOUBLE
(Dvoynik)

Author: Fyodor Dostoevski (1821-1881)
First published: 1846
Genre: Novel
Locale: St. Petersburg
Time: The 1840's
Plot: Fantasy

Yakov Petrovich Golyadkin, Sr. (YAH-kov peh-TROH-vihch gol-YAD-kihn), the assistant to the chief clerk in a government office in St. Petersburg. From the outset, Yakov Petrovich reveals himself to be an insecure and mentally unstable individual who longs to be a success in his personal and professional life but who fails in both. After he makes a fool of himself as an uninvited guest at the birthday party of the woman he desires, Klara Olsufievna, he rushes into the street in a state of distress. There he repeatedly encounters a mysterious individual who, he realizes to his dismay, is his identical physical double. After quelling his anxiety about the appearance of this double, Yakov Petrovich allows the man to spend the night in his apartment. The next day, however, he begins to perceive that the double, labeled by the narrator as Golyadkin, Jr., has begun to worm his way into Yakov Petrovich's office and threatens to take over Yakov Petrovich's place there. Increasingly horrified at the skill of Golyadkin, Jr., in currying favor with Yakov Petrovich's superiors and at the man's continued disdain for Yakov Petrovich's own attempts to make friends with him, Yakov Petrovich launches into a frantic, confused campaign of spying and letter writing to try to protect his own position and to uncover the motives of those he believes are plotting against him. After he conceives of a wild scheme to aid Klara Olsufievna in escaping from her family, he is taken into custody and whisked off to a mental asylum.

Yakov Petrovich Golyadkin, Jr., the cunning and treacherous double of Yakov Petrovich Golyadkin, Sr. A gregarious figure who knows how to combine poses of concerned sincerity with genial good humor, he displays an unerring ability to gain the favor of Yakov Petrovich's superiors while casting Yakov Petrovich himself into situations of public humiliation. His appearance in the novel reflects both Yakov Petrovich's insecurity over his position in society and his unresolvable internal conflicts over what kind of image he should present to the outside world.

Klara Olsufievna Berendeyeva (KLAH-rah ohl-SEW-fyehv-nah beh-rehn-DEH-yeh-vah), the daughter of a man who had once been Yakov Petrovich's benefactor. Although she is the object of Yakov Petrovich's affections, her own romantic interests are directed toward another official, Vladimir Semyonovich.

Andrei Filipovich (fee-LEE-poh-vihch), the head of the government office in which Yakov Petrovich works and the uncle of Vladimir Semyonovich.

Krestyan Ivanovich Rutenspitz (chrehst-YAN ee-VAH-noh-vihch rew-tehn-spihtz), Yakov Petrovich's doctor. It is Yakov Petrovich's visit to this doctor at the beginning of the story that reveals Yakov Petrovich's mental instability, and it is this doctor who conducts the deranged man to the mental asylum at the end.

Karolina Ivanovna (kah-roh-LEE-nah ee-VAH-nov-nah), a German woman in whose apartment Yakov Petrovich once lived and whom he once courted, perhaps with dishonorable motives. Yakov Petrovich denies that he promised to marry her to avoid paying the rent that he owed her.

Petrushka (peh-TREW-shkah), Yakov Petrovich's servant. He is a taciturn man whose drunkenness only compounds Yakov Petrovich's confusion over what intrigues may be transpiring around him.

— *Julian W. Connolly*

THE DOUBLE-DEALER

Author: William Congreve (1670-1729)
First published: 1694
Genre: Drama
Locale: London, England
Time: The seventeenth century
Plot: Comedy

Jack Maskwell, the double-dealer, whose villainy can be admired only because of its audacity. A pensioner of Lord Touchwood, he plots to become his benefactor's heir and marry an heiress. Toward this end, he pretends to be a friend of Mellefont, Lord Touchwood's nephew and heir. He also becomes Lady Touchwood's lover, both for his sensual delight and for an opportunity to put her in a position where she will be a willing tool against the innocent Mellefont. All of Maskwell's evil machinations appear to be so well planned as to bear fruit, but his success causes him to overreach himself, so that he is unmasked as a traitorous friend and as a cuckold-maker. He is motivated only by selfishness and sensuality in his wicked schemes against his friends.

Mellefont, the chief victim of Maskwell's plots. He is a mannerly, virtuous young man who is his uncle's heir and about to marry Cynthia, a rich heiress. He trusts Maskwell: His own honesty blinds him to the dishonesty in his enemy, to the point that he makes Maskwell his confidant and tells him all his thoughts and plans.

Lady Touchwood, Mellefont's aunt by marriage. She is a passionate woman who falls in love with Mellefont, even to offering herself to him in his bedroom. When she is repulsed by the honest young man, her love-turned-hate puts her in league with Maskwell to ruin Mellefont. She then becomes Maskwell's mistress. Her zeal to enter Mellefont's bed, even after being repulsed, proves her undoing, and her husband catches her and reveals her as an adulteress. Sensuality, driven by passions, dominates her nature.

Lord Touchwood, an honest man who, like his nephew, is deceived by dishonest people. When he is misled by Lady Touchwood and Maskwell, he casts off his nephew, believing that Mellefont has tried to seduce Lady Touchwood. He then vows that he will make Maskwell his heir and help that young man marry the rich heiress, Cynthia. With Cynthia's help, however, he discovers the treachery of Maskwell and his wife in time to reconsider his actions and reinstate his nephew.

Cynthia, a beautiful young heiress in love with Mellefont. She refuses to consider Maskwell as a husband because she is sincerely in love with the man she wants to marry. She helps unmask the plot against Mellefont.

Lady Plyant, Cynthia's stepmother, the second wife of Sir Paul Plyant. She pretends to great piety and virtue, even to the point of letting her husband enter the marriage bed only once a year, on their wedding anniversary. She dominates her husband, reading all of his mail and issuing him pocket money as one would give an allowance to a child. Her hypocrisy becomes manifest, however, when Careless, Mellefont's friend, courts her and easily turns her from her virtuous path, revealing her piety to be mere silliness and hypocrisy. That she wishes to be of easy virtue is also indicated by her too ready belief that Mellefont, under cover of marrying Cynthia, will attempt to seduce her. Like her sister-in-law, Lady Touchwood, she is dominated by sensuality.

Sir Paul Plyant, Cynthia's father. A good man but stupid, he accepts his wife's dominance and her supposed piety, not wanting to admit that she fails him as a wife. He wishes his daughter to marry so that she can provide him with a grandson; his wife appears unlikely to produce a son and heir. He is Lady Touchwood's brother.

Ned Careless, a happy, witty young man, Mellefont's good friend. He distrusts Maskwell and tries to warn Mellefont against him. Careless, almost as a joke, undertakes to sue for Lady Plyant's love, in the hope of leading that woman to provide a son for her husband.

Lord Froth, a solemn, stupid nobleman. He tries to appear a bit better than everyone else. He fears especially to demean himself by laughing at other people's jokes.

Lady Froth, a vain, silly woman. She wants to appear as a scholar and poet, but poetical efforts merely show that she has neither taste nor talent.

Mr. Brisk, a would-be wit who succeeds only in being a coxcomb. He strives desperately to be a brilliant conversationalist, only to prove himself a bore.

The Reverend Mr. Saygrace, an absurd clergyman who is Maskwell's willing tool. He would like to be considered a great writer of sermons, as well as a scholar and a wit.

DOWN FROM THE HILL

Author: Alan Sillitoe (1928-)
First published: 1984
Genre: Novel
Locale: England
Time: The summers of 1945 and 1983
Plot: Psychological realism

Paul Morton, a seventeen-year-old Nottingham factory worker. He leaves Nottingham on a six-day bicycle tour in the summer of 1945, then retraces his route by Volvo automobile in the summer of 1983, when he is a successful television scriptwriter separated from his third wife. Along his route, he meets people whom he recalls from his 1945 journey. In 1945, he stays nights in youth hostels, climbs ruins of an abbey, has a sexual encounter, and returns home to begin training as an air traffic controller. In 1983, he climbs the abbey wall and inquires about Alice Sands but declines to retrace the last segment of the tour, down from Broughton Hill.

Alice Sands, the only person whom Paul plans to meet during his bicycle tour. With hazel eyes, auburn hair, and pale skin, she reminds him of the roses in Wishdale Abbey. With Gwen, they have fish and chips, go to movies in Stafford, and visit a castle. Paul never sees her again, though he learns in 1983 that she married a Canadian lawyer, lived for a while in Toronto, and had two children.

Gwen, a friend of Alice. Wearing strong perfume to cover odors acquired from her job in a fish shop, she is an unwelcome third party.

Uncle Fred, Paul's uncle, though in 1983 Paul wonders if Fred in fact is his father. He lived a wild life, was despised by Paul's father, and died in a home for the mentally incompetent. Paul is haunted by memories of Fred.

Albert Colston, Paul's friend in Nottingham. He promises to go on the 1945 bike tour but instead makes up a quarrel with his girlfriend and stays behind.

Janice, Paul's current girlfriend in Nottingham in 1945. Straitlaced and ugly, with buck teeth, she no longer interests him.

Oswestry (Ozzie), a youthful cyclist Paul meets in 1945. Wearing khaki knee shorts, he has fair hair and white hands. He looks at churches and flowers. Paul calls him by the name of the town that is their joint destination.

Joseph, the warden of the Stafford hostel where Paul stays in 1945. He offers Paul a job with Irish laborers.

MacGuinness, a young Irish worker with curly black hair and a red face, who sleeps next to Paul in the Stafford hostel in 1945. He sticks his fork in the hand of a man who tries to steal his breakfast egg.

Eunice, a seventeen-year-old girl with long blonde hair

who works in her grandmother's hostel in Lichfield in 1945. She sleeps with a truck driver in the dormitory and leaves with him the next morning.

Barry "Sheffield" Coutts, one of three young cyclists whom Paul meets in 1945 watching a barge on the Oxford canal. They are from Sheffield, and Paul calls him by that name. Sheffield hates his uncle for making him feel responsible for his mother's death.

Pete Clipstone, who is traveling with Barry Coutts. He has dark curly hair and a pale face. He is impressed with the colors of the barge on the canal, and he dislikes coal mining because his brother was crippled working in mines.

Noah, the third cyclist from Sheffield.

Jack Randall, a friend of the cyclists from Sheffield who has ridden ahead to chase girls. He is the main subject of conversation among the Sheffield cyclists, though it is possible that he does not even exist.

Woman at Blatherdene cottage garden, with whom Paul has a sexual encounter during his tour in 1945. He never learns her name. Then middle-aged, she had two sons in the navy; one disappeared at sea. She leads Paul into her house, where they make love on the hearth rug.

Tom Clifford, a fifty-year-old man on a bicycle whom Paul meets at Kings Cliffe hostel in 1945. He is enthusiastic about a Labour Party election victory and regrets that Napoleon did not invade England in 1804.

Mister Close, an old man whom Paul meets at an Oakham pub in 1945. He recalls days when people walked more.

Ukrainian Man, who has a black, swollen eye and bloated lips. He brings water to Paul, who stops at a farmhouse outside Ab Kebbleby in 1945.

Larry Ragnal, a Nottingham friend with whom Paul stays overnight in 1983. A retired air force officer now in his mid-fifties, he took Paul's job in air traffic control when Paul left for military service. They talk of life in the control tower.

Muriel Fletcher, a television actress Paul dated in 1983. She is the cause of his recent separation. An old man in Stafford compares Alice Sands to her.

Daventry, an unemployed hitchhiker from Daventry whom Paul picks up in Coventry in 1983; he is heading to London for work. A silent young man, he recognizes music by Handel that he used to sing. He refuses the money that Paul offers.

— *Richard D. McGhee*

DOWN THERE
(Là-bas)

Author: Joris-Karl Huysmans (1848-1907)
First published: 1891
Genre: Novel

Locale: Paris, France
Time: Late nineteenth century
Plot: Fantasy

Durtal (dewr-TAHL), a writer. Speaking through Durtal, Huysmans himself is the hero of *Down There*, the first in a series of four novels tracing the author's spiritual journey through skepticism and despair to the final goal of faith. While engaged in compiling the history of Gilles de Rais, Durtal becomes interested in church history and especially in Satanism. He is taken to witness a Black Mass by his mistress, Hyacinthe Chantelouve, who afterward tricks him into committing sacrilege. In disgust, he breaks off their relationship, thus ending this novel, the first of the four.

Gilles de Rais (zheel deh ray), marshal of France murderer, sadist, and Satanist. Durtal's readings from his history of the infamous marshal, youthful companion-in-arms to Jeanne d'Arc, make up large sections of *Down There*. Research into the details of his subject's progress from early religious exaltation, through unspeakable perversion, arrest, trial, and repentance, leads Durtal into his interest in Satanism and from there to the Black Mass and sacrilege.

Hyacinthe Chantelouve (yah-SAHNT shahnt-LEWV), Durtal's mistress, who takes him to a Black Mass and afterward betrays him into committing sacrilege.

Des Hermies (day zehr-MEE), Durtal's friend, whose function in the novel is to listen to the writer talk.

Carhaix (kah-RAY), the bell ringer of Saint-Suspice, with whom Durtal discusses church history and Satanism.

Canon Docre (kah-NOHN dohkr), a renegade priest and a Satanist.

Chantelouve, a Catholic historian and the husband of Hyacinthe Chantelouve.

THE DOWNFALL
(La Débâcle)

Author: Émile Zola (1840-1902)
First published: 1892
Genre: Novel

Locale: France
Time: 1870-1871
Plot: Social criticism

Corporal Jean Macquart (zhahn mah-KAHR), a French peasant serving in the army during the Franco-Prussian War. He is a veteran of many battles who manages to survive honorably during the devastating fighting at Sedan. Captured by the Germans, he escapes with one of his men and bravely makes his way back to join the French Army of the North. In the civil war that breaks out against the Second Republic, he bayonets one of his friends fighting for the other side and is heartbroken.

Private Maurice Levasseur (moh-REES leh-vah-SEWR), a middle-class Frenchman who joins the French army to escape debts and is assigned to Corporal Macquart's squad. Levasseur, who believes in the evolutionary necessity of war, at first despises the corporal but comes to admire Macquart for his bravery and common sense. In the fighting at Sedan, Levasseur saves the corporal's life; later, the corporal helps him to escape the Germans after capture. In the civil war against the Second Republic, Levasseur is killed in night street fighting by his friend Macquart.

Honoré Fouchard (oh-noh-RAY few-SHAHR), a French artilleryman who is helped by Macquart and Levasseur in saving his father from pillaging German soldiers. He is a gallant man who offers to marry his father's servant-girl, who is pregnant by a man suspected of being a German spy. Honoré is killed during the fighting around Sedan.

M. Fouchard, Honoré's father, a farmer. He works with the French partisans against the Germans.

Silvine (seel-VEEN), M. Fouchard's servant-girl, pregnant by one of the hired men. She finds the body of Honoré, who has offered to marry her, on the battlefield and brings it home for burial.

Goliath, M. Fouchard's servant, who seduces Silvine. Goliath becomes a spy for the Germans. When he returns to the farm to renew his affair with Silvine, he is killed by French partisans.

Henriette Weiss, Maurice Levasseur's twin sister. Her husband's death at the hands of German soldiers almost unhinges her mind. She finds her brother in Paris dying of a wound inflicted by Corporal Macquart.

M. Weiss, Henriette's husband, who organizes a band of soldiers and other civilians to fight the Germans. When captured, he is stood against a wall and executed, despite the entreaties of his wife, who sees him shot in cold blood.

M. Delaherche (deh-lah-EHRSH), M. Weiss's employer, a textile manufacturer who finds collaboration with the Germans enables him to reestablish his business.

Captain von Gartlauben, a Prussian officer billeted in M. Delaherche's home. He helps his host collaborate with the conquerors.

Gunther, Maurice Levasseur's cousin, an officer commanding a company of Prussian Guards.

DRACULA

Author: Bram Stoker (1847-1912)
First published: 1897
Genre: Novel
Locale: Transylvania and England
Time: Late nineteenth century
Plot: Horror

Count Dracula, a vampire. A corpse during the day, he comes to life at night. He has lived for centuries by sucking blood from living people. He pursues his victims in many harrowing episodes, and is pursued in turn from England to Rumania. There his body, in transport home to his castle, is overtaken and a stake driven through the heart, making it permanently dead.

Jonathan Harker, an English solicitor. He goes to Castle Dracula to transact business with the count, whose nocturnal habits and total absence of servants puzzle Harker. Harker finds himself a prisoner in the castle, comes one day upon Dracula's corpse, and is occasionally victimized by the vampire. Then the coffin-like boxes are carried away, and Harker finds himself left alone, still a prisoner. Later, after he has escaped, he is able to throw light on certain strange happenings in England.

Mina Murray, Harker's fiancée. She joins in the pursuit of Dracula; in a trance, she is able to tell the others that Dracula is at sea, on his return voyage.

Lucy Westenra, a lovely friend whom Mina visits at the time of Harker's trip to Rumania. She is the repeated victim of Dracula, now in England, who appears sometimes in werewolf guise. Finally she dies and becomes a vampire also.

Dr. Van Helsing, a specialist from Amsterdam called to aid the failing Lucy. His remedies are effective, but a fatal attack comes after he leaves; he then returns to England to still her corpse as well as to hunt Dracula.

Dr. Seward, Lucy's former suitor, who attends her during her illness. Until he makes a midnight visit to her empty tomb, he does not believe Van Helsing's advice that the dead girl's soul can be saved only if a stake is driven through her heart.

Arthur Holmwood, a young nobleman and Lucy's fiancée. As he kisses the dying Lucy, her teeth seem about to fasten on his throat. He goes with Seward and Van Helsing to the empty tomb and joins them in tracking down Dracula.

THE DRAGON CAN'T DANCE

Author: Earl Lovelace (1935-   )
First published: 1979
Genre: Novel
Locale: Port-of-Spain, Trinidad
Time: Early 1960's-1971
Plot: Social

Aldrick Prospect, a thirty-one-year-old man who has never had a regular job and whose only concern throughout the year is the creation of a new costume for his perennial role as dragon during the Trinidad Carnival. Seeing himself as embodying the power of ancestral African warriors and his dispossessed community's potential for rebellion against its oppressors, he deliberately cuts himself off from ordinary ambitions—for love, possessions, a home—to devote himself to the partly mystical and priestly role through which he also asserts his own identity and humanity. He feels the impulse to love and protect Sylvia, but when she offers herself to him, he chooses, despite feelings of guilt, to maintain the emotional isolation and austerity that his role dictates. He gradually becomes alienated from most of his neighbors and is unwilling to act as guardian of the community code or to continue his role as dragon. He acts out his rebellion by scorning his neighbors, betraying his successful friend Philo, and taking part in a foolhardy hijacking of a police vehicle. Released after five years in prison, changed but undefeated, he seeks out Sylvia. Learning of her impending marriage to Guy, he leaves the hill.

Sylvia, a seventeen-year-old girl with special qualities of vitality, beauty, fragility, and desirability. The women of the Calvary Hill slum hope that she can miraculously escape the inevitable and common destiny of sexual exploitation, early pregnancy, and defeat and that her youth and promise will not be destroyed. Unable to establish a relationship with Aldrick based on love and the hope for an ordinary life, Sylvia faces the reality of her fatherless family's poverty and gives herself to Guy in return for gifts, rent, and eventually a place of her own. Seven years later, on the eve of the wedding that will formalize and secure her relationship with Guy, she goes in search of Aldrick.

Belasco "Fisheye" John, a tall and powerfully built man with bulging eyes. He is a "bad John," indulging in violence to vent his bubbling rage. In his mid-thirties, he joins the Calvary Hill steel band more as a fighter than as a musician. Having found a purpose in life and a sense of pride and belonging, he is able to express a humanity that had been hidden. Unable to accept the end of the steel-band wars, he is expelled from the band, returns to his antisocial ways, and is sentenced to seven years in prison for leading an attack on the police.

Miss Cleothilda Alvarez, an aging mulatto who, at Carnival, plays Queen of the Calvary Hill Carnival band. She is a parlor owner and former beauty queen. By virtue of her color, looks, and money, and the credit she extends to her customers, she exercises a condescending and manipulative control over her resentful but compliant neighbors. Gossipy and vindictive, she is superficially transformed at Carnival time into a generous advocate of unity and brotherhood. Forever coquettish, she scorns Philo, her black would-be lover; she loses her superior status when, after many years, she finally accepts him.

Samuel "Philo" Sampson, a forty-two-year-old singer and friend of Aldrick. A pleasant, smiling, boyish man, he becomes affluent when he turns from calypsos of social protest to popular smut. Wanting old friends to understand that he is still one of them, he is confused and hurt when his generosity is rejected.

Boya Pariag, a budding entrepreneur of East Indian descent, a newcomer to Calvary Hill. Shy, introspective, and with a desperate need to belong, he is excluded by his Creole neighbors. Hard work brings him financial success but not, as he had hoped, his neighbors' appreciation of his true self.

Dolly, Pariag's wife through an arranged marriage. She is uncomplaining, patient, and understanding, seeing financial success as protection against prejudice.

Miss Olive, Sylvia's mother. Slow, stout, and six feet tall, she takes in washing to support her seven children. Dutifully suffering Miss Cleothilda's demands and pomposity out of pity as much as respect, she has no heart to expose Cleothilda's weakness.

Guy, a middle-aged property owner and rent collector who makes Sylvia his mistress and later plans to marry her.

— Douglas Rollins

DRAGON SEED

Author: Pearl S. Buck (1892-1973)
First published: 1942
Genre: Novel
Locale: A small village in occupied China
Time: The 1930's-1941
Plot: Historical

Ling Tan, the patriarch of a family that includes five children, three boys and two girls. His story begins as that of a simple farmer who is happy to have his family well provided for through their collective labor. He has a few cattle, pigs, and chickens. Two of his three sons are married, as is his eldest daughter. As the Japanese invade China, his life becomes harsh. The novel is told through his and other peasants' eyes. He becomes clever at hiding food from the Japanese, protecting his children and his neighbors from the invaders and launching attacks against them. His affection and respect for his wife are depicted as genuine. They each know their duties and responsibilities, and they make good decisions for their children and extended families.

Ling Sao, Ling Tan's wife, a benevolent woman not overly critical of her sons and their wives or of her own daughters. She and her husband work together and discuss important decisions. She sees her place as ensuring the biological continuation of the family, finding good wives and trying to provide for grandchildren.

Lao Ta, the oldest son, who is married and has one child as the novel opens. During the occupation, his wife gives birth to another child. He is largely content with his life on the family farm, but with the occupation, his wife is in danger. His wife and children die of disease, and he becomes a wild fighter.

Lao Er, the second son, more dynamic than his brother. He loves his wife deeply and passionately, and he tries to please her. He is also faithful to his parents. He takes her north, away from the invasion, but returns to his parents with his family after Lao Ta's children die. They stay to wage war on the Japanese with his father and brother. His dedication to the resistance and his care of his wife and pride in her accomplishments mark him as an ideal new man of China.

Jade, the wife of Lao Er, intelligent and educated, with a mind of her own. She is the first to really understand the democracy movement and the Japanese invasion. She helps her husband to escape; after they return, she helps him to fight the Japanese. She is as modern a woman as could be found in China in the 1930's, when a limited number of women were educated. She is a fierce fighter and a competent mother and wife.

Lao San, the youngest brother, a teenage boy at the beginning of the invasion. He is more carefree than his older brothers. After being raped by the Japanese because they could find no women in the household, he becomes a bloodthirsty fighter.

His parents worry especially that he and his oldest brother will not return to normal. The whole family contrives to find him a worthy wife. He becomes interested in Mayli, who has returned from life in the United States to be with her people.

Pansiao, the youngest member of the family. She has spent most of her life weaving in a small room in the family house. She gets her opportunity to study when the women must hide with a Christian missionary. When the rest of the family members go back home to fight, she joins other young women at a mission school in the North and starts her education. Her family loyalty is expressed in her quest for a wife for Lao San.

Third Cousin, a partially educated but essentially lazy man. His wife and son cause him a lot of trouble, but they are the ones with spunk and ideas. His wife becomes a spy for Ling Tan's son-in-law, Wu Lien, who collaborates with the Japanese. He tires of his wife's control and becomes an opium addict. With the help of a stolen radio, he passes information to the peasants in a teahouse. He is the mouthpiece through which readers are connected to the world outside the little village and the larger town nearby.

Wu Lien, the husband of Ling Tan's oldest daughter, a well-off merchant in the town who deals in foreign as well as domestic goods. When a general strike is called, along with an embargo on selling foreign goods, he does not comply, and his shop is destroyed. He lives with the Ling family for a while, then manages to make connections with the Japanese and lives in their compound, a seized large family home. A collaborator with the Japanese, even though they killed his mother, he nevertheless keeps silent about the Ling family's guerrilla activities and helps them financially.

— Janice M. Bogstad

A DREAM JOURNEY

Author: James Hanley (1901-1985)
First published: 1976
Genre: Novel
Locale: Chelsea and other parts of London
Time: 1940-1950
Plot: Social realism

Clement (Clem) Stevens, an unsuccessful, fifty-six-year-old artist from the provinces. He lives with Lena in Chelsea, London, five floors up in a once-elegant house, now due for demolition. He and Lena lived there through World War II. Paralyzed by inertia and without contact with the outside world, he spends his days with his rejected paintings, never leaving the house and drinking and smoking heavily, continually reading, fearing that Lena will leave him. He is in poor health. The turning point in his life seems to have been the loss of a canvas during an air raid in the war, when the house was full of occupants. After once venturing out of the house, he dies when an oil stove explodes. The police suspect that he was trying to burn his paintings.

Lena Stevens, a tall woman, aged sixty, with a severe expression and large hands. She uses Clem's surname. She has been Clem's loyal companion for the ten years since they moved into their flat, at the beginning of the war. At first, she believed in Clem's ability, but now she pities his failure and is wearied by his listlessness and helpless dependence. She remains loyal and prepares his meals. Her remaining pleasure consists of shopping expeditions by bus to the distant area of London where they first met. The onset of her breast cancer already was apparent during the war years. After Clem's death, she analyzes the weaknesses that kept them together.

Ivor Cruickshank, a seventy-year-old man of no occupation. Slight in build, dapper, and wearing a goatee, he once was the owner of an art gallery. He bought two paintings from Clem, but his disapproval of certain paintings of an old woman discouraged Clem. Years later, after Clem's death, he visits Lena, whom he has forgotten. He is unlikely to return.

Celia "Cis" Downes, a pretty former model from Bermondsey who tries to call on Clem early in the war and is sent off by Lena. Before leaving, she meets a drunken sailor, steals a painting of herself, and is sick during an air raid.

Richard Jones, an air raid warden in World War II, when he and his wife, Gwyn, occupied a flat in the same house as Clem and Lena. He is very conscientious, and it is he who offers refuge to the drunken sailor and looks after the elderly Frasers. He hears Lena talking to the former model and Clem pacing the floor.

Ephraim Johns, a drunken sailor given refuge by Jones. He is haunted by dreams of ice, having been bombed at sea. He meets Celia in the owners' unoccupied flat and later is killed in an air raid.

Robinson, a man in the Royal Air Force. During the war, he lived in the flat below the Stevenses. On leave, he kept the flat noisy with South American music, drank gin, and took benzedrine. After the war, Lena briefly meets him; he is now gatekeeper at a dog racetrack.

Mrs. Cis Grimpen, the wife of the caretaker who moved in after the war. Tall and stout, it is she who, well-intentioned and interfering, brings to Cruickshank news of Clem's death.

Mr. Grimpen, a tall, heavily built man in his mid-forties. The caretaker after the war of the once-splendid house, he notes the eccentric habits of the Stevenses, the only other occupants.

— W. Gordon Cunliffe

DREAM OF THE RED CHAMBER
(Hung-lou Meng)

Authors: Ts'ao Hsüeh-chin (Ts'ao Chan, 1716-1763), with a continuation by Kao Ê
First published: 1792
Genre: Novel
Locale: Peking
Time: c. 1729-1737
Plot: Domestic realism

Madame Shih, called **the Matriarch**, the widow of Chia Tai-shan and the oldest living female ancestor of the family Chia. In her eighties, she rules with authority and grace her large families in two palace compounds. Although she shows favoritism to her grandson, she is fair in her judgments and unselfish in her actions. She sacrifices her personal wealth to aid her decadent descendants, but she herself never compromises her integrity.

Chia Cheng, her younger son. A man of strict Confucian principles, he manages to keep his integrity in spite of calumnious actions against him. Extremely autocratic and strong-willed, he is puritanic as well. Although he loves his talented son, Chia Cheng cannot condone his frivolous ways or his lack of purpose; hence he disciplines the delicate boy too severely.

Madame Wang, Chia Cheng's wife.

Pao-yu, Chia Cheng's son by Madame Wang and the favorite of the Matriarch. Born with a jade tablet of immortality in his mouth, the boy is thought by all to be favored by the gods and distinguished among mortals. He is extremely handsome, sensitive, and perceptive, though delicate in health. He is also lazy, self-indulgent, effeminate—in short all the things his father does not want him to be—and he lives surrounded by faithful maidservants whose loving care is most touching. His character develops as he associates with his beloved cousin, Black Jade, and her cousin, Precious Virtue. His loss of the jade amulet causes him great pain and trouble, especially when his parents and grandmother decide on the wrong wife for him. When Black Jade dies of a broken heart, he turns to scholarship and distinguishes himself and his family, renewing their fortune before he disappears in the company of a Buddhist monk and a lame Taoist priest. His filial piety in redeeming the reputation and fortune of the Chias atones for all the trouble he caused his family. Precious Virtue, his wife, bears him a son to carry on the family line.

Tai-yu, called **Black Jade**, another of the Matriarch's grandchildren, a girl born into mortality from the form of a beautiful flower. Delicate in health and gravely sensitive, the beautiful and brilliant child comes to live in the Matriarch's home after her mother dies. Immediately she and Pao-yu sense their intertwined destinies, and their mutual love and respect develop to uncanny depths. Given to jealousy and melancholy, she finally wastes away to the point that the Matriarch will not allow Pao-yu to have her in marriage. Black Jade dies when Pao-yu marries Precious Virtue, who is disguised as Black Jade.

Pao-chai, called **Precious Virtue**, the demure and reserved niece of Black Jade's mother, brought into the Matriarch's pavilion as a companion to her favored grandchildren. Obedient to her benefactress' wishes, devoted to the handsome Pao-yu, loyal to Black Jade, and generous to all the many Chia relatives, Pao-chai well fits her name. Her virtues are the more remarkable in the face of the many trials placed before her, especially in giving herself in marriage to one who loves another. She is the model Chinese wife and companion, a great contrast to her brother Hsueh Pan, a reckless libertine.

Hsi-feng, called **Phoenix**, the efficient but treacherous wife of Chia Lien. At first a careful manager of the estate, she eventually indulges her greedy nature, lends money at high interest, and finally brings disgrace upon the Chia family. Her jealous nature causes tragedy and unhappiness among the loving members of the household, but she dies repentant.

Chia Lien, the husband of Phoenix and the son of Chia Sheh by an unnamed concubine, an idle, lecherous man unfaithful to his wife. After the death of Phoenix he marries

Ping-er, called **Patience**, a devoted maid of the household.

Chia-chieh, the young daughter of Phoenix and Chia Lien.

Chia Sheh, the Matriarch's older son and master of the Yungkuofu, one of the two great palace compounds of the Chia family. He is a man of ordinary talents, holds no important official post, and takes little part in the affairs of his household.

Madame Hsing, the wife of Chia Sheh.

Ying-chun, called **Welcome Spring**, the daughter of Chia Sheh by an unnamed concubine. Although the Matriarch and Chia Cheng oppose the match, Chia Sheh marries her to Sun Shao-tsu. Her husband beats her, and she is miserable in her marriage.

Chia Gen, master of the Ningkuofu. A man of no scruples, he carries on an intrigue with his daughter-in-law, Chin-shih. He helps to bring disgrace on the Chia family when he is accused of corrupting the sons of noble families and of turning the Ningkuofu into a gambling resort.

Chia Ging, Chia Gen's aged father. He has renounced the world and retired to a Taoist temple.

Yu-shih, the wife of Chia Gen.

Chia Jung, Chia Gen's son. He involves himself in several family intrigues.

Chin-shih, the wife of Chia Jung. She dies after a long illness, possibly a suicide. Before her death, she carries on an affair with her father-in-law.

Hsi-chun, called **Compassion Spring**, the daughter of Chia Ging.

Chia Chiang, the Matriarch's great-grandson. An orphan, he grows up in the household of Chia Gen and is a close friend of Chia Jung.

Chin Chung, the brother of Chin-shih. He and Pao-yu become good friends. He dies while still a schoolboy.

Chih-neng, a young nun at Iron Sill Temple, in love with Chin Chung.

Cardinal Spring, the daughter of Chia Cheng and Madame Wang. She brings great honor to the Chia family when she becomes an Imperial Concubine.

Chao Yi-niang, Chia Cheng's concubine. Jealous of Pao-yu and hating Phoenix, she secretly pays to have a spell put on them. Both become desperately ill, and their coffins are prepared. Then a Buddhist monk and a lame Taoist priest miraculously appear and restore the power of Pao-yu's jade tablet. Pao-yu and Phoenix recover.

Chia Huan, Chia Cheng's son by Chao Yi-niang. Like his mother, he resents the favoritism shown to Pao-yu.

Tan-chun, called **Quest Spring**, Chia Cheng's daughter by Chao Yi-niang. She marries the son of an important frontier official.

Hsueh Yi-ma, a widow, the sister of Madame Wang. After her husband's death, she goes with her son and daughter to live with the Chia family in the Yungkuofu. Precious Virtue, her daughter, becomes the bride of Pao-yu.

Hsueh Pan, a drunkard and libertine always in pursuit of girls and young men. His purchase of a maid, Lotus, involves him in controversy and a lawsuit. Eventually he marries the quarrelsome Cassia and is unfaithful to her. Cassia dies, accidentally poisoned, while he is living in exile on the frontier. After his return, he makes Lotus his chief wife.

Cassia, Hsueh Pan's selfish, quarrelsome, disobedient wife. While her husband is exiled she tries to seduce his cousin, Hsueh Kuo, but he repulses her. She then tries to poison Lotus, her husband's maid, but drinks the poison by mistake and dies.

Hsueh Kuo, Hsueh Pan's cousin. Incapable of disloyalty, he spurns Cassia's attempts to make him her lover.

Lotus, Hsueh Pan's maid. Stolen from her family while a child, she later attracts the attention of Hsueh Pan, who buys her but soon becomes indifferent to her beauty and grace. Married to her master after his wife's death and his return from exile, Lotus dies in childbirth.

Chen Shih-yin, the father of Lotus. After his daughter has been stolen and he has lost all of his possessions in a fire, he and his wife go to live with her family. One day he disappears in the company of a lame Taoist priest and is never seen again.

Feng-shih, Cheng Shih-yin's wife and the mother of Lotus. After her husband's disappearance, she supports herself as a seamstress.

Lin Ju-hai, the well-born descendant of an ancient family of Soochow, the Matriarch's son-in-law and the father of Black Jade. A widower without a male heir, he decides to give his daughter the education that in those times only sons of noble families received.

Chia Yu-tsun, a scholar befriended by Chen Shih-yin. He becomes Black Jade's tutor in the household of Lin Ju-hai. Later, he is appointed to the post of provincial prefect.

Hsiang-yun, called **River Mist**, a grandniece of the Matriarch. She lives with her Chia relatives for a time, but after Black Jade dies and Pao-yu and Precious Virtue are married she returns to her own family.

Yu Lao-niang, the stepmother of Yu-shih.

Er-chieh, the daughter of Yu Lao-niang by a previous marriage. Chia Lien, enamored of the girl, makes her his secret concubine and installs her with her sister, San-chieh, in a separate house. Phoenix, learning of her husband's second establishment, pretends to be reasonable and without jealousy. Secretly hating her rival, she finds an accomplice in a maid from the other household. The maid insults her mistress and treats her with such abuse that Er-chieh commits suicide by swallowing gold.

San-chieh, the sister of Er-chieh. When Chia Gen and Chia Lien decide to find a husband for her, she announces that the only man she will marry is Liu Hsiang-lien, a handsome young actor. He changes his mind, however, after a formal engagement has been arranged. San-chieh, grief-stricken, kills herself with his sword.

Liu Hsiang-lien, a handsome young actor. Although a female impersonator, he is not effeminate in mind or habits, and he rejects Hsueh Pan's suit when that licentious young nobleman pursues him. He breaks his betrothal to San-chieh after hearing gossip about her, and the girl commits suicide. Conscience-stricken, he cuts off his hair and goes away with a lame Taoist priest.

Hsi-jen, called **Pervading Fragrance**, Pao-yu's devoted maid and concubine. After the disappearance of her master, she wishes only to remain faithful to his memory, but her brother arranges her marriage to a son of the Chiang family. To her surprise, her bridegroom is Chiang Yu-han, once called Chi-kuan, an actor who had been Pao-yu's close friend.

Chiang Yu-han, a young actor whose professional name is Chi-kuan, a friend of Pao-yu. Accused of seducing the handsome player, Pao-yu is beaten severely by his stern father. Chiang Yu-han later marries Pervading Fragrance, his friend's loyal maid.

Golden Bracelet, a maid accused of attempting to seduce Pao-yu. Sent back to her family, she drowns herself.

Liu Lao-lao, a poor relation of Madame Wang. Visiting the Yungkuofu from time to time, she grows prosperous from gifts that the Chias give her.

Pan-er, her grandson, a shy boy.

Exquisite Jade, a pious, fastidious nun living in the Yungkuofu. Bandits who break into the compound seize her and take her away beyond the frontier.

Chia Lan, Pao-yu's young kinsman, who also distinguishes himself in the Imperial Examinations.

Chia Jui, an oaf who tries to force his attentions on Phoenix.

A Buddhist Monk and

A Taoist Priest, mysterious figures, possibly messengers of the Immortals, who appear suddenly and mysteriously in times of revelation or crisis.

Faith,
Ching-wen, called **Bright Design**,
Sheh-yueh, called **Musk Moon**,
Oriole,
Tzu-chuan, called **Purple Cuckoo**,
Autumn Sky, and
Snow Duck, maids in the Yungkuofu.

Chiao Ta, a privileged old family servant.

DREAM ON MONKEY MOUNTAIN

Author: Derek Walcott (1930-)
First published: 1970
Genre: Drama

Locale: A West Indian island
Time: Unspecified, probably the 1960's
Plot: Allegory

Makak, "an old Negro," the hermit of Monkey Mountain. Sixty years old and ugly, he was named for the macaque monkey, which he resembles. He is by trade a wood-gatherer and charcoal burner, but in his dream he is also the king of Africa, following the instructions of an apparition of a beautiful white woman. Partly mad, partly possessed, and partly drunk, he possibly dreams the entire play in Lestrade's cell, after a night of drunkenness in a local tavern. He is arrested for stealing coal and for disorderly conduct. In an elaborate allegorical configuration, he is the Christ figure at the beginning of his public life, performing miracles, collecting followers, and leaving behind exaggerated stories of his wonders, both betrayed and believed, as the Lion of Africa who will lead his black brethren back to Africa, but only after killing their "whiteness." He experiences a sort of apotheosis when he kills the "white" woman who haunted him into this religious and political mission.

Corporal Lestrade, a mulatto guard of the town jail, "doing the white man's work" in jailing and questioning Makak but finally "confessing" to his blackness in the final apotheosis. At first cruel in the use of his power, he forces the villagers into hypocritically agreeing to his absurd statements and pursues Makak to "hunt" him like an animal. The name of his rank suggests his allegorical function as the body of Christ/Makak. Stabbed and left for dead during the breakout, he follows Makak into the mountains, delirious from his wounds' gangrenous infection, and is converted to the African "faith" of Makak. In the epilogue, he is a merciful jailer who frees Makak, releasing him to the care of Moustique.

Moustique, a friend to Makak and a partner in the charcoal business. He is a black man who walks with a limp from "a twist foot God give me." An allegorical composite of all the disciples, he was found drunk by Makak and saved from dissolution. Nonreligious and money-conscious, he disguises himself as Makak to exploit the people but is discovered and killed by the angry mob. At the apotheosis of Makak, he returns from the dead to be judged and to die again. In the epilogue, he remains a true friend to Makak after he awakes from his dream in the cell, leading him away, back to his mountain.

Tigre, a young black thief in jail when Makak is arrested. He breaks out of jail and follows Makak to Monkey Mountain, ostensibly to follow Makak to Africa but actually to steal his money. When he tries to force Makak to lead him to the money, the corporal kills him with a lance. He represents the thief who was damned in the allegorical parallel.

Souris, "the rat," another black thief. He is a partner in Tigre's breakout and equally eager to get Makak's money. Later, he is converted to Makak's African Zionism. He represents the thief who was saved.

Basil, a young man, not only a carpenter but also a charcoal seller, and thus an alter ego of Makak. He is a figure of doom and enlightenment who appears mysteriously from time to time, a nemesis and judge for all the characters.

The Apparition, a beautiful white woman, "like the moon." She entices Makak into his religious proselytizing and is beheaded as a sacrifice at the apotheosis of Makak. She represents the "Roman law" of white Western history.

— *Thomas J. Taylor*

A DREAM PLAY
(Ett drömspel)

Author: August Strindberg (1849-1912)
First published: 1902
Genre: Drama
Locale: Sweden
Time: Late nineteenth or early twentieth century
Plot: Expressionism

Daughter of Indra, incarnated as **Agnes**, a goddess who comes down to Earth in the form of a beautiful woman to find out why humanity is so discontented. Like Christ, she experiences the pain of being human. At first, she is hopeful that love will conquer all, but after she listens to the anguished cries of humanity, experiences the pain of family life, and discovers that reform always will be stifled by the self-righteous, she can look on humanity only with compassion. She finally realizes that human beings are creatures who hopelessly harbor spiritual aspirations but are held down by the weight of their fleshly existence. When she ascends back into the heavens, she throws her shoes into the fire of purification as she leaves a world of never-ending conflicts and contradictions.

The Officer, **Alfred**, a high-ranking military officer and teacher. As the action of the play telescopes in time, he changes from a youthful, effervescent, well-groomed soldier to an aging, weary, unkempt derelict as he hopelessly spends a lifetime waiting for his dream lover, the opera singer Victoria. Restless and self-pitying, he is constantly irritated by the injustice and repetitiveness of life but continues to hold on to the romantic notion that love will cure all ills. When he rescues the Daughter of Indra (Agnes) from the drudgery of domestic life and takes her to Fairhaven, a romantic paradise, he lands in Foulstrand, where he witnesses the everlasting misery of the human condition. In his constant failure to find true love, he represents disillusioned romanticism.

The Attorney, **Axel**, a lawyer. Through his dealings with the crimes and viciousness of humanity, he has acquired a pale, haggard, and discolored face, along with blackened and bleeding hands. Denied his doctorate by the self-righteous academicians, he becomes a Christ figure who suffers rejection because he defends the poor and helpless. More of a realist than the Officer, he sees human beings as flawed creatures trapped between their commitments to odious duties and their desire for life's elusive pleasures, which always result in recriminations. Through their marriage, he enlightens Agnes on the inhuman torments of living in poverty and the constant antagonisms of family life. Later, he continually reminds her of her sacred duty to her child.

The Poet, an erratic visionary who bathes in mud to come down from the ethereal regions of lofty thought and immerse himself in the dirt of life. Caked with mud, he is protected from the stings of horseflies. Being both idealistic and cynical, he sees through life's injustices and hypocrisies and rails against the gods. Although he is an earthbound creature hampered by his bodily existence, he still reaches for spiritual rejuvenation. When those around him are abandoning hope, he realizes that human redemption will come only through suffering and death.

The Quarantine Officer, the overseer of Foulstrand who rehabilitates the overindulgent and the diseased by having them work out their disabilities on instruments of torture and execution. Disguised as a blackamoor, he paints himself to be blacker than he is while indulging in a masquerade to escape from the odiousness of his job. In dealing with profligates and incurables, he has grown callous and indifferent to human misery. He makes the Daughter of Indra and the Officer aware that even love is not immune to corruption.

The Doorkeeper, the guardian of the entrance to the opera house. Wrapped in a shawl of woes, she has spent twenty-six years crocheting a bedspread. Once a famous ballerina, she deteriorated when her lover abandoned her, and now she listens to all the griefs of humanity. She gives the Daughter of Indra the shawl of human miseries and lets her become a doorkeeper so that she can witness human disappointment.

The Billposter, a poster of signs who is overjoyed because he has finally received the fishnet and fish box that he has wanted all his life. He soon becomes dissatisfied with the net and discovers that the box is the wrong shade of green. From him, the Daughter of Indra learns that humans cannot be satisfied.

The Glazier, a worker. He uses his diamond to unlock the cloverleaf door behind which is supposed to be the mystery of the universe.

The Deans of Philosophy, Theology, Medicine, and Jurisprudence, pompous academicians who constantly bicker among themselves as to who has the greater claim to the truth. They open the mysterious cloverleaf door and find nothing behind it. They try to stone the Daughter of Indra when she attempts to teach them.

He and She,

Ugly Edith,

The Coal Heavers, and

The Blind Man, all characters who suffer life's disappointments.

Husband and

Wife, a happy couple who go off to commit suicide because they know that their happiness cannot last.

— *Paul Rosefeldt*

A DREAMBOOK FOR OUR TIME
(Sennik współczesny)

Author: Tadeusz Konwicki (1926-)
First published: 1963
Genre: Novel
Locale: Poland
Time: The 1930's to early 1960's
Plot: Impressionistic realism

Paul, the narrator, an antihero who wanders Poland in an effort to escape his largely undeserved feelings of guilt, to find some meaning in his life and that of his war-ravaged country, and to awake from the nightmare of his unfinished past that includes the death of his parents and his experiences during the war in the Polish underground. Equating belief with surrender, he remains aloof, struggling to be loyal to himself without having to betray anyone else. The novel begins shortly after his attempted suicide and ends with his leaving the remote Polish village alone, his desires for love, forgiveness, and meaning still unfulfilled.

Regina (reh-JEE-nah), an attractive but no-longer-young manager of the village grocery cooperative. She leaves the village in search of a better life only to return and marry Debicki, a railroad foreman. Paul describes her stock of cosmetics as "a secret arsenal of female captivity, of female hope. A laboratory of forgery."

Joseph Car, the "Baptist," a tall, dark leader of a local cult that is a more or less secular, or nonfaith, religion of hope. Car, an epileptic, is, or appears to be, the informer that Paul was ordered to execute during the war but could not, associating him in his mind with his own dead father. Car is the figure Paul would like to forget but cannot.

Justine, Car's wife, an orphan and self-proclaimed enchantress. Paul is drawn by her "lustful softness" but fails to convince her to leave Car and the village and begin a new life with him.

Miss Malvina Korsak (mahl-VIH-nah KOHR-sahk), a sixty-five-year-old woman. She and her brother own the house in which Paul rents a room. One of Car's most ardent followers, she repeatedly urges Paul to join them in their daily prayers. Although she also urges him to forget his past, she keeps her own past very much alive with endless nostalgic references to her previous life "back home in the East."

Ildefons Korsak (ihl-deh-FONS), her brother. He has fought for the czar, the kaiser, the Bolsheviks, and the Poles. More recently, he has been writing a book in which he claims to have put everything everyone has forgotten, but he destroys the manuscript when he discovers that his sister has secretly read it. Like most of the other villagers, he has gotten used to living in the village, which a dam project will soon flood. He does not want to leave and does not know where he will go.

Jasiu Krupa (YAH-syew KREW-pah), known as "the partisan" and suspected of being a Jew. He is a man embittered by the loss of an arm, the murder of his family, dismissal from a position of power in the postwar government because he had no education, and the spurning of his amorous advances by Regina. Vodka and the special painkilling tea he brews are his sole escapes.

Count Pac, a stuttering and long-faced man who denies his aristocratic background and goes out of his way to espouse the new creed of democracy.

Romus (RAH-moos), a slow-thinking, slow-footed villager who is suspicious of anything or anyone that is new, especially Paul, whom he urges to go away.

Szafir (shah-FIHR), the usually reticent local Communist Party official. Trapped with Paul in an abandoned house that they assume will soon be swept away by the swollen Sola River, he divulges his most secret thoughts about the need to help one another and about the burden of regret. Although they survive their ordeal, Szafir dies soon afterward, apparently of consumption, the disease that killed Paul's father.

Huniady (hew-NYA-dih), the pseudonym of the once legendary but now largely forgotten partisan-turned-bandit who, refusing the amnesty that Krupa and the other partisans accepted, lived—perhaps continues to live—alone in the Solec forest.

Father Gabriel, a monk and farm laborer. He invites Paul to visit the monastery to see the collection of old books and liturgical vessels and to find refuge from the flooding river.

Sergeant Glowko (GLOV-koh), an incompetent local policeman. He spends much of his time either hurrying back to his ill-tempered wife or hiding from her.

Korvin, one of the men for whom Paul is searching. Korvin is his code name from the Polish underground, in which he worked first under the command of Paul ("Oldster"), then later, after Oldster disobeyed his superiors and ordered Korvin to murder German prisoners, as Paul's commander. Korvin believed he had to find and kill his brother, a Bolshevik, who betrayed the underground; only in this way will he, Korvin, be able to free himself of his burden of guilt and shame.

Debicki, the foreman of the railroad work crew that includes Paul, Pac, and Krupa. He marries the desperate Regina, mistakenly believing that they will be able to make a new life. The building of the railroad typifies the absurdity of his and the other villagers' situation and that of postwar Poland. The line is completed just as the entire area is about to be flooded by a government dam project.

— Robert A. Morace

DREAMING IN CUBAN

Author: Cristina Garcia (1958-   )
First published: 1992
Genre: Novel
Locale: Santa Teresa Del Mar and Havana, Cuba; New York City
Time: 1972-1980
Plot: Psychological realism

Celia Del Pino (PEE-noh), the aging matriarch of the Del Pino family, a lifelong resident of Cuba, and a loyal Socialist. She proudly volunteers for the revolution and assists by harvesting sugar cane, judging local domestic disputes in the town hall, and watching for invaders from her porch swing overlooking the northern coast. After her husband, Jorge Del Pino, moved to New York to get cancer treatments, she replaced his photo on her nightstand with one of El Líder (Fidel Castro). She dreams of embracing the dictator on a red velvet divan. Celia's passion for the revolution divides her family: She is independent and takes care of herself but is unable to hold her family together. Her children have left, one by one: Lourdes to New York, Javier to Czechoslovakia, and Felicia to insanity. She cares for Felicia's children but ultimately is alone with her deep love of Cuba and the unpredictable sea, her clairvoyant visions, her dreams of long-ago lover Gustavo, and the persistent hope that granddaughter Pilar will return to Cuba, embrace family roots, and sustain their history. Her early life is revealed through her letters written to Gustavo.

Lourdes Puente (LOOR-dehs PWEHN-teh), Celia's first child. During the early years of the revolution, Lourdes miscarried her second child, a son. Angry and sad, she tried to defend her husband's family's ranch before it was confiscated, and she was raped by a soldier. She turns completely against Cuba and communism, embracing exile as a capitalist. With her husband and two-year-old daughter Pilar, she moves to New York, where she opens first one, then another successful Yankee Doodle Bakery. Domineering, compulsive, and fiercely proud to be American, she sends photos of pastries to her mother to emphasize the food shortages and lower standard of living in Cuba. She is never close to Celia, and the revolution drives them further apart. Lourdes finds solace as her father's favorite child and devotes her savings to his comfort during his final years. He repays her devotion by returning after death to accompany her on twilight walks through the city. When she goes to Cuba for Felicia's funeral, she meets her nephew, Ivanito, and gives him money so he can leave Cuba.

Felicia Villaverde (feh-LEE-see-ah vee-yah-VEHR-deh), Celia's second child. She remains in Cuba but is ambivalent about the revolution. She is poetic but unreachable because syphilis, contracted from her violent, unloving first husband, is slowly destroying her brain. Mentally unstable and passionately interested in black magic, she spends weeks inside her dark apartment, dancing in her nightgown to Beny Moré records and feeding her three children nothing but coconut ice cream. In a final attempt to salvage her own life, she becomes a *santera*, an initiate of the African-influenced Santería religion of the region. Ritual sacrifices prove useless, as do prayers and the help of friends. She dies, her body and mind twisted by disease.

Pilar Puente (pee-LAHR), Lourdes' teenage daughter. A rebellious artist, Pilar scoffs at her mother's compulsive patriotism and refuses to work at the bakery. She longs to see her grandmother Celia again, having communicated clairvoyantly and by letter with her since childhood, so she runs away from home toward Cuba. She makes it to the home of her father's family in Miami and is sent back to Brooklyn, where her desire to visit Cuba fades, along with her evening conversations with Celia. She becomes increasingly self-absorbed, angry, and distant from Lourdes and from her family's history until she enters college, where she eventually reembraces her roots. She returns to Cuba with Lourdes, reuniting the remaining family.

Jorge Del Pino (HOHR-heh), Celia's husband. Although deceased before the opening of the story, Jorge still plays a major part in events. He regularly appears as an apparition, and he gives advice to his wife and daughters. Jorge's advice seems to confirm whatever the living characters feel; ironically, the only supernatural character in the novel often comes across as the most rational one.

Ivanito Villaverde (ee-vahn-EE-toh), Felicia's son. Ivanito is five years old when the story opens and thirteen as it closes. Ivanito is the only character for whom the reader feels unquestioned sympathy. When Felicia sets her husband on fire and locks the children in the house, Ivanito is the only one of her children to stand by her. As the youngest character in the novel, Ivanito is the only one who has not yet formed political opinions. He loves and is loved by all the adult members of the family. In this sense, Ivanito is a major focus of attention, symbolizing the human aspects of a complex society torn apart by social, political, and religious differences.

— Mary Pierce Frost

DRINK
(L'Assommoir)

Author: Émile Zola (1840-1902)
First published: 1877
Genre: Novel

Locale: Paris, France
Time: The second half of the nineteenth century
Plot: Naturalism

Gervaise (zhehr-VEHZ), a laundry worker. Deserted by her lover, Lantier, she marries Coupeau, with whom she prospers until her husband is disabled by an accident and takes to drink. When Lantier returns, she begins to degenerate until, worn out by the hardships of her life, she dies alone.

Lantier (lahn-TYAY), Gervaise's lover, who deserts her and their two children only to return later and complete the ruin of her life.

Coupeau (kew-POH), Gervaise's husband. A roofer, he works hard to support his family until, idled by an accident, he takes to drink.

Adèle (ah-DEHL), the prostitute for whom Lantier deserts Gervaise.

Virginie (veer-zhee-NEE), Adèle's sister and the enemy of Gervaise, over whom she finally triumphs by acquiring Gervaise's shop and the favors of Lantier.

Nana, the daughter of Gervaise and Coupeau. Her decision to leave home for the streets causes Gervaise to lose all interest in life and hastens her complete degeneracy and death.

Goujet (gew-ZHAY), a neighbor secretly in love with Gervaise, whom he tries in vain to help.

Claude (klohd) and

Étienne (ay-TYEHN), the children of Gervaise and Lantier.

Madame Boche (bohsh), an older friend of Gervaise.

Madame Fauconnier (foh-koh-NYAY), the proprietor of a laundry, who gives Gervaise work after her desertion by Lantier.

DRUMS

Author: James Boyd (1888-1944)
First published: 1925
Genre: Novel

Locale: North Carolina and London
Time: American Revolution
Plot: Historical

Squire John Fraser, a North Carolina planter, a strict but kind Scotsman determined to educate his son as a gentleman.

Caroline Fraser, his wife.

John Fraser, their son. Educated in Edenton, he returns to his inland farm home when British authority is overthrown in the coastal town. Sent to England on business by his father, he becomes a clerk for an importing firm. He does a favor for Paul Jones (whom he had met at Wylie Jones's home) and later signs as a sailor on Jones's ship when he raids the Scottish coast. John is wounded in a sea battle and, still feverish, he sails for home on a Dutch ship. At first rejected for the militia, he is later accepted and is wounded in a skirmish. No longer a fighter, John rejoices to learn that the British have been defeated.

Sir Nat Dukinfield, a young sportsman and John's friend. He is killed in a tavern brawl while visiting John in a French port.

Captain Tennant, collector of the port at Edenton.

Eve Tennant, his daughter, a coquette who becomes interested in John.

Wylie Jones, a plantation owner who promotes the North Carolina rebellion against the British.

Paul Jones, an adventurous Scottish sailor who takes Wylie Jones's last name and becomes a raiding captain in the American Navy.

Sally Merrillee, John's childhood playmate, a neighbor of the Frasers. She and John fall in love.

James Merrillee, Sally's father, killed in the war. For a time, John manages the Merrillee farm.

Dr. Clapton, an English clergyman who tutors John in Edenton.

Captain Flood, John's friend, a riverboat skipper who takes him up river to Halifax.

Plain Clothes Hewes, a shipbuilder.

Teague Battle, a young lawyer.

Master Hal Cherry, a repulsive rich boy.

General Nathanael Greene, a victorious American commander.

DRUMS ALONG THE MOHAWK

Author: Walter D. Edmonds (1903-   )
First published: 1936
Genre: Novel

Locale: Mohawk Valley
Time: 1775-1783
Plot: Historical

Gilbert (Gil) Martin, a young pioneer, a hard worker ambitious to have a place of his own at Deerfield and willing to continue fighting after each defeat. Seneca Indians burn his first home, and he is wounded in the ambushing of General Herkimer's militia. He works on the land and fights when needed, until the valley is at last safe and he is able to return with his family to Deerfield.

Magdelana (Lana) Borst Martin, his pretty wife. She loses her first baby after the flight from Deerfield to Fort Schuyler but bears a boy, Gilly, the following spring and another boy, Joey, in August of the next year. Recovery from this birth is prolonged, but by the end of the war, she has a baby girl to take to Deerfield with her husband and boys.

Mark Demooth, a captain of the militia, a small, slightly built man rather proud of himself.

John Wolff, a Tory convicted of aiding the British and sent to prison; he later escapes to Canada.

Blue Back, a friendly old Oneida Indian, dirty and paunchy, who likes Gil. He warns the Deerfield residents of a planned raid and later serves as scout and guide for the militia. His young Indian wife is proud of his fertility despite his age.

Mrs. Sarah McKlennar, Captain Barnabas McKlennar's widow, for whom Gil works as a hired hand. Her home is burned by two drunken Indians who take her bed out for her while the fire is burning.

Joseph Brant, an Indian chief who refuses to pledge neutrality in the war.

General Benedict Arnold, General Herkimer's successor, appointed to reorganize the patriot army and lead it against St. Leger's camp.

Jurry McLonis, a Tory who seduces Nancy Schuyler.

Nancy Schuyler, Mrs. Demooth's maid, who bears Jurry's child and is taken by an Indian as his wife.

Hon Yost, Nancy's brother, another Tory who, when arrested, promises to spread in the British camp false reports of American strength.

Clem Coppernol,

The Weavers, and

The Realls, neighbors who help with the Deerfield log-rolling that is interrupted by the Seneca raid.

Mrs. Wolff, John's wife, reported missing after the Seneca raid.

General Nicholas Herkimer, commander of the Mohawk Valley patriots; he is mortally wounded when his men are ambushed and routed.

General Barry St. Leger, British general who leads a combined force of British and Indians against the patriots.

General Butler, British leader of a group of raiding and pillaging parties; he is finally killed and his army routed.

Mrs. Demooth, a snobbish woman who so torments and frightens Nancy about her pregnancy that she leaves. Mrs. Demooth later loses her mind.

Colonel Van Schaick, leader of an attack against the Onondaga towns.

Adam Helmer and

Joe Boleo, two scouts who help Gil build a cabin after Mrs. McKlennar's house is burned.

Lt. Colonel Marinus Willett, leader of an army that pursues and attacks Butler's army, killing him and scattering his men in the wilderness.

DUBLINERS

Author: James Joyce (1882-1941)
First published: 1914
Genre: Short fiction

Locale: Dublin, Ireland
Time: Late nineteenth or early twentieth century
Plot: Social realism

"I," the first-person narrator of the first three stories, often thought of as one character. In "The Sisters" and "Araby," he reveals that he lives with an uncle and aunt. In "An Encounter," he does not mention his home life, but there too he is bright, admired by his teachers, and disdainful of common people, an attitude he learns to reject.

James Flynn, a deceased priest in "The Sisters," and a former teacher of the narrator. Unable to forgive himself for breaking a chalice containing sacred wine, he was found laughing to himself in a confessional. Relieved of his priestly duties, his sisters cared for him until his death from a third stroke.

Mahoney, the boy who ditches school with the protagonist of "An Encounter." Slightly wild, he chases a cat while a perverted old man tries to seduce his friend, but he then runs back as if to aid him.

The Old Josser, a sadistic pederast garbed in priestlike black who approaches the truant boys in "An Encounter," hoping to seduce the protagonist emotionally.

Mangan's sister, the attractive girl on whom the narrator of "Araby" has a crush. Followed to school by the boy every morning, she finally speaks to him, offering a friendly date, but she is not understood.

Eveline, the protagonist of the story that bears her name. She promised her dying mother that she would keep the family together and failed. Her favorite brother Ernest dead, she lives with her threatening father and works at the Stores, hoping for escape. Her new beau, Frank, offers to spirit her away to Buenos Aires but may not be trustworthy.

Little Chandler, a clerk in "A Little Cloud." With a wife and child to support, Chandler dreams of escape. Bright and sensitive, he is too timid to trust his own perceptions. He loves Byron, but his favorite poem is one Byron wrote before his poetic powers matured. He aspires to write poetry but never does. He admires a reporter whose character is flawed.

Farrington, a physically powerful man trapped in "Counterparts" in a world of modern commerce that has no use for his strength. His dehumanizing job in a law office amounts to work as a duplicating machine. His human need for individuality and dignity proves a flaw in him from the perspective of his puny boss, Mr. Alleyne. He regards himself as neglected by his pious wife. His bravado at pubs does not relieve his anguish, so he beats his son.

Maria, the well-intentioned woman of "Clay." She was a nanny for many years and regrets the rift between two of her former charges. Witch- or nutcracker-like, her nose and chin almost touch when she laughs. Lonely and proper, she pretends to like living at the Dublin by Lamplight Laundry, among former prostitutes.

James Duffy, a hermit bank clerk of Chapelizod in "A Painful Case." Disapproving of the world and himself, he "lives at a distance" even from himself. Mozart is his one "dissipation." The walls of his apartment are bare; its color scheme is black and white, with a dash of red. His books are arranged by weight in his bookcase, and he regards his father's death as equivalent to his boss's retirement.

Gabriel Conroy, an educator and literary critic in "The Dead." Gabriel attempts to liberate himself from Ireland but fails. His dead mother chose the presumptuous names Gabriel and Constantine for him and his brother. Her conviction that his wife, Gretta, is beneath him still troubles him. He bristles when he is playfully mocked by Gretta for buying continental galoshes as protection against Irish winters. When Lily, his aunts' servant, speaks generally about untrustworthy men, he perceives that she is attacking him. His colleague, Molly Ivors, incurs his wrath for chiding him gently about his neglect of Ireland. Gabriel, who poses as independent, depends on approval from others and ultimately sees himself as second in Gretta's affection to Michael Furey, a long dead beau of her schoolgirl days.

Gretta Conroy, Gabriel's warm, witty wife, the mother of two. Naïve when she moved from rural Connacht, where young Michael Furey risked his life in a storm to see her, she was regarded by Gabriel's mother as "country cute." Intelligent in her responses to Gabriel's attempts to control her, she appreciates his generosity. When a song stirs her memory, she thinks of Michael with affection.

Molly Ivors, a professor, political activist, and lover of Irish culture. A match for Gabriel intellectually, she would perhaps have seemed to his mother to be an acceptable mate for him.

—Albert Wachtel

THE DUCHESS OF MALFI

Author: John Webster (c. 1577-1580—before 1634)
First published: 1623
Genre: Drama
Locale: Amalfi and Milan, Italy
Time: The sixteenth century
Plot: Tragedy

The duchess of Malfi (MAHL-fee), the sister of Duke Ferdinand and the Cardinal. She is a woman of strong character and deep feeling. Capable of gaiety and affectionate teasing, she is also able to bear danger, grief, and terror with fortitude. Her brothers' attempt to drive her mad fails, and her dignified nobility at her death transforms the character of her murderer.

Ferdinand, the duke of Calabra, the cruel twin brother of the duchess. Arrogant, domineering, and cruel, he forbids his widowed sister to marry again and sets a master spy to watch over her. Finding that she is in love and secretly married, he uses every form of inhuman torture that he can devise to break her mind, then has her murdered. Remorse drives him to madness. In his frenzy, he wounds his brother, mortally wounds Bosola, and receives his death wound from the latter.

The Cardinal, a worldly and evil churchman. Lacking the demon that drives his brother mad, he is completely unscrupulous, killing his mistress dispassionately when she worms from him his secret guilt in the murder of the duchess and her children. His death is a grisly irony, for he has forbidden his followers to enter his room, and they think his howls for help are tests of their obedience.

Daniel de Bosola (boh-SOH-lah), an embittered, satirical villain. A complex character, intelligent and witty but ruthless, he acts as a spy for the evil brothers and betrays the duchess to them. The fortitude and loveliness of the duchess pierce his heart, and after murdering her, he has a strange devotion for her and avenges her. His language is violent and sometimes filthy but emanates a savage poetry.

Antonio Bologna (boh-LOH-nyah), the duchess' steward. Although deeply in love with the duchess, he does not declare himself until she subtly proposes to him. He is a good man, intelligent and loyal, and shrewd enough not to trust Bosola. He is killed accidentally by Bosola after the death of the duchess.

Delio (DEH-lee-oh), Antonio's faithful friend. After the deaths of Antonio and the duchess, he protects their only surviving child.

Cariola (kah-ree-OH-lah), the faithful waiting woman of the duchess, who shares the secret of the duchess and Antonio's clandestine marriage. Fear makes her plead vainly for life, in notable contrast to the dignity of the duchess in facing death.

Julia, the wanton wife of Castruccio and mistress of the Cardinal. She is fascinated by Bosola and entices him into an affair. Her curiosity leads to her death by poisoning at the hands of the Cardinal.

The marquis of Pescara (peh-SKAH-rah), a nobleman of integrity and sensitivity, endowed with a superior ethical sense.

A doctor, employed to treat Duke Ferdinand in his madness. His extreme self-confidence leads him to a beating by the madman.

Castruccio (kahs-TREW-chee-oh), an aged, impotent fool, Julia's husband.

Count Malateste (mah-lah-TEHS-tah), a worthy nobleman, proposed by Duke Ferdinand as a second husband for the duchess.

Silvio (SIHL-vee-oh), a lord.

Roderigo (roh-deh-REE-goh) and

Grisolan (gree-SOH-lahn), attendants to Duke Ferdinand who refuse to answer his cries for help because they are sure that he is testing them.

An old lady, the butt of Bosola's gruesome jesting.

Several madmen, who are sent to the duchess by Duke Ferdinand in the hope of driving her mad.

Three children, the offspring of Antonio and the duchess. Two are murdered; one survives.

THE DUEL
(Duel)

Author: Anton Chekhov (1860-1904)
First published: 1891
Genre: Short fiction
Locale: The Caucasus
Time: The 1880's
Plot: Psychological realism

Ivan Andreitch (Vanya) Laevsky (ahn-DREH-ihch LAH-ehv-skee), a minor official of the czarist government. This slender, neurotic, twenty-eight-year-old intellectual already considers himself a failure. He is living in the Caucasus with another man's wife and, after two years of this scandalous conduct, finds that he has grown tired of her and is going mad in this backwater community. He desperately wishes to abandon his mistress and flee to St. Petersburg, where the social and intellectual life is more compatible with his temperament. He realizes, however, that he is always thinking that a new love affair or change of surroundings will inspire him to do great things. He drinks too much, neglects his work, spends his time playing cards, and generally displays himself as a weakling, a wastrel, and a cad. His behavior eventually involves him in a pistol duel that marks a turning point in his life. Afterward, he becomes temperate, industrious, and mature; he marries his mistress (whose husband has recently died), and they settle down to a humble provincial life.

"Kolya" Von Koren, a zoologist. This broad-shouldered, swarthy, vigorous young man stands in striking contrast to Laevsky. Whereas the latter is a dreamer and romantic, the scientist is a hardheaded realist strongly affected by the ideas of Friedrich Nietzsche and Charles Darwin. He hates Laevsky and believes that individuals like Laevsky should be executed or sent to labor camps to prevent them from infecting society. The real reason for their mutual antagonism, however, is the instinctive biological reaction of two fundamentally different natures. Von Koren lives by his reason, Laevsky by his feelings. Oddly enough, after the sobering experience of their duel, each acquires character traits of the other. Laevsky becomes industrious and responsible; Von Koren becomes more sympathetic and tolerant. When Von Koren's summer field trip ends, the two men part on friendly terms, illustrating the author's thesis that, life being such a mysterious and precarious affair, human beings ought to try to tolerate one another with Christian humility.

Alexandr Daviditch Samoylenko (dah-VIH-dihch sah-moy-LEHN-koh), an army doctor and friend of both Laevsky and Von Koren. This fat, flabby, homely, man affects the brusque manner of a martinet and bully to cover up his tender-hearted, generous nature. Laevsky and Von Koren frequently encounter each other at Samoylenko's home. The army officer likes them both and tries to get them to tolerate each other. In this role, he represents the author's idea of how human beings ought to regard one another.

Nadyezhda Fyodorovna (nah-DEHZH-dah FYOH-doh-rov-nah), Laevsky's mistress. This attractive woman who ran away from her husband to live with Laevsky considers herself a freethinker and an intellectual. Like Laevsky, she has been influenced by the liberal ideas of the 1880's, including those of such men as Herbert Spencer and Henrik Ibsen. She finds herself in a difficult position in the Caucasus, however, among provincial people with conservative ideas. They regard her as a fallen woman, and some men believe they can force her into assignations. Her own attitude toward herself is being undermined by social pressure. She actually succumbs to offers of liaisons with two other men. With no money of her own, she seems well on her way to becoming a common prostitute if Laevsky were to desert her.

Ilya Mihalitch Kirilin (MIH-hah-lihch kih-RIH-lihn), the local police captain. This swaggering, insensitive man is one of Nadyezhda's lovers. His brutal treatment of her shows the extent to which she has fallen in social regard and foreshadows what her future might be like without Laevsky. Just before his duel with Von Koren, Laevsky surprises Nadyezhda and Kirilin in a sordid encounter in a rented room, but he forgives her because of what he has come to understand about universal weakness and human suffering.

— Bill Delaney

THE DUMB WAITER

Author: Harold Pinter (1930-)
First published: 1960
Genre: Drama
Locale: Birmingham, England
Time: c. the 1950's
Plot: Absurdist

Ben, a hired assassin. A senior partner for an unnamed organization, Ben periodically travels around the country murdering people according to the instructions of his superiors. Throughout these gruesome tasks, Ben acts as a responsible professional, a killer who believes in carrying out his job with precision. As a result, Ben often is irritated by the casual actions of his colleague, Gus. Ben perceives Gus and his questions about their mysterious work as dangerous and potentially as violating authority. Tension between these two characters provides both a comic and a serious tone to the character of Ben. The more Gus inquires about his job, the more hostile Ben becomes. Ben is a proud man, afraid to admit the existence of anything that he does not understand. He enjoys his job and resents any suggestion that he is not fully occupied or satisfied with life, both at work and at home; his home life is complete, with its woodwork and model boats. Ben acts cautiously, and he silently carries out his orders without question. Consequently, he could be the "dumb waiter" referred to in the title of the play. Despite his apparent superiority to Gus, however, Ben is threatened by the possibility of change. For example, the mysterious appearance of matches under the door of their basement room and the descent of a dumbwaiter with orders for food that he cannot provide make Ben nervous because he is not in control of his situation. He tries to avoid revealing his fear, not wishing to appear inferior in front of Gus, and attempts to remain calm in the face of an increasingly absurd situation. The discrepancies between what Ben feels and how he expresses himself often are a source of humor and menace in the play.

Gus, a hired assassin. Gus has responsibilities similar to those of Ben, although he is only a junior partner with the anonymous organization. Gus works alongside Ben and assists him in killing. He is a clown figure and the complete opposite of his colleague; nothing seems to function smoothly for him. For example, the toilet refuses to flush, he has difficulty tying his shoelaces, and he fails in an attempt to retrieve a smokeable cigarette from his shoe. Gus is not a professional killer, although he tries to act like one. His failure is a result of his emotional involvement and sensitivity, which are seen as inappropriate for a murderer. For example, because he is haunted by an image of the woman who was their last victim, Gus is unable to settle his mind and lacks confidence in his abilities as a killer. This unease and dissatisfaction in his job prompt him to begin questioning the nature of the organization and the identity of the victim. This gradual emergence of Gus as an individual who confronts the established structure challenges the relationship between the two men and, as a result, lends a darker and more serious side to Gus's character. His insecurities are made apparent through the need for a cup of tea, visits to the bathroom, constant talking, and continual interruptions of Ben. By the end of the play, Gus succeeds in threatening the authority of his superiors and needs to be eliminated.

— Ian Stuart

THE DUNCIAD

Author: Alexander Pope (1688-1744)
First published: 1728-1743
Genre: Poetry
Locale: England and the underworld
Time: Eighteenth century
Plot: Mock-heroic

Dulness, the central character, introduced in the epic's first lines. She is described as a goddess who is the daughter of Chaos and Night and who has ruled over the world and its inhabitants from the beginning of time. Enveloped in clouds, fog, and mist, which magnify her presence and obscure her face, Dulness is also continually surrounded by such allegorical figures as Fortitude, Temperance, and Prudence. In the first book, after surveying and appraising the numerous creators of dull writing, she finally anoints Tibbald as the king of her realm. Dulness, in the second book, presides over the games and contests held between rival booksellers, poets, publishers, and journalists, who all compete for her approval. Because no one can pass her final test—to stay awake while two authors read aloud—Dulness grants her favors to none. The past and future triumphs of Dulness are the subject of the third book, and in the fourth book, Dulness is depicted as a true deity. At the end of the epic, she reigns supreme over the sciences and universities as well as the arts and theatres.

Lewis Tibbald (Cibber), a character modeled on Lewis Theobald, a Shakespearean scholar who embarrassed Alexander Pope in 1726. He is introduced in the middle of the first book, when he is named King of Dulness by the goddess Dulness. In the fourth book, which Pope added to the original poem, Tibbald is replaced by Cibber, who is based on the real Colley Cibber, an eighteenth century playwright and poet laureate. Pope's Cibber is a dull poet who possesses only enough talent to create poor occasional verses. Depicted in all four books of the epic as a pedantic critic, a Grub Street journalist, and a bad poet, the King of Dulness appears only at intervals. As Pope's easy substitution of Cibber for Tibbald indicates, the role the King of Dulness plays in the epic is quite small. The King of Dulness is present as a spectator of, not a participant in, the games described in the second book, and during the third book, his actions are limited to sleeping with his head in the goddess' lap and dreaming of her past and future conquests. In the fourth book, the King of Dulness merely continues to recline in the lap of his queen as she rules the world.

Poetic Justice, a character keenly interested in the affairs of mortals. Poetic Justice assists the goddess Dulness as she searches for one to crown as the King of Dulness.

Elkanah Settle, a character based on the Restoration poet of the same name. During the dream sequence of the third book, Settle shows the King of Dulness the future and the offspring of the goddess Dulness.

John Taylor, who represents the real Water Poet of the Restoration era. He accompanies the King of Dulness and Settle on the journey depicted in the third book of the epic.

The harlot, who appears in the fourth book as the first of many personages who tells of Dulness' victory over the arts. The harlot comes as a representative of the Italian opera, and she rejoices in the banishment of Handel to Ireland and of the new chaos in music.

The specter, who, like the harlot, appears in the fourth book to celebrate Dulness' triumph. Representing education, the specter gleefully assures the goddess that imagination and creativity are no longer allowed in school.

— Traci S. Smrcka

DURING THE REIGN OF THE QUEEN OF PERSIA

Author: Joan Chase
First published: 1983
Genre: Novel
Locale: Sherwood, Ohio
Time: The 1950's
Plot: Domestic realism

Gram (Lil Bradley Krauss), the "queen of Persia" of the title. Having grown up learning to work hard (her mother having died when she was a teenager and her father having been killed in the oilfields of Texas seeking his fortune), she married Jacob Krauss and gave birth to seven children (two sons, stillborn), rearing five daughters (May, Grace, Elinor, Rachel, and Libby). Her marriage became a source of bitterness because Jacob, not acknowledging his desire for her, became an abusive alcoholic.

Grace, the second of Lil's daughters, the one whom Gram counts on to work with her whenever she is on the farm. Grace earned a teaching degree and then married Neil against her mother's wishes. Grace and her daughters, Anne and Katie, spend most of their time on Lil's farm, not living with Neil. Putting her faith in her sister Elinor's Christian Science beliefs, Grace struggles against her cancer for nearly two years, eventually dying in the big farmhouse.

Neil, Grace's husband, a writer. Working as a salesman, he never earns enough money to buy a home without his mother-in-law's help. He is the spirit of mischief with Anne and Katie and a constant antagonist to Lil, who blames him for Grace's cancer coming back after surgery.

Elinor, the daughter who "gets away." The family sacrificed to provide her with piano lessons. Elinor, fulfilling her mother's expectation that she move away from the farm, works for an advertising agency in New York. Every return to the farm includes her giving clothes and jewelry to her nieces. Having become a Christian Scientist, she directs Grace's recovery regimen as Grace battles breast cancer that surgery did not stop. She provides the link to a yearned-for miracle, maintained until the coffin lid is closed at Grace's funeral.

Celia, one of the narrators. Her initiation to womanhood provides the framework for the opening section of the novel. Her sexuality results in boys gathering on the front porch like male dogs seeking a female in heat. Her cousins spy on her dates, awakening their own desires as well as reinforcing the new separation between them and Celia. Her marriage and move to Texas result in a suicide attempt, which sends her back to her family in Ohio for treatment and recovery.

Jacob Krauss, or **Grandad**, the farmer who courts Lil by bringing her family piano to her house. He appears incapable of expressing affection. He drank and battered Lil until her brother provided money that lifted the family out of poverty. His response to Lil's good financial fortune was to withdraw further from the family. His rage against Lil's selling some pastureland results in his driving an Amish man and his son off the road, wrecking their wagon and possibly injuring them. The young cousins were afraid when they were in the house alone with him.

— *Janet Taylor Palmer*

DUSTY ANSWER

Author: Rosamond Lehmann (1901-1990)
First published: 1927
Genre: Novel
Locale: Cambridge, England; the English countryside; and France
Time: The first quarter of the twentieth century
Plot: Bildungsroman

Judith Earle, the protagonist, an only child who lives in the country. Only eighteen years old at the beginning of the novel, she has little experience of the world but a great need for love. Throughout her childhood, she was fascinated by the Fyfe cousins, who frequently visited next door. During and after her time at Cambridge, she continues to see them, reaching out first to one, then to another, for love, security, and a sense of her own identity. At the end of the novel, two have died, and Judith has broken with the others. When her lesbian lover from college also abandons her, Judith finally is free to live her own life.

Julian Fyfe, a musically talented child, later a composer and music critic. Six years older than Judith, he is tall and thin, with an ugly face and a sarcastic manner. Perhaps because he is so detached from others, he is insecure about his relationships; he insists that he bores even himself. When he meets Judith in France, he tells her that he has loved her for ten years and persuades her to be his mistress; however, his brother's death intervenes. At the end of the novel, he adopts his brother's son, Michael Peter, who also is musical.

Charles (Charlie) Fyfe, Julian's younger brother. A tall, handsome, blue-eyed boy, he pretends courage but actually has many fears and weaknesses. It is Charles who gets sick easily, and it is Charles who is afraid of the dark and of blood. Although Judith adores him, Charles marries Mariella. Before their baby is born, he is killed in the war.

Mariella Fyfe, Charlie's wife. Graceful and polite but somewhat remote as a child, she seems to care deeply only for dogs. She grieves briefly for Charlie, but she later admits that it is Julian whom she really loves. Realizing that she cannot be a devoted mother to her child, she turns him over to Julian to be reared.

Martin Fyfe, another cousin. An earnest boy, red-cheeked, athletic, and always hungry, he is the butt of the jokes that his subtler cousins devise. After going to Cambridge, he takes over the family farm. Since childhood, he has loved Judith. When she agrees to marry him after she has been rejected by Roddy, Martin is ecstatic. Within a few days, however, Judith realizes that she does not love him and breaks the engagement. Martin later dies in a boating accident.

Roddy Fyfe, the cousin who seems most different, probably because of his homosexuality. A thin, pale, dark-haired boy, he is secretive and unpredictable. Although he studies art in Paris, he is essentially apathetic about a career and everything else, preferring to drift. After years of flirtation, Judith has a brief encounter with him; however, when she writes him a love letter, he makes it clear that she was only a diversion and that it would be better if they stay apart.

Jennifer Baird, Judith's friend at Cambridge who becomes her lesbian lover. A pretty, fair-haired girl with sparkling blue eyes, Jennifer enchants the unsophisticated Judith. When Judith discovers that Jennifer has been having a relationship with another woman throughout their own time together, she will have nothing more to do with her. Although she is bright, Jennifer has neglected her college work. Depressed over the loss of Judith and realizing that she faces disgrace, she has a nervous breakdown and is sent home. Later, she makes a date with Judith but fails to keep it.

Geraldine Manners, Jennifer's lover. A masculine but handsome woman in her thirties, she makes Jennifer happy because she does not draw strength from her. Eventually, she is jettisoned by the fickle Jennifer.

Mabel Fuller, an English student at Cambridge. An unclean, untidy young woman in her twenties, she is attracted to Judith and attempts to own her. Although Judith tries to be kind to Mabel, she refuses to be possessed by her. Judith is sure that Mabel will fail in her final examinations.

Tony Baring, Roddy's lover. A man with a sensitive, sensuous face, feminine hands, and a lisp. It is he, not Judith, whom Roddy visits in Cambridge. Baring becomes a Fellow at Cambridge.

Michael Peter Fyfe, the son of Charlie and Mariella. A tall, nervous boy, he is naturally musical. From babyhood, he senses his mother's indifference and Julian's love for him. He is sent to live with Julian.

Mrs. Earle, Judith's mother, a widow. Handsome, elegant, and witty, she evidently loved Judith's father but quickly adjusted to his death and became friendly with other men. The kind of woman who dislikes women, she could not hide her disappointment when her daughter was born. After Judith has graduated from Cambridge, Mrs. Earle approves of her, and they have a pleasant summer together in France.

— *Rosemary M. Canfield Reisman*

DUTCHMAN

Author: Amiri Baraka (Everett LeRoi Jones, 1934-)
First published: 1964
Genre: Drama
Locale: New York City
Time: Early 1960's
Plot: Political

Clay, a twenty-year-old, middle-class black man, a college-trained intellectual from New Jersey. He wears a three-button Ivy League suit and tie and passes time by reading a newspaper. He appears to be in control of himself and his environment, amenably aware of sex but not of race, as evidenced when a white woman enters a subway car and coquettishly sits down beside him. He is both embarrassed and fascinated by the woman. Clay is pigeonholed by the woman as being the assimilated African American who wants to pretend that people cannot see his blackness and that black and white people are free of their history. When Clay is insulted, taunted, and goaded by her, however, he loses control of both himself and his situation. Clay's character is both real and symbolic. Symbolically, he represents black America, Adam, and the legendary "Flying Dutchman" of the play's title who was doomed to sail forever unless saved by the love of a virtuous woman.

Lula, a thirty-year-old white woman. Tall, slender, and beautiful, with long, straight red hair, she wears loud lipstick, bright, skimpy summer clothes, sandals, and sunglasses. Clay perceives her as a white, bohemian-type liberal. Recognizing that beneath the surface of the supposedly assimilated black man is a savage spirit chafed by years of oppression, she begins to goad Clay with insults, seeking to uncover his true nature. Although she seduces the outward man, she wishes to seduce and control the inner man as well. She continues to taunt and embarrass him in front of others who have entered the subway car, goading him to show his raw, animal nature. Like Clay, Lula is both real and symbolic. Symbolically, she represents white America and its attempted seduction and consequent destruction of black manhood by assimilation or annihilation; she also represents Eve to Clay's Adam, eating and offering him an apple just as the biblical Eve did. She, too, can be viewed as the legendary "Flying Dutchman, cursed to sail forever with a crew of living dead and compelled to carry out an endless ritual of seducing and destroying.

— *Bettye Choate Kash*

THE DWARF
(Dvärgen)

Author: Pär Lagerkvist (1891-1974)
First published: 1944
Genre: Novel
Locale: Unnamed Italian city-states
Time: The Renaissance
Plot: Parable

The Dwarf, the narrator. He is twenty-six-inches tall but of good physical proportions, save for a slightly oversized head, and of exceptional strength. His wrinkled and beardless face, bristly red hair, and broad but low brow make him look older but less diabolical than he is. He is addressed once as **Piccolino**, but this instance may be a descriptive mode of address (it means "little fellow" in Italian) and not his actual name. His service to the Prince consists largely in doing the Prince's dirty work. His penchant is for treachery, violence, bloodshed, and evil. He is incapable of love, and he never laughs. In his admiration of the Prince's amoral pursuit of power, he personifies Machiavellianism. His own brutality is manifest in his killing of two dwarfs; beheading a kitten; poisoning a rival of the Prince, along with the rival's personal attendants and a courtier who loves the Princess; and causing the beheading of the young man loved by the Prince's daughter, who then, grief-stricken, drowns herself.

The Prince, the ruler of an Italian state. He is modeled on Cesare Borgia, duke of Romagna and the exemplar for Niccolo Machiavelli in his book *The Prince* (1560). He is unscrupulous in his quest for power. He dispenses with the services of the Dwarf after the deaths of his daughter and wife. When the Dwarf refuses under torture to disclose the nature of his consultations with the Prince's wife, the Prince has him chained in a dungeon; the Dwarf is confident, however, that the Prince cannot be without his Dwarf for long.

Messer Bernardo, a painter, inventor, and scientist, identifiable as being based on Leonardo da Vinci. He paints a portrait of the Prince's wife that corresponds to da Vinci's "Mona Lisa" and previously painted a *nattvard* (Eucharist) in the refectory of the Franciscan monastery of Santa Croce, equivalent to da Vinci's "Last Supper" in the refectory of the monastery of Santa Maria delle Grazie.

Princess Teodora, the Prince's wife. She uses the Dwarf as a means of exchanging letters with her lover, Don Ricardo, after whose death she turns to God and uses the Dwarf as her scourge. She is the one person the Dwarf would love, as he himself says, if he were capable of love; he remains devoted to her, in any case. The Prince shows his love for her as she grows ill and dies.

Don Ricardo, a courtier, friend, and fellow brothel-patron of the Prince, whom he cuckolds. When the Prince has the Dwarf serve poisoned wine to Lodovico Montanza and his attendants, the Dwarf, in excess of his instructions, takes it upon himself to poison Don Ricardo as well.

Angelica, the sweet, innocent daughter of the Prince. She loves Giovanni Montanza and commits suicide after his death. She is as incapable of evil as the Dwarf is incapable of love.

Giovanni Montanza, the son of Lodovico. The Prince, thanks to the Dwarf's information, finds him in bed with Angelica and beheads him on the spot. Subsequently, the Dwarf recalls his own earlier beheading of Angelica's pet kitten.

Boccarossa, a leader of mercenary soldiers who hires out first to the Prince and then to the enemies of the Prince. The Dwarf admires him.

Lodovico Montanza il Toro, an enemy of the Prince, evocative of the Milanese Ludovico Sforza il Moro. He and his retinue are murdered by poisoned wine at a banquet given by the Prince, ostensibly in celebration of a truce.

Ercole Montanza, the brother of Lodovico and uncle of Giovanni. He musters the followers of his murdered brother and, with the purchased help of Boccarossa and his mercenaries, seeks to defeat the Prince.

Fiammetta, the mistress of the Prince. She dies, along with many others, during the plague, which, in its severity, brings about the end of the fighting.

— *Roy Arthur Swanson*

THE DYNASTS

Author: Thomas Hardy (1840-1928)
First published: 1903-1908
Genre: Drama

Locale: Europe
Time: 1806-1815
Plot: Historical

Napoleon Bonaparte, who is portrayed as a man driven by an inscrutable fate and conscious of his ability to master Europe. He is a great leader, at times impatient with his subordinates' abilities. Above all, he wants to found a new dynasty to rank with the established royal families of Europe. Disappointed in his negotiations with Tsar Alexander for the hand of a Russian princess, he turns to the defeated Emperor Francis of Austria, who gives him the hand of Marie Louise as his second wife after Napoleon has divorced the unfortunate Empress Josephine because of her failure to provide an heir. Even though he is defeated by the Austrians and Prussians at Leipzig, Napoleon does not lose his sense of destiny. Exiled to Elba, he returns for the famous Hundred Days, only to be defeated a second time at Waterloo. His efforts are finally compared by the Spirit of Years, who sees all of history, to the struggles of an insect on a leaf. Napoleon disrupted many lives and caused great slaughter, all for nothing.

Josephine, Napoleon's first wife, who cannot believe it is truly her fault that she bears no children, even though Napoleon points to bastard children as proof of his own potency in the marriage bed. Despite her protests and tears, for she truly loves her husband, Josephine is forced to consent to make way for Marie Louise.

Marie Louise, the princess of Austria and a pawn of circumstances and politics. She is married to Napoleon to help save Austria from conquest. Eventually, she bears a son to Napoleon, though almost at the sacrifice of her own life. After Napoleon is defeated and exiled to Elba, Marie Louise and her small son, styled as the king of Rome, go to her native Austria for asylum.

George III, the king of England. He is shown first, in 1805, as a robust monarch watching preparations being made along the English coast to meet the expected French invasion. Later, King George is shown at the age of seventy-two, shortly before his death, at the mercy of his physicians, who bleed him, drug him, and give him cold-water treatments in cruel, though well-meaning, fashion. From the state of a monarch, he is reduced to the condition of a pathetic mental case who stands as a living symbol between the prince regent and the British throne.

Tsar Alexander of Russia, who is portrayed as a self-seeking monarch who looks down on Napoleon as an upstart, despite the friendship he expresses for Napoleon and the French at the famous meeting between Alexander and Napoleon on a raft in the middle of the River Niemen.

Emperor Francis of Austria, a monarch forced, against his judgment as a father, to deliver Marie Louise as Napoleon's second wife. This alliance is concluded after Napoleon has dictated bitter terms following the defeat of the Austrian and Russian forces at Austerlitz.

Sir William Pitt, the energetic prime minister of England who struggles to save his country and Europe from Napoleon. In 1805, Pitt works against isolationist members of Parliament to provide for the defense of England. Later, he works even harder to enlist the Continent against Napoleon. Weakened in health, he continues his political struggles, even though George III refuses to permit a coalition government.

Charles James Fox, the prime minister after Sir William Pitt. Fox tries to negotiate with Napoleon, even to warning

Bonaparte of an attempt at assassination. Unfortunately for Fox, his sincere efforts at negotiation are used by Napoleon to screen his plotting against Prussia.

Lord Horatio Nelson, the famous British admiral who defeated the naval forces of Napoleon at the Battle of Trafalgar and thus saved his country from invasion. A man of great courage and hardiness, he paces the deck of his flagship in a bright uniform until cut down by a musket shot during the battle.

Admiral Villeneuve, Napoleon's naval planner, who works against the odds of poor ships and equipment to forge a fighting navy for his master. When his best efforts meet defeat at Trafalgar, he stabs himself to death at an inn.

The Immanent Will, the force that the playwright saw as the power or energy behind the workings of the universe. Because it is blind and uncreative in any rational sense, the force is called It.

The Spirit of Years, the oldest of the allegorical spirits, introduced to give the play a sense of panorama and perspective. The Spirit of Years is the leader among the other spirits, chastening them and dampening their enthusiasms when necessary.

The Spirit of Pities, a spirit of the universal spirit of human nature. This allegorical figure is an idealized human spectator, the chief commentator on the events described.

The Spirit Sinister, a savage allegorical spirit who rejoices in the carnage and the evil displayed during the Napoleonic era.

The Spirit Ironic, an allegorical spirit who comments on the irony, sometimes tragic and sometimes humorous, as the events of the drama unfold.

E

EACH IN HIS OWN WAY
(Ciascuno a suo modo)

Author: Luigi Pirandello (1867-1936)
First published: 1924
Genre: Drama
Locale: Italy
Time: The 1920's
Plot: Play of ideas

Donna Livia Palegari (LEE-vee-ah pah-leh-GAH-ree), an elderly woman. A mouthpiece of conventional morality and behavior, Donna Livia is a caricature of ignorant self-righteousness. She is outraged because her son defended the infamous Delia Morello in an argument, for she fears he may have fallen in love with a woman of such ill repute. Oblivious to the complexities of human motivation presented by the situation at hand, Donna Livia (and thus the decorum she represents) appears ridiculous and meaningless.

Diego Cinci (dee-AH-goh CHEEN-chee), a young friend of Doro Palegari. Diego's perspective, revealed in lengthy speeches, seems to be the one closest to that developed by the play itself. Tolerant of multiple viewpoints and positions, Diego defends Doro Palegari's actions to Donna Livia and attempts to show the others the problematic nature of human behavior and the absurdity of human action.

Doro Palegari (DOH-roh), the son of Donna Livia. Doro, in support of the notorious Delia Morello, argues with Francesco Savio, who conceives of Delia as a self-serving femme fatale. On meeting Delia, who accepts both Palegari's and Savio's interpretations of her story, Doro changes his position. Unfortunately, Savio also alters his point of view, so that the characters are again at odds with each other. They decide to settle their differences in a duel.

Delia Morello (deh-LEE-ah moh-REH-loh), an elegantly dressed young woman with a questionable past and reputation. Delia represents the complex, contradictory nature of human identity and reality. Delia left her lover, artist Giorgio Salvi, to run away with Michele Rocca, his sister's fiancé. Following her departure, Salvi committed suicide. Her former lover, a Russian, also killed himself. The subject of Delia's character becomes a matter of interpretation, even for Delia herself. According to Doro's narrative, she is a victim who acted any way she could in a difficult situation, but in the eyes of others she is a manipulative, selfish woman who acted with malice in a sadistic plan to destroy a sensitive artist. Delia sincerely agrees with each story, perceiving the truth of her self and her situation in both. Finally, she is offered a new explanation: She did it all out of an irresistible love for Michele Rocca. Accepting this reality, she rushes into Rocca's arms.

Francesco Savio (frahn-CHEHS-koh SAH-vee-oh), the opponent of Doro Palegari. Savio disputes Palegari's valiant justification of Delia's actions, only to change his opinion, praising the generosity of Doro's defense and asking for Doro's forgiveness. Now on the reverse sides of the argument, Savio and Palegari agree to duel. Their fighting seems ridiculous, however, for they can change their minds on the issue with the least provocation. In fact, there appears to be no one true, or absolute, interpretation of Delia's motivation.

Michele Rocca (ROHK-kah), the man who ran away with Delia, who was the lover of his fiancé's brother. About thirty years old, with dark hair and complexion, Rocca fits the stereotype of the passionate, angry lover. At first, he insists that he abhors the "treacherous" Delia. Moreover, he claims to have stolen her from Salvi for the artist's own good, to prove Delia's lack of virtue. Nevertheless, he is easily convinced that his actions were really prompted by a deep, unrealized love for Delia.

Prestino (prehs-TEE-noh), a friend of Francesco Savio. Prestino, along with other companions, supports Savio in his upcoming duel, which is thwarted by the union of Delia Morello and Michele Rocca.

Delia Moreno (moh-REH-noh), the "real life" counterpart to Delia Morello. Appearing in the theater lobby during the choral interlude, this character is the supposed "real life" Delia who angrily protests the playwright's onstage depiction of her life. Like the "fictional" Delia, Delia Moreno also falls for her Michele Rocca, Baron Nuti, reenacting the play's ending.

Baron Nuti (NEW-tee), a parallel character to Michele Rocca. Like Rocca, Nuti proclaims his desire for Delia Moreno during the final choral interlude.

Stage manager, a theater employee.

Leading lady, the actress who plays Delia Morello in the play.

Five drama critics,
authors,
a would-be literary figure, and
Spectators, who support or oppose Pirandello. All are characters who appear in the choral interludes, commenting on, criticizing, and interpreting the play, thus further blurring the boundaries between illusion and reality, representation and life.

— *Lisa S. Starks*

EARTH
(La Terre)

Author: Émile Zola (1840-1902)
First published: 1887
Genre: Novel
Locale: La Beauce, France
Time: The 1860's
Plot: Naturalism

Fouan (fwahn), a proud, tough, suspicious old peasant whose waning powers lead him, like King Lear, to divide his land among his children. Without land he loses their fear and respect, and they strip him of the rest of his possessions until he is powerless. Humiliated everywhere, he moves from home to home. Finally his youngest son, fearing Fouan will report him for murder, smothers and burns him.

Rose, his simple, submissive wife, who dies after being hit by the youngest son, leaving Fouan in solitude.

Hyacinthe (yah-SAHNT), called **Jésus-Christ**, their older son, the amiable village loafer who loves drinking and poaching. He offers Fouan the irregular life of his home, but his father leaves when he learns that Hyacinthe is after his bonds.

Fanny, the daughter, a self-righteous, competent housekeeper whose insults and restrictions on her father drive him to leave for good.

Buteau (bew-TOH), the younger son, a brutal, greedy, lustful man. After rejecting his land inheritance out of pride, he accepts it and marries his cousin for her land, vowing never to lose any of it. He tries to keep his sister-in-law from claiming her share and makes violent attempts to rape her. When she does claim her land, he and his wife are evicted, but they return, rape, and kill her. The land reverts to them. In the end, Buteau's vicious greed has caused the death of his parents and sister-in-law.

Delhomme (deh-LOHM), Fanny's husband, a man whose avarice is checked by a crude sense of justice but who supports his wife's policy with regard to her father.

Lise (leez), a cheerful girl who marries Buteau after bearing his child and then becomes coarse, sullen, and greedy. She makes an enemy of her sister, helps Buteau rape her, and then accidentally kills her in a fight.

Françoise (frahn-SWAHZ), Lise's sister, a sensitive, attractive girl disgusted by Buteau to the point that she moves to her aunt's house, accepts a husband whom she does not love, and claims her land. When Buteau finally ravishes her, she realizes she loves him. Dying, she wills him her land.

Jean Macquart (zhahn mah-KAHR), a former soldier, tradesman, and farmhand. A manly, kind person, attracted to Françoise, he finds himself drawn into a violent feud with Buteau and a loveless marriage. When his wife wills her land to Buteau, he decides to become a soldier again.

Hourdequin (ewr-deh-KAHN), a gentleman farmer, Macquart's employer and friend, a man oppressed by ill-used farm equipment and a promiscuous mistress. In the end, his misfortunes overcome him.

Jacqueline (zhahk-LEEN), his loose mistress, an illegitimate girl who sleeps with all the farmhands.

La Frimat (free-MAH), an old woman gardener who takes in Buteau and Lise when they are evicted.

La Grande (grahnd), Fouan's sister, a vicious old woman who commands fear, delights in family feuds, and takes in Françoise for a short time.

Old Mouche (mewsh), Lise's father and Fouan's brother, an old peasant who die and leaves his land to his daughters.

La Truille (TRWEE-yeh), Hyacinthe's lively, promiscuous illegitimate daughter and housekeeper.

Jules (zhewl) and

Laure (lohr), the children of Buteau and Lise. They mistreat Fouan.

Maître Baillehache (mehtr bahy-AHSH), the notary who supervises the division of Fouan's land.

Grosbois (groh-BWAH), a fat, drunken surveyor.

M. Charles (shahrl), a sentimental, retired brothel-keeper.

The Abbé Godard (goh-DAHR), the local priest, invariably angry at the peasants but generous to the poor.

Bécu (bay-KEW), the local constable and Hyacinthe's drinking companion.

Lequeu (leh-KYOO), the local schoolmaster, an anarchist who advocates total destruction when, finally, he breaks out of his reserved manner.

Canon (kah-NOHN), a communist tramp whom Hyacinthe takes home with him.

Palmyre (pahl-MEER), an old farm woman who dies while working for Buteau.

Hilarion (ee-lah-RYOHN), her idiot, crippled brother, killed while trying to rape La Grande.

Macqueron (mah-keh-ROHN), the local innkeeper and merchant who is elected mayor.

EARTHLY POWERS

Author: Anthony Burgess (John Anthony Burgess Wilson, 1917-1993)
First published: 1980
Genre: Novel
Locale: Various locations in Europe and the United States
Time: The 1970's, with flashbacks
Plot: Satire

Kenneth Marchal Toomey, a homosexual and best-selling author. His struggle with homosexuality and his search for truths beyond Catholic moral values are the twin forces driving his life. From the vantage point of his eighty-first birthday (celebrated in his Malta retreat), he looks back on his sixty-year exile from England's conventional sexual values and on a career as an internationally renowned novelist and playwright. For much of that time, he has been careful to ensure public acceptance by writing from a heterosexual point of view; only late in life has he had the courage to declare his true preferences. In recalling the major episodes of his life, he emerges as a man dominated by his inner struggle to reconcile his homosexuality with Catholic moral values. He must also come to terms with his suspicion that, despite a fertile imagination and verbal brilliance, he possesses only a second-rate talent. Although he meets adversity with consistent detachment bolstered by a brittle wit, at bottom Toomey is a tender and caring man, deeply committed to his private code of love and fidelity. His trust in even the most mendacious of his lovers makes him a natural victim. With a single exception, his love for other men has been cheapened by them, and his fidelity betrayed. Love and fidelity nevertheless remain the prominent threads running through his character: intense love for his difficult sister and fidelity to some form of the Catholicism that would place him among the damned. In the end, even when the evidence of evil perpetrated by earthly powers has brought disillusionment with the world, he embraces the values of platonic love and spiritual peace in his final years with his sister.

Hortense Campanati, Kenneth's sister, an internationally famed sculptor. An attractive, bright young woman (ten years younger than Kenneth), Hortense is more at home with her Catholic values than he, and she often criticizes his sexual morality. She learns to incorporate the dark side of life into her religious beliefs. Like her brother, Hortense has her share of suffering with which to come to terms: the breakup of her marriage, the loss of an eye, and the deaths of her lover, son, and granddaughter within a short period of time. She has the resilience of character to retain both dignity and inner peace through it all, becoming the most important influence on her brother as well as an artist with a reputation of her own.

Carlo Campanati, a brother of Domenico. He is an Italian priest who eventually becomes Pope Gregory XVII. He maintains a tough, uncompromising belief in the essential goodness of people and the externality of evil. Physically bulky, Carlo becomes more so over the years as he indulges his gargantuan appetites for both wine and food. His habits, including a love of gambling, seem ill suited to a man of God; however, he is a canny fighter against evil, with a recognized ability to exorcise demons. As an important force in the Vatican during the late 1930's, Carlo also fights demons among the earthly powers, carrying on a private (at times heroic) resistance to Benito Mussolini and to the Nazi occupation during the war. Years later, when he has become Gregory XVII, he reveals a depth of human understanding in addition to the toughness, making use of television and personal appearances throughout the world to spread his message of human goodness in partnership with divine love, as embodied in a militant and enlightened Christian socialism.

Domenico Campanati, a composer, the younger brother of Carlo. At the time he marries Hortense, he is a conventionally handsome young opera composer. In his marriage, he shows an emotional shallowness and histrionic nature (including wife-beating and desertion) matched only by his artistic sterility. In his compositions, he produces imitations of fashionable trends. Later, in his Hollywood years, he writes flashy but empty film scores. His single attempt at grand opera results in nothing more than dismal blasphemy. In the end, crippled and disillusioned, he abandons all faith in love, God, and his own musical abilities.

Raffaele Campanati, a brother of Domenico and Carlo. A highly principled businessman who has set up in Chicago, he opposes the gangsterism of the Prohibition era and pays with his life. His agonizing death brings Carlo to his hospital bedside, providing the occasion for a miracle that plays a decisive role in Toomey's life.

Philip Shawcrosse, a medical doctor and tough-minded idealist Toomey meets during his stay in Malaysia. He represents the novelist's single experience of pure, disinterested masculine love. It is Shawcrosse's good nature and dedicated philanthropy that cause him to fall victim to a Malaysian sorcerer.

Ralph Pembroke, Toomey's secretary and lover. A black nationalist and would-be poet, he is less successful at poetry than at the political activism to which his lack of racial assurance drives him. Having left Toomey, he becomes minister of culture in the emerging African nation of Rukwa.

Geoffrey Enright, Toomey's last secretary-lover. A congenital misfit, he combines a verbal dazzle comparable to Toomey's with utter heartlessness. After he makes his employer unwelcome in more than one Mediterranean refuge, Toomey dispatches him to the United States on an information-gathering mission that provides one of the story's chief ironies.

John Campanati, one of Hortense and Domenico's twin children, a professor of anthropology. After the war, in which he serves as a gallant army photographer in the Italian campaign, John shows his dedication to anthropology by visiting Rukwa to study the language of East African religious rituals. His death as a victim of unspeakable sacrificial rites growing out of Catholic ecumenicism provides one of the final challenges to Toomey's belief in contemporary religious developments.

— *Paul Kistel*

EAST OF EDEN

Author: John Steinbeck (1902-1968)
First published: 1952
Genre: Novel
Locale: California
Time: 1865-1918
Plot: Regional

Adam Trask, a settler in the Salinas Valley. He marries Cathy Ames in Connecticut and moves west, where he and their twin sons, Caleb and Aron, are deserted by her.

Cathy Ames, Adam Trask's innocent-appearing but evil wife. Deserting Adam and their twin sons, Caleb and Aron, she becomes the proprietress of a notorious brothel.

Aron Trask, smugly religious, idealistic twin son of Adam Trask and Cathy Ames. Unable to face the knowledge of his parents' past, he joins the army and is killed in France.

Caleb Trask, impulsive twin son of Adam Trask and Cathy. Rejected in an effort to help his father, he takes revenge by revealing to his brother Aron the secret of their mother's identity. He later accepts responsibility for the disillusioned Aron's death.

Abra Bacon, Aron Trask's fiancée. Disturbed because she feels unable to live up to Aron's idealistic image of her, she finally turns to the more realistic Caleb Trask.

Charles Trask, Adam Trask's half brother.

Samuel Hamilton, an early settler in the Salinas Valley.

Liza Hamilton, Samuel Hamilton's wife.

Lee, Adam Trask's wise and good Chinese servant.

Faye, proprietress of a Salinas brothel. Her death is engineered by Cathy Ames as she seeks to gain full control of Faye's establishment.

Will Hamilton, business partner of Caleb Trask.

EASTWARD HO!

Authors: George Chapman (c. 1559-1634) with Ben Jonson (1573-1637) and John Marston (1576-1634)
First published: 1605
Genre: Drama
Locale: London, England
Time: c. 1605
Plot: Comedy

Touchstone, a blunt, honest goldsmith. The pretensions of his daughter Gertrude and his wild apprentice, Quicksilver, irritate him, while the duty and devotion of his daughter Mildred and his steady apprentice, Golding, gratify him. Although he is stern, he is too good-hearted to deny mercy to the repentant sinners.

Mistress Touchstone, his somewhat simple wife. Dazzled by her social-climbing daughter and her knighted son-in-law, she too irritates Touchstone. When Gertrude comes to grief, Mistress Touchstone urges her to beg her father's forgiveness.

Gertrude, Touchstone's haughty and ambitious daughter. She scorns her father and patronizes her mother and sister. When her husband runs off with another woman and is jailed, her pride has a fall, but even in her plea for her father's pardon, she cannot completely avoid impudence.

Mildred, Touchstone's dutiful daughter. She is kind and friendly even to her contemptuous, self-centered sister. With her father's support, she marries Golding.

Francis Quicksilver, Touchstone's idle and prodigal apprentice. He keeps a mistress, gambles, and wastes his little substance in riotous living. He joins Sir Petronel in a plan for a Virginia voyage. When shipwreck ends the voyage almost at its very beginning, he is imprisoned for theft and sentenced to death. He becomes sincerely repentant, and Touchstone forgives him and secures his release.

Golding, Touchstone's diligent apprentice. Good without being self-righteous or priggish, he rises rapidly in the world and becomes an alderman's deputy. He persuades Touchstone to visit the prison and manipulates the angry old man into forgiving his prodigal son-in-law and his prodigal apprentice.

Sir Petronel Flash, a newly made knight. He dazzles Mistress Touchstone and Gertrude, whom he marries and deserts for Winifred. Imprisoned with Quicksilver, he also repents and receives forgiveness, returning to his wife.

Security, an old usurer, also imprisoned but released by Touchstone's bounty.

Winifred, Security's attractive young wife, who runs off with Sir Petronel but returns to Security.

Sindefy, Quicksilver's mistress and Gertrude's maid. At Golding's urging, Quicksilver agrees to marry her.

EAT A BOWL OF TEA

Author: Louis Chu (1915-1970)
First published: 1961
Genre: Novel
Locale: The Chinatown districts of New York and San Francisco
Time: 1941-1949
Plot: Domestic realism

Wang Ben Loy, the individual at the center of this comic novel. He is a young waiter in a restaurant in New York's Chinatown, and he resembles the sympathetic and underdog youth of classic comedy. Born in a Chinese village and reared there until the age of seventeen, Ben Loy has been brought up with the traditional Confucian values and is thus a filial son. Although as the novel opens he is in his twenties, holds a job, has done his hitch in the army during World War II, and is a married man, he still regards his father with some awe. His one character flaw is his sensuality, which leads him to patronize prostitutes. Retribution for this occurs when he becomes impotent with his wife, who cuckolds him. Through love and forgiveness, he is able to work out his atonement and rehabilitation.

Wang Wah Gay, Ben Loy's father. He has been a sojourner in America for some thirty years. He started out as a laundryman but now owns and operates a gambling joint in New York's Chinatown. Wah Gay fits the classic comic mold of the parent who tyrannizes the younger generation. He exercises a rigid, traditionally Confucian domination over Ben Loy, deciding when to transplant him from his native village to New York and determining whom he is to marry. He gives his son no quarter to develop his own individuality or to pursue his own happiness. Although Wah Gay insists that Ben Loy should be a good Confucian son, he himself is not a good Confucian father, for he makes his living from gambling.

Mei Oi, Loy's sympathetic bride, an attractive young woman who loves her husband and wants to be a mother. She grew up in her native Sunwei village in Kwangtung Province, China, where she was nurtured and sheltered by her family and the societal structure of her clan. Confronted with the freedoms of New York, the impotence of her husband, and the blandishments of a sweet-talking seducer, she naïvely falls.

Lee Gong, Mei Oi's father, a longtime friend and former coworker of Wah Gay. He, too, is a Chinese émigré in the United States, and he too is cast in the mold of overbearing parent.

Ah Song, Mei Oi's lover and father of her child. An idling playboy, Ah Song preys on Chinatown women gullible enough to give credence to his tales, puffing up his wealthy connections in Canada and belittling their husbands. He is a known philanderer and is treated as a contemptible villain by the men of Chinatown. His philandering ways are repaid by his losing an ear when the irate Wah Gay attacks him and by his being exiled from Chinatown by the clan association.

Wang Chuck Ting, the uncle of Wah Gay and elder statesman of the Wang clan in Chinatown. Wealthy and politically well connected, he is a wheeler-dealer who can find a person a job, an apartment, or a contact in the police department. When the enmity between Wah Gay and Ah Song threatens to spill out to the authorities beyond Chinatown, Chuck Ting steps in to contain their dispute within Chinatown, then stage manages the Chinatown judiciary system to achieve a resolution to the conflict.

The Wah Que Barber Shop's customers, who make up an entity that resembles the chorus in Greek drama. These men, who are the remnants of the original bachelor society of Chinatown, hang out in the barber shop and exchange tidbits of gossip, comment on the doings of the principal characters, and act as the mirrors of public opinion in Chinatown.

— C. L. Chua

EATING PEOPLE IS WRONG

Author: Malcolm Bradbury (1932-)
First published: 1959
Genre: Novel
Locale: A provincial English university
Time: An academic year during the 1950's
Plot: Wit and humor

Stuart Treece, the head of the English department at one of Britain's provincial "redbrick" universities in an "anywhere city." In his late thirties, he specializes in the literature of the eighteenth century but recently has become interested in Victorian poetry and has published a book on A. E. Housman. Although in many ways suited to provincial life, Treece feels that he may be missing out on something. He is made uneasy by his unprestigious academic appointment, his degree (from London University rather than an Oxbridge school), and his war service (in the London fire brigade). Having spent his "formative years" in the heyday of British socialism, he also is uneasy with his place in a modern world in which his brand of moral scrupulousness is decidedly out of fashion. By limiting his possessions, he hopes to keep his character undefined and free, but the result is not freedom but lack of substance; he becomes "a person without a firm, a solid centre." Wracked by doubts and later by guilt, he cannot pass a simple road test, communicate with his students effectively, or convince Emma Fielding to accept his proposal of marriage. A representative of debilitated liberal humanism in a posthumanist age, he lacks sufficient will to make the leap from thought to action and ends up curiously alone in a crowded National Health hospital ward, suffering from exhaustion and loss of blood.

Louis Bates, who gives up a teaching position in a girls' school to pursue, at the age of twenty-six, what he assumes is higher education. A member of England's lower middle class, he proves difficult for the establishment, even at this provincial university, to define or accept. Ill mannered but enthusiastic, he is "a curious mixture of the promising and the absurd." Trying too hard to be accepted, he only makes it more apparent just how self-centered and anomalous he is. Fond of comparing himself to William Shakespeare, William Blake, Percy Bysshe Shelley, and others, the pompous Bates may have genuine literary talent and does manage to have his poetry published. Rejection and self-pity finally drive him to attempt suicide.

Emma Fielding, a twenty-six-year-old postgraduate student who still has not completed her thesis on fish imagery in Shakespeare. Although one of the "upstart middle class," she sees herself as having no future and is in fact in retreat from the present. As scrupulous as Treece, her perfectionism precludes her actual participation in the world. Looking like a photograph of Virginia Woolf, she finds herself pursued by the very men who would appeal most to a woman with a saint complex wanting nothing more than to minister to the afflicted. By the novel's end, she has only the guilt that she, like Treece, feels for the small parts they have played in Bates's suicide attempt.

Eborebelosa, one of the novel's several foreign students. His education is being financed by a terrorist group. Claiming that he is despised in England because he is black, he spends much of his time locked in closets and toilets until Treece tells him to face his problems and the world more directly and to stop expecting others to treat him in the royal fashion he believes is his due as the son of a West African tribal chief. Eborebelosa courts Emma (according to tribal custom) and is rejected. He is later attacked and beaten by a group of teddy boys.

Carey Willoughby, a critic, poet, and novelist, one of England's Angry Young Men. A contemptuous and utterly self-centered man, he has included an especially unflattering portrait of Treece in one of his novels. Believing what Treece and the others only passively suspect, that Bates does possess talent, Willoughby helps him get his poetry into print.

The Bishops, the elderly and solidly middle-class couple in whose Georgian home Emma rents an apartment. They are among the people Emma "collects" (eats).

The vice-chancellor, an official at Treece's university, trained in business and "full of bonhomie." He advocates practical education and equates a university with its buildings. Contemporary novels confuse him because they lack the concluding resolution that he requires.

Dr. Viola Masefield, the department's assertive and determinedly fashionable lecturer in Elizabethan drama. Her attempt to seduce Treece ends when he hears the room "booming with moral reverberations."

Jenkins, a sociologist who accepts whatever clothes and ideas are currently in fashion; these ideas include group dynamics and social engineering. Treece does not feel himself to be part of Jenkins' schemes and overall patterns, but he does listen as Jenkins explains just how inconsequential academics such as themselves have become.

— Robert A. Morace

THE EBONY TOWER

Author: John Fowles (1926-   )
First published: 1974
Genre: Novel
Locale: Manoir de Coëtminais, in Brittany; and Orly Airport
Time: Two days in September, 1973
Plot: Love

David Williams, an artist and art critic, formerly a teacher and lecturer. At the age of thirty-one, David is a painter whose small-scale abstracts sell well because they "[go] well on walls." David has been commissioned to write the introduction to *The Art of Henry Breasley* and is visiting Breasley's home in Brittany, Coëtminais. Without his wife, David is faced by a double challenge at Coëtminais. On one hand, Breasley's contempt for abstract painting challenges the vitality and honesty of David's identity as an artist. On the other, the intellectual, imaginative, and sexual attraction David begins to feel for Diana challenges his comfortable conformity as a person—as husband, as father, and as "normal" English intellectual. Having hesitated and thus lost Diana, David knows as he drives to Paris and meets Beth at Orly Airport that his choice—rather, his failure to choose—has doomed him, artistically and personally, to a life of unchanged mediocrity.

Henry Breasley, an elderly and famous British painter, expatriate, and bohemian. Born in 1896, Breasley went into self-imposed exile by 1920. A London exhibition of Spanish Civil War drawings in 1942 established him both as a great artist and as a difficult man. Breasley acquired the Manoir de Coëtminais in 1963 and withdrew into a nearly reclusive life in which he could maintain his view of himself and his art without constant challenge from current artistic trends. In Coëtminais, Breasley is painting a series of huge canvases, described by him as "dreams" and as "tapestries." In contrast to David Williams, Breasley is verbally inarticulate, violently opposed to abstraction in art (he sees it as a retreat from real human facts and needs and calls it the "ebony tower"), and contemptuous throughout his life of social and moral conventions. Breasley's ostentatious obscenity is largely a defense against his fear of old age and diminishing emotional and physical—though not conceptual—power. David recognizes that Breasley has a real connection to the past that is lost to David and all of his generation.

Diana (The Mouse), formerly an art student at Leeds, then at the Royal College of Art, and now companion to Henry Breasley. She has lived at Coëtminais since the previous spring. She is a slim woman in her early twenties, with brown and gold hair and level eyes, both honest and reserved. The end of a love affair and her belief that the Royal College did not allow her to develop her full range of artistic talent induced Diana to drop out of school and go to Coëtminais. She is learning much from Breasley, but he has asked her to marry him, and she is beginning to wonder whether she is quite normal, whether she can develop her considerable artistic gifts at Coëtminais, and whether it is too late to leave Coëtminais and return to the real world. In David, whose art she admires, she finds a knight in shining armor, yet one who cannot save her. She refuses to let David take her to bed because she knows that their attraction for each other is potentially much more than physical. Diana is David's missed chance to become alive again as an artist and a person.

Anne (The Freak), Diana's friend and formerly an art-education student at Leeds, now living with Diana and Breasley at Coëtminais, where she shares with Diana the nursing and sexual chores that are expected of female companions by Breasley. Unlike Diana, Anne is neither emotionally nor sexually naïve. Her wild looks and talk hide a rare ability to give of herself. She worries that Diana will not have the assertiveness to leave Breasley and asks David to talk with Diana. She later berates him for not taking Diana to bed.

Beth Williams, a former student and the wife, since 1967, of David Williams. Beth is an illustrator of books for children. In contrast to Diana, Beth seems to David to represent all in his life that is unfree and conventionally responsible. Beth has not accompanied him to Coëtminais because their daughter Sandy has suddenly become ill with chicken pox. She flies to Paris to meet David after the conclusion of his visit with Breasley.

Mathilde and

Jean-Pierre, elderly servants to Henry Breasley. Mathilde, Breasley's cook and housekeeper, had been cared for by Breasley when her husband was serving time in prison for murder. She had modeled for the painter and, possibly, been his mistress. Because of Breasley's kindness to Mathilde and Jean-Pierre, they serve him now with fierce devotion.

— Jonathan A. Glenn

ECCLESIAZUSAE
(Ekklesiazousai)

Author: Aristophanes (c. 450-c. 385 B.C.E.)
First performed: 392 B.C.E.?
Genre: Drama
Locale: Athens
Time: Early fourth century B.C.E.
Plot: Utopian

Praxagora (prak-SA-goh-ruh), a housewife of Athens who has become disgusted with the dishonesty of public officers, the fickleness and greed of the people, and the mismanagement of domestic and foreign affairs. She encourages a number of her female friends to disguise themselves as men, pack the assembly, and vote for her proposal that the government of the state be turned over to the women. Although not above occasional vulgarity, she is quick-witted and courageous. An accomplished orator, she carries her plan to success and finds herself designated dictator. She quickly institutes a program of reform, evidently based on the playwright's knowledge of an early version of Plato's *Republic*. In Praxagora's utopian society, crime will become impossible because property will be held in common; meals will be taken in communal dining halls, marital restrictions will be abolished (with the proviso that the old and ugly have first claims on desirable sexual partners), and courtesans will be done away with so that honest women may have their choice of young men. Praxagora fears that her reforms are too extreme for adoption, but she is assured that "love of novelty and disdain for the past" among the Athenians will secure the cooperation of the people.

Blepyrus (bleh-PI-ruhs), Praxagora's husband, some years her senior. He, like his neighbors, dabbles in thievery, lechery, and bearing false witness, but he is reasonably good-natured, if a little dense. Pleased that his wife has been elevated to the dictatorship, he plans to bask in her reflected glory.

Chremes (KRAY-meez), a friend of Blepyrus who brings him the news that the assembly has voted to turn the rule of Athens over to the women.

A man, a neighbor of Blepyrus who awakens to find that his wife and his clothing, in which she went disguised to the assembly, are missing from his house.

Two citizens, one of whom hastens to deliver his property to the common store, as has been decreed. The other wishes to retain his property but still to get his part of the common feast.

A young girl, who desires her lover.

A young man, the lover, who because of the new law must be relinquished to the first old woman.

The first old woman, who is ugly, but who must relinquish the young man to the second old woman.

The second old woman, who is even uglier, but who must share the young man with the third old woman.

The third old woman, who is as ugly as it is possible to be.

A group of women, who go disguised as men with Praxagora to the assembly. Each is prepared to speak in favor of women's sovereignty, but each betrays herself in a practice session, one by bringing wool to card, another by calling for neat wine to drink, and another by swearing by the two goddesses. Praxagora is finally chosen as their spokesperson.

THE ECHOING GROVE

Author: Rosamond Lehmann (1901-1990)
First published: 1953
Genre: Novel

Locale: London and Reading, England
Time: The 1930's and 1940's
Plot: Social realism

Rickie Masters, a well-to-do English businessman. A large, handsome man with brown hair and striking blue eyes, he has a boyish quality that makes him attractive to women. After marrying Madeleine Burkett, he falls in love with her younger sister, Dinah Burkett. After he breaks off the affair with Dinah, he feels unable to love anyone. Eventually, he develops ulcers, which cause his death in 1944.

Madeleine Burkett Masters, the wife of Rickie Masters. A graying woman in her early forties when the story begins, shortly after Rickie's death, she has always been considered a beauty. She is tall and slender, with a rather loud voice and a frequently irritable manner. She has been a devoted mother and still grieves for her eldest son, Anthony, who was killed in North Africa during the war. After meeting Dinah at their mother's deathbed, she becomes reconciled with her sister, who consoles Madeleine in the loss of her longtime lover. At the end of the story, Madeleine agrees to leave her daughter Clarissa in Dinah's care so that she can visit her surviving son, Colin, in South Africa.

Dinah Burkett Hermann, an artist and a Marxist, Madeleine's younger sister and Rickie's mistress. A small woman with classic features and large, dark eyes, she strikes men as mysterious. After her child by Rickie dies at birth, Dinah gives up the desire to live and is brought back only by Rickie's devotion. After Rickie breaks off the affair, she marries Jo Hermann, whom she loves deeply but who is killed in the Spanish Civil War. Eventually, she sinks into poverty, into an affair with a former convict, and into self-destroying alcoholism. Robbed and abandoned by her young lover and spurned by Rickie, she finally turns to Dr. Ernest Selbig, who drinks with her, makes love to her, and persuades her to continue living. In her reconciliation with her sister and in their developing friendship, she finds a new peace.

Jo Hermann, a Cockney Jewish intellectual and Marxist. A short, plump man whose bright eyes twinkle behind his horn-rimmed glasses, he gives Dinah both friendship and a secure love during their brief marriage. He is killed in the Spanish Civil War.

Rob Edwards, a former convict and thief who lives with Dinah for a time. A good-looking young man with green eyes, yellow hair, and a long, pale face, he is a rebel against society. When he meets the conventional Madeleine briefly at Dinah's, he cannot forget her and later goes looking for her, ostensibly to get Dinah's address. Instead, he encounters Rickie, who finds himself strangely attracted to Rob. Their intimacy is limited to an evening of conversation, during which they discuss their fear of being destroyed by the women they love. Rob later is killed aboard his navy vessel.

Jocelyn Penrose, a young schoolmaster. Short but strong, he is fair-skinned, with a gentle, quiet manner. Originally introduced into the household as a friend of Colin, he becomes Madeleine's lover during Rickie's absence in 1940. When he breaks off the affair so that he can marry another woman, she is devastated; fortunately, her sister is present to comfort her.

Dr. Ernest Selbig, a psychiatrist. He is a sallow-skinned, heavy, elderly man, elegantly dressed. A Jewish refugee from Germany, he carries with him the memory of killing his mistress in a suicide pact when the Nazis gained power and the guilt of his having failed to die. Befriending the poor and troubled, he takes in Rob and becomes Dinah's friend and lover, even persuading her not to kill herself. Ironically, he poisons himself.

Georgie Enthoven Worthington, an American, the wife of Jack Worthington and a member of the Masters circle. A quiet, subdued woman with brown hair and large gray eyes, she loves and respects her husband but is infatuated with Rickie. They make love only once, in her basement during a night of bombing. Three days later, Rickie dies. Georgie is killed by a car during a blackout.

Mrs. Burkett, the mother of Madeleine and Dinah. A woman with thin hair and pink cheeks, she has a strong sense of duty, as well as a keen understanding of the limitations of both men and women. She continues to feel close to Rickie, despite his weaknesses, and it is she who arranges for his burial. She urges her daughters to forgive each other, but she sees them estranged for fifteen years before her death brings them together.

— Rosemary M. Canfield Reisman

THE ECSTASY OF RITA JOE

Author: George Ryga (1932-1987)
First published: 1970
Genre: Drama
Locale: A city
Time: Late 1960's
Plot: Social realism

Rita Joe, a simple, romantic young American Indian woman. She moves to the city to escape the stagnation of life on her reservation, but things go wrong: She loses her job and is arrested repeatedly for a variety of offenses, such as vagrancy and prostitution. At the mercy both of a legal system she does not understand and of people who view her as inhuman, Rita ends up serving time in prison. Her dreams of a good life conflict with memories of a life that was simpler but one that was dominated by white people's ideas about religion and education. Figures from Rita's past appear and reappear, serving to highlight the conflicts between Native American concerns and the ways of the white culture. Despite pleas from her father to come home, Rita stays in the city. Chronically hungry, tired, and ill from living on the streets, she is finally raped and murdered.

Jaimie Paul, an idealistic, impetuous young American Indian. He argues with the chief of his tribe that life on the land holds no future and that Indians must adopt white people's ways if they are to get ahead. Like his childhood friend Rita, Jaimie opts for the comforts and fast pace of life in the city. Once there, he gets a job and rejoices in the good life it promises. Jaimie does not succeed in bridging the gap between the two cultures either; he loses his job and starts to drink. He balks at accepting charity; his dignity compels him to refuse free food and clothing despite the fact that he is starving and penniless. Frustrated and angry, he assaults Mr. Homer and ends up doing a short prison term. Following his release from jail, he and Rita go out on a date to celebrate. He is beaten and thrown in front of a train while attempting to defend her from the Murderers.

David Joe, an Indian chief, Rita's father. He is a dignified, sorrowful man who despairs about the future of his people on the reservation as well as about the fate of the young people who flock to the city. He speaks thoughtfully, using figurative language that articulates the dilemmas facing Indians.

Singer, a fixture onstage throughout the play. She is an earnest sort whose music is supposed to complement the action, although it is evident that she does not entirely comprehend the issues about which she sings. Her lyrics frequently provide ironic commentary on the drama.

Magistrate, the official who presides over Rita's trial. He is determined to be stern but fair in his judgment of Rita, although her lack of understanding of her predicament exasperates him. He would like to be kind to Rita because she reminds him of a poignant experience he once had in "Indian country," but his sense of duty gets the better of him, and he sentences her to jail.

Mr. Homer, a socially responsible white man. Although he runs a social service agency for American Indians, his charitable acts thinly disguise his real attitude of fear and condescension toward them.

Father Andrew, the church representative. He has known Rita since she was a child and visits her in prison. His clichéd words provide her with little comfort, and he leaves her angry and resentful of his unyielding ideas about God.

Eileen Joe, Rita's younger sister. She appears mostly in Rita's dreams. She brings back memories of simpler times, when she and Rita went berry picking together or when they comforted each other in the face of a violent storm. Eileen also tries to live in the city but eventually returns to the reservation.

Old Indian Woman, a character who represents the ways of the past. She appears with Eileen in Rita's dreams to convey information to Rita about her sickly father.

Miss Donohue, a teacher from Rita's past who serves as a witness against her during the trial. She is a peevish spinster who becomes exasperated when Rita cannot seem to keep her mind on Wordsworth.

Three Witnesses, also called **Three Murderers**, interchangeable characters who hover on the fringe of the action throughout the play. Although they sometimes act as witnesses against Rita in her trial, they usually lurk menacingly in the background, stepping forward only at the end to murder both Jaimie and Rita.

— Susan Whaley

EDEN END

Author: J. B. Priestley (1894-1984)
First published: 1934
Genre: Drama
Locale: Eden End, in northern England
Time: October, 1912
Plot: Naturalism

Stella Kirby, an actress in her early thirties. She has not achieved the success she had dreamed of when she left her home in Eden End, in northern England, some years before. Her unexpected return creates upheaval for the rest of the household. To the prodigal daughter, Eden End has seemed a safe haven, but she soon learns that she no longer belongs in the innocent world of her youth. She foresees that the future may hold even more disappointments for her, but, reunited with the husband from whom she has been estranged, she goes off bravely to face that uncertain future.

Dr. Kirby, a widower, an ailing general practitioner about sixty years old. He is aware of the seriousness of his heart condition and his imminent death. Naïvely believing his daughter Stella to be a success, he admires her for having had the courage to pursue her dream. He had wanted to be a London specialist but had settled for something less at his wife's urging. He is optimistic about a future that he will not live to see, unaware that England will soon be plunged into a shattering war that will disrupt the lives of all of his children.

Lilian Kirby, Stella's younger sister, who acts as housekeeper for her father. She is in love with Geoffrey Farrant and jealous of her sister, whom Farrant still loves. Lilian, who hides her emotions in sarcasm, arranges for Stella's estranged husband, Charles Appleby, to visit Eden End.

Geoffrey Farrant, a former army officer who retains his military bearing despite a slight limp. In his late thirties, he now manages a nearby estate but decides to try a new life in New Zealand, to Lilian's dismay, once he learns that Stella is married.

Charles Appleby, Stella's estranged husband, a second-rate actor, about forty years old, who dresses in loud Harris tweeds. There is evidence of charm and good breeding about him but also signs that he drinks too much. He has weathered many disappointments in his career and in his relationships with women but will carry on, because he recognizes that the wonders and beauty of life outweigh its inevitable setbacks and pain.

Wilfred Kirby, Dr. Kirby's youngest and most unsophisticated child, about twenty-four years old. Sunburned and mustached, he is home on leave from a position with the British West Africa Company in Nigeria. Disappointed to learn that the barmaid he fancies flirts with all of her customers, he is looking forward to getting back to work in Africa, just as he had looked forward to coming home. For Wilfred, anticipation gives way to disenchantment.

Sarah, the seventy-year-old North Country nurse who has remained with the Kirby family long past the years of her usefulness. She indulges her former charges as if they are still children. As the representative of a simpler way of life that is coming to an end, she makes no attempt to cope with such gadgets as the newly installed telephone.

— Albert E. Kalson

THE EDGE OF THE STORM
(Al filo del agua)

Author: Agustín Yáñez (1904-1980)
First published: 1947
Genre: Novel

Locale: Near Guadalajara, Mexico
Time: Spring, 1909-Spring, 1910
Plot: Social realism

Don Dionisio (dee-oh-NEE-see-oh), a parish priest who gives unity to the separate chapters describing the people and festivals of a small Mexican town. He is stern and upright, yet understanding and compassionate. He can combine the best of the contrasting philosophies of his two priestly associates.

Padre Reyes (RREH-yehs), his liberal and progressive assistant. He enjoys seeing the parishioners marry and shocks Padre Islas with his earthy talk. He has advanced ideas about such things as the value of life insurance, though he cannot convince any of the town of its value.

Padre Islas (EES-lahs), Don Dionisio's narrow-minded and unbelievably conservative associate. Unable to meet the townspeople on a personal basis, he scurries along the sun-baked streets with eyes averted. As the sponsor of the church organization for unmarried girls, he exerts tremendous influence on the community by urging the girls to stay pure by remaining single, and he threatens them with damnation for even wholesome thoughts about the men of the town. After achieving a reputation for saintliness, he ends up in an epileptic fit on the church floor, after which he is separated from the priesthood.

María, an orphan niece of Don Dionisio who rebels against the drab life of the community and secretly reads newspapers from Mexico and the forbidden *The Three Musketeers*. Her final rebellion takes the form of running away with the widow of Lucas González, a woman of doubtful reputation, to follow the revolutionary army fighting against dictator Porfirio Díaz.

Marta, the other niece of Don Dionisio, twenty years old and unmarried, who follows the monotonous village pattern, working in the hospital, looking after children, and accepting the social and religious restrictions.

Damián Limón (dahm-mee-AHN lee-MOHN), who has returned from the United States, "where Mexicans are treated like dogs." He retorts that at least they get paid in money instead of promises, as in Mexico. Through the machinations of a political boss, he gets a light, six-year sentence after killing Micaela Rodríguez, following a scandalous love affair. Then, managing to escape while on his way to jail at the capital, he brazenly returns to María. She helps him escape again to join the revolutionary army.

Timoteo Limón (tee-moh-TEH-oh), Damián's father, a prosperous landowner. He dies of a heart attack following a violent quarrel with Damián over his will.

Micaela Rodríguez (mee-kah-EH-lah rrohd-REE-gehs), a spoiled only child who learned about freedom while on a visit to Mexico City and tries to reproduce the gay life of the capital in her little town. She shocks the town with her indecent dress and shameless flirtations. In the end, stabbed to death by jealous Damián, she dies forgiving him and putting the blame for her death on her own actions.

Gabriel (gah-bree-EHL), a young man reared by Don Dionisio. His religious life is upset by four talks with Victoria, a young widow from Guadalajara who is visiting the town.

Luis Gonzaga Pérez (lew-EES gohn-SAH-gah PEH-rehs), once a talented seminary student. Being convinced by Padre Islas of the evil of his natural desires toward the opposite sex, he ends up drawing pictures on the walls of his cell in an insane asylum.

Lucas Macías (lew-KAHS mah-SEE-ahs), a fortune-teller whose prophecies concerning Halley's Comet upset his fellow villagers. Just before his death, receiving news of Madero's revolt, he declares in the words of the title: "The rains are coming [the edge of the storm]. We'll have a fine clearing shower."

Mercedes Toledo (toh-LEH-doh), a young girl of the town.

Victoria, a young widow visiting from Guadalajara.

THE EDIBLE WOMAN

Author: Margaret Atwood (1939-)
First published: 1969
Genre: Novel
Locale: Toronto, Canada
Time: Late 1960's
Plot: Social realism

Marian MacAlpin, a conventional young woman who works in a dull job and is engaged to Peter, a rising young attorney. As the date of her wedding approaches, she loses her appetite, first for red meat and then for all foods. Her behavior becomes increasingly erratic, and at one point she spends a night with Duncan, who seems to be completely unemotional. Marian discovers that she is rebelling against the conventions that have trained her to expect that the best life can offer her is marriage to a financially and socially successful man. The lives of her friends present her with the possible roles of mother, helpmate, companion, and feminist rebel, but she rejects them all. In the end, she breaks her engagement and finds herself alone.

Ainsley Tewce, Marian's roommate. She is a radical feminist who decides to have a baby outside marriage and unemotionally chooses Marian's friend Len Slank to be the father. Once pregnant, she panics and decides she must marry, but she rejects Len and chooses an ordinary young man to be her husband. In the end, she blames Marian for rejecting the conventional life.

Peter, a rising young attorney. He proposes to Marian because all the young men he had played games with have married and have thus betrayed him. Getting married is the thing to do; everyone else does it, so he might as well. He is thoroughly conventional and wants Marian to be the perfect wife, playing the roles of hostess, mother, and mistress and giving all of her attention to him. He is baffled when Marian's behavior becomes strange, but he offers her no help.

Joe and

Clara, friends of Marian, a couple who exist for no apparent reason except to reproduce themselves. Joe earns a living and tends the children while Clara happily produces one child after another. They provide a look at one kind of life, one that Marian decides she must reject.

Duncan, a young graduate student whom Marian meets at a Laundromat and with whom she develops a friendship. Like Marian, he cannot adapt to the expectations of conventional society, but Duncan simply refuses to care. He is bored with his studies but will not leave them. He depends on his roommates to see that he is fed and kept healthy, and he declines to make choices. Even when he and Marian make love, Duncan shows no emotion and indicates no desire for a more serious relationship. Like other characters, he represents one of the choices available to Marian, a choice that she rejects.

Leonard (Len) Slank, a friend of Marian and Peter. He claims that he wants to live unencumbered by a wife and family, but when he learns that Ainsley is pregnant with his child, he is upset that she chooses not to marry him.

Lucy,

Emily, and

Lillie, called the **Three Virgins**, women who work in the office with Marian and whose hopes for a conventional marriage are slowly fading. When Marian breaks her engagement with Peter, Lucy moves in on him.

— *John M. Muste*

EDITH'S DIARY

Author: Patricia Highsmith (1921-)
First published: 1977
Genre: Novel
Locale: Brunswick Corner, Pennsylvania
Time: 1955-1975
Plot: Psychological realism

Edith Howland, the protagonist. As the novel opens, Edith moves with her husband, Brett, and their ten-year-old son, Cliffie, from New York City to Brunswick Corner, Pennsylvania. She and Brett open the *Brunswick Corner Bugle*, a local newspaper that fails shortly afterward. After Cliffie is grown, but while he is still living at home, Brett divorces Edith to marry Carol Junkin, his secretary. Edith and her friend Gert Johnson revive the *Bugle*. Edith also writes left-wing articles and fantasy short stories. Edith takes up sculpture and continues to write in her diary, which contains a blend of fact and fantasy (especially about Cliffie). As the novel progresses, Edith becomes increasingly obsessed with politics, especially U.S. foreign policy in Vietnam, as she descends into madness.

Brett Howland, Edith's husband. Also a journalist, he works for the *Trenton Standard*. He is portrayed as a typical middle-class father who loves his wife and son, but he is incapable of dealing with Cliffie's emotional immaturity, which occasionally borders on psychosis. Brett eventually falls in love with his secretary, Carol, divorces Edith, marries Carol, and moves back to New York, where he begins a new family. He all but despises his son and is unable to deal effectively with his invalid Uncle George, whom he leaves under Edith's care after the divorce.

Cliffie Howland, Edith and Brett's emotionally disturbed son. He is at once both the most apathetic and the most amoral character in the novel. As a child, he attempts to smother Mildew, the family cat, ruins a Christmas turkey by gouging the breast, "playfully" aims a rifle at his father on a camping trip, and jumps into the Delaware River in the middle of winter. As an adult, he becomes a heavy drinker, gets caught cheating on his college entrance examinations, hits a pedestrian with his car after getting drunk, dumps the contents of Uncle George's bedpan all over the room when Edith is at her great-aunt Melanie's deathbed, and finally, murders George by giving him an overdose of codeine. Able to hold only temporary or part-time jobs, he becomes the town clown.

George, Brett's wealthy, invalid uncle who comes to live with the Howlands after they move to Pennsylvania. As the novel progresses, George, a retired lawyer who suffers from a mysterious back ailment, becomes increasingly bedridden and dependent on painkillers, especially codeine. George refuses to move to a nursing home after Brett divorces Edith.

Melanie, Edith's wealthy great-aunt, who serves as Edith's touchstone for emotional support and values. Melanie's twice yearly visits put even Cliffie on his best behavior; he thinks he may inherit money from her. Her death is seen as the one of the last key events leading to Edith's mental instability.

Gert Johnson, Edith's close friend and partner on the *Bugle*. Edith admires Gert's Bohemian lifestyle and thinks they share the same political outlook. The friendship becomes strained as Derek, Gert's son, is drafted and sent to Vietnam and Cliffie mysteriously escapes military service. Gertie continually pressures Edith to tone down her editorials for the *Bugle* and eventually conspires with Brett to get Edith to see a psychiatrist.

Carol Junkin, Brett's secretary, lover, and second wife. She bears Brett a daughter.

Dr. Francis Carstairs, George's doctor. At Brett's insistence, he tries to get Edith to see a psychiatrist. Carstairs suggests that George's death was caused by an overdose but suspects suicide rather than murder. He does not order an autopsy.

Debbie Bowden, the imaginary wife Edith creates for Cliffie in her diary. Edith fantasizes that Debbie and Cliffie, whom she pictures as a successful engineer, have two children, Josephine and Mark.

— *Pat Miller*

EDMUND CAMPION: Jesuit and Martyr

Author: Evelyn Waugh (1903-1966)
First published: 1935
Genre: Novel

Locale: Oxford and London, England; Rome, Italy; and Prague
Time: 1564-1581
Plot: Biographical

Edmund Campion, an Englishman born in 1540 in London. He studied at Oxford University, where he became a very learned and respected professor of Latin and Greek. In 1566, he receives the honor of being asked to deliver a speech welcoming Queen Elizabeth I to Oxford. Queen Elizabeth I and her advisers believe that Campion will have a distinguished career as a leading clergyman in the Church of England because of his intelligence and persuasiveness as an orator. He surprises his colleagues at Oxford and disappoints the queen by his decision to leave England and convert to Catholicism, which was then persecuted in England. In 1571, he begins studying for the priesthood at the Catholic seminary in Douai, France, but after two years he decides that his spiritual development would be served better by his entering the Jesuit order. He travels to Rome, where he is accepted by the Jesuits. He is assigned to their novitiate in Prague, where he continues his study of theology. He is ordained in Prague in September, 1578. He teaches philosophy, theology, Greek, and Latin at a Jesuit school in Prague, for which he also writes several edifying Latin plays. Two years after his ordination, his superiors decide to send him back to England as a missionary. Saying Mass was a capital offense in England at the time, and many Catholics were arrested and executed for their refusal to convert to the Church of England. Campion fully understands the dangers ahead of him as he crosses the English Channel in June, 1580. Campion's tasks are to hear confessions, say Mass, and give communion to Catholics. Until July, 1581, he successfully avoids arrest. He travels extensively around England, says Mass, and hears confessions in secret, as well as using an underground printing press to publish tracts in which he defends Catholic dogma. Queen Elizabeth I wants to silence this eloquent priest, and she uses all the power of her government to find Campion. After his arrest, he is taken to the Tower of London, where he is tortured several times on the rack, but he refuses to reconvert to the Church of England. Campion is indicted on the capital charge of treason because he refuses to recognize Queen Elizabeth I as the spiritual head of the church in England. At the beginning of his trial, he states that paupers like himself are entitled to the services of a lawyer in capital cases, and he further argues that his guilt has to be proven "beyond a reasonable doubt." Judge Christopher Wray rejects both arguments because he is afraid that the jury might not convict Campion and the other seven priests who are being tried with him. The judge does everything possible to ensure a guilty verdict. During his trial, Campion defends himself and the other priests eloquently, but they all are condemned to death. Campion is executed in London on December 1, 1581. He accepts his martyrdom with dignity and grace. His courageous acceptance of torture and death inspired generations of English Catholics to remain faithful to their beliefs. Pope Paul VI canonized Campion on October 25, 1970.

Queen Elizabeth I, the queen of England from 1558 to 1603. She hears Campion deliver a speech at Oxford University in 1566 and signs his death warrant in 1581. At the beginning of this novel, the author imagines that as she lay dying in 1603, Queen Elizabeth I may well have thought about the eloquent orator whom she had heard at Oxford thirty-seven years earlier.

— *Edmund J. Campion*

EDWARD II

Author: Christopher Marlowe (1564-1593)
First published: 1594
Genre: Drama
Locale: England and France
Time: The fourteenth century
Plot: Historical

Edward II, the headstrong, dissolute king of England. In his attempts to please his sycophantic favorites, Gaveston and Spencer, he neglects his responsibilities to the state, alienates Queen Isabella, and provokes rebellion among his nobles, who deprive him of his crown and eventually of his life. He responds to his dethronement with histrionic protests that are echoed by William Shakespeare's Richard II. Like Richard II, Edward II expresses a longing for a quiet life of contemplation.

Piers Gaveston (pihrz GAV-ehs-tuhn), Edward's ambitious favorite. He deliberately plans to corrupt his weak monarch with music, poetry, and "Italian masks," and to enrich himself at the expense of the English lords, whom he views with unceasing scorn. He overestimates Edward's power to protect his friends and falls into the hands of his bitter enemies, Mortimer and Warwick, who have him killed.

Hugh Spencer, Gaveston's protégé and successor in Edward's favor. He urges the king to stand firm against the seditious barons and sends messengers to thwart Isabella's pleas for aid from the French king. Loyal to Edward to the end, he flees with him to Ireland, where he is captured. He is returned to England and hanged.

Queen Isabella, Edward's neglected wife. She remains loyal to her husband during his first infatuation with Gaveston, although it grieves and repels her. To please Edward, she even appeals to Mortimer to allow Piers to return from exile. The king's continual rejection of her and her failure to win help from the king of France, her brother, drive her into the arms of Mortimer. She becomes a far less sympathetic figure as Mortimer's mistress and accomplice in his rise to power, and her imprisonment by her son for conspiring in her husband's murder seems just and inevitable.

Edmund Mortimer, the leader of the forces arrayed against Edward. He is enraged by the king's submission to the flattery of Gaveston, whom he hates bitterly, and he insists on the use of force to rid the realm of his enemy. Although he begins his campaign to free his country from evil influences, he becomes trapped by his own ambition and resorts to regicide to secure the regency for himself and Isabella. He retains a certain grandeur in his death, boasting that Fortune raised him to the heights before she hurled him down.

The duke of Kent, Edward's brother Edmund. He participates temporarily in Mortimer's campaign against Gaveston after his advice and service have been rejected by Edward, but he comes to regret his disloyalty and tries unsuccessfully to rescue his brother from his murderers. He is beheaded by order of Mortimer, who fears his influence with young Prince Edward.

Prince Edward, later King Edward III, the precocious young heir to the throne. He is pathetically eager to win his father's love and offers to help win aid from France to do so. Although he is not strong enough to prevent Kent's execution, he musters a group of loyal lords to assist him in condemning Mortimer for his father's death.

Old Spencer, the father of the king's favorite. He supplies military aid for Edward's defense and meets defeat with his son and the king.

Baldock, Hugh Spencer's tutor, who rises and falls with his pupil. He accepts his fate philosophically, telling Spencer, "All live to die, and rise to fall."

Sir John of Hainault, the kindly nobleman who aids Isabella and Prince Edward after the French king has rejected their suit.

Gurney and

Matrevis, Mortimer's henchmen, Edward's prison guards and murderers.

Lightborn, a hired assassin who devises the means of Edward's death.

Lancaster,

Warwick,

Pembroke,

Elder Mortimer,

The archbishop of Canterbury,and

The bishop of Winchester, leaders of the rebellion against Gaveston and Spencer.

The bishop of Coventry, an outspoken prelate who is sent to the tower for voicing his opposition to Gaveston.

Arundel, a nobleman loyal to Edward.

Beaumont,

Levune,and

Trussel, messengers.

Rice ap Howell, Old Spencer's Welsh captor.

Leicester and

Berkeley, Edward's guardians, relieved of their charge by Mortimer, who finds them too lenient.

Edward's niece, the daughter of the duke of Gloucester, married by her uncle to Gaveston.

EFFI BRIEST

Author: Theodor Fontane (1819-1898)
First published: 1895
Genre: Novel
Locale: Germany
Time: The second half of the nineteenth century
Plot: Domestic realism

Effi von Briest (fon breest), only child of Ritterschaftsrat von Briest and his wife. Married at sixteen to Baron von Innstetten, she goes with her husband to a small town on the Baltic Sea. Bored and depressed by the formal stiffness of her new home, she is attracted to Major von Crampas. With this relationship a burden on her conscience, she is happy to move to Berlin, her husband's new post. There old letters from von Crampas come to light. She is divorced by her husband, socially ostracized, and dies at her parents' home believing that her husband, in divorcing her, has done the right thing for his honor.

Baron von Innstetten (fon IHN-shteht-tehn), Effi's formal, disciplined husband. Discovering a packet of love letters written six years before by Major von Crampas to Effi, he avenges his honor by killing von Crampas in a duel and divorcing his wife.

Major von Crampas (fon KRAHM-pahs), Effi's carefree, witty admirer, who is killed in a duel by Baron von Innstetten.

Annie von Innstetten, the daughter of Baron von Innstetten and Effi.

Roswitha (rohz-VEE-tah), Effi's maid and faithful friend.

Ritterschaftsrat von Briest (RIH-tehr-shahfts) and

Frau von Briest, Effi's parents.

EGMONT

Author: Johann Wolfgang von Goethe (1749-1832)
First published: 1788
Genre: Drama
Locale: Brussels
Time: The sixteenth century
Plot: Tragedy

Count Lamoral Egmont, who was born in Flanders and who serves the Spanish as a capable general and an excellent statesman. When Philip II, the main instrument of the Inquisition, sends the duke of Alva to The Netherlands to prevent disorders that have arisen as a consequence of Dutch displeasure with Spanish rule, Egmont freely speaks his mind in spite of warnings given by trusted friends such as Count Oliva. He urges Alva to use patience and tact in his affairs with the burghers. Alva, however, accuses Egmont of treason and orders his execution.

William of Orange, the founder of the Dutch Republic, an intelligent, cautious man admired by Charles V but hated by Philip. There is outward harmony between Egmont and William, and Alva tries to trap them both. William, however, keeps his distance, is not so outspoken as is Egmont, and escapes the latter's fate.

Margaret of Parma, Philip's half sister, named by him as regent of The Netherlands. She is firm but not cruel toward the Protestants. She does what she can to keep order, but she knows that she is only the titular head of Holland and that Alva actually will rule.

The duke of Alva, the cruel emissary of Philip II. He has no patience with the Dutch commoners' claims for their rights and believes that force has to be used to keep them in line. He garrisons an army and turns Holland into a police state.

Clärchen, a commoner of lowly station who loves and is loved by Egmont. When he is arrested, she attempts to rally the people to rescue him. When she fails, she goes to her house and drinks poison.

Fritz Brackenburg, a citizen who loves Clärchen. Clärchen's mother supports his suit, but the young woman has eyes only for Egmont.

Machiavel, Margaret's shrewd, wise, and capable secretary.

Ferdinand, Alva's natural son, who is given a small part to play in the plan to trap William and Egmont. He actually sympathizes with Egmont.

Silva, the official who reads Egmont's sentence to him in prison.

THE EGOIST: A Comedy in Narrative

Author: George Meredith (1828-1909)
First published: 1879
Genre: Novel
Locale: England
Time: The nineteenth century
Plot: Social satire

Sir Willoughby Patterne, a nobleman whose pattern of egocentricities includes duplicity, austerity, snobbery, and sententiousness. Though he has played on the heartstrings of his most devoted Laetitia Dale, he learns through two broken engagements that all his barren heart can hope for is the solace of the good woman whom he has converted to egoism. Finally, Sir Willoughby is forced to abandon double dealing, to come down from the pedestal where he has viewed himself only in a favorable light, to bend his pride for the sake of a young cousin and a former servant whom he has wronged, and to accommodate himself to the understanding that his wife sees through him and cannot therefore love him. He will, of course, continue to be an egoist, though a more enlightened and flexible one.

Laetitia Dale, his silent admirer for many years and finally his public scourger. A longtime tenant of Sir Willoughby's in a cottage where she nurses her invalid father and writes for a living, she finally sickens of Patterne's self-centered ways, particularly toward his kinsman and her student, young Crossjay Patterne, whose life is being forced into the wrong mold. Always gentle, amenable, and trustworthy, Laetitia finally tires of being a confidante and becomes defiant in her refusal of the nobleman's hand after all others have failed him. Her warmth of admiration has been chilled by observation; her youth has gone in yearning; her health has suffered from literary drudgery. She makes her own terms for becoming Lady Patterne, to which Sir Willoughby agrees.

Clara Middleton, the betrothed of Sir Willoughby and his severest critic. At first attracted by the force of his personality, she soon discovers in him the tendency to manipulate lives and to order life. Feeling stifled and caged, she begs for her release, which the egoist cannot grant since he has only recently been jilted by Constantia Durham. Despairing of gaining her father's permission to break the engagement, she tries to escape to the home of her best friend and maid of honor. In this desperate but abortive effort, she is aided by the sensitive scholar-cousin of Sir Willoughby, Vernon Whitford, whom she will later marry. She, too, defends young Crossjay against the benevolent tyranny of the egotistical nobleman.

The Reverend Dr. Middleton, Clara's father, a retired clergyman, learned scholar, and warm-hearted wit. Dr. Middleton becomes more enamored of Sir Willoughby's fine wine and library than his daughter feels necessary, but he humorously involves himself in the plot to remake the egoist after he learns that the two-faced lover wishes to abandon his spirited daughter for the more complacent Laetitia.

Vernon Whitford, a poor relation of the Patternes and a writer who has taken in young Crossjay Patterne out of sympathy when his wealthy cousin refuses to aid the boy. Almost morbidly shy with women, Vernon finally asserts himself in league with Clara and Laetitia to save his young charge from education as a "gentleman."

Colonel Horace De Craye, the Irish cousin and best man at a wedding that does not come off, partly because of his machinations. The best friend of Sir Willoughby, Colonel De Craye has long been suspicious of the nobleman's lack of nobility. He finds it easy to side with Clara, with whom he is in love, and all the others who wish to thwart the egoist.

Crossjay Patterne, the penniless son of a Marine hero who is not welcomed at Patterne Place. Though not scholarly by nature, the youth is irrepressibly happy and loving, strangely in contrast to his distant, rich relative. He loves most his guardian, Vernon Whitford, and Clara Middleton, his benefactress.

Constantia Durham, Sir Willoughby's betrothed, who jilts him ten days before their wedding date.

Harry Oxford, a military man with whom Constantia elopes.

1876

Author: Gore Vidal (1925-)
First published: 1976
Genre: Novel

Locale: New York City and Washington, D.C.
Time: 1875-1877
Plot: Historical

Charles Schermerhorn Schuyler, the narrator, a journalist and historian who returns to the United States with his daughter, Emma. His fortune having been destroyed recently, he is forced to take journalistic assignments to support himself and his daughter. His ultimate goal is to secure the presidency for Samuel Tilden and, consequently, to earn a diplomatic post in France for himself. Although he finds enough energy to visit several houses of prostitution, his advancing age causes him much illness. He seems to respect deeply his daughter's intellect, and he frequently relates her observations of people and events as well as his own. He dies at the end of the novel. His death is recorded by the character William Cullen Bryant in a special dispatch to *The New York Evening Post*.

Emma Schuyler, the thirty-five-year-old daughter of Charles Schuyler. Having been reared in France and later married to a French prince, she is widowed when the novel begins. Creditors and her mother-in-law's demand for money leave Emma almost penniless after her husband's death. What money she has left, she must use to support her two children, who remain in France. Although engaged to John Day Apgar for a large part of the novel, she eventually marries William Sanford three months after his wife's death during childbirth.

John Day Apgar, Emma's suitor and fiancé. He is replaced in her affections by William Sanford.

James Bennett, the publisher of the *New York Herald*, for which Schuyler writes. He has a habit of beginning to drink as early as nine in the morning. He is a comic yet likable character.

William Cullen Bryant, a renowned American poet and editor of *The New York Evening Post*, a newspaper that often publishes Schuyler's work. Older than Schuyler, Bryant is much more physically fit and walks to his office daily.

Charles Nordhoff, a journalist with whom Schuyler frequently comes into contact.

William Sanford, a millionaire whom Emma interests in politics and who is married to Denise Sanford. After his wife's death in childbirth, he marries Emma.

Denise Sanford, William Sanford's wife and a close friend of Emma. Having been told that she cannot bear children safely, she abstains from pregnancy. After receiving advice later that she may possibly bear a child without harm to herself, she becomes pregnant, carries the baby to full term, and then dies in childbirth, leaving behind her newborn daughter, Blaise Delacroix Sanford, and her husband.

Ulysses S. Grant, a Union Army hero of the Civil War who is serving a second term as U.S. president. There is talk of his running for a third term, but eventually Grant decides not to run, realizing that the citizens no longer adore him as they did in the past. Schuyler often speculates about Grant's possible involvement in what some might call criminal activities.

Samuel Tilden, the Democratic candidate for president whom Schuyler supports. He wins the nation's popular vote but loses in the electoral college because of a discrepancy over the counting of votes in three Southern states.

James Garfield, a Republican congressman of whom Schuyler is fond. The narrator finds that he trusts Garfield in spite of his better judgment.

— *Sally Bartlett*

THE EIGHTH DAY

Author: Thornton Wilder (1897-1975)
First published: 1967
Genre: Novel
Locale: Chicago and Coaltown, Illinois; Hoboken, New Jersey; and Chile
Time: 1880-1905
Plot: Family

John Barrington Ashley, later **James Tolland**, a mining engineer falsely convicted of murder in Coaltown, Illinois, who escapes to Chile. He is "neither dark nor light, tall nor short, fat nor thin, bright nor dull"; that is, he is a typical Midwesterner. He is a creative tinkerer, a hard worker, and an active humanitarian of great energy of mind and body who deplores sloth and despair. Although he is areligious, he has faith and aids others in their religious pursuits and beliefs. He is the personification of charity, and he embodies the best virtues of Protestantism—responsibility, industry, frugality, love, dedication, and sacrifice. His constructive practicality, idealism, and moral consciousness set him apart from the ordinary, though paradoxically he is presented as a typical American of his time. Like Job, he overcomes humiliation, suffering, and the afflictions of his flesh and family, though he has to resume his life in Chile, where he is known as James Tolland, a Canadian engineer.

Beata Ashley, John's wife, a woman of German descent from a Hoboken, New Jersey, family. She is somewhat aloof, serene, and unable to become intimate with neighbors, the result of having been brought up as "royalty." She is cultured (she plays the piano competently) and conventional, though she eloped with John and had four children in nineteen years without having been married. Her efforts at respectability preclude spontaneity and a practical solution to keeping her family without her husband's income.

Lily Ashley, their eldest daughter, beautiful, assured, elegant, and wise in the ways of the world. She reads wisely and well. She does housework by day and devotes evenings to the study of music, eventually becoming a famous concert singer. Her emotional vulnerability is suggested by her bohemianism in eloping with a boarder, Malcolm Ladislas, who is a salesman and drummer. She is practical, however, and supports herself and her son by singing in churches and on social occasions. She is without vanity, has a wry wit, and is fearless, self-confident, and admirable.

Roger Ashley, John and Beata's son, who is almost eighteen years old at the time of the trial. He leaves for Chicago, where he becomes a prominent young journalist known by his nom de plume, Trent Frazier. He has little sense of humor. He is a man of faith, indomitable in his efforts to eradicate injustice and suffering. He reads constantly and is not too proud to take menial jobs. He is not a paragon of virtue: He has affairs with girls of many races and nationalities before, at the age of twenty-four, marrying Félicité Lansing.

Sophia Ashley, John and Beata's second daughter and her mother's principal support. Like her siblings, she has big ears and feet. She is resourceful (she prevails on her mother to turn their home into a boardinghouse), faithful, dedicated to self-improvement, and committed to the relief of others in need.

Constance Ashley, the youngest daughter, who is appropriately named: She is stalwart in her observance of self-imposed behavioral rules, such as speaking only French on Thursday evenings. She is tranquil in disregarding social conventions regarding rank, wealth, status, class, or color. She becomes an internationally famous suffragette, marries a Japanese man, and is witty, though humorless.

Breckenridge (Breck) Lansing, the incompetent manager of the Coaltown mines, whose death erroneously is charged to John Ashley, his friend and coworker. He is a genial, handshaking, big, blond, gregarious socialite from a Baptist family in Iowa and had failed in attempts at a career in the Army and in law, medicine, and the church. He became an agent in St. Kitts (West Indies) for his father's patent-medicine and cosmetics business, and he met his wife on the island. He is as incompetent as a father as he is as a business administrator, and he belittles his son George's athletic abilities and his cultural aspirations. He is lacking in understanding of his wife and children, delights in being prominent, and has an inordinate pride in his patriotism, religiosity, and social importance.

Eustacia Sims Lansing, Breck's Creole wife from St. Kitts. Coaltown gossip links her to John Ashley as lovers, prejudicing the trial jury against him. She is plump, dark, voluble (her voice is like a parrot's), and a mimic. She is a miserable woman.

Félicité Lansing, their older daughter, who tells Roger that her brother killed their father to stop him from killing John Ashley and to protect his mother. She aspired to be a nun and kept a diary in Latin. She dresses with taste and distinction. She loves her brother and mother passionately, but she is laughterless and has a sense of deep suffering. She has left behind a stormy childhood and has become a woman of taste and distinction.

Anne Lansing, Breck and Eustacia's younger daughter, who has the white complexion of her father rather than her mother's Creole color. As a child, she was given to tantrums and rudeness, but she has become faithful, charitable, and hopeful.

Mrs. Wickersham, an English widow and proprietor of the Fonda, a hotel where John Ashley lives. When he is recognized by a guest, she helps him to escape by faking his funeral. She is authoritarian, "the newspaper of the Andes," and the chief local humanitarian, running a hospital, a school, and an orphanage. A good judge of character, she senses Ashley's innocence.

—Alan L. McLeod

EINSTEIN ON THE BEACH: An Opera in Four Acts

Authors: Robert Wilson (1941-) and Philip Glass (1937-)
First published: 1976
Genre: Drama
Locale: A railroad platform, a courtroom, a spaceship, and elsewhere
Time: The twentieth century
Plot: Abstract

Sixteen chorus members,
a violinist, and
four lead actors, each of whom wears a costume based on a photograph of Albert Einstein: baggy pants, suspenders, a short-sleeved shirt, and sneakers. The violinist actually resembles and represents Einstein, who played the violin; the other cast members perform actions and use props in ways that are loosely suggestive of Einstein's habits, appearance, and work. In the first scene of act 1, for example, a female dancer carries a pipe (Einstein smoked a pipe), a man scribbles equations on a blackboard, and a boy standing on a tower carries a glowing plastic tube and launches paper airplanes. The performers' speeches contain references to numbers, stars and planets, light, gravity, and limitlessness, and two of the lead actors appear as astronauts in the penultimate scene, which seems to represent a nuclear apocalypse. No performer takes a fixed role; instead, the performers, music, sets, and lighting work together to create images and scenes to which the audience can assign meaning. Nevertheless, the four lead actors (two women, an old man, and a boy) do appear and reappear in various recognizable "parts." In two scenes reminiscent of a trial, the old man and the boy sit on the judge's bench, one woman is a defendant, and the other woman is a witness. The chorus stands in the jury box. In the second of these scenes, however, the "defendant," after moving from a stool to a bed, rises and assumes the appearance of Patricia Hearst in a famous photograph of a bank robbery. Later in the scene, she reappears with her arms chained and seats herself again on the stool. In a third trial scene, the judge, defendant, witness, and jury are absent; only the image of the bed that stood before the judge's bench remains. The man who plays the "old judge" in the first two trials is a conductor in two scenes that include a train, and he is a bus driver at the close of the piece. The two leading women appear in five scenes, called "Knee Plays," that are placed between the acts; in these joining, or "joint," scenes, they sit, stand, or lie side by side downstage. They tap on a table, recite speeches or random numbers, work a control board of flashing lights, or twist and turn as if in a vat of liquid. Their actions and words may recapitulate or extend moments in the previous act, and they may also evoke Einsteinian associations for the audience. The chorus members, besides singing numbers and solfège syllables to the score, create some recognizable "characters" as well: the man scribbling equations, a Victorian couple pantomiming a love scene and murder, two prisoners, and a photograph of Einstein sticking out his tongue. Even the musicians come on stage near the end to help create the "atomic explosion." The spectator in the audience, who supplies meaning to the abstract action, is the piece's final character.

— *Jocelyn Roberts Davis*

THE ELDER STATESMAN

Author: T. S. Eliot (1888-1965)
First published: 1959
Genre: Drama
Locale: London, England, and Badgley Court, a nursing home
Time: The 1950's
Plot: Ghost

Lord Claverton, formerly **Richard Ferry**, the "elder statesman" who occupies the center of this drama. He has spent his life climbing the social ladder, first through marriage to Lady Claverton, whose name he adopted, and then through politics and public service. Unfortunately, this climbing has led him to discard or step on people as he has found necessary and has resulted in his becoming a hollow man. As a young man, he ran over a corpse with his car and never faced the police to clear himself. He also had a brief affair with Maisie Batterson, whom he later refused to marry, at the price of a lawsuit that was settled out of court. At the beginning of the drama, he is disillusioned about his accomplishments as a public servant. As he encounters his ghosts from the past—including Fred Culverwell, Maisie Batterson, and Michael Claverton-Ferry—he learns to confront his own hollowness, confesses his sins, and becomes a more real person. In the end, he becomes like Oedipus at Colonus as he was translated from this life to the next.

Monica Claverton-Ferry, Lord Claverton's daughter, whose name means "nun" in Italian. She represents selfless love as she postpones her engagement and marriage to help her dying father. Monica proves herself to be deeply loving of her father when she discovers his past failures and still accepts him. She represents Lord Claverton's capacity for genuine love.

Michael Claverton-Ferry, Lord Claverton's son, who has been badly spoiled by his mother. He is a very manipulative and irresponsible spendthrift, continually excusing his own failings as the product of other people's shortcomings, especially his father's. In the course of the drama, he reveals his utter contempt for his father. He seeks to leave England, where his father is well known, and escape to some place, like San Marco, where he can learn how to live by his wits in a less than scrupulous society. Michael represents the irresponsible, selfish side of his father.

Charles Hemington, the fiancé of Monica Claverton-Ferry. Charles is a very patient and helpful man. He supports Monica and Lord Claverton in facing the latter's ghosts, and he creates with them a triangle of love.

Federico Gomez, formerly Fred Culverwell, a college

friend of Lord Claverton. As a young man in Oxford, Fred was poor and greatly enamored of Richard Ferry's expensive habits of smoking and drinking. In an effort to support his expensive habits, Fred took to stealing and forgery, which eventually led to his imprisonment and exile from England. In the South American country of San Marco, Fred changed his name to Señor Gomez and became well established, probably through corrupt activities. His effort to blackmail Lord Claverton into befriending him once again is cunningly sinister. In seeking to tutor Michael Claverton-Ferry, Señor Gomez exacts a terrible revenge on Lord Claverton.

Mrs. Carghill, formerly **Maisie Batterson** and also known as **Maisie Montjoy**, a long-forgotten girlfriend of Lord Claverton. She once filed a lawsuit against Richard Ferry for refusing to marry her after suggesting an engagement. As an act of revenge, she keeps all of his love letters and reads them over and over, dreaming of a time when she can use them to blackmail Lord Claverton emotionally. She joins Señor Gomez in acting out revenge through corrupting Lord Claverton's son, Michael.

— Daven M. Kari

ELECTIVE AFFINITIES
(Die wahlverwandtschaften)

Author: Johann Wolfgang von Goethe (1749-1832)
First published: 1809
Genre: Novel
Locale: Germany
Time: The eighteenth century
Plot: Love

Edward (EHD-vahrd), a wealthy nobleman. He lives an idyllic life on his estate with his wife, Charlotte, until the arrival of Ottilie, for whom he develops a passion which, in his immaturity, he does little to control. He and Ottilie are finally united in death.

Charlotte (shahr-LOHT-teh), Edward's wife. She lives happily with her husband until his friend, the Captain, comes to live with them, and she and the Captain fall in love. A mature person, she controls her passion and resolves to adhere to the moral code. She is united with the Captain after Edward's death.

Ottilie (oh-TEE-lee-eh), Charlotte's young protégée, who comes to live on Edward's estate. She develops for her host a passion that he encourages. Finally, in despair over her situation, she dies of self-imposed starvation. She is soon followed by Edward, and the lovers are united in death.

The Captain, Edward's friend. Living on Edward's estate, he and Charlotte fall in love. Controlling his emotions, he plays an honorable role and is finally united with Charlotte after Edward's death.

Otto, the infant son of Edward and Charlotte.

Herr Mittler, a self-appointed marriage counselor who tries and fails to bring about a reconciliation between Edward and Charlotte.

Luciana (lew-chee-AH-nah), Charlotte's daughter by a former marriage.

Nanny, Ottilie's young friend.

ELECTRA
(Ēlektra)

Author: Euripides (c. 485-406 B.C.E.)
First performed: 413 B.C.E.
Genre: Drama
Locale: Argos
Time: After the fall of Troy
Plot: Tragedy

Electra (ee-LEHK-truh), the daughter of Agamemnon and Clytemnestra. On his return from the Trojan War, Agamemnon was slain by Clytemnestra and Aegisthus, her lover, who now rules in Argos. For his own safety, Orestes, Electra's brother, was smuggled out of the kingdom. Electra remained, was saved from death at the hands of Aegisthus by Clytemnestra, and was married to a poor farmer by Aegisthus. The farmer, out of respect for the house of Agamemnon, has never asserted his marital rights. In her first appearance, Electra is thus a slave princess, unwashed and in rags, longing for attention and some emotional outlet, morbidly attached to her dead father and powerfully jealous of Clytemnestra. Orestes appears and, posing as a friend of the exiled brother, discusses with Electra the conduct of their mother and Aegisthus. In her speech to him, she betrays herself as a woman whose desire for revenge has, through continuous brooding, become a self-centered obsession. Her motive for the murder of Clytemnestra has become hatred for her mother rather than love for her father, and she is an ugly and perverted being. Her expression of joy in the thought of murdering her mother causes Orestes not to reveal his identity until an old servant recognizes him. Electra takes no part in plotting vengeance on Aegisthus but arranges the murder of her mother. She sends a message that she has been delivered of a son and needs Clytemnestra to aid in the sacrifices attending the birth. When the body of Aegisthus is brought in, Electra condemns him. The language in her speech is artificial and stilted; it contrasts sharply with her passionate condemnation of Clytemnestra shortly afterward. Electra never realizes that she is committing exactly the same atrocity for which she wishes to punish her mother. She leads her mother into the house and guides Orestes' sword when he hesitates. It is only after the deed is committed that she feels the burden of what she has done. At the end of the play, she is given by the gods in marriage to Pylades.

Orestes (oh-REHS-teez), Electra's brother. He returns secretly from exile under compulsion from Apollo to kill Aegisthus and his mother. Guided by the oracle, he does not share Electra's extreme lust for revenge. He kills Aegisthus by striking him in the back as he is preparing a sacrifice to the Nymphs and then, driven on by Electra, stabs his mother when she enters the house of Electra. The gods reveal that he will be pursued by the Furies of blood-guilt for his actions but that he will find release at Athens before the tribunal of the Areopagus, where Apollo will accept responsibility for the matricide.

Clytemnestra (kli-tehm-NEHS-truh), the regal mother of Electra. She took Aegisthus as her lover before Agamemnon returned from Troy. Together, the pair plotted the murder of the husband. Her attempt to justify the murder on the grounds that Agamemnon had sacrificed her daughter Iphigenia is unsuccessful. Her cruelty, vanity, and sordid private affairs alienate her from any great sympathy, but she did save the life of Electra and has enough affection to answer Electra's request that she help in the sacrifice to celebrate the birth of her daughter's son. She is murdered by Orestes, at his sister's urging.

A farmer, a Mycenaean to whom Aegisthus gave Electra in marriage. He understands and accepts his station in life with nobility. Electra acknowledges her gratitude for his understanding behavior.

Pylades (PIHL-eh-deez), a mute character. He is the faithful friend who accompanies Orestes during his exile and is given Electra as a wife by the gods.

An old man, a former servant in the house of Agamemnon who is still faithful to Electra. Summoned by her, he recognizes Orestes and helps to devise a plan for the murder of Aegisthus.

Castor (KAS-tohr) and

Polydeuces (pol-ih-DEW-seez), the Dioscuri, brothers of Clytemnestra. They appear at the end of the play to give Electra in marriage and to foretell the future of Orestes.

ELECTRA
(Elektra)

Author: Hugo von Hofmannsthal (1874-1929)
First published: 1904
Genre: Drama
Locale: The inner courtyard of the palace at Mycenae, Greece
Time: Antiquity
Plot: Tragedy

Electra (ee-LEHK-truh), the daughter of Clytemnestra and the murdered king Agamemnon. Consumed by grief for her dead father, Electra has dedicated herself to perpetuating his memory by observing daily the appropriate rites for the dead, hoping that eventfully, when her brother Orestes returns, she can assist him in exacting rightful revenge. In the meantime, humiliated and abused by her mother and Aegisthus, she has lived abjectly in the palace like the lowest of servants. She is sustained through her suffering by wrathful hatred and graphic fantasies of vengeance, which she frequently expresses openly to those around her. Confronting her sister Chrysothemis, she screams out contempt for her complacent acceptance of injustice and asserts her own independent will to resist. With her mother, after a pretense of cordiality, she unleashes her hatred in furious words, threatening her with eventual terror and death. When Orestes at last returns, she is unable at first to recognize him; once his identity is established, she rejoices at his determination to punish the criminals immediately. Her joy is expressed in a frenzied dance that she performs while her brother slaughters the guilty within the palace. She then falls to the floor and remains rigid, probably also dead, her extreme exultation having likely cost her her life.

Clytemnestra (kli-tehm-NEHS-truh), the widow of Agamemnon and mother of Electra, Chrysothemis, and Orestes. She is now the wife of Aegisthus. After helping her lover, Aegisthus, to slay her husband years before, she sent her son into exile, forbade her daughters to marry, and treated them like servants, abusing them physically and mentally. She is obsessed, however by overwhelming feelings of guilt for her crimes. Her sleep is troubled regularly by terrible nightmares for which no relief has yet been found. Never daring to murder her own children, she still fears the just retribution that they may exact from her when Orestes returns. She pleads one evening with Electra to suggest a remedy for her frightening dreams, but her daughter derides her with taunts and threats of Orestes' violent revenge to come some day. Joyfully greeting a stranger whom she believes carries news of her son's death, she welcomes him into the palace, then she discovers that he is actually Orestes. With a piercing cry, she dies at the hands of her son.

Chrysothemis (krih-SOTH-eh-mihs), Electra's sister and Clytemnestra's youngest daughter. Unlike Electra, who mourns for the losses of the past, she wishes to try to forget the cruel murder of her father and allow her mother's crimes to pass unpunished so that she may marry, bear children, and enjoy the pleasures of ordinary family life. She tries to persuade Electra to abandon the project of revenge and settle instead for a happy private life within an admittedly corrupt state. She mourns the loss of her brother, however, when false news of his death is received. After his acts of revenge are accomplished, she is left alive, ready to begin a new life that the retribution accomplished by her brother has made possible.

Orestes (oh-REHS-teez), the brother of Electra and Chrysothemis, brought up in exile, ignorant of his family background. Informed of these circumstances and instructed by the gods to return to Mycenae to exact revenge on the murderers of his father, Orestes returns to his birthplace to perform the terrible but required deeds. He encounters Electra, and when their identities become known to each other, they rejoice at their reunion and plan their revenge. Having been invited inside the palace, Orestes slays first his mother, then the returning Aegisthus, thus fulfilling the commandment of the gods.

Aegisthus (ee-JIHS-thuhs), the consort of Clytemnestra and ruler of Mycenae. Having slain Agamemnon, with the assistance of Clytemnestra, many years earlier, he claimed both the kingdom and the wife of the dead king and established himself firmly on the throne. Showing no shame or remorse, he revels in his newly acquired power and wealth. He is thought by the palace servants to be harsh and cruel. While out in the fields, he hears that messengers have arrived, bearing news of Orestes' death. Returning to the palace, he is met by Electra, who lights his way to the door. Once within, he is slaughtered by the waiting Orestes.

— *Raymond M. Archer*

ELECTRA

Author: Sophocles (c. 496-406 B.C.E.)
First published: 418-410 B.C.E.
Genre: Drama
Locale: Outside the royal palace in Mycenae, Greece
Time: c. 1250-1200 B.C.E.
Plot: Tragedy

Electra (ee-LEHK-truh), daughter of the slain king, Agamemnon, and his devious wife, Clytemnestra, who spends her virginal life—her name, a variation on *A-lectra*, means unbedded—mourning the death of her father. Electra, witnessing her father's murder at the hands of Clytemnestra and Aegisthus, with whom Clytemnestra conspires in the killing of her husband, vows to avenge her father's death, plotting carefully to bring Clytemnestra and Aegisthus to account, which, with the help of her brother, Orestes, she eventually succeeds in doing.

Orestes (oh-REHS-teez), Electra's brother, son of the slain king, Agamemnon, and his adulterous wife, Clytemnestra. The god Apollo has given Orestes a mandate to avenge his father's murder, which he sets out to do as soon as he becomes an adult. In order to gain an advantage, Orestes, Paedagogus, and Orestes' friend, Pylades, implement the deception that Orestes has been killed in a chariot accident. Orestes, now disguised as a Phocian, returns to Mycenae, ironically bringing what are purported to be his own ashes to his mother. Electra does not recognize her brother, who eventually reveals himself to her. He and Pylades leave the stage, where Electra and the Chorus hear Clytemnestra's death shrieks. Aegisthus arrives, relieved by his misconception that Orestes is dead. Entering a room to find evidence of Orestes' demise by viewing his ashes, he is astounded to discover Clytemnestra's lifeless body. He dies immediately afterward at the hands of Orestes, who has, by killing the two, fulfilled Apollo's mandate.

Clytemnestra (kli-tehm-NEHS-truh), widow of King Agamemnon, adulterous lover of his successor, Aegisthus, with whom she has murdered her former husband, father of her children, Orestes, Electra, and Chrysothemis. When news reaches her of Orestes' death, Clytemnestra is simultaneously grieved that her son is dead and relieved that the threat he poses no longer overshadows her.

Aegisthus (ee-JIHS-thuhs), King Agamemnon's cousin who murders and succeeds him as king. Aegisthus has lured Clytemnestra, his lover, into helping him to kill the king, clearing the way for him to succeed Agamemnon as king of Mycenae.

Paedagogus (pee-dah-GOH-guhs), Orestes' faithful servant and teacher, who helps the orphaned prince plot his vengeance against Aegisthus and Clytemnestra for murdering his father, King Agamemnon. The killing of the two murderers fulfills Apollo's command.

Pylades (PEE-lah-deez), Orestes' faithful friend, who, along with Paedagogus, helps Orestes hatch the plot to avenge his father's death by ambushing and killing Clytemnestra and Aegisthus.

Chrysothemis (kree-sah-THEE-mihs), sister of Orestes and Electra, Clytemnestra's daughter. She wishes to honor her supposedly dead brother, but she is weak and, when she learns of the plot to bring Aegisthus and Clytemnestra to account, shrinks from involvement in it. Chrysothemis wants only to live comfortably and without conflict.

The Chorus of women of Mycenae, who represent the social conscience and moral outlook of the citizens of the city-state of Mycenae.

— *R. Baird Shuman*

THE ELEGY OF LADY FIAMMETTA
(Elegia di Madonna Fiammetta)

Author: Giovanni Boccaccio (1313-1375)
First published: 1343-1344
Genre: Novel
Locale: Naples
Time: The fourteenth century
Plot: Psychological

Fiammetta, a passionate, intelligent, and sensitive lady of Naples. In reality Maria d'Aquino, reported to be the daughter of King Robert of Anjou, she is pictured by Boccaccio telling the story of her betrayal as a warning to others of the tribulations of love. Married and universally admired, she catches the eye of Panfilo (Boccaccio); overcome by love, she is obsessed by his image and finally admits him to her bedroom. Completely absorbed in her lover, she imagines that no other gentlewoman has known the true meaning of passion. Finally betrayed by him, she is sure that no other has been so unfortunate.

Panfilo, a poet, in reality Boccaccio, who is writing the story of his pursuit of Maria d'Aquino to show that it was not she who left him but, indeed, he who deserted her. At a church festival, Panfilo catches the eye of Fiammetta and, later, at a series of meetings in society, instructs her in the subtle art of revealing love to one while conversing with many. He finally gains access to her bedroom. After they have spent many passionate nights together, he wearies of Fiammetta. To extricate himself, he tells her that he must make a four-month journey to visit his dying father. Despite her protests and entreaties, he leaves her forever.

ELLEN FOSTER

Author: Kaye Gibbons (1960-   )
First published: 1987
Genre: Novel

Locale: The southeastern United States
Time: The mid-1980's
Plot: Bildungsroman

Ellen Foster, the protagonist and narrator. Eleven years old when the story begins, Ellen never reveals her original last name. She has taken the name Foster to identify with her chosen family, whom she knows, at first, only as "the foster family." Unusually perceptive and resourceful, Ellen, like many abused children, tries to be self-sufficient. Throughout her struggles, she never compromises her integrity. Ellen's strength, however, is sometimes a disguise for real suffering. Her hatred of her abusive father and her desire to find a loving family motivate her even in the darkest times.

Bill, Ellen's father. An abusive alcoholic, he is the epitome of what Southerners call "trash." A shiftless farmer, his main interests in life are liquor and making other people suffer. After driving Ellen's mother to suicide, Bill attempts to make Ellen his substitute wife. Ellen's hatred of him is mixed with a certain twisted loyalty that is typical of abused children.

Starletta, Ellen's friend. Starletta is black and seems a little younger than Ellen. Ellen feels superior to her but loves her loyally. Starletta and her family are, at first, Ellen's only refuge from her own wretched home life. Ellen and Starletta's friendship is marred by Ellen's unself-conscious racism. Learning the emptiness of prejudice may be the greatest challenge Ellen must face.

Julia, Ellen's art teacher. A transplanted Northerner who gleefully recalls her hippie days in the 1960's, Julia is the only person who cares enough about Ellen to notice her bruises and realize that she is being abused. Julia and her husband, Roy, have themselves appointed as Ellen's guardians for a time.

Ellen's maternal grandmother, a wealthy woman who has always controlled others with her will and her money. Ellen's grandmother transfers her hatred of Ellen's father to Ellen. She takes Ellen in, partly out of family duty but mostly for revenge. She forces Ellen to work in the cotton fields and constantly compares her to her hated father. She also blames Ellen for her mother's death.

Nadine, Ellen's aunt. A complacent, insensitive widow, Nadine spoils her daughter Dora and treats caring for Ellen as an unpleasant duty. After Ellen's grandmother dies, Nadine grudgingly takes in Ellen. Her attempts to treat Ellen kindly are well intentioned but ultimately hypocritical. When Ellen refuses to act the part of the humble orphan, Nadine rejects her.

Ellen's foster mother, a court-approved foster parent to several girls, including a teenage single mother and her baby. When Ellen spots her in church, she decides at once that the woman will be her new mother. This woman provides Ellen with everything her family of origin could or would not. Although she admits to some faults, she appears almost too good to be true in her unconditional love for her foster children, perhaps only because she is in such marked contrast to Ellen's relatives.

— Elizabeth L. Rambo

ELMER GANTRY

Author: Sinclair Lewis (1885-1951)
First published: 1927
Genre: Novel

Locale: Midwestern United States
Time: 1915-1925
Plot: Satire

Elmer Gantry, a brawny football hero and indifferent scholar at Terwillinger College. After his inadvertent conversion to Christianity, Elmer makes a successful, plagiarized speech that serves him for years. His call to the Baptist ministry is achieved with the aid of whiskey. After two years at Mizpah Theological Seminary, Elmer is given a small church, where he seduces (and forgives) Lulu Bains. Postponing an Easter meeting to drink with friends, he is asked to leave Mizpah. Later, he finds a job as an assistant to evangelist Sharon Falconer, who becomes his lover. After her death, a Methodist bishop helps him become a Methodist preacher. Elmer marries and gradually advances to larger congregations until he reaches the metropolis of Zenith. He remains obsessed with practical results, money, and power. After forming the Committee on Public Morals, Elmer raids Zenith's red light district and acquires a number of honors. Eventually, he decides to unite all the moral organizations in America, with himself as head. As national director of morality, he will dictate what America should say and think. At the novel's end, having survived all misadventures, Elmer looks forward to making America a truly moral nation under his guidance.

Frank Shallard, the son of a Baptist minister and Elmer's fellow student at the seminary. Elmer accuses him of liberalism because he questions the Baptists' self-appointed role as guardians of Christianity. In fact, Frank is a good, decent man who is weakened by doubt. He longs to share with humanity and resents being set apart as a parson. During World War I, he enlists in the Army, then returns to a church in Zenith. When he bravely attacks Prohibition, big business, and hypocrisy in the pulpit, he becomes the antithesis of Elmer Gantry, who sets the stage for his downfall. After Frank speaks out against Fundamentalist influence in the schools and society, he is beaten into blindness by fanatics.

Sharon Falconer, a former stenographer who becomes a charismatic evangelist and Elmer's first real passion. She is beautiful and powerful as well as a shrewd judge of character. She is also delusional, calling herself the right hand of God and declaring that she is above sin. When Sharon invites Elmer to her home in Virginia, she seduces him in an incredible scene, invoking ancient goddesses and offering herself to him before an altar. After she adds faith healing to her repertoire, she buys a New Jersey pier for her summer meetings. During her first service on the pier, Sharon is trapped in an accidental fire. Bearing the cross and oblivious to Elmer's pleas, she urges the congregation to follow her to safety. She dies as Elmer escapes the flames.

Lulu Bains, a deacon's daughter at Elmer's first church. Kittenish Lulu is seduced by Elmer, who later resents her demands. When Lulu becomes pregnant, they announce their engagement, but Elmer arranges for her to be discovered in a compromising situation with another man, whom she is forced to marry. In later years, their attraction is rekindled. Elmer visits her on a pretense, and she becomes his mistress as he rationalizes his infidelity to his wife. After Elmer drops Lulu in favor of Hettie Dowler, she takes to drink.

Cleo Benham, the virginal daughter of one of Elmer's wealthy parishioners. Elmer realizes that she would make a fine wife for a bishop, although she does not excite him. Seized by ambition, he marries her and then loses interest. Cleo remains patient and loyal.

Jim Lefferts, an intelligent freethinker who rooms with Elmer at Terwillinger College and is his only friend. Jim, who does not live up to his promise, is offered as a negative example in Elmer's oft-repeated sermon.

Dr. Bruno Zechlin, a classicist and scholar at Mizpah Theological Seminary. He is admired by Frank Shallard and hated by Elmer. An atheist and sincere doubter, Zechlin counsels Frank to stay in the church in order to liberate it from within. He is forced into retirement by Elmer.

The Reverend Andrew Pengilly, an ascetic small-town pastor. A man of genuine faith, he finds God in nature and in the Bible. He inspires Frank Shallard; later, he hosts Elmer on the lecture circuit. When Elmer boasts of his church programs and growing congregation, the shrewd Pengilly asks, "Why don't you believe in God?"

T. J. Rigg, a famous criminal lawyer and Elmer's parishioner in Zenith. Rigg believes religion is useful in controlling rebellious workers, but he is open-minded and is seldom troubled by his conscience. Elmer believes he can be honest with Rigg, his first real friend since Jim Lefferts. Rigg suggests and supports Elmer's crusade against vice.

Hettie Dowler, a former secretary who approaches Elmer about a job and becomes his second mistress. Hettie and her husband plan to blackmail Elmer and nearly succeed.

— *Joanne McCarthy*

ELSEWHERE, PERHAPS
(Ma'kom a'her)

Author: Amos Oz (1939-   )
First published: 1966
Genre: Novel
Locale: Kibbutz Metsudat Ram, near the Israeli-Jordanian border
Time: Early 1960's
Plot: Social realism

Reuven Harish (originally Harismann), the most complex figure in the book, who seems to assume many different character roles. This diversity may be governed by the intellectual distance that separates him from the simpler, earthier image of most of the other characters. He is not only a poet but also a principal teacher responsible for the educational program within the kibbutz. A second aspect of Harish's existence is his function as guide for tourists who visit Kibbutz Metsudat Ram. Through Harish, the novel reveals the totality not only of the social and material foundations of kibbutz life but also of its inner emotional experiences. Having lost his wife to an urbane lover (and cousin) who, after a brief visit to Kibbutz Metsudat Ram, took her back to the material comfort and moral decadence of postwar Germany, Harish accepts the modest responsibility of caring for his two children. Although he is hurt by the loss of his wife, he finds solace and carnal satisfaction, but no real emotional security, in the plain person and austere home environment of Bronka Berger, the wife of a rough-hewn truck driver, with whom he shares secret hours.

Noga Harish, also called **Stella Maris** (for her maternal grandmother) and **Turquoise**, the sixteen-year-old daughter of Reuven. Because of her lithe body and skills as a dancer, Noga is chosen to play the part of the fertile vine in an important annual kibbutz ceremonial celebration. There are at least two mysterious sides to young Noga. One suggests a reflection in her of the lascivious charms of her mother, who caused scandal in the kibbutz by abandoning her husband and two children to run off with another man. The other is a childlike image that is apparent in the first stage of her relationship with truck driver Ezra Berger, who does small favors for her. This latter image disappears as Ezra not only becomes her lover but also causes her to become pregnant. Eventually, after taunting, then shunning, her original suitor, the young Rami Rominov, Noga returns not to their love but to the symbol of kibbutz community continuity that their union seems to represent.

Ezra Berger, a truck driver and husband to Reuven Harish's lover, Bronka. Berger represents, more than any other character, the sweat and toil of kibbutz existence. His needs in his conjugal home are basic. The rhythm of his life seems to be dominated by the regularity of his twice-daily runs to the city and continual reference to the wisdom of biblical adages. Even when Berger's simple favors for Noga Harish turn into a relationship of intimacy and scandal, the impression is not that the visibly anomalous seduction was motivated by a desire to punish Noga's father for his affair with Berger's wife. Once Noga discovers her pregnancy, Ezra ceases to be a focal figure. In fact, somewhat ironically, Fruma Rominov, the mother of Noga's original suitor, takes over some of the responsibilities of caring for the young girl as Berger returns to his regular double schedule of truck runs.

Bronka Berger, the wife of Ezra and lover of Reuven Harish. Although Bronka shares with Reuven a certain attraction to higher cultural and intellectual interests, the monotony of her childless marriage to Ezra is, like her husband's job itself, nearly mechanical. Late at night, after Reuven has left, Bronka faithfully leaves a warm cup of tea for her returning husband. Weekly, she provides him with an impeccably clean change of work clothes. Beyond these duties, Bronka's most important function seems to be acting as an intermediary between Reuven and the wife who left him to marry the partner of her brother-in-law in Munich. Letters to Bronka's husband from his brother Zechariah often contain messages from Reuven's former wife, which Bronka passes on to her lover.

Zechariah Siegfried Berger, the brother of Ezra who, instead of dedicating himself to the idealized re-creation of Israel through the experiment of Zionism following World War II, returned to Germany. To the disgust of Israeli Jews, men such as Zechariah are able to extract considerable profit from investments in the reconstructed but artificial economy of postwar Munich. He runs a nightclub in partnership with the man who tempted Eva Harish away from Reuven and took her to Germany. When Zechariah visits Kibbutz Metsudat Ram, he is disdained: He bears expensive German-made gifts and dresses as if he were immune to the dust and sweat of the kibbutz. He befriends Noga Harish, however, in her time of embarrassed need and tries to convince her, though not without hopeful self-interest, that she should rejoin her mother abroad.

Avraham Rominov, or **Rami Rimon**, the eighteen-year-old suitor of Noga Harish. Rami represents the image of the necessary preparedness of Israeli youth for confrontation with the enemy. Rami must also prepare himself psychologically for the possibility of being rebuffed by Noga. He does this initially by conjuring up an image of himself as a soldier-martyr whose death will bring remorse to the girl who played with his emotional vulnerability. This morbid tendency even pushes him so far that he risks death in a solitary bout of Russian roulette. When he is actually called for military service, he throws his entire energies into the process of physical training, making certain to reject publicly his mother's signs of maternal worry and care for her son's welfare.

— *Byron D. Cannon*

EMBERS

Author: Samuel Beckett (1906-1989)
First published: 1959
Genre: Drama
Locale: At the edge of the sea
Time: Unspecified
Plot: Absurdist

Henry, an aging man afflicted with hemorrhoids who lives by the "cursed" sea and who talks to himself in the hope of drowning out its sound. An isolated figure incapable of bringing anything he does to completion, he conjures up people from his past, including the father he longs both to escape and to resurrect. He imagines these others and tells himself stories no longer solely for company but more especially to have someone who knew him in the past and who can therefore understand what he is now, the "washout" his father judged him to be. Henry would like his life to be dramatically interesting—a series of narrative "thuds"—rather than this "sucking." His day at the shore, spent resurrecting the dead and telling one of his unfinished, unfinishable stories, ends with Henry's realization of what he is and what he has: nothing.

Henry's father, described as "an old man blind and foolish." Unlike Henry, he loved the sea. Whether he drowned while taking his evening swim or ran off to escape his family is not clear.

Ada, Henry's wife. Whether Ada is physically present in this radio play or is, like the father, a voice that Henry imagines is left in doubt. Originally attracted by Henry's smile and his laughter, she slowly grew critical of his habit of talking to himself, as he did of her small talk. She appears to have been a methodical, imperious woman and is now estranged from Henry emotionally and perhaps also in space and time.

Addie, Henry and Ada's daughter, born late in their marriage. Forced by her mother to take music and riding lessons, she is (or was) quite attached to and dependent on Henry, who claims to want nothing to do with her and who blames her for coming between him and Ada.

Bolton, a character in one of Henry's stories. He is pictured in his dark house, listening to the sound of the fire dying down, waiting in the dark. "A grand old man . . . in great trouble," he waits patiently, silently, and purposelessly.

Holloway, a burly man described as a "fine old chap," apparently a doctor. Bolton summons him, in the dead of night, to his house. Although he demands to know why he has been summoned, Holloway never does learn the reason.

The music teacher and

the riding master, two of the instructors to whose discipline Ada required Addie to submit.

Horse, whose hoofbeats are heard four times, causing Henry to wonder whether a horse could be trained to mark time.

Sea, beside and against the incessant, meaningless sound of which Henry speaks his own incessant, meaningless monologue.

— *Robert A. Morace*

THE EMBEZZLER

Author: Louis Auchincloss (1917-)
First published: 1966
Genre: Novel
Locale: Primarily New York City and its suburbs
Time: c. 1905-1960
Plot: Social

Guy Prime, the embezzler of the title. He tells the first version of this story. He sets down a memoir just before his death in 1960, hoping his daughter will read it and show it to his three grandchildren, who have never known him. Born in the 1880's to socially pretentious but shallow parents in New York City, Guy combines fine looks and a gregarious personality. A popular member of the Harvard class of 1907, he befriends the impoverished Rex Geer and saves Rex's college career at a critical moment simply by learning (by honest, if unusual, means) that Rex is about to win an important prize.

Later, Guy introduces Rex to his family and friends, as well as to the rich banker Marcellus de Grasse, who hires both young men. Their friendship is shaken when Rex proves to be the better banker but fails to win Guy's cousin Alix Prime, even though Guy tries to help in that endeavor. Guy quits his banking job with de Grasse, then meets and marries Angelica Hyde in Europe. They have a daughter, Evadne, and a son, Percy. Guy sets himself up as a Wall Street broker. Success follows success until, in the Great Depression, Guy fails adequately to retrench. He begins borrowing from funds held in trust to shore up failing projects, thus becoming an embezzler. Exposed, convicted, investigated by New Deal reformers, and imprisoned in 1936, he expatriates himself to Panama in 1941. He lives out his days as a gregarious merchant with a young Panamanian wife and children.

Reginald (Rex) Geer, the second narrator of the story. If children and grandchildren must see Guy's memoirs, he will add his version. The son of a Vermont parson, Rex is a brilliant but isolated student until Guy befriends him. After graduation, he shares Guy's apartment in New York until his rejection by Alix Prime. Rex then concentrates on work, rising rapidly in the world of investment banking. He marries Lucy, a perfect wife in every respect until, in middle age, her crippling illness contributes to Rex's brief infidelity. Rex tries to save Guy from the consequences of his embezzlements by covering them with loans, but Guy continues gambling with other people's money after promising to stop. Rex blames Guy for his own humiliation and for the New Deal's investigation and regulation of Wall Street.

Angelica Hyde, the third and concluding narrator. She corrects Rex as well as Guy. She is educated in a convent and unhappily attached to her endlessly touring mother. Angelica falls in love with Guy during a Mediterranean cruise, only to discover after their marriage that Guy insists on her playing a role to aid his conquest of Wall Street and New York society. Alienated at last by Guy's manipulations and infidelities, she contents herself with an extravagant country estate and equestrian sport. Her affair with Rex begins because he allows her to teach him to ride. It ends when Guy goads Angelica into begging Rex to divorce Lucy. Angelica becomes Rex and Lucy's devoted friend, however, after Guy's conviction. After Lucy's death, Angelica and Rex marry.

Lucy Ames, later **Lucy Geer**, a girl who grows up next door to Rex in Vermont. She moves to New York City to find work. Rex, recovered from Alix and properly established in business, marries her. They have a son, George, and a daughter who dies in infancy. Severely crippled in middle age, Lucy becomes a moral force for restoration after Guy's arrest. She provides a cottage and a vocation for the near-penniless Angelica.

Mrs. Lewis Irving Hyde, a cultivated and worldly-wise woman who contrives the marriage of her daughter Angelica to Guy. An upper-class Catholic, she passes to Angelica high intelligence and an independent spirit. In 1934, she intervenes to keep Angelica from leaving Guy, not for her daughter's sake, she says, but for the sake of Lucy and Rex.

Marcellus de Grasse, the senior partner of an old and successful banking firm. He cultivates Guy but discovers that Guy's friend Rex has the finer intelligence and firmer character. A man of wide knowledge, searching intellect, and personal integrity, he stands for the best of the older world of finance.

Evadne Prime, Guy and Angelica's daughter. She inherits her parents' beauty and intelligence and has better luck—or judgment. Her marriage to George Geer and their three children give vitality and continuity to the marriage of Angelica and Rex.

George Geer, a son who combines the virtues of his parents, Rex and Lucy. He is already established in the world of finance when he discovers his prospective father-in-law going bankrupt. He stands by all concerned.

— Robert McColley

THE EMIGRANTS
(Vor egen stamme)

Author: Johan Bojer (1872-1959)
First published: 1924
Genre: Novel

Locale: Norway and the United States
Time: Late nineteenth century
Plot: Regional

Erik Foss, an emigrant to the United States. He returns to Norway to lead a band of his people to a new start in America, even helping them with money. His feet are frosbitten while he searches for cattle in a prairie blizzard, and he dies as a result.

Morten Kvidal, one of the emigrants. He assumes the leadership of the group after the death of Erik Foss and leads them for many years. He returns briefly to Norway to bring a wife, Bergitta, to Dakota. He becomes a railroad agent, helps his people become Americans, and shows them how to prosper in their adopted land. Blinded by an exploding lamp, he returns as an old man to Norway. He feels that he is still a Norwegian, though his children are Americans.

Ola Vatne, a Norwegian laborer in love with his employer's daughter. After serving a term in prison for burning his employer's barn, he migrates to America with Erik, taking his wife Else with him. A drunkard and gambler, he cannot succeed without help from his friends.

Else Vatne, Ola's wife. She marries him against her father's wishes after he is released from prison.

The Colonel, Else's father, who dismisses Ola when he discovers the love between his daughter and the man.

Per Föll, a big, hardworking emigrant. He is jealous of his wife, knowing her too well. His jealousy drives him mad, and he is placed in an institution.

Anne Föll, Per's wife, admired by Morten Kvidal's young brother. She is pregnant by another man when Per marries her.

Bergitta Kvidal, Anne's sister and Morten's wife.

Kal Skaret, a hardworking, efficient emigrant who succeeds well in the Dakotas.

Karen Skaret, Kal's hardworking, efficient wife.

THE EMIGRANTS OF AHADARRA: A Tale of Irish Life

Author: William Carleton (1794-1869)
First published: 1848
Genre: Novel
Locale: Ireland
Time: The 1840's
Plot: Regional

Hycy (Hyacinth) Burke, a well-to-do, dissolute young man. Determined to seduce Kathleen Cavanagh, he is publicly snubbed; he resolves to have revenge on her and on Bryan M'Mahon, who loves her. A series of maneuvers designed to bring about Bryan's financial ruin finally causes Hycy, himself, to be exposed as a robber, an accomplice of whiskey smugglers, a counterfeiter, and a plotter against Bryan and his family. He is given two hundred pounds by his father with orders to leave the country and stay away.

Bryan M'Mahon, an honest farmer. In love with Kathleen Cavanagh, he is the object of Hycy's plan of revenge for Kathleen's snub. When, as a result of Hycy's plottings, Bryan is near financial ruin and dishonored in the sight of Kathleen and his neighbors, his friends manage to expose Hycy and restore Bryan to his rightful place in the community.

Kathleen Cavanagh, a young girl in love with Bryan. Scorning the blandishments of Hycy, she is, inadvertently, the cause of his attempts to ruin Bryan. When evidence against Bryan seems overwhelming, she reluctantly believes him guilty, but she regains her trust and affection when he is cleared.

Nanny Peety, a beggar girl who lives with the Burkes and who resents Hycy's attempts to seduce her.

Kate Hogan, Nanny's aunt. She is the wife of one of Hycy's smuggling associates.

Patrick O'Finigan, master of a hedge-school. He, Nanny, and Kate are friends of Bryan and Kathleen. They bring in evidence against Hycy that clears Bryan of the charges against him.

Jemmy Burke, Hycy's father. When he discovers his son's true nature, he forces Hycy to leave the country.

ÉMILE: Or, Education
(Émile: Ou, De l'éducation)

Author: Jean-Jacques Rousseau (1712-1778)
First published: 1762
Genre: Novel
Locale: France
Time: The eighteenth century
Plot: Novel of ideas

Jean Jacques Rousseau (zhahn zhahk rew-SOH), the author, who assumes the role of a tutor in this work, which is less a novel than a treatise on education. With the imaginary Émile as a pupil, he illustrates his theories of education as he tries them out on his student. The tutor prescribes for the child's surroundings, diet, and hygiene and gives him the freedom to learn the natural limits of his powers. For the adolescent Émile, he provides an education of the intellect, and for his maturing pupil, a moral education and the study of human relationships. The tutor, all through the life of the pupil, follows a philosophy of learning designed primarily to create neither a noble savage nor a cultivated gentlemen but rather a man living freely and fearlessly according to his nature.

Émile (ay-MEEL), an imaginary French orphan who is used as a child-symbol in the illustrations of Rousseau's theories of education. Fulfilling Rousseau's requirements for an ideal subject for experimentation, he grows to manhood under his teacher's guidance. As a prospective father, he announces his determination to educate his child according to the theories of his beloved tutor.

Sophie (soh-FEE), a woman-symbol used by Rousseau to enable him to discuss marriage problems with his pupil Émile.

EMILIA GALOTTI

Author: Gotthold Ephraim Lessing (1729-1781)
First published: 1772
Genre: Drama
Locale: Guastalia and Sabionetta, fictional principalities of Italy
Time: Early eighteenth century
Plot: Tragedy

Emilia Galotti (gah-LOHT-tee), the beautiful daughter of a soldier. She is betrothed to Count Appiani. Lecherous Prince Hettore Gonzaga, though engaged to marry the princess of Massa and in love with his mistress, Countess Orsina, desires Emilia. The prince's wily chamberlain, the Marquis Marinelli, suggests to the prince that Count Appiani be sent on a mission to another province, thus leaving Emilia unprotected from the designs of the prince. When Count Appiani refuses to go on the mission, he is assassinated. Emilia is abducted and taken to the prince's palace. When her father sees that his daughter's chastity is about to be violated, he stabs her and presents her body to the lustful prince.

Prince Hettore Gonzaga (eht-TOH-ray gohn-ZAH-gah), the lascivious ruler of Sabionetta and Guastalla. He covets Count Appiani's betrothed. Led on by his wicked chamberlain, the prince agrees to Marinelli's treacherous plot to kill Count Appiani and take Emilia by force. In the end, however, he loses the love of his mistress, Countess Orsina, and is left with only Emilia's dead body at his feet.

Odoardo Galotti (oh-doh-AHR-doh), Emilia's father. Unable to protect his daughter from the machinations of Marinelli, he takes her life rather than have her violated by the carnal prince. After stabbing his daughter, he throws the dagger at the prince's feet and gives himself up to the guards.

Claudia Galotti, Emilia's mother. Frantic when she and her daughter are abducted while on the way to Emilia's wedding, she accuses the Marquis Marinelli of plotting Count Appiani's murder.

The Marquis Marinelli (mah-ree-NEHL-lee), Prince Gonzaga's evil chamberlain. He contrives the treacherous plan to remove Count Appiani so that the prince can seduce Emilia.

Count Appiani (ahp-pee-AH-nee), Emilia's betrothed. When he refuses to be beguiled into leaving Emilia on the day of their wedding, he is assassinated.

Countess Orsina (ohr-SEE-nah), the prince's mistress. When he spurns her, she first plans to stab him; instead, she gives the dagger to Odoardo Galotti. Galotti uses this knife to stab his daughter.

EMMA

Author: Jane Austen (1775-1817)
First published: 1816
Genre: Novel
Locale: Surrey, England
Time: Early nineteenth century
Plot: Domestic realism

Emma Woodhouse, the younger daughter of the wealthy owner of Hartfield and the most important young woman in the village of Highbury. Good-hearted, intelligent, but spoiled, she takes under her protection Harriet Smith, a seventeen-year-old girl of unknown parentage who is at school in the village. Given to matchmaking, Emma breaks up the love affair between Harriet and Robert Martin, a worthy farmer, because she thinks Harriet deserves better; Emma persuades her to fall in love with the vicar, Mr. Elton. To her dismay, Elton proposes to her rather than to Harriet and is indignant when she refuses him. Next, Emma becomes interested in Frank Churchill, an attractive young man who visits his father in Highbury, and thinks him in love with her; but it develops that he is secretly engaged to Jane Fairfax. Emma had never really cared for Churchill, but she thinks him a possible match for Harriet. She becomes really concerned when she discovers that Harriet's new interest is in Mr. Knightley, an old friend of the Woodhouse family. She now realizes that Knightley is the man she has always loved, and she happily accepts his proposal. Harriet marries her old lover, Martin, and the matrimonial problems are solved.

George Knightley, a landowner of the neighborhood, sixteen years Emma's senior, and an old family friend. Honorable, intelligent, and frank, he has always told Emma the truth about herself. When she thinks that he may marry someone else, she realizes that she has always loved him and accepts his proposal.

John Knightley, George's brother, married to Emma's older sister.

Isabella Knightley, nee Woodhouse, John Knightley's wife and Emma's sister, a gentle creature absorbed in her children.

Henry Woodhouse, father of Emma and Isabella, kindly and hospitable but an incurable hypochondriac.

Mr. Weston, a citizen of Highbury who has married Anne Taylor, Emma's former governess.

Anne Weston, nee **Taylor**, Emma's former governess, a sensible woman whom Emma regards highly.

Frank Churchill, Mr. Weston's son by a former marriage. He has been adopted by and taken the name of his mother's family. His charm attracts Emma briefly, but she is not seriously interested. He is secretly engaged to Jane Fairfax.

Jane Fairfax, a beautiful and accomplished orphan who visits her family in Highbury. Emma admires but cannot like her, finding her too reserved. The mystery of her personality is solved when it is learned that she is engaged to Churchill.

Mrs. Bates and

Miss Bates, grandmother and aunt of Jane Fairfax. Poor but worthy women, they are intolerably loquacious and boring.

Harriet Smith, the illegitimate daughter of a tradesman. Young, pretty, and impressionable, she is taken up by Emma Woodhouse, rather to her disadvantage, for Emma gives her ideas above her station. She is persuaded to refuse the proposal of Robert Martin and to believe that Mr. Elton, the vicar, is in love with her. When Elton proves to be interested in Emma, Harriet is deeply chagrined. After considering the possibility of Harriet as a match for Churchill, Emma finds to her dismay that Harriet is thinking of Knightley. This discovery makes Emma realize how much she has always loved him. After Emma and Knightley are engaged, Harriet is again proposed to by Robert Martin; she happily marries him.

Robert Martin, the honest young farmer who marries Harriet Smith.

Reverend Philip Elton, vicar of the parish. A conceited, silly man, he proposes to Emma Woodhouse, who has thought him in love with Harriet Smith. Emma's refusal makes him her enemy.

Augusta Elton, née **Hawkins**, the woman Elton marries after being refused by Emma. She is vulgar, pretentious, and officious.

THE EMPEROR JONES

Author: Eugene O'Neill (1888-1953)
First published: 1921
Genre: Drama
Locale: An island in the West Indies
Time: Early twentieth century
Plot: Expressionism

Brutus Jones, emperor of an unnamed island in the West Indies. A large, powerful, and street-smart man, he was for ten years a Pullman porter in the United States. He killed his friend Jeff in a fight over a game of dice and knocked out a guard to escape from prison. He fled as a stowaway and went to the island, where he used his urban ways and vague hints about his violent past to establish himself as emperor of the island. Luck also played a part: When Lem hired a gunman to kill Jones early in his reign, the gun misfired. Jones has convinced the natives that he has a powerful magic and that he can be killed only with a silver bullet. Jones knows that he will not be able to maintain his position for long, but he does not care. He lives well in a rich and gaudy palace. He has stolen a fortune from the natives and put it safely in a foreign bank. Even when the revolt comes sooner than he expects, he shrugs and simply begins his carefully planned evacuation. As he tells Smithers, he has hidden food at the edge of the Great Forest and he has memorized the trails, so that he can make his way easily—even in the dark—to the other side of the island, where a French gunboat is at anchor. Once he reaches the forest, however, Jones is unnerved by the sound of the native drums, which beat insistently throughout the night. As fear overtakes him, he stumbles through the forest, encountering Little Formless Fears, the ghost of Jeff, his comrades on the prison chain gang, a slave auction, an African witch doctor, and the Crocodile God, all representing the stripping away of his layers of intelligence and "civilization." He learns nothing from these encounters but becomes instead a more primitive man, driven only by his fear. In the morning, it turns out he has traveled all night in a circle. Lem's soldiers simply wait for him where he entered the forest and shoot him dead.

Henry Smithers, a Cockney trader who has found his way to the island. Rough and crooked, he has made his money in legal and illegal trade around the world. He is in an uneasy alliance with Jones. The two men believe themselves to be superior in every way to the island natives, whom they consider unintelligent and uncivilized. At the beginning of the play, Smithers is also feeling smug toward Jones, because he knows about the runaways before the emperor does. He does not press his advantage very far: He clearly fears Jones, who is bigger, stronger, and more violent than he is. After Jones leaves, he searches the palace for anything he might take and sell for cash. At the end of the play, Smithers has cast his lot with Lem, following him around as the chief hunts for Jones. He does not believe Jones will be caught: The natives are too stupid. When they do catch and kill Jones, Smithers clings to his beliefs, scoffing at the idea that the natives could be responsible for Jones's downfall.

Lem, a native chief who despises Jones. Displaced when Jones claimed the title of emperor, Lem has been quietly gathering power while Jones looted the island. Although Jones and Smithers both believe that the native population of the island is unintelligent, when Lem appears at the end with his soldiers, it is clear that he knows exactly what he is doing and how he can bring down Jones. He believes Jones's story about the magic of the silver bullets but uses it against him. He has his people melt down coins to make silver bullets, outsmarts Jones to find him, and then has Jones shot.

An Old Native Woman, who is left behind when the younger subjects of the emperor run away. Before she leaves, she tells Smithers that everyone is abandoning the emperor, whom she clearly still fears.

Jeff, a dice-throwing pal of Jones back in the United States. It was for killing Jeff, after he had caught Jeff cheating at dice, that Jones was sent to prison. In his terror as he runs in circles through the jungle, Jones meets the ghost of Jeff and wastes one of his bullets trying to kill him again.

— *Cynthia A. Bily*

EMPIRE OF THE SUN

Author: J. G. Ballard (1930-)
First published: 1984
Genre: Novel

Locale: Shanghai, China
Time: 1941-1945
Plot: Social realism

Jim, the protagonist, a British schoolboy entering adolescence. An intelligent, curious, self-reliant, and somewhat rebellious eleven-year-old from a privileged background, Jim is obsessed with aviation, in particular, warplanes. When Japan enters the war against the Allies, he is separated from his parents. He wanders through the disorder of war-torn Shanghai, learning to survive by using his wits. After meeting Basie on the waterfront, he and the American sailor are taken to a prison camp, where he learns much more about survival in the "university of life." He adapts to conditions in the camp with a readiness not found among the European adults. By the end of the war, he has witnessed many scenes of social upheaval and apocalypse, including the flash of the atom bomb exploding at Nagasaki.

Basie, an American merchant seaman and profiteer. A man in his thirties with an easy manner, a bland, unlined face, and soft hands that he keeps powdered, he is articulate, observant, opportunistic, manipulative, and devious. Basie needs to have people working for him at all times and tries to exploit every event for his own benefit. In the prison camp, he uses Jim as a coolie, but he does teach Jim the necessity of satisfying one's own needs and provides the boy with information about the outside world.

Dr. Ransome, a British doctor in the prison camp. A sandy-haired, long-legged, strong man in his late twenties, he is opinionated, self-confident, somewhat bossy, and interested in helping others. He intercedes on behalf of the other prisoners in disputes with the Japanese guards and encourages the inmates to improve their welfare by growing a garden and building a sewage system. Dr. Ransome also tries to preserve English values in the camp. After taking an interest in Jim, he attempts to educate the boy in such subjects as mathematics, Latin, and poetry.

Mr. Maxted, an English architect and entrepreneur who represents for Jim a Shanghai that existed before the war. He is a dapper, middle-aged, slightly eccentric man who does not adapt well to life in the camp.

Mrs. Vincent, the wife of a former stockbroker, a pale, nervous, exhausted young woman with thinning blonde hair. She is indifferent or hostile to Jim, but he is attracted to her as he matures.

Private Kimura, a Japanese soldier and camp guard who is not much older than Jim and who becomes the boy's friend.

— *Seth Bovey and Jean McConnell*

THE END OF THE AFFAIR

Author: Graham Greene (1904-1991)
First published: 1951
Genre: Novel

Locale: London, England
Time: 1939-1946
Plot: Psychological realism

Maurice Bendrix, the narrator, a cynical novelist usually addressed by his surname. Bendrix always sees the worst in people. Suffering from sudden, inexplicable rejection by his mistress and obsessed with her memory, he decides to hire a private detective to investigate her after her husband confides to Bendrix his fear that she may be having an affair. On learning that she is innocent and even saintly, he tries to revive their love. When she flees him into death, he is left with her memory, her example, and his friendship with her husband, factors that are at war with his characteristic cynicism when the novel ends.

Sarah Miles, Bendrix's mistress and the wife of a civil servant. A beautiful, long-haired woman with a great intensity of feeling, she is overcome when Bendrix appears to have been killed in a London blitz. She makes a vow that if he is allowed to live, she will discontinue their relationship, and she keeps this vow. The suffering that results finally leads her to true piety as well as to death by neglected pneumonia. After her death, she appears to work miracles, and her possessions seem curative. She is perceived by her loved ones as a saint, and her influence for good grows.

Henry Miles, a highly placed British civil servant. Although he takes his wife for granted, he does love her in his way. He is too innocent to be aware of her affair with Bendrix while it is going on, almost literally under his nose. After Sarah's death, he turns to Bendrix for friendship and support.

Alfred Parkis, the private detective hired by Bendrix. He is solemn and not particularly intelligent but kindly and conscientious. He takes his job very seriously, and, although he misses the obvious inductions, he is able to steal Sarah's diary and present it to Bendrix.

Lancelot Parkis, his twelve-year-old son, who likes to take part in his father's investigations and be given ices. After Sarah's death, a book she gave him apparently cures him of a serious illness.

Richard Smythe, a rationalist lecturer and counselor. A tall, ugly man with a face marred by birthmarks, he is approached by Sarah for counsel that will help her set aside her vow. Instead of his converting her from tentative and fearful belief to atheism, however, her goodness converts him. After her death, his birthmark is cured, apparently by her agency, and he becomes one of her disciples.

Father Crompton, a Roman Catholic priest. He is stern and dogmatic in argument but compassionate in the face of suffering and loss. He wants Sarah to have a Catholic funeral, but Bendrix, partly out of spite against a God whom he believes has robbed him, refuses.

Mrs. Bartram, Sarah's mother, an eccentric old lady who is always borrowing money. She fills in Sarah's background for Bendrix. Appearing for the first time at Sarah's funeral, she explains that Sarah had been baptized as a Catholic at the age of two.

— *Janet McCann*

THE END OF THE ROAD

Author: John Barth (1930-)
First published: 1958
Genre: Novel

Locale: Wicomico, Maryland
Time: 1951-1955
Plot: Existentialism

Jacob Horner, the narrator of the novel, a thirty-year-old academic who has completed his course work and passed the oral exams for a master's degree in English at The Johns Hopkins University. Stricken by an inexplicable paralysis in the Baltimore bus station, Horner is rescued by the Doctor, who puts him through a course of bizarre therapies and then dispatches him to teach grammar at the Wicomico State Teachers College on the eastern shore of Maryland. Horner, a thoroughly existentialist man, has no fixed beliefs and no real persona; as he admits, his life is a succession of roles, many of them contradictory. He is capable of holding two conflicting ideas simultaneously. Horner responds to the immediate situation and, left to himself, is capable of sinking into mere existence because he has no true inner self.

Joe Morgan, a man in his early thirties who teaches ancient, European, and American history at Wicomico State Teachers College. Described by Horner as a "tall, bespectacled, athletic young man, terribly energetic," Morgan clearly is a star at the backwater college. He has a bachelor's degree in literature and a master's in philosophy from Columbia University, and he has completed all work toward his Ph.D. in history, except for his dissertation, at The Johns Hopkins University. In contrast to Horner, Morgan has a definite philosophy, which he claims is thoroughly pragmatic and which he pursues to its ultimate, logical conclusions, even when those conclusions conflict with morality or convention. Because he insists on living "coherently," with every action and event rationally explained, Morgan has a certain rigid inflexibility of mind and spirit.

Renée (Rennie) Morgan, Joe's wife and mother of their two young sons. A large-framed woman with short blonde hair and brown eyes, she is athletic. A particularly fine horsewoman, she teaches Jacob Horner to ride. She felt as if she were "nothing at all" until she met Joe Morgan. Although Joe was at first drawn to her self-sufficiency, he systematically, if perhaps unconsciously, transformed her thinking into a replica of his own philosophy. She lacks his strength of will; for this reason, and perhaps out of an unrealized need for revenge, she commits adultery with Jacob Horner.

The Doctor, a mysterious African American medical man. He is small, dapper, and in his mid-fifties, bald and with a greying mustache. The Doctor finds Horner in a state of paralysis in a Baltimore bus station and insists that the younger man undergo a series of unconventional therapies at "The Farm," a facility the Doctor operates. These include mythotherapy, in which the patient uses the events of everyday life to invent a story and create a character that he or she will play. Mythotherapy appeals to Horner's existentialist view and is cited by him repeatedly as the cause of his actions.

Peggy Rankin, an English teacher who is about forty years old. Horner picks her up one afternoon while at the beach. After casually seducing her, Horner drifts out of her life until he is sexually aroused. He contacts her when he needs to find an abortionist after Rennie Morgan becomes pregnant. Peggy at first allows him back into her life, even though she feels humiliated and used; later, she rejects him completely.

— *Michael Witkoski*

THE END OF THE WORLD NEWS

Author: Anthony Burgess (John Anthony Burgess Wilson, 1917-1993)
First published: 1982
Genre: Novel
Locale: New York City and elsewhere in America, Vienna, Western Europe, and Australia
Time: The 1890's through 1938, 1917, and 1999-2000
Plot: Science fiction

Lynx, a rogue planet from another solar system. It is the same size as Earth but ten times the density. The snuffling intonations of its radio signals and its predatory dance of approach and retreat from Earth make its name chillingly appropriate. The increasingly horrific natural upheavals caused on Earth by Lynx's strengthening gravitational pull before the two planets' final collision provide a terrifyingly violent and alien setting for the novel's events.

Dr. Valentine Brodie, the husband of Dr. Vanessa Frame Brodie. He is thirty-eight years old, handsome, and bearded, with the beginnings of a beer belly. A poet as a youth, Val is now a respected science-fiction writer and a university lecturer in literature. A romantic (as his name coyly implies), Val has turned increasingly to Manhattan's seedy lowlife to find vitality and occasional sexual solace as an antidote to the shortcomings of his marriage and to his perception of the scientific world's sterility. With the approach of Earth's annihilation, Val mourns the passing of the vibrancy and even the dirt of human life but finally chooses survival aboard the spaceship *America* with the physically and scientifically elite group assembled to perpetuate humankind. Vanessa, a group leader, insists that Val be included because she loves him; at first, he dreads the prospect, but when he misses the group's departure for the ship, he draws on unplumbed depths of courage and loyalty and on a newly aroused visionary strength to find his way to Vanessa and his new life as recorder of both Earth's last days and this new phase of human existence.

Dr. Vanessa Frame Brodie, a beautiful woman in her early thirties with ice-blue eyes and a perfect body. An eminent scientist and a natural leader for the *America* group, she possesses such a coldly brilliant intellect that her emotions are eclipsed; her clinical approach to sex with her husband, Val, obscures her actual deep love for him. When Val finds the spaceship, it is a less remote, more vulnerable, and more receptive Vanessa that welcomes him aboard.

Robert Courtland van Caulaert Willett, a fiftyish unemployed actor. His natural habitat is the seedy Manhattan bars that Val frequents, and the two become fast friends there. Willett revitalizes Val with his Falstaffian physical proportions and gargantuan appetite for drink, his passion for the richness of the English tongue, and his roaring, exuberant love of life. Willett is also sensitive, however, and, like Val, mourns the imminent passing of the hurly-burly of life on Earth. Unlike Val, he chooses to perish with Earth, rejecting a chance to join the group aboard *America* after he and Val undergo their remarkable odyssey to find the ship. Recognizing that his place is with the past, Willett leaves the spaceship and waddles off to embrace annihilation.

Edwina Duffy-Goya, a woman in her twenties, a lecturer in devotional poetry who is interested in the connection between religion and sex. A devotee of charismatic evangelical preacher Calvin Gropius, Edwina sets out to attach herself to him when Earth's rapidly approaching end finds her a pregnant widow. As a fiercely determined woman, she is disappointed in the weak man behind the Gropius image but meets his kind, decent son Dashiel and in him finds the husband and father for her child who suits her vision of the future. Having fought their way aboard *America*, Dashiel, Edwina, and her newborn son join the progenitors of the new breed of humans.

Paul Maxwell Bartlett, the head of the enterprise aboard *America*. A brilliant scientist and writer in his forties, handsome, physically splendid, and possessing no apparent vices, he sees himself as destined to lead the group into the new life. Once in command at the spaceship compound, however, Bartlett's desire to lead becomes a wish to subjugate all to his increasingly mad vision. He is finally shot by one of the rebellious group members.

Dr. Sigmund Freud, the father of psychoanalysis. He is portrayed over the course of almost fifty years as he develops his theory of the unconscious mind, finding fame, notoriety, disciples, and betrayers. Although his brilliance is clear, so are his less admirable qualities: his inability to contemplate disloyalty among his followers; his refusal, ironically, to address the sexual problems in his own marriage; his imposition of his other neuroses on his long-suffering family; his tendency to let his loyal supporters deal with the problems of entrenched Viennese anti-Semitism that dogged his career; and even his inability to stop smoking the cigars that caused his hideous, agonizing, and finally fatal mouth cancer. A pain-wracked, regretful Freud embarks on a train to London on the eve of World War II.

Lev Davidovich Bronstein, also known as **Leon Trotsky**, a Russian revolutionary. Trotsky's 1917 visit to New York, during his American sojourn as editor of the radical journal *Novy mir*, is treated in Broadway musical form. The austere intellectual and hero of the Russian Revolution is portrayed as an anxious, lovesick visionary.

— Jill Rollins

END ZONE

Author: Don DeLillo (1936-)
First published: 1972
Genre: Novel
Locale: Western Texas
Time: c. 1970
Plot: Allegory

Gary Harkness, a star halfback for Logos College in western Texas. The talented Gary, in his early twenties, goes to Logos College after personal anxieties had destroyed his athletic career at Syracuse, Pennsylvania State, Miami, and Michigan State universities. He seems cursed by a terminal case of spiritual sloth generated by his sense of the world's meaninglessness, a despair that is intensified by his preoccupation at Logos with vivid hallucinations of nuclear catastrophe. Only in the structured patterns enacted on the football field does he find any order in existence ("sport is a benign illusion, the illusion that order is possible"). After the high excitement of Logos' most crucial football game, Gary feels overwhelmed by his nihilism and gives up to endure hospitalization.

Taft Robinson, Logos' only black student, a brilliant football star recruited from Columbia University. Taft not only has a sprinter's speed and runs the hundred in 9.3 seconds but also is a bright and reflective young man who rooms alone and sometimes finds his gift for sports to be a burden. He is one of Gary's closest friends.

Anatole Bloomberg, a three-hundred-pound left tackle on offense. Anatole is Gary's good friend and roommate who shares the alienation of Gary and Taft, all three of them being loners by nature as well as northerners who find themselves in western Texas. Anatole has come to Texas to "unjew" himself, as he puts it. He suffers from bed-wetting and refuses to expose his flesh to the Texas sun. Much of his malaise is caused by the "enormous nagging historical guilt" that he confides he feels as a Jew.

Myna Corbett, Gary's classmate in Mexican geography who becomes his close friend. The 165-pound Myna shares much of Gary's nihilism. She is blessed with half a million dollars but cursed with blotches on her face. She swathes herself in gold chains, Victorian shawls, and patchwork skirts. She refuses to lose weight and take care of her face on the grounds that her physical condition relieves her of the responsibility of being beautiful.

Emmett Creed, the head football coach at Logos. The mythic Creed, known to the press as Big Bend, is a "man's man" who was voted All-American in college, flew a B-27 in World War II, and played halfback for the Chicago Bears before achieving a series of triumphs in various coaching jobs. For Creed, football is "only a game," but "it's the only game." He exhorts his players to "Write home on a regular basis" and "Don't ever get too proud to pray." Under his hard exterior, Creed has much in common with Gary, who observes that "He seems always to be close to a horrible discovery about himself."

Bing Jackmin, a field-goal kicker. Bing is one of the most notable of Gary's teammates and contributes some of the most beguiling and amusing small talk in the novel. Gary notices that his eyes seem crazed by sun or dust or inner visions.

Major Staley, the commander of the Air Force ROTC unit at Logos. The thirty-eight-year-old major teaches a course in aspects of modern war, and Gary sits in on the major's fluent disquisitions on missiles and megatons.

Esther and

Vera Chalk, friends of Myna and Gary. The Chalk sisters compliment Myna's neatness and her breadless organic picnic sandwiches with raw carrots and celery tonic. They find numerological mysteries that bind numbers and raw vegetables, and they think of seventeen when they munch their carrots.

— Frank Day

ENDGAME: A Play in One Act
(Fin de partie)

Author: Samuel Beckett (1906-1989)
First published: 1957
Genre: Drama
Locale: Indeterminate
Time: Indeterminate, perhaps after a future catastrophe
Plot: Absurdist

Hamm, a man who is blind and unable to walk. He appears to be middle-aged, and he sits in an armchair mounted on castors, parked in the middle of the stage. He wears a dressing gown, a brimless hat, and a pair of dark glasses. A whistle hangs from his neck, a blanket covers his knees, and thick socks swathe his feet. At the beginning of the play, his red face is covered with a large, blood-stained handkerchief, which, he explains, stanches the flow dripping from a hole in his head, a wound that makes him dependent on painkillers. Hamm dominates his parents and his servant Clov, to whom he issues arbitrary and contradictory orders. Whenever Clov becomes frustrated and threatens to leave, Hamm entices him to stay by provoking conversation. Hamm considers himself a storyteller and a poet, and, in the course of the play, he composes part of his autobiography.

Clov, Hamm's servant and possibly his adopted son. A younger man than his employer, Clov cannot sit down, and he walks stiffly because of the pain in his legs. He shares Hamm's red complexion, and he acts as a codependent to Hamm's capricious addict's behavior. Clov makes up for his employer's deficiencies by acting as Hamm's eyes and legs, caring for Nagg and Nell, and cleaning up the room where they all live. He grudgingly obeys all of Hamm's orders, and although he feels resentful and victimized by his situation, he feels helpless to leave it.

Nagg, Hamm's father, an old Irishman with a white face who wears a nightcap. He and his wife, Nell, got their legs cut off in a tandem bicycle accident, and ever since they have been living near their son in a pair of trash cans, with the stumps of their legs embedded in sand. Nagg considers himself a great comical storyteller and a philosopher who has come to terms with disappointment and the loss of nearly all of his physical pleasures and abilities.

Nell, Hamm's mother. She is an elderly, white-faced Irishwoman wearing a lace cap who lives in a trash can next to her husband, Nagg. She is more serious than Nagg, and she scolds him for joking about the sorrow of life. She often drifts off into elegiac recollection. Nell insists that she will abandon Nagg, just as Clov threatens to leave Hamm. When she dies, she becomes the only character in the play to carry out her threats and change her situation.

— *Pamela Canal*

ENDYMION: A Poetic Romance

Author: John Keats (1795-1821)
First published: 1818
Genre: Poetry

Locale: Mount Latmos, the Garden of Adonis, caverns, a place under the ocean, Neptune's palace, the sky, and the Cave of Quietude
Time: Antiquity
Plot: Narrative

Endymion (ehn-DIHM-ee-uhn), a shepherd on Mount Latmos who distances himself from the other shepherds (and, hence, earthly matters) because of a dream in which he meets his idealization of feminine perfection. He sets out on an epic journey to find the dreamlover, exploring dreamworld regions of mythology. The character is based on the character from Greek myth who was a beautiful youth in love with Diana (in *Endymion*, she is named Cynthia), the virgin goddess of the moon. Embodied in Endymion is the young poet—his imagination and heart vainly seeking that which can satisfy him. According to Greek legend, Endymion's favorite time is spent in the moonlight, where the moon is the witness to his all-consuming melancholy and ardor. Endymion's story, both in Greek myth and as retold by Keats, is one of poetic aspiration, the search for idealized love, and a life spent more in dreams than in reality. *Endymion* ends with the youth finding immortal love with his beloved, with whom he disappears into the realm of myth.

Cynthia, Endymion's dreamlover, the idealization of feminine perfection, whom Endymion chases through his dreams and the dreamworld to find the best love of all—the love that brings immortality. John Keats based Cynthia on the Roman goddess Diana, who was later identified with the Greek Olympian gods and goddesses. Diana was the goddess of the moon and hunting, the protectress of women and their chastity, and—in her earliest incarnations—the great mother goddess of Nature. During Endymion's quest for Cynthia, Keats incorporates other aspects of the myth of Diana into the character. For example, when Endymion encounters the two streams of Arethusa (AR-uh-THEW-zuh), and Alpheus (al-FEE-uhs), Keats demonstrates two lovers divided by Diana/Cynthia. Arethusa was a wood nymph with whom the river god, Alpheus, was madly in love. Alpheus pursued Arethusa until Diana changed her into a fountain; in this form, she fled to the lower parts of the earth and remained at Alpheus' side. They were never able to merge because Diana kept them separate. Keats's version of Diana is far from the chaste and cold moon goddess of Greek myth. Keats eroticizes her considerably, making Endymion's encounters with her more physical than spiritual (again differing from original myth). Cynthia's love for Endymion is far from platonic. When the lovers meet, they kiss, caress, sigh, pant, entwine, and faint; Cynthia even speaks of melting into Endymion. Cynthia's earthly form in Keats's poem is the Indian Maiden.

Glaucus (GLOH-kuhs), a mortal condemned by Circe (SUR-see) to spend one thousand years beneath the sea joining drowned lovers in a crystal mausoleum because he witnessed her enchanting and deforming other men. He is also a character from Greek mythology. According to the original myth, Glaucus began life as a fisherman who bid farewell to the earth and plunged into the waters, where the gods received him favorably. His appearance changed drastically—his hair became sea green, his shoulders broadened, and his lower torso assumed the form of a fish tail. Glaucus fell in love with the beautiful maiden Scylla (SIHL-uh), a favorite of the water nymphs, who was repelled by his appearance. He consulted with the enchantress Circe, who told him to pursue a more willing object of affection. Glaucus does not listen to Circe, and she turns her wrath on Scylla and casts a spell on her that roots her to a spot in a bay on the coast of Sicily. Circe's temper grows, and she begins to take pleasure in devouring hapless mariners who come within her grasp. In Keats's *Endymion*, Scylla is transformed but not drowned. Glaucus learns that his destiny is to collect the bodies of drowned lovers for one thousand years, after which a youth will appear and help him. Endymion fulfills this prophecy and aids Glaucus, restoring him to youth and Scylla to life, along with the other drowned lovers.

Peona (PEH-oh-nuh), Endymion's sister, who represents the embodiment of the cautious, unbelieving mortals not gifted with the vision (or imagination) of the poet. Her approach to life is far more pragmatic than her brother's. She cautions Endymion to give up on his dreamlover and, instead, seek a real woman who can satisfy his earthly desires. Such a woman would not satisfy Endymion's spiritual needs. Once Endymion fades from Peona's view with his dreamlover, Cynthia, Peona's worldview is forever altered.

— *Thomas D. Petitjean, Jr.*

ENDYMION: The Man in the Moon

Author: John Lyly (c. 1554-1606)
First published: 1591
Genre: Drama
Locale: Ancient Greece
Time: Antiquity
Plot: Comedy

Endymion (ehn-DIHM-ee-on), who is hopelessly in love with the goddess Cynthia. To keep his true love secret, he pretends to be in love with Tellus. After being put into an enchanted sleep at the instigation of his jealous deceived sweetheart, he is awakened by Cynthia. He vows to spend his life in platonic devotion to her.

Cynthia, the goddess of the moon. Chastely above mortal passion, she is moved to pity by Endymion's enchanted sleep, awakens him, and accepts his platonic worship. She has been interpreted as an idealized portrait of Queen Elizabeth I.

Tellus (TEH-luhs), the goddess of the earth. Loving Endymion, she is angered at what she considers his treachery to her. Imprisoned by Cynthia, she learns to love her jailer, Corsites, and releases Endymion to his moon-worship. She has been interpreted as a portrait of Mary, Queen of Scots.

Eumenides (ew-MEH-nih-deez), Endymion's faithful friend and confidant. He is able to learn the secret of Endymion's enchantment because he is a faithful lover. Unselfishly, he asks for the secret to save his friend instead of for his own success in love.

Semele (SEH-meh-LEE), a witty, sharp-tongued girl, delighted with flouting her lover, Eumenides. She is finally moved by Cynthia's request and Eumenides' faithfulness to accept him.

Corsites (kohr-SI-teez), Tellus' jailer, who is in love with his prisoner.

Sir Thopas (TOH-puhs), a fantastical braggart of the literary family that contains Falstaff, among many others. Scornful of love and bloodthirsty in language only, he strangely falls in love with Dipsas, the hideous, elderly enchantress. Disappointed in his expectations there, he accepts Bagoa.

Dares (da-reez),

Samias (SA-mee-uhs), and

Epiton (EH-pih-ton), witty and mischievous pages who delight in making sport of Sir Thopas.

Dipsas (DIHP-suhs), a malicious old enchantress, the estranged wife of Geron. She aids Tellus by casting Endymion into an enchanted sleep for forty years. Cynthia's benign influence reforms her and restores her to her husband.

Bagoa (beh-GOH-uh), Dipsas' assistant. She pities Endymion and confesses her part in the spell. After she is turned into a tree by Dipsas, Cynthia restores her.

Geron (JEH-ron), Dipsas' aged husband, who helps Eumenides find out that the cure for the spell on Endymion is a kiss from Cynthia.

Floscula (FLOS-kuh-luh), Tellus' friend, who warns her against love inspired by witchcraft.

ENEMIES: A Love Story
(Sonim, de Geshichte fun a Liebe)

Author: Isaac Bashevis Singer (1904-1991)
First published: 1966
Genre: Novel
Locale: New York City and upstate New York
Time: Postwar 1940's
Plot: Domestic realism

Herman Broder, a refugee from Poland, where the Nazis have destroyed his family. He lives in Brooklyn and makes a living by ghostwriting for a rabbi, though he tells his wife, Yadwiga, that he is a traveling book salesman so that he can spend time with his lover, Masha Tortshiner, in her apartment in the Bronx. He observes Jewish dietary laws but otherwise has largely forsaken his Jewish faith, having become utterly fatalistic. Perhaps it is this fatalistic attitude, coupled with a smoldering eroticism, that makes him attractive to the three women who love him.

Yadwiga Broder, a Polish peasant girl, Herman's second wife and his savior. She hid Herman in the barn of her parents' farm during the Nazi occupation of Poland. She fell in love with Herman when she worked for his family as a servant and has been devoted to him ever since. She worships Herman and after her conversion tries hard to be a good Jewish wife. Extremely shy and unable to speak much English, she avoids her kindly neighbors and lives only for Herman, with whom she finally has a child.

Masha Tortshiner, Herman's lover, separated from her husband, Leon, who refuses to give her a divorce. Neurotic, beautiful, and demanding, she wants Herman to divorce Yadwiga and marry her. She is not above tricking him into consent.

Shifra Puah Bloch, Masha's deeply religious mother, who is pained by her daughter's behavior but bears it stoically. She keeps a kosher home and likes Herman, despite her disapproval of the affair with her daughter. Her dying effort is to prevent Herman and Masha from running away together to California after Yadwiga has become pregnant.

Tamara Broder, Herman's first wife, believed to have been killed by the Nazis after her two children were taken by them and murdered. Miraculously, she survives the war and the camps and turns up at her uncle's home on the East Side of New York City. She has retained her good looks, despite everything, but accepts her fate and her husband's and does not wish to interfere with his new life. Her generosity grows even to helping Yadwiga care for her child when, at the end, Herman disappears. The two women live together, and she operates a bookstore left to her by her uncle.

Leon Tortshiner, Masha's husband, who for a long while refuses to agree to a divorce. When he does, he also reveals to Herman the kind of woman Masha is, including giving Herman an account of her infidelity. Outraged, Herman refuses to have anything more to do with her and returns briefly to Yadwiga and to a religious life. Even Leon's revelations are insufficient, however, to keep Herman from Masha.

Rabbi Milton Lambert, a sophisticated, modern rabbi who supports Herman by paying him to write speeches for him. He arranges for Masha to run an old people's home in New Jersey, where Shifra Puah also can live, after Herman and Masha break up. The arrangement does not last long, however, before Masha returns to the Bronx and calls Herman.

Reb Abraham Nissen, Tamara's uncle, who runs a bookstore in the Jewish section of the Lower East Side of New York. When Tamara comes to America after her ordeal, he places an ad in the personals column of a Yiddish newspaper to find Herman and arrange a reunion. After he dies, Herman briefly runs the bookstore, until Masha calls him; Tamara then takes over the store and helps support Yadwiga and her child.

— *Jay L. Halio*

AN ENEMY OF THE PEOPLE
(En folkefiende)

Author: Henrik Ibsen (1828-1906)
First published: 1882
Genre: Drama
Locale: Southern Norway
Time: Late nineteenth century
Plot: Social criticism

Dr. Thomas Stockmann, the medical officer of the Municipal Baths, a conscientious man of science and the enemy of illness and deceit. Stockmann discovers that the healing waters, the principal source of income for the town, are polluted, causing typhoid fever and gastric illnesses to the users. Because of his discovery, he incurs the censure of the town and is proclaimed an "Enemy of the People." Stockmann is the one honest man in public life in the town. When he realizes that all of his associates would prefer to conceal the fact that the baths are polluted, he is at first amazed and then infuriated. Denied all means of spreading his information through the press or in public meetings, he at last calls a meeting in the home of a ship captain, Captain Horster. Before Stockmann can speak, however, the group elects a chairman, Aslaksen, who permits Stockmann's brother, Peter, the mayor of the town, to make a motion forbidding the doctor to speak on the matter of the baths because unreliable and exaggerated reports might go abroad. Aslaksen seconds the motion. Stockmann then speaks on the moral corruption of the town and manages to offend everyone, including his wife's adoptive father, Morten Kiil, a tanner whose works are one of the worst sources of water pollution. Morten Kiil buys up the bath stock the next day and proposes that the doctor call off the drive because he has made the purchase with money that Kiil had planned to leave Mrs. Stockmann and the children. Stockmann rejects the suggestion. He thinks of leaving the town and going to America, but when Captain Horster is discharged for permitting Stockmann to speak in his house, he cannot sail on Horster's ship, and he decides to remain in the town, educate the street urchins, and bring up his own sons to be honest men. He says that only the middle class opposes him and that the poor people will continue to call on him. In his decision, he is cheered by his young schoolteacher daughter, Petra, and by Mrs. Stockmann and one of the boys. Although Stockmann is not an especially personable character, he is an excellent representation of the frustrations that confront the reformer.

Peter Stockmann, the mayor of the town and brother of Dr. Stockmann. Peter Stockmann is a typical, willfully blind public official who would rather poison the visitors of his town than cut its income. Under the pretense of concern for the town, he is able to win others to his side. He ruins his brother but suggests that he will reinstate him if he recants.

Hovstad, the editor of the *People's Messenger*. At first, Hovstad supports Dr. Stockmann and plans to print his article about the baths. When he learns that public opinion is against Stockmann, however, he deserts him until he hears that Morten Kiil has bought up the bath stock. He then offers to support Stockmann again because he thinks that Stockmann will cash in on the baths and he wants to be in on the deal. Hovstad starts off as a forthright newspaperman and is a disappointment when he abruptly changes character and sides.

Aslaksen, a printer. Aslaksen starts out as a volunteer supporter of Stockmann's proposal to clean up the baths. As chairman of the Householder's Association, he promises the support of the majority in the town, but as soon as matters become difficult, and when Dr. Stockmann grows more emotional than Aslaksen thinks is in keeping with his idea of moderation, he turns against the doctor. He goes with Hovstad to try to cash in on the profits that they think Stockmann expects to make with Morten Kiil.

Petra, the daughter of Dr. and Mrs. Stockmann. Petra, an earnest young woman, is the first to discover Hovstad's insincerity. Petra, a teacher, refused to translate an English story for Hovstad to print because its theme is that a supernatural power looks after the so-called good people in the world and that everything happens for the best, while all the evil are punished; she has no such belief. When Hovstad tells her that he is giving his readers exactly the kind of story they want, Petra is distressed. When he blurts out a few minutes later that the reason he is supporting Dr. Stockmann is that he is Petra's father, Petra tells him that he has betrayed himself and that she will never trust him again. Because she supports her father, she loses her job. Her employer tells her that a former guest in the Stockmann home has revealed Petra's emancipated views. Petra is her father's true child.

Mrs. Stockmann, the doctor's wife and his loyal supporter. At first, she does not want her husband to go against the wishes of his brother, but she soon gives her full approval. She is presented as a woman without a strong personality.

Morten Kiil, a tanner, Mrs. Stockmann's adoptive father. Although described by other characters as an "old badger," a man of wealth whose influence and money Dr. Stockmann hates to lose because of his wife and children, Morten Kiil seems to live more by reputation than by representation in the play. He goes against Dr. Stockmann and buys up all the bath stock with money he had intended to leave to Mrs. Stockmann.

Captain Horster, a ship's captain who befriends Dr. Stockmann. He is the only person outside the Stockmann family who remains loyal to the doctor. He allows Stockmann to attempt his public speech about the baths to an audience assembled in his house.

Ejlif and

Morten, the two young sons of the Stockmanns.

Billing, a sub-editor. He agrees with Aslaksen and Hovstad.

LES ENFANTS TERRIBLES

Author: Jean Cocteau (1889-1963)
First published: 1929
Genre: Novel
Locale: Paris, France
Time: The 1920's
Plot: Psychological

Paul (pohl), a sensitive, imaginative adolescent living insulated from the real world. With his sister Elisabeth, he inhabits the Room, the one material reality of their two lives, and with her plays the Game—a willful withdrawing into the world of the imagination. With the appearance of outsiders, this world is threatened; in the fight to recapture it, Paul is destroyed.

Elisabeth (ay-lee-zah-BEHT), Paul's older sister. Utterly absorbed in her brother and their life together in the dream world of the Room and the Game, she is terrified by, and retaliates against, any threat to their isolation. Finally, in a successful effort to separate Paul from Agatha, whom he loves, she brings about her brother's destruction and her own.

Agatha (ah-gah-TAH), Elisabeth's friend, whose devotion to Paul threatens the dream world of the brother and sister and finally brings about its destruction.

Gérard (zhay-RAHR), a friend of Paul and Elisabeth. He is persuaded by Elisabeth to marry Agatha, whose devotion to Paul threatens Elisabeth's domination of her brother.

Dargelos (dahr-zheh-LOH), the school hero, worshiped by the fragile Paul for his strength and beauty.

Mariette (ma-RHEHT), the nurse who loves and cares for Paul and Elisabeth.

Michael, an American to whom Elisabeth transfers her dream world when her dominance over Paul is threatened. He marries Elisabeth only to be killed a few hours after the wedding.

THE ENGINEER OF HUMAN SOULS
(Příběh inženýra lidských duší)

Author: Josef Škvorecký (1924-)
First published: 1977
Genre: Novel
Locale: Toronto, Canada
Time: Winter, 1976-Spring, 1977
Plot: Psychological realism

Daniel Smiricky (SMIH-rzhihts-kee), a forty-eight-year-old Czechoslovakian writer employed as a literature professor at Edenvale College in Toronto. Often preoccupied with memories of his lost youth and lost homeland, Smiricky lives the pains of the exile: grief, social discomfort, linguistic disorientation, and political fear. Self-absorbed and dependent on women but without one, Smiricky struggles to find a professional, social, and political place for himself in Western culture. His journeys through the academic, literary, and émigré communities provide a spectrum of ideologies, ethics, and emotions that counterpoint and contextualize his own views. With the acquisition of a beautiful nineteen-year-old girlfriend, Irene, he seems to be quieting the ghosts of his wartime past and starting life anew.

Irene Svensson, an affluent student at Edenvale College. A voluptuous blonde with a Cadillac, Irene becomes Smiricky's lover and accompanies him to Paris during reading week. She asserts that she intends to marry him.

Larry Hakim (hah-KEEM), a sophomore in Smiricky's American literature class. Intensely ideological, this Iranian youth engages his professor in several heated discussions of the political implications of the works of Joseph Conrad and William Faulkner. Hakim's rabid fanaticism challenges Smiricky to articulate more fully his own politics and his political readings of the works being examined.

Nadia Jirouskova (jih-ROOS-koh-vah), a teenage girl impressed into labor in the Messerschmitt factory in Nazi-occupied Czechoslovakia. A frail peasant girl, she worked beside Smiricky in the factory and inspired his boyish attempts at heroism and succumbed to his boyish charms. Although dead of tuberculosis at the age of twenty-one, she still provides tender and vivid memories for Smiricky.

Veronika Prst, a student at Edenvale. A young Czechoslovakian exile overcome with melancholy, Veronika chooses impulsively to return to her homeland regardless of conditions there. Other émigrés often consider, and often debate, doing as she did.

Milena "Dotty" Cabricarova (kah-bree-KAH-roh-vah), a Czech émigré in Toronto. Always quirkily dressed and seemingly scatterbrained, Milena is Smiricky's dearest personal friend in Toronto, although they see each other infrequently. She marries a businessman and happily adjusts to life in the West.

Prema Skocopole (PREH-mah SKOH-koh-poh-leh), a teenage leader of the resistance to Nazis in Kostelec, Smiricky's hometown. The self-appointed commander of a tiny, fragmented, and boyish underground movement during the German occupation, Prema survived the war and immigrated to Australia. He continues to write to Smiricky for thirty years. A brief return to Kostelec convinces him that he must stay in permanent exile.

Jan Prouza, a poet friend of Smiricky who chose to remain in Czechoslovakia after the Russian invasion in 1968. Smiricky followed Prouza's battles with censorship from afar. Exhausted by his struggle against the constraints of Socialist Realism, Prouza committed suicide in August, 1972.

Vachousek (VAH-choo-sehk), a Czechoslovakian foreman at the Messerschmitt factory during the occupation. Years later, Smiricky discovers that Vachousek was a prominent resistance leader, while in the factory and for decades afterward. He was captured and executed in the 1970's. Smiricky regards him as a true hero.

— *Virginia Crane*

ENOCH ARDEN

Author: Alfred, Lord Tennyson (1809-1892)
First published: 1864
Genre: Poetry

Locale: England
Time: Late eighteenth century
Plot: Sentimental

Enoch Arden, a fisherman. He marries his childhood playmate Annie and has seven happy years of marriage with her. He is then injured, and their prosperity vanishes in his months of recuperation. He sells his fishing boat to set up Annie as a trader to support their three children in his absence, then sails on a merchantman. Shipwrecked on a desert island, he worries constantly about his family. Years later, he gets back to England. There, learning that Annie is happily married and the mother of a new baby, he does not reveal his identity until he is on his deathbed.

Annie Lee, his wife. A poor businesswoman and burdened by grief, her difficulties continue until, more than ten years after Enoch's disappearance, another former childhood playmate asks her to marry him. She insists that they wait another year and a half, and even then she is not thoroughly happy and at peace until their child is born.

Philip Ray, Enoch's friend, secretly in love with Annie since childhood. Only well after Enoch's presumed death does he disclose his love. A miller's son, he is well-to-do.

Miriam Lane, a widowed tavernkeeper. Enoch takes lodgings with her on his return. It is she who tells him about Annie and Philip and to whom he relates his story on his deathbed.

THE ENORMOUS ROOM

Author: e. e. cummings (1894-1962)
First published: 1922
Genre: Novel

Locale: France
Time: 1917
Plot: Autobiographical

e. e. cummings, an American ambulance driver. Arrested because of his close friendship with W. S. B. but never charged with any specific offense, he is imprisoned at La Ferte for three months. Naturally observant and interested in people, he sees in his fellow prisoners varied traits, ranging from humanity's best to its most animalistic and depraved. Gifted with a satiric sense of humor, he endures the imprisonment without going insane, as do many of the unfortunates.

W. S. B., also known as **B.**, his American friend. He is arrested by French military police for writing letters suspected by the censor. He is transferred from La Ferte to another prison before cummings is released. W. S. B. is actually William Slater Brown.

Apollyon (ah-pohl-YOHN), head of the French prison, a gross, fiendish man who reminds cummings of Ichabod Crane and who questions him about why he is in prison, though cummings himself does not know. Apollyon is despised by the prisoners.

Rockyfeller, a livid, unpleasant-looking, impeccably dressed Rumanian who causes an uproar the night he arrives at La Ferte.

The Fighting Sheeney, Rockyfeller's revolting bully-boy, a former pimp.

Joseph Demestre (deh-MEHSTR), called **The Wanderer**, a strong man of simple emotions whose wife (or possibly mistress) and three small children are in the women's ward of the prison. Toward his six-year-old son, who sleeps with him, he shows deep love and understanding. Until sent away, he is cummings's best friend.

Zoo-Loo, a Polish farmer who, ignorant of French and English, communicates by signs. He is a wizard at hiding money from the guards, and he is kind to cummings and B.

Surplice, a friendly, inquisitive little man who finds everything astonishing and whose talk makes even small things seem important and interesting.

Jean le Nègre (zhahn leh nehgr), a gigantic, simple-minded black man given to practical jokes and tall tales. Arrested for impersonating an English officer, he becomes a favorite with the women prisoners. After a fight over Lulu's handkerchief and the resultant punishment, Jean becomes quiet and shy. When B. is sent away, Jean attempts, with scant success, to cheer cummings with funny stories and whopping lies.

Count F. A. de Bragard, a Belgian painter of horses, a neat, suave gentleman with whom cummings discusses painting and the arts. Before cummings leaves, the count has withdrawn from the other prisoners, his mind finally breaking under the strain of the sordid prison life.

Lulu, Jean's favorite among the women prisoners; she sends him money and a lace handkerchief.

Judas, a corpulent, blond, large-headed, mop-haired, weak-chinned prisoner who nauseates cummings.

M. le Gestionnaire (gehs-tyohn-NAYR), a fat, stupid man with an enormous nose and a Germanic or Dutch face; he reminds cummings of a hippopotamus.

THE ENTERTAINER

Author: John Osborne (1929-1994)
First published: 1957
Genre: Drama
Locale: An English coastal town
Time: 1956
Plot: Protest

Archie Rice, the title character. He is an actor, singer, and comedian in an archaic and dying institution, the English music hall. He is known as the "professor" by his fellow artists. His career has never afforded more than a meager livelihood and a shabby sort of gentility, a remnant from the better times when his father, Billy Rice, was a very successful showman. At fifty, he is dapper, friendly, and superficially a gentleman. Despite his self-deprecating claim of being selfish and unfeeling, he is affectionate toward his family, especially his daughter, Jean, and his father. He brings the gag man's enthusiastic buoyancy into his domestic conversation to mask an entrenched cynicism and self-pity. At times, he is inattentive and unresponsive, even evasive. Seeking solace for his failure, he drinks excessively and womanizes openly, tormenting his long-suffering wife, whom he both pities and resents. His plan to divorce her and marry a much younger woman is thwarted, and his emotional string runs out with the deaths first of his son Mick, and then of his father. He is unable to accept a proffered chance for a new life in Canada. As the play's ending makes clear, he will end his days either in jail for tax fraud or in poverty, soullessly repeating his music-hall routines before progressively smaller and less appreciative audiences.

Billy Rice, the family patriarch, a retired music-hall showman. He is a dignified man in his seventies, fastidious in manner and dress and both slim and sprightly. Although at times grouchy and stubborn, he inspires fondness in Archie and love in his granddaughter, Jean. Despite his nostalgic ramblings about past glories and his mistrust of contemporary trends, he knows that the music hall is doomed and thinks Archie is a fool for following in his footsteps. He is also mindful of his familial responsibilities. It is Billy who quashes Archie's plans to divorce Phoebe and marry the younger woman. He tries to make amends for his interference by going back onstage with Archie, but the ordeal soon kills him. His death leads to the dissolution of the family.

Jean Rice, Archie's daughter by his first wife. At the age of twenty-two, she is a wise, loving, and thoughtful woman whose selflessness contrasts with her father's selfishness. Her attractive character compensates for her physical plainness. She has a special bond with her grandfather, who is sensitive to her warmth, humor, and intelligence. She is also well educated and responsive to social causes. To the chagrin of her fiancé, Graham Dodd, she has even participated in protest demonstrations. Blaming Archie for Billy's death, at the play's end she decides to sacrifice marriage and respectability to care for Phoebe, her stepmother.

Phoebe Rice, Archie's wife and stepmother to Jean. About ten years older than Archie, she is a rather wretched, pathetic character. She covers her faded good looks with badly applied makeup and supports her unwillingness to face reality with calculated deafness. She fidgets and chats nervously, afraid of getting trapped in confrontations, which depress her. She is basically resigned to her fate, even accepting Archie's flagrant philandering although she obviously is deeply wounded by it. Mostly passive, she evokes Archie's meanest traits, as is evidenced in his curtness toward her and his cruel, music-hall jokes.

Frank Rice, Archie and Phoebe's son, and half brother to Jean. A somewhat pallid young man of nineteen, he is prone to sickness. As a conscientious objector, he served time in jail for refusing military service. He now plays a piano in a bar. Although somewhat shy and retiring, he is drawn into Archie's routines as a straight man or "feed," a role that suits them both because it alleviates the need for a more genuine rapport. Frank's need for familial love and affection is filled largely by Jean, but he will leave her to care for his mother when he seeks a new beginning in Canada.

William (Brother Bill) Rice, Archie's brother, a successful, highly regarded barrister. He is a wealthy man who has from time to time bailed Archie out of financial difficulties. After the death of their father, he offers Archie passage to Canada, temporary support, and the settlement of Archie's debts, but with the stipulation that he will do nothing should Archie refuse. There is no real understanding or bond between them, and Archie's rejection of his offer merely baffles him.

Graham Dodd, Jean's fiancé, a respectable, well-educated, and somewhat stuffy young man whose self-assurance is punctured by Jean's decision to break off their engagement. As is the case with Brother Bill, little is seen of him, and his character is not extensively delineated.

— *John W. Fiero*

ENTERTAINING MR. SLOANE

Author: Joe Orton (1933-1967)
First published: 1964
Genre: Drama
Locale: England
Time: The 1960's
Plot: Black humor

Kathy (Kath), a dowdy Englishwoman in early middle age. An outwardly respectable symbol of bourgeois life and values, Kath is a woman with an illegitimate child in her past. She lives with her father in a small home, and her passion for the young lodger she takes in forms one of the play's central story lines. Although she makes frequent protestations regarding her own morality and honor, she is at heart selfish and easily able to rationalize her less-than-respectable actions. This attitude typifies the play's portrait of the British middle class.

Mr. Sloane, an attractive, ruthless, and utterly amoral young man. Sloane is the catalyst for the play's action, arriving as a lodger in Kath's home in the opening scene and establishing volatile relationships with each of the other characters. Although his background is mysterious and probably criminal, he clearly is a member of the working class and, therefore, an intruder in the social norm of Kath's household. A figure of menace and violence throughout the play, Sloane appears to be an avaricious manipulator, successfully exploiting the other characters' weaknesses for his own ends. The story's conclusion finds him caught in a trap of his own device.

Ed (Eddie), Kath's selfish, bullying brother. Ed is a pompous, greedy hypocrite with a keen interest in young men. He is trying to take control of his father's finances when the play opens. His initial misgivings over his sister's new lodger vanish when Sloane appears agreeable to Ed's broad hints of a close future relationship. Ed, more than any of the play's other characters, makes a constant show of outward concern for notions of morality and social convention, yet he, like Sloane and Kath, is thoroughly unscrupulous in matters of self-interest.

Kemp (Dadda), Kath and Ed's father, an elderly pensioner. Kemp is the play's true victim, an old man saddled with two greedy children and a vicious young intruder whose presence eventually leads to Kemp's death. From the time of their first meeting, Kemp sees the menace that Sloane represents, but his son's and daughter's shared attraction to the young man leaves him at Sloane's mercy. His death at Sloane's hands provides the means by which Kath and Ed finally are able to trap Sloane into doing their bidding.

— *Janet Lorenz*

ENVY
(Zavist')

Author: Yury Olesha (1899-1960)
First published: 1927
Genre: Novel
Locale: Moscow
Time: The 1920's
Plot: Satire

Nikolai Kavalerov (nih-koh-LAY kah-vah-LEH-rov), a homeless drunk, the narrator of the first part of the novel. Kavalerov, a twenty-seven-year-old drifter, "a fat-bellied little guy," has a difficult time finding his place in postrevolutionary Soviet society. His main problem is that he sees no chance for individual success, unlike in the West. Fighting for tenderness, pathos, and individuality, he cannot adjust to the mechanical, practical, and despiritualized world around him and become a cog in the machine; in fact, he does not understand anything about mechanics and is afraid of machines. It is in this world, however, that he longs for glory. Because of this personality split, he develops a strong envy of those who are successful. As a result, he becomes a bystander, a typical superfluous man of Russian literature and a jester at those who have succeeded. He develops a false superiority complex out of his inferiority, belittling everything in impotent rage.

Andrei Babichev (bah-BEE-chehv), the director of the Food Industry Trust. Andrei is an example of the success for which Kavalerov yearns. An inventor of the "Quarter," a cafeteria offering a two-course meal of nourishing, clean, and cheap food for a quarter, he takes pride in being practical and efficient. He has no respect for good-for-nothings like Kavalerov, whom he literally picked out of the gutter in the hope of reforming him. Even though Kavalerov calls him a belly-worshiping glutton and a greedy, jealous, petty, and suspicious bureaucrat, Andrei clearly represents a successful doer who is not devoid of at least some humanitarian impulses.

Ivan Babichev, the older brother of Andrei, a somewhat crazed dreamer and an opponent of the trends of the twentieth century. A direct opposite of his brother, Ivan is a "fat little preacher" of civil disobedience who belongs to the prerevolutionary Russia and who tries to organize an army of all the unhappy and frustrated individuals like Kavalerov. He lives in a world of fantasy, for he believes that fantasy is the beloved of reason. To achieve his quixotic goals, he has invented in his imagination a universal machine to kill all machines, naming her Ophelia, for the Shakespearean character who went out of her mind with love and despair. He also wants to organize a conspiracy of feelings and to lead "the last parade of the ancient, human passions," because he complains that many emotions such as pity, tenderness, pride, love, and compassion have been declared banal. Like his pupil Kavalerov, he ends up sharing the bed of an elderly widow, thus admitting his defeat.

Volodya Makarov (voh-LOH-dyah mah-KAH-rov), a star athlete and engineering student. Even though he is ten years younger than Kavalerov, Volodya can be considered his foil in that he has succeeded where Kavalerov has failed. He calls himself a human machine and a heavy-industry man and wants to be like Thomas Edison. He is envious of the machine and desires to become a cog in it, without allowing for any individuality. A protégé of Andrei, Volodya imitates him in every way and shares his goals. He is the new Soviet man and, as such, shows only contempt for the likes of Ivan and Kavalerov.

Valya, Ivan's daughter. Valya is loved by both Kavalerov and Volodya; Ivan and Andrei fight for her affection as well. The beautiful and healthy sixteen-year-old girl represents the future of the Soviet Union. The fact that in the end she chooses Volodya and shuns her father, despite her love for him, tips the author's hand in predicting the eventual victors in the struggle between the old and the new.

Annie Prokopovich (pro-koh-POH-vihch), an elderly widow with whom both Kavalerov and Ivan sleep. Annie symbolizes the humiliation and defeat of both men, especially the former because of his youth.

— *Vasa D. Mihailovich*

EPITAPH OF A SMALL WINNER
(Memórias Póstumas de Bras Cubas)

Author: Joaquim Maria Machado de Assis (1839-1908)
First published: 1881
Genre: Novel

Locale: Rio de Janeiro, Brazil
Time: 1805-1870
Plot: Satire

Braz Cubas ("Bras" in the original), the somewhat spoiled son of a typical upper-class Brazilian family. A cynical egoist afflicted by the countercurrents of sentimentalism and melancholy, Braz describes his own death at the beginning of the first-person narration and then relates the rest of his life as flashbacks. In each of his major social or intellectual enterprises, Braz aspires to external fame and internal satisfaction, but his accomplishments are only mediocre and superficial. A classicist in a romantic environment, he seeks sex, philosophical wisdom, and humanitarianism in personal conduct but succeeds only partly in each of these quests. In tune with his sentimentalism, he affirms "the voluptuousness of misery." His philosophy and humanitarianism soon decline into cynicism, iconoclasm, and pessimism. His first liaison is with Marcella, a licentious Spanish woman of the world who becomes his mistress but makes him pay dearly for every privilege. He becomes engaged to a girl from his own class, Virgilia, in a match contracted with solid political prospects in view. He is almost immediately supplanted by another young man in both the marital and the political arenas. Within a short time, however, he and Virgilia become lovers, but she refuses to abandon her marriage, upon which her social position depends. He arranges for them to meet clandestinely in an outwardly respectable love nest, the permanent residence of an elderly female acquaintance. Braz's conscience temporarily attacks him over the use of this older woman to gratify his illicit desires, but his cynicism almost immediately leads him to conclude that "vice is the fertilizing flower of virtue." When Virgilia's husband eventually receives a letter informing him of his wife's infidelity, he visits the love nest to confirm the accusation. Braz conceals himself in the bedroom rather than admit his guilt. He reasons that the husband no longer cares about Virgilia but remains married merely because of public opinion. When the husband accepts a post as governor, taking Virgilia with him, Braz in a brief instant of regret reflects on the nature of romantic melancholy. He almost immediately orders an expensive meal at a gourmet restaurant as a way of keeping Virgilia out of his mind. When he reaches middle age, Braz becomes engaged to a girl half his own age, but is not greatly disturbed when she dies of yellow fever. When he learns that the girl's father is disappointed because only a handful of those invited came to her funeral, Braz remarks that formality, or superficial attention to social routines, is the basis of most displays of grief and feelings. He becomes a member of the Chamber of Deputies and recognizes that vanity has been an essential ingredient in all of his expressions of the sentiment of love. He accepts the theory of Helvetius that self-interest is the mainspring of all human action, but he adds vanity as another element. On his deathbed, Braz muses that his life has been filled with negatives. One major negative however, had a contrary positive element concealed: His lack of progeny denied the instruments of transmitting the universal legacy of misery. Because of this childlessness, he regards himself as a small winner in the lottery of life.

Virgilia, who seems to be an exact match for Braz in social class, breeding, and character, perhaps explaining why she becomes his mistress rather than his wife. She becomes pregnant and allows Braz to believe he is responsible, but a miscarriage removes the problem. Shortly after her husband's death, she visits Braz on his deathbed. She is still beautiful but is unable to revive his sentimental attachment.

Lobo Neves, Virgilia's husband.

Marcella, Braz's avaricious mistress, who shares her favors with another man until Braz outdoes him in expensive gifts. She then rejects him in turn. Years later, she encounters Braz after an attack of yellow fever has left her pock-marked. She pretends to be poor but engages in business as a goldsmith to gratify her greatest vice, greed.

Quincas Borba, a boyhood friend of Braz, equally spoiled and even more handsome. In middle age, he is transformed into a penniless beggar and offers to teach Braz his philosophy of misery. After inheriting a large fortune, he expounds another system, humanitism, a variation of the doctrine of the best of all possible worlds in which vanity and self-love are ruling principles.

— *A. Owen Aldridge*

EQUAL DANGER
(Il contesto: Una parodia)

Author: Leonardo Sciascia (1921-1989)
First published: 1971
Genre: Novel

Locale: Imaginary Spanish cities
Time: The 1970's
Plot: Detective and mystery

Inspector Rogas, an investigator, the protagonist. His intelligence and his culture set him apart from the other members of the police force. He is thorough and persistent in his investigation, examining each event or piece of evidence with patience. His search for the assassin, assigned to him by his superiors, extends beyond the execution of his duties; it becomes for him an intellectual and personal challenge as he realizes the cleverness of his opponent. The investigation carries him dangerously close to truths that are best left undiscovered, and he meets with strong opposition to his exposing them.

Cres, the supposed assassin. Although he plays a central role, he is glimpsed only once. He is elusive, mysterious, and virtually untraceable; in short, he is very present yet invisible.

Most important, he is clever and calculating, able to predict what the police's next move will be and to evade it. Like Rogas, he is exact and thorough in his work; if he is indeed the assassin, he leaves no trace.

Nocio, a writer. Dramatic and sarcastic, he speaks openly and readily about his troubles. He is embittered and resentful at the low regard in which his books are held by the fashionable revolutionaries. After having thought of himself as a revolutionary in his country, he believes that he is now being displaced by a young class of pseudointellectuals, who spew ideology without understanding it and without really believing it. Both in his professional life and in his own home, he has become angrily subservient for fear of being labeled a reactionary.

Galano, the editor of a revolutionary political magazine. Cold and detached, he exudes smugness and superiority toward those who are not a part of his intellectual circle. He loudly denounces capitalist wealth and the middle-class lifestyle and thought. At the same time, however, he readily and very willingly accepts all the comforts and advantages that he criticizes. Although he represents a private sector of morality, he enjoys the support of high government officials, who recognize the power and the influence of both the man and the magazine he publishes.

President Riches, the president of the Supreme Court. He is arrogant and self-assured. He firmly believes that during the time he has presided over the court, no wrongful judgment has ever been passed. Indeed, he maintains that judicial error does not exist; the individual no longer exists. One person answers for humanity, and humanity is responsible for one person.

The minister, a high government official. Pompous and formal, he is very much an opportunist. By his own admission, he uses his power to offer protection to individuals and to political groups. He recognizes the inherent weakness and corruption of his government, and, functioning on the premise that only hatred commands respect, he pursues that goal.

Cusan, a writer. Intelligent and perceptive, he is also an old and loyal friend of Rogas. He is a sympathizer of the Revolutionary Party. His support is of a predominantly ideological and certainly idealistic nature, and he is not aware of the political intricacies and intrigues that are involved. Rogas confides in him all his suspicions and his findings, thus involving him more than he would like.

— *Susan Briziarelli*

THE EQUATIONS OF LOVE

Author: Ethel Wilson (1888-1980)
First published: 1952
Genre: Novel
Locale: Vancouver, other parts of British Columbia, and Toronto
Time: Mid-twentieth century
Plot: Psychological realism

Myrtle Johnson, a middle-aged domestic servant who is married to Mort. Myrtle, an unattractive woman, controls not only Mort but also her employer, as well as most people with whom she has frequent contact. She does this by portraying herself as the eternal victim and by manipulating others into assuming guilt for her current complaint or discomfort. With eyelids half closed and a smirk on her lips, she manages to make others feel insecure and unworthy, regardless of their achievement or good fortune. When the police bring the news to her that Mort and his drunken friend have accidentally drowned together, Myrtle, assuming that Mort also was drunk, becomes furious that her husband has disgraced her. Her cousin, Victoria May Tritt, who saw Mort and his friend immediately before the accident, redeems Mort in Myrtle's eyes by telling her the truth, that Mort definitely was not drunk. Myrtle uses the story of Mort as a hero who attempted to save his friend to retain her position of dominance over those who remain in her circle.

Mortimer (Mort) Johnson, Myrtle's enslaved husband. In middle age, he is short and stocky, once strong but now flabby, with kind brown eyes. Mort works, when he will, as a laborer. He is the type who calls himself a landscaper when he is hired to dig soil, a plumber when he is paid to haul pipe, and a horse-breaker when his work is near a stable. He is sensitive to his lowly position in life and works at a job no longer than he can retain his delusion of importance. When Mort's friend Eddie stumbles off the end of a dock into dark water, Mort jumps in to save him. He is pulled under by the struggling Eddie. Both men drown in a matter of a few minutes, before anyone is aware of their desperate situation.

Victoria May Tritt, an unmarried cousin of Myrtle Johnson. Victoria May lives alone in Vancouver and has a job in a small notions shop. In her room, while sitting in a straight chair under a bare bulb that hangs from the center of the room's ceiling, she reads the film magazine that she buys once a week. Victoria is very lonely, having no one except Myrtle, of whom she is afraid. Her timidity prevents her from seeking any real solution to her loneliness. Instead, she creates a comforting, familiar routine for herself, and the mechanics of her daily existence become virtually all there is to her life. It takes considerable gathering of courage for her even to drop in on the Johnsons for a visit. She considers the Johnsons, who are the only couple she knows, to be the ideal. It is Victoria May who is witness to Mort's sobriety on the night of his tragic death, and it is she who reports his "heroism" to Myrtle.

Lilly Waller, a youngster, abandoned first by her mother and then by her father, who grows up a vagrant in the streets of Vancouver. Lilly learns as a child to gain advantage from her look of innocence and neglect, and she also discovers that through fabrication and deceit, she can conveniently avoid what might be the unpleasant results of her behavior. Thrown out of her foster home for staying out all night, she rents a room and takes a job as a waitress in a Chinatown restaurant, where she is pursued by an Asian named Yow. Later, Lilly runs away to work (under the name of May Bates) in a mining camp café, moves in with a transient miner, and becomes pregnant with his child. Even before he leaves to return to his wife and family, Lilly decides to assume a new identity. She will be the widowed Mrs. Walter Hughes and will make a new, respectable life for herself and her baby daughter, Eleanor.

Wanting more for Eleanor than for her to be a maid's daughter, Lilly finds new employment as a housekeeper in a small hospital in the Fraser Valley. She remains there for more than twenty-five years as the respectable Mrs. Hughes, having told her daughter and all who inquire that her husband, whose family had been people of means, had died at their ranch as a result of injuries inflicted by one of his stallions. Yow's appearance causes Lilly to run away to Toronto, where she plans a complete change in her appearance, after which she can return to Vancouver and live near Eleanor, who has married and has three sons. Lilly obtains a wig, applies cosmetics, and effects a complete change in her style of clothing. In Toronto, she meets the recently widowed and very lonely Mr. Sprockett from Winnipeg. He proposes to Lilly on their second evening of dining together. Lilly accepts but tearily insists on revealing to him her deepest secret (lest, she says, he might learn the truth and think less of her for deceiving him): that the hair that he sees on her head has not grown there but is, instead, an "adaptation." Mr. Sprockett is impressed with Lilly's candor, and they begin plans for their wedding.

Eleanor, the illegitimate daughter of Lilly. Sweet, forthcoming, and demonstrative, she is unlike her mother in looks and in temperament. Eleanor, a romantic, relishes the life around her and appears in sharp contrast to Lilly, who has, through necessity, become withdrawn, stiff, and inhibited. Eleanor is reared by Lilly to emulate the good manners and soft-spoken ways of Mrs. Butler, whom Lilly had served during Eleanor's earliest years. Eleanor completes her schooling in the Fraser Valley, then is accepted to nurse training at a hospital in Vancouver, where she meets Paul Lowry, a young lawyer. They marry and establish a home where Lilly visits infrequently, as she is uncomfortable with their refined ways. Eleanor is what Lilly has made her: a respectable, educated young matron.

— *P. R. Lannert*

EQUUS

Author: Peter Shaffer (1926-   )
First published: 1973
Genre: Drama
Locale: Great Britain
Time: The 1970's
Plot: Psychological realism

Martin Dysart, a British child psychiatrist in his mid-forties. He is suffering doubts about the value of his profession as well as about the worth of his existence. After working with Alan Strang for several weeks and learning about the boy's intense religiosity, Dysart discovers that he envies the boy his passionate ability to worship a deity, even if it is one derived from the boy's imagination. He believes that he can purge Alan of his destructive religious beliefs, but he deeply doubts the beneficence of making the boy normal.

Alan Strang, a part-time employee at an appliance store and at Harry Dalton's stable. At the age of seventeen, he still lives with his parents. Having been torn between his Christian mother's intense religiosity and his father's equally intense atheism, at the age of twelve Alan created his own religion, the gods of which are horses ruled by Equus. Alan is taught for years by his mother that biological sex without spiritual love is sinful and that God's eyes are everywhere and always watching him. When Alan's first sexual experience occurs in Dalton's stable, the temple of Alan's gods, his guilt is so great that he stabs out the eyes of six horses.

Dora Strang, Alan's mother, a housewife married to Frank. In her mid-fifties, she is extremely religious and has devoted years to reading the Bible to Alan and indoctrinating him into Christianity, against her husband's expressed disapproval. Her God is essentially a punitive and unforgiving one, and her faith is based on fear.

Frank Strang, Alan's father, a printer married to Dora. In his mid-fifties, he is an atheist who considers vulgar his wife's religious beliefs, as well as the religious instructions she has imposed on Alan, and he blames these for Alan's blinding of the horses. When Alan was twelve years old, Frank ripped from his son's bedroom wall a picture of the crucified Christ and replaced it with a picture of a horse, from then on the object of Alan's religious faith.

Hesther Salomon, a magistrate in the British legal system. In her mid-forties, she is a friend of Dysart who, troubled by the savagery of Alan's crime against the horses and believing that Dysart is equipped to cure the boy of his mental illness, persuades the court to allow her to place Alan in the psychiatric hospital where Dysart works. It is she who persuades the already overworked doctor to take Alan as a patient. She becomes Dysart's confidante, listening and responding to his personal and professional doubts and complaints.

Jill Mason, an employee at Dalton's stable. In her mid-twenties and living with her mother, Jill learns of Alan's love of horses and is instrumental in getting him a part-time job at the stable. She is physically attracted to Alan, communicates this to the boy one evening, and, after persuading him to go with her to see a pornographic film, attempts to seduce him in the stable. It is on this occasion, after they have taken their clothes off and laid down together in the hay, that Alan hears the horses, his gods, stamping their hooves (in disapproval of his sexual behavior, he believes). He chases Jill away by threatening to stab her with a hoof pick, then turns on the horses with the pick and blinds them.

— *David A. Carpenter*

THE ERASERS
(Les Gommes)

Author: Alain Robbe-Grillet (1922-   )
First published: 1953
Genre: Novel
Locale: An unnamed northern French city
Time: Probably after World War II
Plot: Detective and mystery

Wallas, a detective who arrives in a provincial city in northern France to investigate the latest in a series of political murders. He is large and in his forties, and he has shaved his mustache for this mission. His previous assignment had been the investigation of various theosophical societies. He had applied to the bureau for which he now works and had almost been refused because his forehead measures only forty-nine square centimeters instead of the fifty that the chief, Inspector Fabius, required. He has been given his first solo assignment and is to investigate the murder of Daniel Dupont. During his investigation, he frequently wonders what Fabius would have done, even going so far as to imagine himself to be Fabius. While trying to find a killer, Wallas also keeps trying to find a certain type of eraser he once saw, hence the title of the book.

Inspector Laurent, the man normally in charge of murder investigations in the city. He is not pleased with having his case usurped by an outsider, although he does his best to hide it. The most noticeable physical aspect of Laurent is that he is bald. Even though he does much less field investigation than does Wallas, Laurent figures out the truth of the matter by sheer reasoning ability, just as Inspector Fabius would have.

Daniel Dupont, a fifty-two-year-old, internationally respected university professor. He is the latest target of a gang that is murdering prominent people for unknown reasons. He lived alone, attended only by an elderly female servant. Dupont had no real attachment either to his students or to his wife.

Evelyn Dupont, Daniel's former wife. A buxom, exuberant, Mediterranean-type woman, she is rather out of place in this northern city. She had married Dupont, who was much older than she, out of admiration for him. She could not long endure the isolation in which Dupont lived, however, and left him. According to her, Dupont was incapable of any sort of human attachment. He was completely alone and did not suffer from it. She now runs a stationery store. Wallas meets her by accident when he goes into her store to buy an eraser. Wallas is at first intrigued, then annoyed, by her suggestive laugh.

Garinati, a small man who was charged with the assassination of Dupont. He was given very specific, literally step-by-step, directions on how to proceed with the murder but failed to carry them out. As a result, Dupont was only wounded in the attempt and took refuge with a friend, Dr. Juard. Garinati tries to undo his mistake but cannot.

Dr. Juard and his wife, the owners of an obstetrics and gynecology clinic. Dupont turns to Dr. Juard for medical attention after being wounded by Garinati and asks the doctor to hide him from the gang trying to kill him. Juard assists Dupont even though he is a member of the gang. When Inspector Laurent asks him why Dupont would seek the services of a gynecologist, Juard replies that he is a surgeon and that he treated many such wounds during the war.

— *Robert R. Brock*

EREC AND ENIDE
(Érec et Énide)

Author: Chrétien de Troyes (c. 1150-c. 1190)
First transcribed: c. 1164
Genre: Poetry
Locale: Arthurian England
Time: The sixth century
Plot: Arthurian romance

Erec (eh-REHK), a fair and brave knight of the Round Table. In a town where he is lodging, he meets his host's daughter, the beautiful damsel Enide. He returns with her to King Arthur's court and makes her his bride. So enamored is he of the fair lady that he neglects all knightly pursuits in favor of dalliance with her. When the report reaches him that the people think him a coward, he sets out with Enide on a journey of knight-errantry during which he bears himself with such bravery that he returns to King Arthur's court with honor. On his father's death, he becomes king of his own land.

Enide (eh-NEED), the most beautiful damsel in Christendom, Erec's bride. After she hears reports that Erec's dalliance with her has caused him to be suspected of cowardice, she taunts him about the change that love has made in him. When he angrily sets forth on a journey to prove his valor and her love, she accompanies him, bravely shares his adventures, and returns triumphant with him to King Arthur's court.

Guivret the Little (gweev-REHT), a knight who challenges Erec to combat and, after a brave fight on both sides, becomes his friend and benefactor.

Count Galoin (gah-LWAN), a nobleman so smitten by Enide's beauty that he desires to make her mistress of all his lands. His plot to take Erec's life is thwarted by Enide; the defeated count gallantly praises the lady's prudence and virtue.

Evrain (ehv-RAYN), a king whose land is delivered from thralldom by Erec.

King Arthur, the leader of the Round Table.

Guinevere (gwehn-eh-VEER), his queen.

King Lac, Erec's father.

Sir Gawain (gah-WAYN) and

Sir Kay, knights of the Round Table.

Yder (ee-DUR), a haughty knight challenged and defeated by Erec.

Cadoc of Tabriol (kah-DOHK), a knight rescued from giants by Erec.

EREWHON: Or, Over the Range

Author: Samuel Butler (1835-1902)
First published: 1872
Genre: Novel
Locale: Erewhon and England
Time: The 1870's
Plot: Utopian

Strong, a young farmworker who journeys into Erewhon; he discovers there a civilization partly the reverse of and partly similar to that of England. Somewhat like Jonathon Swift's Gulliver, Strong seems a thoughtful, observant, inquiring, and sometimes rather naïve traveler. He should not be identified with the author, since Butler used him only as a convenient mouthpiece to convey the satire in the novel.

Kahabuka (Chowbok), an old native, a sort of chief with a little knowledge of English and a great thirst for grog, with which Strong bribes him for information about the land beyond the mountains. In England, upon his return, Strong finds Chowbok posing as a missionary, the Reverend William Habakkuk.

Senoj Nosnibor, a citizen and leading merchant of Erewhon "recovering"—as if from sickness—from a serious case of embezzlement. He is assigned to instruct Strong in Erewhonian customs. His name is an anagram of "Jones Robinson."

Arowhena, his beautiful younger daughter, with whom Strong falls in love. She helps him to escape from Erewhon, after which they marry and she is baptized into the Anglican Church, though she retains some of her former beliefs in Erewhonian deities.

Ydgrun, Erewhon's main goddess, both an abstract concept and a silly, cruel woman. A law of Ydgrun enforces conformity to the point of intolerability. Her devotees, including priests, worship her in heart and deed rather than in words. Her name is an anagram of "Grundy."

Zulora, the handsome older daughter of Nosnibor. She wishes to marry Strong, who develops a dislike for her.

Yram, the jailor's pretty daughter, who is attracted to Strong. She teaches him the Erewhonian language and explains to him some of the customs of the land. Her name is an anagram of "Mary."

The Straighteners, specialists who treat Erewhonians suffering from "ailments" such as petty theft and embezzlement. They resemble twentieth century psychiatrists.

Mahaina, a homely woman, reputedly a drunkard, whose supposed drinking may perhaps be what would today be called a compensation for an inferiority complex.

Thims, a cashier at a musical bank and a friend of Strong. His name is an anagram of "Smith."

Giovanni Gianni, captain of the ship that rescues Strong and Arowhena.

ESMOND IN INDIA

Author: Ruth Prawer Jhabvala (1927-   )
First published: 1958
Genre: Novel

Locale: New Delhi, India
Time: c. 1957
Plot: Social realism

Shakuntala (shah-kewn-TAH-lah), a nineteen-year-old, upper-class, recent college graduate, the daughter of Har Dayal and Madhuri. Shakuntala enjoys the luxuries of home and of being out of school with an as-yet-undefined future. Attractive, yet careless about her dress and appearance, romantic, headstrong, and slightly bohemian, Shakuntala rejects her mother's conventional values and shares her father's vaguely artistic inclinations. By the end of the novel, she has become Esmond Stillwood's mistress, having cast herself at him because of his romantic good looks and his seemingly vast knowledge of and interest in Indian culture.

Esmond Stillwood, a thirtyish English lecturer on Indian art and culture. The husband of Gulab and father of Ravi, Esmond also is the lover of Betty and later of Shakuntala. Unhappily married, Esmond finds himself turning from mental to physical cruelty toward his wife, who cannot master his British traditions and way of life any more than he can truly understand her deeply Indian culture. By the end of the novel, it is clear that Stillwood will desert India, Gulab, Shakuntala, and even Ravi to return to England on Betty's money.

Gulab (GEW-lahb), Esmond Stillwood's wife, Uma's daughter, and Ravi's mother. Beautiful, idle, fatalistic, and deeply sensual, Gulab embodies an ancient Indian tradition and way of life. Once engaged to Amrit, Gulab jilted him and stubbornly married Stillwood. Although she tries to conform to Esmond's household rules and is never overtly critical of them, she reverts to her way of doing things the moment he is out of sight, both in the food she eats and in her affectionate and deeply physical way of nurturing their child. Although her mother, Uma, has attempted to persuade her to leave Esmond, Gulab does not do so, despite his cruelty and infidelity, until, overcome by Gulab's beauty, their servant makes advances toward her. Only then does she feel justified in leaving, because of her husband's failure in his primary duty: to protect her.

Har Dayal (hahr DAY-ahl), a wealthy and successful government official. He is the husband of Madhuri; father of Shakuntala, Amrit, and Raj; and lifelong friend and admirer of Ram Nath. Willingly dominated by his wife's hard-nosed values, Har Dayal stayed out of the main revolutionary movement in which his friend Ram Nath had been jailed and had become a hero. Har Dayal thrived after Indian independence because of his personal warmth, his unwillingness to offend, and his ability to popularize culture. He is close to his daughter, Shakuntala, who idealizes him, but feels his friend Ram Nath to be the greater man, even though Ram Nath is poor and Har Dayal is, by worldly standards, a success.

Madhuri (mah-DEW-ree), Har Dayal's wife and the mother of Shakuntala, Amrit, and Raj. The center of her wealthy, comfortable, and luxurious household, Madhuri is its dominant and very conservative, traditional force. Deeply concerned that her children marry properly, she holds a grudge against Ram Nath's family for Gulab's jilting of Amrit, though Amrit is happily and suitably married to Indira. Madhuri is worried that Shakuntala's bohemian tendencies may lead her to marry Narayan, Ram Nath's son. The match would be unsuitable because of his poverty and his family. She does not yet know, at the novel's close, of Shakuntala's relationship with Esmond.

Ram Nath, a hero of the independence movement. He is the father of Narayan, the brother of Uma, and an old friend of Har Dayal. An intellectual and once an activist, Ram Nath feels extraneous in and remote from the new India, in which his more adaptable and worldly friend, Har Dayal, is such a success. His family's wealth spent on the revolution, Ram Nath lives in comparative poverty, regretting only that his wife, Lakshmi, must suffer with him without understanding his principles. When Narayan requests that his father find him a suitable wife, Ram Nath focuses on Shakuntala, who has charmed him by enthusiastically espousing idealism. Ram Nath's request, however, is rejected as unsuitable by his old friend, Har Dayal, a rejection that pains Har Dayal more than it does Ram Nath.

Lakshmi (lahk-SHMEE), Ram Nath's wife. Thoroughly conventional in her views, Lakshmi does not share her husband's, her son's, or even her sister-in-law Uma's idealism. Although bothered by the loss of status induced by her poverty, Lakshmi in her way makes the best of her lot by feeling superior to her neighbors while fully participating in their lives.

Uma (EW-mah), Ram Nath's sister, Gulab's mother, and Ravi's grandmother. Uma is the widow of a revolutionary hero. Energetic, superstitious, religious, and, like her brother, idealistically dedicated to the principles of the revolution, Uma runs a rather open household, with all kinds of people temporarily or permanently living there. Uma deeply loves her family and is distressed by Gulab's unhappy marriage and Ravi's unsuitable upbringing.

Ravi (RAH-vee), Gulab and Esmond Stillwood's young son. Ravi loves his mother and grandmother but fears his father.

Amrit, the older son of Har Dayal and Madhuri, brother of Shakuntala and Raj, husband of Indira, and jilted fiancé of Gulab. Amrit is, like his father, Cambridge educated, but he has no interest in the arts. A businessman, Amrit is dedicated to his work; to orderly, material comfort (in this attribute, he resembles his mother); and to his wife. He was not made unhappy by Gulab's defection and is completely satisfied by his marriage and his life. Essentially kind like his father, Amrit has no higher strivings and therefore tends toward smugness.

Indira (ihn-DIHR-ah), Amrit's thoroughly conventional and suitable new wife. Madhuri is increasingly pleased with her and compares Shakuntala unfavorably to Indira. If not as beautiful as Gulab, Indira is healthy, dresses neatly, and adores her husband and her mother-in-law. Shakuntala finds her dull company.

Betty, a well-off, good-looking, agreeable Englishwoman who is Esmond's mistress but is liberated enough sexually not to mind his affair with Shakuntala, whom she views as naïve but agreeable company. A hedonist, Betty seems to have no particular occupation, nor any desire for one, and no particular reason for being in India except that, for a time, it has amused her to be there.

Bachani (bah-CHAH-nee), Uma's lifelong servant, devoted to Uma and also to Gulab and Ravi.

Narayan (nah-RAH-yahn), Ram Nath's son. By choice and conviction a village doctor, the intellectual Narayan never appears in person in the novel, although his request that his father find him a wife and his values are central to the plot.

Raj, Har Dayal and Madhuri's son. Like Narayan, Raj, who is studying in Cambridge, never appears in the novel in person, but his lack of communication followed by his engagement to a suitable English girl form a subplot.

— *Ellen M. Laun*

ESTHER WATERS

Author: George Moore (1852-1933)
First published: 1894
Genre: Novel

Locale: England
Time: Late nineteenth century
Plot: Naturalism

Esther Waters, an uneducated servant girl, sturdily built but graceful; she is rather sullen-looking except when she smiles. As she grows older, she becomes stout but retains a natural dignity despite her unhappy life. Her devoutness, though it causes mockery among the Barfield servants, brings her comfort. Pregnant and disgraced, Esther loses her job and is later left alone when her mother dies and her stepfather moves to Australia. She experiences hard times until Miss Rice employs her before her marriage to the reckless William Latch. Her love for and pride in Jackie provide some joy in an otherwise sad life.

William Latch, son of the cook at Woodview. He is strong but shallow-chested. His forehead is low and narrow, his nose long, chin pointed, cheeks hollow and bloodless, and eyes lusterless. He is an inveterate gambler. Taking advantage of Esther's innocence, he seduces her by promising to marry her. Annoyed by Esther's sulking, he elopes with Peggy, who later leaves him. Chancing upon Esther several years later, he persuades her to marry him instead of Fred. Though he prospers for a while, gambling ruins him, and tuberculosis finally kills him.

Mrs. Barfield, Esther's mistress at Woodview, a deeply religious woman who is Esther's friend as well as her employer. Though she dismisses Esther after her pregnancy is discovered, it is to Mrs. Barfield that Esther returns after William's death, and she proudly introduces Jackie to her before he leaves for army service.

Sarah Tucker, another servant at Woodview who is jealous of William's attentions to Esther.

Jackie, Esther's son, whom she loves deeply and of whom she is very proud.

Fred Parsons, Esther's betrothed, colorless but honest, dependable, and religious. Against her good judgment, Esther turns from a planned marriage to Fred to the uncertainty of one to William because Jackie prefers him.

Miss Rice, a writer and a later employer of Esther, who is sympathetic regarding her plight before her marriage to William.

Mrs. Latch, William's ill-tempered mother, who makes working conditions unpleasant for Esther at Woodview.

Peggy Barfield, Mr. Barfield's cousin, with whom William elopes.

Mr. Barfield, master of Woodview, formerly a famous steeplechase rider, now a portly and well-to-do owner of a stable of racehorses. When Esther returns to Woodview years later, Barfield has died after losing most of his money because of racing debts.

ETHAN FROME

Author: Edith Wharton (1862-1937)
First published: 1911
Genre: Novel
Locale: Starkfield, Massachusetts
Time: Late nineteenth century
Plot: Psychological realism

Ethan Frome, a farmer frustrated in his ambition to become an engineer or a chemist and in his marriage to a nagging, sour, sickly wife. He falls in love with his wife's good and lovely cousin, Mattie Silver, who comes to live with them. When his wife finally drives the girl away, Ethan insists on taking her to the station. Ethan and Mattie decide to take a sleigh ride they have promised themselves and, in mutual despair over the impending separation, they resolve to kill themselves by running the sled against a tree. They are not killed, only permanently injured, and Ethan's wife is to look after them for the rest of their lives.

Zenobia Pierce Frome (Zeena), Ethan's wife, a distant cousin who nursed his mother during a long illness. The marriage is loveless, and Zeena is sickly and nagging.

Mattie Silver, Zeena's cousin, who comes to live with the Fromes. She returns Ethan's love, and once when Zeena spends a night away from home, she and Ethan spend a happy evening together, not making love but sitting quietly before the fire, as Ethan imagines happily married couples do. Mattie feels that she would rather die than leave Ethan, but in the crash she suffers not death, but a permanent spine injury and must submit thereafter to being nursed by Zeena.

Ruth Varnum and

Ned Hale, a young engaged couple whom Ethan observes stealing a kiss. On his night alone with Mattie, he tells her wistfully about it; it is as close as he comes to making advances.

EUGENE ARAM

Author: Edward Bulwer-Lytton (1803-1873)
First published: 1832
Genre: Novel
Locale: England
Time: Mid-eighteenth century
Plot: Detective and mystery

Eugene Aram, a character based on a real-life scholar and scientist. He is in love with Madeline Lester. In his confession, opened after his execution, he explains that he robbed for money to continue experiments of value to the world. He claims that his killing of Geoffrey was an accident.

Geoffrey Lester, a dissipated wanderer who abandons his family, later receives a legacy from a friend in India, and becomes Mr. Clark. His disappearance starts a search. When his grave is discovered, Aram is revealed as his murderer.

Rowland Lester, an English gentleman who adopts his brother's forsaken family.

Madeline Lester, the daughter of Rowland. Because of her love for Aram, she dies of grief when his crime is discovered.

Ellinor Lester, another daughter of Rowland. She is in love with her cousin, Walter.

Walter Lester, the son of Geoffrey, who tracks down his father's murderer. Though originally in love with Madeline, he marries Ellinor.

Houseman, a rogue and the accomplice of Aram. He blackmails Aram for the support of his daughter, whose eventual death nearly drives him mad.

Bunting, Walter's servant, who helps in the search for Geoffrey.

EUGENE ONEGIN
(Evgeny Onegin)

Author: Alexander Pushkin (1799-1837)
First published: 1833
Genre: Poetry
Locale: Russia
Time: Early nineteenth century
Plot: Impressionism

Tatyana Larin (tah-TYAH-nah LAH-rihn), also called **Tanya Larina** (TAHN-yah LAH-rihn-uh), the reserved and withdrawn older daughter of the well-to-do, upper-middle-class Larin family, of whose marriage her parents despair. She falls in love at first sight with Eugene Onegin and, unable to write grammatical Russian, sends him a passionate letter written in French. Although he fails to encourage her, she turns down several other proposals of marriage. When her family takes her to Moscow, she picks up beauty hints at a ball and attracts the attentions of a retired general who persuades her to marry him. Years later, she again sees Onegin, who falls in love with her and writes her passionate letters. She reads them and preserves them to read again, but she gives him no encouragement and remains faithful to her general to the end of her life.

Eugene Onegin (ehuh-GEH-nihy oh-NEH-gihn), the hero of this narrative poem, with many resemblances to its author. Brought up in the aristocratic tradition, he is a brilliant, witty man of the world. Successful in many light love affairs, he is bored with living. City life, with its opera and ballet, has lost its appeal. A stay on the country estate willed to him by his uncle wearies him after several days. He is finally persuaded by his friend, Vladimir Lensky, to accompany him on a visit to the Larin family. There, he finds the conversation dull, the refreshment too simple and too abundant, and Tatyana unattractive. Visiting her later, after receiving her passionate love letter, he tells her frankly that he would make her a very poor husband because he has had too many disillusioning experiences with women. He returns to the lonely estate and the life of an anchorite. When Vladimir takes him under false pretenses to Tatyana's birthday party, Onegin gets revenge by flirting with her sister Olga, who is engaged to Vladimir. His jealous friend challenges him to a duel. Onegin shoots Vladimir through the heart.

Olga Larin (OHLY-guh), also called **Olenka** (oh-LEHN-kuh), the pretty and popular younger daughter of the Larin family, betrothed to Vladimir Lensky. At a ball, she dances so often with Onegin that her fiancé gets angry. Although she assures him that she means nothing by her innocent flirtation, he challenges Onegin to a duel and is killed. Later, she marries an army officer.

Vladimir Lensky (vlah-DIH-mihr LEHN-skihy), a German-Russian friend of Onegin, brought up in Germany and influenced by romantic illusions of life and love. Although his reading of Friedrich von Schiller and Immanuel Kant sets him apart from most other young Russians, he and Onegin have much in common. He tries to get his friend interested in Tatyana Larin by inviting him to her big birthday party, which he describes as an intimate family affair. In resentment, Onegin avoids Tatyana and devotes himself to Olga. After the challenge is given, he is too proud to acknowledge his misjudgment and is killed.

M. Guillot (gihl-YOH), Onegin's second in the duel.

Zaretsky (zah-REHT-skihy), Lensky's second.

The prince (called **Gremin** in the operatic version), a fat, retired general and Onegin's friend. Seeing Tatyana at a ball in Moscow, he falls in love with her and proposes. She accepts. Later, he invites Onegin to his house, and Onegin meets Tatyana again.

EUGÉNIE GRANDET

Author: Honoré de Balzac (1799-1850)
First published: 1833
Genre: Novel
Locale: Saumur, France
Time: Early nineteenth century
Plot: Naturalism

Eugénie Grandet (ew-zhay-NEE grahn-DAY), the young heiress to a fortune, who lives in the world but is not of it. Reared without a childhood in the penurious surroundings of Saumur, a provincial French town, Eugénie for a brief period lives in the love of her cousin, newly orphaned and a guest in the Grandet home. Strong of character and handsome in appearance, she pledges herself to young Charles Grandet and remains true to him throughout her life. As an obedient daughter of parents and Church, she tries to live righteously but defies her father in the matter of love. Her kind ministrations to both her dying parents, her lifelong devotion to her one loyal friend, and her constancy of memory make her one of the most steadfast and pitiable of heroines. Her good deeds and her loving devotion to the poor whom she serves give her life tragic beauty.

Monsieur Grandet, her father, one of the most miserly figures in all literature. The author of the family tragedy, Goodman Grandet, as Balzac satirically calls him, is unyielding in his niggardliness without seeming to realize his great fault. He appears to be trying to clear his brother's good name by not allowing him to fall into bankruptcy, but in reality he profits from the delaying action. His towering angers at the least "extravagance" finally put his devoted wife on her deathbed, and his unrelenting love of gold destroys the loving confidence of his daughter. Shrewd and grasping in his business deals, he has no redeeming features. Ironically enough, his fortune is finally put to good purposes through his daughter, who makes restitution for his wrongs.

Madame Grandet, his long-suffering wife, whose piety is taxed by the burden of her husband's stinginess. Accustomed to her hard lot and strengthened by her religion, Madame Grandet bows under her heavy yoke of work and harsh treatment until she takes up the cause of her daughter's right to love and devotes herself to the memory of that love. Still she prays for reconciliation, and when it comes she dies happy, without knowing her dowry is the reason for the deathbed forgiveness.

Charles Grandet (shahrl), the dandified cousin of the heroine, who loses his fortune through his father's suicide but who regains a fortune through unscrupulous dealings financed, ironically, by Eugénie's gift of money to him. Heroic only in his unselfish grief for his father and generous only once in bestowing his love, Charles reveals a twisted mind tutored by a corrupt society. Outwardly prepossessing, inwardly vacillating, he chooses to disregard the one fine thing that was given him, a dowry of unselfish love, and bases his life on treachery, lechery, and adultery.

Nanon (nah-NOHN), the faithful servant who loyally defends the indefensible in her master because it was he who raised her a full step in the social order. Large and mannish, Nanon manages the entire Grandet household with such efficiency as to cause admiration from the master, himself efficient and desperately saving. Her devotion to him, however, does not preclude rushing to the defense of his wife and daughter, the victims of his spite. Finally she marries the gamekeeper, and together they rule the Grandet holdings for their mistress Eugénie.

Monsieur Cruchot (krew-SHOH-), a notary and petty government official who becomes husband in name only to Eugénie. He feels that by marrying the name and inheriting the fortune his own name will become illustrious. His untimely death ends the reign of self-seeking misers.

Monsieur de Grassins (grah-SAHN), the provincial banker sent to Paris to act for M. Grandet at the time of his brother's bankruptcy. Attracted to the gay life in the capital, he fails to return to Saumur.

THE EUNUCH
(Eunuchus)

Author: Terence (Publius Terentius Afer, c. 190-159 B.C.E.)
First performed: 161 B.C.E.
Genre: Drama
Locale: Athens
Time: The fourth century B.C.E.
Plot: Comedy

Thaïs (THAY-ihs), a Rhodian courtesan living in Athens. She is wooed by Phaedria, whom she loves, and by Thraso, a braggart captain. Thaïs encourages Thraso's love because she wishes him to make her a present of a young slave girl. This girl, Pamphila, had been reared as Thaïs' sister. In fact, she is an Athenian citizen. Thaïs wants to restore the girl to Chremes, Pamphila's brother. After Thraso gives her Pamphila, Thaïs goes to Thraso's house. She quarrels with him and returns home to find that Pamphila has been ravished by Chaerea, who entered Thaïs' house disguised as a eunuch. Pamphila is restored to Chremes and promised in marriage to Chaerea, who loves her. Thaïs reaffirms her love for Phaedria.

Phaedria (FEED-ree-uh), the son of Laches, who loves Thaïs. Hurt because Thaïs excludes him from her house while admitting Thraso, Phaedria listens to her explanation and agrees to leave Athens for two days until Thraso has given Pamphila to the courtesan. Unable to stay away so long, Phaedria returns to find that his brother Chaerea has disgraced him by attacking Pamphila.

Thraso (THRAY-soh), a rich, pompous, and conceited soldier, a foreigner who formerly had been in the service of an Asiatic king. He is used by both Thaïs and his parasite Gnatho for their own ends. When, after being deserted by Thaïs, he asks that Pamphila be returned to him, his demand is refused. When he takes a gang of thugs to storm Thaïs' house and recover Pamphila, he is thwarted by the revelation that Pamphila is an Athenian citizen and, therefore, cannot be held as a slave.

Chaerea (KEE-reh-uh), Phaedria's younger brother, a sixteen-year-old youth. Seeing Pamphila on the street as she is being taken to Thaïs' house, he falls in love with her. With the aid of Parmeno, he impetuously enters Thaïs' house in the garb of a eunuch and ravishes Pamphila. After Pamphila's identity is revealed, Chaerea receives his father's permission to marry her.

Parmeno (PAHR-meh-noh), Phaedria's outspoken and intelligent servant. Having been sent by Phaedria to deliver to Thaïs a eunuch and an Ethiopian girl, Parmeno meets Chaerea. He sympathizes with Chaerea's infatuation with Pamphila and agrees to introduce him into Thaïs' house disguised as the eunuch.

Gnatho (NA-thoh), Thraso's parasite. Gnatho is a scheming cynic who detests his patron. At the end, with a view to his continuing prosperity, Gnatho asks Thaïs and Phaedria not to have Thraso banished for his effrontery in besieging Thaïs' house. He persuades them to allow Thraso to continue to pay court to Thaïs, because Thraso's money can supply luxuries that Phaedria could not otherwise afford.

Chremes (KRAY-meez), a young Athenian, the brother of Pamphila.

Dorus (DOH-ruhs), an old eunuch. Phaedria had bought Dorus to present to Thaïs. Chaerea enters Thaïs' house in Dorus' clothes.

Laches (LA-keez), an old Athenian, the father of Phaedria and Chaerea. When Laches learns that Pamphila is an Athenian citizen, he approves his son's marriage to her because he is glad to save the family from disgrace.

Antipho (AN-tih-foh), the young man to whom Chaerea relates what he had done in Thaïs' house.

Pamphila (PAM-fihl-uh), a sixteen-year-old girl. The sister of Chremes, Pamphila had been kidnaped while a child and sold into slavery in Rhodes. She had been reared there as Thaïs' sister.

Sophrona (so-froh-nuh), an old nurse in Thaïs' household.

Pythias (PIH-thee-uhs) and

Dorias (DOH-ree-uhs), Thaïs' female attendants.

Sanga (SAN-guh), Thraso's cook.

Donax (DOH-naks),

Simalio (sih-MA-lee-oh), and

Syriscus (sih-RIHS-kus), servants of Thraso. Thraso takes them with him to storm Thaïs' house.

EUPHUES AND HIS ENGLAND

Author: John Lyly (c. 1554-1606)
First published: 1580
Genre: Novel
Locale: England
Time: 1579-1580
Plot: Didactic

Euphues (YEW-fyew-eez), the hero of *Euphues, the Anatomy of Wit*, grown older and wiser, who travels to observe customs in England.

Philautus (fih-LOH-tuhs), his friend. He suffers torments for the love of Camilla, but he soon turns to Frances, who is readier to return his affection.

Camilla (ka-MIH-luh), a gay, modest Englishwoman. She answers Philautus' amorous epistles with elegant, firm refusals and devotes her own energies to secret adoration of Surius.

Lady Flavia (FLAY-vee-uh), her friend, a gracious woman who uses her greater maturity to put her young guests at ease. It is at her suggestion that the witty young people debate the nature of love, in the manner of the noble ladies and gentlemen in Baldassare Castiglione's *Book of the Courtier*.

Frances, her niece, Philautus' "violet," whose gaiety and quick wit console him for Camilla's hard-heartedness.

Surius (SEW-ree-uhs), an exemplary young Englishman, brave, eloquent, and witty, whose gifts make him the object of Camilla's love.

Fidus (FEE-duhs), a wise innkeeper who welcomes Euphues and Philautus in Canterbury, apologizing profusely for the poverty of his house and bristling when they presume to praise his queen. He lectures them on the nature of government, drawing examples from his bee hives, then describes his experiences as courtier to Henry VIII.

EUPHUES, THE ANATOMY OF WIT

Author: John Lyly (c. 1554-1606)
First published: 1578
Genre: Novel
Locale: Naples and Athens
Time: The sixteenth century
Plot: Didactic

Euphues (YEW-fyew-eez), a witty, well-born young man. He disregards Eubulus' good advice about the traps which lie in the path of an indiscreet youth, and finds himself betraying his friend Philautus for the favors of a fickle young woman. He recognizes the value of the wisdom of age when she casts him off for another gallant.

Philautus (fih-LOH-tuhs), his friend, a clever, courteous young gentleman. He trusts Euphues at first and is furious to learn that his "friend" has stolen the affections of his bride-to-be.

Lucilla (lew-SIH-luh), a bright, attractive girl whose interest shifts quickly from one young man to another. She debates her motives before she turns from Philautus to Euphues, but she forsakes the latter with no qualms.

Don Ferardo (feh-RAHR-doh), her father, a wealthy nobleman of Naples. He tries to deal wisely with his willful child, but he is so heartbroken by her fickleness that he dies, leaving his estate to be squandered by Lucilla and the foolish Curio.

Curio (KEW-ree-oh), a Neapolitan gentleman "of little wealth and less wit" who draws Lucilla's attentions from Euphues to himself.

Eubulus (YEW-buh-luhs), a wise old man. He laments the waste of Euphues' natural gifts and advises him to govern his wit with wisdom.

Livia (LIH-vee-uh), Lucilla's companion, a young woman of more character and virtue than her friend.

THE EUSTACE DIAMONDS

Author: Anthony Trollope (1815-1882)
First published: 1873
Genre: Novel
Locale: London, England, and Scotland
Time: Late nineteenth century
Plot: Social realism

Lizzie Eustace, a wealthy and beautiful young widow who is much the center of attention in London society. Prior to her brief marriage to Sir Florian Eustace, she was the impoverished daughter of Admiral Greystock, an elderly and dissolute retired naval officer who was, as the narrator states, "in his later life much perplexed by the possession of a daughter." Lizzie is nineteen when her father dies, and it is painfully evident that she has grown up to become a self-centered, amoral person, bored with the Victorian virtues intended as a guide for the conduct and training of proper young women. Whereas other young women seek to prepare themselves for husbands of virtuous character and position in the community, Lizzie is obsessed with a romantic ideal and longs for a Byronic hero, a dark and subtly dangerous "corsair" to carry her off into a vaguely outlined life of ecstasy and excitement. Her selfishness and her many failed attempts at manipulating others take on comic rather than sinister proportions in the course of the novel.

Frank Greystock, a young barrister and newly elected member of Parliament for the conservative party. Frank's father is a clergyman, the dean of Bobsborough, and the family is not wealthy. Frank therefore is faced with the necessity of marrying someone with the financial means to further his career. The apparent dilemma lies in the fact that Frank loves Lucy Morris, a young and rather plain governess who is as loyal and virtuous as she is penniless. When Lizzie, besieged by the family lawyer seeking the return of the Eustace Diamonds, can find no champion for her interests, she turns to Frank, who chivalrously takes up her cause. Their close proximity during the time Frank helps and counsels her causes him to give at least passing consideration to the expediency of marriage to his wealthy cousin. Lizzie makes her best effort to seduce him away from Lucy Morris, but ultimately she fails. The combination of his personal integrity and his love for Lucy keeps Frank from subverting his affections and principles simply to advance his career.

Lucy Morris, the governess to the Fawn family and a childhood friend of Lizzie Greystock Eustace. She is in every significant aspect the polar opposite of Lizzie. A favorite in the Fawn household, she is as highly regarded by Lady Fawn as one of her own daughters. Though not a striking beauty like Lizzie, Lucy, according to the narrator, has a smile that makes all the old and middle-aged men fall in love with her. She is dutiful, sweetly social and genial, bright, and energetic. In short, she is a paradigm of the young Victorian woman. When she discovers that she has fallen in love with Frank Greystock, she is resigned to the fact—or so she believes at the time—that someone with Frank's bright future will never marry a governess. Nevertheless, she knows that she can never love anyone else. Her role in the novel is to be an example of the virtues of constancy and fidelity.

— Richard Keenan

EVA LUNA

Author: Isabel Allende (1942-)
First published: 1987
Genre: Novel
Locale: An unnamed South American country
Time: Mid- to late twentieth century
Plot: Magical Realism

Eva Luna (EH-vah LEW-nah), the narrator. The child of a servant, after her mother's death she is put out to work. Exploited and abused by her various employers and by the godmother who appropriates her earnings, Eva finds her refuge among the lowly and the outcasts. From her mother, Eva Luna learned to invent stories. These not only enable her to escape from the harshness of real life but also eventually to make her way in the world. At first, she simply tells stories to entertain people, but after learning to read and write, Eva becomes a scriptwriter for a successful television series. Eva uses her program to attack her country's oppressive government. In a guerrilla camp, Eva meets Rolf Carlé, who appears to be the man of her dreams. After defeating her old fear of love, she attains her fulfillment as a woman.

Rolf Carlé (kahr-LAY), an Austrian. The youngest child of a schoolmaster who went to war shortly after his birth, Rolf survives the Russian occupation only to discover that in fact his worst enemy is his father, who has returned to torment his family. After the schoolmaster is murdered by his students, Rolf realizes that he is as guilty as they are and becomes ill. Sent to South America to live with distant relatives in a European settlement called La Colonia, Rolf becomes part of a happy household. Rolf leaves to pursue work as a filmmaker. In the course of making a documentary, Rolf meets Eva Luna and falls in love. Back in La Colonia with her, Rolf discovers that their joy in each other has driven away the ghosts that haunted him for so long.

Consuelo (kohn-SWEH-loh), Eva Luna's mother. A child of unknown parentage reared by missionaries and nuns, she is a quiet, unassuming person who spends most of her brief life as the servant of one eccentric master. It is unclear whether her single sexual encounter is prompted more by her own curiosity or by pity for a man who supposedly is dying. Consuelo's bequest to Eva Luna is the gift of creating imaginary worlds through storytelling.

Elvira (ehl-VEE-rah), the cook who becomes a second mother to Eva. At heart a revolutionary, Elvira encourages Eva to stand up to her employers. Because her worst fear is of ending up in a pauper's grave, Elvira keeps her coffin handy and frequently sleeps in it.

Melesio (mehl-leh-SEE-oh), also called **Mimi** (mee-MEE), a Sicilian forced to emigrate because his family disapproved of his feminine characteristics. When Eva Luna first meets him, he is a teacher by day and a singer dressed in women's clothes by night. Melesio proves his courage by leading the Revolt of the Whores, but he is arrested and thrown into prison, where he very nearly dies. He encourages Eva to write for television.

Huberto Naranjo (ew-BEHR-toh nah-RAHN-hoh), also known as **Comandante Rogelio** (koh-mahn-DAHN-teh rroh-HEH-lee-oh), a tough, daring street boy, later a Marxist guerrilla fighter. Although he is briefly Eva's lover and always her friend, Huberto's relationships with women are inevitably superficial, because his macho attitude denies women equality while granting them protection. Huberto's victories bring about a change of government.

Riad Halabí (ree-AHD ah-lah-BEE), a kindly, intelligent shop owner. Riad seems to be loved by everyone but his wife, Zulema. After admitting to Eva that he loves her, Riad points out that the vicious gossip attending Zulema's death has made a marriage between them impossible.

Zulema (sew-LEH-mah), Riad's wife through an arranged marriage. A self-centered woman, she decides at first glance that she hates both her husband and his town. She refuses to be pleased by anything except the jewels he gives her and the stories Eva tells. After the sudden departure of her husband's cousin, whom she has seduced, Zulema is inconsolable and shoots herself.

EVA TROUT: Or, Changing Scenes

Author: Elizabeth Bowen (1899-1973)
First published: 1968
Genre: Novel
Locale: Various English country settings, London, Chicago, and Paris
Time: 1959-1967
Plot: Psychological realism

Eva Trout, a large, clumsy, naïve English girl with only a weak sense of selfhood. At the age of twenty-five, she becomes heiress to the fortune of her father, Willy Trout, when he commits suicide. In Eva's infancy, her mother was killed in a plane crash as she fled from her husband's homosexual relationship with Constantine. Just before receiving her inheritance, Eva lives with a former teacher, Iseult, and unintentionally disrupts her marriage. Morally and spiritually homeless all her life and emotionally crippled by a childhood devoid of normal love—she cannot even cry—Eva first purchases a derelict mansion in England as a home and then leaves for America to create a family for herself by buying a baby,

Jeremy, on the black market. Because she cannot accept her own sexuality, she cannot herself bear a child. Inarticulate and unwilling to communicate with others, she lives for some eight years in isolation with Jeremy, who proves to be a deaf-mute, in a world restricted to television and film images. Finally reaching out for fuller humanity, she emerges and takes him to England to receive training in speech. He shoots Eva as she is departing on a mock wedding journey, but her death is an apotheosis. Having inveigled her longtime friend Henry into a fake marriage for the sake of Jeremy's future, Eva discovers in the moment before death that Henry would willingly marry her for herself, and in knowing herself to be loved she finally discovers her selfhood. Psychically whole at last, she dies crying tears of joy.

Iseult Arble, Eva's former teacher, dark haired and of pleasing appearance. Formerly an inspiring teacher who fancied herself an intellectual, she has since married the unintellectual but physically appealing Eric. Believing that she has demeaned herself, she especially dislikes Eva as a reminder of a more personally meaningful past. Sixteen-year-old Eva, through her adulation at boarding school, taught Iseult the extent of her power over others; in retrospect, Iseult knows that she used it to manipulate the girl and feed her own ego even as Eva knows that Iseult encouraged, then abandoned, her pupil's growth. She steals Jeremy from Eva, and he kills Eva with the gun planted by Iseult in Eva's luggage because Eva had dared to meddle with Eric.

Constantine Ormeau, Eva's guardian for a time and her father's former business partner and lover. He feels obligated to look after Eva not only because of his long relationship with her father but also because his infidelity drove Willy to suicide. He despises women. Although Eva, who regards him as her father's murderer, dislikes and fears him, it is his advice to Eva to do something purposeful with her life that ultimately leads her to rejoin the world after her years of seclusion and refusal of humanity.

Henry Dancey, Eva's friend and lover, a minister's son twelve years her junior. He first becomes involved with Eva shortly before she receives her inheritance, executing small commissions for her. When she returns to England for Jeremy's training some eight years later and he is a student at Cambridge, still somewhat awed by her but very devoted, he agrees to pretend to be leaving on a wedding journey with her, then arrives at the train ready to leave with her in truth.

Eric Arble, Iseult's husband, a ruddy and clean-shaven man who works as an automobile mechanic and foreman. To Iseult's chagrin, he has failed as a fruit farmer, a more romantically appealing occupation. He takes a casual interest in Eva when she stays with the Arbles and blames her for the breakup of his marriage.

Jeremy Trout, Eva's adopted son, an American, and a deaf-mute. He plays a symbolic role in the novel as the alienated self that the loveless Eva became because her longings to comprehend were constantly frustrated, so that she ceased to want to communicate with any reality outside herself.

— *Harriet Blodgett*

EVAN HARRINGTON

Author: George Meredith (1828-1909)
First published: 1861
Genre: Novel
Locale: England
Time: The nineteenth century
Plot: Social satire

Evan Harrington, the son of a tailor, who proves his character in upper-class society. He is a young man who accepts the responsibility of doing good for those he loves, though the gesture on occasion works against his own interest. Apprenticed to Mr. Goren, a tailor, Evan Harrington eventually marries a woman of the upper class and manages to provide abundantly for her.

Rose Jocelyn, the heiress who finally becomes Harrington's wife. She is genuinely kind and fair, but she is set against Harrington on one occasion when he lies to her for her own good. When Harrington can tell her the truth, all things between them are put right again.

Ferdinand Laxley, a young man of the upper class who dislikes Harrington for two reasons: He is the son of a common tradesman, and he loves Rose, the girl Laxley is trying to win. Laxley is pugnacious, and he challenges Harrington to a duel. In the end he is, ironically, disgraced for revealing a secret of which he has no knowledge.

Louisa, the countess de Saldar, Harrington's sister, who has married a titled man. She works energetically to find a good marriage for her brother. It is she who brings about Laxley's downfall by writing an anonymous letter she knows will be attributed to Laxley.

Juliana Bonner, Rose's plain, crippled cousin, who loves and defends Harrington until her death. She leaves him Beckley Court, the Jocelyn estate; but he refuses the bequest and returns Beckley Court to Lady Jocelyn, Rose's mother.

Harriet Cogglesby, Harrington's sister, who is married to Andrew Cogglesby, a brewer whose fortunes are up and down.

Caroline Strike, another of Harrington's sisters; she is married to Major Strike. Harriet and Caroline play less important roles in the novel than does Louisa, the third sister.

Jack Raikes, Harrington's old school friend.

Tom Cogglesby, Andrew's brother.

Harry Jocelyn, Rose's brother.

George Uploft, a man who allegedly ran away some time before with Louisa. Harrington's father, Old Mel, supposedly caught the pair and stopped the elopement.

Mrs. Melchisedek Harrington, the mother of Evan, Caroline, Louisa, and Harriet. She ends her days as Tom Cogglesby's housekeeper.

Mr. Goren, a London tailor to whom Harrington is apprenticed.

EVANGELINE

Author: Henry Wadsworth Longfellow (1807-1882)
First published: 1847
Genre: Poetry
Locale: French Canada and the United States
Time: Mid-eighteenth century
Plot: Pastoral

Benedict Bellefontaine (behl-fon-TEHN), a farmer of Grand-Pré, in French Canada, who dies after the British fleet captures and burns his village.

Evangeline Bellefontaine (ay-vahn-zheh-LEEN), his lovely daughter, betrothed to Gabriel Lajeunesse. After he is exiled by the British, she roams the United States from Louisiana to the Ozark Mountains and Michigan in search of him. Finally, she becomes a Sister of Mercy in Philadelphia, and there she finds him dying. Soon afterward, she dies and is buried beside him.

Gabriel Lajeunesse (ga-bree-EHL lah-zhew-NEHS), Evangeline's sweetheart, deported from Acadia by the British. After years of hunting and trapping, he ends up in Philadelphia. There, he is struck down by yellow fever and dies in an almshouse. Evangeline finds him in time to comfort him in his dying moments.

Basil Lajeunesse (bah-ZEEL), Gabriel's father, a blacksmith who becomes prosperous in his new home but is unable to keep track of Gabriel.

Father Felician (fay-lee-SYAHN), the priest at Grand-Pré who buries Benedict and comforts Evangeline.

Baptiste Leblanc (bahpt-TEEST leh-BLAHN), the son of a notary. Unable to persuade Evangeline to marry him, he loyally follows her in her search for Gabriel.

A Shawnee Indian woman, who tells tribal legends to Evangeline.

Mowis, a legendary Indian bridegroom made of snow who dissolves in the sunshine.

Lilinau, another legendary Indian, who follows her phantom sweetheart into the woods and disappears forever.

EVA'S MAN

Author: Gayl Jones (1949-   )
First published: 1976
Genre: Novel
Locale: Primarily New York
Time: Mid-1940's to 1980
Plot: Psychological realism

Eva Medina Canada, a deeply disturbed forty-three-year-old black woman who is incarcerated in an insane asylum after having murdered and sexually mutilated her lover, Davis Carter. The novel traces her response to the repeated requests of the asylum psychiatrists and her roommate, Elvira Moody, to explain why she committed this grisly act. Eva herself is not so much sincerely trying to understand this murder as she is browsing through memories that come back to her, some repeatedly and some with distortions, but most of which focus on her sexual history. As a girl, she learns to keep quiet after some very early encounters with sexuality, and the silence she maintains on these occasions recurs throughout her life when she is faced with problems. For example, when the police question her, as a teenager, about stabbing Moses Tripp, she lets Moses talk but says nothing herself. After being judged insane for the murder of Davis Carter, she is locked up with Elvira Moody, also a murderer. The novel ends with Eva acquiescing, after much resistance, to Elvira's desire to make love to her but with little reason to believe that Eva's memories will ever coalesce into understanding of her actions on her part.

Davis Carter, Eva's lover, the man she murders. He has been married, has been a gambler, and tells her that he presently works with horses. The tall, dark-skinned, and good-looking Davis reminds Eva a bit of what her husband might have been like as a younger man. He does not physically abuse Eva, but—as had her husband, James—he keeps her confined, not even allowing her to comb her hair. He continues to have sex with her after she develops a kidney infection. His comment that she eats food as if she is making love to it seems to plant the idea of emasculating him in her mind.

James Hunn, also called **Hawk**, Eva's husband, whom she meets in a police station after she has stabbed Moses Tripp and Hunn has been in a car accident. He visits her while she is in the reformatory and later in jail; eventually, she marries him. According to Alfonso, he once killed a man in a fight over a woman. In his two-year marriage to Eva, he lets her out of the house only to go to classes and even tears the telephone out of their house so she cannot make calls. She marries him when she is eighteen years old and he is fifty-two.

Elvira Moody, Eva's roommate, who has a more violent history than Eva but who controls herself better. She killed three men by giving them bad whiskey. Her constant questioning and propositioning of Eva provide much of the impetus for Eva's remembering. The novel ends with Elvira finally making love to Eva.

Alfonso, Eva's cousin from Kansas City, with whom she goes out a few times and who makes a pass at her. Alfonso habitually beats his wife, Jean, and only his brother Otis can stop him.

Tyrone, a short jazz musician who has an affair with Eva's mother and who badgers the twelve-year-old Eva with sexual propositions until Eva's father puts a stop to the affair.

Marie Canada, Eva's mother, a woman who conducts her affair with Tyrone very openly, having him join her, and Eva, for dinner every night while Eva's father is at work, so that Eva's father learns about the affair long before he puts a stop to it.

Miss Billie, a neighborhood woman who befriends Eva's mother when they first move to New York from Columbus, Georgia. When Eva begins school, she gives Eva a wooden bracelet, which Eva loses when she is eight.

The Queen Bee, a neighborhood woman whose male lovers all die under mysterious circumstances.

— *Thomas J. Cassidy*

THE EVE OF ST. AGNES

Author: John Keats (1795-1821)
First published: 1820
Genre: Poetry

Locale: A castle
Time: The Middle Ages
Plot: Romance

Madeline (mahd-LEHN), a young virgin, first shown preoccupied at a ball given in the castle of her noble father. Eager to carry out the ritual of St. Agnes' Eve and thereby see her future husband in a dream, she leaves the revelry and retires to her room where, falling asleep, she dreams of Porphyro, the son of an enemy house. Waking to find him beside her bed, she is at first frightened. After he tells her, "This is no dream, my bride," she steals with him out of the castle, past the sleeping, drunken wassailers, and away into the stormy night.

Porphyro (POHR-fih-roh), her gallant young knight, who comes from his home across the moors, slips into the castle full of his enemies, and with the aid of Angela, an understanding old nurse, goes to Madeline's chamber before she prepares for bed. After she is asleep, he emerges from the closet where he has hidden himself, sets a table loaded with exotic foods, and wakes his beloved with a song, "La belle dame sans mercy," to the accompaniment of Madeline's lute. He persuades his beloved to leave her home of hate and flee with him.

Angela, an old woman, Madeline's nurse and Porphyro's friend. Convinced, after Porphyro has revealed his plan, that the young lover's intentions are honorable, she hides him in Madeline's bedchamber and provides the dainties for a feast. She dies "palsy-twitched."

The Beadsman, an aged supplicant who at the beginning of the poem is telling his rosary with cold-numbed fingers in the castle chapel. He closes the story by sleeping, forever unsought, "among his ashes cold."

EVELINA: Or, The History of a Young Lady's Entrance into the World

Author: Fanny Burney (Madame d'Arblay, 1752-1840)
First published: 1778
Genre: Novel

Locale: England
Time: The eighteenth century
Plot: Sentimental

Evelina Anville, a pretty, unaffected seventeen-year-old girl whose letters, principally to the Reverend Arthur Villars, her guardian, make up the book. They tell of her party-going, her love affairs, and her many admirers in the London and Bristol social sets. Evelina's mother was Caroline Evelyn, who died shortly after Evelina's birth; her father, Sir John Belmont, a profligate young man, had deserted Caroline, his wife, when he was disappointed in the fortune he expected to receive from his marriage. After much maneuvering to avoid the advances of unwelcome suitors, and upon being legally identified as Miss Belmont, Evelina finally marries Lord Orville.

The Reverend Arthur Villars, Evelina's devoted guardian since her mother's death. He guides and counsels her by letter, in answer to her voluminous messages to him at his Dorsetshire home. At first, Mr. Villars advises Evelina against being deceived by Lord Orville, only to give his blessing when he learns of his charge's happiness.

Lord Orville, a young nobleman of good family. He is the quintessence of the well-bred young man and the ardent, jealous lover.

Sir Clement Willoughby, an obnoxious admirer of Evelina, always persisting in his effort to win her. He writes letters to Evelina and Lord Orville, signing their respective names, trying to alter their affections for each other.

Mme Duval (dew-VAHL), Evelina's maternal grandmother. She instigates Evelina's visit to London, where she has come after twenty years of residence in Paris. Given to double superlative, she attributes her double negative and speech habits to the French influence. Blunt, indelicate, and severe, she is a vulgar old woman. Annoyed by Evelina's independence, she declares she will not leave Evelina an inheritance.

Macartney, a young, indolent poet whom Evelina meets early in her London visit. She befriends him, saving him from suicide on one occasion. Macartney is a source of jealousy on the part of Lord Orville. He learns that he is the illegitimate son of Sir John Belmont and marries Polly Green, the daughter of a designing nurse who substituted her own infant for Sir John's child.

Sir John Belmont, Evelina's father. He repents for his many years of unkindness to his legitimate daughter when he reads the deathbed letter written by Evelina's mother and delivered to him by Evelina. He bequeaths Evelina thirty thousand pounds.

Captain Mirvan, a coarse practical joker. Surly and officious, he never smiles except at another's expense. He and Mme Duval, in their grossness, turn many a genteel function into a brawl with their uncouthness and fighting.

Mrs. Mirvan, his wife. An amiable, well-bred woman, she introduces Evelina to many social affairs.

Maria, their daughter, Evelina's only close friend. They confide in each other, sharing happiness and heartaches.

Lady M. Howard, Mrs. Mirvan's mother and the mistress of Howard Grove, the scene of Evelina's first visit away from home. She intercedes for Mme Duval with Mr. Villars so that Evelina may visit London.

M. Du Bois (dew bwah), Mme Duval's friend from Paris. Insipid, he is the brunt of many of Captain Mirvan's practical jokes.

Polly Green, the supposed daughter of Sir John Belmont. Her mother, overhearing Villars' pledge that he would not part with the infant Evelina, delivered her own child to Sir John, as his daughter. Polly marries Macartney.

Mr. Branghton, Mme Duval's nephew, the keeper of a shop and rooming house where Macartney lives. The Branghtons are a gauche, quarrelsome family.

Tom, his son, an admirer of Evelina.

Biddy and

Polly, Branghton's daughters. Proud and conceited, they cause Evelina and Maria many anxious, unpleasant moments.

Mrs. Selwyn, a wealthy neighbor of Mr. Villars. She takes Evelina on a visit to Bristol Hot Wells.

Mrs. Beaumont (BOH-mont), the hostess of Clifton Hill, where Mrs. Selwyn and Evelina are entertained. Mrs. Beaumont would have Evelina believe that good qualities originate from pride rather than from principles.

Lady Louisa Larpent, Lord Orville's sister. Sullen and arrogant, she tries to divert her brother's attentions from Evelina. She attends the wedding willingly after Evelina's heritage has been established.

Lord Merton, a nobleman of recent title and Lady Louisa's fiancé. At Mrs. Beaumont's party, Merton becomes drunk and offends Evelina with his attentions.

Mr. Lovel, a fop who demeans Evelina by constant references to her background. His reckless driving in his phaeton makes for much conversation at social functions.

Mr. Smith, a neighbor of Branghton. Verbose, he irks Evelina with his prolonged speeches on her beauty and his devotion to her.

Jack Coverley, a gay young man who adds humor to the long philosophical conversations engaged in by party guests. His droll wit is seldom aimed at others and is never malicious.

Mrs. Clinton, Mr. Villars' housekeeper. She attends Evelina on her first visit away from Berry Hill, Dorsetshire.

The Misses Watkins, two sisters at Mrs. Beaumont's party. They chide Evelina in their contempt for her attractiveness to young men.

EVERY MAN IN HIS HUMOUR

Author: Ben Jonson (1573-1637)
First published: 1601; revised, 1605, 1616
Genre: Drama
Locale: London, England
Time: Late sixteenth century
Plot: Comedy

Knowell, an old gentleman. A kind and generous father, he is somewhat inclined to formality and overstrictness in governing his son. After being tricked into a ridiculous situation by his son Edward, Wellbred, and Brainworm, he good-humoredly forgives them and confesses that he has brought on his discomfiture by his own meddlesomeness.

Edward Knowell, Old Knowell's son. A bright young student, he troubles his father by too much attention to poetry, "that fruitless and unprofitable art." With his friend Wellbred, he finds enjoyment in the foibles of his associates. He is much taken with Kitely's lovely sister Bridget; with Wellbred's and Brainworm's help, he marries her.

Brainworm, Knowell's witty, mischievous servant. A literary descendant of the witty slave of Roman comedy, he is the prime mover of the dramatic action. Having, as he says, "a nimble soul," he appears in various disguises, aids his young master, and befools his old one. His wit arouses Justice Clement's admiration and earns his pardon.

Wellbred, Dame Kitely's younger brother. A gay, somewhat impish young bachelor, he writes to Edward Knowell an uninhibited letter that is intercepted and read by Old Knowell, who is shocked at its flippant disrespect. When the old gentleman endeavors to separate this baneful influence from his son, Wellbred, aided by Brainworm, tricks the old man. He also arranges Edward's marriage.

Captain Bobadill, a braggart captain. He is fond of quoting snatches of Elizabethan plays, particularly from *The Spanish Tragedy*. His fund of anecdotes of his pretended military career is boundless. He is foolish and cowardly but not vicious. One of the distinctions of the role is that Charles Dickens acted it in a nineteenth century performance of the play.

Master Matthew, a poetaster. A suitor of Mistress Bridget, he pours out plagiarized verse at the slightest excuse, pretending that it is extemporaneous. He is a great admirer of Captain Bobadill, who condescends to show him fencing skills and delivers critical comments on current plays.

Master Stephen, a country gull, the nephew of Old Knowell. A foolish, self-important youth, he admires Bobadill's bluster and far-fetched oaths and tries to imitate him. He provides much amusement for his Cousin Edward and Wellbred. His stupidity and dishonesty lead him into difficulties with Downright and the law.

Kitely, a pathologically jealous husband. Comically obsessed with the mistaken idea that his wife is faithless, he is ridiculous in his efforts to have her spied on and to guard her. His jealousy makes him an easy dupe for his brother-in-law Wellbred, who sends him on a wild-goose chase while Edward Knowell and Bridget are getting married. He is apparently cured of his jealousy by Justice Clement.

Dame Kitely, an attractive young woman who enjoys company. Her brother Wellbred sends her and her husband separately to Cob's house to catch each other in supposed unfaithful conduct.

Downright, a blunt country squire, Wellbred's half brother. Humorless and fiery-tempered, he irritates and insults many people, including Captain Bobadill, who threatens him and gets a beating in exchange for threats.

Justice Clement, an ebullient, jovial eccentric. Shrewd enough to see through the plots that have confused Old Knowell and Kitely, he is so much amused by Brainworm's pranks and so pleased with the young married couple that he asks forgiveness for them and obtains it. Although he is disgusted with the sham soldier, the sham poet, and the country gull, he indicates that they shall have clemency—in harmony with his name.

Oliver Cob, a water bearer, Captain Bobadill's landlord. He is a mixture of stupidity and native wit. After being beaten by Captain Bobadill, he sets the law on him. Discovering the quarrelsome gathering at his hovel, he believes Kitely's accusation that his wife is the bawd for Dame Kitely and Old Knowell and gives her a beating.

Tib, Cob's foolish wife. Angry and sullen after her undeserved beating, she finally allows Justice Clement to pacify her and accepts Cob again as her loving and obedient husband.

Mistress Bridget, Kitely's charming sister. A romantic heroine without sharply individualized traits, she is attracted to Edward Knowell and consents to her brother-in-law's plan for her to become Knowell's wife.

Thomas Cash, a foundling, Kitely's protégé and employee. He is caught in the middle of the mutual jealousies of Kitely and Dame Kitely, but he escapes damage.

Roger Formal, Justice Clement's gullible clerk, who allows Brainworm to get him drunk and steal his gown and his identity.

EVERY MAN OUT OF HIS HUMOUR

Author: Ben Jonson (1573-1637)
First published: 1600
Genre: Drama
Locale: Probably London
Time: Early seventeenth century
Plot: Comedy

Macilente, a malcontent. Morbidly envious of his fellows, he rages at the flourishing folly of the times and plays malicious tricks on his associates. When they have all been discomfited, he is cured of his envy.

Carlo Buffone, a foulmouthed jester. His indiscriminate verbal assaults lead to his having his mouth sealed by hot sealing wax in his beard.

Deliro, a wealthy, doting husband. He is finally driven out of his uxoriousness by suspicion that his wife is unfaithful.

Fallace, Deliro's wife and Sordido's daughter. Enamored of Fastidious Brisk, she behaves so foolishly that she loses her husband's love.

Sordido, a miserly farmer. He consults the almanac, hoards grain, and hopes for bad weather. A good harvest by his neighbors causes him to attempt suicide.

Sogliardo, Sordido's social-climbing brother. He pays Carlo to teach him to be a gentleman, but the lessons are unsuccessful.

Fungoso, Sordido's foolish son. He tries in vain to keep up with Fastidious Brisk's fashionableness.

Fastidious Brisk, an affected courtier. He changes the style of his clothes so rapidly that an imitator is always at least an hour out of fashion. He ends up in a debtors' prison.

Puntarvolo, an old-fashioned knight. He acts romantic scenes with his wife and wagers a sum at five to one odds that he, his wife, and his dog will return safely from a Continental tour. He loses when Macilente poisons his dog. He angrily seals Carlo's lips to silence his taunts.

Shift, a cheap rascal who pretends to be a criminal. He is too cowardly for real crime.

Saviolina, an affected court lady, Fastidious' mistress.

EVERYMAN

Author: Unknown
First extant version: 1508
Genre: Drama
Locale: Indeterminate
Time: Indeterminate
Plot: Morality

God, who has decided to have a reckoning of all men.

Death, who is summoned to receive God's instructions to search out Everyman. Death agrees to give Everyman some time to gather companions to make the journey with him.

Everyman, whom Death approaches and orders to make the long journey to Paradise to give an accounting for his life.

Good-Deeds, the one companion who can and will make the entire journey with Everyman. Everyman finds Good-Deeds too weak to stir, but after Everyman accepts penance, Good-Deeds is fit for the journey.

Knowledge, the sister of Good-Deeds. Knowledge offers to guide Everyman but cannot go with him into the presence of his maker.

Confession, who lives in the house of salvation. Confession gives penance to Everyman.

Discretion,
Strength,
Beauty, and
The Five Wits, companions who go part of the way with Everyman.

Fellowship,
Kindred, and
Goods, to whom Everyman turns for companions. All offer to help but refuse when they learn the nature of the journey.

A messenger, who appears in prologue to announce a moral play to the audience. He warns that people should look to the end of their lives.

A doctor, who appears at the end to remind the audience that only Good-Deeds will avail at the final judgment.

EXCELLENT WOMEN

Author: Barbara Pym (Mary Crampton, 1913-1980)
First published: 1952
Genre: Novel
Locale: London, England
Time: Late 1940's
Plot: Social

Mildred Lathbury, the protagonist and narrator, the daughter of a deceased clergyman. She works part-time for an organization that aids impoverished gentlewomen. A pleasant-looking, quiet woman in her early thirties, Mildred is one of the "excellent women" actively performing good works at St. Mary's Anglo-Catholic Church in London. She is very witty and shrewd, although both of these traits are evinced primarily through interior soliloquies and seldom show in her exterior manner toward others. Mildred has a mild romantic interest in Julian Malory, whose vanities and foibles she readily recognizes, and briefly develops an interest in Rocky Napier. Mildred embodies the excellent traits of unmarried women of a certain age who provide cohesion to churches and other small British communities while making clever observations on the banalities of these groups.

The Reverend Julian Malory, the forty-year-old rector of St. Mary's Church. A tall, ascetically handsome, vain man, Malory lives with his unmarried sister Winifred and delights in the affection and services proffered by the women of his parish. His devotion to high church frills and the Boys' Club shields him from complex interaction with women until he is smitten by love for Allegra Gray. Their engagement is broken off when Allegra tries to evict Winifred from his house, thereby causing Malory to retreat to his snug world of celibacy and incense.

Winifred Malory, a drab, forty-two-year-old unmarried woman who makes a home for her brother, Julian. A friend of Mildred, she is emotionally needy and becomes the victim of Allegra Gray's machinations before returning to the status quo with her brother at the end of the novel.

Allegra Gray, an attractive clergyman's widow in her mid-thirties who becomes Julian Malory's fiancée. Allegra attempts to detach Julian from his sister and an adoring throng of excellent women but finally gives up the unequal struggle and leaves the area.

Rockingham (Rocky) Napier, a demobilized naval officer and neighbor of Mildred Lathbury, living in the flat below hers. When his wife, Helena, leaves him temporarily, Rocky uses his facile charm to coax Mildred into helping him with household chores. Like Julian, Rocky is accustomed to collecting goods and services from women.

Helena Napier, an anthropologist and Rocky's wife. A slovenly and heedless, though pleasant, woman, Helena is devoted to her obscure anthropological studies and provides quite a contrast to her more social and dapper husband.

Everard Bone, an anthropologist, a colleague of Helena who evinces some interest in Mildred. A handsome, clever man of little warmth, Everard is seen by Mildred as similar to clerical types such as Julian, who expect female adulation as their due and give little in return. Mildred is not taken with Everard, although Helena is for a short period of time.

Esther Clovis, an administrative assistant for the learned society with which Helena Napier and Everard Bone are associated. A thin, middle-aged, colorless, and efficient woman, Esther is yet another excellent woman on whom men depend for assistance but not romance.

Dora Caldicote, a teacher and Mildred's good friend from their school days. Dora and Mildred's trip to their school reunion introduces the reader to the breeding ground of the excellent woman, the British girls' school.

— Isabel B. Stanley

THE EXECUTIONER'S SONG

Author: Norman Mailer (1923-)
First published: 1979
Genre: Novel
Locale: Utah, Oregon, and California
Time: April, 1976-January, 1977
Plot: New journalism

Gary Gilmore, the protagonist, a convicted murderer executed at the age of thirty-five for two brutal, unprovoked murders. Gilmore is a rough-featured criminal who has spent most of his life in prison. He is highly intelligent, with an artistic bent. He also has quasi-religious convictions. A complicated person, he shows little remorse for his crimes but insists that the state of Utah execute him for the murders he committed, even though he clearly is afraid to die. Gilmore's steadfast request that his death sentence be carried out makes him the focus of enormous publicity.

Nicole Baker Barrett, Gilmore's nineteen-year-old lover. She is a beautiful woman who already has been married twice. She does not seem to know how to control her life. She is nearly as self-destructive as Gilmore and almost succeeds in killing herself after she and Gilmore make a suicide pact. Although Gilmore manipulates her in various ways, there is no question that he loves her and that they share a bond that cannot be broken by his imprisonment. Nicole becomes Gilmore's inspiration, his reason for writing more than a thousand pages explaining his feelings about her and about his life.

Brenda Nicol, Gilmore's good-hearted cousin who helps to get him released from prison shortly before the period in which he kills two men. Brenda believes that if she can provide Gilmore with a secure environment and a good job, he will not lapse into criminal behavior. She soon discovers, however, that he cannot take responsibility for his own life and that he does not know how to cope with the stresses of his job and his desires for material possessions such as a fancy truck. Eventually, she cooperates with the authorities in tracking down and apprehending him.

Bessie Gilmore, Gilmore's loving mother. She comes from solid Mormon stock and tries to rear her son properly; however, she has misgivings about him even when he is a little boy. She has a premonition, in fact, that he will be executed. Through it all, mother and son remain loyal to each other, with Gilmore rejecting the probing questions of professionals who seek to trace his criminality to his upbringing. At the end of the novel, Bessie wonders what will become of her and her family, and whether her son's execution portends the fatal decline of the Gilmores.

Dennis Boaz, Gilmore's doggedly loyal lawyer. He is intent on providing Gilmore with precisely the representation he requests—even if that means that his client will die.

Lawrence Schiller, a photographer and producer, the main instigator of the Gilmore story. Schiller works feverishly to establish his rights to materials such as Gilmore's letters to Nicole, tape recordings, and other documents from which the author will work in assembling the book. In many ways, Schiller is the most problematic character. He views Gilmore as a commercial property, yet he also feels close to the convicted murderer and to his family and friends. His motivations, to say the least, are mixed, but it is clear that without his shrewd and indefatigable efforts, the novel of Gilmore's life story could not have been assembled or narrated in such depth.

— *Carl Rollyson*

THE EXILE TRILOGY
(Señas de identidad, Reinvindicación del conde Don Julián, and Juan sin tierra)

Author: Juan Goytisolo (1931-)
First published: 1966-1975
Genre: Novels

Locale: Spain, France, and Morocco
Time: The 1930's-1970's
Plot: Magical Realism

Marks of Identity, 1966

Álvaro Mendiola (AHL-vah-roh mehn-dee-OH-lah), a heavy-drinking, thirty-two-year-old photographer and maker of documentary films, loosely based on the author. After a voluntary exile of ten years in France, he returns to Spain to reconstruct his past, which is bound up inextricably with contemporary Spanish history. His conflict in this journey is his conflict with Spain—he can feel his full identity only in Spain, where he was born and reared, but he cannot live there, tolerating a Fascist regime and a narrow-minded, self-righteous culture. From his childhood home, he revisits his life. He was a pious child who grew into a spiritually indifferent adult, the son of a fading *hidalgo* family with a now-dissolved colonial estate in Cuba. He matures slowly, goes to school, and becomes associated loosely with political radicalism. More a poet than an activist, he is depressed and alienated by totalitarian culture and eventually leaves Spain to live and work in France. There, he meets Dolores, who becomes his lover. In 1958, he releases a documentary on emigration from Spain, which is impounded by the Spanish Civil Guard, on the ground that it is "anti-Spanish." Around this time, he experiences a fainting spell on a Paris street, the first indication of a heart condition that threatens his life and eventually prompts his return to Spain.

Antonio Ramírez Trueba (rah-MEE-rehs trew-EH-bah), a school friend of Álvaro, a Marxist law student who is arrested for having Communist sympathies and is imprisoned, then later kept under extended house arrest in his hometown. He functions as an alter ego to Álvaro.

Dolores, Álvaro's lover, the daughter of émigrés living in Mexico. She meets Álvaro in Paris at a boardinghouse, where Álvaro, who is eavesdropping, learns that she is behind on her rent. He pays her rent, she finds out, and after an initial misunderstanding, they become lovers. She cares for him during his convalescence in Barcelona.

Count Julian, 1970

Count Julián (hew-lee-AHN), also called **Ulbán**, **Ulyan**, and **Urbano**, a famous traitor and ally of the Moors, a figure from history. The author appropriates Julián's legendary persona and projects into it his intense hatred for Spain. Julián, in the novel, is an émigré living in Tangier, whence he launches an imaginary counter-*reconquista*, leading the Muslims back across the Straits of Gibraltar and into Spain. He stalks the boy Alvarito (the embodiment of Spain's ideal), rapes and murders him, disgraces him, makes a slave of him, blackmails him, causes him to commit suicide, and merges with him. Julián becomes more and more present as the werewolf-like alter ego of the author, as he wanders Tangier's streets and passes from image to image.

Don Álvaro Peranzules (peh-rahn-SEW-lehs), also called **Seneca** (SEH-neh-kah), a metaphorical figure representing Spain. He is a great poet and a propagandist for the Christian Gentleman, the intellectual and social straitjacket of Spanish culture. He is alternately a celebrated statesman and a skid-row Tangier pimp, plastically taking on all the qualities Julián despises as emblematic of Spain.

Alvarito (ahl-vah-REE-toh), a beautiful, aesthetic boy who undergoes the perfect pious, upright, and narrow Spanish upbringing. He corresponds to the narrator as a child. He aspires to sainthood and is a metaphorical figure for the hopes and ideals of Spanish culture. He will be seduced and destroyed by Julián, raped, murdered, driven to suicide, and enslaved. He is also the image of Julián as a child, his own innocent faith ravaged by the society that instilled it. He will merge with Julián at the end of a protracted psychic struggle.

Juan the Landless, 1975

The narrator, a voice speaking in space. The author has exiled himself from Fascist Spain and has exiled himself from the standards of European narrative, eschewing plot, character, and unities of time and place. The sourceless voice of this novel retains nothing of its own, except the driving force of the author's own outrage and his vital need for freedom. Juan the Landless is, for that reason, a characterless character, having divorced himself from all the contouring conditions that a point of origin, a culture, and a homeland impose. He moves further into the Muslim world of Morocco and closes his trilogy with a gradual shift from Spanish (here translated), with increasingly poor spelling, into transliterated Arabic, and then into Arabic characters.

— *Michael Cisco*

EXILES

Author: James Joyce (1882-1941)
First published: 1918
Genre: Drama
Locale: Merrion and Ranelagh, suburbs of Dublin
Time: 1912
Plot: Naturalism

Richard Rowan, an intellectually independent and emotionally self-reliant Irish writer. In his desire not to bind or be bound, even in love, he refuses ever to advise his common-law wife Bertha, or to ask anything of her. When she accuses him of neglect, he is faced with a conflict between personal integrity and love with its consequent feelings of guilt. His conflict is resolved when he can accept Bertha's desire to revive her relationship with Robert Hand, and Bertha is able to accept her lover's friendship with Beatrice Justice.

Bertha, Richard Rowan's common-law wife. Feeling neglected by her lover's refusal to influence her or to bind her in any way, and mistaking his friendship for Beatrice Justice for a love affair, she turns to Robert Hand, who has loved her in the past. Finally, she realizes that she can never betray Richard, but her expressed desire to meet Robert freely helps her to accept Richard's account of his relationship with Beatrice.

Robert Hand, a newspaper editor. He is dominated by the ideas and personality of Richard Rowan. Formerly in love with Bertha, he woos her again when she feels neglected by Richard. He falters when he faces the demand to accept moral responsibility.

Beatrice Justice, Richard Rowan's devoted and admiring friend.

Archie, the young son of Bertha and Richard Rowan.

EXIT THE KING
(Le Roi se meurt)

Author: Eugène Ionesco (1912-1994)
First published: 1963
Genre: Drama
Locale: The throne room of a king
Time: Modern era
Plot: Absurdist

Bérenger the First, the king. Costumed in a deep crimson coat and a crown, and carrying a scepter, Bérenger is both a human and a mythic figure. He stole fire from the gods, invented gunpowder, and split the atom. He built Rome, New York, Moscow, and Geneva and wrote tragedies and comedies under the name of Shakespeare. On this day, however, he is dying, and his kingdom and all nature are likewise coming to an end. Bérenger struggles mightily against death, passes through many stages, and finally fades into the mist.

Queen Marguerite, Bérenger's first wife. Queen Marguerite's cloak is a bit shabby and her expression is severe, for she is the older wife, no longer loved. She constantly forces the reality of death on Bérenger and assumes some of his power as she leads him to his death. She disappears into nothingness at the play's end.

Queen Marie, Bérenger's second wife, who is first in his affection. Younger and more beautiful than Marguerite, Queen Marie wears jewels, and her cloak comes from a high-class fashion designer. Marie loves Bérenger and implores him to live, but her power over him diminishes as he moves away from her toward death. Seemingly at Marguerite's command, Queen Marie is the first of the characters to disappear.

The Doctor, who is also the king's surgeon, executioner, bacteriologist, and astrologer. The Doctor is dressed in red, wears a pointed hat with stars on it, and carries a telescope. He joins with Queen Marguerite in insisting that Bérenger will die. As the death nears, however, he backs out of the room, bowing and scraping and excusing himself.

Juliette, the domestic help in the palace and also a registered nurse. An overworked and blunt-speaking serving woman, Juliette nevertheless shows sympathy for the dying king and tries to help him. "We'll stay with you," she affirms just before she disappears.

The Guard, who is stationed in the royal palace. An overworked and overly earnest figure carrying a halberd, the Guard turns all action into official proclamations. The Guard lists all the king's deeds and is exceedingly loyal. "I swear we'll never leave you, Majesty," he says just before he disappears.

— *Barbara Lounsberry*

EXODUS

Author: Leon Uris (1924-   )
First published: 1958
Genre: Novel
Locale: Primarily Cyprus, Palestine, and Israel
Time: Late 1940's
Plot: Historical

Barak Ben Canaan, also called **Jossi Rabinsky**, one of the pioneer settlers and political leaders in Palestine. Although he stands more than six feet tall and has bright red hair, he is a gentle giant with a quiet, meditative personality. Growing up Jewish in a Russian ghetto, he quickly learns how to defend himself physically, but he prefers to exercise nonviolent methods whenever possible. His restraint and wisdom become powerful tools that help him negotiate with the United States for Israel's statehood and, later, with individual countries for arms.

Akiva, also called **Yakov Rabinsky**, Barak's younger brother, another pioneer settler and military leader in Palestine. Although considerably smaller than Barak physically, Akiva is easily stirred and fights at the slightest provocation.

He even carries stones in his pockets to throw at people who threaten him. When Simon Rabinsky, his father, is killed in a riot, Akiva stabs to death the man he believes is personally responsible. Barak arrives too late to prevent the murder, but he is observed at the scene and is accused of the crime. The brothers flee Russia together and walk across the continent to Palestine. As other Jewish settlers arrive, Barak and Akiva organize them into communal kibbutzim. Barak barters with the Arabs for land while Akiva develops a strike force called the Guardsmen. Akiva's tendency toward violence eventually results in a fifteen-year silence between the two brothers, and only when Akiva is about to be hanged by British soldiers does Barak attempt to help him.

Ari Ben Canaan, a Palmach military leader. Like his father, Barak, Ari is a handsome man more than six feet tall. Cunning and resourceful, he serves as an invaluable leader for the Jewish secret army, the Palmach, by smuggling refugees and weapons into Palestine in addition to planning and instituting brilliant military strategies. As a boy, he is taught by his father how to defend himself by using a bullwhip; he is also told never to use the weapon in anger or revenge but only in defense. Ari follows that advice throughout his life, as evidenced by his joining the Palmach, the Jewish army, rather than the Guardsmen, his uncle's terrorist group. He becomes so dedicated to his work, however, that he ignores his emotions and refuses to acknowledge his grief for his dead friends or to proclaim his love for Kitty Fremont.

Katherine (Kitty) Fremont, an American nurse. Having blonde hair and a sad smile, she is an attractive middle-aged woman mourning the deaths of her husband, Tom Fremont, and their only daughter, Sandra Fremont. She meets Ari on Cyprus, and he persuades her to use her nursing skills with the children of a Jewish internment camp who are trapped on the island. While trying to decide if she should accept the position, Kitty meets Karen Hansen Clement, a young Jewish refugee who reminds her of her dead daughter, Sandra. Wanting to adopt Karen and whisk her away to America, Kitty follows her to Palestine, and together they work with children who have survived the German concentration camps. By Karen's example, Kitty rediscovers a selfless love within herself and is able to overcome her grief. As one of the only Christian characters in the novel, she provides a commentary on Jewish-Arab tensions.

Karen Hansen Clement, a Jewish refugee and Palmach soldier. Unselfish and tender, she is first depicted as a child giving her doll to her father to protect him. Smuggled out of Germany before the beginning of World War II, Karen is forever separated from her family but is quickly adopted by the Clements in Denmark. They rear her as their only child and attempt to provide a stable and loving home for her, but, after the war, she travels alone throughout Europe in an attempt to locate her original family. She discovers the atrocities committed in Germany against the Jews and against her relatives in particular, and she decides to live as a free Jew in Palestine. During her trek, she encounters Kitty Fremont and, from her, acquires formal nursing training. They live together in Gan Dafna, an orphanage, until Karen decides that she can be of greater assistance in Nahal Midbar, a frontier settlement. Her brutal murder by Arabs on Passover night serves as the final horror of the novel.

Dov Landau, a Jewish survivor of the Warsaw ghetto rebellion. A small-framed blond youth, he is deeply embittered by the time he meets Karen in an internment camp on Cyprus. At ten years of age, he is the youngest member of the Redeemers, an underground organization in Poland that attempts to fight Nazi occupation. From the Redeemers, Dov learns how to forge passports and to survive in sewers, two skills that help save his life on numerous occasions. When captured by Nazis during World War II, he escapes death in Auschwitz by forging money for the German government. After the war, he joins the Maccabees, a terrorist group in Palestine, and is instrumental in several raids against various Arab factions. Only through Karen's tenderness and promises is Dov able to forget his wrath and to find goodness in his own life.

Jordana Ben Canaan, a Palmach leader in Gan Dafna, a Jewish orphanage. With flaming red hair like her father, Barak, she is also tall and shapely, but as a Palmach leader, she has no time for feminine frills. Immediately, she resents Kitty's presence in the orphanage, viewing her as an outsider who competes for Ari's attention.

Bruce Sutherland, a British military commander. With a roll around his middle and a whitening of his temples, at the age of fifty-five Brigadier Sutherland resigns from his command post in Cyprus and moves to Palestine. Having led one of the first armies into Bergen-Belsen, a German concentration camp, and then been assigned to maintain peace at the internment camp in Cyprus, the half-Jewish general suffers from chronic nightmares.

— *Coleen Maddy*

THE EXPEDITION OF HUMPHRY CLINKER

Author: Tobias Smollett (1721-1771)
First published: 1771
Genre: Novel
Locale: England, Scotland, and Wales
Time: Mid-eighteenth century
Plot: Social satire

Matthew Bramble, a Welsh bachelor who, while traveling in England and Scotland, keeps track of his affairs at Brambleton Hall through correspondence with Dr. Richard Lewis, his physician and adviser. Bramble, an eccentric and a valetudinarian, writes at great length of his ailments—the most pronounced being gout and rheumatism—and gives detailed accounts of his various attacks. With the same fervor that he discusses personal matters—health and finances—he launches into tirades on laws, art, mores, funeral customs, and the social amenities of the various communities he and his party pass through on their travels. As various members of the entourage become attracted to one another and are married, and the group plans to return to Brambleton Hall, Bramble senses that his existence has been sedentary. In his newfound interest of hunting, he changes from an officious, cantankerous attitude toward the affairs of others. He writes Lewis that had he always had something to occupy his time (as he has in hunting), he would not have inflicted such long, tedious letters on his friend and adviser.

Tabitha Bramble, his sister. She is the female counterpart of her brother in telling her correspondents of the annoyances of everyday life. Hers is a more personal world than her brother's, people being of more importance than ideas and things. With little likelihood of a change in interests, Tabitha does return home a married woman.

Jerry Melford, the nephew of Matthew and Tabitha, whose letters to a classmate at Cambridge, where Jerry is regularly a student, give a more objective account of incidents of travel and family. With the articulateness of the scholar and the verve of youth, Jerry describes the lighter side of everyday happenings. In his final correspondence, he admits to his friend that in the midst of matrimonial goings-on he has almost succumbed to Cupid. However, fearing that the girl's qualities—frankness, good humor, handsomeness, and a genteel fortune—may not be permanent, he passes off his thought as idle reflections.

Lydia Melford, his sister. The recipient of her letters, Miss Letitia Willis, is the object of Jerry's "idle reflections." Lydia, just out of boarding school, is concerned in her letters with the styles and movement of the young in various stops the party makes. Her primary concern, however, is with the presence or absence of young men. Lydia, it is learned, is carrying on a correspondence with a young actor, with Miss Willis acting as a go-between. A duel between the young man and Jerry is averted, but he continues to show up at various stages of the journey in various disguises. Lydia marries him after he has proved himself a young man of rank and wealth.

Winifred (Win) Jenkins, the maid, and the fifth of the letter writers whose correspondence makes up the story. Her correspondent is another servant at Brambleton Hall. Winifred's spelling exceeds all other known distortions of the English language. She sees people riding in "coxes," visits a zoo where she sees "hillyfents," looks forward to getting back "huom," and closes her letters with "Yours with true infection." Yet such ineptness does not hamper her personal achievements; able to make herself attractive, she is won by the natural son of Matthew Bramble. In the last letter in the book, Win makes her position clear to her former fellow servant, for she plans to return home as a member of the family rather than as a domestic. She reminds her correspondent that "Being, by God's blessing, removed to a higher spear, you'll excuse my being familiar with the lower servants of the family; but as I trust you'll behave respectful, and keep a proper distance, you may always depend upon the good will and purtection of Yours W. Loyd."

Humphry Clinker, the country youth later revealed as Matthew Loyd, the illegitimate son of Matthew Bramble. Clinker, a poor, ragged ostler, is taken on the trip by Bramble after a clumsy coachman has been dismissed. Clinker proves to be the soul of good breeding, a devout lay preacher, and a hero in saving Bramble from drowning. Quite by accident, he hears Bramble addressed as Matthew Loyd, at which time Clinker produces a snuff box containing proof of his parentage. Bramble explains his having used the name Loyd as a young man for financial reasons and accepts Clinker as his son when "the sins of my youth rise up in judgment against me." Clinker, under his legal name, marries Winifred Jenkins.

George Dennison, the young actor who successfully follows the party in pursuit of Lydia's hand. George has masqueraded as an actor, Wilson, to avoid an unwelcome marriage being forced on him by his parents. His status in rank and wealth are proved by his father's and Bramble's recognition of each other as former classmates at Oxford.

Lieutenant Obadiah Lismahago, a Scottish soldier who joins the party at Durham. Lismahago's shocking stories of the atrocities he suffered as a captive of the American Indians entertain the party and win the devotion of Miss Tabitha. Lismahago's manner of doing things is best illustrated by his wedding present to Tabitha: a fur cloak of American sables, valued at eighty guineas.

Mr. Dennison and

Mrs. Dennison, country gentry and George Dennison's parents.

EXPLOSION IN A CATHEDRAL
(El siglo de las luces)

Author: Alejo Carpentier (1904-1980)
First published: 1962
Genre: Novel
Locale: Caribbean islands and Europe
Time: 1789-1808
Plot: Social realism

Victor Hugues (ewg), a robust self-made French entrepreneur and revolutionary living in the Caribbean. He is a man of action who likes to be in charge, whether it is in the Havana household he enters on a trip from his home in Saint-Domingue (future Haiti) in 1789, or, later, as an agent of various French governments in Caribbean colonies. Victor helps organize the business of his recently orphaned young Cuban hosts and familiarizes them with the latest liberal ideas. An opportunist, he adapts to the successive stages of the French Revolution, from initial libertarianism through various phases of repression. He is modeled on the historical personage of the same name.

Sofía (soh-FEE-ah), a wealthy young woman brought up with her brother, Carlos, and male cousin Esteban in a wealthy Havana home situated next door to the retail establishment of her father, who has died just before the action of the novel begins. A spirited woman, she becomes imbued with Enlightenment ideals and stays loyal to them throughout. Sofía's maturation into womanhood is encouraged by Victor's advances, to which she eventually yields before he leaves Cuba. She breaks off their later intimate relationship in French Guiana because she is disgusted with Victor's repression of the black people there. Sofía finally goes to Spain to be near Esteban, who loves her and has been imprisoned there. At

Sofía's urging, they join the revolutionary crowd on the day of the Napoleonic massacre in early May, 1808, and are not heard from again.

Esteban (ehs-TEH-bahn), the initially frail, asthmatic younger cousin of Sofía and Carlos who from early childhood has lived with them. He has a penchant for the imaginative and the fantastic. After his cure, Esteban blossoms into an inquisitive, intellectual young man who is, however, never as independent and self-willed as Sofía. In the Caribbean and in France, under Victor's tutelage, he becomes an enthusiast of the revolution. Later, he becomes disillusioned when the revolution and Victor lose their ideals. Esteban's experiences make up the longest part of the novel. He loves Sofía. He saves her when she is pursued because of her beliefs by the authorities in Cuba and is finally united with her in Madrid.

Carlos, Sofía's brother, a teenage boy when his father dies. His strongest boyhood interest is the flute. When he is orphaned, he is obliged to replace his father in the retail business, for which he initially has no taste. Carlos develops into a successful businessman and over the years retains his enthusiasm for the ideals of the French Revolution. It falls to him, traveling in Madrid, to piece together the fate of Sofía and Esteban from accounts of those who knew them there.

Dr. Ogé (oh-HEH), a broad-shouldered mulatto from Saint-Domingue who is a friend of Victor Hugues. Ogé combines traditional beliefs in biblical myths and mystical doctrines with the progressive liberal credo. He practices folk medicine and cures Esteban of his asthma. A freemason like Hugues, Ogé has to leave Cuba with him to escape monarchist repression. Returning to Port-au-Prince, Ogé learns that his brother Vincent (a historical figure) has been killed by the French in the 1789 rebellion there. Ogé encourages Hugues and Esteban to leave Saint-Domingue for their own safety, but his farewell embrace is stiffer than usual: White and black will no longer mix there.

Don Cosme (kohs-MEH), who is also called the **Executor** because of his role in looking after the financial affairs of Sofía and Carlos' deceased father. He initially acts as guardian for the orphaned young people but is effectively displaced in this surrogate father's role by Victor. Don Cosme is a conventional religionist and monarchist, opposed to Hugues's progressivism. When Carlos takes over the retail business, he dismisses Don Cosme, replacing him with Jorge.

Jorge (HOHR-heh), a slim, handsome Cuban of Irish descent, educated in England, who marries Sofía and works in the family business with Carlos. He brings some decorum into the hitherto disorderly household. Jorge falls ill in an epidemic and, despite his fragile constitution, fights desperately for weeks against fever and asphyxia, which finally kill him.

Caleb Dexter, a North American sea captain and master of the *Arrow*, a freemason and a friend of Hugues and Ogé. The captain is a realist: Against the lovesick Esteban's pleas, Dexter respects Sofía's wishes and agrees to take her from Cuba to French Guiana to be with Hugues after her husband dies.

— *John Deredita*

THE EYE OF THE STORM

Author: Patrick White (1912-1990)
First published: 1973
Genre: Novel
Locale: Sydney, Australia, and Brumby Island, near Australia
Time: The first seventy years of the twentieth century
Plot: Psychological realism

Elizabeth Hunter, once a beautiful and socially poised woman, now in her eighties and slowly dying in her mansion on Moreton Drive in Sydney, Australia. Elizabeth, the wealthy widow of a successful grazier, or sheep rancher, has dominated people all of her life through the force of her charm and personality. Various affairs in her younger days inflicted emotional hurt on her solid and unimaginative husband, and her two children, Dorothy and Basil, have led rather emotionally impoverished lives, feeling more resentment than love toward their mother. A transcendent religious experience during a hurricane when she was stranded on Brumby Island has transformed Elizabeth's vision, however, and as she approaches death, she finds some love and understanding from her night nurse, Mary de Santis.

The Princess de Lascabanes (lahs-kah-bah-NAY), formerly **Dorothy Hunter**, Elizabeth's daughter. She has lived her life in the shadow of her charming and socially accomplished mother, and, despite a marriage to a rather seedy continental aristocrat, she remains unfulfilled and in middle age has become peevish and unattractive. In her inner life, she is haunted by unhappy memories of being bested in competitions with her mother (as when she lost the chance to enjoy a flirtation with a Norwegian biologist because of his infatuation with Elizabeth's charm in the Brumby Island incident). For solace, she flees to an obsessive reading of Stendhal's *The Charterhouse of Parma*, in which she can enjoy the fantasy of imagining herself as the duchess of Sansererina. To find revenge, she schemes to have her aged mother placed in a nursing home in Sydney. Unlike her brother, Sir Basil, she feels little remorse over her bitter resentment of her widowed mother.

Sir Basil Hunter, a famous Shakespearean actor who finds himself in middle age facing crises both in his career and in his emotional life. Although Sir Basil longs to play King Lear as the crowning performance of his career, his recent efforts have been panned by critics, and he faces financial troubles as well as a fear of sexual impotence. His mother's fortune would help him finance his own production of William Shakespeare's *King Lear*, but he is perceptive enough to realize that having her committed to a Sydney nursing home probably would hasten her death. Basil's psychological awareness enables him to perceive the blend of love and pretense in Elizabeth's expressions of affection for him. Unlike Dorothy, he suffers from an ambivalent combination of love and hate for his talented mother. On a sentimental return to his family home in the grazing country, Basil places his bare feet in the mud in a momentary surrender to childhood memory. Obsessed by loneliness and narcissism, he commits a perverse act of incest with his embittered sister while they spend the night in the house where they lived as children. Basil and Dorothy's incestuous night seals an unholy bargain between them: Although committing Elizabeth to a nursing home without the care of Sister de Santis will be tantamount to murder, it will gratify their need for revenge.

Flora Manhood, Elizabeth's day nurse. She is a pretty young woman from the working class who feels both pity and resentment toward her employer. A child of the 1960's, the restless Flora longs for a satisfying relationship with her lover, Col, who, she fears, wants to dominate her. As a reaction, she moves, somewhat unconsciously, toward a lesbian relationship with a friend, until she realizes with a shock where this friendship is leading. The death of Elizabeth, near the end of the novel, shocks her and raises her to a new level of moral awareness.

Lotte Lippmann, Elizabeth's cook. Lotte is a German Jewish emigrant who survived various tragedies in Europe. She loves Elizabeth, much as the night nurse does, but she is somewhat inarticulate in expressing her feelings.

Arnold Wyburd, Elizabeth's solicitor, an aging friend of the family who has served Elizabeth for many years. In his youth, he was fortunate enough to be chosen as one of her lovers for a short time. In his old age, he tries to protect his elderly employer's interests and to resist, in his dry and discreet way, the efforts of her two children to have her committed to a nursing home.

Mary de Santis, Elizabeth's night nurse. Mary is both a loyal and faithful servant and a loving friend. An emigrant from Greece, Mary cherishes memories of her parents' love for each other and of the somber and tragic character of the icons in Greek Orthodox churches. Her devout Greek Orthodox faith has sustained her through some difficult times. A rather plain middle-aged woman, she continues to lead a rich inner life. Aware that Elizabeth has been influenced by a powerful mystical experience, Mary sees Elizabeth's death as both tragic and an initiation into a form of religious mystery. When Elizabeth dies of a heart attack at her home, Mary is at first numbed by grief. On her final morning at the mansion, however, an encounter with the pigeons in the yard takes on numinous overtones, and she experiences a moment of epiphany that affirms her acceptance of life and death.

— *Edgar L. Chapman*

EYELESS IN GAZA

Author: Aldous Huxley (1894-1963)
First published: 1936
Genre: Novel

Locale: London, southern France, and Mexico
Time: 1902-1935
Plot: Social realism

Anthony Beavis, a sociologist who, for much of his life, intellectualizes everything and puts his energy into his scholarly work. In 1933, he realizes that he loves Helen Ledwidge, his mistress, whom he has not allowed to get emotionally involved with him. Anthony's detachment stems partly from guilt he feels at contributing to his friend Brian's suicide. Brian killed himself after learning that his fiancée, Joan, fell in love with Anthony after Anthony kissed her on a bet. From a lonely, motherless schoolboy, Anthony turns into a pacifist who is trying to live according to love, courage, self-sacrifice, and patience. Anthony has changed after meeting James Miller, a charismatic doctor and anthropologist.

Helen Ledwidge, a woman with clear gray eyes, ruddy brown curls, and an embittered expression. When she was young, Helen had an abortion after an affair with Gerry Watchett, her mother's secret lover. Helen later marries Hugh Ledwidge, who wants her to be not a good wife or a sexual partner but a poetic muse. Helen is squeamish about raw meat, sick kittens, and blood and gore. When a dog falls out of an airplane onto her and Anthony, who are naked on a rooftop, she breaks off the affair with him. After leaving Anthony, she falls in love with Ekki Giesebrecht, an idealistic communist who is kidnapped back to Germany by Nazis. Helen says that when he was with her, Ekki made her kind, truthful, and happy. At the end of the novel, Helen and Anthony are friends.

Mary Amberley, Helen's mother. She has spent her life as a pleasure-seeker. She began a two-year affair with Anthony when he was twenty years old and she was twenty-nine. Mary dared Anthony to kiss Joan, Brian's fiancée, and she threatened not to talk to him again if he failed to do it. Her favorite lover was Gerry Watchett, who mismanaged her money for his gain. With her money gone, living in Paris, she ends up drinking and taking morphine, telling lies, and living in squalor.

James Miller, a doctor and an anthropologist. He is Anthony's "Jesus-avatar," according to Mark Staithes. James is a pacifist who lives out his nonviolent principles, even when a heckler punches him repeatedly. James has a Gestalt philosophy, and he advocates meditation. When Mark's leg becomes gangrenous, James amputates it, operating in the bush.

Brian Foxe, A stammerer, Anthony's best friend at boarding school and afterward. Sensitive and having the courage of his convictions, Brian is kind even to the school's scapegoats such as Goggles Ledwidge. Brian loves Joan, but he wants to be chaste, so he tries to stay away from her. He usually resists kissing her. When Anthony reads Brian's suicide letter, it reveals that Brian thought of himself as a collection of fragments that he was tired of holding together.

John Beavis, Anthony's father, a philologist and a pedant. His wife Maisie dies young, and he ritualizes his grief. After a few years, however, he marries Pauline Gannet, and they have two daughters. He also grieves when his brother James dies. When he is not elected president of the philological society, he begins to look like an old man.

Joan Thursley, the daughter of a poor vicar. Slender and shy, she likes bird-watching, as Brian does. Joan has bright hazel eyes and a wide mouth. Engaged to Brian, she does not understand why he does not want to kiss her and why he makes her feel guilty.

Mark Staithes, a short, broad-shouldered man with a deeply lined face and a savage manner. As a schoolmate of Anthony, Mark was the head of the football eleven and a bully. Mark, who once wrote advertisements, buys a perfume factory. He takes up asceticism for its own sake. He goes to San Cristobal to risk his life and to help his friend Don Jorges try to effect a coup d'état in a Mexican province.

Hugh Ledwidge, Helen's husband. He writes *The Invisible Lover* about his idealized love for her, but he prefers her at a distance. He enjoys writing letters to her but he has a horror of her body, especially when she is sick.

Gerry Watchett, a brutal aristocrat who lost his money. He was a college acquaintance of Anthony. Gerry is a virtuoso lover, Mary's favorite. He seduces Helen when she is young and gets her pregnant. Gerry gets a commission for steering Mary into bad stock purchases.

Ekki Giesebrecht, a young man with pale flaxen hair and a ruddy open face who is a friend of Hugh Ledwidge. He is an idealistic communist, very serious about his mission. He becomes Helen's lover but is betrayed by the journalist Holtzmann and kidnapped from Basel, Switzerland. He probably is killed.

James Beavis, the brother of Anthony's father. He converts to Catholicism before his death. He is a homosexual who cannot admit that truth to himself. A first-rate actuary, he is happy during the war, visiting wounded soldiers. He dies of an inoperable tumor.

— *Kate M. Begnal*

EZRA

Author: Bernard Kops (1926-   )
First published: 1980
Genre: Drama
Locale: Italy and Washington, D.C.
Time: 1945-1958, with flashbacks
Plot: Expressionism

Ezra Pound, the internationally recognized poet. During the thirteen-year span of the play's action, which begins when he is sixty years old, he becomes increasingly irrational and, eventually, unhinged. He is trapped in a prison that represents both his real prison (and, later, madhouse) and the limitations of a practical and political world on the imagination of a genius poet. His expansive temperament and misguided trust in Benito Mussolini (whose country he had adopted), together with his love of classical Roman culture, collide with the political realities of World War II, causing him to broadcast anti-Semitic sentiments in support of the Axis war effort. He relives his arrest, trial, and acquittal (on grounds of insanity). The other characters are figments of his deranged mind, visiting him in moments of decreasing lucidity, from his imprisonment in Italy as a traitor to the United States to his release from an American insane asylum.

Antonio Vivaldi, the eighteenth century composer. In Ezra's imagination, Vivaldi is a companion to Mussolini. Musical but taken by dance-hall ditties of the war era, he represents a purer, more artistically viable time that, although Ezra fails to realize it, passed away long ago. His music "The Four Seasons" underscores the action. The actor playing the role transforms himself into other characters, including Amprim, the interrogator, and several comic and musical figures from the period.

Benito Mussolini, called **Il Duce**, the dictator of Italy during World War II. Mussolini is portrayed as personal, almost chummy, his image filtered through Ezra's fantasies into a playful, childish companion dedicated to returning Italy to its Golden Age. He begins the play dead, hanging upside down with his mistress, but addresses Ezra and takes on, with Vivaldi, several comic and musical characters such as Abbott and Costello and the Andrews Sisters.

Claretta Petacci, Mussolini's mistress, an exotic seductress who also transforms herself into Ezra's lover, Olga, and their child, Mary. She represents young sexual females in the lives of Ezra and Mussolini.

Dorothy Pound, Ezra's wife. Solicitous and forgiving, she champions her husband against his detractors. She represents the faithful, unquestioning love of the mother and wife, and she is with Ezra at the play's end.

— *Thomas J. Taylor*

F

A FABLE

Author: William Faulkner (1897-1962)
First published: 1954
Genre: Novel

Locale: The Western Front in France
Time: 1918
Plot: Allegory

The Corporal, a Christlike soldier. Accompanied by his twelve squad members, the Corporal brings about a cease fire along the entire Western front by preaching peace on earth. His story bears a strong yet often subtle resemblance to the life of Christ, the Passion, and the Crucifixion as events unfold that correspond in some degree to the birth, the betrayal, the denial, the Last Supper, and the death of Christ. Refusing an offer of freedom, the Corporal is executed between two murderers and buried at his sister's farm. Shellfire destroys the grave, but, ironically, his body is recovered and placed in the Unknown Soldier's tomb. These events suggest resurrection and immortality of a sort.

The Marshal, commander-in-chief of the Allied armies in France. As a young man stationed in the Middle East, he had seduced a woman and fathered a son who turns out to be the Corporal. The old man never seems surprised by the turn of events and apparently is omniscient. He offers the Corporal an opportunity to escape but must order his execution when he refuses.

General Gragnon, the French division commander. When his regiment refuses to attack the German line, he arrests the entire three thousand and insists upon his own arrest. While in prison, he is executed by a brutal American soldier named Buchwald.

The Quartermaster General, the Marshal's former fellow student. After the Corporal's execution, he loses faith in the cause for which the Marshal stands.

The Runner, a former officer. Sympathizing with the Corporal's aims, he is crippled in a surprise barrage while fraternizing with the Germans. At the Marshal's funeral, he throws a medal obtained at the Corporal's grave at the caisson and shouts his derision and defiance.

Marthe, the Corporal's younger half sister.

Marya, the Corporal's feeble-minded half sister.

Polchek, the soldier in the Corporal's squad who betrays him.

Pierre Bouc, the soldier in the Corporal's squad who denies him.

The Corporal's Wife, a former prostitute.

Buchwald, the American soldier who executes General Gragnon.

The Reverend Tobe Sutterfield, an African American preacher.

David Levine, a British flight officer who commits suicide.

FACE

Author: Cecile Pineda (1942-   )
First published: 1985
Genre: Novel

Locale: Brazil
Time: Probably the 1980's
Plot: Psychological realism

Helio Cara, the protagonist and central character of the novel. Helio starts out in the novel as a barber in the huge Brazilian city of Rio de Janeiro. By no means a successful or extraordinarily happy man, Helio nevertheless has the rudiments of life: a job, a girlfriend, and basic acceptance by others. All of this is jeopardized when he falls off a cliff and severely damages his face. Forced to wear a white handkerchief over his face to conceal injuries that other people find repulsive, Helio at first tries to go on with his life as if nothing had happened, but his coworkers and his girlfriend repudiate him, unable to adjust to or to cope with his injury. Helio petitions the city's medical establishment for aid, but he is told that although his face can be physically repaired, his medical insurance will not cover the cost of making him look attractive once again. Helio decides to return to the town where he was born. Motivated to a new brilliance, Helio self-reliantly proceeds to reconstruct his own face using a mixture of medical guides, folk medicine, and the ingenuity of his own mind. At the end of the novel, Helio has repaired the damage to himself, both physical and psychological, and is ready to meet the challenge of living in society once again.

Lula, Helio's mistress, who had been living with him at the time of the accident. Lula leaves Helio even though she still has some tenderness for him; the burden of coping with his injury is too much for her.

Luis and

Mario, Helio's coworkers at the barbershop. After the accident, they feel empathy for him that is a vestige of their former camaraderie, but they realize that because of the prejudices of their customers, Helio cannot be kept on at the shop.

Cardoso, a barber. Helio's former boss at the shop, Cardoso had taught the younger man to read and had generally acclimated him to the ways of the overwhelming metropolis of Rio de Janeiro.

Senhora Cara, Helio's mother. She dies just before the accident. Helio is bitter toward her for having remarried shortly after his father's death.

Julião, Helio's stepfather. Helio resents Julião for taking the place of his father. Long before Helio's face is injured, he suffers psychically from the trauma of his mother's marriage to Julião.

Godoy, a doctor and hospital administrator. Godoy tells Helio of the insuperable obstacles facing his effort to have his face repaired courtesy of government funding. Later, after Helio has succeeded in convincingly reconstructing his face, Godoy sends Helio a letter at his shack in the hinterlands, presumably offering further help in the treatment.

THE FAERIE QUEENE

Author: Edmund Spenser (c. 1552-1599)
First published: Books 1-3, 1590; books 4-6, 1596
Genre: Poetry
Locale: England
Time: The Arthurian Age
Plot: Allegory

Gloriana, the Faerie Queene, an idealized portrait of Queen Elizabeth. Although she does not appear in the extant portion of the poem, many of the knights set out on their quests from her court, and they often praise her virtue and splendor.

Prince Arthur, the legendary British hero, who represents Magnificence, the perfection of all virtues. He rides in search of Gloriana, who had appeared to him in a vision, and, on his way, aids knights in distress.

The Red Cross Knight, the hero of book 1, in which he represents both England's patron, Saint George, and Christian man in search of holiness. He sets out confidently to rescue Una's parents from the dragon of evil, but he is attacked by forces of sin and error that drive him to the point of suicide. He is restored in the House of Holiness by the teachings and offices of the church and, refreshed by a fountain and a tree, symbolizing the sacraments of baptism and communion, he triumphs in his three-day combat with the dragon.

Una (EW-nah), the daughter of the King and Queen of the West, Adam and Eve; she personifies truth and the church. She advises her knight wisely, but she cannot protect him from himself. Deserted, she is aided by a lion and a troop of satyrs. She is finally restored to the Red Cross Knight, who is betrothed to her after his victory over the dragon.

The Dwarf, her companion, Common Sense.

Error, the Red Cross Knight's first adversary, a monster who lives in the wandering wood.

Archimago (ahr-chih-MAH-goh), a satanic figure who uses many disguises in his attempts to lure the knights and ladies of the poem into sin and disaster.

Duessa (dew-EHS-seh), his accomplice, whose attractive appearance hides her real hideousness. She represents variously Falsehood, the Roman Catholic Church, and Mary, Queen of Scots.

Sans Foy,

Sans Loy, and

Sans Joy, Saracen knights who attack Una and her knight.

Fradubio (frah-DEW-bee-oh), a knight betrayed by Duessa and transformed into a tree.

Kirkrapine (KURK-rah-peen), a church robber, slain by Una's lion when he tries to enter the cottage where she has taken refuge.

Abessa (AH-beh-sah), his mistress.

Corceca (KOHR-seh-kah), her blind mother.

Lucifera (lew-SIH-feh-rah), the mistress of the House of Pride.

Malvenu (MAHL-veh-new), her porter.

Vanity, her usher.

Night, the mother of falsehood, to whom Duessa appeals for help.

Aesculapius (ehs-kew-LAY-pee-uhs), the physician of the gods.

Sylvanus (SIHL-vah-nuhs), the leader of the satyrs who rescue Una from Sans Loy.

Satyrane (SA-tih-rayn), a valiant, gentle knight who is half nobleman and half satyr.

Despair, an emaciated creature who drives warriors to suicide with his sophistic recitals of their sins.

Trevisan (TREH-vih-san), one of his intended victims.

Dame Coelia (CHEE-lee-ah), a virtuous matron who lives in the House of Holiness.

Fidelia (fih-DAY-lee-ah),

Speranza (speh-RAN-zah), and

Charissa (cha-RIHS-sah), her daughters, Faith, Hope, and Charity.

Contemplation, a holy hermit who gives the Red Cross Knight a vision of the City of God, then sends him back into the world to complete his quest.

Guyon (GWEE-on), the Knight of Temperance, the sternest of the Spenserian heroes, who must violently destroy Acrasia's power and all of its temptations that lead men to intemperance.

Palmer, his faithful companion, who stands for Reason or Prudence.

Acrasia (ah-KRAY-zee-ah), the Circe-like mistress of the Bower of Bliss. She lures men to their ruin in her world of debilitating luxuriance and turns them into animals.

Amavia (ah-MAY-vee-ah), the desolate widow of one of her victims.

Ruddymane, her baby, whose hands cannot be cleansed of his dying mother's blood.

Medina (meh-DEE-nah),

Perissa (peh-RIHS-sah), and

Elissa, sisters who personify the mean, the deficiency, and the excess of temperance.

Sir Huddibras (HEW-dee-brahs), a malcontent, Elissa's lover.

Braggadocio (brahg-ga-DOH-chee-oh), a vainglorious braggart who masquerades as a knight on Guyon's stolen horse.

Trompart, his miserly companion.

Belphoebe (behl-FEE-bee), a virgin huntress, reared by the goddess Diana, who cannot respond to the devotion offered by Prince Arthur's squire, Timias. She is another of the figures conceived as a compliment to Elizabeth.

Furor, a churlish fellow whom Guyon finds furiously beating a helpless squire.

Occasion, his mother, a hag.

Phedon (FAY-don), the maltreated squire, who falls into Furor's hands through his jealousy of his lady, Pryene, and his friend Philemon.

Pyrochles (PIH-roh-kleez) and

Cymochles (SIH-mah-kleez), intemperate knights defeated by Guyon.

Atin (AT-ihn), Pyrochles' servant.

Phaedria (FAY-dree-ah), a coquette who lures knights to her island, where she lulls them into forgetfulness of their quests.

Mammon, the god of riches, who sits in rusty armor surveying his hoard of gold.

Philotime (fih-LOH-tih-mee), his daughter, who holds the golden chain of ambition.

Alma, the soul, mistress of the castle of the body where Guyon and Prince Arthur take refuge.

Phantastes (FAN-tahs-teez) and

Eumnestes (ewm-NEHS-teez), guardians, respectively, of fantasy and of memory.

Maleger (mah-LEE-gur), the captain of the shadowy forces who attacked the bulwarks of the House of Alma.

Verdant, a knight released by Guyon from Acrasia's clutches.

Grille, one of Acrasia's victims. He reviles Guyon and the Palmer for restoring his human form.

Britomart (BRIH-toh-mahrt), the maiden knight, heroine of the book of Chastity. She subdues the forces of lust as she travels in search of Artegall, with whom she fell in love when she saw him in a magic mirror. Her union with him represents the alliance of justice and mercy as well as Spenser's ideal of married chastity, which surpasses the austere virginity of Belphoebe.

Malecasta (mal-eh-KAS-teh), the lady of delight, beautiful and wanton, who entertains Britomart in Castle Joyous.

Glauce (GLAW-see), Britomart's nurse, who accompanies her as her squire.

Merlin, the famous magician, whom Glauce and Britomart consult to learn the identity of the knight in the mirror.

Marinell (MA-rih-nehl), the timid son of a sea nymph and Florimell's lover.

Cymoent (SIH-mehnt), his mother.

Florimell (FLOH-rih-mehl), the loveliest and gentlest of the ladies in Faerie Land. She is pursued by many evil beings, men and gods, before she is wed to Marinell.

Timias (TIH-mee-as), Prince Arthur's squire, who is healed of severe wounds by Belphoebe. Although he falls in love with her, he can never win more than kindness as a response.

Crysogene (krih-SAW-jeh-nee), the mother of Belphoebe and Amoret, who were conceived by the sun.

Argante (ahr-GAHN-tee), a giantess, one of the figures of lust.

Ollyphant (AW-lee-fant), her brother and lover.

A Squire of Dames, Argante's prisoner.

Snowy Florimell, Braggadocio's lady, a creature made by a witch with whom Florimell had stayed.

Proteus (PROH-tee-uhs), the shepherd of the sea, who rescues Florimell from a lecherous fisherman.

Panope (PAN-oh-pee), an old nymph, his housekeeper.

Paridell (PAR-ih-dehl), a vain, lascivious knight.

Malbecco (mal-BEHK-koh), a miserly, jealous old man.

Hellenore (HEHL-leh-nohr), his young wife, who runs away with Paridell.

Scudamour (SKEW-dah-mohr), the knight most skilled in the art of courtly love. He wins Amoret at the court of Venus, but she is taken from him almost immediately.

Amoret (AM-ohr-eht), his beautiful bride, who is taken prisoner at her own wedding by Busirane, who represents her own passions and the confining forces of the rigid code of love in which she has grown up.

Busirane (BEW-sih-rayn), her captor.

Venus, the goddess of love and a personification of the creative force in nature, Amoret's foster mother.

Adonis (uh-DON-ihs), her lover.

Diana, the divine huntress, the virgin goddess who raises Belphoebe.

Ate (AH-tay), Discord, a malicious old woman who stirs up strife.

Blandamour (BLAN-dah-mohr), a fickle knight.

Sir Ferraugh (FEHR-raw), one of the suitors of Snowy Florimell.

Cambello (kam-BEHL-loh), one of the knights of friendship.

Canacee (KA-nah-see), his sister, a wise and beautiful lady who is won by Triamond.

Cambina (kam-BEE-nah), Cambello's wife.

Priamond (PREE-ah-mond),

Diamond, and

Triamond (TREE-ah-mond), brothers who fight for the hand of Canacee. The first two are killed, but their strength passes into their victorious surviving brother.

Artegall (AHR-teh-gahl), the knight of Justice, Britomart's beloved.

Talus (TAH-luhs), the iron man, his implacable attendant, who upholds justice untempered by mercy.

Aemylia (eh-MEE-lee-ah), a lady imprisoned with Amoret by a villainous churl and rescued by Belphoebe.

Corflambo (kohr-FLAHM-boh), a mighty pagan who corrupts his enemies by filling them with lust.

Poeana (pee-AH-nah), his rude, tyrannical daughter.

Amyas (ah-MEE-ahs), the Squire of Low Degree, Aemylia's suitor.

Placidas (PLAH-see-dahs), another squire loved by Poeana. Encouraged by Prince Arthur, Placidas marries Poeana and reforms her.

Druon (DREW-on) and

Claribell, pugnacious companions of Blandamour and Paridell.

Thames (TAH-mees) and

Medway, the river god and goddess whose marriage is

attended by the famous waterways of the world.

Neptune, the sea god to whom Marinell's mother pleads for Florimell's release from Proteus.

Grantorto (gran-TOHR-toh), a tyrant who holds Irena's country in his power. He is the emblem of the political strength of the Roman Catholic Church.

Irena, his victim, who appeals to the Faerie Queene for help.

Sir Sanglier (SAHN-glee-ayr), a cruel lord who is chastened by Talus.

Pollente (pohl-LEHN-tay), a Saracen warrior who extorts money from travelers.

Munera (MEW-neh-rah), his daughter, the keeper of his treasury.

Giant Communism, Artegall's foe. He tries to weigh everything in his scales, but he learns, before Talus hurls him into the sea, that truth and falsehood, right and wrong, cannot be balanced.

Amidas (AH-mih-dahs) and

Bracidas (BRA-see-dahs), brothers whose dispute over a treasure chest is settled by Artegall.

Philtera (FIHL-teh-rah), Bracidas' betrothed, who weds his wealthy brother.

Lucy, Amidas' deserted sweetheart, Bracidas' wife.

Sir Turpine (TUR-pih-nay), a knight whom Artegall discovers bound and tormented by Amazon warriors. He refuses aid to Calepine and Serena.

Radigund (RA-dih-guhnd), the queen of the Amazons. She captures Artegall and dresses him in women's clothes to humiliate him, then falls in love with him and tries unsuccessfully to win him.

Clarinda, her attendant, who comes to love Artegall as she woos him for her mistress.

Dolon (DOH-lon), Deceit, a knight who tries to entrap Britomart.

Mercilla (mur-SIHL-lah), a just and merciful maiden queen whose realm is threatened by a mighty warrior.

The Souldan, her enemy, thought to represent Philip of Spain. He is destroyed by the brilliant light of Prince Arthur's diamond shield.

Malengin (mah-LEHN-gihn), an ingenious villain who transforms himself into different shapes at will. Talus crushes him with his iron flail.

Belgae (BEHL-jeh), a mother who loses twelve of her seventeen children to the tyrant Geryoneo and appeals to Mercilla for help.

Geryoneo (jeh-ree-OH-nee-oh), her enemy, the power of Spain, who is slain by Artegall.

Burbon, a knight rescued by Artegall as he fights Grantorto's men to rescue his lady, Flourdelis (France).

Sir Sergis, Irena's faithful adviser.

Calidore (KAH-lih-dohr), the knight of Courtesy, sent to destroy the Blatant Beast, malicious gossip.

Briana (bree-AH-nah), a proud lady who abuses the laws of hospitality by demanding the hair and beards of ladies and gentlemen who pass her castle.

Crudor, the disdainful knight for whom she weaves a mantle of hair.

Tristram, a young prince reared in the forest who impresses Prince Arthur with his instinctive courtesy.

Aldus (AL-duhs), a worthy old knight.

Aladine (AL-ah-deen), his son.

Priscilla, Aladine's lady.

Serena, a noble lady, severely wounded by the Blatant Beast.

Calepine (KAH-leh-peen), her knight.

Blandina, Sir Turpine's wife, who tries to assuage his cruelty.

The Salvage Man, a "noble savage," another untaught practitioner of courtesy.

Matilde, a childless noblewoman who adopts a baby rescued by Calidore from a bear.

Mirabella, a proud, insolent lady.

Disdaine (dihs-DAYN) and

Scorne, her tormentors.

Pastorella, a nobleman's daughter who grows up with shepherds. Calidore falls in love with her and with her rustic life.

Meliboee (MEHL-ih-bee), her wise foster father, who warns Calidore that happiness is not to be found in one place or another but in oneself.

Coridon (KOHR-ih-don), Pastorella's shepherd admirer.

Colin Clout, a shepherd poet who pipes to the graces on Mount Acidale.

Sir Bellamour, Calidore's friend and Pastorella's father.

Claribell, his wife.

Melissa, her maid, who discovers Pastorella's true identity.

Mutability, a proud Titaness who challenges the power of Cynthia, the moon goddess.

Cynthia, her rival.

Mercury, the messenger of the gods.

Jove, the king of the gods.

Mollana, a nymph and an Irish river.

Faunus (FAW-nuhs), a satyr who pursues her.

Dame Nature, a great veiled figure who hears Mutability's arguments and judges, finally, that order reigns in all change.

FAHRENHEIT 451

Author: Ray Bradbury (1920-)
First published: 1953
Genre: Novel
Locale: North America
Time: The twenty-first century
Plot: Science fiction

Guy Montag, a fireman in an era when that job entails burning books. Although he has enjoyed burning books for ten years, his enthusiasm wanes after he smuggles a book out of the home of an old lady whose house and book collection are burned. Convinced that books can prevent humankind from making the mistakes that lead to wars, he joins forces with Faber to arrange for the duplication of books and to eavesdrop on the firemen. After his house and books are burned, Montag kills Captain Beatty and follows the railroad tracks out of town. With the assistance of Faber, he eludes the Mechanical

Hounds that pursue him and is taken in by a group of former college professors, all of whom have memorized books. Although Montag initially believes that he does not belong with these people, the destruction of the city jogs his memory, and he is able to recall part of the Book of Ecclesiastes and the Book of Revelation. Like the others, he plans to pass down what he has memorized to others.

Mildred Montag, Montag's wife. Instead of thinking, as Montag and Clarisse do, she escapes from her stifling existence by driving at excessive speed or by listening to the thimble radios in her ears and watching the wall-to-wall circuit television. Out of frustration, she swallows an entire bottle of sleeping pills and has to have her blood replaced. Because she cannot understand Montag's appreciation of literature, she turns him in to the firemen. Montag mourns her after she dies in the atomic explosion.

Clarisse McClellan, Montag's sixteen-year-old neighbor. Psychiatrists classify her as insane because she thinks more than the average citizen does. Montag realizes that he is unhappy after he meets her, and he continues to walk her to the corner on a daily basis because, unlike his wife, she gives him her full attention. She disappears, possibly the hit-and-run victim of joy-riding teenagers.

Captain Beatty, the Chief Burner and Montag's superior. Having dismissed Montag's disenchantment with book burning as a phase through which all firemen pass, Beatty provides him with a history of the events that led up to the censorship and burning of all books. Although he has memorized quotations from books he has read, Beatty uses them to refute Montag's defense of books. After forcing Montag to set fire to his own books and house, Beatty provokes Montag into incinerating him with a flamethrower.

Mrs. Phelps, a friend of Mildred. She is a childless, superficial woman who is happy because she lets her husband, who has just gone off to war, do all the worrying. Although she seems to be cold, she sobs uncontrollably while Montag reads "Dover Beach."

Mrs. Bowles, a friend of Mildred. Selfish and shallow, she has had three unhappy marriages, twelve abortions, and two Caesarean sections. Incapable of showing or feeling love, she calls Montag's poetry "mush" and turns him in to the firemen.

Granger, the leader of a group of former college professors with photographic memories. The author of a book dealing with the relationship between the individual and society, he has inherited his grandfather's disdain for the status quo. He and his colleagues memorize books and then burn them to escape harassment from the firemen.

Faber, a college professor. He is a self-confessed coward who reluctantly helps Montag by communicating with him through a small two-way radio that he has placed in Montag's ear. Faber teaches Montag that it is not books that he needs but the meanings in books. After helping Montag escape the Mechanical Hounds, he feels alive for the first time in years.

The Mechanical Hounds, eight-legged robots. These insidious creatures are programmed by the firemen to track down and kill fugitives. Montag burns one and eludes another by altering the chemical index of his perspiration.

— *Alan Brown*

THE FAIR
(La feria)

Author: Juan José Arreola (1918-   )
First published: 1963
Genre: Short fiction

Locale: Zapotlán el Grande, in Jalisco, Mexico
Time: Mid-twentieth century
Plot: Social realism

Juan Tepano (hwahn teh-PAHN-noh), the oldest of five *tlayacanques* (Indian tribal officials). His designation as Primera Vara (first staff) identifies him as charged with ecclesiastical matters. He provides information about the history and problems of Zapotlán el Grande, the city of thirty thousand inhabitants that is the focus of the action (variously presented by some seventy characters, beginning with Tepano, in first- and third-person narratives and in dialogues). He works in the fields with his people, who, though nominally landowners, actually are tenant farmers subject to eviction. Tepano and his fellow officials are involved in the conflict of legal issues over land possession between the Indians and the Spanish-lineage upper-class residents.

Don Manuel, a shoemaker who lets his business suffer in his unsuccessful attempt at farming. He provides an account of the working of his farm from seedtime to harvest. His inefficacy as a farmer is surpassed only by that of the Indians, who nevertheless agitate for the repossession of their ancestors' land.

Don Salvador, called **Don Salva**, a storekeeper in love with his beautiful employee, Chayo. His determination to propose marriage to her is defeated by his timidity and, finally, by her being seduced and impregnated by Odilón.

Don Fidencio (fee-DEHN-see-oh), a candlemaker. His oldest daughter is Chayo, whose illegitimate pregnancy disgraces him. He produces, however, the major attraction of the Fair, a two-hundred-peso candle (almost three meters high and one-half meter in diameter), which had been commissioned by María Palomino.

Odilón (oh-dee-LOHN), the handsome playboy and ne'er-do-well son of Don Abigail. His technique of seducing women includes the false promise of marriage. He callously deserts Chayo after she conceives his child.

Don Faustino (fows-TEE-noh), the *presidente municipal* (highest municipal official). Disappointed in his prayers to Saint Joseph, he does not share his constituents' devotion to the patron saint of Zapotlán, in whose honor the Fair is held every October. He legislated the limitation of the city's brothels to a single area and the licensing of prostitutes after medical examination. Despite his avowed disbelief in Saint Joseph, Don Faustino does all that he can to ensure the success of the Fair "con permiso de José" (with Joseph's concurrence).

Gaspar Ruiz de Cabrera (rrew-EES deh kah-BREHR-ah), the *Licenciado*, the investor and moneylender who sponsors the Fair. Carrying meat that he has purchased for his evening meal, he suffers a fatal heart attack in the street.

Don Abigail (ah-bee-GIL), a brother of the *Licenciado*, with whom he was not on speaking terms, and the father of Odilón. He is made executor of his brother's estate.

Father Zavala (sah-VAH-lah), a parish priest. He carries out the preparations for the Fair after the death of the *Licenciado*, calling first on Don Atilano, the fireworks manufacturer, to produce a huge fireworks display. The *castillo*, as the display is called, is vandalized on the last night of the Fair and explodes all at once instead of going off in sections. Father Zavala becomes ill during the Fair and is removed to Guadalajara; an assistant priest replaces him.

Don Alfonso, a member of the Tzaputlatena Atheneum, a cultural society. He wins approval for his suggestion to have the society invite a different literary celebrity every fortnight to address the group. The first is Palinurus, an alcoholic poet from Guadalajara. The second is a boring and offensive historian from Sayula, after whose presentation the invitations are terminated and the project abandoned.

Alejandrina (ah-leh-hahn-DREE-nah), a poet from Tamazula who, without invitation, presents herself to the Atheneum and proves to be popular. She writes erotic poetry, sells beauty cream, and exploits the Atheneum to further her commercial activities.

Poet, a married member of the Atheneum who falls in love with Alejandrina and, much to the actual displeasure of his wife, Matilde, and the ostensible displeasure of town gossips, has an affair with her. She deserts him after he ceases to be of use to her; his taking third prize at the Fair for his poetry leaves him dissatisfied in the absence of his inspiration.

Cousin of Chole (CHOH-leh), a printer's apprentice. In his regular confessions to Father Zavala, he discloses his pubescent curiosity about sex, his nascent desires, and his fantasies, one of which he writes in story form and gives to the priest.

Diarist, a lovesick seventeen-year-old who fails to consummate his love for the fourteen-year-old María Elena. His diary entries trace his pursuit of the elusive, tentatively responsive, but ultimately cool girl, who, after her fifteenth birthday, tells him to call on her in a year's time if his love is serious. That it most likely is not is attested by a diary entry disclosing four earlier infatuations.

Doña María La Matraca (mah-TRAH-kah), a beekeeper who becomes the city's leading brothel madam. She sells Don Fidencio the beeswax for his nine-foot candle.

Celso José (SEHL-soh hoh-SEH), a homosexual employee of Doña María. He treats her rheumatism by applying stinging bees to her leg.

Concha de Fierro (KOHN-chah deh fee-EH-rroh), a prostitute whose vagina is impenetrable. As a challenge to all males, she becomes the main attraction at Leonila's brothel. She is finally deflowered by Pedro Corrales, the bullfighter, who then marries her.

Paulina (paw-lee-nah), called **la Gallina sin Pico** (gah-YEE-nah seen PEE-koh), a prostitute at Doña María's brothel. She terminates her pregnancy by committing suicide.

Urbano (ewr-BAH-noh), the bell-ringer, prone to drunkenness, who frequently rings thirteen peals. He cradles the dying *Licenciado* in his arms.

Don Isaías (ee-SIS), a Protestant whose name reflects his constant use of biblical language, whether in conversation or imprecation or regarding defecation.

Don Farias (fah-REE-ahs), a former worker who has become a successful businessman. He lends support to the *tlayacanques* and the Indians. He also purchases on credit the gold that will be fashioned into crowns for Jesus, Mary, and Joseph at the Fair.

Pedro Bernardino (PEH-droh behr-nah-DEE-noh), an elderly tribal official who is working for the rights of the Indian community. He proudly stands up to Don Abigail, whose respect he wins.

Coyón (koh-YOHN), a companion of Leonides, who tagged him with his nickname, which means "chicken." He is imprisoned for fatally stabbing Leonides, who calls him "Coyón" once too often.

Don Mucio Galvez (MEW-see-oh GAHL-vehs), a *tlayacanque* falsely accused of writing anonymous seditious letters. He is one of the litigants in the suit for Indian rights.

Félix Mejía Garay (FEH-leeks meh-HEE-ah gah-RI), a *tequilastro* (assistant to a *tlayacanque*) who, along with Don Mucio, is falsely accused of writing anonymous seditious letters and who presses the suit for Indian rights.

Indian Sahuaripa (sah-wah-REE-pah), a snake charmer at the Fair who takes in hand a hognose snake that a man offers to sell to him. The snake bites him fatally and slips away uncaught.

José Mentira (mehn-TEE-rah), a snake hunter who kills all of Sahuaripa's snakes after the snake charmer dies.

Don Adolfo, a member of the Tzaputlatena Atheneum, at whose home the poetry awards are made, no one having showed up at the Velasco Theatre, where they were scheduled to be made.

— *Roy Arthur Swanson*

THE FAIR MAID OF PERTH

Author: Sir Walter Scott (1771-1832)
First published: 1828
Genre: Novel

Locale: Scotland
Time: 1396
Plot: Historical

Catharine Glover, the Fair Maid of Perth. Agreeing to be Henry Gow's valentine, she nevertheless refuses to agree to marry him because of his propensity for quarreling. Finally, becoming reconciled to the brave Henry's warlike impulses, she does marry him, and he vows to take up arms again only in defense of his country.

Simon Glover, her father.

Henry Gow, an armorer of Perth. He is in love with Catharine Glover. Of a fiery spirit, his offer of marriage is refused by Catharine because of his quarrelsomeness. Involved bravely in the Highland wars between the clans Quhele and Chattan, he finally wins her hand.

Conachar (Eachin MacIan), the son of the chief of Clan Quhele and an apprentice to Simon Glover. In love with

Catharine Glover, he flees when he meets his rival for her hand, Henry Gow, in battle. Ashamed of his cowardice, he takes his own life.

Robert III, king of Scotland.

The Duke of Albany, King Robert's brother James,

The Earl of March, and

The Earl of Douglas, called **The Black Douglas**, noblemen involved in a struggle for power over Robert III and Scotland.

The Duke of Rothsay, heir to the Scottish throne. He is starved to death by Sir John Ramorny and Henbane Dwining.

Sir John Ramorny, the duke of Rothsay's master of horse and, later, his murderer.

Henbane Dwining, an apothecary and physician to Sir John Ramorny, with whom he kills the duke of Rothsay.

Oliver Proudfute, a Perth burgher and friend of Henry Gow. He is murdered while masquerading in Henry's clothes to frighten away assailants.

Father Clement, confessor to Catharine Glover.

Bonthron, the murderer of Oliver Proudfute, whom he mistakes for Henry Gow.

Louise, a glee-maiden.

Lady Marjory, the duchess of Rothsay.

Sir Patrick Charteris, the provost of Perth.

A FAIRLY HONOURABLE DEFEAT

Author: Iris Murdoch (1919-　　)
First published: 1970
Genre: Novel
Locale: London, England
Time: Late 1960's
Plot: Philosophical

Julius (Kahn) King, a Jewish American biochemist in his mid-forties. He has quit working on his biological warfare experiments and has gone to England to renew old acquaintances. Distinguished looking, with pale hair and violet-brown eyes, he is a cynical observer of the human condition and decides to exploit the weaknesses he sees in the relationships he encounters. His former lover, Morgan Browne, becomes his willing yet unwitting associate in the attempt to break up the homosexual relationship between Axel Nilsson and Simon Foster. King's real goal is to break up the marriage between Hilda and Rupert Foster, Morgan's sister and brother-in-law. He steals love letters written by Rupert to Hilda and by Morgan to himself, blots out certain specifics, and then sends them to Rupert and to Morgan, hoping to inspire a romance between the two. He drives a wedge between Axel and Simon; plays havoc with Hilda's emotions and those of Peter Foster, her son; and uses Tallis Browne, Morgan's estranged husband, as a foil. To Julius, people are puppets, life is ritual, philosophy and theology are empty exercises in futility, and it is his right to alter and interfere in others' lives. As the Foster marriage begins to break up, Julius is persuaded by Tallis to tell Hilda the truth about his tricks, but it is too late: Rupert dies by "misadventure" in the family swimming pool. As the novel ends, Julius, who spent part of the war in the Belsen concentration camp, is in Paris, content with the notion that life is good.

Morgan Browne, a philologist in her mid-thirties who is a disciple of Noam Chomsky. While on a brief academic expedition to America, Morgan met Julius King and had a stormy two-year love affair with him. She is married to Tallis Browne but is irritated by his inability to do anything to her satisfaction. She returns to England to be with her sister Hilda and Hilda's husband, Rupert. Her pursuit of Julius leads to a variety of complications, including her own "innocent" affair with Rupert, her asking Tallis for a divorce, and ultimately her awareness of Julius' unfeeling disregard for her and for everybody except himself. At the end of the novel, she and Hilda have moved to California, where she has accepted an academic appointment.

Rupert Foster, a man in his mid-forties, married to Hilda for twenty years. Rupert is a civil servant and part-time philosopher who believes in the goodness of people and the healing power of love. He has worked for years on a philosophical opus bringing all of his beliefs into focus. He is a steady and positive influence on those around him until the letter stolen by Julius comes to him, leading to a secret meeting with Morgan as innocent lovers, not in-laws. He hopes to convince Morgan, and everyone else, that love can solve all problems, but Hilda finds out about the affair and leaves him. This and other effects of Julius' trickery drive him to an overdose of alcohol and pills and his death in the swimming pool.

Hilda Foster, a woman in her early forties. Plump, sweet, and emotionally uncomplicated, she is a nearly perfect mate for Rupert and is devoted to her sister Morgan. Julius' tricks drive her away from Rupert. When Julius tells her the truth, she tries unsuccessfully to telephone Rupert and to drive back from Wales to be with him, but the telephone is broken and the car will not start. At the novel's end, she has reconciled with Morgan and moved to America with her and with her son, Peter.

Peter Foster, Hilda and Rupert's son. A plump, good-looking Cambridge dropout, he denies the values of his upbringing and has become a pseudo-Marxist. A surly youth, he has moved in with Tallis Browne, living in filth and stealing objects from department stores. He falls in love with Morgan, catches Morgan and his father together, destroys Rupert's book manuscript, and finally is arrested for a shoplifting binge. He goes to California with Hilda and Morgan to undergo psychiatric treatment.

Axel Nilsson, a civil servant in his mid-forties and a longtime friend of Rupert and of Julius. He is a silent, gloomy, and morose person, and he and Simon are living a homosexual life together. Julius almost destroys the relationship by threatening Simon, who ultimately tells Axel the truth. They are vacationing on the Continent, reunited, as the novel ends.

Simon Foster, Rupert's brother, a man in his early thirties. A longtime practicing homosexual, he and Axel form a stormy relationship. Simon is a chatterbox, an interior designer, a gourmet cook, and a frightened young man. He is slim, graceful, childlike, and pleasure loving. He hates violence, and he hates the idea that Axel might leave him. Julius almost destroys him, but, by telling Axel the truth, Simon survives, his love intact.

Tallis Browne, Morgan's husband, a sloppy, untidy, unsuccessful, financially insecure lecturer and champion of social causes. He has patiently awaited Morgan's return, for he still loves her even though she scorns him. Julius meets him, and they become acquaintances. He shows flashes of manliness when he hits a bully who is assaulting a Jamaican and when he literally forces Julius to confess to Hilda the trick he has played on everyone. He lives in squalor with his father, Leonard, and with Peter. At the end of the novel, he is left with the decision whether to tell his father that it is cancer, not arthritis, that is Leonard's illness. Despite Julius' attempt to clean up the house, Tallis allows it to turn back into the dump that it was earlier.

Leonard Browne, Tallis' father, an elderly, cranky, and cynical man. His only positive quality seems to be his feeding of the pigeons in the park. His has been a hard and unhappy life, and his feelings about doctors, life, and his son are colored by his experiences.

— William H. Holland, Jr.

FAITH AND THE GOOD THING

Author: Charles Johnson (1948-　　)
First published: 1974
Genre: Novel
Locale: Rural Georgia and Chicago, Illinois
Time: The 1930's or the 1940's
Plot: Philosophical

Faith Cross, a beautiful young black woman in search of the "Good Thing" who undergoes a spiritual odyssey from the superstitions of backwoods Georgia to the harsh realities of urban Chicago. Initially sweet and naïve, she is rapidly stripped of the illusions nurtured in her by the sheltered environment of her youth. Soon after her arrival in the city, she is robbed and raped, and she progressively hardens in her life to become an alcoholic and a drug-addicted prostitute. Successively rejecting the religion of her youth and several philosophical theories to which she is introduced by her male acquaintances, she tries to find the Good Thing in a materialistic marriage to an ambitious newspaper writer, only to be disappointed once again. The deteriorating marriage finally dissolves after Faith becomes pregnant by another man. Faith is once again alone in resigned despair. Shortly after giving birth to a baby girl, Faith is fatally burned. At her death, she returns to her childhood home and is transformed into a witch who finally realizes the truth of the Good Thing.

The Swamp Woman, a one-eyed, grotesquely misshapen witch who tells Faith that she must go to Chicago and to whom Faith returns at the novel's end. She lives in a shack filled with books and objects associated with necromancy, including a magic urn in which Faith sees her fate. The Swamp Woman tells Faith the story of the legendary Kujichagulia, who pursued and finally discovered the Good Thing only to be killed by the gods for his forbidden knowledge; his wife, Imani, follows him in his quest but is instead pitied by the gods and initiated into the mysteries of essential truth. The Swamp Woman reveals herself to be Imani, still questioning, still exploring, but able to lead Faith to knowledge of the Good Thing. At the end of the novel, the Swamp Woman unzips her skin and steps out of it to put on Faith's former body.

Isaac Maxwell, Faith's husband. An ambitious journalist who believes that money constitutes the Good Thing, Isaac is an odd-looking yet vain man who wears a toupee. Yellow-skinned, with a weak chin, he suffers from severe asthma. He views Faith as one of the possessions that can guarantee him the good life, at one point even bartering his wife's body for a promotion. He is devastated when, after a year of marriage, he learns of her sordid past, and he moves out of their bedroom; when she informs him of her pregnancy, he demands that she move out of the house. Self-absorbed, he has all along loved not Faith but only an image of her that is an extension of himself. Isaac visits the burned Faith in her hospital room right before she dies, but she orders him out. Significantly and characteristically, he leaves a twenty-dollar bill on her bed.

Alpha Omega Holmes, Faith's high school suitor, who reappears as a former convict in Chicago. He is tall, muscular, gentle, and unambitious, and he reminds Faith of her father. Without Faith's knowledge, her mother had driven him away, and she was bewildered at his abandonment. Isaac chooses Alpha for a newspaper project and brings him home to dinner, unaware of his former relationship with Faith. Alpha has become an artist; as he tells Faith, only the act of painting makes him feel free. They resume their affair, even though she recognizes his irresponsibility, exemplified by his lying to her in the same tall-tale style as her father. After she reveals her pregnancy to him, she is not surprised when he abandons her once again.

Arnold Tyler Tippis, the first person Faith meets in Chicago. After buying her a drink, he sexually assaults her but pays her twenty dollars, thus initiating her into prostitution. A college graduate and former dentist who has been through psychoanalysis, he continues to visit Faith, primarily to talk. She later encounters him working as a theater usher and finally as a male nurse who shows kindness to her in her last moments.

Dr. Richard M. Barrett, a former philosophy professor. He is a small, dumpy, dirty man, with red eyes. He robs Faith on her arrival in Chicago but later seeks her out to apologize and return her possessions. He shares with her his Doomsday Book, which supposedly contains his understanding of truth, but at his death she finds the pages to be blank. He haunts her periodically after his death.

Lavidia Cross, Faith's mother. She is strong-willed and superstitious. Her dying injunction to Faith to find the "Good Thing" initiates the plot.

— Caren S. Silvester

THE FAITHFUL SHEPHERDESS

Author: John Fletcher (1579-1625)
First published: 1629
Genre: Drama
Locale: Thessaly
Time: Antiquity
Plot: Tragicomedy

Clorin (KLOH-reen), the faithful shepherdess. She lives in a sacred grove beside the tomb of her dead lover, mourning him and cultivating herbs to heal injured shepherds. She finds her chastity a magical defense against all evils of the wood, and her healing arts are effective only when she has purged her patients of lust.

Thenot (tay-NOH), a disillusioned shepherd who loves Clorin for the virtue and constancy that he finds in her alone. He languishes in this passion, which by its very nature cannot be satisfied, until Clorin mercifully decides to free him from it by offering to return his love and forsake her dead sweetheart. His illusions shattered, he leaves her, resolving to choose a lady for her beauty and convinced that no woman can be loved for her merit.

Perigot (pay-ree-GOH), a virtuous young shepherd who gives extravagant assurances of his undying love for Amoret. Deceived by Amaryllis' transformation, he is horrified to hear her offer herself to him, and he twice wounds the real Amoret, who appears soon afterward, for deceiving him. Clorin restores his faith in his beloved, and they are happily reconciled.

Amoret (AM-oh-reht), Perigot's sweetheart, whose beauty and innocence win the devotion of a river god and a satyr as well as the love of her shepherd swain. Although she cannot understand Perigot's treatment of her, she quickly forgives him and again promises him her hand and heart.

Amaryllis (am-eh-RIHL-ihs), a passionate shepherdess who desires Perigot and has herself magically disguised as Amoret to win him for herself. His misery awakens her sympathy, and she tells him the truth before she flees the Sullen Shepherd, whose help she had enlisted by promising him her love. She is rescued and cleansed by the Priest of Pan.

Cloe (KLOH-ee), another lustful shepherdess who makes assignations with both Daphnis and Alexis, hoping to compensate for the shyness of the one by the boldness of the other. She, like Perigot, is purified by Clorin's teaching.

Daphnis (DAF-nihs), her shy, modest admirer. Blind to her desires, he assures her of his virtuous affection.

Alexis (uh-LEHK-sihs), Cloe's more passionate suitor. Wounded by the Sullen Shepherd, he is healed of both his injury and his lust by Clorin.

The Sullen Shepherd, who is almost the personification of blind desire. He professes love to Amaryllis and aids her in separating Perigot and Amoret, but he confesses secretly that any woman satisfies him and that he is willing to use any trick to win one.

A satyr, a gentle creature of nature who worships Clorin and brings her gifts of fruit from the wood. He searches the forest to bring to her those who need her help and carries out the mystic rites that purify her grove.

The Priest of Pan, the guardian of all the shepherds. He rescues Amaryllis, then goes to Clorin's grove to find the rest of his flock, bless them, and send them to their homes with a hymn to Pan.

An old shepherd, his companion, who notes disapprovingly the disappearance of the young shepherds and shepherdesses into the wood.

The God of the River, Amoret's protector, who raises her from the fountain where the Sullen Shepherd has dropped her. He begs her to leave her mortal life and join him in his crystal streams.

THE FAKE ASTROLOGER
(El astrólogo fingido)

Author: Pedro Calderón de la Barca (1600-1681)
First published: 1633
Genre: Drama
Locale: Madrid, Spain
Time: The seventeenth century
Plot: Farce

Don Diego (dee-EH-goh), a wealthy nobleman. In love with María but spurned by her, he directs his servant, Morón, to try to learn how best to approach the lady. When Don Diego repeats to his friends Morón's gleanings concerning María's activities, the servant spreads the story that his master is an astrologer with knowledge of past and future. Don Diego's supposed occult powers bring him only trouble, as his false prophecies spread confusion and turn everybody against him. He even succeeds in uniting María and his rival, Juan de Medrano.

Morón (mohr-OHN), Don Diego's servant, who is in love with Beatriz. His master instructs him to pump Beatriz concerning her mistress, María. Morón finds his beloved in danger of exposure when Don Diego passes on the information obtained from her. To protect Beatriz, Morón explains that Don Diego's knowledge comes through his powers as an astrologer.

María (mah-REE-ah), a young girl loved by Don Diego and Juan de Medrano.

Juan de Medrano (hwahn deh meh-DRAH-noh), an impoverished young nobleman in love with María and preferred by her to Don Diego.

Beatriz (beh-ah-TREES), María's maid, loved by Morón, to whom she reveals the details of Juan de Medrano's visits to her mistress.

Don Carlos, Juan de Medrano's friend.

Doña Violante (vee-oh-LAHN-teh), a woman in love with Juan de Medrano.

Leonardo (leh-oh-NAHR-doh), María's father.

FALCONER

Author: John Cheever (1912-1982)
First published: 1977
Genre: Novel
Locale: Falconer Prison, near New York City, and Southwick, Connecticut
Time: Early 1970's
Plot: Social realism

Ezekiel (Zeke) Farragut, a forty-eight-year-old veteran of World War II, college professor, drug addict, and convicted murderer. He is articulate, sensitive, masculine, and sex-crazed. Zeke's story is one of imprisonment, drug withdrawal, homosexual love, fratricide, and affirmation of life. The story begins at the time of Zeke's imprisonment in Falconer, a one-hundred-year-old prison in what is evidently New York state. While there, he is mistreated by guards who deny him methadone while he is withdrawing from heroin. He falls in love with Jody, another prisoner, whom he takes as a homosexual lover. Finally, he escapes from Falconer by zipping himself into the body bag of a fellow inmate who has died, thereby getting himself carried out of the prison.

Eben Farragut, the older brother whom Ezekiel murdered. Eben already is dead when the story opens, but Zeke tells his story to Jody, and he also discusses his brother with his wife during her visits. Eben was given to psychological violence toward his younger brother. As a youth, he once encouraged Zeke to swim against an incoming tide. The attempt would have meant death, but Zeke was warned in time by a passing stranger. Eben also had taunted Zeke with the fact that their father had tried to force their mother to have an abortion before Zeke was born. There is also turmoil created by Eben in regard to the two brothers' wives. Zeke murdered Eben by striking him some twenty times with a fire iron, a fact that he later denies.

Jody, Zeke's homosexual lover. Handsome, youthful, masculine, and resourceful, Jody becomes the full object of Zeke's love and life while he is in Falconer. Jody has a secret place in the prison where the two lovers meet, whenever possible, for their trysts. Jody escapes from Falconer by disguising himself as an altar boy when a cardinal comes to the prison to give Communion. A few months after his escape, Zeke learns that Jody has married a woman and established a new life for himself. Zeke also learns that Jody had other lovers while in prison.

Marcia Farragut, Zeke's wife. Serious in attitude, devout in her marriage, and a good mother to their son, Peter, Marcia visits Zeke twice while he is in Falconer. On both occasions, she seems to miss her husband and is unable to understand the murder. She does not know whether she will divorce Zeke, as state law permits. She evidently has had a lesbian affair with a friend, which perhaps helps account for her acceptance of her husband's homosexual lover.

Chicken Number Two, one of the inmates in Falconer. Chicken is a jewel thief who strangled an old woman for eighty-eight dollars. He is tattooed from head to foot. It is Chicken's corpse that Zeke removes from a body bag as a means of escaping from the prison.

Cuckold, another inmate. Cuckold is always telling colorful stories of his wife's ubiquitous infidelities. These stories, often violent and predatory in nature, abet the masculine brutality of the novel.

Tiny, the prison trusty most often in charge of Zeke. Tiny is brutal and effectual, clearly as given to evil and violence as those he oversees in his cell block. His worst self is revealed when he withholds methadone from Zeke, then takes pleasure in watching Zeke try to kill himself.

— *Carl Singleton*

THE FALL
(La Chute)

Author: Albert Camus (1913-1960)
First published: 1956
Genre: Novel
Locale: Amsterdam and Paris
Time: The 1950's
Plot: Philosophical realism

Jean-Baptiste Clamence (zhahn-bah-TEEST klah-MAHNS), the narrator and the only speaking person in this novel. Every word of this book is spoken by this character, to the unidentified listener. Clamence describes himself as formerly a lawyer in Paris, not a judge-penitent. As a lawyer, he did not accept bribes and was not involved in shady dealings. His courtesy was famous and undeniable; he was a person of incredible politeness and manners. Only near the end of the novel does the reader learn the narrator's definition of judge-penitent: the one who announces the law. His profession after being a Parisian lawyer consists of indulging in public confession as often as possible. He describes himself as bursting with vanity, and in the course of the novel he reflects on every facet of his life that he finds meaningful. The narrator says that his love for life is his only true weakness. He calls himself a prophet and happens to have a name strikingly similar to Saint John the Baptist. The bulk of this text consists of Clamence scrutinizing his life on the premise of two important events. The first is that he heard laughter behind him and could not discover its source; the second is that a woman jumped off a bridge into the river Seine and he made no effort to help her.

The unidentified listener, who is explained to the reader only so far as Clamence makes observations about him. The narrator attaches himself to this unidentified listener, and single words of the listener occasionally are repeated by the narrator, thereby making the modest and vague insinuation of dialogue that continues throughout the text. The listener is much like the narrator. They are about the same age, in their forties, and the listener is well dressed and appears sophisticated. The listener has smooth hands, which causes Clamence to exclaim that he is a bourgeois, though a cultured one. Because Clamence amuses the listener, Clamence assumes his listener is open-minded. The listener is considered again only briefly as Clamence repeats answered questions and at the ends of the days, which are chapters.

The proprietor of Mexico City, who is spoken of by the narrator in the opening pages, as a means of stage setting. Mexico City is the bar in Amsterdam where half of the novel takes place. The proprietor of Mexico City does not enter as a true character, as there are no true characters in this novel except the narrator. The proprietor speaks only Dutch, and even that very grudgingly. He frequently snubs patrons and does not serve people if he has a whim not to. The business of this bar owner is to entertain sailors of all nationalities. The narrator speaks of this man as a barbarian and as having extremely low intelligence.

Unknown laughing voice, a voice Clamence hears behind him; when he looks, he is unable to find its source. The laughing voice is found to be the narrator laughing at himself, a psychological trick that forces him to analyze his conscience.

Woman who jumps off the bridge, who is mentioned in a story told by the narrator to the unidentified listener. The narrator walked by her one night, "a slim young woman dressed in black," as she was standing on a bridge, looking over the railing into the river. The narrator continued past her and later heard a splash in the water, followed by several cries and screams. Then there was silence. The narrator did not interfere in the woman's life in any way. In the closing sentences of the novel, the narrator wishes for the same opportunity again, so that he might have a second chance to save them both.

— Beaird Glover

THE FALL OF THE HOUSE OF USHER

Author: Edgar Allan Poe (1809-1849)
First published: 1839
Genre: Short fiction
Locale: The House of Usher
Time: The nineteenth century
Plot: Gothic

Roderick Usher, a madman. Excessively reserved in childhood and thereafter, Usher is the victim not only of his own introversion but also of the dry rot in his family, which because of inbreeding has long lacked the healthy infusion of vigorous blood from other families. His complexion is cadaverous, his eyes are lustrous, his nose is "of a delicate Hebrew model," his chin is small and weak though finely molded, his forehead broad, and his hair soft and weblike. (The detailed description of Usher's face and head in the story should be compared with the well-known portraits of Poe himself.) In manner Usher is inconsistent, shifting from excited or frantic vivacity to sullenness marked by dull, guttural talk like that of a drunkard or opium addict. It is evident to his visitor, both through his own observation and through what Usher tells him, that the wretched man is struggling desperately but vainly to conquer his fear of fear itself. His wide reading in his extensive library, his interest in many art objects, his playing the guitar and singing to its accompaniment, his attempts at conversation and friendly communication with his guest—all seem piteous efforts to hold on to his sanity. The battle is finally lost when Madeline, risen from her grave and entering through the doors of the guest's apartment, falls upon Usher and bears him to the floor "a corpse, and a victim to the terrors he had anticipated."

Madeline, his twin sister, a tall, white-robed, wraithlike woman who succumbs to catalepsy, is buried alive, escapes from her tomb, confronts her brother in her bloodstained cerements, and joins him in death.

The Narrator, Usher's visitor and only personal friend. He is summoned to try to cheer up Usher but is himself made fearful and nervously excited by the gloomy, portentous atmosphere of the Usher home. Having witnessed the double deaths of Usher and Madeline, the narrator flees in terror and, looking back, sees the broken mansion fall into the tarn below.

FAMILY

Author: J. California Cooper
First published: 1991
Genre: Novel
Locale: The rural South
Time: The 1840's through the early twentieth century
Plot: Historical realism

Clora, the narrator, born a slave to a woman who kills herself and her master. Truly omniscient, Clora is a phantom, a time-traveler who poisoned herself rather than continue living as a slave. She stays on to look after her favorite child.

Always, Clora's favorite daughter, who loved all natural life as a child only to become embittered by slavery and to turn into an acquisitive, proud, and assertive woman, one who prospers through hatred and ambition.

Sun, another of Clora's children, born so light-skinned that he is able to escape north with the help of his half sister, Loretta. He "passes," marries the daughter of an immigrant Frenchman, and becomes a successful businessman.

Peach, Clora's other surviving daughter. She is pretty and good-natured, and she learns the skills of homemaking as a personal maid to Loretta. She is sold to a Scotsman, who marries her and takes her away to live in affluence in Europe.

Sue Butler, the wife of Doak Butler, who buys Always and fathers her child. Sue is the mistress of the farm that Always tends with Doak's disabled brother Jason and his slave Poon. Sue is important as a foil in this novel.

Loretta Butler, Doak's second wife and the half sister of Always. She had helped Sun to escape north, but his refusal to send for her, to take her away from the poor, rural South, leaves her angry and mean-spirited. Joy comes to her in the guise of a child, Apple, whose father is Sephus, Always' son. In the confusing, incestuous family of this novel, Loretta becomes the aunt and mother of her half sister's grandchild.

Doak, Jr., the true son of Always. She swaps the boy, originally named Soon, with her master's son. He returns from the war to find his inheritance endangered. Always trades some of Doak, Sr.'s gold for her life and land of her own. Eventually, Doak, Jr.'s hatred of Always leads him to allow the Ku Klux Klan to ravage her land and livestock. He has, by this time, become the richest landowner in the county.

— William Eiland

THE FAMILY AT GILJE
(Familjen paa Gilje)

Author: Jonas Lie (1833-1908)
First published: 1883
Genre: Novel
Locale: Norway
Time: The nineteenth century
Plot: Domestic realism

Captain Jäger, a Norwegian army officer in command of the mountain post near Gilje. He wants his favorite daughter, Inger-Johanna, to be a society woman and sends her to live with his sister in the city. He is bitterly disappointed when the girl refuses a good marriage because she loves a radical student. The captain's health fails rapidly after this disappointment, and he dies.

Inger-Johanna Jäger, the captain's charming and favorite daughter. She falls in love with a radical student, Arent Grip, who teaches her to look beneath the symbols of success to the inner human nature. Because she loves the young man, she refuses to marry Captain Rönnow and instead becomes a schoolteacher. When her beloved is fatally ill, she goes to nurse him.

Mrs. Jäger, the captain's wife.

Thinka Jäger, a pliant daughter who marries Sheriff Glucke as her father wishes. She really loves a young clerk her father will not consider as a husband for her. She makes a considerate wife, but she is a sad woman.

Jorgen Jäger, the captain's son. He has aptitude as a mechanic and migrates to America, where he does well for himself.

Captain Rönnow, a suitor for Inger-Johanna's hand in marriage. She refuses to marry him, though the captain has her father's approval, because she does not love him.

Arent Grip, a radical student who loves Inger-Johanna and is loved by her. He is a failure in the world, becoming by turns a drunkard and an ascetic, always wandering about the country. After twenty years of aimless roving, he returns and is nursed during his final illness by Inger-Johanna.

Gülcke, the sheriff, a widower who marries Thinka, though she loves a younger man.

FAMILY HAPPINESS

Author: Laurie Colwin (1944-1992)
First published: 1982
Genre: Novel
Locale: New York City
Time: Late twentieth century
Plot: Love

Polly Solo-Miller Demarest, the main character, the only daughter of Henry Solo-Miller and his wife, Constanzia Hendricks, who is always called Wendy. Polly (whose real name is Dora) is the wife of Henry Demarest and mother of Pete (age nine) and Dee-Dee (age seven and a half). Polly, in her early thirties, is employed part-time as coordinator of research in reading projects and methods. She is a competent, devoted wife and mother as well as an amiable and accommodating daughter to her parents. She mediates between her two brothers. Polly has one other role: mistress of the successful but reclusive painter Lincoln Bennett. This affair began several months before the book opens. Polly's anguish over the conflicts in her feelings about Henry Demarest and Lincoln Bennett forms the crux of the novel.

Lincoln Bennett, Polly's lover, whom she met at a gallery showing of his paintings. He lives alone in his studio. He is a naturally loving man, but he has given up expecting to find happiness in love because he cannot endure living with anyone. He has known the Solo-Millers for some time and considers them smug, snobbish, and unappreciative of Polly, the only one of the family who is completely selfless, kind, and tenderhearted. He is the only person who recognizes and values these qualities in her.

Henry Demarest, Polly's husband, so absorbed in his work that he appears unaware of the devotion and skill with which Polly manages his household and the love she lavishes on him without expectation of gratitude or return of passion. He loves Polly, as Lincoln does, but Henry never asks her about herself, is always distracted and preoccupied, and is sometimes snappish and surly. He acknowledges that he needs Polly and insists that he loves her when she asks him if he does, whereas Lincoln Bennett wants to know everything about her life and her feelings but does not want her to live with him. Like Henry, Lincoln sees his work as the most important part of his life.

Wendy Solo-Miller, Polly's mother. Having reared a perfect daughter, Wendy continues to remind Polly constantly of her duties as a mother, frequently criticizing her for holding a job that takes her away from home and children three days a week, even though Wendy herself, when her children were small, spent at least as much time on various volunteer projects. Scatterbrained and demanding, especially of Polly,

Wendy has no notion of Polly's feelings, worries, and disappointments, because Polly herself never reveals them, rightly believing that no one is interested.

Henry Solo-Miller, the patriarch of the family. Although he is a successful lawyer, Henry is no more aware of other people than he needs to be. He has crotchets and idiosyncrasies, such as insisting that all food be washed with soap and water. For the most part, he leads a detached life, centered on the family, often disapproving but uninvolved in any real sense. The Solo-Millers are an old Jewish family that is more old American than Jewish, descended from people who settled in America before the American Revolution.

Paul Solo-Miller, the older son, is forty-three years old, unmarried, respected as a lawyer, often silent, preoccupied, and somewhat ill-tempered.

Henry Solo-Miller, Jr., the younger son, is considered a lout, yet his place in the family is never questioned. He is married to a Czech refugee named Andreya Fillo. They are both aeronautical engineers, behave like ill-mannered children, and have a child substitute named Kirby, a large untrained tickhound.

Karlheinz von Waldau and **Beate**, twins, who are forty-four years old. Beate, a psychoanalyst, has lived in New York for eighteen years. Karlheinz, or Karlo, who still lives in Switzerland, is a composer and has come to New York to perform a new work.

Martha Nathan, Polly's office friend, a free-lance computer expert.

Marty Rensberg, a divorcée with two daughters. At one time, the family thought that she was going to marry Paul, but their relationship came to an end. She is a successful antique dealer.

— *Natalie Harper*

FAMILY HAPPINESS
(Semeynoye schastye)

Author: Leo Tolstoy (1828-1910)
First published: 1859
Genre: Novel
Locale: A country estate, St. Petersburg, and a spa in Baden
Time: The 1850's
Plot: Psychological realism

Marya (Masha) Alexandrovna (ah-lehk-SAN-drov-nah), the narrator, a young noblewoman. She tells about her life from the age of seventeen, shortly after the death of her widowed mother, until she is about twenty-three, some four or five years after her marriage. A modest, intelligent woman as yet unaware of her great beauty, she lives with her sister and a governess on the family estate, Pokrovskoe. She falls in love with her legal guardian, Sergey Mikhaylych, a man more than twice her age. In time, he returns her love, and their romance culminates in marriage. Living with her husband and his mother on their estate, Nikolskoe, proves confining to the young woman. On a trip with Sergey to St. Petersburg, she is introduced to high society, becomes fully conscious of her attractiveness to men, and gradually is drawn to the worldly vanities of the capital. Three years later, while spending the summer in Baden, Masha only barely resists committing adultery with a handsome foreigner. Frightened, she returns to her marriage, which, after all, she had not meant to test so severely. Although her life with Sergey will never be quite the same, the marriage, now with two children to strengthen it, will be a sufficiently happy one.

Sergey Mikhaylych (sehr-GAY mih-KHAY-lihch), a serious, responsible landowner of the noble class. Already thirty-six years old at the time of his engagement to Masha, he is a tall and robust man with a perfectionist personality. He understands that his young wife is likely to find the demands of marriage difficult; therefore, he sets out deliberately to allow her as much freedom as possible. In learning her limits, so to speak, she is better able to become a reliable partner in marriage. It is also true that Sergey's "granting" of freedom is merely part of the overall control exercised by an older husband over a young wife. Sergey is able to forgive his wife's flirtation, knowing that the end of idealized romance in their marriage is by no means the end of the marriage itself.

Katerina (Katya) Karlovna (kah-teh-REE-nah kahr-LOV-nah), the elderly governess who has brought up Masha and her sister. She is given a place in the Nikolskoe household.

An Italian marquis, a visitor at the resort of Baden. He is bold, handsome, and passionate, but coarse and "animal" as well. Attracted to Masha at the resort, he nearly succeeds in seducing her.

Tatyana Semyonovna (tah-TYAH-nah seh-MYOH-nov-nah), Sergey's mother. She dies about two years after the marriage of her son to Masha, thereby suggesting the promise of greater independence for Masha in the future.

Sonya, Masha's younger sister. She remains at the end of the tale as she was at the beginning, a companion to Masha.

— *Donald M. Fiene*

THE FAMILY OF PASCUAL DUARTE
(La familia de Pascual Duarte)

Author: Camilo José Cela (1916-)
First published: 1942
Genre: Novel
Locale: Extremadura, Spain
Time: Early twentieth century
Plot: Social realism

Pascual Duarte (pahs-KWAHL DWAR-teh), a peasant of Extremadura, Spain, who has a murderous destiny. He tries to alleviate the tensions and hostility of his life by acts of ferocity. His first acts of violence—the killing of animals, tavern fights, and even the murder of his wife's lover, El Estirao—seem to occur spontaneously in moments of rage, but the murder of his mother is premeditated. He also shoots his grandmother and may be responsible for the death of the village patriarch, Don Jesús González de la Riva, during an uprising at the start of the Spanish Civil War. His life story, written as he awaits execution, is an attempt at least to explain, if not to justify, his cruelty. He claims to have made his peace with God and humanity and is ready to die, but his end is as ignominious as his life. His courage fails him, and he must be dragged to the scaffold, crying out that no one has the right to judge him.

Pascual's mother, whose name is not given. A drunkard, slovenly and illiterate, she is the devil incarnate in her son's eyes. Pascual is accustomed to her constant belittlement and scorn of him. It is her cruelty toward her handicapped young son Mario, Pascual's brother, that serves as the catalyst for Pascual's growing resentment and hate. These emotions and her treatment of his second wife finally incite him to murder.

Rosario (roh-SAHR-ee-oh), Pascual's beautiful younger sister, who is the only softening influence in the family. She is adored by her parents and by Pascual. Their lives are shattered when she runs away and becomes a prostitute. She returns home, ill with fever, and almost dies. The family nurses her back to health, but she soon leaves again, unable to break away from her abusive relationship with El Estirao, a pimp. Rosario is the only one who seems to have genuine affection for Pascual. When he returns home after serving his sentence for killing El Estirao, he finds Rosario gone. This loss leads him to his final condemnation.

Mario, Pascual's handicapped little brother. Retarded, unable to walk, and unloved and scorned by his mother, Mario spends his days groveling in the dirt like an animal. In fact, he is treated worse than a dog by everyone except Rosario. In a horrifying moment, his ears are eaten by pigs. He is found drowned in a vat of oil, perhaps murdered by his mother's lover, Rafael, who may be his biological father.

Esteban Duarte Dinaz (ehs-TEH-bahn DWAR-teh dee-NAHS), Pascual's father. Esteban is a drunken bully who once served time in prison. Proud of his own ability to read and write, he tries to better his son's condition by sending him to school. Two days before Mario is born, he is bitten by a rabid dog. Locked in a closet, he dies mad. His wife laughs when she sees the fearful expression on the face of the corpse.

El Estirao (ehs-tee-ROW), Rosario's pimp and lover. He is called El Estirao (meaning "stretched" and "pulled taut") because of the upright, rigid manner of his walk. He is admired by the men of the village for his cockiness, self-assurance, and pride. He is a bully who lives off women. When Pascual abandons his family for a time, he has an affair with Pascual's wife. Pascual kills him but has to admit that the man is not a coward.

Lola, Pascual's first wife. She marries Pascual after discovering she is pregnant as the result of what could be seen as Pascual's rape of her. After the miscarriage of this first baby and the death in early infancy of a second, her sorrow and resentment drive Pascual away. She has an affair with El Estirao and becomes pregnant. Astonished at Pascual's return to the village, she confesses what she has done and then dies mysteriously in his arms. Her death may be caused by grief, shame, or fright, or Pascual himself may be responsible.

Esperanza (ehs-peh-RAHN-sah), Pascual's timid second wife. His mother's treatment of her convinces Pascual that he must murder the older woman before she also poisons his second marriage.

Don Manuel, the curate of the village and the only one who believes that Pascual has potential. He helps Pascual to arrange his marriage to Lola.

— Charlene E. Suscavage

THE FAMILY REUNION

Author: T. S. Eliot (1888-1965)
First published: 1939
Genre: Drama
Locale: England
Time: The twentieth century
Plot: Symbolic realism

Amy, Dowager Lady Monchensey, an old member of the English aristocracy. She is determined to preserve the family estate, Wishwood, as it has always been and use it as a means to keep the family together. Like most people who are used to giving orders, she believes that her desires eventually will be fulfilled, in this case her wish that her oldest son will return to take over the estate and marry her ward. As she dies, she begins to see that she has been living in an unreal world; some of the things happening around her then begin to make sense.

Harry, Lord Monchensey, Amy's son. Having returned home for the first time in eight years, he finds his family still trying to deny any change in the world. While he was gone, he had murdered his wife, and he is currently searching for some satisfactory way of life. In the few hours that he spends at Wishwood, he finds that the ghosts that have been following him are not his at all, but his father's, and that he is really pursuing them. He soon leaves to seek out the deeper reality that he has just glimpsed.

Agatha, Amy's sister. Many years prior to the action of the play, Agatha fell in love with her sister's husband but convinced him that he must not murder Amy because of her pregnancy. At the time of the play, Agatha is making her first visit to Wishwood in thirty years. She is the only one of the older members of the family who has any sense of reality or who is aware of the changes that have taken place around them. She helps Harry to glimpse reality and advises him to leave immediately.

Downing, Harry's servant and chauffeur. Although he has seen the Eumenides, he realizes they have nothing to do with him and is therefore able to treat the subject with equanimity. He has complete faith in his master's ability to cope with the situation.

Mary, Amy's niece and ward. Although she is aware of Lady Monchensey's plans for her marriage to Harry, she knows that this will not do. Upon Harry's return, she finally finds the courage to leave the estate and enlists the aid of Agatha in carrying out her plans.

Ivy and

Violet, Amy's other two sisters. They understand nothing of what is going on around them, not even that they are old and no longer a part of a moving world. Their chief interest in life is Amy's will.

Colonel the Honorable Gerald Piper and

the Honorable Charles Piper, brothers of Amy's deceased husband. Much like Amy's sisters, they are living in the past, but they retain their confidence that they can meet the challenges of a changing world.

Dr. Warburton, an old friend of the family who is called in to try to diagnose Harry's trouble.

The Eumenides (ew-MEHN-ih-deez), the evil spirits that Harry believes are following him. They are seen by him and Downing, as well as by Agatha and Mary.

Denman, a parlor maid.

Sergeant Winchell, a policeman in the local village.

FAMILY VOICES

Author: Harold Pinter (1930-)
First published: 1981
Genre: Drama
Locale: England
Time: The 1980's
Plot: Psychological realism

Voice 1, a man, younger than twenty-one years of age, who has recently moved to the city and away from his biological family. He has become part of a new family, the Withers, in which the relationships are based on heterosexual and homosexual needs and power plays. He recounts, through a series of monologues, the happenings in their house, which appears to be a brothel and from which only he is able to leave. These monologues are filled with so much ambiguity and so many lies and contradictory statements that it is impossible to verify any truth within the play. In attempting to break away from intense Oedipal relationships, he remains confused and torn about his own sexuality and identity.

Voice 2, the mother of voice 1. She still lives in a rural community. Feeling deserted and isolated, in the past as well as in the present, she associates herself with the symbols of an "indifferent fire," winter, and eternal night. Her feelings for her son are equally contradictory, ranging from love with sexual undertones to hatred to a final giving up on him. She relinquishes her physical hold, but the psychological link that she has forged will tie her son to her emotionally in ways that neither of them ever will be able to accept. The core of this family unit will remain twisted and bitter.

Voice 3, the presumably dead father of voice 1. Alternately declaring himself not dead and then dead, he finally admits that he is ensconced in a "glassy grave" where the absolute silence is broken only by the frightening sound of a dog. He is one of the living dead; his actual demise registers no more on those around him than his life did. More than any of the other characters, he talks in a vacuum; no one pays any attention to him, and he is always the odd man out in the mother-son relationships. At the end of the play, he holds out the promise of special knowledge, but like many of the fathers created by the playwright in other works, he can never reveal his secret.

— *Lori Hall Burghardt*

FAR FROM THE MADDING CROWD

Author: Thomas Hardy (1840-1928)
First published: 1874
Genre: Novel
Locale: Wessex, England
Time: 1869-1873
Plot: Psychological realism

Gabriel Oak, a sturdy young English farmer. Refused as a husband by Bathsheba Everdene, he also loses his farm through ill luck. Disheartened by these events, he becomes a shepherd and is taken on at the farm just inherited by his beloved. Although the girl proposes to manage the farm herself, she soon puts more and more of its affairs into the hands of Gabriel Oak, whose skill and loyalty she can trust. Saying no more of love or marriage, Gabriel watches the courtship of Bathsheba by Mr. Boldwood, a well-to-do farmer of the neighborhood. He also watches when she is courted by Sergeant Francis Troy and becomes the latter's wife. During this time, although disappointed in love, Gabriel is so successful at managing his beloved's farm that he becomes the manager of Mr. Boldwood's farm as well. When Bathsheba's marriage ends tragically and Mr. Boldwood is imprisoned for murder, Gabriel still loyally serves both. He finally decides to leave England. When he informs Bathsheba of his intention, she suddenly realizes that she loves the loyal young farmer. She reveals her love for him, and they are married.

Bathsheba Everdene, a vain and unpredictable young woman of great beauty, loved for many years by Gabriel Oak. Despite her personal weaknesses, she is a practical woman after taking over the farm inherited from her uncle. She hires Gabriel as a shepherd but soon makes him the bailiff in all but name. She rejects the proposal of Mr. Boldwood, a well-to-do neighbor, but she readily falls to the audacious lovemaking of Sergeant Troy. Though she loves him, she distrusts his character; she travels to Bath to break the engagement with him, but her trip results in their marriage. The marriage is unfortunate, for her husband is a wasteful, disloyal man who has married her without love, attracted by her beauty and her money. After being revealed as the seducer of one of the farm girls, he disappears and is presumed dead. His wife gradually admits Mr. Boldwood as a suitor once again, but Troy suddenly reappears to claim his wife and her fortune. His effort is cut short by a blast from a shotgun in the hands of Mr. Boldwood. For Bathsheba, who loved her wastrel husband despite his faults, the shock is deep, but as the months go by, her emotional wounds heal. Given an opportunity, she recognizes the worth of Gabriel Oak, whom she marries. She has learned by bitter experience what to value in a man.

Francis Troy, an arrogant, selfish man. Reared as the son of a doctor and his French wife, Troy is reputedly the son of the doctor's wife and a nobleman who was her lover. Though given a good education, Troy enlists in a regiment of dragoons and becomes a sergeant. A handsome man and a pleasant one when he wants to be, he has many successes with women, including Bathsheba Everdene, who becomes his wife; he is attracted by her beauty, wealth, and position. With her money, he buys himself out of the army, leads a pleasant, wasteful life, and almost ruins his wife's farm. One of his earlier victims appears and, with her infant, dies. For Troy, who really loved the woman, the shock is great. After a violent scene with his wife, he disappears and is presumed dead, although he actually lives a hand-to-mouth existence as an actor in a cheap company. Tiring of that life, he returns to claim his wife. His brutal and surprising reappearance is cut short when he is killed by Mr. Boldwood, his wife's suitor.

Mr. Boldwood, a confirmed bachelor of middle age who falls in love with Bathsheba Everdene and courts her, only to lose her to another man. His love endures and, after her husband's disappearance, he courts her again. His patient courtship, about to succeed, is ended by the reappearance of Francis Troy, who brutally tries to force his wife to go to her home with him from a Christmas party at Mr. Boldwood's house. Boldwood, outraged by Troy's behavior, shoots Troy and kills him. Mr. Boldwood is convicted of murder and sentenced to hang, but his sentence is commuted to imprisonment when evidence is brought forward that he is mentally deranged.

Fanny Robin, a pretty servant in the Everdene household. She foolishly allows herself to be seduced by Francis Troy while he is in the army. Though he promises to marry her, she finds herself deserted and expecting a child. She returns to her home community just in time to have her baby, only to die along with the infant. Their deaths, caused in part by Troy's refusal to help the girl when he finds her on the road in need, reveal him for what he is.

Jan Coggan, a worker on the Everdene farm, a good friend to Gabriel Oak.

Lydia (Liddy) Smallbury, Bathsheba's loyal and trusted maid.

FAR TORTUGA

Author: Peter Matthiessen (1927-   )
First published: 1975
Genre: Novel

Locale: Various locations in the Caribbean Sea
Time: April and May, 1965
Plot: Impressionistic realism

Raib Avers, the captain of the *Lillias Eden*, a turtle fisherman and sailor. He is a resident of Grand Cayman in the Caribbean, as are most of the rest of the crew. Unforgiving and coarse, the fifty-four-year-old Raib is more comfortable with sails than with his new diesel engines, more attuned to an older, simpler time and bitter in the face of the modern world. As the story begins, he is sailing out late to an exhausted turtling ground in a half-renovated ship with a ragged crew, a bad radio, no life preservers, and no cook. He taunts and bullies the crew until they begin to assert themselves. He makes a desperate attempt to sail out of a dangerous reef and is fatally wounded in the ensuing crash. The ship sinks.

Junior (Speedy) Bodden, an inexperienced crewman determined to learn from his first voyage. A black Honduran, he is a hardworking example to the crew and has the captain's hard-earned respect. He dreams of returning to his piece of farmland on Grand Cayman. Acknowledging changing ways, he is determined to survive and, indeed, is the lone survivor of the shipwreck.

Byrum Powery Watler, an experienced crewman, though a listless and lazy sower of discord. He is a modern sailor who wants everything on the ship to be up to date, who shows no respect toward the captain, and who tells stories about the backgrounds of the captain and others.

Vemon Dilbert Evers, a crewman most noted for his drinking, though he is an experienced turtler. He is bitter and comes to his work slowly in the beginning, but he develops as a tutor for Speedy, who needs teaching and learns quickly.

William Parchment, the first mate of the *Lillias Eden*, an experienced sailor and turtler. Even the captain claims that Will is the best turtler aboard. He is the most reliable and knowledgeable among the crew, and he supports and defends the captain. One of a handful of survivors of a shipwreck, he knows the power of the sea.

Wodie Greaves, a crewman who is wanted for murder. A superstitious and yet joyful and natural man, he regales the crew with examples of his sense of the supernatural. He angers the captain when he tells the crew that he feels they are bound for their deaths.

Miguel Moreno Smith, the ship's engineer. Sulky and explosive, he imagines himself a fine singer of love songs, but he rarely completes one without cursing. An opportunist, he turns against the crew when the ship is boarded by thieves.

Athens Ebanks, a crewman, Byrum's sometime partner. He and Byrum provide much of the rumor about Captain Raib and Desmond Eden.

Desmond Eden, the captain of the *Davy Jones* and Raib Avers' degenerate half brother. He has their father, Andrew Avers, aboard his ship until the ships meet; then Raib Avers takes him aboard.

Jim (Buddy) Eden Avers, a crewman and Raib Avers' seventeen-year-old son, though Raib barely acknowledges his presence. He admires his father but is not a sailor; with his books and seasickness, he is more a scholar. He takes responsibility for Andrew Avers, his unacknowledged grandfather.

Andrew Avers, Desmond Eden and Raib Avers' father, the former captain of a turtling vessel. He is taken aboard the *Lillias Eden* after having a stroke as a crewman aboard Desmond Eden's ship. Once aboard the *Lillias Eden*, he refuses to eat or speak. He is lashed to the mast, with a conch shell in his hands, until he dies.

— *John S. Nelson*

FAREWELL FROM NOWHERE
(Prochanie iz niotkuda)

Author: Vladimir Maximov (Lev Samsonov, 1930-1995)
First published: 1974
Genre: Novel
Locale: The Soviet Union
Time: Late 1930's through early 1950's
Plot: Autobiographical

Vladimir (Vlad) Samsonov, a Russian youth. Vlad is, for the most part, modeled on the author and is the main character. At the beginning of this coming-of-age story, he is a small Jewish boy growing up in the Moscow suburb of Sokolniki. He becomes aware, early in life, of his background and of the resulting disadvantages. He spends his life trying to adjust to his precarious position while holding on to his tenuous yet deep-rooted family ties. As a schoolboy, he merges his individuality with the collective and renounces his dissident father, a concentration camp convict. Later, he is forced to leave home and his mother, who is surprisingly glad to get rid of him and whom he never forgives for that. Vlad finds love and support in his grandfather Saviely, which unfortunately does not prevent him from spending long years wandering and searching for his true self. In his life as a delinquent, sleeping in railroad stations and shantytowns and serving time in jail, reformatories, and juvenile detention centers, two things keep Vlad alive: love for books and the goodness of some of his fellow tramps. Although several times he is on the verge of giving up in despair and committing suicide, he survives primarily because of his urge to be a poet and because of his constant thinking of home, to which he wants to return in triumph. He also benefits from his ability to adapt quickly and painlessly to new situations, from being mature for his age, and from some qualities that make others, especially his peers, like him and want to help him (most of them affectionately call him "kid"). Prone to falling in love, which often leads to misfortune and disappointments, he finds little happiness with women, being always aware of a wall dividing him from others. This pronounced egotism leads at times to a persecution complex and makes him dream of being pursued. At the same time, he is always looking for fairness and justice, and he often wonders why people cannot live in peace with one another. Expressing his love-hate feelings for Russia, he vows to return in the hope that the country will finally understand and embrace its stepchildren, the Jews.

Alexei Samsonov, his father, who plays a brief but important role in Vlad's life. Through his incarceration, Alexei personifies for the young boy the persecution of his race and the basic injustice of the system in which they are forced to live. In the short time the father spends with his precocious son, he teaches him a few important lessons, the primary one being that when a man betrays another, he betrays himself. By repenting his betrayal, Vlad makes up for his father's seemingly futile life, suffering, and early death in World War II, when he and many others were abandoned to their fate by their officers.

Fedosya Samsonov, Vlad's mother. She is an apathetic woman, seemingly going to pieces under the blows life has dealt their family. She is largely absent in Vlad's life, except for her indifference toward him, which, in turn, contributes to his misery but also to his resolve not to submit to fate's cruelty.

Saviely Mikheyev, Vlad's grandfather, a retired railroad worker. Representing the Russian half of Vlad's background, Saviely symbolizes the split in Vlad's psyche that leads to his love-hate relationship with his country. An unsociable man who has never had any dealings with his children and never had any friends, he nevertheless provides, through his love for Vlad, the only mooring for the young boy adrift in a sea of seeming indifference and hopelessness.

Sergei, a young delinquent, one of many such characters Vlad meets on his wanderings. Developing a strong liking for Vlad, he becomes his protector in the underground world and even from the police. From him, Vlad learns love and respect for others, as well as loyalty to his friends. Vlad sees that through all the murk and filth of existence, Sergei always possessed the divine gift of conscience, which keeps hope alive and makes life worth living.

Boris Essman, an artist from Vlad's Krasnodar days. Essman provides friendship and moral support at the time when Vlad desperately tries to get on the right track. Like so many gifted young people of that time, Boris was prevented from fulfilling his potential, thus deserving the epitaph of a master craftsman who never lived to see his own church spire, a tragic fate Vlad is able to avoid.

— *Vasa D. Mihailovich*

FAREWELL, MY LOVELY

Author: Raymond Chandler (1888-1959)
First published: 1940
Genre: Novel
Locale: Los Angeles and Bay City, California
Time: Late 1930's
Plot: Detective and mystery

Philip Marlowe, an intelligent, wisecracking private investigator about forty years old. Although Marlowe presents a hard-boiled, cynical exterior, it is really a cover for his somewhat sentimental and romantic nature. It is Malloy's heartfelt search for his old girlfriend and his obvious love for her even after eight years in prison that inspire Marlowe to investigate. Marlowe's cynicism is belied when, despite Velma's cold-blooded and self-serving murder of Malloy, Marlowe can still attribute her later suicide to the selfless motive of wishing to spare her husband the embarrassment of a murder trial and its ensuing publicity.

Anne Riordan, a beautiful auburn-haired writer in her late twenties. Her father was fired from his job as police chief of Bay City because he refused to give in to corrupting influences. As a result, Anne is interested both in mysteries and in seeing that justice is done. She helps Marlowe figure out elements of the case and serves as a confidant to whom he can tell his theories about the mystery.

Mrs. Lewin Lockridge Grayle, formerly **Velma Valento**, the beautiful young wife of a rich investment banker many years older than she. Her husband allows her to go out with other men, one of whom is Lindsay Marriott. Mrs. Grayle, then known as Velma Valento, also was at one time Moose's girlfriend; she hid her shady past when she married a wealthy man. Mrs. Grayle is behind the murders of both Mrs. Florian and Marriott and kills Moose to keep him silent. After Moose's murder, she flees, but she kills herself when she is caught.

Moose Malloy, a former convict whose search for his lost love sets the series of tragedies in motion. He is a huge and slow but physically powerful man who dresses in loud outfits that call attention to his appearance. His love for Velma (Mrs. Grayle) is pure and perfect. He dies still unable or unwilling to believe that Velma framed and double-crossed him.

Lieutenant Nulty, a tired policeman. He is the detective in charge of the investigation of Moose's murder of the club manager, which begins the police involvement in the case.

Lieutenant Randall, the police officer in charge of the investigation of Marriott's murder and the person to whom Marlowe gives much of the information that he uncovers.

Lindsay Marriott, the escort of a number of beautiful wealthy women. He is also, however, a finger man for a gang of jewel thieves who rob the women.

— James Baird

THE FAREWELL PARTY
(La Valse aux adieux)

Author: Milan Kundera (1929-)
First published: 1976
Genre: Novel
Locale: Czechoslovakia
Time: The 1960's
Plot: Farce

Klima, a rich and famous jazz trumpeter. Klima is a polite and gallant gentleman who loves his wife immensely yet needs to be with other women occasionally. For him, these affairs strengthen the erotic passion of his marriage. Deep down, he dreads all women and feels doomed to fall victim to the power that pregnancy gives them over men. This fear is realized when Ruzena makes her paternity claim on him. He is generally a calm, reasonable, and clear-thinking man, but in trying to persuade Ruzena to have an abortion, his nerves overcome him and cause him inadvertently to say and do things he later regrets. A clever and imaginative liar, Klima ultimately is a bumbler and muddles through only by luck and the intervention of others. Professionally, he loves playing the trumpet but is not truly comfortable with his fame as an artist. Too much attention worries him.

Ruzena, a nurse at a health and fertility spa in the mountains. Ruzena is a forthright and hard-edged young woman, a moderately attractive blond in a desolate rural existence. She envies the wealthy married women she attends and fears that she will have to settle for a life with Franta, whom she loathes but tolerates. She likes power and longs for excitement. She spends one night with Klima and convinces herself that he is therefore responsible for her pregnancy, which offers a way out of her current existence. At first, she is determined to have the baby. She is swayed by those around her, however—her friends one way and Klima the other—and ends up confused and indecisive, not knowing what she wants or whom she can trust.

Bartleff, an older American patient at the spa. Bartleff is a jovial bon vivant who, in spite of serious illness, energetically loves and affirms life. He is married to a younger woman who recently bore him (he assumes) a son. He is intelligent and well read, especially in religion and philosophy, and he paints striking religious pictures as a hobby. Talkative, generous, and often theatrical, he usually is the center of attention.

Kamila Klima, Klima's beautiful wife. Kamila was on the road to a successful singing career when illness cut it short, and now her beauty is pervaded with an air of sadness. She is devoted to her husband but does not trust him and has learned to exploit her moods and sickliness to get his sympathy. Plagued by jealousy and constant suspicions, she sets out to catch Klima in his philandering. Despite her certainty, she is terrified of the truth.

Dr. Skreta, the doctor who runs the health and fertility spa. Dr. Skreta is a middle-aged gynecologist with a supercilious attitude toward almost everything. A blatant chauvinist, he theorizes at length about women and treats his patients in a ridiculously offhand manner. He is a dominant person and a schemer who imposes his will on others. Dr. Skreta detests stupid people and is secretly populating the countryside—and eventually, he hopes, the world—with his own progeny by injecting a special fertility drug—his sperm—into women who believe themselves barren but who, he knows, suffer only from their husbands' inadequate virility. He is much more interested in what is practical and expedient than in what is moral. He also is an amateur drummer.

Franta, a local mechanic and Ruzena's boyfriend. Franta is pathetically in love with Ruzena. His possessiveness and jealousy drive him to extremes of both violent rage and superhuman patience. He proudly believes that he is responsible for Ruzena's pregnancy and is determined that she bear the child.

Jakub, a forty-five-year-old political dissident who has come to the spa to bid Dr. Skreta and Olga farewell. Jakub is an intellectual who thinks exhaustively, reads symbolic meaning into everything, and takes moral questions very seriously. Although prone to sentimental and dramatic perceptions and at heart very compassionate, he has learned to conceal his inner states. Having endured persecution and imprisonment, he is extremely cynical about human nature. His true solace is a poison pill, procured years ago from Dr. Skreta, by which he has maintained control over his own death and which, now that he has permission to emigrate, he no longer believes he needs. Despite his comprehensive moral ruminations, Jakub is a notorious procrastinator and freezes at the moment of action. He has mixed feelings about leaving his homeland and about his ward, Olga, whom he loves paternally but sometimes considers an unwanted burden.

Olga, a young, frail patient at the spa. Olga's father was wrongly executed when she was seven years old, and she was adopted and reared by Jakub. She loves Jakub dearly but resents the patronizing way he treats her and wants to be recognized for the woman she has become. She is very intelligent and strongly committed to principles such as freedom and moral rectitude. Her anxiety, uncertainty, and weakness, however, keep her from being the calm, elegant, self-assured, and daring modern woman she imagines herself to be. Olga often becomes detached from life, one who observes rather than one who experiences. A silent and private woman, she is fascinated with death.

— B. P. Mann

A FAREWELL TO ARMS

Author: Ernest Hemingway (1899-1961)
First published: 1929
Genre: Novel
Locale: Northern Italy and Switzerland
Time: During World War I
Plot: Impressionistic realism

Lieutenant Frederic Henry, an American who has volunteered to serve with an Italian ambulance unit during World War I. Like his Italian companions, he enjoys drinking, trying to treat the war as a joke, and (it is implied) visiting brothels. Before the beginning of a big offensive, he meets Catherine Barkley, one of a group of British nurses assigned to staff a hospital unit. Henry begins the prelude to an affair with her but is interrupted by having to go to the front during the offensive; he is wounded, has an operation on his knee, and is sent to recuperate in Milan, where he again meets Miss Barkley, falls in love with her, and sleeps with her in his hospital room. When Henry returns to the front, he knows Catherine is pregnant. In the retreat from Caporetto, Henry is seized at a bridge across the Tagliamento River and realizes he is about to be executed for deserting his troops. He escapes by swimming the river. At Stresa, he rejoins Catherine and, before he can be arrested for desertion, the two lovers row across Lake Como to Switzerland. For a few months, they live happily at an inn near Montreux—hiking, reading, and discussing American sights (such as Niagara Falls, the stockyards, and the Golden Gate) that Catherine must see after the war. Catherine is to have her baby in a hospital. Her stillborn son is delivered by Caesarian section; that same night, Catherine dies. Lieutenant Henry walks back to his hotel through darkness and rain. As developed by Hemingway, Henry is a protagonist who is sensitive to the horrors and beauties of life and war. Many of his reactions are subtly left for the reader to supply. At the end of the novel, for example, Henry feels sorrow and pity for the dead baby strangled by the umbilical cord, but the full, unbearable weight of Catherine's death falls upon the reader.

Catherine Barkley, the nurse whom Frederic Henry nicknames "Cat." She had been engaged to a childhood sweetheart killed at the Somme. When she falls in love with Henry, she gives herself freely to him. Although they both want to be married, she decides the ceremony would not be a proper one while she is pregnant; she feels they are already married. Catherine seems neither a deep thinker nor a very complex person, but she enjoys life, especially good food, drink, and love. She has a premonition that she will die in the rain; the premonition is tragically fulfilled at the hospital in Lausanne.

Lieutenant Rinaldi (rih-NAHL-dee), Frederick Henry's jokingly cynical friend. Over many bottles, they share their experiences and feelings. Although he denies it, Rinaldi is a master of the art of priest-baiting. He is very fond of girls, but he teases Henry about Catherine, calling her a "cool goddess."

The Priest, a young man who blushes easily but manages to survive the oaths and obscenities of the soldiers. He hates the war and its horrors.

Piani (PYAH-nee), a big Italian soldier who sticks by Henry in the retreat from Caporetto after the others in the unit have been killed or have deserted. With other Italian soldiers he can be tough, but with Henry he is gentle and tolerant of what men suffer in wartime.

Helen Ferguson, a Scottish nurse who is Catherine Barkley's companion when Frederic Henry arrives in Stresa. She is harsh with him because of his affair with Catherine.

Count Greffi, ninety-four years old, a former diplomat with whom Frederic Henry plays billiards at Stresa. A gentle cynic, he says that men do not become wise as they grow old; they merely become more careful.

Ettore Moretti (EHT-toh-ray moh-REHT-tee), an Italian from San Francisco serving in the Italian army. Much decorated, he is a professional hero whom Frederic Henry dislikes and finds boring.

THE FATHER
(Fadren)

Author: August Strindberg (1849-1912)
First published: 1887
Genre: Drama
Locale: Sweden
Time: Mid-nineteenth century
Plot: Psychological realism

The Captain, a captain of cavalry who is the chief sufferer in this domestic tragedy. He was rejected by his mother and consequently sought a mother/wife in marriage. Driven to raving madness by his wife, he is straitjacketed and suffers a stroke.

Laura, his wife. Accepting the maternal side of her relationship with her husband, she loathes her role as wife and takes vengeance on her husband by destroying him. In her efforts to prove him mad, she resorts to forgery and to misrepresentation of his scientific interests, which in fact she does not understand. She also exploits a suspicion that she has planted in his mind, that their daughter is not his.

Bertha, their daughter and a chief object of conflict.

Margaret, the Captain's old nurse. She tries to reassure him periodically; it is she who at last calms him enough to slip a straitjacket on him.

Dr. Ostermark, the new village doctor, to whom Laura goes with her "evidence" of her husband's insanity.

Auditor Safberg, a freethinker with whom the Captain intends to board Bertha so that she will be educated away from the influence of her mother and of her grandmother, who is bent on teaching her spiritualism.

Nojd, a trooper in difficulties because he impregnated a servant girl. His relatively trivial problem suggests to Laura the weapon she successfully uses against her husband.

Emma, the servant girl in trouble.

Ludwig, who Nojd claims may well be the father of Emma's child.

The Pastor, Laura's brother, before whom Nojd is called. His sympathy for Nojd is greater than the Captain's. Later, when the Pastor sees through Laura's scheme, she dares him to accuse her.

FATHER MELANCHOLY'S DAUGHTER

Author: Gail Godwin (1937-   )
First published: 1991
Genre: Novel
Locale: Romulus, Virginia, and Charlottesville, North Carolina
Time: 1972-1988
Plot: Domestic realism

Margaret Gower, the protagonist and narrator. Margaret's father, Walter, is an Episcopal priest; her mother, Ruth, abandoned the family when Margaret was six years old. Walter is a victim of frequent bouts of depression, and as Margaret grows older, she gradually assumes her mother's old role of caretaker for him. Sharing her father's introspection, as well as his faith in God and in the church, she tries to find a path into the confusing world of adulthood. She is, in turns, insightful and naïve about herself and those close to her. A generally reliable narrator, she has a keen sense of character and an inclination to see people kindly. For all of her insight into those around her, she avoids the obvious truth about her mother's reasons for leaving.

Walter Gower, Margaret's father and the rector of St. Cuthbert's Church in Romulus, Virginia. He is a wise man with a deep faith in God and a sometimes unbelievable capacity for patience and forbearance. The "Father Melancholy" of the book's title, he suffers from frequent and severe depressions, which he calls "the Black Curtain." When the Curtain is open, he is an inspiring priest and mentor, as well as a caring father. When it is closed, he becomes strongly dependent—emotionally and physically—first on his wife, then on his daughter.

Ruth Gower, Margaret's mother. As a college student in her early twenties, Ruth had fallen in love with Walter, sixteen years her senior, and married him. By the time their daughter Margaret is six years old, Ruth has become bored with her marriage and her life, largely because of the overpowering neediness of her husband. On an impulse, she takes off with an old school friend, Madelyn Farley, who is returning to New York. With Madelyn and her painter father, Ruth explores her own artistic talents and takes her first paying job. She makes ineffective attempts to stay close to Margaret but dies in an auto accident before Margaret is old enough to understand what Ruth is trying to do.

Madelyn Farley, a set designer, Ruth's old friend. Madelyn is artistic and self-confident. She seem exotic and bold to Ruth, and rather rude and self-absorbed to Walter and Margaret. Madelyn shows Ruth the world of the theater, introduces her to other artists (including Madelyn's father, a famous but ill-mannered painter), and encourages Ruth's own meager artistic talents. She blames Walter and religion for Ruth's unhappiness until she learns that Ruth was incapable of happiness.

Old Farley, a famous landscape painter, Madelyn's father. Like Madelyn, Old Farley has devoted himself entirely to his art, leaving no room in his life for human attachments. He is constantly rude and angry, and he seems not to notice Madelyn's attentions to him.

Adrian Bonner, the pastoral counselor at the larger Episcopal church in Romulus. In his forties, Adrian is intelligent and kind. Margaret is attracted to him, in the same way that her mother was attracted to the much older Walter in her own youth. Like Walter, Adrian is a burdened man—he is a victim of child abuse. His strongest attachment is to Walter, who becomes his mentor.

— *Cynthia A. Bily*

THE FATHERS

Author: Allen Tate (1899-1979)
First published: 1938
Genre: Novel
Locale: Northern Virginia and Georgetown
Time: 1860-1861
Plot: Historical realism

Lacy Buchan (BUHK-an), the narrator of the novel. Now sixty years old and a bachelor, he was fifteen in April of 1860, when his mother died. He remembers the events of that year, the one before the beginning of the Civil War. The narrator is an educated, pensive man who wants to understand what happened to his family and why. The boy was torn between the tradition represented by his father and the more exciting lifestyle of George Posey. During the year in which the action of the novel takes place, Lacy falls in love with his brother-in-law's sister, Jane, but he does not have the courage to tell his brother, Semmes, who proposes to her. Lacy is confused by events; as an adult, he is confused by the meaning of the events. On the whole, he is an observer who joins the Confederate Army to be a man of action like his brother-in-law but generally finds himself watching and trying to understand or explain rather than change what is happening.

Major Lewis Buchan, Lacy's father. Major Buchan is a traditional but impractical man. His plantation, Pleasant Hill, is not profitable. He tries to free some of his slaves, but the man he has chosen to manage his affairs, his son-in-law, sells them instead. The major seems past his prime, unable to run his life or help his children. When discussions about the North and the South arise, he assumes that his sons are Unionists, as he is. When his son Semmes becomes a Confederate, the major disowns him. To him, honor is everything. When Union soldiers give him a half hour to get out of his house before they burn it, he refuses to tell them he is on their side; instead, he hangs himself in the house.

George Posey, Lacy's brother-in-law. Lacy sees George as a knight in shining armor. George, however, is pragmatic, not noble. He sells slaves his father-in-law wants to free; he even sells his own half brother, Jim, to buy a mare. Although he is able to win the bride he wants, he does not try to make their marriage succeed. George spends large sums of money to help his Confederate regiment, even though his rival, John Langton, is elected its captain.

Susan Posey, Lacy's sister and George's wife. Lacy blames Susan for manipulating the situation with him, his brother Semmes, and Susan's sister-in-law, Jane. She wants to manage Jane's affairs rather closely because Jane's father is dead and her mother is not capable of helping the girl. After Jim apparently rapes Jane, Susan is torn between wanting him killed and wanting to protect him. After her husband kills her brother Semmes, Susan's hair turns white and she becomes insane.

Jane Posey, Lacy's sister's fifteen-year-old sister-in-law. Lacy loves Jane for what he calls her vitality, but she perceives his love for her as boyish and agrees to marry his brother Semmes. Jane lives in a sheltered but impersonal household in which she is waited on by servants and escorted to a convent for music lessons. Her mentor is Susan, but neither Susan nor Jane's mother could protect her from her half brother, the slave Yellow Jim, of whom she had become afraid.

Yellow Jim, the Poseys' slave and Jane and George's half brother. Jim, son of the Poseys' cook, manages their household and even takes care of Jane. George sees him as "liquid capital" and sells him to buy an expensive horse. Insulted by an overseer who wants to make him a field hand, he runs away and returns to the Poseys. Insulted again when he overhears Jane say that she fears him, he later loses control and assaults her. When George's wife, Susan, urges him to run away, he refuses and stays to be killed by Jane's fiancé, Semmes Buchan.

— *M. Katherine Grimes*

FATHERS AND SONS
(Ottsy i deti)

Author: Ivan Turgenev (1818-1883)
First published: 1862
Genre: Novel
Locale: Russia
Time: 1859
Plot: Social realism

Yevgeny Vassilyitch Bazarov (ehv-GEH-nihy vah-SIH-lihch bah-ZAH-rof), a nihilistic young medical school graduate and Arkady Kirsanov's closest friend. Arrogant and ruthless, Bazarov believes only in the power of the intellect and science. As a revolutionary, he feels himself far superior to Nikolai Kirsanov and his brother. To him, they are hopelessly antiquated humanitarians. He tells them: "You won't fight—and yet you fancy yourselves gallant chaps—but we mean to fight. . . . We want to smash other people."

Arkady Kirsanov (ahr-KAH-dihy kihr-SAH-nof), Nikolai's son and Bazarov's naïve young disciple. For a time, he worships his leader and echoes everything that Bazarov says; however, Arkady lacks the necessary ruthlessness required for a revolutionary spirit. He is unable to believe, as Bazarov does, that a good chemist "is twenty times as useful as any poet." After Bazarov's death, he marries Katya and settles down to a prosaic life on the family estate.

Nikolai Petrovitch Kirsanov (NIH-koh-li peht-ROH-vihch), Arkady's gentle, music-loving father. Possessing a liberal, well-meaning spirit, he is happy to free his serfs and to rent them farm land. In his ineffectual way, he attempts to run the estate profitably. Unfortunately, the newly freed serfs take every opportunity to cheat him out of his rent.

Pavel Kirsanov (PAH-vehl), Nikolai's brother. A dandified patrician, he has little liking for Bazarov or his revolu-tionary ideals. Believing strongly in the aristocratic way of life, he considers Bazarov a charlatan and a boor. In his own heart, however, Pavel knows that the new must supplant the old. Finally, dissatisfied with provincial life, he moves to Dresden, where he is much sought after by the aristocrats.

Katya Loktiv (KAH-tyah lohk-TIHF), Anna Odintsov's attractive young sister. Although she is shy and somewhat afraid of her sister, Katya becomes interested in Arkady. When he asks her to marry him, she readily accepts his proposal and shortly afterward becomes his wife.

Anna Odintsov (AHN-nah oh-DIHN-tsof), a haughty young aristocrat, a widow. Because of her beauty, even the unsentimental Bazarov falls in love with her. At first he interests her, but he is never able to pierce her cold exterior for long. She does show some feeling for him as he is dying and even brings a doctor to his deathbed. Unable to help him, she unbends enough to kiss his forehead before he dies.

Vasily Bazarov (vah-SIH-lihy), a village doctor, the father of young Bazarov. Like the other fathers, he is unable to bridge the gulf between his generation and his son's; in fact, he has no desire to do so. Doting on his son, the old man thinks Yevgeny to be beyond reproach.

Arina Bazarov (ah-RIH-nuh), Yevgeny Bazarov's aging mother. In her way the old woman, although quite superstitious, is clever and interesting. She also loves her son deeply. When he dies, she becomes, like her husband, a pathetic, broken figure.

Fenitchka Savishna (feh-nih-CH-kuh sah-VIHSH-nuh), Nikolai's young mistress. At Pavel's urging, Nikolai finally marries her and thereafter lives a happy life with the gentle, quiet girl.

FAULTLINE

Author: Sheila Ortiz Taylor (1939-)
First published: 1982
Genre: Novel
Locale: Los Angeles, California
Time: The 1980's
Plot: Social realism

Arden Benbow, the mother of six children born during her twelve-year marriage to Whitney Malthus. The marriage ends in divorce after Arden meets and falls in love with Alice Wicks and realizes how oppressive and controlling Malthus has always been. Malthus vindictively sues Arden for custody of the children on the grounds that as a lesbian, she is an unfit mother. Arden's goodness and caring love are testified to by most of the people who know her, and they celebrate with her when she wins custody rights. Much of what she has learned about life came from her irrepressible Aunt Vi. Arden was born on the San Andreas faultline in Southern California, and she knows life is tenuous and always subject to change. She believes that life should be lived with enthusiasm and joy rather than with a selfish or narrow-minded hostility to others. Whether it is releasing the overabundance of rabbits she has into a wilderness area, rearing her children, or hosting a party, she does it with energy and style.

Violet Groot, Arden's **Aunt Vi**, the woman of "furious activity" who is an inspiration for Arden and many others. Aunt Vi's husband tries to control her, but she will not be kept down. She works in a variety of jobs, from yo-yo painter to cake icer to bookie. Mr. Groot has a mistress and quickly puts Vi in a hospital after she suffers a minor stroke. Unwilling to end her life institutionalized, she enlists the help of a young orderly, Mario Carbonara. She invites her niece Arden—then a young woman just out of college—to travel with her and Mario to Mexico, and Vi makes friends wherever they go. She especially impresses Ruby, a former stripper from San Francisco who runs a trailer park where they stay. When Mr. Groot sends private investigator Michael Raven after them, Vi wins him over as well. Mr. Groot eventually sends another investigator, Luther P. Grinwall, who arrives the night Aunt Vi dies. She has almost finished writing a gothic romance novel, and Arden writes the final three pages. Vi's philosophy was that life might end with marriage but not with death. Thirteen years later, when Arden and her family and friends celebrate the custody victory, they fondly celebrate the death of Aunt Vi, whose life-enhancing spirit continues to live in them.

Whitney Malthus, the man Arden marries because of his persistence but who turns out to believe that women are his inferiors and that a wife should have no life of her own. His male ego is hurt when Arden leaves him to live with a woman, and he irately claims it is an oxymoron, an impossible contradiction, for a lesbian to be a fit mother. It is ironic that Malthus always thinks he knows everything and that his high-paying job is as a city planner, because he cannot plan adequately for himself and his family or deal with changing realities. He does not provide his share of financial support and does not know how to treat his children, who adamantly choose to stay with their mother.

Wilson Topaz, a tall black dancer who is discriminated against because of both his color and his homosexuality. He answers Arden's ad for a babysitter and immediately knows he has found family and acceptance as well as inspiration.

Alice Wicks, the woman who comes to love and share her life with Arden. She had married because society expected it of her, but she finds happiness with Arden and they celebrate with their own "wedding" ceremony.

Mario Carbonara, formerly Homer Rice, a hospital orderly whose life is changed by meeting Vi, who inspires him to develop a new self. During the trip to Mexico with Vi and Arden, Mario and private investigator Michael Raven fall in love. Years later, they celebrate with Arden and Alice in a double "wedding."

Ellison Granville Todd, the assistant registrar at the college where Arden and Wilson Topaz had been students. He is pretentious and full of self-importance, and his own words convict him as a bigot. Like Malthus, he cuts himself off from what life is meant to be.

— Lois Marchino

FAUST

Author: Johann Wolfgang von Goethe (1749-1832)
First published: 1790-1833
Genre: Drama
Locale: The world
Time: Indeterminate
Plot: Philosophical

Faust (fowst), a perpetual scholar with an insatiable mind and a questing spirit. The middle-aged Faust, in spite of his enthusiasm for a newly discovered source of power in the sign of the macrocosm, finds his intellectual searches unsatisfactory and longs for a life of experiences in the world of humans. On the brink of despair and a projected suicide, he makes a wager with the Devil that if he ever lies on his bed of slothfulness or says of any moment in life, "Stay thou art so fair," at that moment he will cease to be. He cannot be lured by the supernatural, the sensual, or the disembodied spiritual, but he does weaken in the presence of pure beauty and capitulates to humanitarian action. He displays himself as a sensual man in his deep love for Gretchen (Margarete), only to be goaded to murder by her brother, who sees not selfless love in their actions, but only sin. Faust aspires to the love of Helen of Troy, but he is disconsolate when she appears. As an old man, he returns to his early vision of being a man among men, working and preparing for a better world to be lived here on earth. His death is not capitulation, though he thinks at this point man can cry "stay," and he has never taken his ease or been tempted by a life of sloth. His death is his victory, and his everlasting life is to be lived resourcefully among the creators.

Mephistopheles (mehf-ih-STOF-eh-leez), the Devil incarnate and Lucifer in disguise of dog and man. Portrayed here as a sophisticate, cynic, and wit, he is persuasive and resourceful. He works magic, manages miracles, and creates spirits and situations for Faust's perusal and delectation. His persistence is the more remarkable for the ability of Faust to withstand and refute these offerings, though Mephistopheles often expresses resentment. Somehow more attractive than God and the archangels, he powerfully represents the positive force of evil in its many and attractive guises.

Gretchen, sometimes called **Margarete**, an innocent, beautiful young maiden. A foil for the Devil, Gretchen remarkably personifies womanly love without blemish or fear. She gives herself to Faust, who swears he cannot molest her, with an earthy abandon and remains for a time unearthly innocent in her raptures, until the forces for morality convince her that she has sinned deeply and that she must pay first by destroying her child and then by being sacrificed to the state, suffering death for her transgressions. Brooding over her brother's death, she refuses solace from her lover.

Valentin (VAHL-ehn-teen), a soldier and Gretchen's brother, killed by Faust with the aid of Mephistopheles.

Wagner (VAHG-nur), Faust's attendant, an unimaginative pedant. Serving as a foil for Faust, Wagner expresses himself in scholarly platitudes and learns only surface things. He aspires not to know all things but to know a few things well, or at least understandably; the unobtainable he leaves to Faust. He serves as the Devil's advocate, however, in the temptation of Faust by helping Mephistopheles create Homunculus.

Homunculus (hoh-MUHNG-kyew-luhs), a disembodied spirit of learning. This symbol of man's learning, mind separated from reality, interprets for Mephistopheles what Faust is thinking. The spirit discloses Faust's near obsession with ideal beauty, and thus Faust is given the temptress, Helen of Troy.

Helen of Troy, who appears as a wraith at first and then with form. Representing the classical concept of eternal or ideal beauty, Helen very nearly succeeds where Gretchen failed. She finally seems to Faust only transitory beauty, no matter how mythological and idealized. After this final experience, Faust denounces such hypothetical pursuits and returns to deeds.

Dame Marthe Schwerdtlein (MAHR-teh SHVEHRDT-lin), Gretchen's neighbor and friend, an unwitting tool in the girl's seduction.

FEAR OF FLYING

Author: Erica Jong (1942-   )
First published: 1973
Genre: Novel
Locale: Vienna and elsewhere in Europe, with flashbacks including New York City
Time: The early 1970's
Plot: Social realism

Isadora Wing, the protagonist and narrator. Isadora is a twenty-nine-year-old Jewish poet, the daughter of secular Jews. Her mother gave up painting to have a family, and her father is portrayed as somewhat distant. Isadora is torn between two contradictory impulses: the need for security and a supportive husband and the desire for freedom, adventure, and sexual exploration. Isadora is a writer and intellectual but also a highly sexual being who often says that men's bodies are nice.

Bennett Wing, Isadora's husband, to whom she sometimes refers as a father figure. Bennett is an orthodox Freudian who views all adult actions and feelings as having their genesis in childhood experiences, in particular in the relationship of the young child to his or her parents. Before he and Isadora make any important decisions, he insists that they discuss matters with their respective psychiatrists. Isadora sees him as silent and withdrawn. He has a beautiful body and is expert at providing sexual satisfaction, but he will not talk to her or tell her he loves her.

Adrian Goodlove, a British Laingian psychiatrist whom Isadora meets in Vienna when she goes there for a psychological conference with her husband. Isadora is attracted to his blond good looks and casual manner. He advocates a life of spontaneity and existential freedom. He tells Isadora that she should not be afraid of what is inside her and proposes that they go off together. He turns out to be a disappointment, both as a companion and as a lover.

Judith Stoloff White, also known as Jude, Isadora's mother. The daughter of a painter who painted over her canvases when he ran out of canvases himself, Jude gave up her art to become a wife and mother. She is fond of telling her four daughters that they are the reason she is not a great painter. To Isadora's chagrin, she dresses eccentrically (for Jude, the greatest sin is being ordinary), but she is also Isadora's greatest booster and admirer, praising her high school compositions and listening tirelessly to her poems.

— *Charlotte Templin*

FELIX HOLT, THE RADICAL

Author: George Eliot (Mary Ann Evans, 1819-1880)
First published: 1866
Genre: Novel
Locale: Rural Midland England
Time: 1831-1833
Plot: Social realism

Felix Holt, the radical, an energetic and intelligent young man who objects to his mother's business—selling patent medicines—as fraudulent. Formerly apprenticed to an apothecary, he now works as a watchmaker in order to feel himself closer to the people. A political radical, Felix supports Harold Transome in the first Parliamentary election after the passage of the 1832 Reform Bill, but he objects to the bribery and rabble-rousing in which others indulge. As he fears, the workers riot on Election Day. Trying to disperse the riot, Felix inadvertently kills a constable. He is tried, convicted, and sentenced to four years in prison, but a petition to Parliament secures his release. He marries Esther Lyon.

Harold Transome, the younger son of Mrs. Transome and apparently the heir to Transome Court. Harold has been away in Smyrna for fifteen years, building up a fortune as a merchant and banker. He returns and decides to run for Parliament as a Radical, an allegiance that shocks his Tory mother. He is honest and committed but loses the election. When he discovers that his mother's lawyer, Matthew Jermyn, has been cheating the estate for years, he decides to sue Jermyn. Jermyn attempts to avoid the suit by uncovering the fact, through an old will, that Esther Lyon is really the heiress of Transome Court. Harold invites Esther to his home and falls in love with her, but she rejects his suit and gives up her rights to the property. He abandons his plans to sue Jermyn when he learns that the latter is his father. At first crushed and furious, he is reconciled to his mother by Esther.

Rufus Lyon, another radical, the Dissenting minister of the Independent Chapel in Treby Magna (the Chapel is referred to as "Malthouse Yard"). He had found a destitute Frenchwoman, Annette Ledru, on the street with her infant daughter. He brought them home, later married Annette, and cared for Esther, the daughter, as his own after Annette died. Some papers that Felix finds in the woods lead to Lyon's discovery of the identity of Esther's father. Lyon regards Felix as an exceptional young man.

Esther Lyon, the sensitive and poetic daughter of Annette Ledru and Maurice Christian Bycliffe, brought up by Rufus Lyon. Educated in France, she teaches French in Treby Magna. At first, she and Felix argue about the relative importance of the aesthetic and the political, but she finds him entirely honest and vital. She soon falls in love with him and remains entirely loyal through his trial and short prison sentence.

Mrs. Arabella Transome, Harold's mother, who has long held Transome Court together despite legal and financial problems, an incompetent husband, and a mentally impaired older son. She places all her faith in Harold, her illegitimate son by Matthew Jermyn. Despite her disapproval of her son's politics and his disapproval of Jermyn, the two value and appreciate each other.

Matthew Jermyn, the florid and insinuating lawyer who has mismanaged the estate for his own benefit. He also handles Harold's political campaign and is not above offering bribes.

Mr. Johnson, a London lawyer hired by Jermyn to stir up rabble-rousing activity among the new electorate. He also helps Jermyn in various shady financial operations. Johnson accuses Felix of leading the riot.

Philip Debarry, the successful Conservative candidate in the election. An honorable man, he intercedes on Felix's behalf after the trial.

Henry Scaddon, alias **Maurice Christian Bycliffe (Christian)**, the servant to Philip Debarry, an unsavory character who had, in order to escape the law, changed identities with Maurice Christian Bycliffe, Esther's father, just before Bycliffe's death. Papers in Christian's purse, tossed away as a practical joke and discovered by Felix, reveal the assumed identity.

Mrs. Holt, a poor widow who makes a living selling patent medicines. Later, her son Felix cheerfully supports her. She is a member of Mr. Lyon's Chapel.

The Reverend John Lingon, rector of Little Treby and Mrs. Transome's brother. He is very fond of his nephew Harold and supports his political campaign.

Sir Maximus Debarry, the owner of Treby Manor and Philip's father. Although Sir Maximus is an arch-Tory, he helps petition Parliament to gain Felix's release from prison.

The Reverend Augustus Debarry, his brother and a strong Tory.

Peter Garstin, a mine owner and a Liberal candidate for Parliament.

Sir James Clement, a poor baronet and a Liberal candidate for Parliament.

Mr. Chubb, the politically interested publican of the Sugar Loaf at Sproxton.

Tucker, the constable Felix inadvertently kills during the riot.

Mr. Spratt, a local Tory whose life Felix saves in the riot.

The Reverend Theodore Sherlock, a diffident young rector put to writing political speeches.

Thomas Transome, also called **Tommy Trounsem**, an old and alcoholic bill-paster trampled in the election riot.

Lady Debarry, the wife of Sir Maximus.

Mrs. Jermyn, Matthew's socially pretentious wife, who hates tobacco.

Miss Louisa Jermyn, her daughter, who takes French lessons from Esther Lyon.

Mr. Scales, the butler to the Debarrys, who tosses away the sleeping Christian's purse as a practical joke.

Denner, Mrs. Transome's faithful maid and confidant.

Hickes, Denner's husband, Mrs. Transome's butler.

Dominic, Harold Transome's servant, whom he brings back from Smyrna.

Lyddy, Rufus Lyon's trusted maid.

Mr. Transome, Mrs. Transome's old, paralyzed husband.

Durfey Transome, Mrs. Transome's retarded older son, who dies at an early age.

Harry Transome, Harold Transome's attractive young son, whose mother, a native of Smyrna, is dead.

Mr. Sircome, a local miller and businessman.

Mr. Crowder, a local citizen.

Miss Harriet Debarry, the oldest daughter of the Debarrys.

Miss Selina Debarry, the Debarrys' "radiant" daughter.

Job Tudge, an independent child in Treby Magna, friendly with Esther and Felix.

Felix Holt, Jr., the oldest child of Esther and Felix.

FEMALE FRIENDS

Author: Fay Weldon (1931-)
First published: 1974
Genre: Novel
Locale: London and rural England
Time: Late 1960's or early 1970's, with flashbacks
Plot: Psychological realism

Chloe Evans Rudore, a wife and mother of five (only two of them her biological children). Nearly forty years old, tall, and very slender, with short dark hair, she grew up in a room behind the Rose and Crown, a bar in the British village of Ulden, where her mother, Gwyneth, cleaned and served customers. There she learned never to stand up for herself, but rather to understand and forgive whenever ills befell her. This upbringing left her somewhat lacking in self-esteem. As the novel begins, she is on her way to London to meet her friends Marjorie and Grace, both of whom are urging her to end her husband's affair with the Rudores' French housekeeper. Chloe, however, is almost relieved that her tyrannical husband has found a replacement for her.

Marjorie, a producer at the British Broadcasting Corporation. She is about forty years old and very smart. She has a pear-shaped body, frizzy hair, oily skin, and sad, astonished eyes. She was evacuated from London to Ulden during World War II and essentially was abandoned there by Helen, her socialite mother, to be reared by the Songford family. As a girl, she thought that if she were good, her mother might retrieve her. As an adult, she is still playing the role of the good, capable daughter by shouldering other people's burdens. Chloe claims that Marjorie "invites trouble, in order to face it." Despite this knack, Marjorie often seems to lack the ability to cope with her own misfortunes.

Grace Songford, a high-strung and beautiful woman more than forty years old, with green eyes and red hair. She has some money of her own, but for the most part, she lives off men. As the novel begins, she is sharing a half-finished flat with Sebastian, a twenty-five-year-old actor. As a girl, Grace took Marjorie's fashionable, yet heartless, mother Helen as a role model instead of her own subservient and cowed mother. Her thoughtlessness was tempered somewhat when she married, but after an ugly divorce from her architect husband, she was left completely disillusioned with domestic life. She manages to survive her defeat in a bitter custody fight by affecting no interest in her children. When she has a child fathered by Patrick Bates, she gives the boy to Chloe to rear.

Patrick Bates, a forty-seven-year-old painter with brilliant blue eyes, coarse reddish hair, and a way with women. Chloe, Marjorie, and Grace first met him in Ulden when he was twenty-two and serving as the entertainment officer at the local air force camp. Each of the girls lost her virginity to him, and he never entirely leaves their lives, although only Grace carries on a long-term affair with him. As he grew rich and famous from his painting, he grew nasty and stingy in equal measure. Midge, his despairing wife, eventually committed suicide, and he danced on her grave. As the novel begins, Chloe has not seen him for nine years, Marjorie has taken responsibility for his laundry, and Grace is his occasional lover.

Oliver Rudore, Chloe's husband and a screenwriter of B films. The slight, muscular, and hairy man rules at home with a set of idiosyncratic rules and habits. For a time, in the early 1960's, Oliver and Patrick were drinking and whoring buddies, to the disgust and despair of their wives.

Françoise, Chloe and Oliver's French housekeeper. Stocky and lascivious-looking, the twenty-eight-year-old woman has been sharing Oliver's bed for the past nine months as the novel begins.

— *Liz Marshall*

THE FEMALE MAN

Author: Joanna Russ (1937-)
First published: 1975
Genre: Novel
Locale: Several versions of Earth
Time: 1969 and the future
Plot: Science fiction

Joanna, a writer who frequently is the first-person narrator. She struggles to make a career for herself as a single, liberated woman. Her characteristics of independence, assertiveness, and self-reliance have caused others to label her as masculine when, in fact, she is simply a strong, capable person. Despite her liberated mind-set, Joanna is not comfortable when confronted by the lesbian relationship between Janet and Laura. Joanna is what her configuration of genes produces, given the environment of the United States in the late 1960's. She realizes that to succeed in her culture, she must become a female man, because all the traits that are rewarded are those that are traditionally applied to, and lauded in, men. Joanna believes that she is invisible in her world because all the positions of power, influence, and authority are held by men. Joanna is searching for a way to bring meaning to her life without effacing herself in her male-dominated culture.

Jeannine Dadier, a twenty-nine-year-old unmarried librarian who desperately wants to find the "right" man and get married. She, like the other "J" characters, has the same set of genes as Joanna. In her world's version of reality, World War II did not occur and the Great Depression has continued to the present (1969). She has an unhappily conventional relationship with a thickheaded man named Cal. She spends her time catering to his needs and picking up his dirty underwear. She is tentative and shy, scared of her own shadow and frightened by any display of strength on the part of a woman, even though she at first secretly wishes to be like Janet Evason. At the conclusion of the book, Jeannine decides that she wishes she could be like Jael. In this allegorical story of Joanna's search for identity and meaning, Jeannine represents woman as the oppressed.

Janet Evason, a woman from Whileaway (Earth's far future), where no men exist. She is another result of the genetic program she shares with Jael, Joanna, and Jeannine. She has been sent to Joanna's time as a spy to learn what these times were really like. Janet is a completely self-contained person. In her world, there is no question that women can accomplish whatever they set their minds on doing. They are trained to be independent by the time they reach their early teens. Women give birth without the aid of men. Janet is a free spirit who pursues pleasure without guilt, in particular where love and sex are concerned. She seduces and befriends Laura, a teenager. Whileaway has sent her as an emissary to its past, where she frightens the other women with whom she comes in contact. Despite her world's protestations to the contrary, her culture has adopted as its own the male characteristics that it decried: aggressive, domineering behavior. For example, dueling is one of the preferred ways to resolve conflicts.

Alice-Jael Reasoner, a woman who lives several hundred years prior to Janet Evason's time on Earth. She is a trained assassin who seeks out and destroys chauvinistic men. Jael reveals to Janet that, contrary to the other woman's belief that a plague wiped out all the males on Earth, it was the war between the sexes that occurred during Jael's lifetime that was responsible for the destruction. Her character represents the radical feminist-female separatist answer to male oppression: destruction of the oppressors.

Laura, a teenage girl with whom Janet Evason has a lesbian relationship. She earlier had experienced feelings for other women but had never acted on them. She is an uninhibited person who serves as a foil character to whom the other four women react.

— *Melissa E. Barth*

FENCES

Author: August Wilson (1945-   )
First published: 1985
Genre: Drama

Locale: An American industrial city
Time: 1957-1965
Plot: Domestic realism

Troy Maxson, a garbage collector who is fifty-three years old at the outset of the play. He is a large man with powerful hands, a forceful personality, and a lust for life. After fighting with his father and leaving home at the age of fourteen, he became a thief to survive. He became an excellent baseball player while serving a fifteen-year sentence for murder. Embittered because racist practices prevented him from playing major league baseball, he later insists that his son Cory abandon his dream of playing football and learn a trade. Troy loves his wife, maintains a cool distance from his children, and actively protests discrimination at his workplace. He entertains and inspires his friend Jim Bono with his combination of jovial vulgarity and wisdom, and he seeks to rediscover lost passion with a mistress, Alberta. Unapologetic after fathering a child with her, he becomes isolated from his family in the years preceding his death in 1965.

Rose Lee Maxson, Troy's wife, forty-three years old at the beginning of the play. She admires her husband's strengths and tolerates his faults but comes to regret her lack of assertiveness in his presence. Although her arguments with Troy rarely progress beyond chiding, she strongly opposes him in her support of Cory's interest in football, and she virtually severs communication with him after discovering that he has impregnated his mistress. She agrees to rear the child after Alberta dies giving birth.

Cory Maxson, Troy and Rose's son, a promising high school football player in 1957. His desire to please his demanding and uncompromising father turns to hatred and contempt when he learns of Troy's romantic entanglement. After failing to best his father in a series of confrontations, Cory leaves home. He returns on the day of Troy's funeral in 1965, wearing the uniform of a Marine corporal. He admits that he plans to marry soon and resists attending the burial ceremony.

Gabriel Maxson, Troy's brother, seven years younger. He received a head injury while serving in World War II. As a result, he has a metal plate in his head. Subject to a recurring delusion that he is an incarnation of the archangel Gabriel, he carries an old trumpet wherever he goes. When the play commences, he has moved from Troy and Rose's house to board with Miss Pearl. Later, Troy pays fifty dollars to free him from jail after he has been arrested for disturbing the peace. The question of whether Gabriel should be committed to a hospital is a source of contention between Rose and Troy, who has profited from the compensation dispensed to Gabriel because of his injury. At the end of the play, Gabriel tries to usher Troy into heaven, blowing his trumpet and performing an eerie dance.

Lyons, Troy's oldest son by a previous marriage, a thirty-four-year-old at the beginning of the play. Something of a dilettante, he dabbles in the jazz scene, sporting a trim goatee, a sport coat, and a buttoned-up white shirt without a tie. He visits Troy on Fridays to borrow money. Around the time of his father's retirement in 1961, his relationship with Bonnie comes to an end; later, he is sentenced to three years of imprisonment for cashing other people's checks.

Jim Bono, a fellow garbage collector who has been a loyal friend of Troy since they met in prison. Because he admires Troy and Rose, he is especially concerned about his friend's dalliance. In the years after Rose rejects her husband, he appears to have lost some faith in him as well. His own marriage to Lucille seems stable.

Raynell, a seven-year-old in 1965. She is the daughter of Troy and Alberta.

— David Marc Fischer

FERDYDURKE

Author: Witold Gombrowicz (1904-1969)
First published: 1937
Genre: Novel
Locale: Poland
Time: Mid-1930's
Plot: Farce

Johnnie, the narrator, a writer. At the age of thirty, Johnnie finds himself trapped behind an adult "face" created by others. Realizing this when critics attack his first book, he regresses to adolescence, becoming embroiled against his will in the novel's bizarre plot as though in a dream of immaturity. Abducted and returned to school by the pedantic Professor Pimko, he is powerless to convince anyone that he does not belong there or to assert a truly mature individuality. Passive and irresolute in general, Johnnie rarely articulates his feelings, acting furtively instead. Boarding at the home of the Youthfuls, for example, he falls in love with Zutka but wages a campaign of irrational behavior against her charms, finally bringing about a general brawl. In a world in which meaningful relationships are impossible, once Johnnie subverts the social forms that prevent genuine human contact, escape is his only recourse. At the novel's end, he runs away from his uncle's estate.

Professor T. Pimko, an educator. A ridiculous, bald little man in striped pants and tailcoats, he is so self-assured and overbearingly pedantic that he renders Johnnie helplessly boyish. He leads Johnnie off to school and later to the Youthfuls' home. Pimko's authority is shattered only after he is smitten by Zutka.

Pylaszczkiewicz (pee-LAHSH-kah-vihch), called **Siphon**, Johnnie's schoolmate. Leader of the idealistic, purist faction at school, he engages in a duel of grimaces with Mientus. Victorious, he is then physically assaulted and his innocence violated through his ears, with fatal results.

Mientus, Johnnie's schoolmate. Leader of the school faction denying youth's innocence, he is the most innocent of all, though he spouts obscenities and engages in the duel with Siphon that freezes his face in an ugly grimace. Obsessed with a privileged boy's notions of stable-lad purity, he runs off with Johnnie to the country, where his repeated attempts to fraternize with the servant Bert disrupt the social system.

Kopeida, Johnnie's schoolmate and rival for Zutka. Extremely self-possessed, he stands aloof from the factional strife at school and resists Johnnie's friendly approaches. Later, drawn to Zutka's bedroom by a forged note, he loses his composure.

Zutka Youthful, Johnnie's beloved. Sixteen years old, slim, and athletic, she is the model of the stylish modern schoolgirl, ignorant, insolent, and passionate for life. With her seductive thighs reducing all men to slavish adolescents, she glories in youth's dominance, a tyranny Johnnie can ridicule and ruffle but not undermine.

Mrs. Mary Youthful, Zutka's mother. Cultivated, fat, and high-minded, she is involved in all the right causes and embraces all the right ideas. Wielding modernity in her eagerness to be a sister rather than a mother, she encourages Zutka's youthfulness in the most mindless ways and despises Johnnie's self-conscious posing.

Mr. Victor Youthful, an engineer and architect. Tanned, informal, and vacuous, he at first vies with his wife in spouting platitudes and urging his daughter to be modern. Johnnie's odd behavior reduces him to a depraved, gibbering buffoon, but he sobers up when he catches Pimko and Kopeida in Zutka's room.

Aunt Hurlecka (huhr-LEH-skah), Johnnie's aunt. An oblivious woman of suffocating kindness, she constantly doles out sweets and reminiscences to keep everyone childish.

Uncle Edward, an estate owner. Tall, thin, and delicate, he is the epitome of the bored, pampered, and insensitive aristocrat who responds to others in terms of class. His own social position rests on the exploitation of indispensable servants he despises and fears, and his brutal treatment of Bert at the end results in a rebellion.

Alfred, Johnnie's cousin. A budding young aristocrat whose identity is determined by family and class, he shows little interest in Johnnie until the latter slaps Bert. His ludicrous involvement with an older peasant woman points out the childishness of the landed gentry.

Isabel, Johnnie's cousin, an ordinary girl seemingly incapable of discussing anything except her innumerable ailments. Her youthful passions are aroused in the end when Johnnie abducts her to cover his flight.

Bert, a stable boy. This rustic youth attracts Mientus' attentions, a violation of social form that causes Bert to mock his "betters" and the system. His eventual defense of Mientus precipitates the novel's final outbreak of chaos.

Philifor and

Anti-Philifor, rival professors. Characters in an absurdist fable, they represent the dialectical struggle between synthesis and analysis. Anti-Philifor's attempt to dissolve his rival's wife into her parts is countered by Philifor's synthesizing of the higher self of the other's mistress, all of which leads to a duel in which the women's extremities are shot off.

— Philip McDermott

FIASCO
(Fiasko)

Author: Stanisław Lem (1921-   )
First published: 1986
Genre: Novel

Locale: Saturn's moon Titan and the planet Quinta
Time: The future
Plot: Science fiction

Angus Parvis, a spaceship pilot. Twenty-nine years old, slight, and fair-haired, Parvis arrives in confusion on Titan, a moon of Saturn, with a load of mining equipment. He discovers that his friend and teacher, Pirx, has become lost on a mission between two bases. Going out to rescue him, Parvis also becomes lost. He attempts to save himself from death by instantaneous freezing.

Mark Tempe, a spaceship pilot. Tempe may be either Angus Parvis or Pirx. He was found on Titan one hundred years after he was frozen, his body repaired and restored to life aboard the *Euridyce*, an interstellar ship bound for Quinta. The ship's mission is to contact the only intelligent beings that have detected in the universe since humanity began searching with radio telescopes. After his restoration, he is assigned to help pilot the exploratory vessel that is to land on Quinta. When the mission becomes increasingly violent in the face of the Quintans' apparent lack of interest in communication, Tempe joins forces with Father Arago to urge forms of peaceful contact. He is the only human to land on the planet. Continued misunderstandings lead to his being destroyed by his own superiors when he fails to stay on a schedule of radio contacts.

Father R. P. Arago, a Dominican monk. He is elderly, with almost white hair, but tall, lean, and sinewy, and of dark complexion, with gray, piercing eyes. His role in the mission to Quinta is to guarantee humane behavior in the attempts to communicate. Throughout the fiasco of their attempts, he argues for trust, peacefulness, and risk of selves to preserve the aliens. Once on the scene, Captain Steergard and most of his advisers become increasingly aggressive in their demands that the Quintans respond to them. Arago alone maintains the position agreed on by all the leaders at the beginning of the mission, that if the Quintans do not wish to communicate, they should be left in peace.

Steergard, the captain of the Quinta mission. Trained as a military and spaceship commander, Steergard finds that his training and his mammalian instincts combine to determine his actions once he arrives on Quinta. At the first sign of danger, he begins to think in terms of attack and defense. From that moment, his interpretation of every scrap of evidence about the Quintans is placed in the context of warfare, civil war on the planet, and probable hostility of various kinds toward his mission. His way of seeing becomes the controlling mechanism of the plot; every event becomes part of a militaristic interpretation of the entire series of events.

Lauger, an eminent physicist and member of the Quinta mission. As they travel toward Quinta, he explains various concepts to Tempe. He describes the difficulties of finding and contacting intelligence in outer space. His theories suggest that there is a narrow frame of time within which intelligent civilizations are ripe for contact with one another. He argues that they may easily arrive at Quinta too early or too late for meaningful contact and, therefore, that they must be prepared to leave the Quintans without communicating successfully. Because he is not part of the staff of the contact vessel, the *Hermes*, he is not able to influence directly the events that lead to the fiasco.

— *Terry Heller*

THE FIDDLER'S HOUSE

Author: Padraic Colum (1881-1972)
First published: 1907
Genre: Drama

Locale: The Irish Midlands
Time: Early twentieth century
Plot: Naturalism

Conn Hourican, a talented old fiddler who is fond of traditional melodies. He lives in the countryside of the Irish Midlands. Conn clearly loved his past existence on the open roads and feels hemmed in by the house he and his two daughters inherited. He is a passionate, simple man rather than an abstract thinker, and he feels trapped by the conventions of his farming community. Conn perceives that those living around him are unhappy because they do not live life adventurously.

Maire (Mary) Hourican, the pretty eldest daughter of Conn Hourican. A single woman who has chosen to be her aging father's helper, she shares his love of adventure. Calm and steady in temperament, she has some interest in a local suitor, Brian MacConnell, but cannot summon sufficient interest to marry him. Generously, she allows her sister Anne and Anne's husband-to-be to have rights to the house until they can afford one of their own. She decides to join her father for a life on the open roads of Ireland.

Anne Hourican, Conn Hourican's youngest daughter. Anne is nineteen years old and is in love with James Moynihan, her ardent suitor. Her life revolves around thoughts of marriage to him.

Brian MacConnell, the quiet, intense young farmer who loves Maire Hourican so much that he is trying to build a home for them to live in after their hoped-for marriage. She does not want to marry him at present, content as she is to follow her father's itinerant lifestyle. Taking things well, he wishes her good fortune in her travels.

James Moynihan, the good-natured son of a local farmer and "councillor" who asks for Anne Hourican's hand in marriage. James is a persistent and, finally, successful suitor, though he cannot provide Anne a home in which to live. With Maire's offer of her home, James and Anne can get married.

— *John D. Raymer*

THE FIELD OF VISION

Author: Wright Morris (1910-1998)
First published: 1956
Genre: Novel
Locale: A small Mexican town
Time: The 1950's
Plot: Psychological symbolism

Walter McKee, a successful businessman from Lincoln, Nebraska. On vacation in Mexico with his wife, grandson, and father-in-law, McKee spends his time reminiscing about his boyhood exploits with Gordon Boyd. McKee had witnessed Boyd's charisma and great potential and had been sorely shaken to find Boyd down and out in New York. McKee's obsession with, and absorption into, his friend's life has left him unable to understand the direction and nature of his own life. At a bullfight, McKee is thrilled by the sense of community and daring of the matadors but saddened by the tedium of his own life in comparison. During the bullfight, his wife is appalled by the gore and forces him to take her to the car. In the process, McKee loses sight of his grandson, Gordon. Fearful that this will solidify his wife's contempt, McKee searches for the boy and finds him in the ring. Saddened by the fact that his family witnessed his incompetence, McKee resolves to go on because he lacks the courage to change.

Gordon Boyd, McKee's childhood friend, who has been in competition with him since that time. Boyd essentially exploited McKee's naïve love and turned him into an adoring fan. Boyd effectively directed McKee's life, choosing his wife for him while also making known his love for her. Although Boyd wrote and produced a successful play, he was unable to follow up his potential and collapsed into a paralyzing nostalgia. Unlike McKee, however, Boyd became a compulsive drifter and layman philosopher, seeing through and mocking conventional morality. Boyd has nothing with which to replace it and, like McKee, is trapped in his own past. At the bullfight, Boyd exploits McKee's inadequacies by stealing the attention of his grandson and luring the child into the bullring. Despite his antics, Boyd fails to dishearten McKee or prod Lois into accepting his romantic attention.

Lois McKee, who accepts her life with McKee because he is a provider. Although Lois recognized the early competition between Boyd and her husband, she lacked the courage to fulfill her desire to elope with Boyd. In fact, Boyd's simple seduction terrified Lois into a life of suffocating self-control with McKee. She has succeeded in repressing almost everything in her personality. Mexico, the bullfight, and the close proximity of Boyd scare her into nervous collapse and a hasty retreat to the hotel.

Leopold Lehmann, Boyd's psychologist. He is strictly an observer of the McKee family drama, lending a tolerant understanding of conflicting human passions. As an Austrian immigrant, he holds an outsider position that is the perfect vantage point on American psychological culture. Lehmann is accompanied by his strange transsexual partner, Paula Kahler, and is fascinated by her ability to transform her identity completely from man to woman. Although Lehmann is a tragically lonely figure, he has learned to tolerate difference as the only real defense against loneliness.

Tom Scanlon, Lois' father, who is both eccentric and bordering on senility. Shaped by a harsh life on the plains, he has a furious independence. Scanlon usually chooses not to speak and directs most of his attention to his great-grandson. By imparting frontier anecdotes to the boy, Scanlon hopes to win him into his nineteenth century world.

— *Paul Hansom*

THE FIELDS

Author: Conrad Richter (1890-1968)
First published: 1946
Genre: Novel
Locale: Northwest Territory, later Ohio
Time: Early nineteenth century
Plot: Regional

Sayward Wheeler, called **Saird**, a strong pioneer woman who wants many children; but after having eight, she decides that seven living and one dead are enough, and she leaves her husband's bed. She lives through a period when the forest disappears as the pioneer settlement grows. She contributes her share to this growth and donates land for a meeting house. She realizes that she has neglected her husband and that he has been sleeping with the schoolteacher in the community. When the schoolteacher must quickly marry another man because she is going to have Portius' baby, Sayward is very much ashamed and is reconciled with her husband.

Portius Wheeler, a backwoods lawyer and schoolteacher, Sayward's husband. He has a hand in making Ohio a state and in making his community thrive and grow. Having no desire to return to his family in Boston, he tells them so. Portius wants to move his family into the new town, but Sayward refuses to be parted from the country. Portius has an affair with the schoolmistress but later returns to Sayward.

Genny Scurrah, Sayward's sister, who is a fine singer and who helps Sayward deliver her first child.

Wyitt Luckett, Sayward's brother, who realizes that he is a woodsman, as was his father. When he finds that all the game is gone from the woods, he moves on west.

Resolve Wheeler, Sayward's eldest son. He breaks his leg on a trip with his father and, while recuperating, he discovers that he has a great love of learning and books. When he returns home, he again breaks his leg in order to have time to read.

Sulie Wheeler, Sayward's daughter, who is named after Sayward's lost sister. The young Sulie is burned to death.

Mistress Bartram, a schoolteacher, to whom Portius turns when Sayward refuses to sleep with him. Because she is pregnant with Portius' child, she is married rather hurriedly to Jake Tench.

Jake Tench, the man who builds the first keelboat in the township.

Judah MacWhirter, a neighbor of the Wheelers who is bitten by a dog and dies of rabies.

Guerdon Wheeler,
Kinzie Wheeler,
Huldah Wheeler,
Sooth Wheeler,
Libby Wheeler,
Dezia Wheeler, and
Mercy Wheeler, Sayward and Portius' other children.

FIESTA IN NOVEMBER
(Fiesta en noviembre)

Author: Eduardo Mallea (1903-1982)
First published: 1938
Genre: Novel
Locale: Buenos Aires, Argentina
Time: Mid-1930's
Plot: Social realism

Eugenia Rague (eh-ew-HEHN-ee-ah RRAH-geh), a highly respected woman in the society of Buenos Aires. She achieved her position by being very rich rather than by aristocratic birth. She looks down upon all who are beneath her class but also resents authentic aristocrats. She acquires paintings and sculptures as a means of acquiring the admiration of members of high society. She is puritan almost to the point of fanaticism, incapable of pardoning human weaknesses, domineering, and ambitious; the role she plays in her family is more that of tyrant than that of matriarch. She does not worry about Marta, whom she believes she is able to control, but she feels doubts about Brenda, whom she considers weak and unpredictable.

Marta Rague, Eugenia's twenty-seven-year-old daughter. She has traveled extensively, visited the most renowned museums, heard the most famous musicians in concert, and loved intensely, giving herself to those whom she thought were seeking pleasures beyond the mere physical. These activities have left her bored and fatigued.

Lintas (LEEN-tahs), a painter whom Eugenia Rague met at an exhibition. She invites him to her fiesta to get his opinion on the authenticity of three paintings. The painter informs her that the paintings are fakes. During dinner, Marta and Lintas exchange glances that leave both intrigued. Later, after dancing and chatting, they realize that both of them belong to a complex world, full of conflicts, far removed from the fatuous reality that they are living at that instant. After conversing for many hours about life, society, reality, love, and hate, Marta bids farewell to Lintas. She has undergone a transformation: In place of disillusion and boredom, she feels a desire to serve.

Brenda Rague, Eugenia's younger daughter. She leads her own life. As a consequence of her adventures, she has had two abortions, unknown to her mother.

The poet, whose story runs parallel with the overall plot. The nameless character symbolizes those persecuted by association. He has read books prohibited by the regime, has family ties with an executed revolutionary, and has seen innocent people assassinated. He is taken away from his home, beaten, and finally riddled with bullets by a patrol.

THE FIFTH HORSEMAN

Author: José Antonio Villarreal (1924-   )
First published: 1974
Genre: Novel
Locale: Northern Mexico
Time: 1893-1915
Plot: Historical realism

Heraclio Inés (ehr-AH-clee-oh ee-NEHS), the youngest of five brothers born into a family of horsemen, a fact that places him above the peasants in the oppressive social structure of the Hacienda de la Flor but below the owner, Don Aurelio Becerra, his godfather. After mastering his craft and the code of honor that attends it, Heraclio casts off the rigid authority of his family in order to fulfill his individual potential, something that the prevailing sociopolitical tradition in Mexico would deny him. In an assertion of his independence, Heraclio enters into a passionate affair with Don Aurelio's daughter. When threatened with exposure and violence, Heraclio kills a man; thereafter, seeking refuge from the brutality of the rural police, he joins a group of bandits and, eventually, the forces of Pancho Villa. Democratically at one with the people and moved always by his growing sense of justice, Heraclio fights hard for the revolution only to see the cause fail as Mexico falls once again into the grips of easy compromise and corruption. In his last revolutionary act and in order to preserve his integrity, Heraclio executes a traitor. Defeated but not broken, he then leaves Mexico for exile in the United States.

David Contreras (kohn-TREHR-ahs), the illegitimate peasant son of Don Aurelio and a healer. David befriends Heraclio while the two herd sheep together, but he begins to turn against Heraclio when Heraclio leaves the flocks in order to learn the craft of the horsemen. Rejected by his natural father and condemned by the social system to a life of peonage, David becomes embittered. After Heraclio sleeps with David's half sister, Carmen Becerra, David's bitterness turns to hatred, a hatred that finds its only outlet in lawless violence. Unable to kill Heraclio, the focus of his frustration, David kills Heraclio's wife and child, acts of brutality for which Heraclio, in turn, kills David.

Carmen Becerra (beh-SEH-rrah), Don Aurielo's daughter, who is passionately in love with Heraclio. Like both David and Heraclio, however, she is trapped by the rigid social and political stratification of a system that condemns her to marry the corrupt Domingo Arguiú, a Spanish aristocrat. To Carmen's credit, she attempts to break the barriers that restrain her in order to fulfill her love for Heraclio, but in the end, denied anything beyond a temporary physical relationship, she fails.

Marcelina Ortiz (mahr-seh-LEE-nah ohr-TEES), the innocent young woman Heraclio marries. Bearing the same name as Heraclio's dead mother, Marcelina represents the continuing embodiment of the pure wife and virtuous Mexican mother. In clear terms, she stands for the sanctity of home and hearth. In a better Mexico, the Mexico for which Heraclio fights, she would not only survive but also prosper. The destructive Mexico into which she is born, however, kills her and her baby.

Xochitl Salamanca (hoh-chee-TEEL sah-lah-MAHN-kah), a circus performer who meets Heraclio amid the chaos of the revolution. When Heraclio extracts her from the clutches of Pancho Villa, she becomes his wartime wife and lover. More a symbol than a fully drawn character, Xochitl represents the spirit of the revolution, waxing strong during the period of Villa's victories but dying of smallpox in the sick world that follows in the wake of Villa's defeat.

Teodoro Inés (teh-oh-DOHR-oh), Heraclio's older brother. Teodoro takes over as head of the family after the death of his father. Proud and brutal within his own family, Teodoro grovels willingly before Don Aurelio, places the landowner on the level of a god, thereby ensuring the survival of the oppressive social system.

FIFTH OF JULY

Author: Lanford Wilson (1937-   )
First published: 1978
Genre: Drama
Locale: The Talley Place, near Lebanon, Missouri
Time: July 4-5, 1977
Plot: Psychological realism

Kenneth (Ken) Talley, Jr., the current owner of the Talley Place, which has been in the family for generations. A Vietnam veteran who lost both legs in the war, he is resisting returning to his former life as a schoolteacher because he fears that the students will not accept his disability. Although he and his partner Jed have put three years into fixing up the home and gardens, Ken is prepared to sell the Talley Place to John and Gwen and start a new life somewhere else. Ken, his sister June, John, and Gwen shared a communal life back in the 1960's. Ken was in love with John, who chose Gwen instead. Ken learns that John lied to Gwen all those years ago, setting in motion the events that led to John's marriage and Ken being drafted and then injured. When Ken learns the truth about his past, he is better able to face his future. He and Jed resume making plans for the garden and for Ken to teach in the fall.

John Landis, Gwen's controlling husband and Ken's best friend since high school. Ken has always been attracted to John, and they slept together once years ago. Unable to handle commune life—or perhaps unable to accept his own feelings for Ken—John lied to get rid of Ken and married the wealthy Gwen. Now he manages her copper business, without her knowing it, and encourages her singing career. He and Gwen want to buy the Talley Place to use as a private recording studio. He does not believe that she has any real talent; he only wants her to be distracted so that she will not interfere with the business. When he and Ken talk over the old days, he reveals by the force of his denial that he blames himself for Ken's injury. When his plans for buying the Talley Place fall through, he becomes angry and knocks Ken to the floor. Ken does not accept his apology, and John leaves.

Gwen Landis, John's self-absorbed wife. She took so many drugs in the 1960's that she has permanently damaged her brain. She cannot focus on any thought for more than a few minutes and flits from one subject to another as she tries to converse. She has an immense inherited fortune, over which John has taken control without her knowledge. She would like to be a singer and hopes to have her own recording studio. Everyone assumes that she is chasing an empty dream, but near the end of the play she receives a genuine offer from a major recording studio.

June Talley, Ken's sister, another former member of the commune. She also was in love with John in those days, but of the four of them she was the first to realize the emptiness of the life they were living and the first to leave. Soon after moving to St. Louis on her own, she gave birth to Shirley, a daughter John has never acknowledged or supported. She has been a bad mother because she has no sense of direction herself, but she is the most sensible of the four friends, and she speaks frankly and kindly to Ken about his fears. When John tries to take Shirley to live with him and Gwen, June's motherly love turns fierce, and she sends him away.

Jed Jenkins, Ken's lover and friend. Jed says little and defers to Ken when others are around. When they are alone, Jed is the strong one, supporting Ken physically and emotionally.

Sally Talley Friedman, June and Ken's aunt. She became something of a family outcast after she married Matt Friedman, a Jewish man, in the 1940's. With this younger generation that includes her gay nephew and single-mother niece, she feels part of a family again. She has returned to the Talley Place to scatter the ashes of Matt, who always liked the area, and to attend the funeral of another man from town. At the end of the play, she comes up with the money to buy the Talley Place herself and keep it in the family.

— Cynthia A. Bily

THE FIFTH QUEEN

Author: Ford Madox Ford (Ford Madox Hueffer, 1873-1939)
First published: 1980
Genre: Novels
Locale: England and France
Time: 1539-1542
Plot: Historical

The Fifth Queen, 1906

Katharine (Kat) Howard, the fifth wife of Henry VIII. Devoutly Catholic, the nineteen-year-old is the most learned woman in England. Her knowledge of Greek and Latin and the moral precepts she has embraced from the ancients (along her great beauty) attract the attention of the king when she is brought to her uncle, the duke of Norfolk, at a time of riot and unrest in her home county. Named for Katharine of Aragon, Henry's first queen, the fearless Katharine becomes lady-in-waiting to their daughter, Lady Mary. In that position, she is thrown into close association with the king while simultaneously abetting Lady Mary's scheme to reinstate Catholicism in England.

Henry VIII, the king of England. He is massive and powerful, and his ability to be gentle and his great wit inspire Katharine's respect and love.

Thomas Cromwell, the Lord of the Privy Seal who arranged the marriage of Henry and Anne of Cleves to cement the Protestant alliance.

Lady Mary, the daughter of Henry VIII. Aloof and bitter, Mary despises her father for having poisoned her mother and declared her to be illegitimate.

Nicholas Udal, a tutor to Lady Mary and former tutor to Katharine Howard, a master of Greek and Latin in his time. Udal's character is suspect.

Margot Poins, a maidservant to Katharine. The large blonde woman is also Udal's betrothed.

Thomas Culpepper, a cousin of Katharine. Culpepper takes Katharine to London to save her from the poverty and violence of her home. The red-haired Culpepper's mad love for his cousin alternately saves and damns her.

The Privy Seal, 1907

Katharine (Kat) Howard, now the beloved of the king. She is caught up in the intrigues that fill Henry's court, but she remains the voice of conscience. Katharine's love for Henry and her realization that she has the chance to return England to Catholicism enable her to accept his proposal of marriage once she is certain that his marriage to Anne of Cleves is unconsummated.

Henry VIII, who, once assured that Cleves has abandoned the Protestant cause, divorces Anne and prepares to marry Katharine.

Thomas Cromwell, whose plot to keep Henry under his influence crumbles with Henry's marriage to Katharine. Katharine's recognition that he had the best intentions for Henry's reign cause her to oppose his execution, but she is unsuccessful.

Nicholas Udal, who marries an innkeeper in Paris in hopes that Catholicism will not be restored to England, nullifying the marriage.

Thomas Culpepper, who goes to Paris as an assassin to win his fortune so that he can wed Katharine.

The Fifth Queen Crowned, 1908

Katharine (Kat) Howard, who lives in seeming bliss with Henry for more than a year. When her plan to reunite England with the Church of Rome and return the treasures taken over from it becomes a real possibility, the Protestant and Catholic nobles who have benefited from the separation conspire to discredit her. She is convicted of adultery and beheaded on February 13, 1542.

Henry VIII, who is deeply in love with Katharine, who wishes to effect his salvation by returning him to Catholicism. Henry comes very close, even drafting a letter of reconciliation to the pope. He is, however, easily influenced. He listens to the slander against his wife and reluctantly agrees to her execution.

Nicholas Udal, who is cast into prison when he asks the king to divorce him from the Englishwoman he married in Paris so that he can become chancellor of the realm and marry Margot Poins. Despite his less than sterling character, Udal refuses to lie about Kat's innocence.

Lady Mary, who is swayed by the purity of Katharine's faith to reconcile with her father and marry the duke of Orleans; however, Katharine is denounced soon thereafter.

Margot Poins, who faithfully serves Katharine until Udal's marriage to the innkeeper in Paris forces her into a nunnery. When tortured to confess Katharine's lewdness, she instead cries out that Katharine is virtuous.

Hal Poins, the guard of Katharine's chamber. He takes part in the conspiracy against Katharine because the king refused to grant Udal a divorce to marry Hal's sister Margot.

Thomas Cranmer, the archbishop of Canterbury, influential in the break with Rome. Conscience-stricken Cranmer dons a hair shirt when reconciliation with Rome seems near.

Thomas Culpepper, who is caught in Kat's chamber, drunk, when Henry returns from a trip to Scotland. Although Henry recognizes the innocence of this meeting on Katharine's part, this scene begins the scandal culminating in Katharine's downfall.

Mary Hall, a twin to Lascelles, a conspirator against Katharine. She was a maid in the home of Katharine's grandmother when Kat was a child. Mary lies about Katharine's youthful escapades, leading to Katharine's beheading.

—Jaquelyn W. Walsh

THE FIFTH SON
(Le Cinquième Fils)

Author: Elie Wiesel (1928-   )
First published: 1983
Genre: Novel

Locale: New York City and Reshastadt, Germany
Time: The 1950's to the 1980's
Plot: Historical realism

The narrator, a young Jewish man, born in New York City in 1949 and living in a Hasidic section of Brooklyn. Reared and educated as an Orthodox Jew, he was silent and often gloomy as a young child. Later, during adolescence, as he studies to become a writer and teacher, he sets out on a quest to uncover the inaccessible mysteries of his father's painful experiences in Germany during the 1940's. The narrator deeply loves his father, considering him the most important influence in his life. Since childhood, the narrator has felt cut off from his father's thoughts; he has ached to share the older man's wisdom and pain. In his quest, however, he is able to learn of his father's past from the latter's notes, written to his dead firstborn son, and from the discourses of his father's two old friends.

Reuven Tamiroff, the father of the narrator, a librarian living in Brooklyn, New York. After surviving World War II in Davarowsk, Germany, along with his wife, Reuven settled into a quiet life of books and scholarship on his beloved philosopher, Paritus. When his wife's mental breakdown in the mid-1950's forces her to live in a hospital, Reuven rears his son, the narrator, alone, showing him love and attention, taking him nearly everywhere he goes, and allowing him to visit with the one old friend who visits their home. He cannot speak of his past; the secrets of his life in the ghetto and the concentration camps are so terrible that they cannot be put into speech. To help overcome his grief, he writes loving letters to his dead six-year-old son, who was murdered by the Angel, a Nazi officer in Germany.

Simha-the-Dark, the only close friend of Reuven, both in Germany and, later, in Brooklyn. A clever metaphysical man who earns his comfortable living as a merchant "selling shadows," Simha meets with Reuven on the last Thursday of each month to argue philosophical issues. The issue that most occupies the two men is the justification of acts of vengeance against acknowledged enemies. This subject looms over all other problems for them because of their own vengeful assassination of the Angel in 1946, which, twenty years later, they discover to have been unsuccessful. Even with his troubled past, Simha is able to live according to Jewish law, which requires that each person live in joy, although that joy may be incomplete. He pleases those around him with mesmerizing anecdotes illustrating his quiet wisdom.

The Angel, **Richard Lander**, the military governor of the ghetto and town of Davarowsk, Germany, during World War II. A mediocre actor, Lander speaks with a false and cruel kindness, apparently enjoying the duplicity of creating trust in the Jews of the ghetto, only to annihilate them later at his whim. He survives the bomb attack by Reuven and Simha but, twenty years later, is confronted by the narrator and must exist knowing that his identity has been discovered.

Lisa Schreiber, the young woman the narrator meets at City College and whom he comes to love. Vibrant and popular, she is attracted to the shy narrator and invites him to spend the evening with her. Her father is a well-to-do banker, and Lisa has an independence that allows her to help the narrator in many ways in his quest for the Angel. She charms Reuven, and, although she and the narrator separate during their adult lives, she is the love of the narrator's young life.

Ariel, the brother of the narrator, born eleven years before him in Germany. He is executed by the Angel at the age of six; however, Reuven continues to write him letters years after his death. He was a beautiful, strong, and brilliant child hunted down and killed specifically to punish Reuven, the leader of the Jews in the ghetto.

Rachel Tamiroff, the mentally disabled and hospitalized mother of the narrator. When the narrator was six years old, she lost her sanity (she said that she was "missing something") and has spent the remainder of her life in a hospital in upstate New York. The narrator recalls her anguish and her solemn beauty, but not until he is a young man does he learn that his brother Ariel was also six years old when he was murdered by the Angel.

Bontchek, another friend who experienced the Holocaust with Reuven. He did not participate in the attempted murder of the Angel. An oversized man, he meets Reuven by accident in the New York Public Library, where Reuven works, after a separation extending back to the end of the war in Germany. He often meets with the narrator, taking him to the theater and concerts and explaining the mysteries of his father's life. Even though he has had an intimate friendship with Reuven and Simha, he is not invited to the Thursday evening discussions. Only later is it revealed that this is because he did not participate in the assassination attempt on the Angel.

— *Vicki K. Robinson*

FILE NO. 113
(Le Dossier no. 113)

Author: Émile Gaboriau (1832-1873)
First published: 1867
Genre: Novel

Locale: Paris, France
Time: 1866
Plot: Detective and mystery

Monsieur Lecoq (leh-KOHK), a brilliant detective and master of disguise. He clears Prosper chiefly to shame Gypsy, who was formerly his mistress.

Prosper Bertomy (prohs-PEHR behr-toh-MEE), a trusted bank clerk who has one of the two bank keys and is therefore suspected of a robbery there. After being cleared, he marries Madeleine.

M. André Fauvel (ahn-DRAY foh-VEHL), a Paris banker who possesses the other key to his bank.

Valentine (vah-lahn-TEEN), Fauvel's wife. As a young woman, she had an affair with a young neighbor, Gaston de Clameran, and secretly bore a son in England. The child is now dead. Her husband is unaware of her indiscretion.

Louis de Clameran (lwee deh klah-meh-RAHN), Gaston's younger brother. He coaches Raoul to impersonate Valentine's dead son. He goes mad in prison.

Raoul de Lagors (rah-EWL deh lah-GOHR), an impostor claiming to be Valentine's son and now living with her as her "nephew." He forces her to provide Fauvel's key. Lecoq unmasks him by means of a scratch on the bank safe.

Madeleine (mahd-LEHN), Fauvel's niece, who is in love with Prosper but is willing to marry Louis de Clameran in order to silence him about Valentine's indiscretion.

Chocareille (shoh-kah-REE-yeh), called **Gypsy**, an ex-criminal and now the mistress of Prosper.

Fanferlot (fahn-fehr-LOH), a detective secretly married to Mme Alexandre.

Mme Alexandre (ah-lehk-SAHNDR), the manager of the Archangel Hotel, where Gypsy is hidden.

Cavaillon (kah-vay-YOHN), a friend of Prosper who carries Prosper's warning note that puts the police on Gypsy's trail.

IL FILOSTRATO

Author: Giovanni Boccaccio (1313-1375)
First transcribed: c. 1335
Genre: Poetry

Locale: Troy
Time: c. 1200 B.C.E.
Plot: Love

Troilo, a Trojan knight during Troy's siege by the Greeks, a son of King Priam. Although Troilo has always mocked love, when he sees Griseida at the temple of Pallas, he is overpowered by her beauty and immediately falls in love with her. At first he keeps his love secret, but at last he allows her cousin Pandaro to act as go-between. Soon she returns his love, and Troilo rejoices in the delights of an intense, though secret, love affair. During that time, he continues to fight bravely for Troy. When Griseida must leave Troy to go to the Greek camp in a prisoner exchange, Troilo is devastated. He tries to persuade her to run away with him, but at last he reluctantly lets her go, believing her promise to return within ten days. He waits for her in agony, and when she does not return within the appointed time, he writes her several letters. Finally, he can no longer believe her deceptive replies. His sister, Cassandra, tells him that Griseida now loves Diomede. When Troilo finds a brooch he once gave Griseida on Diomede's cloak, the reality of her betrayal sinks in. He fights Diomede several times on the battlefield, then is killed by the Greek warrior Achilles.

Griseida, a beautiful young widow living in Troy during the siege. When her cousin Pandaro brings her word that the young warrior Troilo has fallen love-victim to her beauty, Griseida is unsure that she wishes to be involved in a love affair because of the possibilities of scandal. She feels especially vulnerable to gossip because her father has just left Troy to join the Greeks. At last, moved by Troilo's compelling love letter, she agrees to meet with him. She later finds that she returns his passion. It is she who arranges for their first night together. When she is ordered to the Greek camp, she agrees to the exchange, pointing out to Troilo that to elope with him would make scandal inevitable. Once among the Greeks, Griseida soon finds herself being courted by Diomede. She writes Troilo a series of insincere letters, assuring him of her return, but in fact she has thrown her lot in with Diomede, her new lover.

Pandaro, a Trojan warrior, Griseida's cousin, Troilo's friend and confidant. Although he is unsuccessful in love, Pandaro is eager to advance his friend's affair. He acts as adviser and go-between for the couple, urging Griseida to entertain Troilo's courtship. Pandaro frequently reminds Troilo of the need for secrecy as an aid to increasing Griseida's passion. When Pandaro finds Troilo deep in grief at the prospect of Griseida being sent to the Greeks, Pandaro suggests that it might be better to find a new love than to mourn her loss. Pandaro is the first to conclude that Griseida will never return.

Diomede, a Greek warrior, a hardy fighter. He courts Griseida and wins her affections after she is exchanged to the Greeks. Diomede first approaches Griseida on her fourth day in the camp. With his usual sense of how to advance his self-interest, he assures her that the Greeks are bound to win this war and tells her about his own nobel origins. When Griseida says that she is mourning her dead husband, Diomede does not believe her.

Calchas, Griseida's father, a Trojan priest who foretells Troy's fall. At the story's beginning, Calchas has deserted Troy for the Greek camp. When he has a chance, he asks that Griseida be included in a prisoner exchange. Griseida describes Calchas to Troilo as avaricious, claiming that she will be able to use that quality to bribe him into allowing her to return to Troy.

—Ann Davison Garbett

THE FINAL MIST
(La última niebla)

Author: María Luisa Bombal (1910-1980)
First published: 1934
Genre: Novel

Locale: Southern Chile
Time: Late 1920's
Plot: Surrealism

The protagonist, whose name is never revealed, a woman who very subjectively narrates her own feelings of frustration and loneliness. She posits that they are a result of her husband's disinterest in her, in particular, and society's treatment of women, in general. Afraid of old age and incapable of expressing her true feelings to a despotic husband, she lives an existence permanently tainted and defined by a withdrawal into herself. She consciously opts for a fantasy world in which her repressed sexuality finally finds an outlet. It is only then that her love and observation of her own body become positive traits. Her marriage is a failure from the very start, and every contact with her husband is a constant reminder of that fact. The logical world limits and closes her within a boringly repetitive and senseless world, and her dream lover liberates her. Her mental activity establishes different mechanisms for self-realization only when Regina, her husband's sister-in-law, shows her how a woman can truly respond to her own innermost desires. The protagonist's flights of fantasy and reliance on reason and practicality, however, condemn her to the passive existence she had at the start of the novel. She never becomes aware that such constraints can be fought, for they are imposed by a society in which women have at most an unreasonable facsimile of life. She does not fight what by her own description will be a future full of petty and frivolous worries and undertakings.

Daniel, her extremely sarcastic and bright husband, who possesses boundless cynicism. His wife's passivity makes her an easy mark for his irony and his desire to control every one of her actions. Insultingly, he constantly reminds the protagonist that she will never be more than a weak substitute for his first wife. His arrogance is never undone, even though his everyday concerns are banal and positively bourgeois.

Regina, Daniel's sister-in-law. She is the barometer of activity, beauty, and self-expression for the protagonist. Regina, a lover of the arts, talkative, and full of life, has taken a lover. She is thus capable of venting her passion much more concretely than is the protagonist. Her fulfillment, like the protagonist's, is postulated as something that cannot come exclusively from her relationships with men; nevertheless, even Regina's attempted suicide is a source of anger and envy for the protagonist.

The protagonist's lover, who is unnamed. He is not her reason for being, like Regina's lover was. More than a concretely described character, he is a representative of the "otherness" in a man for which the protagonist longs. In her mind, he is presumably wealthy and stimulatingly erotic. His mundane end is attributed by his servant to a fall he suffered because of his blindness.

— *Will H. Corral*

FINAL PAYMENTS

Author: Mary Gordon (1949-)
First published: 1977
Genre: Novel

Locale: New York City
Time: Early to mid-1970's
Plot: Domestic realism

Isabel Moore, a product of a sheltered Catholic upbringing. She nursed her widowed father in his long final illness. Thirty years old at the time of her father's death, Isabel finds herself with unaccustomed freedom from his constant needs. She must come to terms both with her lost faith and her lost youth. She takes a job with a social services agency surveying the living arrangements of people who care for the elderly in their homes, a position that makes her look into a variety of homes, both loveless and loving. Simultaneously eager to experience life and made uncertain by her inexperience, Isabel takes two married lovers and then, in revulsion, leaves them both to care for Margaret Casey, the Moores' former housekeeper. When she realizes that she will never be able to meet the old woman's demands, Isabel frees herself once more to return to life and her lover Hugh Slade.

Margaret Casey, the Moores' elderly former housekeeper, now retired. Margaret had once hoped to marry Joseph Moore, until thirteen-year-old Isabel, frightened at that prospect, fired her. Now she tyrannizes the adult Isabel, attempting to cause guilt about the firing so that Isabel will support her financially or even take her in. Tyranny comes easily to Margaret, as she is a selfish and unhappy old woman who is incapable of being pleased by Isabel's efforts to care for her.

Eleanor, Isabel's closest friend since elementary school days. Fashionable and sensitive, Eleanor is a now a career woman who, sharing Isabel's background, both understands and cares deeply for her friend. She takes her clothes shopping, cooks for her, gives her perfect gifts, and ultimately comes with Liz to rescue her from her martyrdom with Margaret Casey.

Liz Ryan, the wife of a politician and mother of two children, the other of Isabel's closest friends from the past. She is frankly pleased that her husband John's infidelity reduces his interest in her. Liz has a lesbian lover and startles Isabel by introducing Isabel to her. She tends to cut short Isabel's leanings toward self-pity, and she accompanies Eleanor to rescue Isabel.

John Ryan, Liz's faithless husband, a politician of considerable charm and influence. At first, Isabel is attracted by John's crudely insistent sexuality, but almost immediately she feels diminished by it and rejects him in favor of Hugh.

Hugh Slade, Liz's veterinarian and Isabel's second lover. Attractive, gentle, and undemanding, he has had a series of love affairs in response to his dying marriage to Cynthia. His Quaker upbringing makes Isabel's past seem exotic to him. As their affair progresses, their love grows into mutual understanding and respect. At the end of the novel, he has moved out of Cynthia's house, and a possible reconciliation with Isabel is implied.

Cynthia Slade, Hugh's wife. At the age of forty-eight, she feels threatened by Hugh's potential defection to a younger woman. Her verbal attack on Isabel at Ryan's office precipitates Isabel's decision to leave Hugh so that she can care for Margaret Casey.

Father Mulcahy, an elderly priest and longtime friend of Isabel, simple and faithful (despite his alcoholism) in his love for her. His visit to her at Margaret's house helps Isabel decide to leave. When she decides to return to the church, he is the one priest to whom she can make confession.

Joseph Moore, Isabel's father. Before his stroke, he was a professor of medieval literature. His involvement in the Catholic church was passionate, intellectual, and relentless in the demands it made on his own spiritual state and on others'. Learning of his secretly paid pension to Margaret Casey at first makes Isabel angry with his memory; later, it helps send her to care for the old housekeeper.

— *Ann Davison Garbett*

THE FINANCIAL EXPERT

Author: R. K. Narayan (1906-   )
First published: 1952
Genre: Novel

Locale: Malgudi, in southern India
Time: Late 1940's
Plot: Regional

Margayya, the owner of a small business, in his thirties. A wizard with numbers, crafty, and unscrupulous, Margayya earns a modest living as a financial consultant from a spot under a banyan tree in the Indian town of Malgudi. Eventually, he becomes a wealthy moneylender and banker, but when he assaults an old associate, he loses his reputation, his business, and his fortune.

Meena, Margayya's wife, his uncomprehending confidant and his scapegoat. Although she is frightened by his rages and his irrational schemes, she accepts the various changes in her fortune with docility. The only time she asserts herself is when she thinks that Margayya has driven their son Balu to suicide; then her fury and her grief frighten him into going to Madras to find Balu.

Balu, Margayya and Meena's son, who is first seen as a spoiled, uncontrollable baby. He is later a failure at school, a runaway, and even, after his marriage, a wastrel. Ironically, it is his childish destruction of his father's account book that drives Margayya from the banyan tree to a new business venture and wealth. At the end of the book, it is an attempt to stop Balu's debauchery that causes Margayya's downfall.

Dr. Pal, a self-styled journalist, author, and sociologist. A lean, confident thirty-year-old when he first appears, Dr. Pal has a seemingly intellectual patter that awes Margayya. Periodically, he turns up to direct Margayya's life. At first, his influence on Margayya is benign. It is Dr. Pal who sells him the sexually explicit book whose publication becomes the basis of Margayya's fortune; it is he who moves Margayya into the fortunately situated office and pushes him into banking; and it is he who arranges an appropriate if inaccurate horoscope so that Balu can marry the girl whom Margayya has selected. At the end of the story, however, it is Dr. Pal who encourages Balu's debauchery and who takes revenge for the assault by spreading the rumors that ruin Margayya.

Brinda, Balu's wife, a beautiful, sweet seventeen-year-old, the daughter of a man who owns a small tea estate. At first, she is as delighted with her young husband as Margayya is with her and her station. When Balu mistreats her, however, she confides in her father-in-law. These complaints lead to his attack on Dr. Pal. In the collapse of his fortunes, Margayya is comforted by the fact that Brinda's baby will now be living with him.

Madan Lal, the principal printer in Malgudi. A large, red-faced man who is aware of his own importance, he is so fascinated by the sex manual that Margayya has bought from Dr. Pal that he stops work to read it and then arranges to publish it.

Guru Raj, a dark, talkative, and polite blanket merchant, the friend of Dr. Pal. He rents an office to Margayya.

Arul Doss, the head servant at the Cooperative Bank. An old Christian, wrinkled, with a white mustache, he has the air of authority that derives from his uniform and his position. When he brings Margayya word that he must leave his place near the bank, Doss frightens Margayya and his clients, even though he himself laughs at Margayya's boldness.

The Inspector, a Madras policeman. A kindly man, he befriends Margayya on the train and finds the runaway Balu for him.

Sastri, Margayya's accountant. A tired old man, he occasionally remonstrates with his employer about his unkindness to customers. He has no real status, however, until Margayya entrusts to him the search for an appropriate wife for Balu.

— Rosemary M. Canfield Reisman

THE FINANCIER

Author: Theodore Dreiser (1871-1945)
First published: 1912; revised, 1927
Genre: Novel

Locale: Philadelphia, Pennsylvania
Time: c. 1850-1874
Plot: Naturalism

Frank Algernon Cowperwood, the "financier," primarily interested in acquiring a fortune. Energetic and skillful, he begins by dealing successfully in soap when he is about thirteen years old. His uncle gets him a job in a grain commission house. Cowperwood's skill leads him into the brokerage business. He then marries Lillian Semple, the attractive widow of a business associate, five years older than he. Branching out into city railways and loans, he becomes involved with local politicians in Philadelphia. The daughter of a contractor becomes Frank's mistress. When his speculations in municipal railways and city loans are brought to light in the turmoil following the Chicago fire of 1871, he is apprehended and sent to jail. Released in thirteen months, he rebuilds his fortune during the panic of 1873. He then decides to move to Chicago.

Lillian Semple Cowperwood, his wife. A beautiful, passive woman, she becomes inadequate for Cowperwood. She knows of his affair with Aileen Butler but tolerates it until he decides to go to Chicago. Then she divorces him.

Henry Worthington Cowperwood, Frank's father, who began as a bank clerk, later becoming teller, head cashier, and finally president. He is forced to resign when his son becomes involved in the City Treasury scandal.

Edward Malia Butler, a Philadelphia contractor. For a time, Cowperwood is his financial adviser, thereby meeting his daughter Aileen. When Butler discovers, through an anonymous letter, that his daughter is Frank's mistress, he hires detectives to trail his daughter, but he is unable to break up the affair. Through powerful political friends, he helps to ruin Cowperwood and send him to jail.

Aileen Butler, his daughter, strongly attracted by Cowperwood's personal and financial magnetism. She remains loyal to him despite her awareness of her father's objections. She visits him in jail and goes to Chicago as his mistress.

George W. Stener, the city treasurer, appointed because he could easily serve as a dupe for the politicians. Through weakness and fear, he refuses to lend Cowperwood the additional city money necessary to cover his speculations.

Nancy Arabella Cowperwood, Frank's mother, happy with the elegant house he builds for her.

Seneca Davis, her wealthy brother, a former planter in Cuba. He encourages his nephew early in his career.

Anna Adelaide Cowperwood, Frank's sister. She becomes a clerk in the city water office.

Joseph Cowperwood, Frank's brother, whom he hires to work in the brokerage business.

Edward Cowperwood, another brother and a faithful employee.

Frank Cowperwood, Jr., Frank's son.

Lillian Cowperwood, Frank's daughter and favorite child.

Mrs. Edward Butler, Aileen's religious mother, who never knows of her daughter's affair.

Nora Butler, Aileen's younger sister.

Owen Butler, the older brother of Aileen, a hard, cruel man who is a member of the state legislature.

Callum Butler, his younger brother, a clerk in the city water office and an assistant to his father.

Harper Steger, Frank's friend and defense counsel.

Alfred Semple, Lillian's first husband.

Henry A. Mollenhauer, a rich coal dealer, the most vicious politician in Philadelphia. A city profiteer, he opposes Cowperwood bitterly during the scandal in order to get his railway shares.

Edward Strobik, president of the Philadelphia city council, a henchman of Mollenhauer.

Senator Mark Simpson, a state senator who joins Mollenhauer and Strobik in their financial dealings.

Albert Stires, Stener's secretary, the city clerk who issues the check that later gets Frank in legal trouble.

Van Nostrand, the state treasurer.

Senator Terence Relihan, another crooked politician.

Judge Wilbur Payderson, the judge at Cowperwood's trial. To please the politicians, he hands down the maximum sentence.

Dennis Shannon, the district attorney who prosecutes Frank.

Mary Calligan (Mamie), Aileen's school friend, now a teacher, with whom Aileen lives when she leaves her family.

Mrs. Katherine Calligan, Mary's mother, a widow and a dressmaker.

Alderson, the Pinkerton detective who uncovers Aileen's and Frank's trysting place.

Judge Rafalsky, the jurist who writes the dissenting opinion, in Frank's favor, at the appeal.

Judge Marvin, another dissenting judge.

Stephen Wingate, who acts financially for Frank while the latter is in prison.

Warden Desmas, warden at the Philadelphia prison in which Frank is kept. He treats Frank very well.

FINN CYCLE

Author: Unknown
First transcribed: Possibly eleventh century
Genre: Poetry
Locale: Ireland
Time: Third century
Plot: Folklore

Finn, an Irish legendary hero, the leader of the King's warriors known as the Fianna Erinn. *The Finn Cycle* is composed of a series of ballads celebrating the brave exploits of this third century hero and his band of warriors; their virtues and their weaknesses; the eventual diminution of their powers; the dissolution of the band; and the waning of a heroic age.

Cumhal, the former leader of the Fianna Erinn and Finn's father.

Murna, Finn's mother.

Goll Mac Morna, the leader of the rival clan and, later, Finn's strong and loyal warrior.

The Lord of Luachar, a chieftain slain by Finn in his first heroic exploit.

Finegas, a sage from whom Finn learns wisdom and the art of poetry.

Conn, the ruler of Ireland, who makes Finn captain of his band of warriors known as the Fianna Erinn.

Oisin, Finn's son. He is a warrior poet. After his father's death, he is taken to an enchanted land where none grows old. After more than two hundred years, homesick for Ireland, he returns and finds the land populated by weaklings, and the heroic age long since passed.

Oscar, Finn's grandson, the fiercest fighter of the Fianna Erinn.

Dermot, the ladies man,

Keelta, the warrior poet,

Conan the Bald, the gluttonous and slothful trickster, and

Mac Luga, the one skilled in courtesy, Finn's men.

The Dark Druid, a sorcerer who changes his beloved into a deer. She is released from the spell by Finn and becomes his wife. When Finn is called away to war, the Dark Druid recaptures the girl and takes her away, this time forever.

Vivionn, a giantess.

Fergus, a minstrel whose music restores peace between quarreling clans.

Grania, the daughter of the king of Ireland. She is married to Finn in his old age.

Niam, a fairy princess who takes Oisin to an enchanted land where none grows old.

FINNEGANS WAKE

Author: James Joyce (1882-1941)
First published: 1939
Genre: Novel
Locale: Chapelizod, Dublin, Ireland
Time: Early twentieth century
Plot: Fantasy

Finnegan, the title character, whose name is derived from Finn MacCool, for two hundred years the legendary captain of Ireland's warrior heroes; the name change is coined in a Joycean pun "Mister Finn, you're going to be Mister Finnagain." Finnegan, a hod carrier, has fallen from a ladder and is apparently dead. The fall is symbolic of the various falls (with implied corresponding resurrections) of humankind. At the wake, Finnegan's friends become noisy and unrestrained, and in the course of the festivities, at the mention of the Irish word for "whiskey" (usquead-baugham!), Finnegan sits up, threatening to rise. The mourners soothe him back. With Finnegan's demise, a new day is structured, and the hod carrier is supplanted by a man who has arrived to start life as Finnegan's successor.

Humphrey Chimpden Earwicker, also **Here Comes Everybody** and **Haveth Childer Everywhere**. HCE, the newcomer, is a tavern keeper. In keeping with the metamorphosis, his initials are a carry over from Finnegan's vocation of "hod, cement, and edifice." Another connection between the two men lies in Earwicker's emerging from Howth Castle and Environs, to which locale Finnegan's interment fades in the story. HCE has wandered widely, leaving his progeny along the way, from Troy and Asia Minor, through the lands of the Goths, the Franks, the Norsemen; he has traveled in Britain and Eire; he has Germanic and Celtic manifestations; up through history he becomes Oliver Cromwell. In short, he is Here Comes Everybody and Haveth Childer Everywhere, representing civilization. At present, he is Earwicker, HCE, a sympathetic character, harrowed by relentless fate. In Phoenix Park (the Garden of Eden), he is caught exhibiting himself to several girls. This impropriety and the Dubliners' resentment of HCE as an intruder give rise to rumors that plague Earwicker, as the scandal takes on aspects of troubled times throughout history. The tumult in Earwicker's soul is consistent with the struggles of all battles in the past. The trials and tribulations of HCE continue until, after a description of the shadows on a windowblind of him and his wife in copulation, HCE turns from his wife. He is now the broken shell of Humpty Dumpty. The hopes of the parents are in the children. The cycle of man is ready to start anew.

Ann, also **Anna Livia Plurabelle**, HCE's wife. Just as Earwicker becomes Adam, Noah, Lord Nelson, a mountain, or a tree, so is ALP (as Ann is referred to generally throughout the book) metamorphosed into Eve, Isis, Iseult, the widow who serves at the wake, a passing cloud, a flowing stream. In this last transformation, as the River Liffey (which flows through Dublin), Ann plays her most important role. At the source, as a brooklet, she is a gay, young girl. Passing her husband's tavern, she is comely, matronly. Flowing on through Dublin, she becomes the haggard cleaning woman, carrying away the filth of the city. She finally moves on to the ocean, from which she rises again in mist to become rain and start again as a mountain stream. As Earwicker's wife, Ann plays the part of the motivator of her husband's energies. She is the housekeeper. She is the mother of his children. Among the various polarities spelled out in the book, Ann is love, opposed to war as depicted by Earwicker.

Kevin, also **Shaun the Postman**, **Chuff**, **Jaun**, and **Yawn**, one of their sons. In his domestic role as Kevin, he is the extrovert, the man of action. He is the political orator, the favorite of the people, policeman of the planet, bearer of the white man's burdens. He is the aggressor and the despoiler. As the symbolic Shaun, he is the Postman delivering to humankind the great message discovered and penned by his brother Jerry. Shaun, whose advice is "Collide with man, collude with money," enjoys the rewards of the carrier of good tidings. Shaun is one of the opposites in another polarity stressed by Joyce, the opposites being the principals in the Brother Battle.

Jerry, also **Shem the Penman**, **Dolph**, and **Glugg**, Kevin's twin brother. As the polar extreme of his brother, Jerry acts on in-turned energy. The books he writes are mortifying in that they lose the lines of good and evil; they are rejected by the decent. Erratic in his introversion, he vacillates between vehement action and unselfish forgiveness. His uncontrolled love is as dangerous as his wanton hate. Among the domestic scenes, the personalities of the two boys are shown, as Glugg (Shem) loses to Chuff (Shaun) in their fights for the approval of girls. Also, as Dolph and Kevin working at their lessons, Dolph, the studious one, helps his brother with a problem; Kevin indignantly strikes Dolph, who forgives.

Isobel, HCE and ALP's daughter and sister of the twins. In the domestic scene she behaves as the child of an average family—playing, studying, and brooding on love. Symbolically, Isobel figures in episodes involving Swift and Vanessa, Mark and Iseult. Identifying her with Tristram's Iseult, HCE has illicit desires for Isobel; also, he envisions her as the reincarnation of the wife. These thoughts keep him young. Among the myriad other characters—local and historical—that are intermingled in this poetic, convoluted account of birth, conflict, death, and resurrection are two significant groups:

Twelve Stately Citizens, who are variously a jury sitting in judgment on HCE, constant customers of Earwicker's tavern, leading mourners at Finnegan's wake, and the twelve signs of the zodiac.

Four Old Men, who are intermittently four senile judges, the four winds, the four recorders of Irish annals, the four phases of the Viconian cycle: theocratic, aristocratic, democratic, and chaotic. This last phase, marked by individualism and sterility, represents the nadir of man's fall. Yet humankind will rise again in response to the thunderclap, which polysyllabic sound Joyce uses to introduce his story.

THE FIRE-DWELLERS

Author: Margaret Laurence (1926-1987)
First published: 1969
Genre: Novel
Locale: Vancouver and the fictional prairie town of Manawaka
Time: A summer in the late 1960's
Plot: Domestic realism

Stacey Cameron MacAindra, a Vancouver housewife who grew up in the small prairie town of Manawaka, Manitoba. Thirty-nine years old, of medium height, and dark-haired, Stacey is beset by middle-age spread and is developing a penchant for gin and tonics. She and her husband, Mac, are the parents of four children: touchy, beautiful Katie, age fourteen; reserved, tense Ian, age ten; vulnerable, lonely Duncan, age seven; and happy Jen, a two-year-old who has yet to speak. Jen's silence until the novel's end mirrors the novel's theme of problems of communication. Stacey faces encroaching middle age with doubt, with regret for her lost youth, looks, and vitality; with longings for lovers she never had; and with deep fears that she cannot express to her often fractious family. In the running interior monologue with which she guides herself through the minefields of daily life, however, she also reveals a sardonic, self-deprecating humor that allows her to acknowledge both her shortcomings and her strengths. She can thus grapple with her fears for herself and particularly for her family in a world that she regards as dangerous and crazy. Having weathered a summer of crises, both internal and external, Stacey emerges at her fortieth birthday with a new sense of acceptance and serenity but not capitulation.

Clifford "Mac" MacAindra, a forty-three-year-old, auburn-haired, good-looking salesman for Richalife, a vitamin company. He was forced to take the job, which he dislikes, after the unplanned birth of Duncan. Reserved to the point that he scarcely speaks to his wife, Stacey, he makes love to her only in a perfunctory way. His heavy smoking betrays his inner tension and self-doubt, yet he is conscientious and a good salesman. He has a single unsatisfactory extramarital encounter with an uncertain young female employee at Richalife. He later confesses this affair to Stacey. Often a grim husband and a surly father, Mac nevertheless makes evident his love and loyalty for his family.

"Buckle" Fennick, an aging truck driver and Mac's wartime buddy. Sensing that he is wearing out his welcome in the MacAindra household and aware of Stacey's present vulnerability, Buckle retaliates, proferring to Stacey his showy "macho" sexuality and then contemptuously denying it to her (a practice that had lost him his wife, Julie). Saddled with his monstrous, blind, alcoholic mother and weary of his unfulfilling life on the road, Buckle plays "chicken" on the highway one last time and loses, dying in the ensuing truck accident.

Luke Venturi, a twenty-four-year-old science-fiction writer and free spirit. Brown-haired and brown-eyed, he sports the same Indian-design sweater each time Stacey sees him. After their first chance encounter, Stacey seeks out Luke twice more to talk and make love in the A-frame beach house where he is staying alone. He gives Stacey a sympathetic ear, a renewed confidence in her desirability, and a sexual experience outside her marriage. Their brief relationship makes two things finally clear to her: She is not the Stacey Cameron of first youth, and her commitment to her family takes precedence over any desire for personal freedom.

Vernon Winkler, also known as **Thor Thorlakson**, the messianic head of Richalife and Mac's boss. Although he is in his mid-thirties, he wears a mane of coiffed silver hair, and surgery has given him a smooth young face and thrusting jaw. Thor has stony blue eyes in which Stacey reads an unmistakable and puzzling hostility despite his unctuous, friendly manner. This hostility is also expressed in his constant, worrisome needling of Mac. When Stacey encounters Valentine Tonnerre, a now-derelict Métis woman from Manawaka, and learns that Thor is actually Vernon Winkler, the childhood object of derision in Manawaka, her relief is enormous. Soon after, Thor transfers to Montreal, and Mac becomes the Vancouver manager of Richalife.

Matthew MacAindra, Mac's elderly father, a retired United Church minister and widower. He is becoming increasingly helpless as his sight fails. Both Mac and Stacey dread his moral rectitude and fear his disapproval, but when he becomes dependent on them and moves in with them, the family opens up to receive him with increasing tolerance and love.

Tess Fogler, Stacey's next-door neighbor, a childless housewife who often looks after Jen. Always envious of Tess's tall, cool elegance, Stacey realizes remorsefully after Tess's attempted suicide that her own inner turmoil has made her insensitive to the anguish often betrayed in Tess's little eccentricities.

— *Jill Rollins*

FIRE FROM HEAVEN

Author: Mary Renault (Mary Challans, 1905-1983)
First published: 1969
Genre: Novel
Locale: Macedon, the Greek peninsula, and Athens
Time: 351-336 B.C.
Plot: Historical

Alexander III of Macedon, later known as **Alexander the Great**, the son of Philip II and Olympias of Epirus. Nearly five years old at the beginning of the novel, he is twenty at the time of his father's assassination, when this narrative closes. (The story continues in *The Persian Boy* [1972], which covers the period of Alexander's conquests in the east.) Physically smaller than his fellow Macedonians, he combines the fiery spirit of his mother with his father's canniness on the battlefield. From early childhood, he is repelled by his father's coarseness, seeing him as something of a Polyphemus (Philip's injured eye contributes to this perception). His hardy constitution, physical courage, athletic self-discipline, and lightning reflexes provide the perfect instruments for his keen and sensitive personality. Like Achilles in Homer's *Iliad*,

Alexander is capable of affection and loyalty—as seen particularly in his relationship with his lover Hephaistion—but he is also wary of intrigue and increasingly distrustful of his obsessive mother, Olympias. He is obsessed with the idea, suggested to him by his mother, that he is the son not of Philip but of some god, perhaps Zeus himself, Dionysus, or the demigod Herakles.

Philip II, the king of Macedon, Alexander's battle-scarred father. Black-bearded and blind in one eye from a wound received in the battle of Methone, he has the roughness of the mountain warlords from whom he is descended, tempered by military and diplomatic genius and a genuine love of Athenian culture. Philip and his son share only a few occasions of personal closeness, but Philip is at pains to provide Alexander with the best available teachers (including Aristotle), and he recognizes his son's abilities in war, giving him a key role in the Battle of Chaironea, which establishes Macedonian control over Greece and sets the stage for his planned conquest of the Ionian coast. All of this is cut short by his assassination at the age of forty-six, the last event of the novel.

Olympias of Epirus, Alexander's mother, only twenty-one years old at the beginning of the novel. Strange, turbulent, uncanny, and obsessive, she practices witchcraft, snake-handling, and the particularly violent Bacchic maenadism of her native Epirus. Although usually motivated by hatred, she is highly possessive of Alexander and insanely jealous of Philip's many infidelities and politically motivated marriages. Her control over Alexander slips as the boy grows into a man, but Alexander accompanies her into self-imposed exile after the Battle of Chaironea, when Philip marries Eurydike, the daughter of Attalos. The rift eventually is smoothed over, and an uneasy truce is made until Philip's assassination. Because one of Olympias' driving forces is the wish to see Alexander as king of Macedon, she is a beneficiary of and likely participant in the plot to kill Philip, but the details of her complicity are unclear.

Hephaistion (heh-FI-stee-ehn), the son of Amyntor, Alexander's older companion and lover. This novel follows the tradition that casts their relationship in the mold of Greek aristocratic pederasty, an idealized love in which physical sex is combined with genuine solicitude of the older partner toward the younger and modest acquiescence on the part of the younger recipient of these attentions. Hephaistion and Alexander take their cues from Plato's *Symposium* and a now-lost play of Aeschylus, the *Myrmidons*, which represents the Homeric Achilles as the sexual partner of his older companion Patroclus. Like Patroclus, Hephaistion is of lower rank and lacks the conspicuous talents of young Alexander, but he is his only true confidant.

Ptolemy (TOL-eh-mee), known as the son of Lagos although actually a bastard son of Philip and thus Alexander's half brother. Some dozen years older than Alexander and a member of the Companion Cavalry, he becomes Alexander's sworn blood brother.

Antipatros (an-TIHP-ah-trohs), one of Philip's key generals, a Macedonian of ancient stock. Appointed adviser to young Alexander, who is made regent during Philip's campaign in Thrace, he is startled by his charge's independence. He is deeply loyal to Philip's interests but described as loving the king before the man.

Aristotle of Stagira, the son of the physician Nikomachos. A scientist, philosopher, and tutor of Alexander and his official circle of Companions, he establishes his school in Mieza, where Alexander receives his higher education. The school emphasizes the scientific and ethical aspects of the curriculum. Alexander is portrayed as not ready to accept Aristotle's low opinion of "barbarians."

Lysimachus of Akarnania (li-SIHM-eh-kehs), an old friend and palace retainer of Philip, one of Alexander's earliest mentors. A book lover, he cultivates Alexander's well-known love of Homer and *The Iliad*, in appreciation of which Alexander nicknames him Phoinix, after Achilles' companion and tutor in that epic.

— Daniel H. Garrison

FIRE ON THE MOUNTAIN

Author: Anita Desai (1937-   )
First published: 1977
Genre: Novel

Locale: Kasauli, India
Time: The 1970's
Plot: Domestic realism

Nanda Kaul, the aged protagonist. The widow of a university vice chancellor and once at the hub of a large, demanding family and a hectic social life, she now lives in seclusion in Carignano, a desolate old house on the ridge of a mountain in Kasauli. Aloof, indifferent, and irritable, she frequently lapses into a reminiscent mood and wants no intrusion or distraction to violate her privacy. Her cloistered life is upset when her great-granddaughter Raka is sent to spend the summer with her. Tired of a long life of duties and responsibilities, Nanda wants to be left alone; therefore, she does not pay much attention to the child. She manages to stay detached until she observes that the child, instinctively withdrawn into a world of her own, completely ignores her great-grandmother. Challenged by Raka's indifference, Nanda reluctantly comes out of her self-imposed quietude and makes a desperate, though futile, attempt to attract the child to her by telling her fantastic stories about her own childhood. In a final climactic moment, when she hears the news of the rape and death of her longtime friend Ila Das, her psychological defenses suddenly break down. Before she collapses, she splutters the truth that all the stories she told Raka were fabricated, that her husband never loved her and had carried on a lifelong affair with a Christian woman whom he loved but could not marry, that she always felt alienated from her children, and that she was forced into this life of self-exile.

Raka, Nanda's great-granddaughter who arrives at Carignano to spend the summer. A recluse by nature, this frail, convalescent, crop-haired girl with protruding ears and enormous eyes has the knack of slipping away into her own private world, ignoring her great-grandmother completely. Haunted by the nightmarish memories of a drunken, violent father and an unhappy, battered mother, she shuns human company and spends her time roaming the desolate hills and ravines like a bird or a lizard. When she hears the news of her mother's mysterious illness, the old horrors revive and she feels a strong urge to visit the burned house. After that, she steals some matches and sets the forest on fire, thus bringing the story to a climax.

Ila Das, Nanda's longtime friend, a lonely, unmarried woman. Formerly a lecturer in home science at Mr. Kaul's university, she now works as a welfare officer in the Kasauli area. An awkward, clumsy, deformed, and shriveled old woman, with a shrill and hideous voice, she is the object of ridicule and derision from everyone in society, including schoolchildren. During her brief visit to Carignano for tea, she nostalgically evokes memories of Nanda's seemingly glamorous past as the vice chancellor's wife. On her way home, she is raped and murdered. The shocking news of her tragic end shatters Nanda.

Ram Lal, the old cook and caretaker at Carignano. He becomes Raka's friend, provides her with information about the surrounding area, warns her against visiting the burned house on the hill alone, and tells her stories about witches and ghosts to ignite her imagination.

— *Chaman L. Sahni*

THE FIREBUGS: A Learning-Play Without a Lesson

Author: Max Frisch (1911-1991)
First published: 1958
Genre: Drama
Locale: The house of Gottlieb Biedermann, in an unidentified city
Time: The 1950's
Plot: Absurdist

Gottlieb Biedermann, a solid citizen and the millionaire manufacturer of a dubious hair tonic. His name suggests a respectable, unimaginative bourgeois who adheres rigidly to the social and ethical standards of his class (*bieder* means upright, worthy, or gullible). He accordingly believes in hanging as the proper punishment for the arsonists who are at large in the city, according to the newspapers. When a suspicious looking stranger suddenly appears in his living room, Biedermann yields without a struggle to his thinly veiled threats, face-savingly disguised as appeals to humane principles. Far from expelling the stranger, Biedermann allows him to order a meal and then to install himself in the attic. Biedermann's vaunted firmness shows itself only in the case of Knechtling, a dismissed employee with a legitimate claim, whom he drives to suicide. With the intruder, later joined by two companions, Biedermann extends his cowardice and self-deception to protecting his "guests" from police investigation, explaining that the gasoline canisters they have brought into the house contain hair tonic. Finally, he provides the matches with which the arsonists, who have barely troubled to conceal their intentions, light the fuses when the outskirts of the town are in flames. Eisenring suggests that a troubled conscience prevents him from reporting the arsonists to the police. The dinner party that Biedermann arranges in rough proletarian style to suit Schmitz, but at which the criminals order all the appurtenances of bourgeois elegance, is an effective parable of Biedermann's compliant nature. He consistently disregards the arsonists' increasingly clear announcements of their intentions and ends. In the epilogue, in hell, he still refuses to face the plain truth. His entire existence has been founded on the assumption that words are used to conceal the truth.

Sepp Schmitz, the principal arsonist, who installs himself in Biedermann's attic. His appearance suggests a mixture of prison and circus. His aspect and manner are threatening, and in conversations with Biedermann he refers to his training as a wrestler while genially allowing Biedermann to pretend that humane feelings prompt his hospitality. Schmitz, however, expends no great efforts on the support of this pretense, and his terrorism grows more obvious as the play proceeds and as he introduces accomplices and material for arson.

Babette, Biedermann's wife, who copies her husband slavishly in attempting to placate Schmitz. She is assigned unpleasant tasks by her husband; for example, she has breakfast with Schmitz while Biedermann leaves the house. Her only mode of resistance is to reproach her husband for the good nature that allows him to take in strangers.

Willi Eisenring, Schmitz's accomplice, who suddenly turns up in Biedermann's attic. He wears evening dress; he was head waiter at the Metropol "until it burned down." He joins Schmitz in intimidating Biedermann under a genial exterior. He openly works with gasoline and fuses in Biedermann's attic and utters the principle that truth is the best disguise.

Chorus of firemen, a comic attempt to clothe proceedings in the dignity of Greek tragedy.

A Ph.D., who turns up with a revolutionary ideology at the same time as the gasoline arrives. He repudiates his former beliefs only when the town is burning. He has little to say but makes a telling point.

— *W. Gordon Cunliffe*

FIREFLIES

Author: Shiva Naipaul (1945-1985)
First published: 1970
Genre: Novel
Locale: Port-of-Spain, Trinidad
Time: The 1960's
Plot: Social satire

Vimla "Baby" Lutchman, the protagonist, a cousin to the Khojas and the least important member of the Khoja family. A visionary but passive woman, with a taste for commerce, she is not a deep thinker. She relies instead on instinct and suspicion. Never a very pretty girl, though she does have a beautiful, aristocratic nose, she grows fat soon after being married. Her marriage is arranged, and she immediately moves from being controlled by her family to being physically dominated by her husband. Despite her husband's occasional brutality, his lack of interest in their marriage, and his affair with Doreen James, Baby remains devoted to him and their sons, and she never really questions the role into which she has been placed; hence, the marriage is relatively happy. Of limited intelligence and insight, she tends to accept the advice of Govind Khoja without thought. After her husband's sudden death, however, she starts to rebel a bit, cherishing her newfound independence and freedom. Baby remains quite superstitious throughout her life, always attempting to interpret her dreams and looking for signs and portents. Slowly losing control, she is forced to sell her house. Rather than go back to the domination of living with one of the Khojas, Baby chooses to live with an old friend and help run a country store. After finally getting the opportunity to run a business, she finds that she has lost interest in this dream.

Ram Lutchman, Baby's husband, first a bus driver and then an employee in the ministry of education. Not a particularly good-looking man, Ram is poorly educated and comes from a poor background; therefore, he was glad to make such a good marriage. He does not find his wife very attractive, however, and during the early years of their marriage he visits prostitutes and beats his wife regularly. Through the aid of Govind Khoja, his situation begins to improve, but Ram only grows to hate the Khojas, both for their interference in his own life and for their influence on his wife. Ram tends to develop obsessions (such as Doreen, gardening, swimming, photography, and Christmas) on which he thrives for a while and then, with their inevitable failure, abandons. Ram is suspicious of other people's motives and has a tendency to be sneaky and to steal things. As he ages, he realizes that he is not very close to his family and makes some futile attempts to bring them all closer together, but he finds it to be too much of an effort. He dies of a heart attack rather suddenly, while tending his garden, the only one of his obsessions that ever grew into anything.

Bhaskar Lutchman, the Lutchmans' firstborn son. An ugly, quiet, and obedient boy, he is in no way extraordinary. Solitary and not at all close to either of his parents or to his brother, he is very well behaved in the classroom and studies hard, but he is not much of a student. After struggling to get into medical school, he suffers a nervous breakdown and is sent home in failure. His repeated failures drive him to a mocking cynicism and make him unwilling to put much effort into anything. He eventually marries and moves to England.

Romesh Lutchman, the Lutchmans' secondborn son. A handsome and lively boy who suffers from his nerves and tends to have violent and hysterical fits of rage and weeping, he is quite unpredictable. Despite his high intelligence, Romesh hates school, preferring to spend his time either hanging out with friends or going to the cinema. Early in life, he separates himself from the rest of his family, coming to despise their weaknesses. Eventually, he leaves school and home. Developing criminal tendencies and carrying on his father's hatred of Govind Khoja, he campaigns enthusiastically against Khoja in the election. One night, he gets drunk and breaks into the Khojas' house, terrorizing them both and showing Govind to be the coward he really is. After serving his time in jail, he moves to New York City and, eventually, marries a Puerto Rican heiress.

Govind Khoja, the head of one of Trinidad's most important families and Mrs. Lutchman's cousin. The only son of the family, Govind takes himself and his position quite seriously. Being fairly well-read and a disciple of Jean-Jacques Rousseau, he has managed to convince himself that he is highly intelligent, much more so than the rest of his relatives and friends, and hence is the only person capable of leading the family. The dissension within the family grows after his mother's death and his rather miserly distribution of the inheritance. He decides that it is time to separate himself from the family and take his message to the people. He futilely runs for political office, forming his own political party. After losing the election and being attacked by Romesh, he retires once more to his library, where he can remain insulated from the real world.

— *Susan V. Myers*

THE FIRM

Author: John Grisham (1955-)
First published: 1991
Genre: Novel
Locale: Memphis, Tennessee
Time: The 1980's
Plot: Legal

Mitchell (Mitch) Y. McDeere, a brilliant young attorney recruited directly from Harvard Law School by Bendini, Lambert & Locke. Having grown up with a shaky family background, Mitch is ambitious and eager to attain the affluence that will separate him from his past. Mitch is shaken and terrified when he learns that the Bendini firm is being examined by the Federal Bureau of Investigation (FBI) for Mafia-related activities and that several attorneys died when they tried to leave the firm. Mitch comes up with a scheme that allows him and his wife to escape the firm as well as free his brother Ray from prison.

Abigail (Abby) McDeere, Mitch's wife, who quickly becomes suspicious of the firm's overzealous interest in the attorneys' personal lives. Her suspicions are confirmed when Mitch tells her about the firm's true nature. In spite of her fear, Abby stands by Mitch and helps him formulate his plans.

Raymond (Ray) McDeere, Mitch's brother, an inmate at Brushy Mountain State Prison. Although Ray's personality is somewhat violent and reckless, he cares deeply about his family and is far brighter than his rough background would suggest.

Wayne Tarrance, an FBI special agent assigned to infiltrate the Bendini firm. Although he wishes the McDeeres no particular harm, Tarrance is willing to risk their lives to bring down the Bendini firm. When Mitch, Abby, and Ray finally go on the run, Tarrance betrays them by launching a massive manhunt and informing the media that the McDeeres are dangerous criminals.

Avery Tolar, a partner at the Bendini firm who is assigned to mentor Mitch and becomes oddly protective of him. Avery is the "rogue" of the Bendini firm because he drinks and womanizes, both of which are strictly against the firm's rules. When Avery learns that Mitch is about to turn the firm in to the FBI, he seems almost relieved and simply waits at his girlfriend's apartment until DeVasher's men eventually find and kill him.

Tammy Hemphill, Eddie Lomax's street-smart secretary. When Eddie is killed, Tammy contacts Mitch and works with him to obtain the incriminating documents needed by the FBI to bring down the Bendini firm.

Eddie Lomax, a private detective. Lomax was Ray McDeere's cellmate in prison and became a loyal friend because of Ray's protection of him from other inmates. Mitch hires Eddie to investigate the deaths of several former associates at the Bendini firm. Eddie is soon killed by DeVasher's men as a result of his probing questions.

Oliver Lambert, the senior partner at Bendini, Lambert & Locke. Although Oliver considers himself a gentleman, he is deeply entrenched in the firm's illegal activities, including the "elimination" of attorneys who try to leave the firm or contact the authorities.

DeVasher, the head of security at Bendini, Lambert & Locke. DeVasher is a ruthless man who maintains contact between the firm and its Mafia owners. DeVasher takes a sadistic pleasure in eavesdropping and spying on the McDeeres and other attorneys.

Lamar Quin, a senior associate and Mitch's closest friend at the firm. When the attorneys are enlisted to search for the missing McDeeres, Lamar demonstrates his empathy for the McDeeres' plight by pretending not to see Ray at a convenience store rather than alerting DeVasher's men. Because Mitch eventually turns over incriminating files to the FBI, Lamar's action indirectly results in his own incarceration.

F. Denton Voyles, the director of the FBI. Like Wayne Tarrance, Voyles is more concerned about making a spectacular Mafia bust than with how the McDeeres will be affected.

Kay Quin, Lamar Quin's wife. Kay tries to become close to Abby, who is put off by Kay's cheerful acceptance of the firm's meddling ways. Like most of the attorneys' wives, Kay is oblivious to the firm's illegal activities.

Joey Moralto, the head of the crime family for which the Bendini firm works.

— *Amy Sisson*

THE FIRST CIRCLE
(V kruge pervom)

Author: Aleksandr Solzhenitsyn (1918-)
First published: 1968
Genre: Novel
Locale: Suburban Moscow
Time: December 24-27, 1949
Plot: Historical realism

Gleb Vikentyevich Nerzhin (vih-kehn-TEE-yeh-vihch NEHR-zhihn), a thirty-one-year-old *zek* mathematician who turns to history and writes secretly and frantically. He is the most autobiographical of the *zeks*. He is a friend of Rubin, and the virgin Simochka has a crush on him, but the affair is interrupted by an unexpected visit from his wife, Nadya, who has had to live a lie for five years about her husband and now needs to disown him to save her job and her dissertation, though she loves him more than physical life. They both sense that he has thrived spiritually and intellectually on circle life. At the end of the novel, he is transported to an unknown, but probably horrible, camp.

Lev Grigoryvich Rubin (gree-goh-REE-yeh-vihch REW-bihn), a *zek* philologist whose talents are crucial to the voice encoder. He narrows voiceprints of five suspects to two, including the guilty party, Volodin. A Jew with a thick black beard and an odd gait and stance caused by a shell fragment in his side, he was an assistant professor before the war and knew every German writer who had ever published. Thirty-six years old, like his best friend, Nerzhin, he was given ten years for knowing Germans at the end of the war. Unlike Nerzhin, he is a Communist. Although he has trouble reconciling prison life and Party ideals, he is the spokesman for progressive ideology and calls Stalin "the Robespierre and the Napoleon of our Revolution wrapped up into one." Although he momentarily thrills to the thought that he might be inventing a new science, "phonoscophy," he realizes that his talent is wasted. He blames the waste on those who do not allow him to use his talents.

Dimitri Aleksandrovich Sologdin (dih-MIH-tree ah-lehk-SAN-droh-vihch soh-LOG-dihn), a thirty-six-year-old *zek* designer. He is in his second term and not likely to be released. He volunteers to cut wood for the kitchen for the exercise, though it is hard to convince Security that he does not have ulterior motives. He is a permanent character among the *zeks*. Secretly, he designs an absolute voice encoder, which he hopes to trade for his freedom.

Anton Nikolayevich Yakonov (nih-koh-LAY-yeh-vihch yah-KOH-nov), the colonel of engineers of the State Security Service and chief of operations at the Mavrino Institute research laboratory. More than fifty years old but still in his prime, he is tall, with a large frame, but moves swiftly. He has a princely manner. He had been a young radio engineer in 1932 and was arrested because he might have been "polluted" on a foreign assignment. He was one of the first *zeks* in one of the first *sharaskas*. He has bad relations with his deputy, Major Roitman, and is fearful of being returned to "The Pit" (prison).

Joseph V. Stalin, originally **Iosif Vissarionovich Dzhugashvili**, the secretary general of the Communist Party, 1922-1953, and premier of the Soviet Union, 1941-1953. He is called many other names that demonstrate his facility for being the best at everything. His aide Sasha calls him Ios Sarionich. The familiar portrait of the youthful, steely-eyed, mustachioed, short-haired strongman is everywhere. Stalin created the "first circle" (or *sharaska*) as a scientific center that would be staffed by prisoners (*zeks*) with scientific expertise. Stalin triggers action in the novel by demanding action (as opposed to optimistic progress reports) on the voice decoder.

His progressive paranoia makes it increasingly urgent for security personnel to be able to identify voices on every telephone call. Unlike his portrait, he is an old, mistrustful man in ill health who cannot sleep at night. He decides to live until the age of ninety so that he can finish drawing up plans to guide the "simple people" who he believes love him but who have so many shortcomings.

Lieutenant General Aleksandr "Sasha" Nikolayevich Poskrebyshev (poh-skreh-BIH-shehv), the chief of Stalin's personal secretariat and the closest person to Stalin for fifteen years. A balding man, he has the air of a simpleton yet knows how to treat subordinates, even Stalin's daughter.

Innokenty Artemyevich Volodin (ee-noh-KEHN-tee ahr-teh-MIH-yeh-vihch vo-LOH-dihn), a thirty-year-old state counselor in the Ministry of Foreign Affairs. He is expecting an assignment to Paris, where he could escape his wife, Dotnara Makargin. At the beginning of the novel, Volodin places a telephone call to warn the doctor who had treated Volodin's mother patiently for years. In increasing fear, Volodin turns to the letters of his late mother and the philosophy of one of her favorites, Epicurus. Volodin is trapped by Rubin's reading of voiceprints, and three chapters at the end of the novel record the details of Volodin's arrest.

Major General Pyotr Afanasyevich Makargin (pyohtr ah-fah-NAH-syeh-vihch mah-KAHR-gihn), a prosecutor and a good father to his three daughters.

Serafima (Simochka) Vitalyevna (seh-rah-FIH-mah vih-TAHL-yehv-nah), a Ministry of State Security (MGB) lieutenant and a free worker assigned to watch the *zeks* in the acoustics lab. Excessively small, she is not pretty, and Nerzhin was the first man to kiss her.

Major Adam Veniaminovich Roitman (veh-NYA-mih-noh-vihch ROYT-man), Yakonov's deputy, a Stalin Prize winner. Thirty years old, he is nearsighted, fits his uniform awkwardly, and is genuinely pleased by every success in the laboratory. *Zeks* like Roitman, and he loves his wife of five years and his three-year-old son, but his happiness is suddenly threatened by anti-Semitism, a strange twist because Jews had supported the Russian Revolution.

Rostislav "Ruska" Vadimich Doronin (RO-stih-slav vah-DIH-mihch do-ROH-nihn), a twenty-three-year-old, blue-eyed, and boyish *zek* vacuum specialist. Clara Makargin finds it hard to see in him "a bloodhound of imperialism." Summoned by Security to become an informer, he becomes, instead, a double agent and fingers the real informers.

Boris Sergeyevich Stapanov (sehr-GAY-yeh-vihch stah-PAH-nov), called **The Shepherd**, the new Communist Party secretary at Mavrino. Although his family had been landless farm laborers, he had four years of elementary school and two years of Party School, and he had won two medals during the war. A casual question regarding what he is doing about Jews galvanizes him into identifying and investigating them.

Victor Semayonovich Abakumov (seh-MYO-noh-vihch ah-bah-KEW-mov), the minister of state security. Tall and athletic, with black hair combed back, he plundered millions in 1945. As an intimate of Stalin, he can only await death.

Lieutenant Colonel Klimentiev (klee-MEHN-tyehv), the head of Mavrino Special Prison. He has shiny black hair and a pomaded mustache, and he never smiles on duty. He supervises 281 *zeks* and 50 guards in a businesslike, not bureaucratic, way. Outside Mavrino, he is fairly human, as when Nadya Nerszhin asks for a visit with her husband.

Foma Guryanov Oskolupov (gew-RYA-nov oh-sko-LEW-pov), the head of the Special Equipment Section of the Ministry of State Security. Corpulent and a man of action, not an intellectual, he knows how to manipulate the expertise of others. When the list of suspects is narrowed to two, he orders the arrest of both because he believes that both must be guilty of something, if not the crime in question.

Major Myshin, also called **The Snake**, a Mavrino Prison security officer. Plump and purple-faced, he competes with Major Shikin, the Mavrino Institute security officer. Their passion for security delays progress.

Hippolyte Mikailich Krondrashev-Ivanov (HIH-poh-liht mih-KHAY-lihch kohn-DRAH-shehv-ee-VAH-nov), a resident *zek* painter. He is a fifty-year-old on a twenty-five-year sentence for being caught in a group listening to a novelist read from his novel. He does large paintings that no one except Nerzhin likes, for ministries and officials' apartments. They are popular because they cost nothing and look better in gold frames.

Captain of the Combat Engineers Shakagov (shah-KAH-gov), a man with a B.S. in mathematics. He served four years on the front lines, where he "learned the value of a can of soup, an hour of quiet, the meaning of true friendship, of life itself." He dates Nadya Nerzhin and supports her when he discovers that her husband is a prisoner.

Vladimir Erastovich Chelnov (eh-RAH-stoh-vihch CHEHL-nov), a professor of mathematics and former member of the Academy of Sciences. He called Stalin "a loathsome reptile" and is now serving his eighteenth year. He answers "*zek*" instead of "Russian" on questionnaires and is the only *zek* not required to wear coveralls. He is shifted from *sharaska* to *sharaska* as his expertise is needed.

Colonel Yakov Ivanovitch Mamurin (YAH-kov ee-VAH-noh-vihch mah-MEW-rihn), called **The Man in the Iron Mask**, a former chief of special communications and creator of Mavrino Institute. He was fired because Stalin heard static on his telephone line. Now that he is a *zek*, authorities are not sure how to treat him. They fear that they will meet the same fate.

Spiridon Danilovich Yegorov (spih-rih-DON dah-NIH-loh-vihch YEH-goh-rov), a fifty-year-old, red-haired, vigorous *zek* janitor at Mavrino. Nerzhin seeks his folk wisdom.

Andrei Andreyevich Potopov (an-DREH-yeh-vihch po-TAH-pov), called **The Robot**, a *zek* electrical engineer. He was the designer of the Dnieper Hydroelectric Power Station and a prisoner of war in Germany. He is a workaholic.

Issak Moiseyevich Kagan (ee-SAK moy-SEH-yeh-vihch KAH-gan), the *zek* director of the battery room. Short, dark, and shaggy, he tries to live an obscure life and to pass through "The Era of Great Accomplishments" sideways. A paid informer, he is one of five exposed by Ruska Doronin.

Dushan Radovich (DEW-shan RAH-doh-vihch), an orthodox Marxist Serb and former member of the Comintern. Parchment-faced, he has physical ailments that save him from prison even though his ideology and his nationality make him a double loser in Stalinist Russia.

Illarion Pavlovich Gerasimovich (ee-lah-rih-ON PAV-loh-vihch geh-rah-SIH-moh-vihch), a *zek* physicist specializing in optics. Short, narrow-shouldered, and wearing a pince-nez like a spy in a poster, he says that the only likely path to invulnerability is to kill within oneself all attachments and to renounce all desires.

Bobynin (boh-BIH-nihn), the *zek* boss of laboratory seven at Mavrino. Forty-two years old, he is a big man with short, red hair who is on a twenty-five-year term. He is not intimidated by Abakumov because he already has lost everything.

Arthur Siromakha (see-roh-MAH-khah), a *zek* mechanic in laboratory seven. A wilted young man with sad eyes, he is "The King of Stool Pigeons," and *zeks* shun him.

Valentine (Valentulya) Martynich Pryanchikov (mahr-TIH-nihch PRYAN-chih-kov), a thirty-one-year-old *zek* radio engineer and former German prisoner of war. He is frail and thin. He is dedicated to his work on the voice encoder and innocently shocks Abakumov with the simple fact that success is not in sight, certainly not within the month that Abakumov has promised his superiors.

Junior Lieutenant Nadelashin (nah-deh-LAH-shihn), a Mavrino prison guard. Clean-shaven and moon-faced, he is called "Junior" by the *zeks*. He is notable for never swearing.

Larisa Nikolayena Emina (la-RIH-sah nih-koh-LAH-yehv-nah eh-MIH-nah), a thirty-year-old free employee and assigned spy in the design office. Her husband is a lieutenant colonel in the MGB and a dullard. She is large-bosomed and friendly. She and Sologdin have an assignation on a Sunday when no one else is in the design room.

Grigory Borisovich Adamson (grih-GOH-ree boh-RIH-soh-vihch AH-dahm-son), a *zek* engineer in his second term whom Nerzhin had known in another camp. Loyal to the old Revolution, Adamson was exiled when Stalin changed the Party.

Ivan Salivanov Dyrsin (sah-lih-VAH-nov DIHR-sihn), a *zek* engineer. He was denounced by neighbors for listening to German radio broadcasts. He did not have a radio, but it was argued that he might have had a radio because he was a radio engineer and he might have built one. Two radio tubes found in his apartment were enough to convict him.

— Frederic M. Crawford

FIRST LOVE
(Pervaya lyubov)

Author: Ivan Turgenev (1818-1883)
First published: 1860
Genre: Novella

Locale: Moscow, a summer home near the Neskutchny gardens, and St. Petersburg
Time: 1833
Plot: Psychological realism

Vladimir Petrovich Voldemar (vlah-DIH-mihr peh-TROH-vihch VOL-deh-mahr), the romantic sixteen-year-old protagonist and the thoughtful forty-year-old narrator. The youthful Vladimir meets Zinaida during the summer of his sixteenth year while staying with his family at their summer home. He immediately becomes infatuated with her and tries to live this first love according to the dictates of the romantic novels he has read. He dreams of winning Zinaida's love with acts of heroism and idealizes the object of his affection. He eventually discovers that his father has become Zinaida's domineering lover. Disillusioned and confused by this revelation, particularly by the vision of his father reprimanding Zinaida with a riding crop as though she were an unruly mount, the young Vladimir cannot comprehend the brutal passion his father and Zinaida share. As the novella's narrator, the middle-aged Vladimir is able in retrospect to sympathize with the lawless lovers, but it is obvious that he has never experienced such love.

Piotr Vassilich Voldemar (pyohtr vah-SIH-lihch), Vladimir's dashing father and Zinaida's lover. Known for his skill at breaking horses, Piotr Vassilich is equally adept at managing people. A complete believer in the power of will, Piotr feels constrained neither by the responsibilities of family nor by conventional codes of behavior. Without his idealistic son's knowledge, he initiates a brutally passionate affair with Zinaida. His single-minded pursuit of passion eventually consumes him, and on his deathbed he warns Vladimir against its destructive power.

Princess Zasyekin (zah-SYEH-kihn), the impoverished and widowed mother of Zinaida. Ugly and vulgar, she is a materialistic and quarrelsome opposite of her daughter. Princess Zasyekin shamelessly tries to use her daughter's beauty to repair her own diminished wealth and social standing.

Zinaida Alexandrovna Zasyekin (zih-nah-IH-dah ah-lehk-SAN-drov-nah), the beautiful twenty-one-year-old daughter of the impoverished Princess Zasyekin. Part saint and part temptress, Zinaida shares characteristics with both Vladimir and his father. Like Piotr, she is a willful character. She mercilessly uses her beauty to humiliate her numerous suitors and seems to enjoy exercising her power over them. Like Vladimir, she is a romantic, and she secretly yearns to give herself completely to a domineering man. This fantasy becomes incarnate in Piotr, who establishes her as his mistress. She eventually marries a man named Dolsky and dies in childbirth just before the middle-aged Vladimir decides to see her again.

Maria Nikolaevna Voldemar (MAH-ryah nih-koh-LAH-yehv-nah), Vladimir's long-suffering mother. Meek and passive, Maria Nikolaevna is unsuccessful in her feeble attempts to control her husband's wanton behavior.

Victor Yegorich Byelovzorov (yeh-GOH-rihch byeh-loh-ZOH-rov), a dashing young hussar. Handsome and athletic, Byelovzorov is the most persistent of Zinaida's suitors, repeatedly proposing marriage and announcing his willingness to sacrifice his life in her honor.

Count Malevsky (mah-LEHV-skee), a handsome, clever, and insincere nobleman who courts Zinaida. The anonymous letter he writes to Maria Nikolaevna describing Piotr's infidelity results in the Voldemars' early departure from their summer home. It also reveals Malevsky's essential cowardice.

Lushin (LEW-shihn), a cynical and intellectual doctor. The least fawning of Zinaida's admirers, Lushin tries unsuccessfully to insulate himself from the humiliations to which she subjects all her suitors. More than the others, he understands Zinaida, but like the others, he ultimately is unable to resist her charms.

Meidanov (MAY-dah-nov), a poet. Another of Zinaida's suitors, Meidanov demonstrates his love by composing lengthy poems dedicated to her.

— Carl Brucker

FIRSTBORN

Author: Larry Woiwode (1941-)
First published: 1982
Genre: Short fiction
Locale: New York City
Time: Early to mid-1960's
Plot: Love

Charles, Katherine's husband, a radio advertising executive and father. He recalls the birth and immediate death of his firstborn son, Nathaniel, from the perspective of several years later. Through his recollections, he comes to reconcile the death, to release the years of grief, and to place his own role and the role of his son within the birth-death experience. Charles is a man of feeling but not of fortitude and conviction. When a young internist describes how some men take to their own beds when their wives become pregnant, Charles and Katherine privately assent to the behavior. During the birth of Nathaniel, Charles's powerlessness makes him deferential, and he is ordered out of the delivery room, despite his promise to Katherine that he will not leave her. He has difficulty articulating his sentiments, and, following his son's death, he succumbs to the high-pressured recommendations of Dr. Harner, who urges him to sign the child over for hospital research before seeing Katherine. The death settles in Charles as an ache that takes years to soothe. Finally, after the birth of four healthy children, he fully accepts his son's death and feels free of his memories and his burden as he begs God's forgiveness. Through a freshly acquired awareness of Nathaniel's power to secure his parents' marriage, Charles experiences his own rebirth.

Katherine, Charles's wife and a mother. Her pregnancy and experience of childbirth metaphorically produce a marriage rather than a child. Whereas prior to the pregnancy, she had an affair and was uncommitted to Charles, her birth experience joins her with the child and then with her husband. She is more intuitive and expressive than Charles. When she tries to convey to him the lesson of the dead child, that "time and events can never destroy actual love," she quickly recognizes that whereas she understands now, he will do so only later. Although the loss of the child depresses her, unlike Charles she immediately senses the significance of Nathaniel's arrival and his capacity to unite them. Although Katherine feels betrayed by Charles because he signed over the child's body without consulting her, Nathaniel's death becomes the seed of a new commitment in their marriage.

Nathaniel, the firstborn son of Charles and Katherine. Although he is never seen by either of his parents, his presence nevertheless floods their lives, and he functions as the catalyst in reuniting them. His entry in the story parallels a scene in the excerpt from Leo Tolstoy's *War and Peace* that Charles reads to Katherine as she labors in his birth.

Dr. Harner, Katherine's obstetrician. Young, heavy, and balding, he is an insensitive and pragmatic physician who provides no emotional support to his patient and her husband. In fact, he avoids personal interaction by safely deferring to his medical assessments, and he responds to patient questions either humorously or cavalierly.

— Barbara A. Looney

THE FISHER KING

Author: Anthony Powell (1905-)
First published: 1986
Genre: Novel
Locale: On board the *Alecto*, near the British Isles
Time: The 1980's
Plot: Psychological realism

Saul Henchman, a society photographer. Wounded in World War II, Henchman is short and frail, and he requires crutches. He and his assistant, Barberina Rookwood, join a cruise around Great Britain on the liner *Alecto*. Among the small circle of passengers, he is the subject of gossip and speculation, chiefly concerning his relations with the beautiful Barberina. Valentine Beals, one of the circle, tries to associate Henchman with the Arthurian legend of the Fisher King. The Fisher King was a king wounded in battle and unable to do anything other than fish; spied by the knight Percival, he was invited to join the knight in his castle. At a banquet, a spear and a cup were brought to the table by a page and a maiden. If Percival had asked what these objects meant, the Fisher King would have been healed, but he did not, showing indifference to their appearance. Henchman proves to be like the Fisher King, in that the indifference to his feelings by others causes him to lose Barberina.

Barberina Rookwood, Henchman's assistant, in her early twenties. Barberina gave up a promising ballet career to care for Henchman, whom she believes to be a genius. Her beauty attracts many admirers on the *Alecto*, the most ardent of whom is Gary Lamont, a press tycoon. Less imposing is the frail Robin Jilson. Although Lamont is very pressing, Rookwood has little respect for him and instead falls in love with the helpless Jilson.

Valentine Beals, a writer of historical romances. Formerly an employee at a whiskey distillery, he has found success writing popular novels. Fascinated by Henchman, he associates him with the Fisher King legend. He follows Henchman and Rookwood around, becoming obsessed with their lives, to the extreme boredom of his wife, Louise. Beals is the only passenger on the *Alecto* who even approaches friendship with Henchman.

Gary Lamont, an up-and-coming newspaper tycoon possessed by a need to exert his will. Short and leathery looking, he falls in love with Barberina and attempts to seduce her. He is unattractive and is crude in his advances. Although he fails with Barberina, his consolation is that his empire grows during the voyage.

Dr. Lorna Tiptoft, a doctor and the daughter of Sir Dixon and Lady Tiptoft, passengers on the cruise. She is plain and humorless, and Beals associates her with another character from the legend, the Loathly Lady, who chides Percival for not asking about the spear and the cup. She takes young Jilson under her wing and cares for him in a domineering way.

Robin Jilson, an ailing young man for whom Barberina Rookwood feels pity and whom she seeks to help. She falls in love with him, primarily because he draws on her need to care for helpless men, and she loses her interest in Henchman. Eventually, Jilson is taken over by Lorna Tiptoft.

Mr. Jack, a melancholy drunkard who is a fixture in the ship's bar. Known by no other name, Mr. Jack looks like an overgrown schoolboy, though he is clearly at least in his seventies. Untidy, he has seen better days, yet he has a certain faded panache. In the end, Henchman finds him a suitable replacement for Barberina.

— *Philip Brantingham*

THE FISHER MAIDEN
(Fiskerjenten)

Author: Bjørnstjerne Bjørnson (1832-1910)
First published: 1868
Genre: Short fiction
Locale: Norway
Time: Early nineteenth century
Plot: Pastoral

Petra, known as the fisher maiden. She is the illegitimate child of Pedro Ohlsen and Gunlaug. As a child, she is brought back to her home village by her mother. When she grows up, she acquires three suitors who fight over her. She leaves the village for Bergen because she is attracted to the stage. She is later forgiven by Hans Ödegaard, who has felt that she ruined his life when he was her suitor.

Hans Ödegaard, the village pastor's son. He teaches Petra to read and falls in love with her. To his father's sorrow, he is indifferent to a career as a clergyman. Though he feels his life is ruined by Petra's having other suitors, he gets over his despair and marries a girl named Signe, daughter of a clergyman.

Pedro Ohlsen, a dreamer and a flute player. He has an affair with Gunlaug that results in Petra's birth. His father and grandfather leave him a fortune, which he in his turn wills to Petra upon his death.

Gunlaug, an audacious and bewitching woman, the mother of Petra. She helps her daughter escape from the village after the village is aroused by the girl's having three suitors.

Gunnar, a poor sailor. He is one of Petra's three suitors.

Yngve Vold, a rich shipowner, one of Petra's three suitors. When he announces that he plans to marry Petra, he is beaten by both Gunnar and Hans.

Signe, a friend of Petra. She loves Hans and plans to marry him. She is a suitable wife because she is a pastor's daughter of unimpeachable reputation.

FISKADORO

Author: Denis Johnson (1949-)
First published: 1985
Genre: Novel
Locale: The Florida Keys
Time: Early twenty-first century, after a nuclear holocaust
Plot: Science fiction

Anthony Terrence Cheung, a musician and small-scale cultivator of sugarcane. As the "manager" of the Miami Symphony Orchestra and a leading member of the Twicetown Society for Science, he is at the center of the two organizations devoted to the conservation of civilization in Twicetown (formerly Key West) during the period of the Quarantine. He hopes that he and his aged grandmother will live to see the end of the Quarantine, when the Cubans will sail north to reestablish contact with the inhabitants of the radiation-polluted remnants of the United States. At the climax of the book, after the Miami Symphony Orchestra has given its belated first performance to an audience of "Israelites"—dreadlocked worshipers of the god Bob Marley—he sees an approaching ship that might signal the end of the Quarantine.

Marie Wright, Anthony Cheung's grandmother, perhaps the oldest living person in the world. In her youth, she lived in Saigon and was fortunate to escape from the city when it fell in 1974. She lives almost entirely in her memories, and when she accompanies her grandson to the climactic concert, the terrible experiences she underwent after the helicopter taking her away from Saigon crashed into the sea come flooding back into her mind. The recapitulated moment of her rescue overlaps Cheung's vision of the ship that might represent a new salvation.

Fiskadoro, a teenage boy who inherits a clarinet from his father, Jimmy Hidalgo, and asks Cheung to teach him to play. After his father is lost at sea, he is kidnapped by the swamp-people, an ill-assorted company who have reverted to preliterate tribalism and have improvised a new rite of passage involving memory-twisting drugs and genital mutilation. After undergoing this rite, the much-changed Fiskadoro is returned to his own people, but the only connections with his past that he retains are his name—which is derived from the Latin *pescatore*, although he insists that it means "harpooner" rather than "fish-man"—and his clarinet, which he now plays better than he did before. He is the only other musician to play alongside Cheung for the Israelites.

Cassius Clay Sugar Ray, Cheung's mulatto half brother, known as Martin before his conversion to Islam. He is an entrepreneur and would-be merchant adventurer who sometimes trades with the poisoned mainland. He tries, unsuccessfully, to find the source of the memory-twisting drugs that the swamp-people use in their rites. He takes the Society of Science—which meets regularly to read from the few books to have survived the holocaust—a copy of a disturbing text that describes the effect of the atom bomb dropped on Nagasaki.

Belinda, Fiskadoro's mother. Jimmy Hidalgo's death leaves her bereft. Her three children drift away from her, and she develops an untreatable breast cancer. She prays for salvation, mostly to the powerful voodoo loa Atomic Bomber Major Colonel Overdoze, but she dies shortly before Fiskadoro's debut with the Miami Symphony Orchestra.

William Park-Smith, a black man with bleached blond hair who claims to be an Australian. He is the "musical director" of the Miami Symphony Orchestra and the president of the Twicetown Society of Science, collaborating with Cheung in trying to preserve a few threads of knowledge and civilization within the reemergent tapestry of superstitious religion.

— *Brian Stableford*

FIVE WOMEN WHO LOVED LOVE
(Kōshoku gonin onna)

Author: Ihara Saikaku (Hirayama Tōgo, 1642-1693)
First published: 1686
Genre: Short fiction

Locale: Japan
Time: The seventeenth century
Plot: Love

The First Story

Seijuro, a handsome young man apprenticed to a shopkeeper. Reluctantly, he returns the love of his master's sister. They elope and are discovered. Wrongly convicted of stealing money (actually mislaid), Seijuro is executed.

Onatsu, the shopkeeper's sister, who is in love with Seijuro. After his execution, she goes mad for a time and later enters a nunnery.

The Second Story

Osen, the young wife of a cooper. Wrongly accused of adultery by Chozaemon's wife, she takes impulsive revenge by actually giving herself to him. Discovered by her husband, she commits suicide.

Chozaemon, a yeast maker and Osen's partner in adultery, suspected and real. When his guilt is discovered, he is executed.

The Third Story

Osan, a wife whose scheme to punish her maid's reluctant lover by taking the maid's place in bed runs counter to plan. She falls in love with him herself; after a period of hiding together in a distant village, they are found and executed.

Rin, Osan's maid. She is a party to the scheme by which her lover is supposed to be punished.

Moemon, a clerk and Rin's reluctant lover, who is the victim of the substitution. He falls in love with Osan. When caught, they are executed.

The Fourth Story

Oshichi, a young woman. Having taken refuge in a temple after her house burned down, she falls in love with Onogawa, whom she meets there. Later, unable to see him, she decides to arrange another meeting by setting a fire. Discovered, she is burned at the stake.

Onogawa Kichisaburo, a young samurai whom Oshichi loves. Learning of her death, he contemplates suicide but finally becomes a monk.

The Fifth Story

Gengobei, a Buddhist monk and a former pederast.

Hachijuro, now dead, a boy whom Gengobei loved.

Oman, a young girl in love with Gengobei. Disguising herself as a boy, she wins Gengobei's love. He leaves the priesthood to live with her and later to marry her.

THE FIXER

Author: Bernard Malamud (1914-1986)
First published: 1966
Genre: Novel

Locale: Around Kiev, in the Ukraine, Russia
Time: Shortly before World War I
Plot: Historical realism

Yakov Bok, a poor fixer, or handyman. A tall, nervous man with a strong back and work-hardened hands, this orphan—whose mother died in childbirth and whose father was killed not more than a year later in a pogrom, a mass destruction of

Russian Jews—holds a pessimistic philosophy of life. Taught his trade at the orphanage, he was apprenticed at the age of ten and has, during his thankless life, served in the Russian army and taught himself Russian as well as some history, geography, science, and arithmetic. He considers himself a freethinker and professes no interest in politics. At the beginning of the novel, he feels trapped by his run-down village and lowly job. Even his wife has deserted him. Claiming that he wants his rewards now, not in heaven, he sells all he owns except for his tools and a few books, then journeys to Kiev to find new opportunities. In the city, his basic humanity embroils him in a series of events that lead to his being falsely accused of the ritual murder of a Christian boy. Escaping the symbolic entrapment of his village, he finds himself literally imprisoned for more than three years. During this period of physical and mental suffering, he fights to understand the reasons for his cruel and undeserved fate. Through reading, reflection, and dialogue with a few people with whom he has contact, this man who once hid his Jewishness comes to accept his irrational suffering as a means of identifying himself as a Jew and as a human being. No longer fearful, he concludes that his long-sought freedom is in truth a state of mind that must be pursued actively. At the novel's conclusion, he drinks in the cheers of the crowds lining the streets as he goes to trial, a hero of the downtrodden. With a newfound spirit, he proclaims, "Where there's no fight for it there's no freedom."

Raisl (RI-suhl), Bok's wife of almost six years. Faithless and childless, she has deserted Bok at the beginning of the novel for a stranger she met at the village inn. She visits Bok in prison to get him to sign a paper acknowledging his paternity of a child she conceived by another man. Her plea leads Bok to ponder the nature of responsibility and its role in defining oneself as a human being.

Shmuel (shmew-EHL), Bok's father-in-law. A skinny man with ill-fitting clothes, he is a peddler with the ability to sell the seemingly worthless. His philosophy of life is that God will always provide. He visits Bok in prison, where he attempts unsuccessfully to get his son-in-law to open his heart to God and accept at least partial responsibility for his troubles. He later dies of diabetes.

Zinaida (Zina) Nikolaevna (ZIHN-ay-dah nih-koh-LAYV-nah), a lonely unmarried woman. About thirty years old, sharp-faced, and slightly built, she is marked by a crippled leg, the result of a childhood illness. From Bok's first appearance in her father's house as a handyman, she attempts to seduce him. Failing, she later falsely accuses him of attempted assault.

Nikolai Maximovitch, a semiretired businessman. A fattish man of about sixty-five, with a bald head and melancholy eyes, he runs his late brother's brickworks. Unaware that Bok is a Jew, this anti-Semite hires him to manage the brickyard. Later incensed by Bok's deceptions, he turns on Bok and testifies against the man who saved him from smothering in the snow after passing out from the effects of alcohol.

B. A. Bibikov, the investigating magistrate for cases of extraordinary importance. A man of medium height with a large head, dark gray hair, and a darkish beard, he is a lover of Baruch Spinoza who claims that he depends on the law. He possesses great compassion and plans to get Bok's story to journalists in the hope of saving an innocent man. He is hanged mysteriously in what is termed a suicide by authorities.

Attorney Grubeshov, a prosecutor of the Kiev Superior Court. A heavy man with a fleshy face, thick eyebrows, and hawk eyes, he relentlessly pushes for Bok's conviction of the ritual murder of the Christian boy. His obsession with Bok's guilt blinds him to reason.

— *Harold Blythe*

THE FLAGELLANTS
(Les Flagellants)

Author: Carlene Hatcher Polite (1932-)
First published: 1966
Genre: Novel

Locale: New York City
Time: The late 1960's
Plot: Social realism

Ideal, the heroine, a headstrong young black woman who was reared in a Southern black community. Ideal abandons both her career and her financially stable marriage to live with Jimson, the beautiful man of her dreams. She eventually grows to resent their poverty and Jimson's apparent lack of interest in finding employment. Ideal complains that Jimson's behavior places her in the problematic role of the black matriarch, forced to be stronger than the man she supports. In some ways, Ideal draws her identity from Jimson's dependence. When he finally finds a job with the Bureaucratique, Ideal feels abandoned and becomes obsessed with the notion that he is involved with another woman, whom she refers to as "The Byzantine Lady Under Glass," from the title of one of Jimson's poems. Although she truly loves Jimson, Ideal finally asks Jimson to leave because she realizes that they are destroying each other.

Jimson, the hero, a black poet who responds to Ideal's demands that he seek employment by telling her that as an artist, it is a waste for him to squander his mental energy working for the white society. Jimson grows to resent what he perceives as Ideal's attempt to play the part of the dominant matriarch in their relationship. At the end of the novel, finally confessing to a love affair with another woman, Jimson tells Ideal that he has cheated on her because, like all black women, she is never satisfied with her man's achievements and because he longs to be with a woman who will simply accept him as he is.

Adam, Ideal's first husband, an older man whom Jimson vilifies for his weakness and his inability to be a worthy romantic and sexual partner for a strong woman like Ideal. To Jimson, Adam represents the emasculated, passive role black men are forced into by black matriarchs.

Papa Boo, Jimson's grandfather, who has taught his grandson that whereas black people from West Indian or African backgrounds are tolerated in American society because they provide an exotic element, American blacks are below consideration.

Rheba, a white librarian with a "pitiful lackluster birdface" who hires Jimson to work for her, attempting to become his confidante. Rheba's desperate bid to learn about Jimson's life so that she can identify with his experiences as a black man fails when Jimson, regarding her as another suffocating matriarchal figure, resigns from his job.

Johnny Lowell, Jimson's sharp-dressing, manicured, West Indian supervisor at the Bureaucratique, a social service organization where both men work. A master at the business of looking busy while doing nothing, Lowell depresses Jimson by making it clear that the purpose of their job is not to promote peace and social good but to exploit the company's benefits as much as possible.

— *V. Penelope Pelizzon*

THE FLANDERS ROAD
(La Route des Flandres)

Author: Claude Simon (1913-)
First published: 1960
Genre: Novel

Locale: Northeastern France, Nazi Germany, and Paris
Time: 1940-1945
Plot: Love

Georges (zhohrzh), the narrator, a young cavalry soldier and prisoner of war. He is obsessed with Corinne de Reixach as a means of determining whether her husband's death was an accident of war or a suicide. The product of a solid classical education but little real-life experience, Georges possesses a cultivated contempt for authority and scorns his parents' intellectual and aristocratic pretensions. With the French army en route and in an attempt to reestablish a sense of order, Georges becomes obsessed with solving the mystery of de Reixach's death.

Charles de Reixach (shahrl deh ri-SHAHK), a distant cousin of Georges, the commanding officer of Georges's squadron and the cuckolded husband of Corinne. He is elegant, controlled, distant, meticulous in dress and manner, and cordial to his men. This forty-two-year-old aristocrat presents an impenetrable expressionless face that defies access to his inner thoughts and motivations and makes him an enigma to Georges. De Reixach is killed by a sniper's bullet, a death he may have chosen as a result of his humiliation at his wife's infidelity.

Corinne de Reixach (koh-RIHN), Charles's wife, the object of Georges's obsession, and Iglésia's lover. Twenty years younger than her husband, Corinne is seen as a parvenue with a reputation for promiscuity. Blonde and possessing an ideal, translucent beauty, she is a fascinating and disturbing woman/child whose shameless clothes and actions scandalize the aristocratic class. Corinne's whims continually challenge her husband's traditions and values, as well as his ability to control and satisfy her. After the war, Corinne remarries and has a brief affair with Georges.

Iglésia (ih-GLAY-zee-ah), who in peacetime was employed as a jockey by de Reixach and during the war was de Reixach's orderly in the cavalry squadron. He is incarcerated as a prisoner of war with Georges. Some fifteen years older than the other cavalry soldiers, Iglésia is small of stature, with bow legs, sallow skin, and a mournful, hawkish face. Iglésia displays an unquestioning loyalty toward his employer that does not extend beyond de Reixach's death. Naturally taciturn and uncommunicative and interested only in discussing horses, Iglésia presents a challenge as a source of information for Georges about both Charles and Corinne.

Blum (blewm), Georges's Jewish comrade in arms and fellow prisoner of war. Blum is slight of build, with large, protruding ears and a narrow girlish face that belies his stubbornness and savvy. The son of an overworked family of clothiers and thus well versed in the requirements of survival, Blum, though the same age as Georges, possesses a much more practical experience of life's hardships and injustices. A partner in Georges's attempts to solve the mystery of de Reixach's demise, he is also critical of Georges's obsession with finding the "truth" of a past event that has little or no bearing on their present situation. Blum dies of tuberculosis in the prison camp.

Pierre, Georges's father. A corpulent intellectual whose own parents were illiterate peasants, Pierre idolizes knowledge and reveres the written word as the ultimate source of humankind's progress and salvation. He spends his days reading and writing, physically detached from the world and its events. He unwittingly inspires Georges's disdain for the impotence and inefficacy of intellectual pursuits and naïve idealism.

Sabine (sah-BEEN), Georges's mother, a poor relation to the de Reixach family. Horrified at growing old, the red-haired Sabine tries to hide her advancing age behind brightly colored clothes and an ever increasing quantity of jewelry. Although Sabine's marriage to the bourgeois intellectual Pierre excludes her from lofty social circles, she retains her admiration of the prestige of aristocracy. Heir to the family home, documents, and portraits, she is the unofficial family historian. It is she who, through her ceaseless chatter, fills Georges's childhood with family stories and legends.

Reixach, an eighteenth century ancestor of Charles de Reixach (and thus also of Georges) whose portrait hangs in the family gallery. His populist sympathies compel him to drop the aristocratic particle "de" from his name. His political views lead to family and personal embarrassment and prompt his suicide, a scandal that the family tries to hide. Ironically, his portrait is marred by a crack in the paint at the level of his temple, which seems to memorialize the suicide. This portrait feeds Georges's curiosity about de Reixach by proposing an ancestral prototype of suicide.

Wack, a fellow cavalry soldier. An Alsatian peasant, anti-Semitic, simple, and stubborn, with a fool's face, Wack is a know-it-all and is constantly baited by his comrades. Wack is shot off his horse in an ambush that precedes de Reixach's death.

— *Kathleen A. Johnson*

FLAUBERT'S PARROT

Author: Julian Barnes (1946-   )
First published: 1984
Genre: Novel

Locale: France and England
Time: Early 1980's
Plot: Experimental

Gustave Flaubert (gew-STAHV floh-BEHR), the famous nineteenth century novelist. He is the object of obsession of Geoffrey Braithwaite. He is a blond giant, a Norman who thinks of himself as being like a bear. By the age of thirty, however, his good looks have begun to crumble as the result of syphilis treatments that leave him increasingly balding and stout. He is also prone to recurrent epileptic fits. The son of a successful Rouen surgeon, Flaubert has failed in law school and begun a confirmed bachelor's life, devoted to writing while he lives on an inheritance from his father and tends to his niece and mother (with occasional interruptions for travel to exotic places). Flaubert's primary traits are his pessimism and his pronounced misanthropy. He dislikes humanity in general, with its stupidities and its intrusive technology, and the bourgeoisie in particular. He also fears any woman who might make permanent demands on him. The closest he can come to a normal love relationship is his off-and-on affair with Louise Colet, carried out on occasional railroad trips. Flaubert has little or nothing in his life beyond writing. After the failure of his first work, he achieves nothing remarkable in literature until the publication of his masterpiece *Madame Bovary* when he is thirty-six years old. Inept at handling money, he loses whatever he manages to make from his writing. At the cost of years of effort, he produces three more books that have some success; however, when he dies of a stroke at the age of fifty-five, he is impoverished as well as exhausted and obscure.

Louise Colet (lweez koh-LAY), Flaubert's long-suffering lover and literary friend. A writer herself, she is well known in the literary circles of Paris when she meets him at the age of thirty-five; he is eleven years younger. Although she is married, they have an affair for two years before ending it for a time. As much as Louise loves him, she finds his behavior, particularly his need to humiliate her, unbearable at times. By the time he is thirty years old, she thinks of him as old before his time. She endures many forms of neglect and abuse from him, but three years after they part, she takes up with him again. Louise is mature, self-confident, artistic, amorous, and patient. Flaubert tries to limit her social life, treats her like his student, and dismisses her writing. She endures four more years of fleeting hotel trysts before they part company for good.

Geoffrey Braithwaite, a retired medical doctor. His ruling obsession is collecting trivia about Flaubert's life and traveling in France to puzzle out enigmas such as the "true" identity of the stuffed parrot Flaubert used as his model in a story. Fond of talking, he delivers monologues to people encountered in such places as Flaubert's birthplace of Rouen or on a cross-channel ferry. Once, he even runs into a fellow literary detective, an American academic named Winterton who seems to have evidence of a previously unknown romantic entanglement in Flaubert's life. Geoffrey seems remarkably phlegmatic and undemonstrative, indifferent even to the memory of friends who died alongside him in the Normandy invasion. His literary passion for the long-dead Flaubert never quite masks his uneasiness about his late wife's pathetic adulteries. A serious man, always faithful to his wife, Geoffrey feels permanently damaged by her death. Although she may or may not have attempted suicide, it is certain that he turned off her life support system at the end. Geoffrey reluctantly finishes his monologue and turns to the "pure story" of his wife's betrayals, divulging as little personal information as possible. He believes that a relationship with a literary immortal ultimately is more interesting, as well as more rewarding. The truth eludes Geoffrey at the end, however; having tracked down a roomful of parrots, he can be no surer of the "true" parrot's identity than of the reasons for his wife's infidelity and death.

Ellen Braithwaite, the recently deceased wife of Geoffrey. In her husband's view, she was a clumsy, absentminded woman, as likely to snatch at illicit pleasures as to attend a winter sale in July. She is barely discreet in her "secret" life with other men, and Geoffrey's friends know all about her infidelity. Having borne Geoffrey's children and seen them through school, she falls into a "mood" that remains with her for the next five years, until her mysterious death at the age of fifty-five.

— *Paul Kistel*

THE FLIES
(Las moscas)

Author: Mariano Azuela (1873-1952)
First published: 1918
Genre: Novel

Locale: Mexico
Time: April, 1915
Plot: Historical realism

General Malacara (mahl-ah-KAH-rah), the highest ranking individual among the throng of former federal officials fleeing the capital by train. Like the other refugees who share the hospital car, he is a social parasite and a self-serving opportunist whose loyalty evaporates when his political faction loses control. His only concerns are escape, survival, and realignment. Because he is the most promising link to the protection of Francisco Villa, once the train is under way, everyone courts his favor. He makes promises of help only in the hope of gaining some advantage, and he rarely delivers. He is a debauched libertine. In spite of the perilous circumstances, he initiates a drunken party and publicly cavorts with Cachucha and Manuela, women young enough to be his granddaughters.

Marta Reyes-Téllez (RREH-yehs-TEH-yehs), a strong-willed, essentially silly, middle-aged widow who knows how to take care of her family. Even though she has never worked, she understands better than do her employed children the moral flexibility and hypocrisy required to secure and protect a government job. She believes that she and her family, because of their social and political connections, are morally superior to virtually all others.

Matilde Reyes-Téllez (mah-TEEL-deh), the older daughter of Marta. She arrogantly but mistakenly assumes that her place in society and her self-professed artistic talent will guarantee both her safety and her future.

Rosita Reyes-Téllez (roh-SEE-tah), the younger daughter of Marta. She uses her charms to manipulate men, but she lacks a will of her own.

Rubén Reyes-Téllez (rew-BEHN), the youngest of Marta's children. He always follows his mother's orders and Matilde's lead. A manly but utterly gullible youth, he is attracted to those in powerful positions and allows their opinions to determine his behavior. His naïveté and simplistic machismo allow his mother and older sister to coerce him to remain in Irapuato, in spite of the extreme danger, to arrange the family's future with the new administration.

Quiñones (keen-YOHN-ehs), a friend of Rubén who understands even less than Rubén of the social rules by which those in power expect their underlings to abide. An arrogant braggart, he demonstrates his careless disregard for Villa's rules and for the well-being of others when he openly criticizes Villa knowing that some of Villa's soldiers can hear him.

Dionacio Ríos (dee-oh-NAH-see-oh RREE-ohs), a prosecuting attorney for Villa's government.

Señor Rubalcaba (rrew-bahl-KAH-bah), a corpulent federal schoolmaster. Like the novel's other displaced functionaries, he is utterly bereft of the will to act. More disposed to irony than to anger, he can only sigh with resignation when soldiers make off with his beloved companion, Miss Aurora of the fourth grade.

Don Sinforoso (seen-foh-ROH-soh), the blustery former mayor of Turicato. Until he learns that military men are in grave danger, he claims to be a colonel in the federal army.

THE FLIES
(Les Mouches)

Author: Jean-Paul Sartre (1905-1980)
First published: 1943
Genre: Drama

Locale: Argos, Greece
Time: Antiquity
Plot: Existentialism

Zeus (zews), the principal Greek god. He knows that people are completely free, that the gods are in fact powerless over them, and that only those who accept the laws of the gods can be controlled through remorse. Because of this, he successfully breaks the brother-sister alliance between Orestes and Electra and destroys her once-defiant spirit by instilling fear and anguish in her heart. This is also why he warns the compliant Aegistheus of his planned assassination, even though fifteen years earlier he did not warn Agamemnon (a-guh-MEHM-nahn). Electra and Aegistheus have accepted his edicts, but with Orestes, Zeus finds his apparent omnipotence and his blandishments to be useless as he tries to convince the young hero to pledge his total allegiance to the divine order. While admitting defeat in this instance, he reminds Electra of his unshaken power over her and all those who accept the gods' laws.

Orestes (uh-REHS-teez), the son of King Agamemnon and Queen Clytemnestra. If at first he is a disinterested observer of the human scene, he soon is concerned, upon his return to Argos from exile, by the virtual enslavement of the people caused by the guilt they feel concerning the murder of his father years ago. Following his encounter with Zeus and Electra, he becomes increasingly dissatisfied with his rootlessness and searches for the type of commitment that will allow him full expression of his identity. He then decides to avenge his father's death by killing his mother and her new husband, thereby affirming his free will utterly and irrevocably. Despite his tutor's wishes and the gods' threats, he commits himself to the human community and assumes the burden of their remorse as well as the responsibility for his own double crime. Unregretful, he wants to leave the kingdom with his sister; when she rejects him, he is more than willing to embark on a new life, his freedom intact. Pursued but unstung by the flies, he strides out into the light in magnificent isolation.

Electra, the daughter of Agamemnon and Clytemnestra. Since discovering the murder some fifteen years earlier, she has been a slave in the palace, doing all the menial labor. This dissenter is full of hatred for her mother and constantly rebels in limited ways against the powers that be, going as far as performing a sacrilegious dance of joy in a vain act of defiance. Above all, she has dreamed of punishing the royal couple. Her bad faith is underscored when she, terrified by the horror of Orestes' act, finally refuses her brother's form of freedom and authenticity by repenting to Zeus and accepting the same guilt imposed on her compatriots, which she had all along attacked.

Aegistheus (ih-JIHS-thuhs), the murderer of Agamemnon and the new king of Argos. Although this crime has become a public burden, he has succeeded, usually through fear and sometimes through terror, in convincing the citizens that they are guilty and that public penance and mourning alone can appease the angry gods who have sent a plague on the city. Indeed, to the crowd's cries of mercy, he replies that the dead know no pity as he and his queen, Clytemnestra, look down on the wretches assembled in the main temple. In a further clever act, he directs their anger at Electra by reminding them of her cursed heredity and later by casting her out of Argos. He has been able to rule thanks to his elaborate hoax. Without it, he, like Zeus, might have been overthrown by his people. It is understandable, therefore, that Orestes, a free man by choice, kills him in righteous justice.

Clytemnestra (klit-uhm-NES-truh), the widow of Agamemnon, whom she murdered with the help of her lover, Aegistheus. Even though she displays repentance as part of her overall behavior, she is happy that her late husband is dead. Now married to Aegistheus, she always takes his side and approves of everything he does. She too dies at Orestes' hand, screaming and cursing her two children.

The tutor, the rationalistic, cosmopolitan philosopher and teacher of Orestes. Besides teaching Orestes to view the world and humanity with amused skepticism—while also imparting history, archaeology, and culture to him—he reveals to him the secret of his birth and family ties.

The Furies, or the flies, the terrible Greek goddesses who relentlessly harass unpunished criminals.

The high priest, the main religious personage. His chief role consists of seconding Aegistheus' secular authority through moral censure and threats of divine retribution.

— Pierre L. Horn

FLIGHT TO CANADA

Author: Ishmael Reed (1938-)
First published: 1976
Genre: Novel
Locale: The United States and Canada
Time: Around the time of the Civil War, with anachronisms
Plot: Social satire

Raven Quickskill, a slave who escaped from Swine'rd, the Virginia plantation of Arthur Swille. Quickskill initiates the action of the novel, even though he is not physically present during most of the book, because the event that sets the action in motion is his escape to Canada. Quickskill's poem "Flight to Canada" makes him famous and causes him to be a target of the Nebraska tracers, a group of slave catchers employed by Swille and other slave owners. When Quickskill discovers that Uncle Robin has inherited the Swine'rd Plantation after the death of Arthur Swille, he returns to America and begins planning a new life as a writer who will write his own life story in an attempt to displace the works of such dissembling white writers as Harriet Beecher Stowe, author of *Uncle Tom's Cabin*.

Princess Quaw Quaw Tralaralara, a Native American who is Yankee Jack's wife and Quickskill's lover. She is also a show business personality, performing as a trapeze artist and dancer. The princess becomes incensed at Yankee Jack when she discovers that he killed her father in the raid in which she was carried off to become his spouse. She gets to Canada by walking a tightrope backward over Niagara Falls, but she quarrels with Quickskill and leaves him.

Arthur Swille, Quickskill's master. He controls not only the slaves on his plantation but also much of the politics of the United States from his quarters on his baronial plantation. His life is enlivened by romantic fantasies based on the works of Sir Walter Scott, Edgar Allan Poe, and other Romantic writers. Poe is a frequent houseguest. Swille begins each day by drinking two gallons of slave mothers' milk brought to him by Uncle Robin. Swille dies when his wife, parodying the end of "The Fall of the House of Usher," pushes him into a fireplace and he burns to death.

Yankee Jack, the princess' husband. He is a robber baron figure who plunders the country, particularly its minorities, to maintain his expensive lifestyle and his taste for art and fine cuisine.

Uncle Robin, the main house slave at Swine'rd. He seems to be Swille's right-hand man, but he is actually manipulating the plantation owner and turning things to his own advantage. Swille leaves the plantation and his fortune to Uncle Robin in his will. Uncle Robin reveals to Quickskill that he actually wrote the will to benefit himself. He also says that he had been fooling Swille; the mothers' milk was actually a solution of coffee creamer.

Mammy Barracuda, the Aunt Jemima figure to Uncle Robin's Uncle Tom. She keeps the female part of the plantation in line, beating Mrs. Swille and giving her an injection of Valium when the mistress of the house prefers to lie in bed instead of dressing in crinolines, arranging flowers, and making vapid comments in a Southern drawl.

Stray Leechfield, an escaped slave with whom Quickskill flees to Canada. He has no interest in Quickskill's plans to emancipate the rest of the slaves and improve the race but instead tries to make money in the pornographic film business.

40s, another slave, with a missing leg, who escaped to Canada with Quickskill. He hides out in a houseboat and prepares to defend himself with a shotgun.

Abraham Lincoln, the president of the United States. He plays all sides of the Civil War and the emancipation issue. He sneaks behind Confederate lines to borrow money from Swille to keep the war going but tells Uncle Robin that he should write Swille's will to benefit the slaves. The nation watches Lincoln's assassination on television as part of the coverage of the play *Our American Cousin*.

— James Baird

THE FLOATING OPERA

Author: John Barth (1930-)
First published: 1956
Genre: Novel
Locale: Maryland's eastern shore
Time: The 1920's and 1930's
Plot: Psychological realism

Todd Andrews, a fifty-four-year-old lawyer living alone in the Dorset Hotel in Cambridge, Maryland. An expensive dresser, cigar smoker, and chronicler of his own life, he suffers heart and prostate trouble. He fancies that he resembles actor Gregory Peck. Never married, he enjoys an intimate relationship with Jane Mack, his best friend's wife. He claims he is not a philosopher, yet he makes a habit of applying his own eccentric notions to his own and other people's lives, often with grim results. He passes through various "poses" through the years (including misanthropic hermitism, cynicism, and Buddhist "sainthood") until one day in 1937 he decides to kill himself because he has come to believe that life has no intrinsic value. Foiled in his attempt at self-destruction, he accepts the proposition that perhaps there are, after all, relative values.

Harrison Mack, a pickle magnate. His meeting with Todd in 1925 changes his life dramatically. A large, muscular, amiable, handsome, and intelligent man, he professes Marxism in his youth and is disinherited. Inspired by Todd, he also takes on various poses, one of which results in his encouraging his wife to sleep with Todd. He adheres to what he regards as sophisticated moral and social values but lacks the inner strength to accept the consequences of some of these values.

Jane Mack, Harrison's wife, about twenty-six years old when she commences her affair with Todd in 1932. Beautiful and athletic, she is described by Todd as a woman who leaves nothing to be desired. Her problem is a too-rigid adherence to values imposed on her by her husband, which results in her own partial loss of identity.

Captain Osborne Jones, an eighty-three-year-old retired oyster dredger living in the Dorset Hotel. Crippled by arthritis and other afflictions, he is nevertheless full of life and has few philosophic ideas or preconceptions. A survivor, he complains but goes on, enjoying what life he has left. Todd admires him enormously.

Mr. Haecker, a seventy-nine-year-old retired high school principal living in the Dorset Hotel. Devoid of family and ailing, he attempts a Stoic-like acceptance of old age, citing Cicero as his mentor. When Todd tells him that his stoicism is hypocritical, that he really despises old age, he attempts to kill himself. Unlike Captain Osborne, he suffers from dread, idealistic delusions, and despair.

Thomas T. Andrews, Todd's father. Although in absentia, he exerts a powerful influence over his son. Todd spends much of his own life trying to discover why his father committed suicide in 1930, refusing to accept that he could have done so because of mere bad luck or financial ruin from the stock market crash of October 29, 1929. He was an uncommunicative man who nevertheless made it clear that he expected his son to succeed. He remains a mystery throughout the novel.

Colonel Henry Morton, the owner of a tomato cannery and the richest man in Cambridge, Maryland. He is somewhat vulgar and is corrupted by power. His life becomes a torment when Todd gives him a gift of five hundred dollars with no strings attached. He attempts to offer Todd various jobs and new business because he cannot understand the gift. Only after he finds Todd in a compromising situation with his wife does he proceed to shun Todd altogether.

Betty June Gunter, a poor, scrawny, blonde seventeen-year-old high school student when she first meets Todd, whom she befriends so that she can confess her love for an older man. When, finally, she allows Todd to seduce her, Todd laughs as he catches a glimpse of their lovemaking. She never forgives him. Later, in 1924, having become a prostitute, she attempts to kill him with a broken bottle in a brothel.

Captain Jacob Adam, the tough, wiry, leather-faced proprietor of Adam's Original & Unparalleled Floating Opera, a circuslike, showboat extravaganza. Part charlatan and part genuine businessman, he runs a floating opera that grotesquely depicts life itself.

Jeannine Mack, the young, blonde, charming daughter of Jane Mack and either her husband, Harrison, or Todd. Her convulsions during Captain Adam's extravaganza interrupt Todd's suicide and lead him to conclude that relative values are possible in a world of no intrinsic value.

— *Louis Gallo*

THE FLOATING WORLD

Author: Cynthia Kadohata (1956-   )
First published: 1989
Genre: Novel
Locale: The United States
Time: The 1950's and the 1960's
Plot: Bildungsroman

Olivia Ann, the protagonist and narrator. Olivia is the oldest of four children. She tells about her cross-country adventures from the West to the South and about her teenage life in Gibson, Arkansas, where her family settles. She relates her adolescent view of her relatives and of the key events in her own life, including the death of her grandmother, her first job, and her first sexual encounter. In her episodic reminiscences, Olivia sketches out her life from the time she is twelve until she is a young adult, all the while living in a "floating world."

Obasan, Olivia's grandmother. Obasan is a powerful figure in Olivia's life, both as a tormentor and as a role model. Resentful of Obasan's domineering and abusive nature, Olivia never refers to her by the affectionate term for grandmother, "Obachan," but always by the more formal reference "Obasan." In contrast to the stereotype of Japanese women as obedient and demure, Obasan has had three husbands and seven lovers. She feels compelled to relate the stories of her life and loves to Olivia, who inherits her grandmother's journals after her grandmother's death. Olivia, who ignores Obasan's pleas for help while she is dying, always carries the guilt with her that somehow she killed her grandmother.

Laura, Olivia's mother. At the age of seventeen, Laura becomes pregnant with Olivia. Because her lover, Jack, is married, Obasan arranges for Laura to marry Charlie-O. Married to a man she cares for but does not love, Laura often seems restless and lost in her "floating world." During her marriage, she has an affair, but she decides to stay with her family.

Charles (Charlie-O) Osaka, Olivia's stepfather. Charlie-O takes his family across the country to Arkansas, where he invests in a garage business. Although an apparently happy man, Charlie-O feels frustrated and helpless in the face of much of what happens to him: his wife commits adultery, he gambles too much, and he cannot ensure that his children will be happy.

Tan, Olivia's first lover. Both Tan and Olivia work at a hatchery, and they become teenage lovers. They separate when Tan's father relocates to accept a job in Indiana. Olivia unsentimentally regards their love life as a "prodigious adventure."

Andy, Olivia's second lover. Andy, a small-time criminal, is Olivia's lover in Los Angeles.

Walker,
Peter, and
Ben, Olivia's three younger brothers. Of the three, the family feels most protective of Walker. With his penchant for wandering, Walker seems the most fragile, the most likely to get "lost."

— *Sandra K. Stanley*

THE FLOUNDER
(Der Butt)

Author: Günter Grass (1927-)
First published: 1977
Genre: Novel
Locale: Germany and Poland
Time: The neolithic period to the late 1970's
Plot: Magical Realism

The narrator, a writer. He has lived many lives in the past, in particular as the husbands or lovers of a series of cooks, whose lives mirror important points in human history. The relationships between the narrator and these women illustrate the relationship between the sexes, in which men strive for dominance but remain subject to the will and cooking skill of women. The narrator, in his present life, is the weak and philandering husband of the pregnant harridan Ilsebill. He attempts to gratify himself sexually with the members of the Feminist Revolutionary Tribunal and the last two cooks, Sibylle Miehlau and Maria Kucorra, but in actuality he is used by them.

Ilsebill, the narrator's wife. She advances through nine months of pregnancy during the book, finally delivering a daughter near the conclusion. She is named Ilsebill for the wife in the Brothers Grimm tale "The Fisherman and His Wife." The narrator's wife, who like the fisherman's wife always wants more, is an insatiable virago.

The Flounder, a seemingly omniscient godlike entity, actually a turbot with bony, pebblelike bumps. The Flounder allows himself to be caught by a fisherman in the neolithic period. He wishes to serve as a guide and adviser to weak males to enable them to overcome matriarchy and to develop their assertive, dominating, and culture-producing, if destructive, traits. The Flounder, who is released, can be summoned readily and repeatedly comes back to give the narrator, in his many existences as generalized "man," advice on how to deal with women. Despairing of progressively impotent man as an agent of progress, the Flounder finally allows himself to be caught by three radical feminists, Sieglinde "Siggie" Hunyscha, Susanne "Maxie" Maxen, and Franziska "Frankie" Ludkowiak. Although he offers to serve as an adviser to women, they choose to place him on trial for his crimes against women. During the course of the trial before the Women's Revolutionary Tribunal in Berlin, the story of the eleven cooks, embodying the history of male dominance and the hidden contributions of women, is told. The Flounder repents of his wrongdoing and agrees to serve as adviser to women. Although he is found guilty of crimes against women, he is, to the disgust of the Revolutionary Party, allowed to live. After being forced to witness a banquet in which fellow flounders are consumed, he is released into the Baltic Sea.

Awa, an enormously fat, three-breasted living Baltic fertility goddess from the Stone Age. She is the first cook. She and the women keep the men satisfied and subservient by suckling them. She forbids the narrator, then called Edek, to use her gift of fire to smelt metal as the Flounder had taught him or to count above 111, the number of her dimples. When she dies, Awa, as she had instructed, is stuffed, roasted, and eaten.

Wigga, the Iron Age cook. When she forbids a certain hallucinogen, dream wurzel, men lose their innocence. The unsuckled men become restive and resent the farming initiated by Wigga. She orders her people to stay close to the source of fish for her soups and not to follow the wandering Germanic hordes. Although she rails against the fire-eating Goths, she makes the men gather the iron pots that they discard when they move on. She dies of blood poisoning when she cuts herself on a rusty roasting spit left behind by the Goths.

Mestwina, a cook and priestess for the Pomeranian people living in the Wicker Bastion on Fisherman's Island, later incorporated into Danzig. Through her cooking, she wins the heart of Bishop Adalbert of Prague, who had come to practice proselytizing on the Pomeranians before turning to the more difficult Prussians. She accidentally drops a string of amber beads into his fish soup. They dissolve, transforming the dish into a pagan love potion. After Adalbert orders the destruction of the Pomeranians' fish head offerings to the Flounder god, Ryb, she kills her lover with a cast-iron spoon. She is then baptized by force and beheaded. Her death brings an end to matriarchy.

Dorothea Swarze, of Montau, the beautifully ethereal wife of the master sword maker Albrecht Slichting. This frigid fourth cook, who extends the Lenten fare throughout the year, lusts for Jesus. Among the living, however, she can relate only to beggars and lepers, and she neglects her children and husband. After an enlightening encounter with the Flounder, she chooses, in her quest for freedom, to be walled up in a small cell in the Marienwerder Cathedral, where she eventually dies.

Margarete Rusch (rewsh), or **Fat Gret**, the belly-laughing fifth cook, convent cook, and then cooking abbess of Saint Bridget's whose irrepressible sexual appetite equals her love for food. She cultivates her abundant fat for the physical warmth she happily shares with men. She dismisses male controversies and endeavors with laughing disdain. After cooking the last meal for her father, blacksmith Peter Rusch, who had been involved in an artisanal conspiracy against the city government of Danzig, she dispatches the two men responsible for his death. She smothers Eberhard Ferber, the former patrician mayor, during lovemaking and feeds Abbot Jeschke to death. She dies a similar death, choking on a pike bone during a royal banquet.

Agnes Kurbiella (kewr-BEE-lah), the curly haired, childlike, and allegorically empty but warm Kashubian sixth cook, who never speaks but always smiles. At the age of thirteen, Agnes had been gang raped by the Swedish soldiers who had killed her parents during the Thirty Years' War. She becomes cook, mother, inspiration, and sexual partner to the painter Anton Möller and the poet, diplomat, and spy Martin Opitz. Agnes gives her love unconditionally but never loses her memory and love for one of her Swedish assailants, Axel. After the death of Opitz, Agnes bears a daughter, Ursula, with whom, years later, she is burned at the stake in Moscow for witchcraft. After her death, Axel Ludstrom, the Swedish ambassador to the czar, orders the destruction of the file of Kurbiella, long suspected of being a Swedish agent.

Amanda Woyke (VOY-keh), a serf whose face has the beauty of a potato, with an earthy sheen and happy glow. She is the seventh cook, on the Royal Prussian State Farm at Zuckau, and popularizes the potato in Prussia. She bears seven daughters, fathered (between the campaigns of Frederick the Great's wars) by August Romeike, a Prussian soldier. After the Seven Years' War, Romeike is placed in charge of the farm, to the disgust of Amanda, who thinks that his administration is inefficient and counterproductive. After her first three daughters die of starvation, Amanda becomes totally committed to the promotion of the potato. She corresponds with Benjamin Thompson, Count Rumford, and through him her West Prussian potato soup becomes the foundation stone of the soup kitchen.

Sophie Rotzoll (ROHT-zohl), the eighth cook, a thin, angular, and boyish revolutionary. She remains a virgin. Her only love, Friedrich Bartholdy, a stuttering Danzig schoolboy, is condemned to death for a Jacobin conspiracy during the time of the French Revolution. The death sentence is commuted to life imprisonment, but despite all the pleading and cooking of Sophie, he is not released for thirty-eight years. Enraged at the failure of the Napoleonic governor of Danzig, Rapp, to release her beloved and enraged also at his sexual advances, Sophie prepares a dinner spiced with poisonous mushrooms. Rapp, warned by the Flounder, abstains, but the dinner leads to the death of his guests. Rapp does not punish Sophie, however, and eventually she is able to spend her virginal old age with the released but spent Friedrich.

Lena Stubbe (SHTUHB-eh), a dedicated Socialist, author of an unpublished "Proletarian Cookbook," and long-suffering wife successively to two physically strong but emotionally weak anchor makers. The first is killed in the Franco-Prussian War; the second, as a middle-aged volunteer, in World War I. Lena cooks a soup flavored with a noose and nail that cures suicidal depression. After the death of her second wife-beating husband, she cooks at a series of soup kitchens until, at the age of ninety-three, she is sent to the Stutthoff concentration camp for her political comments. She cooks in the concentration camp until she is beaten to death for attempting to prevent the Kapos from stealing the prisoners' meager rations.

Sibylle Miehlau (MEE-low), called **Billy**, the author's former fiancée, a gorgeous lawyer. After cooking a Father's Day picnic meal in 1962 for her three confused feminist and lesbian friends, Siggie, Maxie, and Frankie, who long to be male and assimilate the stereotypically worst male characteristics, Billy is gang raped by seven black-jacketed cyclists and then crushed by their motorcycles.

Maria Kucorra (KEW-kohr-ah), a beautiful, curly headed blonde distant cousin of the narrator who works at the canteen of the Lenin Shipyard in Gdansk. Her fiancé, Jan Ludkowski, an employee of the shipyard's publicity department, a trade unionist, and a member of the Communist Party, is shot in December, 1970, by the police of the Polish Workers' Republic as he attempts to address striking workers in front of the shipyard. After his death, Maria bears twins, whom she names Mestwina and Damroka. At the end of the novel, after using the narrator for a very impersonal act of intercourse, she wades into the Baltic Sea and summons the Flounder, who counsels her.

— Bernard A. Cook

THE FLOWERING PEACH

Author: Clifford Odets (1906-1963)
First published: 1954
Genre: Drama
Locale: The Near East
Time: Biblical times
Plot: Allegory

Noah, the patriarch, past the age of seventy when the play begins. He later becomes a stronger, younger man of fifty with "eagle bright" eyes and reddish hair, then returns to an old man at the end of the play. He is very authoritarian and acts as the ruler of his family, but he is obedient to God. He demands the obedience of his sons and banters with his wife. He bitterly disagrees with his son Japheth, who wants to do things in his own way. To obey God, Noah is willing for people to think that he is crazy and to mock and ridicule him for building an ark and saying that God will destroy Earth with a flood. He is made younger by God so that he has the strength to do what must be done. His chief weakness is his unbending, impatient authoritarianism. When he becomes old Noah again at the end of the play, these attitudes have vanished, replaced by gentle humor, friendliness, and open affection. Having lost Esther, the love of his life, he grants her dying wish to marry Japheth to Rachel and Ham to Goldie, establishing new laws for a new world.

Esther, Noah's wife, a practical Jewish mother. She bosses her daughters-in-law, chides her sons for disrespect toward their father, chides Noah with loving banter about things with which she disagrees, breaks up arguments within the family, and maintains her own sanity by keeping occupied with daily chores. She mistrusts Leah but loves the delicate, hesitant Rachel, lamenting Rachel's unhappy marriage to Ham and encouraging her to have self-confidence. She takes the children's side against Noah when Ham wants to marry Goldie and Japheth wants to marry Rachel, but she reminds them that she loves Noah. She feels inadequate when Noah becomes younger and she remains old, but she carries on. She dies just before the ark lands and tells Noah to marry the children as they wish "for the sake of happiness in the world."

Japheth, the youngest son of Noah, in his early twenties, proud, private, thinking, slow, and shy. Noah subconsciously identifies with him. Japheth loves and respects his father but stands up for his own beliefs, which often are at odds with Noah's beliefs. He is the most capable of the sons and the one to whom Noah turns for comfort in his darkest moments. Refusing to marry Goldie, whom Noah says God has chosen for him, Japheth loves his brother's wife, Rachel. Willing to die to protest what he thinks is an avenging and destructive God, he plans to die in the flood, but he is knocked out by Noah and carried on board the ark by his brothers. Going against his father's wishes, he saves the ark and its inhabitants from sinking by patching holes and steering it with a rudder. At the end of the play, it is he who finds the young flowering peach tree, the symbol of new life.

Shem, the eldest son of Noah, heavy and shrewd, sometimes to the point of foolishness, looking like a "weighty, worried boxer dog." He is an entrepreneur, always looking for a good business deal, even making fuel briquettes from animal dung on the ark and hoarding them for future use. He tries to arbitrate in the arguments between Noah and Japheth. He says and does what is expedient, getting someone else to do the work whenever possible; for example, he gives Ham liquor to do his work on the ark. It is he, however, with whom Noah decides to live in the new world.

Ham, the middle son of Noah, a neurotic, restless, and high-strung man, filled with malice and jealousy that masquerade as humor and good fellowship and even as honesty. He taunts and mocks, but he knows how to charm, especially Shem, for whom he works. He married Rachel to please his father, but he mocks and belittles her and has an affair with Goldie before Noah finally permits a divorce between him and Rachel and marries him to Goldie.

Leah, Shem's wife. She is smug and plump, with a prim, small, disapproving mouth; contentious and judgmental; and haughty and disapproving. She is a fit and sometimes prodding mate for Shem. She assists her husband in his business dealings and attempts to boss others. Stubbornly smug, she is mistrusted by Esther and reluctantly obeys her mother-in-law. She likes luxury and will work hard to get it.

Rachel, the wife of Ham, nervous and unsure, bright and hopeful, with a delicate, tentative, and hesitant air. She loves and obeys Esther, tolerates and obeys Ham, and carries unspoken love for Japheth. Finally, she leaves Ham and admits her love for Japheth.

Goldie, the proposed wife for Japheth, attractive, chatty, informal, and easygoing, with a sense of humor. She is poor and has no mother, but she has a kind heart. She saves Japheth's life when drunken townspeople beat and try to burn him. Ham is attracted to her, but Noah accepts her as a mate for Japheth. Esther, after initial reluctance, welcomes her and teaches her how to do chores. She loves Ham.

— Bettye Choate Kash

FOGO MORTO

Author: José Lins do Rego (1901-1957)
First published: 1943
Genre: Novel
Locale: Paraíba, Brazil
Time: 1848-1900
Plot: Historical

José Amaro (zhew-ZAY ah-MAH-rew), a crippled saddlemaker. Embittered by his failures, he hides his sense of inferiority and his cowardice under a cloak of scorn, especially for the district's wealthy plantation owners. Finally, disillusioned in his fight against the aristocrats, deserted by his family, and friendless, he commits suicide.

Antonio Silvino (ahn-TOH-nyew seel-VEE-new), a bandit who inspires the admiration but later the disillusionment of José Amaro.

Captain Victorino Carneiro da Cunha (veek-toh-REE-new kahr-NAY-rew dah KEWN-yah), a penniless lawyer who is connected with the best families but censures their misuse of power. Regardless of the cost to himself, he fights courageously against cruelty and injustice.

Colonel Lula César de Holanda Chacón (LEW-lah see-ZUR deh oh-LAHN-dah shah-KOHN), the owner of the Santa Fe sugar plantation. Deserted by his emancipated black slaves because of his cruel treatment in the past, Holanda Chacón sees his sugar refinery doomed to become a place of dead fires.

Colonel José Paulino (pow-LEE-new), the owner of the Santa Clara plantation. Paulino's humane treatment of his field hands causes Santa Clara to prosper in contrast to doomed Santa Fe.

Leandro (lay-AHN-drew), a kindly black hunter and friend of Amaro.

Sinha (SEE-nyah), Amaro's wife.

Lieutenant Mauricio (mow-REE-syew), a cruel army officer.

Captain Tomás Cabral de Malo (toh-MAHS kuh-BRAHL deh MAH-lew), the father-in-law of Holanda Chacón.

Quinca Napoleon (KEEN-kuh), the prefect of Pilar, a victim of Silvino.

Laurentino (low-RAYN-tee-new), a house painter and neighbor of Amaro.

Floripes (floh-REE-pehs), the black overseer of the Santa Fe plantation and an enemy of Amaro.

Torcuato (tohr-KWAH-tew), a blind man accused of being a spy and beaten by Lieutenant Mauricio.

THE FOLKS

Author: Ruth Suckow (1892-1960)
First published: 1934
Genre: Novel

Locale: Iowa
Time: Early twentieth century
Plot: Domestic realism

Fred Ferguson, a bank employee in Belmond, Iowa. Born and reared on a nearby farm, he has worked hard for what he has: a pleasant home, a good job, and the respect of his church and his community. Fred does not see that society is changing. If he is one of the last of his social class to hire domestic help, upgrade his house, or buy a car, it is not that he is consciously resisting the lure of materialism but simply that he likes things as they are, especially when the old ways save him money. Only late in life, when he returns from his first long trip away from home to find his church closed and his bank shaky, does Fred see that his world and his values are rapidly disappearing.

Annie Ferguson, Fred's wife. Reared in a poor but easygoing German family, Annie resents being forced into the mold of the Fergusons, whom she sees as being ruled by Scotch stinginess, and having to fit into the role of the perfect wife and mother, thereby losing her own identity. Even though the children she loves are soon grown and gone, leaving her with a husband who does not understand her, Annie thinks of herself as fortunate. After she has finally accomplished her heart's desire by taking a trip to California, she finds that her old passion for Fred has returned.

Carl William Ferguson, their older son, who tailors his behavior to win the approval of others. Adored by his mother, Carl always tries to be a "good boy." In high school, however, when he leads the student body at a pep rally, he gains a new self-confidence, and he is certain that he will accomplish great deeds. Although he is drawn to strong-willed women, after graduation from college he marries his high school sweetheart, the colorless, passive Lillian White. Carl becomes a school principal, then a superintendent. When two of his teachers are threatened with dismissal for the sin of smoking, Carl comes to their defense. This seemingly courageous act is actually motivated by his own yearning to escape from dull respectability and his unresponsive wife. When one of the women Carl likes finds a new job for him, Lillian attempts suicide, and Carl buckles. Realizing that he lacks the will to rebel, he accepts his own mediocrity and takes another position.

Margaret Ferguson, their older daughter, a born rebel. Margaret regularly flouts authority, as when, against her mother's orders, she goes home with a classmate from the wrong side of town. Margaret dislikes the girls who remind her of Annie and of her sister, Dorothy. She thinks of them as "Eves," destined for obedient domesticity, and of herself as an exotic, defiant Lilith. Margaret always chooses a dangerous but interesting direction for her life. She is expelled from college for helping a friend to elope. After going to New York, ostensibly to take a library course, she changes her name to Margot and becomes involved, first, with bohemians in Greenwich Village, then with a married man, Bruce Williams, who eventually leaves her. When Bruce finds that he cannot live without her, Margaret takes him back as her lover, as usual preferring passion to prudence.

Dorothy Ferguson, Fred and Annie's younger daughter, who is much like Annie. Even as a small child, Dorothy buries her feelings for the sake of domestic tranquillity, for example, hiding her tears when Margaret deliberately fastens her hair too tightly. At school, Dorothy is popular because she is so sweet and "feminine." She marries the handsome Jesse Woodward and expects to live happily ever after. When her parents visit her in California, they find Dorothy cheerful and uncomplaining, despite the fact that Jesse's financial problems have forced his family to leave their comfortable home for a tiny rented house.

Bunny Ferguson, Fred and Annie's younger son. Annie enjoys her affectionate "baby" more than any of her other children; however, Bunny secretly feels detached from his family. Instead of attending a church college, he goes to the state university. One summer, he works out West, and because he sees immigrant workers badly treated, he starts questioning his family's capitalistic values. At the university, he is fascinated by a fellow student, Charlotte Bukowska, an avowed Marxist. When Bunny brings her home as his wife, Fred and Annie are shocked and disappointed, and Charlotte makes no secret of her dislike of them. Although Bunny seems to accept Charlotte's view of life, on a visit to the old home place, he reveals his feelings for the land and for the past.

— Rosemary M. Canfield Reisman

FOMA GORDEYEV

Author: Maxim Gorky (Aleksey Maksimovich Peshkov, 1868-1936)
First published: 1899
Genre: Novel

Locale: Russia
Time: Late nineteenth century
Plot: Psychological realism

Foma Gordeyev (FOH-muh gohr-DEH-yehf), the son of a tough trader who owns barges and tugs and speculates on the exchange. Foma, wishing to know the meaning of life, has trouble accepting capitalistic views; he denounces local moneyed dignitaries by shouting reminders of their unsavory pasts for all to hear at a ship launching. He is hustled off to an insane asylum. Released, he is a drunken, broken man who wanders about the town, out of his mind and in rags. He is befriended only by his godfather's daughter, a childhood friend, who gives him a small room.

Mayakin (mah-YAH-kihn), Foma Gordeyev's godfather, in whose house Foma lived until he was six years old. Mayakin takes a personal interest in his godson's life and fortune. He advises, and intervenes; finally, he takes a power of attorney over Gordeyev's holdings and sends Foma to a mental hospital after he makes his outraged speech exposing the lives of respectable townsmen.

Liuboff (LEW-bof), Mayakin's daughter, Foma's friend from childhood. She never understands him but tries to do so by discussing ideas with him. She gives him sanctuary after his release from the asylum.

Ignat Gordeyev (ihg-NAHT), Foma's father, a ruthless, thoroughgoing trader who makes his fortune by hard work and cunning. He falls under the influence of a woman who persuades him to give much of his wealth to charity. He dies a foolish, confused man.

Smolin (smoh-LIHN) and

Ezhoff (ehzh-OHF), Foma's school friends. Ezhoff was poor but intelligent; Smolin, fat, rich, undistinguished. Ezhoff becomes a quick-witted journalist who makes revolutionary speeches to laborers. Foma and Ezhoff do not argue about politics; they simply drink together. Smolin becomes a sharp trader, the betrothed of Liuboff.

Sasha (SAH-shuh), a river girl who, along with her sister, fascinates Foma. He has a wild, carousing affair with her, but she abandons him because his philosophical speculations bore her.

Madame Medynsky (meh-DIHN-skihy), the guiding hand in Ignat's philanthropic ventures. She is cosmopolitan and sophisticated, and willing to bestow her favors where they will do the most good. Foma, deeply attracted to her, is disappointed when he thinks she does not take him seriously.

Natalya (mah-TAH-lyah), a handsome young woman, Ignat's second wife and Foma's mother. She dies soon after his birth.

Aunt Anfisa (ahn-FIH-suh), the relative who cares for Foma after he leaves Mayakin's house. Her fantastic adventure stories greatly impressed him when he was young.

FONTAMARA

Author: Ignazio Silone (Secondo Tranquilli, 1900-1978)
First published: 1930
Genre: Novel
Locale: The Abruzzi region in southern Italy
Time: Early 1930's
Plot: Social realism

Berardo Viola (beh-RAHR-doh vee-OH-lah), the biggest and strongest of the Fontamarans and, accordingly, the most respected. A peasant with no land, Berardo has nothing to lose and is thus free to retaliate against the government's cruel and unfair treatment of the *cafoni* (peasants). Driven by an inherent sense of Christian brotherhood, he becomes the first peasant to sacrifice his life for his fellow people.

Giovà (jee-oh-VAH), short for **Giovanni**, one of the narrators. Giovà personifies the typical Fontamaran peasant. He works his arid land for endless hours because he has to provide for his wife and son. His land and his family are of primary importance to him; people outside his family matter little. Giovà has a quick temper, but he is resigned to the political oppression and social injustice that, for years, have caused the *cafoni* to live in abject poverty. As a consequence, he is unwilling at first to join in the retaliation initiated by Berardo.

Matalè (mah-tah-LAY), short for **Maddalena**, Giovà's wife and the second narrator. Matalè is characteristic of the Fontamaran peasant women. She is quick to anger and to criticize. She openly denounces Marietta Sorcanera's moral lassitude, but she is secretly envious of her new apron and curled hair.

Giovà's son, the third narrator. He accompanies Berardo to Rome. Unlike Berardo, but typical of others his age, the young man has no vision of a "higher calling" to altruism and self-sacrifice. He is quick to sign the government papers attesting Berardo's "suicidal tendencies."

The contractor, a newcomer to the Abruzzi region who became rich by speculating on the price of wheat. Although an outsider, he is soon appointed *podestà* (mayor) of the town. He uses his position to further exploit the peasants.

Don Circonstanza, a lawyer and self-proclaimed "Friend of the People." As his name implies, his loyalty to the Fontamarans varies according to circumstances; in fact, the lawyer has swindled the peasants on numerous occasions.

Don Abbacchio (ahb-BAHK-kee-oh), the corrupt priest who personifies the church's compliance with the Fascist state following the signing of the Concordat in 1929. Like Don Circonstanza, Don Abbacchio is unworthy of the title of respect *(don)* that precedes his name.

The Mystery Man, an agent of the revolutionary underground who befriends Berardo. It is the Mystery Man who brings the duplicating machine to Fontamara and later helps the three narrators to escape the attack on the village.

Marietta Sorcanera (sohr-kah-NEH-rah), the owner of the local café. Marietta is the widow of a war hero and consequently has a pension that allows her to purchase a few luxuries. Since her husband's death, she has had three of four children out of wedlock.

General Baldissera (bahl-dees-SEH-rah), the town cobbler, who repeatedly sings a song about his namesake's campaign in Africa. He was required by the Federation of Tradesmen and Artisans to secure working papers. This leads him to question whether the peasants are at peace or war, because "interferences with personal liberty are possible only in wartime." His question makes a big impression on the *cafoni*.

Elvira, a seamstress who is in love with Berardo. She witnesses the rape of Maria Grazia, which leaves her in a state of shock. Elvira accompanies Maria Grazia on her pilgrimage to the shrine of Our Lady of Libera. There she prays that the Virgin Mary help Berardo, who is in prison. Immediately, she is seized with a high fever; shortly thereafter, she dies at home.

Maria Rosa, Berardo's mother, who thinks Elvira's death may have saved her son, as his salvation was "to be restored to his destiny."

Michele Zompa, a peasant who irritates a government bureaucrat named Pelino by recounting a dream and his view of the sociopolitical hierarchy in southern Italy.

Sciarappa (skee-ah-RAHP-pah), a peasant who emigrated to America, where, he says, "the streets are paved with gold." Sciarappa returned to Fontamara, where he repeatedly tells the peasants to "shut up."

Venerdì Santo (veh-nehr-DEE) and

Ponzio Pilato (POHN-zee-oh pee-LAH-toh), two peasants who obviously took part in an Easter pageant—hence, their nicknames, "Good Friday" and "Pontius Pilate."

— *Lucille Izzo Pallotta*

FOOL FOR LOVE

Author: Sam Shepard (Samuel Shepard Rogers, 1943-)
First published: 1983
Genre: Drama
Locale: The Mojave Desert
Time: Late 1970's
Plot: Expressionism

The Old Man, who may or may not be the ne'er-do-well father of Eddie and May by different mothers. Of indeterminate age, he is not a living character and exists only in the minds of Eddie and May, who communicate directly with him at their discretion. The Old Man, dressed in Western clothing, complete with Stetson hat, sits in a rocking chair throughout the play and sips whiskey that he pours from a bottle into a Styrofoam cup. He claims to be married to country singer Barbara Mandrell and stares at what he says is her picture on an empty wall in the rundown motel where all the action takes place. The patriarch does not seem to like his children very much; he says of them, "I don't recognize myself in either one a' you. . . . You could be anybody's. Probably are." He is a specterlike figure, a kind of perverse Greek chorus who argues with Eddie and May until the end, when they leave and he is left alone, staring at the empty wall. It is possible that he is the only real individual and has invented the whole episode, with the other characters being figments of his imagination.

Eddie, an ornery rodeo stuntman in his late thirties. He is dressed in his working clothes, and his smell indicates his need of a bath. The cowboy is the former lover and half brother of May. Eddie is obsessed with May. To find her, he has traveled 2,480 miles with his pickup truck and horse trailer. For fifteen years, he has had an intense love-hate relationship with May, usually breaking it off because he is always chasing someone new. Women seem to find him attractive and irresistible. A mysterious and unseen lady known as "the Countess," said by May to be his latest conquest and her reason for leaving him, arrives in a Mercedes Benz and waits for Eddie outside the motel. Eddie has bought some property in Wyoming and has come to take May there. He is a violently self-centered man who is obsessed with pursuing May for himself. Eddie wins May back at the end but then inexplicably leaves her for the enigmatic Countess.

May, the attractive half sister and former lover of Eddie. She is in her early thirties and has had a turbulent fifteen-year relationship with Eddie. Tired of his continual infidelities, particularly with the wealthy Countess, she apparently has left him for good and now lives in a dingy motel on the edge of the Mojave Desert. May works as a short-order cook and is putting her shattered life together. When Eddie unexpectedly shows up, May is both pleased and disgusted by his sudden intrusion and his passionate pursuit, but she cannot forget their stormy emotional past or their mutual attraction and revulsion. She knows they are inextricably bound together, but she has no illusions about Eddie, or about the Old Man. Her outburst at Eddie's drunken lies to Martin about their relationship forces her version of the truth to be revealed and precipitates Eddie's exit, a departure that she knows will be final.

Martin, an easygoing, solidly built maintenance man in his early thirties. A native of the area, he arrives at the motel to pick up May for their first date. Thinking that May is in trouble when he hears screams, Martin makes a dramatic entrance by kicking open the door and tackling Eddie to the ground. Martin is interested in developing a relationship with May. He is a simple, amiable individual who is puzzled by the contradictions between the stories told by May and by Eddie. He remains a largely uninteresting and undeveloped character, but his presence delineates the incestuous bond between Eddie and May. Martin remains confused by all that occurs from the moment he arrives until the end, when he watches May leave the motel.

— *Terry Theodore*

THE FOOL OF QUALITY: Or, The History of Henry, Earl of Moreland

Author: Henry Brooke (1703?-1783)
First published: 1765-1770
Genre: Novel
Locale: England
Time: The eighteenth century
Plot: Didactic

Henry (Harry) Clinton, the second son of the earl of Moreland, put out to nurse when an infant. Educated to be perfect, he is liberal and friendly, impressing even the king and the court. At his father's death, his older brother being already dead, he becomes the earl of Moreland and uses his fortune and position to help many people.

Mr. Fenton, a wealthy elderly gentleman who becomes young Harry Clinton's benefactor. He, too, is a Harry Clinton, the uncle of the hero. After he makes himself known to his brother the earl, he is known as Mr. Clinton.

Ned, a beggar lad who becomes Harry's companion as a boy. He turns out to be of good family and is returned to his parents, from whom he had been stolen as a baby.

Lady Maitland (Fanny Goodall), Mr. Fenton's cousin. Years before, they had been in love. She is married to Louisa d'Aubigny's brother and is thus Mr. Fenton's sister-in-law.

The Earl of Moreland, Harry's father. He is remorseful for his treatment of his son and brother and is happy when they are restored to him.

Louisa d'Aubigny, Mr. Fenton's second wife. She dies after a fall.

Eloisa, daughter of Mr. Fenton and Louisa d'Aubigny. Thought lost at sea, she is rescued and becomes the wife of the emperor of Morocco.

Abenaide, daughter of the emperor of Morocco and Eloisa Fenton. She appears in England disguised as a page. Later she appears in her true form and marries Harry, now the earl of Moreland.

FOOLS CROW

Author: James Welch (1940-   )
First published: 1986
Genre: Novel
Locale: Montana Territory
Time: 1868-1870
Plot: Historical realism

Fools Crow (earlier called **White Man's Dog**), a Pikuni Blackfeet youth. He is considered to be unlucky because in eighteen winters he has captured no horses and has no wives. His first vision quest has failed. With the aid of the healer Mik-api, Fools Crow acquires courage and strength, distinguishing himself in the horse-raiding party and later the war party against the Crows. In his coming of age, Fools Crow evolves from an uncertain young man to a generous, brave, and selfless hero. He becomes a hunter, warrior, healer, and leader of the Pikunis. Ultimately, he is chosen to foresee and to witness the near destruction of his tribe.

Rides-at-the-door, Fools Crow's father, a wise man and adviser to the chief of the Lone Eaters. Years ago, he took as wife the mother of Fools Crow and her younger sister. When he takes a young third wife out of kindness to her father, it is an unfortunate choice, because she is treated like a servant by the older wives and like a daughter by Rides-at-the-door. After his son Running Fisher is found with the young wife, Rides-at-the-door blames himself for failing them both. Because he is a just man, he does not punish her according to custom but releases her from the marriage, gives her four horses, and sends her back to her father. He is pained that Running Fisher has not become a man like Fools Crow. Rides-at-the-door is a quiet, thoughtful model of manhood who lives by honor. He listens, speaking rarely, but his voice is respected in council and his advice is valued.

Fast Horse, Fools Crow's boastful friend. Fast Horse invites him on the horse raid and arranges for a ceremonial sweat to give them strong medicine. On the journey to the Crow camp, Fast Horse dreams that the spirit Cold Maker tells him that their raid will be successful if he will uncover an ice spring now blocked by rocks. When he cannot find the spring, the ambitious Fast Horse becomes sullen. This failure colors his life. Although his loud boasts during the raid cause Yellow Kidney to be captured and mutilated, Fast Horse denies any responsibility. He angrily blames all of his misfortunes on Cold Maker. In the end, he joins the outlaw band of Owl Child.

Yellow Kidney, the courageous Pikuni warrior who leads the horse-raiding party against the Crow camp. He is a good judge of young men, rightly mistrustful of Fast Horse and one of the first to perceive the steadiness of Fools Crow. Fools Crow learns much from this man. When Yellow Kidney is captured and maimed, he survives under incredible conditions, but he returns to the Lone Eaters camp a changed man—he has lost his spirit. As Fools Crow's father-in-law, he has a final happy vision of his future grandson before his death.

Running Fisher, Fools Crow's younger brother. Formerly a confident youth, he loses his courage when the Pikuni war party encounters a solar eclipse, but he cannot speak of this. He covers his shame with arrogance. When Running Fisher is discovered with Rides-at-the-door's young wife, he becomes a man at last, accepting his banishment with dignity and regret.

Feather Woman, the legendary Pikuni woman who married Morning Star and is the mother of Scarface, who taught the Pikuni the sacred Sun Dance. Feather Woman is the gentle guide of Fools Crow on his final vision quest, painting for him scenes from a time to come.

— *Joanne McCarthy*

A FOOL'S ERRAND

Author: Albion W. Tourgée (1838-1905)
First published: 1879
Genre: Novel
Locale: Warrington Place, Verdenton, in the southern United States
Time: 1860's-1870's
Plot: Fiction of manners

Colonel Comfort Servosse, the central character, who tries to help the South during the aftermath of the Civil War. Born in Michigan and schooled there as a lawyer, Servosse has little idea of the cultural opposition he will face as a Northerner trying to live in the same area of the South where he had served in the Union Army as it demilitarized the defeated Confederate Army. Colonel Servosse is identified repeatedly by the narrator as a fool because of his ambitions to change quickly an old culture. Convinced of the need for education for black people and of land reforms to enable emancipated slaves to buy small farms, Colonel Servosse sets about promoting both, doing the latter at his own expense. As he struggles to help the powerless blacks and the outnumbered Unionists, he often finds himself threatened with violence and isolation from all but a few of his neighbors. In the end, he earns the respect of his Southern neighbors but comes to recognize that in taking the advice of so-called wise men from the North, he has become a fool whose ideals cannot be fully realized in the South.

Metta Ward Servosse, the wife of Colonel Servosse. Metta recognizes that her husband's quest to fight in the Civil War and rebuild the South with equality for all is doomed to failure, but she still supports his efforts. She bravely shares his isolation from most of their neighbors and writes many informative letters to her sister, Julia.

Lily Servosse, the daughter of Colonel Servosse. Her heroic ride one night saves her father and Judge Denton from an impending raid by the Ku Klux Klan. By the end of the novel, she is being courted by Melville Gurney, the man she shot in the arm the night of that ride. Because of her respect for authority, she refuses to marry Melville until his father grants permission.

Colonel Ezekiel Vaughn, a self-proclaimed colonel. He sells Warrington Place to Colonel Servosse for nearly $5,000 in gold; the 600-acre property is worth far less than half this amount. Ezekiel also heckles and opposes Colonel Servosse for his radical views, but in the end he comes to respect his character.

Squire Nathaniel Hyman, a gossipy neighbor who lives one mile from Warrington Place. He gradually comes to accept some of Colonel Servosse's views concerning the need to treat black people with respect. Squire Hyman's son, Jesse, is whipped by the Klan for holding such views and flees to the West. Ironically, Jesse is helped by one of the very abolitionist ministers whom Squire Hyman had sent a mob to whip before the Civil War started.

Thomas Savage, a man who tries to bushwhack Colonel Servosse one night but ends up being caught in the trap set for the colonel. Colonel Servosse nurses Thomas back to health, and afterward Thomas becomes a staunch friend.

John Walters, one of the white leaders who champions the political causes of the black community. Because he is a long-term member of this Southern community and a Unionist from the Civil War days, he is greatly despised by his neighbors. He is elected to office but later is brutally murdered by the Klan for daring to help educate black people and organize them politically. John leaves behind a young wife and two daughters; the daughters are playing on the front lawn of their house only a few yards away from John when he is murdered.

Jerry Hunt, one of the elderly leaders in the black church who reveals in a prayer meeting, attended by several members of the Klan, his knowledge about which people killed John Walters. In an effort to silence this report, the Ku Klux Klan raids Jerry's home one night. Klan members hang him on a tree forty steps from the Temple of Justice in the middle of Verdenton.

The Reverend Enos Martin, a longtime ministerial friend of Colonel Servosse who encourages him to try reforming the South. At the end of the novel, he commiserates with the colonel about what he then perceives as his fool's errand.

John Burleson, a member of the Ku Klux Klan whose open defection triggers a widespread renouncing of the Klan and its violence. He and other Klan members are given a general amnesty by the state legislature.

Melville Gurney, the son of General Gurney and the suitor of Lily Servosse. Because his father is an adamant opponent of Colonel Servosse's politics, Melville has difficulty obtaining permission for marriage to Lily, even though General Gurney respects Colonel Servosse as a person.

— Daven M. Kari

"FOOLS SAY"
("Disent les imbéciles")

Author: Nathalie Sarraute (1900-)
First published: 1976
Genre: Novel

Locale: Unspecified
Time: Indeterminate
Plot: New Novel

A mixed group of voices, most of them unidentified. This New Novel, as such, does not contain characters in a traditional sense, just as there is no plot in a traditional sense. The text is one long narrative, delineated by shifts in speakers, most not identified well enough to individualize. Most of the speakers are identified only by pronouns. Many are referred to in the third person (he, she, it, they); few have the distinction of a "we" or "I."

The grandmother, also called **Grandmama**, an elderly woman with silver and gold hair. Her thin hands are covered with tan age spots, and her eyes look like blue enamel. She is physically frail, though a spark of life still exists within her. When her grandchildren call her "sweet," she inwardly rebels against such a confining description; her reaction shows only in her eyes, however, and it is up to one of her grandchildren, her favorite grandson, to stop the others from saying the detested word.

The grandson, a young boy. He becomes upset when the other grandchildren continually say, as they caress their grandmother, "She is sweet . . . couldn't you just bite her." He is teased by her relatives, who say that he is developing an "undershot" jaw and that soon he will be as ugly as his Uncle François.

Mr. Varenger, an old man who walks stooped over. He resents what he sees as the patronizing attitude of the young toward the old.

The young newlywed girl, who suddenly realizes that her husband is a miser. Distraught over whether to leave him or merely ignore this flaw, the girl is goaded by two formless voices into making a decision.

— T. M. Lipman

FOR COLORED GIRLS WHO HAVE CONSIDERED SUICIDE/ WHEN THE RAINBOW IS ENUF: A Choreopoem

Author: Ntozake Shange (Paulette Williams, 1948-)
First published: 1977
Genre: Drama

Locale: Outside various U.S. cities
Time: The 1960's and 1970's
Plot: Social realism

Lady in Red, the dominant character in this work (she has the largest number of lines). She recites the most violent and emotionally moving poems in the drama, including those that demonstrate the brutality and anguish endured and experienced by African American women. Like all the other characters in the drama, she has a feminist point of view. She recites poems titled "no assistance," "latent rapists," "one," and "a nite with beau willie brown." In "no assistance," she berates a lover who has failed to assist her in developing and maintaining a relationship; in "latent rapists," she points out that rapists often are known to their victims; in "one," she portrays the image of a glittering seductress who cries herself to sleep after her romantic activities; and in "a nite with beau willie brown," she tells the story of a crazed Vietnam veteran who throws his children out the window. Her pieces address the major themes of the drama.

Lady in Orange, a poet and a dancer. With a feminist outlook, she expresses a love of the arts of poetry, song, and dance in the poems "i'm a poet who" and "no more love poems #1." The first poem declares that she is a poet who wants to write, sing, and dance but who cannot communicate with people anymore. In the second poem, she declares that she needs love even though the world considers her to be evil and a nag, thereby expounding on a primary theme in the drama, the misunderstanding of women and failures of communication between men and women.

Lady in Yellow, who represents youth and liveliness. She recites "graduation night," a selection about a fun night of dancing, parties, and lost virginity, and "no more love poems #3," about the unfortunate dependence of women on sources outside themselves for love. The author uses this poem to affirm the drama's assertion that strength must be found inside oneself and in the friendship and support of other women.

Lady in Green, called **Sechita**, a dancer in a poem that is strong with images of Egyptian royalty and mixed with references to New Orleans "conjurin." Sechita has performed in many places and has taken her mystical and magical aura along with her sometimes tattered appearance. She recites the lively and amusing poem "somebody almost walked off with alla my stuff," which affirms the need to find strength within oneself.

Lady in Purple, who expresses the need for mutual support and understanding among women in the poem "pyramid." In "no more love poems #2," she begs her lover to allow her to love him, furthering the theme of unrequited love found throughout the drama.

Lady in Blue, who is given somber pieces, as symbolized by the color she wears. The poem "i used to live in the world" portrays an isolated character trapped by a six-block section of Harlem, her universe, thus demonstrating the tragedy of a woman without supportive female companions. In "sorry," she points out the uselessness of the word, along with all the ramifications of the word when used as an excuse after inflicting pain on someone. In "no more love poems #3," she asserts her need for love. These poems demonstrate the tragedy that isolation and pain cause in the lives of black women.

Lady in Brown, dressed in a neutral color not of the rainbow. She introduces the choreopoem by reciting the first major poem. She deals with the earthly matters of the world that her color denotes through her recitations of "dark phases," a poem about the pain and misunderstanding that often accompany the youth of black women, and "toussaint," a piece with historical, social, and cultural significance as well as one denoting the pride that comes from learning about the contributions of black people throughout history.

— Betty Taylor Thompson

FOR WHOM THE BELL TOLLS

Author: Ernest Hemingway (1899-1961)
First published: 1940
Genre: Novel

Locale: Spain
Time: 1937
Plot: Impressionistic realism

Robert Jordan, an American expatriate schoolteacher who has joined the Loyalist forces in Spain. Disillusioned with the world and dissatisfied with his own country, Jordan has come to Spain to fight and die, if necessary, for a cause he knows is vital and worthwhile: that of the native peasant free souls against the totalitarian cruelty of Francisco Franco and his Fascists. He is, however, aware of the contrast between his ideals and the realities he has found among narrow, self-important, selfish, bloodthirsty men capable of betrayal and cruelty as well as courage. He also finds love, devotion, generosity, and selflessness in the persons of Anselmo, Pilar, and especially Maria. The latter he loves with the first true selflessness of his life, and he wishes to avenge her cruel suffering and someday make her his wife in a land free of oppression and cruelty. With bravery, almost bravado, he carries out his mission of blowing up a bridge and remains behind to die with the sure knowledge that in Maria and Pilar his person and ideals will survive. Successful for the first time in his life, in love and war, he awaits death as an old friend.

Maria, a young and innocent Spanish girl cruelly ravaged by war and men's brutality. Befriended by Pilar, a revolutionary, Maria finds a kind of security in the guerrilla band and love in her brief affair with Robert Jordan. As his common-law wife, almost all memory of her rape and indignities disappear, and at a moment of triumph for their forces it looks as if they will live to see their dreams of the future fulfilled. Elemental in her passions and completely devoted to her lover, she refuses to leave him and must be forced to go on living. The embodiment of Jordan's ideals, she must live.

Pilar (pee-LAHR), the strong, almost masculine leader of the guerrilla group with whom Jordan plans to blow up the bridge. Although a peasant and uneducated, Pilar has not only deep feeling but also a brilliant military mind; she is somewhat a Madame Defarge of the Spanish Civil War. Her great trial is her murderous, traitorous husband, whom she loves but could kill. Without fear for herself, she has sensitive feelings for Maria, who is suffering from her traumatic experiences as the victim of Fascist lust and cruelty behind the lines. Greatly incensed by inhumanities, Pilar valorously carries out her mission in destroying the bridge, the symbol of her vindictiveness.

Pablo (PAHB-loh), Pilar's dissolute, drunken, treacherous husband, a type of murderous peasant for whom nothing can be done but without whom the mission cannot be successfully carried out. A hill bandit, Pablo feels loyalty only to himself, kills and despoils at random, and is given to drinking and whoring at will. Nevertheless, he displays a kind of generosity, even after he has stolen the detonators and peddled them to the enemy, when he comes back to face almost certain death and to go on living with the wife whom he loves and fears. This admixture of cunning, cruelty, and bravado finally leads the band to safety. Pablo represents that irony of ways and means that war constantly confuses.

Anselmo (ahn-SEHL-moh), the representative of peasant wisdom, devotion to duty, high-mindedness, selfless love for humanity, and compassion for the human condition. Hating to kill but not fearing to die, Anselmo performs his duty by killing when necessary, but without rancor and with a kind of benediction; he dies as he lived, generously and pityingly. While the others of the guerrilla band are more of Pablo's persuasion, brutally shrewd and vindictive in loyalty, Anselmo tempers his devotion to a cause with a larger view. Aligned with Pilar and Jordan in this larger vision, he displays disinterested and kindly loyalty that is almost pure idealism, all the more remarkable for his age, background, and experience. The benignant, almost Christ-like Anselmo dies that others may live and that Robert Jordan may know how to die.

El Sordo (SOHR-doh), a Loyalist guerrilla leader killed in a Fascist assault on his mountain hideout.

General Golz (gohlz), the Russian officer commanding the Thirty-fifth Division of the Loyalist forces.

Karkov (KAHR-kof), a Russian journalist.

Andrés (ahn-DRAYS), a guerrilla sent by Robert Jordan with a dispatch for General Golz.

André Marty, the commissar who prevents prompt delivery of the dispatch intended for General Golz.

Rafael, a gypsy.

Agustín (ah-gews-TEEN),

Fernando (fehr-NAHN-doh),

Primitivo (pree-mee-TEE-voh), and

Eladio (eh-LAH-dee-oh), other members of the guerrilla band led by Pablo and Pilar.

THE FORBIDDEN FOREST
(La Forêt interdite)

Author: Mircea Eliade (1907-1986)
First published: 1955
Genre: Novel
Locale: Romania
Time: 1936-1948
Plot: Psychological realism

Stefan Viziru (shteh-FAHN vee-ZEE-rew), a tall, slender but sturdy, and handsome thirty-four-year-old political economist. He earned his doctorate in political science in Paris and is working for the Romanian Ministry of National Economy. Although happily married, with a young child, he is obsessed with his entrapment in time. He tries unsuccessfully to use his talents as a painter to project himself into cosmic time. He experiences cosmic time when he meets his ideal love, Ileana, in the Forest of Baneasa, the setting of his childhood; he spends the remainder of the novel searching for Ileana so he can reenact that timeless moment of bliss. He finally encounters Ileana in a forest near Paris, where they prepare to enter cosmic time together, through death.

Ioana Viziru (YWAHN-ah), the twenty-six-year-old wife of Stefan. Beautiful, intelligent in practical ways, and utterly devoted to her husband, she cannot understand his fixation with the burden of time. An excellent wife and mother, she dies with her baby Razvan during a bombing raid.

Ileana Sideri (eel-YAH-nah see-DEH-ree), a beautiful, tall, dark-haired woman in her twenties who falls in love with Stefan. Although she initially mistakes him for the famous author Ciru Partenie, they nevertheless have a brief but passionate affair. He then leaves her even though she begs him to stay; they meet later in Portugal, where they undergo another painful separation. He spends the remainder of the novel searching for her as the embodiment of ideal love. They enter into a final union, both actual and mystical, in the concluding scene of the book.

Petre Biris (PEH-treh bee-REEZ), an indigent, witty, and tubercular professor of philosophy and Stefan's closest friend and confidant. He is preoccupied with the higher concerns of philosophy, particularly those of an existential nature, and considers himself a devoted disciple of Martin Heidegger. He is also the world authority on the works of Ciru Partenie, a famous Romanian novelist and dramatist whom he has never met. He, like Ileana, mistakes Stefan for Partenie but quickly indulges Stefan in his crisis over time, calling him a Proustian who cannot be an artist and a normal human being simultaneously. He loves to play intellectual games and falls passionately in love with the beautiful Catalina, but to no avail. He dies of tuberculosis.

Spiridon Vadastra (SPEE-ree-dohn vah-DAHS-trah), formerly known as **Spiru Gheorghe Vasile** (SPEE-rew GYOHR-geh vah-SEE-leh), a young, highly ambitious lawyer and one-eyed confidence man, an articulate and enormously clever picaresque character. He changed his name because he is ashamed of his destitute family background. He dreams of becoming Romania's greatest pianist and writes outrageous letters to Henry Ford, hoping to curry his favor and become his country's conduit to the American Dream. An obvious embodiment of Hermes the trickster, he supports whoever is in power, switching sides after the war from Communism to Anglo-American capitalism. Ostensibly killed in a bombing raid in London during the war, he reappears in Paris to spy on Stefan six years later.

Gheorghe Vasile, Vadastra's father, a retired secondary school teacher of literature and history. A witty, pleasant drunk who misses nothing, he wants to preserve Romanian culture, especially from the barbarian Russians, so he hides his valuable books and art treasures in a tomb near his town just as the Russians are taking over.

Ciru Partenie (KEE-rew pahr-TEH-nee), a famous novelist and dramatist in his mid-thirties. Romania's principal existential writer, he bears an uncanny resemblance to Stefan and is constantly mistaken for him. He is killed in a cross fire when mistaken for Stefan. The opportunist Bibicescu attempts to capitalize on his work by finishing his last play, *The Wake*.

Dan Bibicescu (bee-bee-CHEHS-kew), a brilliant, idiosyncratic playwright, actor, director, and opportunist in his thirties. He is a disciple of the famous British director Gordon Craig and wants desperately to become the director of the National Theater of Romania. He builds his career on the unfinished work of Partenie and is so driven by ambition that he casually switches political positions to attain his goal. He dies at the end of the novel.

Bursuc (BUR-suhk), a middle-aged, amoral, opportunistic theology student who will do anything to retain his favored position. Although he believes in nothing, he becomes a monk just before the Russians invade Romania as a means of furthering his career. He spends the majority of the novel exhorting people, especially Stefan, to repent of their sins and preparing them for the Second Coming of Christ.

Anisie (AHN-zee), an elderly spiritual guide for Stefan. Having had a near-death experience, he has devoted himself to menial tasks and has learned to live in the present moment without distraction from memory or desire. He teaches Stefan to begin to find a way out of profane time and into sacred, or cosmic, time.

Stella Zissu (STEH-lah ZEE-zew), Anisie's Dionysian counterpart. She becomes the sexual temptress of Stefan and helps to release him from his inhibitions. Stefan recognizes her as the embodiment of Circe or Calypso because she is young, tall, and red-haired, and she possesses alluring forest-green eyes.

Catalina (kah-tah-LEE-nah), an attractive young actress who is in love with Bibicescu. Although the object of Biris' devoted attention, she shares in the pseudomythic roles that Bibicescu mistakes for life. She takes him to task when he misuses Partenie's final, unfinished play for his own advancement. She dies of a hemorrhage at the end of the novel.

Irina Ivascu (ee-REE-nah ee-VAHS-kew), the young, dark-haired, attractive, and dedicated wife of Vadastra. Unlike her amoral husband, she is a highly moral and devoutly religious woman who is helpful and caring toward Stefan. Possessing prophetic powers, she warns Stefan that he must live life fully and drop his obsession with time and death.

Misu Weissman, a middle-aged, wealthy Jewish supporter of Bibicescu's plan to establish a National Theater of Romania. A practical but intelligent man, he helps Stefan during his final journey to Paris but dies shortly thereafter.

— *Patrick Meanor*

THE FORCED MARRIAGE: Or, The Jealous Bridegroom

Author: Aphra Behn (1640-1689)
First published: 1671
Genre: Drama
Locale: France
Time: The seventeenth century
Plot: Romance

The king, who by the power of his authority sets the plot in motion, although he is not a major figure in the play. He is a wise and just ruler, beloved by his people, who obey him out of reverence rather than fear. He is grateful to his generals for the successful war they have waged and rewards them liberally. He is a devoted father to his son and daughter.

Prince Philander, the king's son, one of the two heroes of the play. He is young and brave and always obedient to his father's wishes, even when they are in conflict with his own personal happiness. He is loyal to his friends to the point of self-sacrifice. He is secretly betrothed to a general's daughter.

Alcippus (ahl-SIHP-uhs), the second hero of the play, a young soldier who, because of his military triumphs, is promoted to the rank of general. He is modest enough to point out that an older man already occupies that position, but the latter's wish to retire and hand over his authority to Alcippus persuades the young man to accept the honor. Alcippus is a close friend of Prince Philander, and both are in love with the same woman. In the beginning of the play, neither man is aware of the other's passion.

Erminia (ehr-MIH-nyuh), the daughter of the general. She is in love with the prince, who returns her feelings. They have not yet declared themselves openly in fear that the king would oppose the match because Erminia is not of royal blood.

Galatea (gah-lah-TAY-uh), the daughter of the king and sister of Philander. She is equally as brave, as beautiful, and as loyal as her friend and rival in love, Erminia. Galatea loves Alcippus, who is not aware of her feelings, especially because he covets Erminia.

Orgilius (ohr-GIH-lee-uhs), an old general and father of Erminia. He is a bluff and honest soldier, ready to resign his place in favor of the young Alcippus, whom he believes to be the best man to lead the army. His relationship with his daughter suggests that of Polonius to Ophelia in William Shakespeare's *Hamlet, Prince of Denmark*: Both fathers warn their daughters against entanglements with royalty because their lesser station in life would make a lawful marriage impossible. Although with very different results, both girls obey their fathers.

Alcander (ahl-KAHN-dur), a friend of Prince Philander. He is in love with a lady of the court named Aminta, who returns his affection. These two provide an echo of the love story involving the major figures.

Olinda (oh-LIHN-dah), the maid of honor to Princess Galatea. She is Alcander's sister and staunch ally.

Pisaro (pih-ZAH-roh), a friend of young General Alcippus. He acts as a counterbalance to Alcander. When the two principals, Alcippus and Philander, finally quarrel over Erminia, Pisaro defends Alcippus, and Alcander defends Philander, thereby extending the dispute until it threatens to engulf the country in a civil war.

Cleontius and
Labree, male servants.
Lisette and
Isillia, female servants. The servants also take sides, contributing to the intrigue. There is little attempt to give them individuality; they are all stock figures popular in seventeenth century theater and opera. The focus is not so much on character as on trickery, and the theme is a standard one of the time, love versus honor.

— *Mildred C. Kuner*

FOREIGN AFFAIRS

Author: Alison Lurie (1926-   )
First published: 1984
Genre: Novel
Locale: London, England
Time: The early 1980's
Plot: Satire

Vinnie Miner, a fifty-four-year-old unmarried professor who specializes in children's literature at Corinth University in New York. Vinnie is an Anglophile and is in London to study the rhymes of schoolchildren. She meets another American, Chuck Mumpson, whom she at first snubs but whose kindness eventually inspires in her a more generous view of men and of transatlantic cultural values.

Fred Turner, Vinnie's colleague in the Corinth English Department. He also is studying in London. Fred is separated from his wife, Roo, and is struggling with his research on John Gay, which he hopes will win him tenure. Fred is an innocent American in this comic reprise of Henry James's theme of the New World coping with the Old.

Chuck Mumpson, a retired sanitary engineer from Tulsa whom Vinnie meets on the plane to London. Chuck's hearty mid-America ways are an embarrassment to the Anglophile Vinnie, but she comes to feel differently about him. Chuck searches for aristocratic roots in Wiltshire but comes up with only a mad hermit among his forebears.

Ruth (Roo) March, Fred Turner's wife and the daughter of Vinnie's bête noire, the critic L. D. Zimmern. Roo is a free spirit who goes by the name March because of her identification with Jo March of the novel *Little Women*. She and Fred are estranged over their disagreement concerning revealing photos of Fred's anatomy she had exhibited.

Rosemary Radley, a television star from the *Tallyho Castle* series. Rosemary admits to being thirty-seven years old, probably about a decade less than her true age. In her flutter of feminine pastels, her actor's genius at role-playing, and her coquettish response to Fred's (successful) courtship, she is the complete opposite of the straightforward Roo.

Edwin Francis, a children's book editor, writer, and critic. He is Vinnie's oldest friend in London. Edwin is gay, suffers the depredations of the young male parasites he takes in, and fusses prissily over his food, feigning a resistance to desserts that his short but plump person belies.

Lady Billings, a beautiful society hostess known to her friends as **Posy**. Posy hosts mildly debauched weekends when her husband is away, entertaining friends such as Rosemary and Edwin while cohabiting with her "cousin" William Just, known affectionately as Just William to those who are privy to the pretense.

Debby Vogeler and
Joe Vogeler, graduate school friends of Fred now studying in London. Fred relies on them for a decent meal when he is hungry, which is much of the time given his scant funds. In return, he endures their worries about their infant son's slowness in speaking and their rude putdowns of Roo.

Fido, the imaginary "medium-sized dirty-white long-haired mutt" who accompanies Vinnie in her imagination. Usually silent and inconspicuous, in moments of Vinnie's self-pity, Fido fawns and clamors for notice.

— *Frank Day*

THE FOREIGN GIRL
(La Gringa)

Author: Florencio Sánchez (1875-1910)
First published: 1910
Genre: Drama
Locale: The province of Santa Fe, Argentina
Time: About 1905
Plot: Social realism

Don Nicola (nee-KOH-lah), an ambitious first-generation immigrant farmer from Italy, a foreigner, or *gringo*. He works hard to improve his farm and his family's life. He increases his acreage and builds a new farm on Don Cantalicio's land when the latter fails to make good on his debt. Don Nicola dislikes the creoles, or native ranchers, considering them lazy good-for-nothings who do not know how to work or earn money. He refuses to let his daughter Victoria see Don Cantalicio's son Próspero, fearing that Próspero is little more than a fortune hunter. When he discovers Próspero's interest in his daughter, he fires him and throws him out. When Próspero returns two years later, established in a profession, Nicola approves the match.

Don Cantalicio (kahn-tah-LEE-see-oh), a *criollo*, or a native of Argentina. He used his farm as collateral to borrow money from Don Nicola, whom he despises for being one of the foreigners "taking over" Argentina. Once a gentleman farmer who grazed cattle and raised horses, he has not adapted to the times. His penchant for town life and his gambling losses make it impossible for him to repay his debt. He is not only unable to pay the debt and interest, but he also refuses to turn over the land in place of the money. He postpones the inevitable by bringing a suit against Don Nicola. He loses the suit, but the final agreement requires Don Nicola to pay him an additional sum of money, which Don Cantalicio uses to establish himself in another town. Two years later, he returns to his old farm, which has been radically altered and modernized under Nicola's ownership. His resentment of Nicola—and of foreigners in general—deepens. He gallops away, passing by the new threshing machine. His horse panics and throws him off. Injured, he is carried to the farmhouse, where he resists care from anyone but Victoria. His right arm is amputated as a result of the accident. Though resistant in the beginning, he finally gives Victoria and Próspero his blessing to marry, accepting the *gringa*, though not the *gringos*.

Victoria, the hardworking elder daughter of Nicola. She falls in love with Próspero. Her mother catches her kissing him, and he is forced to leave. Two years later, they become betrothed. Their union will forge the new race of native and gringo.

Próspero (PROHS-peh-roh), Cantalicio's son, who is hardworking and ambitious. Unlike his father, Próspero realizes that the old days are gone and is prepared to adapt to the new world. He works for Nicola until he is fired, then moves to a nearby town, where he works hard to earn enough money to marry Victoria. He returns to Santa Fe and to Nicola's new farm as the man in charge of the threshing machine, and he asks for Victoria's hand in marriage.

María, Nicola's wife. She dislikes and distrusts the native Argentines even more than her husband does. She does not want Victoria to marry Próspero; she judges the son by the father, whom she considers an old scoundrel.

Horacio (oh-RAH-see-oh), the son of Nicola and María. Trained in engineering in Buenos Aires, he returns to Santa Fe and helps his father modernize the new farm. Like his sister Victoria, he is sympathetic to both foreign and native views, though dedicated to modernity.

Rosina (roh-SEE-nah), another daughter of Nicola and María, about twelve years old. As industrious as the rest of the family despite her young age, she rises early to work on the farm.

— *Linda Ledford-Miller*

THE FORK RIVER SPACE PROJECT

Author: Wright Morris (1910-1998)
First published: 1977
Genre: Novel
Locale: Near the border of Kansas and Nebraska
Time: Late 1970's
Plot: Realism

Kelcey, a middle-aged writer. The fact that his wife calls him a "tease" suggests the fact that he has a tentative attitude toward life; he is always willing to alter his opinions. His curiosity propels him to the ghost town of Fork River and leaves him open to Harry Lorbeer's vision of the past and the future. Although he is devoted to his young wife, when she leaves him he is neither bitter nor vengeful. Instead, he is content to wait patiently for what will happen, perhaps a tornado, perhaps a visitation from outer space.

Alice Calley Kelcey, Kelcey's wife. A small, pretty woman with brown eyes and dark brown hair, she is shy but stable in character. Much younger than Kelcey, she nevertheless seems happy with him, attached to her home and to her garden. Her very openness and generosity, which led her to fall in love with Kelcey, draw her to O. P. Dahlberg. Finally, Alice disappears with Dahlberg, leaving a cryptic note for her husband.

Harry Lorbeer, a proprietor of the Fork River Space Project. A part-time plumber, usually attired in bib overalls, he is short, plump, and balding. He drives a gaudy hippie van. The youngest child and only son of a railroad magnate who once lived in Fork River, Harry is now the mysterious guru of a mysterious faith that sees the only possible salvation of the world in some contact with forces beyond it.

O. P. Dahlberg, also known as **Peter O. Bergdahl**, a house painter. A boyish, clean-cut man in his late thirties, he is not prepossessing. He is pockmarked, bowlegged, and awkward, with an unexpectedly high voice. Secretive and indifferent almost to the point of being insulting, he will not volunteer any information about himself to Kelcey. At second hand, Kelcey learns that Dahlberg was a young genius and later a writer of science fiction, that his real name is Peter O. Bergdahl, and that he is a lifelong resident of the Fork River area. Evidently, Dahlberg confides more in Alice, with whom he eventually falls in love, courting her in conversation and in trips to a salvage store and to a fair, trips that arouse Kelcey's suspicions. Kelcey does not suspect anything serious, however, until he reads the note from Alice indicating that she has run away with Dahlberg.

Miss Ingalls, a librarian. A quiet, prim woman in late middle age, she kindles with excitement when she has an inquiry about local history. She discovers the works by Peter O. Bergdahl, including the story that seems to attribute the decline of Fork River to a visit by an unidentified flying object.

Dr. Rainey, the local weather expert. A large, suntanned man with a booming voice, he appears ill at ease in the formal clothes that his indoor job demands. A happily married man with four children, he is conventional in manner but is open-minded about what space may hold, from aliens to black holes, and he is willing to speculate about the Fork River mystery.

— *Rosemary M. Canfield Reisman*

THE FORSYTE SAGA

Author: John Galsworthy (1867-1933)
First published: 1922
Genre: Novels
Locale: London and rural England
Time: 1886-1920
Plot: Family

The Man of Property, 1906

Soames Forsyte, the son of James Forsyte and the grandson of the founder of the family fortune, Jolyon Forsyte ("Superior Dosset"). Soames cannot understand why his wife, whose every material need is met, is not happy with him. When he finds out about her affair with Philip Bosinney, Soames sues him, determined to drive him bankrupt. Asserting his marital rights, he rapes Irene.

Irene Heron Forsyte, Soames's beautiful wife. After marrying Soames, she discovered that she found him sexually repellent. In the architect Philip Bosinney, she finds a man she can love. After the rape, she leaves Soames; however, when Bosinney is run over after she has told him about the rape, she feels responsible for her lover's death. Near collapse, she returns home.

Jolyon Forsyte (Old Jolyon), an eighty-year-old man who is especially fond of children. Because of his love for his little granddaughter June Forsyte, he sided with his daughter-in-law against his only son, Young Jolyon. After not seeing him for fourteen years, however, Old Jolyon seeks out his son, reestablishes their old relationship of total trust, and becomes close to the two young grandchildren he has never known. To please June and to spite his brother James, he buys the house at Robin Hill, which Bosinney had built for Soames.

Jolyon Forsyte (Young Jolyon), the son of Old Jolyon, a painter, who like his father is not a typical Forsyte. When he left his wife for another woman, young Jolyon and his father became estranged. After they begin to see each other again, they soon become as close as before.

June Forsyte, Young Jolyon's daughter by his first wife. After her engagement to Bosinney has been formally announced, June is humiliated by his well-known involvement with Irene. Because she still loves Bosinney, she urges her grandfather to help him extricate himself from his financial difficulties.

"Indian Summer of a Forsyte," 1922

Jolyon Forsyte (Old Jolyon), now eighty-five years old. He lives contentedly at Robin Hill with his son and his three grandchildren. After a chance encounter with Irene, who has left her husband, Old Jolyon befriends her. During June's absence, she often comes to visit him. He is happily anticipating her arrival at the time of his death.

In Chancery, 1920

Soames Forsyte, who yearns for a son to carry on the family name. Soames decides that he must obtain a divorce from Irene. He has selected a young, practical French woman, Annette Lamotte, as a suitable wife for him and the future mother of his child. He cannot, however, stay away from Irene, whom he still considers his property. A detective's report on her involvement with Young Jolyon prompts Soames to sue for divorce, naming Young Jolyon as co-respondent. Soames marries Annette, and they have a daughter.

Irene Heron Forsyte, Soames's estranged wife, who is determined to get away from Soames. In Young Jolyon, she has a dependable, understanding friend and, in time, a devoted lover. After the divorce, she marries Young Jolyon and moves to Robin Hill. They have a son, Jon.

Jolyon Forsyte (Young Jolyon), a widower. Appointed by his father as trustee of the large bequest to Irene, Jolyon feels compelled to protect her from Soames and his unwelcome attentions. Traveling together in Europe, Young Jolyon and Irene realize that they love each other.

Jolyon Forsyte (Jolly), the older son of Young Jolyon. He is a student at Oxford when the Boer War breaks out. When Val accuses him of being pro-Boer, he enlists. He dies of disease in South Africa.

Winifred Dartie, Soames's sister, who is deserted by her spendthrift husband and begins divorce proceedings. When he returns, she takes him back.

Publius Valerius (Val) Dartie, their son. He marries Holly Forsyte. He is wounded in South Africa and returns home.

Holly Forsyte, Young Jolyon's daughter and Val Dartie's wife.

"Awakening," 1922

Jolyon Forsyte (Jon), the son of Young Jolyon and Irene. At the age of five, he is aware of his parents' love for each other and his mother's beauty.

To Let, 1921

Soames Forsyte, whose wife cares nothing for him and who loves only his daughter. He is appalled by the idea that she might marry Irene's son.

Fleur Forsyte, Soames's daughter. She is determined to marry Jon, but she has to settle for Michael Mont.

Jolyon Forsyte (Young Jolyon), who writes Jon a letter describing Soames's mistreatment of Irene but dies before Jon finishes reading it.

Irene Forsyte, who, seeing that Fleur has inherited Soames's selfishness, begs Jon not to marry her.

Jolyon Forsyte (Jon), who has loved Fleur since he first met her. He nevertheless breaks off their engagement, telling her that he must respect his father's last wishes.

— *Rosemary M. Canfield Reisman*

FORTITUDE

Author: Sir Hugh Walpole (1884-1941)
First published: 1913
Genre: Novel

Locale: England
Time: Late nineteenth century
Plot: Love

Peter Westcott, the son of a harsh father and an invalid mother. Having been sent for a time to school, and now reading law in an office, he finds his home life intolerable after the death of his mother, and he leaves Cornwall to accept a job in an acquaintance's London bookshop. In London, he writes a novel that proves successful, and he marries; but his subsequent books are failures, his small son dies, and his wife leaves him. At last, ready to give up the struggle, he returns to Cornwall. There he meets an old friend who is dying, and from her he learns fortitude.

Clare Elizabeth Rossiter, whom Peter marries. He blames her for the death of their son. In spite of Peter's efforts to preserve their marriage, Clare leaves him for another man.

Stephen Brant, a farmer with whom Peter becomes friendly as a boy and from whom Peter learns much about life. It is through Stephen that Peter meets the bookseller who employs him. When the political activities going on in the bookshop prove dangerous, Stephen comes to take Peter away. Clare disapproves of Stephen.

Nora Monogue, whom Peter meets in London. She encourages him to write. Much later, the dying Nora admits that she has always loved him; her dying request is that he go back to London and continue writing. Through her, he learns fortitude.

Jerry Cardillac (Cards), Peter's idol at school. After Peter's marriage, Clare becomes interested in Cardillac; later, she leaves Peter to join Cardillac in France.

Emilio Zanti, a London bookseller who gives Peter a job. Clare disapproves of him.

Bobby Galleon, Peter's schoolfriend, the son of a famous writer. After Peter has been instrumental in the expelling of the school's best bowler, Bobby alone does not join in hissing him.

Jerrard, the best bowler in school. On the eve of a big game, Peter finds him forcing whiskey down the throat of a small boy and reports him. Jerrard is expelled, the game is lost, and Peter is hissed in school.

Zachary Tan, the operator of a curiosity shop to which Stephen Brant takes young Peter. There he meets Emilio Zanti.

Mr. Aitchinson, in whose office Peter reads law for a time.

Gottfried Hanz, an employee in Mr. Zanti's bookshop. Peter works as Hanz's assistant.

Mrs. Brockett, in whose lodging house Peter lives while working in the bookshop and while writing his first novel.

Mrs. Launce, whom Peter meets after his introduction to literary circles. She is instrumental in bringing Peter and Clare together.

Stephen Westcott, the son of Peter and Clare. His early death is a final blow to Peter's happiness.

THE FORTRESS

Author: Sir Hugh Walpole (1884-1941)
First published: 1932
Genre: Novel

Locale: England
Time: The nineteenth century
Plot: Historical

Judith Paris, who has returned with her illegitimate son to live with her nephew's widow. She continues to resist the persecution of another nephew's son.

Jennifer Herries, the widow of Judith's nephew Francis. A principal in an old quarrel, she is now its victim. The strain of her nephew's persecution is too much for her, and she dies.

Walter Herries, the son of Judith's nephew William. Determined to drive Jennifer and Judith out of their home, he offers first to buy it. When they refuse, he does his best to drive them away by persecution. To this end, he builds a great mansion, called the Fortress, on a hill overlooking their house.

Elizabeth Herries, Walter's beautiful and kind daughter. She loves Jennifer's son John but agrees not to see him because of family hatred. She goes to live with London relatives until her father's command that she marry a detested suitor drives her to take employment as a governess. There her employer's pursuit causes her to marry John. They are happy until John is killed by Elizabeth's brother. Learning that her father, who has resisted all her overtures, is seriously ill, Elizabeth storms the Fortress, nurses him back to health, and even succeeds in effecting a semblance of reconciliation between him and Judith on Judith's hundredth birthday.

John Herries, the son of Jennifer. A parliamentary secretary, his future seems bright; but he is dogged by his wife's brother, whose hatred makes John feel powerless. At last he confronts Uhland, who shoots him.

Uhland Herries, Walter's lame, pampered, and rancorous son. After shooting John, he kills himself.

Adam Paris, Judith's illegitimate son. Robust and rebellious, he leaves for London at twenty-two and becomes involved in the Chartist movement. He marries and returns to his mother's house to live.

Caesar Kraft, Adam's guide in London. He urges moderation on the Chartists, is blamed for the failure of a procession, and is killed in a riot.

Margaret Kraft, his daughter. She marries Adam and at first, with him and his mother, feels herself an outsider. Adam comes to understand her needs and gives her first place over Judith.

Benjie Herries, the son of Elizabeth and John.

Mr. Temple, a fat and rich lawyer who is Elizabeth's suitor. He is favored by her father and brother.

Christabel Herries, Walter's weak mother.

Reuben Sunwood, whose death is an addition to the trouble between Judith and Walter.

FORTUNATA AND JACINTA
(Fortunata y Jacinta)

Author: Benito Pérez Galdós (1843-1920)
First published: 1886-1887
Genre: Novel
Locale: Madrid, Spain
Time: 1869-1875
Plot: Social

Juanito Santa Cruz (hwah-NEE-toh SAHN-tah crewz), the protagonist in a realistic four-volume novel of bourgeois life in Madrid in the 1870's. He is without morals or scruples.

Bárbara Santa Cruz (BAHR-bah-rah), Juanito's mother and the proprietor of a dry-goods store established by the family in the previous century. She spoils her son.

Plácido Estupiña (PLAH-see-doh ehs-tew-peen-YAH), a part-time smuggler and her adviser.

Fortunata (fohr-tew-NAH-tah), a lively, attractive lower-class woman who becomes Juanito's mistress. Later she marries Maximiliano. She dies of exposure while seeking revenge for Jacinta and herself.

Petusin (peh-tew-SEEN), the illegitimate son of Juanito and Fortunata.

Jacinta (hah-SEEN-tah), Juanito's placid, beautiful cousin, chosen by his mother to be his wife. She cannot have children.

Maximiliano Rubín (mahks-ee-mee-lee-AH-noh rrew-BEEN), the ugly, schizophrenic orphan son of a goldsmith. He marries Fortunata.

Lupe (LEW-peh), Maximiliano's aunt, who warns Fortunata against the marriage.

Juan Pablo Rubín (hwahn PAHB-loh), one of Maximiliano's brothers, a loafer.

Colonel Evaristo Feijóo (eh-vahr-EES-toh feh-ee-HOH-oh), an elderly protector of Fortunata.

Guillermina Pancheco (gee-yehr-MEE-nah pahn-CHAY-koh), at whose house Jacinta learns of her husband's infidelity.

The Widow Samaniego (sah-mahn-ee-EH-goh), the owner of a drugstore, who employs Maximiliano.

Aurora (ow-ROH-rah), her flashy daughter, who attracts Juanito. They become lovers.

Moreno Isla (mohr-EH-noh EES-lah), whose proposition is refused by the faithful Jacinta.

FORTUNE MENDS
(Mejor está que estaba)

Author: Pedro Calderón de la Barca (1600-1681)
First performed: 1631
Genre: Drama
Locale: Vienna
Time: The seventeenth century
Plot: Comedy

Carlos Colona (koh-LOH-nah), the son of the governor of Brandenburg. He is attracted to a veiled lady, Flora. His efforts to speak to her cause a quarrel with her fiancé, Licio, whom Don Carlos kills in the ensuing duel. He seeks asylum in the house of his father's friend, Don César, who is the father of the veiled Flora. After a series of adventures involving disguises, recognitions, escapes, pursuits, fights, and problems of honor, Don Carlos wins Flora's hand.

Don César (SEH-sahr), Flora's father and an old friend of Carlos Colona's father. When Don Carlos, after killing Licio in a duel, seeks asylum in his house, Don César faces the dilemma of having to choose between the obligations of friendship, which demand that he aid the young man, and the obligations of a magistrate, which require that he arrest and execute him.

Flora (FLOH-rah), Don César's daughter. Veiled, she attracts the attention of Carlos Colona, who kills her fiancé, Licio, in a duel. When Don Carlos arrives at her house as a fugitive seeking asylum, she hides him. After many complications, her identity becomes known, everyone's honor is satisfied, and she and Don Carlos are married.

Laura, Flora's friend, who is loved by Arnaldo.

Arnaldo, Laura's suitor.

Dinero (dee-NAY-roh), Carlos Colona's servant.

Fabio (FAH-bee-oh), Laura's brother.

Silvia, Flora's servant.

THE FORTUNES OF NIGEL

Author: Sir Walter Scott (1771-1832)
First published: 1822
Genre: Novel
Locale: England
Time: Early seventeenth century
Plot: Historical

Nigel Olifaunt, lord of Glenvarloch, a gallant young Scotsman who comes to England to collect payment for injustices committed against his noble family. Naïve and impressionable, he becomes involved in gambling and ribaldry in the ordinaries and gaming houses of the town. This experience leads to his association with ruffians and life in Alsatia, the haunt of bully-boys, thieves, and murderers. A brave youth, he kills a robber in his rooming house and saves the life of Martha Trapbois, his landlord's daughter. Imprisoned for carrying arms in the presence of King James, he languishes while his faithful servant negotiates for the money owed the Glenvarlochides, as the king calls them. On his return to Scotland, he is accompanied by his bride, Margaret Ramsay, an English commoner now known to be of noble Scottish descent.

James I, king of England, whose conduct makes him a portentous clown among the Stuarts. His folly, insensibilities, and erudition are interwoven to make him a comedic character, to the detriment of the suspense of the story.

Richard (Richie) Moniplies, Nigel's faithful page. His capabilities and fortitude make Nigel's expedition a success. Richie's impudence is offset by better qualities, to justify his winning the wealthiest woman, although of low birth, in the story. Money becomes Richie more than rank or station.

Lord Dalgarno, a spendthrift Scotsman who knows the ways of London. Befriending the newly arrived Nigel, Dalgarno introduces him to the seamy side of life, only to desert him in time of reverses and to report Nigel's unbecoming behavior to court circles. The villain Dalgarno marries Martha Trapbois, a usurer's daughter, for her large sum of money, but deserts her and takes another man's wife with him when he starts back to Scotland. Richie murders him.

Master George Heriot, an old goldsmith and confidant of the king who is involved in most of the political intrigue surrounding Nigel's efforts to regain family property and Dalgarno's rascality to prevent Nigel's success.

Reginald Lowestoffe, a young, profligate law student who befriends Nigel in Alsatia. He aids Richie in avenging Nigel against Dalgarno.

Margaret Ramsay, the beautiful young daughter of a London clockmaker. Enamored of Nigel because of his handsome appearance and his ill fortune at the hands of Dalgarno, she goes before the king in the disguise of a page to plead for Nigel's release from the Tower of London. Through Heriot's efforts, Margaret and Nigel are married, Margaret's noble heritage having been established to save the union from that of nobleman and commoner.

Martha Trapbois, the uneducated but wise daughter of a moneylender in Alsatia, in whose house Nigel lives in his exile from society. Nigel saves her life during a robbery and flees with her when she takes her father's great money chest. She is intercepted on her way to John Christie's rooming house by Dalgarno, who marries her for her wealth. After Dalgarno's murder, she marries Richie Moniplies.

Lady Hermione, a descendant of the House of Glenvarloch and long an isolate in the house of George Heriot, after her criminal abduction from her Spanish husband. Approached for counsel by Margaret Ramsay, Lady Hermione encourages the young woman to leave no stone unturned in winning and keeping her lover, Nigel.

Andrew Skurliewhitter, the scrivener who handles all court papers. An accomplice to Dalgarno, he lacks courage to complete the thefts that will accomplish Dalgarno's purposes, and he disappears from the scene and the story when Dalgarno is murdered.

Dame Nelly Christie, the housewife who elopes with Dalgarno when he flees with money and papers to Scotland. A simpering woman, she pleads to become Dalgarno's loving wife rather than his loving lady. She is apprehended by her husband at the scene of Dalgarno's murder.

John Christie, her husband, a ship chandler who acts as a news carrier from his rooming house.

Sir Mungo Malagrowther, a confidant of the King. As Nigel's adversary, he adds considerably to the young nobleman's difficulties.

Dame Ursula Suddlechop, a barber's wife who acts as a matchmaker, her activity bordering on sorcery. She predicts marriage between Margaret Ramsay and Jenkin Vincent, as well as other unfulfilled prophecies.

Jenkin Vincent, a young apprentice to the clockmaker. Thwarted in his desire for Margaret, he is sent, through the efforts of George Heriot, on an important business mission to Paris. It is assumed that he returns to London and establishes a prosperous business with his fellow apprentice.

Frank Tunstall, another apprentice to the clockmaker, introduced into the plot only as a possible suitor to Margaret.

David Ramsay, Margaret's father. An ingenious, whimsical mechanic, he becomes a successful horologist.

The Duke of Buckingham, a favorite of King James, at odds with Nigel when he appears at court to sue for money due his family.

Prince Charles, the son of King James. His chief function seems to be to point up the foolish behavior of the king.

Lord Huntinglen, Dalgarno's father. A righteous man, he would have the Glenvarlochs compensated. In the manner of the old nobility, he deplores his son's villainy.

Trapbois, Martha's father, a usurer, murdered by accomplices of the scrivener, who thinks that Trapbois was able to steal Nigel's mortgage papers while Nigel lived in the Trapbois house in Alsatia.

Captain Colepepper, a cowardly criminal who flees any danger but may be talked into any villainy. He and the scrivener plot against Dalgarno as Dalgarno plots against Nigel.

De Beaujeu, a gaming-house keeper whose establishment, as a rendezvous, is a focal point for much of the action in the novel.

THE FORTUNES OF RICHARD MAHONY

Author: Henry Handel Richardson (Ethel Florence Lindesay Richardson Robertson, 1870-1946)
First published: 1930
Genre: Novel
Locale: Ballarat and Melbourne, Australia; and England
Time: Late nineteenth century
Plot: Historical realism

Australia Felix, 1917

Richard Mahony, one of many Englishmen lured to Australia to seek a fortune in the gold fields. He is never truly happy or at ease in his adopted country. Trained as a doctor, he abandons his profession to make a living as a shopkeeper in a rough mining community. His success is only marginal until after his marriage. At his wife's urging, he returns to medical practice. He has never been skilled at dealing with people, being introspective, sensitive, critical, and at times brutally honest. With the help of his wife's charm, however, he gradually attracts a practice of well-to-do patients. Unfortunately, even this achievement leaves him unsatisfied; he is always looking for something and someplace better, moving his family from location to location.

Mary Turnham, who becomes Richard's wife. When he marries her, she is very young and working as a family helper at Beamish's Inn. She admires Richard greatly, although it is her personality that enables him to become a success. She likes most people and is inclined to think well of them. She remains loyal to Richard, at first from admiration and respect and later as a defense against recognizing his weaknesses. She eventually realizes that some of his desires are foolish, even destructive.

Purdy Smith, Mahony's boyhood friend from Dublin. In Australia, they are close at first because of these memories. Purdy sides with the workers and the rebels, however, eventually finding his former friend too distant and aristocratic. Richard, on the other hand, dismisses Purdy as coarse and vulgar. The friendship between the two is further harmed when Purdy falls in love with Mary.

John Turnham, Mary's older brother, the first of the family to go to Australia. He quickly became successful. After the death of his first wife, he rejects his children, sending them to live with Mary and Richard. He goes on to become a successful politician.

Tilly Beamish Ocock, the daughter of the inn owners who employed Mary Turnham. She is jovial and a little vulgar. Her relationship with Purdy brought Mary and Richard together. Her rather vulgar manner is toned down after her marriage to Mr. Ocock, an older man who is the Mahonys' neighbor.

Henry Ocock, the lawyer son of Mahony's neighbor. He is arrogant and supercilious, seeming to lack warmth. As Mahony's wealth increases, the relationship between the two improves. When his father meets Tilly at the Mahonys' and subsequently marries her, Henry is furious.

Sarah (or **Sara** or **Zara**, depending on her choice of name), Mary's sister. She always insists on being the height of fashion. She flits from place to place, relying on her charm and glamour to pave her way.

The Way Home, 1925

Richard Mahony, a rich man, having made a fortune on stocks. He is dissatisfied with his life, however, dragging his wife to England to fulfill his dream of returning home. As always, the reality is less satisfactory to Mahony than either his dreams or his memories, and the couple return to Australia. Having placed his fortune in the hands of an unscrupulous speculator, he loses the bulk of his money. He becomes fascinated with spiritualism.

Mary, who is rejected as coarse and provincial by the British society her husband longs to join, even though she was considered a prominent beauty in Australia. He is both protective and ashamed of her lack of social awareness. When they return to Australia, she is delighted. Soon afterward, she has a son and then twins.

Tillie Ocock Smith, Mary's source of emotional and financial support. She is loud but is lavish with money and generous with her spirit. Richard dislikes her intensely because of her common behavior.

Purdy Smith, who is married to Tilly. He settles down but is not reconciled with his old friend. His advice causes Mahony's ruin.

Sarah, who is no longer able to survive by her glamour. She marries Hempel, Mahony's former clerk, whom she once despised.

Ultima Thule, 1929

Richard Mahony, who is plagued by the loss of both his money and his prominent position in the medical community. He squanders the rest of his savings trying to recoup. Eventually he goes mad, burning all of his papers, thus placing his family in total financial ruin. He becomes childlike, dependent on Mary for everything.

Mary, who becomes a postmistress in the outback to support herself, her children, and Richard after Richard loses the family wealth. She rescues him from a state-run asylum, treating him at home until his death.

Henry Ocock, who helps Mary in her desperate quest to rescue Richard and to support herself and her children.

— *Mary E. Mahony*

THE FORTY DAYS OF MUSA DAGH
(Die vierzig Tage des Musa Dagh)

Author: Franz Werfel (1890-1945)
First published: 1933
Genre: Novel

Locale: Near Antioch, Syria
Time: 1915
Plot: Historical

Gabriel Bagradian, a loyal Armenian, although he is an officer in the Ottoman reserves. Married to a Frenchwoman and long a resident of Paris, he has returned to his native village, Yoghonoluk, in order to settle some business affairs managed by his older brother Avetis, who has just died. Gabriel has never been able to forget his Armenian home and ancestry. The mountain, Musa Dagh, is as dear to him as if it were a relative. War is imminent, and the Turkish plan is to exile all the Armenians of the district. After Gabriel assumes leadership of the community, the Armenians vote to defend Musa Dagh and take their position on that natural fortress. Their bravery is unmatched, but they have little food and insufficient ammunition for a siege. After forty days, the last attack is planned by Gabriel, and they have set fire to the mountainside. Three days of starvation have weakened the people, and they fly a flag of distress, which the French boat in the harbor sees. Immediately, it fires a protective barrage, which stops the Turks from their planned advance. After the survivors have been placed aboard the French ship, Gabriel climbs the mountain for one last farewell beside his son's grave. A Turkish sniper shoots him, and he falls across the grave of his son; the last of the Bagradians lies on the bosom of Musa Dagh.

Juliette, Gabriel's French wife. A woman with strong love for her own country, she finds her husband's patriotism difficult to share. However, she falls in love with the country home in Yoghonoluk, and she enjoys its gardens and the refurbishing of the house. She also makes smart costumes for the servants, who enjoy her devoted care of the home. As Gabriel is drawn into political problems and has less time for his family, Juliette allows herself to respond to the charms of an adventurer. After the terrors of the defense of Musa Dagh, and after she is consumed by fever, she is carried, a raving madwoman calling only for her son, to the French ship.

Gonsague Maris, a Greek adventurer with an American passport, a onetime journalist who seduces Juliette. In the hue and cry aroused by his perfidy, he escapes down the mountainside.

Stephan Bagradian, Gabriel's adolescent son, deeply aware of his Armenian heritage and admiring of his father. Stephan tries to accompany his friend Haik, a hardy young scout, on a trip to ask aid of the American consul. He turns back, ill, and is shot by the Turks.

Samuel Avakian, Stephan's competent tutor. He has the long, narrow face of an intellectual but the guarded look of the Armenian patriot.

Ter Haigasun, the Gregorian priest of the village and one of the three members of the council that plans the defense of Musa Dagh.

Sarkis Kilikian, a deserter from the Turkish army, an Armenian patriot.

Iskuhi Tomasian, the sister of a pastor, deeply in love with Gabriel Bagradian.

Agha Rifaat Bereket, old Turkish friend of Avetis Bagradian. He is a religious mystic.

Dr. Johannes Lepsius, a German pastor in charge of rescue work.

THE FOUNDATION PIT
(Kotlovan)

Author: Andrei Platonov (Andrei Platonovich Klimentov, 1899-1951)
First published: 1969
Genre: Novel

Locale: A provincial city and nearby village in Russia
Time: Early 1930's
Plot: Satire

Voshchev (VOH-shchehv), a former machinist, now a laborer in the crew digging a foundation for a multiple housing unit in the Soviet Union in the early 1930's. At the age of thirty, he lost his job because of a tendency to "stop and think." Amid the changes in the Soviet Union designed to build the new society after the revolution, he feels the need to understand the "sense of the action" and the enduring meaning of life. He sees suffering everywhere, and his main quality is compassion. He strikes the death blow to the activist as punishment for the activist's error in believing that he had a monopoly on truth. Voshchev, the truth-seeker, deserts his search when Nastya dies.

Prushevsky (prew-SHEHV-skee), an engineer and intellectual with an "excited" heart. He is only twenty-five years old, but he is "gray" because, as a scientist and rationalist, he regards the world as dead matter, a perception that limits and depresses his imaginative mind. It was his idea to build a great communal building, for which the foundation pit is being excavated by the powerful labor of the crew. The building will eliminate exactly those individual relationships in which the engineer is deficient, those that bind people together. He has the memory of a lost love, a glimpse of a woman whom he never saw again; it provides his only feelings. This man without love can build only the structure that will unmake humankind itself. His lack of feeling leaves him in despair, wishing for suicide.

Chiklin (CHIH-klihn), the brigade leader of the diggers. He is very strong, hardworking, and generous. An older man, he has a "small stony head," thick with hair; he is a worker, not a thinker, and cannot express in words what he feels. Devoted to the revolution, he too has encountered the one woman for him and lost her. Unlike the engineer, he goes in search of her and finds her dying, cared for only by a young child, her daughter, Nastya. He takes Nastya under his protection as his hope for the future. When the girl dies in spite of his efforts, he digs her grave deep enough to allow her never to be troubled by the earth. Chiklin is a sledgehammer in his strength, the emblem of the proletarian defender of the revolution, but he too is left without faith at the end of the novel. He continues digging as the only way to bear his despair.

Zhachev (ZHAH-chehv), a legless man, wounded in the "capitalist" World War I. Intelligent and caustic, Zhachev, with "brown, narrow eyes," is verbally aggressive and hostile. He suffers from the "greed of the deprived," extracting food and services from everyone, exploiting their guilt at his disability. He forgets his own needs in his devotion to the girl Nastya, whom he tries tenderly to protect as what will live and thrive when he dies.

Nastya, a young orphan girl adopted by the digging crew. She is the daughter of the beautiful bourgeois woman whom both Prushevsky and Chiklin have loved from afar, having seen her in her youth and never forgotten her. She is all the beauty of the old regime that they have missed and that the revolution lets die. Nastya represents for all the men the claims of the future for which they labor and suffer, an ideal Communist state envisioned but, as yet, far from achieved. Her presence at the foundation pit and the *kolkhoz* (collective farm) in the process of being established gives them hope and their labor meaning. She is pitiless in her commitment to the revolution, scolding backsliders and excoriating bourgeois remnants for their behavior. Her death is symbolic of their loss of hope, and it is a counterpoint to the establishment of the collective farm at the cost of the pain and death of the *kulaks*.

The activist, a man who is so much the Party official that he gets no name. He has been sent to liquidate the landowning peasants and establish the *kolkhoz*. He follows government directives to the letter, ignoring his own feelings and ideas. In his zeal, he even goes beyond the requirements in his callous devotion to the Party's aims. When the Party deserts him, sending an order canceling all he has achieved and calling him a class enemy as he has called others, his disillusionment is complete. He takes his coat from the feverish Nastya, signaling his alienation from the dream. Chiklin strikes him as a traitor to the revolution, and Voshchev finishes him off for his having sucked all meaning in life into his own commitment.

— *Martha Manheim*

THE FOUNDATION TRILOGY

Author: Isaac Asimov (1920-1992)
First published: 1963
Genre: Novels

Locale: Primarily the planets Trantor, Terminus, and Kalgan
Time: Years 1-377 of the Foundation Era
Plot: Science fiction

Foundation, 1951

Hari Seldon, a psychohistorian who is the founder of both the First Foundation and the Second Foundation. Originally a mathematician working at a university on the imperial planet of Trantor, Seldon developed the discipline of psychohistory, which he uses to predict the end of the Galactic Empire. Seldon is arrested by the Empire because of his predictions, but he manages to outwit its rulers, who allow him to form the two Foundations. These Foundations are the chief organs of the Seldon Plan, which is intended to save the Galaxy from twenty thousand years of barbarism. Seldon dies shortly thereafter but reappears in video recordings to instruct later generations.

Salvor Hardin, the first mayor of Terminus, the remote planet where Seldon has set up the First Foundation. Hardin chafes under the rule of the Encyclopedists, who think that the only purpose of the Foundation is to prepare an Encyclopedia. When Hardin realizes that the neighboring planet Anacreon is about to annex the Foundation and that the declining Empire will do nothing to prevent this, he seizes political power in Terminus. His theories about the Foundation's imperial mission proven, Hardin outwits the rulers of Anacreon and paves the way for the Foundation's growing regional power.

Hober Mallow, the mayor of Terminus approximately eighty years after Hardin. A merchant trader from the planet Smyrno, Mallow is mistrusted by the Foundation's elite, who resent the fact that he relies on trade rather than their religion of science to establish Foundation power in neighboring regions. Mallow exposes the Foundation elite as authoritarian and dishonest, and he becomes mayor himself after defeating the rival power of Korell.

Foundation and Empire, 1952

Bel Riose, an imperial general who attempts to reconquer the Foundation. Riose is a young and confident leader who wins many military victories. His success, however, arouses the suspicion of the Emperor that Riose plans to take over the throne, and he is recalled and arrested, leaving the Foundation stronger than ever.

The Mule, a mutant with unusual emotional powers who seizes control of the planet Kalgan and begins a war against the Foundation. The Mule is astoundingly successful and eventually attacks the planet Terminus itself, defying assumptions that the Seldon Plan will protect the Foundation forever. The Mule can defy the Seldon Plan because he is a mutant and thus not provided for by the plan. After conquering the Foundation, the Mule embarks on a desperate search to find the Second Foundation. He tries to use his emotional power to find the secret but is foiled by the sudden intervention of Bayta Darell.

Bayta Darell, a young woman from the Foundation who marries a member of the dissident Independent Traders and, with him, escapes the Mule's sack of Terminus. Bayta had first encountered the Mule's power on Kalgan, and by the time she is in the old Imperial Library on Trantor, she has come to understand the Mule in such a way as to defeat him.

Second Foundation, 1953

The Mule, who, after being defeated by Bayta, tries to search for the Second Foundation through more conventional means. He uses his emotionally converted lieutenant, Han Pritcher, to attempt to trick a suspected Second Foundationer into revealing the nature of his people. The Second Foundation, though, manages to outwit and defeat the Mule through an ingenious stratagem. The Mule dies shortly thereafter.

Arcadia Darell, the granddaughter of Bayta Darell. She lives in the revived, post-Mule Foundation and becomes interested in the Second Foundation when her father, Toran, leads a group of prominent Foundation intellectuals who try to look for it. Arcadia persuades her uncle, Homir Munn, to take her along to Kalgan with him. On Kalgan, she is almost seduced by the lascivious Lord Stettin. Arcadia flees to Trantor after guessing where the Second Foundation really is, a guess borne out by events occurring after her reunion with her father.

The First Speaker, the principal leader of the Second Foundation. Wielding tremendous power by means of his ability to control others psychologically and to envision the future, the First Speaker conceals his identity so as to arrange events according to the will of the Second Foundation and to ensure that the Seldon Plan will continue.

— *Nicholas Birns*

THE FOUNTAIN OVERFLOWS

Author: Rebecca West (Cicily Isabel Fairfield, 1892-1983)
First published: 1956
Genre: Novel
Locale: The Scottish countryside and London
Time: Late nineteenth century
Plot: Psychological realism

Rose Aubrey, the narrator, the middle child (with her twin, Mary) in the Aubrey family. The novel covers the period from her young girlhood to her first engagement as a professional pianist. Rose defines herself through her musical identity and her family affection. She inherits psychic gifts from her mother. Her parents' eccentricity develops her survival skills of selective vision and creative lying. She adores her parents and deals realistically with the strains they place on her; she is convinced that everything will be all right in the end.

Clare Keith Aubrey, Rose's mother, a concert pianist who abandoned her career to be married and have children. She has the ferocity of genius in her family devotion as well as in her music. A highly principled intellectual, she is gifted with second sight but unable to deal with practical life except through savage self-discipline and sacrifice. The constant strain makes her gaunt, nervous, and outwardly ridiculous.

Piers Aubrey, the brilliant, unstable father of the family, a journalist and political writer. He loses jobs suddenly and gambles family funds on the stock exchange. He is infinitely kind to Aunt Lily yet often completely disregards his family's welfare. He has a talent for fine carpentry and makes his children enchanting gifts. His charm and genius win their adoration, yet he abandons them. His absence ironically ensures their financial security, because it allows Clare to sell family portraits whose true value she had concealed from Piers.

Mary Aubrey, Rose's twin, a complement and opposite to her. She is beautiful, with a greater and more spontaneous musical talent than Rose's. Her personality is more reserved; she does not share Rose's warm temper and emotional expressiveness. The twins are constant conspirators, however, in the management of their family life.

Cordelia Aubrey, the oldest of the children, a source of pain to the family in her plan to be a violinist. Endowed with beauty, great energy, and no musical taste, she wishes to please the outer world and escape her parents' inconvenient genius. She enters into a precocious concert career, but the cruel assessment of a bitter master violinist breaks her resolve and leaves her bedridden, with hope of eventual music-free happiness.

Richard Quin Aubrey, the adored younger brother of the Aubrey girls.

Constance, a childhood friend of Clare Aubrey, unhappily married to her cousin Jock. She shares Clare's understanding of life but is a physical opposite of her: tall, substantial, calm, and as beautiful as an ancient Roman statue. She is gifted with the practical skills Clare lacks.

Rosamund, Constance and Jock's only child, a friend of the Aubrey children. She is beautiful and tranquil like her mother, and she is able to understand and manipulate other people. She stammers and seems slow, with no outward brilliance, but she is an expert at chess and meets life with practical equanimity.

Beatrice Beevor, the misguided teacher who launches Cordelia on her concert career in defiance of Mrs. Aubrey's qualms.

Queenie Phillips, the darkly beautiful, tyrannical mother of a schoolmate of the Aubrey girls, fascinated by Rose's psychic gift. Queenie murders her prosperous businessman husband. Her death sentence at the hands of an insane old judge provides Piers Aubrey with a major legal cause and personal victory.

Lily Moon, called **Aunt Lily**, Queenie's small, ugly, blonde sister, a former barmaid who was rescued and befriended with her niece by the impoverished Aubreys. A tragicomic figure, she inspires the Aubreys' affection while trying their nerves.

— *Anne W. Sienkewicz*

THE FOUNTAINHEAD

Author: Ayn Rand (Alice Rosenbaum, 1905-1982)
First published: 1943
Genre: Novel
Locale: New York City
Time: 1922 to the 1930's
Plot: Social morality

Howard Roark, the hero, a maverick architect apparently modeled on Frank Lloyd Wright. He refuses to compromise with mediocrity and conventional fashion, insisting on pursuing his personal vision whatever the cost. The story follows Roark from his architectural school days to the novel's climax, his trial for dynamiting a public housing project whose builder had compromised his design. Roark's credo is, "I don't build to have clients; I have clients so I can build."

Peter Keating, Roark's classmate in architectural school. The two are antithetical personalities. Keating rises in the architectural profession through manipulating people rather than through creative design. His yearning for commercial success leads him to play up to anyone who can assist his career, and several times he begs for Roark's assistance. The result is the atrophy of what talent he had to begin with. By the novel's end, he has become an empty shell.

Ellsworth M. Toohey, the influential columnist on architecture for the *Banner* newspaper and the novel's villain. Toohey's ambition is to advance his power by exploiting the weaknesses of others. Without any talent of his own, he exploits his position to stir up popular hostility against the superior few in the name of "selflessness." Accordingly, Roark becomes his number one target.

Gail Wynand, newspaper publisher who turned the *Banner* into a crime-and-scandal sheet to appeal to the vulgar masses. A disappointed idealist, he first tries to corrupt Roark to confirm his pessimism about human nature. He is won over by Roark's spirit and becomes his defender. Toohey, however, has so undermined Wynand's position that he is forced to backtrack from his support for Roark. Although Wynand regains his wealth and power, his doing so at the expense of his integrity leaves him a tragically broken man.

Dominique Francon, the novel's heroine. The daughter of a financially successful architect who is Peter's first boss, she despises her father's mediocrity and is cynical about the possibility of anybody having sufficient backbone to resist the pressures for conformity. She first allies with Toohey to destroy Roark because his work is "too good" for a corrupt society: she later tries to domesticate Roark via sexual seduction. She marries Peter Keating, then Gail Wynand. Her efforts to dominate Roark backfire, and at the novel's conclusion they are married.

Henry Cameron, an embittered and neglected architectural genius apparently modeled on Frank Lloyd Wright's mentor, Louis Sullivan. He is the one person whom Roark admires.

Austen Heller, a popular newspaper columnist. He is Toohey's opposite in values. He gives Roark his first major commission, is responsible for bringing Roark's work to public attention, and remains Roark's friend and defender through the novel.

Steven Mallory, a sculptor who becomes one of Roark's closest friends because of their shared respect for the talented individual. Even more than Roark, he suffers professionally because of his independence. His statue of a nude Dominique is a masterpiece symbolizing the indomitability of the human spirit.

— *John Braeman*

THE FOUR HORSEMEN OF THE APOCALYPSE
(Los cuatro jinetes del Apocalipsis)

Author: Vicente Blasco Ibáñez (1867-1928)
First published: 1916
Genre: Novel

Locale: Argentina, Paris, and the front lines of World War I
Time: Early 1900's
Plot: Historical

Julio Madariaga (HEW-lee-oh Mah-doh-ree-AH-gah), a tough, virile Spaniard who immigrates to Argentina. Madariaga makes a fortune buying land no one wants and converting it into fine ranch land, stocked with cattle bred from a prize-winning bull that is now stuffed and placed at the entrance to his parlor. Madariaga kills or tames the Indians, seduces the local women, and leaves progeny wherever he roams. Despite the large numbers of illegitimate offspring left on his doorstep, the death of his only legitimate heir leaves him inconsolate. His granddaughter, Chichi, however, roams the range with him. Madariaga dies in the saddle and leaves his heirs a fortune.

Julio Desnoyers (HEW-lee-oh day-noh-YAY), the spoiled, handsome son of millionaire Marcelo Desnoyers. He is a hot-footed tango dancer and the heartthrob of numerous Parisian ladies. Julio becomes enamored of Marguerite Laurier, but when the war makes her husband a hero, his war injuries recall her to her first love and duty. Heartbroken and angered by Parisian comments about his avoidance of war duties and by the end of his clandestine affair, Julio joins the French army and serves heroically, winning the respect of comrades and the praise of superiors. He rises in the ranks for his bravery in the trenches but is killed shortly before the war's end.

Marguerite Laurier (mahr-geh-REET loh-RYAY), the beautiful, adulterous lover of Julio Desnoyers, whose not-so-secret trysts with him begin on the dance floor and end in his Montmartre study. Discovery by Marguerite's husband, Etienne Laurier, lead to marriage plans. Her husband's uniform and heroism, however, make her embarrassed by her lover's failure to join the war effort. She takes nurses' training and then, after learning of her husband's possible blindness, decides that duty and self-sacrifice are wartime necessities. When Julio finally tracks her down, she confesses that she loves both men, though in different ways; she chooses the man who needs her most. When Julio comes home from the front, handsome in his uniform and medals, she, though pregnant, looks at him longingly before fleeing temptation.

Argensola (ahr-gehn-SOH-lah), Julio's manservant and confidant, who reads widely all the books about which Julio, as a man of the world, has to be conversant. He provides compact summaries of their contents for his master's edification. He keeps Julio's cupboard full by raiding the family larder and wine cellar; introduces Julio and his father to the Russian political philosopher Tchernoff, whose analysis of current events and world movements impresses them both; and, while Julio is at war, employs Julio's studio for his own affairs.

Don Marcelo Desnoyers (mahr-SAY-loh), the husband of Luisa Madariaga, the overseer and heir of Madariaga's ranch, and the millionaire father of Julio and Lusita. Most of the story is from the perspective of Marcelo, first as he experiences the splendor of Argentina, with its multicultural population and its potential for growth and development; then as a Frenchman returning to his motherland and savoring the sights and sounds of Paris; next as a father concerned for the welfare of his son and daughter; then as a patriot, outraged by the barbarisms of the Germans and proud of the French stand against them. As a landowner and victim, Desnoyers observes the French retreat, the German advance, and the French resurgence at the Battle of the Marne. He is shocked at the sadism and perversions of German officers. Later, he witnesses the nightmare of trench warfare as he searches proudly for his heroic son, only to learn of his death shortly after their encounter. As an old man, he realizes the futility of his wealth and, through his personal loss, the depth of his nation's suffering. He finds meager hope in the possibility of grandchildren, though ones who would not bear his family name.

Lusita "Chichi" Desnoyers Lacour (lew-SEE-tah "CHEE-chee" day-noh-YAY lah-KEWR), the darling of her grandfather. Chichi is a wild, free-spirited youth who grows into a purposeful, determined young woman, in love with the son of Senator Lacour. Although he is scarred, maimed, and without a hand, she firmly undertakes his nursing and acts on survivalist instincts to counter death by bearing children to make a new future.

Karl Hartrott, a timid, servile sneak, of dubious origin, taken into Madariaga's household under protest. Hartrott betrays Julio Madariaga's hospitality by absconding with his daughter and then returning with their children to beg support. Inheriting wealth exposes him as a pretentious, arrogant social climber, fawning over aristocracy and enamored of German theories of racial superiority and the right to conquest.

Elena Hartrott, a wholehearted supporter of German culture, philosophy, and will to power, trapped by the war in Paris. Her loss of several sons in the same battle in which Julio dies evokes some sympathy, but overall she is irritating.

Gina Macdonald

THE FOURTEEN SISTERS OF EMILIO MONTEZ O'BRIEN

Author: Oscar Hijuelos (1951-   )
First published: 1993
Genre: Novel
Locale: Cuba and the states of Pennsylvania, New York, California, and Alaska
Time: The twentieth century
Plot: Family

Emilio Montez O'Brien, the youngest child and only son of Nelson O'Brien and Mariela Montez O'Brien. Reared and coddled in a household dominated by fifteen women, he serves in Italy during World War II. Following some success on the New York stage, he moves to Hollywood, where he makes forty-two B-films in five years. A vain philanderer, he is seduced by a Montana fan who marries him and soon ends his career in scandal. He flees to Alaska, where he finds true love with Jessica Brooks. Their joyous marriage ends in a fire that kills Jessica and their baby, Mary. Emilio overcomes drinking and depression to take up his father's old profession, becoming "photographer to the stars" in Hollywood.

Margarita Montez O'Brien, the eldest of the fifteen O'Brien children, born in 1902 on the ship taking her parents away from Cuba. Margarita's erotic fantasies are first aroused when a barnstorming aviator is forced to stay at the O'Brien house. Her marriage to the wealthy but abusive Lester Thompson ends in divorce after sixteen years. One of the few siblings to maintain their mother's language, she becomes a Spanish teacher. Still spry at the age of ninety, Margarita does volunteer work for the library, where she meets a gentle pilot named Leslie Howard and marries him, finally fulfilling her adolescent dream of love with a handsome flier.

Nelson O'Brien, patriarch of the clan. Nelson emigrates from Ireland with his sister Kate in 1896. When she dies shortly thereafter, Nelson goes off to Cuba to photograph the Spanish-American War. When the fighting concludes, he sets up a studio in Santiago. When Mariela Montez sits for a portrait, Nelson begins wooing her. Shortly after their marriage, Nelson and Mariela move to Pennsylvania. Nelson continues to work as a photographer and, with the help of his many children, operates the Jewel Box Movie Theater. Outwardly cheerful, Nelson, a secret tippler, suffers from deep depressions.

Mariela Montez O'Brien, the matriarch of the clan. Soon after their marriage, Nelson takes her back to Cobbleton, a town that mystifies and terrifies the young Cuban woman. Mariela never masters English, becoming even more monolingual with age. After Mariela's death, her daughter Margarita discovers a cache of notebooks in which her mother reveals a complex emotional life unsuspected by the rest of the family.

Katherine Anne (Kate) O'Brien, Nelson's sister. She dies of pneumonia soon after she and her brother settle in Pennsylvania.

Gloria Montez O'Brien, the youngest O'Brien daughter. She suffers from an embarrassing crush on her brother, Emilio.

Isabel Montez O'Brien, the second O'Brien daughter. She marries a Cuban pharmacist and settles in Santiago, Cuba.

Lester Thompson, Margarita's wealthy and abusive first husband. He meets her while she is working in her family's theater. They are divorced after sixteen years of marriage.

Betsy MacFarland, Emilio's first wife. Claiming to be an ardent fan of his films, she seduces him. Their brief marriage ends in scandal, causing Emilio's departure from Hollywood.

Jessica Brooks, Emilio's beloved second wife. He meets her in Alaska, where she is running a restaurant. Their joyful marriage is ended by a fire that kills Jessica and their baby.

Leslie Howard, a courtly octogenarian pilot. Margarita meets him in the local library and marries him when she is ninety.

THE FOX

Author: D. H. Lawrence (1885-1930)
First published: 1923
Genre: Novella
Locale: The Midlands of England
Time: During World War I
Plot: Psychological realism

Ellen (Nellie) March, a co-owner of a Berkshire farm. Strong, authoritative, and almost masculine, Nellie is the decision maker on Bailey Farm, where she does most of the outdoor work. The stability on the farm between Nellie and Jill, the farm's vaguely fragile co-owner, is upset by two events in the story. The first is the appearance of a fox that frequently disturbs the quietude by stealing and murdering chickens. The second is the appearance of Henry Grenfel, a young soldier who soon decides to marry Nellie. The woman is thereafter torn between her desire for stability with Jill Banford and her attraction to the prospects of marrying Henry and going to Canada. In the end, she is left with Henry, but there is little hope for joy in this union.

Jill Banford, the other owner of Bailey Farm and best of friends to Nellie March. Nerve-worn and delicate, but warm-hearted, Jill functions in the novella as the losing vortex of the love triangle. Jill is taken aback by Nellie's prospects of marriage to Henry Grenfel, and she works constantly to thwart this outcome. At the end of the story, however, in what is seemingly a convenient accident, she dies when a tree being felled by Henry strikes her on the head. Her death ensures that Nellie will marry Henry.

Henry Grenfel, a young soldier who used to live on Bailey Farm with his grandfather. Henry, about twenty years old, is foxlike in every respect: He has ruddy, fair, and sharp features, and his mannerisms, which are quick, cunning, and animal-like, are becoming to a fox. He returns to the farm only to discover his grandfather gone; however, he quickly ingratiates himself with the two owners by doing odd chores and bringing home game for food. As a human animal, he predatorily kills the fox that is robbing the henhouse, pursues Nellie with operant male aggression, and works to effect the death of Jill so he can conquer Nellie.

The fox, the robber of the henhouse. An aggressive predator that simply takes what it wants, the fox is the symbol of the unleashed and unvarnished masculine ego at its worst. It plunders, rapes, robs, and murders at will. In so doing, it holds a domineering control over Nellie and Jill, although an indirect one. The fox appears in Nellie's dreams until it is shot by Henry, who then assumes the same predatory role more clearly.

Captain Berryman, Henry's commanding officer. Another figure of masculinity, Berryman gives Henry a twenty-four-hour leave after he realizes that the young soldier must be excused because of "problems with a woman."

Mr. Banford, Jill's father. Old and ineffectual, Banford stands in direct contrast to Henry. When Henry returns to the farm on leave, he discovers Banford attempting to cut down a tree, vaguely rendered as a phallic symbol. Henry immediately fells the tree, killing Banford's daughter in front of him.

— Carl Singleton

FOXFIRE: Confessions of a Girl Gang

Author: Joyce Carol Oates (1938-)
First published: 1993
Genre: Novel
Locale: Hammond, a small city in upstate New York
Time: 1952-1956
Plot: Psychological realism

Madeleine (Maddy) Faith Wirtz, the novel's narrator. Maddy lives quietly in New Mexico, where she works as an astronomer's assistant. Thirty-five years earlier, she was a member of FOXFIRE and the historian of that gang's violent exploits. Now, in 1989, the fifty-year-old Maddy is transcribing the notebooks in which she recorded the adventures of the girl gang in the early 1950's.

Margaret Ann "Legs" Sadovsky, FOXFIRE's first in command and the inspiration for most of its adventures. Sixteen years old when she brings the gang of misfit girls together, Legs is the product of a broken home. Her mother died when she was born, and her father (who may not be her biological parent) is an abusive alcoholic. Legs transcends her own awful beginnings to bring this gang of girls together into the only community they may ever know.

Elizabeth (Rita) O'Hagan, a slightly overweight young girl in the gang. Her sexual abuse at the hands of Mr. Buttinger, her ninth grade math teacher, precipitates the first act of FOXFIRE. The youngest of nine O'Hagan children, Rita was gang raped two years earlier by the Viscounts. Eventually, she will be banned from the gang for dating a boy.

Betty "Goldie" Siefried, the first lieutenant of FOXFIRE, who at the age of fifteen is five feet, ten inches, tall. She has been kept back in school so is in Maddy's class, "towering above everyone except the tallest boys."

Loretta (Lana) Maguire, the fifth of the founding gang members, a tall, good-looking platinum blonde with one weak eye.

Violet "Snow White" Kahn, one of several girls who join FOXFIRE later. Her beauty is used as a lure in some of the gang's worst crimes.

Whitney Kellogg, Jr., a Hammond industrialist whose attraction for Violet is used in his own kidnapping but whose religious conversion helps foil the plot.

— David Peck

THE FRAGMENTED LIFE OF DON JACOBO LERNER
(La vida a plazos de Don Jacobo Lerner)

Author: Isaac Goldemberg (1945-)
First published: 1976
Genre: Novel
Locale: Peru, primarily Lima and Chepén
Time: 1923-1935
Plot: Psychological realism

Jacobo Lerner, a Jewish businessman. After leaving Russia as a young man, he settles in Peru, where he attempts to start a business and marry a nice Jewish girl. He has to abandon his first store, however, because in a moment of weakness he gets a Catholic girl pregnant, and he cannot marry her. Eventually, he becomes prosperous as the owner of a brothel. He cannot marry the woman he loves because she is already his brother's wife; her sister, his second choice, breaks their engagement. When he becomes ill, those very people to whom Jacobo has been so generous are interested only in the financial implications of his death. At the age of forty-two, he dies.

Bertila Wilson (behr-TEE-lah), the mother of Jacobo's son. A shy girl of seventeen when she first meets Jacobo, she is so ignorant that she believes all of his invented adventures and is easily seduced. After Jacobo refuses to take in their son, she turns against the child.

Efraín Wilson (eh-frah-EEN), the illegitimate son of Jacobo Lerner and Bertila Wilson. A sensitive, confused boy, he is loved only by his great-aunt Francisca, who has told him that his father is dead. When he becomes aware of his Jewish background, however, he is abandoned by her and by the priest. Eventually, he goes mad and is kept in seclusion.

León Mitrani (leh-OHN mee-TRAH-nee), a grocer. A friend of Jacobo from the time of their youth in Russia, León precedes him to Peru. A former Bolshevik, in old age León turns back to Judaism. Hated by his blind, Catholic wife and disliked by the neighbors whom he reviles in his prophetic outbursts, he loses his trade. After he is killed by a careless doctor, his casket is lost somewhere on the road.

Moisés Lerner (moh-ee-SEHS), Jacobo's brother. Smug and hypocritical, he conceals the fact that he cheated Jacobo in a business they owned jointly and that later Jacobo saved him from bankruptcy.

Sara Brener Lerner (BREH-nehr), Moisés' wife. A chatty woman who admits that she cannot make up her mind, she is constantly balancing the opinion of the Jewish community against the possibility of financial gain. Realizing that Jacobo loves her, she is interested only in using him, whether to marry him off to her sister or to make a profit by taking in his son.

Miriam Brener Abramowitz, Sara's widowed sister. To regain her social position as a married woman, she is willing to marry Jacobo even though she does not love him. When she learns that he owns a brothel and supports a mistress, however, she breaks the engagement. Unknown to her, she is thereafter supported by Jacobo.

Juana Paredes (HWAH-nah pah-REH-dehs), Jacobo's Peruvian mistress. A woman whose main concern is her family, she has made sure that Jacobo feels responsible for her widowed sister and her sister's seven children. When he is dying, her primary concern is that she will get enough money for herself and for them.

Francisca Wilson, Efraín's great-aunt and foster mother. A devout Catholic, she loves him deeply until he discovers his own Jewish heritage; she then turns against him and consigns him to hell.

Samuel Edelman, a traveling salesman. A friend of Jacobo, he visits Mitrani and checks on Efraín; however, when he discovers that the boy has gone mad, he resolves not to tell the dying Jacobo.

— *Rosemary M. Canfield Reisman*

FRAMLEY PARSONAGE

Author: Anthony Trollope (1815-1882)
First published: 1861; serial form, 1860-1861
Genre: Novel

Locale: England
Time: The 1850's
Plot: Domestic

Mark Robarts, vicar of Framley in Barsetshire, a living he gained at the age of twenty-five through his friendship with the Lufton family. At a house party given by Sowerby, a man of whom Lady Lufton disapproves, he foolishly signs a note for four hundred pounds. When the note falls due, Sowerby has him sign another note he cannot pay. Sowerby is able, through political connections, to get Robarts a prebendal stall at Barchester. His friends feel that he has become too worldly. Events finally reach the point where Robarts is subjected to a sheriff's inventory because he is unable to meet his financial obligations. At the last moment, Lord Lufton appears and assumes responsibility for the debt.

Fanny Robarts, Mark's wife. She remains loyal to her husband through all his financial difficulties.

Lucy Robarts, the sister of Mark Robarts, who comes to live at Framley Parsonage when her father, a doctor, dies. Although quiet and shy, Lucy soon gains the love of the highly eligible young Lord Lufton, but his mother disapproves of the "insignificant" match. Although Lord Lufton proposes, Lucy honorably refuses until such time as his mother may approve. Lucy then goes to nurse Mrs. Crawley, the wife of a neighboring clergyman, stricken with typhoid fever. At the end of her stay at Hogglestock, Lady Lufton relents, and Lucy marries Lord Lufton.

Lady Lufton, the matriarchal ruler of Framley Court. Although she has made a pact with the mother of Griselda Grantly that their children will wed, she does not force her point of view once she sees that her son is not in love with Griselda. She pays her son's gambling debts and forgives Mark Robarts' folly in money matters.

Lord Ludovic Lufton, a close friend of Mark Robarts and a persistent suitor for Lucy's hand.

Nicholas Sowerby, the squire of Chaldicotes, an improvident and parasitical young man greatly in debt to the duke of Omnium. He uses both Mark Robarts and Lord Lufton in his financial dealings. At the suggestion of his sister, he proposes to Miss Dunstable, a very wealthy woman, in an effort to regain his fortune. Miss Dunstable wisely refuses the offer of marriage but buys Chaldicotes and allows Sowerby to live there.

Harold Smith, the brother-in-law of Sowerby and a member of Parliament who becomes Petty Bag when Lord Brock is made prime minister. His influence secures the prebendal stall for Mark Robarts.

Mrs. Harold Smith, the sister of Sowerby and good friend of Miss Dunstable.

Martha Dunstable, the wealthy heiress to a patent medicine fortune, humorously accustomed to refusing young men who seek her for her money. She admires Dr. Thorne, whom she marries, and they later live at Chaldicotes.

Dr. Thomas Thorne, a bachelor physician at Greshamsbury. Without worldly interests, he marries Miss Dunstable, but not for her money.

Mary Gresham, Dr. Thorne's niece, married to Frank Gresham, master of the hunt in Greshamsbury.

Lady Scatcherd, the widow of Sir Roger Scatcherd, a poor stonemason who became wealthy. She is friendly with Dr. Thorne.

Susan Grantly, the wife of Archdeacon Grantly of Barchester. Eager to get her daughter Griselda married, she defeats her arch-adversary, Mrs. Proudie, because Griselda marries Lord Dumbello, while young Olivia Proudie makes an unsuitable marriage.

Mrs. Proudie, the aggressive wife of the bishop of Barchester. Her efforts toward social position and elegance are constantly foiled.

Olivia Proudie, the oldest daughter of the bishop of Barchester; she marries a widower with three children.

Reverend Tobias Tickler, the widower who marries Olivia Proudie.

Griselda Grantly, the attractive daughter of Archdeacon Grantly. Her marriage to Lord Dumbello makes her the future marchioness of Hartletop.

The Duke of Omnium, the wealthiest landowner in Barsetshire. Although usually indifferent to politics, he exercises himself to remove Sowerby from Parliament.

Lord Brock, briefly prime minister of England.

Lord Supplehouse, an opportunistic politician who writes letters to the newspaper against Harold Smith.

Lord Dumbello, an unprepossessing nobleman who wins Sowerby's seat in Parliament with the help of the duke of Omnium.

Mr. Fothergill, agent of the duke of Omnium and a man of business, instrumental in Sowerby's defeat.

Tom Tozer, a shady moneylender who holds Mark Robarts' notes.

The Reverend Josiah Crawley, the clergyman at Hogglestock parish. He lectures Mark Robarts concerning the danger of worldliness in a parson.

Mrs. Crawley, his wife, who becomes ill with typhoid fever and is nursed back to health by Lucy Robarts.

Grace Crawley, the bright and charming oldest daughter of the Crawleys.

The Reverend Francis Arabin, dean of Barchester and an old school fellow of austere Mr. Crawley.

THE FRANCHISER

Author: Stanley Elkin (1930-1995)
First published: 1976
Genre: Novel
Locale: Various U.S. locations from the South to the West
Time: Primarily the 1970's
Plot: Picaresque

Ben Flesh, the franchiser (actually the franchisee), born in 1928. His parents die in 1944, and no one bothers to tell him. Two years later, he enrolls in the Wharton School of Business under the G.I. Bill. During his junior year, he inherits from his godfather the prime interest rate, the ability to use money at low cost. He subsequently uses it over the next three decades to buy various franchise operations in an effort not to make money but instead to homogenize the country, to cater to what he perceives is the American public's "esperanto of simple need," including his own need for family, his need to belong. Alone, unattached, and oddly without identity, he tries to turn the entire country into his home, buying the names of others in order to become those others, only to realize that what he has is not a life, only an itinerary. While endlessly crisscrossing the country by car, he discovers that he has multiple sclerosis (MS) and that the nation is suffering from an analogous energy shortage. Eventually, he decides to sell or mortgage all of his franchises for the sake of his Travel Inn, the newest, biggest, and, it turns out, least successful of all of his businesses. As interest rates rise in the 1970's, his business interests suffer. The novel ends with Ben more cheerful than ever; his euphoria, however, is a symptom of his disease.

Julius Finsberg, Ben's godfather. Having cheated Ben's father out of his share of their theatrical costume business, the now-wealthy Julius tries to make amends by giving the godson he has never seen the prime interest rate.

Estelle Finsberg, the fecund dancer whom Julius marries late in his life. Her death in the 1970's makes Ben the nominal head of the Finsberg clan.

Patty,
LaVerne,
Maxene,
Cole,
Owen,
Oscar,
Ethel,
Lorenz,
Jerome,
Noel,
Gertrude,
Kitty,
Helen,
Sigmund-Rudolf,
Mary,
Moss,
Gus-Ira, and
Lotte, the Finsberg children, eighteen in all, four sets of triplets and three of twins. Each is named for either a composer of or a singer in musicals, and each will die as the result of some grotesque and absurdly fatal malady, including bedwetting, cradle cap, lead-filled bones, baldness, and inability to menstruate or defecate. Ben becomes the lover of each of the Finsberg women and confidant of each of the men.

Nate Lace, a liquidator. He has recently purchased the Nittney-Lion Hotel in Harrisburg, Pennsylvania, from the inventory of which he sells the television sets Ben needs for his Travel Inn. He takes literally the businessman's maxim that a handshake is as good as a contract.

Flight Lieutenant Tanner, an Englishman suffering from Lassa fever—an incurable, generally fatal disease—whom Ben meets in a Dakota hospital. Tanner's British manner of speaking irritates the linguistically less fastidious, more exuberant Ben, as much as Tanner's being strapped to a wheelchair and perspiring blood disturbs him. Tanner is in turn critical of Ben's whining, advising this owner of a local ice cream franchise to "Be hard, Mr. Softee." Ben later speaks of Tanner as his friend but forgets his promise not to make a sad story out of Tanner's death.

Clara, a dance instructor at Ben's Fred Astaire dance studio. In her late thirties, she is attractive but without prospects now that Ben has decided to close the franchise.

"Doctor" Wolfe, the owner of a K-O-A campsite whom Ben meets at a conference in Miami. Married to a victim of MS, Wolfe, though not a doctor, is the first to diagnose Ben's disease. Wolfe ends his diagnosis with a laugh.

Roger Foster, the owner of an airport limousine service. He likes to dress up as Colonel Sanders of Kentucky Fried Chicken fame to enhance his own life and those of others, including Ben, who is completely fooled by Foster's impersonation.

A young hitchhiker, who is wary of Ben's friendliness and trust and therefore turns down an offer to manage one of Ben's franchises. He learns too late Ben's lesson: that opportunity knocks only once and has nothing to do with merit, only with luck.

An old hitchhiker, who was just released from prison, where he spent the last twenty years. His speech, clothing, and luggage appear weirdly out of date. He is precisely the kind of loser in whom Ben likes to invest his trust. Claiming that "the ordinary is all we can handle," he too rejects Ben's offer, offering instead his own piece of advice, that Ben "get a reality."

A nice young man, who speaks in public service announcements. Ben also picks him up as a hitchhiker.

— *Robert A. Morace*

FRANKENSTEIN: Or, The Modern Prometheus

Author: Mary Wollstonecraft Godwin Shelley (1797-1851)
First published: 1818
Genre: Novel
Locale: Europe
Time: The eighteenth century
Plot: Gothic

Victor Frankenstein, a native of Geneva who early evinces a talent in natural science. Having concluded his training at the university at Ingolstadt, he works until he discovers the secret of creating life. He makes a monster from human and animal organs found in dissecting rooms and butcher shops. The monster brings only anguish and death to Victor and his friends and relatives. Having told his story, he dies before his search for the monster is complete.

The Monster, an eight-foot-tall synthetic man endowed by its creator with human sensibilities. Rebuffed by man, it turns its hate against him. Its program of revenge accounts for the lives of Frankenstein's bride, his brother, his good friend, and a family servant. Just after Victor dies, the monster appears and tells the explorer that Frankenstein's was the great crime, for he had created a man devoid of friend, love, or soul.

Robert Walton, an English explorer who, on his ship frozen in a northland sea of ice, hears the dying Frankenstein's story and also listens to the monster's account of, and reason for, its actions.

Elizabeth Lavenza, Victor's foster sister and later his bride, who is strangled by the monster on her wedding night.

William Frankenstein, Victor's brother, who is killed by the monster while seeking revenge on its creator.

Henry Clerval, Victor's friend and a man of science who is killed by the monster to torment Frankenstein.

Justine Moritz, a family servant tried and condemned for William's murder.

FRANKENSTEIN UNBOUND

Author: Brian W. Aldiss (1925-   )
First published: 1973
Genre: Novel
Locale: Texas and Switzerland
Time: 2020 and 1816
Plot: Science fiction

Joseph (Joe) Bodenland, a liberal presidential adviser deposed by right-wing extremists. He is transported by a timeslip from the twenty-first to the early nineteenth century. He is a grandfather but becomes young again when the timeslip takes him back to 1816. He finds himself at Lake Geneva, near the Villa Diodati, where he meets Lord Byron, Percy Bysshe Shelley, and Shelley's mistress, Mary, who is in the process of writing the novel *Frankenstein*. Attracted to Mary, he has a brief affair with her. Having come from the future, Bodenland can foretell the ecological damage that will be wrought by technology run amok, by the conquest of nature symbolized by Frankenstein's experiments. Consequently, he kills Frankenstein and destroys both Frankenstein's monster and his mate.

Victor Frankenstein, a Swiss scientist. Unlike the Frankenstein of Mary Shelley's novel, who is an idealistic man of sensibility, this Frankenstein is a cynical, abrasive, and bitterly proud individual. Mary Shelley's Frankenstein destroys the monster's mate on which he is working, lest he create a race of monsters, and then pursues the male monster after it murders his bride, Elizabeth. In this novel, unlike Shelley's, Victor does not marry Elizabeth, nor is she killed. He completes the monster's mate and brings her to life. When he then proposes creating a third monster to fight the first two, Bodenland kills him.

Mary Wollstonecraft Godwin, the author of *Frankenstein*, the eighteen-year-old mistress and future wife of Percy Bysshe Shelley. When Bodenland encounters her, she is still in the process of writing her novel, which she insists is fiction. At the same time, however, some of the events in it, altered by the author of *Frankenstein Unbound*, are occurring in a parallel world. Mary has a brief, idyllic affair with Bodenland before he returns to Geneva to try to persuade Frankenstein not to proceed with his monster making.

George Gordon, Lord Byron, the well-known English Romantic poet, who is twenty-eight years old in this novel. In self-imposed exile from England because of his dissolute life and several sex scandals, the handsome, dashing, and cynical Byron is currently the lover of Mary's half sister, Claire.

Percy Bysshe Shelley, the well-known English Romantic poet, who is twenty-four years old in this novel. He is the author of *Prometheus Unbound*, from which the title *Frankenstein Unbound* was derived. A religious and political radical, Shelley deserted his wife, who drowned herself, and is currently the lover of Mary Godwin, whom he will later marry. A session in which Byron, Shelley, and Mary told tales of terror on a tempestuous night resulted in Mary writing *Frankenstein.*

The Frankenstein monster, a creature cobbled together from cadavers and brought to life by Victor Frankenstein. In the original novel by Mary Shelley, the monster is a highly articulate person of sensibility, benevolent until turned to rage and violence by repeated rejection. The monster of *Frankenstein Unbound* lacks sensitivity and is a coarse brute who mates violently with his bride.

The monster's mate, whom Victor Frankenstein destroys in *Frankenstein* before her completion. In *Frankenstein Unbound*, she is brought to life, mates with the monster, and flees with him, pursued by Bodenland, who kills them both. In a sinister touch, Victor gives her the face of Justine Moritz, an innocent maidservant hanged for the murder of Victor's brother, who was actually killed by the monster.

Elizabeth Lavenza, Frankenstein's betrothed. In *Frankenstein*, she is a gentle, sorrowful person killed by the monster on her wedding night. In *Frankenstein Unbound*, she is abrasive, has Bodenland arrested, and then disappears from the action, unharmed by the monster.

— *Robert E. Morsberger*

FRANNY AND ZOOEY

Author: J. D. Salinger (1919-   )
First published: 1961
Genre: Short fiction
Locale: New England and New York City
Time: November, 1955
Plot: Philosophical realism

Frances (Franny) Glass, the youngest of the seven extraordinary Glass children and focus of the "Franny" section of the book. She is a bright twenty-one-year-old college student and gifted actress who is in painful conflict with herself and the world. She is uneasy with the superficiality of her surroundings and their clash of egos. Her profound wish is for a spiritual dimension that would give her life a substance beyond all the posturing, grasping, and self-absorption that threatens to engulf her. Repressing her own feelings, she observes and feels guilty about her own disingenuousness. She is disgusted by her culture's artistic, educational, and religious forms of pretentiousness. In contrast to her pedantic boyfriend, she sees her deceased brother Seymour as the apotheosis of the pure poet. While having lunch at a fashionable restaurant with her boyfriend, she breaks out in a cold sweat and faints in the restroom. She feels that she is losing her mind and experiences an acute spiritual and psychological crisis. As a young woman who espouses self-effacement, she fears that as an aspiring actress she may be heading down the path of narcissism. A breakdown follows, and she quits the theater. She recuperates at her family's apartment in Manhattan with the help of her brother Zooey.

Lane Coutell, an Ivy League undergraduate and Franny Glass's boyfriend. He is shallow, pretentious, intellectually pedantic, and arrogant. He views Franny as an attractive object that enhances his own ego. Zooey Glass refers to Lane as a "big nothing." He is too self-absorbed to take note of Franny's impending breakdown.

Zachary Martin "Zooey" Glass, the youngest Glass son, a handsome and successful television actor. His honesty, talent, and unwavering standards of behavior leave most of those he encounters feeling stunned and Zooey himself with an ulcer. Before they are able to read, he and Franny receive an education in the great mystical and religious traditions from their older brothers Buddy and Seymour; Franny and Zooey both are haunted by the remnants of this early education. Zooey's lack of sympathy for the failings of others makes him a very unlikely person to help Franny during her breakdown. He cannot help challenging her motives for breaking down and her choice of the family couch as the stage for what he views as theatrical behavior. He calls Franny and pretends to be Buddy; in his own way, Zooey tries to comfort and guide his sister through her spiritual crisis. Exhorting Franny to return to her chosen profession of acting, he asks that she do it for God, if necessary.

Buddy Glass, Franny's favorite brother. He is a writer and recluse, the chief chronicler of the family saga. He is the author/compiler of the "Zooey" section of the book. Salinger's fiction is that Buddy is the actual author of some of Salinger's work, thus reinforcing the notion that the Glasses are flesh-and-blood creatures. In his preface to "Zooey," Buddy reveals that Zooey, Franny, and Mrs. Glass have separately advised him on reconstructing their stories. Each also finds fault with Buddy's finished product. Buddy refers to "Zooey" not as a long short story or novella but as a "prose home movie," an artistic creation designed for in-house viewing, a form of discourse in which events are captured by Buddy's camera eye and translated into images that the subjects themselves might watch and critique. For the Glass children, the obsession with self-consciousness, in the task of overcoming the entanglements of the ego, constitutes the stories' major dilemma. The Glass children's burden evokes their brilliance.

Seymour Glass, the eldest child of Les and Bessie Glass. He entered Columbia University when he was fifteen years old and by twenty-one is a professor of English; he also is a gifted poet and a mystic who attempts to answer the essential questions of Being. He commits suicide in 1948. This act is at the emotional and spiritual core of "Zooey," although it occurs seven years before the story takes place. The abiding mystery surrounding Seymour's death is whether his artist's soul is too pure for this world or instead he is a psychotic, shattered victim of the horrors of World War II. The end of Seymour's life—which focuses past and present—is at the tragic center of his siblings' lives.

Bessie Glass, the mother of the seven Glass children. In "Zooey," realizing that her husband is ineffectual, she tries to help Franny recover from her nervous breakdown.

— *Genevieve Slomski*

FRATERNITY

Author: John Galsworthy (1867-1933)
First published: 1909
Genre: Novel
Locale: London
Time: Early twentieth century
Plot: Social criticism

Ivy Barton, the girl around whom the story revolves. She is a lower-class country girl who is transported to the city to serve as a model for an artist, Bianca Dallison. Through no fault of her own, she causes trouble because she is pursued by the husband of the Dallisons' seamstress and befriended by Bianca's husband. Ivy Barton is finally abandoned by Hilary Dallison, who throws a handful of money on her bed in a rented London room and leaves her forever.

Hilary Dallison, a prosperous writer who found Ivy and brought her to London to pose for a painting by his wife, Bianca. His emotions for Ivy are a mixture of pity and love, but at the end he chooses his own way by refusing to befriend Ivy and by deciding not to return to Bianca, a woman with whom he has not lived as a husband for several years.

Bianca Dallison, Hilary's artist wife, who, though she refuses Hilary his marital prerogatives, still becomes extremely jealous when another woman attracts his attention, as Ivy does.

Mr. Hughs, a lecherous, suspicious ne'er-do-well who pursues Ivy, spies on her, and spreads gossip about her and Hilary. Finally, for beating his wife and wounding her with a bayonet, he is sent off to prison for a short time.

Mrs. Hughs, the Dallisons' seamstress, who lives a hellish existence with her husband. Nevertheless, she is still jealous of him; when she sees that he is enamored of Ivy, she tells the story to Bianca's sister, who makes the news known to the whole family. While her husband is in prison, Mrs. Hughs loses her baby because she is too nervous to nurse him.

Stephen Dallison, Hilary's brother, who tries to make Hilary see what his attentions to Ivy are doing to his reputation.

Mr. Sylvanus Stone, Hilary's father-in-law, who is writing a book on the brotherhood of man. His subject leads him to make philosophical remarks intended to instruct the reader on the subject of the classes in British society. Ivy works as a copyist for Mr. Stone.

Cecilia Dallison, Hilary's rather bland sister-in-law, whose chief concern seems to be the Dallison reputation in the community.

Thyme Dallison, Stephen and Cecilia's daughter, who helps the plot along by guessing that her uncle Hilary has bought the new clothes she sees Ivy wearing.

FREDDY'S BOOK

Author: John Gardner (1933-1982)
First published: 1980
Genre: Novel
Locale: The United States and Sweden
Time: The 1970's and the early sixteenth century
Plot: Symbolic realism

Jack Winesap, the first-person narrator of the realistic part of the text. Visiting a college, Winesap accepts a dinner invitation from Professor Agaard. Winesap endures Agaard's testy behavior and takes an interest in the book that his son, Freddy, is rumored to be writing. Freddy secretly shows Winesap his book; it is this "book within the book" that constitutes the remainder of the novel.

Sten Agaard, a professor of Scandinavian history and father of Freddy. Agaard is a wizened, older man of vinegary disposition and considerable social awkwardness. Despite these drawbacks, he often has keen insights into the fallacies of academia and its politics, and he is a devoted father. His embittered cynicism makes him an outcast among his peers and a problematic parent for Freddy.

Freddy Agaard, a semi-invalid and the only child of Professor Agaard. A young adult, Freddy is more than eight feet tall, obese, and extremely strong. He has childlike facial features and an extremely gentle, retiring nature. Freddy also has a predisposition toward sudden and largely unpredictable tantrums, during which he is capable of inflicting considerable damage. Freddy, therefore, has jailed himself in his father's house, where he pursues his remarkable but unshared talents in art and prose. The greatest of his achievements is "Freddy's Book," a tale of the turbulent and violent times surrounding Gustav Vasa's accession to the Swedish throne in the early 1520's. Crafted as a symbolic realist saga, Freddy's book is a sensitive and insightful investigation into the nature of the human heart, of good and evil, and of existence itself.

Gustav Vasa, the king of Sweden and one of the main characters of Freddy's book. Vasa and his friend Lars-Goren Bergquist are committed to regaining Sweden's independence by throwing off the yoke of their Danish overlords. In the process, Vasa is confronted by the Devil, who inspires the would-be king with plans for revolt and conquest. Although headstrong and often hotheaded, Vasa is neither greedy nor deceitful; rather, one ally characterizes him as being so utilitarian and driven by purpose that he is not really a human but an animal, a creature that has no inclination for contemplation of ideals or ideas. Vasa does have values: Although he accepts the Devil's counsel, he hates the demon and plans to slay the Devil once Sweden has been stabilized.

The Devil, a creature of infinite shapes and illusions. One of the most unusual characters in the book, he is able to assume any shape and uses this power to sow discord. Although never violent himself, he preys on the fears, desires, and lusts of humans, using these drives to encourage them into acts of destruction, betrayal, and degradation. Although he is a master of lies and rhetoric, the Devil has one weakness: He has a short attention span when it comes to the petty and inane conversations and plots of human beings. Ultimately, this proves to be his downfall, because such "inane" thoughts motivate and compel those who are sent to kill him.

Lars-Goren Bergquist, a knight known throughout Sweden as a just and fair man; he is Vasa's primary assistant. Lars-Goren thinks slowly but very well and clearly, and he fears nothing except the Devil. Consequently, when the Devil approaches Vasa and begins to influence the king-to-be, Lars-Goren is mute with fear. He continues to serve as Vasa's moral compass and also exerts a gradual but powerful influence over the cynical Bishop Brask. Most of Freddy's book follows the affairs and thoughts of Lars-Goren, the one character who is happy in his station, gladly accepting his lot in life and his pastoral existence.

Hans Brask, a cynical bishop and unreliable ally of Vasa and Lars-Goren. He is blessed with a gift for rhetoric and intellectual accomplishment. These strengths become the bishop's greatest weaknesses. Brask's ability to pierce façades, expose self-delusion, and investigate the disparities between idealistic dreams and the grim realities whereby people pursue them makes it impossible for him to believe in anything. Ironically, Brask is paralyzed by his own intellect. Condemning Lars-Goren at first, Brask eventually begins to gravitate toward the knight, uncertain of what is drawing him in that direction. It is fairly clear that Brask is drawn by Lars-Goren's steady dedication to justice and the intelligent faith that undergirds it.

— Charles E. Gannon

FREE FALL

Author: William Golding (1911-1993)
First published: 1959
Genre: Novel
Locale: Southeastern England
Time: 1917-c. 1950
Plot: Bildungsroman

Sammy Mountjoy, the narrator and protagonist, a well-known artist who has risen from abject poverty through his talents. In the novel, he is not concerned about his rise to fame, instead recounting his moral and spiritual development. He finds such development not in the gradually unfolding events of his life but in certain specific moments, recounted as memories. The most significant of such moments is when he lost his innocence and thus the freedom of choice; further, he took on guilt and experienced the bondage of the will. He feels his life is therefore divided into a before and an after. The before consists of his school life. The after begins at his high school graduation, which therefore becomes a graduation into slavery, a slavery that lasts up to his experience of despair in a cell of a prisoner-of-war camp. He owns this part of his life and feels guilt for it, even though he recognizes that he could have lived no other way. This prison experience has symbolically broken the prison of his own self-centeredness, so he can perceive the glory of life. This is where he is living as he writes the book. He realizes that others, like Beatrice, are trapped as a result of his past, and he must continue to bear responsibility.

Beatrice Ifor, the daughter of respectable shopkeepers. She attends Sammy's high (grammar) school and then trains to be a teacher near Sammy's art college in London. Even though she is pious and conformist, she is seduced by Sammy, who sees her as mysterious, nunlike, and secret. After trying to relate to her, he is appalled by her passivity, the role she adopts as victim, and her doglike devotion. Sammy's desertion of her is probably the main cause of her insanity.

Rowena Pringle, a teacher at the high school, specializing in history and religious education. She is a complex character, pious and fastidious, maintaining discipline through fear and emotional manipulation. She delivers spellbinding accounts of Bible stories. She has an inveterate hostility to Sammy, based, it is suggested, on her own repressed sexuality—she wants to marry the vicar. She accuses Sammy of dirty-mindedness to the headmaster.

Nick Shales, a brilliant and popular science teacher at the high school. He respects his students and relates closely to them. He, too, has risen from poverty and has become a socialist idealist. He believes in a rational, ordered world, and his exemplary life wins Sammy over both to his politics and to his atheism.

Ma, a fat, shapeless earthy woman at the bottom of the social pile. She has occasional work, frequents the pub, and makes up all sorts of stories as to the identity of Sammy's father.

Father Watts-Watt, a high church Anglican vicar, paranoid and battling to suppress his pedophilia and sexual fantasies. He is unable to relate to anyone, including Sammy, whose guardian he becomes on the death of Sammy's mother.

Dr. Halde, a university professor of psychology. He has been enrolled in the Gestapo to interrogate prisoners. He appears rational and urbane, his morality relativistic—the tempter figure. His methods do not win the approval of the army officers running the camp, but they open Sammy's eyes to his own nature.

— David Barratt

THE FREEDOM OF THE CITY

Author: Brian Friel (1929-)
First published: 1974
Genre: Drama
Locale: Derry City, Northern Ireland
Time: 1970
Plot: Social realism

Michael Joseph Hegarty, an unemployed young man who is engaged to be married and has plans for an education and a career. Twenty-two years old and of average looks and build, he is serious, even humorless. A very proper man, he has a staunch belief in the civil rights movement in Northern Ireland and fears its contamination by radicals and troublemakers. He trusts the British military forces not to use violence without provocation.

Elizabeth (Lily) Doherty, a cleaning woman, wife of a disabled worker, and mother of eleven children. She is physically worn but still shows traces of her youthful good looks. At the age of forty-three, she is sensible but still imaginative, and she joins Skinner in joking and play-acting when they take refuge in the mayor's parlor of the Guildhall. Her squalid life of overcrowded poverty is revealed in contrast with the opulence of the mayor's rooms.

Adrian Casimir Fitzgerald, called **Skinner**, a restless, keen-witted young man who has no home and often is in trouble with the police. Twenty-one years old and of very lean build, Skinner is the first to realize where they are when he, Lily, and Michael run for shelter. He is also the one who correctly assesses the situation and knows that the military will react violently. Although seemingly irreverent and careless, he is highly concerned with determining meaning and motive, pressing the other characters to explain why they participated in the march. He flirts with Lily and taunts Michael, persistently showing disrespect for the trappings of the mayor's rooms.

Dr. Dobbs, a sociologist who appears at intervals to offer an analysis of the effects of poverty and class. He alternates between making pompous statements and astute observations.

Liam O'Kelly, an Irish television reporter who gives periodic news reports on the action of the play. He presents the official media view of the Irish Republic.

The Judge, a nameless official who conducts the "investigation" that runs parallel to the main action of the play. He is the representative of British justice in Northern Ireland.

Ballad Singer, who appears at intervals to sing (and invite others to join in) impromptu verses composed on the "occupation" of the Guildhall and the deaths of Lily, Michael, and Skinner. The songs are of the traditional romantic and patriotic type, emphasizing martyrdom.

The priest, an unnamed cleric who gives last rites to the victims and sermonizes twice in the play. He vacillates, speaking out against both British authority and Irish militancy.

Brigadier Johnson-Hansbury, who commands the British and local Protestant forces outside the Guildhall and represents the British military presence in Northern Ireland. He is responsible for the shootings and testifies that the victims were armed. His testimony helps create the official version of the incident.

— *Heidi J. Holder*

FREEDOM OR DEATH
(Ho Kapetan Michales)

Author: Nikos Kazantzakis (1883-1957)
First published: 1953
Genre: Novel
Locale: Meghalo Kastro, Crete
Time: 1889
Plot: Historical

Captain Michales (meh-KAH-lehs), a Cretan patriot who dies fighting the Turks. Nothing matters to him except liberation of the island. When everyone else abandons the battlefield, he alone fights on, not listening to his wife, daughter, or elders. He is subject to drinking fits during which he commits atrocities against Turkish civilians. In the last moments of his life, raising aloft the severed head of his nephew Kosmas, he roars, "Freedom or—," but a bullet pierces his brain before he can finish the slogan.

Nuri Bey (BAY), the childhood friend and "blood brother" of Michales. He is married to a beautiful and voluptuous woman lusted after by many men, including Michales and Polyxigis. Nuri tries to win back his wife's affection in various ways. In a show of strength, he kills Michales' brother Manusakas but receives a knife wound that leaves him sexually impotent for the rest of his life. Demoralized, he wants to die in a fight or in war. When Michales comes to avenge his brother, he finds Nuri in such pathetic condition that he refuses to kill him. Losing this opportunity to die with some semblance of honor, Nuri commits suicide.

Eminé (eh-mee-NAY), the lusty Circassian wife of Nuri. She sings enchanting songs that leave men in rapture. Michales and Captain Polyxigis vie for her affection. She chooses Polyxigis and, after Nuri's suicide, marries him. She converts to Christianity from her original religion of Islam. Turks, enraged by her objectionable behavior, including marrying a Greek infidel, capture her and plan to make an example of her. Michales punishes himself for leaving his vitally important battle post to rescue her by going back and fighting to the death. Eminé is an important influence throughout the novel.

Captain Polyxigis (pah-LIHKS-ih-jihs), a courageous and important officer in the fight against the Turks. He is present when Eminé serenades her guests with rapturous love songs. Although Michales is in many ways more attractive, Polyxigis wins Eminé's love. She gives herself to him while married to Nuri. Nuri's suicide opens the way for Polyxigis and Eminé to marry.

Kosmas (KAHZ-mahs), a Europeanized nephew of Michales, an intellectual and a socialist who returns to his homeland with a Russian-Jewish bride. He has idealistic visions of revolution and freedom but is open-minded and kind-hearted. The fact that he has taken a Jewish wife is an indication of his liberalism. Under the influence of Michales, Kosmas is transformed into a revolutionary and fights alongside his uncle. Inexperienced in warfare, he is wounded, captured by the Turks, and beheaded. His youthful sacrifice inflames Michales' already burning desire for martyrdom.

Noemi (noh-EE-mee), the kindly and gentle wife of Kosmas, European in a cosmopolitan tradition. She endures the abuse of Kosmas' mother and sister. She becomes pregnant but has a miscarriage after Kosmas has left to try to bring Michales back. Kosmas' family makes a variety of unfavorable interpretations of this miscarriage.

Tityros (Tih-TEE-rohs), Michales' brother, an ineffectual schoolteacher who tries to become a more powerful member of his family. He is a weakling and feels this keenly. To acquire some semblance of power and control in his household, he poisons his young brother-in-law and in so doing drives his own wife, Vangelio, to commit suicide. These deaths affect him profoundly, and he experiences a sort of epiphany. He finds salvation in becoming a *Pollikaria*, fighting the Turks and preaching the revolution.

Sefakas (SEH-fah-kahs), Michales' father and Kosmas' grandfather, a patriarchal figure who can leap unaided onto his horse even after his hundredth birthday. He is a wise and respected member of Michales' household. Although proud of Michales and a patriotic Cretan, he is weary of his son's zealotry and continually questions the wisdom of war and killing. His questions are deep and thought-provoking. He dies right before his son is killed. His body is carried through town with the utmost reverence. The members of his family sense that a new beginning should come because of his death and erroneously believe his death might somehow bring about Michales' return from war.

— *Chogollah Maroufi*

THE FRENCH LIEUTENANT'S WOMAN

Author: John Fowles (1926-)
First published: 1969
Genre: Novel
Locale: Lyme Regis, Dorset, England
Time: 1867-1869
Plot: Symbolic realism

Charles Smithson, the protagonist, thirty-two years old in 1867, an amateur paleontologist and a gentleman of leisure. He lives somewhat passively and complacently in the expectation of inheriting a baronetcy from his uncle and marrying the daughter of a rich middle-class businessman. He unexpectedly falls in love with the mysterious Sarah and has an affair with her that jars him out of his conventionalized view of the world. He breaks off with Ernestina, who sues him for breach of promise and ruins his reputation, only to find that Sarah has disappeared by the time he returns to their meeting place. After searching fruitlessly for several years, he finds her, at which point the novel offers two different endings. In the first, she introduces him to the daughter conceived at the time of their one sexual encounter; the implication seems to be that they will have a future together. In the second, they part after a bitter argument that convinces Charles that he had been manipulated from the start and that she had never really loved him.

Sarah Woodruff, the mysterious and melancholy "French lieutenant's woman," about twenty-five years old, who becomes Charles's obsession. Born into a farming family of modest means, she nevertheless had obtained a sufficient education to make her living as a governess but is now a social outcast because of the affair she is supposed to have had with a French officer. In fact, she did not have an affair and is still a virgin but allows the rumors about her to persist for reasons that are never fully made clear to the reader. The narrator's pretended inability to read her mind (he is "omniscient" with regard to all the other characters in the novel) makes it impossible for the reader to determine whether she was genuinely in love with Charles and forced apart from him by circumstances, or simply using him in some way. The novel's multiple endings support both hypotheses.

Ernestina Freeman, Charles's fiancée, who is about twenty-one years old in 1867. She is the pampered only child of a wealthy merchant, pretty and fashionable but also naïve and very conventional.

Sam Farrow, Charles's valet, a Cockney in his early twenties with aspirations above his social class. He eventually betrays Charles to Ernestina's wealthy father by disclosing Charles's liaison with Sarah, primarily to ensure his financial future and to be able to wed Mary, the maid of Ernestina's aunt, prospects jeopardized by Charles's erratic behavior and his uncle Bob's remarriage late in life. Sam is rewarded with a job at Mr. Freeman's department store and rises in the ranks to be in charge of window displays.

Uncle Bob, Charles's rich, titled, and eccentric relative, whose estate he expects to inherit. The inheritance is blocked unexpectedly when the sixty-seven-year-old uncle marries a middle-class woman young enough to have children, which will pass the line of inheritance to them and leaves Charles untitled and much less wealthy than anticipated.

Dr. Grogan, a bachelor in his sixties, a freethinking physician who is, like Charles, a reader of Charles Darwin and a follower of the new scientific advances of the latter half of the nineteenth century. He is the primary advocate within the novel of the view that Sarah may be psychologically unstable or even a manipulative schemer rather than a victimized innocent.

Mrs. Poulteney, a wealthy and elderly widow, a sanctimonious hypocrite known for her acts of charity but actually sadistic and intolerant. She takes Sarah in as a companion, ostensibly out of charitable motives but really with the selfish end of furthering her own chances to reach heaven with a good deed.

— *William Nelles*

FRENCH WITHOUT TEARS

Author: Terence Rattigan (1911-1977)
First published: 1937
Genre: Drama
Locale: The south of France
Time: The 1930's
Plot: Comedy

Kenneth Lake, one of a number of students attending a summer foreign-language school on the French Riviera, in an idyllic existence upper-class students enjoyed in pre-World War II England. He is about twenty years old and good-looking in a vacuous way. He joins his friends in romantic frolics that involve the "ladies of the town." The circle of students, of which he seems to be the leader by virtue of his droll wit, is untouched by the domestic or foreign problems looming on the English horizon.

Alan Howard, another of the students, about twenty-three years old. He is dark, saturnine, and serious. The only student to resist the seductive Diana, he makes it clear that his ideal woman will be able to converse intelligently on various subjects, will possess all the masculine virtues and no feminine vices, should be just attractive enough to be desirable and to remain faithful to him, and will be in love with him. He is interested in becoming a writer despite his parents' wish that he follow in his father's footsteps as a diplomat; he thus serves as the author's surrogate. The play ends with his departure for London, Diana following closely on his heels.

Diana Lake, Kenneth's sister, a beautiful seductress about twenty years old who lives up to her mythical name. She joins her brother and his fellow students at the French-language school merely because her parents are in India. She snares males as different as Kit, Commander Rogers, and Brian. Pursuing Alan despite his resistance to her charms, she is a delightful shadow of the Shavian woman who pursues her man until he catches her. Her foil in the romantic intrigue of the play is the more stable and slightly less attractive Jacqueline Maingot, who, in this happy world, finally convinces Kit that he is not in love with Diana.

Jacqueline Maingot (zhahk-LEEN mahn-GOH), the attractive daughter of Monsieur Maingot, about twenty years old. She assists her father in his instructional duties and serves as a complicating factor in the romantic interest of the plot. Straightforward and serious, she confronts the wily Diana, who is bent on making victims of the males. Jacqueline resents Diana, whom Kit prefers. Eventually, Kit comes to his senses and admits his real love for Jacqueline.

Monsieur Maingot, the affable host and instructor of French for English students. His ferocious face and dark beard belie the affable earnestness with which he conducts the instruction of his pupils.

Kit Neilan, who is about twenty-two years old, fair, good looking, and easily ensnared by Diana's charms. He eventually comes to his senses, admitting to loving Jacqueline without having known it.

Brian Curtis, a thickset, carelessly dressed Scotsman about twenty-three years old. He is immodest and a zestful participant in the youthful pranks of the students. He takes advantage of "the green light" given him by Diana at one point but receives only a "sharp buffet on the kisser"; he laughs about the experience afterward.

Commander Rogers, a sober man of about thirty-five, with a dark complexion. Studying French in preparation for an interpretership, he is a stereotype of the admirable, stiff-upper-lipped Englishman. His ensnarement by Diana ends when she admits her love for Alan.

Lord Heybrook, a bright young schoolboy of fifteen. Awaited by Diana as her next possible conquest, he appears at the very end, only to disappoint her, his age causing her to pursue Alan to London.

Marianne, the requisite maid in a farce.

— *Susan Rusinko*

FRIAR BACON AND FRIAR BUNGAY

Author: Robert Greene (1558-1592)
First published: 1594
Genre: Drama
Locale: England
Time: The thirteenth century
Plot: Historical

Edward, the pleasure-loving prince of Wales. Delighted by the charms of the milkmaid, Margaret, he sends his friend Lacy to woo her. He is filled with jealousy when he learns that the courtier has won her for himself, but he quickly overcomes his anger and has their marriage solemnized with his own.

Lacy, the earl of Lincoln, a gracious young courtier who disguises himself as a farmer to visit Margaret. He feels no disloyalty in winning her love for himself, because he wishes to marry her and he knows that Edward's attentions would be fleeting.

Margaret, the fair maid of Fressingfield, whose youth and charm win the love of both the prince and Lacy. She is notable chiefly as one of the first romantic heroines in English drama.

King Henry III, Edward's father, who follows the prince to Oxford with his court.

Ralph Simnell, the king's rotund fool, Edward's companion. He revels in his opportunity to masquerade as the prince in Oxford.

Friar Bacon, the wise necromancer of Brasenose College, the only man capable of defeating Vandermast in a battle of wits. He breaks his magic mirror and renounces his studies when he sees the tragedies brought about by his skills.

Miles, his servant, a poor scholar. Notoriously stupid, he lets the friar sleep through his one chance to master his art, when the Brazen Head speaks. For his negligence, he is carried off to Hell on a devil's back, bragging about his mount.

Friar Bungay, another necromancer, inferior to Bacon, who magically prevents him from marrying Margaret and Lacy.

Jaques Vandermast, a learned doctor, brought by the emperor of Germany to dispute with Oxford's wisest men.

Elinor of Castile, the attractive young princess who is betrothed to Edward.

Burden, a spokesman for a group of learned doctors who visit Friar Bacon at Oxford to inquire about his proposed Brazen Head.

FRIDAY: Or, The Other Island
(Vendredi: Ou, Les Limbes du Pacifique)

Author: Michel Tournier (1924-)
First published: 1967
Genre: Novel

Locale: Speranza, an island off the coast of Chile
Time: 1759-1787
Plot: Mythic

Robinson Crusoe, a Quaker mariner from York, England. At the age of twenty-two, as a tall, red-haired, slender young man, he leaves his family to seek a fortune in the New World, but this ambition is thwarted by a shipwreck off an island on the South American coast. Robinson is the only human survivor. At first, he rails against his fate and his haven. He names the island "Desolation," and he builds a ship, the *Escape*, but cannot launch it. Robinson then experiences the first in a series of rebirths of personality and philosophy that occur during his twenty-eight-year ordeal. He rechristens the island "Speranza," and his pious, obsessive nature comes to the fore. He cultivates more crops than he could possibly need, and he legislates and codifies his existence. Robinson believes that he can even stop time when he chooses to shut off his water clock. He is, during this phase, a dry and avaricious man, yet he is ethical, successful, and moral by societal standards. After discovering a cavern on the island, Robinson adopts a more Earth-oriented, nonconventional outlook, and he develops a sensual nature. The island literally becomes his mistress; he copulates in the cave, in a tree, and in the soil itself. When this period of emotional and physical awareness is interrupted by the arrival of Friday, Robinson returns to the psyche that loves order, until Friday inadvertently blows up the island's buildings. Then, Robinson adopts a persona inspired by his Araucanian (South American Indian) companion. He lives in the present and enjoys nature but does not exploit it, he allows his hair to grow and his skin to darken, and he appears to be years younger. At this point, Robinson achieves a happiness based on harmony with his environment, particularly with the sun. When Friday leaves and Jaan appears, Robinson is on the threshold of a new life that will allow him to blend the multiple facets of the self he has developed.

Friday, an Araucanian native. A slender, extremely dark, and lithe young man, Friday is brought to the island for sacrifice by his fellow tribesmen. By accident, Robinson saves him; then, he is named by and becomes a companion to Robinson. Friday has an insouciant manner; he is equally content to follow Robinson's orders, nature's will, or his own whims. He feels at ease with animals, even those (such as vultures) that society abhors, but he is not averse to torturing or even killing them for his own ends. After he accidentally destroys Speranza's civilized ambience, Friday in many ways becomes the master of Robinson. Rather than take advantage of this situation, he shares his knowledge and cultural myths in a matter-of-fact way. Friday consistently possesses a dual nature. He is skilled in the ways of the island, enjoys the fairness of one-to-one combat with nature, such as in a battle with the goat Andaor, and is seemingly content. He has a simple inquisitiveness that can be callous. He is capable of being companionable, but his allegiance is easily seduced. Perhaps this is a result of his naïveté, which in the end proves dangerous. He abandons Robinson to go on board the *Whitebird*, a ship that discovers them. Although it is clear to Robinson, Friday does not understand that his fascinating new friends have destined him for the slave trade.

Jaan Neljapäev, a galley boy on the *Whitebird*. The twelve-year-old, fair-haired, and blue-eyed youth, born in Estonia, is an often-whipped and ill-rewarded servant of the ship's cook. When he serves Robinson's dinner, he senses his kindness. Later that night, when he sees Friday board the ship, he takes Friday's canoe and literally takes his place. Robinson renames him "Sunday."

Captain Pieter Van Deyssel, the skipper of the brig *Virginia*. A bulky, sardonic, Epicurean man, this Dutch commander accurately prophesies Robinson's future via the tarot cards during the fateful storm of September, 1759.

— *Katherine C. Kurk*

FRITHIOF'S SAGA
(Frithiofs saga)

Author: Esaias Tegnér (1782-1846)
First published: 1825
Genre: Poetry

Locale: Scandinavia
Time: The eleventh century
Plot: Epic

Frithiof, the Viking hero of this nineteenth century reshaping of a tale of ancient Scandinavia. After the death of his father and of the king his father served, Frithiof is humiliated by the new brother-kings, who refuse him their sister's hand in marriage. Frithiof is at last outlawed but acquires riches and glory as a sea fighter. He goes in disguise to the kingdom of the man now married to the woman he has consistently loved. He saves the lives of both king and queen, and the good king gives up his queen to Frithiof and makes him war-guardian of the kingdom. Frithiof succeeds to the throne after the king dies and later defeats his old enemies, the brother-kings, in battle.

Helge, one of the brother-kings. When Frithiof returns from a difficult journey to collect tribute money, he finds Helge's wife wearing the ring of gold he once gave to Ingeborg. In the resultant struggle, the temple is burned and Frithiof is outlawed. After Frithiof himself becomes king, the brother-kings wage war on him and Helge is slain.

Halfdan, the brother of Helge and co-ruler of the kingdom. At last, he is made to swear fealty to Frithiof.

Ingeborg, the sister of Helge and Halfdan, loved by Frithiof. Although she and Frithiof exchange vows and gold rings, she is forced to marry King Hring. She remains in love with Frithiof and, as a result of Hring's generosity, is at last united with him.

Hring, a Scandinavian king. Victorious in battle against the brothers, he extracts their promise to give him Ingeborg as a wife. Much later, when Frithiof appears disguised in the kingdom, Hring recognizes him but pretends not to until Frithiof has proved himself.

King Bele, the father of Helge and Halfdan. Dying, he warns them against losing Frithiof's friendship.

Thorsten Vikingsson, Frithiof's father, who has helped King Bele in the past. Dying, he requests his son to help the brother-kings.

Yarl Angantyr, the ruler of the Faroe Islands. The brother-kings send Frithiof to collect tribute money from him.

THE FROGS

Author: Aristophanes (c. 450-c. 385 B.C.E.)
First performed: 405 B.C.E.
Genre: Drama
Locale: The Underworld
Time: The fifth century B.C.E.
Plot: Satire

Dionysus (di-oh-NI-suhs), the god of wine and revelry, who combines in a farcical fashion many of the defects that the playwright ridiculed in his fellow Athenians—cowardice, egoism, lechery, effeminacy, and laziness—but is, nevertheless, the patron god of the drama. Inspired by a reading of Euripides' *Andromeda*, he resolves to journey to Hades to bring the tragic poet back to Athens. To facilitate his entry to the Underworld, he disguises himself as his kinsman Herakles, who had earlier made the dangerous trip. This is a ludicrous idea, because the two are of totally different natures, and Dionysus is terrified of the monsters he sees, or thinks he sees, along the way. Eventually, with the aid of a chorus of initiates into the Mysteries of Dionysus and Demeter, souls who enjoy a favored place in Hades, he enters the realm of Pluto. There he learns that the chair of tragedy, which Sophocles had refused to take from Aeschylus, the elder poet, has been usurped by Euripides, who, upon his arrival in the Underworld, gained the support of the rabble. Aeschylus has challenged Euripides, and Dionysus finds that he has been chosen to judge between them. He has each poet recite lines from his dramas, a situation that allows Aristophanes ample opportunity to parody the defects of each and to have Dionysus make critical comments, some incisive, some obtuse. At last, scales are produced. Because Aeschylus' verses are the weightier and because he has displaced Euripides in the affections of the god, Dionysus chooses Aeschylus to accompany him to the upper world. The chair of tragedy is left to Sophocles, and Euripides is contemptuously dismissed.

Xanthias (ZAN-thee-uhs), Dionysus' slave, who has been compared with Sancho Panza. He has a highly comical sense of the many wrongs his master visits upon him but too broad a humor to take them very seriously. He is not above taking mild revenge when the opportunity offers itself, and on several occasions he exhibits a shrewdness that makes Dionysus appear all the more foolish.

Euripides (ew-RIH-pih-deez), the tragic poet, presented in a very unfavorable light as a debaser of poetry and the drama, a purveyor of corrupt ideas and empty rhetoric, a sentimentalist, a weakener of the public morality, and a self-seeking pleaser of the mob. He is allowed, however, to make some telling criticism of Aeschylus' tragedies before he is defeated.

Aeschylus (EHS-kih-luhs), a tragic poet considerably more dignified than Euripides but not above shrewdness in argument against his opponent. He takes credit for stiffening the moral fiber of his countrymen, but he must bear charges of deficiency in dramatic action and the use of pompous language. His style at its best, however, is deemed far superior to anything Euripides can offer.

Herakles (HEH-ruh-kleez), the demigod, who advises Dionysus on his journey to Hades.

Charon (KAY-ruhn), the ferryman of the dead, who makes Dionysus row across Acheron. He will not admit Xanthias to the ferry, however, and the slave, loaded with baggage, is forced to walk around the lake.

Pluto (PLEW-toh), the god of Hades.

Aeacus (EE-uh-kuhs), usually one of the judges of the Underworld, here presented as Pluto's porter.

A Landlady of Hades and

Plathané (pla-tha-NAY), her servant, who attack Dionysus. They mistake him for Herakles, a great glutton, who had robbed them of food.

A Chorus of Frogs, who mock noisy spectators at the theater. At the entrance to Hades, they sing of the rain and the marshes.

A Chorus of Initiates, who praise the gods of the Mysteries, advise the citizens of Athens, and sing a farewell when Dionysus and Aeschylus return to the upper world.

FROM BAD TO WORSE
(Peor está que estaba)

Author: Pedro Calderón de la Barca (1600-1681)
First published: 1636
Genre: Drama

Locale: Gaeta, Italy
Time: The seventeenth century
Plot: Comedy

César Ursino (SEH-sahr ewr-SEE-noh), a fugitive from justice. Preparing to marry Flérida Colona, he is also having assignations with a veiled lady who has fired his imagination. She is Lisarda. A series of adventures involving mistaken identities follows and ends in César's marriage to Flérida.

Lisarda (lee-SAHR-dah), the daughter of Juan de Aragón. Veiled, she has been meeting César Ursino, the fiancé of Flérida Colona. Finally, following a succession of adventures during which a mistaken identity threatens her reputation, she is compelled, to save her honor, to give up César to Flérida and to marry Don Juan.

Flérida Colona (FLAY-ree-dah koh-LOH-nah), who is loved by César Ursino and finally becomes his bride after a series of complications brought about by his attraction to the veiled Lisarda.

Don Juan, César Ursino's friend and the suitor with whom Lisarda must be satisfied when César is paired off with Flérida Colona.

Camacho (kah-MAH-choh), César Ursino's servant, who marries Celia.

Celia (THAY-lyah), Lisarda's servant and Camacho's bride.

Juan de Aragón, the governor of Gaeta.

FROM CUBA WITH A SONG
(De donde son los cantantes)

Author: Severo Sarduy (1937-   )
First published: 1967
Genre: Novel

Locale: Cuba
Time: Primarily the 1950's
Plot: Experimental

Mortal Pérez (mohr-TAHL PEH-rehs), a common name from Dolores Rondón's epitaph ("come, mortal, and see") turned into a character. He is a blond Spaniard who speaks Castilian Spanish and who always possesses some attribute of power. He starts as an old general, when, in "By the River of Rose Ashes," he falls in love with and relentlessly pursues Lotus Flower. At first a voyeur, he ends as a would-be assassin. In "Dolores Rondón," he is a politician rising from provincial obscurity to national prominence as a senator. His fall comes when it is revealed that the Hawaiian dancer he procured for the president is a mulatto woman from his province. In "The Entry of Christ in Havana," he is a young elusive lover ardently desired by Auxilio and Socorro. Later, he is identified with the wooden statue of Christ found by them in the Cathedral of the Cuban Santiago and is taken triumphantly to Havana. He disintegrates on the way and, finally, dies.

Auxilio (owk-SEE-lee-oh) and

Socorro (soh-KOH-rroh), metaphysical twins in perpetual transformation. (Both names mean "call for help" in Spanish, but they appear as "Help" and "Mercy" in some translations.) They start looking for God, only to find all the principal characters in a "self-service" grocery store. In "By the River of Rose Ashes," they are chorus girls (at the burlesque Chinese opera in Havana), transvestites, and, occasionally, prostitutes. They also help the old general with his passion for Lotus Flower. In "Dolores Rondón," they act as the magic twins, or tricksters, of Afro-Cuban religion. They reveal the senator's fraud. In "The Entry of Christ in Havana," they are two Spanish women in love with Mortal, whom they pursue from the origins of European lyric in Arabic poetry through the discovery of the New World. Having arrived in the Cuba of the early colonial days, they learn music in the Cathedral of Santiago, where they find a wooden statue of Christ, with whom they identify their elusive lover. In a triumphant procession, they take the statue to Havana. They are received by gunfire from helicopters.

Lotus Flower, a transvestite who is an actress in the Chinese burlesque opera house in Havana and is pursued desperately by the general Mortal Pérez.

Dolores Rondón (rrohn-DOHN), a young mulatto woman from the provinces, mistress and wife of the senator Mortal Pérez. Her new high life enters into conflict with Afro-Cuban religion, and the offended deities cause the fall of the senator. She returns to the province and dies in poverty, summarizing her life in an epitaph she writes for her tomb as a lesson to all mortals.

The Great Bald Madame, **Death**, a character presented as the final essential ingredient of the cosmic jigsaw puzzle.

Myself, a personal pronoun turned into a character. It represents the authorial voice, which later splits into a dialogue between Narrator One and Narrator Two.

The Director, who stages the show at the burlesque opera house. He seems to be another incarnation of Myself.

The reader, who struggles with Myself and the Director for the proper meaning and the realism of the work.

— Emil Volek

FROM HERE TO ETERNITY

Author: James Jones (1921-1977)
First published: 1951
Genre: Novel

Locale: Hawaii
Time: The months before the bombing of Pearl Harbor in 1941
Plot: Naturalism

Private Robert E. Lee Prewitt, a soldier stationed with the U.S. Army in the Hawaiian islands. He is rebellious and proud, but he loves the Army and is a good soldier. He is also an excellent bugler and boxer. He requests a transfer into Captain Holmes's company (G Company) because the company commander of the Bugle Corps replaced him as first bugler. Holmes and the sergeants of G Company pressure Prewitt, in increasingly forceful ways, to box on the company team. Prewitt, who once blinded a friend while sparring, refuses, despite the fact that boxing would ensure that he has an easy time and offer a promotion to corporal and the job of first bugler for G Company. He later goes absent without leave after killing the sergeant who beat a friend of his to death in the stockade. He is shot while attempting to return to his company after the Japanese attack Pearl Harbor.

Alma Schmidt, who now calls herself **Lorene**, a prostitute at the New Congress Club who becomes Prewitt's lover. Formerly a waitress in Oregon, she came to Hawaii after her boyfriend married someone else. Prewitt wants to marry her. He even offers to box, so that he can become a sergeant and get posted back to the mainland United States. Lorene refuses. She does not want to marry a soldier. Her goal is to make enough money to be able to go back to Oregon, buy herself and her mother a house, live an ordinary middle-class life, and be "proper."

Sergeant Milton Anthony Warden, the first sergeant of Prewitt's company. Thirty-four years old, efficient, and cool-headed, he, not Captain Holmes, really runs the company. He is tough but fair with his men, and they respect him. He begins an affair with Karen Holmes and soon falls in love with her. She wants him to become an officer so that he can get a post on the mainland; she could then leave her husband and marry him. He despises officers, but he agrees. When it comes to the point of applying for the commission, however, he cannot bring himself to do it; like Prewitt, he is "married" to soldiering. He and Karen finally separate.

Captain Dana "Dynamite" Holmes, Prewitt's company commander and the company's boxing coach. He has been cheating on his wife for years, and they are estranged. Self-centered and concerned with his status, Holmes links his company's boxing success to his chances to become a major; as a result, he tacitly encourages the men on the boxing team to give Prewitt "the treatment" until he agrees to fight. Finally pushed to the limit, Prewitt enters a fight with a sergeant who taunts him once too often. Holmes sees them fighting and does nothing to stop them, not realizing that the regiment's colonel is watching. Because of this incident, Holmes is forced to resign. He and his wife return to the mainland.

Karen Holmes, Captain Holmes's wife. She is beautiful but cold in her manner, and she has a "reputation." After becoming her lover, Warden confronts her with the stories he has heard about her past. She lashes back with her own story: Her husband, who began sleeping with other women soon after they were married, gave her gonorrhea, and she had to undergo a hysterectomy. After that, she says, she had an affair of her own. She loves Warden, but when he refuses to apply for an officer's commission, she realizes that they can never marry. She leaves Hawaii with her husband.

— *Jocelyn Roberts Davis*

FROM THE RIVER'S EDGE

Author: Elizabeth Cook-Lynn (1930-)
First published: 1991
Genre: Novel
Locale: On and near the Crow Creek Indian Reservation in South Dakota
Time: 1967
Plot: Regional

John Tatekeya (tah-TAY-kee-yah), a Dakota cattle rancher on the Crow Creek Indian Reservation in South Dakota. Tatekeya has watched with sadness and regret as his culture changed through assimilation with the white culture. The Missouri River, harnessed by a series of dams for water power, now covers some valuable Dakota lands, and Christianity has made inroads, with many Dakota replacing the traditional worship of the Four Winds. Tatekeya, in his sixties, longs for the old days and ways but realizes they are gone. He struggles to live by the old values but finds it difficult in the midst of so many changes. A successful rancher until almost half of his herd is stolen, Tatekeya decides to seek redress in court. He soon discovers that the justice sought in a court of law is contrary to his own values. As his own flaws of laziness, drunkenness, and unfaithfulness are brought out in court, Tatekeya finds himself, rather than the defendant, on trial. Although Tatekeya wins his case, he feels that he loses when Jason Big Pipe, a neighboring Dakota and a relative through ritual, testifies falsely against him. Realizing that American legal justice is not what he wants, Tatekeya risks a mistrial to discover the motives of the Big Pipe brothers. Family and cultural ties are more important to Tatekeya than the verdict.

Aurelia Blue, Tatekeya's lover for many years. Although she is more than thirty years younger than Tatekeya, Blue also longs for the old Dakota ways and culture. She is a solitary woman who cares for her elderly grandparents. She, by nature, feels the loneliness of existence and comes to accept the idea that nothing—not even attempting to hold on to old values—can assuage her loneliness or provide her with peace. She realizes that her relationship with Tatekeya must end and accepts Jason Big Pipe's attentions despite his betrayal of her lover in court.

Rose Tatekeya, Tatekeya's wife, who after thirty years of marriage moves into town to live with her married daughter. She stops attending the trial once her husband's relationship with Aurelia Blue is mentioned in court. Once the trial is over, she returns to her husband to continue their life together. Theirs was a traditional arranged marriage, one of the last in their community, and they respect each other and the bond that their marriage symbolizes.

Benno, a Dakota who appears in the novel only through Tatekeya's memory. As a child, Tatekeya hunted geese with Benno, who was an old man at the time. Tatekeya remembers Benno as a teacher and singer and as a man of ethical influence. He epitomizes for Tatekeya the old ways and the ideal. Benno, holding fast to tradition, refused to choose or accept an allotment of land when the Missouri River Power Project took over the Dakota land.

Jason Big Pipe, a young man related to Tatekeya; his grandfather and Tatekeya's father participated in a ceremony making them brothers. Jason Big Pipe testifies falsely against Tatekeya at the trial and successfully woos Aurelia Blue after the trial begins. Once the case is over, Big Pipe reveals to Tatekeya that he testified falsely to protect his own brother, who had taken part in the cattle theft. Despite his false testimony, Big Pipe also reveres Dakota values, including the importance of responsibility to family and to communal life.

Walter Cunningham, Tatekeya's lawyer, a district attorney born to Quaker parents in New Haven, Connecticut. He occasionally represents Native Americans but does not understand how the trial undermines Tatekeya's values. Cunningham underestimates Tatekeya's intelligence and moral code.

— *Marion Boyle Petrillo*

FROM THE TERRACE

Author: John O'Hara (1905-1970)
First published: 1958
Genre: Novel
Locale: Pennsylvania, New York City, and Washington, D.C.
Time: The first half of the twentieth century
Plot: Social

Raymond Alfred Eaton, a boy who, especially after the death of his older brother, is emotionally neglected by his father and is disillusioned by his mother's increasingly apparent alcoholism and infidelities. He develops a strong sense of self-sufficiency while boarding at Knox Preparatory School, while attending Princeton University, and while serving with the Navy during World War I. He becomes a handsome and remarkably poised young man, exhibiting a genuine charm balanced by a polite reserve. He falls in love with Victoria Dockwiler and then Norma Budd, but his willfulness causes both relationships to end abruptly and badly. In these relationships and his two marriages, his faith in the long-term value of behaving sensibly comes close to being a rationalization of a selfish insensitivity. Likewise, in his professional relationships, his propriety isolates him in his successes. His self-assurance allows him to underestimate those who are more unself-consciously calculating. A staunch Republican, he is determined not to be used politically. He does not recognize until too late that his enemies are able to force him from MacHardie and Company and possibly to compromise the integrity with which he has handled his duties as assistant secretary of the Navy. Although financially secure, he ends up without a position and without purpose. After a long recovery from a hemorrhaged stomach ulcer and after Natalie gives birth to a stillborn son, he is reduced to a pitiful willingness to serve on meaningless social committees and to perform demeaning errands for his former associates.

Samuel Eaton, Alfred's father, a hard-nosed and unimaginative businessman. He devotes himself to the management of his steel mill. Devastated by the death of his first son, he alienates his wife and Alfred. Almost perversely, he dies on the day of Alfred's wedding to Mary St. John.

Martha Eaton, Alfred's mother. She reacts to Samuel's selfish grief by becoming an alcoholic and by having affairs with a neighbor named Miller, who commits suicide, and with a Philadelphian named Frolick, whom Alfred beats. In her later years, in moments of lucidity, she accuses Alfred of being like his father.

William Eaton, Alfred's older brother. He seems more readily personable and athletic than Alfred. At the age of fourteen, he dies of spinal meningitis.

Sally Eaton, Alfred's sister. She is his confidant, keeping him informed about family matters. She marries Harry van Peltz, has several children, and is widowed at a relatively young age.

Constance Eaton, Alfred's sister. For many years, she carries on an affair with a man who will not divorce his wife for her.

Victoria Dockwiler, Alfred's first love. A beautiful, assertive woman, she resents his attempts to monopolize her. To spite him, she goes for a drive with Peter van Peltz, and they are both killed in a wreck.

Norma Budd, Alfred's first lover. Seven years older than Alfred, her delight in him as a boy becomes a deeper rapport with him as he matures. After Victoria Dockwiler's death, she becomes his mistress. Alfred alienates her by objecting to her obvious promiscuity. She is later murdered by a married lover who then commits suicide.

Alexander (Lex) Thornton Porter, who for a long time was Alfred's closest friend. Through several misadventures with upperclassmen, they form such a bond at Princeton that Alfred becomes, in effect, a member of Lex's wealthy, indulgent New York family. Charmingly arrogant and impulsively energetic, Lex shows his lack of business sense in their partnership in the Nassau Aeronautical Corporation. Later, Lex marries Clemmie Shreve, one of Alfred's former lovers, without knowing the extent of that involvement. They open a dude ranch in Wyoming and seem happy until he reenters the military after Pearl Harbor; in his absence, she becomes promiscuous. Wounded in both world wars, he returns from the second clearly dissipated. While on his way to a hospital for further surgery on his wounded leg, he is killed, along with one of his mistresses, in a train wreck.

James MacHardie, Alfred's employer. He hires Alfred after Alfred saves MacHardie's grandson from drowning. A shrewd speculator with regimented habits, he sees much of himself in Alfred.

Creighton Duffy, James MacHardie's son-in-law. A Wall Street lawyer and, eventually, an influential member of the Roosevelt Administration, he resents what he sees as Alfred's arrogance, especially because Alfred has saved his son's life and is clearly a favored associate of his father-in-law. He encourages Alfred to go to Washington, D.C., but then helps to undermine Alfred's future with MacHardie and Company.

Tom Rothermal, a boy from a hardworking, lower-middle-class family in Port Johnson, Pennsylvania. He borrows money from Alfred to finish his college education. He works for various public utilities until he becomes a prominent, left-wing labor organizer. He makes no attempt to disguise his loathing for those who have inherited wealth, but he is ambitious to make himself financially secure through stock speculations. He joins Creighton Duffy, whom he despises, in undermining Alfred professionally and politically.

Mary St. John, Alfred's first wife. She marries Alfred because of her strong sexual attraction to him and because she believes that he will become a financial success. Disenchanted by his sometimes lengthy absences on business trips for MacHardie and Company, she becomes promiscuous. Eventually, she regards Alfred as a hypocrite because he will not agree that love is a passing emotion and that sexual gratification, within and outside a marriage, is a basis for whatever contentment is to be had. Strikingly beautiful even in middle age, she grants him an easy divorce and plans to find a new husband before she starts to lose her looks.

Jim Roper, a young man from a middle-class family in Wilmington, Delaware. He is unofficially engaged to Mary St. John when she rejects him for Alfred Eaton. After working his way through medical school, he pursues Mary and convinces her to have an affair with him. He takes up a psychiatric practice, has many lovers from among his patients, and becomes a sort of avant-garde celebrity in New York City. Eventually, he discovers that he is a homosexual and begins to choose lovers for Mary instead of committing adultery with her himself.

Jack Tom Smith, a Texas oilman who becomes acquainted with Alfred in the Navy. He seems at first straightforwardly unpretentious, but as he becomes older, his crassness about his great wealth becomes more apparent. After Alfred's illness, he invites Alfred and Natalie to use his house in California and offers Alfred a position in his corporation. He has for a long time admired Alfred's breeding, but when he sees Alfred losing his self-assurance, he uses an ill-timed snub by Alfred as an excuse to attack Alfred's self-esteem.

Natalie Benziger, a resident of Gibbsville, Pennsylvania, who is ten years younger than Alfred. When they meet, she agrees with Alfred that it is love at first sight and carries on an intermittent affair with him, meeting him in hotels in various cities where he has business or where she has a social engagement. The lack of a clear future depresses her to the point of breaking off the affair. She marries Ben Eustace, a former Pennsylvania football star, whose alcoholism is fueled by the knowledge that she will never love him as she loves Alfred. After he slaps her during one of their arguments, she moves to New York City and works in a clothing shop to be near Alfred. When they finally marry, she is warily ecstatic, but when it becomes clear that he will not recover his self-assurance, she begins to despise him.

— Martin Kich

THE FRUIT OF THE TREE

Author: Edith Wharton (1862-1937)
First published: 1907
Genre: Novel
Locale: The United States
Time: Late nineteenth century
Plot: Social realism

John Amherst, an assistant mill manager. Concerned with the low standard of working conditions at the mill, he endeavors to convince Bessy Westmore, the owner, of the necessity for improvement. Impressed by her apparent interest in the project, he marries her, only to be disillusioned by her unwillingness to make any sacrifice in the cause. On her death, he marries Justine Brent.

Bessy Westmore, a mill owner and John Amherst's first wife. Selfish and self-indulgent, she disillusions her husband by her lack of interest in the working conditions at the mill. She is paralyzed by an injury and dies of an overdose of morphine she has begged from her nurse, Justine Brent.

Justine Brent, the nurse who becomes John Amherst's second wife. As a companion to Bessy Westmore, she nurses Bessy after she is paralyzed by an accident. She gives in to her patient's pleading for release from pain and administers an overdose of morphine, an act that is to plague her life as John Amherst's wife.

Dr. Wyant, Bessy Westmore's physician, who guesses the truth about her death and uses the knowledge to blackmail Justine Brent.

Mr. Langhope, Bessy Westmore's father.

Cicely Westmore, Bessy Westmore's daughter.

Dillon, a millhand whose injury brings to the fore the miserable working conditions at the mill.

Mrs. Harry Dressel, a friend of Justine Brent.

FRUITS OF THE EARTH

Author: Frederick Philip Grove (Felix Paul Greve, 1879-1948)
First published: 1933
Genre: Novel
Locale: The prairies, near Winnipeg, Manitoba, Canada
Time: 1900-1920
Plot: Historical

Abe Spalding, a successful pioneer. Standing six feet, four inches, he is a giant both literally and figuratively within the district that bears his name. More than a hardworking farmer, Abe possesses intelligence and foresightedness that help him survive a series of problems ranging from drought and flood to family disgrace and death. Only thirty years old when the novel opens, Abe devotes the next twenty years to building a legacy for his family. Eventually, after surviving numerous crises, he realizes not only that his material affluence is ephemeral but also that it is unwanted by his offspring. As each child moves away from home, Abe feels that the family heritage he has fought to establish is slowly slipping away. With that insight comes the realization that his life has been pointless, and he slips into a depression. By the closing pages, however, he has found a new purpose for his life: He leads a battle against the post-World War I decadence growing in Spalding District.

Ruth Spalding, Abe's wife. The daughter of small-town merchants, she has difficulty adjusting to the life of a prairie wife. Not even capable of milking cows, she resents Abe's preoccupation with the farm and with district politics. As her slim figure becomes "plump" and, later, "stout," she sequesters herself inside their shack and isolates herself from the community. With four children to rear, she badgers Abe to build a larger house and refuses to acknowledge his financial concerns about losing the farm. After twelve years of marriage, he is able to save enough money to build her dream house. Ironically, one of their children is killed when the construction is completed, and their palace becomes a shell rather than a home. When Frances, their youngest daughter, becomes pregnant out of wedlock, Ruth decides to handle the situation on her own and, perhaps for the first time, realizes how dependent on her husband she has been.

Charlie Spalding, their oldest child. A perceptive and sensitive boy, he is the only family member able to establish a close bond with Abe. His tragic death in a farming accident when only twelve years old has a profound impact on Abe, causing him to question his values and his goals.

Jim Spalding, their second-oldest child. Tall and muscular, he prefers a detailed rather than a holistic approach to life. Jim is labeled, by the principal, as disrespectful when he challenges a fact asserted by one of his teachers. Ruth forbids him to leave school, so he manages to get expelled and moves to Somerville, where he pursues his ambition of becoming a car mechanic.

Marion Spalding, their third child. A tall, feminine version of Charlie, she moves to a boarding school, where she studies to become a teacher. During her visits home, Abe becomes increasingly disturbed by her glowing appearance, believing that she has engaged in immoral sexual behavior. When an aspiring young lawyer asks Abe for permission to marry Marion, Abe demands that they wait one year before the ceremony takes place.

Frances Spalding, their youngest child. She resembles her brother Jim in disposition though not in appearance; she is short. Like her sister, she studies to become a teacher. Frances becomes romantically involved with McCrae, a married farmhand. When Ruth learns that Frances is pregnant, she tricks McCrae into confessing so that he can be brought to trial.

Nicoll, Abe's first neighbor and closest friend on the prairie. Described as medium-sized, middle-aged, bearded, and deliberate, he often acts as an intermediary between Abe and the other farmers. Nicoll deeply admires Abe and is responsible not only for getting the district named after him but also for getting Abe elected as a councilman. When Ruth confronts McCrae about Frances, Nicoll serves as a witness.

Charles Vanbruik, a retired physician. An educated man of slight build, he originally serves as an antipode to his brother-in-law Abe. After Abe endures the death of his oldest son, Charlie, he turns to the doctor for advice and companionship.

McCrae, a farmhand. Supercilious and arrogant, he belongs to a gang of men who seduce young girls. When Abe leaves town on business, Ruth has McCrae arrested for raping her daughter Frances, but McCrae manages to beat the charge.

— *Coleen Maddy*

FULL MOON

Author: P. G. Wodehouse (1881-1975)
First published: 1947
Genre: Novel
Locale: Blandings Castle, an estate in Great Britain
Time: Mid-twentieth century, after World War II
Plot: Farce

Clarence Threepwood, the ninth earl of Emsworth, the vague and woolly-headed master of Blandings Castle, somewhere in Shropshire. In the opinion of his younger brother Galahad—who has had ample opportunity to form a reasoned judgment—his IQ is about thirty points lower than that of a not-too-agile-minded jellyfish. He is ruled by whichever of his ten sisters happens to be in residence at Blandings, in this case Lady Hermione Wedge. The widowed father of Freddie Threepwood, he is devoted chiefly to his black Berkshire sow, the Empress of Blandings.

The Hon. Galahad Threepwood, the fifty-six-year-old younger brother of Clarence. He has headquarters in Duke Street, St. James, and subsists on a younger son's allowance from the Threepwood estate. He is one of the great London figures at whom the world of the stage, the race course, and the rowdier restaurants point with pride. Although strongly disapproved of by his sisters, he is the only genuinely distinguished member of his family. He masterminds a scheme to put the Empress of Blandings in Veronica's bedroom as a means of breaking down Tipton Plimsoll's shy reserve and concocts a variety of schemes to keep Bill Lister at Blandings until his union with Prue Garland is accepted by her family.

William Galahad "Blister" Lister, the godson of Galahad Threepwood, son of a sporting journalist and a Strong Woman on the music-hall stage. A painter of limited talent, he has just inherited from his uncle a pub on the outskirts of Oxford. His broad nose, prominent ears, prognathous chin, and heavily muscled body give him the general aspect of a kindly gorilla. He is in love with Prudence Garland, but his suit is determinedly opposed by her mother, Lady Dora, and by Lady Hermione Wedge. With the aid of Galahad, he appears at Blandings in various aliases, two of them artists commissioned to paint a portrait of the Empress of Blandings.

Tipton Plimsoll, a rich young American educated in England. He has just inherited from his uncle Chet Tipton (a longtime crony of Galahad Threepwood) a controlling interest in Tipton's Stores, with branches in every small town throughout the Middle West. Tall and thin, with a beaky nose and horn-rimmed spectacles, he is by virtue of his enormous wealth the welcome suitor of Veronica Wedge.

Prudence Garland, the only daughter of Lady Dora and Sir Everard Garland, K.C.B. Trim, slim, and blue-eyed, she is in love with Bill Lister and has been exiled to Blandings Castle to prevent further developments along that line.

Veronica (Vee) Wedge, the only daughter of Lady Hermione and Colonel Egbert Wedge. Twenty-three years old, she is the least intelligent but most beautiful girl registered among the collateral branches in the pages of Debrett's Peerage. Once engaged to her cousin Freddie Threepwood, she is courted successfully by the American millionaire Tipton Plimsoll.

Lady Hermione Wedge, the sister of Lord Emsworth and chatelaine of Blandings Castle. She is the wife of Colonel Egbert Wedge and mother of Veronica. Unlike her numerous tall and stately sisters, she is short and dumpy and looks like a cook. Her self-appointed mission is to encourage the courtship of her daughter by Tipton Plimsoll and to discourage the courtship of her niece Prudence Garland by Bill Lister.

Colonel Egbert Wedge, the husband of Lady Hermione for twenty-four years and father of Veronica. He is the retired colonel of a cavalry unit.

Lady Dora Garland, a relict of the late Sir Everard Garland, K.C.B., and one of Lord Emsworth's tall and beaky sisters. She lives on the fourth floor of Wiltshire House, Grosvenor Square, London. Acutely alive to the existence of class distinctions, she vigorously opposes the courtship of her daughter Prudence by Bill Lister, to prevent which she ships Prue off to Blandings Castle.

The Hon. Freddie Threepwood, the younger son of Lord Emsworth, who has inherited his father's intelligence but shows much of his uncle Galahad's energy and enterprise. Once engaged to his cousin Veronica, he is now a vice president of Donaldson's Dog-Joy in Long Island City and happily married to Niagara "Aggie" Donaldson. Back in England to build the English end of the dog biscuit business, he is headquartered at Blandings Castle while calling on Shropshire gentry to generate large orders for Donaldson's Dog-Joy.

The Empress of Blandings, a black Berkshire sow who is the apple of Lord Emsworth's eye. She was twice in successive years a popular winner in the Fat Pigs Class at the Shropshire Agricultural Show. Placed in Veronica Wedge's bedroom, she elicits a scream that brings Veronica and Tipton Plimsoll together.

— *Daniel H. Garrison*

THE FUNERAL: Or, Grief à-la-mode

Author: Sir Richard Steele (1672-1729)
First published: 1702
Genre: Drama
Locale: London, England
Time: Early eighteenth century
Plot: Comedy of manners

The earl of Brumpton, a British nobleman. Believed dead, he recovers immediately after the funeral but is persuaded by his faithful servant to remain "dead" until his survivors reveal their true characters.

Lady Brumpton, his young wife by a second marriage. Having gotten him to disown his only son, she is delighted with her presumed widowhood and large fortune. She plots to ruin the earl's two young wards, but counterplots are successful. Even after the earl's reappearance, she hopes to regain his favor, but when it is revealed that she has a still-living first husband, she loses everything.

Lord Hardy, the earl's son by a first marriage. An officer in the army, he remains steadfast in his loyalty to his father even after his disinheritance. In love with one of his father's wards, he is at last united with her and reinstated as his father's heir.

Mr. Campley, Lord Hardy's friend and junior officer. He is in love with the earl's other ward, whom he helps to escape in disguise from the Brumpton mansion.

Lady Sharlot, who is loved by Lord Hardy. She hides in the earl's empty coffin, which Lord Hardy's soldiers take by force from the Brumpton mansion.

Lady Harriot, Lady Sharlot's sister and the earl's other ward. He gives his blessing to her marriage with Mr. Campley.

Trusty, Lord Brumpton's faithful servant and the only person present at the earl's recovery. He recognizes the opportunity to prove Lady Brumpton's falsity.

FUNERAL GAMES

Author: Mary Renault (Mary Challans, 1905-1983)
First published: 1981
Genre: Novel
Locale: Greece, Egypt, and Asia Minor
Time: 323-286 B.C.
Plot: Historical

Alexander the Great, the charismatic Macedonian conqueror of Asia. He dies in Babylon at the age of thirty-two. (Later references to Alexander will be to this person, Alexander III.)

Alexander IV, the son of Alexander and his Asiatic wife Roxane. Inheriting her dark complexion but his father's keenness, he learns Macedonian ways under his Greek pedagogue, Kebes, and shows promise of ability to inherit his father's kingship but is poisoned in boyhood by Kassandros.

Antigonos (an-TIHG-uh-nuhs), who is nicknamed **One-Eye**, having lost an eye fighting in Phrygia for Alexander. He is promoted from general to satrap of Phrygia to commander in chief in Asia and is the founder of the Antigonid dynasty.

Antipatros (an-TIHP-ah-trohs), the regent of Macedon at the time of Alexander's death. He retains the regency well into old age, despite the hatred of Alexander's mother, Olympias. On his deathbed, he appoints Alexander's staff officer Polyperchon guardian of the kings, passing over his own son, Kassandros.

Bagoas, Alexander's Persian boy, brought to him at the age of sixteen by a Persian general involved in King Darius' murder. He is twenty-three at the beginning of this narrative. He later accepts the protection of Ptolemy in Egypt.

Eurydike (yuhr-IH-dih-kee), a descendant on both sides from Macedonian royalty, named **Adeia** until her betrothal to Philip III. A tall, fresh-faced, athletic girl of fifteen at the time of Alexander's death, she tries to use her marriage to Alexander's mentally retarded half brother as a stepping-stone to power but finds herself out of her depth.

Kassandros, the eldest son of the Macedonian regent Antipatros, a lifelong enemy of Alexander but deeply envious of his magic. Although he conspired to poison Alexander, his father Antipatros passes him over for the regency. Ambitious for the throne, he is a successful contender in the power struggle that follows the death of Alexander. He is an unsympathetic figure.

Kleopatra, Alexander's sister, the Queen of Molossia and widow of Alexandros, King of Molossia. Her betrothal to Perdikkas ends with his death.

Meleager, a phalanx commander since Alexander's first command. He has risen no higher, however, having been appraised by Alexander as a good soldier if one did not stretch his mind. An enemy of Perdikkas, he is the first to exploit Philip III as a pretext for seizing power after Alexander's death.

Olympias, the mother of Alexander and widow of Philip II of Macedon. She is the daughter of King Neoptolemos of Molossia. She attempts to manipulate events in favor of Alexander IV.

Perdikkas (puhr-DIHK-uhs), the second in command to Alexander after the death of his beloved Hephaistion. Perdikkas receives Alexander's ring on the great king's deathbed. He uses his betrothal to Kleopatra to support his claim to the succession and is opposed to Eurydike's betrothal to Philip III. Unsuccessfully, he attacks Ptolemy's forces in Egypt and is killed in a mutiny of his officers.

Philip III, the son of Philip II by a minor wife and first named **Arridaios** before his exploitation by various opportunists seeking to profit from his royal ancestry. He is epileptic and mentally impaired and is protected by Alexander. His physical resemblance to Alexander's father aids his claim to the succession. A pathetic figure, he is married to Eurydike and becomes her puppet.

Ptolemy (TOL-eh-mee), a staff officer of Alexander and reputedly his half brother, later king of Egypt and founder of the Ptolemaic dynasty. Able but not brilliant or overly ambitious, he is the only genuinely successful one of Alexander's successors. Author of a history of Alexander, he establishes a stable regime in Egypt and lives into old age.

Roxane, Alexander's young widow, the mother of Alexander IV. Murderously ambitious for her son, she poisons her pregnant rival Stateira but eventually dies by poison with her son.

Stateira, Alexander's second wife, whom he married at Susa, and the daughter of Darius III. Nearly six feet tall, she has inherited much of her famous mother's beauty. Pregnant at the time of Alexander's death, she is poisoned by her rival Roxane before she can bear a claimant to the succession.

— *Daniel H. Garrison*

FUNNYHOUSE OF A NEGRO

Author: Adrienne Kennedy (1931-)
First published: 1969
Genre: Drama
Locale: New York City
Time: The 1960's
Plot: Surrealism

Sarah, also referred to as **Negro**, a student and poet who has retreated to the room that contains her treasures. She is a pale black woman who wants either to deny her black heritage or to die. Wearing black clothes and an executioner's rope, Sarah has masses of frizzy hair, one clump of which she carries with her, but only blood for facial features. She verbalizes the internal conflict between her ancestries as a trap from which she cannot extricate herself despite surrounding herself with white friends to guard against recognition of her black birthright. Sarah sees her father as God but cannot reconcile his rape of her with her image of him as Christ and believes that she split her father's head with the ebony mask. Sarah's "funnyhouse" is the only safe place she knows, and her "selves" are the only ones with whom she interacts lovingly, but they are deceptions. Finally, her father overcomes her, and Sarah is found hanging in her room.

Patrice Lumumba, also called **Man** and **Wally**, one of Sarah's selves. He sees himself not as the murdered savior of the black race but as a now-crucified Judas who has betrayed mother, wife, and child. A large black man with a shattered head, Lumumba has no identifiable face; the area of his face is covered by blood and skull fragments. He carries an ebony mask. Like Sarah, Patrice Lumumba wants to barricade himself with friends and externals against his black heritage. He is Sarah's father, who raped her mother because she would not voluntarily consummate the marriage. Lumumba, although in conflict between his guilt and fear and his need to fulfill his mother's expectations of him as a savior, pleads with Sarah to accept him and to help him save their race. Sarah's escape to her mother exacerbates the denial of her African ancestry. Sarah's father has died violently but continues to return. He appears to embody the part of Sarah that relates to the time she spent with her family in Africa.

Duchess of Hapsburg, one of Sarah's selves, mirrored by both Victoria Regina and Jesus. She empathizes with Sarah's fear and challenges the father's right to return. The duchess reinforces Sarah's belief in her room as a safe place. Concealed behind an alabaster facial mask, she carries a red paper bag of her kinky hair and futilely attempts to return it to her head while simultaneously reflecting Sarah's need for Raymond to hide her so that she can escape the suffering of her father's world. Failing to resolve the conflict, the duchess, hanging from a chandelier and decapitated, is discovered by an impotent Jesus. She is the female embodiment of white European tradition.

Queen Victoria Regina, one of Sarah's selves, who denies her place in the black world she believes to be evil. In facial appearance, she is a twin to the duchess. Queen Victoria is dressed in a royal but poor-quality white satin gown. The queen is interested in the motivations behind events. With understanding, she unmasks pieces of Sarah's essence for the duchess and for Sarah herself. Ultimately powerless, Victoria

Regina represents the repulsiveness of a white-distorted reality, and she witnesses Sarah's death.

Raymond, the **Funnyhouse Man**, a tall, anorexic-looking Jewish poet dressed in black. He initially displays a dispassionate attitude toward Sarah, whom he sees as a sadistic, suffering liar. He opens and closes the blinds in Sarah's bedroom just as he opens and closes insights into her life. Raymond first states that her father shot himself but contradicts himself after Sarah's suicide with the statement that Sarah's father is "married to a white whore" and living as Sarah's selves have fantasized. Raymond has the insane laugh of a funnyhouse greeter. He may be Sarah's boyfriend. He appeals to the part of Sarah that denies her African American background.

Sarah's Landlady, called the **Funnyhouse Lady**, whose real name is **Mrs. Conrad**, a lanky white busybody who increases her own sense of importance by revealing intimacies about Sarah such as details of her hair loss when traumatized and of her father's suicide. The Funnyhouse Lady also has the insight to know, however, that Sarah sees only her room and her own perceptions as truth and that she has defined the rest of the world as "they." Mrs. Conrad responds with false sympathy and genuine hostility to Sarah's suicide. The landlady's identifying characteristic is the inappropriate laugh of an insane funnyhouse greeter.

Jesus, one of Sarah's selves. He reinforces her internal conflict by being caught between the white mother and the black father. An impotent, hunchbacked, pale Negroid dwarf, he carries a red paper bag containing his hair. Jesus, betrayed by his own spiritual belief system and his need to deny being black, decides to kill Lumumba in the name of white royalty because God cannot be his father if his father is black. He is the embodiment of Sarah's religious background.

The Mother, Sarah's mother. Once symbolized by a dove but now consumed by rage because of her rape by a man she loved, Sarah's mother mumbles and sleepwalks in a white nightgown while she holds a bald head. She is bald, has been institutionalized, and has died because she allowed a black man to touch her. Even though Sarah shows her constant devotion, her mother denies Sarah's existence because Sarah is black.

— *Kathleen Mills*

THE FUTILE LIFE OF PITO PEREZ
(La vida inútil de Pito Pérez)

Author: José Rubén Romero (1890-1952)
First published: 1938
Genre: Novel
Locale: Michoacan and Morelia, two provinces in Mexico
Time: The 1920's and 1930's
Plot: Picaresque

Jesús Pérez Gaona (heh-SEWS PEH-rehs gah-OH-nah), or **Pito Perez** (PEE-toh), the protagonist, a thin, long-haired, drunken rogue dressed in rags. He works as a street peddler in Morelia. During his vagabond life, he has assumed various occupations, such as druggist's assistant, sacristan, jailer's secretary, and general store clerk. His adventures inspire his incisive and satirical observations of human nature. He firmly believes that society's injustice and hypocrisy have made him a loser. He feels fully justified to lie, cheat, and steal his way through life. He considers his shamelessness to be a sign of his honesty, and he observes that people can relax only when they have no reputation to maintain.

José de Jesús Jiménez (hoh-SEH deh heh-SEWS hee-MEHN-ehs), a corpulent and lethargic druggist. He is Pito Perez's first master. Pito fled when the druggist discovered Pito's love affair with the druggist's wife. Under the druggist's tutelage, Pito learned the tricks of the pharmaceutical trade.

Father Pureco (pew-REH-koh), the dim-witted priest of La Huacana, who employed Pito as his sacristan. Pito supplied him with Latin phrases to embellish his sermons, as his parishioners appreciated him much more when they did not understand what he was saying. Pito left his service because he received no salary and was not allowed to drink liquor.

José Vásquez (VAHS-kehs), a jailer and champion drinker. He and Pito were drinking companions. Pito became his secretary but promptly left that position when Vásquez proved to be dictatorial and self-serving. Pito left Vásquez's employ with great disdain for representatives of the law.

Pito Perez's Uncle, the bearded owner of a general store. He fired Pito for misusing the store's earnings. Pito extended credit to customers without keeping records and used the store's income to finance dances on the outskirts of Morelia.

Irene (ee-REHN-eh), the tall, dark, and slender child of a poor family. She was Pito's neighbor and first love. Pito serenaded her for a year on his flute until he found out that his brother, Francisco, already was courting her.

Chucha (CHEW-chah), Pito's olive-skinned cousin whose father owns the general store where Pito worked. She charmed Pito into allowing her to take money from the store's cash box. Pito asked his friend, Santiago, to request her hand in marriage for him. Instead, Santiago asked to marry her himself. From this incident, Pito learned that his bad luck in life extended to the pursuit of romance.

Soledad (soh-leh-DAHD), a happy, seductive woman who plays the guitar. Pito kept the account books for her and her mother's business. Pito's romance with her ended abruptly when she married the town's new tax collector.

Caneca (kah-NEH-kah), a female skeleton that Pito calls his wife. Pito claims that she is the perfect mate because she is faithful to him, makes no demands, and has no bodily functions or odors.

Narrator, a rich poet who convinces Pito to tell his life story in exchange for *aguardiente* (liquor). The book comprises the narrator's memories of his conversations with Pito.

— *Evelyn Toft*

G

G.

Author: John Berger (1926-   )
First published: 1972
Genre: Novel

Locale: Italy, England, and Trieste
Time: Late nineteenth century through the beginning of World War I
Plot: Historical

G., the protagonist. Though described as an "ugly, intense young man," he is very successful with women; he is seduced by his cousin Beatrice at the age of fifteen. As he gets older, his complexion grows sallower and his face thinner, making his nose appear larger. G. is a cynic who does not believe in "the Great Causes." He does what he wants, ever in search of more conquests and new experiences. Although people assume that he must be an idealistic dreamer because of his actions (for example, he becomes a spy in Trieste for the Allied side), he seems to be the exact opposite, except that, at the end, he does take Nuša the passport he promised her, heedless of his own safety. It is uncertain if this gesture is merely a way of ensuring Nuša's seduction. G. is killed because his actions have become so arbitrary as to indicate that he is a traitor, though he is not, because he holds no allegiances.

Laura, G.'s mother. A short woman with fair hair and a somewhat retroussé nose, Laura is described as being the opposite of her lover Umberto's wife, Esther. Laura enjoys being unconventional: She married at the age of seventeen but two years later, in public, told her husband never to come back. The idea of having a child out of wedlock seems to her to indicate self-sufficiency rather than disgrace. Once she has the child, she is not interested in rearing him, but she will not allow Umberto to rear him either. Instead, Laura deposits G. at her cousins' farm in England. Later, however, Laura takes G. to meet his father in Italy.

Umberto, a wealthy Italian candied-fruit merchant, G.'s father. Umberto is devoted to his mistress, Laura, though he never allows her to meet him in Livorno, where his wife lives. He does not see his son until G. is eleven years old, and he dies in 1908. G. adopts the guise of a wealthy Italian candied-fruit merchant when he is in Trieste, an identity that would have been his had he been Umberto's legitimate son.

Jocelyn, Laura's cousin. A large, handsome man with pale blue eyes, he is the last remnant of an English upper-class family. He is a bachelor but maintains an incestuous affair with his sister, Beatrice. He and Beatrice are G.'s guardians while G.'s mother, Laura, is away, and it is on their farm that G. is reared.

Beatrice, Jocelyn's sister. Five years younger than her brother, Beatrice breaks away from him when she marries and moves to Africa. After she is widowed, however, she returns to the family farm, where she seduces G. Beatrice stays in G.'s memories for the rest of his life, though he does not attempt to look her up when he returns to England as an adult.

Charles Weymann, a friend of G. He is the pilot on one of the first night flights ever made, on which G. is his passenger. A small, dapper man with blue eyes and a bow tie, Weymann cannot understand why G. does not want to learn how to fly; in general, he is disgusted by G.'s increasingly cavalier behavior.

Geo Chavez, an aviator friend of Weymann and G. He is a small young man with dark eyes and full lips. He becomes the first person to fly an airplane across the Alps, though he is fatally injured in a crash landing. His character corresponds to a historical figure, Jorge "Geo" Chavez, a Peruvian flyer. Chavez and G. are in the same hospital after G. is shot by a cuckolded husband.

Nuša (NEW-sheh), a Slovene girl born in the Karst. G. meets her in Trieste, in the garden of the Museo Lapidario, also called Holderlin's garden. Her brother, Bojan, is a member of the Young Bosnians, the group responsible for the assassination of Archduke Francis Ferdinand in Sarajevo, an act credited with being responsible for the beginning of World War I. Nuša decides to go along with G.'s invitation to a fancy ball so that she can obtain G.'s passport, with which her brother can escape to France.

Marika von Hartmann, the Hungarian wife of an Austrian banker. G. is fascinated by her mouth and nose, and it is on this basis that he decides to have an affair with her. She is a large-boned woman with a thick, muscular neck, and she walks unsteadily: Her gait resembles that of a camel. She still wishes to have an affair with G. even after he shows up at the ball with the peasant girl Nuša, who is dressed as an upper-class woman.

Wolfgang von Hartmann, Marika's husband. A stout, wealthy man, he gives permission to G. and Marika to have an affair but is then offended when G. flaunts his connection with Nuša. Finding himself emotionally outmaneuvered by G., von Hartmann tries to have G. arrested by the Austrian government for espionage.

— T. M. Lipman

GABRIELA, CLOVE AND CINNAMON
(Gabriela, cravo e canela)

Author: Jorge Amado (1912-)
First published: 1958
Genre: Novel
Locale: Ilhéus, Bahia, Brazil
Time: 1925-1926
Plot: Social realism

Gabriela, a mulatto girl from the backlands. She comes to Ilhéus, in the Brazilian province of Bahia, to escape the drought. Her physical charms, including cinnamon-colored skin that always smells of cloves, and her ingenuous personality make her irresistible to everyone she meets. She is hired by Nacib Saad, the owner of a local bar. She lacks formal education, but her ability to prepare delicious Bahian dishes and her beauty soon make the bar popular. Gabriela and Nacib become lovers, a situation that pleases the girl. For her, sex is a natural part of life that should be shared with whomever she chooses. She and Nacib marry, making her a member of an exclusive social circle. The trappings of affluence restrict her physically and emotionally. Their marriage is annulled after Nacib finds Gabriela in bed with another man, but soon the estranged lovers are reunited and resume the same type of relationship they enjoyed before their marriage.

Nacib Saad, the Syrian owner of the Vesuvius Bar. He passionately loves Gabriela and wants to be the only man in her life. He marries her but soon notes that her passion is not as intense as it was before the marriage. When he finds her with Tonico, he wants to kill her, as any betrayed Brazilian husband should. He cannot do so, and in failing, he reflects the modern attitude gradually taking hold in tradition-bound Ilhéus.

Mundinho Falcão, a young businessman from a prominent family in Rio de Janeiro. As the political rival of Ramiro Bastos, Mundinho represents progress in Ilhéus. He hires an engineer to devise a plan to remove a sandbar and obtains accreditation for the local school. Such contributions turn the community toward a more modern way of life.

Ramiro Bastos, a wealthy old cacao planter who has controlled local politics for decades. His influence in government has been valuable in the past, but he finds himself challenged by the young, dynamic Mundinho Falcão. Bastos represents the traditional patriarchal system of Ilhéus.

Tonico Bastos, the son of Ramiro Bastos. He lacks his father's political talents. A regular at the Mount Vesuvius Bar, he works as a notary public. In this capacity, he prepares the documents for Gabriela's marriage to his best friend, Nacib. Known as a ladies' man, Tonico struggles to keep his affairs secret from his wife.

Malvina, the daughter of cacao planter Melk Tavares. She reads "controversial" books and insists that she does not want the kind of traditional marriage that her parents have. Her love affair causes gossip and precipitates a brutal beating by her father. Unable to tolerate such a repressive atmosphere, Malvina leaves Ilhéus.

Colonel Jesuino Mendonca, a planter whose murder of his wife and her lover becomes the talk of Ilhéus. According to tradition, he acted honorably and should not be punished. As progress spreads throughout the area, however, tradition is replaced by justice, and he receives a prison sentence.

GALILEO
(Leben des Galilei)

Author: Bertolt Brecht (1898-1956)
First published: 1943
Genre: Drama
Locale: Florence, Padua, Rome, and Venice
Time: 1609-1637
Plot: Historical

Galileo Galilei (gah-lee-LAY-oh gah-lee-LAY-ee), a forty-five-year-old lecturer at the University of Padua and a subject of the Republic of Venice. He lives with his daughter, Virginia; his housekeeper, Mrs. Sarti; and her bright son, Andrea, whom he enjoys instructing in his research in astronomy and physics. He is fat, self-indulgent, sensuous, and crafty, a glutton for both old wine and new ideas, a hedonist but also a great teacher as well as scientist. Frustrated by his meager pay, which he must supplement by private tutoring, Galileo accepts the invitation to improve his material circumstances at the court of Florence, dominated by the Medici. In Florence, Galileo's research confirms the Copernican cosmology of a sun-centered universe. Ordered to avoid further inquiry into astronomy, Galileo obeys for eight years. When the progressive Cardinal Barberini becomes the new pope, however, Galileo obsessively resumes his work on sunspots. As his subversive ideas become popular, the Inquisition first warns and then imprisons him. In 1633, threatened with torture, Galileo recants. Although he secretly continues his work, he regards himself as a traitor to both science and society at large. He believes that had he held out against the Inquisition, scientists might have developed something like the physicians' Hippocratic oath, a vow to use their knowledge only for the good of humankind.

Andrea Sarti (AHN-dreh-ah SAHR-tee), Mrs. Sarti's son, who is eleven years old in the first scene and thirty-nine in the last. He is an ardent pupil of Galileo, enjoying a father-son relationship with him. In the recantation scene, Andrea leads Galileo's disciples in passionately affirming their faith in the truth of his discoveries and the courage of their master. After Galileo's disavowal of his work is announced, the distressed Andrea greets his returning teacher with contemptuous insults. In his last meeting with Galileo, Andrea refuses to accept Galileo's self-revilement, then successfully smuggles Galileo's masterwork across the Italian border. He ends the play by introducing some boys to scientific reasoning, just as

Galileo began by initiating Andrea into the scientific method.

Virginia, Galileo's daughter. She is a pious devotee of church dogma who has neither interest in nor understanding of her father's work. In turn, Galileo shows little concern for her welfare: He insults Virginia's reactionary fiancé to the point of causing the young man to break the engagement. During the abjuration scene, she prays fervently that Galileo will see the error of his challenge to the church's guidance. The Inquisition places Virginia in charge of her father's submissive conduct for the remainder of his life. She is forty when the play concludes.

Mrs. Sarti, Galileo's housekeeper. She braves even the plague to care for him. She is shrewd, salty, practical, and wholly devoted to his welfare.

Ludovico Marsili (lew-doh-VEE-koh MAHR-see-lee), the smug, spoiled son of reactionary, rich, landowning aristocrats. He briefly becomes Galileo's private pupil in Venice and enters an eight-year engagement with Virginia. He abruptly terminates it, however, when he witnesses Galileo's defiance of the Inquisition's strictures against conducting astronomic research.

Cardinal Barberini (bahr-BEHR-ee-nee), a liberal mathematician who befriends and impresses Galileo during a masked ball in Rome. When Barberini becomes Pope Urban VII, however, he finds himself subject to the pressures of both the Inquisition and the aristocracy allied with the church. He reluctantly yields to the Inquisition's insistence that Galileo be interrogated. Although the new pope refuses to sanction Galileo's torture, he does permit the showing of the instruments of physical coercion to the scientist. That suffices to frighten Galileo into disavowing his research.

— *Gerhard Brand*

THE GAMBLER
(Igrok)

Author: Fyodor Dostoevski (1821-1881)
First published: 1866
Genre: Novel
Locale: German watering places
Time: Mid-nineteenth century
Plot: Psychological realism

Alexey Ivanovitch (ah-lehk-say ih-VAH-no-vihch), a young, impoverished nobleman, the tutor in a decadent, aristocratic Russian household where he falls in love with the stepdaughter of the family. Boorish and insolent in response to the patronizing impoliteness of his sponsor, he causes his own dismissal but remains in the German gambling resort town to be near his beloved Polina, who makes use of his devotion to send him on errands and to win for her at the roulette tables. Although perceptive and cultured, Alexey is addicted to the tables, so much so that he wins a fortune in order to relieve Polina of financial worries. When she refuses to accept his gift, she leaves him so despondent that he takes up with a French adventuress who impoverishes and then discards him. Even after he hears that Polina, ill at the time, really loves him and wishes him to return, he goes again and again to the salons, for by this time his gambling has become compulsive.

Polina Alexandrovna (poh-LIH-nuh ah-lehk-SAHN-drov-nuh), the stepdaughter of a Russian general. Beautiful in a strange way, Polina is the mistress of a false marquis, an adventurer who practices usury and who is ruining the General by attaching his real estate in order to keep the Russian in gambling money. Her influence on Alexey is so great that he not only gambles for her, literally and figuratively, but also obeys her slightest whim. She in turn is under the spell of the false marquis. Mr. Astley, who is also in love with Polina, finally takes her to Switzerland for her health.

The General, the son-in-law of a wealthy old lady and the stepfather to Polina. Formerly a colonel, he had bought his preferment upon retirement. In desperate straits financially and madly in love with Mlle Blanche, a French adventuress, he sees health and prospects grow dimmer each day that his aged aunt lives. He is a mixture of suspicion and haughtiness; his whole life is built on pretense. Although he never finishes a sentence, his ideas are so simple and self-centered that no one misunderstands him. His two children mean no more to him than the dim memory of Victoria, his dead wife. After years of anticipation while waiting for his inheritance, he lives only a few months longer than the dowager, who has gambled away most of her fortune in the meantime.

Antonida Vassilievna Tarasevitcheva (ahn-toh-NIH-duh vahs-SIH-lyehv-nuh tah-rahs-SEH-vih-cheh-vah), the General's aunt, a sprightly seventy-five-year-old aristocrat and autocrat who rules her family with wicked glee. She is called "Grandmother" by her family, and she is confined to her chair, where she sits like a ramrod and issues orders in a stentorian voice. Fond of Polina, she loathes the General and threatens to cut him off for his chicanery. Suddenly possessed, almost overwhelmed, by gambling fever, she loses a fortune at the gaming tables. Her keen wit and cunning intuition make her a delightful eccentric, tender to those she loves, a terror to the others.

Mr. Astley, an English businessman with an inherent nobility of nature and an actual title, which he conceals because of almost morbid shyness and diffidence. Desperately in love with Polina, he aids the young tutor out of a generous nature and takes in the despondent girl when she is abandoned by the gambler and her family. His shyness is offset by a fierce sense of independence. An observer of human foibles, he also declares himself on the side of the genuine, those of strong character and the finer motives.

Mlle de Cominges, called **Mlle Blanche**, a woman with many invented names, an adventuress on the grand order and of shady dealings. In spite of her outward appearances, she has a sense of loyalty, even generosity, toward those she loves or pities. The false marquis is her accomplice and a thoroughly despicable one.

The Marquis de Grieux (deh gree-OO), a self-styled French nobleman and an alleged kinsman of Mlle Blanche. He lends the General money with which to gamble and in the end succeeds in ruining the reckless nobleman. Polina is in love with him, much to Alexey Ivanovitch's distress.

THE GAMES WERE COMING

Author: Michael Anthony (1932-   )
First published: 1963
Genre: Novel
Locale: Southern Trinidad, British West Indies
Time: January to April during a year in the early 1950's
Plot: Social realism

Leon Seal, a competitive cyclist who has quit his job to devote himself to preparing for the fifteen-mile race at the Southern Games. In his early twenties, big and powerfully built, he obeys his father's instructions and pays exceptional attention to the training and care of his body. He ignores the Trinidad Carnival celebrations and willfully turns his back on his emotional life by severely limiting contact with his girlfriend, Sylvia. Disciplined, cold, and calculating in his quest for personal glory, Leon naïvely misreads the complexity of Sylvia's personality and her potential for an identity independent of him. Controlled and cautious in his own behavior, Leon allows his ambition to blind him to Sylvia's physical and emotional condition and her manipulation of him; in promising to marry her if he wins the race, he may have committed himself unknowingly to rearing another man's child.

Sylvia, Leon's girlfriend, a store clerk. A tall, attractive twenty-one-year-old, she is quiet and easygoing, the product of a poor but respectable upbringing. She is in love with Leon but hurt, frustrated, and confused by his recent neglect of her. Never particularly interested in sports, she is increasingly taken with the spirit of the Trinidad Carnival, with its undercurrent of abandon and immorality. Resentment and a desire for retribution combine with loneliness, boredom, and a shaken sense of self-worth to make Sylvia vulnerable to the advances of her married employer, Imbal Mohansingh. When she becomes pregnant, Sylvia wants an abortion but accepts her friend May's suggestion and decides to try and trick Leon into accepting the baby as his own.

Dolphus Seal, Leon's preadolescent brother. Observant, imaginative, and reflective, he is equally excited by two approaching events: the Southern Games and the Carnival. He cannot decide whether to become a cyclist or a steel band musician. When he thinks of the games, he imagines himself like Leon: big, strong, and powerful. Steel band music makes him feel tender, artistic, and emotional. He takes great pride in Leon's growing prowess and celebrity but is sometimes bitter and resentful that Leon is too preoccupied to recognize him publicly and allow him some reflected glory.

Fitz Seal, Leon's father and trainer. A big, powerful oil refinery worker in his early fifties, he is a reformed rum-drinking, dancing Carnival man who has imparted a strong sense of order and discipline to Leon and oversees his preparations for the race. He likes Sylvia but wants Leon to keep her away during his training. Embarrassed by shows of emotion, he is superficially severe and undemonstrative to his children; however, his wife knows him to be gentle and loving. A perfectionist who only grudgingly gives praise, he is sustained by his son's admiration and boasts of Leon's abilities to others.

May, a friend of Sylvia who works in a café. She brazenly admits to having illegitimate children and having had several abortions. Surprised by Sylvia's innocence and naïveté, May is annoyed by her air of moral and social propriety and feels a vindictive satisfaction when Sylvia becomes pregnant. May refuses help in finding an abortionist but suggests that Sylvia pass the baby off as Leon's.

Imbal Mohansingh, Sylvia's employer and owner of a small clothing and dry goods store. Nearing fifty and married, he is amazed at his success in seducing Sylvia.

Melda Seal, Leon's mother. Good-natured, with a lively sense of humor, she is amused by Dolphus' antics. She has great affection for her husband and knows the real man behind the reserved exterior. She senses that there is a problem between Sylvia and Leon despite his denial.

Ironman Hamille, a great cyclist from the same club as Leon and a rival in the fifteen-mile race. He no longer has the necessary dedication and discipline and fails to stay the distance. He is attracted to Sylvia and tries unsuccessfully to form a liaison with May.

Mr. Grays, an athletics coach who is proud of his own past glory and strongly believes in dedication and the brotherhood of sportsmen.

— *Douglas Rollins*

THE GAOL GATE

Author: Lady Augusta Gregory (1852-1932)
First published: 1909
Genre: Drama
Locale: Galway, Ireland
Time: 1906
Plot: Tragedy

Mary Cahel, one of two characters who provide most of the dialogue and dramatic action. She is the mother of Denis Cahel, who is being held in Galway Jail. She is a strong-minded woman with a deep sense of family pride. Like many of the common people of the time, she cannot read. She goes to Galway bearing a letter that she has not opened, in order to find out from the authorities at the jail what it says about her son, who was arrested for firing a gun. She is concerned about his possible punishment and about his good name, and therefore that of the family. It has been rumored in their village that he informed on his companions to save himself.

Mary Cushin, Denis' wife, who goes on the long journey to Galway with her mother-in-law. She was prepared to ask a neighbor to read the letter for them, but she could not overcome Mary Cahel's fear of the letter's contents and how they might be used by the person who read the letter. Mary Cushin is torn between fear that Denis may have been executed and hope that he will be released when they arrive at the jail.

Terry Fury and

Pat Ruane, Denis' friends, who also were arrested.

The gatekeeper, who tells Mary Cahel and Mary Cushin that Denis has been hanged and that the letter gave them permission to visit him before his sentence was carried out.

— *James L. Hodge*

THE GARDEN

Author: L. A. G. Strong (1896-1958)
First published: 1931
Genre: Novel
Locale: Ireland
Time: Early twentieth century
Plot: Impressionistic realism

Dermot Gray, an Anglo-Irish boy who spends his holidays with his maternal grandparents in Ireland. To him, his grandparents' cottage at Sandycove is home, beloved as his home in England is not. After a happy childhood and a comparatively painless adolescence, Dermot is killed in World War I.

Mrs. Gray, his mother. To her also, the cottage in Ireland is home.

Mr. Gray, his father. He confuses Dermot, who does not know whether he will react to something with patience or anger. Dermot is afraid of his father, who is sickly, and is also afraid for him.

Eithne, Dermot's younger sister. As she grows older, she shares in his pleasures and excursions; when Dermot and her beloved cousin are killed in the war, she feels torn apart but comforts herself with the belief that the young men are together and surely happy.

Granny, Dermot's grandmother. As a very young child, Dermot confuses her garden with the Garden of Eden.

Grandpapa, his grandfather, a wise and loving man.

Ben McManus, Dermot's uncle, a boisterous retired mariner who is also a strict Puritan.

Aunt Patricia McManus, Ben's wife. They live a happy-go-lucky life in a seaside house containing such wonders as a telescope and the dried jaws of a whale.

Con McManus, one of their four children. Much older than Dermot, he is boyish and exuberant. When Eithne is fourteen, he falls in love with her. He and Dermot are killed only a day apart.

Eileen McManus, Con's sister, a lovely and lively girl whom Dermot adores.

Paddy Kennedy, a disabled lad hired by Granny to teach Dermot to fish.

Long Mike Hogan and

Peg-leg O'Shea, Paddy's pals. From them and Paddy, Dermot learns a great tolerance for poor people.

GARDEN, ASHES
(Bašta, pepeo)

Author: Danilo Kiš (1935-1989)
First published: 1965
Genre: Novel
Locale: Northern Yugoslavia
Time: Late 1930's and early 1940's
Plot: Impressionistic realism

Eduard "Sam" Scham, a railway official, poet, and world traveler. The character of Eduard is seen through the eyes of his son, Andi; the perceptions are necessarily subjective and biased. What comes through is a portrait of an eccentric, an incorrigible dreamer, and a man of many talents. He is a poet and a philosopher whose abilities are unfulfilled and squandered, partly because of his circumstances and his Jewish background, but partly because of his several character flaws. A railroad inspector, he is drawn to his profession by an insatiable urge to travel, which, in turn, reveals a basic instability and restlessness. As a Jew, he is persecuted, at first subtly but later, during World War II, openly. He also is a drunkard, a man who cannot hold on to steady relationships, whether with family members or with friends. Eduard's aloofness to Andi is especially revealing. Despite his obvious love for his son, he frequently calls him "young man," as if he were a stranger. Eduard also is aloof from his wife, without being unfaithful. An amateur philosopher, he adopts a fatalistic point of view that makes it somewhat easier for him to accept his final tragic fate. He lives his life as a free spirit, as a misplaced wanderer from some mysterious, exotic land. Even though he fades away into nothingness in the pogrom, he remains alive forever in his son's memory and, even more poignantly, in his imagination.

Maria Scham, Eduard's wife, a perfect example of an understanding and forgiving wife. An intelligent and well-educated woman, she seems to know her husband better than he knows himself. She is thus able to tolerate many of his idiosyncrasies and weaknesses, weighing the pluses against the minuses and realizing that one's personality cannot and should not be changed. Whatever she is missing in her relationship with her husband, Maria compensates for by devoting herself to her children, especially Andi. A rock of granite, she is often the only safe mooring onto which her family can hold. It is primarily through her tales of the past that Andi develops an artistic inclination and a sublime sense of beauty in life and nature, despite the accompanying ugliness and sorrow.

Andreas (Andi) Scham, their eleven-year-old son, the narrator of the story. Although he is too young to understand fully the problems facing his parents, especially his father, he senses instinctively an almost mystical bond with his father. Moreover, Andi develops traits similar to those of his father, such as the inclination toward poetry and a desire to travel. On the other hand, he acts his age as he plays, fantasizes, suffers bouts of anxiety and insecurity, and lives in his own world. From his mother, he has inherited sensitivity and confidence; from his father, wild imagination and the desire to excel. Both parents have imbued him with an artistic inclination that results in his first attempts at writing poetry. What Andi loses through the physical absence of his father, he gains by developing a myth about Eduard that sustains him throughout his life.

Anna Scham, Eduard and Maria's daughter and Andi's older sister. Although still a child herself, Anna is able to cope slightly better with the threatening events swirling around the family. She is apparently just as affected by the predicaments, yet Andi, preoccupied with his own perception of events, seems hardly to notice her presence. As a result, Anna is left undeveloped as a character and used primarily as a prop to bring Andi's world into a sharper focus.

— *Vasa D. Mihailovich*

THE GARDEN OF EARTHLY DELIGHTS

Author: Martha Clarke (1944-)
First produced: 1984
Genre: Drama
Locale: A landscape painted by Hieronymus Bosch
Time: Biblical creation and the fifteenth century
Plot: Surrealism

Tree-Man, who appears during the opening measures of music, a man in a gray body suit who trudges slowly and stiffly to center stage, holding bare tree limbs overhead. He remains onstage, silently watching the unfolding scene between Adam and Eve in the Garden of Eden. He stalks offstage glumly at the end of the scene but reappears throughout the piece to survey the ensuing decadence and eventual desolation. Throughout the piece, his presence is ambiguous, but he seems to watch the events with the natural gaze of a choral commentator.

Adam and

Eve, the biblical characters, representing the first man and woman on Earth. Wearing skin-colored body suits, Adam and Eve perform a lyrical, gently danced duet in the first scene. Eve's long hair, hanging straight to her waist, is choreographed into the dance sequence. Adam uses it to manipulate her movements by wrapping it around himself and pulling her from the floor by it. The dance follows the couple's short-lived innocence in the Garden of Eden to their encounter with the serpent that ends their innocence and symbolically sends humanity from paradise. They are transformed into lumbering, awkward, bent-over animals as they slowly exit.

The Serpent, based on the serpent in the biblical creation myth. Wearing a white body suit and clutching an apple between her thighs, the serpent slinks onstage toward Adam and Eve in their opening duet. Her movements are coquettish as she reaches between her legs for the famous apple, with which she tempts Eve and Adam. As they exit in shame, she exits in smug triumph.

Peasants, seven men and women in various medieval costumes representing farmworkers, town gossips, the village idiot, a nun, and town laborers. They broadly enact the seven deadly sins in a quick series of pantomimed scenes, using potatoes as props. Alternately humorous and cruel acts are performed clownishly, but the implications of the peasants' coarse behavior often are frightening.

Angels, musicians or actors who are flown in over the heads of the other performers at various times throughout the piece. Two play harp and flute over Adam and Eve in the Garden of Eden; one floats and somersaults over a group in the Garden of Earthly Delights section; and another holds her head as she sails over the group of peasants in the Seven Deadly Sins section. They are dressed in white body suits, and the mechanisms of their flying, such as the harnesses and wires, are clearly visible.

Demons, musicians and actors who use onstage musical instruments to torture one another and to set up a cacophony of sounds signaling humanity's damnation and descent into hell. In the final scene, demons fly, tumble, and plummet through the air; crash their heads into drums and keyboards; beat each other with drumsticks and cymbals; and stab one another with violin and cello bows.

— *Diane Quinn*

THE GARDEN OF THE FINZI-CONTINIS
(Il giardino dei Finzi-Contini)

Author: Giorgio Bassani (1916-)
First published: 1962
Genre: Novel
Locale: Ferrara, Italy
Time: Primarily Fall, 1938, to Summer, 1939
Plot: Social realism

Micòl Finzi-Contini (mee-KOHL FEEN-zee-kohn-TEE-nee), a young and wealthy Jewish woman of twenty-three, accustomed both to the adoration of her family and friends and to having her own way. She is unenthusiastically working on a graduate thesis about Emily Dickinson. Anti-Semitic feelings, propaganda, and regulations in her hometown of Ferrara, Italy, force her to socialize with other Jews, rather than with Gentiles of her own social and economic station. She lives with her parents, brother, and grandmother on the large ancestral estate belonging to her father's family. Micòl is having an affair with Giampiero Malnate. Although she speaks publicly about Malnate as boring and unattractive, she secretly meets him at night in a farmer's hut in the park of the estate.

The narrator, a young, middle-class Jewish man who has decided to take an advanced university degree. He finds himself involved, at a transitional phase in his life, with the wealthy Finzi-Contini family. They have fascinated him since his childhood, when he watched them during Sabbath services at the local synagogue. When the Fascists come to power and restrictions are placed on the Jewish population of Ferrara, the narrator becomes friendly with the Finzi-Contini children. He has never socialized with them because they have been tutored at home and have kept apart from the less wealthy Jews in town. What begins for the narrator as a pleasant interlude of tennis and camaraderie grows into an obsession with Micòl and the subsequent realization that she does not love him. Micòl's father offers him the free run of his large Renaissance library in which to do research. The narrator accepts because it places him in daily contact with Micòl. As he learns the distressing fact that she will never return his love, he also discovers the manifestations of economic and racial prejudice that exist within the Jewish community.

Alberto Finzi-Contini, Micòl's brother, a young man in his early twenties. He is passive and unsure of himself; bored with his existence, he is too much of a follower to risk interest in anything. He has a materialistic bent and shows some talent in reproducing antique furniture. He takes little pleasure in his possessions or designs beyond showing them off to others. Although he has been led to believe that he is superior to others by virtue of his family position, he suspects that this may not be true. He develops a malignant lymphogranuloma during the year and becomes more passive and quiet as the disease takes its course.

Giampiero Malnate (jee-ahm-pee-EHR-oh mahl-NAH-teh), a twenty-five-year-old Gentile. He is tall, hairy, and overweight. He wears glasses with thick lenses and has steel-gray eyes. He is the oldest of the group of tennis players invited to play at the Finzi-Contini estate after the Ferrara tennis club is closed to Jews. An acquaintance of Alberto from Milan, he has recently been certified as a chemist and works at a factory producing synthetic rubber. Malnate is a Communist, which leads him to believe that he is hard-boiled and practical. In reality, he is trusting and uncomplicated. After Micòl forbids the narrator to come to the estate because of his obvious obsession with her, Malnate becomes his friend and discusses Communist ideas with him. When he finds out about the narrator's infatuation with Micòl, he shows a brotherly concern for him.

Professor Ermanno (ehr-MAHN-noh), the father of Alberto and Micòl, a gentleman and a scholar. He is considerably shorter than his wife and wears light-colored linen suits and a panama hat with a black ribbon. He has a great love of literature, and he quotes from great works while peering through his pince-nez. He believes that he has a mission to pass along his knowledge, which makes him generous enough to allow the narrator the use of his library. He is a historian of Italian Jewry and wants to maintain his ancestral way of life. He is blind to the actual political conditions in Ferrara and takes refuge in his books. He depends on Micòl to deal with the everyday household chores. He is disappointed in his children, whom he wishes were more like the narrator.

— *Stephanie Korney*

THE GARDEN PARTY
(Zahradní slavnost)

Author: Václav Havel (1936-)
First published: 1963
Genre: Drama
Locale: Czechoslovakia
Time: The 1960's
Plot: Social realism

Hugo Pludek, an amateur chess player and, later, liquidator of the Liquidation Office and Inauguration Service. Young, commanding, and insightful, Hugo attends the garden party of the Liquidation Office looking for a career; his penetration of the bureaucratic paranoia allows him to move up quickly in politics, treating his confrontations as moves in a chess game.

Maxy Falk, the Inaugurator of Parties, Conferences, and Celebrations. A young man with a sense of humor, he is trying to reform the dogmatic institution of the Inauguration Service. He keeps the clerk and secretary of the garden party on their toes, until Hugo decides to liquidate the Service.

Director, the head of the Liquidation Office, a womanizer and a bureaucrat. While in the act of liquidating the Inauguration Service, he discovers that his own office is next on the liquidation list. Losing a verbal duel with Hugo, he "hits the sack," climbing into the wastebasket with the Secretary.

Secretary, who works at the garden party and in the Liquidation Office. Unmarried, she is an attractive woman with an ongoing relationship with the Director and a budding relationship with the Clerk. Alternately emotional and businesslike, she carries out the liquidation of property, including the Director's clothes.

Clerk, who also works at the garden party and in the Liquidation Office. Young and unmarried, he is enamored of the Secretary. Falk invites him to relax, "undress if you like," precipitating his struggle between obeying the "party" line and thinking for himself. Before he can reform completely, the liquidation of his office is announced.

Albert Pludek, Hugo's father, middle-aged and middle class, possibly once a director in the theater. Hopeful for his son's prospects, he spouts meaningless aphorisms as wisdom and sends his younger son, Peter, to the basement or the attic to avoid contact with visitors.

Berta Pludek, Hugo's mother, a former actress. Equally middle class and hopeful, she wants Hugo to date Amanda. She appears whenever Hugo mentions "Mummy."

Amanda, a young woman, a beginning actress in a postmodern self-signifying theatrical device, both a character in the play and simply an actress in Havel's play. Her task is to deliver telegrams from Albert Pludek's childhood chum, now in a position of importance in the bureaucracy. Berta Pludek cheers her up, remarking that bit parts are a way to start in show business.

Peter Pludek, Hugo's nearly silent younger brother. He is shuttled into hiding whenever visitors are expected. He says one word, "Goodbye," and exits with Amanda.

— *Thomas J. Taylor*

THE GARDENER'S DOG
(El perro del hortelano)

Author: Lope de Vega Carpio (1562-1635)
First published: 1618
Genre: Drama
Locale: Naples
Time: Late sixteenth century
Plot: Comedy of manners

Diana (DYAH-nah), the countess of Belflor, who is like the gardener's dog that will not eat the food or let anyone else enjoy it. Investigating the story of a man seen escaping from the top story of her palace, she discovers that her secretary, Teodoro, has been seeing Marcela, one of her ladies in waiting. At first, she gives permission for their wedding, but then she changes her mind and in a letter dictated to Teodoro hints at her affection for him, though his blood is not noble. Meanwhile, she is courted by two nobles and consents to marry Ricardo, even while alternately encouraging and rejecting Teodoro. At last, angered by Teodoro, she wounds him with a knife. His announcement that he is leaving Naples for Madrid makes her decide to marry him; in addition, his servant has concocted a plan to make him one of the nobility. Although she is assured by Teodoro that the scheme is false, Diana decides that happiness is found in a union of souls, not of social classes, especially if they conceal the truth of his lowly status, so they marry.

Teodoro (tay-oh-DOH-roh), the secretary of Countess Diana. He loves Marcela, one of her ladies in waiting, but he turns to Diana, then back to Marcela, and again to his employer when her jealousy is aroused by seeing him embrace Marcela. At last, he tells Marcela to marry Fabio, but at his next rebuff by Diana, because of his lowly birth, he announces his departure for Spain. Too honorable to make false claims about noble blood, he refuses to let his servant Tristan persuade Count Ludovico to claim him as a long-lost son. Diana nevertheless takes him for her husband.

Tristan (trees-TAHN), the shrewd, picaresque servant of Teodoro. He protects his master by hurling his cap at a candle when Teodoro is almost discovered leaving Marcela's chamber at night. Reluctantly, he advises his master to marry her; however, when Teodoro yearns for the countess, Tristan invents a noble lineage for him. On another occasion, when two nobles, Federico and Ricardo, want Teodoro killed, Tristan accepts their gold to commit the murder, then confesses the plot to his master. At the end, when everybody is getting married, he is paired off with Dorotea, a member of the countess' household.

Marcela (mahr-THAY-lah), a good-hearted young woman who is looking, like most young women in Spanish comedies, for a husband. After her off-and-on engagement to Teodoro, she is satisfied to get Fabio instead.

Count Federico (fay-day-REE-koh), a mercenary noble who knows Diana's wealth and comes wooing her. When he learns of Teodoro's wound, he decides the man must have offended her, and he pays to have the secretary assassinated.

The Marquis Ricardo (rree-KAHR-doh), a money-seeking suitor whom Diana at one time decides to marry as the lesser of two evils.

Fabio (FAH-byoh), a gentleman of Naples who is tossed from Anarda to Marcela as a possible husband, then ends in Marcela's possession.

Anarda (ah-NAHR-dah), one of Diana's ladies in waiting. She accuses Marcela of harboring a man in her room and hints that the man is Teodoro, in revenge for Marcela's encouragement of Fabio, who is courting Anarda.

Dorotea (doh-roh-TAY-ah), another member of the countess' household, who at the end becomes a consolation prize for Tristan.

Count Ludovico (lew-doh-BEE-koh), an elderly nobleman who, having lost a son named Teodoro twenty years earlier, is easily convinced by Tristan that his master is the missing boy.

Octavio (ohk-TAH-byoh), Diana's squire.

Celio (THAY-lyoh), a servant of the Marquis Ricardo.

Leonardo (lay-oh-NAHR-doh), a servant of Count Federico.

GARGANTUA AND PANTAGRUEL
(Gargantua et Pantagruel)

Author: François Rabelais (c. 1494-1553)
First published: 1567
Genre: Novel
Locale: France
Time: Renaissance
Plot: Mock-heroic

Gargantua (gahr-GAHN-tew-ah), an affable prince, a giant—as an infant, more than two thousand ells of cloth are required to clothe him—who has many adventures. He travels over Europe and other parts of the world, fighting wars from which all prisoners are set free, straightening out disputes in other kingdoms, and helping his friends achieve their goals.

Pantagruel (PAHN-tah-grewl), Gargantua's giant son, who once got an arm out of his swaddling clothes and ate the cow that was nursing him. Pantagruel was born when his father was four hundred years old. Accepting with good nature the responsibility of aiding the oppressed, he spends a good deal of his time traveling the earth with his companion Panurge. In their travels, they visit a land where all citizens have noses shaped like the ace of clubs and a country in which the people eat and drink nothing but air.

Panurge (PAHN-urzh), a beggar and Pantagruel's companion, who knows sixty-three ways to make money and two hundred fourteen ways to spend it. He speaks twelve known and unknown tongues, but he does not know whether he should marry. Finally, he decides to consult the Oracle of the Sacred Bottle to find the answer to his question. The trip to the island of the Sacred Bottle is filled with adventures for Panurge and Pantagruel. The oracle, when finally consulted, utters one word, "trinc." Panurge takes this pronouncement, translated as "drink," to mean that he should marry.

Friar John of the Funnels, a lecherous, lusty monk who fights well for Gargantua when the latter finds himself at war with King Picrochole of Lerne. To reward the friar for his gallantry, Gargantua orders workers to build the Abbey of Thélème, which has been Friar John's dream. There, men and women live together and work to accumulate wealth.

Grandgousier (grahnd-gew-SYAY), the giant king who is Gargantua's father.

Gargamelle (GAHR-gah-mehl), Gargantua's mother, who, taken suddenly in labor, bears Gargantua from her left ear.

Picrochole (PEEK-roh-shohl), king of Lerne, who invades Grandgousier's country. His army is repulsed by Gargantua with the aid of Friar John and other loyal helpers. The prisoners captured are all allowed to go free.

Anarchus (ahn-AHRK-uhs), king of Dipsody, who invades the land of the Amaurots. His army is overcome by Pantagruel, who makes the king a crier of green sauce.

Bacbuc, the priestess who conducts Panurge to the Sacred Bottle and translates the Oracle's message for him.

Ponocrates (poh-noh-KRAY-teez), Gargantua's teacher in Paris.

Holofernes (HOH-loh-furnz) and

Joberlin Bridé (zhoh-behr-LIHN bree-DAY), Gargantua's first teachers.

GARGOYLES
(Verstörung)

Author: Thomas Bernhard (1931-1989)
First published: 1967
Genre: Novel

Locale: The Austrian Alps
Time: After World War I
Plot: Psychological realism

The narrator, a student home for the weekend. The narrator is surrounded by derangement (the meaning of the original German title) and death both at school, where the students suffer fits of suicidal melancholy, and at home, where his mother died an early and inexplicable death some time before and his sister frequently attempts suicide. His life is one of almost total estrangement and solitude, again both at school, where he has severed all relations with colleagues so as to progress with his scientific studies, and at home, where there is little if any communication among the narrator, his father, and his sister. The narrator has written a long letter to his father about their problematic familial relations, and he hopes to be able to discuss this letter with his father while home; however, the father, who is a doctor, receives an emergency call. The narrator accompanies his father on his rounds and is exposed to a series of increasingly insane and diseased patients, culminating in the visit to Prince Saurau. The rounds provide a type of disquieting response to the narrator's letter. His questioning of, and even attempt to halt, the natural process of disintegration and decay through science is proven useless. Alienation, solitude, and death are revealed to be universally human conditions that even the science of medicine cannot reverse. The objectivity and distance with which the narrator initially relates the day's events eventually are replaced by involvement and perhaps even obsession as the narrator loses himself within the prince's monologue and narrates page after page of his disjointed ramblings.

The doctor, the narrator's father. Well known and dedicated, the doctor spends twenty-two-hour days seeing to the needs of his patients but heals not a single one of them. After years of working in an area marked by cases of insanity and brutality, the doctor has come to the conclusion "that everything is *fundamentally sick and sad*." The early death of his wife has forced him to acknowledge death as a fact of nature. During his rounds, the doctor conveys little emotion and seems distanced from the misery around him. He lives in a solitude broken only by a weekly visit to a broker friend. His relationship to his children is weak and worsening. In particular, the doctor worries about his extremely withdrawn, fearful, and sensitive daughter. The fact that he does not worry about his son, oblivious to the narrator's decreasing ability to resolve or at least repress problems in his studies, indicates how little the father knows his son. The doctor is unable to open his heart to either son or daughter, although at times, usually in the presence of a third person, he can speak of them with seeming emotion and concern.

Prince Saurau (SOW-row), the landlord of Hochgobernitz. Incurably insane, the prince, who is the final and by far most important patient seen by the doctor, epitomizes many of the human traits introduced in prior patient visits. Of all the patients, the prince suffers from the highest degree of disease and mental confusion. The isolation characteristic of the narrator, the doctor, and all the doctor's patients is absolute in the prince, who lives high atop a mountain. The only visitor received is the doctor, and although the prince lives in Hochgobernitz with his two sisters and two daughters, he describes the distance between them as being hundreds of thousands of miles, so far that they can no longer hear one another. The prince's alienation from his family has developed into a hatred of all society and of the Austrian state. The relationship between the prince and his son approximates that between the doctor and the narrator. Both sons are pursuing scientific studies away from home, and both their courses of study preclude friends of any kind. The prince, similar to the doctor, knows very little of his son, who only writes when in need of money and who intends to undo his father's work and destroy Hochgobernitz.

Woman from Gradenberg, an innkeeper's wife who is brutally and senselessly murdered, precipitating the emergency call that prevents the anticipated discussion between father and son.

Bloch (blohkh), a real estate broker. Jewish, with exquisite taste and suffering from terrible headaches and insomnia, Bloch is the doctor's only friend.

Frau Ebenhöh (frow AY-behn-heh), a widow soon to die. Like the prince, she is afraid that her mentally backward son will sell her home and possessions after her death.

The industrialist, who is retired and suffering from diabetes. Described as not yet mad, the industrialist is working on a philosophical manuscript that he creates and destroys anew every day. To prevent distractions from this work, his lodge and grounds have been emptied of everything, including pictures, books, people, and even the forest game.

Teacher von Salla, a country schoolteacher fired for having engaged in sexual relations with a pupil. After serving his jail sentence, the teacher developed an astonishing gift for pen drawings expressing the grotesque, demoniac, and self-destructive forward momentum of human existence. The teacher died in the doctor's presence.

The miller, who suffers from a gangrenous leg ulceration and is bedridden with his wife, who is suffering from water on the feet. Their two sons and a Turkish worker are in the process of killing all the exotic birds housed in an aviary behind the mill because of the birds' unrelenting screeching since the death of their owner, the miller's brother. All the inhabitants of the mill are feebleminded.

Krainer (KRI-nuhr), the disabled and insane son of upstanding parents who work on the Saurau estate. Formerly a gifted musician, Krainer can no longer speak intelligibly and has become so dangerous that he must be restrained by a cagelike covering over his bed. Krainer and his sister, the sole person who still cares for him, remind the doctor of his own son and daughter.

— Linda C. DeMeritt

THE GATES OF THE FOREST
(Les Portes de la forêt)

Author: Elie Wiesel (1928-)
First published: 1964
Genre: Novel
Locale: Hungarian forests and villages, Paris, and Brooklyn
Time: The 1940's and early 1950's
Plot: Psychological realism

Gregor, whose real name is **Gavriel**. He is an orphaned seventeen-year-old Hungarian Jew who successfully escaped the Nazis during World War II. Clever and resourceful, and entirely committed to the underground partisan movement in Hungary, Gregor is both a loyal friend and someone who elicits intense love and loyalty in others. He is introspective and philosophical, a young man who has learned to love solitude and night, and not to live "outside his body." As a result, he develops great resourcefulness in his quest for survival. In each of the four sections of the book, Gregor narrowly escapes capture while many of the people whom he loves and respects are lost. He shares his refuge in a cave with Gavriel; he plays the part of a deaf-mute nephew of the family's old Christian housekeeper, Maria; and he works as a Jewish partisan acting the role of the anti-Semitic Christian lover of Clara, a fellow partisan. Finally, years later, he faces his future as a New York City newspaper writer locked in a less-than-successful marriage with Clara. He acquires strength and self-awareness after a private audience with the Rebbe, the spiritual leader of the Hasidim in Brooklyn, and after a mysterious conversation with Gavriel in the hall of the Hasidim.

Gavriel, the enigmatic Jew who lives with Gregor for several days in a cave in a forest in Hungary. About thirty years old, taller than Gregor, and slightly stooped, Gavriel has no name but accepts the true Jewish name of Gregor after Gregor offers it to him. A man of a thousand voices and a thousand names from another place and time, Gavriel laughs at war and killing. It is he who tells Gregor of the true fate of the Jews and saves the life of his young companion with his own surrender to Hungarian soldiers.

Maria, the Christian housekeeper to Gregor's family before they are killed. The old woman lives alone in a small cottage in a Christian village in Hungary. Wise and strong, she devises the false identity for Gregor of a deaf-mute idiot son of her harlot sister Ileana and is able to give Gregor refuge in her home for a few months.

Lieb the Lion, the courageous Jewish childhood comrade of Gregor. After Gregor leaves Maria's home and goes into hiding in the forest, he surprisingly meets Lieb, who has become the leader of the Jewish underground partisans. Loyal and strong, he helps Gregor in a vain effort to locate Gavriel in a local prison that is in a town that is supposedly *Judenrein*. In the process, Lieb is captured by Hungarian soldiers. Like Gavriel, he is a victorious human being, able to laugh at his own torture.

Clara, the young lover of Lieb. A beautiful fellow partisan, she joins Lieb and Gregor in their attempt to find Gavriel. With courage and cleverness, she acts the part of the lover of Gregor as they become friendly with Janos, a simpleminded, anti-Semitic guard at the prison. After Lieb's death and a chance meeting with Gregor in Paris after the war, she agrees to marry Gregor even though they both acknowledge that she still loves Lieb. Because of this lack of love, their marriage is never joyful. Despite the ghosts that haunt their lives, they decide to fight the past in what Gregor calls a "bitter, austere, and obstinate battle."

— Vicki K. Robinson

A GATHERING OF OLD MEN

Author: Ernest J. Gaines (1933-)
First published: 1983
Genre: Novel
Locale: Southern Louisiana
Time: The 1970's
Plot: Psychological realism

Mathu, a black man, now in his eighties, built like an "old post in the ground." He is the one black man on Marshall's Plantation who has never been afraid to stand up to the whites. He has great personal dignity and has even earned the grudging respect of some white men, including Sheriff Mapes.

Candy Marshall, the daughter of the original owners of the plantation. Candy was half reared by Mathu after the death of her parents. A strong and independent woman of about thirty, she is determined to protect Mathu and the rest of "her" people. She must learn that there is something patronizing in her assumption that the grown black men and women on the plantation are hers and that it is her duty to protect them.

Sheriff Mapes, a big, powerful, often brutal man. Mapes is to some extent free of the rigid racism of the past. Although he treats most of the old men with amused contempt and is not above slapping them when he does not get the answers he wants, he gradually becomes aware that something he has not seen before is happening among these old men.

Fix Boutan, father of a man who has been killed and patriarch of the Cajun Boutan family. Known in the past for his brutal mistreatment of African Americans, Fix is moved powerfully by a sense of family, and he is capable of listening to those in his family who tell him it is time to abandon the old ways.

Gil Boutan, Fix's son and Beau's brother. He is the "Salt" of "Salt and Pepper," the white and black running backs on the football team of a now integrated Louisiana State University. He is bitter at the death of his brother, and he has always resented the air of superiority that people like Candy assume toward Cajuns. Both his concern for his own future and his sense of all that has changed tell him that he cannot participate in any violence against black people.

The old men, each an individual with his own story. They all share in the same experience, an experience of growth into a full sense of themselves as men as they are granted a last chance to take a stand after a lifetime of giving in.

— *W. P. Kenney*

THE GAUCHO MARTÍN FIERRO
(El gaucho Martín Fierro *and* La vuelta de Martín Fierro)

Author: José Hernández (1834-1886)
First published: 1872 and 1879
Genre: Poetry
Locale: Argentina
Time: The nineteenth century
Plot: Adventure

"The Departure of Martín Fierro," 1872

Martín Fierro (mahr-TEEN FYEH-rroh), the central character. He sings of his misfortunes and adventures on the Argentine pampa (open plain), where he can live by his skills and enjoy nature's beauty. Born to sing, he celebrates the life and character of the gaucho, whom he typifies. He is fearless and quick in a fight, and he is truthful in speech. His greatest joy is to live free. The life of the gaucho is not easy. Fate and corrupt officials are responsible for the many injustices he and his kind have suffered. His own misfortunes began when a judge took him from his wife and children, sending him away to the army to fight the Indians. Forced to perform hard labor without pay and treated brutally by those in charge, he deserts after two years, returning home to find his family and possessions gone. He soon kills a black man in a barroom brawl, then a drunken bully. With his new companion, Cruz, he sets out for the wildlands, breaking his guitar as a final gesture.

Cruz (crewz), who, with several other policemen, attempts to arrest Martín for murder. Admiring Martín's bravery, Cruz helps him escape. A gaucho himself, he too has endured many hardships with an unbroken spirit. Like Martín, he enjoys the freedom of the outlaw life and is convinced that the gaucho is persecuted and doomed to suffer unremitting hardships. It is better, he says at the end, to wander free in the highlands.

The Return of Martín Fierro, 1879

Martín Fierro, whose fortunes have not improved; his songs sustain him. Now he tells of his life among the Indians, his friend Cruz with him. Although the Indians are skilled hunters and fighters, they are lazy, ruthless, and brutal. They treat women and children with savage cruelty. Gallantly, Martín rescues a woman in the desert, killing the Indian who has beaten her and slaughtered her infant. When he meets two of his sons after ten years away from them, he displays a fatherly regard and gives them advice that reflects his own principles: be a good friend; hold firm to faith in God; be good to the poor and aged; do not look for trouble; be truthful, lawful, and hardworking; treat women with respect; and sing always from the heart. He is proudest of his minstrel skills and wit, which he displays in a singing match with a black man, who turns out to be the brother of the black man he killed. A fight is averted—perhaps age and experience have tempered his fiery spirit. The wildlands beckon again, so he bids his companion farewell and goes on his separate way.

Cruz, who lives with Martín in captivity for two hard years among the Indians. His humanity is evident in his tending of an Indian chief stricken with smallpox. This charitable act costs Cruz his life, for he contracts smallpox himself and dies.

The oldest son of Martín Fierro, who tells Martín of his childhood spent in extreme poverty and of his years in prison, falsely accused of murder. Like his father, he remains strong in spirit and independent, going his separate way with his father's advice.

The second son of Martín Fierro, who had his inheritance taken away by a crooked judge. The judge also placed him in the care of a scoundrel of a tutor, who cruelly mistreated him. The son does not abandon him as the old rascal is dying. Left homeless and poor, he falls for a widow, who gives him a hard lesson in unrequited love before he is shipped off to the army. After his sad tale is told, he sets off on his own with a new name.

Don Vizcacha (veez-KAH-chah), a mangy, drunken, thieving, cowardly wife-murderer who is put in charge of the second son. His advice on how to survive in a ruthless world contrasts sharply with Martín's: Be selfish, sly, and suspicious of everyone, and keep the knife ready. His wickedness catches up with him at last as, raving and cursing God, he expires.

Picardia (pee-KAHR-dee-ah), whose life has been one of gambling and cheating. When he learned that he is Cruz's son, he mended his ways in honor of his father and joined the army. In the end, he goes his separate way with a new name and a better understanding of honor and virtue.

— *Bernard E. Morris*

GAUDY NIGHT

Author: Dorothy L. Sayers (1893-1957)
First published: 1935
Genre: Novel
Locale: Oxford and London, England
Time: June, 1934-May, 1935
Plot: Detective and mystery

Harriet Vane, a thirty-two-year-old mystery writer who, four years earlier, was accused falsely of poisoning her lover and was tried for murder. Intelligent, introspective, and fiercely independent, Harriet is asked to investigate a series of disturbing poison pen letters and acts of vandalism at her alma mater, the University of Oxford. When she seeks the assistance of her friend and longtime suitor, Lord Peter Wimsey, she is forced to reexamine her life and her relationship with Wimsey. As Harriet reenters the cloistered university atmosphere after ten years in London, she brings a worldly perspective to the school's sheltered, intellectual, and often inbred way of life.

Lord Peter Death Bredon Wimsey, an aristocratic amateur detective and Harriet's persistent suitor. His investigative talents resulted in Vane's acquittal on the charge of murder. Described in the book as "fair and Mayfair," Wimsey is a brilliant and perceptive sleuth who masks his true nature with a show of frivolous elegance and surface charm. During the course of his courtship with Harriet, Wimsey has come to see himself through her eyes and has made determined attempts to achieve a higher level of emotional honesty in his life. A deeply sensitive man, he loves Harriet for her intelligence and her spirit, and their work together on the Oxford mystery brings them to a new realm of understanding that will decide the fate of their romance.

Letitia Martin, the dean of Shrewsbury College, Oxford. An intelligent, capable woman, she is a brisk, no-nonsense figure throughout the book as she tries to cope with the disturbing series of events that have unsettled the college and led its members to doubt one another. It is the dean who turns to Harriet for help when her beloved school is threatened by a public scandal.

Helen de Vine, the college's new research fellow. De Vine is a brilliant scholar with a keen mind and a remote, analytical nature. Forthright and unyielding, she is interested less in human beings than in facts and is therefore less effective in her interactions with students than in her scholarship. She serves throughout the novel as a touchstone for Harriet in her own struggle toward an honest assessment of her feelings for Peter.

Miss Lydgate, an excellent scholar and Harriet's former tutor. A warmhearted and endearing woman, Miss Lydgate combines breadth of knowledge with an unwavering and somehow innocent belief in the inherent goodness of each individual. Sympathetic to her students' problems, she is a figure of integrity and wisdom.

Miss Hillyard, a history tutor who dislikes Harriet. Bluntly outspoken, Miss Hillyard is also bitterly antimale, an attitude that seems based on some unhappy past experience. The history tutor's attitude serves a cautionary purpose for Harriet.

Lord Saint-George, an Oxford student and Wimsey's nephew. An engaging young man with more than a passing resemblance to his uncle, Saint-George is perpetually short of money and in need of a loan from Wimsey. The car accident he suffers offers Harriet the excuse she needs to write to Wimsey.

Annie Wilson, a widow with two children who works as a maid, or "scout," at the college. Annie is an uneducated woman who believes that a woman's place is caring for her husband and children, and she warns Harriet darkly of unnatural goings-on at the college.

Padgett, the college's longtime porter. Padgett is a fixture at Shrewsbury College, greeting visitors and helping out with any problems that arise.

— *Janet Lorenz*

GAZAPO

Author: Gustavo Sainz (1940-   )
First published: 1965
Genre: Novel
Locale: Mexico City, Mexico
Time: Mid-1960's
Plot: Comic realism

Menelao (meh-neh-LOH), a restless, confused, and somewhat fearful teenager who resists both parental and religious dicta. Much of the novel focuses on the sexual awakening of Menelao and Gisela, his girlfriend, and on the seemingly aimless activities of Menelao and his group of friends. It is evident that he struggles with many factors in his life. His mother and father were divorced when Menelao was four years old, and he does not see his mother again until he is in high school. Ambivalence marks his relationships with both his mother and his father. Menelao is living in his mother's apartment, and he would prefer that she not return to Mexico City. His relationship with his father is also troubled, with much of the friction between the two growing out of the dislike that Menelao and his stepmother, Matriarca, feel for each other. None of the adults in the novel sanctions or understands the relationship between Menelao and Gisela, and even Menelao's friends view it one-dimensionally. Brief, interspersed passages, however, suggest that Menelao seeks more than merely sexual satisfaction from Gisela. His activities—the meetings with Gisela and with friends, the fights with a rival, Tricardio, and the interactions with his parents and with other adults—are all recounted, usually ambiguously, through conversation, tape, and letter.

Gisela (hee-SEH-lah), Menelao's girlfriend, who awakens sexually over the course of the novel. She is seemingly timid and naïve, but her bathing in front of an open door and her confident swimming in the presence of a floundering Menelao intimate strong latent feelings. Her parents and her two aunts disapprove of Gisela's relationship with Menelao, fearing, it seems, Gisela's loss of innocence.

Vulbo (VEWL-boh), one of Menelao's friends. Bold in his pursuit of Nacar, Vulbo is one of the few teenagers who openly defies adult authority. When Nacar's mother tells Vulbo that her daughter already is involved with a soldier, Vulbo ignores the mother's wishes. His pursuit of Nacar, told and retold throughout the novel, is one of the major narrative threads.

Mauricio (mow-REE-see-oh), Menelao's roommate. Mauricio, like Menelao, enjoys using audiotape to record the gang's activities. These stories are altered even as they are told and retold. At times, even the experiences themselves are recorded. Mauricio notes the dreamlike quality of life, an outlook that the novel's disjointed, sometimes surreal narration reflects. His relationship with the chorus girl Bikina is not surprising, considering his preoccupation with sex and sexual intrigue.

Tricardio (tree-KAHR-dee-oh), a switchboard operator at the Bank of Commerce and Menelao's chief rival. Known for being a voyeur and a seducer of female servants, he fights Menelao after Menelao learns that Tricardio surreptitiously has seen Gisela bathing. Typically, however, ambiguity marks even the interactions of Tricardio, Menelao, and Gisela; Menelao does seem to feel some kinship with his rival, and, as Mauricio notes, Gisela does appear to find Tricardio interesting.

Matriarca (mah-tree-AHR-kah), Menelao's stepmother. Much of Menelao's difficulty at home is caused by the friction between the meddlesome Matriarca and her stepson. Noting the difference between his father's behavior at home and his behavior away from his wife, Menelao blames Matriarca for turning his father against him.

Nacar (NAH-kahr), Vulbo's beautiful neighbor. Vulbo pursues Nacar over the course of the novel, thinking for some time that she is an ingenue. He learns, however, that she was married at the age of fourteen and widowed, with a child, at sixteen. Currently, she is involved with a soldier, with whom Vulbo must contend throughout the book.

Menelao's mother, a frail woman now hounded by creditors. Menelao is staying in his mother's apartment while she is in Cuernavaca escaping bill collectors. Throughout the novel, she threatens to return to Mexico City; eventually, she does, disrupting her son's plans with Gisela.

Menelao's father, a husband loath to go against his wife's wishes, even at the risk of losing his son. Glimpses of the father away from his wife show him to be concerned about his son.

Aunt Cripla (KREEP-lah) and

Aunt Icrista (ee-KREES-tah), Gisela's aunts. Aunt Cripla, a Protestant, and Aunt Icrista, a Catholic, loom, specterlike, throughout the novel, passing judgment on many of the actions of Menelao's group.

Fidel (fee-DEHL),

Jacobo (ha-KOH-boh),

Arnaldo (ahr-NAHL-doh), and

Balmori (bahl-MOHR-ee), Menelao's friends. They are differentiated by the fact that the first wears dark glasses, the second stutters, the third is the only male in his family, and the fourth is somewhat morbid.

— *Tom Rash*

GEMINI
(Les Météores)

Author: Michel Tournier (1924-)
First published: 1975
Genre: Novel
Locale: Various locations in France and elsewhere
Time: 1918-1961
Plot: Philosophical

Édouard Surin (ay-DWAHR sewr-AHN), a handsome, elegant, irresistible man who divides his time between running the textile factory he inherited from his wife's father and getting away from the boredom of the country to the excitement of a big apartment in Paris. There, he keeps a mistress while maintaining his affectionate feeling for the wife and many children he leaves behind. Outwardly happy and content with his double life, he secretly longs for a heroic end to it all. As an infantry captain in World War II, he leads an assault on a Belgian town held by the Nazis but is afterward captured. In prison, his health worsens, and he is diagnosed as a diabetic and dismissed from the army. In Paris, he finds a resistance group to join, and his dream of a heroic death is revived, but it is his wife who is recognized as a resistance fighter and sent away by the Germans. Édouard wanders through the displaced persons camps of Europe looking for her and wearing a sandwich board with her picture on it. Four years later, he dies quietly, nearly blind.

Maria Barbara Surin, Édouard's wife and mistress of the big family house, La Cassine. She is the mother of a large brood, the last of whom are identical twin boys that only she can tell apart. Motherhood for Maria Barbara is a blissful state, and into her happiness she incorporates the retarded children of St. Brigitte's, a home (beside the textile factory) run by nuns. She has no interest in accompanying her husband to Paris, and so domestic and homebound does she seem that no one suspects that she is an active member of a resistance group that includes sixteen recruits from the children's home and the factory. One morning, German officers arrive to take her away, and she never returns.

Alexandre Surin (ah-lehk-SAHNDR), the brother of Édouard and uncle of the twins. He is never allowed to meet his nephews because of his shocking behavior as a homosexual dandy who runs the family garbage disposal empire at close proximity to seedy young male employees and to the municipal dumps he supervises. He wears a waistcoat with six pockets, each holding a medallion of pressed garbage from the six cities he serves, and he carries a walking stick with a hidden dagger that he calls "fleurette," the name bestowed on him while a schoolboy by a club of youthful homosexuals.

Paul Surin, one of the identical twins known jointly as Jean-Paul. The unique closeness of "twinship" is essential to Paul, and all relationships are either twin or nontwin, that is, complete or incomplete. When Jean tries to escape the suffocating "ovoid" condition of their twinship (they sleep as two fetuses, head to feet), by bringing his fiancée to La Cassine, Paul manages to discourage the young woman, and she leaves hastily. After Paul loses an arm and leg trying to escape to West Berlin through a tunnel that collapses, he turns for solace, bedridden and alone, to a mystical communion with meteorological mysteries.

Jean Surin (zhahn), the restless twin who wants to escape Paul. After his fiancée's departure, he becomes a vagabond, moving from Paris to Venice to Djerba to Japan to Vancouver and across Canada, then to Berlin, where he rejoins the "non-twin," Urs Kraus, a German artist he met in Japan.

— *Lucy Golsan*

A GENEROUS MAN

Author: Reynolds Price (1933-   )
First published: 1966
Genre: Novel
Locale: Warren County, North Carolina
Time: Early to mid-twentieth century
Plot: Bildungsroman

Milo Mustian, a teenage boy struggling to become a man. Fairly short, with red hair, he looks exactly like his cousin Tom Ryden. Only fifteen years old, Milo is proud and cocky, as he demonstrates by bragging about his sexual encounter with Lois Provo, a girl he met at the Warren County Fair. As the oldest child in a household without a father, he shoulders numerous responsibilities and finds himself involved in two separate hunts. The first is a search for his brother Rato, the family dog, Phillip, and an Indian python, Death. The other is a quest for his own identity and for understanding of the world around him.

Lois Provo, Milo's girlfriend. Sixteen years old, with long black hair, she is Milo's first paramour and also one of his first close friends. She travels along the eastern seaboard of the United States with her aunt/mother Selma Provo as part of the fair. Together, she and her mother take care of forty-six snakes, the main attraction being Death, an eighteen-foot python.

Selma Provo, Lois' mother, masquerading as her aunt. A short, plain woman around fifty years of age, she has spent the last sixteen years tending snakes and telling lies. Trying to shield Lois as well as herself from the truth, she concocts a story that her sister Edith Provo died giving birth to Tom Ryden's illegitimate daughter, Lois. Milo discovers that Edith never existed and that Selma actually is Lois' mother rather than her aunt.

Rosacoke Mustian, Milo's younger sister. Like Milo, Rosacoke assumes many family responsibilities, including cooking, washing, and tending her baby sister. Although only eleven years old, she already has resigned herself to a life of drudgery and misery. Lois reads her palm and indicates that Rosacoke will meet a man, bear his child, and then marry him.

Horatio (Rato) Mustian, Milo's younger brother. Mentally slow, Rato is quiet and withdrawn and prefers animals to people. When Phillip, the family dog, becomes ill, Rato attempts to carry the creature several miles to get him to a veterinarian. A sensitive individual, he removes Phillip's muzzle even though the dog supposedly is dangerous because of an illness.

Phillip, the family dog. Diagnosed with everything from worms to rabies, he is supposed to be shot, but he escapes from Rato at the county fair and begins chasing Death, Lois' python. When Rato and Phillip fail to return home, a posse begins to search for them and Death.

Death, an eighteen-foot python given by Tom Ryden as a gift to Lois and Selma Provo. Death has a monetary value of five hundred dollars, but he also takes on a symbolic meaning as the posse becomes obsessed with finding him.

Rooster Pomeroy, the town sheriff and posse leader. Easily distinguished by his large bulk and his stained panama hat, he pairs himself with Milo during the hunt and continually offers the boy advice on handling women. Ironically, Rooster has nothing to crow about, for he and Kate Pomeroy, his wife, are experiencing marital problems. He eventually sends Milo to his house, fairly sure that the youth and his wife will end up in bed together.

Kate Pemberton Pomeroy, Rooster's wife. A twenty-seven-year-old woman with huge black eyes, she is haunted by her past. After seducing Milo, she reveals that years ago she had met Tom Ryden, Milo's look-alike cousin, in a jail cell. Tom had asked her to bear his child, but she refused. Since that time, she has attempted suicide twice at the realization of the passion she has lost.

Tom Ryden, a shiftless wanderer. Physically a middle-aged version of Milo, Tom is believed by everyone to have been killed in World War II. Although he does not make his brief appearance until two-thirds of the way into the novel, his relationships to Lois, Selma, and Kate cause interesting plot twists. Milo is forced to kill him in self-defense when he begins to lose his mind and attacks the boy.

— *Coleen Maddy*

THE "GENIUS"

Author: Theodore Dreiser (1871-1945)
First published: 1915
Genre: Novel
Locale: Alexandria and Chicago, Illinois, and New York
Time: 1889-1914
Plot: Naturalism

Eugene Witla, a sensitive young man with vaguely artistic aspirations. Haunted by an ideal of beauty, he is led to become an artist and to fall in love with many women. Finding no enduring peace in his search for beauty, he seeks it in social and financial success with the same negative results. After years of dryness, his impulse toward beauty is reawakened by his infant daughter, around whom he begins to weave impossible dreams for their future together.

Angela Blue, a young schoolteacher seduced by and later married to Eugene. In an attempt to save their marriage, she has a baby against all medical advice, and she dies in childbirth, leaving her husband with a daughter who revives his interest in artistic endeavor.

Angela Witla, the daughter of Eugene and Angela. She becomes her father's inspiration for a renewed interest in his artistic life.

Stella Appleton, Eugene's first love.

Margaret Duff, Eugene's first mistress.

Ruby Kenny, an artist's model and mistress of Eugene.

Miriam Finch, a sculptress Eugene meets in New York.

Christina Channing, a singer. She and Miriam become friends of Eugene and help educate him in the ways of the New York artistic world. Christina becomes Eugene's mistress briefly.

Anatole Charles, an art dealer and exhibitor of Eugene's paintings.

Frieda Roth, a young woman attractive to Eugene.

Carlotta Wilson, a gambler's wife with whom Eugene has a passionate affair.

Daniel Summerfield,
Obadiah Kalvin,
Marshall P. Colfax, and
Florence J. White, Eugene's associates in the publishing and advertising businesses. White is jealous of Eugene's rise in the company and cheerfully helps Mrs. Dale get him fired.

Suzanne Dale, a young woman with whom Eugene falls in love. Her influential mother takes her away and has Eugene fired from his job.

Mrs. Emily Dale, a wealthy socialite, mother of Suzanne.

Thomas Witla, Eugene's father.

Sylvia and
Myrtle Witla, Eugene's sisters.

Mrs. Johns, a Christian Science practitioner.

THE GENTLEMAN DANCING-MASTER

Author: William Wycherley (1641?-1715)
First published: 1673
Genre: Drama
Locale: London, England
Time: The seventeenth century
Plot: Satire

Mr. James Formal, known as **Don Diego**, the father of Hippolita. Engaged in trade with the Spaniards, he is so enamored of their gallantry and pride that he attempts to imitate their manners and confines his daughter to her house in true Spanish fashion. Blinded by his pride, he allows himself to be duped by Hippolita and her allies to the point where, to save face, he must pretend to have been a willing collaborator in her plans to wed Mr. Gerrard.

Hippolita, the daughter of Mr. Formal. Although she is engaged to her cousin, Mr. Paris, and confined to her home by her father, she manages to become enamored of Mr. Gerrard, whom she sees from her balcony. Through a series of ruses, she, Mr. Gerrard, and her maid, Prue, contrive to deceive her father and her fiancé and bring about a wedding between her and her beloved.

Mr. Paris, the nephew of Mr. Formal and the approved suitor of Hippolita. Fresh from Paris, he affects French manners to the point of absurdity, and his silliness causes him to be the willing dupe of Hippolita in her love affair with Mr. Gerrard.

Mr. Gerrard, a young gentleman about town who courts Hippolita while disguised as a dancing master. His suit is aided by Mr. Formal's fierce Spanish pride in his ability to protect his daughter under his own roof. Mr. Gerrard marries the lady under the deceived parent's nose.

Mrs. Caution, Mr. James Formal's sister and Hippolita's duenna.

Prue, Hippolita's resourceful maid and ally.

Mistress Flirt, a prostitute by whom Mr. Paris is undone.

Mr. Martin, Mr. Gerrard's friend and ally.

THE GENTLEMAN USHER

Author: George Chapman (c. 1559-1634)
First published: 1606
Genre: Drama
Locale: Italy
Time: The seventeenth century
Plot: Comedy

Duke Alphonso, an elderly widower who is in love with Margaret. Under the influence of a sinister favorite who calls himself Medice, he banishes his son for attempting to marry Margaret. Although he is hot-tempered, the duke is generous and finally forgives the young couple.

Prince Vincentio (veen-chehn-TEE-oh), the duke's son.

Rather than lose Margaret, he makes a private marriage contract with her, gaining access to her by flattering her father's gentleman usher. Seriously wounded by Medice, he recovers, receives his father's forgiveness, and is united with Margaret.

Margaret, Count Lasso's daughter. Thinking Vincentio slain by his father's orders, she disfigures her face and denounces the duke for his tyranny, bringing about his repentance and reformation.

Count Lasso (LAHS-soh), Margaret's tyrannical father, who wishes her to marry the duke.

Cortezza (kohr-TAYZ-zah), Lasso's sister, who steals a letter from Margaret's jewel box and betrays the young lovers to the count and the duke.

Bassiolo (bahs-see-OH-loh), the count's pompous gentleman usher. Susceptible to flattery, he aids Vincentio in sending a letter to Margaret and in bringing the lovers together. He also is forgiven by his angry master.

Count Strozza (STROHZ-zah), Vincentio's friend. Medice treacherously has him shot with an arrow, but he recovers to unmask Medice and furnishes a physician to heal Vincentio and Margaret.

Medice (meh-DEE-cheh), the duke's malicious parasite, an impostor. Responsible for most of the misfortune befalling the other characters, he is terrorized into confessing his crimes and his real identity and is banished by the duke.

GENTLEMEN IN ENGLAND: A Vision

Author: A. N. Wilson (1950-   )
First published: 1985
Genre: Novel

Locale: Victorian England
Time: 1880
Plot: Satire

Horace Nettleship, a geology professor at London University who specializes in volcanoes. Bald and quiet, with gray whiskers, Horace has chosen to be consumed by his work so as to ignore the reality that he has lost his Christian faith in God and humanity. In addition, because of his retreat into his research, he gradually loses the affection of Charlotte, his wife. Their relationship is reduced to public formalities; when at home, they communicate with each other by addressing their comments to their children, Lionel and Maudie.

Charlotte Nettleship, Horace's angry and discontented wife. Only thirty-nine years old, she is dissatisfied with the drudgery of her daily life and is angry that she was allowed to marry in her naïveté at the age of eighteen. Although she views Horace as a worthy and honest man, through the years she has come to realize that she does not like him. Bored with her own life, she looks for the excitement and romance that she believes her husband does not provide in their relationship. Mistaking the attention that Timothy Lupton, a family friend, displays toward Maudie as intended for herself, Charlotte convinces herself that Timothy is her lover and plans a rendezvous with him on the Continent.

Lionel Nettleship, Horace and Charlotte's oldest child, who is away from home to study at a university. Influenced by various students as well as driven by his own inner longings, Lionel explores the doctrine of the Catholic church and undergoes what he believes is a spiritual conversion. After shocking his family, in particular his father, by announcing in a letter to his sister Maudie that he intends to become a priest, he retires to a monastery for a few weeks, during which time he witnesses unspeakable atrocities and injustices committed by the young men and boys who reside there. This experience causes him to question his own beliefs and results in confusion and loss of faith.

Maudie Nettleship, Horace and Charlotte's teenage daughter. Described as a doe with brown eyes and chestnut hair, the sixteen-year-old still lives at home and finds herself caught in the tension between her parents. Throughout the novel, she learns how to manipulate each parent so as to achieve her desires, but she fails to comprehend completely that her parents are using their relationships with her to hurt each other. This dynamic climaxes when Maudie, who has a racking cough, is forced at the last minute by her mother to stay home rather than attend an important ball for which she has spent the previous year preparing. She pleads with her father to overturn the decision, but he is forced to acknowledge his powerlessness over his wife.

Timothy Lupton, a bohemian painter who becomes obsessed with Maudie. He has dark eyes and thick blond hair and whiskers, and his artistic temperament makes him very attractive to women. He becomes so engrossed with Maudie that she appears in all of his works, but she does not return his affections. Instead, Charlotte misinterprets his attention to the family as devotion to her and even approaches Horace for a divorce so that she can be with Lupton.

Father Cuthbert, a charismatic monk who encourages Lionel in his spiritual pursuits. Standing only five feet, six inches tall, he is described as a Roman emperor with a sharp nose and beady eyes. Although physically small, he captivates large audiences with his emotionally charged speeches.

Doctor Jenkinson, a master at Oxford. Whereas Father Cuthbert provides emotional impetus for Lionel, Doctor Jenkinson offers intellectual stability. Lionel turns to him after his monastic experience, and they discuss faith on a philosophical level.

— *Coleen Maddy*

GEOGRAPHY OF A HORSE DREAMER: A Mystery in Two Acts

Author: Sam Shepard (Samuel Shepard Rogers, 1943-   )
First published: 1974
Genre: Drama

Locale: England
Time: The 1970's
Plot: Mythic

Cody, a clairvoyant who, in his dreams, foresees the results of horse races before they occur. Kidnapped from Wyoming and taken to England by criminals who exploit his talent, he is, as the play begins, suffering from the loss of his powers, which he regains in the course of the action. Sensitive, misunderstood, and a conduit for energies beyond his control, Cody clearly is in the mold of the Romantic artist.

Santee and

Beaujo, criminal underlings who are Cody's keepers. Outfitted like gangsters of the 1940's, Santee and Beaujo follow a pattern well established on stage and screen. Santee is the "bad" guard, harsh in his treatment of their prisoner and contemptuous of Cody's gift; Beaujo is the "good" guard, sympathetic and somewhat in awe of Cody.

Fingers, a gambler, Santee and Beaujo's chief. Tall, slender, and full of affectations, Fingers is an artist manque; he appears to be excessively eager to establish a rapport with Cody.

The Doctor, Fingers' lieutenant. The stage directions specify that he should resemble the cinematic villain Sydney Greenstreet; with his black bag, his unpredictable violence, and his chilling amorality, the doctor lives up to his prototype.

Jasper and

Jason, Cody's brothers. Appearing only at the conclusion to rescue their brother, shotgunning his captors, these hulking figures in cowboy garb are borrowed from the mythology of the Old West.

— *John Wilson*

GERMINAL

Author: Émile Zola (1840-1902)
First published: 1885
Genre: Novel
Locale: France
Time: The nineteenth century
Plot: Naturalism

Étienne Lantier (ay-TYEHN lahn-TYAY), a French laboring man who becomes a miner and falls under the influence of Marxism, which he believes is the workers' only hope. He organizes the miners, only to lose his popularity when a strike is settled and the people go back to work. His suffering, even the loss of his lover in a mine disaster, only persuades him that he must continue his revolutionary work. He is the illegitimate son of Gervaise Macquart.

Catherine Maheu (kah-teh-REEN mah-HEW), a girl who works as a miner. She is loved by Lantier, even though she takes another man as her lover. She eventually becomes Lantier's lover after they are trapped together in the collapsed mine. She dies before help reaches them.

Vincent Maheu, an elderly miner nicknamed "Bonnemort" because of his many escapes from accidental death in the mines.

Maheu, Vincent's son, the father of seven children. He becomes Lantier's friend and works with him in the mine. He is killed by soldiers during a strike at the mine.

Maheude (mah-HEWD), Maheu's wife.

Zacharie Maheu (zah-kah-REE), a young miner who marries his mistress after she presents him with two children.

Philomène Levaque (fee-loh-MEHN leh-VAHK), Zacharie's mistress and, later, his wife.

Souvarine (sew-vah-REEN), a misogynist who becomes Lantier's friend.

M. Hennebeau (ehn-neh-BOH), one of the mine owners. He refuses to make any concessions to the miners and imports strikebreakers to operate the closed mines.

Paul Négrel (nay-GREHL), nephew of M. Hennebeau. He feels compassion for the miners and leads a rescue party to save them after a mine collapses and traps Lantier and others below the surface of the ground.

Chaval (shah-VAHL), a miner who seduces Catherine Maheu. He is jealous of his rival, Lantier, and their mutual animosity ends in a fight below the surface of the ground in which Chaval is killed.

Dansaert (dahn-SEHRT), head captain of the mine in which Lantier works.

Cécile Grégoire (say-SEEL gray-GWAHR), daughter of a mine owner, fiancée of Negrel Hennebeau.

Maigrat, a rapacious storekeeper who lends money to the women who grant him amorous favors.

M. Grégoire, a mine owner who justifies low pay for the workers by believing they spend their money only for drink and vice.

Jeanlin Maheu (zhahn-LEHN), an eleven-year-old child who works in a mine until he is crippled in an accident. He murders a mine guard, but his crime is hidden by Lantier.

Alzire Maheu (ahl-ZEER), a sister of Catherine. The little girl dies of starvation during the strike.

Pluchart (plew-SHAHR), a mechanic who persuades Lantier to become a Marxist.

GERMINIE LACERTEUX

Authors: Edmond de Goncourt (1822-1896) and Jules de Goncourt (1830-1870)
First published: 1865
Genre: Novel
Locale: Paris
Time: The nineteenth century
Plot: Naturalism

Germinie Lacerteux (zhehr-mee-NEE lah-sehr-TEW), an orphan reared by her sisters. Set to work as a waitress at the age of fourteen, she is soon seduced and bears a stillborn child. After a series of jobs she becomes the maid of Mlle de Varandeuil. Because she is naïve, people take advantage of her, even members of her family. She has a desperate need for love, physically and psychologically, which proves her undoing many times. She becomes an alcoholic. She dies of pleurisy after standing hours in the rain in hopes of seeing Jupillon, her former lover.

Mlle de Varandeuil (vah-rahn-DEW-yeh), an old maid with few friends or acquaintances and little money. She becomes Germinie's employer. She does not see Germinie's weaknesses, even her drunkenness, for she is too old to want to hire a new servant. She learns of the frustrations in Germinie's life only after her death.

M. Jupillon (zhew-pee-YOHN), loved by Germinie, though he is ten years her junior. He takes advantage of her and becomes her lover. They have a son who lives only a few months. Though he leaves Germinie for another woman, he still takes her hard-earned money to buy his way out of military service.

Mme Jupillon, M. Jupillon's mother. She owns a dairy store near where Germinie is employed by Mlle de Varandeuil. She takes advantage of Germinie's willingness to help in the store.

M. Gautruche (goh-TREWSH), another of Germinie's lovers. She wants him only as an object for her affections. To his surprise, she refuses to marry him when he proposes, and they part forever.

GETTING OUT

Author: Marsha Norman (1947-   )
First published: 1979
Genre: Drama
Locale: Louisville, Kentucky
Time: Late 1970's
Plot: Psychological realism

Arlene Holsclaw, a young woman in her late twenties, just released from an eight-year prison term for accidentally killing a cabdriver during a robbery. Although physically free, Arlene is psychologically captive to the dehumanization and abuse suffered since early childhood, and her struggle to overcome her past and the self-destructive behavior it engendered forms her central conflict. Arlene, who is driven by her desire to acquire custody of her son and who is fighting to live a normal life and be treated respectfully, encounters people from her past who, in refusing to acknowledge her as a human being, make difficult her struggle to achieve self-fulfillment and self-love. Her strength and courage, both in confronting these ghosts from her past that have molded her into a hostile, cynical, and dispassionate woman and in rejecting their inhumanity toward her, enable her reconciliation with the past and her resignation to live free from the psychological prison and conditioning of her youth.

Arlie Holsclaw, Arlene as an abusive, volatile, and trouble-making teenager, recalled in flashbacks. Arlie is the psyche of Arlene, reliving those painful childhood experiences that shaped and molded Arlene into a displaced, lonely, and bitter child. The memories Arlie enacts, all depicting her life of victimization, particularly the sexual molestation by her father as well as dehumanized treatment of her in prison, are those incidents that robbed her of self-esteem and that she must now confront and exorcise if she is to survive psychologically and emotionally.

Bennie, a retired prison guard who accompanies Arlene home after her release from prison. While he was Arlie's guard in prison, Bennie manipulated her and viewed her as subhuman, an animal in need of taming. Now, Bennie still regards Arlene as his possession, and his initial unwillingness to accept her as a free human being is manifested by his attempt to rape her. He offers Arlene a friendship that she ultimately rejects because it is founded on the typical patriarchal master-slave relationship to which she has been subjected all of her life.

Mrs. Holsclaw, usually called **Mother**, Arlene's mother, a cabdriver. She is a callous, uncaring mother whose neglect of her children resulted in their life of crime. Although aware that her husband sexually molested Arlene, she did nothing to stop it, and now, at Arlene's release from prison, she does not ask Arlene's forgiveness for her injury to her but only offers criticism and indirect refusals to allow Arlene back into her home.

Ruby, a thirty-year-old short-order cook, a former convict who lives in Arlene's apartment complex. Ruby is a pragmatist who, like Arlene, has been victimized by others and has successfully overcome her past. She helps Arlene accept the cruelty in the world, realize the possibility of self-improvement, and understand the need for self-acceptance.

Carl, an escaped convict and small-time hustler who is Arlene's former pimp and the father of her child, though he does not know the latter. He tries to tempt Arlene, with the lure of big money, to travel with him to New York and to return to crime and prostitution.

Ronnie, a juvenile offender who is beaten by Arlie for sexually taunting her.

Principal, a woman in her fifties, another maternal-authority figure whom Arlie defies and who in turn punishes Arlie by coldly admitting that her mother wants her put away somewhere.

Evans and
Caldwell, prison guards who bring Arlie food and break up her fights. Their depersonalized treatment of her and their sexual innuendoes exemplify other degrading experiences Arlie has suffered at the hands of men who control her life.

Warden, another authority figure in Arlie's life who controls her by vague references to parole but affords her no direct help or comfort.

Doctor, a prison physician whose only assistance to Arlie is sedation.

— B. A. Kachur

A GHOST AT NOON
(Il disprezzo)

Author: Alberto Moravia (1907-1990)
First published: 1954
Genre: Novel
Locale: Rome, Capri, and the coast of southwestern Italy
Time: The 1950's
Plot: Psychological

Riccardo Molteni (mohl-TEH-nee), a screenwriter. When he was an impoverished theater critic, Molteni lived happily with his wife, Emilia, although he always yearned to do more for her. When a film producer named Battista hires him to write a screenplay, he does so and is a success. From the moment he begins his new career and acquires more money, however, Emilia gradually turns away from him and rejects him. Insecure and puzzled by Emilia's cold behavior, Riccardo is driven frantic by her rejection. He seeks ways to recapture her love and return to the old days when they were happy. He does not give up his screenwriting or his affluence and loses Emilia.

Emilia Molteni, Riccardo's wife, a former typist. A beautiful young woman, she was content when she and Riccardo lived simply and together in spirit. She secretly comes to resent Riccardo's new job, their new apartment, and his extravagance, but she refuses to admit that her feelings have changed and continues to deny her indifference to him, even though it makes him unhappy and insanely jealous. Emilia is unable to adapt to the new level of affluence that Riccardo has earned for her.

Signor Battista, the film producer who gives Riccardo his first job as a screenwriter. Battista is a middle-aged man, short and sometimes called "the big ape." He has found rich success in the Italian film industry of the postwar era. Materialistic and vain, he nevertheless pretends to be interested in films only as art. He considers using Homer's *The Odyssey* as the subject of a film and views the various events in the story as opportunities to titillate film audiences. Battista symbolizes the crass and sensational aspects of the Italian film industry and films in general. In his speech, Battista also represents "culture" as traduced by commerce, and he becomes upset with anyone who hints that he is materialistic.

Herr Rheingold (RIN-gold), a German film director called in to direct the film of *The Odyssey* that Battista proposes. Silver-haired and with the "Olympian" features of a great thinker, he is a man of the past, having reached fame in the 1930's as a director of German films in the colossal style. Rheingold disagrees with Battista that Homer's poem can provide the basis of a sensational film. Instead, Rheingold wants to make the film a psychological study of a man who is unhappy with his wife and hesitates to return home. This view in a way harmonizes with Riccardo's worry over his own dilemma about Emilia. Thus, Riccardo often agrees with Rheingold during script discussions, though he does not agree with Rheingold's personal interpretations of the story.

Pasetti (pah-SEHT-tee), the director of Molteni's first film. A maker of small commercial films, Pasetti nevertheless professes great admiration for the arts and presents himself as a cultured man. He lives with his devoted wife, and Riccardo envies him tremendously for this domestic bliss, although he dislikes Pasetti's pretensions. Pasetti is typical of the kind of entertainment people with artistic ambitions who filled the Italian film business in the 1950's. Pasetti also displays the pettiness of the little tyrant when he pretends to withhold Riccardo's check temporarily. It is this gesture that makes Molteni despise and envy the director.

— *Philip Brantingham*

THE GHOST SONATA
(Spöksonaten)

Author: August Strindberg (1849-1912)
First published: 1907
Genre: Drama
Locale: An apartment house in Sweden
Time: The early 1900's
Plot: Expressionism

Arkenholz (AHR-kehn-hohlts), a student. The unshaven young man's appearance is less an indication of slovenliness than of the fact that he is a man of action. The student was a hero in a disaster, a house collapse, that occurred just before the time of the play. Throughout, his vigorous, life-affirming qualities are in contrast to those of the mostly anemic, old, or quite literally dead characters who appear in this dream play. The "student" aspect of his character is at least as important. As the central character, his chief function is to observe the events around him, contemplate the various intrigues and disclosures of corruption, and thereby learn what life and death truly entail. At the end, he shares his conclusions with the audience.

Hummel (HUHM-mehl), an old man. Hummel has white hair and a white beard, wears glasses, and uses a wheelchair. Rather than the grandfatherly figure his appearance would suggest, Hummel is a sinister character who generally goes by "**the old man**" rather than his surname. "The old man" may recall "old Nick" and other sobriquets for the devil, an appropriate association because Hummel operates in a context of vampirism and the satanic. He seems to have had a hand in the lives (or deaths) of most of the characters in the play, and he entangled Arkenholz's father in shady dealings in the past. He seems intent on ensnaring Arkenholz as well, at least early in the play. If Arkenholz is the student, Hummel is the teacher; Arkenholz's wisest decision is to reject the teachings of his master.

The Girl, a friend of Arkenholz. Unnamed, like most of the characters, the Girl ostensibly is the daughter of the Colonel, who lives in the imposing house that dominates the setting of the play, but really is the daughter of Hummel. She appears wearing first a riding outfit, then a dress. From their first meeting, Arkenholz and the Girl seem destined for each other. Unlike many of the other characters, she survives long enough to share with Arkenholz some of the secrets of the house and to witness his final illuminating vision. Although spiritually innocent, she is contaminated by the tradition of corruption represented by Hummel and the house itself, and at the end she moves toward death.

The Milkmaid, an apparition. The Milkmaid is seen only by Arkenholz, but she is much feared by Hummel, whom the Milkmaid implicates in her death. She—like most of the characters in the play except for Arkenholz, Hummel, and the Girl—has no personality as such but serves to personify some facet of experience.

The Colonel, the ostensible father of the Girl and husband of the Mummy. As is true for many of the characters, the Colonel's past is more important than what he does or does not do in the play. According to Hummel, the Colonel beat his wife, who left him, then returned to marry him a second time.

The Mummy, the Colonel's wife and mother of the Girl. White and shriveled, she is a sort of walking death, broken not by age so much as by the lies of her life. She lied to her husband about her age when they first met, for example. More important, her daughter was fathered not by her husband but by Hummel. Early in the play, she can hardly speak, only parroting phrases of others. By the end of the penultimate scene, though, she has worked up enough rage to tell everyone the truth about Hummel, thereby causing his death.

The Dead Man, a consul. The Dead Man's corpse awaits burial throughout the play. Sometimes, the Dead Man walks around, generally to check on his funeral arrangements.

— Dennis Vannatta

THE GHOST WRITER

Author: Philip Roth (1933-)
First published: 1979
Genre: Novel
Locale: The home of E. I. Lonoff, in the Berkshires
Time: 1956
Plot: Comic realism

Nathan Zuckerman, an established Jewish novelist. He recalls a visit, twenty years earlier, to the home of a famous older writer. At the age of twenty-three, Zuckerman was serious about his work and longed for the kind of reclusive life devoted to his craft that his mentor E. I. Lonoff was leading in the Berkshires. As is characteristic of people in his chosen profession, Zuckerman lives more in a life of fantasy than in reality. He quarreled with his own father, who objected to a story by Zuckerman that was not flattering to Jews, and he goes to visit Lonoff to find sanction from a literary father. The most significant fantasy in which Zuckerman engages while at Lonoff's home occurs when he meets a mysterious young woman, Amy Bellette, whom he fantasizes is Anne Frank, the girl who became famous posthumously as a result of her diary about her experiences while in hiding, with her family, from the Nazis during World War II.

E. I. Lonoff, who is described by Zuckerman as the most famous literary ascetic in America. Lonoff has little time for anyone or anything but his writing. At the age of fifty-six, he has the devotion to his craft of Henry James, the mysterious seclusion of J. D. Salinger, and the perceptive awareness of Jewish experience of Bernard Malamud or Isaac Bashevis Singer. Nothing ever happens to him, he says; his life consists of "turning sentences around," and he considers anything else a waste of time.

Hope Lonoff, the famous writer's neglected wife. Not a master of renunciation like her husband, Hope is starved for love and attention. She has spent the thirty-five years of her married life primarily trying to keep quiet and out of Lonoff's way as he pursues his religion of art. Primarily, says Zuckerman, she has the obedient air of an aging geisha. Helplessly, she watches as one of Lonoff's former students, Amy Bellette, tries to persuade him to leave for Europe with her. Finally tiring of what she calls Lonoff's rejection of life, she packs her bags at the end of the story and leaves.

Amy Bellette, a mysterious and beautiful young Jewish immigrant. Because all that is known of Amy Bellette is what Zuckerman tells the reader, and because he has created such a significant fantasy life, it is difficult to say exactly who she is. It is known that she emigrated from England to become one of Lonoff's students at a local college. She now works for the Harvard Library, which is trying to persuade Lonoff to donate his manuscripts to its archives. The fantasy that Zuckerman makes up about her—that she is really Anne Frank and that he wishes to marry her to exonerate himself from the accusations of his father that he is indifferent to Jewish survival—is by far the most interesting aspect of her character.

Victor Zuckerman, Nathan's father, a podiatrist. "Doc" Zuckerman strongly objects to the image of the Jewish people he sees in Nathan's first short story. He claims that non-Jews will not perceive it as art but only as a story about "kikes."

Leopold Wapter, a prominent Jewish leader in Newark, New Jersey. At the request of Nathan's father, Judge Wapter writes Nathan a long letter expressing his objections to his story and urging him to see the play *The Diary of Anne Frank*.

— Charles E. May

GHOSTS
(Gengangere)

Author: Henrik Ibsen (1828-1906)
First published: 1881
Genre: Drama
Locale: Rosenvold, Norway
Time: The nineteenth century
Plot: Social realism

Mrs. Helen Alving, a widow, the mother of an ailing only son. Although she reads liberal books and has extraordinarily liberal views concerning the possible marriage of her son and his illegitimate half sister, whose identity is known only to Mrs. Alving, she is an outwardly severe woman whose life has been governed by duty. As a young wife, she had fled from her profligate husband, whom she had married for his money, to seek refuge with the parish pastor, Mr. Manders, with whom she had fallen in love. Mr. Manders righteously had sent her back to her husband, and they maintained the appearance of a home for the remainder of his life. With her husband's money, which she now loathes, Mrs. Alving has built an orphanage in memory of her husband. On the advice of Mr. Manders, she decides not to insure the building because to do so would be to show lack of faith. When the building burns, Mrs. Alving is indifferent. Although Mrs. Alving promises her son Oswald that she will administer some fatal pills to him when his mind goes, she is unable to do so at the conclusion of the play. Her revulsion and terror are unrelieved.

Oswald Alving, an art student afflicted with a disease, apparently syphilis, contracted or inherited from his father. He reveals to his mother that his mind is being blotted out by the disease, which doctors have told him was acquired early in his life. Because Mrs. Alving had sent Oswald away from home at seven years of age so that he would not realize his father's true nature, he believes he has brought the disease on himself. In addition, he has inherited his father's joy of life, now left behind with his art and his free-living companions abroad. Faced with mental oblivion, he comes home but finds no solace except in the contemplation of a possible marriage and departure with Regina, a young servant, in whom he recognizes the joy of life they have both inherited from their father. Incapacitated by the knowledge of his destiny, Oswald can no longer paint. He tries drink but gets little relief. After he tells his mother of his condition and his hope of marrying Regina, Mrs. Alving decides that she must tell them that they have the same father. This knowledge devastates Oswald. Shortly after he shows his mother the pills, which he says Regina would have been willing to give him, his mind goes, and he plaintively asks his mother to give him the sun.

Regina Engstrand, a servant, ostensibly the daughter of a carpenter. Her mother, Joanna, now dead, had been a maid in the Alving household. Mr. Alving was Regina's father. Unaware of her identity, Regina feels that she is above Engstrand, who wants her to return to him and help him run a "home for homeless sailors." Regina, ambitious to marry Oswald and improve her station even before the idea has occurred to Oswald, detests Engstrand, who drinks and accuses her mother of immoral behavior. When Regina discovers that she is Oswald's half sister, she leaves for the "Alving Home," the sailors' refuge that Engstrand will finance with money from the Alving estate, money that Mr. Manders has secured for him. When Mrs. Alving tells her that she is going to her ruin, Regina shows no concern.

Mr. Manders, the pastor of the parish. When Mr. Manders reproves Mrs. Alving for deserting her husband and for sending her young son away to become a freethinking artist, she reveals the true nature of Mr. Alving, her reason for sending Oswald away, and the identity of Regina. After young Helen Alving's flight to him, Mr. Manders, fearful of his reputation, had never gone again to the Alving house. He is present now only to advise her about the business of the orphanage, but he proves a poor counselor. When the orphanage burns as the result of his snuffing a candle carelessly at prayer services and throwing it on a heap of shavings, his remorseful cry is, "And no insurance!" Manders, a self-righteous man, reproves Mrs. Alving for her liberal reading and unwise behavior and Oswald for his unconventional views, but he is completely taken in by the rascal Engstrand, who, Manders thinks, wants to reform. He pays Engstrand to assume blame for the orphanage fire.

Jacob Engstrand, a carpenter paid to marry Joanna, Regina's mother. Engstrand is a drinking man of no consequence, a rascal. Regina thinks at first that it would be improper for her to live in his home, even though at the time she thinks of him as her father. Engstrand suggests the fatal prayer service at the orphanage and later claims to have seen the candle fall in the shavings. Because he uses the occasion to get the Alving money from Manders, he may be lying. For the reward of the money paid him, he gladly assumes responsibility for the fire.

GIANTS IN THE EARTH: A Saga of the Prairie
(I de dage *and* Riket grundlægges)

Author: O. E. Rölvaag (1876-1931)
First published: 1924-1925
Genre: Novel

Locale: The Dakotas
Time: Late nineteenth century
Plot: Regional

Per Hansa, as his friends call him, born **Peder Hansen** and later renamed **Peder Holm** to fit his new life in the Dakota Territory. A strong, self-reliant man who came to America to be near his best friend, Per Hansa saves his small Norwegian pioneer community by his ingenuity and perseverance in the face of great odds. Though beset by family problems, the powerful man turns his wilderness tract into the finest farmland, superior to all the other farms in the region. He is loving, cheerful, and even-tempered, except for a few black and angry moods caused mostly by his wife's piety on the one hand and her lack of wifely respect on the other. He goes to his certain death in a blizzard for the spiritual comfort of his best friend.

Beret, his beautiful, pious, superstitious wife, who sees the giants or trolls of destruction come out of the untamed prairie. She often confounds her enterprising husband with sharp criticism of his seemingly dishonest acts, such as removing claim jumpers' stakes from their land. She suffers from a mental disorder brought on by childbirth and depression over their hard life; after a traveling preacher sets her mind at ease, however, she becomes the loving wife of former years, with only her dark piety causing discord. It is she who persuades the dying friend that he needs the ministrations of the preacher; thus she sends her husband out into the blizzard that claims his life.

Ole Haldor,
Hans Kristian,
Anna Marie, and
Peder Seier, their four children, the latter born on Christmas day of their first year in the wilderness. Ole and Hans are useful to their father and mother, while the younger sister keeps them all cheered by her sunny looks and disposition. The new arrival, is born with a caul, a sign of future greatness that the mother hopes will mean he will become a minister.

Hans Olsa, born **Hans Olsen**, who later changes his name to **Hans Vaag**, after his wife's birthplace. Hans Olsa, the leader of the community and the great friend of Per Hansa, is as steady as he is strong. Only once is he roused to anger, when an Irish claim jumper curses him; and then one sledge-hammer blow with his great fist fells the man, and a great swoop of the Norwegian's arms throws the poor fellow into his own wagon. Hans performs christening ceremonies, fills out legal papers, opens up new lands, and generally manages the pioneering community's business. His wife Sorïne cares for the Hansa child while Beret is ill, looks after the bachelor Solum brothers when they are teaching the neighborhood youngsters, and ministers gently to the needy immigrants. Their daughter is a favorite among Per Hansa's boys. Hans Olsa loses his life as the result of exposure and frostbite, and he dies waiting for the preacher he knows his friend Per will bring safely through the blizzard.

Sorïne, Hans Olsa's devoted wife.

Sofie, their daughter.

Syvert Tönseten, the foolish, garrulous justice of the peace. Although his wife Kjersti is a favorite of the group, Tönseten is embittered because he has no children and because he is never consulted on matters of importance. While Kjersti is beloved for her secret generosity, Syvert is laughed at for his pompous ways. He keeps the Solum brothers from leaving the community, but he offsets the value of keeping them on as schoolteachers by displaying his own authority in the classroom.

Henry Solum and
Sam Solum, Norwegian American brothers who come with the wagon train from Minnesota. Henry shows good sense and courage at all times, though Sam develops these pioneer qualifications as he grows to manhood. They speak English and thus act as interpreters for the group.

THE GIFT
(Dar)

Author: Vladimir Nabokov (1899-1977)
First published: 1937-1938
Genre: Novel

Locale: Berlin
Time: 1926-1929
Plot: Parody

Fyodor Konstantinovich Godunov-Cherdyntsev (FYOH-dohr kohn-stahn-TIH-noh-vihch GOH-dew-nov-chehr-DIHN-tsehv), a young Russian émigré writer who lives in Berlin. As the novel begins, Fyodor recently has published his first volume of poetry, a collection of works about childhood. The collection contains several gems of precise description but is destined never to receive the approval of a broad general audience. Over the course of the novel, Fyodor probes the possibility of using a variety of topics as the subject of a new written work: the suicide of Yasha Chernyshevski, the adolescent son of Fyodor's friends, Alexander and Alexandra Chernyshevski; the life and disappearance of his own father, the famous Russian explorer and naturalist Konstantin Godunov-Cherdyntsev; and the life and public image of Nikolay Chernyshevski, a famous nineteenth century critic. During this time, Fyodor meets Zina Mertz and falls in love with her. The novel concludes after the publication of Fyodor's controversial treatise on Nikolay Chernyshevski, a work that exposes the enormous fallacies in the critic's theories on art but that also depicts the man as eminently human. Despite the generally unfavorable reviews his work receives, Fyodor is pleased, and as the novel ends, he looks forward to spending the night with Zina, oblivious to the fact that both he and she are locked out of their apartment.

Zina Mertz, a young woman who lives with her mother and stepfather, Marianna Nikolaevna and Boris Ivanovich Shchyogolev. A quiet and sensitive soul, she responds deeply to Fyodor's aesthetic talents and serves as his supporter and muse during his work on Chernyshevski.

Konstantin Kirillovich Godunov-Cherdyntsev (kohn-stahn-TIHN kih-RIH-loh-vihch), Fyodor's father, a famous explorer who never returns from an expedition to the Far East during the period of the Russian Revolution and Civil War.

Nikolay Chernyshevski (nih-koh-LAY chehr-nih-SHEHV-skee), a radical nineteenth century Russian journalist whose ideas on the relationship between art and life proved influential for succeeding generations of utilitarian critics.

Yasha Chernyshevski, the son of Alexander and Alexandra Chernyshevski, an impressionable youth who becomes caught up in a complex emotional triangle with two friends, Rudolf Baumann and Olya G., and who kills himself as part of a triple suicide pact. The other two, however, are horrified by his act and decide not to kill themselves.

Koncheyev (kohn-CHEH-yehv), an émigré poet whose work Fyodor very much admires. Fyodor conducts two imaginary conversations with Koncheyev on the subject of Russian literature and Fyodor's own writing.

Alexander Yakovlevich Chernyshevski (yah-KOV-leh-vihch), an émigré Russian who has become mentally unbalanced after the death of his son. Fyodor imagines how this man might perceive the ghost of his son appearing at regular intervals in their apartment.

Boris Ivanovich Shchyogolev (ee-VAH-noh-vihch SHCHO-goh-lehv), Zina Mertz's stepfather, a narrow-minded individual who relishes long-winded conversations about world politics, during which he reveals a tendency toward ethnic bigotry.

— *Julian W. Connolly*

THE GIFT OF THE MAGI

Author: O. Henry (William Sydney Porter, 1862-1910)
First published: 1905
Genre: Short fiction

Locale: New York City
Time: Early twentieth century
Plot: Moral

Della, or **Mrs. James Dillingham Young**, a young housewife in New York City. Deeply in love with her husband, Della is distraught that Christmas Day is imminent and she has but a pittance to spend for a gift for him. Her husband's salary of $20 a week leaves little after living expenses are paid. Although her love for her husband is enough to sustain her even in this abject poverty, not being able to honor her husband with a worthy Christmas gift is simply too much to bear. She is overcome with tears of helplessness, but they pass as inspiration moves her to a creative solution to her dilemma. Della's one prideful possession in the midst of her humble circumstances, her long, lustrous hair, may be the means to secure a present that she can wholeheartedly give her beloved. Her willingness to sacrifice for him bespeaks the depth of her love.

James Dillingham Young, Della's husband. Jim is a thin, serious young man of twenty-two who bears the burden of supporting his wife and himself on only $20 a week. Times had once been better for Jim. In brighter days, he had brought home $30 a week. A drop in their income has not changed the fact of their love for each other. Ever punctual, Jim may be so in part because of the one treasure he possesses, a beautiful gold watch that had belonged to his father and his grandfather before him. Slightly embarrassed by its inglorious fob, an old leather strap, Jim often checks the time furtively. He sacrifices the watch to buy combs for Della's hair as his Christmas gift to her.

Madame Sofronie, the proprietor of the shop that sells "hair goods of all kinds." A large, impassive woman, she offers Della $20 when Della seeks to sell her hair.

— *Kim Dickson Rogers*

GIGI

Author: Colette (Sidonie-Gabrielle Colette, 1873-1954)
First published: 1944
Genre: Novel

Locale: Paris, France
Time: 1899
Plot: Social satire

Gilberte (zheel-BEHRT), known as **Gigi** (zhee-ZHEE), a charming fifteen-year-old girl who is being educated by her great-aunt and her grandmother to become a successful courtesan. Gigi has the legs and feet of a ballet dancer: heronlike legs, with high-arched insteps, perfect oval-shaped kneecaps, and slender calves. Her eyes are dark blue, and her hair of ash-blonde ringlets has magnificent fullness. She looks like Robin Hood, a carved angel, or a boy in skirts; she least resembles a nearly grown girl. She dresses in typical French schoolgirl fashion, wearing a serge coat and blue sailor hat. Her nature is both gentle and independent. She is playful and irreverent, traits that charm Gaston, the thirty-three-year-old millionaire who at first sees her as an enchanting child and who later decides that he wants her as his mistress. She, however, has her own ideas about what she wants to do with her life. She does not want to be a typical courtesan who will please a man for a while and be discarded for the next woman, nor does she want to become the dull wife of a boring clerk. She wants to marry the kind of man who will love her forever and treat her in the lavish, glamorous way a man is expected to treat only his mistress, never his wife.

Madame Inez Alvarez (ee-NEHS AHL-vah-rehs), Gigi's grandmother, who is in charge of rearing her. She took the name of a Spanish lover, now dead, and calls herself Inez. She has a heavy Spanish face and resembles the nineteenth century writer George Sand. She has a creamy complexion, an ample bust, hair lustrous with brilliantine, and too-white face powder on her heavy cheeks. She teaches Gigi decorum. Madame Alvarez once had an affair with Gaston's father and thinks that Gaston would be the perfect first wealthy admirer for her granddaughter. She creates the perfect ambience for Gaston's visits; offering good conversation and chamomile tea, she demands nothing in return.

Andrée (ahn-DRAY), Gigi's mother, the second lead singer in the state-controlled theater. She lives with her mother, Inez Alvarez, and Gigi. Her life is a sober one of work and very little amusement. Madame Alvarez makes it very clear that Gigi is not to turn out like Andrée; she must profit from the example of her mother's bad judgment and unfortunate marriage and prepare herself well for the life of a courtesan who will be kept in grand style by wealthy admirers.

Aunt Alicia, Gigi's maternal great-aunt, a former courtesan who helps her sister, Madame Alvarez, in Gigi's education. She is seventy years old and still quite beautiful, combining robust health with a pretense of delicacy. She has fastidious taste and teaches Gigi how to eat daintily and to cultivate discriminating taste in jewelry, knowing which stones are appropriate to accept as gifts and which stones should be refused. Her philosophy of life is that she, her sister, and her niece are not ordinary women; they do not marry and should not marry. She agrees with her sister that Gigi should agree to become Gaston's mistress.

Gaston Lachaille (gahs-TOHN lah-SHI), a handsome millionaire, heir to the Lachaille sugar fortune. Gaston is a thirty-three-year-old, self-indulgent dandy with a long nose and dark eyes who carries massive gold or silver cigarette cases, wears a dark sable-lined topcoat, and drives a pretentious Dion-Bouton motorcar. He is, in a word, "smart." He has just been jilted by his mistress and is looking for a replacement. He spends much time at the flat that Gigi shares with her mother and grandmother. Madame Alvarez consoles him and flatters him. At first, he sees Gigi as a charming child, one whom he spoils with gifts. The plot of the novel turns on the change in his perception of Gigi, when he recognizes in her a potential mistress and makes an arrangement with her grandmother to that effect. When Gigi refuses his offer, her attitude angers him, confuses him, and, finally, wins his heart.

— Anne Callahan

GIL BLAS
(Histoire de Gil Blas de Santillane)

Author: Alain-René Lesage (1668-1747)
First published: 1715, 1724, 1735
Genre: Novel
Locale: Spain
Time: The seventeenth century
Plot: Picaresque

Gil Blas of Santillane (heel blahs, sahn-tee-YAHN), a rogue who serves a series of masters and finally ends up a country gentleman.

Blas of Santillane, his father, married to an elderly chambermaid.

Gil Pérez (PEH-rehs), Gil's uncle, a fat canon who gives Gil forty pistoles and a donkey and sends him to the University of Salamanca.

Antonia (ahn-TOH-nyah), a farmer's daughter who becomes Gil's wife. She and their baby daughter die.

Dorothea (doh-roh-TEH-ah), Gil's second wife, with whom he spends his remaining days in Lirias on an estate given him by Don Alfonso.

Scipio (SKEE-pee-oh), Gil's servant, who tries to arrange a marriage with the rich daughter of a goldsmith, an effort ruined by Gil's arrest.

Captain Rolando (rroh-LAHN-doh), a leader of robbers who capture Gil on his way to Salamanca.

Donna Mencia (MEHN-see-ah), a prisoner of the robbers who is rescued by Gil.

Fabricio (fah-BREE-see-oh), Gil's schoolmate, who advises him to go into service.

Doctor Sangrado (sahn-GRAH-doh), one of Gil's masters, whose universal remedy is bleedings.

Don Matthias (maht-TEE-ahs), another master, whose fashionable clothes Gil borrows to impress a "fine lady." She turns out to be a serving maid.

Arsenia (ahr-SEHN-ee-ah), an actress who employs Gil for a short time after Don Matthias is killed in a duel.

Aurora (ow-ROH-rah), a virtuous woman whose love affair with Lewis is furthered by Gil.

Lewis, a college student desired by Aurora. They eventually marry.

Don Alphonso (ahl-FOHN-soh), whom Gil gets appointed governor of Valencia.

The Archbishop, who angrily discharges Gil for criticizing his sermons.

The Duke of Lerma, the prime minister, whom Gil serves as a confidential agent.

Count Olivarez (oh-lee-VAHR-ehs), the new prime minister, who tries unsuccessfully to keep Gil at court.

THE GILDED AGE: A Tale of Today

Authors: Mark Twain (Samuel Langhorne Clemens, 1835-1910) and Charles Dudley Warner (1829-1900)
First published: 1873
Genre: Novel
Locale: The United States
Time: Late 1840's to early 1870's
Plot: Social satire

Colonel Beriah Sellers, an improvident opportunist of Missouri and an operator on a grand scale.

Squire Hawkins, of Obedstown, Tennessee, persuaded by Sellers to move to Missouri, where his affairs fail to prosper.

Nancy Hawkins, his wife.

Emily, their daughter.

George Washington, their son.

Henry Clay, an orphan adopted by Hawkins during his journey.

Laura, the survivor of a steamboat accident, who is also adopted by Hawkins. She is fraudulently married by Colonel Selby, who already has a wife. When she sees him later, she shoots him. At the trial, she pleads insanity and is acquitted, only to die of grief.

Colonel Selby, of the Union army.

Major Lackland, who boasts of knowing about Laura's missing father.

General Boswell, a real-estate man who employs Washington Hawkins.

Louise Boswell, the general's daughter, in love with Washington.

Philip Sterling, a young New York engineer who is building the railroad in Missouri.

Harry Brierly, his friend, in love with Laura.

Ruth Bolton, who is in love with Philip and eventually becomes his wife. She wants to study medicine.

Eli Bolton and

Margaret Bolton, Ruth's Quaker parents of Philadelphia. They are shocked by her modern ways.

Alice Montague, whom Ruth visits in New York.

Senator Dilworthy, who investigates Seller's request for congressional funds to improve the area. The senator's bill to establish a university for blacks on Hawkins' land is defeated when his attempt to buy votes is exposed.

GILES GOAT-BOY

Author: John Barth (1930-   )
First published: 1966
Genre: Novel

Locale: New Tammany College
Time: Indeterminate; resembles the 1960's
Plot: Fantasy

George Giles, known as **Goat-Boy** and **Billy Bocksfuss**, a young man seeking his identity and vocation at New Tammany College. At first, George believes he is a kid and that his name is Billy Bocksfuss. George was conceived by a mating between the artificial intelligence running the East and West Campuses and a human female. The book covers his life from adolescence to his thirty-third year, during which time he learns that he is not a goat, learns to walk erect (with a stick because he is lame when not on all fours), learns to control his sexual impulses (relative to goat standards), and learns that it is difficult to distinguish between saintly and sinful (Passed and Flunked) behavior. The vocation he chooses is that of hero. His adventures, sexual and otherwise, surround his quest to become a Candidate for Graduation, to become a Graduate, and to demonstrate that he is a true Grand Tutor, or great teacher. He must also determine his true and proper relationship to Anastasia Stoker, or Stacey, with whom he falls in love as soon as he approaches the campus. After several near lynchings, George becomes accepted by a small number of disciples, but he leaves a document saying that he expects to have been consumed by lightning at the age of thirty-three and a third, hung (ritually and by his own choice) on an old oak tree. A postscript, supposedly questioning the validity of that document, says he simply disappeared.

Max Spielman, the Goat-Boy's Moishian (Jewish) keeper and adviser. He is a scientist who discovered EAT (Electroencephalic Amplification and Transmission), which is used to attack political or philosophical opponents by destroying their minds. He used the process during a time of crisis (Campus Riot II) and throughout the time of the story is torn with remorse. Having ensured George's entry to the Campus, he allows himself to be falsely arrested and executed. George reveres Max as a foster father as well as a moral and intellectual guide.

Anastasia (Stacey) Stoker, the adopted daughter of Virginia Hector (also known as Lady Creamhair), the real mother of George. She sexually provokes George Giles as he enters the campus, though she claims to have been helping to subdue Croaker, a Frumentian (or African) exchange student. Anastasia is unable to refuse her body as a source of consolation to anyone desiring it. She and George learn the nature of true love, and she bears his child.

Maurice Stoker, the husband of Anastasia Stoker and half brother of Chancellor Lucky Rexford. He is head of Main Detention and the Power House. He represents a model of Flunked behavior in small matters (farting) as well as large (hosting orgies and encouraging his wife in promiscuous behavior). He is temporarily converted to Passed behavior, but George finds him more charming in his natural mode.

Peter Greene, a capitalistic Huck Finn, good old boy patriot, and family man. He is a devoted admirer of Anastasia who talks about and endures a series of difficulties related to his sexual potency. He champions the Goat-Boy's enemy, Harold Bray, a false Grand Tutor, but maintains his naïve good nature and is a friend to George throughout.

Leonid Alexandrov, a Nikolayan (Russian) defector. He has the power to unlock anything, and his personality is filled with love; his father, Classmate X (Chementinski), turns out to be Max's compatriot. Leonid's mission is to earn his father's love at any cost, but he is also a great friend to Max and George.

Virginia Hector, also known as **Lady Creamhair**, George's mother, who unintentionally arouses him while teaching him that he is a human. It is later that he discovers that she is his mother and not Anastasia's. She was inseminated by the West Campus Automatic Computer (WESCAC) with the Grand-Tutorial Ideal, Laboratory Eugenical Specimen (GILES).

Dr. Eierkopf, a scientist who created George, in the sense that he was in charge of the Cum Laude project that developed the GILES. He serves during the story to control Croaker mentally as Croaker provides for him physically. Eierkopf is continually doing research on eggs.

Harold Bray, the false Grand Tutor. He continually succeeds in convincing the majority of West Campus that he is the Grand Tutor. At the time of Max's shafting (execution), he reveals himself as a horrible, green phallus.

G. Herrold,
Croaker, and
O. B. G.'s daughter, three black characters. They provide sexual or other assistance to George; to the impotent scientist, Dr. Eierkopf; and to Peter Greene, respectively. G. Herrold and Croaker sacrifice themselves. G. Herrold is the one who saved the Goat-Boy from WESCAC, at the cost of his own sanity, though not of his sexuality. Croaker carries George and Eierkopf on his shoulders, the only way in which he remains tame. O. B. G.'s daughter is considered by Peter Greene to be an inveterate tease.

Kennard Sear,
Hedwig Sear,
Lucky Rexford,
Reginald Hector, and
Ira Hector, each of whom represents a philosophical, political, and personality type significant in George's growth and experience.

Mary Appenzeller,
Redfearn's Tommy,
Hedda-of-the-Speckled-Teats,
Brickett Ranunculus, and
Triple T., all goats, who serve as Billy Bocksfuss' friends and family.

— *Anna R. Holloway*

THE GILGAMESH EPIC

Author: Unknown
First published: c. 2000 B.C.E.
Genre: Poetry

Locale: The ancient world
Time: Antiquity
Plot: Adventure

Gilgamesh, the king of Uruk, a demigod. He is the wisest, strongest, and most handsome of mortals. In earth-shaking combat, he overcomes Engidu, who has been fashioned by Aruru to be his rival. After the battle, the heroes become inseparable friends and companions through a series of heroic exploits. After Engidu dies, the grieving Gilgamesh seeks for and finds his friend in the land of the dead.

Engidu, a demigod formed by Aruru to be a rival to Gilgamesh. Vanquished by Gilgamesh, he becomes the hero's inseparable companion and goes with him to conquer Khumbaba. Accidentally touching the portal of the gate to Khumbaba's lair, he receives a curse from which he even- tually dies. Allowed to meet the grief-stricken Gilgamesh in the underworld, he reveals to his friend the terrors of death.

Utnapishtim, a mortal who possesses the secret of life. After Engidu's death, Gilgamesh receives from Utnapishtim the secret—a magic plant—only to lose it on his homeward journey.

Aruru, a goddess who fashions Engidu from clay.

Anu, the chief of the gods.

Ninsun, a goddess and adviser to Gilgamesh.

Ishtar, a fertility goddess who is in love with Gilgamesh.

Siduri, the divine cupbearer.

Ur-Shanabi, the boatman on the waters of death.

Ea, the lord of the depths of the waters, who grants to Gilgamesh a meeting with the dead Engidu.

Khumbaba, a fearful monster.

THE GINGER MAN

Author: J. P. Donleavy (1926-)
First published: 1955
Genre: Novel

Locale: Dublin, Ireland, and London, England
Time: Late 1940's
Plot: Picaresque

Sebastian Balfe Dangerfield, a former American soldier attending Trinity College law school after World War II. He is a twenty-seven-year-old who is less concerned with academic pursuits than with drinking, brawling, wenching, and thieving his way through Dublin. He assumes a series of personae in hopes of escaping detection and entrapment. Although he longs for wealth and respectability, his chaotic life ensures poverty. Just as a fortune seems within his grasp after his father's death, Dangerfield learns that the will stipulates holding his inheritance in a trust for twenty years.

Marion Dangerfield, Dangerfield's disenchanted British wife. Tall and slender, with long, blond hair, she frequently quarrels with her husband over his dissolute ways. Although she leaves him repeatedly, they always reunite, until finally she prevails on his father to send her money. She then escapes to her parents in Scotland.

Kenneth O'Keefe, a former Harvard student who is Dangerfield's best friend. Twenty-seven years old and destitute, O'Keefe is frustrated by his poverty and sexual privation. He leaves for France with great expectations, later returns to Dublin, and then embarks for the United States. His many humorous letters of defeat and travail punctuate the narrative.

Christine, a twenty-five-year-old laundry worker and former psychology student at London University. With fair skin, dark hair and lips, and a mellow voice, she is attracted to Dangerfield and has an affair with him before Marion leaves. Eventually, she tires of his exploitative ways and will have nothing more to do with him.

Lilly Frost, an unmarried Roman Catholic woman who rents a room from the Dangerfields. A botanist for a seed company, she is thirty-four years old, with a medium build and large teeth. After his wife leaves him, Dangerfield seduces and then uses and humiliates Frost until she is forced to return to a corrupt aunt. Because of her Catholicism, she is wracked with guilt, for which Dangerfield has little sympathy.

Mary Maloney, a young woman dedicated to rearing her brothers and serving her abusive father. She is short and stocky, with green eyes and long, black hair. Dangerfield is immediately attracted to her. After Mary and Dangerfield sleep together, she vows to leave her father and join Dangerfield in London. In London later, and after he berates her, she loses weight and begins a career in films and resumes her fitful romance with Dangerfield.

Percy Clocklan, a short, bullish man who is one of Dangerfield's drinking companions. He invites Dangerfield to the party where Dangerfield meets Mary. Later, Clocklan is believed to have committed suicide by jumping from a mail ship. A destitute Dangerfield meets him on the streets of London, where the now-wealthy Clocklan outfits and takes care of Dangerfield.

Egbert Skully, a former landlord of Dangerfield who hounds him through most of the novel for back rent and repairs on a damaged house. Middle-aged and dressed in black, Skully is symbolic of death and entrapment, and Dangerfield goes to hilarious lengths to avoid the man.

— *David W. Madden*

GIOVANNI'S ROOM

Author: James Baldwin (1924-1987)
First published: 1956
Genre: Novel
Locale: Brooklyn and New York, New York; southern France; and Paris
Time: Late 1940's or early 1950's
Plot: Social morality

David, an American living in France. David is in his mid- to late twenties, and he is a selfish and self-deceiving man. The story is told through his recollections on the eve of the morning that Giovanni is to be executed for murder. As a boy, David had a mutually fulfilling sexual encounter with another boy, Joey, but felt ashamed and left early the next morning. He ignored Joey the rest of the summer. As a penniless young man living in Paris, he becomes involved with a woman, Hella Lincoln. He also becomes involved in another homosexual relationship, this time with Giovanni, an Italian bartender. David ends this relationship as cruelly as he did his first homosexual encounter, and he becomes engaged to Hella in an effort to deny his true sexuality. All of David's actions ultimately become ruled by his homosexual desire or his desire to escape his homosexuality.

Giovanni, an Italian living in Paris. A passionate, good-looking homosexual whom David meets, Giovanni is attractive to—but is not attracted by—the men at the bar where he works. He is, however, attracted to David, whom he comes to love deeply. When David moves out on him, he searches frantically for him and is devastated to find that David has moved in with Hella and that he is denying that their relationship ever happened. Unemployed and broke, he becomes Jacques's companion but leaves when Jacques stops giving him money. When he goes back to Guillaume's bar to apply for his old job, Guillaume once again makes a pass at him, to which he submits. When Guillaume tells him afterward that he still cannot have his job back, Giovanni beats him in a fit of rage and kills him. Giovanni is arrested a week later. He pleads guilty to murder and is sentenced to death.

Hella Lincoln, an American woman living in Paris who becomes David's girlfriend. She is attractive but deeply concerned with trying to find her identity as a woman. She decides that the thing she most wants is to start a family. Although David and Hella's relationship is fairly casual, Hella accepts David's marriage proposal. Later, Hella feels used and enraged when David leaves her and she discovers him with another man. She leaves for the United States a few days later.

Jacques, a wealthy American living in Paris. A middle-aged homosexual, Jacques is accustomed to buying sexual favors from young boys. He takes David out to the bar, where they meet Giovanni. While David is living with Giovanni, Jacques lends David money. After David leaves, Giovanni becomes Jacques's companion and financially dependent on him, until Jacques stops giving him money.

David's father, a resident of Brooklyn, New York. After his first wife's death, he reared David with the help of his sister, Ellen, though he did not get on well with her. He refuses to send David money until David promises to come home.

Guillaume, the owner of the bar at which Giovanni worked. Ugly and accustomed to having sex with young boys, Guillaume's sexual harassment of Giovanni causes Giovanni to quit. He finally seduces Giovanni by hinting that he might get his job back but finally refuses to rehire him, causing Giovanni to kill him in a fit of violent rage.

Sue, a large, wealthy young American woman living in Paris. David, while trying to erase his memory of Giovanni, seduces her. She is largely aware of how he is using her.

Joey, a boy on Coney Island with whom David had a deeply and mutually fulfilling sexual encounter but ignored afterward.

— Thomas J. Cassidy

THE GIRL

Author: Meridel Le Sueur (1900-　　)
First published: 1978
Genre: Novel
Locale: St. Paul, Minnesota
Time: The 1930's
Plot: Social realism

The Girl, the unnamed narrator, daughter of poor, rural Minnesotans. She makes her way to the twin cities, "Sodom and Gomorrah," as her mother calls them, and finds work in a speakeasy called the German Village. There, she falls in love with Butch. They become involved in a bank robbery that results in Butch's death. The Girl, who is pregnant, returns to her women friends who live in a warehouse in St. Paul and help each other through collectives and by pooling their resources. She gives birth to a daughter.

Clara, a prostitute. Frail and loving, she befriends the Girl, who is unacquainted with the city. Clara is full of hope and imparts optimism to the Girl as they walk the bitter winter streets of St. Paul. Ironically, Clara, who knows the streets, is a dreamer of dreams derived from magazines or films, and all the time she is showing the Girl how to survive, she is dying. She dies as the Girl gives birth to a daughter named Clara.

Butch, a man with a dream. He wants to own a gas station, and he wants to love the Girl and to have a family. All of his dreams are thwarted because he cannot find work. His brother Bill is killed for "scabbing" during a strike, and in desperation, he goes along with Ganz, who plans to rob a bank. The plan is a fiasco. Butch is shot but escapes long enough to die in the arms of the Girl.

Belle, Hoinck's wife. Married to Hoinck for more than thirty years, she has a heart as big as her body. She serves and nurtures him, as well as her women friends, amid the chaos and poverty overshadowing their lives. She dispenses bootleg liquor along with her homemade "booya," a rich, nourishing stew. When Hoinck is killed in the bank robbery, she moves with her women friends to the warehouse and continues to sustain others.

Ganz, the "stool," betrays through greed. He and his lawyer, Hone, use and manipulate the downtrodden. He rapes the Girl and shoots Hoinck and Butch. During the robbery, Butch shoots him.

Amelia, a woman who frequents the speakeasy distributing leaflets of the Workers Alliance. She also serves others through her labor, whether peeling carrots or midwifing. Faithful and helpful, she is a bulwark against the ravages of poverty. She helps see the Girl through her delivery.

Emily Schaffer, the Girl's mother, who has given birth to eleven children. She lives a life of poverty yet imparts a sense of "it's good to live" to the Girl.

Hoinck, Belle's husband. He is a bootlegger and works in a speakeasy. He has tried honest occupations, from selling handmade toys to street preaching, but he failed at all of them. He is shot in the back during the bank robbery.

— Alice L. Swensen

THE GIRL GREEN AS ELDERFLOWER

Author: Randolph Stow (1935-)
First published: 1980
Genre: Novel
Locale: Suffolk, England
Time: Early 1960's
Plot: Symbolic realism

Crispin Clare, a twenty-five-year-old anthropologist who has experienced a physical and emotional breakdown. Suffering from malaria, he attempted to commit suicide. Recuperating in isolation at The Hole Farm in Suffolk, England, where his ancestors lived, Crispin attempts to accomplish in writing a goal that he cannot verbalize. Between visits and games with his cousin's children, Clare reads Latin tales of twelfth century England. When he writes, the children, the locals, and Crispin's visitors dissolve into a mysterious blend of medieval legend, superstition, folk tales, and twentieth century culture: Medieval children play Monopoly, and a twelfth century merman is enchanted by a transistor radio. Fascinated by a mysterious young woman seen locally, whom he associates with the medieval "girl green as elderflower," Clare writes his way back to health. He grapples with his past through the visit of his friend Matthew Perry, with the present through the children, and with the problem of good and evil through his contact with the disaffected American priest Jim-Jacques Maunoir.

Alicia Clare, the recent widow of Crispin Clare's cousin Charles. At forty-three (the age of soon-to-be-inaugurated President Kennedy), Alicia is youthful and attractive in a manner reminiscent of Pre-Raphaelite paintings, with hair that gives red glints in the firelight. As the mother of the adolescent Marco and his younger brother and sister, Lucy and Mikey, she appears with them in various forms in the tales that Crispin tells. Alicia is the stable force in Crispin's world, busying herself with household duties, yet needing adult conversation.

Marco (Mark) Clare, the tall nineteen-year-old son of Alicia and Charles Clare. With dark hair that, like Alicia's, has a hint of copper, Mark is troubled by adolescent woes, yet he is an insightful young man. He weaves in and out of Crispin's life and tales—in the present arranging a disappointing meeting with a girl at Crispin's house, in the past appearing as a tall boy in the tale of a family with whom a twelfth century spirit child (cursed by her mother into a kind of half-damnation) becomes familiar.

Mikey Clare, Alicia and Charles's ebullient six-year-old son. Genuinely fond of Crispin, whom he telephones frequently and urges to play games, Mikey appears with the other children in Crispin's story of the spirit child and is suggested, as the boy christened Michael, in the tale of the green children who emerged from the earth.

Lucy Clare, the brown-haired ten-year-old daughter of Alicia and Charles. A considerate, pleasant, sensible child, Lucy urges Crispin to play at the Ouija board and helps her mother serve tea. Lucy appears in all of Crispin's time-transcending tales—as the girl with whom the spirit child is most familiar in the first tale, as the constable's daughter in the tale of the wild man from the sea, and as the child of the injured warrior to whose home the green children come in the third tale.

Amabel, an uncanny seven-year-old friend of the Clare children who seems to communicate with the twelfth century spirit child through the Ouija board. Amabel is very fair, with pale hair, eyes of mixed hazel and green, delicate features, and a small voice that leads Mark to call her "Tinkerbell." She has an uncanny sensitivity to the tarot cards. She appears in Clare's tales of the wild man from the sea and in the tale of the green children as the girl who becomes the wife of the Jewish peddler.

Jim-Jacques Maunoir (moh-NWAHR), a French Canadian priest from Maine. Disillusioned as a priest, he seems nevertheless to be in control of himself. He, too, appears in Clare's tales. In the final tale, he provides the consolation to the peddler's widow that grief is love, that the world is wider than it may seem, and that God's garden is ongoing and includes an infinite variety of experiences.

Matthew Perry, Crispin's old school friend who comes to visit. Troubled by his tendency toward homosexuality and by his Jewishness, Perry consoles Crispin as he recalls his illness. Perry appears as the hanged and tortured merman in Crispin's tale of the wild man from the sea and as the peddler in the final tale.

A pale blonde stranger, a possibly Swedish or Welsh woman who appears in the local pub, in the local church, and on the road. Resembling Amabel's pale beauty, she weaves in and out of present and past. She is thought by the locals to be "lascivious" and is suggested in the tale of the green children as the girl who later becomes Earth Mother and wife to the Jewish peddler.

— Mary Ellen Pitts

A GIRL IN WINTER

Author: Philip Larkin (1922-1985)
First published: 1947
Genre: Novel
Locale: A provincial town and a village in England
Time: Mid-1930's and early 1940's
Plot: Psychological realism

Katherine Lind, a foreign girl visiting in England. Twenty-two years old, Katherine is a refugee from an unnamed European country. Her home near the Rhine has been invaded by the British. Katherine is pale, with dark hair and a shield-shaped face. She has dark eyes, high cheekbones, and a wide mouth with full lips. She has returned to England, having previously spent a three-week summer holiday with the Fennels in Oxfordshire six years earlier. Lonely and isolated for the nearly two years she has been back in England, she lives above a chemist's shop and works as a temporary assistant librarian. She has not notified the Fennels of her return, but when she reads that Jane's child has died, she writes a letter of sympathy. Asked to escort Miss Green to the dentist, Katherine takes her afterward to her own apartment, where a note from Robin has been delivered. Prevented from keeping her appointment with Robin because she mistakenly picked up the wrong handbag at the chemist and feels obliged to retrieve Miss Green's purse, Katherine vows to live without the pain and disappointment that such a reunion likely would bring. Katherine recognizes that she has lost the romanticism of youth and settles instead for self-protective pessimism.

Robin Fennel, Katherine's English pen pal. Dark and slight, Robin possesses long eyelashes and bowlegs. Idolized by Katherine, he treats her as would a schoolboy, with courteous reserve and consideration but not romantically. When she is saved by him from toppling into the water, Katherine falls in love with him, even though his sister claims he is dull and ordinary. On the last night of Katherine's summer visit, Robin awkwardly kisses her. When war breaks out, he joins the army and spends fourteen months as an artilleryman. Having not seen Katherine for six years, Robin writes her to say he will call on her that afternoon. He slips away without leave from his military post with the intention of sleeping with Katherine, leaving a friend to cover his absence. He attempts to force kisses on her but cannot arouse an amorous response from her.

Jane Fennel, Robin's older sister. She left school at the age of sixteen and went to technical college to learn shorthand and typing. She then worked at an insurance office for a year and subsequently for her father. When Katherine meets her, Jane is without an occupation and always acts as chaperon to Katherine and Robin. She is a small and bony young woman who is rude to Katherine during her stay at the Fennels' home. Although Robin has been Katherine's pen pal, it is actually Jane who encouraged Robin to invite Katherine to stay with the family for the summer. Although she lacks Katherine's romantic illusions, she agrees to marry Jack Stormalong to escape the boredom of home. Jane's daughter, Lucy Katherine, is named in part for Katherine Lind, but the child is born with a defective heart and dies.

Jack Stormalong, a young, fast-talking friend of the Fennels. About twenty-five years old, Jack stands more than six feet tall and drives a sports car. He has short, wavy, oily hair and blue eyes, and his front teeth protrude. He has been tiger hunting in India, and his visit to the Fennels removes Katherine as the center of attention.

Lancelot Anstey, Katherine's fussy and irritable boss, the head librarian. Thin and about forty years old, Anstey has a narrow face and oiled hair. A widower—his wife died five years previously—he smokes a pipe and is a boorish and pompous man. Katherine discovers that he is secretly courting Miss Parbury when she finds an unsigned letter in his handwriting in Miss Parbury's purse.

Miss Green, a junior librarian about sixteen years old. She has the reputation of a gossip at work. Although she lives with her mother, when she suffers from a toothache she is directed to a dentist by Katherine, who is quite considerate of Miss Green's suffering.

Miss Veronica Parbury, the owner of the handbag that Katherine mistakenly picks up when buying aspirin for Miss Green. About thirty years old, she lives with her invalid mother who has had a stroke.

Miss Holloway, a library cataloger. She has crisp black hair and horned spectacles. She is Katherine's well-informed but unemotional colleague.

Rylands, the previous head of the library. Young and well-educated with a university degree, he left the library to become a soldier.

— *Jerry W. Bradley*

GIRL, 20

Author: Kingsley Amis (1922-1995)
First published: 1971
Genre: Novel
Locale: London, England
Time: Late 1960's
Plot: Comic realism

Douglas Yandell, the narrator and coprotagonist. He is a bachelor and a classical music critic for a London newspaper, occupations to which he devotes himself equally. Thus, he has divided loyalties—or rather, divided antagonisms—toward London society. He stands out, by comparison, as a committed antiquarian. About him he sees indolence and habits of taste that are not simply bad but perversely opposed to human enjoyment. His habit of analysis comes with his critic's vocation, and his bachelor's avocation makes him appreciate laxness. The events of the novel make him doubt himself and his conviction that he is a holdout and a dissenter. The time seems ripe for him to form an alliance with Penny; these two lost souls, in their aimlessness, might help each other find direction. Penny, however, has found another, more desperate, solution. Douglas, newly aware that he is sick, ends the novel with no prospects of recovery.

Sir Roy Vandervane, the other protagonist, a fiftyish symphony conductor. Successful and well respected, he constantly struggles to keep up with the times and to increase his already considerable celebrity. There is nothing serious about him, besides his talent for music, but his energy, affability, and undisguised enthusiasm for low pursuits give him charm. Roy is dissatisfied with the respectability of married life and takes up with a seventeen-year-old mistress, despite her not-to-be-ignored, thoroughgoing faults. He feels that the taboos involved are a boon to his vigor. When his sincere attempt to betray classical music to ingratiate himself with youth ends in the smashing of his Stradivarius violin, he is chastened. The incident stirs his sentimental attachment to what the violin represents: excellence and the difficult, painstaking effort that is made to look easy. He does not learn this lesson well enough, however, and soon is increasing his efforts to curry favor with youth and accept its love for the easy made to look easy. By the end of the novel, he has made an open break with his wife, thus causing the disintegration of his family, and is making plans to marry his young lover.

Penny Vandervane, Roy's daughter by another marriage. She is a lost youth, with a well-developed horror of the entertainments, diversions, and purposes that the London society of her time offers, yet cynical about all of its alternatives. She feels compelled to do nothing, despises anything that by chance or design she happens to do, and is disgusted by her own idleness. Only her family and its troubles animate her. When the family dissolves, she solves the problem of having a life to live by taking heroin. By the end of the novel she has, in effect, begun a long suicide.

Gilbert Alexander, the Vandervanes' West Indian factotum. Although he has adopted a fashionable left-wing activist's personality and speaks in Third-World-liberationist cant, he is the novel's foremost social conservative. He works quietly and with bewildering efficiency as a Vandervane family partisan. He cannot save the Vandervane family; he cannot even save Penny, whose lover he has been and for whom he reserves his most personal attention. When the Vandervanes' situation becomes hopeless, he quits the battlefield. He takes for himself Douglas' girlfriend, winning her by offering demands and interference where Douglas offered merely freedom and independence.

Sylvia Meers, Roy's young mistress, a monster of youth. She makes herself master of every social situation by being eagerly insulting. She has enough native intelligence to give her insults sting, and she also draws on her complete shamelessness and an utter confidence in the virtues of youth. Her enthusiasm for railing against bourgeois mores and manners runs only slightly ahead of her enthusiasm for bourgeois privileges and luxuries. All the characters in the novel work against her affair with Roy, but she keeps her hold on Roy by the purity of her lewdness. At the book's close, they are making plans for their marriage.

— *Fritz Monsma*

A GLANCE AWAY

Author: John Edgar Wideman (1941-   )
First published: 1967
Genre: Novel
Locale: A town in the Allegheny region of the United States
Time: Easter Sunday, in the early 1950's
Plot: Psychological realism

Edward (Eddie) Lawson, a thirty-year-old black drug addict whose jobs have included moving pianos and sorting mail for the post office. His high forehead, with its taut, shiny skin, shows his skull beneath, with a palpitating vein that in anger thrusts itself forward. Eddie returns home on Easter morning from a drug rehabilitation program to find himself an outsider both at home and in his old community. He feels that he is somehow responsible for his mother falling down the stairs on the day he returns home. He tries to come to terms with his anger and guilt, getting little support except from another outsider, Robert Thurley.

Robert Thurley, a middle-aged professor of comparative literature. An unhappy marriage, alcoholism, and frustration from teaching uninterested students all have turned Thurley to homosexual encounters with young black men. He encounters Eddie both before and after Eddie returns from his rehabilitation program. He is impressed by Eddie's intensity and somehow feels connected to Eddie. On Easter day, he tries to save Eddie from returning to drugs. His nonsexual encounter with Eddie leads to a rediscovery of the dignity within himself.

William "Brother" Small, Eddie's best friend and a man of the streets. An albino black man with horsey features, pink eyes, pimples, a bald head, and a lispy voice, Brother is ugly even in his own repulsive world of drinking and drugs. His very ugliness excites Thurley, and they become friends. They both feel responsible toward Eddie because he lives life more intensely than they do.

Martha Lawson, Eddie's mother. Skinny Martha is still a young girl when she has her first son, Eugene, named for her father. She favors Eugene over her second son, Eddie. After Eugene is killed and her alcoholic husband, Clarence, dies, she ages rapidly. The weight of her steel crutches and her anger at Eddie cause her to topple down the stairs on the evening of Eddie's return home.

Alice Small, a ballet dancer who is Brother's sister and Eddie's girlfriend. After Alice returns from winning a ballet scholarship, she tries to integrate Eddie into a more cultured world by taking him with her to her ballet lessons so he can watch. When she finds out that Eddie has slept with one of her white ballet friends, Clara, she cannot forgive him. When he returns from rehabilitation, a confrontation between them ensues from which Eddie backs down.

DaddyGene, Martha's father and Eddie's grandfather. He is an alcoholic, half-black, half-Italian who worked as a paperhanger. He takes the children to church, which makes a deep impression on Eddie.

Eugene Lawson, Eddie's older brother. As the first-born child, Eugene is his mother's favorite. Even after he is killed in the war, his mother waits at the gate for his return.

Bette Lawson, Eddie's younger sister. Her young life consists of taking care of her mother. She already has started to become like her mother by waiting up for Eddie and questioning him. She is sometimes Brother's lover.

Tiny, called **Twinkletoes** because he would dance at the Tioga Street Sanctified in the Name of Jesus Christ Church. Huge, with rolls of black fat, Tiny could cast off the weight of his world and dance on a cloud of grace. He made a lasting impression on Eddie and his sister Bette. Talking about Tiny's dancing created an almost mystical link between brother and sister.

— Sandra Willbanks

THE GLASS BEAD GAME

(Das Glasperlenspiel: Versuch einer Lebensbeschreibung des Magister Ludi Josef Knecht samt Knechts hinterlassenen Schriften)

Author: Hermann Hesse (1877-1962)
First published: 1943
Genre: Novel
Locale: Castalia
Time: Possibly the year 2400
Plot: Bildungsroman

Joseph Knecht, **Ludi Magister Josephus III**, an elite student of Castalia who is, at the age of forty, appointed Master of the Game, an instrument of transformation and perfection. The novel's narrator recounts Knecht's story as a legend rather than as strict biography and traces Knecht's development from his teenage years at the schools Eschholz and Waldzell, to his years as Master of the Game, and, lastly, to his brief entry into the *vita activa* before his death. The existential experiences of his life gradually bring him closer to full self-realization ("awakening"). A compassionate individual and open-minded thinker, the protagonist becomes the leader and prototype of all who cultivate the realm of the mind. He displays the most positive of virtues and qualities, and after much study and learning he eventually is able to integrate the ideals of Castalia (mind and contemplation) with those of the temporal world beyond (nature and life). Focused and goal-directed, the self-reliant Knecht exhibits freedom from personal ambition and yet an intense desire for success as he proceeds down the path of self-analysis and ultimate fulfillment. Knecht's tranquil, cheerful, and radiant manner is free of somberness and fanaticism. His adherence to the ideals of Castalia is superseded by his altruism and preeminent quest for the truth achieved through genuine self-realization. As the meaning of his name in German signifies, Knecht is a servant. He ultimately stands in service to humanity, which is symbolized through his self-sacrifice in ensuring young Tito's safe emergence from the water as he himself dies.

The Music Master, one of the twelve demigods of the Board of Educators for Castalia. He exercises supreme authority in musical matters. Old and kindly, he functions as Knecht's lifelong friend and wise mentor. He imparts to Knecht an appreciation of the importance of meditation and of finding truth within oneself. A saintly figure, the Music Master embodies serene cheerfulness and dignity and, in contrast to the other characters with the exception of Knecht, achieves harmony within the world. Through him, Knecht learns that the only path to truth and fulfillment is through oneself.

Plinio Designori (PLEE-nee-oh deh-zeen-NYOH-ree), a hospitant at Waldzell, combative friend of Knecht, and future man of the world as politician and government official. Older than Knecht, the handsome, fiery, and well-spoken Designori is a non-Castalian from the outside world who embraces anticlerical views. His dedication to the temporal world (nature) is, however, one-sided, as is revealed when his self-confidence is threatened by the difficulties that he encounters in rearing and relating to his son Tito. Designori thus represents a viewpoint equally as limited as those of the players of the Game, who pursue life abstractly and make no attempt to integrate the complementary poles of mind and nature.

Fritz Tegularius (teh-gew-LAH-ree-ews), a friend of and later assistant to Knecht. He is one of the most gifted and brilliant of the players and is referred to as the sublime acrobat of the Glass Bead Game. An eccentric individualist who refuses to adapt to society, he reveals deficiencies of health, balance, contentment, and self-confidence. A classical philologist, Tegularius possesses a rare intellectual gift, but his exaggerated aestheticism leads him to despair. In his neglect of meditation, he embodies a deteriorating Castalia that places too much emphasis on outward form and ritual and too little on the contemplative and integrating factors necessary for achieving harmony and the *unio mystica*.

Father Jacobus, the foremost historian and monk of the Benedictine Order. A scholar, seer, and sage who is an activist and practical statesman influential in Rome, he is responsible for teaching young Knecht the importance of history. In contrast to the sterile pursuit of the history of ideas and art as frequently practiced in Castalia, Jacobus posits a historical perspective full of chaos and of conflict between good and evil, yet one that preserves faith in order and meaning. In interacting with Knecht, he attempts to enlighten but not proselytize, and thus he displays a genuine sense of understanding the value and importance of the individual's independence in fostering his or her own development.

Thomas von der Trave, the Master of the Game prior to Knecht. A great exponent of classical form and irony, he represents the ultimate master and Castalian. Thomas, who is famous, well-traveled and cosmopolitan, and gracious and obliging, fanatically guards the Game against all contamination of its traditional principles.

Carlo Ferromonte, a fellow student and friend of Knecht who rises to the second-highest rank of the Board, a hardworking, practical pedantic devoid of any mystical proclivities. He supports the side of natural life as opposed to Knecht and Castalia's cultivation of the mind. Ferromonte contributes to Knecht's awakening in warning him of the dangers and risks of a sterile life based solely on mind. In returning to the outside world, Ferromonte expresses his gratitude for the benefits that life in Castalia has afforded him but demonstrates that, for him, remaining there is an escape from real life.

The Elder Brother, the founder of the Chinese hermitage where Knecht once briefly studied. He pursues Oriental studies with an ardor that reveals flight from reality rather than acceptance of it.

Tito (TEE-toh), the temperamental son of Plinio and Madame Designori, who experiences a love-hate relationship with his father. When Knecht is summoned to tutor him, Tito gradually recognizes his noble and innate aristocratic qualities and leadership potential. His emergence from the water as the fully awakened Knecht dies symbolizes his first step along the path of achieving his full potential.

Bertram, the deputy of the Magister Ludi, who lacks luck but not talent or goodwill. He provisionally administers the annual Game in the stead of the ailing Thomas.

Plinius Ziegenhals (PLIH-nee-ews ZEE-eh-gehn-halz), a scholar and historian of literature during the earlier bourgeois Age of the Feuilleton. He is credited with establishing the Order of the Glass Bead Game.

Bastian Perrot, an eccentric, clever, sociable, and humane musicologist, most likely a member of the Journeyers to the East. He invents the abacus-like bead-strung wires from which the Glass Bead Game derives its name.

Lusor "Joculator" Basiliensis (bah-sihl-ee-EHN-sihs), the Swiss musicologist who brought the Game to the verge of its capacity for universal application. He represents the quintessence of intellectualism and art and is responsible in the history of the Game for developing it to integrate mathematical and musical principles.

Otto Zbingden, the sixty-year-old headmaster of Waldzell, an eccentric who inspires fear. Through his notes, much of the documentation concerning Knecht's development has been preserved.

Alexander, a master of meditation and deputy of the Order who eventually becomes the new president. He is a strong-willed, disciplined individual with whom Knecht discusses his request for leave from Castalia. As a representative of the status quo, Alexander defends a Castalia that in Knecht's mind is in need of rejuvenation.

— *Paul F. Dvorak*

THE GLASS KEY

Author: Dashiell Hammett (1894-1961)
First published: 1931; serial form, 1930
Genre: Novel
Locale: New York City and its environs
Time: The 1930's
Plot: Detective and mystery

Ned Beaumont, a tall, lean, narrow-eyed, mustached, cigar-smoking gambler and amateur detective. He finds Taylor Henry's body, collects the money Bernie owes him, is tortured by O'Rory, disbelieves Madvig's confession, witnesses O'Rory's murder, receives Senator Henry's confession, and gets Janet.

Paul Madvig, his blond, heavy-set, ruddily handsome friend and the city's political boss, in love with Janet. Though innocent, he confesses to Taylor's murder.

Senator Henry, Madvig's distinguished, patrician-faced candidate for reelection; he is the real murderer of his son, Taylor, who is killed during a violent quarrel.

Janet Henry, his brown-eyed daughter, who hates Madvig and falls in love with Ned.

Shad O'Rory, Madvig's rival, a gangster and ward boss who has Ned brutally beaten for refusing to help frame Paul. He is killed by Jeff.

Opal Madvig, Madvig's blue-eyed, pink-skinned daughter, who had been meeting Taylor secretly. She attempts suicide.

Bernie Despain, a gambler Ned suspects of having murdered Taylor. He owes Ned money, which he finally pays.

Taylor Henry, Senator Henry's son, found dead in the street.

Jack Rumsen, a private detective hired by Ned to trail Bernie.

Michael Joseph Farr, the district attorney, stout, florid, and pugnacious.

Jeff, O'Rory's apish bodyguard, who beats Ned and later strangles O'Rory.

THE GLASS MENAGERIE

Author: Tennessee Williams (Thomas Lanier Williams, 1911-1983)
First published: 1945
Genre: Drama
Locale: St. Louis, Missouri
Time: The 1940's
Plot: Psychological realism

Amanda Wingfield, a middle-aged woman and an incurable romantic. Deserted by her husband and forced to live in dreary lower-middle-class surroundings, she retreats from reality into the illusory world of her youth. She lives for her children, whom she loves fiercely, but by her constant nagging, her endless retelling of romantic stories of her girlhood, and her inability to face life as it is she stifles her daughter, Laura, and drives away her son, Tom.

Tom Wingfield, Amanda's son, through whose memory the story is seen. With literary ambitions, he is trapped by his dreary surroundings, the care of a nagging mother and a disabled sister, and the stifling monotony of a job in a warehouse. He finally rebels and makes his escape.

Laura Wingfield, the disabled daughter of Amanda Wingfield. So shy that she finds ordinary human relationships almost unbearable, she is totally unequipped for the romantic role in which her mother has cast her. She takes refuge among her glass figurines, the "glass menagerie" that is the symbol of her fragility and her retreat from reality.

Jim O'Connor, a former high school hero whom Laura Wingfield has admired from afar. He works with Tom Wingfield, who invites him to dinner. Jim brings Laura her one moment of confident happiness but then, in his honest manner, Jim tells her that he is engaged to be married.

A GLASS OF BLESSINGS

Author: Barbara Pym (Mary Crampton, 1913-1980)
First published: 1958
Genre: Novel
Locale: London and its environs
Time: Mid-1950's
Plot: Comic realism

Wilmet Forsyth, a beautiful and perceptive but idle woman whose only occupation is wife to her civil servant husband. At the age of thirty-three, she is tall, dark, elegant, and obsessed with trivia and social proprieties. Secretly reproving herself for her aimless and self-indulgent existence, she longs for romance and excitement, represented for her by the dashing and mysterious Piers Longridge, and for purpose, which she seeks in St. Luke's parish society. As the story progresses, Wilmet gradually involves herself in church activities and a variety of lives. Her roles as confidant and adviser to Mary Beamish, as benefactor to Wilfred Bason, and as friend to Piers Longridge allow her to develop an understanding of human complexities. By the end of the novel, she is able to look beyond surface appearances in others and appreciate the blessings in her own life.

Rodney Forsyth, a middle-aged, successful civil servant, Wilmet's husband. Viewed through his wife's eyes, he is a good husband and a reliable, conscientious man but is without imagination or spontaneity. Late in the story, he demonstrates, through a near-romance with a professional colleague, that he is also dissatisfied with his overly comfortable existence. Wilmet comes to perceive his ability for impulsive action, his wry sense of humor, and his own insecurities.

Sibyl Forsyth, Rodney's intelligent and strong-minded mother. Nearly seventy years old and of independent means, she maintains an active life in social welfare and intellectual activities that contrasts sharply with Wilmet's idleness. Her confidence, humor, and clear sense of self provide her daughter-in-law with both security and a sense of her own incompleteness. Sibyl's marriage to her friend, Professor Root, provides the stimulation necessary for Wilmet and Rodney's relationship to mature.

Arnold Root, an elderly professor and Sibyl's intellectual companion. As active and carefree as his friend, he decides to cement their long-term relationship through marriage.

Mary Beamish, a dowdy woman in her thirties with a strong sense of religious and social responsibility. After years of caring for an ailing mother and participating in all manner of church and social welfare activities, Mary still seeks her calling. She unsuccessfully tests her vocation in a convent and comes to understand that her useful way of life needs only marriage to Father Marius Ransome to be complete.

Father Marius Ransome, the young and very handsome assistant priest at St. Luke's. With a sense of humor and a taste for good living that, he realizes, may be inappropriate for a man of his vocation, he accepts his own humanity and acquires sufficient confidence to marry Mary and become vicar of his own parish.

Father Oswald Thames, the domineering vicar of St. Luke's. At seventy, he is a man of independent means who is overly conscious of his position as spiritual and social guide. Wilmet learns the value of tolerance through his good-humored acceptance of Wilfred Bason's minor indiscretions, which she finds shocking.

Wilfred Bason, a pompous and effeminate kleptomaniac who is installed as housekeeper for St. Luke's priests after he loses his job in Rodney's office. His penchant for malicious gossip and his need to "borrow" things not belonging to him finally are understood as a desire for acceptance by others.

Piers Longridge, a charming and attractive man in his mid-thirties and the brother of Wilmet's best friend. He has never settled down to either a career or marriage. These facts, combined with a poor showing at the university and a tendency to drink too much, make him an unsatisfactory and vaguely sinister figure to the conventional Forsyths and Talbotts. He provides Wilmet a focus for both of her longings, for purpose and excitement: She decides to reform him and daydreams about an illicit romance between them.

Rowena Talbott, Wilmet's contemporary and best friend. She is content with her role as wife and mother but, like Wilmet, vaguely yearns for the excitement of a lost youth.

Harry Talbott, Rowena's husband, a successful businessman. A solidly conventional man, he rejects Piers as a ne'er-do-well and attempts to initiate a covert flirtation with Wilmet.

— *Gwendolyn Morgan*

GLENGARRY GLEN ROSS

Author: David Mamet (1947-   )
First published: 1983
Genre: Drama
Locale: Chicago, Illinois
Time: 1982
Plot: Psychological realism

John Williamson, a man in his early forties, the office manager for a disreputable real estate company. He receives the blame for all the other characters' problems and failures because he rates their sales and awards and then leads potential buyers to the more successful, thus creating a situation of better salespeople always getting the better leads. He appears incompetent and more concerned with office procedure than with sales. Roma claims that Williamson got the position because he is the boss's nephew. Although he demonstrates an inability to string a customer along, Williamson is not above accepting bribes from his employees or acting ruthlessly. At the end, he catches Levene in his own boast and solves the robbery.

Shelly Levene, a desperate, failing salesman in his fifties. Levene becomes pathetic and foolish in his attempts to regain his salesmanship. Constantly referring to his past successes, he blames his present state on bad luck and Williamson's bad leads. His one moment of triumph becomes a cruel joke when Williamson delights in telling him that his large sale was to a notoriously insane couple whose checks are no good and about whom Williamson warned everyone through memos. Worse, Levene also falls victim to Dave Moss's scheme and robs the office. At the end, Levene is the play's only pathetic figure whose luck has failed him.

Richard Roma, a caricature of the sleazy, smooth salesman; he is in his early forties and is slick and self-absorbed. Completely amoral, he demonstrates the technique by which he has become top salesman of worthless Florida property when he cons James Lingk with a deceptively sincere-sounding contemplation on everyone's need to seize the moment. Roma is the salesman that Levene must have been in his prime. Later, in the middle of the robbery investigation, Roma teams with Levene to dissuade Lingk from backing out of the sale. Ironically, at the end, Roma, impressed by Levene's recent sales but ignorant of Levene's confession, displays his own greed and gullibility when he tells Williamson that he wants a share of whatever Levene has coming to him, or he will tell the boss of Williamson's incompetence.

Dave Moss, a bigoted salesman in his fifties, always looking for an angle to get leads. He sees no problem in resorting to robbery yet is sharp enough to seek out weaker colleagues to perform the actual crime. Persuasive and threatening, he tests his plot on George Aaronow but succeeds with the more desperate Levene.

George Aaronow, a gullible salesman in his fifties who acts as Moss's foil in the robbery plot. He questions the ethics of the act but also is interested in its success. Surprisingly, he does not succumb to Moss's threat and perform the crime. It is not clear if Aaronow saves himself because of any stronger sense of morality or simply by luck.

James Lingk, a man in his early forties who is a caricature of a naïve customer. He is suckered by Roma and saved by his wife. He provides the comic counterpoint to the play's ending by apologizing to Roma for being forced by his wife to cancel the deal.

Baylen, a rough policeman in his early forties who ineptly investigates the office robbery. He provides opportunity for a variety of jokes on police incompetence by the other characters.

— *Richard Stoner*

THE GO-BETWEEN

Author: L. P. Hartley (1895-1972)
First published: 1953
Genre: Novel
Locale: Primarily Brandham Hall in Norfolk, England
Time: 1900, within framing chapters set in 1952
Plot: Love

Leo Colston, a bachelor librarian in his sixties and self-proclaimed "foreigner in the world of the emotions." Colston's discovery of the diary he kept in the summer of 1900, the year he turned thirteen, precipitates release of the repressed memories of the people and events that led to his withdrawal from emotional relationships. The young Leo, imaginative, sensitive, and eager to please, his values and vision determined by the self-centeredness of a child, visits the estate of a schoolmate. Interpreting the kindness of the young adults there as affection for him, Leo feels humiliated when he realizes that their attention to him derives from their use of him as a messenger. Leo's complicity in the tragic result of their love affair causes him to repress the incident and his own emotions.

Marian Maudsley, a young woman engaged to the aristocrat Hugh but in love with the farmer Ted. A spirited, attractive, and sympathetic but somewhat self-centered woman, Marian is torn between her love for Ted, who is socially beneath her, and her family's wish that she marry Hugh, the impoverished but noble man whose family estate the wealthy Maudsleys now own. Marian responds to Leo's discomfort by buying him a suitable set of clothes and a bicycle. Her interest is not quite unselfish, however, as she involves Leo in her affair with Ted by asking the boy to carry messages of assignations between them.

Ted Burgess, a young tenant farmer on the estate. Virile, physically attractive, and passionate, Ted would be a suitable mate for Marian, except that he has insufficient income and is of a lower class. He, too, is kind to Leo. He allows his love for Marian to override his reluctance to involve Leo in their affair. Ted serves as a father figure for Leo in the matter of sex, so his suicide, after he and Marian are witnessed by Marian's mother and Leo, intensifies Leo's reaction to the whole business.

Hugh, Viscount Trimingham, an impoverished noble heir to the estate occupied by the Maudsleys. Hugh's virtues are those of the responsible aristocracy: good taste, good manners, and a highly developed sense of duty. He has recently returned from the Boer War with a disfiguring scar on his face. Whereas Ted's love for Marian is inseparable from his sexual passion, Hugh's love for her is inseparable from his obligation to restore the family estate to the family name. Hugh always does "the right thing." He is also kind to Leo and uses Leo to convey messages to Marian but without anything illicit behind them. Eventually, he marries Marian even though she is pregnant with Ted's child.

Mrs. Maudsley, Marian's mother. The principal proponent of Marian's marriage to Hugh, she invites Leo to visit so that he will be a companion for her son while she arranges the engagement. Her excessive need to be in control causes a conflict of wills between herself and her daughter and results in her nervous breakdown after she discovers Marian with Ted.

Marcus Maudsley, Leo's schoolmate. Marcus is a schoolboyish snob with good manners and a desire to know successful people. Impressed by the name of Leo's home, Court Place, Marcus cultivates Leo's friendship at school. At his mother's suggestion that he invite a companion home, he chooses Leo. Marcus' attack of the measles provides Leo with the freedom to wander the estate and be useful to Marian and Ted.

Edward Trimingham, the grandson of Marian and Ted who, in the frame story, is the current Viscount Trimingham. In his twenties, he refuses to marry the woman he loves because he believes that his family has been cursed since that summer. Although he still lives in the house, it is rented to a girls' school. Marian asks Leo again to carry a message for her and thus again to become involved in her affairs. That Leo does so implies his willingness to come out of his shell.

— *William J. McDonald*

GO DOWN, MOSES

Author: William Faulkner (1897-1962)
First published: 1942
Genre: Novel
Locale: Mississippi
Time: 1859-1941
Plot: Psychological realism

Isaac McCaslin (Uncle Ike), the grandson of Lucius Quintus Carothers McCaslin and heir to his plantation. Isaac, whose father dies while he is young, has two father figures: Sam Fathers, once a slave of Isaac's grandfather, and Cass Edmonds, a cousin sixteen years his elder. Sam Fathers teaches Isaac to hunt and to appreciate nature. As a child, Isaac longs for his tenth birthday, when he will be old enough to go on hunting trips to the wilderness. When Isaac turns twenty-one, he tells Cass that he is relinquishing his patrimony. He argues with Cass, who has been handling the responsibilities of the land, saying that no one should own land. Isaac's objections run deeper: At the age of sixteen, he read the commissary ledgers that reveal his grandfather's sexual relationship with Eunice and Tomasina, both slaves. He believes he must relinquish his patrimony in order to be free of the miscegenation, the incest, and the repudiation of black family members. Isaac leaves the plantation and lives an ascetic life in Jefferson as a carpenter. He continues to hunt with the men who took him to the wilderness, and as he ages, he continues that relationship with their sons and grandsons. Isaac marries, but the marriage is barren and unsuccessful because his wife cannot forgive him for not accepting his birthright.

Lucas Beauchamp, the grandson and great-grandson of Lucius Quintus Carothers McCaslin, descended through McCaslin slaves. He is allotted $1,000 at the age of twenty-one, which allows him to leave the land if he wants to begin a life elsewhere. The money is left to him by Isaac's father and twin brother, who decided to multiply the $1,000 legacy the original McCaslin left to his own son Turl, Lucas' father, who refused the legacy. As soon as Lucas turns twenty-one, he demands not only his $1,000 but also the same sum left to his brother James, who left the McCaslin land without it. Lucas marries Mollie, a city woman. Cass provides him with a house and acres of land to farm, and Lucas rears his family there. Throughout his time on the land, he refuses to accede to demands made on him by any of the Edmondses as they oversee the land. He is proud of his McCaslin blood.

Carothers (Cass) McCaslin Edmonds, the great-grandson of Lucius Quintus Carothers McCaslin, descended through his daughter. Cass, like Isaac, is introduced to the wilderness by Sam Fathers. He oversees the McCaslin land while Isaac is too young and inherits it when Isaac relinquishes it. He is a father figure to Isaac, but they quarrel when Isaac relinquishes his patrimony. Cass believes it is Isaac's responsibility to take over the family land despite whatever sins Isaac sees as coming with it. Cass argues that one cannot give up responsibilities but must discharge them.

Theophilus McCaslin (Uncle Buck), Isaac's father. He and his twin brother Amodeus (Uncle Buddy) move the McCaslin slaves into the plantation house after their father's death in 1837 and triple the legacy their father left to his son Turl by providing $1,000 to each of Turl's children.

Sam Fathers, who was sold with his mother as a slave to Lucius Quintus Carothers McCaslin. He is part Indian, part black, and part white; he associates most with his Indian heritage. He is Isaac and Cass's mentor, teaching them regard for the land and all the creatures on it. He teaches Isaac to hunt and is with him when he kills his first deer. Sam Fathers lives as a blacksmith on the McCaslin land until Isaac is nine, then moves to the Big Bottom, where the McCaslin family hunts.

Zachary (Zack) Edmonds, Cass's son and Lucas' contemporary. He is reared on the land with Lucas, and when young they are almost like brothers. By the time Zack inherits the McCaslin land, he treats Lucas as an inferior rather than as a brother. When Zack's wife dies in childbirth, he appropriates Mollie, Lucas' wife, to care for his infant son. Eventually, Lucas demands Mollie's return. Zack complies, seemingly never before having considered the injustice done to Lucas.

Carothers (Roth) Edmonds, Zack's son. He and Lucas Beauchamp's son Henry are reared as brothers until, at the age of seven, Roth decides that as a white boy he is superior to his black friend and relative. Years later, Roth, a bachelor in his forties, refuses to recognize a son he has by a member of the Beauchamp family. He is a cynical voice repudiating Isaac's more optimistic one.

— *Marion Boyle Petrillo*

GO TELL IT ON THE MOUNTAIN

Author: James Baldwin (1924-1987)
First published: 1953
Genre: Novel
Locale: Harlem, New York City
Time: 1935
Plot: Social realism

John Grimes, a fourteen-year-old boy who, everyone says, is destined to be a preacher and a great leader of his people. He is insecure, intelligent, and ambivalent in the love/hate relationship with the Reverend Grimes, who has taken over as his father, and his church. John is a pubescent artist who finds within himself a terrible conflict over his religious heritage. The novel relates what happens on his fourteenth birthday, a day only his mother remembers. The final chapter finds John writhing on the floor of a sanctuary, his soul the prize in a battle he does not comprehend.

Roy Grimes, John's younger half brother. He is indifferent to religion and expected to be in trouble; he does not disappoint. Roy is the favorite of the Reverend Gabriel Grimes, whereas John is the child of his mother's heart—and sin.

The Reverend Gabriel Grimes, a tyrannical, puritan man, the husband of Elizabeth and father of three of her children, but not of John. Gabriel cannot love John because he cannot forgive the circumstances of his birth; he idealizes his "natural" son, Roy. John represents a child whom Gabriel had conceived with a lover out of wedlock, then abandoned. John thus serves as a reminder of the failure of his own flesh. John also symbolizes for the preacher the former sinfulness of his second wife, Elizabeth.

Brother Elisha, a seventeen-year-old preacher in the storefront church of John's family, the Temple of the Fire Baptized Congregational Church. He is a young, handsome man, consumed by religious fervor, and he is the object of John's spiritual and physical longing.

Florence Grimes, Gabriel's sister and the only person who will stand up to him. She hates him and knows the secrets of his dissolute youth and his fall from grace even after he professed himself saved. In many ways, she is his conscience and his scourge.

Elizabeth Grimes, perhaps the most complex character. She has no conflict with her faith. She is a true believer in the sense that she bears the cross of her past sin—John's conception—as well as the burdens of her poverty, blackness, and hidden hatred of white people, a loathing brought on by her lover's suicide. Richard, John's real father, represented for her a choice between God and lust, a corruption to which she had gladly succumbed. The two leave the South, but before they can be married, yet after Elizabeth is pregnant with John, Richard is jailed for a crime he did not commit. After being acquitted, he cannot live with his understanding that as a black man he is truly "invisible," denied his humanity. He slashes his wrists, despite Elizabeth's great love for him. After his death, Elizabeth is lonely, poor, and guilt-ridden; she turns to Gabriel, who promises to become a true father to John.

— *William Eiland*

THE GOALIE'S ANXIETY AT THE PENALTY KICK
(Die Angst des Tormanns beim Elfmeter)

Author: Peter Handke (1942-   )
First published: 1970
Genre: Novel
Locale: Vienna and a small Austrian village
Time: Late 1960's
Plot: Psychological realism

Joseph Bloch, a construction worker and former soccer goalie. Bloch is a young man when viewed from all perspectives except the game of soccer, which he used to play quite well. Unfortunately, his soccer days are behind him; this is unfortunate because he cannot accommodate himself to the far more complex and unpredictable world of an everyday reality that does not abide by the clear-cut rules of sport. Bloch's paranoia is signaled in the novel's opening paragraph, when he assumes that he has been fired because only the foreman looks at him when he walks into the construction shack. His murder of a theater cashier a day later is merely an extension of this first irrational thought. Throughout the rest of the novel, this formerly great goalie is, ironically, without a goal: He has no genuine destination or purpose in life. The reader follows his wanderings, witnesses his descent into ever deeper psychosis, and wonders how long it will be before his murderous impulse overtakes him again.

Gerda, a theater cashier. Because all characters are seen through Bloch's paranoid-psychotic eyes, it is difficult to view them as discrete, independent entities. For example, the reader is less "astonished" at the naturalness with which the cashier handles Bloch's money than is Bloch himself, yet it is this quality (which Bloch does not possess) that attracts him to her, ultimately leading to her death. She is a product of an existential age, as is Bloch, and in a small way at least—by her foolishness and loose morals—she contributes to her own demise. She lets the peculiar-acting and strange-looking Bloch (he has just been mugged) follow her down a dark street, and when he touches her, she embraces him with a ferocity that surprises even him. She takes this disheveled stranger into her apartment and into her bed. One indication of how little human warmth is involved in this sexual encounter is the fact that she does not bother to tell Bloch her name until the next morning. Shortly afterward, he murders her.

Girl in restaurant, whom Bloch encounters shortly before he meets Gerda. She personifies the rootlessness, heedlessness, and lack of morals of most of the characters who people Bloch's bleak world. With hardly any effort, Bloch manages to pick her up in the restaurant, and she accompanies this total stranger as he tries to find a doorway in which they can have a sexual encounter. No doorway is available, so they ride up and down in an elevator; afterward, Bloch leaves her.

Hertha, Bloch's girlfriend. It is possible that Hertha exists only in Bloch's imagination. He "remembers" that she lives in the border town to which Bloch flees after the murder, but he makes no effort to locate her. In the middle of a conversation with his landlady, however, he begins to call her "Hertha" in his mind, though never aloud. She responds to him in a friendly fashion, but she is efficient, practical, and responsible—unlike the rootless women whom Bloch encounters elsewhere—and perhaps this saves her. Nothing comes of their relationship, although Bloch talks to her more than to anyone else in the novel.

A policeman, who in a short scene with Bloch describes the task of catching a suspect in terms strikingly similar to those used by Bloch to describe the task of a soccer goalie.

— Dennis Vannatta

GOAT SONG
(Bocksgesang)

Author: Franz Werfel (1890-1945)
First published: 1921
Genre: Drama
Locale: A Slavic countryside
Time: Late eighteenth century
Plot: Allegory

Gospodar Stevan Milic, a farmer and the father of two sons, both grown. One is a monster, hidden since birth. He crawls on all fours like a goat and screams terribly. A physician wants Stevan to have him placed in a home, but Stevan refuses because this will mean revealing his secret. The monster's escape worries Stevan so much that people think him mad. In a struggle between the villagers and nearby vagabonds, the monster, now bound and hidden behind the church altar, is regarded as a saint. The vagabonds murder and plunder, thinking that they are appeasing the monster. At last, Stevan is forced to claim the monster as his son before everyone. Later, with both sons dead, Stevan feels young. Their guilty secret disclosed, he and his wife find each other again.

Mirko Milic, his normal son. When he attacks the leader of the vagabonds, he is killed by a guard.

Stanja Vesilic, who is betrothed to Mirko. The marriage has been arranged by the parents, and Stanja comes to stay in the Milic house for a month, as is the custom. Because the vagabond leader says that the monster is to be released only to Stanja, she takes a knife to go into the sanctuary to cut the monster's bonds. After Mirko's death, she insists on staying with Stevan and his wife. At the end of the drama, she reveals that she is carrying the monster's child.

Mirko's mother, Stevan's wife. She always yearns secretly for the misshapen son she has not seen since birth. When Mirko is killed, she is happy, though she does not understand why she wants her good son dead.

Juvan, a student and the leader of the vagabonds. Knowing the truth about the monster, he uses his knowledge to work the vagabonds into a frenzy, thus forcing the landowners to bargain. He sends Stanja in to release the monster. Later, condemned to hang, Juvan tells Stanja that he loves her; her sacrifice to the monster has changed him from an animal knowing only lust to a man capable of love. Although she wants to die with him, Juvan insists that she live.

The monster, Stevan's malformed son. Hidden in a hut since birth and now grown, the human monster is released by a physician who visits him. He is captured by vagabonds, who are in the area demanding land from the farmers, and they install him as a god behind the church altar. The vagabonds force Stevan to acknowledge his afflicted son and then sacrifice Stanja to him before they are dispersed by soldiers. The monster escapes from the church and is later found burned to death in the woods.

GOD BLESS THE CHILD

Author: Kristin Hunter (1931-   )
First published: 1964
Genre: Novel
Locale: An unspecified northern city
Time: The 1950's and the 1960's
Plot: Social realism

Rosalie (Rosie) Fleming, a young black woman driven by her need for love and escape from her ghetto beginnings. During her childhood, the father she adores abandons the family, leaving Rosie with her mother, whom she cannot fully love because she partially blames her for the father's desertion. Rosie turns to her grandmother for solace and love, and her needs go unmet. Instead, Rosie's sense of inadequacy increases; she cannot match her grandmother's romanticized vision of white people, whom the grandmother idolizes, mimics, and serves as a live-in domestic. At an early age, Rosie learns to despise herself and her roach-infested home, which cannot compare to the immaculate, fairy-tale image presented in her grandmother's stories about whites. Once she is old enough, Rosie leaves school and doggedly trudges toward her warped dream. After she is physically worn and wasted, Rosie finally questions all that she has worked for and believed.

Lourinda Baxter Huggs, Rosie's grandmother. She is a devoted servant and admirer of her white employers. Of Southern origins and Creole heritage, Lourinda reveres the chivalric idea of a noble South with benevolent white masters and happy black servants who know and relish their place. After decades of service to a white family, Lourinda considers her employers more her family than she does her own daughter and granddaughter, who cannot possibly attain the gentility Lourinda values above all else. She imparts her twisted love to Rosie, and soon her poisonous dreams capture and consume Rosie's imagination.

Queenie Fleming, Rosie's weary, alcoholic mother. Queenie was once pretty, but her exuberance and vitality have vanished. Unable to rise above racial and sexual conditions, Queenie, a beautician, dreams of finding a good man. Instead, she settles for a hustler who cons her for money. Queenie is able to see through her mother's pretension but is unable to produce more than sporadic outbursts of impotent rage against her mother's ludicrous values. Because Queenie knows how difficult life is for a black female, especially an unattractive one like Rosie, she treats her daughter roughly to make her tough and able to survive. She succeeds, but she alienates

Rosie. Queenie is finally presented with an opportunity to help and possibly reclaim her daughter. The ensuing failure is too much for the already ailing Queenie, who dies.

Dolores (Dolly) Diaz, Rosie's friend since childhood. Dolly envies Rosie's impoverished life, which appears glamorous and exciting. Whereas Rosie is common, strong, and independent, Dolly is prim, repressed, and weak. They are also opposites in appearance. Rosie is skinny and dark, with coarse, short hair; Dolly, on the other hand, has light skin and long, "good" hair. Dolly's preoccupation with her own internal conflicts make her unable to save Rosie. In time, she comes to see the folly of Rosie's life and her own.

— Kenneth D. Capers

GOD BLESS YOU, MR. ROSEWATER: Or, Pearls Before Swine

Author: Kurt Vonnegut, Jr. (1922-   )
First published: 1965
Genre: Novel
Locale: Rosewater, Indiana, and Pisquontuit, Rhode Island
Time: 1964-1965
Plot: Social satire

Eliot Rosewater, the forty-six-year-old president of the Rosewater Foundation. Eliot describes himself as "a drunkard, a Utopian dreamer, a tinhorn saint, an aimless fool." The wealthy alcoholic, who has inherited millions of dollars, distributes money to the denizens of Rosewater, Indiana, as they telephone the Rosewater Foundation to ask for help. Eliot is certifiably insane and bumbles his way through life as the satirical figure of the liberal do-gooder. A member of the volunteer fire department, Eliot foils attempts by crooked lawyers to put an end to his unrequited generosity. He, a sexual eunuch, is accused erroneously of fathering fifty-seven illegitimate children in Rosewater. He absurdly claims them all as his own, thus ensuring the survival of the Rosewater Foundation with its fifty-seven heirs.

Sylvia Du Vrais Zetterling Rosewater, Eliot Rosewater's wife. A Parisienne beauty who comes to hate Eliot, his ways, and his philanthropy, she sincerely tries to live in his world for some time but gives up both on loving Eliot and on living with him. She secures a divorce and goes to a nunnery in Belgium. Her continental manners and demeanor are unadaptable to the American Midwest and to Eliot in particular.

Norman Mushari, a shyster lawyer and the antagonist. Mushari, a graduate of Cornell Law School, seeks to earn millions of dollars for himself by proving Eliot Rosewater insane, at which point he will cash in on his control of Fred Rosewater, Eliot's distant cousin and heir apparent. Mushari surfaces periodically throughout the novel, always working to undermine Eliot. Mushari represents the central strain of greed in the American character. That his advances are finally thwarted by Eliot offers no comfort.

Kilgore Trout, a science-fiction novelist and a stock clerk in a trading stamp redemption center. Eliot admires Trout, calling him the greatest prophet of the time. Although he cannot write well, his ideas reinforce Eliot's own theories about society. Trout is described as a modern-day Christ figure, but beyond the fact that he continues to sacrifice himself for the arts (as manifested in his poorly written, ill-conceived novels), there is no purposeful reason for this appellation.

Lister Ames Rosewater, Eliot's father, a conservative senator who never worked a day in his life. Arrogant, ruthless, and debauched by wealth, Lister stands in opposition to Eliot's liberal character and misdirected social largesse. Lister is horrified that Eliot would help those who do not deserve help because they have not helped themselves, and he fails to recognize his own good luck by birth.

Fred Rosewater, Eliot's distant cousin and heir to the presidency of the Rosewater Foundation. Bumbling, silly, and obtuse, the insurance salesman from the East Coast is no more competent or stable than Eliot, but Mushari can control Fred and thus keeps him as his own pawn. Fred is not aware, for most of the novel, of Mushari's designs for him.

— Carl Singleton

GOD ON THE ROCKS

Author: Jane Gardam (1928-   )
First published: 1978
Genre: Novel
Locale: Northeastern England
Time: The 1930's and after World War II
Plot: Psychological realism

Margaret Marsh, an eight-year-old girl. Precocious, inquisitive, and outspoken, Margaret enjoys climbing trees and exploring the grounds of the big manor house on her outings with Lydia, a servant. Her surprisingly exhaustive knowledge of biblical texts (inculcated by her fundamentalist father) is of limited help in answering her larger questions about God and life. Her candid observations of an adult world she only partially understands provide the novel's primary point of view.

Elinor Marsh, Margaret's mother, aged thirty-six. Large and maternal, she nevertheless retains her youthful beauty. She is eager to be a friend to Margaret and tries (rather unsuccessfully) not to let her new baby boy distract her attention from her daughter. Initially attracted to Kenneth Marsh because of the intensely religious "goodness" he exudes, she leaves him when she discovers him in the arms of Lydia. She flees to a former fiancé, Charles Frayling, whose acquaintance she has recently renewed; from this union, she bears a son. Eventually, she marries the local vicar, Father Carter.

Kenneth Marsh, Margaret's father, who works in a bank. A neat, controlled, fervently religious man, Marsh belongs to a denomination called the Primal Saints. Marsh denounces sin energetically, but the attractions of the serving girl Lydia, who he initially argues has been sent to them by God that they may redeem her, prove too tempting for him. He is discovered by both Margaret and Elinor attempting to seduce Lydia. Later that day, Kenneth drowns trying to save Margaret after she is caught by the tide far from shore during a storm.

Charles Frayling, a local schoolmaster. Elinor's childhood love, Charles rather neglected her after he went away to Queen's College, Cambridge, but at his graduation he proposed to her. He lacked, however, the will to resist his domineering mother's determined efforts to break off the match with Elinor, who she felt was a social inferior. Now, he lives as a bachelor with his unmarried sister, Binkie. He is a quiet, introverted man whose easy, understanding manner at first makes Margaret suspicious but soon comes to appeal to her greatly. When Elinor flees to him after discovering Kenneth's infidelity, he is taken aback at finding himself in the role of the pursued. He ends up living in Australia, alone.

Binkie Frayling, Charles's unmarried sister. Plain, practical, and studious, she studied economic theory with some distinction at Girton College, Cambridge. She is very active in the local parish, perhaps because she is romantically interested in the vicar, Father Carter. She claims to have had plenty of offers of marriage in her time, but these opportunities, like Charles's, were somehow thwarted by her strong-willed mother. In a painful moment of self-realization, she admits to Father Carter that she hates her mother and, indeed, hates everyone. Even so, she continues to be sensible, understanding, and kind to everyone.

Rosalie Frayling, Charles and Binkie's mother. In her youth, she accepted the proposal of Edwin Frayling, many years her senior. Secretly, she desperately wanted her mother to forbid the marriage, but her mother allowed her to decide for herself. As a consequence of this unwelcome freedom and the resulting unhappy marriage, she completely dominates her own children. She once loved a wounded captain who convalesced at the family manor during World War I; although his wife soon came to fetch the incapacitated captain home, she continues to dream of him. Toward the end of her life, she allows her house to be converted to a lunatic asylum, and now, bedridden, arthritic, and near death, she lives there, cared for by the nurses and sharing a love of painting with Drinkwater, one of the residents.

Beezer-Iremonger, one of the Primal Saints. Gassed at the Somme during World War I, Beezer-Iremonger is not entirely sane. He eventually is revealed to be the wounded captain of Rosalie's youth. He returned north from his home in Surrey, presumably seeking her, but they were never reunited. He drowns trying to save Margaret during the storm.

Lydia, the Marshes' attractive maid. About seventeen years old, Lydia is garish, plump, and coarse, but she has a genuinely caring and affectionate nature and is a real friend to Margaret. Cheerful and brazen, Lydia flirts openly with the young men at the seaside and trysts with the gamekeeper of the manor while Margaret goes off exploring during their outings. She is nevertheless disillusioned and angry when Marsh makes his pass at her. She finds his transgression particularly painful because the evangelistic Marsh, who in fact had her nearly converted to Primal Sainthood, has shattered her budding belief in religion and higher values.

— *Catherine Swanson*

THE GODS ARE ATHIRST
(Les Dieux ont soif)

Author: Anatole France (Jacques-Anatole-François Thibault, 1844-1924)
First published: 1912
Genre: Novel
Locale: Paris, France
Time: 1793-1794
Plot: Historical

Évariste Gamelin (ay-vah-REEST gahm-LAHN), a young painter. Convinced that the success of the Jacobin cause will bring about a new day for France, he becomes an ardent revolutionary genuinely desiring justice for all. Blinded by his passion for the cause, he gradually assumes the role of self-righteous reformer, and finally, as a member of the Grand Tribunal, orders the execution of people in lots without trial. Among them is his closest friend, Maurice Brotteaux. He thus becomes a symbol of the romantic whose devotion to a cause corrupts his humanity.

Maurice Brotteaux (moh-REES broh-TOH), Évariste Gamelin's friend, an atheist and intellectual who lacks Gamelin's faith in the goodness of the masses. Executed without trial by the tribunal of which Évariste is a member, he becomes a symbol of the intellectual who will not abandon his integrity for a cause in which he does not believe.

Élodie Blaise (ay-loh-DEE blehz), the seducer of Évariste Gamelin. Purely physical, without ideals or fidelity to any cause, she survives the Reign of Terror to become the mistress of the non-political Philippe Desmahis.

Jean Blaise (zhahn), a printseller and Élodie's father.

Jacques David (zhahk dah-VEED), a painter and young Évariste Gamelin's teacher.

Pére Longuemare (pehr lohn-geh-MAHR), a monk falsely accused as a thief and given refuge by Maurice Brotteaux, with whom he is finally convicted without trial and executed.

Madame de Rochemaure (deh rohsh-MOHR), a revolutionary opportunist.

Henry (ahn-REE), a dragoon who is the lover of Madame de Rochemaure and Élodie Blaise.

Marat (mah-RAH) and

Robespierre (rohbs-PYEHR), French revolutionaries.

Athenaïs (ah-tay-nah-EES), a prostitute once befriended by Maurice Brotteaux and executed with him.

Madame Gamelin, Évariste Gamelin's mother.

Julie Gamelin (zhew-LEE), Évariste's sister.

Jacques Maubel (moh-BEHL), a young man convicted by Évariste Gamelin for lack of faith in the people and executed.

Philippe Desmahis (fee-LEEP day-may-EES), a non-political engraver who survives the Reign of Terror to become the lover of Élodie Blaise.

GOD'S BITS OF WOOD
(Les Bouts de bois de Dieu)

Author: Ousmane Sembène (1923-)
First published: 1960
Genre: Novel
Locale: Senegal
Time: October 10, 1947-March 19, 1949
Plot: Social realism

Ibrahima Bakayoko (ih-brah-HEE-mah bah-kah-YOH-koh), a locomotive engineer on the Dakar-Niger railroad and union delegate in the strike in progress as the novel begins. A man of physical vigor and stamina, he circulates constantly among groups in Bamako, Thiès, Dakar, and the villages. Intelligent, reflective, perceptive, well-read, and multilingual, he understands the situation of his people: their need to retain their African heritage but also to deal with Western industrialized culture. Compassion tempers his strict sense of justice and hard militant approach. Through his unyielding stand and capacity for articulating the people's position to men in power, he emerges as the leader to whom all look for decisive moves. His firm words transform a negotiating meeting with a company representative into a confrontation reinforcing the strikers' determination to persevere until all demands are met. Facing the initial disapproval of the men, he supports and encourages the women's participation in an organized march from Thiès to Dakar. It is his speech, given in four languages to the public, including civil, religious, and industrial authorities, in the Dakar stadium that brings final victory. At the end of the novel, when demands have been met and workers have returned to work, Bakayoko sets out alone to continue his work elsewhere; for him, this struggle of the oppressed is universal, and he must go on.

Ramatoulaye (rah-mah-tew-LAH-yay), the head of her large family concession in Dakar and sister of El Hadji Mabigé, a prominent and rich Muslim from Dakar. Both inside and outside her concession, she is concerned for others, meeting their needs and reconciling their differences. A woman of dignity, ordinarily quietly going about her affairs, she is capable of heroism when either her principles or the welfare of others is in jeopardy. When strikers' families begin to lack sufficient food and water, she goes to her wealthy brother to ask him to obtain credit for food for the women and children. Outraged at his refusal, she reproaches him soundly for his conduct and attitude, adding a threat to kill his fat, well-cared-for ram, Vendredi, if the animal wanders into her concession. Vendredi does wander in, destroying property and the meager supply of rice. At the risk of her life, Ramatoulaye kills the foraging ram and orders that the meat be prepared and distributed to hungry families. She is arrested and tried; El Hadji is persuaded to withdraw his complaint, and Ramatoulaye is asked to apologize to him. She refuses to do so, instead walking out of the room in silent dignity. She becomes a support and leader in the women's march on Dakar, instrumental in empowering them to become a crucial element in the success of the strike.

N'Deye Touti (ihn-DAY-yay TEW-tee), the niece of Ramatoulaye and a student at the French normal school in Dakar. An attractive young African woman, she is torn between two different worlds: that of her native surroundings and traditions and that of Europe, which she knows through books, film, and school experiences. Her normal life in the concession is colored by dreams of a Prince Charming styled after those encountered in romantic novels and imagined existence in upper bourgeois French settings. Fastidious about her appearance and sensitive to derogatory comments on her French ways, she is sometimes embarrassed by native behavior. Although Daouda Beaugosse would like to marry her, it is Bakayoko whom she admires and to whom she is first attracted by the breadth of his interests and by his personality. Having learned that the French way is to go through the law, she does not join the women in the strike. After the march on Dakar, however, she is among them collecting supplies. She expresses to Bakayoko her desire to become his wife; when he refuses her and leaves on his own route, she sinks into apathy, ceases to care about her appearance, and assumes a man's heavy work hauling containers from the well. Ultimately, in a symbolic action, she burns her school journals, retaining one sheet on which she writes a poem, a death song to her youth. N'Deye moves temporarily out of her African culture but seems to belong to neither world in the end.

Doudou (DEW-dew), the father of five, an adjuster and secretary of the federation of railway workers. As secretary, he has responsibility for the conduct of the strike. It is an exhilarating task at the start, attending meetings and rallying workers, but the weight of this responsibility brings on fatigue and worry as the strike is prolonged and families suffer. At the point where responsibility for rationing food must be assigned, Doudou is relieved not to have to designate the committee, as that decision is reached through consensus. Presiding at the meeting of the delegates with the company negotiator, Edouard, he is indecisive, mildly suggesting a vote on the terms offered. It is Bakayoko who, rebuking Doudou, remains firm. Doudou has, however, strengthened the resistance of the strikers by revealing to them his angry refusal of a bribe from Isnard, a company man. Ultimately, Doudou contracts a work-related illness and dies in Thiès. His colleagues think his death might have been prevented had the company provided access to medical help.

Daouda Beaugosse (dah-EW-dah BOH-gahz), a turner on the Dakar-Niger railway and assistant to Alioune, the local strike committee chairperson. Having received his training in a professional school, learned French, and acquired a taste for elegance, he spends his money on clothes and finds it difficult to mingle with other workers on the job. His attraction to N'Deye Touti causes him to be jealous of Bakayoko, although he admires the latter. Tempted by the opening of a job that requires literacy, he is already contemplating leaving the railway when he attends the meeting at which union representatives are told that their demand for family allocations will not be granted. Taking courage from his feeling of support from the people, Daouda comments that in France everyone has that right. The reply that there is no concubinage in France serves to further anger the strikers. Beaugosse leaves the company for a job as a warehouse stock clerk.

Monsieur Dejean (deh-ZHAHN), the director of the regional office of the Dakar-Niger railway at Thiès. A company man who sees the Africans in his employ not as employees with whom one negotiates but as members of another and inferior race, subject to his authority. He typifies the colonial overlord: comfortably established in the colonies, condescending, authoritative, insensitive, uncomprehending, and obdurate. Assured of his own position, he expects his subordinates to handle the Africans and to penalize a subordinate who is disloyal. During his meeting with the strikers' delegates, he releases his anger by striking Bakayoko before the entire group. In the ensuing struggle, the two men have to be separated by force. Subsequently, Monsieur Dejean leaves Dakar, thereby escaping any violent confrontation, such as that experienced by his colleague Isnard.

Edouard (ay-DWAHR), an inspector for the Dakar-Niger railway. Sincere in his mission as negotiator, believing that he can come to an understanding with the strikers, he has offered his services and been designated as negotiator. He is the only European present at the preliminary meeting. In response to his attempt to explain reasonably why the demands will have to be delayed for study, Bakayoko, in French and in hard terms, reminds him that nothing has been done in the seven years in which Edouard has been there. Edouard understands that he is not wanted but is too stunned to leave the meeting. When Bakayoko invites him to step out for a moment to permit discussion, he disappears, having escaped to warn Monsieur Dejean and the other waiting company delegates that he has failed in his mission and that Bakayoko is to be feared, thereby arousing anticipatory tension that colors the following meeting and leads to an explosion of conflict.

— *Mary Henry Nachtsheim*

GOD'S LITTLE ACRE

Author: Erskine Caldwell (1903-1987)
First published: 1933
Genre: Novel

Locale: Georgia and South Carolina
Time: Late 1920's or early 1930's
Plot: Naturalism

Ty Ty Walden, an eccentric patriarch and sage of the Walden clan. He was a prosperous Georgia cotton farmer with more than one hundred acres, two black sharecroppers, and mules. For the past fifteen years, Ty Ty has been mining for gold on his property. He has destroyed the rich land and the crop with his obsessive search for the precious metal. To ease his conscience, the owner has set aside one acre of the land and dedicated it to God and the church. He frequently moves that acre around the property, however, creating a new location whenever he wishes to dig at the old one. Ty Ty claims not only that gold exists on his land because he has been looking for it all these years but also that he is very scientific about his excavating. His search becomes even more ludicrous when it leads him to kidnap and hold an albino male in the mistaken belief that the hostage will locate the gold for him. Ty Ty loves to philosophize about life: "There was a mean trick played on us somewhere. God put us in the bodies of animals and tried to make us act like people. That was the beginning of trouble." His two greatest joys in life are digging a new hole for the elusive gold and staring at the female members of his family, particularly when they are undressing.

Will Thompson, Ty Ty's son-in-law, who is married to Ty Ty's daughter Rosamond. Will and Ty Ty are much alike in outlook, philosophy, and vitality. Will likes to drink, fight, and womanize. He openly seduces his sisters-in-law, Darling Jill and the previously unobtainable Griselda. Will is not a farmer like the others but a loom-weaving mill worker who has been on strike for a year and a half. The three Walden brothers openly dislike him and derisively call him "linthead." He is the symbolic leader of the strikers and angrily resents the American Federation of Labor's strategy of not coming to terms with management. His fury is fueled by living in a company town and by being powerless to end the strike. Will becomes a tragic hero at the end when he leads the disgruntled workers back into the factory and turns on the equipment. He is shot three times in the back by security guards and is killed. His sacrificial death, the dramatic high point of the novel, stirs the workers to take action and brings the three Walden women who loved him closer together.

Griselda Walden, Ty Ty's beautiful daughter-in-law, who is married to a jealous husband, Buck. Ty Ty says of her repeatedly that she is the prettiest girl in Georgia. Men are attracted to her, but she is put off by all of them except Will Thompson, whom she feels is a real man. Griselda openly offers herself to the eager Will in front of his wife and Darling Jill.

Darling Jill Walden, Ty Ty's attractive and openly promiscuous daughter, who flirts with, and seduces, almost every man she meets. Her interest in lovers is momentary, however, and no man can truly claim her. Darling Jill badly mistreats and embarrasses her amiable suitor, Pluto Swint. Resentful of his corpulent appearance, she tells Pluto bluntly that he must lose his large belly. Attracted to the unobtainable Will, she finally promises to marry Pluto one day, but "I'd have to be a few months gone before I'd do that."

Rosamond Thompson, Ty Ty's other daughter, who is the very patient and long-suffering wife of Will Thompson. She dearly loves her husband and is extremely tolerant of his many love affairs, until she discovers him making love to her sister, Darling Jill, and beats them with a hairbrush. She fires a pistol at her wastrel husband, who leaps out a window and runs naked through the town streets. Rosamond must also suffer Will's open seduction of the willing Griselda. Ultimately, however, she accepts Will's drunkenness, adultery, and inevitable martyrdom.

Pluto Swint, the obese, bald-headed suitor of Darling Jill. He is a candidate for sheriff and worried that he will not be elected. Pluto has absolutely no ambition in life and has done very little work for years. His idea of a good life is to sit around all day and shoot pool, especially if he is elected. He owns a car and manages to get by on the income from a sixty-acre farm that is homesteaded by a black sharecropper. His passion for Darling Jill is overwhelming, and the more she openly abuses him and seduces other men, the more he desires her. Pluto knows that Darling Jill will marry him one day—it is only a matter of time.

— *Terry Theodore*

THE GOLD-BUG

Author: Edgar Allan Poe (1809-1849)
First published: 1843
Genre: Short fiction
Locale: South Carolina
Time: Early nineteenth century
Plot: Detective and mystery

The Narrator, who relates the story of William Legrand's discovery of Captain Kidd's treasure. He fears for a time that his friend is going out of his mind because of Legrand's peculiar behavior when he finds a piece of parchment that eventually leads him to a fortune of more than a million and a half dollars in gold and jewels.

William Legrand, a young man of good family from New Orleans who has taken up residence in a hut on Sullivan's Island, near Charleston, South Carolina, because his family fortune is gone. He spends his time fishing, hunting, and searching for specimens of shells and insects to add to his collection. One day he finds a peculiar new beetle, gold in color, and a piece of old parchment. His behavior becomes very peculiar for about a month. Later, helped in his digging by his servant and the narrator, he uncovers a rich buried treasure. Legrand then reveals that he has played a joke on the narrator and Jupiter: Realizing that they thought he was going crazy, he led them on by acting peculiarly. Legrand's solving of the cryptograph on the parchment shows that he has rare intelligence as well as a sense of humor.

Jupiter, a manumitted slave who once belonged to the Legrand family. After being freed, he stays as a servant and has followed William Legrand to Sullivan's Island. He is devoted and loyal to his master, as much a trusted associate as a servant. Like the narrator, Jupiter is fearful that Legrand is losing his mind.

Lt. G———, an army officer stationed at Fort Moultrie. He is a friend of Legrand and very much interested in entomology. He is fascinated by the gold beetle discovered on Sullivan's Island by Legrand.

THE GOLD-RIMMED EYEGLASSES
(Gli occhiali d'oro)

Author: Giorgio Bassani (1916-   )
First published: 1958
Genre: Novel
Locale: Ferrara and Rimini, Italy
Time: The 1930's
Plot: Social realism

The narrator, a young man of age twenty (at the time of the main events of the story), a member of a middle-class Jewish family of Ferrara and a student of literature at the University of Bologna. He is becoming aware of the impact of Fascism on his family and on all Jews. Sensitive and sympathetic to the trials of other Jews, yet barely grasping what the growing anti-Semitism of the Fascist regime may mean to Italian Jews, he witnesses the torments of Dr. Fadigati, who is in his own way just as much an outsider as the narrator is going to be in Italian Fascist society.

Dr. Athos Fadigati (AHT-ohs fah-dee-GAH-tee), an ear, nose, and throat specialist who came from Venice and settled in Ferrara. Middle-aged and overweight, Fadigati became somewhat of a society doctor, for a time, until his penchant for young men became known. He takes one of the narrator's friends to Riccione, on the Adriatic Sea, for a vacation, and is more or less despised by other families. As an outsider, he attracts the narrator's pity, especially when the boy whom Fadigati takes to the seashore absconds with all of Fadigati's money. The doctor by then has lost much of his fashionable clientele, and eventually he takes his own life.

Eraldo Deliliers (ehr-AHL-doh deh-lee-LEE-ehrz), a young schoolmate of the narrator, a handsome young boy who is admired by all of his classmates. There is a thread of opportunism to his character. When he takes up with Dr. Fadigati, that seems to seal his fate, and even though the narrator sympathizes with him and converses with him at Riccione, Deliliers is interested only in the best opportunities for his own welfare. He leaves Fadigati at Riccione, having stolen all the doctor's money and papers, and ends up in Paris.

Signora Lavezzoli (lah-vehz-ZOH-lee), a leading member of the Lavezzoli family, vacationing at Riccione. Originally from Pisa, she is married to a lawyer who is an expert in civil law. She represents the kind of people who welcome and support the growth of the Fascist state in Italy and who approve of the increasingly severe measures of the Benito Mussolini regime. She despises Dr. Fadigati, and, although she is a friend of the narrator's family, she seems to approve of the coming repression of Jews. Although her husband is no supporter of the Fascists, he says nothing as she praises Mussolini and the government.

The narrator's father, a harried businessman of broad interests who pretends that the changes in Italian society cannot be too bad and who hopes that the Fascists will not be as dangerous as the Nazis in Germany. He treats Dr. Fadigati with respect, despite the contempt of others for the man. The narrator feels pity for his father, who is hoping against hope that all will be well.

— *Philip Brantingham*

THE GOLDEN APPLES

Author: Eudora Welty (1909-)
First published: 1949
Genre: Short fiction

Locale: The fictional town of Morgana, Mississippi
Time: 1900-1940
Plot: Social

King MacLain, the wandering patriarch of Morgana, Mississippi. He periodically reappears in Morgana for sexual encounters with the town's women. "Shower of Gold" is the story of his courtship of and marriage to Snowdie Hudson and the birth of their twin sons. "Sir Rabbit" tells of his sexual encounter with another Morgana woman. In "The Wanderers," an aged King returns to Morgana to be cared for by his wife, but he still displays hints of his earlier rebelliousness.

Mrs. Snowdie Hudson MacLain, the albino wife of King MacLain. Deserted by her husband and left alone to rear her twin sons, Randall and Eugene, Snowdie takes in boarders. The opening story, "Shower of Gold," tells of the birth of Snowdie's twin sons. In the last story, "The Wanderers," Snowdie readies Katie Rainey's body for burial. Her association with birth and death frames the rest of the stories of Morgana.

Randall MacLain, one of King and Snowdie MacLain's twin sons. As children, the twins demonstrate the rebellious streak inherited from their father. "The Whole World Knows" tells the story of Ran's troubled relationship with his wife, Jinny Love. Separated from Jinny Love, Ran has an affair with Maideen Sumrall that ends tragically in Maideen's suicide. At the end of the book, Ran has been elected mayor because of the aura of glamour and revelation his past gives him.

Eugene MacLain, Randall's twin brother and one of the few characters who leave Morgana. Living in San Francisco, Eugene works for Bertsingers' Jewelers and marries his former landlady, Emma Gaines, but their love is replaced by sorrow after the death of their daughter. In "Music from Spain," the habitual Eugene does the unexpected: He slaps his wife, skips work, and spends the day roaming the streets of San Francisco with a Spanish guitarist. Later on, Eugene returns to Mississippi without his wife and dies quietly of tuberculosis.

Katie Rainey, the wife of Fate Rainey, who sells milk, butter, and ice cream in Morgana. Katie Rainey is the narrator of the first story, "Shower of Gold," and her funeral is the collection's final event. She is the gossip and storyteller of the town; her narrative introduces most of the characters and their relationships to one another.

Virgie Rainey, the vital, rebellious daughter of Fate and Katie Rainey. She is the one gifted musician among the town's children. Because Virgie is from a lower-class, Methodist family, she is not awarded the Presbyterian church's music scholarship. "June Recital" tells the story of Virgie's journey from talented, iconoclastic piano student to sexually mature piano player at the local movie theater. Virgie's sexuality and rebellion make her the object of gossip in the small town. Tired of the limitations imposed by Morgana, she escapes to Memphis for a short time but returns home to help her mother after Fate Rainey dies. Milking her mother's cows and typing for a lumber company replace her piano playing. After her mother's funeral, Virgie prepares to go back out into the world. She is a wanderer whose vision encompasses the beauty, tragedy, and mysteries of life.

Miss Eckhart, a German piano teacher who boards at the MacLain house. An outsider because of nationality, religion, and artistic sensibility, Miss Eckhart is tolerated but never accepted by the community. Miss Eckhart passes on to Virgie her love and knowledge of music; the two are linked by their roles as outsiders and wanderers. As a result of the war with Germany, fewer and fewer children in Morgana take lessons from her; eventually, she ends up impoverished on the County Farm. In "June Recital," she tries to burn down the house where she taught music. Her attempted conflagration is an apt symbol of the passionate intensity and loneliness of the artist.

Loch Morrison, one of the narrators of "June Recital" and a Boy Scout. He is another of the visionary characters. In "Moon Lake," as a lifeguard for a girls' summer camp, Loch saves the life of Easter, an orphan, who has almost drowned. Eventually, Loch leaves Morgana for New York City.

Cassie Morrison, Loch's older sister and the other narrator of "June Recital." She is awarded the music scholarship, though she is less talented than Virgie. Like Loch and Virgie, Cassie can see beyond the surface of life into its mystery of mingled beauty and horror; unlike Loch and Virgie, she remains rooted in the conventionality of the small southern town. Although she envies Loch and Virgie their ability to grow beyond Morgana's confines, she chooses to stay in the town, give piano lessons, and tend the flowers that every spring blossom to spell out her dead mother's name.

— *Suzan Harrison*

THE GOLDEN ASS
(Metamorphoses)

Author: Lucius Apuleius (c. 124-probably after 170 C.E.)
First transcribed: Second century
Genre: Novel

Locale: Greece
Time: Early second century
Plot: Picaresque

Lucius (LEW-shee-uhs), a traveler who is turned into an ass, in which form he has several adventures before becoming a man again.

Charites (KAY-rih-teez), a Greek lady abducted from her wedding by the thieves who stole Milo's gold.

Lepolemus (leh-POH-leh-muhs), her resourceful husband. He joins the robbers who stole his wife, makes them drunk and chains them, rescues his wife, and causes the robbers to be killed.

Thrasillus (thrah-SIH-luhs), Lepolemus' friend, in love

with Charites, who blinds him with a pin while he is drunk.

Milo (MI-loh), a rich usurer robbed by thieves who use Lucius (now an ass) to carry their stolen gold.

Pamphile (PAM-fih-lee), his wife, a witch who turns herself into an eagle.

Fotis (FOH-tihs), her buxom and lusty maid, who grants her favors to Lucius and then turns him into an ass.

Aristomenes (a-rihs-TO-meh-neez), a merchant who tells Lucius of Socrates' misfortune.

Socrates (SOK-ruh-teez), Aristomenes' good friend. Beaten and robbed, he is cared for by Aristomenes. At midnight, two hags cut his throat and substitute a sponge for his heart, which they steal. The next day, he dies when the sponge drops out of his severed throat.

Byrrhaena (bih-REE-nuh), Lucius' cousin, a rich gentlewoman.

Cupid (KYEW-pihd), a young god, the son of Venus, who, envious of Psyche's beauty, sends Cupid to make her fall in love with a monster. Instead he takes Psyche for his wife.

Psyche (SI-kee), beauteous young wife of Cupid. Urged by her jealous sisters, she looks upon her sleeping husband's face and he, influenced by Venus, deserts her. Pitied by Jupiter, the pregnant girl becomes immortal, united to Cupid forever.

Queen Isis (I-sihs), who provides for Lucius to eat roses so that he may return to human form.

THE GOLDEN BOWL

Author: Henry James (1843-1916)
First published: 1904
Genre: Novel

Locale: England and the Continent
Time: c. 1900
Plot: Psychological realism

Maggie Verver, the motherless daughter of an American millionaire. For a number of years the Ververs have spent much of their time abroad, where Mr. Verver has devoted himself to acquiring a magnificent art collection for the museum he plans to build in American City. Sharing her father's quiet tastes and aesthetic interests, Maggie has become his faithful companion, and they have created for themselves a separate, enclosed world of ease, grace, and discriminating appreciation, a connoisseurship of life as well as of art. Even Maggie's marriage to Prince Amerigo, an Italian of ancient family, does not change greatly the pattern of their lives, a pattern that she believes complete when Mr. Verver marries her best friend, Charlotte Stant. What Maggie does not know is that before her marriage, the prince and Charlotte, both moneyless and therefore unable to marry, had been lovers. Several years later the prince, bored by his position as another item in the Verver collection, and Charlotte, restless because she takes second place beside her elderly husband's interest in art, resume their former intimacy. Maggie finds her happiness threatened when her purchase of a flawed gold-and-crystal bowl leads indirectly to her discovery of the true situation. Her problem is whether to disclose or conceal her knowledge. Deeply in love with her husband and devoted to her father, she decides to remain silent. Her passivity becomes an act of drama because it involves a sense of ethical responsibility and a moral decision; her predicament is the familiar Jamesian spectacle of the innocent American confronting the evil of European morality, in this case complicated by Maggie's realization that she and her father are not without guilt, that they have lived too much for themselves. In the end her generosity, tact, and love resolve all difficulties. Mr. Verver and his wife leave for America, and Maggie regains her husband's love, now unselfishly offered.

Prince Amerigo (ah-MEH-ree-goh), a young Italian nobleman, handsome, gallant, sensual, living in England with his American wife. A man of politely easy manners, he is able to mask his real feelings under an appearance of courteous reserve. Though he has loved many women, he has little capacity for lies or deception in his dealings with them; he objects when Charlotte Stant, his former mistress, wishes to purchase a flawed golden bowl as a wedding gift to his wife, for he wants nothing but perfection in his marriage. He and Charlotte are often thrown together after she marries his father-in-law, and they become lovers once more. When his wife learns, through purchase of the same flawed bowl, the secret of his infidelity, he tries to be loyal to all parties concerned, and he so beautifully preserves the delicate harmony of family relationships that no outsiders except their mutual friends, the Assinghams, know of the situation. Maggie, his wife, is able to save her marriage because his delicacy in the matter of purchased and purchasable partners makes tense situations easier. After Mr. Verver and his wife return to America, the prince shows relief as unselfish as it is sincere; their departure allows him to be a husband and a father in his own right.

Charlotte Stant, the beautiful but impecunious American who needs a wealthy husband to provide the fine clothes and beautiful things she believes necessary for her happiness. Because Prince Amerigo is poor, she becomes his mistress but never considers marrying him. After the prince marries Maggie Verver, her best friend, Maggie's father proposes to Charlotte. She accepts him and, though Mr. Verver cannot understand her claim of unworthiness, declares herself prepared to be as devoted as possible, both as a wife and as a stepmother to her good friend. Often left in the prince's company while Maggie and her father pursue their interest in art, she resumes her affair with her former lover. When the truth is finally revealed, Charlotte, determined to prove her loyalties to all concerned, persuades Mr. Verver to return with her to America. Her poised and gracious farewell to Maggie and the prince is more than a demonstration of her ability to keep up appearances; it shows the code of responsibility she has assumed toward her lover, her friend, and her husband.

Adam Verver, a rich American who has given over the pursuit of money in order to achieve the good life for himself and his daughter Maggie. In his innocence, he believes that this end may be attained by seeing and collecting the beautiful art objects of Europe. A perfect father, he cannot realize that there is anything selfish in the close tie that exists between himself and his daughter, and he tries to stand in the same relationship with his son-in-law, Prince Amerigo, and Charlotte Stant, his daughter's friend, whom he marries. All he really lives for is to provide for Maggie and his grandson the life of happiness and plenty he envisions for them. When he finally realizes that the pattern of his life has been a form of make-believe, he sacrifices his own peace of mind and agrees to return with his wife to make the United States his permanent home.

Fanny Assingham, the friend of Maggie and Adam Verver, Prince Amerigo, and Charlotte Stant, and the guardian angel of their secret lives. As one who senses the rightness of things, she helps to bring about both marriages with a sensitive understanding of the needs of all, a delicacy she will not allow to be disrupted by Maggie's discovery of her husband's infidelity. She helps to resolve the situation between Maggie and Prince Amerigo when she hurls the golden bowl, symbol of Maggie's flawed marriage and the prince's guilt, to the floor and smashes it.

Colonel Robert Assingham, called Bob, a retired army officer who understands his wife's motives in the interest she takes in the Verver family but who manages to keep himself detached from her complicated dealings with the lives of others.

The Principino (preen-see-PEE-noh), the small son of Prince Amerigo and Maggie.

GOLDEN BOY

Author: Clifford Odets (1906-1963)
First published: 1937
Genre: Drama
Locale: New York City
Time: The 1930's
Plot: Social realism

Joe Bonaparte, a young violinist who becomes a prizefighter. At heart a musician, he has been laughed at and hurt by people against whom he longs to fight back. The fame and money he earns in the ring make retaliation possible but brutalize Joe and change his personality. He falls in love with Lorna Moon, who finally persuades him to give up the ring. That night, they are both killed in an automobile accident.

Tom Moody, Joe Bonaparte's fight manager and part owner.

Lorna Moon, Tom Moody's mistress. Asked by Joe Bonaparte's father to help the fighter find himself, she falls in love with him but feels that she cannot give up Tom Moody, whose wife has at last consented to a divorce so that he can marry her. Finally, in Joe's dressing room after a triumphant fight, she tells him again that she loves him and persuades him to leave the ring. She is killed with him that night in an automobile accident.

Mr. Bonaparte, Joe Bonaparte's father. Hoping that Joe will give up fighting and return to music, he refuses the parental blessing on Joe's career until he sorrowfully sees that his son is totally committed to the ring. When Joe is killed, he claims the body and brings the boy home where he belongs.

Eddie Fuseli, a gambler and part owner of Joe Bonaparte.

THE GOLDEN NOTEBOOK

Author: Doris Lessing (1919-   )
First published: 1962
Genre: Novel
Locale: London, England
Time: The 1940's and 1950's
Plot: Social realism

Anna Freeman Wulf, the protagonist, a sensitive, highly intelligent woman, a writer who labels herself as a "minor talent." Neat, delicate, and prim, she is small, thin, and dark, "with large black always-on-guard eyes," a "pointed white face," delicate hands, and "a fluffy haircut." She must force herself to take the lead, as she is by nature shy and self-effacing. She lives on the royalties of a commercially successful novel about her 1940's experiences in southern Rhodesia and is compiling four notebooks to exorcise her personal demons and to explore the meaning of her life and its relationships. These record her present life (psychoanalysis, friendships, affairs), her African days (the hypocrisies of apartheid, her fear of domesticity), her political change (from liberal to communist to disillusioned idealist), and various drafts and ideas for story lines. Her thirteen-year-old daughter, Jane, produces her sense of emotional stability; past failed relationships with men produce her sense of inadequacy. Ultimately, her real sources of strength are her role as a mother, her sisterhood with a fellow divorcee (Molly), her relationship with the exasperating Saul Green, and the self-knowledge that comes from analyzing herself and her past in her notebooks and from undergoing a process of fragmentation and breakdown that ends in an integrated self.

Molly Jacobs, a worldly-wise Jewish actress, Anna's best friend, both her complementary opposite and her mirror image, "a free woman." Although she is tall and big-boned, Molly appears slight, even boyish, with rough, streaky gold hair, cut like a boy's, and a varied wardrobe. Fluent in half a dozen languages, "abrupt, straightforward, tactless," and frankly domineering, yet full of life and enthusiasm, she is forty years old (in 1957), with an adult son, Tommy. In 1935, when she met Anna, she worked for the Spanish Republican cause while supporting her husband, Richard, a failed artist. She sang, danced, gave drawing lessons, worked as a journalist, and became involved in Communist cultural works. Anna and Molly once shared a house but now live a half mile apart. Both are divorced, rearing a child alone, and sharing basic Communist ideals, following a lifestyle condemned by conventional society. She, like Anna, feels nostalgia and anguish about the Party, and, despite occasional jealousies, she provides a solid relationship (sister/friend) on which Anna can depend.

Tommy Jacobs, Molly's only son by her long-divorced husband, Richard. At age twenty, Tommy looks like his father: round, dark, heavy, and "almost stupid-looking." He moves in slow motion, as if imprisoned by his own nature. Contact with his tycoon father's world of wealth and choices makes him hostile. Tommy's brooding is the subject of much soul-searching by Molly, Anna, and Richard. When his attempted suicide leaves him blind, he plays on their guilt to wield power over them. He seems triumphantly malicious, happy to be the center of attention and determined to cause pain and mayhem while feigning innocent helplessness. He attacks the values, sensibilities, and commitments of all around him, dogmatically and menacingly.

Ella, Anna's fictional creation, her alter ego, a separate entity though similar in appearance (thin, small-boned, with a pointed face) and situation (a failed marriage, a failed affair, self-doubts, depression, and loss). Ella served in a canteen for factory workers and then wrote for a women's magazine, first doing articles on dress and cosmetics and then answering letters to the medical column of a personal, nonmedical nature. Her ongoing novel about a young male suicide allows Anna to explore Tommy's real suicide attempt. Ella's Molly is Julia. Ella's affair with Paul Tanner, a London psychiatrist with a wife and family, parallels Anna's former affair with Paul Blackenhurst, a witty, charming South African. Ella blinds herself to the signs of conflict that should have warned her that her five-year-long, intense relationship with Paul Tanner was doomed; the loss of her lover shatters her ego, reduces her independence, and undercuts her self-confidence. Unlike Anna, she suffered from tuberculosis, has a former army officer for a father, cares nothing about politics, and undergoes no positive transformation. She tries to be hard, cold, and indifferent; to live alone; and to thrust away the pain caused by an empty relationship, but a trip to Paris and involvement with a jovial American, Cy Maitland, "a healthy savage," frees her painfully to re-evaluate her life.

Saul Green, a neurotic, guarded American writer, Anna's most significant lover. Saul is fair, with gray-green eyes, close-cropped hair, broad shoulders, a slight build, and the pallid look of ill health. His initial relationship with Anna is jarring, hostile, and competitive. He drifts into various personalities, but when he begins to discuss shared political and social views, to reveal his hidden side, and even to help her with the theme for her next book ("Free Women"), he enables her to achieve a richer, more emotional, more creative life. Frank, insightful, and sexy, at times he seems to merge identities with Anna.

— *Gina Macdonald*

THE GOLDEN SERPENT
(La serpiente de oro)

Author: Ciro Alegría (1909-1967)
First published: 1935
Genre: Novel

Locale: Marañón River, in northern Peru
Time: The 1930's
Plot: Social realism

Lucas Vilca (VEEL-kah), a young *cholo* (part Indian, part white) from the hamlet of Calemar, located in an Andean valley in northern Peru that is bordered by the mighty Marañón River. Lucas is a ferryman—transporting travelers on balsa rafts—and small coca farmer. As narrator, Lucas voices the *cholos'* deep respect for the land and the river and their identification with nature. He pines for Rogelio Romero's wife, Florinda, after Rogeleio dies, and he invokes the magical aid of the coca leaf to get her. When she becomes his wife, Lucas believes that the coca gave her to him.

Matías Romero (maht-TEE-ahs roh-MEH-roh), the head ferryman and owner of the largest house in the Calemar valley. From his long experience, old Matías tells heroic tales of the raftsmen's exploits. He is attentive to nature's signs and has presentiments before the deaths of his son and of Don Osvaldo Martínez. Don Matías also predicts a disastrous landslide by the look of the slopes of the ravine overhanging Calemar. Rogelio's fate depresses Matías, and he becomes less active, passing the title of head ferryman on to his elder son, Arturo. The old man's eyes, however, still twinkle under the broad rim of his hat as he tells his stories.

Arturo Romero (ahr-TEW-roh), a brawny boatman, the son of Matías. Arturo is smitten with Lucinda at the yearly festival in the town of Sartín and, with rural Andean directness, invites her to return to Calemar with him. They all have to leave Sartín in a hurry when he and his similarly forthright brother Rogelio beat two state troopers who are harassing them. Arturo's prudence is seen on a long raft trip, when he tries unsuccessfully to dissuade Rogelio from taking the rapids at a dangerous water level. He is deeply affected by Rogelio's death there. Arturo's rural naïveté comes out when he chases a puma that has been terrorizing the village and becomes convinced that it is a magic animal because it looks blue to him in the blaze from his shotgun.

Rogelio Romero (rroh-HEH-lee-oh), known as **Roge** (RROH-heh), Arturo's younger brother, a fearless river man from an early age, when he swam across the swollen Marañón to take food to strangers stranded on the other side. Rogelio's courage is not tempered by good judgment, however, and he dies on the Marañón, despite Arturo's warning to wait before taking the raft over a rough spot.

Lucinda Romero (lew-SEEN-dah), Arturo's wife. She has bloomed as a woman in the two years since Arturo last saw her at the Sartín festival, and she captivates him this time with her shining green eyes and graceful figure. In Calemar, she has several miscarriages, but then she legally marries Arturo at the time of the Feast of the Virgin of Calemar. Shortly thereafter, she bears him a son, Adán.

Osvaldo Martínez de Calderón (mahr-TEE-nehs deh kahl-deh-ROHN), a Lima engineer who has come to study the Marañón area for economic development. Blond, educated, and unfamiliar with the region, he is an outsider, but he is received cordially and adapts well. His travels fill him with respect for the natural world of the Marañón. To anesthetize himself against its rigors he begins to chew coca like the natives. Osvaldo dreams of organizing a company to extract the mineral wealth of the region and plans to call the firm "The Golden Serpent," in homage to the color and shape of the Marañón as he has seen it from mountaintops. Ironically, Osvaldo is mortally bitten by a golden serpent, a yellow viper, and is buried in Calemar.

Juan Plaza (hwahn PLAH-sah), a cordial and hospitable old rancher, the owner of the Marcapata hacienda not far from the Calemar valley. Don Juan is white, and he belongs to the highest social class in the Marañón region. With his white beard and bushy eyebrows, he has a biblical look. He is a storyteller and a source of regional lore for Osvaldo Martínez, whom he also helps materially with guides and a horse. He warns Martínez about the cruelty of the mountains, the jungle, and the river.

Mariana Chinguala (mah-ree-AHN-ah cheen-GWAH-lah), a lonely, mature widow who takes in lodgers in her house at the foot of the Calemar valley and cooks for Lucas Vilca. Fashioning an ingenious trap, Doña Mariana kills the marauding puma that has daunted Arturo, and she verifies that it is not blue; it is an unusually bold brown and yellow puma.

Ignacio Ramos (eeg-NAH-see-oh RAH-mohs), an outlaw from Calemar who has to keep moving constantly to avoid being sent to prison for slayings he committed twenty years ago and more. He is something of a mythical figure in Calemar, where they refer to him as Riero, rather than Ramos. His hard face, calm and steady eyes, and determined jaw mirror his spirit of defiance against an unjust legal system that is harsh on poor men such as him. As he tells it to Lucas Vilca (whom he visits one night in a rare appearance in his hometown), the several killings he perpetrated were in self-defense. Ramos lives in the river gorge.

— *John Deredita*

THE GONDOLIERS: Or, The King of Barataria

Author: W. S. Gilbert (1836-1911)
First published: 1889
Genre: Drama
Locale: Venice and Barataria
Time: 1750
Plot: Comedy

The duke of Plaza-Toro, a grandee of Spain. The duke, who always led his regiment from behind, except when it retreated, is eager to place his daughter on the throne of Barataria and to feather his own nest as much as possible.

The duchess of Plaza-Toro, his formidable wife.

Casilda (kah-SEEL-dah), their daughter, married in infancy to the royal heir of Barataria. She is in love with Luiz.

Don Alhambra del Bolero (ahl-AHM-brah dehl boh-LEH-roh), the grand inquisitor of Spain. He is searching for the royal heir, whom he had stolen in infancy and left with a tippling gondolier to rear with his own son. The gondolier could not remember which of the two boys was his own son and which the prince. The Inquisitor decides to torture their former nurse to find out which is which.

Marco Palmieri (pahl-MEE-eh-ree) and

Giuseppi Palmieri (jee-ew-SEHP-pee), gondoliers with republican principles. Each being half a king until the truth can be discovered, they promote everybody in the kingdom to a lord high something-or-other, to the inquisitor's disgust. They are separated from their recent brides and told that one is an unwitting bigamist.

Giannetta (jee-ahn-NAYT-tah) and

Tessa, flower girls, wives of Marco and Giuseppi.

Luiz (lew-EES), Casilda's lover and the duke's attendant, who carries a drum to beat before the duke. He turns out to be the real king of Barataria.

Inez (ee-NEHS), an elderly nurse. She is readily persuaded by torture to confess that Luiz is the king of Barataria, for whom she had substituted her own son, actually the child stolen by the grand inquisitor. Her testimony reunites Luiz and Casilda and the gondoliers and their brides.

GONE TO SOLDIERS

Author: Marge Piercy (1936-   )
First published: 1987
Genre: Novel
Locale: The United States, especially Detroit, and battle zones of World War II
Time: 1939-1946
Plot: Psychological realism

Louise Kahan, also known as **Annette Hollander Sinclair**, a popular writer of women's fiction. She is the former wife of Oscar Kahan and the mother of a fifteen-year-old daughter, Kay. When World War II breaks out, Louise works as a war correspondent and writes about anti-Semitism and the problems of women while resolving the nature of her continued involvement with her former husband.

Daniel Balaban, a child of immigrant Jewish parents living in the Bronx. He trains Japanese-language officers and works as a cryptologist deciphering codes in Japanese.

Jacqueline Lévy-Monot, known by her Jewish name, **Yakova**, and as **Jacqueline Porell**, whose identity she assumes in order to disguise her Jewish heritage. Using the name Gingembre, she escorts Jewish children over the Pyrenees to escape capture by the Germans. As a concentration camp victim, she takes part in the death march from Auschwitz to Bergen-Belsen to Magdenburg and survives to "make the past walk through the present."

Abra, a graduate student at Columbia University and the lover of Oscar Kahan, whom she follows to London as a member of the Office of Strategic Services. Increasingly upset in her role of compliant mistress, she asks what women want in a relationship with another person and in terms of their own self-identity.

Naomi, who is twelve years old at the beginning of the novel. She becomes **Nadine Siegel** when she is sent to the United States as the adopted daughter of her Aunt Rose and Uncle Morris. Her twin sister, Rivka, and her mother die in a concentration camp. Her father, Lapin, is killed on July 20, 1944, in Montagne Noire and is declared a hero of the Resistance movement. Raped by Leib, her friend Trudi's husband, she becomes pregnant with his child. Ari Katz, her future husband, meets Naomi on her return to France as the novel ends with the words "The End of One Set of Troubles Is But the Beginning of Another."

Bernice Coates, the unmarried daughter of Professor Coates. Her life before the war consisted of taking care of her widowed father. She joins the Army Air Corps as a pilot. Following an unrewarding affair with her brother's friend and lover, Zach, she falls in love with another woman. After the war, she assumes the identity of Harry Edward Munster, a former captain in the Army Air Corps, in order to find a job and live with Flo.

Jeff Coates, the artistic brother of Bernice, who works with guerrilla and sabotage groups as a member of the Jewish Resistance in France, where he is known as **Vendôme**. He becomes Jacqueline's lover but takes his own life when he is captured by the Milice.

Ruthie Siegel, who works in a plant, attends school at night, and earns an undergraduate degree before enrolling in graduate school to pursue a career in social work. After the war, she marries her fiancé, Murray, and becomes Mrs. Feldstein.

Duvey Siegel, Ruthie's brother. He works on tankers during the war. A skirt chaser who plays up to Naomi when home on leave, he drowns after a U-boat attack on his ship.

Murray Feldstein, who enlists in the Marines and, before coming home and marrying Ruthie, kills the commanding officer who had insulted and abused him because he is Jewish.

— Sue Brannan Walker

GONE WITH THE WIND

Author: Margaret Mitchell (1900-1949)
First published: 1936
Genre: Novel
Locale: Atlanta and Tara Plantation, Georgia
Time: 1861-1873
Plot: Historical

Scarlett O'Hara, a Georgia belle. Gently bred on Tara plantation and the wife of Charles Hamilton, she finds herself, through the fortunes of war, a widow and the mistress of a ruined plantation with a family to feed. With an indomitable will to survive and an unquenchable determination to keep Tara, she improves her fortunes with the aid of her own native abilities and opportunistic marriages to Frank Kennedy and Rhett Butler.

Ashley Wilkes, Scarlett O'Hara's sensitive, sophisticated neighbor, with whom she fancies herself in love. His genteel sensibilities and quiet resignation are a poor match for Scarlett's practicality and strong will, which she realizes in the end.

Rhett Butler, a cynical, wealthy blockade runner, Scarlett O'Hara's third husband. Knowing Scarlett for the unscrupulous materialist that she is, he nevertheless admires her will to survive and is plagued with a love for her, which he finally overcomes just as she discovers that it is Rhett and not Ashley Wilkes that she loves.

Charles Hamilton, Scarlett's first husband, whom she marries for spite.

Frank Kennedy, Scarlett's second husband, whom she marries for money.

Melanie (Hamilton) Wilkes, Ashley Wilkes's reticent, ladylike wife.

Gerald O'Hara and

Ellen O'Hara, Scarlett's parents.

Bonnie Blue Butler, the daughter of Scarlett O'Hara and Rhett Butler.

Suellen O'Hara, Scarlett's sister.

Miss Pittypat, Melanie Wilkes's aunt.

India Wilkes, Ashley Wilkes's sister.

Mammy, Scarlett's nurse.

THE GOOD APPRENTICE

Author: Iris Murdoch (1919-)
First published: 1985
Genre: Novel
Locale: London, England
Time: The 1980's
Plot: Domestic realism

Edward Baltram, a man who hopes to bring joy and happiness to his beloved friend Mark Wilsden by giving him a hallucinogenic drug hidden in a sandwich. As Mark falls asleep under the influence of the drug, Sarah Plowmain telephones, and Edward goes to her apartment, where they make love. While Edward is away, Mark apparently wakes, then falls to his death from the window of Edward's room. From his euphoric heights of sensual and mind-altered pleasure, Edward is plunged into a mental, emotional, and spiritual hell, blaming himself for Mark's death. The novel portrays the consequences of the other characters trying to help cure or intensify Edward's depression. Edward slowly begins to understand that his pain will never go away but that he can live with it, as others do.

Jesse Baltram, an elderly, bedridden mystic living on the edge of insanity. He is Edward's father as the result of a brief affair with Chloe Warriston. He exerts a powerful influence on Mother May, Bettina, and Ilona, who protect him from the outside world while they wait for him to die. As an artist, his early fame, now diminished through inactivity, will blossom anew at his death. As a lover of many women, his fame continues to burn brightly. His large and remarkable head is out of proportion to his diseased body. He drowns in the small river running near Seegard, fulfilling a vision that Edward had.

Harry Cuno, twice a widower, a man in his mid- to late forties. He married Chloe Warriston knowing that she carried Jesse's child and reared Edward as his own. He lives with his older son, Stuart, from his first marriage. He is having an affair with Midge, Chloe's sister and wife to his best friend, Thomas McCaskerville. Returning from a passionate weekend away from London, he and Midge lose their way, get their car stuck in a ditch, and find themselves at Seegard, where both Edward and Stuart happen to be. Midge ends their affair, and Harry, a writer, sets out for Italy to confer with his publisher, another woman.

Stuart Cuno, a man in his mid-twenties who has had a revelation and has become an advocate of the pure in heart, the "white" existence as opposed to Edward's "black." Tall, bulky, and awkward, Stuart is a source of strength to Edward, Midge, Harry, and Meredith (Midge's son). Estranged from Harry after discovering the affair, and from Edward before Mark's accident, Stuart eventually reconciles with both. The novel ends with father, son, and stepson drinking champagne toasts to one another's health and to the future at home together.

Margaret (Midge) Warriston McCaskerville, a former model married to Thomas and the mother of Meredith, age thirteen. As a child, she once was noticed by Jesse and has been haunted by the memory. She and Harry have attempted to keep their love of two years secret but have been caught once by Meredith and then by Stuart, Edward, Mother May, Bettina, Ilona, and Jesse at Seegard. Jesse thinks that Midge is her sister, Chloe. She finally decides to leave Harry and to tell Thomas the truth, something that Stuart has been urging her to do.

Thomas McCaskerville, the psychiatrist treating Edward for his depression over Mark's death. It is Thomas who arranges secretly for Edward to be asked to visit Jesse at Seegard; who urges Edward to return to the room where Mark died; who quietly arranges to help bring things to a better conclusion; and who is the last to know of the affair between his wife, Midge, and Harry. A quiet, gentle Scotsman of mixed Catholic and Jewish descent, it is his inner strength that provides the stability that the major characters need to survive and to learn to live with pain.

Meredith McCaskerville, the thirteen-year-old son of Midge and Thomas. Wise and observant, he knows of the affair between his mother and Harry but does not speak of it. He and Stuart become close friends. He is very much like his father, with whom he communicates silently. Meredith has a wine-colored birthmark on his cheek.

May Baltram, Jesse's wife of many years, who runs Seegard the way Jesse wants it run. Life at Seegard is quiet, simple, and self-supporting, and Mother May, as she is called, has established and lives by a routine that Edward readily accepts. At Thomas' request, she invites Edward to visit, telling him that Jesse wants to see him. After Jesse's death, she publishes excerpts from her diary, naming names and places and embarrassing Harry, Midge, and others.

Bettina Baltram, May and Jesse's twenty-four-year-old daughter. Like her mother, she is plainly dressed, efficient, cool to Edward, and a conspirator in keeping Edward ignorant of Jesse's condition. She dominates Ilona, her sister. Her future, at the end of the novel, is uncertain.

Ilona Baltram, May's eighteen-year-old daughter, who may not be Jesse's daughter but the product of an affair between May and Max Point, an old friend of Jesse. Quietly bored and frustrated by life at Seegard, she ultimately sees, in Edward, the chance to escape. When Edward sees her in London after Jesse's death, she has lost her virginity and become a stripper in a Soho club. Of the three women at Seegard, she is the most prone to public emotion and the one closest to Edward.

Brenda "Brownie" Wilsden, Mark's sister, who confronts Edward about Mark's death. He tells her the truth. Edward falls in love with her and pursues her, only to discover that she is to marry Giles Brightwalton and move to America.

Jennifer Wilsden, Mark's mother, who writes bitter and inflammatory letters to Edward, accusing him of murder and wishing all sorts of horrors on him. At Brownie's urging, probably aided by a visit from Stuart, she writes a final letter of forgiveness and moves with Brownie to America.

Mark Wilsden, Edward's dear friend and fellow student and the cause of Edward's painful search for peace. He dies from a fall from Edward's window while under the influence of drugs.

Sarah Plowmain, a nineteen-year-old who seduces Edward while Mark is under the influence of the drug. Later, she meets Edward by accident at Railway Cottage, near Seegard, which she shares with her mother and with Brownie. She accuses Edward of fathering her child, but the child is never born.

Elspeth Macrain, Sarah's mother, a vocal feminist writer and friend to and protector of Jennifer Wilsden and Brownie. She reviews Mother May's diaries unfavorably.

Willy Brightwalton, Edward's tutor in French. He is married to Ursula and is father to Giles.

Ursula Brightwalton, the Cuno and McCaskerville family physician. She thinks that pills, taken regularly, will cure Edward's problems.

Giles Brightwalton, Stuart's friend, who is pursuing an academic career in America.

Mr. Blinnet, Thomas McCaskerville's longtime patient, who, by accepting psychiatric treatment, apparently is constructing an alibi for some horrible crime that he may have committed in the past.

Mrs. Dorothy Quaid, a woman who conducts séances. Ilona moves in with her when Jesse dies, and Edward finds her there when he tries to have another séance. Ilona tells him that Mrs. Quaid is dead.

Max Point, an aging, besotted old painter friend of Jesse, now living as a human derelict on a barge, kept alive by a social worker and booze. He and Jesse apparently once were lovers, as were he and May. Ilona is thought to be the child of Max and May. He dies shortly after Jesse does.

Victoria Gunn, a rich twenty-year-old American whose father has bought Jesse's old house in London for her. Edward visits her while trying to find Jesse. She invites him to a party.

— *William H. Holland, Jr.*

THE GOOD COMPANIONS

Author: J. B. Priestley (1894-1984)
First published: 1929
Genre: Novel
Locale: England
Time: The 1920's
Plot: Social realism

Jess Oakroyd, a Yorshireman. A stolid, seemingly dull man, he proves that he is no fool. He sets off, tired of home, to see England. Meeting Elizabeth Trant, he befriends her and joins her, becoming the handyman of The Good Companions. He keeps the group united when they are dispirited. His adventures with the traveling company convince him he wants to go on traveling.

Elizabeth Trant, an "old maid" at thirty-five. She inherits a little money and sets out to see England. She falls in with a traveling vaudeville company, takes them over, and enjoys life for the first time. She meets a doctor who had been her suitor years before and marries.

Inigo Jollifant, a teacher who leaves his job because he is unhappy. He begins to travel; meeting The Good Companions, he joins them as their songwriter. He falls in love with Susie Dean, the comedian.

Morton Mitcham, a banjo-playing professional who becomes one of The Good Companions.

Susie Dean, a pretty young comedian who wants to become a star on the London stage. She cannot understand why Inigo Jollifant prefers writing for the literary journals to his success as a writer of popular tunes.

Jerry Jerningham, a male dancer with The Good Companions. He marries a wealthy woman and uses his influence to get Susie a chance to play in London. He gets places, too, for the other members of the troupe.

Jimmy Nunn and

Elsie Longstaff, members of The Good Companions.

Dr. Hugh McFarlane, Elizabeth's former suitor, whom she meets again and marries.

Mrs. Oakroyd, whose nagging causes Jess to leave home. When she becomes seriously ill, he returns to her; when she dies, he again takes to the open road.

THE GOOD CONSCIENCE
(Las buenas conciencias)

Author: Carlos Fuentes (1928-   )
First published: 1959
Genre: Novel
Locale: Guanajuato, Mexico
Time: Late 1920's to mid-1940's
Plot: Social realism

Jaime Ceballos (HI-meh seh-BAH-yohs), a boy brought up in the household of his aunt and uncle in the provincial Mexican city of Guanajuato. Rebelling against their tight-lipped upper-middle-class conformity, Jaime seeks a deeper, more personal experience of Catholicism than is offered by his family's conventional piety and begins to develop intellectual curiosity and a social conscience. He is, however, unable to put his principles into action. Notably in late adolescence, when he comes across his mother—long removed from the family because of her humbler class origin and unsophisticated attitudes—he cannot bring himself to approach her. Shortly thereafter, he abandons his ideals and resolves to conform to the role of heir to the family fortune. This decision is marked by an act of gratuitous violence: Jaime kills his aunt's house cat.

Asunción Ceballos de Balcárcel (ah-sewn-see-OHN seh-BAH-yohs deh bahl-KAHR-sehl), Jaime's aunt and surrogate mother, the descendant of a mercantile and landowning family of nineteenth century Spanish origin. Back with her husband from England (where they lived for more than a decade to escape the chaotic phases of the Mexican Revolution), she sees to it that Jaime's mother leaves the family circle so that she, Asunción, can rear the boy. Her husband, Jorge, is sterile, as is her relationship with him; surrogate motherhood gives Asunción some measure of fulfillment. In her frustration, she is even drawn to Jaime sexually when he reaches adolescence. Asunción and Jorge seek to control Jaime's development with the help of obliging priests.

Jorge Balcárcel del Moral (HOHR-heh bahl-KAHR-sehl dehl moh-RAHL), Jaime's uncle, a hypocritical landowner and moneylender who acts as the paternal figure in Jaime's life, despite the presence in the house of the boy's biological father. Balcárcel has obtained degrees in economics in England, and back in Mexico he becomes wealthy through political accommodation and privileged business dealings. Outwardly, Balcárcel is a model of stern bourgeois authoritarianism and restraint, but at one key moment Jaime catches him in a brothel, narcissistically dancing on a table with a rum bottle in his arms. This image contributes to the boy's cynical decision to conform.

Rodolfo Ceballos (rroh-DOHL-foh), Jaime's father and Asunción's brother. Portly, weak, and self-indulgent, he is discouraged by his mother from studying law, stands idly by as the family hacienda is confiscated during the Revolution, and ends up routinely running the family haberdashery. Rodolfo marries beneath his class and then capitulates to the Balcárcels' demand that his wife leave the home because she does not fit in with Guanajuato high society. He cedes the Ceballos homestead to Jorge and Asunción and lives like a guest in his own house, having little contact with Jaime. He reaches out to his son shortly before his premature death but is met with indifference by the boy, who blames him for the banishment of his mother.

Adelina López de Ceballos (ah-deh-LEE-nah), Jaime's mother, who is forced to leave her husband's home before her son is born and then to give up the boy to the Balcárcels. Adelina's lower-middle-class background has made her seem vulgar even amid the mediocrity of the provincial gentry. After her separation from Rodolfo, who does not support her, she grows even thinner than she normally was and slips into the lower depths of a town near Guanajuato. It is there that Jaime sees her in a working-class bar she frequents, preaching morality to her prostitute acquaintances.

Juan Manuel Lorenzo, Jaime's schoolmate and best friend, an intelligent boy of full-blooded Indian peasant background studying in the Guanajuato school on a federal scholarship. Juan Manuel encourages Jaime to read and to think about and discuss ideas and social issues. He is more perceptive about Jaime's situation than Jaime himself. Mexico's stratified society pulls the two boys apart at the end of their adolescence, when Juan Manuel goes off to Mexico City to take a job with the railroad and Jaime prepares to study law.

Ezequiel Zuno (eh-SEH-kee-ehl SEW-noh), a fugitive activist miner who takes refuge in the stable of the Balcárcel/Ceballos house, on one of the many days when Jaime has gone there to be alone with his thoughts. Jaime is inspired by Ezequiel's courage and conviction and gives him food and shelter, but the fugitive is discovered by Jorge Balcárcel and led away by soldiers as Jaime, powerless, shouts out to the miner that he did not betray him.

Father Obregón (oh-breh-GOHN), the priest who prepared Jaime for his First Communion and who sincerely tries to counsel him in the crisis of his late adolescence. By pointing out the pridefulness of Jaime's religious feeling, however, and his inability to love others, including his mother, the priest helps to precipitate the boy's turn to conformity.

— John Deredita

THE GOOD EARTH

Author: Pearl S. Buck (1892-1973)
First published: 1931
Genre: Novel
Locale: Northern China
Time: Early twentieth century
Plot: Social realism

Wang Lung, an ambitious farmer who sees in the land the only sure source of livelihood. At the end of his life, however, his third son has left the land to be a soldier, and his first and second sons callously plan to sell the land and go to the city as soon as Wang dies.

O-Lan, a slave bought by Wang's father to marry Wang. She works hard in their small field with Wang; during the civil war, she loots in order to get money to buy more land. She dies in middle age of a stomach illness.

Nung En, their oldest son, who, when he covets his father's concubine, Lotus Blossom, is married to the grain merchant Liu's daughter.

Nung Wen, their second son, apprenticed to Liu.

The Fool, their retarded daughter.

Liu, a grain merchant in the town.

The Uncle, who brings his wife and shiftless son to live on Wang's farm. Secretly a lieutenant of a robber band, he also brings protection.

Lotus Blossom, Wang Lung's concubine, who is refused entrance into the house by O-Lan.

Ching, a neighbor hired by Wang Lung as overseer.

Pear Blossom, a pretty slave taken by Wang after the death of his wife.

GOOD MORNING, MIDNIGHT

Author: Jean Rhys (Ella Gwendolen Rees Williams, 1894-1979)
First published: 1939
Genre: Novel
Locale: Paris, France
Time: The 1930's
Plot: Psychological realism

Sasha Jansen, the narrator and protagonist, a woman whose fading good looks are synonymous in her mind with her fading chances for happiness. Very few details of her childhood are provided. Even her real name is missing: Sasha, she says, is an affectation. Her story begins shortly after she has a chance meeting with an old friend who, shocked by Sasha's appearance, sends her to Paris for a much-needed change of scene. Her routine in Paris becomes a series of solitary outings to clothing shops and bars. She encounters strangers, mostly men, in the bars and cafés, but instead of getting to know these people, she concentrates on her own lack of self-worth, thus effectively ruining these relationships before they begin. What is known of her earlier life is revealed in cinematic flashbacks about an earlier time, five years ago, when she is married to the vagabond Enno, with whom she has a child who dies soon after birth. Her husband drifts in and out of her life, telling her that she does not know how to love, and finally leaves her to endure the agony of the child's death alone. Five years later, she still suffers from these experiences, attributing her sadness not to one thing but to a slow process that took years to produce. Men, even the insignificant men in her life, determine the few decisions made in the novel—the patriarchy pervades her life. Her profound sense of loneliness, isolation, and lack of direction all converge in Sasha's poignant question, "What's happening to me? Oh, my life, oh, my youth."

Enno, the man whom Sasha marries in Amsterdam, a would-be writer. Although he is something of a drifter who is always looking for money, Sasha loves him and trusts him to provide the stability for which she longs. He leaves the pregnant Sasha, presumably to look for work, but ultimately concedes that he has grown tired of her. Their bohemian existence soon loses its glamour for Sasha as well. Enno is the type of person who takes the good times but not the bad.

René (reh-NAY), the gigolo who befriends Sasha during her last trip to Paris. Both he and Sasha project a wounded aura, and this easily recognized sense of vulnerability sparks their initial attraction. He intuits that she is someone with whom he could be at rest—hardly a romantic sentiment. She responds to his youth and finds comfort in his poignantly naïve optimism. She cannot bring herself to trust him, thinking that he is using her for her money. After Sasha has driven René away, she discovers that her suspicion is unfounded. His departure and the emptiness that follow echo Enno's desertion five years earlier.

Nicholas Delmar, a young Russian who befriends Sasha in a bar. He offers to introduce her to his many friends, including Rubin the painter.

The Man Next Door, whose anonymous presence provides one of the few unifying threads throughout the story. Sasha considers him a nuisance who is unworthy of her, yet she accepts his advances after she realizes that she has misjudged René. Their liaison symbolizes the emptiness of Sasha's life and her inability to care about anything. He is the last in a series of men to whom Sasha turns for comfort and fulfillment.

Sidonie, Sasha's acquaintance, who offers her money to provide her with a change of scene after the two old friends meet by chance in London.

— Lagretta T. Lenker

THE GOOD MOTHER

Author: Sue Miller (1943-   )
First published: 1986
Genre: Novel

Locale: Primarily Cambridge, Massachusetts; also rural New England and Chicago
Time: The 1970's
Plot: Psychological realism

Anna Dunlap, the protagonist and first-person narrator. She tells of her struggles to survive after she leaves a loveless marriage, taking her daughter, Molly, with her. An uncertain young woman, Anna gives piano lessons and finds work in a laboratory. Other players in the novel are seen only through Anna's eyes, so that except for Molly, they never become fully rounded characters. The events are narrated about four years after they take place, and from Anna's changing perceptions it is clear that she has grown stronger and wiser.

Brian Dunlap, Anna's former husband. He is fairly content in a tepid relationship with Anna during their marriage. It is Anna who suggests a separation when Brian's law firm transfers him to Washington, D.C. He is a decent man who plays by the rules, which is to his advantage later in the novel, when he sues for custody of Molly. Although he has an affair with another woman while his marriage with Anna is dissolving, society is more tolerant of his indiscretions than of Anna's.

Molly Dunlap, Anna and Brian's three-year-old daughter. She is a bright, once-happy child who struggles to make sense of her parents' divorce and the profound consequences it has on her life. Anna describes her daughter in exquisite and loving detail, using every sense to convey the physical reality of a little girl. Molly is one of the most successfully realized characters in the novel. The child's dialogue is true to the prattle of a child her age as well as a subtle indicator of what is going on in Molly's deeper consciousness.

Leo, Anna's lover, who has a passionate approach to life that no one in Anna's circle has ever displayed. A man of many appetites, he provides the sexual fulfillment Anna never knew in her marriage. He is never fully developed and is almost a stereotype of the artist often depicted in literature, an intense, gifted painter who lives beyond the rules of traditional society. When he does enter the "real" world of the courts in order to help Anna retain custody of Molly, he appears awkward and confused.

Frank McCord, Anna's grandfather and patriarch of her mother's family. He represents the repressive Calvinism that shaped her girlhood. He is slightly contemptuous of the other members of the family and constantly manipulative. An arrogant, self-made man, McCord holds everyone to the same rigid standards to which he holds himself.

Bunny, Anna's mother, who is dominated by Frank McCord and worships achievement as he does. She is ambitious for Anna and pushes her daughter to become a concert pianist. Failing that, she is content to see Anna settled in an emotionally sterile marriage.

— Sheila Golburgh Johnson

THE GOOD SOLDIER

Author: Ford Madox Ford (Ford Madox Hueffer, 1873-1939)
First published: 1915
Genre: Novel

Locale: England, Germany, and the United States
Time: The 1890's through 1913
Plot: Psychological realism

John Dowell, an independently wealthy American who has spent most of his adult life in Europe taking his weak wife from spa to spa. Dowell is so intellectually confused and morally obtuse that for nine years he has been unaware of the duplicity of his closest friends, the Ashburnhams, and his wife. Without passion himself, he fails to realize its power in the lives of others. Dowell assumes surface manners to be the defining characteristics of people; whenever anybody behaves erratically, Dowell is mystified. Not until after the deaths of his wife and Leonora's husband, when Leonora Ashburnham tells him of their adulteries and the accompanying deceits, does Dowell have any inkling of the truths of their relationships.

Edward Ashburnham, the good soldier of the title, an English gentleman who inherited large estates. On the surface, Ashburnham is the model of the English officer and administrator, meticulous in his manners and kind to his tenants. He is, however, unable to control either his financial or his sexual affairs. In public, he and his wife behave so well together that they appear to have a perfect marriage; in private, they rarely speak to each other. Although initiated with the best of intentions, his sexual affairs have drastic consequences for the women involved. This series of failures of the code of the gentleman culminates in his passion for his ward, Nancy Rufford, and his subsequent suicide.

Leonora Ashburnham, the good wife of Edward. Catholic and with a strong will, Leonora does not leave her husband even though they have no conjugal relations and no children. She assumes control of their finances and, to a large extent, their lives. They save money by living in India and on the continent. She is responsible for the subterfuge of Edward's weak heart, and she contributes to his suicide by maintaining her high expectations of him. Because she is the only person in the story who knows what is going on most of the time, perhaps she is most responsible for the tragic results.

Florence Dowell, Dowell's self-indulgent wife. She marries him for his money and his willingness to live in Europe, where nobody will tell him of her past. To prevent his knowing that she is sexually experienced, she fakes a weak heart as an excuse for not having marital relations with him on the ship to Europe. She has a nine-year affair with Ashburnham and kills herself when she discovers that he is falling in love with Nancy Rufford.

Nancy Rufford, an adolescent girl who has been left in the charge of Ashburnham by her father in India. She is a lovely, vulnerable young woman. Even Dowell fancies that he loves her and that, at Florence's death, he is now free to marry her. She learns of Ashburnham's suicide while she is on the ship returning to India, where Ashburnham is sending her in self-defense. Hopelessly infatuated with Ashburnham, she loses her mind. Thus, she becomes another helpless female for Dowell to nurse.

— *William J. McDonald*

THE GOOD SOLDIER ŠVEJK
(Osudy dobreho vojáka Švejka ve svètove války)

Author: Jaroslav Hašek (1883-1923)
First published: 1921-1923
Genre: Novel
Locale: Bohemia and Austria
Time: World War I
Plot: Satire

Josef Švejk (YOH-sehf shvayk), a Czech recruited to serve in the Austrian army during World War I. Švejk's military experience is a series of mishaps that repeatedly land him in jail, yet Švejk avoids serious punishment, even execution, through the same bizarre behaviors that get him into trouble. Švejk is a deceptively complex character, appearing both imbecilic and ingenious, as well as both honest and deceitful. When confronted by bureaucratic red tape and the harsh, often unreasonable conditions in the army, Švejk foils the establishment. Sometimes he makes fools of authorities by complying with irrational demands and carrying out instructions to the letter. Another of his ploys is to digress into a stream of disjointed anecdotes that often enrage his superior officers or convince them he is a fool. He seems always to know what tactic to employ each time he encounters difficulty, when to proclaim his innocence, no matter how guilty he may be, and when to admit guilt, no matter how innocent he may be. He frequently attributes his mishaps to bad luck. Throughout his ordeals, he maintains a cheerful attitude that ultimately disarms his oppressors. As a result, Švejk avoids punishment and delays his progress to the battlefields on the eastern front. At times, Švejk appears honest to a fault, yet he will lie and deceive others in carrying out his duties as batman (military gofer) for his assigned superior. Švejk survives the hostility of the Austrians toward Czech soldiers, avoids combat, and protects others. The author provides little physical description of the character and little of his background. His age is difficult to determine, and aside from brief references to a brother and a lover, his past life remains a mystery.

Otto Katz, a Jewish-born Catholic priest serving as a military chaplain. Katz is a drunkard, a debaucher, and an atheist whose priesthood is merely a way of avoiding combat. Katz, to whom Švejk is assigned as batman, loses the communion chalice and substitutes a sporting trophy, pawns his landlord's furniture to purchase alcohol, and frequents brothels. He loses Švejk, in a card game, to Lieutenant Lukáš.

Lieutenant Lukáš, a Czech officer in the Austrian Army. Lukáš is a strict but just officer who loves animals and dislikes batmen, whom he considers dishonest. After Švejk comes to work for him, he is won over by Švejk's good nature and seeming innocence. Lukáš enjoys an active love life, but one complicated by his relationships with married women, and he relies on Švejk to resolve some of his difficulties. Švejk's penchant for disaster causes Lukáš to regard his batman with mixed emotions.

Colonel Kraus, a German officer in the Austrian army and Lukáš' immediate superior. Kraus is an unyielding man who orders Lukáš and Švejk to the front after Švejk steals Kraus's dog and gives it to Lukáš.

Lieutenant Dub, a Czech who abuses his power and treats his men cruelly. Before the war, Dub was a schoolteacher known for his loyalty to the Austrian emperor and suspected of being an informer. As an officer, he is unyielding, but he is never able to intimidate or defeat Švejk. To the contrary, Švejk, who is assigned to Lukáš, not Dub, is able to embarrass and discredit Dub, once surprising him in a brothel. Dub retains his position, although his power is undermined.

Marek, a classically trained philosopher and Czech volunteer serving a one-year term. Marek's civilian career bears strong parallels to that of the author, Jaroslav Hašek, who, like Marek, edited a publication titled *Animal World* and was fired for inventing animals. Like the author himself, Marek is a political dissident. Marek presents a point of view not available to Švejk, particularly in his satirization of the Austrian army. The friendship between Marek and Švejk is significant because it suggests that the two—Marek, the recognized intellectual, and Švejk, the "patent lunatic"—are kindred souls.

— *K Edgington*

THE GOOD TERRORIST

Author: Doris Lessing (1919-   )
First published: 1985
Genre: Novel

Locale: London, England
Time: The 1970's
Plot: Social realism

Alice Mellings, a would-be terrorist. Although she is in her mid-thirties, she looks like either an overgrown child or a plain woman of fifty. Described as "pudgy" and "clumsy," Alice is a self-effacing woman who relishes being subservient to others. A college graduate and a product of a middle-class family, she shuns her former world, turning to her mother and old friends only for financial assistance. She has been a political agitator for about fifteen years. Directionless herself, she takes pleasure in organizing other people's lives, especially through running a commune of squatters in London. Some of the commune's inhabitants think of themselves as terrorists; others are interested only in free food and lodging. Alice remains at the center of the narrative, which becomes more an exploration of her and the others' characters than a chronicle of terrorist activities.

Jasper, Alice's boyfriend and a would-be terrorist leader, in his early twenties. He is extremely thin, with "pinkish freckled skin" that helps to give him what is described as "an angelic, candid air." Like Alice, he comes from a middle-class family, which he has rejected. Jasper is a homosexual whose interest in Alice stems from his need for mothering, a role that Alice fulfills with delight. Bitterness toward his father appears to be the major motivation for his amateurish terrorism, which finally leads to a car bombing and his rejection of Alice.

Bert, another terrorist and a friend of Jasper. Bert, a dark, thin, bearded man about thirty years old, provides the main leadership for the group. Jasper develops a strong sexual attachment to him, and after the car bombing they leave together to continue their political maneuverings.

Dorothy Mellings, Alice's mother, a woman in her sixties. She is sensible and still attractive. Wanting Alice to have a fuller life than she had experienced as a mother and a housewife, she finds disappointing her daughter's obsessive relationship with Jasper and the others, whom she considers spoiled children, not revolutionaries.

Pat, Bert's girlfriend and a terrorist. She is a forceful and striking young woman, with glossy black hair and white skin. Taking an active part in events, the commanding Pat serves as an antithesis to Alice's sideline role as a provider.

Jim, one of the hangers-on in the commune. A West Indian immigrant, Jim is more interested in drumming than in politics and typifies those who take advantage of the commune for their own convenience. He is the original inhabitant of the house where the group resides, and he has none of the high expectations of the middle-class members of the group.

Roberta, a commune member and terrorist. In her thirties, she is described as "bulky." Although Roberta is involved in the political action, the novel focuses on her tempestuous relationship with Faye.

Faye, Roberta's friend and a terrorist, a young woman about twenty years old, fair-skinned, with an innocent air. In the climactic scene in which the group carries out a bombing, Faye is killed.

Jocelin, another of the terrorists. She is unattractive but efficient with explosives and firearms. More capable and serious than the others, this perpetually angry woman turns into the unofficial leader of the group on its ill-fated bombing expedition.

— Robert L. Ross

THE GOOD WOMAN OF SETZUAN
(Der gute Mensch von Sezuan)

Author: Bertolt Brecht (1898-1956)
First published: 1948
Genre: Drama

Locale: The fictional province of Setzuan, China
Time: Between World War I and World War II
Plot: Moral

Shen Te, a prostitute in the capital of the Chinese province of Setzuan. Later, she assumes the identity **Shui Ta**, supposedly her male cousin and a ruthless businessman. A kind, charitable woman who cannot say "no," Shen Te apparently is the only person left on Earth who fulfills the prerequisites of a "good" human being. Although the three gods in search of such a person reward her with sufficient money to enable her to buy a tobacco shop, she soon finds herself again in a state of destitution when the news of her new possession attracts many alleged relatives and debtors who sponge off her meager means. To survive, Shen Te is forced to play the role of an assumed cousin named Shui Ta, whose ruthless acts enable "him" to increase Shen Te's possessions.

Wang, a water-seller. He has a naïve, unshaken belief in the power of the gods, who appear to him in his dreams at regular intervals during the play and who reveal to him their impotence in the light of Shen Te's social dilemma. Ironically, it is through Wang's incorrect perception of Shui Ta's use of physical coercion toward Shen Te that the three gods are called to serve as judges.

The three gods, nameless deities vaguely resembling a popular concept of the Christian Trinity, and with distinctly human characteristics. The first one is strongly authoritarian, the second one pessimistically cynical, and the third one noncommittally jovial. The three gods appear to be blind to the causes of human misery and, against all proof to the opposite during the final trial scene, they reaffirm their belief in Shen Te's ability both to be good and to survive without the help of Shui Ta.

Yang Sun, an unemployed airman. Yang is a selfish egotist who wants to use Shen Te's money to bribe a prospective employer in Peking. Although he reveals his self-seeking intentions to Shui Ta, Shen Te is willing to marry him because she truly loves him and she wants him to become a mail carrier pilot, symbolizing the stringing of positive bonds between human beings everywhere. Instead of going through with his intention, however, Yang becomes a cruel and merciless foreman in Shui Ta's factory.

Shu Fu, a barber. He is a wealthy capitalist who wants to seize the opportunity of Shen Te's financial dilemma to make her become his wife. Although apparently helping her to become the "angel of the suburbs" by letting her use some of his warehouses as shelters for homeless people, he shows his true character when he breaks Wang's hand with his curling tongs and when, following his realization that he cannot get Shen Te as he had expected, he lets Shui Ta turn his damp and unhealthy warehouses into an exploitative tobacco factory.

Mrs. Yang, Yang Sun's mother. She talks in bourgeois clichés and claims that her son will marry Shen Te out of love, when actually she sees only the opportunity for a financial profit. She calls off the wedding when Shui Ta does not show up in time to clear Shen Te of her financial debt, and she later supports Shui Ta in his ruthless business practices.

A carpet dealer and his wife, who recognize and appreciate Shen Te's innate goodness. Like the old couple Philemon and Baucis in Greek mythology, they become vulnerable to the greed of humans, but here they are not saved by the gods. When Shen Te, as a result of Yang Sun squandering her money, is unable to repay a debt to them of two hundred silver dollars, they cannot pay their taxes and thus lose their shop.

An unemployed man, who moves within the group of people who profit from Shen Te's generosity. He understands her dilemma in calling on the help of Shui Ta. He also expresses social sympathy for Wang when he is hurt, directing Wang to pursue legal action against the barber.

Mrs. Shin, a widower.

Lin To, a carpenter.

Mi Tzü, a property owner.

A family of eight, who like the previous three characters are either previous or new acquaintances of Shen Te. Like a swarm of parasites, they all take advantage of her kindheartedness and her money.

— *Helmut F. Pfanner*

THE GOODBYE LOOK

Author: Ross Macdonald (Kenneth Millar, 1915-1983)
First published: 1969
Genre: Novel
Locale: Southern California
Time: Late 1960's
Plot: Detective and mystery

Lew Archer, the narrator, a Los Angeles private detective called in to investigate what seems to be a minor theft in the home of Mr. and Mrs. Larry Chalmers in the wealthy (fictitious) town of Pacific Point. Archer's investigation uncovers a web of intrigue and changed identities leading back to the shooting death of Eldon Swain fifteen years earlier. By the time the investigation is finished, two more people have been murdered, a man has been killed by the police, the sinister histories of the Chalmers and Swain families have been revealed, and the murderer, Larry Chalmers, has committed suicide. Archer's persistence and his refusal to be diverted from his investigation by his affair with Moira Smitheram lead to the revelations and what seems to be a healing conclusion for the troubled younger characters, Nick Chalmers and Betty Truttwell.

Lawrence (Larry) Chalmers, a wealthy man, supposedly a veteran of World War II. In fact, he was discharged after very brief service because of his mental instability. He supposedly inherited wealth from his mother and has never worked. Despite his apparent love for his son, Nick, it becomes clear that he and his wife are responsible for most of the violence that has made Nick neurotic and suicidal. Larry and Irene had stolen money that her former lover, Eldon Swain, had embezzled, and they had killed John Truttwell's wife when she recognized them. Later, Swain had kidnapped Nick (in fact, his son and not Larry's), and when he was killed, his identity had been covered up by the Chalmers couple. The money Swain embezzled is the fortune that Chalmers supposedly inherited from his mother. Chalmers murders Jean Trask and a sleazy detective, Sidney Harrow, to cover up his crimes, but in the end Archer uncovers the truth, and Chalmers commits suicide.

Irene Chalmers, née **Rita Shepherd**, who was once Eldon Swain's lover. She is the mother of his child, Nick, who is passed off as Larry's son. She shares Larry's guilt in the embezzlement and the killing of John Truttwell's wife.

Nicholas (Nick) Chalmers, a confused young man who runs away when Jean Trask gives him reason to believe that he is not Larry Chalmers' son. When he was a boy of eight, he was kidnapped by Eldon Swain. While escaping, he shot Swain, and now he is almost framed for the murders of Jean Trask and Sidney Harrow. Despite the attempts of his parents and his psychiatrist to keep him from the truth to hide their own crimes, he seems to be on the road to recovery at the end.

John Truttwell, the Chalmerses' attorney, who hires Archer but tries to manipulate his investigation. He tries to prevent the marriage of his daughter, Betty, to Nick Chalmers, who, he thinks, is insane and probably a murderer. He is unaware that his wife's death was murder, not an accident.

Betty Truttwell, John's daughter, a twenty-five-year-old innocent who loves Nick and helps Archer in the investigation.

Jean Trask, the daughter of Eldon Swain. She precipitates the action of the novel when she tries to find the money her father had embezzled. She gives Nick Chalmers evidence that he is Swain's son, setting off his flight that leads to his attempted suicide. Larry Chalmers murders her and tries to frame Nick for the crime.

Dr. Ralph Smitheram, Nick's psychiatrist, who tries to prevent Archer from finding out about the lives of his patients, Larry and Nick Chalmers. In fact, he hides these facts because his practice is built on the money he has blackmailed from Larry Chalmers over the years.

Moira Smitheram, Ralph's wife. She had an affair with Larry Chalmers during the war, when her husband was on combat duty in the Pacific. She has a brief affair with Archer and tries to dissuade him from pursuing his investigation, but in the end she helps him to uncover the truth.

— *John M. Muste*

GOOD-BYE, MR. CHIPS

Author: James Hilton (1900-1954)
First published: 1934
Genre: Novel
Locale: An English boys' school
Time: 1870-1933
Plot: Sentimental

Mr. Chipping, referred to as **Mr. Chips**, a retired schoolmaster, white-haired, semi-bald, fairly active for his age. Unprofound, he prefers detective novels to the Greek and Latin works that he taught for so long. His mind is filled with memories of his dead wife, the many boys he taught at Brookfield, and the many experiences he had there. He is a legend at the school and is remembered with affection. He dies dreaming of the thousands of boys he had taught.

Mrs. Wickett, his landlady.

Wetherby, the head of Brookfield when Mr. Chips came there.

Colley, a Brookfield boy whom Mr. Chips disciplined on his first day at the school. Colley's son and grandson later become pupils of Mr. Chips.

Katherine (Kathie) Bridges Chipping, Mr. Chips's young wife, whom he marries at forty-eight. She is very popular with the boys. She dies in childbirth along with her infant son.

Dr. Merivale, Mr. Chips's physician.

Collingwood, a Brookfield boy who becomes a major and is killed in the war.

Ralston, a young headmaster at Brookfield whom Mr. Chips never likes.

Chatteris, Ralston's successor as headmaster; he and Mr. Chips get on well.

Max Staefel, a former German master at Brookfield, drafted while visiting in Germany and later killed on the Western Front.

Linford, a Brookfield boy, the last to say, "Goodbye, Mr. Chips," the night before the old man dies.

GOODNIGHT!
(Spokoinoi nochi)

Author: Andrei Sinyavsky (as Abram Tertz, 1925-1997)
First published: 1984
Genre: Novel
Locale: The Soviet Union
Time: The 1940's through 1971
Plot: Autobiographical

Andrei Donatovich Sinyavsky (ahn-DRAY doh-NAH-toh-vihch sih-NYAV-skee), a writer later known under the pseudonym **Abram Tertz**. Brought up by a revolutionary father, Sinyavsky studied Russian literature of the late nineteenth and early twentieth centuries. His dedication to phantasmagoric literature flew in the face of the officially accepted Socialist Realism. Sinyavsky eventually had his work smuggled out of the country and published in the West under the pseudonym Abram Tertz. He is eventually arrested and imprisoned. After his release, he discovers that people have changed; they no longer live under the fear that was prevalent during Joseph Stalin's time.

Donat Evgenievich Sinyavsky (DOH-naht yehv-GEH-nih-yeh-vihch), the younger Sinyavsky's father. A love of hunting and disdain for the petty details of everyday life (both remnants of his aristocratic heritage) combine with a strong will and fervent idealism to form this sincere atypical revolutionary. The elder Sinyavsky maintains genuine human compassion for individuals throughout the collectivization and maintains revolutionary idealism despite imprisonment. He participated in political agitation during the revolution, organized famine relief in the 1920's, and eventually was imprisoned for anti-Soviet activity (a completely groundless charge). As a result of his imprisonment in 1951, he later becomes convinced that the authorities have tapped his brain in such a way that they can monitor his thoughts and conversations even at great distances. This belief causes him to fear talking about anything important except when he is convinced that no one is listening.

Maria Vasilievna (vah-SIH-lyehv-nah), the elder Sinyavsky's wife. An archetypal Russian woman with strength that arises from necessity, she patiently bears her husband's imprisonment, rears their son alone, and brings food and comfort to her incarcerated spouse.

Efim Bobko (yeh-FIHM BOB-koh), an orphan. He is grimly serious, nonintellectual, and slowly methodical in saving money. The son of farmers dispossessed during the collectivization, Efim, with his parents' blessing, escapes from the train taking his family into exile and ends up in Moscow. There he tells the elder Sinyavsky that he is merely lost and cannot remember where his home is. Sinyavsky arranges for Efim to live in an orphanage and provides him with a semblance of a home while trying in vain to find Efim's family. Efim grows up in the orphanage, eventually serves in the war, and dies some time afterward from shock and starvation.

Hélène, the daughter of a French diplomat who arranges for her to study in a Soviet university. Her undeceitful nature, coupled with modesty, charms everyone whom she meets. With a keen mastery of Russian, she maintains an idealistic worldview while successfully completing the obligatory courses on Marxism-Leninism. Soviet authorities try to subvert her by coercing Sinyavsky into proposing to her. Sinyavsky reveals the plan to Hélène, and together they orchestrate a quarrel to ensure her safety. Later, she becomes the courier for taking Sinyavsky's manuscripts to the West.

Seryozha (sehr-YOH-zhah), Sinyavsky's childhood friend and hero. A prodigy of artistic talent, he is capable of expressing himself in pointed verse and has a heartfelt appreciation for art. Women in his life quickly discern the cowardly streak in him that leads him to denounce friends and compatriots to the authorities. This untrustworthiness leads Hélène and Sinyavsky to dissemble before him to convince the authorities that they have quarreled.

Viktor Aleksandrovich Pakhomov (ah-lehk-SAN-droh-vihch pah-KHOH-mov), a lieutenant colonel and interrogator for the Komitet Gosudarstvennoi Bezopasnosti (KGB). Pakhomov skillfully utilizes a mixture of humanitarian pleas, threats, lies, suggestions, and logic to bring Sinyavsky to the point of capitulation without having to resort to physical violence.

— Donald E. Livingston, Jr.

GORBODUC

Authors: Thomas Norton (1532-1584) and Thomas Sackville (1536-1608)
First published: 1565
Genre: Drama
Locale: England
Time: Before the Saxon invasion of Britain
Plot: Tragedy

Gorboduc (gohr-BOH-duhk), a king of ancient Britain. After ruling his land wisely for many years, he disregards the advice of his sage counselors, divides the realm between his two sons, and thus brings tragedy on his family and his country. He recognizes the folly of his decision too late, when he learns of the unnatural deaths of his sons. Filled with remorse, he learns that as a human being, he must grieve; the patience prescribed by his advisers is an attribute of gods alone. He is finally murdered by his people, who have fallen into anarchy as a result of the overturning of the natural order of succession and government.

Videna (vee-DAY-na), his queen. She is partial to her older son and disapproves from the beginning the king's resolution to deprive Ferrex of half his rightful inheritance, for she foresees in Porrex the envy and pride that later erupt in his brother's murder. Horrified by Ferrex's death, she curses and disowns her younger child, then wreaks her unnatural revenge on him.

Ferrex (FEHR-ehks), Gorboduc's older son, his mother's favorite. Although he is less malleable than Porrex, he listens to the counselors who encourage him to build an army as protection against the jealous ambition of his brother, thus provoking Porrex's attack.

Porrex (POHR-ehks), Ferrex's brother. Easily convinced by flatterers that Ferrex intends to rob him of his realm, he is enraged to learn that his brother is armed and retaliates by invading his territory and murdering him. Returning grief-stricken to his parents, he finds that Gorboduc will not accept his explanation that he killed Ferrex to save his own life. Banished from his father's sight, he is slain by his own mother.

Arostus, Gorboduc's counselor. He praises the king's decision to give the kingdom to his sons, for he believes that the young men can learn to rule wisely under their father's guidance. After the death of the princes, he moralizes to the king about the uncertainty of human life, but his words give no comfort to his master.

Philander, another of the king's advisers, who later attempts to control Porrex's ambition and anger. Although he does not foresee the inevitable strife that is to arise from the division of the realm, he argues that the princes should learn to govern well from their father's example and suggests that to disrupt the natural order by handing down the crown before the death of the king is to "corrupt the state of minds and things."

Eubulus, Gorboduc's secretary. He pleads with the king to preserve the kingdom intact for the sake of its citizens, for he knows that "divided reigns do make divided hearts." He prophesies the dissatisfactions that arise in both princes. After the death of the king and queen, he counsels the immediate quelling of the popular revolt and argues that no subject has a right to rebel against his prince for any cause. When he hears of Fergus' rebellion, he laments the fate of his country, which will be torn by civil wars until the legitimate heir can be restored to the throne.

Dordan, Ferrex's wise counselor, who attempts to mollify the prince's resentment at being deprived of half his kingdom.

Hermon and

Tyndar, parasites of the two princes. They play on their masters' feelings of resentment and ambition, inciting them to their disastrous combat.

Fergus, the duke of Albany. In league with other noblemen to put down the popular revolt, he decides to try to win the crown for himself by force. His ambition begins a long series of civil wars.

Clotyn, the duke of Cornwall,

Mandud, the duke of Loegris, and

Gwenard, the duke of Cumberland, lords allied to put down rebellion and later to overcome Fergus' army.

Marcella, Videna's lady in waiting, who relates with grief and horror the queen's murder of her remaining son.

GORKY PARK

Author: Martin Cruz Smith (1942-   )
First published: 1981
Genre: Novel
Locale: Moscow, Russia
Time: Late 1970's
Plot: Detective and mystery

Arkady Vasilevich Renko (ahr-KAH-dee vah-SIH-leh-vihch REHN-koh), a senior homicide investigator for the Moscow Militia. Although he is the son of a Russian general known as a war hero, he refuses to use his father's standing to promote his career. He also rejects active Communist Party membership. This decision on principle taints his relationship with his wife, Zoya, and political disagreements facilitate their separation. He investigates a triple homicide in Gorky Park and initially wonders whether the case should be handled by KGB agent Major Pribluda. The brutal murders lack straightforward clues to motive, but he methodically picks apart physical evidence in order to pinpoint a suspect. He interviews Mosfilm wardrobe assistant Irina Asanova, who provides him with a link to the victims. He develops feelings for Irina, although he is unsure of her involvement in the case. He links an American, John Osborne, to the murders and suspects KGB involvement. This notion is reinforced when his colleague, plainclothes detective Pasha Pavlovich, receives a bullet in the back. The loss embitters Arkady, who blames Pribluda for Pasha's death. He becomes more determined to solve the murders and befriends William Kirwill, an American police officer who was the brother of one of the victims; they establish a beneficial "partnership." He alienates Irina when he forces her to face her friends' deaths, but he flies to her rescue when he learns of her abduction by KGB officials. The ensuing confrontation ends in his near-fatal stabbing. After months of recuperation and KGB interrogation concerning Osborne, he agrees to aid in the fur trader's arrest in the United States. Arkady works with the KGB, but only for Irina's sake. Although he loves Irina, he leaves her in America, admitting that he could never be more than Russian.

Major Pribluda (pree-BLEW-dah), a KGB chief investigator and member of the Committee for State Security. He takes over for the Moscow Militia when cases involve foreign affairs. Pribluda holds duty to state far above any individual code of ethics, unlike Arkady. In order to protect KGB interests, he allows Renko to handle the Gorky Park murders, even though the victims appear to have international ties. When Arkady closes in on a suspect, Pribluda stymies his efforts using any means possible, including killing plainclothes detective Pasha Pavlovich to slow the investigation. He interrogates Arkady for months and acquires new respect for his former rival.

William Kirwill, an Irish American police officer from New York. His parents were members of the Marxist movement. He travels to Moscow to find his brother, James, and discovers that James was one of the three victims in the Gorky Park murders. After a scuffle with Arkady, the two become allies, although Kirwill's brutish temperament colors their friendship. Kirwill returns to New York, still tracking Osborne. He hopes to facilitate the defections of Arkady and Irina while avenging James's death. Osborne kills him in the final meeting with KGB agents.

Irina Asanova (ee-REE-nah ah-SAH-noh-vah), a Siberian working in Moscow as a Mosfilm wardrobe assistant. She knew the three Gorky Park victims but assumes that they left the country safely with Osborne's help. Arkady provides her with solid evidence confirming their deaths, but she fails to believe him. She falls in love with Arkady but still maintains a relationship with Osborne, hoping he might smuggle her out of Russia to join her friends. She agrees to help the KGB capture Osborne, but only after Arkady is delivered to America. She survives the final shootout and stays in New York.

Pasha Pavlovich (PAH-sha PAHV-loh-vihch), a plainclothes detective working with Arkady. He aids in the Gorky Park investigation, collecting evidence and following Arkady's lead. While trying to retrieve a paneled chest that could provide clues to the prime suspect's dealings, he is shot by an unknown assailant.

John Osborne, an American, the president of Osborne Furs, Inc., and an informant for the KGB. He successfully smuggles live sables out of Russia and breeds them in America. He secures a second group of sables with the help of two Russians and one American. He later kills his associates and leaves their mangled bodies in Gorky Park. When the KGB closes in on his racket, he agrees to swap six sables for Irina Asanova, knowing that she wants to leave Russia. He is killed by Arkady after the KGB confronts him on his sable farm.

Zoya Renko (ZOH-yah), Arkady's wife, an active Party member. She openly has an affair with a coworker and leaves Arkady when she realizes that he will never climb the political ladder.

Andrei Iamskoy (ahn-DRAY YAHM-skoy), the chief prosecutor overseeing the Gorky Park murder case. Arkady trusts him. Iamskoy works with the KGB, misdirecting leads in the investigation to slow progress. When Arkady pins the murders on Osborne, Iamskoy tries to kill him but is shot by Irina.

— Elizabeth Vander Meer

THE GORMENGHAST TRILOGY

Author: Mervyn Peake (1911-1968)
First published: 1946-1959
Genre: Novels

Locale: The castle of Gormenghast and the world beyond
Time: Unspecified
Plot: Gothic

Titus Groan, 1946

Steerpike, an ambitious kitchen-boy. With great cunning, he employs flattery and deception gradually to increase his status and influence, until he becomes the effective master of Gormenghast. He fosters the antipathy that exists between Flay and Swelter until it explodes into violence, seduces Fuschia into craven dependence, and encourages Lord Sepulchrave's gathering madness. Initially rather pathetic in his smallness and seeming weakness, he becomes increasingly demonic as he masters the hidden byways of the castle. Although his rebellion against the petrifaction of the closed world of Gormenghast never acquires heroic status, he retains enough sympathy to avoid being seen as an outright villain until he begins to be corrupted by the power he has achieved.

Lord Sepulchrave, the master of Gormenghast. He is a deeply melancholy man who needs the order imposed by Gormenghast's many rituals but still has to take frequent refuge in his library. The eventual burning of the library hastens the onset of his madness, in which he seems to himself to be turning into an owl—although the real owls refuse to admit him to their company and punish his ambition horribly.

Gertrude, Sepulchrave's wife, a forbidding individual who prefers the company of her birds and cats to that of humans.

Fuschia, Sepulchrave's shy and reclusive daughter, who is attracted to Steerpike partly because she finds him so fearful. Initially portrayed in a sympathetic manner, she is so ineffectual in becoming a willing partner in her own victimization that she comes to seem rather contemptible.

Flay, Lord Sepulchrave's valet. A skeletal figure obsessively devoted to his master, he flees into the wilderness after a fight with Swelter ends with the fatal stabbing of the cook.

Swelter, the supervisor of the castle kitchens. He is a massively obese and loquacious man, always at odds with his eventual killer.

Sourdust, the master of ritual who instructs Lord Sepulchrave in the regulations that govern the life of the castle. He dies in the library fire, whereupon his place is taken by his son Barquentine.

Alfred Prunesquallor, the castle doctor, a bespectacled aesthete whose friendship assists the first steps of Steerpike's ascent to power.

Titus Groan, the heir to Gormenghast, who comes into his troublesome inheritance while still a baby.

Gormenghast, 1950

Steerpike, who, having completed his rise to power by murdering Barquentine and becoming master of ritual, becomes overconfident in his domination of Fuschia and his control over the young Titus. His malevolent nature finds increasing expression until it is horrifically exposed when he casually revisits the scene of one of his murders—that of Titus' twin aunts Cora and Clarice.

Titus Groan, who becomes increasingly determined and accomplished in his resistance to Steerpike, whose destructively rebellious spirit he matches with a more adventurous one of his own, partly inspired by his forest-reared foster sister, the Thing. It is frank distaste rather than any nobler sentiment that eventually leads him to kill Steerpike, but the deed makes a hero of him nevertheless.

Gertrude, who accepts the responsibilities of her maternal role in respect of Titus, although she makes little real effort to protect Fuschia from Steerpike's increasingly sadistic affections.

Fuschia, whose romantic illusions initially make her easy prey to Steerpike's insincere protestations of love, although she knows what he is well enough to attack him at Nannie Flagg's funeral. She eventually finds sufficient resolve to reject him.

Irma Prunesquallor, the doctor's sister. A vain creature who had earlier responded foolishly to Steerpike's flattery, she now becomes the rather improbable object of the ardent affections of Bellgrove.

Bellgrove, the headmaster of the professors who have been entrusted with Titus' education. He is an imposing man, but his advanced age and temperament make him an unlikely suitor, and his romance with Irma is a scathing parody providing a telling counterpoint to Steerpike's quest to wed Fuschia.

Titus Alone, 1959

Titus Groan, who is now a stranger traveling through a world that is the gaudy and anarchic antithesis of Gormenghast. He struggles to adapt himself to the wilderness of the city but remains helpless in its toils because he still carries the spirit of Gormenghast within him and cannot free himself from his heritage.

Muzzlehatch, a zookeeper who rescues Titus from the menacing Helmeteers and becomes his mentor. When his animals are killed, he seeks revenge against the scientists who are responsible for the zoo's destruction, but he can achieve that revenge only at the cost of his own life.

Juno, Muzzlehatch's onetime lover, who takes Titus under her wing. Her attitude toward him is a mixture of the erotic and the maternal, and his response to her is equally confused.

Cheeta, Juno's rival for Titus' affections. He turns against Titus and becomes a dangerous enemy working for his humiliation and destruction.

— *Brian Stableford*

GOSSIP FROM THE FOREST

Author: Thomas Keneally (1935-   )
First published: 1975
Genre: Novel

Locale: Berlin, Germany, and Compiègne, France
Time: November, 1918
Plot: Historical

Field Marshal Ferdinand Foch (fohsh), commander of the Allied armies and head of the Allied armistice delegation in November, 1918. A small yet physically imposing man of sixty-seven, with disproportionately large head and hands, he is "monumental." The son of a provincial civil servant, educated by Jesuits, he rose quickly through the military, achieving the rank of captain at the age of twenty-six and that of major ten years later. A professor and then director of the École Supérieure de Guerre, he is well known as a military theorist; his teachings and writing stress morale as the greatest strategic and tactical determinant in warfare. Marshal Foch is extremely strong-willed, convinced of his own correctness in every question; he believes that he is the most powerful man in the world. His determination and the sheer power of his will force the Germans to swallow whole the humiliating terms of the armistice.

Plenipotentiary Matthias Erzberger, the head of the German armistice delegation. A liberal politician and idealist with reformist instincts, he leads the left wing of the Catholic Center Party and serves as a cabinet member. Forty-three years old, a happily married family man of country stock, he is big-boned, with delicate eyes behind his pince-nez. He feels inadequate to the task of leading the armistice delegation, believing that there is nothing in his background to qualify him for the endeavor. He is also plagued by visions of his own death, seeing would-be assassins at every turn. Fearing that Germany is on the brink of revolution, he knows that peace is imperative if his country is to survive. His only hope as leader of the German delegation is to wring a small measure of mercy for his famine-threatened country from Marshal Foch, who is not swayed by Erzberger's facts and figures on starving and dying children. Given no alternative, he is forced to sign an armistice agreement that is devastating to Germany.

General Maxime Weygand (mak-seem VEE-gahnd), Marshal Foch's chief of staff, often referred to as "Foch's encyclopedia." He is fifty-one years old, a small, meticulous man devoted to Foch. A career army officer and a lover of horses, his background is uncertain; it is often rumored that he is the illegitimate son of the empress of Mexico. His purpose on the delegation is merely to reinforce Marshal Foch's position at every opportunity.

Count Alfred Maiberling, a member of the German delegation, an aristocrat from a tragic family background and a friend of Erzberger. Once a pleasant diplomat and good companion, he now suffers from severe mood swings, drinks heavily, carries a gun in the lining of his coat, and plays at suicide. He is an ironic and sarcastic observer of events, contributing little of substance to the negotiations.

General Detlev von Winterfeldt, a general of the Royal Prussian Army, representing the German army on the armistice commission. An old, aristocratic gentleman, he is tall, with a thin mustache. Once a military attaché in Paris, he is a Francophile who is vain about his command of French. His beloved French wife is institutionalized for attacking him with a knife. Von Winterfeldt mistakenly believes that his familiarity with the French will give him an advantage in the negotiations.

Captain Vanselow, a captain of the German High Seas Fleet and a recipient of the Iron Cross, although he has never seen battle. He carries his chin tight against his chest. An uncomplicated man with no sense of irony, he is a liberal officer who has never hit a sailor and, in fact, abhors pain and death. He is naïve, shy, and socially inept. The rest of the delegation considers him a "nobody," a mere token representative from the German navy. His hopeless task is to keep the German navy from being completely dismantled.

First Sea Lord Rosslyn Wemyss, Britain's representative to the armistice commission. A square and beefy admiral with an aristocratic presence, descended from a line of naval admirals, he has a rather genial face and wears a monocle. It is his mission to see that the German navy is totally disarmed and disabled by the armistice agreement. He loathes Marshal Foch yet feels inadequate in his overpowering presence.

— *Mary Virginia Davis*

A GRAIN OF WHEAT

Author: Ngugi wa Thiong'o (James Ngugi, 1938-   )
First published: 1967
Genre: Novel
Locale: Kenya
Time: Mid-twentieth century
Plot: Social realism

Mugo (MEW-goh), a farmer, reared by his drunken aunt. He has always felt himself to be an outsider. Naturally self-protective because he is alone in the world, he fears those involved in the revolutionary movement (Mau Mau) that seeks to overthrow the British rulers. He is especially envious of one of his peers, Kihika, who speaks in favor of independence. He also yearns to sacrifice himself for a larger purpose. When he intervenes to stop a pregnant woman from being beaten by a British policeman, he is imprisoned. His silence makes him appear mysterious, and rumors abound regarding his heroic defiance in jail. The villagers claim him as a local hero and are stunned when he finally admits having betrayed Kihika. Wambui and General R. execute him.

Karanja (kah-RAHN-jah), an opportunist and collaborator with the British. He works at the Githima Library and serves as a go-between for Mrs. Dickinson, the librarian and mistress of John Thompson. During the state of emergency, he works himself up to leader of the homeguards (who worked for the British) and is named chief of the village of Thabai. He becomes notorious for his cruelty. After independence, he flees.

Mumbi (MEWM-bee), one of the most beautiful women in the region, Kihika's sister and wife of Gikonyo. During her husband's six-year detention, she gives birth to Karanja's son.

Gikonyo (gee-KOH-nyoh), a carpenter who achieves financial security by becoming a merchant. He and Karanja are rivals for Mumbi, who marries Gikonyo. He is not an enthusiastic follower of the movement, but he is arrested and imprisoned for six years. He becomes disillusioned, confesses, and is released. When he learns that Mumbi has been unfaithful, he loses all hope.

Kihika (kee-hee-kah), who acquired an interest in politics from listening as a child to Warui's stories of British injustice. He left the Christian school when teachers spoke against Kenyan customs. After Jomo Kenyatta is arrested and a state of emergency is declared, he flees to the forest and joins the movement. He captures the Mahee police post and later assassinates District Officer Thomas Robson.

John Thompson, the administrative secretary who, with the country's upcoming independence, is retiring to England. He first went to East Africa during World War II and was impressed by those Africans who appreciated ties with Great Britain. He had a promising career in civil service but never reached Nairobi because of an incident in Rira, in which he caused the beating deaths of eleven detainees. He felt more sympathy for his pets than he did for the Kenyans.

Wambui (wahm-BEW-ee) and

Warui (wah-REW-ee), an aging man and woman active in the movement from its inception. They suspect Karanja of having betrayed Kihika and plot his death. When independence comes, they suspect that very little has really changed.

Gitogo (gee-TOH-goh), a deaf and mute young man who faithfully supports his old mother. The British mistake him for a Mau Mau sympathizer and shoot him in the back.

General R., a tailor, a no-nonsense man of action in the movement. No one knows his real name, but the second R stands for Russia. He and Lieutenant Koina kill Mugo.

— John C. Hawley

GRAND HOTEL
(Menschen im Hotel)

Author: Vicki Baum (1888-1960)
First published: 1929
Genre: Novel
Locale: Berlin, Germany
Time: The 1920's
Plot: Social

Baron Gaigern (GI-gehrn), one of the guests at Berlin's Grand Hotel who, while seeming rich, is actually a gambler and a thief. He tries unsuccessfully to steal from the other guests in the hotel and, for various reasons, fails in each case. As a result of trying to steal jewelry from Elisaveta Grusinskaya, a ballerina, he becomes her lover. While he is trying to steal Herr Preysing's wallet, he is killed, felled by a blow inflicted with a bronze inkstand.

Herr Preysing (PRI-zihng), general manager of the Saxonia Cotton Company and a guest at the hotel. He tries to reestablish his company's financial position by a merger with another company. He hires Miss Flamm as a stenographer and then offers to make her his mistress. He murders Gaigern when he discovers the baron trying to steal his wallet. Because the baron is unarmed at the time, Preysing is held for murder.

Otto Kringelein (KRIHN-geh-lin), a forty-six-year-old junior clerk in Preysing's company and a guest at the hotel. Having been told that he is dying, he is out for one last frolic in the world, inasmuch as he has been a meek, downtrodden man all his life. His personality changes when Miss Flamm flees to him for help when Baron Gaigern is killed. Her friendship and interest in him give Kringelein some purpose in life. He decides to go to England with her.

Miss Flamm, nicknamed "Flaemmchen" by Herr Preysing. She is a beautiful stenographer who works as a part-time photographer's model. When Herr Preysing kills Baron Gaigern, she flees from her employer to ask Kringelein's help and becomes interested in her protector.

Elisaveta Alexandrovna Grusinskaya (eh-lee-sah-VAY-tah ah-lehks-ahn-DROV-nah groo-SIHNS-kah-yah), an aging ballerina. She finds Baron Gaigern in her room. He denies trying to steal from her and becomes her lover, giving her the admiration and self-confidence she desperately needs.

Dr. Otternschlag (OHT-tehrn-shlahg), a retired doctor staying at the hotel. Having been disfigured in World War I, he has no real interest in life. When he tries to commit suicide, he finds, however, that he really wants to live.

The Grand Duke Sergei (SEHR-gay), an aristocrat who gave expensive pearls to Elisaveta Grusinskaya.

Anna Kringelein, Kringelein's wife, left at home in Fredersdorf.

THE GRANDISSIMES: A Story of Creole Life

Author: George Washington Cable (1844-1925)
First published: 1880
Genre: Novel
Locale: New Orleans, Louisiana
Time: 1804
Plot: Regional

Honoré Grandissime (oh-noh-RAY grahn-dees-EEM), a merchant, head of the Grandissimes. Extremely handsome and well-dressed, he is an impressive figure, the flower of the family. His egalitarian views and his opposition to slavery are viewed with suspicion and distaste by other Grandissimes. He represents the peacemaking element as his uncle, Agricola, represents the strifemaking element in the family. Conscience-stricken over his possession of and profit from Aurora's property (given him by Agricola), he returns it and thereby angers his family. He further alienates them by going into partnership with another Honoré Grandissime, a free man of color.

Honoré Grandissime, f. m. c., his older quadroon half brother, a rentier. (To prevent confusion, he is usually distinguished from the white Honoré by the initials f. m. c.—free man of color—after his name.) He has strong feelings about the lot of the Louisianians of mixed blood, but he is feeble of will about fighting the caste system. He hates Agricola and loves Palmyre. After going with Palmyre to Bordeaux following Agricola's death, he vainly courts her and then drowns himself.

Agricola Fusilier (ah-GREE-koh-lah fyew-seel-YAY), Honoré's uncle, a sturdy, bearded old lion careless of his dress. Loving all things French, he scorns Americans and their jargon. He is proud of his Creole blood, contemptuous of all people of color, and fearful of Palmyre. He is mortally stabbed by Honoré f. m. c., whom he has attacked. Dying, he affects to forgive all enemies of the Creole aristocracy, but he dies with his prejudices.

Aurora Nancanou (ah-rohr-AH nahn-kah-NEW), née **De Grapion** (deh grah-PYOH[N]), a beautiful young widow whose husband died in a duel after accusing Agricola of cheating at cards. She is poor but proud, and she superstitiously believes in Palmyre's spellmaking powers. In love with Honoré, she is mindful of the enmity of the Grandissimes toward her own family, the De Grapions. After Agricola, dying, admits to having years before promised a marriage between Honoré and Aurora, she still resists, but she finally accepts her formerly diffident adorer.

Clotilde Nancanou (kloh-TEELD), her lovely daughter, who appears to be a younger sister rather than the daughter of the youthful-looking Aurora. Loved by Joseph, she finally accepts his suit.

Joseph Frowenfeld, a handsome young American immigrant of German ancestry whose family dies of yellow fever, which Joseph survives. He becomes a proprietor of an apothecary shop. A serious student, he has liberal views that are resented by the Creoles. He cannot understand why the caste system for people of varied colors is permitted to continue in Louisiana. Wounded mistakenly while attending Palmyre after she is shot, he recovers and becomes a partner in an expanded drug business supported by capital from Aurora. He falls in love with Clotilde and apparently will marry her.

Dr. Charlie Keene, Joseph's physician and friend, red-haired and freckled. Intelligent and perceptive, he acquaints Joseph with the Creole-dominated society of New Orleans.

Palmyre Philosophe (pahl-MEER fee-loh-SOHF), a freed quadroon slave, formerly Aurora's maid, who hates Agricola and who is wounded after stabbing him. Loved by Honoré f. m. c., she ignores him and hates all men except the white Honoré and Bras Coupé, to whom she was married before he ran away. She passionately desires the love of Honoré, but in vain.

Bras Coupé (brah kew-PAY), a giant African prince captured by slavers and brought to Louisiana. After marrying Palmyre, he strikes his master in a drunken fit and escapes. Returning to get Palmyre, he is captured, imprisoned, and mutilated, and he dies in prison after removing the curse he had put upon Don José's family and land. Bras Coupé is a symbol of the dignity, the native worth, and the tragedy of his race.

Don José Martinez (hoh-SEH mahr-TEE-nehs), Honoré's brother-in-law and Bras Coupé's master.

Governor Claiborne, a young Virginian, governor-general of Louisiana.

Numa Grandissime, father of the two Honorés.

Raul Innerarity, an amateur artist, a cousin of Honoré. He becomes Joseph's clerk.

Achille (ah-SHEEL),
Valentine (vah-lehn-TEEN),
Jean-Baptiste (zhahn-bah-TEEST),
Hippolyte (ee-poh-LEET),
Sylvestre (seel-VEHSTR), and
Agamemnon (ah-gah-MEHM-nohn), kinsmen of Honoré.

Clemence (kleh-MAHNS), Palmyre's voodoo accomplice, shot to death by an unknown marksman after her lynching is interrupted.

THE GRANDMOTHERS: A Family Portrait

Author: Glenway Wescott (1901-1987)
First published: 1927
Genre: Novel
Locale: Wisconsin
Time: 1830-1925
Plot: Family

Alwyn Tower, a young boy deeply interested in the history of his family. He pours over the family albums and pieces together his relatives' stories.

Henry Tower, Alwyn's grandfather. He came to Wisconsin from New York planning, but failing, to become rich. His first and dearly loved wife dies, leaving a baby boy. He marries again to give the child a mother. After the boy dies, Henry loses interest in life, though he has many other children. In his old age, his chief interest is his new garden. He lives to be eighty-two, but to Alwyn he never seems completely alive.

Serena Cannon, Henry's first wife, who dies of a fever.

Rose Hamilton, Henry's second wife, Alwyn's grandmother. Jilted by Henry's brother, her one true love, she marries Henry and gives him many children. She too never seems completely alive to Alwyn, though she appears resigned and not unhappy.

Leander Tower, Henry's brother. Returning from the Civil War, he no longer wants to marry Rose, and he goes to California. Later he returns to Wisconsin. Rose, though she still loves him, remains true to Henry.

Hilary Tower, the younger brother of Leander and Henry. He disappeared in the war, and Leander seems always to be looking for a substitute for him. Old Leander seems happy only when helping a young boy.

Nancy Tower, Alwyn's great-aunt, insane for part of her life.

Mary Harris, another great-aunt whose first husband was killed by Southerners because he was a Northern sympathizer. Her second husband was a drunken sot; often she had to beg for food to stay alive. With her third husband, one of the Tower men, she knows happiness and prosperity for the first time.

Jim Tower, Alwyn's uncle, the son of Henry and Rose. A minister who married a rich woman, he lives in Chicago and has been persuaded by his wife to give up preaching. Living with him and his wife in Chicago, Alwyn gets his only chance for a good education. After his wife's death, Jim goes on living with and humoring the whims of his mother-in-law and his sisters-in-law. Alwyn likes but does not admire Jim.

Evan Tower, Alwyn's uncle, another son of Henry and Rose. He was a deserter from the Spanish-American War who went west under a different name. He comes home sometimes to see his father, but relations between them are so strained that on his last visit, the old man refuses to enter the house while Evan is there.

Flora Tower, Alwyn's aunt, the daughter of Henry and Rose. Afraid of being awakened to love, she refuses to marry. Having nothing to fear from her young nephew, she loves him wholeheartedly. She dies at twenty-nine, appearing to Alwyn happy as she draws her last breath.

Ralph Tower, Alwyn's father, another son of Henry and Rose. He wanted to be a veterinarian, but Jim was the one chosen to be educated. Ralph, resigned rather than bitter, takes over his father's farm.

Marianne Tower, Ralph's wife and Alwyn's mother. Her parents hated each other, and Marianne was lonely until she met Ralph. Their marriage is completely happy; they love each other so much that Alwyn is sometimes embarrassed to see them together.

GRANIA

Author: Lady Augusta Gregory (1852-1932)
First published: 1912
Genre: Drama
Locale: Ireland
Time: Legendary prehistory
Plot: Mythic

Grania, the daughter of an Irish king. Grania is intended to be the bride of Finn. She is young, beautiful, self-controlled, and initially calm about her impending marriage. She nurses a childhood memory of a great warrior whom she once saw in her father's courtyard. This half-fanciful attachment is in contrast to her cool, well-mannered demeanor. The knowledge that this warrior is one of Finn's men provokes her decision to desert Finn. Her sense of dignity remains constant even in poverty and sorrow and supports her when she is, in turn, deserted by Diarmuid.

Finn, a king of Ireland and leader of the Fenian warriors. He is in late middle age, and he plans to take a young wife for the sake of happiness and comfort. Like Grania, he at first seems reasonable and prudent in his affections, yet when he is faced with Grania's passion for Diarmuid, Finn is overwhelmed by jealousy and hounds the fleeing couple for years, devoting all of his energy to the possession of Grania. Despite his rage, Finn shows an astute understanding of the conflicts within himself and within Diarmuid and Grania, and he proves capable of not only cruelty but also compassion.

Diarmuid, one of the chief warriors of the Fenians, known both for his bravery in battle and for his success with women. Perhaps his most prized quality is his loyalty to Finn, which he swears is immutable. It is his sense of honor that causes Diarmuid to leave with Grania; he feels obliged to protect her from the unjust wrath of the jealous Finn. Love and honor are in perpetual conflict within him, however, even after he gives in to his desire for Grania. On his deathbed, he has no memory of her but thinks only of his friendship with Finn.

— *Heidi J. Holder*

THE GRAPES OF WRATH

Author: John Steinbeck (1902-1968)
First published: 1939
Genre: Novel
Locale: The Midwestern United States and California
Time: The 1930's
Plot: Social realism

Tom Joad, Jr., an ex-convict. Returning to his home in Oklahoma after serving time in the penitentiary for killing a man in self-defense, he finds the house deserted, the family having been pushed off the land because of dust bowl conditions and in order to make way for more productive mechanization. With Casy, the preacher, he finds his family and makes the trek to California in search of work. Tom kills another man when his friend Casy, who is trying to help migrant workers in their labor problems, is brutally killed by deputies representing the law and the owners. He leaves his family because, as a wanted man, he is a danger to them, but he leaves with a new understanding that he has learned from Casy: It is no longer the individual that counts but the group. Tom promises to carry on Casy's work of helping the downtrodden.

Tom Joad, Sr., called **Pa Joad**, an Oklahoma farmer who finds it difficult to adjust to new conditions while moving his family to California.

Ma Joad, a large, heavy woman, full of determination and hope, who fights to hold her family together. On the journey to California, she gradually becomes the staying power of the family.

Rose of Sharon Rivers, called **Rosasharn**, the married, teen-age daughter of the Joads. Her husband leaves her, and she bears a stillborn baby because of the hardships she endures. As the story ends, she gives her own milk to save the life of a starving man.

Noah, the slow-witted second son of the Joads. He finally wanders off down a river when the pressures of the journey and his hunger become too much.

Al, the third son of the Joads. In his teens, he is interested in girls and automobiles. He idolizes his brother Tom.

Ruthie, the pre-teen-age daughter of the Joads.

Winfield, the youngest of the Joads.

Uncle John, the brother of Tom Joad, Sr. He is a lost soul who periodically is flooded with guilt because he let his young wife die by ignoring her illness.

Grampa Joad, who does not want to leave Oklahoma and dies on the way to California. He is buried with little ceremony by the roadside.

Granma Joad, also old and childish. She dies while crossing the desert and receives a pauper burial.

Jim Casy, the country preacher who has given up the ministry because he no longer believes. He makes the trek to California with the Joads. He assumes the blame and goes to jail for the crime of a migrant worker who has a family to support. He is killed as a "red" while trying to help the migrant workers organize and strike for a living wage.

Connie Rivers, Rosasharn's young husband, who deserts her after arriving in California.

Floyd Knowles, a young migrant worker with a family, called a "red" because he asks a contractor to guarantee a job and the wages to be paid. He escapes from a deputy sheriff who is attempting to intimidate the workers. Tom Joad trips the deputy, and Jim Casy kicks him in the back of the head.

Muley Graves, a farmer who refuses to leave the land although his family has gone. He remains, abstracted and lonely, forced to hide, hunted and haunted.

Jim Rawley, the kind, patient manager of a government camp for the migrant workers.

Willy Feeley, a former small farmer like the Joads; he takes a job driving a tractor over the land the Joads farmed.

Ivy Wilson, a migrant who has car trouble on the way to California with his sick wife Sairy. The Joads help them, and the two families stay together until Sairy becomes too ill to travel.

Sairy Wilson, Ivy's wife. When the Wilsons are forced to stay behind because of her illness, she asks Casy to pray for her.

Timothy Wallace, a migrant who helps Tom Joad find work in California.

Wilkie Wallace, his son.

Aggie Wainwright, the daughter of a family living in a box car with the Joads while they work in a cotton field. Al Joad plans to marry her.

Jessie Bullitt,

Ella Summers, and

Annie Littlefield, the ladies' committee for Sanitary Unit Number Four of the government camp for migrant workers.

GRATEFUL TO LIFE AND DEATH

Author: R. K. Narayan (1906-)
First published: 1945
Genre: Novel
Locale: Malgudi, in southern India
Time: Late 1930's
Plot: Magical Realism

Krishna, an English teacher. A man in his late twenties, he is bored with his job at Albert Mission College in Malgudi, a fictitious city in southern India. When he rents a house and brings his wife and baby to live with him, however, he is much more contented. When his wife becomes ill, he nurses her devotedly; after she dies, he is devastated. Although his daughter consoles him, he has a glimpse of happiness only when he can contact his wife beyond the grave. Finally, he resigns his position so that he can teach young children at the headmaster's school.

Susila, Krishna's young wife. Tall and beautiful, with sparkling eyes and gleaming hair, she trails a scent of jasmine. Although she is not interested in the books that Krishna gives her, she is a good mother and an excellent manager. After a memorable day, when she and Krishna have gone out looking for a house to buy, she becomes ill. She eventually dies of typhoid fever.

Leela, the daughter of Krishna and Susila. A bright, lively, intelligent little girl, she adjusts fairly well to the loss of her mother, partly because she is enrolled in a play-school. Finally, she asks to live with Krishna's parents, who urge their son to visit her every weekend.

The medium, also called **the Friend**, a plump, cheerful man who talks incessantly. It is he who first writes down messages from the dead Susila to her husband. He later teaches Krishna to summon her to him. The medium is a sensible man; finding that Leela is unhappy after the death of her mother, he suggests that Krishna put her in school, thus indirectly directing Krishna to his new vocation.

The headmaster, a thin, unkempt, long-haired young man. He operates an unusual school for young children where they learn through play. After he makes an error in predicting his own death, he has a kind of rebirth and gets the courage to leave his tyrannical, slatternly wife and their savage children, who then have far more respect for him. He is delighted to have Krishna become his partner in the school.

Brown, the principal of the college. Although he is a good-natured man, Krishna frequently is annoyed with him, simply because he is tired of his job. After urging Krishna, in vain, to remain at the college, Brown arranges a fine send-off for him.

Gajapathy, the assistant professor in English at Albert Mission College and Krishna's superior. His pedantry is irritating to Krishna, who dares not taunt him. Gajapathy cannot understand Krishna's decision to leave his job.

Sastri, the logic teacher at the college. He is also a real-estate developer. It may be at one of his home sites that Susila contracts typhoid.

— *Rosemary M. Canfield Reisman*

GRAVITY'S RAINBOW

Author: Thomas Pynchon (1937-)
First published: 1973
Genre: Novel
Locale: Europe
Time: Mid-1940's
Plot: Historical realism

Tyrone Slothrop, a lieutenant in the U.S. Army toward the end of World War II. Stationed in England, he is sent on a strange mission to locate the staging area both for the V-2 rockets bombarding England and for the prototype of a new rocket, the A4. The A4 is even more destructive than the V-2. The Germans are preparing to launch it in a desperate effort to change the course of the war. Slothrop goes to the French Riviera, to Switzerland, and ultimately to the "Zone," occupied Germany after the hostilities officially have ended. Slothrop is a naïve young man who is never fully aware of what he is doing. As an infant, he had been experimentally conditioned by a famous behaviorist, and the behaviorist psychologist Ned Pointsman tries to make use of that conditioning for his own purposes. Made aware on the Riviera that he is being manipulated, Slothrop escapes from the surveillance that Pointsman and his masters have arranged and roams around Europe in the chaos of the first months of "peace." He is still searching for the rocket, and he finds traces of it in many places but never discovers the rocket itself. After numerous strange adventures, he loses whatever it was that made him unique and becomes completely ordinary, seeming simply to disappear.

Captain Weissmann (Blicero), a German officer, the manager of the project to create the A4 rocket. Physically unimpressive, he is a terrifying figure, in love with death and destruction, sadistic in his bisexual love affairs with the African Enzian, the young soldier Gottfried, and the spy, Katje Borgesius. In the final days before the German surrender, he manages to fire the rocket, with Gottfried as its passenger, but as far as is known the rocket never lands. Blicero apparently is killed as the war ends.

Roger Mexico, a British mathematician and officer. He is the spokesman for the importance of chance and indeterminacy in the lives of humans. He is the most human of the characters in his sense of humor, his love for Jessica Swanlake, his determination to counteract the behaviorism of Ned Pointsman, and his willingness to take risks with his own life to try to save Slothrop from the people who are trying to control his life. In the end, he loses Jessica, but he never gives up the struggle against the forces of repression who dominate the world and seek total control of human actions.

Ned Pointsman, a British scientist and exponent of behaviorism. He is the director of a secret facility called the "White Visitation," where scientists and pseudoscientists are carrying on experiments in psychological and parapsychological warfare that they hope will destroy the Germans' will to fight. A disciple of Pavlov, Pointsman believes that all human behavior can be controlled through conditioning, and he uses Slothrop's early conditioning as a means to direct his actions in the search for the rocket. The failure of Pointsman's efforts to find the rocket using Slothrop dooms his hopes for a Nobel Prize and a knighthood.

Geoffrey "Pirate" Prentice, a captain in the British Army, a secret agent. He has a special talent for living the fantasies of other people, a talent valued by those who direct espionage for the British government. Prentice is in charge of collecting the remains of V-2 rockets fired by the Germans, so that the British can learn as much as possible about the rockets and how to combat their effects. Prentice also directs the activities of the spy Katje Borgesius, who lives with Weissmann so that she can report on his activities. After she escapes to England, and after she has helped seduce Slothrop and warned him of the dangers he faces, she and Prentice both face the reality that in their espionage activities they have killed or caused the deaths of innocent people and therefore cannot hope for redemption of any kind. To atone for their deeds, Prentice and Katje join the Counterforce, a loosely defined group of people who have lived lives like theirs but who now oppose, as much as they can, the forces that have controlled them.

Katje Borgesius, a beautiful Dutch woman who is one of Weissmann's lovers. Later, Pointsman trains her to become part of the pattern that will push Slothrop along in the search for the rocket. On the Riviera, she is Slothrop's lover, performing the role Pointsman has designed, but eventually she gives Slothrop the hint that sends him off on his own journey, outside Pointsman's control. Later, after she and Prentice recognize their guilt, she joins the search for Weissmann and his unit in postwar Germany.

Enzian, a native of Southwest Africa, now chief of the "Zone Hereros," Africans serving in the German army. He is the son of a Herero woman and a Russian sailor. As a young man, Enzian had been Weissmann's lover when the latter was stationed in Africa. When the Herero tribe was decimated, he and other survivors followed Weissmann to Germany. His people are divided between those who seek tribal suicide and those who seek to return to their homeland. Enzian, caught between the two groups, leads them on a search for rocket parts, hoping that they can construct an A4 in which he will be the sole passenger. It is his hope that this action will give his people a new unity and sense of common values. It is never clear whether they succeed in firing the rocket.

Jessica Swanlake, a British WAAF. She is Roger Mexico's lover in the most romantic relationship in the novel, but she associates their affair with the war and its dangers. When the war comes to an end, she chooses to leave Roger for the Beaver, a pipe-smoking nincompoop who promises her domesticity.

Franz Pokler, a German rocket scientist. He is marginally associated with early attempts to develop rockets in the 1920's. During the war, Weissmann controls Pokler, giving him routine assignments and keeping him in line by allowing him yearly visits from a girl who he says is Pokler's daughter. The girl spends the rest of the year in a concentration camp, and Weissmann's implied threat is that she will be killed if Pokler fails to cooperate with Weissmann's scheme. Weissmann's purpose is to use Pokler to make one small part for the A4 rocket. In the end, having performed his task, Pokler is released; Slothrop meets him living quietly in the ruins of a children's village after the end of the war. His daughter also survives.

Leni Pokler, Franz's wife. A Communist, she leaves Franz when the Nazis come to power and with her daughter winds up in a concentration camp during the war. She reappears after the war, in a brothel visited by Slothrop and Major Marvy.

Tchitcherine, a Soviet espionage agent and the half brother of Enzian. He always has been a maverick in the Soviet intelligence system. During a period of exile in Siberia, he underwent a mystical experience that he never fully understands. He is valuable because he has special perceptions that his superiors think will help him find the super rocket before the Western powers do. His own crusade is to find and kill Enzian, whom he has never seen but for whom he nurses a burning hatred. When they finally meet, they fail to recognize each other because of a spell cast by Tchitcherine's lover, a witch named Geli Tripping.

Duane Marvy, an American major and an agent for American industries that are trying obtain German scientists and technology for their own uses. A cruel slob, Marvy runs into Slothrop on several occasions and tries unsuccessfully to kill him, apparently hating him because Slothrop does not share his brutish appetites. He joins the search for the rocket but is frustrated by Slothrop and Enzian. In the end, a British medical team mistakes him for Slothrop and castrates him, a fate intended for Slothrop.

Geli Tripping, a beautiful and benevolent young German witch. She gives shelter and affection to Slothrop at one stage of his travels through Germany, but her real lover is Tchitcherine, whom she saves from his own obsession.

Seaman Bodine, an American sailor. He helps Slothrop escape from the military police at the German port of Cuxhaven. Later, he and Roger Mexico disrupt a dinner party staged by German and British Fascists at which the two of them are intended to be the main course. Bodine represents a kind of innocent and necessary vulgarity.

Greta Erdmann, a onetime German film star whom Slothrop meets in the ruins of postwar Berlin. She is one of his lovers and takes him with her aboard the *Anubis*, a ship sailing the Baltic carrying sensualists whose only desire is to avoid responsibility.

— *John M. Muste*

THE GREAT AMERICAN NOVEL

Author: Philip Roth (1933-)
First published: 1973
Genre: Novel
Locale: The eastern and midwestern United States
Time: 1943-1944, with flashbacks to the early twentieth century
Plot: Social satire

Word Smith (Smitty), the novel's narrator, a longtime sportswriter currently residing at the Valhalla nursing home. Smitty's prologue establishes his credentials as a writer (noting, in particular, his love of alliteration) and as a witness to the events, recounted in the main body of the book, that led to the demise of the Patriot Baseball League, the memory of which has been wiped clean from American history. Smitty appears later in the book in his role as a sportswriter and commentator, and as a defiant witness before Congress' House Committee on Un-American Activities. In the epilogue, Smitty, having been rebuffed by American publishers, likens himself to Aleksandr Solzhenitsyn in the Soviet Union and is attempting to have *The Great American Novel* published in the People's Republic of China.

General Douglas O. Oakhart, the president of the Patriot Baseball League and a stickler for rules. During the 1934 season, Oakhart assigns his best umpire, Mike Masterson, to officiate games pitched by Gil Gamesh, a temperamental rookie phenomenon. This selection accidentally sets in motion events leading to the destruction of the Patriot League. At the close of the 1934 season, Oakhart bans Gamesh from baseball for purposefully injuring Masterson. Ten years later, Oakhart reluctantly reinstates Gamesh as a means of combating an alleged communist insurgency in the Patriot League. Ironically, this campaign leads to the demise of the Patriot League. It also serves as the springboard for Oakhart's subsequent career in politics.

Gil Gamesh, an all-star left-handed pitcher of Babylonian descent, banished from the Patriot League in 1934, at the end of his rookie season. His only problem was a hideous temper. When a missed call by umpire Mike Masterson delays the conclusion of Gamesh's perfect game, the tempestuous lefty hits Masterson in the throat with the next pitch, ending the umpire's career and bringing about his own expulsion from baseball. After disappearing from the scene for a decade, Gamesh reemerges as a Soviet double agent. With the help of Angela Whitling Trust, Gamesh convinces General Oakhart that there is a communist conspiracy afoot in the Patriot League that only he (Gamesh) can expose. Gamesh is named manager of the hapless Ruppert Mundys and, after a tragic shooting, "names names," causing a scandal that brings about the league's downfall. Once again, Gamesh drops out of sight, reappearing at Stalin's side in state-approved photographs before finally being executed by the Soviet secret police.

Ulysses S. Fairsmith, the manager of the Ruppert Mundys during their hapless (and homeless) 1943 season. When the 1943 Mundys are evicted from their home park as part of the war effort, Fairsmith sees this as an opportunity for a spiritually uplifting experience. A deeply religious man, Fairsmith likens the Mundys to the Hebrews of the Old Testament and sees himself as a Mosaic figure. To be sure, Fairsmith has had experience with adversity. He was nearly killed by angry natives while teaching the game of baseball in Africa. That was somewhat disheartening, but the Mundys are so pathetic that, in the end, Fairsmith cannot cope; he stops attending Mundy games and begins to lose his faith in God. A 31 to 0 loss on the final day of the season (after a miraculous winning streak has drawn Fairsmith back to the Mundy dugout) is too much for the old skipper. After the last out is recorded on an incredible baserunning blunder, Fairsmith, feeling forsaken by God, rolls off his rocker and dies on the dugout floor.

Mike Masterson, known as **Mike the Mouth**, the umpire injured by Gil Gamesh. The most famous, and vocal, umpire of his era, Masterson proved his integrity early in his career when he refused to influence illegally the outcome of a ball game, even though gangsters threatened (and later killed) his young daughter. When Oakhart assigned Masterson to Gamesh, the veteran empire did his best to give the young phenomenon his due without sacrificing the rules of the game. Pretty soon, however, the strain of working with Gamesh began to tell. Finally, Masterson completely misses a call because he believes that he has spotted the man who abducted his daughter. Gamesh's next pitch hits Masterson in the throat, ruining his voice. Masterson is not satisfied with Gamesh's expulsion from the game; he wants the left-hander prosecuted for criminal assault. To this end, he travels from ballpark to ballpark with a blackboard, laying out his case before skeptical baseball fans. When Gamesh is reinstated, Masterson attempts an assassination, killing Roland Agni but only wounding Gamesh. The old former umpire then crawls off and dies of a heart attack.

Roland Agni, a star center fielder, definitely out of place on the Ruppert Mundys because he is young, strong, and in possession of all his limbs. Roland winds up with the Mundys because his father thinks that he needs a healthy dose of humility. He stays a Mundy because his draft board thinks that only some hidden malady would have landed so good a physical specimen on so bad a baseball team; they pronounce Roland 4-F. Frustrated, Roland attempts to engineer a trade to a better team. He is rebuffed by Angela Whitling Trust. The Ellis family, scandalously Jewish owners of the Tri-City Greenbacks, are interested in Roland, but the Mundys' asking price is too high. Young Isaac Ellis, a boy genius, gives Roland some spiked Wheaties breakfast cereal to feed the Mundy players and plans to make enough money on bets to purchase Roland's contract. This leads to the Mundy winning streak. On the last day of the season, Agni's conscience prompts him to fail to substitute the charged-up Wheaties. This leads to the 31 to 0 loss and Ulysses Fairsmith's death. Roland reports reluctantly for the 1944 season. Just as he is about to decide whether to risk exposure for the Wheaties incident by turning Gamesh in as a Soviet agent, he is shot to death by Mike Masterson.

Angela Whitling Trust, the owner of the Tri-City Tycoons. Before the death of her husband, Spenser, Angela is best known for her romantic trysts with prominent ballplayers such as Ty Cobb, Babe Ruth, Prince Charles Tuminikar, Luke Gofannon, and Gil Gamesh. After her husband is mortally injured in an accident, he chides her from his deathbed to become "responsible." Angela changes her ways drastically. She takes over the Tycoons, becoming the most conservative owner in the league. She also becomes a vigilant anticommunist, ever alert to the Soviet conspiracy against the foundation of American morale, organized baseball. It is Angela who rebuffs Roland Agni, pointing out that without him the Mundys would completely undermine the image of the Patriot League. It is also Angela who arranges to have Gamesh reinstated so that he can use his Soviet training to counter this conspiracy.

— *Ira Smolensky*

THE GREAT DUNE TRILOGY

Author: Frank Herbert (1920-1986)
First published: 1979
Genre: Novels

Locale: Primarily the planet Arrakis
Time: Far future
Plot: Science fiction

Dune, 1965

Paul Atreides, later known as **Paul Maud'Dib** and **Usul**, the focus of the first two of the three novels and a significant character in all three. He is the son of Duke Leto of Caladan. As a child, he moves with his family to the planet Arrakis, or Dune, where his father has been sent by the emperor to manage a company that mines "spice" from the vast deserts. Paul is trained in the mind-body disciplines of the Bene Gesserit cult. When Duke Leto is killed, Paul and his mother escape to the deserts and are taken in by the elusive Fremen. He thrives and is able to lead them in the defeat and death of the Harkonnens, thus neutralizing the emperor.

Lady Jessica, Paul's mother and concubine of his father, who, for political reasons, never married. She is a Bene Gesserit "witch" but has defied the sisterhood by giving birth to Paul, a son, rather than daughters. She often defies orders and displays decisive strength and intelligence. She becomes a Reverend Mother for the Fremen on Dune by drinking a concentrated spice formula that intensifies her prescience. Soon afterward, she gives birth to a daughter, Alia. She remains with Paul in the seitch until he disappears at the end of the second book.

Thufir Hawat, who has special training and skills in detecting false statements made by others. He is an adviser to Duke Leto. Under the control of the Harkonnen enemies who hold over him the fate of his wife, he colludes with them in Leto's defeat.

Gurney Halleck, one of the two masters at arms to Duke Leto. He is a swordsman and fighter whose loyalty to Leto and Paul is unquestioned. He becomes a smuggler on Arrakis when the Atreides house falls, then rejoins Paul and Jessica when he finds them several years after Leto's death.

Duncan Idaho, the other master at arms. He is secretly in love with Lady Jessica. He is killed saving Jessica and Paul.

Chani, the daughter of the emperor's ecologist on Arrakis, Liet-Kynes. She was reared as a Fremen woman and becomes a concubine to Paul; she bears him a son who is killed in the first book. She is an accomplished fighter.

Baron Vladimir Harkonnen, the stereotypical force of evil, with a grossly huge body maintained by excessive eating, held up by "suspensors" that offset its mass. His hate and his greed for power are primary, and the Atreides are their central object. After regaining power, he puts his cruel son Rabban in a leadership position on Arrakis. He is subject to many assassination attempts, by his own as well as by other's supporters, and is finally killed by Paul on Arrakis.

Feyd Ruatha, the baron's official heir, although only a nephew. He is almost seventeen years old when the novel opens. He is related to Paul through Paul's mother and has been trained in many skills that parallel Paul's, but as a perverted double. He has killed one hundred slave gladiators by his seventeenth birthday, plots against his uncle as well as his uncle's enemies, and seeks power at any cost.

Princess Irulan, the daughter of Emperor Shaddam IV. She is married to Paul as a method for her father to save face after Paul's armies defeat his. She is never his bedmate and becomes a historical chronicler and bitter enemy of Paul and his wife.

Alia, Paul's sister, born with adult awareness and some Bene Gesserit skill because Jessica was pregnant with her when she first consumed the spice drink. Alia is considered an abomination by her Fremen friends as well as by the Bene Gesserit.

Dune Messiah, 1969

Paul Atreides, who consolidates his intergalactic rule and negotiates the several futures his spice-prescience has given him. He has become the focus of a cult, and a movement created in his name intends to bring thousands of worlds under one rule. He loses his eyesight, his throne, and his beloved Chani, then retreats into the desert, leaving the people without a ruler.

Chani, a fierce companion for Paul who counsels him until she dies in childbirth as this novel ends. The children are twins, born somewhat prematurely. Princess Irulan had administered antifertility drugs that accelerated their birth and made them self-aware, like Alia was, in the womb.

Alia, now a young woman to whom Paul looks for counsel and support. She acts as a leader for his religious cult, with a temple built in her honor. She reacts to the ghola Duncan with lust that threatens her religious fervor. Paul leaves her at the head of his religious cult.

Scytale, a Tleilaxu Face Dancer who is employed by the guild of intergalactic navigators, who depend on Dune spice for their craft, and the Bene Gesserit, represented by Mother Gaius Helen Mohiam, to overthrow and perhaps kill Paul/Maud'Dib. As a face dancer, he changes his physical appearance to that of a young Fremen woman and joins Paul's court at the same time as the ghola of Duncan.

Duncan Idaho, who returns to Paul's service as a ghola, a creature of reanimated flesh created by the Tleilaxu. He has become adept in the philosophy of Zensunni and is programmed to kill Lady Jessica and Paul. He is a gift to Paul from the guild of steersmen. He has no memories of his past but gradually develops them. He becomes Jessica's protector and then husband to her daughter, Alia.

Edric, a guild steersman, an intimate part of the plot to overthrow Paul's control of the empire and halt the spread of his religion. His human shape has been altered by the spice and the work of a steersman. He swims inside a tank filled with orange gas when he is not in his spaceship.

Princess Irulan, who is still Paul's wife in name and is part of the plot against him. She feeds a drug to Chani to prevent a pregnancy. Her function at court, under Paul's orders, is to record official proceedings, an employment she finds demeaning but that turns her into a historian of his rule.

Children of Dune, 1976

Alia, whose knowledge of her past lives finally overwhelms her. She has grown into a powerful woman on Arrakis, with a cult of her own. As the wife of Duncan Idaho, she is regent for her twin niece and nephew. She is controlled internally by her ancestor, Baron Harkonnen, whose genetic memories are stored inside her. She, Princess Irulan, and various retainers plot to destroy Jessica and control the twins. She becomes insane early in the book.

Leto II, who was born and was named by Paul at the end of *Dune Messiah*. He is a now nine-year-old child. He and his twin sister possessed adult awareness at birth. Both children avoid the spice in fear that they will become possessed like Alia, but it becomes part of Leto II's training in the desert. When the twins separate to avoid the plot against their lives, Leto II is taken by Gurney Halleck to his seitch, where he is forced into a spice trance. He escapes to travel alone to the legendary pirate seitch and learns the secrets of Arrakis. He becomes a composite being, with endless life, by encasing himself in sandtrout and helping the traditional Fremen, with his great strength and speed, to halt efforts to transform Arrakis' desert.

Ghanima, the twin sister of Leto II, an accomplished fighter and strategist who is often underestimated because of her age. The young twins manage to elude the plot to have them eaten by tigers. Alia sees her as a pawn, planning to marry her to Farad'n and keep control of them both.

The Preacher, a blind mystic who appears early in the novel in the streets of the Arrakis capital. In his public preaching, he attacks the Maud'Dib cult and the practices of Alia's regency for the twins. With his young guide, a son of Namri the Fremen, he travels around Arrakis, even meeting Leto II in the desert. Their meeting confirms the suspicion held by many, Alia and Duncan included, that he is actually Paul.

Duncan Idaho, Alia's husband, who tries to be loyal to her out of a complex love for the woman and for her mother. When Leto II makes it clear that Alia is possessed by one of her past lives, that of Baron Harkonnen, Duncan abandons her. When ordered to provide a plausible plot against Jessica, he takes her to Salus Secundus to become both a prisoner and a teacher for Farad'n, the possible next emperor. He then bows out of the conflict.

Farad'n, the son of Wencias and the dead emperor Saladam IV's nephew. His mother, in grooming him to take back the throne, has instilled in him some of his family's monstrous qualities. He is part of the plot to kill the twins but has some spark of humanity left when Jessica arrives to teach him. He never realizes his aim to become emperor or to marry Ghanima: He will be the royal consort and father of the royal children, but never a husband.

Lady Jessica, who returns from her seclusion on Caladan supposedly to see her grandchildren, Leto II and Ghanima. She quickly discerns Alia's condition and is ready for the kidnapping plot against her. Her talents are central as she weans Farad'n from the plots of his power-hungry mother and trains him in Bene Gesserit mind control to be a worthy mate to Ghanima.

Stilgar, who has risen from simple seitch chief to counselor in Paul's court, then fallen back to aging seitch chief. He remains faithful in his Fremen fashion to the Atreides family, fostering the twins in seitch Tabor. His loyalty extends only as far as he judges it will profit his beloved Fremen culture.

Gurney Halleck, who arranges for the education of Leto II into the Fremen desert pirate culture and his training as a claimant to the throne left by his father.

Princess Irulan, who has stayed on in the capital and become a sort of adviser to Alia. She later goes with Leto II into exile and proves more loyal to Paul's memory.

— Janice M. Bogstad

GREAT EXPECTATIONS

Author: Charles Dickens (1812-1870)
First published: 1860-1861
Genre: Novel

Locale: England
Time: The nineteenth century
Plot: Bildungsroman

Philip Pirrip, called **Pip**, an orphan and the unwanted ward of his harsh sister, Mrs. Joe. Although seemingly destined for a career as a blacksmith, he sees his fortunes improve after he meets a convict hiding in a graveyard. Afterward, through Miss Havisham, he meets Estella, the eccentric old woman's lovely young ward. Thinking Miss Havisham is his benefactor, he goes to London to become a gentleman. Unfortunately for his peace of mind, he forgets who his true friends are. Finally, after Magwitch, the convict, dies and the Crown confiscates his fortune, Pip understands that good clothes, well-spoken English, and a generous allowance do not make one a gentleman.

Miss Havisham, a lonely, embittered old woman. When her lover jilted her at the altar, she refused ever to leave her gloomy chambers. Instead, she has devoted her life to vengeance. With careful indoctrination, she teaches Estella how to break men's hearts. Just before her death, she begs Pip to forgive her cruelty.

Estella, Miss Havisham's ward. Cold, aloof, unfeeling, she tries to warn Pip not to love her, for she is incapable of loving anyone; Miss Havisham has taught her too well. Years later, however, Pip meets her in the garden near the ruins of Satis House, Miss Havisham's former home. She has lost her cool aloofness and found maturity. Pip realizes that they will never part again.

Joe Gargery, Pip's brother-in-law. Even though he is married to the worst tempered of women, Mrs. Joe, he manages to retain his gentle simplicity and his selfless love for Pip. After he marries Biddy, he finds the domestic bliss that he so richly deserves.

Mrs. Georgiana Maria Gargery, commonly called **Mrs. Joe**, Pip's vituperative sister, who berates and misuses him and Joe with impunity. When she verbally assails Joe's helper, Orlick, she makes a mortal enemy who causes her death with the blow of a hammer. Later he tries to do the same for Pip.

Abel Magwitch, alias **Mr. Provis**, Pip's benefactor. When Pip helps him, an escaped convict, Magwitch promises to repay the debt. Transported to New South Wales, he eventually makes a large fortune as a sheep farmer. When he returns illegally to England years later, the escaped felon reveals himself as Pip's real patron. Casting off his distaste, Pip finds a real affection for the rough old man and attempts to get him safely out of England before the law apprehends him once more. Recaptured, Magwitch dies in prison.

Mr. Jaggers, a criminal lawyer employed by Magwitch to provide for Pip's future. He is a shrewd man with the ability to size up a person at a glance. To him, personal feelings are unimportant; facts are the only trustworthy things. Although completely unemotional, he deals with Pip and Magwitch honestly throughout their long association.

Herbert Pocket, Miss Havisham's young relative and Pip's roommate in London. Almost always cheerful and uncomplaining, he is constantly looking for ways to improve his prospects. With Pip's aid, he is able to establish himself in a profitable business.

John Wemmick, Mr. Jaggers' efficient law clerk. Dry and businesslike in the office, he keeps his social and business life completely separate. As a friend, he proves himself completely loyal to Pip.

Biddy, Joe Gargery's wife after the death of Mrs. Joe. A gentle, loving woman, she is a good wife to him.

Compeyson, a complete villain, the man who jilted Miss Havisham and betrayed Magwitch. He is killed by Magwitch as the two struggle desperately just before the ex-convict is recaptured.

The Aged P, John Wemmick's deaf old father. In their neat little home, his chief pleasures are reading the newspaper aloud and listening to his son's nightly firing of a small cannon.

Dolge Orlick, Joe Gargery's surly helper in the blacksmith shop. After an altercation with Mrs. Joe, he attacks her with a hammer. Later he plots to kill Pip, his hated enemy. Only the timely arrival of Herbert Pocket and Startop prevents the crime.

Molly, Mr. Jaggers' housekeeper, a woman of strange, silent habits, with extraordinarily strong hands. A murderess, she is also revealed as Magwitch's former mistress and Estella's mother.

Matthew Pocket, Miss Havisham's distant relative and Pip's tutor during his early years in London. He is also Herbert Pocket's father.

Mrs. Belinda Pocket, a fluttery, helpless woman, the daughter of a knight who had expected his daughter to marry a title.

Alick Pocket,
Joe Pocket,
Fanny Pocket, and
Jane Pocket, other children of the Pockets.

Sarah Pocket, another relative of Miss Havisham, a withered-appearing, sharp-tongued woman.

Uncle Pumblechook, a prosperous corn chandler and Joe Gargery's relative. During Pip's childhood, he constantly discusses the boy's conduct and offers much platitudinous advice.

Clara Barley, a pretty, winning young woman engaged to Herbert Pocket. Magwitch is hidden in the Barley house while Pip is trying to smuggle the former convict out of England.

Old Bill Barley, Clara's father. A former purser, he is afflicted by gout and bedridden.

Mr. Wopsle, a parish clerk who later becomes an actor under the name of Mr. Waldengarver. Pip and Herbert Pocket go to see his performance as Hamlet.

Bentley Drummle, called **The Spider**, a sulky rich boy notable for his bad manners. He is Pip's rival for Estella's love. After marrying her, he treats her cruelly. Pip meets him while Drummle is being tutored by Mr. Pocket.

Startop, a lively young man tutored by Mr. Pocket.

Mr. Trabb, a village tailor and undertaker.

Trabb's Boy, a young apprentice whose independence is a source of irritation to Pip.

Mr. John (Raymond) Camilla, a toady.

Mrs. Camilla, his wife, Mr. Pocket's sister. She and her husband hope to inherit a share of Miss Havisham's fortune.

Miss Skiffins, a woman of no certain age but the owner of "portable property," who marries John Wemmick.

Clarriker, a young shipping broker in whose firm, Clarriker & Company, Pip secretly buys Herbert Pocket a partnership.

Pepper, also called **The Avenger**, Pip's servant in the days of his great expectations.

THE GREAT GALEOTO
(El Gran Galeoto)

Author: José Echegaray y Eizaguirre (1833-1916)
First published: 1881
Genre: Drama
Locale: Madrid, Spain
Time: The nineteenth century
Plot: Social satire

Ernesto (ehr-NAYS-toh), a young playwright taken into the home of his father's close friend Don Julián as secretary. Don Julián has a young and beautiful wife, Teodora, and the presence of the handsome young secretary in the household causes gossip. When Don Julián's brother Severo voices his suspicions, Ernesto, though entirely innocent, moves from Don Julián's house into a garret. The Viscount Nebreda repeats the malicious slander publicly in Ernesto's presence and is challenged to a duel. Before they can fight, Don Julián finds Nebreda, fights him, and is gravely wounded. He is taken to Ernesto's room, where he finds Teodora, who has innocently come to say goodbye before Ernesto leaves Spain the following day. The circumstantial evidence now seems overwhelming. Before he dies, Don Julián slaps Ernesto's face and threatens to kill him in a duel. After his death, Severo claims his brother's house and orders Teodora banished from the premises. When she faints, Ernesto denounces Severo and all gossiping society as no better than an evil panderer determined to bring two innocent people to ruin with vague innuendoes and vicious rumors. The title of the play is derived from Galeoto, the go-between for Lancelot and Guinevere, as referred to in Dante's story of Paolo and Francesca.

Don Julián (hew-lee-AHN), a wealthy businessman who befriends Ernesto. He is then led by slander to suspect an affair between Ernesto and Teodora.

Teodora (teh-oh-DOHR-ah), Julián's young and faithful wife, wrongly suspected by society of being in love with Ernesto. Severo bars her from her dying husband's room and later tries to put her out of the house. When she faints, Ernesto lifts her up and tells Severo that he will take her away.

Severo (seh-VEH-roh), Julián's brother. He voices the rumors of Madrid. He is forced by Ernesto to apologize on his knees to Teodora.

Mercedes (mehr-THAY-dehs), Severo's gossiping wife, who passes on the rumors of scandal to Teodora.

Pepito (peh-PEE-toh), the son of Severo and Mercedes. He carries the news of Julián's duel.

The Viscount Nebreda (neh-breh-dah), who is challenged to a duel by Ernesto for slandering Teodora. Julián, taking up the challenge, is fatally wounded by Nebreda, who, in turn, is killed by Ernesto.

THE GREAT GATSBY

Author: F. Scott Fitzgerald (1896-1940)
First published: 1925
Genre: Novel
Locale: New York City and Long Island
Time: The 1922
Plot: Social realism

Nick Carraway, the narrator. A young Midwesterner who was dissatisfied with his life at home, he was attracted to New York and now sells bonds there. He is the most honest character of the novel and because of this trait fails to become deeply fascinated by his rich friends on Long Island. He helps Daisy and Jay Gatsby to renew a love they had known before Daisy's marriage, and he is probably the only person in the novel to have any genuine affection for Gatsby.

Jay Gatsby, a fabulously rich racketeer whose connections outside of the law are only guessed at. He is the son of poor parents from the Middle West. He has changed his name from James Gatz and becomes obsessed with a need for making more and more money. Much of his time is spent in trying to impress, and become accepted by, other rich people. He gives lavish parties for people he knows nothing about and most of whom he never meets. He is genuinely in love with Daisy Buchanan and becomes a sympathetic character when he assumes the blame for her hit-and-run accident. At his death, he has been deserted by everyone except his father and Nick.

Daisy Buchanan, Nick's second cousin. Unhappy in her marriage because of Tom Buchanan's deliberate unfaithfulness, she has the character of a "poor little rich girl." She renews an old love for Jay Gatsby and considers leaving her husband, but she is finally reconciled to him. She kills Tom's mistress in a hit-and-run accident after a quarrel in which she defends both men as Tom accuses Gatsby of trying to steal her from him; but she allows Gatsby to take the blame for the accident and suffers no remorse when he is murdered by the woman's husband.

Tom Buchanan, Daisy's husband. The son of rich Midwestern parents, he reached the heights of his career as a college football player. Completely without taste, culture, or sensitivity, he carries on a rather sordid affair with Myrtle Wilson. He pretends to help George Wilson, her husband, but allows him to think that Gatsby was not only her murderer but also her lover.

Myrtle Wilson, Tom Buchanan's mistress. She is a fat, unpleasant woman who is so highly appreciative of the fact that her lover is a rich man that she will suffer almost any degradation for him. While she is with Tom, her pretense that she is rich and highly sophisticated becomes ludicrous.

George Wilson, Myrtle's husband, a rather pathetic figure. He runs an auto repair shop and believes Tom Buchanan is really interested in helping him. Aware that his wife has a lover, he never suspects who he really is. His faith in Tom makes him believe what Buchanan says, which, in turn, causes him to murder Gatsby and then commit suicide.

Jordan Baker, a friend of the Buchanans, a golfer. Daisy introduces Jordan to Nick and tries to throw them together, but when Nick realizes that she is a cheat who refuses to assume the elementary responsibility of the individual, he loses all interest in her.

Meyer Wolfshiem, a gambler and underworld associate of Gatsby.

Catherine, Myrtle Wilson's sister, who is obviously proud of Myrtle's rich connection and unconcerned with the immorality involved.

Mr. and Mrs. McKee, a photographer and his wife who try to use Nick and Tom to get a start among the rich people of Long Island.

Mr. Gatz, Jay Gatsby's father who, being unaware of the facts of Jay's life, thought his son had been a great man.

THE GREAT GOD BROWN

Author: Eugene O'Neill (1888-1953)
First published: 1926
Genre: Drama
Locale: The East Coast of the United States
Time: The 1920's
Plot: Expressionism

Dion Anthony, a talented but failed artist and architect. Dion's dilemma is that of the creative and sensitive artist in the crass, materialistic world. In his youth, he starts on the course of ruination through drink and gambling. His dissipation is reflected in the mask this character sometimes carries and sometimes wears throughout this expressionistic play. In the opening scene, his mask shows the defiance and rebelliousness of a "sensual young Pan" and hides the more spiritual, poetic qualities of Dion's face. Seven years later, his mask has hardened into an image of a bitter, mocking Mephistopheles, and his face has become more aged and strained but also more ascetic. At this point, Dion's wife, Margaret, obtains a position for Dion as an architect with Billy Brown, a childhood friend. Although Dion produces successful designs, his disgust over selling out to materialism, to the Great God Brown, helps to complete the ravages on his face and mask. He dies seven years later, his face that of a martyr but his mask completely diabolic in its picture of cruelty and evil.

William A. (Billy) Brown, a successful architect, a good-looking, well-dressed, prosperous businessman. He has always loved Margaret and employs Dion at her request. Brown, however, takes credit for Dion's ingenuity and designs, a betrayal that contributes to Dion's decline. Dion dies in Brown's home, and when Margaret arrives, Brown conceals the body and garbs himself in Dion's clothes and mask. For the next three months, he deceives both Margaret and office draftsmen by wearing his own Billy Brown mask of the smiling, successful executive at work and by wearing Dion's mask at the Anthony home. His own face, however, now shows the strain of living with the demon in Dion's mask, and he comes to realize that he has failed in stealing the mask to acquire the creative spirit of Dion.

Margaret Anthony, Dion's wife. Young and pretty when she marries, she grows increasingly worried over Dion's dissipation. At home, she reveals her face to her husband, but when she goes to Billy's office to ask him to hire Dion, she covers her anxiety with the mask of her character: that of the innocent, hopeful matron. Margaret is thereby able to pretend that things are better at home than they really are.

— *Glenn Hopp*

THE GREAT MEADOW

Author: Elizabeth Madox Roberts (1886-1941)
First published: 1930
Genre: Novel
Locale: Western Virginia and Kentucky
Time: 1775-1783
Plot: Historical

Diony Hall Jarvis, a pioneer wife and a lover of books and learning who is by nature introspective and is often philosophical and poetic in her thoughts. She frequently muses over her own identity and the part she is playing in the settling of a new land. She sees herself and the others creating order out of disorder. Combining the idealist and the practical woman, she trains herself carefully for her mission by learning the homely arts that will be needed to establish enduring order. When, after Berk's return, she is faced with the problem of choosing between her two husbands, she is loyal to the one to whom she first gave herself.

Berk Jarvis, her husband, a strong, adventurous, restless fighting man experienced in enduring the many hardships of pioneer life and the dangers of Indian warfare. Intent on avenging his mother's murder and bringing back her hair, he leaves his wife and child in order to achieve his goal. He represents the early pioneers who opened the wilderness for white American occupancy and who fought the Indians and the British who tried to drive them out.

Evan Muir, married to Diony after Berk's supposed death. Patient, industrious, and capable, he is a symbol of the men who followed the wilderness trail blazers and conquerors. Such men as Evan were needed to establish the settlements and homesteads on a permanent basis.

Thomas Hall, Diony's father, a wilderness surveyor who accepted land as pay for surveying a great tract for a Maryland company. A cultured man, he has encouraged Diony's studies in the arts and philosophy. Though disappointed in Diony's choice of Berk, he permits their marriage.

Elvira Jarvis, mother of Will, Berk, and Jack Jarvis. She is scalped by an Indian.

Betty Hall, Diony's younger sister. In contrast to Diony, who is excited by the prospect of a pioneer life in newly settled country, Betty loves the seaboard towns and the settled life there, and she romantically dreams of going east to live.

Polly Hall, wife of Thomas Hall. A pious Methodist, she opposes Berk and Diony's going into the wilderness because they will be taking land that belongs to the Indians.

James (Jim) Harrod, valorous founder of Harrod's Fort and Harrodstown.

George Rogers Clark, the commander at Harrod's Fort.

Daniel Boone, the famed wilderness pioneer who helped build Harrodstown.

THE GREAT PONDS

Author: Elechi Amadi (1934-)
First published: 1969
Genre: Novel
Locale: Nigeria
Time: 1918
Plot: Social morality

Olumba (oh-LEWM-bah), the principal warrior of the Chiolu village. A short but muscular middle-aged man, he is respected widely as a brilliant strategist in warfare and is equally respected for his skills with the knife and bow. Although he is not yet an elder, his suggestions on tactics in battle and his views on negotiations for peace are frequently followed by the chief and other elders. A devout, even zealous, believer in the gods, he looks up when he walks. He spends much of his time at home in ritual meditation and possesses a vast collection of charms and amulets to protect himself during battle. Olumba's manner before the villagers reflects dignity and an even-tempered judgment, but inwardly he wrestles with fits of anger and despair. His pride as a warrior yields to the best interests of Chiolu when he swears on oath to the gods so that they might judge the rightful village's ownership of fishing rights to Wagaba Pond. As the influenza epidemic strikes both Chiolu and Aliakoro villages, Olumba becomes physically emaciated and mentally disoriented, wrestling with spirits who attempt to kill him. Although he survives a final attack by Wago, his hollowed eyes look out over a village decimated by the deadly virus, making the triumphant judgment of the gods meaningless in the wake of the community's many victims.

Wago the Leopard-Killer (WAH-goh), the principal warrior of Aliakoro village. A skilled hunter renowned for his three leopard skins, he is brave and strong but sometimes so aggressive that he is outwitted strategically in battle. In peace negotiations, Wago shows little respect for the elders of his own village and even less for his enemies, often punctuating discussions with loud boasts, rude insults, and thinly veiled lies. He is an excellent stalker, capable of intense concentration on his prey. The middle-aged Wago's deep-set eyes embody his stubborn determination, regardless of the wisdom of his views. He shows little respect for his gods, preferring to rely on his own strength and swiftness; when his physical abilities fail him or his crude style of negotiation collapses, he resorts to a weird, condescending laughter. Impatient when the gods do not kill Olumba as a result of his oath, Wago pretends to be a leopard and attacks the ailing Olumba, only to be mortally wounded by Ikechi. He escapes to Wagaba Pond and commits suicide by drowning himself, thereby rendering the judgment of the gods insignificant: The Chiolu people will not fish in water polluted spiritually by an act of suicide.

Ikechi (ee-KAY-chee), a young and inexperienced Chiolu warrior who apprentices himself to Olumba. Boyishly impulsive, he is known for his great speed as a runner; in his first battle, he runs down an enemy from Aliakoro and kills him, earning the right to be initiated as a warrior. When courting the chief's daughter Chisa, Ikechi displays his good humor and his respect for tribal customs. In battle, he is anxious, often grinding his teeth, but brave and loyal. When he confronts Wago and warriors in alliance with those of Aliakoro, he flees, using the good sense that Olumba has taught him to exercise should he face odds that he cannot overcome. As Olumba and other villagers become ill with influenza, Ikechi shadows him protectively, saving Olumba's life when Wago attacks him in an effort to thwart the judgment of the gods.

Eze Diali (AY-zay dee-AH-lee), the chief of Chiolu village. Adorned in peacock feathers and exuding dignity even in his walk, the short but nimble old chief commands the love and the respect of his people. Known as a rational and fair-minded leader, Diali seeks and honors consistently the advice of Chiolu's elders and warriors, but he constantly second-guesses his decision to go to war over the fishing rights to Wagaba Pond. Earnestly desiring an end to the war, Diali attempts negotiation several times to bring an end to the killing. As the war continues and the influenza progresses, he becomes frail and ill, but he remains genial and gentle toward his people, often spending long hours playing with his children. Something of a fatalist, Diali resists a temptation to subvert the strength of Chiolu's warriors by pursuing the kidnappers of his own daughter Chisa.

Eze Okehi (AY-zay oh-KAY-hee), the chief of Aliakoro village. Still strong and well preserved, the aged, white-haired leader starts the war with Chiolu, encouraged by the aggressive arguments of Wago. Although determined to win the fishing rights for Wagaba Pond on behalf of his people, Okehi honors the divination of Igwu, who claims that Aliakoro has offended the gods by kidnapping Eze Diali's daughter and Olumba's wife, Oda, who is pregnant. Because the two women have been sold into slavery and their return is unlikely at best, Okehi agrees to Olumba's oath as a means of resolving the five-month war. During the six-month period of Olumba's oath, Okehi's health deteriorates, and Wago's influence dominates the village.

Anwuanwu (ahn-wew-AHN-wew), the *dibia*, or shaman, of Abii village. Far more powerful and learned than Chiolu's *dibia*, Achichi, he is renowned for producing protective amulets and using herbs and roots to develop cures. Especially trained to subvert curses imposed by other *dibias*, Anwuanwu discovers Igwu's curse on Olumba and helps battle Igwu for Olumba's health during his oath.

Igwu (ee-GWEW), the *dibia* of Aliakoro village. A wrestling champion in his early years, the stocky, middle-aged *dibia* uses "male" and "female" drums to perform his divinations. Although he believes that fishing rights are not worth the loss of human lives in warfare, Igwu consents to invoking a deadly curse so that he might subvert the judgment of the gods on Olumba's oath; only Anwuanwu's intervention prevents the death of Olumba in his fall from a palm tree. Despite supporting Aliakoro by provoking Olumba's fall, Igwu fears Wago's aggressive dominance of Aliakoro and causes him to fall ill. Igwu's divinations, however, like those of the other villages' *dibias*, cannot stem the disastrous epidemic of influenza.

— *Michael Loudon*

THE GREAT VALLEY

Author: Mary Johnston (1870-1936)
First published: 1926
Genre: Novel
Locale: Virginia and Ohio
Time: 1735-1760
Plot: Historical

John Selkirk, a Scottish Presbyterian minister. Considered too liberal by his Scottish congregation, he emigrates, with his family, to Virginia's Shenando Valley. After establishing a new home and a new church, he decides to move a day's journey west in spite of rumors of sporadic Indian uprisings. Shortly after the move, he is killed by an Indian.

Jean Selkirk, John Selkirk's wife.

Andrew Selkirk, John Selkirk's son and fellow settler in the Shenando Valley.

Colonel Matthew Burke, a wealthy landowner and developer of the Shenando Valley, from whom John and Andrew Selkirk buy their tract.

Conan Burke, Colonel Matthew Burke's son, who has settled on his father's land. His homestead is attacked by a band of Indians and his family taken captive. He is later reunited with his wife and daughter after their escape from captivity.

Elizabeth Selkirk, John Selkirk's daughter and the wife of Conan Burke. Kidnapped by Indians, she is made the squaw of Long Thunder. She finally escapes with her daughter and, after a long trek through the wilderness, is reunited with her husband.

Eileen Burke, the daughter of Elizabeth Selkirk Burke, with whom she escapes from the Indians.

Andrew Burke, Elizabeth Selkirk Burke's infant son, killed by an Indian.

Stephen Trabue, a driver and guide.

Nancy Milliken Selkirk, Andrew Selkirk's wife.

Mother Dick, an old woman captured by Indians along with Elizabeth Selkirk Burke.

Ajax and

Barb, servants captured along with Elizabeth Selkirk Burke by Indians.

Robin Selkirk and

Tam Selkirk, Elizabeth Selkirk's brothers.

George Washington, a young surveyor.

THE GREAT WHITE HOPE

Author: Howard Sackler (1929-1982)
First published: 1968
Genre: Drama
Locale: The United States, Europe, Mexico, and Cuba
Time: The years preceding World War I
Plot: Historical

Jack Jefferson, a black heavyweight boxing champion. A complex personality, Jack plays many roles in American society in the years preceding World War I. After defeating the white champion, he becomes the object of the establishment's attempts to dethrone him by finding a Great White Hope. Jack is powerful, aware, and moody; he knows what is expected of him outside the ring, but he plays the role of the big, black buck, slow of speech and intelligence and lusting after white women, with obvious irony. He also has a self-destructive bent because he lives openly with his white lover, Ellie Bachman, despite the outrage and vindictiveness of both white and black forces. After being arrested for violation of the Mann Act, Jack escapes to Europe rather than face his sentence. During his exile, Jack deteriorates as a fighter and as a man, unable to establish a stable personality among the many roles he is forced to play: embittered exile, victim of racism, and self-deprecating actor-fighter. He expresses his increasing bitterness toward the persecuted Ellie, who is driven to suicide. In his remorse, Jack accepts the offer from Cap'n Dan to throw the fight against the Kid, the new Great White Hope, in exchange for amnesty. Overall, Jack remains an enigma, defined more by the swirling forces around him than by himself.

Ellie Bachman, the young white woman who becomes Jack's lover and suffers the consequences of living with a black champion in a racist society. Ellie refuses to give up her relationship with Jack, saying that she loves him for his character rather than for the notoriety surrounding him. She proves her love by staying with him throughout his exile, but when she sees how totally Jack is consumed by his struggle against hostile social forces, she advises him to accept the fixed fight with the Kid. Jack belittles her for this advice, causing her to commit suicide. She leads a tragic life in pursuit of a doomed relationship with a complex, tortured man.

Cap'n Dan, a former heavyweight champion who is determined to restore the heavyweight crown to a white man. He convinces the former champion Brady to come out of retirement to fight Jack, but after Brady is easily defeated, Cap'n Dan joins with newsman Smitty, Chicago District Attorney Cameron, federal agent Dixon, and promoter Pop Weaver to have Jack arrested and later to force him to throw the fight with the Kid.

Smitty, a famous sportswriter who is outraged by Jack's success as heavyweight champion and his relationship with Ellie. He is a calculating wordsmith, asking probing questions and writing inflammatory articles in an effort to discredit Jack.

Goldie, Jack's white manager, who is devoted to promoting Jack's career. Goldie sets the fight with Brady for July 4, knowing that Jack's victory will bring him fame and money. Goldie also warns Jack not to flaunt his relationship with Ellie and to recognize the power of the hatred the white establishment has for him. Jack ignores Goldie's advice, and during his exile he becomes estranged from his manager, who finally counsels Jack to accept the offer of amnesty in exchange for losing to the Kid.

Tick, Jack's loyal trainer, who is with him throughout his career as a daily functionary but has no influence over the fighter.

— *Frank Ardolino*

THE GREEK PASSION
(Ho Christos xanastauronetai)

Author: Nikos Kazantzakis (1883-1957)
First published: 1953
Genre: Novel
Locale: Lycovrissi, Anatolia
Time: c. 1920
Plot: Allegory

Priest Grigoris, the priest of Lycovrissi. He is a cruel man who compromises God and the gospels for his own ends. He vents his rage at unexpected times and in inappropriate settings. He indulges his gluttony at his parishioners' expense. He jealously protects his position as sole Christian leader. Without compassion, he orders Fotis, a priest and leader of refugees fleeing Turkish cruelty, to take his people elsewhere. To frighten them, he announces an outbreak of cholera. Grigoris tries every trick to advance his own interests. He accuses Michelis and Manolios of stealing food from Archon Patriarcheas' cellar to feed refugees. His approval of his daughter's marriage to the archon's son is a political move to enhance his political power.

Manolios, the most interesting character in this novel. He is betrothed to the chief magistrate's illegitimate daughter Lenio. He is a handsome, well-liked, and good-hearted shepherd chosen to play Christ in the forthcoming Easter Passion Play. He tries all manner of purification to become worthy of the role. The young shepherd casts away all worldly things and appears saintlike to villagers. Eventually, Manolios takes his role even more seriously, trying to engage in Christ-like projects, one of which is to help Fotis' desperate people. Manolios leads them to the top of Mount Sarakina, where they can settle in caves protected from wind and cold. He camps there and begins his purification process. He remains alone, fighting the desires of the flesh. He is successful in fighting his weaknesses, but his dreams are full of sinful imagery involving the village harlot, Katerina. His face breaks out in putrid sores. He tells his friends that the sores are given by God as punishment for his lewd dreams. He believes he must suffer martyrdom. He offers to give his life to save the elders of the village from being killed by Agha. He falsely claims he is the unknown killer of Agha's pretty boy, but the real killer is exposed and Manolios is released. He evolves from a compassionate Christ to a furious Christ who advocates revolution and revenge. He and some of the refugees storm Lycovrissi. He is badly wounded and later dies.

Captain Fortounas, a rough old sailor, enjoying his pleasant retirement while reminiscing about his seafaring days. His past is his most treasured possession. He and Nadji Nikolis are considered the wise elders of Lycovrissi. Most of the time, Fortounas is too drunk to give worthwhile advice to anyone.

The Agha, the Turkish lord of Lycovrissi. His main preoccupations are with enjoying his oriental splendor, eating rich foods, drinking raki, receiving gifts from his Greek subjects, and leading a sensuous life with beautiful young boys. When Youssoufaki, a dimpled, gentle boy, is killed, Agha imprisons all the town elders and threatens to kill them one by one until the killer is found.

Lenio, the handsome, bright love child of old Patriarcheas. She is engaged to Manolios. Her desire for love and passion is urgent. She waits impatiently to be married but is dismayed to discover that Manolios is taking his role as Christ too seriously and has chosen celibacy for the rest of the year, or perhaps even for the rest of his life. Full of passion, and with her wedding plans unrealized, she fulfills her burning desires with Niolio, an equally passionate and impetuous young lad.

Panayotaros, a red-bearded buffoon known as "plaster-eater," the village saddler. He is a cunning, undisciplined man who has been chosen to play Judas in the Passion Play. He is always waiting to exact revenge and customarily hates almost everyone. Currently, he hates Manolios for teaching virtue to Katerina, the only prostitute in the village. Living up to his Judas character, he betrays Manolios in the raid that ends in Manolios' death.

Michelis, who is chosen to play the role of the apostle John. He is the handsome son of the archon. Unlike his wealthy family, he is deeply sensitive, always questioning the treachery of the oppressors he witnesses on both the Turkish and Greek sides. He is engaged to Mariori, the divinely fair, charming daughter of Priest Grigoris who always hears angels' wings fluttering around her. Michelis, affected by Manolios' passion to imitate Christ, leaves family, future wife, and wealth behind and joins Manolios on Mount Sarakina.

Katerina, Lycovrissi's kindhearted prostitute, chosen to play the role of Mary Magdalene. She is generous with her possessions and her body. With her husky voice and voluptuous beauty, she has attracted many men before she is moved by Manolios' plea and closes her door to transient lovers. She haunts Manolios' dreams so often that he decides to give his life as a gesture of penitence.

— *Chogollah Maroufi*

THE GREEN BAY TREE

Author: Louis Bromfield (1896-1956)
First published: 1924
Genre: Novel
Locale: Middle West
Time: Early twentieth century
Plot: Social

Julia Shane, a wealthy widow, a cynical, proud, stubborn woman who feels separated from both her worldly older daughter and her neurotically religious younger daughter. A Scotch Presbyterian, she scorns Irene's piousness and her desire to be a nun, though in her will she leaves Irene free to make her own choice. In her declining years, Julia spends much of her time recalling the past and reading French novels.

Lily Shane, her older daughter, tall and lovely, with honey-colored hair. She refuses the governor despite his offer to marry her to prevent a scandal, and she later rejects Willie. Lily lives in Paris for ten years before her mother's death, which occurs while Lily is back home on a visit. She returns to Paris, takes a lover, and finally marries a French diplomat, M. de Cyon.

Irene Shane, Julia's frail, blond younger daughter, a pious, introverted teacher of mill hands. After her mother's death, she becomes a Carmelite nun named Sister Monica.

The Governor, a vulgar politician twenty years older than Lily and the father of her son. After Lily's rejection of him, he marries the plain, sturdy daughter of a manufacturer.

Hattie Tolliver, Julia's niece, who cares for Julia during the long illness that ends in her death.

Ellen Tolliver, Hattie's daughter, a talented pianist who marries a traveling salesman, studies music in Paris, and becomes a noted pianist under the name of Lilli Barr.

M. de Cyon, Lily's husband, a dignified French diplomat several years her senior.

William (Willie) Harrison, a millionaire steel mill owner, a mother-dominated young man who wishes to marry Lily. He increasingly resents his mother's bullying and after her stroke longs for her death.

Mrs. Julis Harrison, Willie's dictatorial mother, who suspects the reason for Lily's leaving her hometown.

Madame Gigon, a widow with whom Lily lives in Paris; she dies during the war.

Judge Weissman, a political boss whose Jewishness revolts Julia.

John Shane, Julia's husband, a wealthy man of unknown background who was a political boss until he died of apoplexy.

Jean, the son of Lily and the Governor; he is wounded in the war.

Stepan Krylenko, a big, burly young Ukrainian strike leader. He is befriended by Irene. After he is shot by a mill guard at a strikers' meeting, he is hidden by Lily. He later becomes an international labor leader and dies of typhus in Moscow.

The Baron, Lily's lover, a cousin of Madame Gigon. He is killed in the war.

GREEN CARD

Author: JoAnne Akalaitis (1937-   )
First published: 1987
Genre: Drama
Locale: The United States and a jungle
Time: The 1980's, with flashbacks
Plot: Social

Raye, an Anglo man, forty to sixty years old. Raye takes the part of a nineteenth century Jewish immigrant from Lithuania. He tells how his people were persecuted in Europe and how wonderful America seemed to him on his arrival. Later, he dons a comical wig to portray the overbearing host of the Green Card Show. He also plays a Central Intelligence Agency (CIA) employee who describes the Cambodian people in a patronizing and stereotypical manner.

Jesse, a young Latin man. Jesse plays a nightclub comic who spews out racial slurs for ironic effect, in the manner of Lenny Bruce. Later, he takes the role of an illegal alien from El Salvador who has been arrested by the Immigration and Naturalization Service. He describes the harsh treatment he received at the alien detention center.

Rosalind, a young Asian woman. She acts as a pronunciation guide for Asian names in the second act.

George, a Latin man, twenty to forty years old. He portrays a sleazy television evangelist. Later, he plays an Indian peasant in Central America, and he recounts the persecution his family suffered there.

Jim, an Asian man in his fifties. He plays a CIA employee who narrates a slide show justifying America's support of the right-wing death squads in El Salvador.

Dana, an Asian man, thirty to fifty years old. Dana takes the part of Marshall Ky, a member of the Vietnamese Mafia who later settled in America. He complains about the difficulty of adjusting to life in America. Later, he justifies his takeover of Danang and his attack on the Buddhists. He wonders aloud if it was a mistake to lead the fight against the Communists in Vietnam for the United States, because, when he arrived in this country as a refugee, he received no acknowledgment from the government.

Alma, a Latin woman, twenty to forty years old. As a Mexican maid, she describes the luxury of the homes that she cleans and contrasts that with the poverty in which she lives. She explains that when she comes home after a hard day of tidying up the homes of the rich, she loves to relax by watching television. Later, she plays a Salvadoran refugee who describes the torture she received at the hands of the death squads.

Jessica, an Anglo woman, twenty to forty years old. She walks around the audience, playing a Jewish immigrant describing the work she did in a sweatshop when she first arrived in America. She gives pieces of cake to members of the audience.

Josie, an Asian woman in her twenties. She dresses in an elaborate costume to narrate a puppet show that tells the folktale of the origin of the Vietnamese people.

Mimi, an Anglo woman, thirty-five to fifty years old. Mimi plays a rich American woman describing the charms of Vietnam before the war there.

— *Pamela Canal*

GREEN GRASS, RUNNING WATER

Author: Thomas King (1943-)
First published: 1993
Genre: Novel
Locale: Blossom, Alberta, Canada
Time: Late twentieth century
Plot: Comic realism

Lionel Red Dog, a good-natured underachiever of Blackfoot Indian heritage. All his life, Lionel has stumbled into mishaps. As a child, misidentified as another boy, he narrowly avoided receiving heart surgery instead of his tonsillectomy. As a college student, he was mistaken for a Wounded Knee protester and arrested after he read a paper on cultural pluralism at a conference. On the brink of forty, he sells television sets and stereos in Bursum's electronics store; everyone, including Lionel, thinks the job is a waste of his talents. He has to wear a garish gold blazer at work. The blazer, which becomes increasingly ratty as time goes by, symbolizes Lionel's stalled plans. He dreams of finishing his university degree but has taken no steps to do so beyond talking about it. It is unclear at the book's end whether he will go on selling TV sets, move back to the reserve and live in his uncle's rebuilt cabin, or go back to school; his direction probably will be determined by other people or by fate.

Alberta Frank, a professor of native studies at the university in Calgary. Alberta dates both Lionel and Charlie Looking Bear. She is fond of both but does not want to marry either. A brief, youthful marriage made her wary of too close an involvement with any man. She does, however, feel her biological clock ticking and wants to have a baby. Artificial insemination seems to her the most trouble-free way, but because most clinics reject unmarried applicants and the others have long waiting lists, she is unable to follow through with this idea. Meanwhile, she teaches Native American history to bored white students and plans to travel back to Blossom, where she can attend the annual Sun Dance and help Lionel celebrate his fortieth birthday. By the time she arrives, she is plagued by nausea. Her female relatives are sure she is pregnant. Alberta vehemently denies it for fear of being pulled into the marriage trap.

Charlie Looking Bear, Lionel's cousin, a successful lawyer in Edmondton. Charlie formerly had Lionel's job of selling televisions at Bursum's; he even wore the same unattractive gold jacket. Charlie went on to build a career working in the white man's world, becoming outwardly smooth but inwardly ambivalent about his own identity. Because the Duplessis company wants an Indian lawyer, he represents it, thus working, albeit amicably, against his own uncle Eli's crusade to halt the hydroelectric project on Blackfoot land. Charlie is fired when the dam breaks, and he sets off for Hollywood to find his father.

Portland Looking Bear, Charlie's father, a sometime film actor. Before Charlie's birth, Portland acted in many Westerns, usually as an extra but sometimes in supporting roles as an Indian chief. To his distress, he had to wear a large artificial nose for these roles so he would "look like an Indian." When jobs become sparse for him, he goes back to the Blackfoot reserve in Canada, but after Charlie grows up, he returns to Hollywood, his favorite place in the world, and arduously builds a second acting career.

Eli Stands Alone, who formerly was a professor of literature. He returned to live in his mother's house on the reserve when she died, for reasons even he does not entirely understand. The house is located just below the dam built by the Duplessis company for the Parliament Lake development. Eli files a series of lawsuits and manages to hold up the project's implementation for ten years. The company representative comes by his house every morning and drinks coffee with Eli, cheerfully inquiring whether the old man has changed his mind. When the dam cracks from an earthquake, Eli is swept away in the ensuing flood.

Latisha, Lionel's sister, who owns a restaurant called the Dead Dog that claims to serve dog meat. It actually is beef, but the pretense attracts the tourist trade, and the Dead Dog provides a good living for Latisha and her children. Latisha, who has tossed out her abusive white husband, is an informal community leader who helps crystallize opinion and gives good advice.

Coyote, the trickster of Native American lore. He narrates a separate story interwoven with the main one, questioning the whites' creation story by telling it his own way. Coyote appears to Lionel once, as a funny yellow dog dancing outside the electronics store.

— *Emily Alward*

GREEN GROW THE LILACS

Author: Lynn Riggs (1899-1954)
First published: 1931
Genre: Drama
Locale: Indian Territory before it became Oklahoma
Time: 1900
Plot: Local color

Curly McClain, a footloose, ballad-singing cowboy. When he stops by Laurey's farm to ask her to a "play-party" and she refuses, he asks Aunt Eller to go with him, singing the title song about a rejected lover abandoning the green lilacs for the "red, white, and blue" of a soldier's life. When he notices the handyman Jeeter's unhealthy interest in Laurey, Curly warns Jeeter off by besting him in a gun duel. At the party, when Laurey turns to him for comfort after she has fired Jeeter, he proposes marriage. After Jeeter's accidental death while he is trying to kill Curly and Laurey, Curly is taken from his wedding celebration and held for trial, even though the crowd agrees that Jeeter provoked the fight with Curly that led to his death. Curly escapes jail for one night to go to Laurey and reassure her. He admits that as a cowboy he had few responsibilities, but his marriage to Laurey and the subsequent running of a farm will help him become a responsible citizen worthy of a new state.

Laurey Williams, a young farm owner romantic enough to dream about exotic adventures but reluctant to admit her love for Curly. Despite Curly's promise of a fancy surrey, Laurey refuses to attend the "play-party" with him, accepting Jeeter's offer instead, despite her fears that the handyman has set a neighbor's house on fire as revenge for being denied food. Although Aunt Eller prefers Curly as a suitor, she admits that the farm needs a handyman. When Jeeter accosts Laurey at the party, she fires him. When Laurey turns to Curly for comfort, they admit their mutual love, and Curly proposes marriage. After the wedding and disrupted gathering afterward, Laurey locks herself in her room and refuses to eat.

Aunt Eller Murphy, a fiftyish widowed aunt of Laurey who has acted as guardian for her orphaned niece. A practical woman, she encourages Curly's pursuit of Laurey. After the wedding and tragedy, when Curly is taken away to jail to await trial, Aunt Eller assures Laurey that he is innocent and reminds the girl that a woman's lot in a new land is a hard one by recounting her own life's tragedies. Worried that the marriage has not been consummated, Aunt Eller is delighted when Curly escapes custody temporarily to comfort Laurey. She cleverly defies the law so that the lovers can be together for one night, before Curly turns himself in to the federal marshal the next morning.

Jeeter Fry, the murderous farmhand who threatens Laurey. When Curly confronts Jeeter, Jeeter relates stories of the revenge taken by men on women who rejected them. In one of them, the woman is burned to death on a haystack. When Curly rejects the peddler's attempt to sell dirty pictures, Jeeter inquires about a deadly knife, a "frog-sticker." At the party, Jeeter's unwelcome advances frighten Laurey, and he vows revenge for being fired. After the wedding, the drunken Jeeter disrupts the festivities but is prevented from doing harm by the crowd. Later that evening, the men place Curly and Laurey on a haystack and toss them straw dolls to represent children. After distracting the crowd by setting the hay fields on fire, the enraged Jeeter tries to torch Curly and Laurey's haystack. When Curly jumps down to confront him, Jeeter pulls out the knife. During the ensuing fight, he falls on it and dies.

Ado Annie Carnes, a simple farmgirl with little intelligence and few physical attractions. She believes Laurey's tall tales and allows Laurey to experiment with face whitening to cover Ado Annie's freckles. When the attempt fails, she is flustered and angry, but she rides to the party with Laurey and Jeeter. Ado Annie sits sewing with Aunt Eller when Curly escapes from jail.

A peddler, a philandering Syrian who encourages Laurey's romantic dreams with his exotic merchandise. He provides Ado Annie with a ride to Laurey's farm, soothes Aunt Eller's temper, tempts Laurey with cosmetics, and sells Jeeter the deadly knife.

Old Man Peck, a neighboring farmer who gives the "play-party." He allows Curly to stay with Laurey for their wedding night rather than returning to jail after Aunt Eller argues that Curly and Laurey's love outweighs the law of the land.

—*Anne K. Kaler*

GREEN HENRY
(Der grüne Heinrich)

Author: Gottfried Keller (1819-1890)
First published: 1854-1855; revised 1879-1880
Genre: Novel
Locale: Switzerland and Bavaria
Time: Mid-nineteenth century
Plot: Love

Heinrich Lee (HIN-rihkh), a painter. Losing his father in early childhood and, later, finding it impossible to finish his studies, he sets out to fulfill his dreams of becoming a painter. Studying in Switzerland and then in Munich, and after many discouragements and hardships, he becomes a successful artist and a moderately rich man. He returns to his native town, is elected a county official, and, finally, writes the story of his life.

Frau Lee, Heinrich Lee's devoted, self-sacrificing mother. Having used her slender inheritance to further her son's career, she is all but forgotten by the successful Heinrich and dies just as he finally returns home.

Anna (AH-nah), Heinrich Lee's frail cousin and first love, who dies as a young girl.

Judith (YEW-diht), a widow who loves Heinrich Lee. When Heinrich tells her he wishes to be faithful to Anna's memory, she emigrates to America, but she returns in Heinrich's later years to be near him.

Roemer (REH-mehr), an unstable painter who is Heinrich Lee's teacher.

Ericson and

Lys (lees), painters who introduce Heinrich Lee to favorable contacts in the artistic world of Munich.

Schmalhoefer (SHMAHL-heh-fehr), a secondhand dealer

who sells some of the indigent Heinrich Lee's pictures and offers him a job as a flagpole painter. The young man accepts the work and so impresses his employer with his willingness that Schmalhoefer later leaves him a considerable sum of money in his will.

Count Dietrich zu W . . . berg (DEE-trihkh), the purchaser of Heinrich Lee's paintings and the sponsor of his successful exhibit.

Dorothea (doh-roh-TAY-ah), Count W . . . berg's adopted daughter, who is loved by Heinrich Lee. Doubting his love because he delays so long in speaking of it, she marries another.

THE GREEN HOUSE
(La casa verde)

Author: Mario Vargas Llosa (1936-)
First published: 1965
Genre: Novel
Locale: Piura and the Amazon jungle in Peru
Time: 1920-1960
Plot: Social realism

Don Anselmo (ahn-SEHL-moh), an imaginative individual, a harpist and founder of the original "Green House" in Piura. Along with several others, Anselmo provides residents of this barrio with a much needed sense of pride and self-esteem. He temporarily fills the community's need for a positive self-image. In the novel, the rise and fall of Anselmo and the Green House are paralleled. Even though he and the Green House ultimately are defeated, Anselmo attains heroic stature as a result of his courage, perseverance, and capacity for sacrifice.

The Sergeant, **Lituma** (lee-TEW-mah), a national policeman from Piura who is stationed near the jungle. The story of Lituma's confrontation with Chapiro Seminario, and the latter's death in a macho game of Russian roulette suggested by Lituma, provides a clear illustration of how group values, when put to the test, deprive the individual of the independence of judgment, response, and feeling that are necessary to achieve personal autonomy.

Bonifacia (boh-nee-FAH-see-ah), also called **Wildflower**, an Indian girl of mysterious origins who is taken from her home and reared in a convent. Her one outstanding physical characteristic is her green eyes. Expelled from the convent when she allows the other Indian girls to escape, she is ultimately forced into prostitution as a means of survival. Although largely deprived of her personal and cultural past at the mission, Bonifacia acquires no solid basis on which to fashion an identity or a position in society. Her fate illustrates the role of the church and the military in the conquest and "civilization" of Peru.

Fushía (few-SHEE-ah), a Japanese Brazilian contrabandist who deals in illegal rubber. As the novel's antihero, he embodies both good and evil; he is both victim and victimizer. During Fushía's month-long river voyage from his island to the leper colony of San Pueblo, he seeks answers to vital questions concerning his existence. Although many of his illusions are shattered on this trip, Fushía nevertheless clings to the belief that he can control his final destiny. Gradually and irrevocably, his own distorted view of life and the pressures of his hostile environment destroy him.

Aquilino (ah-kee-LEE-noh), Fushía's friend and boatman. Aquilino engages Fushía in numerous conversations on their river voyage, thereby eliciting the recapitulation of significant events from Fushía's past. Aquilino's primary function in the novel is to act as a moral and spiritual guide to Fushía. As he probes deeper and deeper into Fushía's troubled past, questioning motives and pronouncing ominous judgments, there is an omniscience about him that further emphasizes the mythic quality of Fushía's story. He takes a stoic position concerning Fushía's fate.

— *Genevieve Slomski*

THE GREEN MAN

Author: Kingsley Amis (1922-1995)
First published: 1969
Genre: Novel
Locale: Fareham, in Hertfordshire, and Cambridge
Time: Late 1960's
Plot: Ghost

Maurice Allington, the narrator, the fifty-three-year-old innkeeper of The Green Man in Hertfordshire. He was abandoned, three years earlier, by his first wife after twenty-two years of marriage. She took their ten-year-old daughter, Amy, with her. When the woman died in an automobile accident, however, he recovered custody. Since then, he has not been able to discover much common ground with Amy or to interest his second wife in taking over the role of mother. Moreover, this second marriage is not providing significantly more companionship than did the first. Maurice drinks to excess (more than a bottle of whiskey a day) and typically spends much of his time trying to figure out ways in which to avoid his wife. From the outset of the novel, he lusts after the wife of his physician; as soon as he succeeds in seducing her, he immediately begins plotting a sexual threesome involving his wife and this woman. To make matters worse, his eighty-year-old father, who lives with them, has just suffered a third stroke, and a series of mishaps threatens the operation of the inn. At this point, several apparitions appear, almost exclusively to Allington and apparently somehow related to his state of mind. There are three particular apparitions: a red-haired woman, supposedly murdered by her husband in the 1680's; Dr. Thomas Underhill, the alleged murderer of the woman and at least one other, whose spirit is still trying to work evil even after death; and The Green Man, composed of vegetation and capable of acting out his controller's will.

Joyce Allington, the second wife of Maurice. An attractive, willowy woman of roughly fifty, Joyce is not entirely committed to helping Maurice keep the books for the inn and rear his daughter. In fact, there is little interaction between the couple beyond their weekly sexual bouts, which hardly transcend the physical.

Amy Allington, Maurice's thirteen-year-old daughter. Withdrawn, preoccupied, and alienated like most early teenagers, Amy spends most of her time by herself, listening to mindless music and watching mindless television. She clearly needs and wants parental direction and love, and just as clearly she has little basis for communication with adults. Her isolation makes her vulnerable.

Diana Maybury, the wife of Jack, Maurice's physician. Almost a carbon copy of Joyce Allington, she is nevertheless pursued by Maurice, even though he is unimpressed with either her intellect or her character. She gives in readily, revealing in the process that she hates her husband and is looking for diversion.

Nick Allington, Maurice's twenty-four-year-old son, an assistant lecturer in French literature at a university in the Midlands. Nick is prompt to come to his father's assistance and speaks openly and frankly with him, but their relationship is not particularly close. Nick does understand both his father's use of alcohol to insulate himself and his sister's need of reaffirmation and support.

Lucy Allington, Nick's wife, a student in her mid-twenties. Maurice has, at the outset of the novel, seen little appealing in her, yet she is almost alone in taking his complaints and symptoms seriously. In fact, she is the only woman in the story with whom Maurice really converses; he learns companionship through her.

Dr. Thomas Underhill, the spirit of malice haunting The Green Man. Having discovered that his magic gives him power over others, he begins by using it to extort sexual favors from young girls, then progresses to conjuring up evil powers to destroy those who oppose him.

The Young Man, a final apparition who appears only near the end, when it begins to look as if Maurice alone can oppose the reemergence of Dr. Underhill. Apparently twenty-eight years old, fair, pale, and prosperous looking but otherwise undistinguished, his appearance is accompanied by a suspension of time, molecular motion, and even radiation. He claims in so many words to be God himself; the object of his visitation is to appoint Maurice as God's champion in the upcoming struggle with Underhill.

— *James L. Livingston*

GREEN MANSIONS

Author: W. H. Hudson (1841-1922)
First published: 1904
Genre: Novel
Locale: South American jungles
Time: The nineteenth century
Plot: Fantasy

Abel Guevez de Argensola (ah-BEHL geh-VEHS deh ahr-gehn-SOH-lah), a Venezuelan living in Georgetown, British Guiana. Uninterested in politics, sport, or commerce, he loves the world of nature and the spirit. As a youth he was involved in an abortive Caracas political conspiracy. Fleeing for his life, he disappeared into the Guayana wilderness and lived for some months among the Indians and with Nuflo and Rima. Loving Rima with an etherealized but passionate love, he (with Nuflo) accompanied her in a fruitless search for her mother's people. Maddened and grief-stricken upon learning of Rima's murder, he fled from Runi's village, returned after it was sacked by Managa, gathered Rima's ashes in an urn, and, half-dead, finally reached Georgetown, where he has since lived. Having loved and lost Rima, he understands the loneliness she felt when she longed for her mother's people.

Riolama (rree-oh-LAH-mah), or **Rima** (RREE-mah), a girl of the Venezuelan forest. Daughter of an unknown father and a mysterious young woman whose life Nuflo saved about seventeen years earlier, she has been brought up by the old man, who pretends that he is her grandfather. Slim, less than five feet tall, with delicately small hands and feet, she is like the wood nymphs of ancient legend or like the spirit of nature itself in its beautiful, mysterious aspects. Her abundant dark iridescent hair is cloudlike, her pale skin seems at times almost transparent, and her dark eyes are lustrous. In the forest, she is like a wild creature, but one that fears no harm and will permit no harm to other creatures; there, she utters a beautiful, bird-like language in a lovely, warbling voice. In Nuflo's lodge she is shy and reticent and speaks Spanish, in which she also converses with Abel. When occasionally angered, she reminds Abel of a beautiful wasp, as stinging words issue from her. After the trip to Riolama and the final realization that it was a vain illusion that she would find her mother's people, she confesses her love for Abel. Returning to Nuflo's lodge ahead of Nuflo and Abel, she is found in a tree by Runi's men and is burned to death.

Nuflo (NEW-floh), a white-bearded, brown-skinned old hunter with whom Rima lives. To avoid offending her, he sneaks away to kill forest animals and cook them for himself and his two foul-smelling dogs. A frequent critic of the state of the world, he superstitiously believes that Rima has supernatural powers that she might use to make things better, especially for an old man with many sins on his conscience. He is killed by Indians.

Runi (RREW-nee), a Guayana Indian chief, a friend and later an enemy of Abel.

Kua-kó (KEW-ah-KOH), nephew of Runi and friend of Abel, whom he teaches to use a blowpipe in the hope that he will kill Rima, for the Indians regard her as an evil spirit, a daughter of the Didi. After telling Abel of the burning of Rima, he pursues when Abel flees and is stabbed to death.

Cla-Cla (KLAH-klah), a talkative, wrinkled old woman, grandmother of Kua-kó.

Managa (mah-NAHN-gah), chief of an Indian tribe at enmity with Runi. Abel flees to Managa after killing Kua-kó and incites him to kill Runi and the murderers of Rima.

THE GREEN MOUNTAIN BOYS

Author: Daniel Pierce Thompson (1795-1868)
First published: 1839
Genre: Novel

Locale: Vermont
Time: 1775-1776
Plot: Historical

Captain Charles Warrington, a fictional disguise for the Vermont patriot Seth Warner, who is the protagonist of a homespun American novel that achieved widespread popularity. Owner of land in dispute between New York and New Hampshire, Warrington is an outlaw who sometimes travels as "Mr. Howard."

Lieutenant Selden later identified as **Edward Hendee**, Warrington's friend, who is in love with Jessy Reed.

Colonel Reed, who, after buying a land title in Albany, has expelled the settlers and fortified the region.

Jessy Reed, his daughter, who is captured at her father's fort by Selden. She eventually marries him.

Sergeant Donald McIntosh, who is in charge of the Reed fort's garrison.

Zilpah, Jessy Reed's half-Indian servant, who marries Neshobee.

Munroe, a New York sheriff in pursuit of Warrington.

Neshobee, a friendly Indian who brings Warrington a warning from Mrs. Story that a band of New Yorkers is planning an attack.

Ann Story, a widow who is resisting eviction from her farm. She has built an underground shelter for her family.

Jacob Sherwood, Munroe's guide and a Tory turncoat in the pay of New York. He loves Alma Hendee but does not win her.

Pete Jones, a Green Mountain Boy who captures and beats Sherwood.

Colonel Skene, with whose daughters Jessy Reed takes refuge.

Alma Hendee, whose family farms land on Lake Champlain. She marries Warrington.

Captain Hendee, her father, whose estate had been squandered by Sherwood's father.

Gilbert Hendee, the captain's brother, who is persuaded by Sherwood's father to will Jacob the estate if little Edward Hendee fails to reach maturity.

Ruth, Alma's maid, who marries Pete Jones in a quadruple wedding.

Bill Darrow, the partner of Sherwood, who, when dying, confesses to the kidnapping of Edward Hendee, and identifies Selden as the son of Captain Hendee.

Ethan Allen, the leader of the Green Mountain Boys. He sometimes travels as "Mr. Smith." He brings the news of Lexington and Concord to the Green Mountain Boys.

Squire Prouty, a York justice of the peace captured by the Green Mountain Boys.

Benedict Arnold, who helps capture Fort Ticonderoga.

THE GREEN PASTURES: A Fable

Author: Marc Connelly (1890-1980)
First published: 1929
Genre: Drama

Locale: Lower Louisiana and Heaven
Time: The 1920's and biblical times
Plot: Mythic

God, who is seen through the eyes of an elderly black preacher as the tallest and biggest of the angels. Dressed in evening clothes and speaking in a rich, bass voice in black dialect (which all the characters use), He participates in human activities such as attending fish fries and working in His office. He also makes human mistakes; for example, when in need of some "firmament" to season his boiled custard, He creates too much and wets the cherubs' wings, so He must pass a miracle to get rid of the excess "firmament." He creates Earth to drain off the excess and then creates Adam to farm and enjoy the earth. As an elderly minister's simple view of an Old Testament God, He interacts with the angels and humankind as a God of power, love, and wrath until, at the end of the play, He realizes that He must also be a God of mercy gained through suffering and must send Jesus to earth.

Gabriel, the second-in-command angel and God's principal assistant. He is young, big, beardless, and elaborately winged. He is the one to whom God talks about His frustrations, especially with humankind's sinfulness. Gabriel keeps his trumpet ready to blow whenever God commands. His practicality offsets the idealism and passion of God.

Moses, a shepherd and fugitive from Egypt, living in a cave in the mountains to escape prosecution for killing a man in Egypt. He is about forty years old but ages into an old man two scenes later. He dresses inconspicuously and stutters slightly until God cures this problem. After seeing a burning bush that is not consumed, Moses is told by God that it is a magic trick and that God will teach him to perform such tricks for Pharaoh as a means of coercing Pharaoh into freeing the Hebrew people. Moses requests that his brother Aaron be allowed to go with him; God agrees. They "trick" Pharaoh with plagues until he releases the Hebrews, whom Moses leads to the Promised Land. There he turns them over to Joshua, then dies and goes to Heaven.

Noah, a preacher, a basically good man to whom God appears, first as a fellow preacher, then revealing Himself to be God. Noah first appears in the dress of a preacher, then as a steamboat captain. He rules his family but obeys God, building an ark and taking aboard his family, two animals of each species, and one keg of liquor. When he brings the ark to a successful landing, he is forgiven by both God and his family for getting drunk.

Pharaoh, the ruler of Egypt, wearing a crown and garments like those worn by a high officer in a black lodge ritual. He is vindictive and hates the Hebrews, retaining magicians and wizards to devise means of pestering and intimidating them.

King of Babylon, the equivalent in Babylon to Pharaoh in Egypt, wearing a diamond tiara and an ermine cloak over evening clothes. Like Pharaoh, the king is a tyrant, enslaving the Jews and buying whatever favors he desires, including bribing the Hebrew High Priest to ask God's forgiveness for killing a Hebrew prophet.

Cain, a husky young black man, a field laborer who is discovered to have killed his brother. He takes God's advice to leave the country and find someone to marry and raise a family with, but his choice displeases God.

Cain's girl, who is wickedly pretty and flashily dressed. She is as large as Cain and lives in Nod Parrish. She flirts with Cain, declares herself to be Cain's girl, and takes him home with her.

Zeba, a rouged and very flashily dressed prostitute of about eighteen, the great granddaughter of Seth (the son of Adam), and the girlfriend of both Cain the Sixth and Flatfoot. She is flippant with God, lies to Cain the Sixth, and, appearing with Flatfoot to ridicule Noah for building the ark, incites the jealousy of Cain the Sixth. She represents the depths to which humankind has sunk since God created Adam.

Cain the Sixth, a stylishly dressed, egotistical young man with a quick temper who wears a "box" coat and other flashy garments. He is impudent and dangerous. He kills Flatfoot, whom he finds with Zeba. He appears with gamblers at Noah's ark and touts Noah as foolish. He represents the continuance of degradation from the first Cain.

Aaron, a field hand and brother of Moses. He is a little taller than Moses and slightly older. Like Moses, he appears as an old man two scenes later. As a younger man, he helps Moses play God's "tricks" on Pharaoh and lead the Hebrews to the Promised Land. As an old man entering Canaan, he is commissioned by Moses to care for the Ark of the Covenant.

Hezdrel, a Hebrew soldier in the end of Old Testament times. Appearing in part 2 of the play, he is played by the same actor who played Adam in part 1. Hezdrel is shown standing in the same position that Adam held when first discovered. He is engaged in battle with the Hebrews against the forces of Herod. Hezdrel tells God, who appears to him in the form of a preacher, that he fights unafraid because of his faith in the God of Hosea, a god of mercy. Hezdrel, like Hosea, knows mercy through suffering. This revelation leads to the climax and denouement of the play.

Adam, God's first human creation, a thirty-year-old man of medium height. He is muscular and wears the clothes of a field hand. He talks with God, accepts Eve as a wife, and is drawn to the tree of knowledge, from which God has forbidden him to eat.

Joshua, a scout for the Hebrews, a handsome man about thirty years old. He is assigned by Moses to lead the army into Canaan and to capture the city of Jericho.

Archangel, the principal angel next to Gabriel, older than the other angels, wearing a white beard, darker clothing, and larger wings. He is the head deacon angel, giving Sunday School cards and diplomas to the cherubs and telling the choir what and when to sing.

Noah's wife, an elderly black woman, simply and neatly dressed, representing the good woman: polite, hospitable, and a good wife and mother.

Shem,

Ham, and

Japheth, sons of Noah, obedient and loyal, who help Noah load and sail the ark.

Zipporah, the wife of Moses, somewhat younger than him, dressed inconspicuously. Like Noah's wife, she demonstrates a good relationship between husband and wife, and her conversation with Moses provides necessary expository information.

Flatfoot, a former drug pusher. He is tall, arrogant, and wicked looking, and he is a lover of Zeba. His killing elicits no remorse from the crowd around Noah's ark.

Prophet, a patriarchal, ragged figure who denounces the sins of the Babylonians and their king and of the Hebrews. Preaching repentance, he is killed on orders of the king.

High Priest, a fat voluptuary dressed in elaborate, brightly colored robes. He arrives at the Babylonian "nightclub" with a prostitute, is denounced by the Prophet, and takes a bribe from the king to "pray" for God's forgiveness for killing a Hebrew prophet.

Mr. Deshee, an elderly country preacher in Louisiana who teaches Bible lessons to Sunday School children in a black church. It is his interpretation of God and the Heaven and earth of the Old Testament that forms the play within the play. He introduces the play and provides exposition.

Eve, Adam's wife, twenty-six years old and very pretty. She is dressed like a country girl in a new, clean gingham dress. She appears primarily to complete Adam and imply the entrance of sin.

Head Magician, the henchman of Pharaoh who carries out Pharaoh's dirty work. He is a very old and villainous man, costumed in a robe covered with cabalistic and zodiacal signs.

Master of Ceremonies, the henchman of the king of Babylon who conducts the king's dirty work and runs a type of "nightclub" in Babylon.

— *Bettye Choate Kash*

GREENE'S GROATS-WORTH OF WITTE BOUGHT WITH A MILLION OF REPENTANCE

Author: Robert Greene (1558-1592)
First published: 1592
Genre: Short fiction

Locale: A fictional city resembling London
Time: Late sixteenth century
Plot: Satire

Roberto, the author's persona, a "scholar" educated at university. He is the son of a miserly father who takes great umbrage at his son's superior airs and disapproval of his profitable usury. His father, about to die, announces that he has willed everything to his younger son, Lucanio. Distraught, Roberto plots revenge. After his father's death, he sets up a meeting between Lucanio and a prostitute named Lamilia, knowing that his inexperienced brother will prove easy prey for her confidence schemes. She, however, turns on Roberto, rejecting his claims on a share of the booty. Demoralized and nearly destitute, he becomes a mere observer of his brother's ruination. At the prompting of a player-patron, he takes up a dissolute, bohemian life as a playwright, keeping company with society's scum, rebuffing his wife's efforts to reform him, and drinking and whoring his way to ill health and penury. He is left at the end with the groat that had been his sole inheritance.

Lucanio, Roberto's younger brother and his father's favorite. Although he shares his father's miserliness, he is putty in the hands of the conniving Lamilia. She soon tricks him out of his fortune, leaving him destitute. Roberto offers no solace but does use Lucanio as a "property" in "conny-catching" bunko schemes. Lucanio finally resorts to pimping, a job that even his brother finds degrading.

Gorinius, a usurer and father to Roberto and Lucanio. He is a hypocrite, appearing religious and upright but lacking in compassion for his debtors, driving many of them into exile. He is selfish and proud of his material success. He suffers from gout and an unspecified lingering disease that kills him. On his deathbed, he reveals that he has bestowed all of his money and property on Lucanio because the younger son shares his miserly love of gold. His philosophy is that wealth is a substitute for true character and has been formulated from reading Machiavelli. Gorinius disinherits Roberto because Roberto, university trained in liberal arts, does not value wealth. Gorinius bequeaths to him a single old groat that Gorinius had before beginning his climb to material success.

Lamilia, a shrewd and alluring courtesan who keeps a "hospital" in the unnamed city's suburbs. As planned by Roberto, she seduces Lucanio, feigning maidenly innocence. Through her allure and by cheating at cards and dice, she begins fleecing Lucanio of his inherited wealth. In the absence of Lucanio, she rejects Roberto's claim, as the affair's broker, to part of the money and exposes his scheming against Lucanio to the younger man, who forthwith disowns Roberto as his brother. Within two years, Lamilia reduces Lucanio to beggary.

Player, a wealthy, successful, and self-important actor who becomes Roberto's patron when he talks the destitute profligate into becoming a playwright.

The fox, who, in Lamilia's fable, is a resourceful villain who convinces a badger to entice a ewe to the badger's hole. The fox rips out the ewe's throat and sneaks away, leaving the badger to face the shepherd's dogs.

The badger, who, in Lamilia's fable, is the scapegoat in the fox's scheme. He seduces the ewe with a promise of perpetual amity between "devouring beasts" and the "harmless kind." He is used by the fox as an unwitting accomplice and is left to bear the mortal enmity of dogs.

The bride, who, in Roberto's tale, is a squire's daughter, fickle and proud. She is infatuated with her new husband but quickly disowns him when he is tricked into an assignation with Marian, his jilted girlfriend.

The bridegroom, who, in Roberto's tale, is a gullible farmer's son who, lacking trust in his wife's fidelity, proves foolish enough to be tricked out of her love before it can be consummated. His own unfaithfulness makes him suspicious enough to believe the gentleman's lies.

The gentleman, who, in Roberto's tale, is a former suitor of the bride. Amoral but resourceful, he outwits the bridegroom to win the squire's daughter by trickery.

Mother Gunby, who, in Roberto's tale, is a widow who devises the scheme used by the gentleman to trick the bridegroom. She proves adept at feigning injury over the seduction of her daughter.

Marian, who, in Roberto's tale, is Mother Gunby's daughter. Claiming that she was overcome by the bridegroom's "allurement," she goes along with the ruse to win back her former lover.

The ant, who, in a retelling of Aesop's fable, is a thrifty laborer working to store adequate food for winter.

The grasshopper, who, in the Aesop fable, is a profligate pleasure seeker who fails to prepare for winter and is rebuked by the ant.

GRENDEL

Author: John Gardner (1933-1982)
First published: 1971
Genre: Novel

Locale: The Scandinavian countryside
Time: Early Middle Ages
Plot: Fantasy

Grendel, a thinking monster and the narrator of this modernist retelling of the *Beowulf* legend. A dweller in an undersea cave, Grendel disregards the fearful protests of his mother and repeatedly ventures above into the world of humans. Merely curious at first, Grendel soon learns that humans are dangerous, thinking creatures, better eaten than trusted. He kills an occasional person and conducts periodic raids to amuse himself, but his uncertainty about human nature nags him. He vacillates between the brute existence he sees before him and the idealism humans spout even in the face of their barbaric acts. In search of an answer, he travels to see the Dragon, who insists that humankind's pretensions to meaning are pure illusion. When Grendel later discovers that adopting the Dragon's cynicism has charmed him and made him invulnerable to any weapon, the fierceness of his raids intensifies. Unfortunately, the "charm" isolates him still further from the human community that he plunders but secretly wishes to join, and it makes killing people a tedious and mechanical process, unlike the sporting event it had been when there were risks involved. Grendel's boredom and his disgust with human beings continue intermittently, as do his raids, until the Geat Hero arrives from another land to challenge him.

Grendel's mother, also a monster. Although still fierce in defending her son, Grendel's mother has grown fat, timid, and somewhat senile in her old age. When Grendel is trapped during his first encounter with humans, she rescues him and subsequently tries to dissuade him from leaving their cave to roam aboveground. Although Grendel obviously is attached to her and values her protection, he does not want to be limited to the crude and inarticulate existence that she offers.

Hrothgar (ROHTH-gahr), a minor king, ruler of the Scyldings, a group of Danish warriors. Noted for being an accomplished warrior in his youth, Hrothgar has assembled a loyal band of fighting men (thanes) to protect him and his wealth. He extracts payments from neighboring villages in exchange for protection from outside raids and uses his substantial resources to build Hart, a magnificent tribute hall. Grendel, knowing that Hrothgar's power and position rest on nothing more legitimate than bloodshed and intimidation, delights in waging a personal war against him, undermining both his power and his claim to a divinely ordained prosperity. Hrothgar is able to do nothing to stop Grendel's raids and can only watch as his thanes are killed and his power eroded.

The Shaper, a blind harpist who composes and sings poetry at Hrothgar's court. The Shaper arrives after Hrothgar has established his kingdom, and he proceeds to invent noble accounts of the creation of Hart and of the divine benevolence and intercession that made it possible. Half teary-eyed and half enraged, Grendel fluctuates between being seduced into hope by the Shaper's song and being sickened by its falseness and irony. He witnessed the real circumstances, calculated and brutal violence, that enabled Hrothgar to become a wealthy king. The Shaper enjoys his position not because he speaks the truth but because he tells people what they want to hear. Even on his deathbed, he proclaims visions that the Danes, nearly decimated by Grendel's raids and now vulnerable to attack by other clans, will be restored to their former greatness. Grendel savors the irony as the man dies in mid-sentence.

The Dragon, a huge, fire-breathing beast. Misanthropic and cynical, the Dragon reinforces Grendel's doubts about the Shaper and about human nature in general. He characterizes human beings as counters and theory makers who assemble random facts and ideological schemes that mean nothing, and he maintains that the Shaper merely "invents" significance that does not exist. Omniscient in his knowledge of the past, present, and future, the Dragon suffers from an unrelieved boredom, which he tries to mitigate by hoarding gold and jewels. He explains to Grendel that all existence is arbitrary and temporal and thus includes no absolute truths of meaning and no eternal reality. Grendel leaves, saturated with the Dragon's bleak message, and begins to vent his murderous rage whenever he hears people's songs of hope and self-satisfaction.

Unferth (UHN-furth), Hrothgar's best warrior. Still relatively young and a large, capable fighter, Unferth challenges Grendel during one of the monster's meadhall raids. Prone to theatrics, Unferth is not so much a threat as a comic annoyance. Rather than fight him, Grendel decides to pummel him with a barrage of apples, humiliating him in front of his peers. Unferth surprises Grendel by following him back to his cave, where, prepared to fight to the death, he makes a grandiose speech about the meaning and importance of heroism, then passes out from exhaustion. Grendel returns him unharmed and refuses to kill him in subsequent raids, adding to Unferth's shame and frustration.

Wealtheow (WEEL-thee-ow), Hrothgar's queen. A young redhead of unsurpassed beauty and charm, Wealtheow was a gift offered by her brother, a young king who planned to attack Hrothgar but who changed his mind when he saw the army Hrothgar had assembled. Wealtheow seems less than happy in her new life but accepts the duty graciously and becomes a civilizing force among Hrothgar's people. Like the Shaper's song, Wealtheow's beauty and grace "tease" Grendel out of his bitterness, but only temporarily.

The Geat Hero, **Beowulf**, a huge, well-muscled warrior who has come by ship to rid the Danes of Grendel. As cunning as he is powerful, Beowulf silences the boasts of Hrothgar's men and unnerves the watchful Grendel with his intensity and single-mindedness. Grendel is both afraid of him and eager for their encounter. When they meet, Beowulf uses his shrewdness and strength to make good on his promise to end Grendel's reign of terror.

— *William LaHay*

GRIEVER: An American Monkey King in China

Author: Gerald Vizenor (1934-)
First published: 1987
Genre: Novel
Locale: Tianjin and Beijing, China
Time: The 1980's
Plot: Experimental

Griever de Hocus, a fair-skinned mixed-blood from the White Earth Reservation. He merges through dreams with the trickster of Chinese mythology, the Monkey King. As the combination Native American trickster/Monkey King, he reimagines the world, invents a nonspatial, nontemporal existence, and attacks the hypocrisies of the Chinese as well as his fellow American exchange teachers and the human race in general. He is the son of a gypsy whose "Universal Hocus Crown" caravan stopped long enough at the reservation to sell plastic icons, miniature grails, and a book on health, and for the gypsy to engender Griever. Griever impregnates Hester Hua Dan and is very happy about it, even though he is fondling the breasts of Gingerie a few moments before he learns of Hester's (and their unborn daughter's) death. In true trickster form, he "liberates" prisoners and chickens, is safely smuggled out of danger, and winds up on Obo Island, a land where mythological people exist in real form. Ultimately, the trickster escapes the "terminal state" of China in an airplane bound for Macao. He is the central decentralizing character in an intensely political trickster novel.

China Browne, who also is from the White Earth Reservation. She goes to China to locate Griever. She finds Wu Chou, who shows her a scroll with pictures drawn on it. The pictures on the scroll tell the story of Griever de Hocus. A letter to China from Griever opens the book, and a letter to her closes it.

Matteo Ricci, a rooster, Griever's constant companion and the source of many puns about liberated cocks and their inability to "fit in."

Egas Zhang, the director of foreign affairs at the university where Griever works. He is the totally corrupt father of Hester Hua Dan.

Kangmei, the daughter of Egas Zhang's wife and Battle Wilson, an idealist, poet, and petroleum engineer from Oklahoma. She lives on Obo Island, smuggles Griever to safety, and, at the novel's end, flies off with Griever in an ultralight airplane.

Hester Hua Dan, Egas Zhang's daughter, who has an affair with Griever that results in pregnancy. Griever is ecstatic, but while he is delivering mooncakes to Lindbergh Wang during the Marxmass Carnival, Hester drowns herself to escape her father's anger.

Hannah Dustan, one of the eight American exchange teachers. She cannot tolerate mixed-bloods and believes that people who can be recognized for what they are, such as Jews and Chinese, will do better in the world. Mixed-bloods live in a no-man's land, as far as she is concerned. She is plagued by dreams in which immigrants and children (all mixed-bloods) haunt her, their hands covered with mold. She does not know that Griever is a mixed-blood; otherwise, she would not tolerate him.

Yaba Gezi, "the mute pigeon" of old Chinese mythology, who first appears in Griever's dream. He is rarely spoken of in China, but in Native American mythological style he is part of the dreaming and the waking worlds. Griever meets him in person on Obo Island.

Pigsie, who teaches his pigs to play basketball. He studied the operation of ultralight airplanes in the United States before his lewd and lustful behavior resulted in his fall to the position of colorful swine-herder. His name is taken from the Chinese "comic opera" stories of the mind monkey.

Sandie, who also has a name from the Chinese comic opera. Sandie is the Chinese government's official rat hunter. After studying at the University of California at Berkeley, Sandie became embroiled in politics and was demoted to the rank of rat hunter as a result.

— *N. Jacquelyn Kilpatrick*

GRINGOS

Author: Charles Portis (1933-)
First published: 1991
Genre: Novel
Locale: Mérida and elsewhere in Yucatán, Mexico
Time: Early 1990's, near Christmas
Plot: Adventure

Jimmy Burns, the protagonist and narrator. A native of Shreveport, Louisiana, this former Marine military policeman who saw combat in Korea is now an expatriate, residing at the Posada Fausto in Mérida, in the Yucatán peninsula. Jimmy earns his living as a free-lance teamster and as an occasional tracer of lost persons. At one time, he also was a dealer in illicit Mayan artifacts. He accepts what he believes to be a routine job hauling supplies to an archaeological site, but it leads him into a jungle quest for two missing persons and a confrontation with the Jumping Jacks, a gang of dangerous hippies.

Refugio Bautista Osorio, Jimmy's stalwart friend and Mexican counterpart, a jack-of-all-trades. Refugio teams with Jimmy in his search for the mystical City of Dawn, a search to which the middle third of the novel is devoted. He fights bravely, and lethally, at Jimmy's side in the climactic battle against the Jumping Jacks. Thereafter, he dates all occurrences as either before or after the night he and his gringo friend killed the "pagans."

Rudy Kurle, an investigator of extraterrestrial visitations. He spouts pseudoscientific babble about landings of flying saucers around the world and believes the City of Dawn to be a landing site for visitors from outer space. He takes voluminous notes, which he guards jealously. When he wanders off down the river and disappears, he becomes one of the missing persons Jimmy Burns must find.

Louise Kurle, supposedly Rudy's wife and assistant, a helpful young woman with a degree in human dynamics. She is a social worker without portfolio; it is simply her nature to help everyone. Louise eventually reveals that she is Rudy's sister, not his wife. The subterfuge is a device to avoid unwanted advances from the gringos of Mérida. She helps marriage-shy Jimmy to overcome his fears, and they are married by the end of the novel.

Dan, the leader of the Jumping Jacks, an aging biker and white supremacist. He is burly, bearded, and dressed "like a wrestling act" whose costume has "not quite worked out." He and his gang seek a mystical leader known as El Mago in the City of Dawn. On the way south, he has picked up a female runaway called Red and kidnapped a Mexican boy. He and his two lieutenants—toughs with shaved heads and vacant eyes—eventually are shot to death by Jimmy and Refugio while atop a Mayan temple.

Doc Richard Flandin, a self-styled expert on Mayan culture. He affects Frenchness but grew up in Los Angeles. For forty years, he has been working on his mammoth study of Meso-American civilization, and he takes a perverse delight in the neglect with which academic Mayanists treat his work and theories. Early in the novel, he announces that he is dying of prostate cancer but, after acquiring a young female admirer, he seems no longer to have any inclination to die, or even to be ill.

Alma Kobold, the invalid widow of a talented but neglected photographer of Mayan temples. The bitter, wheelchair-ridden, chain-smoking Frau Kobold also resides at the Posada Fausto. Despite—or, perhaps, because of—Jimmy's many kindnesses to her, she has for many years been sending him anonymous hate letters. She is the cause of the debacle at the City of Dawn, because she wrote an anonymous letter to a flying-saucer newsletter prophesying the appearance of El Mago at Likín (the City of Dawn), a hilltop ruin across the river in Guatemala that she and her husband had photographed many years earlier.

Red, a young girl traveling with the Jumping Jacks. She turns out to be **LaJoye Mishell Teeter** of Perry, Florida, a runaway for whose return a reward of two thousand dollars has been offered. After the Jumping Jacks gang is broken up, LaJoye—characterized by Jimmy as a girl who too easily gets into cars with strangers—is returned to her father.

Beany Girl, another Jumping Jack. She is a tall, slovenly woman who horrifies Jimmy by urinating while in his sight only moments after they meet. He meets her again much later; she is cleaned up, wearing makeup, and using the name **Freda**. She has become the live-in girlfriend of one of his old temple-robbing colleagues. Gallantly, Jimmy does not expose her.

— *Patrick Adcock*

THE GROUP

Author: Mary McCarthy (1912-1989)
First published: 1963
Genre: Novel
Locale: New York City
Time: 1933-1940
Plot: Social

Catherine (Kay) Leiland Strong, of Salt Lake City, an outsider yet the generally acknowledged leader of a group of eight recent graduates of Vassar, class of 1933. During their senior year, the girls shared a coveted suite in South Tower. Although not entirely compatible or equally fond of one another, they developed a close-knit coterie, somewhat dominated by the strong will of Kay, who often shocked them with her audacious ideas, adventurous spirit, uninhibited language, and unconventional behavior. Kay is the first to announce her engagement to be married, to Harald Petersen, a stage manager and aspiring playwright. By some of the group, Kay is suspected of having married Harald out of ambition, as she developed an interest in the theater while at Vassar. The couple live in an impoverished but hopeful state while Harald struggles to establish himself in the theater world and Kay works at Macy's. Harald is unfaithful to her without her knowledge, does not achieve outstanding success as a playwright (no one wants to produce his plays), and becomes a small-time gambler. They quarrel constantly. Shortly before the fifth reunion of the class of 1933, Kay is rumored to be on the verge of both a divorce and a breakdown. She is hospitalized for a while, then goes home to Salt Lake City to live with her parents, divorces Harald, and returns to live alone in New York. By this time, the members of the group have not been in touch with Kay for several years. They gather to arrange a proper funeral for her, dead at the age of twenty-nine after a fall (or leap) from the twentieth floor of the Vassar Club.

Dorothy (Dottie) Renfrew, a member of the group, from Boston. After graduation, Dottie spends a few months in New York, learning about sex. Despite her religious scruples, naïveté, and close relationship with her mother, Dottie deliberately loses her virginity to Dick Brown, a recently divorced painter who lives across the hall from Kay and Harald. Dottie immediately falls in love with Dick, who has forbidden her to do so but is quite willing to continue having sex with her if she will get a diaphragm. She undergoes a painful and humiliating ordeal in obtaining one after arranging to meet Dick later at a bench in Washington Square, but he never appears. The next day, she returns to Boston. Sent by her parents to Arizona for her health, she becomes engaged there to a wealthy mine owner named Brook Latham, an older man and a widower. She admits to her mother that she still loves Dick Brown, and Mrs. Renfrew sympathetically urges her to see Dick once more and to postpone the wedding. Dottie refuses and goes to live in Arizona. She does not return to New York for Kay's funeral.

Helena Davison, a Clevelander and Kay's former roommate. Her parents are very wealthy but plain-living and self-educated. After graduation, Helena plans to teach in a private nursery school, but first she travels to Europe. On her return, she does not look for a job because her father believes that by taking one she would deprive a woman who needs it much more. Helena becomes an art student. She has a droll sense of humor and is well versed in modern literature, music, and art; she is the most accomplished member of the group in many fields. Living in Cleveland, she is not closely connected to any member of the group, but as class correspondent for the *Alumnae Magazine*, she does occasionally see her friends and reports on their activities in a trite, coy style that is a parody of that kind of writing. She imagines writing such a piece when she attends a party to celebrate Harald's sale to a producer of an option on his play. There she discovers, in the kitchen, Harald and Norine Schmittlap Black in a passionate embrace. Norine was a classmate but not a member of the group. Feeling pity and embarrassment for Kay, Helena does not reveal to anyone what she has seen. The next day, Norine asks Helena to visit her; Helena learns of Norine's unhappy marriage to Putnam Blake, who she says is impotent, thus attempting to justify the fact that she and Harald have been lovers for a long while. To the surprise of both women, Helena speaks frankly and gruffly to Norine, who thanks her for telling the truth about her faulty thinking and disgraceful style of life.

Elizabeth (Libby) MacAusland, another member of the group, from Pittsfield, Massachusetts. After graduation, Libby lives in an elegant New York apartment for which her parents pay the rent while she tries hard to find a job in publishing. In the two years that follow, Libby reads manuscripts, reviews books, writes translations, and thinks about writing a novel. She also leads an active social life with several contemporaries in the popular pursuits of the time: skiing, ice skating, picnicking, and attending the theater, operas, and concerts. She persists in her efforts to find steady work in publishing, and at last Gus LeRoy, an editor for whom she has done occasional work, arranges a job for her with a literary agent.

Polly Andrews, a member of the group from Stockbridge, Massachusetts, where her eccentric family, impoverished by the stock market crash, still live on a farm that they managed to keep. Three years after graduation, Polly works as a technician at Cornell Medical Center and lives in a one-room apartment on Tenth Street. A fair, pale girl, Polly has a sympathetic nature that attracts all sorts of people in need of help. She advises the iceman on filing his income tax return, for example, and assists Libby in giving a party, at which she meets Libby's editor, Gus LeRoy. An affair between them ensues and lasts for almost a year. Polly is troubled by Gus's longtime analysis and inability to divorce his wife, from whom he has been separated for some time. Finally, Gus decides to go back to his wife, just as Polly's parents announce that they are getting divorced, and Polly's father comes to New York to live with her. They remodel the top-floor rooms of Polly's lodging house and turn them into a delightful apartment at considerable expense. Mr. Andrews has a serious character flaw: his extravagance and complete disregard of their present slender means. One day, Polly's friend, Jim Ridgeley, a psychiatrist, discovers her giving blood for money, and the whole story of Polly's life up to this point comes out. They fall in love, become engaged, and are married secretly and privately. It is Polly who finds Kay in the hospital after Harald's attack on her. Until Kay's release, Polly spends as much time as she can with her, in her usual compassionate and sympathetic manner, and they have long conversations about Kay's life. Polly never sees Kay again after she leaves the hospital.

Mary "Pokey" Prothero, a New York society girl of limited intelligence, like the rest of her family, who take pride in this trait as a sign of good breeding. Pokey does not advance the action of the novel, but her cheerful, good-natured snobbery serves to bring out that particular characteristic in some of the members of the group. She surprises everyone by learning to fly and going to Cornell to study veterinary medicine, turning out to be not so dim-witted after all. Eventually, she marries a Princeton man and has twins. Pokey's misfortune was having been born rich, but she makes the most of this disadvantage.

Priss Hartshorn, who is known as the group grind and is engaged to Sloan Crockett, a young pediatrician. Priss is a liberal because she comes from an Oyster Bay, New York, family that has always subscribed to liberal principles. She is married in the September following Kay's June wedding, but only four of the group are able to attend. She has three miscarriages before Stephen is born. Priss's story is one of endless conversations with her mother, her friends, and her husband about breast-feeding, toilet training, and other such matters. Priss is an insecure and uncertain mother, largely because she is dominated by the advice-givers and reluctant to assert her own common sense. Toward the end of the novel, Priss meets Norine Schmittlap, who has divorced Putnam Blake and married Freddie Rogers, a banker. After chatting in Central Park for a while, Priss accepts Norine's invitation to have lunch at her brownstone, which is being completely and expensively renovated. Norine's notions of child care are in total contrast to Priss's anxious ideas; the former is completely permissive and full of psychological jargon, not only about bringing up children and about comparative religion (Freddie is a Jew whose entire family has converted to Episcopalianism), but also about Kay, whom they have not seen in years. Priss takes care to avoid Norine after this brief, unpleasant reunion. Priss and Norine do not meet again until Kay's funeral.

Elinor "Lakey" Eastlake, of Lake Forest, Chicago. Beautiful, intellectual, and wealthy, Lakey usually is taciturn, but on some occasions she is the most critical and outspoken of the group. She is the only one who recognizes the hypocrisy of the others at Kay's embarrassing and humiliating wedding. As sophomores, Kay and Lakey had been very close friends, but Lakey believes that Kay worked her way into the group for social prestige. Lakey spends most of her time abroad, but she returns shortly before Kay dies, accompanied by the ferociously suspicious Baronesse d'Estienne (Maria), with whom, the members of the group gradually realize, she has a lesbian relationship, much to their dismay and disapproval. The baroness accepts the group on occasions when husbands will be present; otherwise, she will have nothing to do with them. It is only Kay, however, divorced and living at the Vassar Club, of whom the baroness seems to be jealous and mistrustful. Later, at Kay's funeral, Harald appears and asks Lakey for a ride to the cemetery in her two-seater. The baroness excuses herself and Harald takes the wheel. Driving very fast, stopping at a bar for a drink or two, he discusses Lakey's feelings (about which he speculates) and his own about each member of the group, when they were in college and later. Harald's coarse, wild talk disgusts Lakey. At his final insult, concerning her relationship with Kay—as he suspects it was but as it in no way is acknowledged by Lakey—he demands to be let out of the car. The novel ends as Lakey follows the cortege and sees him through her rearview mirror, thumbing a ride back to New York.

— Natalie Harper

GROUP PORTRAIT WITH LADY
(Gruppenbild mit Dame)

Author: Heinrich Böll (1917-1985)
First published: 1971
Genre: Novel

Locale: Rhineland, Germany
Time: 1922-1970
Plot: Social realism

Leni Gruyten Pfeiffer (GREW-tehn PFI-fehr), a survivor and mystic. A classic Germanic blond, she is forty-eight years old at the time of the book's main action. She has lived in the same apartment building all her life, in the one piece of property left after a wartime scandal erased her family's wealth. She lives almost without resources, and her parents have been dead for years; she has few relatives except for her son Lev, who is currently in jail. She reacts to these troubles with serene indifference. Leni combines a sensual approach to life (fascination with bodily organs, as well as excretory functions) with Catholic mysticism. Her highly sensual nature transforms even the act of eating breakfast rolls into an erotic experience, yet she believes herself to be on intimate terms with the Virgin Mary (whom she sees nightly on her television screen). These mystical tendencies are sharpened in her teens by her close relationship with Sister Rahel. Through all of her troubles, Leni continues to paint her picture and fight off creditors, a lonely but serene woman, giving and taking love. When eviction is threatened, an impromptu committee of her friends pools forces to keep her where she is. This effort comes just in time, as she has a new love, a Turkish worker whose baby she is going to bear.

Sister Rahel (RAH-hehl), also called **Haruspica** (hah-REW-spih-kah), a nun in Leni's boarding school. A brilliant woman of Jewish origin, Sister Rahel converted to Catholicism after a career as a biologist, physician, and philosopher. She is demoted to a combination cleaning woman and nurse after her teaching permit is suspended as a result of suspicions about her "mystical materialism." In this role, she has earned her reputation as "excremental mystic" because of her skill at divining the health of boarding school girls from inspections of their stool. She teaches the ability to Leni, who becomes her disciple in this and other lessons on the miraculous nature of the body. Because of nervousness about Sister Rahel's racial identity, the school finally moves her to a tiny attic closet, where she eventually dies, perhaps starved to death. Buried on cloister grounds without a gravestone, she returns to haunt the church that rejected her. Her ongoing miracle of winter-blooming roses leads to calls for her canonization.

Boris Lvovich Koltovsky (LVOH-vihch kohl-TOHV-skee), a Russian prisoner of war, the father of Leni's child, Lev. Thin and bespectacled, unworldly, and naïve, he is an introspective youth who speaks fluent German and is fond of reading the work of German poets, even though his father is Russian. (He was a Soviet trade emissary in Berlin.) A graduate highway engineer, he is captured while building roads for the Russians. He is spared the grim fate awaiting Russian war prisoners by the intervention of a high-ranking German who has him sent to work in Pelzer's wreath factory. There, he meets and falls in love with Leni. The end of the war brings little opportunity for freedom. Allied soldiers catch him with forged German papers and send him to work in French mines, where he dies in a mining accident.

Hubert Gruyten, Leni and Heinrich's father, a leading German industrialist during the war. He is a man fascinated by power for its own sake, a gambler for whom the game is more important than its rewards. Negligible as an architect, he is a genius as an organizer, finding a role as a construction manager and strategist on a vast scale. Even so, before the war his contracting business seems headed for bankruptcy, but in 1933 he begins to smell concrete (lots of it) in the Reich's future. Having bought up the best experts on fortifications, he makes enormous money with the Siegried Line. Shortly after the beginning of the war, his son Heinrich's execution causes him to lose interest in his business. Soon a self-destructive urge produces his "notebook enterprise," a phony construction firm that he sets up with rosters of fictional Russian workers. Its discovery results in the "Dead Souls" scandal. In the aftermath, he barely escapes with his life. His sentence of hard labor takes all drive from him, even after he is freed at the war's end. Always a brooder, he can no longer rise above day work as a plasterer and wrecker. In this role, he dies when he falls off a beam and is impaled.

Heinrich Gruyten (HIN-rihkh), Leni's brother. Constantly in boarding schools or on vacations around Europe until the war starts, Heinrich is a lovable but unrealistic idealist, an embodiment of Western culture with keen interests in architecture, music, and the classics. He is fit to become almost anything except a soldier. Although his father has the power to keep him out of the army, Heinrich insists on being drafted. Within months, he and his cousin Erhard undertake a fatal adventure, going absent without leave to Denmark and attempting to sell an antiaircraft cannon. The action seems intended as a grim parody of his father's success in the war industry. Heinrich dies an idealist martyr's death, with his last words before the firing squad a pungent curse on Germany that perhaps aims at opening his father's eyes to the evils of aiding the war machine.

Walter Pelzer (VAHL-tehr PEHL-tsehr), a former Nazi, Leni's employer during the war. Always an opportunist, by the time of the war Pelzer has built up large real estate holdings by investing money from gold teeth and other effects of German and American soldiers killed in World War I. He quits the Storm Troopers to run the flower nursery and wreathmaking workshop inherited from his father. Pelzer, who thinks of himself as a decent man, remains puzzled by his failure to convince others that he is not a monster.

— *Paul Kistel*

GROWTH OF THE SOIL
(Markens grøde)

Author: Knut Hamsun (Knut Pedersen, 1859-1952)
First published: 1917
Genre: Novel
Locale: Norway
Time: Late nineteenth century
Plot: Social realism

Isak, a sturdy Norwegian peasant, the rough-hewn, monumental hero of the novel. Starting out on his own, he clears some isolated forest land and builds a sod hut. He sends out word by way of some Lapps that he is looking for a woman, and eventually a robust, harelipped woman comes to live with him. Together they acquire livestock, better living quarters, sufficient crops, and a happy life blessed with four children. Then she is sent to jail for killing her newborn harelipped baby, and Isak is unhappily forced to live without her for five years. After her release, he is forced to make some adjustments to her new ideas, but things tend to go on as productively as before. He sells some ore-bearing property; he builds a sawmill and a grain mill; he buys farming machinery; his children, for the most part, thrive; and he is made a Margrave—all the result of his fidelity to the soil and a fruitful way of life.

Inger, Isak's hardy, loving, spirited wife. She admires her husband a great deal and lives contentedly with him, bearing his children and helping with the work. A rather primitive person but a woman of deep feeling, she gains some refinement in prison and has an operation that mends her harelip. After her return to Isak, she finds that their coarse way of life is hard on her, but because their relationship is based on mutual love and respect, they continue to live and prosper together.

Eleseus, Isak and Inger's first child, a relatively weak man who becomes a village clerk. After an abortive romance, he goes from job to job, always with a taste for luxury and a penchant for failure. In the end, he leaves for America.

Sivert, the second child, a high-spirited, active boy. He takes naturally to the rough pioneering life of his parents and at last is fit to take his father's place.

Leopoldine, the third child, a girl born in prison. She grows up on the farm and becomes an attractive, marriageable young woman.

Rebecca, the last child, born in Inger and Isak's middle age, a likable, affectionate little girl.

Oline, a relative of Inger, a malicious and thieving old woman. Her gossip leads to Inger's arrest for child murder; because Isak has no one else to help him, she is given the management of the household while Inger is in jail. An expert on domestic intrigue, she steals and lies. Later, her gossip leads to the arrest of another woman on the same charge. She dies when she is no longer wanted by anyone.

Geissler, a good friend of Isak and Inger, a mysterious, powerful man with a deep respect for men of sense and worth. He manages the sale of Isak's mining property, secures a pardon for Inger, helps Isak irrigate his land, and always turns up to offer assistance. A lonely person, he has no real roots of his own.

Axel Ström, Isak's nearest neighbor, a hardworking and sensible man who nevertheless has hard luck. After Barbro, his servant, murders her child by him and goes away to Bergen, Oline saves his life and forces him to take her on as his housekeeper. Finally Barbro, whom he really cares for, comes back, and they marry.

Barbro, Axel Ström's servant, a shallow, frivolous woman who dislikes responsibility. Arrested for child murder, she is acquitted and placed with Fru Heyerdahl, the wife of the sheriff's officer. After a time, Barbro decides that life with Axel will be better than her present position.

Brede Olsen, Barbro's father, a shiftless man unable to manage his jobs, his farm, or his boardinghouse.

Aronson, a well-to-do shopkeeper whose store fails when the mines close down. He buys it back when the mines reopen.

Os-Anders, a Lapp tramp who spreads Oline's rumors.

Heyerdahl, a rather feckless man who takes over Geissler's job as sheriff's officer when he is fired.

Fru Heyerdahl, his outspoken wife; she defends Barbro at her trial and then tries to take her in hand.

Gustaf, a light-hearted miner with whom Inger has a slight romance in her middle age.

Uncle Sivert, Inger's supposedly rich uncle; he has almost nothing to leave to anyone when he dies.

Jensine, Inger's maid, a girl to whom Sivert takes a liking.

GUARD OF HONOR

Author: James Gould Cozzens (1903-1978)
First published: 1948
Genre: Novel
Locale: An Air Force base in Florida
Time: Three days during World War II
Plot: Psychological realism

Major General Ira N. (Bus) Beal, commanding general of Ocanara Air Force Base. Brooding unhappily over troubles of his own, he appears unaware of the seriousness of certain tensions that have developed on the huge base until an accident occurs during a parachute jump. General Beal immediately arouses himself from his melancholy and directs rescue operations with all his old skill and resourcefulness.

Colonel Norman Ross, General Beal's air inspector and resourceful assistant in the complicated running of huge Ocanara Air Force Base.

Lieutenant Willis, a black pilot who violates the right of way and nearly collides with a plane piloted by General Beal. He is struck and hospitalized by Lieutenant Colonel Benny Carricker.

Lieutenant Colonel Benny Carricker, General Beal's copilot, who strikes and hospitalizes Lieutenant Willis, thus triggering a series of problems and tensions, including a near riot, at Ocanara Air Force Base.

Brigadier General Nichols, assistant to the commanding general of the Air Force. A sympathetic and tolerant man, he understands the problems of Ocanara Air Force Base at a glance.

Mr. Willis, Lieutenant Willis' father.

Sal Beal, General Beal's wife.

Cora Ross, Colonel Ross' wife.

Lieutenant Edsell, a writer assigned to Special Projects.

Lieutenant Lippa, a WAC in love with Lieutenant Edsell.

Captain Nathaniel Hicks, an officer in Special Projects.

Second Lieutenant Amanda Turck, a WAC.

Colonel Mowbray, an officer on Ocanara Air Force Base.

Chief Warrant Officer Botwinick, Colonel Mowbray's assistant.

THE GUARDIAN OF THE WORD
(La Maître de la parole)

Author: Camara Laye (1928-1980)
First published: 1978
Genre: Novel
Locale: Ancient West Africa
Time: The thirteenth century
Plot: Adventure

Sundiata, a great warrior, brave and resolute but humane. Sundiata's life follows a pattern common to mythic heroes in many cultures, African and otherwise: the auguries at birth (in this case, a violent storm), an inauspicious youth (he is unable to walk until the age of ten), exile from his homeland (to escape jealous relatives), many tests of bravery and manhood, encounters with supernatural persons and events, and an eventual triumphal return to his homeland. In addition to having courage and prowess, Sundiata is clever and resourceful, an able military tactician and leader of men, and lucky. Like all national heroes, despite the formidable odds against him, Sundiata seems destined to triumph from the outset. This "lucky" or "destined" quality imparts to Sundiata an almost supernatural or godlike aura, also characteristic of the mythic hero. At the same time, he is warm, humane, loyal, and loving, and he elicits these qualities from others.

Babu Condé (kohn-DAY), the narrator, a griot (traditional storyteller). Not an active participant in the story that he tells, Babu is nevertheless its most important character, perhaps because his method of telling and attitude toward his materials are crucial to the reader's apprehension of these materials. Babu narrates from a religious perspective (Islamic) about an ancient people who had not yet embraced that religion, although they were on the verge of doing so. More important, he narrates from a modern perspective, discussing his characters in a psychological depth that would have been unfamiliar to Sundiata's contemporaries and describing certain practices with a modern frankness. Still, it is obvious that Babu addresses his subject not only with respect but also with reverence. Most evident of all is the griot's love of storytelling itself, of the joys of language. It is not mere coincidence that the title of the work refers not to a participant in the action but to Babu, who is indeed the "guardian of the word."

Sumaoro (sew-MOW-roh), a tyrant. Although both he and Sundiata desire to rule, Sumaoro is the young warrior's opposite in almost every other respect. Sumaoro is arrogant, brutal, cruel, and venal. He achieves his ends through force and terror, and he takes great delight in abusing his power. Although there is an almost supernatural quality about him—he is invulnerable to all but one rather strange weapon, the identity of which he guards carefully—the reader believes that he is destined to fail, just as surely as Sundiata is destined to triumph. His fall comes about through his venality, so the climax truly can be said to be a triumph of good over evil.

Sogolon Condé, Sundiata's mother. Sogolon is ugly and a hunchback, yet still she manages to bewitch the king into marrying her. "Bewitch" is the proper term, for Sogolon possesses the power to cast spells, which she does frequently over the course of the work. Rather than being an evil temptress, however, Sogolon appears more the frightened, confused child during her courtship, wedding, and torturously long honeymoon, long because the king is unable to consummate his marriage. Of the two parents, it is Sogolon who has the greater influence on her son and on the plot of the story.

Maghan Kön Fatta, Sundiata's father, king of the Manden. Maghan Kön Fatta is a great hero himself, but his major contribution to the tale of Sundiata is to die, leaving the field of battle to his two wives, Sogolon and Fatumata Béreté.

Fatumata Béreté (beh-reh-TAY), Maghan Kön Fatta's first wife. Fatumata is the stock older wife of African literature. Suspicious, spiteful, jealous, and shrewish, she gains her way by treachery and is never to be trusted. It is she who sends Sogolon fleeing from her homeland, with Sundiata in tow, thus setting events on their course.

— Dennis Vannatta

GUERRILLAS

Author: V. S. Naipaul (1932-)
First published: 1975
Genre: Novel
Locale: An unnamed Caribbean island
Time: The 1970's
Plot: Satire

James (Jimmy Ahmed) Leung, a half-Chinese leader of a black power agricultural commune. Physically neat and compact, with a magnetic personality, he was a celebrated black activist in England, deported for rape and indecent assault. Feeling himself loveless, rejected, and lost, he dreams of being seen as a famous and controversial savior of the common people. Bisexual, with a confusion of passions, hates, and paranoid delusions, he has a philosophy and program that are both ill-formed and clothed in empty rhetoric; he is, nevertheless, a threat to the island establishment, which attempts to placate him with token support. After the police kill a former follower, he attempts to lead a popular uprising, which is put down by the authorities. Having constructed an impressive but bogus public persona, he takes refuge in a pathological fantasy life that, when it spills over into reality, results in destruction, rape, and murder.

Peter Roche, a white South African doing public relations work for an old island company once engaged in the slave trade. Arrested, tortured, tried, and imprisoned in South Africa as a pro-black saboteur, he has published an autobiography. That book results in notice of him and a death threat in England, as well as bringing him a mistress (Jane), a job, and an ambivalent reception on the island. A small, ordinary looking, sad-faced man of forty-five, a rootless refugee who has lost the idealistic vision and optimism that prompted his earlier actions, he finds himself passive and without function. Willing to make compromises on many levels, he tries to support the commune despite his awareness of Jimmy's elaborate pose and instability. Realizing that Jane has been killed, Roche seeks to protect himself by hiding evidence of her fate on the island before fleeing himself.

Jane, Roche's English mistress. Attentive to her clothes and pale complexion, at twenty-nine years of age she is divorced. After many disappointing affairs (including the one with Roche), she is always watching for a man who will give meaning to her life. Lacking commitment or convictions of her own, she mouths the ideas and phrases of others without regard to coherence, contradiction, or the sensitivities of her audience. Affecting an attitude of being the victim, perpetually irritated and harassed, she is secure in her sense of class privilege and ability to leave situations that might prove unpleasant. Typically and irresponsibly disregarding the consequences of her actions, she embarks on a sexual adventure with Jimmy. Having left her escape until too late, she eventually is raped and murdered.

Meredith Herbert, a black solicitor, radio broadcaster, and sometime government minister. He is a friend of Roche. Tough, cynical, and ambitious, he feels contempt for Jimmy, a former schoolmate, but recognizes his dangerous potential. In turn friendly, secretive, hostile, and manipulative, he reveals some of his class, race, and political antagonisms in a public attack on Roche.

Harry de Tunja, an affluent local businessman and a friend of Roche and Jane. Middle-aged, genial, asthmatic, and from an old Jewish family, he has been deserted by his wife. He seems firmly rooted on the island but feels threatened and has made contingency plans to live in Canada.

Bryant, a young man at the commune and Jimmy's homosexual lover. Thin, with very black skin and a twisted and deformed face, he wears his hair in pigtails to show his aggression. Abandoned as a child, he is insecure, aimless, fearful, and highly emotional. Following Jimmy's order, he chops Jane to death with his cutlass.

Mrs. Grandlieu, an elderly member of the brown-skinned planter elite. She gives cocktail parties and dinners for important people and uses low-class forms of the local idiom to remind prominent black people of their place.

Adela, Roche's live-in maid. A plump, young, healthy devotee of an American faith-healing evangelist, she sullenly makes known her disapproval of Roche and Jane's alcohol consumption and unmarried cohabitation.

Knolly Stephens, a gang leader whose death precipitates a riot. An inspiration to other boys at the commune, he returns to the city and is shot by the police.

— Douglas Rollins

A GUEST FOR THE NIGHT
(Oreach nata lalun)

Author: Shmuel Yosef Agnon (Shmuel Yosef Czaczkes, 1888-1970)
First published: 1939
Genre: Novel
Locale: Eastern Galicia and Palestine
Time: Late nineteenth and early twentieth centuries
Plot: Philosophical

The Guest, the narrator of the story, a forty-year-old writer. He returns to the town of his birth, after the destruction of his home in Israel, in an effort to put together the fragmented pieces of his life and his religious faith. He finds the town ruined by continuous pogroms that have caused many to flee and by extreme poverty among those who remained. He undertakes the responsibility of heading the Beit Midrash (the house of study) and finds in that self-imposed duty a reconnection with the Almighty and joy in life. He is both generous and stingy, gregarious and solitary, responsible and lazy. At the end of the novel, he prepares to reunite with his wife and children and return to Israel.

Daniel Bach, a skeptic whose personal misfortunes have destroyed his faith that the Almighty is concerned with the suffering of his people. While he served in the army, his family moved from place to place seeking sustenance, and although he returned from the war uninjured, he soon lost one leg trying to board a moving train. In spite of the opposition of their religious beliefs, he and the Guest become close friends.

Reb Hayim (hah-YEEM), who in his youth as the scholarly son of a great rabbi attains renown as a wise man. He becomes proud and vain, ignoring his four daughters and treating his wife as a maidservant. After serving in the army and spending many years in a prisoners' camp, he returns to his hometown a transformed person. Utterly humble and self-effacing, he performs the menial tasks of the Beit Midrash and gives his wages to the widow of Hanoch, whose fatherless children he teaches the Torah. At his death, he is called a saint.

Yeruham Freeman, a day laborer who holds a festering grudge against the Guest, whose resettlement in Israel inspired him to follow. He is shamefully expelled from the country for engaging in communist activities; after returning to his hometown, he marries the innkeeper's daughter. Eventually, he and the Guest become fast friends. As the Guest departs for Israel, he places the key to the Beit Midrash into the hand of Freeman's infant son.

Rachel Zommer, the innkeeper's younger daughter. Beautiful and independent, she marries Yeruham and gives birth to the first child, a son, to be born in the town of Szibucz for several years.

Dr. Jacob Milch, called **Kuba**, a boyhood friend of the Guest who, after attending the university, returned to Szibucz to minister to the poor. The absence of an air of superiority and his modest fees earn for him contempt rather than gratitude. When the Guest's money runs out, he goes to live with Dr. Milch.

Erela "Hannah" Bach, Daniel's daughter. Betrothed to Yeruham Freeman, who abandons her to marry Rachel, she is a plain-looking children's Hebrew teacher, an argumentative rationalist who scoffs at matters of faith. At the end of the novel, she marries Dr. Milch, and they prepare to resettle in Israel.

Nissan Zommer, the owner of the inn where the Guest lodges. A quiet man, he rejoices in the commandments, though he follows them imperfectly.

Mrs. Zommer, the innkeeper's wife. Unobtrusive in her kindness and concern, she prepares special vegetarian dishes for the Guest and worries about his comfort. Courageous and durable, she managed to keep food in her children's mouths through the hardest of times.

Babtchi, the innkeeper's elder daughter, an assertive, outspoken, and rather disrespectful young woman. She wears her hair bobbed and smokes cigarettes. Courted by three suitors, by the end of the novel she has married none of them and turns her attention to her sister Rachel's child.

Ignatz, the half-Jewish town beggar whose nose was blown off in the war, leaving a repulsive hole in his face.

Reb Shlomo Bach, an old cantor, Daniel's father, who goes to Israel even though his son Yerumin was killed there. Unquestioning in his service to God, he does not judge any work of the Almighty as either good or bad. In Israel, he becomes rejuvenated working in the fields alongside the young.

Penhas Aryeh (PEHN-hahs AHR-ee-eh), a writer for the Orthodox newspaper *Agudat Israel*, a "new man," shallow and hypocritical, who does not know Torah or practice its commandments yet uses it to argue against the communists.

— Lolette Kuby

GUEST THE ONE-EYED
(Borgslægtens historie)

Author: Gunnar Gunnarsson (1889-1975)
First published: 1912-1914
Genre: Novel

Locale: Iceland
Time: c. 1900
Plot: Domestic

Ketill Ørlygsson, the devious, blasphemous, and dishonest son of Ørlygur à Borg. As a parish priest eager for the family property at Borg, he seeks to destroy his father's good name by accusing him of being the father of Runa's child. After Ketill himself is revealed as the father, he repents of his sins and becomes a homeless and compassionate wanderer. Regarding himself as a guest on earth, and losing an eye while saving the life of a child, he becomes "Guest the one-eyed." Finally, the old self of Ketill destroyed, he returns to Borg as Guest and is forgiven by his family.

Ormarr Ørlygsson, Ketill Ørlygsson's honest, intelligent, and artistic brother, who sacrifices his own concerns to marry Runa.

Ørlygur à Borg, a well-to-do landowner and the father of Ketill and Ormarr. Falsely and publicly accused by his son Ketill of the crime of lust, he is killed by the knowledge of his son's depravity.

Gudrun (Runa), the daughter of a poor farmer and the mother of Ketill's son, Ørlygur the Younger.

Pall a Seyru, Runa's father.

Ørlygur the Younger, the son of Ketill and Runa.

Snebiorg (Bagga), an illegitimate girl engaged to marry Ørlygur the Younger.

THE GUIDE

Author: R. K. Narayan (1906-   )
First published: 1958
Genre: Novel

Locale: India
Time: Mid-twentieth century
Plot: Social realism

Raju, the protagonist and at times the narrator, the son of a poor shopkeeper from the village of Malgudi. His character undergoes various transformations as he goes from shopkeeper to guide ("Railway Raju"), to lover, to impresario (manager of Rosie's career as a dancer), to prisoner, to impostor (fake guru), to perhaps genuine swami or mahatma (the highest of the Hindu spiritual leaders). Raju is clever, and although he succumbs to the temptations of luxury when Rosie succeeds as a dancer, he does offer her the chance to do what she has always wanted, and his love for her appears to be genuine. On the other hand, his forgery of her name, even if it is not for profit but to sustain their relationship, is unwise, and his initial willingness to assume the role of a guru simply to be fed suggests he may be just another con man. Readers must decide for themselves about the reality and depth of Raju's transformation by the end of the novel.

Raju's mother, a traditional Indian woman who defines herself in terms of her domestic role. She is developed more fully as a character than is her husband, about whom she complains frequently. Her initial, albeit reluctant, acceptance of the low-caste Rosie into her house and Rosie's affection for her indicate that she is a positive character. Raju's failure to heal their relationship or to build her a new home when he becomes wealthy tends to undercut his character. When she calls in her imperious brother to deal with Rosie, she reveals the weakness of the traditional Indian woman, who relies on domineering males to resolve problems.

Rosie, a traditional (temple) dancer and therefore of a lower caste. She has a master's degree in economics and married as a means of improving her status. She has the ambitions and dreams, as well as the passion, of a genuine artist. Her unusual name may suggest that she is something of a nonconformist, which would make her love of traditional dance ironic. She is, in fact, a great dancer. She shows her strength of character when she resists Raju's demands that she avoid the company of other artists and when she dances to raise money for his defense. Unlike Raju, she has little interest in wealth. She feels guilty about having deceived her husband, despite his ill treatment of her, and she is all too easily manipulated by Raju, who goes so far as to change her name. By the time of his imprisonment, their relationship has cooled. Significantly, she does not return to Raju or to her estranged husband at the end, but is apparently doing quite well for herself.

Marco, the name by which Raju identifies Rosie's husband (with Marco Polo). He is an archaeologist and art historian who is deeply devoted to his work and has little time for his wife. He also has no tolerance of her desire to dance. A cold sort of man, as he is seen by Raju, Marco appears to be a dry scholar. His icy treatment of Rosie before, during, and after the affair causes him to emerge as the least sympathetic character in the novel. That he should be so obsessed with the art and culture of southern India (the subject of his research and book) is ironic in the light of his lack of interest in his wife's art and his failure to recognize her dancing as art.

Gaffur, the taxi driver who assists Raju with his tours. He functions as a sort of social conscience for Raju. He is usually seen winking knowingly, often through the rearview mirror. He attempts to dissuade Raju from continuing with the dangerous relationship, but his conventional views are of no avail.

Velan, a simple villager from Mangal, on the outskirts of Malgudi. He reveres Raju for no particular reason other than the fact that he is at the temple and is willing to listen to him. He may be said to embody the universal need for spiritual leadership; that is, he may represent humanity in search of a guide. Both Rosie and Raju undergo profound transformations of character, but Velan (like Gaffur, Marco, and Raju's mother) remains essentially unchanged. He retains faith in Raju until the end. Depending on how one reads the last chapter (and perhaps the last paragraph in particular), one could say that his faith is rewarded (that is, Raju does become a holy man) or that it is mocked (that is, Raju goes from deceiving Marco to deceiving everyone).

— *Ron McFarland*

GULLIVER'S TRAVELS

Author: Jonathan Swift (1667-1745)
First published: 1726
Genre: Novel
Locale: England and various fictional lands
Time: 1699-1713
Plot: Social satire

Lemuel Gulliver, a surgeon, sea captain, traveler, and the narrator of these travel accounts, the purpose of which is to satirize the pretentions and follies of humans. Gulliver is an ordinary man, capable of close observation; his deceptively matter-of-fact reportage and a great accumulation of detail make believable and readable a scathing political and social satire. On his first voyage, he is shipwrecked at Lilliput, a country inhabited by people no more than six inches tall, where pretentiousness, individual as well as political, is ridiculed. The second voyage ends in Brobdingnag, a land of giants. Human grossness is a target here. Moreover, Gulliver does not find it easy to make sense of English customs and politics in explaining them to a king sixty feet high. On Gulliver's third voyage, pirates attack the ship and set him adrift in a small boat. One day he sees and goes aboard Laputa, a flying island inhabited by incredibly abstract and absent-minded people. From Laputa he visits Balnibari, where wildly impractical experiments in construction and agriculture are in progress. Then he goes to Glubbdubdrib, the island of sorcerers, where he is shown apparitions of such historical figures as Alexander and Caesar, who decry the inaccuracies of history books. Visiting Luggnagg, Gulliver, after describing an imaginary immortality of constant learning and growing wisdom, is shown a group of immortals called Struldbrugs, who are grotesque, pitiable creatures, senile for centuries, but destined never to die. Gulliver's last journey is to the land of the Houyhnhnms, horse-like creatures in appearance, possessed of great intelligence, rationality, restraint, and courtesy. Dreadful human-like creatures, called Yahoos, impart to Gulliver such a loathing of the human form that, forced to return at last to England, he cannot bear the sight of even his own family and feels at home only in the stables.

GUY MANNERING: Or, The Astrologer

Author: Sir Walter Scott (1771-1832)
First published: 1815
Genre: Novel
Locale: Scotland
Time: The eighteenth century
Plot: Historical

Captain Brown (Harry Bertram), a young Scottish aristocrat whose life took a turn when he was kidnapped in his sixth year. He becomes an officer and, while stationed in India, falls in love with Julia Mannering. The Mannerings, old friends of the Bertrams, do not recognize Brown as young Harry Bertram. Through a chain of events—an interview with a Dutch smuggler and a secret revealed by an old gypsy—Bertram has his identity and inheritance restored and becomes eligible to marry Julia.

Colonel Guy Mannering, a British gentleman and a friend of the Bertrams who, being a student of astrology, predicts dire events for Harry Bertram: the boy's fifth, tenth, and twenty-first years will be especially dangerous, he says. His predictions are more or less accurate. Mannering, finally, is happy to see his friend's son, Harry Bertram, whom he has known as Captain Brown, restored to his inheritance, and he blesses his daughter Julia's alliance with Bertram.

Gilbert Glossin, a crooked lawyer who sets in motion the machinery of the novel. It is he who arranges to have Harry Bertram kidnapped; with Harry out of the way, the lawyer is able to buy the Bertram estate, Ellangowan, inexpensively. He is finally unmasked and, while in prison awaiting trial, is killed by one of his partners in crime.

Charles Hazlewood, a young gentleman who loves Lucy Bertram, Harry's sister. Once mistaking Captain Brown for a bandit, he tries to shoot him. He himself is wounded, however, when, as he and Brown wrestle for the weapon, it is discharged. He marries Lucy Bertram.

Meg Merrilies, an old gypsy woman who played a role in the kidnapping. When young Bertram is twenty-one, she confesses her part, thus disclosing a smuggler and Glossin as her confederates; the smuggler then kills Meg before he is taken to prison.

Dirk Hatteraick, a Dutch smuggler and murderer who killed the revenue officer with whom young Bertram was riding the day Dirk and Meg kidnapped him. Later, he shoots Meg and, while Glossin's cellmate, kills him. Before the law can send him to the scaffold, Hatteraick hangs himself.

Julia Mannering, Guy Mannering's daughter, who finally becomes Harry Bertram's wife.

Lucy Bertram, Harry Bertram's sister, who marries Charles Hazlewood.

Godfrey Bertram, Laird of Ellangowan, who is Lucy and Harry's father. He dies seventeen years after Harry's kidnapping, leaving Lucy an orphan.

Sir Robert Hazlewood, Charles's father.

Dominie Sampson, the faithful tutor to the Bertram children.

GUY OF WARWICK
(Gui de Warewic)

Author: Unknown
First transcribed: c. 1240
Genre: Poetry
Locale: England, Europe, and the Middle East
Time: The tenth century
Plot: Romance

Guy, a knight of Warwick. He is the son of the steward of Rohaud, the earl of Warwick, and principal cupbearer to the earl. Guy falls in love with his master's daughter, Felice la Belle. To satisfy his lady's demand that he become the foremost knight in the world, he enters into adventures that bring about the deaths of many brave knights. He marries Felice only to become beset with qualms of conscience over the mischief he has caused to satisfy a lady's whims. He ends his life as a penitent pilgrim.

Rohaud, the earl of Warwick, Guy of Warwick's master, and the father of Felice la Belle.

Felice la Belle, the daughter of Rohaud. Loved by Guy of Warwick, she demands, as the price of her hand, that he become the greatest knight in the world.

Herhaud of Ardern, Guy of Warwick's mentor and companion in knight-errantry.

Otous, the duke of Pavia, who is defeated by Guy of Warwick.

Segyn, the duke of Louvain, who is assisted in battle by Guy of Warwick.

Reignier, the emperor of Germany. In an unlawful attempt to take the lands of Segyn, he is captured by Guy of Warwick, who brings about a rapprochement between the enemies.

Ernis, the emperor of Greece, who is assisted by Guy of Warwick against the Soudan of the Saracens.

Loret, Ernis' daughter, promised to Guy of Warwick for his services in battle.

Morgadour, a knight enamored of Loret. He is a traitor to Guy of Warwick.

Tirri, a knight and friend of Guy of Warwick. He is rescued by Guy from his persecutor, Otous.

Athelstan, the king of England.

Anlaf, the king of Denmark.

Colbrand, a Danish giant slain by Guy of Warwick.

THE GUYANA QUARTET

Author: Wilson Harris (1921-   )
First published: 1985
Genre: Novels
Locale: Guyana
Time: The twentieth century
Plot: Allegory

Palace of the Peacock, 1960

The Dreaming I, the narrator, a younger brother of Donne. He accompanies Donne on the quest and participates in the mystical experience that unites the dead and the living. He alone survives to tell the story.

Donne, an estate owner, the lifelong protector of the narrator. A brown-skinned man, he is the captain of the crew that is traveling into the mountains to get laborers for the estate he is building in the interior of Guyana. Donne is tough, decisive, and harsh. His brutality toward his mistress, Mariella, echoes his brutality toward all the natives, and the narrator's initial dream or vision indicates that eventually Donne was or will be killed by the natives, or by Mariella as their representative.

Cameron, a member of the crew, whose red face and kinky hair indicate his mixed Scottish and African ancestry. Although he is quiet and long-suffering, he is frustrated because he has never been able to accumulate enough money to realize his dreams of landownership. In a quarrel, he is stabbed in the back by one of the Da Silva twins.

Schomburgh, a crew member of German and Amerindian background. Although he is in his fifties, he is agile and a good bowman. After the death of Carroll, his son, Schomburgh dies in his sleep.

Carroll, the youngest crew member and the son of Schomburgh. A strong, stocky black boy of seventeen, he is popular because of his good nature and fine singing voice. The first crew member to die, he is drowned in the War Office rapids.

Vigilance, the stepbrother of Carroll. A black-haired Indian, he serves as lookout for the rest of the crew. It is he who comes to understand the duality of his crewmates. He disappears mysteriously with Mariella.

Wishrop, the assistant bowman on the crew. A man of forty, he has lived a violent life, claiming to have killed his wife, her lover, the priest who had married them, and the Arawak woman who aided him during his flight from the Venezuelan authorities. Like Carroll, he is drowned.

Jennings, the crewman responsible for the boat's engine. A young, serious man, he is rebellious and quarrelsome. He dies in a fall.

Mariella, an old Arawak woman, the mistress of Donne. Silent and patient, even when she is mistreated and beaten by Donne, she represents all the objects of the exploiters' quest. She disappears, but the narrator knows that she will destroy Donne.

Da Silva, a Portuguese man whose twin is also a member of the crew. A tall, thin man, he plans to marry the mother of his child. In a quarrel, he kills Cameron. He falls off a cliff and dies.

The Far Journey of Oudin, 1961

Oudin, a mysterious man with whose death the novel begins. A dark, childlike person, when plied with drink he becomes the slave of Ram, the moneylender, even his willing tool to the scheme to steal cattle from Mohammed. When Ram has him abduct Mohammed's niece, however, Oudin keeps her for himself.

Beti, Oudin's wife for thirteen years. Black-haired and once attractive, she is the daughter of Rajah, a poor man, and the niece of Mohammed. Even though Ram could have given her wealth, she prefers young Oudin and elopes with him. At his death, in an effort to cheat the moneylender, she eats the contract that her husband made with Ram.

Ram, the moneylender. A man who is loathed by everyone, he devotes his life to destroying Mohammed, with the help of Oudin. He is impotent and compensates for this with his acquisitiveness.

Mohammed, a landlord, the descendant of an Indian immigrant to Guyana. A tall, thin man, he is unscrupulous about making money but careless of his property. When he learns that his father has left an inheritance to an illegitimate child, Mohammed schemes to get rid of his half brother and to change the will. Eventually, he falls into the clutches of the moneylender.

Muhra, Mohammed's wife. When, after a succession of daughters, she miscarries a male child, she is convinced that Mohammed's evil deed has caused her misfortune.

Hassan, a brother of Mohammed. Round-faced and secretive, he works on his brother's bus. He is the first of Mohammed's brothers to die.

Kaiser, Mohammed's twin brother. He is shorter and thinner than Mohammed, whom he envies and resents. He dies in a fire in the rum shop, which may, like Hassan's death, be a working-out of the curse on the brothers for killing the heir.

Rajah, Mohammed's cousin and Beti's father. A poor man, always hungry, he is a compulsive thief. He is struck by lightning.

Mohammed's father, who came from India. He has a black face and a white beard. It is his changing of his will in favor of a mentally deficient, illegitimate son that leads to Mohammed's evil deed.

The Whole Armour, 1962

Cristo, a fugitive. A twenty-one-year-old black man, he has a graceful, restless body and a devoted mother. He has returned to Guyana after completing his education and finds himself a stranger there. After killing his girlfriend's lover, he takes refuge with Abram but then is suspected of killing his benefactor. When he returns to prove his innocence, he is ambushed, tried, and executed.

Magda, a prostitute. She is a strong black woman, roughly forty years old, whose eyes indicate her Chinese blood. Convinced that her son Cristo killed Abram, she urges him to flee and, in hopes of saving him, offers herself to a police sergeant so that the police will delay their search.

Abram, a half-caste old man who lives alone. When Cristo is with him, Abram dies of an apparent heart attack and later is savaged by a jaguar.

Sharon, Cristo's girlfriend, who appears white but has black ancestors. A slender, attractive woman, she seems to attract both men and death. Because of her infidelity, Cristo kills her lover. Later, her fiancé is killed, her father hangs himself, and Cristo, the father of her child, is executed. Her confusion about her identity causes her to behave promiscuously.

Peet, Sharon's father. A coconut farmer with dark, slanting eyes and a ragged beard and mustache, he is frequently drunk and violent. When he attacks Magda, she knocks him down, but when he starts a fight with Mattias Gomez, the outcome is tragic: Mattias falls on Peet's knife. When Peet hangs himself, further suspicion descends on Cristo.

Mattias Gomez, Sharon's fiancé after Cristo goes into hiding. A man in his late twenties, he is pale-skinned and black-haired, of Portuguese and Syrian descent. Mattias is the bookkeeper for his father, a wealthy store owner. When the drunken Peet accuses him of seducing Sharon and starts a fight, Mattias accidentally falls on Peet's knife and is killed.

The Secret Ladder, 1963

Russell Fenwick, a government surveyor. A tall man of mixed African, English, and French blood, he took his job to help support his elderly mother. Because his kindness is interpreted as weakness, he causes rebellion in the crew and the natives.

Weng, Fenwick's foreman. Of Chinese and Amerindian extraction, he is the best hunter in the group. He intimidates the crew and thus controls them.

Jordan, the cook and storekeeper. A large, baby-faced man, he is disliked for his stinginess. He warns Fenwick that his softness will lead to disaster.

Dominic Perez, an older member of the crew. A stocky Portuguese man, he dotes on his young wife and insists on having her with him. After her complaint to Fenwick gets him fired, he threatens to kill her.

Catalena Perez, the wife of Dominic. A big-breasted young woman with blue-black eyes and long lashes, she is regularly beaten by her husband, perhaps for her infidelity, perhaps simply because of his jealousy. When she is captured by the natives and stripped, she expects to be raped and murdered. She is saved by chance, however, and runs away with Bryant.

Bryant, a thin young African, a member of Fenwick's crew. He feels a special kinship with Poseidon, whom he identifies with his own grandfather, and cannot forgive himself for the fact that the old man is killed when he falls after Bryant attacks him.

Poseidon, the old man who leads the natives in defying Fenwick and the government. A man with white, kinky hair and ragged clothes, he is the grandson of an escaped slave. His defiance is motivated by Jordan's cheating him and by his perception of Fenwick's character, as well as by fear of government intrusion. When, in a sudden burst of virility, he attempts to rape Catalena, he is knocked down by Bryant and dies.

Chiung, a Chinese crewman. A man in his forties or fifties, he is disliked by Weng, as well as by the natives, whom he cheats. After Fenwick loans him a raincoat and cap, Chiung is attacked by native assassins. When they realize that they have the wrong man and take the news to their camp, the natives abandon Catalena, and she is able to escape.

— Rosemary M. Canfield Reisman

GUZMÁN DE ALFARACHE
(La vida y hechos del pícaro Guzmán de Alfarache)

Author: Mateo Alemán (1547-c. 1614)
First published: Part I, 1599; Part II, 1604
Genre: Novel
Locale: Spain and Italy
Time: The sixteenth century
Plot: Picaresque

Guzmán de Alfarache (gewz-MAHN deh ahl-fah-RAH-chay), a rogue who early learns he must trick or be tricked. He lives by his wits in Spain and Italy until caught and sentenced to life imprisonment as a galley slave. Winning a pardon by revealing the slaves' conspiracy to seize the vessel, he determines to lead an exemplary life.

Don Guzmán, his father. Cheated by a partner in Genoa, he recovers most of his money in Seville. When he becomes rich, he buys an estate in San Juan de Alfarache and takes a mistress, whom he eventually marries. Addicted to gambling and high living, he dies penniless.

A muleteer, who teaches Guzmán the world's crookedness.

Two friars, who hire animals from the muleteer.

A constable, who arrests and severely beats Guzmán, thinking he is a thieving page.

An innkeeper, who hires Guzmán and teaches him to cheat travelers.

A captain of soldiers, with whom Guzmán plans to travel to Italy.

Don Beltrán (behl-TRAHN), Guzmán's uncle in Genoa, who orders the servants to beat his nephew. The boy gets revenge by tricking him out of jewelry.

A cardinal, who thinks the fake sores on Guzmán's legs are real and who gives him money and a job. He soon discharges Guzmán for stealing.

The French ambassador, who hires Guzmán for intrigues.

Sayavedra (sah-yah-BAY-drah), a supposed friend who rifles Guzmán's possessions but later helps him cheat the rich of Florence.

Alexandro Bentivoglio (ah-layk-SAHN-droh behn-tee-BOH-glyoh), a thieves' fence.

Guzmán's first wife, who is not the heiress she pretends to be.

Guzmán's second wife, who helps him rob wealthy men and then deserts him for an Italian sea captain.

Soto (SOH-toh), a fellow galley slave of Guzmán who plots the seizure of the ship. In revenge for a previous wrong committed against him by Soto, Guzmán reports the plot, and Soto is executed. The grateful ship's captain frees Guzmán from the oars.

H

HADJI MURAD
(Khadzi-Murat)

Author: Leo Tolstoy (1828-1910)
First published: 1911
Genre: Novella

Locale: The Caucasus Mountains
Time: November, 1851-April, 1852
Plot: Historical realism

Hadji Murad (KHAH-jih MEW-rahn), a Turkish Caucasian warrior-leader, formerly a Russian-appointed governor of Avaria and more recently the insurgent Shamil's chief representative there. With widely separated black eyes, a shaven head, a slender frame, muscular arms and small, sunburned hands, and a limp as a result of a fall over a precipice during an escape from Akhmet Khan, the turbaned Hadji Murad cuts an impressive figure astride a horse. Intimidating when serious and disarming when smiling, Hadji Murad is fearless, uncomplicated, devoutly religious, and instinctively optimistic. The narrative revolves around his decision to join forces with the Russians in an effort to defeat Shamil, who holds his aged mother, two wives, and six children captive. The politically naïve Hadji Murad, caught between the Russians and their Caucasian foes, appears doomed from the outset to a tragic end.

Shamil (shah-MIHL), the spiritual and military leader (imam) of the Chechen Caucasian Turks. A tall, slender, powerful, plainly clad, and charismatic figure, Shamil is dedicated to an ascetic Muslim faith and to the defeat of the "infidel" Russian foreigners. Russia's most formidable regional foe of the day, Shamil is a calculating, realistic leader who, though he regrets Hadji Murad's defection, realizes that victory is impossible without his former associate's death. His threat to kill or blind Hadji Murad's son Yusuf succeeds in drawing Hadji Murad into a fatal rescue attempt.

Prince Mikhail Semenovich Vorontsov (seh-MYO-noh-vihch voh-ROH-tsov), the aging, aristocratic Russian commander in chief at Tiflis. Vorontsov's ambition, wealth, connections, abilities, and kindness toward inferiors have brought him great success. Still agile and mentally alert at more than seventy years of age, although readily susceptible to flattery, he is the only sirdar (commander) to whom Hadji Murad is willing to surrender himself. Vorontsov does not act on Hadji Murad's request for an exchange of prisoners of war for the latter's family members in Shamil's custody, nor does he believe the latter's declaration of loyalty to the czar. He treats Hadji Murad well nevertheless and allows him to move about the region in an effort to find a way to secure his family's release.

Prince Semen Mikhailovich Vorontsov (seh-MYON mih-KHAH-ih-loh-vihch), the Russian commander of the Kurinsky regiment stationed at Vozdvighensk and the commander in chief's son. A fair-haired and long-faced colonel with a beautiful wife, Vorontsov has the good fortune to be the person whom Hadji Murad contacts to arrange for his reception by the Russians.

Marya Dmitrievna (dmih-TRIH-ehv-nah), the housekeeper and mistress of Major Petgrov Ivan Matveyevich. The daughter of a hospital assistant, she is thirty years old, fair-haired, freckle-faced, and full-figured, with a radiant smile. Hadji Murad likes her simplicity of manner and gives her a gift after leaving Major Matveyevich's custody. When Kamenov shows Hadji Murad's head to her, the major, and Captain Butler, Dmitrievna calls everyone around her butchers.

Princess Maria Vasilyevna Vorontsova (vah-SIH-lyehv-nah voh-RON-tsoh-vah), the wife of the younger Prince Vorontsov. A well-known, big-eyed, dark-browed beauty and flirt from St. Petersburg, with a Junoesque figure, she has a six-year-old son by her first husband. The Vorontsovs think they are living in Spartan conditions at the front, whereas others have never seen such a luxurious lifestyle at the Vozdizhensk fort.

Captain Butler, the commander of the Fifth Company, a tall, good-looking young man recently transferred from the Guards in St. Petersburg because of the debts caused by his compulsive gambling there. Butler loves the mountains and life at the front. Party to emperor Nicholas' command in January, 1852, that raids be carried out in Chechnya, he meets Hadji Murad. They come to like each other. At a farewell dinner for General Koslovsky, Butler drinks to excess and subsequently at Captain Poltoratsky's gambles himself back into debt. He makes unpleasant advances to Marya Dmitrievna. He takes part in the devastating raid on the village of Mahket and is with Marya when Kamenov shows Hadji Murad's head.

Nicholas I, the czar of Russia. Cold, lackluster, intimidating eyes look out from the czar's long white face with its tremendous sloping forehead. He has fatty cheeks, side-whiskers, and a mustache, and he wears a wig to cover the bald crown of his head. A large man with a protruding stomach, he is haughty, wrathful, and full of thoughts of his own greatness. He takes pleasure in being relentlessly cruel. He assumes that all of his policies end up making sense merely because they emanated from him. He gives free rein to Prince Vorontsov in the latter's dealings with Hadji Murad.

Captain Count Mikhail Tarielovich Loris-Melikov (tah-rih-YEH-loh-vihch LOH-rihs-MEH-lih-kov), the aide-de-camp to the elder Prince Vorontsov. Because he speaks the "Tartar" tongue (the Turkic language of northern Caucasus), Loris-Melikov is assigned to Hadji Murad during the latter's stay at Tiflis and there records Hadji Murad's life story, which includes Hadji Murad's assassination of Shamil's predecessor Hamzad and his falling out with Shamil.

Yusuf (YEW-sewf), Hadji Murad's eighteen-year-old son. Confined in a dungeon at Shamil's stronghold at Vedeno, this broad-shouldered young man, who is taller than his father, is a ploy in Shamil's plan to kill Hadji Murad. Although he craves freedom and the easy life that were once his as an overlord's son, and although he admires Shamil, Yusuf attempts suicide when he learns that Shamil is using him to get to his father.

Sado (SAH-doh), a Chechen villager who is a steadfast friend to Hadji Murad. He shelters the latter in his hut in Mahket despite Shamil's prohibition of support for the renegade leader. He sends his brother Bata on Hadji Murad's behalf to pass along the latter's message to the Russians that he wishes to join them against Shamil. The Russians destroy Sado's hut and kill his young son, but he begins rebuilding his life thereafter. Sado, Peter Avdeev, and Eldar exemplify the author's sympathy for and faith in the nobility of the Russian peasantry (as opposed to the author's disdain for the false heroics of the pampered educated elite).

Peter Avdeev (av-DEH-ehv), a Russian soldier fatally wounded in an exchange of fire with Chechen Turks who had been pursuing Hadji Murad after his escape from Sado's hut. He is an excellent worker and farmhand. Avdeev had volunteered for military service in place of his indolent older brother Akim because Akim was married, with four children. Poltoratsky had ordered the exchange of fire only as a diversion. Avdeev's peasant family back home mourns his death.

Eldar, one of Hadji Murad's four closest followers. A sturdy-limbed, heavy-chested, shaven-headed, handsome young man, Eldar is unquestioningly loyal to his leader and, along with the cheerful Khan Mahoma, the equally dedicated Hanefi, and the virulently anti-Russian Gamzalo, dies at the hands of the Russians with Hadji Murad.

— *Michael Craig Hillmann*

THE HAIRY APE

Author: Eugene O'Neill (1888-1953)
First published: 1922
Genre: Drama
Locale: At sea and on land
Time: Early twentieth century
Plot: Expressionism

Robert Smith, known as **Yank**, the chief coal stoker on a ship bound for Europe. A Neanderthal type with a strong back and hairy, powerful arms, Yank is a man of apparent personal confidence who sees himself as doing the real work of the world, in contrast with the ineffectual, wealthy tourists who travel above deck in first class. He is an honest laborer, proud of his vitality and usefulness in the world of industry, sure that he "belongs" in a way the idle rich never could. His pride is crushed, however, when Mildred Douglas, an empty-headed society social worker, sees him at work in the hold and calls him a beast. Thwarted in his attempts at revenge on her for this insult, he goes to his death in the cage of the Central Park Zoo ape that he has come to see as his brother.

Mildred Douglas, the daughter of the president of the board of directors of the shipping lines and a passenger on Yank's ship. A delicate, haughty twenty-year-old, Mildred has dabbled in social work in the slums of New York City, almost as a voyeur looking with fascination at how the poor survive. She exhibits a certain vacuity in the face of life; she is stubborn, unfeeling, and even cruel. By flirting with the ship's stewards and through outright lies, she gets permission to see the stokers at work in the hold, only to faint with horror at the sight of Yank's blackened, sweaty body and his menacing glance in response to her screams.

Aunt, a traveling companion to Mildred. She is a pompous, fatuous dowager, pretentious in dress and actions. Her demeaning comments serve to goad Mildred on in her foolish demand to observe the stokers at work.

Paddy, a fellow stoker. He is an old sailor, yearning for the bygone days of sailing ships, when men stood tall in the clean wind and sun rather than huddled below decks shoveling dusty coal to feed the raging fires of the hellish furnaces.

Long, another stoker. Like Yank, Long is angered at the insult of being exhibited before Mildred as a lower-class social phenomenon. He accompanies Yank to upper Fifth Avenue in an attempt to convince him that Mildred, on whom Yank is so eager to have vengeance, is no more than a representative of the entire class of the callous wealthy and that it is the class that he must fight rather than the individual.

Second Engineer, a young officer on Yank's ship. Having been forced into taking Mildred on the tour of the ship's stokehold by her lies to the captain, he is witness to her crushing treatment of Yank when she calls him a hairy beast.

Secretary of the Industrial Workers of the World, a labor organizer concerned with fair wages and good working conditions for the common laborer. Yank approaches him with a plan to sabotage the Douglas steel plant as an act of revenge on Mildred Douglas. The secretary rejects his plan forcefully. Once again, Yank is shown that he does not "belong," even among the common laborers with whom he so closely identifies himself.

— *Gabrielle Rowe*

THE HAM FUNERAL

Author: Patrick White (1912-1990)
First published: 1965
Genre: Drama

Locale: London, England
Time: 1919
Plot: Expressionism

The Young Man, a tenant in the Lustys' house, a poet and a dreamer. Although his true name is never revealed, the Young Man is called both "Jack" and "Fred" by the Landlady, the former because he reminds her of the infant son she lost and the latter because he brings to mind a lover she once had. The Young Man spends copious amounts of time either lying on his bed staring at the ceiling or with his ear pressed against the door of the room across the hall, waiting to commune with the Girl, who inhabits the room. He is penniless and, despite his pretensions to a literary life, he has written only one poem, which he later discards. Instead, he talks a considerable amount about life and art, using sophisticated vocabulary, until he meets his silent, taciturn Landlord, who jolts the Young Man out of his stagnation with simple, profound truths. The Landlord dies, however, before the Young Man can question him. The Young Man takes on the responsibility for notifying the Lustys' relatives and inviting them to the funeral. When the Landlady attempts to seduce him, the Young Man cruelly spurns her advances in favor of listening to the musings of the ever-unseen, wraithlike Girl. Finally, with the Girl's help, he reconciles the needs of both body and soul and leaves the house in search of wholeness.

The Landlady, **Alma Lusty**, a blowsy, overripe woman tending to slovenliness. She is a gregarious creature who particularly craves the attention of men. It comes as something of a surprise that she has been married to the grim, stonelike Landlord for almost twenty years. She delights in material comforts and still mourns the death of her son, Jack, in his infancy. Alma feels some guilt for an affair she once had, which may or may not have produced the child she lost. She is attracted to the Young Man, both as a son-substitute and as a lover, but until the Landlord's death she offers him only friendship. She believes her lodger to be a little bit crazy. Although she finds a poem he discarded, she admits she could not read his educated words. After her husband dies, Alma shows real remorse and vows to serve ham following his funeral, ham being the most elegant repast she can think of to honor his memory. After the wake, Alma tries to seduce the Young Man. He rejects her and leaves, but not without first making peace. Alone at the end, as at the beginning, Alma is a survivor.

The Landlord, **Will Lusty**, a fat, slovenly man who neither moves nor speaks. He harbors resentment toward his wife for her affairs and lives mostly in the past, in a time when he used to run a sweets shop. His occasional pronouncements make it evident that there is much going on inside Will's head. He is the real philosopher of the play, seeing life in things such as tables and reveling in the simple fact of being. Following his silent, unglamorous death, it is his funeral and the echo of his mysterious words that dominate the action.

The Girl, **Phyllis Pither**, the Young Man's insubstantial anima. She is serious, with her expression remote but radiant. Dressed in white, with long, fair hair, she plays the part of the poet's muse. Although the Young Man yearns to see and touch her, she will not (in fact, cannot) permit him to do either. Instead, they talk through the door to her room. She provides him with moral balance by urging him to reconcile the disparate, conflicting halves of himself. The Girl, however, is a phantom; her real-life counterpart is a drab, mousy woman named Phyllis Pither.

Two ladies, formerly prostitutes, now bag ladies. When the Young Man meets them, they are methodically going through garbage bins, eating rejected scraps of food, reading discarded letters, and chatting about life. The Young Man's affected manner and obvious disgust offend them, as does the sight, once they near the bottom of the bin, of a dead fetus.

Four relatives, all of whom inhabit one house. They are beckoned to the ham funeral by the Young Man. They prove less than sympathetic toward the widow, making vulgar jabs at her character, all the while devouring her ham.

— *Susan Whaley*

THE HAMLET

Author: William Faulkner (1897-1962)
First published: 1940
Genre: Novel

Locale: Mississippi
Time: Late nineteenth century
Plot: Psychological realism

Flem Snopes, a character who epitomizes an economic force that moved into the South shortly after the Civil War. Snopes is cunning, ruthless, cruel, and devoted to self-aggrandizement through the power that comes with owning property. His business ethics are an abomination; his contempt for the ignorant townspeople he cheats is complete. Flem Snopes, along with his many relatives, is a symbol of economic rape that Faulkner presents throughout the stories and novels he has written about a mythological Mississippi county.

Eula Varner, a sexually precocious rural beauty who becomes Mrs. Flem Snopes after she becomes pregnant by one of three suitors who leave the region when her condition becomes known. Flem marries Eula, not out of compassion but because he is anxious to get established in the community, and she is the daughter of the hamlet's wealthiest man.

Will Varner, Eula's father, the leading citizen of Frenchman's Bend and the town's largest property owner.

Henry Armstid, a local farmer distinguished by his stupidity and bull-headedness. He is twice duped by Flem Snopes.

He buys a worthless horse from him and later, with two other men, buys a piece of property on which Snopes has led them to believe buried treasure will be found. Armstid's blind pride prevents him from learning anything from the crooked transactions. At last, disappointed because he finds no treasure on the property, he loses his mind.

V. K. Ratliff, a sewing-machine salesman who knows everything about everybody in the countryside. Flem Snopes bilks him out of some money by selling him and Armstid a worthless piece of property.

Ab Snopes, Flem's father, a newcomer to the hamlet, who rents a farm from Will Varner. He is suspected of being an arsonist, and he is known to be an unscrupulous horse trader. Poetic justice is served when he, trying to cheat a horse trader, is himself roundly cheated.

Jody Varner, Will Varner's son and heir.

Isaac Snopes, a mentally deficient boy whose peculiar erotic behavior toward a cow causes a town scandal.

Mink Snopes, one of the Snopes clan convicted of murder and sent to prison for life.

Jack Houston, the citizen who impounds Mink Snopes' stray cow and is murdered following a dispute over the cost of feeding the animal.

Labove, a schoolteacher who attempts to seduce Eula Varner, fails, and leaves Frenchman's Bend forever.

Mrs. Henry Armstid, a shy, uneducated woman who lives in abject poverty with Armstid and their four children.

Pat Stamper, an extremely shrewd horse trader who buys a worthless horse from Ab Snopes, paints it and fattens it with a bicycle pump, then sells it back to him.

Buck Hipps, a Texan who, in collusion with Flem Snopes, sells a group of wild spotted horses to the credulous farmers of the Frenchman's Bend area.

Hoake McCarron, one of Eula Varner's more gallant suitors and the father of her unborn child.

Eckrum (Eck) Snopes, a member of the Snopes tribe who receives a wild horse as a gift from Buck Hipps.

Vernon Tull, a townsman who is injured when Eck Snopes's wild horse collides with his wagon.

Odum Bookwright, a naïve citizen who, along with Ratliff and Armstid, is taken in by Flem Snopes on a property deal.

THE HAMLET OF STEPNEY GREEN: A Sad Comedy with Some Songs

Author: Bernard Kops (1926-)
First published: 1959
Genre: Drama
Locale: The East End of London
Time: The 1950's
Plot: Comedy

David (Davy) Levy, the twenty-two-year-old son of Sam and Bessie Levy, his Jewish parents. He is tall and intelligent, but he has no regular job, and his great ambitions are to be a crooner and to "make people happy." His intelligence is undirected, and his musical ability is unlikely to make him popular. He appears dissatisfied, melancholy, and quixotic. He rejects not only his father's plans for him but also Hava's love. He wants to shock the older generation; for example, he appears in a teddy boy outfit at his father's funeral as a mark of protest. Parallels to William Shakespeare's Hamlet appear both in his character and in his desire to avenge his father's death. He becomes quite unbalanced in his behavior at the Kaddish and also later, when his mother talks of remarrying. Like Hamlet, he does not really achieve anything by revenge, but unlike Hamlet, he drops his quest for revenge. The play ends with his declaring his love to Hava and accepting his mother's remarriage, to Solly Segal, as revenge enough.

Sam Levy, a Jewish pickled-herring seller in the East End of London. He is sixty-five years old and appears to be a hypochondriac. He suffers a heart attack at the end of act 1 and dies. For the rest of the play, he appears as a ghost visible only to David. He is portrayed as very confused in his values and, especially, in what he wants for David. At times, he upbraids David for not settling down, yet sometimes he urges David to find himself. Sam believes that his own confined life and less than happy marriage contributed to his death. As a ghost, he not only contributes to David's bizarre behavior but also breaks up the séance organized by his wife by indicating that he is happy for her to marry Solly. In the end, he realizes that David's desire for revenge has gotten out of hand and substitutes an aphrodisiac for the poison David plans to use. He thus brings about a happy resolution.

Bessie Levy, the fifty-two-year-old wife and widow of Sam. A plump woman fond of wearing cheap jewelry, she is much younger than her husband and still attractive. She has no strong character of her own and appears more as the object of David's and Sam's conflicting emotions. She has little sympathy for Sam's hypochondria but nevertheless seems to have been a loyal wife and caring mother, though she seems ready enough to marry Solly after only eight months of widowhood. She takes life as it comes.

Solly Segal, a Jewish friend of the Levy family. At sixty years of age, he is retired and a widower. He is very much a pragmatist, as is his equivalent in Shakespeare's play, Claudius, and he has little patience for either David's or Sam's inner conflicts and uncertainties. He seems a natural partner for Bessie: Both are uncomplicated people who refuse to see life as a tragedy. It is his courting of Bessie so soon after Sam's death that triggers David's bizarre behavior. He tries to dissuade his daughter, Hava, from being interested in David.

Hava Segal, an eighteen-year-old who is "beautiful and sure of herself." She makes a strong initial impact, having just returned from an Israeli kibbutz, but she is not a rebel like David. In fact, she went to Israel to try to forget David, her childhood sweetheart, but in vain. She is, at heart, a homey girl, which is perhaps why David rejects her at first. At the end, however, he comes to his senses, and her quiet persistence is rewarded in the burst of celebratory love that concludes the play.

Mr. Stone and

Mrs. Stone, both in their fifties and both described as fat, foolish, and jovial. They are childless and neighbors to the Levys. He is a taxi driver. Their world is completely trivial.

hey represent the mundaneness of life that the playwright sees as part of the reality that needs to be celebrated.

Mr. White,

Mr. Black, and

Mr. Green, three salesmen who appear at the funeral, the first two to sell tombstones, the last to discuss life insurance. By the last act, they have switched jobs. They spend much of their time playing cards, oblivious to both the comedy and the tragedy that goes on around them.

— David Barratt

HAMLET, PRINCE OF DENMARK

Author: William Shakespeare (1564-1616)
First published: 1603
Genre: Drama
Locale: Elsinore, Denmark
Time: c. 1200
Plot: Tragedy

Hamlet, the prince of Denmark, generally agreed to be William Shakespeare's most fascinating hero. No brief sketch can satisfy his host of admirers or take into account more than a minute fraction of the commentary now in print. The character is a mysterious combination of a series of literary sources and the phenomenal genius of the playwright. Orestes in Greek tragedy is probably his ultimate progenitor, not Oedipus, as some critics have suggested. The Greek original has been altered and augmented by medieval saga and Renaissance romance. Perhaps an earlier *Hamlet*, written by Thomas Kyd, furnished important material; however, the existence of such a play has been disputed. Hamlet is a mixture of tenderness and violence, a scholar, lover, friend, athlete, philosopher, satirist, and deadly enemy; he is larger than life. Torn by grief for his dead father and disappointment in the conduct of his beloved mother, Hamlet desires a revenge so complete that it will reach the soul as well as the body of his villainous uncle. His attempt to usurp God's prerogative of judgment leads to all the deaths in the play. Before his death, he reaches a state of resignation and acceptance of God's will. He gains his revenge but loses his life.

Claudius (KLOH-dee-uhs), the king of Denmark and husband of his brother's widow; he is Hamlet's uncle. A shrewd and capable politician and administrator, he is courageous and self-confident, but he is tainted by mortal sin: He murdered his brother and married his queen very soon thereafter. Although his conscience torments him with remorse, he is unable to repent or to give up the throne or the woman that his murderous act brought him. He has unusual self-knowledge and recognizes his unrepentant state. He is a worthy and mighty antagonist for Hamlet, and they destroy each other.

Gertrude, the queen of Denmark, Hamlet's mother. Warm-hearted but weak, she shows deep affection for Hamlet and tenderness for Ophelia. There are strong indications that she and Claudius were engaged in an adulterous affair before the death of the older Hamlet. She loves Claudius, but she respects Hamlet's confidence and does not betray him to his uncle when he tells her of the murder, of which she has been obviously innocent and ignorant. Her death occurs after she drinks the poison prepared by Claudius for Hamlet.

Polonius (peh-LOH-nee-uhs), the lord chamberlain under Claudius, whom he has apparently helped to the throne. An affectionate but meddlesome father to Laertes and Ophelia, he tries to control their lives. He is garrulous and self-important, always seeking the devious rather than the direct method in politics or family relationships. Hamlet jestingly baits him but apparently has some affection for the officious old man and shows real regret at killing him. Polonius' deviousness and eavesdropping bring on his death; Hamlet stabs him through the tapestry in the mistaken belief that Claudius is concealed there.

Ophelia (oh-FEE-lee-ah), Polonius' daughter and Hamlet's love. A sweet, docile girl, she is easily dominated by her father. She loves Hamlet but never seems to realize that she is imperiling his life by helping her father spy on him. Her gentle nature being unable to stand the shock of her father's death at her lover's hands, she loses her mind and is drowned.

Laertes (lay-UR-teez), Polonius' son. He is in many ways a foil to Hamlet. He also hungers for revenge for a slain father. Loving his dead father and sister, he succumbs to Claudius' temptation to use fraud in gaining his revenge. This plotting brings about his own death but also destroys Hamlet.

Horatio (hoh-RAY-shee-oh), Hamlet's former schoolmate and loyal friend. Well balanced and with a quiet sense of humor, he is also thoroughly reliable. Hamlet trusts him implicitly and confides in him freely. At Hamlet's death, he wishes to play the antique Roman and die by his own hand, but he yields to Hamlet's entreaty and consents to remain alive to tell Hamlet's story and to clear his name.

The ghost of King Hamlet, who appears first to the watch, then to Horatio and to Hamlet. He leads Hamlet away from the others and tells him of Claudius' foul crime. His second appearance to Hamlet occurs during the interview with the queen, to whom he remains invisible, causing her to think that Hamlet is having hallucinations. In spite of Gertrude's betrayal of him, the ghost of murdered Hamlet shows great tenderness for her in both of his appearances.

Fortinbras (FOHR-tihn-bras), the prince of Norway, the son of old Fortinbras, who was the former king of Norway. Fortinbras is the nephew of the present regent. Another foil to Hamlet, he is resentful of his father's death at old Hamlet's hands and the consequent loss of territory. He plans an attack on Denmark, which is averted by his uncle after diplomatic negotiations between him and Claudius. He is much more a man of action than a man of thought. Hamlet chooses him as the next king of Denmark and expresses the hope and belief that he will be chosen. Fortinbras delivers a brief but emphatic eulogy over Hamlet's body.

Rosencrantz (roh-ZEHN-kranz) and

Guildenstern (GIHL-dehn-sturn), the schoolmates of Hamlet summoned to Denmark by Claudius to act as spies on Hamlet. Although they are hypocritical and treacherous, they are no match for him, and in trying to betray him they go to their own deaths.

Old Norway, Fortinbras' uncle. Although he never appears on the stage, he is important in that he diverts young Fortinbras from his planned attack on Denmark.

Yorick (YOHR-ihk), King Hamlet's jester. Dead some years before the action of the play begins, he makes his brief appearance in the final act when his skull is thrown up by a sexton digging Ophelia's grave. Prince Hamlet reminisces and moralizes while holding the skull in his hands. At the time, he is ignorant of whose grave the sexton is digging.

Reynaldo (ray-NOL-doh), Polonius' servant. Polonius sends him to Paris on business, incidentally to spy on Laertes. He illustrates Polonius' deviousness and unwillingness to make a direct approach to anything.

First clown, a gravedigger. Having been sexton for many years, he knows personally the skulls of those he has buried. He greets with particular affection the skull of Yorick, which he identifies for Hamlet. He is an earthy humorist, quick with a witty reply.

Second clown, a stupid straight man for the wit of the first clown.

Osric, a mincing courtier. Hamlet baits him in much the same manner as he does Polonius, but without the concealed affection he has for the old man. Osric brings Hamlet word of the fencing match arranged between him and Laertes and serves as a referee of the match.

Marcellus (mahr-SEHL-uhs) and

Bernardo, officers of the watch who first see the ghost of King Hamlet and report it to Horatio, who shares a watch with them. After the appearance of the ghost to them and Horatio, they all agree to report the matter to Prince Hamlet, who then shares a watch with the three.

Francisco, a soldier on watch at the play's opening. He sets the tone of the play by imparting a feeling of suspense and heartsickness.

First player, the leader of a troop of actors. He produces *The Murder of Gonzago* with certain alterations furnished by Hamlet to trap King Claudius into displaying his guilty conscience.

A priest, who officiates at Ophelia's abbreviated funeral. He refuses Laertes' request for more ceremony because he believes Ophelia has committed suicide.

Voltimand (VOL-tih-mahnd) and

Cornelius (kohr-NEEL-yuhs), ambassadors sent to Norway by Claudius.

A HANDFUL OF DUST

Author: Evelyn Waugh (1903-1966)
First published: 1934
Genre: Novel
Locale: England
Time: The twentieth century
Plot: Social satire

Anthony Last, called **Tony**, a young Englishman whose dream is to restore his Hetton Abbey to its feudal glory. He does not suspect his wife's infidelity until she informs him of it and asks for a divorce. Agreeing at first, he becomes angry at her family's greed for alimony and refuses to give her a divorce. To get away, he goes on an expedition to the jungles of South America. There he contracts a fever and is nursed back to health by a trader who keeps Tony a permanent prisoner, forcing him to read and reread aloud the works of Charles Dickens interminably. Finally, Tony is declared officially dead. His abbey passes on to a cousin; his wife moves on to a new husband.

Brenda Last, Tony's wife. Bored with their life, she takes a room in London and has an affair with a selfish young man who loses interest when Brenda can obtain neither money nor a divorce. After Tony is declared dead, she marries another of his bachelor friends.

John Beaver, a worthless young bachelor whose social success consists chiefly in his availability as an extra man. He has an affair with Brenda but later discards her.

Mrs. Beaver, his mother, an interior decorator. She rents Brenda the one-room flat from which Brenda conducts her affair with John; after Tony's disappearance, with Brenda unable to get his money, she refuses Brenda's application for a job.

John Andrew Last, Brenda and Tony's son. He is killed while fox hunting, when his mount is struck by a runaway horse. Receiving the news of his death, Brenda at first thinks that John Beaver is being discussed. Learning that her son is the one who is killed, she is relieved;, thus realizing how much she cares for Beaver, she resolves to get a divorce.

Jock Grant-Menzies, Tony's friend, whom Brenda marries after Tony's disappearance.

Dr. Messinger, the explorer with whom Tony sets out on his travels. Deserted by their Indian guides, he and Tony venture down a jungle river in hopes it will lead them out. Dr. Messinger leaves the delirious Tony on shore and goes on for help, but the boat capsizes, and he drowns.

Todd, an illiterate trader who loves Dickens' novels. After finding Tony and nursing him back to health, Todd keeps him a prisoner so that he can spend his life hearing Tony read Dickens over and over.

HANDLEY CROSS: Or, The Spa Hunt

Author: Robert Smith Surtees (1803-1864)
First published: 1843; enlarged, 1854
Genre: Novel
Locale: England
Time: The nineteenth century
Plot: Satire

Michael Hardy, who before his death had been leader of the hunt in Sheepwash Vale.

John Jorrocks, a wealthy but lower-class grocer and a lover of fox hunting. He is invited to come to Handley Cross to revive fox hunting.

Julia Jorrocks, his wife.

Belinda Jorrocks, his pretty niece, who adds to his popularity.

Pigg, a Scot of puny appearance but enormous appetite, hired by Jorrocks as a huntsman.

Dr. Swizzle, whose discovery of the curative powers of a local spring makes Handley Cross a fashionable watering place.

Dr. Mello, another shady doctor who nightly pours Epsom salts into his own spring.

Captain Doleful, a lean, hypocritical soldier on half pay who thinks Handley Cross should have social life and a hunt club. It is he who invites Jorrocks to Handley Cross.

Mrs. Barnington, the leader of the social set in Handley Cross.

Fleeceall, a social secretary who helps Doleful select Jorrocks.

The Earl of Bramber, the owner of Ongar Castle, where Jorrocks mistakenly becomes an overnight guest and ends up sleeping in the bathhouse.

THE HANDMAID'S TALE

Author: Margaret Atwood (1939-)
First published: 1985
Genre: Novel
Locale: The fictional Gilead
Time: The future
Plot: Psychological realism

Offred, a Handmaid to Fred, one of the Commanders in the Republic of Gilead. Deprived even of her name, she is known only in reference to her master, as "of Fred." Having already proven her fertility by giving birth to a daughter before the revolution, this thirty-three-year-old woman functions as a surrogate womb for Serena Joy, the infertile wife of the Commander. Other than her role as substitute womb, Offred has no standing in the community; she is a faceless entity, forced to wear a nunlike habit of red (for fertility), the headpiece of which prevents her from looking anywhere except straight ahead. Offred, like all women in Gilead except the wives of the Commanders, is allowed no recreation other than shopping for the household; thus, she spends many hours alone in her room staring at the walls. No women in Gilead are permitted to learn to read, nor are the Handmaids allowed to form friendships with anyone of either gender. Prior to the revolution, she had been a wife and mother, as well as working to support herself. Eventually, she forms quasi relationships with Nick and the Commander. Her one goal is to escape from Gilead and go north to Canada in search of her husband and child.

The Commander, **Fred**, one of the leaders of the Republic of Gilead, the husband of Serena Joy, the "owner" of Offred, and the employer of Nick. A conservative man caught up in the strictures of his country's social, political, and moral system, he leads an empty life. Eventually, he turns to Offred for companionship, even though Handmaids should mean nothing to those in power. He plays Scrabble with her and gives her reading material, despite the injunction against women being literate. Eventually, he takes Offred to a club/brothel, where he has her dress like a prostitute. Even though he does not acknowledge it, Gilead's ultraconservative structure has failed him on the most basic, interpersonal levels.

Serena Joy, the Commander's wife and a onetime television evangelist. Like the other Commanders' wives, she cannot bear a healthy child because of the toxic wastes, pollution, and fallout that have contaminated the globe. Serena Joy leads an idle life as a symbol of the Commander's social rank: His power and status allow him to maintain an essentially useless person in relative luxury. Serena Joy is neither the Commander's friend nor his companion; marriage in the Republic of Gilead is a sham. Nor is she really a sexual being; rather, she only symbolically copulates with the Commander. It is the Handmaid, Offred, who receives his sperm and who would bear his child should she conceive. She encourages Offred to have sex with Nick and thus conceive a child.

Ofglen, another Handmaid, a companion of Offred and a member of the underground. She helps Offred to escape.

Moira, a college friend of Offred, a feminist separatist, and now a rebel in Gilead. Refusing to be co-opted by the system, she escaped from the Red Center, where women are trained to be Handmaids. She nearly made it to Canada before being caught and offered a choice: deportation to the Colonies or life as a prostitute. She now works in the brothel where the Commander takes Offred.

Offred's mother, an early feminist who favored the right to abortion. Offred's mother reared her as a single parent and taught her daughter to value herself as a woman. Offred's mother is now a prisoner in one of the Colonies, where women who will not bend to the system in Gilead are sent.

Aunt Lydia, one of the women in charge of training the Handmaids at the Red Center. She is a cross between a mother superior and a prison warden; it is her responsibility to teach women how to behave. She and the other Aunts essentially brainwash Handmaids into accepting their role as captive possessions by telling them that, if they willingly sacrifice their wombs, future generations of women will be free.

Nick, the Commander's chauffeur and, later, Offred's paid lover. He is an uncultured member of the working class whom, unbeknown to her husband, Serena Joy pays to have sex with Offred so she will conceive a child that Serena Joy and the Commander can claim as their own.

Luke, Offred's husband before the revolution that brought the Republic of Gilead into existence. Offred believes that he and her daughter managed to escape to Canada, where they are alive and well. Despite Offred's eventual escape from Gilead, her reunion with them is never confirmed in the novel.

— Melissa E. Barth

HANDS AROUND
(Reigen)

Author: Arthur Schnitzler (1862-1931)
First published: 1900
Genre: Drama

Locale: Vienna, Austria
Time: The 1890's
Plot: Social

The Prostitute, **Leocadia**, who begins and ends the sexual roundelay. She loses what little dignity she has left when she gives herself, free of charge, to the uncaring Soldier on the banks of Vienna's Danube Canal. In a later sexual encounter with the Count, she is more self-assured, more hopeful, and more "professional."

The Soldier, **Franz**, an unfeeling, swaggering macho type. He treats his second sex partner, the Maid, no better than his earlier one as he takes her on a meadow at an amusement park.

The Maid, who surrenders herself to the Soldier. She finds that yielding to the blasé young gentleman of the family she works for produces no change in the master-servant relationship.

The Young Gentleman, **Alfred**, who turns out to be quite an aesthete as he prepares the seduction of a young married woman. He finds himself temporarily impotent, possibly because she is "respectable" and his socioeconomic equal.

The Young Wife, **Emma**, the quintessential unfulfilled woman. Yearning for a son, in addition to her daughter, she wistfully remembers her wedding night in Venice as she listens to her husband smugly moralizing about the unhappiness of unfaithful wives.

The Husband, **Karl**, a domineering philistine who priggishly preaches the virtues of morality and the benefits of carefully rationed conjugal intercourse even as he prepares to commit adultery.

The Sweet Girl, called in various translations **Sweet Young Lady**, **Sweet Young Thing**, **Sweet Young Miss**, **Little Miss**, and **Little Darling**, an earthy, naïve, pleasure-loving girl from the lower class who is by turns prudish and promiscuous. She is always eminently realistic.

The Poet, a pretentious, pompous man convinced of his own sophistication and superiority. Having failed to impress the Sweet Girl with his complexity and celebrity, he gets his comeuppance from the Actress, who does want him as a sex partner but ridicules the fanciful vaporings of this poseur.

The Actress, a worldly, hard-boiled, capricious, cynical, rather misanthropic woman. She is a take-charge type who uses sex for her enjoyment and prestige and to cement professional and social relationships.

The Count, a hedonistic but inhibited aristocrat. When he calls on the Actress one morning, he soon finds himself drawn into her bed. He again becomes a reluctant sex partner after following the Prostitute to her shabby room in a drunken stupor, but the next morning he is revealed as a kindly person and sensitive soul as he muses about the meaning of life, permanence, and happiness.

— *Harry Zohn*

HANDY ANDY

Author: Samuel Lover (1797-1868)
First published: 1842
Genre: Novel

Locale: Ireland
Time: The nineteenth century
Plot: Love

Andy Rooney, a naïve, mischievous Irish boy. Eventually, Andy inherits the estate and the title of his father and goes to Parliament.

Mrs. Rooney, his mother.

Oonah, a cousin of Andy whom he marries.

Squire Edward Egan of Merryvale Hall, who hires Andy as a stable boy.

Mrs. Egan, his wife.

Murtough Murphy, an attorney and political boss.

Sir Timothy Trimmer, the aging holder of a political office.

The Honorable Sackville Scatterbrain, a candidate for Trimmer's post.

Lord Scatterbrain, Sackville's uncle, the secret father of Andy, who finally acknowledges him.

Squire O'Grady, of Neck-or-Nothing Hall, a supporter of Scatterbrain.

Gustavus O'Grady, his son and heir.

M'Garry, an apothecary who becomes involved in one of Andy's mistakes and almost causes a duel.

Edward O'Connor, a poet and a brave gentleman. He fatally wounds Squire O'Grady in a duel.

Fanny Dawson, who is in love with O'Connor.

Major Dawson, Fanny's father, who dislikes O'Connor.

Mr. Furlong, who is on O'Grady's side. He is forced to marry Augusta.

Augusta, the daughter of Squire O'Grady, innocently involved with Furlong.

Larry Hogan, who tries to blackmail Squire Egan.

Father Phil, Andy's confessor.

James Casey, who fails to turn up for his wedding.

Matty Dwyer, who is in love with Casey.

Jack Dwyer, her father, who will settle for Andy as a son-in-law.

Shan More, to whose cave the kidnapped Andy, disguised as Oonah, is taken.

Bridget, Shan's sister, who takes Andy, disguised as Oonah, to bed with her. The next morning, lamenting her lost honor, she forces Andy to marry her. He is later freed by the discovery that she is already married to a convict. Thus, Andy at last can marry Oonah.

HANGMAN'S HOUSE

Author: Donn Byrne (Brian Oswald Donn-Byrne, 1889-1928)
First published: 1925
Genre: Novel

Locale: Ireland
Time: Early twentieth century
Plot: Regional

James O'Brien, Lord Glenmalure, called **Jimmy the Hangman** for his record as a judge. He marries his daughter to John D'Arcy and dies the same night.

John D'Arcy, an ambitious, tricky man of little character. Lord Glenmalure hopes he will become a great politician, but he does not. He is a weak character who takes to gambling. Challenged to a duel by the Citizen for deserting the Citizen's sister, D'Arcy cheats by shooting before the signal. He burns down his wife's house and dies when he jumps from a window to escape the flames.

Dermot McDermot, a serious young Irishman, D'Arcy's cousin. He mistrusts the loyalties of D'Arcy. He falls in love with Connaught and tries to prevent the Citizen from killing D'Arcy, Connaught's husband. When Hangman's House is burned by D'Arcy, McDermot builds a cottage on the site, hoping Connaught will return.

Connaught, Lord Glenmalure's daughter, who marries D'Arcy. After her husband's weak character becomes apparent, she falls in love with McDermot. She leaves Ireland for England but returns after her husband's death to live in the cottage built for her by McDermot.

The Citizen, an Irishman who is an officer in the French army. He returns to try to prevent civil war in Ireland. He seeks revenge for his sister Maeve, deserted by D'Arcy. He fights a duel with D'Arcy and is wounded. After D'Arcy's death, he returns to France and his regiment.

Tricky Mick, D'Arcy's father, an old friend of Lord Glenmalure.

Maeve, the Citizen's sister, married to and deserted by D'Arcy. After the desertion, she and her little son die.

The Bard of Armagh, Connaught's famous race horse. D'Arcy kills the horse after he bets heavily against the animal in a race and loses a small fortune.

HAPGOOD

Author: Tom Stoppard (Tomas Straussler, 1937-)
First published: 1988
Genre: Drama

Locale: London, England
Time: The 1980's
Plot: Play of ideas

Elizabeth Hapgood, a thirty-eight-year-old British female intelligence operative. She is involved in a spy mission attempting to locate a mole or "sleeper" who is passing secrets to Russia. Her code name is "Mother," although she is also addressed as "Betty" by her "sister" Celia. Hapgood is the mother of a son by Kerner, a German-Russian spy, and also has had a long-standing relationship with Blair and a lesser one with the enigmatic operative Ridley. The leading character in a geometrically complicated web of intrigue and contradictions, Hapgood, along with every other character in the shadowy world of spying, is a potential "joe," the term for an operative who turns into a double or triple spy. Uncertainties multiply about whether her sister (also a Hapgood), who calls herself Celia, is really a sister, possibly a twin, or merely "Mother" in a double role. Torn between her two mother roles, she remains an enigmatic character whose conflict is resolved by the safety of her son and the intended return of Kerner to Russia.

Joseph Kerner, a fortyish Russian scientist and spy who has been "turned" by Hapgood and, therefore, is her "joe." He was born in Königsberg, the birthplace of philosopher Immanuel Kant. His triple-spy role is merely a working out of his intellectual gymnastics, which combine Kant's philosophical ideas with current atomic theories. Those theories involve the random nature of life and, therefore, of spies, who are like the electron, which can be here and there at the same moment. The particle world, as a result, becomes the dream world of the spy. Like "Mother," his real name, Joe, takes on the double significance of a "joe." His interest in physics supersedes his political preference. Although he sees the West as morally superior "in the fact that the system contains the possibility of its own reversal," he will accept the offer of transportation back to Russia. For him, spying is a metaphor for all people as they, in their dreams, meet their "sleepers": "the priest is visited by the doubter, the Marxist sees the civilizing force of the bourgeoisie, the captain of industry admits the justice of common ownership."

Paul Blair, a man about forty-eight years old and in good physical shape. He has been a longtime friend of Hapgood and, possibly, her lover. Hapgood can depend on him when all else fails. He might have been young Joe's father had not Hapgood, in one incident with Kerner, become pregnant. His role is that of a trustworthy and reliable friend of Hapgood, on both personal and professional levels, even when he suspects her as a mole.

Ernest Ridley, a spy in his mid-thirties who remains enigmatic to the end. His role involves a series of deliberately confusing costume disguises and, possibly, the existence of his twin. In the past, he, too, may have had a romantic liaison with Hapgood, and he is still attracted to her.

Ben Wates, a black American spy, about forty-five years old, who is the first black man to "make it to the seventh floor at Langley," the home of American intelligence activities. Turning up in London, he is not very much liked or trusted by the English, partly as a result of earlier operations in Athens in which a Russian and an American had been killed by the English.

Celia Hapgood, an artist's or photographer's model, not

listed in the opening list of characters. It is uncertain whether she is a disguise of "Mother," a sister, or a twin. The possibility exists that she is the delinquent side of Hapgood's double character.

Maggs, in his twenties, a young, calm, and professional secretary to Hapgood and a minor functionary in the events. He attends mostly to seeing that all beepers and telephones are in working order.

Merryweather, a minor operative, twenty-two years old, involved in the highly confusing opening incidents in which documents are transmitted in and out of cubicles in a bath-house.

Joe, the eleven-year-old son of Hapgood and Kerner. He attends a public school and is the object of a kidnapping attempt by the Russians, but in the end he is safe.

— *Susan Rusinko*

HAPPY DAYS

Author: Samuel Beckett (1906-1989)
First published: 1961
Genre: Drama
Locale: A barren plain of scorched grass
Time: Indeterminate
Plot: Absurdist

Winnie, a woman described in the play as "well preserved" and "plump," with a "big bosom." She is about fifty years of age. In the first act, she is buried up to her waist in earth. By the opening of the second act, she has been sucked, or sunk, downward so that only her head is visible. Winnie can best be characterized by her abundant optimism, which lies in sharp contrast to her desolate situation. Such an attitude to life is both courageous, because Winnie keeps her spirits high, and tragic, in that she is in an impossible situation. Consistent with her desire to appear cheerful, Winnie takes great pride in her personal possessions. Each one is endowed with a special meaning, even Brownie, the revolver she keeps in her bag. Winnie delights in seemingly banal conversation that helps her through the day, from the bell that wakes her to the bell for sleep. Following in a set pattern, almost like a ritual, Winnie cleans her teeth and glasses, applies lipstick, brushes and combs her hair, perhaps trims her nails if necessary, and then talks to her husband, Willie, who is beside her. Consequently, Winnie's language is vital as she clings to her words and memories, which, especially in the second act, are almost the only things left for her. Despite Winnie's attempts at remaining optimistic, many of the quotations that occur throughout her long monologue betray sadness and regret. This is most apparent in her singing of the Waltz Duet from Franz Lehar's *The Merry Widow*.

Willie, Winnie's husband. Willie remains hidden for the majority of the play, with only his bald head visible behind the slope. Unlike his wife, Willie is mobile. At the end of the second act, he appears on all fours to crawl up the mound toward Winnie. This appearance shows Willie "dressed to kill" in top hat, morning coat, and striped trousers, holding white gloves in his hand. He climbs a little way toward his wife but, unable to sustain the effort of looking up at her, he drops his head to the ground. Slowly, Willie climbs to the summit of the hill. With a hoarse cry to his wife ("Win"), he gazes at her, with an outstretched arm. It is not clear why Willie makes this effort. It may be to embrace Winnie for a last time, or it may be to kill her, himself, or both of them.

— *Ian Stuart*

HARD TIMES

Author: Charles Dickens (1812-1870)
First published: 1854
Genre: Novel
Locale: England
Time: Mid-nineteenth century
Plot: Social realism

Thomas Gradgrind, a retired hardware merchant and the founder of an experimental school where only facts and proved scientific laws are taught. A firm believer that "two and two are four, and nothing over," he is the father of five unhappy fact-finders and the husband of an ailing, dispirited woman quite worn out from the facts of life. While he is essentially a kind and good man, his excessive attention to the scientific and the practical and his total neglect of the imaginative and the speculative make him a kind of bumbling ogre. Through Gradgrind's theories and activities, Dickens projects his sharp criticism of nineteenth century industry and culture.

Louisa Gradgrind, his older daughter, called **Loo** by her husband, a wealthy, elderly industrialist to whom she was married according to her father's calculated mathematical theories. A sensible young woman, trained to have respect for hard facts by Mr. M'Choakumchild, master of the model school, she has no nonsense about her and therefore makes a proper wife for unsentimental and callous Josiah Bounderby. She cannot wonder, speculate, or love. Her two thwarted rebellions, an attempt in her girlhood to see a circus and a planned elopement from her unhappy marriage, fail because she lacks courage. Resisting the temptation to run away with another man, she returns to her father's house and stays there when she cannot bring herself to return to her husband's bed and board within the time limit he sets.

Thomas Gradgrind, the younger son. Although trained in the same school of hard facts, he is filled with melancholy and a lack of ambition that lead him to a determination to sample life's vices. Loved and protected by his sister, he becomes a drunkard, a sensualist, and finally a thief, stealing one hundred and fifty pounds from his brother-in-law's bank, where he is employed as a clerk. For a time, he is able to throw suspicion on an innocent man, but eventually his guilt is revealed. Easily led, he accepts the overtures of cynical James Harthouse, who uses the relationship of weak brother and protective sister as a wedge in his attempted seduction of Louisa. Tom is given another chance to face the facts, something he has rebelled against, when his sister and Sissy Jupe give him an opportunity to flee the country, away from Bounderby's wrath and the law's long arm.

Malthus Gradgrind,

Adam Smith Gradgrind, and

Jane Gradgrind, the other Gradgrind children, all victims of their father's harsh training.

Josiah Bounderby, a wealthy industrialist, the friend of Thomas Gradgrind and Louisa's husband. The owner of a Coketown (Manchester) factory, he is exceedingly proud of the fact that he is a self-made man. He advises Mr. Gradgrind against taking Sissy Jupe into his home or allowing her to attend the experimental school. In the end, he loses his wife and the respect of his friends—everything but his money.

Cecilia Jupe, called **Sissy**, the daughter of a circus clown. Deserted by her father, she grows up in the Gradgrind home, a companion to Louisa. Unsuccessful in learning facts, she is constantly forced to face them and is turned from her foster home to work in Bounderby's factory. A sensitive, loving girl, she is convinced that her father has not abandoned her, that the Gradgrinds have been generous, and that people are generally trustworthy. She proves her own trust by supporting confused Louisa, persuading Harthouse to leave the neighborhood, and helping Tom Gradgrind escape from the law.

James Harthouse, a cynical political aspirant and a shrewd observer of human nature and behavior. Handsome, smooth-spoken, he attempts the seduction of lonely, unloved Louisa. Sissy Jupe saves her friend from folly when she visits the young politician and persuades him the planned elopement would bring unhappiness to all concerned, including himself.

Mrs. Sparsit, a woman of aristocratic pretensions and closed mind, formerly Bounderby's housekeeper. Deposed from her position of authority after his marriage, she embarrasses the self-made industrialist by producing his respectable mother and thus proving that his story of his rise from rags to riches is a hoax.

Mrs. Pegler, the mother of Josiah Bounderby, a figure of mystery after her appearance in Coketown. The truth, finally revealed, is that she had reared her son in modest but comfortable circumstances and given him an education. Ashamed of his real background, the son has paid her a pension to stay away from him so that she cannot disprove his story that he lifted himself from the gutter.

Stephen Blackpool, a poor, honest weaver in Bounderby's factory. The victim of a drunken wife and the factory system, his life is a hard one. During a labor disturbance at the factory, he refuses to join the rebellious workers or to side with his employer. Discharged, he leaves Coketown to look for work elsewhere. During his absence, he is accused of the robbery committed by Tom Gradgrind. Louisa and Sissy find the miner in an abandoned mine shaft, into which he had fallen while returning to prove his innocence. He is brought to the surface alive but severely injured, and he dies soon afterward.

Mrs. Blackpool, his wife, a confirmed drunkard.

Rachel, a worker in Bounderby's factory, hopelessly in love with Stephen Blackpool.

Bitzer, a typical product of Mr. Gradgrind's school. Acting as Bounderby's agent, he tracks down Tom Gradgrind and arrests him, only to lose the culprit when Tom makes his escape with the aid of a circus owner, a performer, a trained dog, and a dancing horse.

Mr. M'Choakumchild, the master of Mr. Gradgrind's model school, also a believer that facts are facts.

Mr. Sleary, the proprietor of a circus troupe. A friend of Sissy Jupe, he helps Tom Gradgrind to flee the country.

E. W. B. Childers, a circus performer billed as "The Wild Huntsman of the North American Prairies." He aids Mr. Sleary in the plan for Tom Gradgrind's escape from Bitzer.

Emma Gordon, Sissy Jupe's friend, a member of the circus troupe.

Master Kidderminster, a young boy with a strangely aged face, the member of the circus troupe who assists E. W. B. Childers in his high-vaulting act.

Josephine Sleary, the lovely daughter of the circus proprietor.

Slackbridge, a trade union organizer.

Lady Scadgers, the eccentric, incredibly obese bedridden aunt of Mrs. Sparsit.

Signor Jupe, the circus clown who deserts his daughter.

HARLAND'S HALF ACRE

Author: David Malouf (1934-)
First published: 1984
Genre: Novel
Locale: South Queensland, Australia
Time: Early 1900's to the 1980's
Plot: Impressionistic realism

Frank Harland, an Australian painter. At first a gawky country boy, Harland develops into an awkward, reticent, and eccentric man, described as "leathery" in appearance. His acute sensitivity sets him apart, so that he comes to epitomize the artist struggling against a bourgeois society. The novel traces his development as a painter, and the other characters acquire importance only as they contribute to or detract from that process. Although a fully realized character, Frank emerges as the quintessential Australian artist who constructs his art from the Australian myth and landscape.

Phil Vernon, a lawyer and longtime friend of Frank. Phil is the first-person narrator of parts of the book and represents the ordinary world that revolves around family, established social circles, and business. A child when he first meets the then-unknown artist, Phil finds that his otherwise conventional life is enriched through connections with Frank, whom he understands more fully than most.

Clem Harland, Frank's father. Clem, who is called a soft, round man, fails as a farmer and landowner but succeeds as a master storyteller. This dreaming, talkative, impractical man influences Frank's own vision as an artist.

Tam Harland, Frank's brother. Slow-witted and overweight, Tam devotes his life to taking care of Frank, whose work he does not understand but whose greatness he senses.

Walter "Knack" Nestorius, a Polish refugee and friend of Frank who fled to Australia during World War II. Knack is a gigantic, balding man of near sixty. From this displaced antique dealer and pianist who later commits suicide, Frank learns about European art and culture.

Edna Byrne, Knack's Australian girlfriend. Plump, with bleached hair, she is a good, simple sort of woman in her thirties. Frank feels at ease with her, and she acts as a buffer to the complexities of Knack's world.

Aunt Roo, Phil's aunt. She is an attractive woman, young when first introduced and middle-aged when the novel concludes. Although she considers herself an unfulfilled artist (an actress, she dabbles in the arts), she rejects Frank until he receives international acclaim.

Gerald Harland, Frank's nephew. About the same age as Phil, this son of Frank's immoral sister is a worthless young man, described as athletic in build and "defiantly careless" in attitude. Frank places great hope in Gerald, who disappoints him by failing to restore the disintegrated family.

Pearsall Harland, Frank's youngest brother. He is a drunken and violent failure. His ruined life helps to symbolize the loss of family that so deeply affects Frank.

— *Robert L. Ross*

HARP OF A THOUSAND STRINGS

Author: H. L. Davis (1894-1960)
First published: 1947
Genre: Novel
Locale: The American prairie country, Tripoli, and Paris
Time: Late eighteenth and early nineteenth centuries
Plot: Historical

Melancthon Crawford, an American trader and one of the men who names a Western town. A slave of the Tripolitan pirates, he escapes with two companions, returns to America, founds a trading post, and makes a small fortune. Because of his eccentricities, his relatives return him to Pennsylvania as an old man, thus making sure he will not give away the money they hope to inherit from him.

Commodore Robinette (ro-bee-NEHT), a former slave with Crawford. He turns out to be a philanderer and ends up as a fugitive from the authorities for participation in an insurrection.

Apeyahola, called **Indian Jory**, a Creek Indian. He is Crawford's other companion in the escape from Tripoli. He ends up as a fugitive from the law after killing a man in Georgia.

Jean-Lambert Tallien (zhah[n]-lahm-BEHR tahl-LYA[N]), a man who tells his story to the three escaping Americans in Tripoli as they hide in a warehouse. He was once a leader in the French Revolution but has fallen because of a woman.

The Marquis de Bercy (deh behr-SEE), benefactor of Tallien while the latter is a young man.

Anne-Joseph Théroigne (an-zhoh-SEHF tay-ROYN-yeh), a woman in love with René de Bercy. She later becomes a revolutionist and is stripped, beaten, and driven insane by a mob for helping the man she loves. She is exposed as a traitor to the mob by Tallien.

René de Bercy (reh-NAY), son of the marquis de Bercy. He is Tallien's rival for the love of Countess Thérèse de Fontenay. He scorns Tallien's offer of escape to England and is among a group of pursuers killed by Tallien's order during the French Revolution.

Father Jarnatt (zhahr-NAHT), a priest who befriends and protects Tallien when he is sought by a mob of peasants for injuring the son of the marquis.

Countess Thérèse de Fontenay (tay-REHZ deh fon-teh-NAY), loved by Tallien, who marries her and protects her during the French Revolution. While Tallien tells his story to the Americans in the warehouse, she enters with another man. She identifies herself to the Americans but not to Tallien.

Captain Belleval (behl-VAHL), an officer who incurs Tallien's jealousy by befriending Thérèse de Fontenay.

M. de Chimay (deh she-MAY), a wealthy French aristocrat and merchant. He comes to the warehouse accompanied by Thérèse de Fontenay to transact business with Tallien.

M. Ouvrard (ew-VRAHR), Thérèse de Fontenay's onetime lover, a wealthy, influential banker.

HARRIET SAID

Author: Beryl Bainbridge (1933-   )
First published: 1972
Genre: Novel
Locale: Formby, England
Time: Mid-twentieth century
Plot: Psychological realism

The narrator, a thirteen-year-old middle-class English girl. Home for the summer from the boarding school to which she has been sent as a "problem child," she resumes her interrupted friendship with a neighbor girl, Harriet, whom she admires and to whom she feels inferior. Plain and heavyset, she is flattered when a married man in their seashore town, Mr. Biggs, shows a sexual interest in her. Under Harriet's guidance, she plots the seduction of this man, toward whom she has ambivalent feelings of fascination and disgust. She is vaguely repelled by his physical evidences of middle age and reacts with contempt at his fear and helplessness when they are locked in a church one night. Several nights later, however, she allows him to consummate their relationship on a deserted dune. Her indifference toward his feelings and her possibly destructive effect on him parallels her curiously detached attitude toward her parents, toward whom she admits an inability to feel love. Two weeks before the end of her vacation, she and Harriet pay a call on Mr. Biggs; when his wife comes home unexpectedly, the narrator, although intending only to stun her, inadvertently kills her at Harriet's command.

Harriet, the fourteen-year-old friend of the narrator, whom she dominates with alternating fondness and cruelty. She dictates what the narrator must write in their joint diary, a journal of their sexual fantasies and experiences. Although she masterminds the narrator's relationship with Mr. Biggs, she is somewhat jealous of his obvious attraction to her friend, prompting her decision that he must be humbled. She orchestrates a voyeuristic excursion to the Biggses' house and later maliciously and sadistically locks the narrator and Mr. Biggs in the church. When at one point she comes upon Mr. Biggs lying prostrate in his parlor, weeping at the feet of the narrator, she laughs viciously at his humiliating posture. Extremely self-assured, she is adept at manipulating adults, even her parents, and uses this talent to triumph in her psychological warfare against the Biggses. When her friend murders Mrs. Biggs, Harriet succeeds in forcing the drunken and defeated Mr. Biggs to take the blame.

Peter Biggs, whom the girls nickname the **Tsar**, a fifty-six-year-old married man who pursues the narrator. He is both physically and psychologically weak. Balding and frail, he allows himself to be dominated by his wife, whom he married thirty years earlier because, as he explains to the narrator, she won a house in a church raffle. His approaches to the narrator are at first tentative as he tries to drive a wedge between her and Harriet, whom he intensely dislikes but is forced to accept as the inescapable companion of his paramour. Ironically, he does not perceive that the narrator is not completely a naïve dupe of Harriet, and he succumbs to her schemes. He seems unable to resist his impulses. Even after several embarrassing consequences resulting from their clandestine meetings, such as having to explain away an injured arm suffered in the escape from a church through a window, he persists in his infatuation. His matter-of-fact sexual conquest of the narrator does not provide him with the satisfaction he anticipated. The gradual recognition of his powerlessness in all of his relationships leads to self-loathing and total disillusionment, which make inevitable his acceptance of sole guilt in his wife's death.

Mrs. Biggs, a fat, middle-aged woman who is openly suspicious of the girls' actions. When they peer into the Biggses' parlor window one evening, they witness Mrs. Biggs sexually dominating her feebly resistant husband, a scene that fills Harriet with scorn for both partners and thus provokes the subsequent action of the novel. She is killed by the narrator.

— *Caren S. Silvester*

THE HASTY HEART

Author: John Patrick (John Patrick Goggan, 1905-1995)
First published: 1945
Genre: Drama

Locale: The Assam/Burma border
Time: Early 1940's
Plot: Comedy

Lachlen (Lachie) McLachlen (LO-kee), a twenty-one-year-old Scottish soldier fighting for the British in the Burmese campaign of World War II. Small, slightly built, feisty, proud, solitary, independent, and surly, Lachie was orphaned as a child, has no family or friends, and has never trusted or been friendly with anyone. He yearns for companionship but is afraid to open himself up to people for fear of being rejected and deserted. When a piece of shrapnel destroys one of his kidneys, leaving the remaining kidney defective, Lachie is doomed to die within six weeks. Unaware of his condition, Lachie is placed in the convalescent ward of a military hospital so he can have friends around him when he dies. Lachie is so suspicious and unfriendly at first, however, that the men of the ward must struggle to be kind and comforting. A surprise birthday party and the gift of a kilt touch him deeply, and he becomes gregarious, attempting to befriend all the men and proposing marriage to the attractive young nurse of the ward, Margaret. When he discovers that he is going to die, Lachie becomes angry again, accusing the men and Margaret of merely pitying him.

Yank, an American from the deep South, the putative leader of the men in the convalescent ward. In his late twenties, Yank stutters when he gets excited, and when he loses his temper he recites the books of the Bible to recover his composure. Blond, wholesome, and easygoing, but prone to anger, Yank dislikes Scotsmen and the sound of bagpipes. He is frequently driven to anger by Lachie's behavior but leads the attempts to befriend him.

Margaret, the attractive twenty-one-year-old British nurse who runs the ward. Compassionate and kind, she has an easy and assured manner with the men and is patient with Lachie's unpleasant behavior. After Lachie proposes to her, she is unsure whether her acceptance of him is based on real romantic interest or on pity.

Digger, another patient in the ward, a dark Australian of about thirty, good-natured, gregarious, athletic, and thickly muscular. He is a paratrooper and the boxing champion of his regiment.

Tommy, the comic butt of most of the jokes and taunts in the ward, a short, exceedingly fat British Cockney with a thick accent. Lazy and fun-loving, he responds to everyone's good-natured taunting with childlike playfulness.

Kiwi, another patient in the ward, a very tall, blond New Zealander in his middle twenties who will make a bet on anything to ease the boredom of confinement.

Blossom, the least talkative patient, a huge African Basuto who knows only one word of English, his name. When Blossom offers the departing and angry Lachie a gift of beads, unaware of Lachie's impending death, the act proves that pure human concern unalloyed by pity is possible.

The Colonel, the medical officer and surgeon who places Lachie in the ward, asking the men to befriend Lachie to make his last days pleasant.

Orderly, a young British man who helps Margaret in the ward.

— *Terry Nienhuis*

HAVELOK THE DANE

Author: Unknown
First published: c. 1350
Genre: Poetry

Locale: England and Denmark
Time: The tenth century
Plot: Romance

Havelok, the son and heir of the king of Denmark. Exiled and reared in England by an old fisherman, he is a typical hero of the popular romances, renowned for his strength, his athletic prowess, his size, and his gentle nature rather than for his intellectual acumen.

Goldeboru, his wife, the lovely heiress to the English throne. Unwillingly married to an unknown kitchen boy, she rejoices to find him in reality a king, and she supports him in his successful attempts to regain his own throne and hers.

Athelwold, Goldeboru's father, the brave, just, and devout king of England. He entrusts his young daughter to his noblemen on his deathbed.

Godrich, a treacherous lord, named regent and Goldeboru's guardian by Athelwold. He marries the rightful queen to Havelok to secure the throne for himself and ultimately is burned at the stake for this act of treason.

Birkabeyn, the good king of Denmark, whose only fault is his lack of judgment in leaving his three children in Godard's hands at his untimely death.

Godard, the Danish regent, who murders two of his charges and sends the third, Havelok, to be drowned. His tyrannical reign is brought to a close by Havelok's return.

Grim, Havelok's loyal guardian, an old fisherman who rears the prince as one of his own children.

Ubbe, a powerful Danish lord. He protects Havelok and Goldeboru when they arrive in his country, and he rallies the gentry and nobility to the cause of their rightful ruler.

HAWAII

Author: James A. Michener (1907-1997)
First published: 1959
Genre: Novel

Locale: Primarily Hawaii
Time: 814-1954
Plot: Historical

Tamatoa VI, the chief of the Bora Borans, whose name means "the warrior." In his thirties, he is a burly and serious man. He leads his people during a time in which the gods are changing; he recognizes that he must change himself if his people are to be saved. He devises a plan, with his brother Teroro, to migrate with his people to a land in the north known only through myth and legend. Although he is following a dream, he is very practical about organizing the supplies for the trip. He successfully leads his people and their traditional gods to the northern land, Hawaii, in an arduous sea voyage that shakes his self-confidence.

Teroro, the navigator of the ceremonial canoe used to transport the Bora Borans to Hawaii. Handsome and impetuous, he takes revenge against the priests of the new gods despite objections from his brother. It is Teroro who discovers the meaning of the new fixed star that appears after the canoe crosses the equator. Using the star for navigation, he returns to Bora Bora for his wife and additional settlers.

Marama, Teroro's wife. She cannot accompany him on his northern journey because she is thought to be barren and, therefore, not useful to the new settlement; however, she conceives his child the night before he leaves. She is stately, resourceful, wise, and compassionate. As a priest's daughter, she sees the essentials of a situation and always gives good advice. When she returns with Teroro to the new colony, she brings flower seeds and plants with her for cultivation there. She becomes the seeress for the new settlement.

Malama Kanakoa, the ruler of Maui when the missionaries arrive. She is a large woman and very progressive. She recognizes that the white men have more power than the Hawaiians and equates Christian conversion with this power. She learns English and establishes a new civil code of laws to match the tenets of Christianity that she finds beneficial to her people. She pretends to accept more of Christianity than she really does as a means of placating the missionaries. On her deathbed, she asks her husband, Kelolo, to bury her according to traditional and ancient ceremonies.

Kelolo Kanakoa, Malama's husband, who never accepts Christianity despite the missionaries' efforts. He is devoted to Malama. When he establishes a police force, he becomes its chief. He welcomes his son Keoki's reversion to the ancient gods. As keeper of his family's history, he recognizes that the coming of the missionaries is the end of his way of life. After the death of his son and his wife, he takes his gods with him in a canoe for a trip to Bora Bora, knowing that he will never return.

Keoki Kanakoa, the son of Malama and Kelolo who converted to Christianity in the United States. Educated at Yale, he is a powerful speaker and convinces many missionaries to travel to his pagan homeland to take the word of Christ there. He has a simple and direct faith in the goodness of Jesus. He is hurt by Abner Hale's refusal to ordain him as a full minister and reverts to the ancient beliefs of his family. He marries his sister, Noelani, in the traditional rites. He contracts measles and dies without reconciling with the Christian faith.

Noelani Kanakoa, the daughter of Malama who is groomed to be the next ruler of Maui. Although she is not interested in the Christian faith, she is very interested in the power and money of the white men. She knows that the royal Hawaiian families have lost their power. After Keoki dies, she marries Rafer Hoxworth because she believes that he is the kind of strong man who will shape her country's history.

Kelly Kanakoa, an attractive Hawaiian beach boy and nightclub singer. Kelly makes his living by squiring American divorcées around Hawaii. Although he is a descendant of the royal Hawaiians Malama and Kelolo, he owns no land and has no money. He marries Judy Kee despite objections that he is not good enough to marry into a prominent Chinese family.

Abner Hale, a thin, sallow, and unattractive man who becomes the leader of the first group of missionaries to go to Hawaii. He is a strict Calvinist from a pious and penurious New England family. He has not known any women physically before he is required to marry Jerusha Bromley to be accepted to the Hawaiian mission. He believes that his will and God's are the same, which leads him to profess a proud and unbending form of Christianity that is at odds with the relaxed Hawaiian culture. He truly likes Malama, whom he teaches, but he views Hawaiians in general as abominations to God. He continues to rave against nonwhite cultures his entire life and dies separated from his family.

Jerusha Bromley, a compassionate New England woman who marries Abner Hale in a burst of Christian zeal after she comes to believe that she has been spurned by her true love, Rafer Hoxworth. She accompanies Abner to Hawaii, where she teaches Malama to read and begins a school for the Hawaiian children. She grows to love Abner despite her dislike of his fire-and-brimstone religious policies, and she eventually convinces him to soften his preachings.

Rafer Hoxworth, a rough and cruel whaling captain who becomes rich and influential through his commercial dealings and his marriage to Noelani. He never forgives Abner for taking Jerusha away from him and encourages the marriage of his daughter and Abner's son as a form of revenge. He expects and needs to have control over all situations and takes what he wants, regardless of the consequences. After Noelani's death, he becomes more interested in his grandchildren and encourages Whipple Hoxworth, his grandson, to be as bold and daring as he was in his youth.

Whipple Hoxworth, Rafer's grandson, who is known as **Wild Whip** for his womanizing and brawling. He is a visionary and a doer. He chooses agriculture over commerce and the family business. He brings an improved type of pineapple to the islands for cultivation as a cash crop. He designs a way to bring water from the wet side of the mountains to the dry side and turns thousands of unproductive acres into fertile fields. He has a great concern for beauty and brings various flowers and plants back from his travels. He is responsible for the diversification of the agricultural economy.

John Whipple, one of the first missionaries to come to the islands at the behest of Keoki Kanakoa. Although he begins as a missionary, he returns to medicine after finding missionary work as defined by Abner Hale to be too restrictive and hypocritical. He joins with the captain of the ship that took him to Hawaii in a merchandising and trading venture that grows into one of the most powerful and richest firms in the islands. He is responsible for bringing the Chinese into Hawaii, both to work on the sugar plantations and as a means to rejuvenate the Hawaiian race.

Micah Hale, the son of Abner and Jerusha and the husband of Rafer Hoxworth's daughter Malama. After a youth spent in the United States, to be educated away from pagan Hawaii, he returns to the islands with Rafer and his family. He becomes a partner in the firm of Hale and Hoxworth and works for the political and economic acceptance of Hawaii by the United States. He is somewhat less rigid than his father, but, as he grows older, he reverts to the Calvinist teachings of his childhood. He disapproves of the behavior of the younger generation.

Char Nyuk Tsin, also known as **Woo Chow's Auntie**, a Chinese woman who is taken to Hawaii to be sold into prostitution but becomes the unofficial wife of Kee Mun Ki instead. She is unattractive but strong and tenacious. She is very loyal to Kee, bearing him four sons who are destined to become important in Hawaiian politics and business. She never loses sight of her goal to own land and works indefatigably toward that goal. She is ambitious for her children. She acquires a degree of fame and respect for following Kee to the leper colony when he contracts the disease. She cares for him and for other lepers and brings a modicum of order to what had been a lawless and brutal life for the victims of leprosy.

Kee Mun Ki, a gambler and wheeler-dealer who goes to Hawaii to make his fortune. He marries a girl from his home village and requires the sons that he fathers by Char Nyuk Tsin to send money and respect back to his official wife. He contracts leprosy and spends the last years of his life in a leper colony, where he continues his success at gambling.

Africa Kee, a son of Char Nyuk Tsin. He becomes a lawyer and one of the Golden Men. The term "Golden Men" was invented to describe a type of intercultural man that had developed in Hawaii. Africa is modern and American in style, but he understands the ancient Oriental ways.

Hong Kong Kee, a grandson of Char Nyuk Tsin. He is appointed to high positions in government and business in recognition that Oriental peoples are controlling more and more of Hawaii's commerce.

Kamejiro Sakagawa, an émigré from Japan who goes to Hawaii to make his fortune. He is singled out by Whipple Hoxworth for his toughness to help him dynamite a tunnel through the mountains to bring water to the fields. When money troubles plague him, he becomes receptive to the ideas of labor organizers and loses his job on the plantation. After being accused of dynamiting a plantation home, he is blacklisted from plantation work. He opens a barbershop and allows his daughter to work there, in contrast to traditional Japanese ideas.

Ishii, or **Oshii**, the husband of Reiko, Kamejiro's daughter. He is a zealous supporter of Japan during World War II. He informs the Sakagawas that Japan has attacked Hawaii before that event occurs.

Goro Sakagawa, the son of Kamejiro, who begins his success by becoming a high school football star. He volunteers for service in the American Army immediately after the attack on Pearl Harbor. He becomes a respected war hero, rising to the rank of lieutenant. After the war, he returns to Hawaii and is instrumental in organizing agricultural laborers.

Shigeo Sakagawa, the youngest son of Kamejiro, who knows much about the Japanese attack on Hawaii because of his job as a telegram delivery boy. He becomes a captain in the U.S. Army and later becomes a lawyer and political leader.

— *Stephanie Korney*

A HAZARD OF NEW FORTUNES

Author: William Dean Howells (1837-1920)
First published: 1890
Genre: Novel
Locale: New York City
Time: The 1880's
Plot: Social realism

Basil March, an unsuccessful Boston insurance man who accepts the editorship of a literary magazine in New York. His adventures with the magazine's promoters, financial backers, and staff members constitute the story. Though March has little self-confidence, the magazine thrives. Eventually he has a chance to buy the publication, in partnership with the promoter, a happy circumstance that will make him not only financially successful but also spiritually fulfilled.

Mr. Dryfoos, a rustic who had made a fortune from his natural gas holdings. It is he who finances the magazine March edits. He lives a harassed existence: His womenfolk are socially ambitious; he cannot approve his daughter's choice in suitors; his son, determined to be a minister, makes a bad businessman; and a socialist on the magazine's staff plagues him on political issues. Dryfoos finally solves his problems by selling the magazine to March and the promoter, Fulkerson, and taking his family on an extended trip to Europe.

Henry Lindau, March's tutor, a German socialist who becomes the magazine's foreign editor and reviewer. His clash with Dryfoos results in Lindau's dismissal from *Every Other Week*, Dryfoos' periodical. While demonstrating with the workers in a streetcar strike, Lindau is set upon by the police and beaten so severely that he eventually dies. He receives a proper funeral by a contrite Dryfoos.

Conrad Dryfoos, Dryfoos' son and the ostensible publisher of *Every Other Week*. While defending the one-armed Lindau from the police who are beating him, he is struck by a stray bullet and killed.

Mr. Fulkerson, the promoter who invites March to accept the editorship of the magazine. He is happy when he and March buy the magazine, because in this act he sees a secure future for himself and the girl he wants to marry, a Southern belle whose Virginia colonel father loves to extol the merits of slavery.

Christine Dryfoos, Dryfoos' daughter, who is bent on entering society and who finally has her way. First, however, she loves a young man to whom her father objects, but whom she rejects when her father later approves of him. In Europe, her fondest dreams come true when she becomes engaged to a penniless French nobleman.

Mrs. March, March's wife, who, though reluctant to leave Boston, persuades her husband to take the editorship in New York.

Angus Beaton, the art director of *Every Other Week*, who loves Christine and is paid for his trouble when, despite her love for him, she scratches his face and forcibly ejects him from her father's house.

HE WHO SEARCHES
(Como en la guerra)

Author: Luisa Valenzuela (1938-　　)
First published: 1977
Genre: Novel
Locale: Barcelona, Spain; Mexico; and Argentina
Time: The 1970's
Plot: Social morality

AZ, the protagonist and main narrator, known by his initials and also called **Pepe** (PEH-peh) but not given a full name. He is an Argentine semiotics professor and psychoanalyst living in Barcelona. Although he is married, he is obsessed with a woman referred to only as "she," whom he purports to analyze without her knowledge. Visiting her late at night in a number of disguises, including female costumes, AZ has sexual relations with her, secretly tapes her conversations and associations, and transcribes them as part of his narration. Professionally pompous (often lapsing as narrator into the royal "we"), he pretends to himself that his love interest in her is all in the line of psychoanalytic duty. AZ becomes so involved with the woman that his own identity begins to merge with hers, especially when he loses track of her and leaves Barcelona to search for her in Latin America. AZ's quest is as much for self as for the other, and he also theorizes that he is searching for death. AZ feels a typically Argentine alienation from his Latin American identity, but his return to Latin America and Argentina brings him closer to his nationality: He is absorbed by the ritual magic he witnesses in Mexico and by the guerrilla operation he joins in Buenos Aires while standing in line with a multitude of his compatriots, who are expecting a miracle. Sometime after the miracle (the revelation of "her" radiating light from a glass coffin), AZ, who has been relatively apolitical, is tortured by the authorities because of his previous association with "her."

She, a curly-haired Argentine living in political exile in Barcelona and working as a cabaret waitress and prostitute. She has been at least marginally involved in guerrilla activity in Argentina, has been tortured, and is herself capable of violence. At times, she suspects that AZ is spying on her for an intelligence agency, and she plans his murder, keeping a .32 pistol under her pillow. AZ and others perceive her as a femme fatale and associate her with darkness. Like AZ, she has a shifting identity, appearing in many guises, principally through the use of wigs. She is aware of his deception but continues to receive him until she disappears. She writes compulsively, as if she (like AZ) were trying to reach an understanding of herself by setting down her thoughts and impressions. She collects carved hands and hand symbols from every religion and from all over the world, because she sees in them a relationship to the cosmos. This enigmatic woman is last seen, dramatically and miraculously, in Buenos Aires. Going to the head of the queue, AZ sets a charge that bursts the walls of a fortress. She is seen within, luminous in a glass coffin on a white dais, an image reminiscent of the historical Eva Perón, who was publicly displayed in the 1970's in a mausoleum.

Beatriz (beh-ah-TREES), also called **Bea** and **Bé**, AZ's jealous but faithful wife. She becomes aware of his infidelity and is eventually reduced to helping him dress for his sexual-analytical exploits and anxiously waiting for him to return home. She also helps AZ by transcribing his tapes of his encounters with the woman. Bea is blonde, a kind of opposite of the darker woman with whom AZ is fascinated. Whereas "she" is worldly, unconventional, and perceived as menacing, Bea is an inoffensive homebody, a repressed, banal, bourgeois wife.

Alfredo Navoni (ahl-FREH-doh nah-VOH-nee), a guerrilla who was the Argentine woman's lover when they both were involved in activism. She remembers her time with him as more real than her time in Barcelona. When he went underground, he abandoned her. She tells AZ two of Navoni's dreams as if they were her own, although she could not have learned them from Navoni himself: They are private, violent dreams that reveal Navoni's violent fascination with her. The first is a dream of sexual hunger transmuted into the terms of a feeding frenzy: Navoni appears disguised as a ravenous tiger and then a wolf. The second, seen through male eyes, is her striptease on a railroad track and her explosion into a thousand colored flashes as a train hits her.

— *John Deredita*

HEADBIRTHS: Or, The Germans Are Dying Out
(Kopfgeburten: Oder, Die Deutschen sterben aus)

Author: Günter Grass (1927-)
First published: 1980
Genre: Novel

Locale: Germany and Asia
Time: 1979 and 1980
Plot: Social realism

The narrator, probably Günter Grass himself, born in 1927 in Danzig. The first-person narrator is on a sponsored lecture tour of China and India with his wife, Ute. A sympathetic observer, he nevertheless retains his commitment to German affairs and to the coming elections. The crowds in Shanghai lead him to imagine a grotesque world in which the Germans, in danger of dying out according to alarmist, patriotic politicians at home, would be as numerous as the Chinese. He finds a parallel between the stultification of China through the cultural revolution and that of Germany through Nazi ideology. He imagines his own situation if he had been born ten years earlier and had been active in the Nazi era. These speculations and others of their kind lead to the narrator conceiving the idea for a book or film to be called *Headbirths*—a reference to Zeus—and to be prepared with the help of film director Volker Schlöndorff. The author duly presents his characters but constantly returns to his own doings and preoccupations, including the West German elections with the politician Franz Joseph Strauss and the nuclear power plant near Broksdorf. These matters preoccupy characters Harm and Dörte Peters. The author also refers to personal affairs, such as the death of a fellow writer. Without doubt, the narrator tends to lose the thread, unlike Ute, who knits a scarf all the way through Asia.

Harm Peters (PEE-tehrs), a high school teacher from Itzehoe, Germany, born in 1945. He is Dörte's husband. He has taken part in the student movements of the 1960's, is an active member of his local socialist party, and now undertakes an Asian tour with Dörte in a spirit of social responsibility. He and Dörte are full of scruples about bringing a child into the world. The Asian tour does not help them to find a solution, nor do their phases of willingness in this matter often coincide. As Harm's participation in this decision is, in any case, subordinate, the author tries to give him a compensatory subplot that involves a German liver sausage destined for a friend in Bali. The plot is abandoned, however, and Harm carries the sausage home. A bout of dysentery allows Harm to feel that he is sharing native life. His interests resemble those of the author, and his reform plans include allowing the Germans to die out, a scheme not generally acceptable to the high school students. Returning home in 1980, a year after his creator, Harm is sucked up in election issues.

Dörte Peters (DEHR-teh), a high school teacher from Itzehoe. She is blonde, was born in 1948, and is Harm's wife. She and Harm are similarly principled. Her scruples about bringing a child into a violent, overcrowded, and polluted world pursue her on her Asian tour with her husband. Admirable as these scruples are, there is something ludicrous about her hope of finding spontaneity of decision in an overpopulated Indian fishing village. On Bali, she hangs a wishing slip on a tree in the native fashion and visits a temple cave full of darkness and bats. Finally, she even toys with the idea of picking up a gentle Balinese youth to be the anonymous father of her child, but this cinematic solution, from a Vicki Baum novel, is rejected as not in character. Undecided as ever, Dörte and her husband return to their native land and its concerns (for example, the nuclear power plant) and to their pupils' questions.

Dr. Konrad Wenthien (VEHN-tee-ehn), a tour guide in Asia to the Sisyphus Tourist Bureau. He is a master of languages and full of expert lore extending from religious rites in Bombay to cockfighting in Bali. It is he who takes Harm and Dörte to spend a night in a Bombay (or Bangkok) slum. Although Dörte finds him a "creep," it is to Wenthien that she turns in the matter of the Balinese beach boy. Wenthien's answer to the central question of overpopulation is contained in ironic visions of a peaceful Asian invasion of Europe, or of an impassable wall.

— *W. Gordon Cunliffe*

HEADLONG HALL

Author: Thomas Love Peacock (1785-1866)
First published: 1816
Genre: Novel
Locale: An estate in Caernarvonshire in North Wales
Time: The 1810's
Plot: Satire

Mr. Escot, a philosopher of the "deteriorationist" school. Heavily influenced by the ideas of Jean-Jacques Rousseau, he believes that the condition of humankind has been corrupted by civilization and luxury and is physically degenerate in comparison with conditions of prehistoric ancestors. As with all of his fellow guests at Headlong Hall, however, he does not allow his doom-laden judgments to detract from his enjoyment of the weekend's entertainments. Nor does his pessimism inhibit his ardent courtship of the lovely Cephalis Cranium, during the course of which he must exercise courage and cunning to outshine his rival, the erudite Mr. Panscope.

Mr. Foster, a philosopher of the "perfectibilian" school. As a fervent believer in progress, arguing that the inexorable advancement of technology coupled with the refinement of morals will lead eventually to the perfection of human society, he is diametrically opposed to Mr. Escot on every issue. In matters of everyday conduct, however, he and Mr. Escot are very much alike. His simultaneous marriage to Caprioletta Headlong—Cephalis Cranium's dearest friend—ensures that their lives will continue to mirror each another.

Mr. Cranium, a determinist who believes that the characteristics of individual people can be read in the bumps on their skulls (the author does not use the term "phrenology"). When Mr. Escot saves him from drowning, he is inclined to withhold credit on the grounds that his rescuer was simply following his innate tendencies, but he gladly gives consent for his daughter's marriage when Mr. Escot presents him with an unusually interesting skull to add to his collection.

Squire Headlong, the landowner who is host to the house party attended by the miscellaneous amateur philosophers, artists, and men of letters. He is the provider who spares no expense in laying on good food, good wine, and all manner of scientific and artistic apparatus. His sole concern is to ensure that everything goes well. When he decides that the party needs a fourfold wedding to round it off, he immediately assents to his sister's marriage to Mr. Foster, then allocates one of the two daughters of the violinist Cornelius Chromatic to the painter Patrick O'Prism while proposing to the other himself.

Marmaduke Milestone, a landscape gardener who chooses to substitute lawns and flower beds, suitably embellished by pagodas, Chinese bridges, and artificial fountains, for the wilderness that surrounds Headlong Hall. His demonstration of the use of gunpowder in clearing difficult ground causes the accident in which Mr. Cranium nearly drowns.

Mr. Panscope, an expert in all the sciences who determines his beliefs by taking census of the gross weight of intellectual authority, from the Greek philosophers to contemporary scientists. He is, however, willing to descend to mere flattery in order to persuade Mr. Cranium to promise his daughter's hand in marriage, without bothering to consult the young lady regarding her wishes.

Mr. Nightshade and

Mr. MacLaurel, poets who dabble in literary criticism to the extent of being leaders of an entire critical coterie. They are accompanied at Headlong Hall by two further members of the coterie, Timothy Treacle and Geoffrey Gall. Apart from enjoying the food and wine, none of these four takes any active part in the weekend's events, all of them being perfectly content to stand on the sidelines and pass comment on the conduct of others.

The Reverend Doctor Gaster, a religious fundamentalist who attempts (ineffectually) to arbitrate the disputes of Mr. Escot and Mr. Foster by continual reference to the Scriptures.

Mr. Jenkinson, an intellectual liberal who attempts (absurdly) to arbitrate the disputes of Mr. Escot and Mr. Foster by continually arguing that there is merit on both sides.

— *Brian Stableford*

THE HEALERS

Author: Ayi Kwei Armah (1939-)
First published: 1978
Genre: Novella
Locale: The Asante empire area and the Cape Coast of Ghana
Time: 1873-1874
Plot: Historical

Densu Ansa (DEHN-sew AHN-sah), a leading youth of Esuano at the age of twenty, an orphan since birth. A critically reflective person, he could have won the chosen-year games of competition and could have become king-elect, but, compassionately, he refused to kill a tethered pigeon in the final shooting contest. Actually, he prefers the work of the ascetic healers to the manipulative world of the court. He escapes the machinations of his evil guardian, Ababio, who would exploit Densu as a figurehead ruler. Densu, choosing truth and honorable service, is successful in joining the community of healers.

Damfo (DAHM-foh), the leader of a community of healers in the forest and a mentor to Densu. Wise and compassionate, he aids people in seeing, hearing, and knowing themselves, as well as in understanding truly and acting truly. An enemy of manipulation, his method is inspiration. He seeks to instill unity, wholeness, and spirituality through his consultative treatments.

Ababio (ah-bah-BEE-oh), a corrupt, power-hungry court retainer whose tools are force, fraud, and deceit. As Densu's guardian, Ababio wants Densu to replace Appia in the line to the throne. Ababio, who has Appia killed, wants a straw king whom he can manipulate. Eventually, Ababio becomes the local king of Esuano of the Asante empire. Later, he is arrested for his crimes.

Araba Jesiwa (ahr-AH-bah jay-SEE-wah), the mother of the murdered crown prince, Appia. About fifty and a friend to Densu, she is beautiful and regal but compassionate. Internally, she suffers periodically from depression, which Damfo is able to treat. Childless at the age of twenty-eight, she initially consults Damfo, who leads her to see that she made the wrong choice in marriage. She breaks from her upper-class husband and happily marries the craftsman Kofi Entsua, who becomes Appia's father. Kofi Entsua dies accidentally a few years after their marriage. Araba Jesiwa is brutally maimed in the attack in which Appia is killed, and Densu, painstakingly, heals her.

Asamoa Nkwanta (ah-sah-MOH-ah ihn-KWAHN-tah), the greatest of the Asante generals, strong, dependable, and loyal to the nation. Holding the title of Osajefo, the highest title for bravery among warriors, he acquires later the greatest title among fighters: Srafo Kra, the Warriors' Soul. He suffers deep depression because his favorite nephew has been murdered treacherously by an Asante prince. Healed in mind and attitude by Damfo, Asamoa Nkwanta reunites and readies the Asante army to repel an English invasion. He is betrayed by the royal family, however, who, rather than see him emerge as a strong and influential victor, negotiate a humiliating truce with the English.

Anan (ah-NAHN), an intellectually curious companion of Densu, about Densu's age. "Seeing" (understanding where once there was ignorance) makes Anan happiest. When Densu is arrested and falsely accused of murdering Appia, Anan is instrumental in protecting and saving Densu. Anan, wounded in the escape, dies.

Ajoa (ah-JOH-ah), the wise and beautiful eighteen-year-old daughter of Damfo. When Densu was eight years old and she six, her expressive eyes drew him to her. When her parents were separated, she chose to live with her father, becoming an invaluable aide and spiritual companion to him. She and Densu are betrothed at the novel's end.

Sir Garnet Wolseley, an English general, now lame in one leg. He casts an indirect presence over the events of the action, in speaking through decrees and official statements. He has massed a tremendous force, which moves relentlessly toward a dubious victory over the Asante.

Captain Glover, a vain white freebooter who demands exaggerated deference from his black men. The Africans manipulate him by pretending to cater to his vanity. When Wolseley countermands him, Glover comes to see the buffoonery of his vainglorious pretensions.

Efua Kobri (ay-FEW-ah KOH-bree), the queen mother of the Asante, a manipulative power behind the throne. She advises her son, King Kofi Karikari, to make peace with the invading whites rather than allow Asamoa Nkwanta to resist and possibly defeat them, for then the people might elevate Asamoa Nkwanta to the throne.

Ama (AH-mah), Damfo's former wife, the mother of Ajoa. After about seven years, she grows tired of Damfo's ascetic forest life, leaves him, and returns to the town of Esuano, which has more of the commotion and festivity that suit her taste. She takes a new husband, Esuman, an apprentice healer, who accompanies her from Damfo's camp.

Nyaneba (nyah-NAY-bah), a fellow healer and friend to Damfo. With a small, neat body, she has the voice of an old woman, which she is, but the quick motions of a girl. She hosts Damfo's party in its flight from Ababio's henchmen who seek Densu's death.

Esuman (ay-SEW-man), the corrupt healer who quit the hard life in the forest to seek profit in the town of Esuano. He presides over Densu's trial-by-ordeal, involving the drinking of a poisonous potion as a test of guilt or innocence, from which Densu escapes, with Anan's help.

Appia (ahp-PEE-ah), the elected crown prince. He is twenty years old, capable, and serious-minded. As a result of winning the chosen-year athletic and mental competitions of his age group, he becomes next in line to the throne of Esuano. Ababio has him killed.

Buntui (bewn-TEW-ee), a slow-witted but powerful wrestler of Densu's age group. Becoming a thuggish lackey of Ababio, Buntui kills Appia and maims Araba Jesiwa. He eventually is hanged for theft during the English-led sack of the Asante capital of Kumase.

Collins, an irreverent, heavy-drinking white man who came to Esuano and taught Densu English when Densu was twelve years old. Collins was likely murdered, after two years in Esuano, at the instigation of Ababio and a newcomer white priest.

Warner, an arrogant, manipulative white priest who came to Esuano when Densu was fourteen years old. He wanted Densu as a lifetime servant, but Densu avoided this role.

— *James H. Randall*

THE HEART IS A LONELY HUNTER

Author: Carson McCullers (1917-1967)
First published: 1940
Genre: Novel
Locale: A small Southern mill town
Time: The 1930's
Plot: Psychological realism

John Singer, a tall, immaculate, soberly dressed mute who mysteriously attracts troubled people to him. He considers Mick pitiful, Jake crazy, Dr. Copeland noble, and Biff thoughtful; they are all welcome to visit or talk to him. Ironically, he himself longs to talk manually to his insane mute friend Spiros in the asylum but cannot penetrate Spiros' apathy and craving for food. Singer shoots himself, leaving his other four friends variously affected by his death.

Mick Kelly, a gangling, adolescent girl always dressed in shorts, a shirt, and tennis shoes until she gets a job in a five-and-ten-cent store. A passionate lover of music, she finds relief from her loneliness by talking to Mr. Singer and listening to his radio. After his death, the loneliness returns, along with a feeling that she has been cheated, but by whom she does not know.

Biff Brannon, a café proprietor, a stolid man with a weakness for cripples and sick people and an interest in human relationships. Having watched Mr. Singer with Jake and Mick, he is left after Singer's death puzzled and wondering whether love is the answer to the problem of the human struggle.

Jake Blount, a frustrated, idealistic workingman who tries to rouse his fellow workers; a squat man with long, powerful arms. He believes that Mr. Singer is the only one who understands him. After Singer's death, Jake joins in a free-for-all and later, evading the police, leaves town.

Dr. Benedict Mady Copeland, the only black physician in town; an idealistic man devoted to raising the standards of his race. Trying to see the judge about Willie, he is severely beaten by white men and jailed but is released on bail. Still sick from the beating, he broods over Singer's death.

Portia, his daughter, the Kellys' maid, a devout Presbyterian who worries over her father's and Mick's lack of religious belief.

Willie, Portia's brother, sentenced to hard labor for knifing a man. After brutal punishment for an attempted escape, he loses both feet from gangrene.

Spiros Antonapoulos, Mr. Singer's mute Greek friend, a fat, dreamy, slovenly man who works for his cousin. Spiros is interested in food, sleep, and drink, and sometimes in prayer before sleeping. After becoming insane and a public nuisance as well as a petty thief, he is put into an asylum.

Charles Parker, Spiros' cousin, a fruit-store owner, who has taken an American name. Finally fed up with Spiros' insane actions, he has him committed to the asylum.

Alice, Biff's complaining wife, with whom he has little communication.

Highboy, Portia's husband.

THE HEART OF A DOG
(Sobache serdtse)

Author: Mikhail Bulgakov (1891-1940)
First published: 1968
Genre: Novella

Locale: Moscow
Time: Early 1920's
Plot: Satire

Professor Philip Philippovich Preobrazhensky (fih-LIH-poh-vihch preh-oh-brah-ZHEHN-skee), a sixty-year-old doctor with a pointed goatee and fluffy gray mustache. He examines his privileged patients and conducts research in rejuvenation in his luxurious Moscow residence. A connoisseur with a love for opera, cigars, and other luxuries, he disdains the recently empowered proletariat and repeatedly exerts his influence to protect his apartment from the Kalabukhov house management committee, which wishes him to give up two of his seven rooms. As part of his research, he brings a stray dog into his apartment and cares for it, preparing it for an operation in which a human cadaver's pituitary gland and testes are transplanted into the canine's body. After the animal begins to take on the characteristics of a human being, the doctor's patience is sorely tested by its unruly behavior.

Polygraph Polygraphovich Sharikov (SHAH-rih-kov), called **Sharik** (SHAH-rihk), a pathetic stray dog at the onset of the story. At the mercy of Moscow weather and the generosity of the city's inhabitants, the perennially embattled two-year-old mutt has managed to decipher store signs in his search for food. As a beneficiary of Professor Preobrazhensky's kindness, Sharik is pleased to become part of the household but horrified to find himself dragged into the examination room. Within a month of his operation (during which he receives the body parts of Klim Grigorievich Chugunkin, a twenty-five-year-old barfly and thief), he becomes a short, small-headed, continually hungry cigarette smoker able to dress himself and converse. Ill-mannered as well, he briefly disappears from the apartment after being discovered in the female servants' room. With his rough clothing, low forehead, shaggy eyebrows, and passionate hatred of cats, he registers as a citizen and obtains the position of director of the subsection for purging Moscow of stray animals (especially cats) of the Moscow Communal Property Administration. After returning to the apartment, he again offends his hosts by trying to coerce his typist, Vasnetsova, into moving in with him. A violent battle in the examination room precedes his apparent reversion, under mysterious circumstances, to his former state.

Dr. Ivan Arnoldovich Bormenthal (AHR-nol-doh-vihch bohr-MEHN-tahl), a charismatic and devoted supporter of his mentor, the professor. After assisting in the first operation on Sharik, he moves into the apartment. Sharing a room with Sharikov, he develops an intense feeling of animosity toward the uncouth upstart.

Darya Petrovna Ivanova (peh-TROV-nah ee-VAH-noh-vah), the cook, who sports a powdered nose and fair hair drawn back over her ears. After expelling Sharik from her kitchen, she succumbs to the dog's ingratiating manner. She nevertheless considers Sharikov to be a plague on the household. Formerly married, she is romantically involved with a fireman and may be infatuated with Bormenthal.

Zinaida (Zina) Prokofievna Bunina (zih-nah-EE-dah proh-KOH-fyehv-nah BEW-nih-nah), the maid and doctor's assistant, a pretty young woman with a shy disposition. She is especially overwhelmed by Sharikov's wild behavior.

Shvonder (SHVON-dehr),
Vyazemskaya (VYAH-zehm-skah-yah),
Petrushkin (peh-TREWSH-kihn), and
Sharovkyan (shah-ROV-kyan), members of the house committee. The chairman, Shvonder, a dark man with a shock of thick, curly hair, supplies Sharikov with a volume of Friedrich Engels' correspondence and helps him secure his job. Vyazemskaya, a woman, is the director of the Cultural Department.

Fyodor (FYOH-dohr), the doorman, who helps to contend with the disruptions within the Kalabukhov house and earns gratuities through his efforts.

— *David Marc Fischer*

HEART OF AZTLÁN

Author: Rudolfo A. Anaya (1937-)
First published: 1976
Genre: Novel
Locale: The American Southwest
Time: The 1950's
Plot: Social realism

Clemente Chávez (kleh-MEHN-teh CHAH-vehs), the patriarch of the Chávez family. A man tied to "the sacred earth," he is forced to sell his three acres in Guadalupe and move to the city of Santa Fe. He takes a job at the railroad but soon loses it during a dispute over working conditions. Unable to support his family and uncomfortable with the new ways of city life, Clemente believes his wife has taken his authority from him and turned his children against him. He drinks to numb his pain and confusion, until one night he is rescued from death by Crispín. Revived by the legend of Aztlán, Clemente gradually charts a new course. Though timid at first, he involves himself in the workers' efforts to improve their working condition. Clemente is not the leader the workers seek, but after his son Benjie's injury, he has an epiphany and becomes a leader.

Jasón Chávez (hah-SOHN), Clemente's son. Like his father, Jason is tied to the land and the mythology of their people. He too seems about to lose himself in the whirl of city life, but he meets Cristina Sánchez, the daughter of the man whose death he witnessed at the rail yard, and finds new peace. Although he is younger than his brother Benjie, Jason defends him against drug dealers and gang members. He even keeps quiet when he is falsely accused of having impregnated Cindy, the girl that Benjie impregnated. Jason saves Benjie's—and perhaps Cristina's—life at the end of the novel.

Benjie Chávez, Clemente's son and Jason's brother. On arrival in Barelas, a Chicano barrio of Santa Fe, Benjie immediately begins living the high life. He becomes involved with a fast crowd and begins selling marijuana and "junk" (heroin) for them. Frankie and Flaco, two drug dealers, want the money he owes them, but Jason steps in to defend his brother. This is a short-lived victory, however, because Flaco's friend Sapo swears to kill Benjie.

Sapo (SAH-poh), also called **Lawrence**, a bully who is especially mean when he is high on heroin. Holding Cristina as hostage, Sapo (whose name means "toad") forces Benjie to climb the ladder of the water tank. Shooting wildly, Sapo hits Benjie in the hand. Benjie falls to the ground, alive but paralyzed.

Adelita Chávez (ah-deh-LEE-tah), Clemente's wife, who adjusts more easily to city life than he does. A strong matriarchal figure, Adelita seems to be a bridge for her family between the old and new life.

Crispín (krees-PEEN), a man with a blue guitar. Known only as Crispín, he plays magical melodies. He is said to be able to play the song of life and death and thus bring someone back to the living. He is the repository of ancient knowledge and seems to have mystical connections with the gods.

— *Linda Ledford-Miller*

HEART OF DARKNESS

Author: Joseph Conrad (Jósef Teodor Konrad Nałęcz Korzeniowski, 1857-1924)
First published: 1899
Genre: Novella
Locale: The Belgian Congo
Time: Late nineteenth century
Plot: Psychological realism

Marlow, the narrator and impartial observer of the action who becomes the central figure of the story. Because he is an observer and never centrally involved in the action of the story, he survives to tell the tale. He tells his listeners about his childhood passion for maps and about his declared intention to go, someday, to the heart of Africa. This thoroughly British Everyman describes how, years later, he signs on for the journey, with the help of his aunt. An accident has befallen the steamer that he was to have commanded, and the previous captain was murdered. Because of the damage done to his intended vessel, Marlow waits months for repairs that eventually allow him to command his steamboat. He then makes the difficult and perilous trip upriver to retrieve a sick agent, Kurtz, who dies on board shortly after being rescued. Marlow's voyage into the heart of Africa becomes, symbolically, a journey into the core of his being as well as into the evil at the center of human experience. After talking with Kurtz, with whom he identifies, he is able to see deeply into his own being. Even after returning to Brussels, Marlow is haunted by the memory of Kurtz.

Kurtz, a powerful and intelligent man who manages an inland trading station in the Belgian Congo. His fame is based partly on the fact that he brings in more ivory than all the others put together, and his station is surrounded by heads on stakes. After having arrived in the Congo with high ideals and a self-imposed mission to "civilize" the natives (he was entrusted with making a report for the International Society for the Suppression of Savage Customs), he is instead converted by them to savagery and is destroyed by the dark and weak aspects of his own personality. He represents the dark continent, that is, a continent that has been subjected to the evils of colonialism. Kurtz's awareness of his downfall and his conviction that evil is at the heart of everything is revealed in a long talk that he has with Marlow. After Kurtz falls into a fever and dies, Marlow becomes the custodian of his papers and last wishes.

The District Manager, an avowed enemy of Kurtz who wishes that the climate would do away with his rival. He believes that Kurtz's new methods are ruining the entire district. His only interest while in the Congo is in collecting as much ivory as possible, and he is oblivious to the fate of the natives. His only desire is to get out of the country.

Russian Traveler, an admirer and disciple of Kurtz. He later tells Marlow about Kurtz's ultimate corruption and about his grave illness.

Kurtz's Fiancée, a woman who Marlow wishes to retain the belief that Kurtz is good and powerful.

— *Genevieve Slomski*

THE HEART OF MIDLOTHIAN

Author: Sir Walter Scott (1771-1832)
First published: 1818
Genre: Novel
Locale: Scotland
Time: Early eighteenth century
Plot: Historical

David Deans, a moderately prosperous Scottish farmer in the early 1700's. A vigorous, stern Presbyterian, he is hurt and stunned when his younger daughter is charged with child murder, and he finds comfort only in the devotion of his older daughter Jeanie, who indirectly gets him a more fertile farm while obtaining a pardon for her sister. Although David cannot wholly approve of Jeanie's fiancé, he is reconciled to the marriage.

Jeanie Deans, a rather plain and simple girl who shows much moral earnestness and courage when she refuses to lie to save her sister from a death sentence and then goes to London at great risk to present her case before the queen. Her force and warmth impress the duke of Argyle and the queen, who obtain a pardon for her sister, give her father a better farm, and give her betrothed a good clerical position. As a result, she is able to marry, and eventually she bears three children.

Effie Deans, Jeanie's spoiled, pretty younger sister. When Effie's illegitimate child disappears, she is arrested and sentenced to hang for child murder. Released through the steadfast efforts of Jeanie, she marries her betrayer, the criminal known as Geordie Robertson, and when he later acquires a title under his rightful name of George Staunton, she becomes a court beauty. Years after, she and her husband return to Scotland, where he is killed by a young outlaw who is really his long-lost son. Effie then retires to a convent.

Reuben Butler, Jeanie's betrothed, a sensible, educated, somewhat pedantic young minister. Unable to marry because of his impoverishment, his difficulties are cleared away when he gives Jeanie a hereditary claim on the duke, is given a church on one of the duke's estates, and earns the respect of David.

Geordie Robertson, in reality **George Staunton**, a reckless, profligate young man who seduces two girls but tries to redeem his past by offering to turn himself in as the leader of the Porteous riot in return for Effie's freedom. Jeanie, however, makes this offer unnecessary. After Effie has been pardoned, he marries her and achieves a respectable life, first in the West Indies, later in the English court. When he willfully returns to seek his illegitimate son, the outlaw son kills him in a robbery attempt.

Meg Murdockson, a vicious old woman who serves as Effie's midwife, tries to destroy the child, and testifies that Effie killed the baby. Motivated by her desire for revenge because Robertson loves Effie instead of her own daughter, whom he had also seduced, she tries everything in her power to destroy Effie, including a murder attempt on Jeanie. Finally, after confessing her evil deeds, she is hanged as a witch.

John, duke of Argyle, a skilled, honorable Scottish statesman in the court of King George II. He shows his generosity by giving Jeanie a hearing with the queen and by aiding her father and Reuben Butler. He becomes a family friend.

The Laird of Dumbiedikes, a member of the gentry and Jeanie's clumsy suitor. He pays for Effie's defense and Jeanie's trip to London.

Madge Wildfire, Meg Murdockson's daughter, crazed after Robertson betrays her. She helps Jeanie escape Meg and is later harried to death by a mob.

Ratcliffe, the ex-criminal keeper of the Edinburgh jail. He treats Effie well and suggests to Jeanie that she seek a pardon from the queen.

Queen Caroline, the touchy, powerful queen who, affected by Jeanie's simplicity, secures her sister's pardon and gives Jeanie fifty pounds.

The Reverend Mr. Staunton, Robertson's righteous father. He shelters Jeanie after her escape from Meg Murdockson and gives her an escort to London.

The Whistler, Effie and Robertson's illegitimate son. After killing his father, he escapes to the wilds of America.

Bartoline Saddletree, a stupid, pompous, meddlesome lawyer who tries to take over Effie's case.

Mrs. Saddletree, his generous, motherly wife, who employs Effie as a servant during her pregnancy.

John Porteous, an officer who needlessly fires into a crowd of citizens at a hanging and is afterward killed by a mob led by Robertson.

Andrew Wilson, Robertson's partner in crime, a smuggler hanged by Porteous.

Archibald, the duke's groom of chambers, who escorts Jeanie back to Scotland.

Duncan of Knock, the brusque, lively protector of the duke's estate on which David Deans is placed.

David Butler,

Donald Butler, and

Euphemia Butler, Jeanie and Reuben Butler's three spirited children.

THE HEART OF THE MATTER

Author: Graham Greene (1904-1991)
First published: 1948
Genre: Novel
Locale: British West Africa
Time: During World War II
Plot: Psychological realism

Major Scobie, "Ticki" to his wife, a police chief in a British-controlled West African colony. He is a man whose merit is frequently overlooked and whose capacities for sensitive reaction are underestimated. Thus, when he learns he is not to be chosen district commissioner, he feels the slight more for his wife than for himself. He is scrupulous in his dealings, and he has a reputation for honesty earned in fifteen years of hard work. His scrupulousness is a result of religious convictions that force him to view every problem as a moral conflict; the tendency also diminishes his powers of decision. Compromising with his principles under the hysterical pressure of his wife, who feels that she must leave the colony, he borrows money from Yusef, a suspected Syrian smuggler. Another threat of compromise arises when, during his wife's absence, he meets Helen Rolt, a young widow who is among the survivors of a torpedoed British ship. Greatly in need of friendship and encouragement, she becomes Scobie's mistress, but it is desperation as much as love that binds him to Helen. An honest man, he cannot conceal from himself the fact that he is an adulterer. The same honesty forces him to recognize that he has profaned the act of communion by sharing the rite with his returned wife; this act is another step toward damnation. He reaches the end of his rope when he discovers that he is under official surveillance because of his relationship with Yusef. He commits suicide after fabricating the hoax of a serious heart condition, even though he knows that his act points toward complete damnation.

Louise Scobie, the major's wife, essentially a weak woman whose pretenses and lack of perspective set her apart from the colony. She is ambitious for her husband, and she has suffered the loss of her only child. Her lack of perception appears after her husband's suicide; she remarks to the priest that her husband was a "bad Catholic" and speaks of Scobie's defects. She has no sense of the utter despair that her husband had reached before his act.

Helen Rolt, a young woman rescued after a British ship has been torpedoed by a German submarine. She becomes Scobie's mistress and cannot understand why his religion prevents divorce and remarriage. Her recent widowhood makes her seek the security of a second marriage—if not to Scobie, then to a young officer who is attracted to her.

Wilson, a counter-intelligence agent sent to investigate the smuggling of industrial diamonds to Nazi Germany. He sees in Scobie a man who neglects his wife, deals with Yusef, a patently suspicious character, and is in love with another woman. He hates Major Scobie because he has himself fallen in love with Louise Scobie.

Yusef, a wily Syrian merchant. He loves Scobie as a fellow human being beset with problems, but he hates Scobie because he is honest and perhaps because he recognizes Scobie's tarnished but still superior moral strength.

Father Rank, a priest of less than saintly demeanor who sees more deeply than the colony knows. He has compassion for Scobie and sees in him the lonely man forced by his conscience to choose among the evils that face him. It would not have shocked him to know that Scobie's angina was feigned and that his suicide was the surrender of a soul endlessly tormented. As he says, a priest knows only sins; a man does not confess his virtues.

Tallit, a Syrian involved with Yusef. He is capable of great double-dealing.

Ali, Scobie's favorite "boy," who loses his life.

HEARTBREAK HOUSE: A Fantasia in the Russian Manner on English Themes

Author: George Bernard Shaw (1856-1950)
First published: 1919
Genre: Drama
Locale: Sussex, England
Time: 1913
Plot: Play of ideas

Captain Shotover, the master of Heartbreak House. This eighty-eight-year-old eccentric retired sea captain is constantly cranky, impressively wise (a visionary), and generally drunk (three bottles of rum a day). Although a realist, Shotover has built his Sussex home in the form of a ship, strives to attain the seventh degree of concentration (perfect tranquillity), and spends much of his time experimenting with death-dealing inventions, especially dynamite. Shotover is a remnant of the culture and leisure that flourished in Europe, particularly England, before World War I.

Lady Ariadne (Addy) Utterword, Captain Shotover's younger daughter, age forty-two. The wife of Sir Hastings Utterword, she is a handsome blonde who, although seemingly scatterbrained, is quite competent. On her return to Heartbreak House after an absence of twenty-three years, neither her father nor her sister recognizes her. As an alternative to the confusion she finds, Lady Utterword exudes a conservative prestige (implying the British Empire's element of foreign rule) and is concerned only with horses and hunting.

Mrs. Hesione (Hessy) Hushabye, the captain's elder daughter, perhaps forty-four years old, the wife of Hector Hushabye. Dark and statuesque, Hesione is the epitome of domesticity, an exemplar of the power of a woman's love and the authority in her home. She invites young Ellie Dunn to visit Heartbreak House so that she can discourage the ingenue from marrying Boss Mangan. At the end of the play, she is much less the paragon of domestic virtue, as boredom provokes her to anticipate and exult in the excitement and destruction.

Hector Hushabye, Hesione's husband, a dandy in his fifties. He is heroic but shy. A man capable of brave deeds, Hector, now tamed (domesticated) by his wife, refrains from action and resorts to concocting tales of high adventure. He reasons that people need to hear such stories so as still to believe in heroes. In the end, it is he who defiantly turns on the lights in the house.

Ellie Dunn, a pretty, young singer betrothed to Boss Mangan but secretly in love with Marcus Darnley, a mysterious older gentleman later revealed to be Hector Hushabye. This ingenue finds the atmosphere at Heartbreak House puzzling, for she notes that guests are not greeted, the elderly servant addresses everyone as "love" or "ducky," relatives are treated as strangers, and strangers are welcomed as if they are old friends. Incredibly naïve, Ellie is fooled by Hector Hushabye's amorous antics and deluded by Boss Mangan's apparent wealth. Ellie first sees Captain Shotover as unpredictable, later as very wise, and finally as a drunkard. Disillusionments destroy her romantic bent. Coupled with a newly acquired knowledge of her power over men, these disillusionments convert her into a "modern" girl. Finally, unable to discover alternate values, something "real" to respect, Ellie gratefully embraces the impending destruction and doom.

Mazzini Dunn, Ellie's father. A rather elderly, earnest man, Dunn asserts the philosophy of a nineteenth century liberal; he believes in progress but is not a moving force to be reckoned with as a result of his sentimentalism. He is now a tool of the capitalistic Boss Mangan and, as such, has promised his only child, the pretty young Ellie, to this elderly industrialist. Poverty-stricken and a little pathetic, Dunn remains the ineffectual "good" man.

Alfred "Boss" Mangan, the fifty-five-year-old, apparently rich mogul whom the unsuspecting young Ellie is engaged to marry. Jaded, suspicious, pedestrian, manipulating, and deceitful, he is the overbearing boss of Ellie's subjugated father and the cast of capitalistic exploitation. He is exposed to have none of the millions of dollars to which he constantly alludes; the monies actually belong to others. He is killed while hiding in the cave containing the captain's dynamite.

Billy Dunn, who is not related to Ellie or Mazzini. He was once a pirate and is now a burglar. He is captured when he attempts to rob Heartbreak House. Billy had stolen from the captain many years earlier and is afraid of him. Although he insists on being turned over to the law, Billy finds himself a servant in the household, put to this by his captors. Consistently paralleled with the Boss by deeds and by intentions, Billy dies in the cave with Mangan.

Randall Utterword, the brother-in-law of Ariadne and younger brother of Sir Hastings Utterword (who is referred to in the play but never appears). This Utterword is a gentleman, both in looks and in manner; he is callow and without talents, yet a tower of pride. He is a snob, sustaining a high regard for caste. He fancies himself to be in love with his sister-in-law.

Nurse Guiness, Captain Shotover's elderly servant, secretly married to the thief Billy Dunn. She is casual and impudent in her station, always calling the gentry "ducky."

Sir Hastings Utterword, Ariadne's husband, referred to but never on stage. A governor of colonies, he craves the routine, especially administrative duties. He encourages his wife's flirtations because these keep her occupied and in good humor.

— *Cynthia Jane Whitney*

HEARTBREAK TANGO
(Boquitas pintadas)

Author: Manuel Puig (1932-1990)
First published: 1969
Genre: Novel

Locale: Argentina
Time: Primarily 1937-1939, 1949, and 1968
Plot: Psychological realism

Juan Carlos Etchepare (eht-cheh-PAH-reh), a ladies' man who is suffering from tuberculosis. Although Juan Carlos is the center of the novel, the reader cannot with total confidence know his personality and character. The novel begins after his death, and the reader must reconstruct Juan Carlos through unreliable sources: the letters and memories of persons who loved him too much and understood him too little, his brief comments remembered years after the fact, and a few of his love letters, the sincerity of which is at least suspect. Tall, dark, and handsome, Juan Carlos is in a sense a walking cliché. He saw himself as a ladies' man of the Hollywood matinee variety, as did many of the women whom he encountered. Beneath the arrogant playboy exterior is a sensitive, frightened man who becomes more frightened and more in need of true understanding and compassion as he approaches death. The reader's task in untangling events is not so much to understand what really happened as to understand who Juan Carlos really was.

Nélida (Nené) Enriqueta Fernández (NEH-lee-dah neh-NEH ehn-ree-KEH-tah fehr-NAHN-dehs), a married woman who had been in love with Juan Carlos. Compared to most of her friends stuck back in the dusty hinterlands town of Coronel Vallejos, Nené has done well for herself in life. She has married a successful businessman and moved to the big city (Buenos Aires). Nené is a study in frustration. She—and the reader through her eyes—sees the mediocrity of her emotional and material life. Her constant thoughts of Juan Carlos are an attempt to recover a time of romance that is quite likely more glorious in her imagination than it was in reality. Her letters to Juan Carlos' mother, which compose a substantial portion of the novel, are not so much an effort to cleanse herself of guilt as they are an attempt to share a hallowed memory.

Celina Etchepare (seh-LEE-nah), Juan Carlos' sister. Celina is about the same age as Nené and comes from approximately the same socioeconomic background. It seems natural that the two should be good friends; such is not the case. Celina so fiercely defends her brother's reputation from the attacks in Nené's letters that she seems almost to be motivated by jealousy. Strangely, considering her defense of her brother's honor, she is no saint herself, having probably been involved in more affairs than Juan Carlos.

Francisco Catalino Páez (kah-tah-LEE-noh PAH-ehs), a police officer and friend of Juan Carlos. If Juan Carlos is the suave playboy, Francisco is his cruder but no less lecherous sidekick. Francisco gets his way with women largely by intimidation and brute force, and he pays for this with a violent death.

Antonia Josefa Ramírez (hoh-SEH-fah rah-MEE-rehs), also known as **Big Fanny**, a servant girl. Big Fanny is a poor girl with few options in life or in love. Her big "romance" is a hopeless, squalid one with Francisco. Both are largely inarticulate. Francisco expresses himself best physically; Big Fanny, when things are bleakest, responds with violence.

Donato José Massa (doh-NAH-toh hoh-SEH MAH-sah), Nené's husband. Massa is a local auctioneer who catches Nené "on the rebound" from Juan Carlos. Massa's move to Buenos Aires with his wife is an attempt to move up in the world, but his small dreams and minor successes cannot measure up to his wife's memories of Juan Carlos.

Leonor Saldívar de Etchepare (leh-oh-NOHR sahl-DEE-vahr), Juan Carlos' mother. Leonor offers another perspective on Juan Carlos.

— Dennis Vannatta

HEARTBURN

Author: Nora Ephron (1941-)
First published: 1983
Genre: Novel
Locale: New York City and Washington, D.C.
Time: The 1970's
Plot: Farce

Rachel Samstat, the narrator/protagonist, a thirty-eight-year-old cookbook writer and mother married to Mark Feldman, a syndicated columnist who is having an affair with another woman. Rachel (modeled on Ephron herself) discovers the affair when she is seven months pregnant. She flees to New York City when Mark informs her that he is in love with Thelma Rice. Despite the humiliation, Rachel still loves Mark, a feeling she cannot understand or justify but one she views with comic detachment as she reexamines her two failed marriages, her relationship with her parents and friends, her cookbooks, and her pregnancy, all the while suffering from "terminal heartburn." Rachel suspects that her cooking is to blame for Mark's affair because cooking has become her way of saying "I love you," and it is not sufficient for a man who is very sexual. She earns the reader's sympathy with her self-deprecating humor as she deals with the vagaries of life in two of America's largest cities. Rachel is the only fully rounded character in the novel.

Mark Feldman, Rachel's husband, a syndicated columnist loosely based on Carl Bernstein, the celebrated Watergate investigator. He has a black beard with a small white stripe on the left side of his chin. His affair with Thelma Rice has been going on since Rachel became pregnant, and he was unfaithful to Rachel even before their marriage. Mark not only lies to his wife about his affair but also pursues couples therapy with the other woman. He tells Rachel he loves Thelma but insists that Rachel stay with him until the birth of their second child (another son) for the sake of appearances.

Thelma Rice, Mark's lover. Her extramarital affairs are legendary in Washington. She is married to Jonathan, a State Department official who bugs his own house to eavesdrop on her affairs. He tries to convince Rachel to take Mark back because he wants Thelma to stay with him. Thelma becomes angry with Rachel over a rumor Rachel starts about Thelma having a sexually transmitted disease, but she sees nothing wrong in wrecking other people's marriages.

Julie Siegel and

Arthur Siegel, Rachel and Mark's best friends. They are traveling and eating companions and try to patch up the broken marriage.

Vera Maxwell, Rachel's fifty-eight-year-old therapist. She is beautiful, caring, happily married, and always right. Vera forces Rachel to face Mark's betrayal and start over.

The Samstats, Rachel's parents. He is an entertainer and she an agent who became wealthy by investing in Tampax. Bebe, the wife, thinks she finds God in a man named Mel, who believes he truly is God and robs her of every cent she has. Rachel's father marries the maid and later ends up in a mental hospital.

Richard Finkel, Rachel's tall, red-haired producer and former lover, whose wife is also having an affair. He drunkenly and loudly proposes to Rachel in Central Park and then falls into the seal pond.

Betty Searle, Rachel's best friend, who helps her through the hard times with Mark.

— Linda L. Labin

HEAT AND DUST

Author: Ruth Prawer Jhabvala (1927-)
First published: 1975
Genre: Novel
Locale: Satipur and Khatm, India
Time: 1923 and 1975
Plot: Philosophical

Olivia Rivers, a young Englishwoman recently married, living in Satipur in 1923. Bored with the company of other English officials and their wives and neglected by Douglas, her hardworking husband, Olivia is also uncomfortable with the foreignness of India itself. Over a period of several months, she becomes romantically involved with the Nawab, the local native Indian ruler. When she becomes pregnant, she has an abortion because she is not sure whether her husband or the Nawab is the father of the child. After leaving her husband, she remains in India as the mistress of the Nawab, dying in the late 1950's without ever returning to England.

Anne, an Englishwoman in her late twenties who narrates Olivia's story. The granddaughter of Douglas Rivers and his second wife, Tessie, Anne goes to India in the 1970's to discover the story of her grandfather's first wife. Through her diary, Anne also relates her own life in India. Like Olivia, Anne becomes pregnant, but after initially choosing an abortion, she decides instead to have the child. She follows Olivia's life to the house in the Himalayas bought for her by the Nawab. At the close, Anne, nearing the time for her own delivery, has decided to join an ashram even higher in the mountains.

Douglas Rivers, a young, dedicated English official serving in India as his ancestors had done before him. Upright and controlled, taking a paternal attitude toward the Indians, Douglas is the pillar around which Olivia's changing feelings revolve. After Olivia's desertion, Douglas obtains a divorce and marries Tessie, a sister of Beth Crawford. After Indian independence, he retires to England, where he dies.

The Nawab, a local Indian prince and ruler of Khatm. About thirty-five years old, the Nawab is married, but his wife suffers from mental illness. Although outwardly generous, the Nawab is self-centered, and he generally gets whatever he desires. He becomes for Olivia the romantic, all-consuming figure that her nature needs. He lavishes attention on her and enjoys her company in the knowledge that it embarrasses the British. Later, he loses both political and economic power, and he dies in his mother's arms in New York in the early 1950's.

The Begum, mother of the Nawab, an elusive but powerful influence on her son. Her presence in the palace at Khatm is always implicit, and it is to her that Olivia turns when she decides to get an abortion. The Begum seems to be the most influential woman in the Nawab's life.

Harry, an Englishman who had met the Nawab in London and had accompanied him back to India. He is a houseguest of the Nawab and is fond of him and grateful for his indulgences, making it difficult to leave. He is ill and does not like the food and climate of India. Weak and vacillating, Harry often expresses a desire to escape the seductiveness of the Nawab and his palace and return to his mother in England, but he is able to do so only after Olivia commits herself to the Nawab.

Beth Crawford, the wife of the chief British official of Satipur in 1923. As with most of the English, her family has deep roots in India. Sure of herself and her situation, she has mastered the life required of her position. Her sister, Tessie, becomes Douglas Rivers' second wife.

Major Minnies, the official political adviser to the Nawab. Sympathetic to the Nawab, he also paternally perceives him as a child who has not grown to his responsibilities. More understanding of Olivia's changing feelings than are the others, he later writes a book warning Westerners about allowing India to seduce them and their different values.

Dr. Saunders, the chief British medical official in Satipur in 1923. Less sympathetic and more judgmental than Minnies, he treats Olivia for complications from her abortion and condemns her for allowing India to corrupt her. His wife, Joan, is the English figure most brought down by India: Her environment has lost the battle to Indian foreignness.

Inder Lal, Anne's Indian landlord in Satipur, about twenty-five years old. A mid-level bureaucrat, frustrated and fearful of his position, feeling that India is inferior to the West, and unhappy with his illiterate and traditional Indian wife, he allows himself to be seduced by Anne, thus fathering her child.

Inder Lal's mother, who, like the Begum, is a strong influence on her son. She chose his wife, runs his home, and even decides the proper treatment for her daughter-in-law's mental problems.

Ritu, the young and uneducated wife of Inder Lal. Dominated by her mother-in-law, Ritu suffers, as did the Nawab's wife, from mental illness.

Chidananda (Chid), a young Englishman who has converted to Hinduism. He stays with Anne briefly, and she becomes his reluctant lover. Although initially he appears to have stripped himself of his Western past, ultimately India proves too much for him; he becomes ill and desperately wishes to return to England.

Maji, a holy woman in Satipur. It is to her that Anne turns when she decides to get an abortion. Anne changes her mind, however. Later, she believes that her decision was a result of Maji's influence.

— *Eugene S. Larson*

THE HEAT OF THE DAY

Author: Elizabeth Bowen (1899-1973)
First published: 1949
Genre: Novel
Locale: London, England
Time: 1942-1944
Plot: Psychological realism

Stella Rodney, an attractive English widow. She is unbelieving when told that her lover is a Nazi sympathizer. Because she cannot keep her knowledge to herself in fairness, she tells her lover the accusations. He shocks her by revealing that the accusations are true. Even after this revelation, she still tries to shield him from the authorities.

Robert Kelway, Stella's lover and, although a veteran of Dunkirk, a Nazi sympathizer. After he reveals his nature to Stella, he climbs out to her roof, from which he jumps and falls to his death.

Harrison, an intelligence agent. He informs Stella of her lover's Nazi propensities. At first he seems affectionate, but after the war, he seems relieved that she is planning to marry someone else.

Roderick Rodney, Stella's son, a soldier in the British army. He is an enthusiastic young man. His mother looks after his estate, inherited from a cousin in Ireland, while he is in the service during World War II.

Louie Lewis, a soldier's wife. A clumsy, cowlike person, she on impulse tries to pick up Harrison. Later, she intrudes herself upon Stella and Harrison while they are dining out.

Francis Morris, Stella's relative who bequeathed his Irish estate to Stella's son.

HEAVEN'S MY DESTINATION

Author: Thornton Wilder (1897-1975)
First published: 1934
Genre: Novel
Locale: Middle West
Time: 1930-1931
Plot: Social satire

George Marvin Brush, a traveling salesman for a textbook company. He tries hard to live a clean, Christian life. Having undergone a religious conversion, he tries to live up to unattainable ideals, often irritating people by his priggishness and his insistence that other persons ought to live better lives. He is a believer in "ahimsa," a theory requiring that he react in the exact opposite way to what others expect in a given situation. This belief and its practice often plunge him into trouble.

Roberta, a farmer's daughter seduced at one time by George Brush. He marries her to salve his conscience, even though she really wants nothing more to do with him. Exasperated by the conditions of their marriage, she finally leaves her husband, whom she heartily dislikes, and returns to her parents' farm.

Doremus Blodgett, a traveling salesman for a hosiery company. He is infuriated by George's righteousness and idealism until he learns that George has not lived entirely untouched by sin.

Mrs. Margie McCoy, Blodgett's mistress, who travels with him posing as a cousin.

Herb, a newspaper reporter in Kansas City who becomes George's friend. Herb tries to help George see that he must let other people live in their own ways. At Herb's death, he leaves a child for George to care for.

Elizabeth, Herb's daughter. She is adopted by George and complicates her foster parents' married life, as both of them compete for her affection.

George Burkin, a movie director. He and George meet in jail. Burkin is in jail for being a Peeping Tom and George for graciously helping a robber hold up a store. Burkin tries to convince George that he has never grown up.

Lottie, Roberta's sister, who tries to persuade George that the answer to his problem with Roberta is a marriage and an immediate divorce.

Morrie,
Bat, and
Louie, three of George's friends in Kansas City. They play enormous practical jokes on George. Once, angered by his priggishness, they almost beat him to death.

Mrs. Crofut, keeper of a brothel. She is passed off to George as a genteel society matron. When her identity is revealed, George refuses to believe the truth about her and her bevy of beautiful "daughters."

Mrs. Efrim, the owner of the store George helps a man rob.

HEDDA GABLER

Author: Henrik Ibsen (1828-1906)
First published: 1890
Genre: Drama
Locale: Norway
Time: Late nineteenth century
Plot: Social realism

Hedda Gabler Tessman, the daughter of General Gabler. She is the exciting but unenthusiastic bride of George Tessman, who holds a scholarship for research into the history of civilization. Back from a six-month wedding trip during which George studied civilization, Hedda is dangerously bored. She keeps as her prize possession her father's pistols, with which she plays on occasion. She also plays with people: with George's Aunt Julia, whose new bonnet Hedda pretends to think belongs to the servant; with George, who has bought her a villa that she pretended to want and who now must buy her a piano because her old one does not suit her new home; with an old school acquaintance, Thea Elvsted, who has rescued Hedda's talented former lover, Eilert Lovberg, from drink; with Eilert Lovberg, whom she cannot bear to see rescued by Mrs. Elvsted; and with Judge Brack, who outmaneuvers her and pushes her over the brink of endurance to her death. Hedda is a complete egocentric, caring for no one and careless of life for herself and for others. Badly spoiled, she seems to find her only pleasure in making others miserable. She finds Eilert Lovberg more amusing than anyone else, even though she had dismissed him when she was free. When she realizes that he has destroyed his career, she gives him a pistol and tells him to use it—beautifully. When the pistol discharges accidentally and injures him fatally in the boudoir of Mademoiselle Diana, and when Judge Brack convinces her that he knows where Eilert got the pistol, Hedda takes its mate, goes to her room, and shoots herself in the temple, but not before she has seen Mrs. Elvsted quietly gain a hold on George Tessman.

George Tessman, Hedda's husband, a sincere, plodding young man dazzled by his bride but devoted to his work. When Hedda burns Eilert's manuscript, which George has found, she tells George that she did so to keep Eilert from surpassing him, but in reality she burned it because Eilert wrote it with Mrs. Elvsted and they call it their "child." George's surprised horror at her deed turns to warm delight when he thinks that Hedda loves him enough to destroy the manuscript for his sake. When Mrs. Elvsted says that she has notes for the manuscript, George says that he is just the man to work on someone else's manuscript and that they can put the book together again. Sincerely delighted that he can help restore the lost valuable book, he plans to work evenings with Mrs. Elvsted, to the disgust of Hedda, who in cold, calm rage and despair shoots herself.

Eilert Lovberg, a former suitor of Hedda who has written a book in the same field as Tessman's. He could easily win the appointment that Tessman expects, but he decides not to compete with him. Since Hedda broke up their association, after it threatened to become serious, he has been living with the family of Sheriff Elvsted, teaching the Elvsted children and writing another book. His manuscript completed, he comes to town. In his writing and in his reform from his old wild ways, he has been inspired by Mrs. Elvsted. Eilert shows the effects of hard living. As soon as Hedda has an opportunity, she reasserts her control over him, destroying his confidence in Mrs. Elvsted and persuading him to resume his drinking. Hedda says that he will return "with vine leaves in his hair—flushed and fearless." Instead, he returns defeated, having lost his manuscript. He tells Thea Elvsted that all is over between them, because he has destroyed the manuscript, but he has merely lost it and is ashamed to tell her so. After leaving Judge Brack's party, he had gone to the rooms of Mademoiselle Diana, a redheaded entertainer whom he had known in his riotous days. There, missing his manuscript, he had accused Diana and her friends of robbing him. When the police appeared, he struck a constable and was carried off to the police station. Released the next day, he goes in despair to Mademoiselle Diana's rooms to look for his lost manuscript. The gun discharges there, killing him. Wanting the manuscript desperately because he claimed it contained his "true self" and dealt with the future, he had planned to deliver lectures on it after Tessman's appointment had gone through.

Judge Brack, a friend of the family, a sly man whom Tessman trusts. Hedda agrees to the apparently harmless arrangement to keep her entertained. After Eilert Lovberg's death, Judge Brack tells Hedda that he knows the true story, but there is no danger if he says nothing. When Hedda protests that she will now be his slave, a thought which she cannot bear, he replies that he will not abuse the advantage he now holds. He is incredulous when he hears that Hedda has killed herself.

Thea Elvsted, the wife of Sheriff Elvsted, a sweet-faced woman with blonde hair, born to inspire men, although, unfortunately, not her husband. She rescues Eilert, works with him, preserves his notes, seeks to preserve him, and after his death and Hedda's will no doubt inspire Tessman. When Eilert comes to town, Mrs. Elvsted, who is in love with him, follows him because she is afraid that he will relapse into his old ways. Because she and Hedda had known each other in school, she comes to see Hedda. Mrs. Elvsted had been afraid of her when they were girls because Hedda sometimes pulled her hair and threatened to burn it off. She confides to Hedda the story of her love for Eilert and thus helps to bring about his death and Hedda's.

Miss Juliana Tessman (**Aunt Julia**), Tessman's aunt, who is eternally hoping for an offspring for Hedda and George. Her constant, veiled remarks about sewing and the use for the two empty rooms are lost on George and ignored by Hedda. Aunt Julia had reared George with her sister, Rina, who is now dying. She serves in the play to remind George of his past and to irritate Hedda. She is a sweet, good woman who loves her nephew and wants to help the helpless.

THE HEIDI CHRONICLES

Author: Wendy Wasserstein (1950-   )
First published: 1988
Genre: Drama
Locale: New York City and Chicago
Time: 1965-1989
Plot: Social morality

Heidi Holland, an art history professor and essayist who teaches at Columbia University. After attending Miss Crain's School in Chicago in the mid-1960's, she pursues her education as an undergraduate at Vassar and a member of the art history graduate program at Yale in the early 1970's. Throughout her professional career, she advocates greater recognition for female artists, demonstrating at the Art Institute of Chicago in 1974, writing the book *And the Light Floods in from the Left* in the late 1970's, directing the group Women's Art in 1982, and arranging a show on Lila Cabot Perry in 1984. Although she has a deepening friendship with Peter Patrone and long-standing relationships with Susan Johnston and Scoop Rosenbaum, she feels lonely and stranded in 1986. Dissatisfied with social standards that discourage both women and men from recognizing and achieving their full potential, Heidi hopes that Judy, the Panamanian infant she adopts in 1988, will live in a more encouraging milieu than the one in which she came of age.

Scoop Rosenbaum, a man whom Heidi meets at a 1967 Eugene McCarthy fund-raiser in New Hampshire. Dressed in blue jeans and a work shirt, the Exeter graduate and Princeton dropout informs her that he is the editor in chief of *The Liberated Earth News* and displays a penchant for assigning grades to potato chips, music, people, and whatever else strikes his fancy. Describing himself as arrogant, difficult, and very smart, he simultaneously attracts and repels Heidi, with whom he carries on a sexual relationship while a Yale law student in 1970 and United States Supreme Court clerk in 1974. A junior associate at Sullivan Cromwell in 1977, he marries Lisa Friedlander, explaining to Heidi that, although he will always love the "A+" Heidi, the "A-" Lisa will prove to be a less competitive and, hence, more satisfactory wife. After becoming the influential editor of *Boomer* magazine, Scoop has an affair with his graphics assistant in 1980. By 1982, he and Lisa have two children, Maggie and Pierre. Increasingly estranged from Heidi in the 1980's, Scoop visits her in 1988 with a silver spoon for Judy. He uses the occasion to tell Heidi that he has sold *Boomer* and decided to campaign for a congressional seat.

Susan Johnston, Heidi's boy-crazy high school girlfriend. By 1970, she is a member of the Huron Street Ann Arbor Consciousness Raising Rap Group. She announces to the group that, instead of starting a women's legal journal, she wishes to work within the system and accept a job with *The Law Review*, but she later leaves her clerkship alongside Scoop at the Supreme Court in 1974 to move to a women's health and legal collective in Montana. In 1980, having attended business school, she accepts a position in Los Angeles as an executive vice president for a new production company. By 1984, she is a power broker, uninterested in Heidi's emotional distress and unappreciative of the serious nature of her work, who callously proposes that her friend act as a consultant in creating a situation comedy about three female artists in a Houston loft.

Peter Patrone, a boy Heidi meets at a high school dance. He charms her with his cynical attitude toward the proceedings and remains in touch with her while a student at Williams

College. Pursuing a career in medicine in Chicago in 1974, he reveals to Heidi that he is a homosexual and that he is involved with fellow doctor Stanley Zinc. A pediatrics resident at Bellevue in 1977, Peter earns the title of "The Best Pediatrician in New York Under Forty" from *Boomer* and becomes chief of pediatrics at New York Hospital by 1982. Concerned about the AIDS crisis, by 1987 he has started a special unit for AIDS-stricken children, using funds supplied by Susan Johnston's production company. Although Peter and Heidi occasionally squabble, the two establish a strong friendship over the years. In 1988, he helps Heidi adopt Judy.

Lisa Friedlander, an award-winning illustrator of children's books. Married to Scoop, she is happy to stay at home and care for their children but is distressed by her husband's infidelity.

Denise, Lisa's younger sister, who works for the talk show *Hello New York* from 1980 to 1982. Heidi, Scoop, and Peter appear on the show as a cross section of baby boomers. By 1984, she is a story editor for Susan.

Jill,

Fran, and

Becky Groves, women who attended a meeting of the Huron Street Ann Arbor Consciousness Raising Rap Group in 1970. Jill is a forty-year-old wife and mother, Fran is a thirty-year-old lesbian physicist, and Becky Groves is a seventeen-year-old newcomer who is unhappy with her demanding live-in boyfriend.

April Lambert, the hostess of *Hello New York*. She is married to David Lambert, who owns sixty buildings in Manhattan in 1982.

— *David Marc Fischer*

HEIMSKRINGLA

Author: Snorri Sturluson (1179-1241)
First transcibed: c. 1230-1235
Genre: Short fiction
Locale: Norway
Time: Legendary times to the twelfth century
Plot: Folklore

Odin, an Asian conqueror who finally settles in the Scandinavian peninsula. From him, later rulers of the northland claim descent.

Mime, Odin's friend, a spy killed by a neighboring people. Receiving the head, Odin preserves it with herbs and sings incantations over it; thereafter, it speaks and discovers secrets for him.

On Jorundsson, king of Sweden. He extends his life by sacrificing a son to Odin every ten years. His people refuse to permit his tenth son to be sacrificed, and he dies of extreme old age.

Halfdan the Black, king of Norway. A good king, he dies young. His quartered body is sent to separate provinces to spread his good influence.

Harald the Fairhaired, Halfdan's son. Challenged by a girl who refuses his advances because of the smallness of his territory, he conquers all of Norway and marries her.

Aethelstan, king of England. He and Harald constantly try to trap each other into acknowledging the other's mastery, but each rules his own kingdom until death.

Hakon the Good, Harald's son. Sent by Harald as foster son to Aethelstan, Hakon returns to Norway at Harald's death, and becomes king of Norway. A Christian, he does not force Christianity on his followers, but many are converted.

Eric Blood-Ax, Hakon's brother. Slayer of at least four other brothers, he is killed in England.

Tryggve Olafsson, a petty king slain by Eric's sons, who rule Norway after Hakon is killed in battle.

Olaf Tryggvesson, the son of Tryggve, who becomes a Viking chieftain when twelve. Converted to Christianity after his raids on England, he in turn converts all of Norway to Christianity. He dies at the hands of Danish kings in 1000.

Aethelred, king of England. Olaf makes and keeps peace with him.

Olaf Haraldsson the Saint, a descendant of Harald the Fairhaired. He extends the influence of Christianity and persistently tries to establish independence and national union. Slain in 1030 by petty chieftains whose traditional powers he is trying to reduce, he has long-lasting influence. After his death, many miracles are attributed to him.

Magnus the Good, the stepson of Olaf the Saint. He becomes king of Norway; later he is also king of Denmark.

Hardacanute, king of Denmark and king of England. According to peace terms with Magnus, the survivor is to rule the other's country.

Edward the Good, king of England. So sensible and courageous is his reply to Magnus' claim to the English throne after Hardacanute's death, that Magnus is content to let him rule in England.

Harald Sigurdsson the Stern, the brother of Olaf the Saint. He collects great wealth in his plundering travels. Returning to Norway, he is troublesome to his nephew Magnus, who finally gives him half of Norway in return for half his booty.

Ellisiv, the daughter of the Russian king and the wife of Harald the Stern.

Harald Godwinsson, successor to Edward the Good of England. Trying to unthrone him, Harald the Stern meets his death in England.

Magnus, a son of Harald the Stern. Co-ruler of Norway with his brother, he dies young of sickness.

Olaf the Quiet, another son of Harald the Stern. He is a successful ruler of Norway for twenty-six years.

Magnus Barefoot, so called after his return from Scotland in Scottish national costume. The son of Olaf the Quiet, he greatly extends the power of the central government during his ten-year rule of Norway. Not yet thirty, he is killed in Ireland in 1103.

Hakon Magnusson, the nephew of Olaf the Quiet. He shares with Magnus Barefoot in the rule of Norway until his early death from sickness.

Olaf, the youngest son of Magnus Barefoot. He dies young.

Eystein, another son of Magnus Barefoot. Co-ruler of Norway, he is jealous of his brother Sigurd.

Sigurd the Crusader, another son of Magnus Barefoot. He travels for three years to the Holy Land and elsewhere while Eystein rules at home. Surviving his brother, he greatly improves the legal system of his country.

Magnus the Blind, the son of Sigurd and a foolish king. Captured and blinded by Harald Gille, he retires to a monastery.

Harald Gille, from Ireland. Claiming to be Sigurd's half brother, he proves his paternity in an ordeal by hot iron. Proclaimed ruler over part of Norway, he is a cruel sovereign.

Sigurd Slembedegn, a pretender to the throne, by whose order and treachery Harald Gille is killed.

Sigurd and

Eystein, sons of Harald Gille. Constant unrest results from their leadership of separate factions.

Crippled Inge, Harald Gille's most popular son. Surviving his brothers, he rules alone for a time and dies at twenty-six.

Cardinal Nicholas, who comes from Rome in 1152 to establish an archbishopric at Nidaros, shrine of Olaf the Great. Well-loved, he later becomes Pope Adrian IV.

Hakon Sigurdsson the Broad-Shouldered, an untrustworthy claimant to Eystein's part of Norway. He kills Inge and is defeated in battle at fifteen in 1162.

Erling Skakke, a power behind Inge's throne. He gives up power to archbishops and to Denmark and becomes a tyrant in order to secure the Norwegian throne for his son.

Valdemar, king of Denmark. Erling Skakke gives him part of Norway as a fief under the Danish crown in exchange for peace.

Magnus Erlingsson, the son of Erling Skakke. Son of a daughter of Sigurd the Crusader, he is a legitimate candidate for the throne of Norway. He is five years old when his father's supporters make him king.

HELEN
(Helenē)

Author: Euripides (c. 485-406 B.C.E.)
First performed: 412 B.C.E.
Genre: Drama
Locale: Egypt
Time: Seven years after the fall of Troy
Plot: Love

Helen, the wife of King Menelaus of Sparta. Promised by Aphrodite to Paris for his judgment, Helen was rescued by Hermes and supernaturally transported to Egypt. A phantom-image was given to Paris, and Helen was promised that she would return to Sparta to be with her husband, who should know that she did not elope to Troy. She has been protected in Egypt by King Proteus, but he is now dead, and his son Theoclymenus wishes to marry her. She has taken refuge at the tomb of Proteus and, at the beginning of the play, laments her misfortunes. When a Greek, Teucer, appears with the news that Menelaus is reported dead, Helen takes the report as fact. She goes to consult Theonoe, a prophetess who is the sister of Theoclymenus, and learns that Menelaus is alive and will arrive in Egypt. When she returns, Menelaus has appeared. He cannot believe, because he has been wandering for seven years with the phantom-image, that Helen is really in Egypt until one of his men comes to report that the phantom-image has returned to the skies. He and Helen then retell their separate stories, convince the all-knowing Theonoe not to reveal their presence to Theoclymenus, and devise a plan to escape. Helen has Menelaus, ragged and dirty after his wanderings, report his own death to Theoclymenus. She agrees to marry the young king if he will allow her to perform burial rites at sea for dead Menelaus. Once at sea, Helen and Menelaus make their escape. Helen is a romantic figure; she has charm, wit, self-importance, and self-pity combined with loveliness and virtue.

Menelaus (meh-neh-LAY-uhs), the king of Sparta. Shipwrecked on the coast of Egypt, he hides his men and the phantom-image of Helen and sets out in search of aid. He appears, shabbily clothed, and is faced down and treated as a beggar by an old portress at the house of Theoclymenus. She tells him of Helen's presence in the house and of her master's hostility toward all Greeks. Helen enters and, after Menelaus learns that the gods had substituted a phantom-image for his wife, they are reconciled and seek the aid of Theonoe. In his plea before her, Menelaus is the "miles gloriosus," the braggart soldier: he threatens, is highly rhetorical, and even congratulates himself during his speech. After he makes several useless suggestions for their escape, he accepts Helen's plan and carries out his role bravely.

Theoclymenus (thee-uh-KLIM-eh-nuhs), the king of Egypt, a pious and kindly man whose love for Helen has caused him to attempt to make her his wife in spite of his father's oath of protection. He dislikes Greeks because he is afraid they may come to steal Helen. Eager to believe the reports of Menelaus' death and overjoyed because Helen now seems willing to accept his suit, he is easily duped into agreeing to any funeral arrangements she wishes to make. He is kept from pursuit by the intervention of the gods, whose advice he gladly follows.

Theonoe (thee-ON-oh-ee), a prophetess and the sister of Theoclymenus. Helen consults her offstage and learns that Menelaus is not dead. The seeress makes a spectacular entrance and reveals that the final decision in the fate of Menelaus is hers. After hearing from both Helen and Menelaus, she decides, out of self-respect and piety, for Menelaus.

Castor (KAS-tur) and

Polydeuces (pol-ih-DEW-seez), the twin brothers of Helen. They appear at the end of the play to keep Theoclymenus from pursuing Helen and to prevent his punishment of Theonoe for deceiving him.

Teucer (TEW-sur), the famous archer. Traveling to Rhodes because his father, Telamon, has banished him for failing to protect his brother Ajax at Troy, he gives Helen news of the fall of Troy and of the wanderings and reported death of Menelaus.

The portress, a guardian of the house of Theoclymenus. A manly woman, typical of Egypt, she faces Menelaus down when he attempts to beg.

A servant, a simpleminded but faithful servant of Menelaus who brings news of the disappearance of the phantom Helen and who has some bitter things to say against soothsayers.

The Chorus, captive Greek women who are sympathetic to Helen. They render the odes that lift the play above the level of mere comedy.

HENDERSON THE RAIN KING

Author: Saul Bellow (1915-   )
First published: 1959
Genre: Novel

Locale: Primarily Africa
Time: The 1950's
Plot: Picaresque

Eugene Henderson, a fifty-five-year-old millionaire from Danbury, Connecticut. He has been married twice and has five children. At a time when most people would be thinking of retirement and the end of life, Henderson is seized by wanderlust. Although he never precisely explains why he wants to go to Africa, in the course of his adventures it becomes clear that he is the kind of person who is curious about everything and who must find out what is over the next hill, like Odysseus, a classical character with whom he is compared. Before he leaves on his African journey, his restlessness is shown in his attempts to become a pig farmer and then a violinist. When Henderson arrives in Africa, he begins a journey into the continent's interior that also turns out to be a journey to the interior of his life and soul. At the first village he visits, that of the Arnewi, he finds that the cattle are starving because the water cistern is full of frogs. He fashions a bomb, throws it into the cistern, and kills all the frogs, but he also blows a hole in the side of the cistern and loses the village's water. In disgrace, he heads further inland to the country of the Wariki, where he unwittingly passes a series of tests that identify him as the tribal Sungo, or rain king. Henderson appears to be effective as the rain king, because it rains following ceremonies with which he is involved. He becomes friends with Dahfu, the king of the Wariki, and participates with him in rituals that also include a lioness, Atti, who lives in an underground enclosure. The king is killed trying to trap a lion, and Henderson is named king in his place. Henderson deduces that the king's death was a trap and that a similar fate awaits him, so he escapes from the village. In the last scene in the novel, he leaves his flight home at a stop in Newfoundland and, with a young Persian boy he met on the plane, runs around and around the runway. This suggests that his adventures, and his education, are still not over. It also is a reminder that although Henderson has been triumphant in a number of encounters, he has twice fled trouble, and he is running at the novel's close.

Willatale (wihl-lah-TAH-lay), the queen of the gentle Arnewi tribe. She realizes that Henderson has a problem with the concepts of life and death.

Mtalba (ihm-TAHL-bah), Willatale's sister. She wishes to marry Henderson. He runs away, however, after accidentally destroying the Arnewi's water cistern.

Dahfu (DAH-few), the king of the Wariki. He has had a Western education and is therefore able to talk to Henderson about philosophical questions. He reaches the conclusion that meaning and truth come from suffering and that one must face difficulties rather than flee from them. True to his own code, he dies in an attempt to capture Gmilo, a lion said to be his animal father.

The Bunam (bew-NAHM), a priest of the Wariki, the villain of the novel. He is jealous of Dahfu's power and rigs the king's hunting equipment so that Dahfu will fall victim to the lion he is trying to trap. The Bunam represents the dark forces seeking to undermine those of high spirits and dignity.

Romilayu (roh-mee-LAY-ew), the guide whom Henderson hires when he arrives in Africa. He is also Henderson's confidant and friend. Without Romilayu, Henderson would not have been able to reach the places he visited and could not have escaped the Wariki village when faced with treachery and death.

The Persian boy, a passenger on the plane taking Henderson back to America. He represents both newness (through his youth) and mystery (through his country). When Henderson picks up the boy and runs with him around the frozen Canadian airstrip, that act suggests that the future of the human race is bright as long as people have the ability to challenge whatever fate presents to them.

— *James Baird*

HENRY IV
(Enrico IV)

Author: Luigi Pirandello (1867-1936)
First published: 1922
Genre: Drama

Locale: A solitary villa in Italy
Time: 1922
Plot: Psychological realism

Henry IV, an apparent madman who claims that he is the medieval German king Henry IV. In his fifties, Henry lives in a villa in Italy, surrounded by his advisers, who are really his hired companions. Henry is visited by a group of persons from his past: his nephew, di Nolli; his former love, Matilda; and a psychiatrist, among others. During the visit, Henry, who actually recovered from his illness a dozen years ago but has kept up pretenses to remain contented, pretends to fall in love with

Frida, Matilda's daughter, whom he calls his true love. Taunted by Matilda's lover, Baron Belcredi, Henry is gradually driven to violence, and he kills Belcredi in a fit of rage.

Marchioness Matilda Spina (SPEE-nah), a forty-five-year-old widow. She was once the object of Henry's attention before his mental illness. At that time, there was a historical pageant at which everyone pretended to be historical characters. Henry was Henry IV, and Matilda was Matilda of Tuscany. When Henry's horse shied, he fell and struck his head. When he awoke, he thought himself to be Henry IV. Matilda now has a relationship with Baron Belcredi, and she is shocked to see Henry paying attention to her daughter Frida, who looks exactly like Matilda did in her youth.

Marquis Charles di Nolli (dee NOHL-lee), Henry's nephew. Still in mourning for his mother, Henry's sister, the marquis has brought the party to see Henry because his mother believed that Henry was almost cured and should be examined. For this reason, di Nolli has brought the psychiatrist Dr. Genoni. The marquis is also tired of supporting Henry's establishment financially and would like to see Henry declared sane.

Baron Tito Belcredi (TEE-toh behl-CRAY-dee), Matilda's lover, who is a few years younger than she and somewhat of a fop. Facile and witty, he displays contempt for Henry and believes him to be a fake. Jealousy plays a role in this belief, because Belcredi is envious of the grip that Henry's memory has on Matilda. He taunts Henry until the "king" is driven to violence.

Frida (FREE-dah), Matilda's daughter. She is nineteen years old and engaged to di Nolli. Shy and beautiful, she looks exactly like her mother at the time of Henry's accident. Henry is struck by this resemblance and pretends that she is his love. He courts her, though she is afraid of him, until his attentions become real and he cannot bear to part with her.

Landolph, one of Henry's four keepers, who maintain the pretense that they are court advisers. Landolph and the other three—Harold, Ordulph, and Berthold—humor Henry and insist that visitors wear medieval costumes and assume the names of people from King Henry's time. Landolph is astonished when Henry finally admits to them that for the last twelve years he has been cured of his illness but told no one because he felt a certain stability in his pretense. Landolph has believed for all these years that Henry was really insane.

— *Philip Brantingham*

HENRY IV, PART I

Author: William Shakespeare (1564-1616)
First published: 1598
Genre: Drama
Locale: England
Time: 1403
Plot: Historical

King Henry IV, England's troubled ruler. Haunted by his action in the deposition of his predecessor and kinsman, Richard II, and indirectly in that man's death, as well as deeply disturbed by the apparent unworthiness of his irresponsible eldest son, he also faces the external problem of rebellion. He wishes to join a crusade to clear his conscience and to carry out a prophecy that he is to die in Jerusalem.

Prince Hal, later King Henry V. A boisterous youth surrounded by bad companions, he matures rapidly with responsibility, saves his father's life in battle, and kills the dangerous rebel Hotspur.

Sir John Falstaff, a comical, down-at-the-heels follower of Prince Hal, considered by many to be one of William Shakespeare's finest creations. He is the typical braggart soldier with many individualizing traits. As he says, he is not only witty himself but also the cause of wit in other men. He is a cynical realist, a fantastic liar, and a persuasive rascal as well as apparently being a successful combat soldier. His colossal body appropriately houses his colossal personality.

Thomas Percy, the earl of Worcester, a leading rebel against King Henry IV. He conceals the king's offer of generous terms from his nephew Hotspur, thereby causing the young warrior's death. He is executed for treason.

Henry Percy, Sr., the earl of Northumberland, the earl of Worcester's brother. Having played an important part in the deposition of Richard II and the enthronement of Henry IV, he feels that he and his family are entitled to more power and wealth than they receive. He is also influenced to rebellion by his crafty brother and his fiery son. He fails his cause by falling ill or feigning illness before the Battle of Shrewsbury, and he does not appear there.

Henry Percy, Jr., called **Hotspur**, the son of Northumberland. A courageous, hot-tempered youth, he seeks to pluck glory from the moon. He is a loving, teasing husband, but his heart is more on the battlefield than in the boudoir. He rages helplessly at the absence of his father and Glendower from the Battle of Shrewsbury. In the battle, he falls by Prince Hal's hand.

Edmund Mortimer, the earl of March, Hotspur's brother-in-law, designated heir to the English throne by Richard II. Captured while fighting against Glendower, he marries his captor's daughter. King Henry's refusal to ransom him leads to the rebellion of the Percys. He too fails to join Hotspur at Shrewsbury.

Owen Glendower, the Welsh leader. Hotspur finds his mystical self-importance irritating and almost precipitates internal strife among King Henry's opponents. Glendower also fails Hotspur at Shrewsbury.

Archibald, the earl of Douglas, a noble Scottish rebel. After killing Sir Walter Blunt and two others whom he mistakes for King Henry at Shrewsbury, he is prevented from killing the king by Prince Hal. After the battle, Prince Hal generously releases him without ransom.

Richard Scroop, the archbishop of York, a principal rebel. He thinks to make peace with King Henry and take later advantage of his weakness but is tricked by Prince John, Hal's younger brother, and executed.

Sir Walter Blunt, a heroic follower of the king. At the Battle of Shrewsbury, he pretends to Douglas that he is the king, thus bringing death on himself.

HENRY IV, PART II

Author: William Shakespeare (1564-1616)
First published: 1600
Genre: Drama
Locale: England
Time: 1405-1413
Plot: Historical

King Henry IV, the first Lancastrian monarch. Weighed down by the troubles of high office, he is despondent over having deposed his predecessor Richard II and profoundly pessimistic about prospects for the nation when Prince Hal, his successor, becomes king. Beset by rebellions from two quarters, he is inclined to credit exaggerated reports of rebel strength. Following assurances from wise counselors that he will prevail, the king reaffirms his intention to lead a crusade to the Holy Land after peace has been restored. Illness cuts short his plan. As he lies dying, he is reassured by Prince Hal that his counselors will be retained and heeded. He advises Hal to involve the nation in a foreign war to promote domestic unity.

Prince Henry, often called **Prince Hal**, the prince of Wales and later **King Henry V** in the drama. After being dismissed from the king's council for striking the Chief Justice in court, the witty Hal turns his attentions to enjoying himself with Falstaff and his companions at the Boar's Head Tavern. When he hears of the king's illness, he conceals his grief because, he thinks, people would regard sadness on his part as hypocritical. Visiting his father before his death, Hal takes away the crown and must explain to the king's satisfaction why he did something seemingly so callous. Although his response restores the king's confidence, he is compelled to quiet the justifiable fears of others after the king's death. Through magnanimity to the Chief Justice, severity toward Falstaff, and professed allegiance to his father's memory, Hal convinces members of the court that he will become a worthy monarch.

Prince John, Hal's younger brother. A man of few words, he is tough and ruthless. As commander of the king's army, he convinces the rebel leaders to surrender and then sends their leaders to immediate execution.

Westmoreland, the king's counselor and general. Resolute and strong-willed, he upholds the king's position in a meeting with the rebels.

Warwick, the king's cousin, an important counselor. He attempts to calm the king's fears about rebel strength and reassures the king about Hal's intentions. Among the courtiers, only Warwick believes that Hal will reform.

The Lord Chief Justice, a fearless, upright man of justice. In two encounters with Falstaff, he parries the knight's efforts to intimidate him. Having reason to fear the worst from Hal, he stoutly justifies to the new king his earlier role in sending him to prison. Hal rewards him by retaining him in office.

Scroop, the archbishop of York, an elderly, highly respected clergyman and a natural leader. He leads the rebels in northern England. Wise and eloquent, he elicits respect from both followers and adversaries. Professing to oppose the government on principle, he is motivated in large measure by a grudge against the king, who had executed his brother for treason. Tricked into an ambiguous truce, he is beheaded on an order from Prince John.

Earl of Northumberland, a powerful nobleman, first a supporter, then an implacable opponent, of the king. Wild with grief over the death of his son Hotspur in battle against the king's army, he vows revenge, but betrayed by his cowardly nature, he retreats into Scotland rather than join the rebels as he had promised. He eventually is defeated in battle by a force under the sheriff of Yorkshire.

Sir John Falstaff, a comical, corpulent knight, a companion of Prince Hal, often at the Boar's Head Tavern. His moods vary from effervescent, contagious gaiety to maudlin self-pity. A complete hedonist, Falstaff exists only for his own pleasure. He manages to intimidate others through bluster if he cannot outsmart them through his boundless wit. His hopes of favor when the prince becomes king are cruelly belied.

Pistol, a companion of Falstaff, full of bluster, threats, and extravagant rhetoric.

Mistress Quickly, the hostess and owner of the Boar's Head Tavern. She creates conflict with Falstaff through attempting to collect money he owes her, but she surrenders to his wit and provides him with even more entertainment.

Doll Tearsheet, a prostitute at the Boar's Head Tavern, a virago in speech with an explosive temper. She is sentimental about Falstaff.

Poins, a youthful companion of Prince Hal, given to witty pranks. His association with the prince arouses the envy of Falstaff. To Prince Hal, he is a sounding board for common opinion.

— *Stanley Archer*

HENRY V

Author: William Shakespeare (1564-1616)
First published: 1600
Genre: Drama
Locale: England and France
Time: Early fifteenth century
Plot: Historical

Henry V, the king of England from 1413 to 1422, the wild "Prince Hal" of the "Henry IV" plays. Since his accession to the throne, he has grown into a capable monarch whose sagacity astonishes his advisers. The question of state that most concerns him is that of his right, through his grandfather, Edward III, to certain French duchies and ultimately to the French crown. His claim to the duchies is haughtily answered by the Dauphin of France, who sends Henry a barrel of tennis balls, a jibe at the English king's misspent youth. Having crushed at home a plot against his life fomented by his cousin, the earl of Cambridge, abetted by Lord Scroop and Sir Thomas Gray, and having been assured by the archbishop of Canterbury that his claim to the French crown is valid, Henry invades France. After the capture of Harfleur, at which victory he shows mercy to the inhabitants of the town, the king meets the French at Agincourt in Picardy. The French take the impending battle very lightly, because they outnumber the English. Henry spends the night wandering in disguise around his camp, talking to the soldiers to test their feelings and to muse on the responsibilities of kingship. In the battle on the following day, the English win a great victory. The peace is concluded by the betrothal of Henry to Princess Katharine, daughter of the French king, and the recognition of his claim to the French throne. To the playwright, as to most of his contemporaries, Henry was a great national hero whose exploits of two centuries earlier fitted in well with the patriotic fervor of a generation that had seen the defeat of the Spanish Armada.

Charles VI, the weak-minded king of France.

Queen Isabel, his wife.

Lewis, the Dauphin of France, whose pride is humbled at Agincourt.

Katharine of France, the daughter of Charles VI. As part of the treaty of peace, she is betrothed to Henry V, who woos her in a mixture of blunt English and mangled French.

Edward, the duke of York, a cousin of the king, though called "uncle" in the play. He dies a hero's death at Agincourt.

Richard, the earl of Cambridge, the younger brother of York. Corrupted by French gold, he plots against the life of Henry and is executed for treason.

Lord Scroop and
Sir Thomas Gray, fellow conspirators of Cambridge.

Philip, the duke of Burgundy, the intermediary between Charles VI and Henry V. He draws up the treaty of peace and forces it on Charles.

Montjoy, the French herald who carries the haughty messages from the French to Henry.

Pistol, a soldier. He is addicted to high-flown language and is married to Mistress Quickly, formerly the hostess of a tavern in Eastcheap. Later, Fluellen proves him a coward. When he learns of his wife's death, he resolves to return to England to become a cutpurse.

Nell Quickly, formerly the hostess of the Boar's Head Tavern in Eastcheap and now married to Pistol. It is she who gives the famous account of the death of Falstaff. She dies while Pistol is in France.

Bardolph, now a soldier, formerly one of Henry's companions in his wild youth. In France, he is sentenced to be hanged for stealing a pax.

Fluellen, a Welsh soldier, tedious and long-winded. By a trick, the king forces him into a fight with Williams.

Michael Williams, a soldier who quarrels with Henry while the king is wandering incognito through the camp. They exchange gages to guarantee a duel when they next meet. When the meeting occurs, the king forgives Williams for the quarrel.

John, the duke of Bedford and the younger brother of Henry V.

Humphrey, the duke of Gloucester, the youngest brother of Henry V.

HENRY VI, PART I

Author: William Shakespeare (1564-1616)
First published: 1598
Genre: Drama
Locale: England and France
Time: 1422-1444
Plot: Historical

King Henry VI, a simple, peace-loving, and almost saintly monarch. He becomes the pawn of his queen and his powerful noblemen. Although he is aware of their evil, he remains incapable of action against them.

Margaret of Anjou, his strong-minded, articulate queen. She despises Henry for his weakness and allies herself with the duke of Suffolk to become, in effect, the ruler of England.

William de la Pole, the earl of Suffolk, her lover. A staunch Lancastrian, he tries to govern the kingdom through his influence over the queen.

Humphrey, the duke of Gloucester, the Lord Protector, a violent, uncontrollable foe of Cardinal Beaufort.

Henry Beaufort, the cardinal of Winchester, his power-hungry uncle and bitter enemy.

Lord Talbot, later the earl of Shrewsbury, the English military hero who leads his nation to victory over France and Joan of Arc.

Joan la Pucelle, commonly called **Joan of Arc**, the French shepherdess who becomes the leader of the Dauphin's army. She is presented as a witch, possessed by devils.

Charles, the Dauphin of France, who readily accepts Joan's aid and offers himself as her lover.

Richard Plantagenet, who becomes the duke of York, the ambitious leader of the Yorkist party. He is the nephew of Edmund Mortimer. He proclaims his title to the English throne and forces Henry to make him his heir.

Edmund Mortimer, the earl of March, an elderly Yorkist heir who bequeaths his cause to Richard.

The duke of Bedford, Henry VI's uncle, regent of France.

Thomas Beaufort, the duke of Exeter, Henry's great-uncle.

HENRY VI, PART II

Author: William Shakespeare (1564-1616)
First published: 1594
Genre: Drama
Locale: England
Time: 1444-1455
Plot: Historical

King Henry VI, the king of England. Although he is the title character, he is by no means the central character of the play. A deeply religious man, he is an ineffective ruler, easily swayed by stronger personalities, including those of his wife and his advisers. He is unable to deal realistically with political conflict and seems unaware that many members of his court are plotting against him. When France retakes territory the English have held, Henry responds only that it must be God's will. He calls for peace and harmony. Neither does he protest much when Gloucester is brought down. He is aware of his own weaknesses as a ruler and wishes he were not called by God to command. When Richard Plantagenet claims the throne, Henry retreats.

Humphrey, duke of Gloucester, a noble and patriotic son of England. He is deeply upset that Henry has given to the French the territories of Anjou and Maine, in exchange for Margaret, the new queen. He remains loyal to the king and to England, using his popularity and wisdom in the service of holding together the divided country. He is next in line for the throne but has no desire to rule. A trusted adviser and friend to Henry, he is a threat to Margaret and to the Duke of Suffolk's quest for more power. Humphrey's wife faces trumped-up charges of witchcraft and is banished; soon afterward, Humphrey himself is falsely accused of treason and then murdered. After his death, England cannot hold together, and the civil conflict known as the Wars of the Roses begins.

Margaret of Anjou, Henry's new bride, who has come from Anjou. A scheming and ill-tempered woman, she is jealous of Humphrey and intolerant of her husband's helplessness. When Gloucester is brought down and subsequently murdered, she rejoices and gathers a group of noblemen around her to influence the king. Later, when the Duke of Suffolk is arrested for his part in the murder, it becomes apparent that he and Margaret have been lovers.

The duke of Suffolk, an unscrupulous and ambitious man who vies with Humphrey for influence over King Henry. He is the lover of the queen, Margaret of Anjou, and although his passion for her is genuine, he is also attracted by the power he hopes to have through her. He orchestrates the downfall of Humphrey and hires Humphrey's murderers. When Henry learns of Suffolk's treachery, he banishes him from England. Suffolk falls prey to a band of pirates and is killed.

Eleanor Cobham, duchess of Gloucester, who longs for her husband to become king. She consults a conjurer in order to see the future and plot an overthrow. She is betrayed, accused of witchcraft, and banished. Her humiliation is the beginning of Gloucester's downfall.

Richard Plantagenet, duke of York, a claimant to the throne of England. He is a minor figure in the plot against Gloucester but remains in the background, quietly gathering power. From Ireland, where he has gone to put down a rebellion, he plans a military coup using the forces under his command. He orchestrates a rebellion in England, brings his own army to quell it, and then announces his claim to the throne, beginning the civil war.

— *Cynthia A. Bily*

HENRY VI, PART III

Author: William Shakespeare (1564-1616)
First published: 1595
Genre: Drama
Locale: Various locations in England and France
Time: 1455-1471
Plot: Historical

King Henry VI, the helpless and ineffective king of England. A deeply religious man, he is gentle and contemplative, completely incapable of understanding or dealing with treachery. As the play opens, Henry tries to bring a peaceful end to the civil war, but there is no common ground to unite Richard on one side and Margaret on the other. He persuades Richard Plantagenet to let him continue to rule but makes Richard his heir instead of his own son. As killing leads to revenge and more killing, Henry protests eloquently, but he has no power to influence the actions of others. In the midst of battle, Henry wishes for a calm, pastoral life, but he can never find it. After his forces, under Queen Margaret's command, lose at the battle of Towton, he is imprisoned in the Tower of London; later, he is murdered there by Richard, the son of Richard Plantagenet.

Queen Margaret, the ruthless and intelligent wife of Henry, effectively the leader of England's armies. Angered that Henry has disinherited her son Edward in favor of Richard Plantagenet, she arranges for the murder of Richard's son, Rutland. When Richard is captured by her forces at Wakefield, she tortures him with a mock coronation, tells him that she has had his son killed, and then helps stab Richard to death. Although a brave and decisive leader— quite unlike her husband, who has no heart for killing—Margaret loses the battle at Towton. Another loss at Tewkesbury seals her fate. There, she is taken prisoner by Edward, Richard's son, and watches as her own son Edward is killed. Her final speech is an eloquent lamentation.

Richard Plantagenet, duke of York. Although he has defeated the king at St. Albans, he agrees, in an attempt to end the bitter civil war, that Henry may continue to rule until his death if he will agree to pass the throne to Richard or his son. Richard's son, the duke of Gloucester and also called Richard, is unhappy with the new terms, as is Margaret, Henry's wife. Civil war soon breaks out again. York is captured by Margaret's forces and stabbed to death by the queen, who has also had Richard's son Rutland killed.

Edward, earl of March, a son of Richard Plantagenet and later King Edward IV. Although he becomes king, his dishonesty and selfish ambition make him as unsuitable for the role as Henry's gentleness makes him. He states clearly that he would break any oath if it would help him acquire power, and he breaks an arranged marriage to the sister of the French king in order to marry his mistress, setting England and France at war. When his forces encounter Margaret's at Tewkesbury, he captures her and helps kill her son, viciously satisfying his own lust for revenge instead of taking steps to reunify his divided country.

Richard, duke of Gloucester, another son of Richard Plantagenet. Bloodthirsty and ambitious—and aware and proud of his evil nature—he is an admirer of Machiavelli and of Judas Iscariot. In the opening scene, he displays the head of the duke of Somerset, defeated in battle, on his sword. Near the end of the play, while Henry is imprisoned in the Tower of London, Richard murders him with the same sword and swears to use his full capacity for evil to gain the throne.

Edward, Prince of Wales, the son of King Henry and Queen Margaret. More his mother's son than his father's, he is decisive and bold. He joins with his mother to oppose Richard Plantagenet, and he criticizes his father for his ineffectiveness. In the battle of Tewkesbury, he is captured and killed by Richard's son Edward.

— *Cynthia A. Bily*

HENRY VIII

Authors: William Shakespeare (1564-1616) with John Fletcher (1579-1625)
First published: 1623
Genre: Drama
Locale: England
Time: 1520-1533
Plot: Historical

King Henry VIII, the king of England. Possibly because he may be a composite portrait by two authors and possibly because of the difficulty of writing about a controversial political figure so nearly contemporary, King Henry is not one of the more successful creations in the playwright's gallery. At times, he seems to be an allegorical figure of Royalty, like Magnificence in John Skelton's morality play of that title. The injustice of his treatment of Queen Katharine is partly offset by his generous protection of Cranmer against the council's attack.

Thomas Cardinal Wolsey, the cardinal of York and Lord Chancellor of England. A far better dramatic creation than the king, he is drawn as arrogant and stubborn when he is in power and ruthless in hounding the duke of Buckingham to his death and in attempting to force Queen Katharine to submit the decision on her divorce to Henry and Wolsey. He falls through pride but accepts his fall with dignity. His death is reported to Queen Katharine as a good death, and she speaks of him with forgiveness.

Queen Katharine, called **Katharine of Aragon**, the first wife of Henry VIII. Characterized by dignity, firmness, and compassion, she never allows her adversity and her material losses to shake her integrity or reduce her to bitterness. Even her successful rival for the king's affections, Anne Bullen, speaks of her with pity and admiration. The king himself has nothing to say in dispraise of her character or conduct, either before or after the divorce.

Thomas Cranmer, the archbishop of Canterbury, a loyal friend and supporter of King Henry. He is considered a heretic by Wolsey. Saved from the plots of the council by the king, then chosen as godfather for the infant Elizabeth, he delivers a glowing prophecy of the future of his tiny goddaughter. This supposed prophecy and actual eulogy of the late queen is the true end of the play, followed only by the concluding speech of King Henry, in keeping with the contemporary convention of giving royalty the last word on stage.

Anne Bullen (also spelled **Anne Boleyn**), Queen Katharine's maid of honor. She becomes the king's second wife and the mother of Elizabeth. Although she has sympathy for the queen and says that she would not be a queen for all the riches under heaven, she readily consents to be Queen Katharine's successor.

The duke of Buckingham, Edward Bohun, the son of the duke of Buckingham beheaded under Richard III. He is the bitter enemy and victim of Cardinal Wolsey. His role in act 1 is a large one, but it ends early in act 2 as he goes to his death with great dignity and nobility.

The duke of Norfolk, Thomas Howard, the son of "Jockey of Norfolk," who appears in William Shakespeare's *Richard III*. A moderate nobleman, an admirer of Queen Katharine, and a supporter of her plea for relief of the hardship of the commons, he has no love for Cardinal Wolsey. He bears the king's command that Wolsey give up the seal of the Lord Chancellor.

The earl of Surrey, the son of Norfolk and son-in-law of Buckingham. He shares in Wolsey's downfall and heaps recriminations on him.

The duke of Suffolk, Charles Brandon, another enemy of Wolsey. He also shares in the overthrow of the cardinal and taunts him in his adversity.

The Lord Chamberlain, Charles Somerset, earl of Worcester. He is present at the cardinal's party, which is attended by the king and Anne Bullen. He informs the king who Anne is.

Lord Sands, a coltish old gentleman given to flirting. He also attends the cardinal's party.

Sir Thomas Lovell, another guest at the cardinal's party. He is in charge of Buckingham's execution and asks forgiveness from the duke, which is granted.

Cardinal Campeius, an emissary sent from Rome to hear the case for the divorce between King Henry and Queen Katharine. He endeavors in vain to persuade the queen to submit to the judgment of the king and Wolsey in the matter of her divorce.

Capucius, the ambassador from Charles V (Queen Katharine's nephew) to Henry VIII. He visits Queen Katharine just before her death and tries to console her.

The Lord Chancellor, Sir Thomas More, the successor to Cardinal Wolsey. He presides at Cranmer's hearing before the council.

Stephen Gardiner, the bishop of Winchester, a follower of Wolsey and an enemy of Cranmer. He becomes reconciled with Cranmer on the king's command.

An old lady, a friend of Anne Bullen. She and Anne discuss Queen Katharine's case. She may be the officious old lady who announces to the king the birth of his daughter Elizabeth.

Griffith, the gentleman usher to Queen Katharine. He remains faithful to her in her retirement and ill health to her death.

Doctor Butts, Sir William Butts, the king's physician. He is friendly to Cranmer and informs the king of the council's hostility toward him.

The surveyor to the duke of Buckingham, who sells out his master to the cardinal and aids in bringing about the execution.

Thomas Cromwell, Wolsey's loyal servant, to whom he speaks the famous and much-quoted passage on ambition.

Sir Henry Guildford, who welcomes the guests at the cardinal's party.

The duchess of Norfolk, the godmother of Elizabeth. She carries the infant in the ceremonial procession.

The marchioness of Dorset, the second godmother of Elizabeth.

Sir Nicholas Vaux, who is responsible for conducting the duke of Buckingham to execution.

Lord Abergavenny (ab-ur-GEHN-ih), a friend of Buckingham and Norfolk.

HER PRIVATES, WE

Author: Frederic Manning (1882-1935)
First published: 1929
Genre: Novel
Locale: Somme and Ancre in northern France
Time: 1916
Plot: Social realism

Bourne, a private in the Westshire regiment on the Somme front in World War I. As an outsider, evidently Australian, he maintains a detached perspective toward the British around him. Nevertheless, he is sympathetic and grows angry only at meanness, malice, and the dodging of responsibility. Because of his superior education and ability to influence others, he is repeatedly offered promotion. He rejects these offers, primarily because he feels at home with the men in the ranks. At the end, vindictively ordered to lead a night raid on the German trenches, he is shot in the chest and dies while being carried back.

Shem, a Jewish private in the Westshire regiment. He had a safe job in the Army Pay Office in England, which he gave up to go to the trenches in France. After a battle, he forms a friendship with Bourne and Martlow and, although careful to avoid buying their drinks, he does pick up the bill if the others are broke. Early in the disastrous Somme offensive, he is wounded in the foot but manages to crawl back to the British trenches.

Charlie Martlow, a private in the Westshire regiment. The son of a gamekeeper, he is obstinate but generous. He happened to sit beside Bourne and Shem after a battle, through which chance their friendship was formed; this friendship sustains them through all the hardships and horrors of trench warfare. During the Somme offensive, the back of his head is blown off, and he dies in Bourne's arms.

Weeper Smart, a private in the Westshire regiment. Weeper is a nickname imposed on him because he always bears an expression of suffering, at once pitiful and repulsive; Bourne never calls him by it. His face resembles a vulture's, with a narrow forehead; arched eyebrows; loose, pendulous lips; a receding chin; and a large, fleshy nose jutting from between protruding, watery blue eyes. He has thin sandy hair, sloping shoulders, abnormally long arms, and huge hands. He dreads the thought of killing and is haunted by the memory of it. He volunteers to go on the patrol with Bourne. When Bourne is fatally wounded, Weeper carries him back to the British lines.

— *Christopher M. Armitage*

HERACLES
(Hērakles)

Author: Euripides (c. 485-406 B.C.E.)
First transcribed: c. 420 B.C.E.
Genre: Drama
Locale: Thebes
Time: Remote antiquity
Plot: Tragedy

Herakles (HEHR-uh-kleez), the Greek hero who passes, through suffering, from the courage of outward physical strength to internal courage raised against intolerable necessity and based on true friendship. During the first third of the play, he does not appear, but Amphitryon, his father; his wife, Megara; his small sons; and the Chorus attest his heroism and express the increasing fear that he is dead. He has gone to Hades to capture Cerberus, the last of his labors to be performed. He appears suddenly, just before Lycus, usurper of the throne of Thebes, returns to kill Herakles' father, children, and wife. He determines, sure of his physical strength, to march against Lycus and his forces, but Amphitryon persuades him to enter his house and wait for Lycus. He does so. Lycus returns, enters the house to drag out Megara and the children, and is killed by Herakles. Suddenly, Iris and Madness appear to carry out the will of Hera, the queen of the gods and persecutor of Herakles, to make him murder his children in a fit of insanity. The murders, described by a messenger, are terrible. Herakles believes his own children to be those of Eurystheus, and he kills them and Megara. When he turns on his father, however, the goddess Athena appears and knocks him unconscious with a rock. As he awakens, Theseus, the king of Athens, rescued from Hades by Herakles, appears. He has come to aid Herakles against Lycus. Herakles speaks of suicide, but Theseus' taunt that it is a "boorish folly" worthy only of cowards causes him to renounce self-death and to accept Theseus' offer of refuge and honor in Athens. Herakles' last words are that it is a sad error to seek "wealth or strength" rather than fine friends.

Amphitryon (am-FIHT-ree-ehn), the father of Herakles. His opening monologue provides the background and states the plight of Herakles' kin. His defense of his son before Lycus is vigorous and overshadows his plea for exile rather than death. He curses the gods because the plea is not granted, but he then prays to them for deliverance. He tempers Herakles' desire for wholesale vengeance against Lycus and his followers. At the end of the play, he is left to bury Megara and her children.

Megara (MEHG-ah-rah), the wife of Herakles. Driven to hasty refuge by Lycus, she still has hope that her husband is alive and accepts Amphitryon's plea for a delay of death. When Lycus threatens to burn the suppliants, she reveals her true dignity as Herakles' wife: They must willingly accept death, now inevitable, and not beg from Lycus. She requests that she be allowed to enter the house of Herakles and clothe herself and her children for death. When Herakles appears, Megara reveals the circumstances and enters the house with him. She is killed by Herakles in his madness.

Theseus (THEE-see-uhs), the king of Athens. He appears at the close of the play with an army to help Herakles against Lycus. He is the model of what a friend should be. Because he cannot fight for Herakles, he offers to share his sufferings, unafraid of the pollution that contact with a murderer was thought to bring upon an innocent person. He warns Herakles against suicide and offers him refuge, wealth, and honor in Athens. The two leave together.

Lycus (LI-kuhs), the usurper of the throne of Thebes. He had killed Creon, the father of Megara, and taken the throne. A tyrant, he feels it necessary to destroy the family of Herakles. His belief that Herakles is dead contrasts with the remaining hope of Megara and Amphitryon. He is killed by Herakles when he enters the latter's house to drag Megara from the altar.

Iris (I-rihs), the messenger of Hera, queen of the gods. She is sent to carry out Hera's wrath against Herakles as well as her own, and she sees to it that Madness does not rebel against her task.

Madness, who rebels against divine vindictiveness, but to no avail. Although she must obey the goddess' command, she calls on the sun to witness her reluctance. In carrying out her task, she is madness incarnate.

The Chorus of old men of Thebes, friends who are sympathetic to the plight of Megara. They are helpless because of age. In spite of their weakness, they threaten Lycus and attempt to intervene, but his show of force makes them realize there is nothing they can do.

A messenger, who reports Herakles' madness and the murder of Megara and the children.

HERCULES AND HIS TWELVE LABORS

Author: Unknown
First published: Unknown
Genre: Novel
Locale: The Mediterranean region
Time: Antiquity
Plot: Adventure

Hercules (HUR-kyew-leez), the son of Jupiter and Alcmena. He is a mortal. As a child, he is the object of Juno's jealousy. Through her influence, he is commanded to carry out twelve labors, in hopes that he will be killed in accomplishing one of them: (1) he must strangle the Nemean lion; (2) he must kill the nine-headed hydra; (3) he must capture the dread Erymanthian boar; (4) he must capture a stag with golden antlers and brazen feet; (5) he must get rid of the carnivorous Stymphalian birds; (6) he must cleanse the stables of Augeas; (7) he must capture the sacred bull of Minos; (8) he must drive away the carnivorous mares of Diomedes; (9) he must secure the girdle of Hippolyta, queen of the Amazons; (10) he must bring back the oxen belonging to the monster Geryoneus; (11) he must bring back the golden apples of the Hesperides; and (12) he must bring back Cerberus, the three-headed dog of the Underworld.

Jupiter (JEW-pih-tur), king of the gods, Hercules' father.

Alcmena (alk-MEE-nee), a mortal woman, Hercules' mother.

Juno (JEW-noh), Jupiter's wife. Jealous of mortal Alcmena, she hopes to cause Hercules' death and thus be avenged.

Eurystheus (yew-RIHS-thews), Hercules' cousin. Acting for Juno, he assigns the twelve labors.

Rhadamanthus (rad-uh-MAN-thuhs), Hercules' tutor, killed by Hercules when he punishes the boy.

Amphitryon (am-FIHT-ree-on), Hercules' foster father. He rears the boy as a shepherd, high in the mountains.

HEREWARD THE WAKE: Last of the English

Author: Charles Kingsley (1819-1875)
First published: 1866
Genre: Novel
Locale: England, Scotland, and Flanders
Time: The eleventh century
Plot: Historical

Hereward Leofricsson, called **Hereward the Wake**, a handsome, bold, adventurous Saxon thane and outlaw; a high-spirited, rebellious, irreligious youth who later becomes a great knight and leader of the English against the Normans. After his marriage to Alftruda, he again becomes what he was before Torfrida inspired him to heroic stature: a toper and an idle boaster. Though he makes his peace with William, he has many Norman enemies who cause his imprisonment and finally bring about his murder.

Lady Godiva, his mother, who causes him to be declared an outlaw, an action for which she later asks his pardon.

Leofric, lord of Bourne, a Saxon nobleman, father of Hereward, whom he outlaws at Lady Godiva's request.

Torfrida, Hereward's blue-eyed, raven-haired first wife

and mother of his daughter, also named Torfrida. She falsely declares herself a sorceress to gain annulment of her marriage to Hereward. Though he had betrayed her with Alftruda, Torfrida loyally claims his butchered body and buries it. She herself later is put in the same grave.

Alftruda, Hereward's second wife, with whom he commits adultery before marrying her.

Martin Lightfoot, a faithful companion in Hereward's wanderings. He goes mad with grief after Hereward's murder.

William the Conqueror, duke of Normandy and king of England.

Gilbert of Ghent, the stout, hearty guardian of Alftruda and sometime friend of Hereward; the leader of a group of men who arrest Hereward on various charges of enmity to William.

Harold, king of England, killed in the Battle of Hastings.

Abbot Brand, aged, infirm uncle of Hereward. He dies after warning Hereward of English drunkenness, French cleverness, and the doom of those who live by the sword.

Baldwin of Flanders, a powerful ruler of the Lowlands of Western Europe for whom Hereward performs valiant services.

Sir Ascelin, a knight who plots against Hereward and severs his head after his murder.

Ivo Taillebois and

Hugh of Evermue, two Normans who attack Hereward from behind and run him through with lances.

HERLAND

Author: Charlotte Perkins Gilman (1860-1935)
First published: 1915
Genre: Novel
Locale: Utopia, in South America
Time: Early twentieth century
Plot: Social realism

Vandyck (Van) Jennings, a young sociologist and chronicler of the Herlandean adventures. A scientist and linguist, he maintains an open mind and objectivity toward the all-female country he and his two friends discover. The most levelheaded of the three explorers, he is better able to observe and interpret their situation than are the others. He is eager to learn the language and willing to accept the education provided by his tutor, Somel; later, his relationship with Ellador, which begins as a comradely friendship, deepens into love. He enjoys sharing knowledge and experience with her. Although their views of marriage differ markedly, his respect for her as a person contributes to their successful union.

Terry O. Nicholson, a wealthy young pilot, eager to explore and overconfident of his masculine charm. He is unable to accept a society without men or one in which women are equal; he expects a woman to relate to him. Fretting about confinement by the Herlandeans, he organizes an escape attempt and is humiliated to be recaptured by the women. Suave and masculine, he courts and marries Alima, still insisting that women enjoy being mastered, but his childish attempt to force her sexually results in failure and his divorce. He is expelled from Herland.

Jeff Margrave, a young doctor, courteous and curious, interested in all the wonders of science. An opposite to Terry in his attitudes toward women, he is a romantic and an idealist, and he views women as akin to angels, needing protection. He is immediately captivated by the culture of Herland and is soon convinced of its superiority to his own. He worships Celis and what she represents, and he cheerfully accepts the conditions she sets for their marriage.

Ellador, a young woman of Herland, a forester with soft brown hair and eyes. She is logical, intelligent, and strong, and she also possesses the qualities developed in Herland's women: compassion, tenderness, and a high regard for mothering. She accepts Vandyck as a companion, a friend, and finally a husband. Her naïve yet astute questions about life in the rest of the world elicit stark contrasts between Herland and elsewhere. Firmly convinced that sexual activity should occur only to produce children, she cleverly deflects Vandyck's desires with an excess of comradeship.

Alima, another young forester in Herland. A blazing dark-eyed beauty, she is exceptionally strong and proud, as well as a shade more provocative and atavistically female than her friend Ellador. She is very much an individual, accustomed to independence and recognition as a person; consequently, her courtship with Terry is stormy and their marriage a disaster.

Celis, another young forester in Herland, described by Vandyck as a "blue-and-rose-and-gold person." She is at first a little puzzled by Jeff's enthusiastic devotion and desire to serve her, but she is capable enough to help him adjust to a Herlandean marriage. Her pregnancy brings great joy to them both. Their child is to be the first in Herland's history to be conceived by a male and a female rather than parthenogenetically.

Somel, Vandyck's tutor, a sweet, motherly woman and an excellent teacher. She answers Vandyck's questions with candor and thoroughness, and they become good friends.

Moadine, Terry's tutor, a big woman who is calm and friendly. Unfailingly polite, she responds to Terry's rudeness and outbursts with pleasant laughter or grave acknowledgment.

Zava, Jeff's tutor. Like the other tutors, she is friendly, wise, and motherly. Jeff declares that he loves Zava like a jolly aunt.

— *Joyce E. Henry*

A HERO AIN'T NOTHIN' BUT A SANDWICH

Author: Alice Childress (1920-1994)
First published: 1973
Genre: Novel
Locale: Harlem, New York
Time: Early 1970's
Plot: Social morality

Benjie Johnson, a thirteen-year-old black heroin addict. Benjie is rebellious and searches for meaning in his life while purposely disrupting the lives of his friends and members of his family. He believes that he caused his father to abandon him and his mother. Benjie longs for validation, particularly because he feels like an intruder in his own home, where his mother attempts to show love both to him and to her common-law husband, Craig Butler. Benjie rejects and provokes Butler, forcing his mother to choose between them.

Rose Johnson, Benjie's mother. She is thirty-three years old and works odd jobs to support herself, her son, and her aging mother. She meets and falls in love with Craig Butler, who adores her. She is acutely aware that loving Butler exacerbates the friction in her home, because Benjie is jealous and resentful of Butler. Rose is a willful woman who tries to exorcise Benjie's demon, an addiction to heroin.

Craig Butler, a struggling maintenance man who wants to marry Rose as soon as her divorce is final. Butler is faced with Rose's mother, Mrs. Ransom Bell, who constantly chastises him, and with Benjie, who uses his drug addiction to punish Rose for loving a man who is not his father. Butler strives to show his two detractors that he can be a good provider and source of support for the entire family. An easygoing, even-tempered man, Butler gives balance to the Johnson household.

— *Elizabeth Brown-Guillory*

A HERO OF OUR TIME
(Geroy nashego vremeni)

Author: Mikhail Lermontov (1814-1841)
First published: 1840; serial form, 1839
Genre: Novel
Locale: The Russian Caucasus
Time: 1830-1838
Plot: Psychological realism

The First Narrator, the "I" of the novel, who is supposedly the author himself. On a trip, he meets Maksim Maksimich (the second narrator), who tells him of his friendship with Grigoriy Aleksandrovich Pechorin (the third narrator). The first narrator comes into possession of Pechorin's journal and, on the diarist's death, publishes from it three tales just as they were written.

Maksim Maksimich (mahk-SIHM mah-SIHM-ihch), the second narrator. He tells to the first narrator the story of his friendship with Grigoriy Aleksandrovich Pechorin (the third narrator). Later, scorned by Pechorin, he angrily throws away his friend's diary, which he had been saving, and the journal falls into the hands of the first narrator.

Grigoriy Aleksandrovich Pechorin (grih-GOH-rihy ah-lehk-SAHN-dro-vihch peh-CHOH-rihn), the third narrator, the "Hero of Our Time." A companion of Maksim Maksimich at a frontier post in the Caucasus, he later scorns his old friend, who throws away his journal. The diary is rescued by the first narrator, who publishes excerpts from it, thus making Pechorin the third narrator in the novel.

Bela (BEH-luh), a beautiful princess,

Azamat (ah-zah-MAHT), Bela's younger brother, and

Kazbich (kahz-BIHCH), a bandit, three characters in Maksim Maksimich's tale of his friendship with Grigoriy Aleksandrovich Pechorin.

Yanko (YAHN-ko), a smuggler. He is a character in the first tale from the journal of Grigoriy Aleksandrovich Pechorin.

Princess Mary, the daughter of Princess Ligovskoy,

Grushnitski (groosh-NIHTS-kihy), Princess Mary's suitor, and

Vera (VEE-ruh), a former sweetheart of Grigoriy Aleksandrovich Pechorin, three characters from the second tale of Pechorin's journal.

Lieutenant Vulich (VOO-lihch), a Cossack officer in the third tale from the journal of Grigoriy Aleksandrovich Pechorin.

HERSELF SURPRISED

Author: Joyce Cary (1888-1957)
First published: 1941
Genre: Novel
Locale: England
Time: First quarter of the twentieth century
Plot: Social

Sara Monday, an open-hearted, self-indulgent cook whose thoughtless behavior has a way of getting her in trouble. Finally landing in jail, she looks at herself, examines her weaknesses, and resolves, with the help of her newly found self-knowledge, to regain her "character" and keep it when her sentence is over.

Matthew (Matt) Monday, Sara Monday's husband, an ineffectual man dominated by his family. His marriage to Sara emancipates him until his jealousy of Gulley Jimson destroys the self-confidence he has achieved.

Gulley Jimson, an artist who persuades the widowed Sara Monday to live with him after she learns that he has a legal wife and cannot marry her. He mistreats Sara, who leaves him, but he never loses his hold over her, and eventually he is the cause of her arrest and imprisonment for the indiscretions she commits to support him.

Mr. Hickson, an art collector and a friend of Sara and Matt Monday.

Mr. Wilcher, the employer and, later, the lover of Sara Monday. His plans to marry Sara are interrupted by her arrest and imprisonment.

Nina, the supposed wife of Gulley Jimson.

Blanche Wilcher, Mr. Wilcher's niece by marriage.

Clarissa Hipper, Blanche Wilcher's sister.

HERZOG

Author: Saul Bellow (1915-   )
First published: 1964
Genre: Novel

Locale: New York City, Chicago, Ludeyville, and the Berkshires
Time: Early 1960's
Plot: Psychological realism

Moses Elkanah Herzog, an unemployed American professor and intellectual whose major interest is the history of ideas. He is forty-seven years old, with a lined face and graying hair. Descended from Russian Jewish immigrants who were notably unsuccessful in the United States, he has lost his direction in life and spends his time writing letters—which he does not intend to mail—to friends, acquaintances, celebrities, and leaders, past and present. These letters combine his thoughts on a wide variety of subjects including science, philosophy, psychology, world affairs, and human relationships. An idealist, he feels an intense responsibility for civilization and progress, to the degree that he pays little heed to his surroundings or daily living. He finds himself involved in a custody fight for his daughter June against his former wife Madeleine. Somewhat unstable and afflicted with hypochondria, he is passionate, energetic, impulsive, and highly emotional.

Madeleine (Mady) Pontritter Herzog, Herzog's domineering second wife, from whom he is divorced. Her blue eyes, long straight nose, and slender neck give her a classical appearance. Her dark hair is tied in a bun behind, with bangs in front. She exudes self-assurance and exhibits a sense of style. Her adroit handling of Herzog causes him to accept her decisions as if they were mutual.

Daisy Herzog, Herzog's first wife and the mother of his son Marco. She is a conventional Jewish woman with green eyes, golden hair, and clear skin. She is at times shy and stubborn. Herzog reflects that he treated her badly.

Ramona Donsell, a divorced businesswoman, owner of a flower shop, and formerly Herzog's student, who became his mistress. An attractive woman in her late thirties who received her early education in Switzerland, she is an excellent cook and is basically maternal. Although short and full-figured, she has an attractive throat and holds her head high. Brown-eyed with black hair and slightly bowed legs, she is both passionate and energetic.

Valentine (Val) Gersbach, a friend of the Herzogs who became Madeleine's lover and persuaded her to leave Moses. He is a large, middle-aged man with brown eyes, flaming red hair, a thick face, heavy jaws, and one wooden leg. A former radio announcer and disk jockey, he possesses strong masculine tenderness.

Phoebe Gersbach, Valentine's wife. She is brown-eyed, middle-aged, and attractive. Her personality reflects her domesticity, and her dress and manner suggest that she might have been head nurse.

Sandor Himmelstein, a Chicago attorney who represents Herzog in his custody case. A short man, stooped because of a war wound in his chest, he has a proud, sharp, handsome face; a prominent nose; thin gray hair; and sallow skin. A tough negotiator with a confrontational manner, he gives his client blunt advice.

Willie (Will) Herzog, Herzog's successful, conventional elder brother. He provides bail when Herzog is arrested on a weapons charge and gives sympathetic but unaccepted advice that Herzog spend a few weeks in a mental hospital for rest.

Sono Oguki, Herzog's tenderhearted and compliant Japanese mistress after his breakup with his first wife. She has black eyes and a small mouth. She brings him the comforts of excellent cooking, fine music, and luxurious baths. Never having learned English, she converses with him in French.

Lucas (Luke) Asphalter, an old Chicago friend of Herzog. He is a zoologist at the University of Chicago who never completed his doctorate. Nearly bald, he has heavy arched eyebrows and wears crepe-soled shoes. His attempt to revive his pet monkey, Rocco, with mouth-to-mouth resuscitation alarmed Herzog, because the monkey had tuberculosis.

— *Stanley Archer*

HIGH COTTON

Author: Darryl Pinckney (1953-   )
First published: 1992
Genre: Novel

Locale: Indianapolis, Indiana; New York City; the American South; London, England; and Paris, France
Time: The early 1960's through the end of the 1980's
Plot: Bildungsroman

The narrator, who is based on the author. An astute observer of others, the narrator is determined to escape any pigeonhole, racial or other, into which others might be tempted to place him.

Grandfather Eustace, a graduate of Brown and Harvard who, after several business failures, becomes a minister of the Congregational church. He is the member of the narrator's family with whom the narrator has the most complex and intense relationship.

Aunt Clara, who lives in Opelika, Alabama. She is actually the narrator's mother's aunt. She is light-skinned, or "high yellow," and obsessed with blood mixture.

Uncle Castor, a jazz musician, who played with Noble Sissle. He has fallen on such hard times that he must depend on the hospitality of the narrator's family.

Jesse, a security guard at Columbia University. He guides the narrator to parts of Harlem that are outside the normal itinerary of Columbia students.

Jeanette, an alcoholic singer the narrator comes to know in Harlem.

Djuna Barnes, an actual historical figure who wrote *Nightwood* (1936), one of the acknowledged masterpieces of American literary modernism. By the time the narrator works for her as a handyman, that accomplishment is far in the past.

Bargetta, who, like the narrator, is a member of the Also Chosen. He is the narrator's friend at college and his guide to Paris.

— *W. P. Kenney*

A HIGH WIND IN JAMAICA

Author: Richard Hughes (1900-1976)
First published: 1929
Genre: Novel

Locale: Jamaica, the high seas, and England
Time: Early nineteenth century
Plot: Psychological realism

Mr. Bas-Thornton, a plantation owner in Jamaica who sends his children to school in England. On the way, the children, with two of their friends, are taken aboard a pirate ship. Though the children are returned within a few months, their father and mother never realize what the experience has done to them psychologically.

Mrs. Bas-Thornton, his wife.

John, oldest of the Bas-Thornton children. He is killed in a fall from a warehouse when his pirate captors, who have taken the children accidentally and treated them well, are selling their booty at a Cuban port.

Emily, John's sister, an excitable ten-year-old child. She and the pirate captain achieve a strange psychological relationship, though a stormy one. While emotionally upset, Emily slashes one of the pirates' prisoners, a Dutch sea captain, to death with a knife. Months later, she allows the pirate captain to go to his death by hanging for her own crime, without apparently suffering any qualms of conscience.

Edward,
Rachael, and
Laura, other children of the Bas-Thorntons.

Margaret Fernandez, Emily's friend and fellow captive. Margaret voluntarily goes to the captain's cabin to live, being an older girl. She knows that Emily actually killed the prisoner but does nothing to change what happens to the innocent man. She appears to suffer from shock and loss of memory when she finally reaches England.

Harry Fernandez, Margaret's young brother.

Captain Jonsen, the pirate captain. He is not a bad man, so far as the children are concerned. He sees that they are left alone by his men and treated well. He did not intend to keep the children and gives them up voluntarily to a passing ship. Later, he is condemned to hang for the murder Emily committed.

Captain James Marpole, from whose raided ship pirates remove the children. Thinking the children killed, he sails away, leaving them aboard the pirate ship.

A HIGH WIND RISING

Author: Elsie Singmaster (Mrs. E. S. Lewars, 1879-1958)
First published: 1942
Genre: Novel

Locale: Pennsylvania
Time: 1728-1755
Plot: Historical

Johann Sebastian Schantz (YOH-hahn zeh-BAS-tih-ahn shants), called **Bastian** or **Owkwari-owira** (Young Bear), a white boy freed from the Mohawk Indians by Conrad Weiser.

Ottilia Zimmer (oh-TEE-lee-ah TSIHM-mehr), an orphan who is first seen by Bastian among the immigrants in Philadelphia. He locates her later in Lancaster and marries her. She is attacked by Indians and left for dead but recovers and returns to safety.

Margaretta and
Gertraud (GEHR-trowd), their twin daughters, who are later stolen by Indians.

Conrad Weiser (VI-zehr), an Indian agent and interpreter who helps keep the Six Nations loyal to the British.

Anna Eve Weiser (AHN-nah AY-veh), Conrad's wife, who brings up Bastian until he can be taken to Anna Sabilla Schantz.

Anna Maria, the Weisers' daughter, in love with Bastian.

Anna Sabilla Schantz (sah-BIHL-lah), a pioneer matriarch and the grandmother of Bastian.

Margaretta, her daughter, who runs away with an English trader.

Nicholas, Anna Sabilla's paralyzed brother.

Skelet (skeh-LEHT), a sickly, humpbacked Delaware Indian, befriended by Anna, who teaches woodlore to Bastian. Chiefly moved by greed, he repays Anna by rescuing her and the twins during an Indian massacre, and he returns with them to the settlement.

The Reverend Henry Melchior Muhlenburg (MEHL-khyohr MEWL-ehn-burg), who eventually marries Anna Weiser.

Sibby Heil (hil), who is in love with Bastian.

Israel Fitch, a trader who buys Anna Sabilla's carved puppets.

General Edward Braddock, who tries to drive the French out of Ohio.

Shekellimy, a Delaware chief friendly to Weiser.

Sassoonan, another Delaware chief.

Tanacharison and
Scarouady, Indian war leaders when the winds of violence rise in the West.

THE HILL OF DREAMS

Author: Arthur Machen (1863-1947)
First published: 1907
Genre: Novel
Locale: England
Time: Late nineteenth century
Plot: Impressionism

The Reverend Mr. Taylor, an Anglican rector of a rural parish. He becomes unpopular in his parish as his fortunes decline. Because of his misfortunes, he is unable to send his son to Oxford. He becomes a moody man.

Lucian Taylor, the rector's son, a studious, reflective lad who is introverted. When he cannot go to Oxford because his father lacks the necessary money, he wanders about the countryside or studies in his father's library the things he likes: ancient history, the medieval church, and works on magic. Because of his introversion and because he refuses to take a job, he becomes something of an outcast. When he tries to become a writer, his attempts are regarded as foolish, especially when he cannot find a publisher. He makes up an imaginary world from his study of Britain in Roman times, and there he lives. He escapes from his imaginary world when he receives a small legacy, only to become an opium addict. His addiction causes his death.

Mrs. Taylor, the rector's wife. She dies while her son is still in his youth.

Annie Morgan, a farmer's daughter who loves Lucian. She shows him how to escape into a world of imagination. She succeeds so well in showing him that he thinks only of himself and his dream world, even when she is about to go away.

HILLINGDON HALL: Or, The Cockney Squire

Author: Robert Smith Surtees (1803-1864)
First published: 1845
Genre: Novel
Locale: England
Time: The nineteenth century
Plot: Satire

John Jorrocks, "the Cockney Squire," a wealthy London grocer turned sportsman who buys Hillingdon Hall. He wholeheartedly takes part in the community life. He wins election to Parliament against a marquis and leaves Pigg in charge of Hillingdon Hall when he returns to London for sessions of Parliament.

Julia Jorrocks, his wife, who, as patroness of the local school, forces the girls to wear flashy, tasteless uniforms.

Mr. Westbury, the former owner of Hillingdon Hall.

Joshua Sneakington, called **Sneak**, the manager of Jorrocks' estate until jailed for cheating his master.

James Pigg, the new manager.

The Duke of Donkeyton, who wants Jorrocks' political help. He invites the family to dinner and appoints Jorrocks a magistrate.

The Marquis of Bray, the duke's effeminate son, who finds Emma attractive. He cooperates with Jorrocks in an agricultural society and runs for Parliament.

Bill Bowker, who runs against Bray for Parliament until bought off by the duke. The farmers then put up Jorrocks to replace him, and Jorrocks wins the election by two votes.

Emma Flather, a country girl in search of a husband.

Mrs. Flather, her mother.

James Blake, Emma's favorite until she can do better.

Mrs. Trotter, the neighborhood gossip.

HIPPOLYTUS
(Hippolytos)

Author: Euripides (c. 485-406 B.C.E.)
First performed: 428 B.C.E.
Genre: Drama
Locale: Troezen in Argolis
Time: Antiquity
Plot: Tragedy

Hippolytus (hih-POL-ih-tuhs), the son of Theseus by Hippolyta, queen of the Amazons. Because he pays exclusive worship to the virgin goddess Artemis, Aphrodite, the goddess of sexual love, determines to punish him by making Phaedra, the wife of Theseus, fall in love with her stepson. Phaedra is dying of her guilty passion; when her nurse reveals her state to Hippolytus, after swearing him to secrecy, he is horrified. Phaedra kills herself out of shame, but because Hippolytus has shown no pity for her plight she leaves a tablet saying that she has killed herself because Hippolytus had raped her. Theseus, calling down on his son one of the infallible curses granted him by Poseidon, asks that Hippolytus be killed that day; in addition, he pronounces a sentence of exile against him. In the subsequent interview with his father, Hippolytus reveals the same inability to show affection, understanding, and tact that he had exhibited earlier in the interview with the nurse. He cannot reveal the truth, and his defense becomes an unpleasant exhibition of ostentatious purity and a long catalog of all his virtues: his piety, his seriousness, his modesty, and his chastity. His aloofness and self-satisfaction can be related to his illegitimacy, which is emphasized repeatedly; abandoned by his father and ashamed of his mother, he has cultivated his aloofness, revolted against the passion of love, and cut himself off from life itself. Hippolytus is mortally wounded as he prepares to leave the country. A tidal wave delivers a miraculous bull to frighten the horses that draw his chariot, and he is dragged behind the panic-stricken animals. When he is brought before his father, Artemis reveals his innocence. Hippolytus releases Theseus from blood-guilt, and the two are reconciled.

Phaedra (FEE-druh), Theseus' wife and the means of Aphrodite's vengeance on her stepson Hippolytus. She is introduced in the last stages of voluntary starvation, weak and delirious. The nurse is able to wring a confession of her passion for Hippolytus from her, but she fails to forbid absolutely any action on the part of the nurse. After Hippolytus refuses the nurse's plea for help, Phaedra feels that she must kill herself to preserve the honor of her children. It is Hippolytus' shocked brutality that leads her to a desire for personal vengeance. She is not entirely guiltless and hopes that Hippolytus will learn true modesty.

Theseus (THEE-see-uhs), the king of Athens. His hasty temperament causes passion and jealousy to blind him to anything but Phaedra's accusation; he fails to understand, or to make any real effort to understand, his son. In fact, his attack on Hippolytus' virtues is brutal and unfair. His undue haste is his chief weakness.

Aphrodite (a-froh-DI-tee), the goddess of beauty and patroness of love. She speaks the prologue and reveals her plan to punish Hippolytus. Her presence is felt throughout the drama as a personification of one of the forces in conflict that give the play universal significance.

Artemis (AHR-teh-mihs), the virgin goddess and goddess of the chase. She is worshiped by Hippolytus, reveals his innocence to Theseus at the close of the play, and vows revenge on Aphrodite. She is not as clear-cut a representation of one quality as Aphrodite, but she is presented as a form of beauty. Hippolytus' prayers to her reveal his ability to put into words those feelings he cannot express for Theseus or Phaedra.

The nurse, Phaedra's devoted servant. Although cynical by nature, she is at first shocked by Phaedra's confession of passion for Hippolytus. Later, she deliberately tries to persuade her mistress to give way to her passion and abandon her plan of suicide. She reveals Phaedra's passion to Hippolytus but does so in the hope of preventing Phaedra's death.

The Chorus, palace women who announce the arrival of various characters.

A servant of Hippolytus, who, in his attempt to rebuke his master for failing to acknowledge properly the powers of Aphrodite, reveals Hippolytus' insolence to her.

HIROSHIMA

Author: John Hersey (1914-1993)
First published: 1946
Genre: Novel

Locale: Hiroshima, Japan
Time: 1945-1985
Plot: New journalism

Kiyoshi Tanimoto, a Methodist minister whose energy and perseverance help him save lives after the atomic bomb falls on Hiroshima. Initially feeling the pressure of fellow citizens' suspicions because of his American education, Tanimoto works selflessly to help others. His charitable spirit and caring for others are exemplified in his comforting of one of his earlier accusers, Mr. Tanaka, who is dying of wounds suffered in the bombing. Tanaka, an influential, powerful man, is reduced to suffering and seeks redemption from someone earlier perceived as an enemy. Tanimoto's good intentions, however, do not keep him from being perceived as a seeker of personal glory. His willingness to remain in contact with Americans is, like his Christianity, an indication to many of his fellow citizens that he is not truly Japanese.

Father Wilhelm Kleinsorge, a German priest who identifies with the Japanese so strongly that he takes Japanese citizenship and changes his name to Makoto Takakura in the years after the bombing. The days immediately after the bombing prove Father Kleinsorge's dedication to helping people. Those days also allow him to demonstrate strengths of which he had previously been unaware. For example, his practicality overcomes what had been his typical squeamishness when he discusses eating a fish right after helping give water to soldiers whose faces had been horribly burned. His own ability to speak calmly to those same soldiers and comfort them surprises him.

Dr. Terufumi Sasaki, a doctor who works seemingly beyond human endurance in the days after the bombing. A man motivated by challenge and personal need, Dr. Sasaki risks censure by practicing outside regular hospital hours in his small town and pursues marriage to a young woman whose father made clear his opposition to the wedding. Dr. Sasaki does not pursue research into medical effects of the atomic bomb and distances himself from his memories of its aftermath. He attains an understanding of the importance of relationships in his life after he nearly dies of lung cancer. After the near-death experience, his focus is on helping others for the personal satisfaction such help brings, a change from his earlier concern with financial security.

Miss Toshinki Sasaki, a personnel clerk whose left leg was badly broken in the bombing. Her dedication to her family is evident in her arising at 4 A.M. to prepare the day's meals before she left for work the morning the bomb was dropped. In the months following her injury, she waits for healing to occur. Her own strengths, however, emerge in her work with orphans and the elderly in her middle age, when she becomes a Catholic nun, Sister Dominique.

Mrs. Hatsuyo Nakamura, a widow with three small children who keeps her family together after the bombing. Never a rebellious spirit, she is the soul of perseverance, continuing to work while suffering the exhaustion that is part of radiation sickness. Embarrassed as a young woman by baldness that resulted from the radiation, she—at retirement age—takes pleasure in a folk-dance group as well as in her children's successes.

Dr. Masakazu Fujii, a doctor whose home and private

practice building are destroyed by the atomic bomb. Dr. Fujii is hedonistic and proud of his possessions, preferring Scotch to saki and eventually building an American-style home. He took advantage of opportunities afforded by the occupation army and advertised a specialty in treating venereal diseases. His final years are spent in a vegetative state, and his family continues in his individualistic tradition by quarreling over the estate he leaves.

— *Janet Taylor Palmer*

HIS MASTER'S VOICE
(Głos pana)

Author: Stanisław Lem (1921-)
First published: 1968
Genre: Novel
Locale: The desert Southwest
Time: The 1960's
Plot: Science fiction

Peter E. Hogarth, a professor of mathematics. A middle-aged man who has died of an undisclosed illness by the time his memoirs are published, Hogarth is a moralist whose actions contradict his opinion of himself as an evil man. An independent thinker and scientific iconoclast, he proves that a neutrino message sent to Earth by unknown aliens is a circular description of an (unknown) object. Confronted with the military application of this knowledge, he despairs, but he is relieved on learning that such an abuse is not possible. Hogarth comes to think that the message was a test that he (like humankind) failed bitterly.

Dr. Saul Rappaport, a physicist in the vanguard of his science. A skinny Polish Jew with a birdlike head and a bad stomach, Rappaport came to America after barely surviving the Holocaust. He believes that the American government keeps scientists like French farmers keep pigs: to hunt for truffles and feed acorns while the owners collect the prizes. Rappaport defies the idea that future humans should become ultraefficient machines. He disappears after Project His Master's Voice (HMV) ends.

Yvor Baloyne, a linguist and philologist who is science director of the HMV project. Fat, beardless, and essentially timid, he overcomes his frailties with humor and irony. He tries to keep the project funded and independent. After a military intervention, his threatened resignation gives the scientists a last respite. He ends up as an influential professor and dean in America.

Donald Prothero, a physicist. A pipe-smoking second-generation Anglo-American, Prothero is, to Hogarth, the "personification of averageness" yet possesses a "mind of the first order." He discovers a potential military application of the message from the stars and envisions a terrible future war. Relieved at the eventual failure of his experiment, he later dies of cancer.

Dr. Eugene Albert Nye, a government lawyer. Well-groomed and diplomatic, yet not without vengefulness, Nye is instructed to keep an eye on the scientists. Immune to their personal insults, he is removed from the project at Baloyne's insistence, only to be replaced by another man.

Dr. Sam Laserowitz, a confidence artist who is the first to suspect that the series of neutrino emissions may be a message from aliens. After defying attempts at bribery and intimidation, he ends up in a mental hospital, where he commits suicide.

Swanson, a rogue physicist who makes available to Laserowitz and Rappaport the tapes with the interstellar message. Paid off by the CIA, he keeps silent and prospers.

Dr. Michael Grotius, a biophysicist who introduces Hogarth to the project and creates a strange substance by using instructions derived from the partially decoded message.

Dr. Romney, a biologist who first discovers the life-promoting qualities of the message.

Dr. Tihamer Dill, Jr., a shiftless physicist and ultrarealist who makes his peace with authority, ridicules the moral concerns of others, and goes to live in Canada. The hostility of Dill's father toward Hogarth motivated the latter to demonstrate excellence.

Dr. Lerner, a military cosmogonist who postulates that the "message" is nothing but an accidental leftover from cyclical contractions of the universe every sixty billion years.

Dr. Sylvester, an Army astrobiologist, small of stature and with a pasty complexion. He believes that His Master's Voice is an attempt by a dying civilization to influence the next universe.

— *Joss Lutz Marsh*

HIS OWN WHERE

Author: June Jordan (1936-)
First published: 1971
Genre: Novella
Locale: New York City and the African American community of Bedford-Stuyvesant
Time: The mid-1960's
Plot: Psychological realism

Buddy Rivers, the protagonist, a sixteen-year-old living alone while his father remains in serious condition following a traffic accident. The narrative action, which takes place over several months, is presented almost entirely from his perspective and is located primarily within the flow of his consciousness. He has been living with his father since his mother returned to her native Barbados. During the course of the narrative, he becomes friendly with Angela, a young woman who is the daughter of the nurse caring for his father in a hospital. Buddy is immediately attracted to her, sensing that she can appreciate the inner qualities of reflective sensitivity and aesthetic discrimination that he guards behind a protective shield of street wit and brash vitality. He is keenly observant and verbally exuberant, and he has a reputation as a leader at Boys High School. He is also thoughtful, almost philosophical, about the social ills he sees everywhere. His relatively harsh life has compelled him to grow up quickly, but he is neither cynical nor vicious, and he has been inspired by his father's example to want to plan, build, and improve his immediate environment. His relationship with Angela is driven by love and hope, and there seems to be some possibility that they will not replicate the anger and hostility that has torn both of their families apart.

Angela Figueroa, the oldest of five children born to a woman working as a nurse and a man working as a cab driver. She is about Buddy's age and is attracted to the sense of quiet confidence she detects beneath his brashness and verbal virtuosity when he visits his father in the hospital. She is loyal to her parents until their frustrations result in an attempt to control all of her activities. Her rebellion is a matter of necessity, a desperate attempt to preserve a measure of herself as an independent person. She has a quietly ironic way of looking at the world and a poetic vision of beauty she struggles to express. She believes that these latent qualities may begin to emerge in Buddy's company.

Mrs. Figueroa, Angela's mother. She is proud of her work as a healer. She is worn down by the demands of her children and her husband, and she expresses her dissatisfaction by attempting to discipline Angela, overlooking Angela's basic trustworthiness and good sense.

Mr. Figueroa, Angela's father, a cab driver who is often angry at his life. He strives desperately to keep his family together but resorts to alcohol as an escape from his almost constant anger. He beats Angela severely when her "disobedience" overwhelms his self-control.

Mr. Rivers, Buddy's father, an essentially unseen but powerful presence. He is confined to a hospital bed with very serious injuries suffered in a traffic accident. Buddy has been inspired by his ingenious remodeling of their home and by his creative craftsmanship and appreciation of beauty. Buddy carries an image of him as a lonely, handsome man, powerful and short, and he yearns to see him again "alive in action."

Mrs. Rivers, Buddy's mother, a prim and sarcastic woman beaten down by the limits of her life. Failing in a desperate attempt to shape her life, she leaves before the narration begins but remains in Buddy's memory.

— *Leon Lewis*

HISTORY
(La storia)

Author: Elsa Morante (1918-1985)
First published: 1974
Genre: Novel
Locale: Rome and its environs
Time: 1941-1947
Plot: Historical realism

Ida Ramundo (EE-dah rah-MEWN-doh), a widow and schoolteacher, the mother of two children. After the death of her mother, she discovers that she is half Jewish. She is frail and timid, and her life is a daily battle against a threatening and aggressive world. Her general sense of estrangement from society is exacerbated by her suffering from occasional epilepsy-like seizures. Impressionable and imaginative, she is also quite prone to troubling and powerful dreams that continue to haunt her during her waking hours. She worries about her teenage son, but her greatest concern is the care of her infant boy, the product of her rape by a German soldier. She becomes tenacious and unrelenting in her support of his well-being. Her life during the war becomes a constant struggle against the very visible enemies of deportation, hunger, and aggression.

Nino Mancuso (NEE-noh), Ida's teenage son. From the beginning, he shows a reckless disposition and a rebelliousness against any rule or form of constraint. Self-absorbed and egotistical, he has an endearing and carefree quality that he uses to manipulate others. Irresistibly attracted to glamour and adventure, he throws himself wholeheartedly and unquestioningly into various activities, only to become bored or to find something else more enticing. He involves himself in Fascism, antifascism, and later the black market. The only true interest he takes in another human being is that which he shows toward Giuseppe, his young half brother. He is killed while fleeing the police in a van carrying stolen weapons.

Giuseppe Ramundo (jee-ew-SEHP-peh), usually called **Useppe**, the younger son of Ida. Born from the rape of his mother by a German soldier, he comes into the world with a sunny and peaceful disposition. He is exceptionally sensitive, perceptive, and gentle. As he grows older, he displays a love for animals and shows an uncanny ability to communicate with them. His friendliness, innocence, and openness make him instantly popular wherever he goes. He becomes increasingly prone to epileptic seizures, which leave him not only weak and exhausted but also at times confused and taciturn. The effects of the war take their toll on the boy's health and on his psyche.

Davide Segre (dah-VEE-day SEH-gray), alias **Carlo Vivaldi**, an escaped prisoner. He is haunted both by the possibility of being recaptured and by his memories of his past imprisonment and the deportation of family and friends. He discovers that his parents and sister, whom he rejected, were killed in a concentration camp. His restlessness and the fears from which he cannot rid himself prompt him to join forces with Nino in his partisan band. In Nino, he finds a friend and companion. After the war, he dies of a drug overdose.

Bella, a dog. She plays an important part in the story as Giuseppe's good and trusted friend. She is companion, protectress, and confidant to the boy. At times, she appears to him to be his only friend and the only one who knows all of his secrets.

— *Susan Briziarelli*

THE HISTORY AND REMARKABLE LIFE OF THE TRULY HONORABLE COL JACQUE, COMMONLY CALL'D COL JACK

Author: Daniel Defoe (1660-1731)
First published: 1722
Genre: Novel
Locale: England, France, and Virginia
Time: Late seventeenth century
Plot: Picaresque

Colonel Jacque, called **Colonel Jack**, an adventurer who commits many misdeeds. An illegitimate child, he is given to a nurse who dies when Jack is but ten years old. Having to fend for himself, Jack the waif becomes a successful though sometimes conscience-stricken pickpocket. He is tossed by fate into the American Colonies and becomes an indentured servant on a plantation, where he becomes a successful and kindly overseer of slaves. When freed from his period of indenture, he becomes a landowner in Virginia. Leaving his plantation in the hands of his faithful overseer, he returns to England and marries. Unfortunate in love, he attacks his wife's lover and flees to France to become a professional soldier, fighting with the French against his countrymen. After another sojourn in Virginia and many adventures, he finally repents of his life of crime and violence, seeks a pardon from the English crown, and settles down in England, persuaded that only the goodness of God has saved him. He hopes that his life story will make other persons repent of their sins and become good Christians.

Captain Jack, Colonel Jack's thoroughly evil foster brother. He is a witty, intelligent rogue who introduces Jack to the picking of pockets. Captain Jack rebels against indentured servitude, flees to England to resume his criminal life, and is at last hanged as a common criminal.

Will, a pickpocket and a partner in crime of Colonel Jack. Will is a vicious man who murders as well as robs. Will's hanging at Newgate Prison saddens Colonel Jack, even though he knows the punishment is deserved.

Jack's First Wife, an unfaithful woman, as well as a gambler and spendthrift. She turns up years later as an indentured servant and a repentant woman. She and Colonel Jack are remarried and live happily for many years in their old age.

Jack's Second Wife, the daughter of an Italian innkeeper, who is unfaithful to her husband.

Jack's Third Wife, a beautiful and virtuous woman who becomes a drunkard and finally commits suicide. By her, Colonel Jack has three children.

Jack's Fourth Wife, an older woman who provides Jack with a pleasant home and is good to his children. She dies after a fall.

THE HISTORY MAN

Author: Malcolm Bradbury (1932-   )
First published: 1975
Genre: Novel
Locale: Watermouth University in Watermouth, England
Time: Fall semester of 1972
Plot: Social satire

Howard Kirk, a radical professor of sociology at Watermouth University. Thirty-four years old, small, and intense, with a Zapata mustache, he has written two fashionable books and appears frequently on television. Timid and unpolitical when an undergraduate at Leeds University, he has evolved into the epitome of the social activist. Howard loves to argue, lives for confrontation, and manipulates people politically, intellectually, and sexually. He enjoys giving large parties and watching chaos develop. Constantly unfaithful to Barbara, his wife of twelve years, he creates a controversy involving one of his students as a means of seducing Annie Callendar.

Barbara Kirk, Howard's wife. Big, with frizzled yellow hair, the thirty-five-year-old Barbara feels unfulfilled by her roles as wife, mother, and promoter of new causes. She considered herself Howard's equal when they were students but now resents living in his shadow. Barbara's only real pleasure comes from her weekend "shopping" trips to London, actually excuses for rendezvous with Leon, an actor.

Henry Beamish, the Kirks' friend from Leeds University and Howard's colleague at Watermouth. A social psychologist who once caused a stir with a book claiming that television socializes children more effectively than do their parents, he finds himself unable to write a book about charisma, not knowing anything about the subject. He has grown fat and lazy, and he would rather talk about his farm than about intellectual matters. Possessing an instinct for disaster, he is bitten by a dog and sticks one arm through a windowpane at a Kirk party; he injures the other when attacked by student demonstrators.

Flora Beniform, Howard's colleague and longtime lover. A Rubenesque social psychologist specializing in families, she combines sex with research by going to bed with men who have troubled marriages, even taking in Henry when his wife leaves him. Flora forces Howard to discuss his personal life in detail following sex, making him uncertain whether he is having an affair or treatment. She understands Howard better than anyone, holding no illusions about his manipulative charms.

Annie Callendar, a lecturer in English literature, specializing in lyric poetry. Mature and levelheaded at the age of twenty-four, she resists Howard's seductive wiles for weeks before falling victim to his machinations. She is an adviser to Howard's would-be nemesis, George Carmody.

Felicity Phee, one of Howard's students. She seduces Howard at one of his parties. After she is kicked out by her lesbian lover, she becomes the Kirks' live-in baby-sitter. Gradually turning against Howard, she eventually drops him as both lover and teacher.

George Carmody, the only conservative among Howard's students. Clean-shaven and well-dressed, he does not fit in at

Watermouth. When Howard attacks one of his essays, he accuses the sociologist of grading him rather than his work. George takes photographs of Felicity and Howard having sex and shows them to Howard's department head. After Howard accuses him of blackmail, students label George a threat to academic freedom and demand his expulsion.

Myra Beamish, Henry's bored wife. After long threatening to leave Henry, she moves in with the Kirks, only to return to her husband. Seduced by Howard four years earlier, she intends to have him again.

Professor Alan Marvin, the head of Howard's department. Happy to lead a boring and empty life, he is not prepared to be caught in the middle of the Carmody-Kirk turmoil.

Moira Millikin, one of Howard's colleagues, an unorthodox economist. An unwed mother, she brings her infant to classes and parties and becomes pregnant again during the fall term.

Leon, a London actor with whom Barbara Kirk spends occasional weekends when she is ostensibly shopping.

Celia Kirk and

Martin Kirk, Barbara and Howard's children. They emulate their parents by emerging from a school Christmas party with a torn dress and a black eye, respectively.

— *Michael Adams*

THE HISTORY OF HENRY ESMOND, ESQUIRE: A Colonel in the Service of Her Majesty Q. Anne

Author: William Makepeace Thackeray (1811-1863)
First published: 1852
Genre: Novel
Locale: England and the Low Countries
Time: Late seventeenth and early eighteenth centuries
Plot: Historical

Henry Esmond, an orphan believed to be the illegitimate son of the late Thomas Esmond, Lord Castlewood. He is seen first as a grave, observant boy and later as an intelligent, levelheaded young man. The novel, though narrated in the third person, takes the form of his memoirs, beginning when he is twelve years old and continuing until his early manhood and marriage. A lonely boy under the guardianship of his kinsman, Francis Esmond, Viscount Castlewood, Henry spends his adolescence at the Castlewood estate. The untimely death of Viscount Castlewood, fatally wounded in a duel, leads to Henry's discovery that he is the true heir to the Castlewood title. This secret he continues to keep out of affection for his kinsman's widow and her children. For years he believes himself in love with his beautiful cousin, Beatrix Esmond, and for her sake he becomes involved in a Jacobite plot to secure the English throne for James, the young Stuart Pretender, at the time of Queen Anne's death. When events prove that he has been deceived in both Beatrix and the Stuart exile, he realizes that the real object of his affection is Rachel Esmond, the youthful mother of Beatrix. With her he emigrates to America, leaving her son Frank in possession of the title and the Castlewood estate.

Francis Esmond, Viscount Castlewood, a hard-living, pleasure-seeking nobleman, the amiable, though hardly devoted, guardian of young Henry Esmond. Having aided in concealing the secret of Henry's birth, he repents the injustice done the boy and on his deathbed reveals that Henry is the true heir to the Castlewood title.

Rachel Esmond, the viscount's much younger wife, a quiet, attractive woman whose loyalty to her husband never fails, even when he begins to neglect her for drinking and gambling with his reckless, pleasure-loving London friends. Her chief fault, a tendency to possessiveness, is displayed first toward the viscount and later toward Henry Esmond, whom she marries after the plot to put James Stuart on the throne of England has failed.

Beatrix Esmond, the beautiful and lively daughter of Francis and Rachel Castlewood. As fickle and unstable as she is fascinating, lovely but ambitious and scheming, she accepts Henry Esmond's attentions when no more suitable admirer is at hand. Her affair with James, the Stuart Pretender, finally reveals to Henry her true nature.

Frank Esmond, the sturdy, unimaginative younger brother of Beatrix Esmond. He is, by virtue of Henry Esmond's sacrifice, the eventual successor to the lands and title wrongly held by his father, the former viscount.

Father Holt, Henry Esmond's tutor in boyhood. The priest secretly acts as a Jacobite spy, helping to prepare the way for the return of the Stuart Pretender.

Lord Mohun, a London rake with designs on Rachel Esmond. He kills her husband in a duel.

The duke of Hamilton, an impetuous young nobleman engaged to marry Beatrix Esmond. He is killed in a duel in which he fatally wounds Lord Mohun.

The duke of Marlborough, the famous military commander in chief. During the duke's campaigns, Henry Esmond sees service as a soldier in France and Spain.

General John Webb, the officer to whom Henry Esmond serves as aide-de-camp. Webb becomes involved in a bitter controversy with the duke of Marlborough.

Richard Steele, an early friend of Henry Esmond. Steele is presented as a henpecked husband and lovable scapegrace; his status as a literary man is only lightly accented.

Joseph Addison, a leading Whig of the period as well as a prominent man of letters.

THE HISTORY OF MR. POLLY

Author: H. G. Wells (1866-1946)
First published: 1910
Genre: Novel
Locale: England
Time: Early twentieth century
Plot: Love

The Historian, an anonymous first-person narrator, brisk, pleasantly jocular, and rather Dickensian. Although he has no part in the action, he provides humorous commentary on it.

Mr. Alfred Polly, a sensitive, dyspeptic petty tradesman, given to romantic dreams, mispronunciation, and pungent phrases. After starting as a draper's assistant, he was left some money by his father, and acquired a shop and a wife. Fifteen years later, Mr. Polly is bald and chubby, and imagination and good will have been stifled by his neighbors and his wife. He bungles a suicide attempt but unexpectedly becomes a hero when he saves an old woman from the fire he has started. A short time later, he runs away. He wanders until he finds a wayside inn kept by a plump woman who is threatened by her worthless nephew, called Uncle Jim. Mr. Polly shows his pluck by standing up, rather quakingly, to Jim and defeating him in a series of comic fights. Five years later, he returns home, finds himself unneeded, and goes back to the inn for good.

Mrs. Miriam Polly, his dowdy, unimaginative wife, a poor housekeeper and a worse cook, whom Mr. Polly married on the rebound from an abortive romance. Under the illusion that she would be tidy and affectionate, he soon learns otherwise. After he disappears and his supposed corpse is found, she and her sister start a tea shop with the insurance money. She is horrified when her husband returns to the village and is glad to see him go away again.

The Plump Woman, the proprietress of the Potwell Inn, a warm, easy-going, motherly person. Mr. Polly immediately likes her and takes a job as a handyman at the inn. She gives him permission to leave when Uncle Jim shows up, but the devotion she inspires induces Mr. Polly to defend her.

Uncle Jim, a short, tough, mean ex-convict. A comic villain, he teaches the plump woman's granddaughter to swear. He goes after Mr. Polly with beer bottles, an axe, and a gun, but he complains that Mr. Polly does not fight fair when he finds himself dumped in the river. Eventually he runs off, drowns, and gets mistaken for Mr. Polly.

Polly, the plump woman's granddaughter, a sprightly nine-year-old who at first worships Uncle Jim and then comes to admire Mr. Polly.

Aunt Larkins, the mother of Mrs. Polly. She misrepresents her daughters and cries vulgarly at the wedding.

Annie Larkins, her daughter and Mrs. Polly's sister. One of Mr. Polly's kissing cousins, she enjoys vigorous embraces and laughs loudly at all his jokes. Then, as a middle-aged frump, she becomes Miriam's partner in the tea shop venture.

Minnie Larkins, another sister of Miriam. Though ill-bred and common, she almost won Mr. Polly for a husband.

Christabel, a coy, pretty schoolgirl, Mr. Polly's only romantic interest. For ten days he courts her as she sits on the schoolyard wall, but at last her teen-age schoolmates giggle and she runs off, shattering Mr. Polly's dream.

Parsons, Mr. Polly's best friend when he was a draper's assistant. Chubby, imaginative, a lover of poetry, Parsons gets in a battle with the store manager over a window display, is fired, and leaves.

Platt, the third member of the Parsons, Polly, Platt trio, also a clerk.

Mr. Howard Johnson, the cousin who puts Mr. Polly up for a while, urges him to buy a shop, and becomes sullen at the loss of rent when Mr. Polly marries.

Mrs. Johnson, his optimistic, vulgar wife.

Mr. Garvace, the store manager who fired Parsons.

Rusper, a shopkeeper, ignorant but with pretense to knowledge, whose quarrel with middle-aged Mr. Polly ends in a law court.

Rumbold, another obnoxious, mulish neighbor.

Mrs. Rumbold, his mother, the old woman Mr. Polly saves in a fire.

Hicks, a grumpy, gossipy, low-bred neighbor.

Mr. Voules, a fat, stupid man who takes charge of Mr. Polly's wedding.

Uncle Pentstemon, an old, crotchety, offensive relative.

Mrs. Amy Punt, another odious relative.

THE HISTORY OF PENDENNIS:
His Fortunes and Misfortunes, His Friends, and His Greatest Enemy

Author: William Makepeace Thackeray (1811-1863)
First published: 1848-1850
Genre: Novel
Locale: England
Time: Mid-nineteenth century
Plot: Social satire

Arthur "Pen" Pendennis, a young Englishman of semi-aristocratic background whose essential nature is kind and gentle. Throughout the course of the novel, he moves from a childish infatuation with an actress, to an academically and financially disastrous career at the University of Oxbridge, to a dandified life in London, to the career of a journalist, to a seat in Parliament, and to a happy and successful marriage. During this time, he grows more sophisticated and somewhat snobbish, but he still retains the essential goodness of his original character.

Major Arthur Pendennis, Arthur's uncle, a snobbish retired army officer and a man of fashion. Always aware of his friends' social standing, he spends much of his time culling the most advantageous invitations to dinners and balls. Although he is a snob, he is good-hearted and generous in the sense that he does look out for his nephew and tries to get him placed in the most favorable circumstances at all times.

Helen Pendennis, Arthur's mother, a lovely, sensitive woman who adores her young son and spends many heartbreaking moments worrying about him. She dies at the end of the novel but not before she is assured that Arthur will be successful and happy in his life.

Laura Bell, Arthur's adopted sister, the daughter of Francis Bell, Helen Pendennis' cousin and former suitor. A sweet, intelligent woman, somewhat like her aunt in character, she watches Arthur's career and sympathizes with his mother over Arthur's failures. She is loved by George Warrington, Arthur's closest friend, but because of his early and unfortunate marriage, she cannot become his wife. Eventually, she marries Arthur, the man she has really loved all her life.

George Warrington, Arthur's roommate in London. He is reading for the law when Arthur first rooms with him. Later, he takes up a career in journalism and helps Arthur edit the *Pall Mall Gazette*. He is in love with Laura, but because of an unfortunate marriage he cannot marry again. He is intelligent, exceedingly kind, and casual, a good companion for Arthur.

Sir Francis Clavering, a weak and dandified spendthrift baronet, much taken with cards and gambling. After Major Pendennis' discovery that Lady Clavering's first husband is still living, Sir Francis offers Arthur Pendennis his seat in Parliament.

Lady Clavering, a supposed widow who becomes Sir Francis' wife. Although uneducated, she is a good and loving person at heart, and popular in spite of her social gaucheries.

Blanche Amory, Lady Clavering's daughter by her first marriage, a talented, intelligent girl but affected and shallow in character. For a while it seems that she will marry Arthur Pendennis. Later, she is courted by Harry Foker, but he deserts her when he learns that her father is still living. She resigns herself to a charming spinsterhood.

Master Francis Clavering, the son of the Claverings and half brother to Blanche, a spoiled and demanding brat. He remains in the background of the story as an example of the very bad match between Mrs. Amory and Sir Francis.

Captain Edward Strong, a friend of Sir Francis Clavering. He is a cheerful, talented fellow who eventually goes to live at Shepherd's Lane Inn with Colonel Altamont, the shadowy personage who mysteriously figures in the story of the Clavering family.

Colonel Altamont, a supposedly retired army officer who turns out to be Lady Clavering's first husband, whom everyone had believed dead. He turns up to plague his former wife with the realization that her second marriage is bigamous; however, it is proved that he had contracted several previous marriages and therefore has no legal claim on her. He eludes the police and disappears at the end of the novel.

Emily Costigan, also known as **Miss Fotheringay**, an actress with whom young Arthur Pendennis falls desperately in love. An ill-bred, calculating young woman, she finally makes a good marriage with Sir Charles Mirabel and elevates herself into society.

Captain Costigan, her rakish, drunken father. After his daughter marries, he is treated as a poor relation, and he goes to live in Shepherd's Lane Inn. There, his drunken exploits are the topic of local conversation.

Little Bows, a disabled friend of Colonel Costigan and his daughter, who goes to live with the colonel at Shepherd's Lane Inn. He gives music lessons to Fanny Bolton, whom he worships in secret.

Fanny Bolton, the daughter of the proprietor of Shepherd's Lane Inn. For a time, it seems that she will persuade Arthur Pendennis to marry her, but she ends up with one of his acquaintances, Mr. Huxter.

Mr. Bolton and

Mrs. Bolton, Fanny's parents and the owners of Shepherd's Lane Inn.

Mr. Huxter, a crude fellow, a surgeon who marries Fanny Bolton. Arthur refuses to recognize him as a friend.

Lady Rockminster, Laura's kind but somewhat wayward patroness after Helen Pendennis' death. Delighted with the prospect that Arthur will marry Laura, she does everything she can to hasten the match.

Morgan, Major Pendennis' valet, a clever but cruel man. By saving his money, he is able to buy the lodgings where Major Pendennis stays. After a quarrel, he tells Arthur Pendennis about his uncle's scheming to have Blanche Amory inherit her mother's fortune and to force Sir Francis to relinquish his seat in Parliament.

Mrs. Brixham, a widow who is cheated out of her rooming house by shrewd Morgan.

Frosch, the major's new valet, a pleasant young fellow whom Morgan procures for his old master.

Percy Sibwright, a neighbor of Warrington and Arthur at Shepherd's Lane Inn.

Jack Holt, another neighbor, a veteran of Queen Christina's army. He is engaged in organizing a scheme for smuggling money.

Tom Diver, another neighbor. He claims that he knows of a sunken specie ship from which he plans to reclaim the treasure.

Filby, a man of varied careers as a corporal of dragoons, a field preacher, a missionary agent for converting the Irish, and an actor at a Greenwich Fair Booth.

Henry (Harry) Foker, Arthur Pendennis' former schoolmate, a dandified, snobbish young man of London. He almost marries Blanche Amory, but the discovery that her father is still alive breaks up the match.

Anatole, Harry Foker's valet.

George Robert, the earl of Gravesend and Fisherville, Harry Foker's uncle.

Lady Ann Milton, Harry Foker's cousin and intended wife.

Lady Agnes Foker, Harry's mother, who secures for him invitations to parties to which the Claverings are invited.

Mr. Bungay, a publisher who knows little about novels but takes his opinions from professional advisers.

Mr. Bacon, another snobbish publisher, who reads Arthur Pendennis' book.

Lord Steyne, an aristocratic party-giver, constantly courted by Major Pendennis.

Miss Rouncy, the confidential friend of Emily Costigan during the time that they are actresses.

Mrs. Creed, the Costigans' landlady.

Dr. Portman, a clergyman and a friend of the Pendennis family.

Lieutenant Sir Derby Oaks, another suitor of Emily Costigan.

Mr. Garbets, the principal tragedian of the theatrical company.

Mr. Tatham, a lawyer whom Major Pendennis consults on business.

Mr. Dolphin, a great theatrical manager from London who comes to see Emily play and hires her.

Mr. Wenham and

Mr. Wag, Lord Steyne's aristocratic friends, who hobnob with Major Pendennis.

The Reverend F. Wapshot, a teacher at Clavering Grammar School.

Mr. Smirkle, Dr. Portman's cleric and the tutor to young Arthur Pendennis.

Mr. Plummer, the proprietor of the George, a tavern in London frequented by Captain Costigan.

Miss Blandy, the governess to young Francis Clavering.

Mr. Pymsent, Laura's admirer, an acquaintance of Arthur.

Mr. Paley, an industrious law student who is different from Arthur and Warrington because he applies himself to his studies.

Charles Shandon, the friend of George Warrington and Arthur Pendennis, later the publisher of the *Pall Mall Gazette*.

Jack Finucane, the sub-editor of the *Pall Mall Gazette*.

THE HISTORY OF SANDFORD AND MERTON

Author: Thomas Day (1748-1789)
First published: 1783-1789
Genre: Novel
Locale: England
Time: Late eighteenth century
Plot: Didactic

Mr. Barlow, a clergyman charged with the education of Sandford and Merton. He has the boys learn by doing, even insisting that they help in the garden to learn about food. He inspires the boys to learn a great deal. He takes them on excursions to see how the world's work is done, and he tries to inculcate moral virtues as well as knowledge.

Tommy Merton, a headstrong, ill-tempered, and weak lad. He has been pampered by his doting mother and by the family's slaves in Jamaica. Upon arriving in England, he has neither a formal education nor any inclination to study. He is sent to the vicarage to live with Mr. Barlow and be educated. With the example of Harry Sandford and the tutelage of Mr. Barlow, Tommy catches up with his education and becomes a healthy, unselfish, and exemplary youth.

Mr. Merton, Tommy's father, a sensible English gentleman who wants his son to be an educated, virtuous young man.

Harry Sandford, an English farmer's son. He is a sincere lad with a philosophical attitude. He is educated by Mr. Barlow. He makes a good impression on Mr. Merton and causes the latter to send his son to be educated by the same man. At the vicarage, he is a good example for Tommy Merton to follow.

Mrs. Merton, Tommy's doting mother. She is displeased by young Harry's belief that artificiality and the possessions of the rich are unimportant.

Mr. Sandford, a self-sufficient farmer. He refuses to accept Mr. Merton's payment of money for the good example that his son gave Tommy Merton, saying that he fears that the money would only bring trouble to the family.

THE HIVE
(La colmena)

Author: Camilo José Cela (1916-   )
First published: 1951
Genre: Novel
Locale: Madrid, Spain
Time: December, 1943
Plot: Social realism

Martín Marco (mahr-TEEN), a chronically impoverished leftist intellectual and freelance writer of articles for daily newspapers in Madrid, Spain. Martín is first seen being thrown out of Doña Rosa's café for his inability to pay his bill. His nighttime walks through post-civil war Madrid serve as the novel's principal thread, linking the city's dispersed locales and its plethora of lower-middle-class denizens. Martín's republican sympathies oppose him to Francisco Franco's fascist régime, and his obvious disaffection with Spanish life of the 1940's may be a contributing factor to his apparent growing dementia. His aimless café-hopping and frequent association with prostitutes mirror the dispirited inertia and moral lassitude of the era. Although Martín's political leanings tend toward the espousal of a collective responsibility for all Spaniards, he is not above accepting, or even expecting, handouts in the stagnant economy in which all of his fellow citizens must make do. Martín's emergent mental unbalance is most clearly in evidence in the novel's final section. Rambling and disoriented, he visits his mother's grave and contemplates becoming part of the societal establishment he so despises.

Filo (FEE-loh), Martín's kindhearted sister. She and her accountant husband, Roberto González, have five young children. Barely able to make ends meet with the paltry salary Roberto brings home, Filo must also contend with Martín's constant expectation of leftover food as well as the intense mutual dislike the brothers-in-law feel toward one another. On the day before she turns thirty-four, Filo fears that Martín and Roberto will forget her birthday, as they did the previous year, and that she will again feel unimportant and neglected.

Roberto González (gohn-SAH-lehs), Filo's husband, whose salary as an accountant for a perfume shop and a bakery barely keeps his large family clothed and fed. Roberto has always harbored an intense dislike for Martín, whom he considers arrogant and lazy. Martín calls Roberto "that beast" and despises his petty-bourgeois temperament and lifestyle. Roberto must ask his employer for an advance in order to buy Filo a birthday present and his children a new ball. Despite what Martín thinks, Roberto loves his family dearly and does his best to provide for them in hard economic times. Filo defends him as a decent and honorable man.

Doña Rosa, the mean-spirited owner of a café frequented by Martín and many other characters. Doña Rosa, fond of screaming at employees and customers alike, is not above watering down her drinks to save on precious ingredients during Spain's postwar rationing. Doña Rosa's recommendation that her waiters give Martín a sound thrashing for not being able to pay his tab provides a good glimpse into her typical behavior. In addition to having little use for the down-on-their-luck types who, whatever she may think about them, keep her establishment afloat, Doña Rosa is staunchly profascist and greets the news of Adolf Hitler's World War II setbacks with considerable trepidation.

Señorita Elvira (ehl-VEE-rah), an aging prostitute who spends so many listless hours in Doña Rosa's café that she is considered by the clientele to be part of its furniture. Orphaned young, after her father was executed for killing her mother, Elvira took up with a merchant to escape her crushing poverty. Once he started beating her, she left him for a life of prostitution. Elvira's situation is undoubtedly one of the most pathetic and dire of any character in the book. She basically subsists from day to day, dreaming of a quiet death in some hospital room near a radiator.

Doña Ramona Bragado (brah-GAH-doh), a shrewd businesswoman who turns a large cash settlement from a past tryst with a nobleman into a lifelong nest egg. She purchases a dairy with her unethical gains and supplements her steady income by acting as a procuress of impoverished women for financially secure gentlemen.

— *Gregary J. Racz*

HIZAKURIGE
(Tōkaidōchū hizakurige)

Author: Jippensha Ikku (1765-1831)
First published: 1802-1822
Genre: Novel
Locale: Japan's Tokaido highway
Time: Early nineteenth century
Plot: Farce

Yajirobei, or **Yaji** for short. Born into a well-to-do merchant family but now in greatly reduced circumstances as a result of his dissipations, he travels about Japan and becomes involved in a variety of broadly humorous episodes. More quick-witted than virtuous, he is a recognizable type of picaresque traveler. His creation was, however, an innovation and a popular one; previous Japanese travel accounts did not make use of this kind of robust and realistic traveler.

Hana-no-suke, an actor, later renamed **Kitahachi**, or **Kita** for short. Exuberant and shrewd, Kita is Yaji's traveling companion and shares in his adventures.

H.M.S. PINAFORE: Or, The Lass That Loved a Sailor

Author: W. S. Gilbert (1836-1911)
First published: 1878
Genre: Drama
Locale: Portsmouth harbor, England
Time: The second half of the nineteenth century
Plot: Love

Sir Joseph Porter, First Lord of the Admiralty, the pompous ruler of the Queen's Navy. He has reached his exalted station by sticking to his desk and never going to sea. Wherever he goes, he is accompanied by a host of admiring female relatives. A great egalitarian, he believes a British tar (sailor) the equal of every man except himself. He intends to condescend to marry Josephine and makes an official pronouncement that love levels all ranks, but in practice he finds some limitations in this dogma.

Captain Corcoran, the well-bred captain of H.M.S. *Pinafore*. He is hardly ever sick at sea and seldom uses profanity; when his daughter is discovered eloping with a common seaman, he allows a "damme" to slip, greatly shocking Sir Joseph. When he loses his exalted station, he takes his former nurse, Little Buttercup, to be his wife and promises that he will hardly ever be untrue to her.

Mrs. Cripps (**Little Buttercup**), a Portsmouth Bumboat Woman. She confesses that many years ago when she practiced baby-farming, she mixed up Captain Corcoran and Ralph Rackstraw in their cradles, causing a great social upheaval in later years. Her plump and pleasing presence captivates the captain, who proposes to her when he loses his social standing.

Ralph Rackstraw, the smartest lad in all the fleet. He loves the captain's daughter but is painfully conscious of their difference in social station. When he and the captain are discovered to be victims of mistaken identity, he, being the rightful captain, joyfully marries Josephine.

Josephine, the captain's daughter. She would gladly laugh her rank to scorn for love if Ralph were more highly born or she more lowly. Sir Joseph's pronouncement about the leveling power of love convinces her that she should accept Ralph.

Dick Deadeye, a hideously ugly and deformed able seaman. Even the kindhearted Buttercup admits that he is a plain man. Finding that even sweet sentiments cause horror when they come from his lips, Dick becomes embittered, deserts his shipmates, and betrays Ralph and Josephine to the captain. He takes malicious pleasure in the foiling of the young lovers but fades into insignificance in the general rejoicing at the end.

The Boatswain, a British tar who takes pride in being an Englishman. Along with Buttercup and most of his shipmates, he supports the young lovers in their plans to elope.

Cousin Hebe, the leader of Sir Joseph's numerous sisters, cousins, and aunts who follow him adoringly. When Sir Joseph expresses his belief that Josephine's social decline is too great for even love to level her rank with his, Cousin Hebe decides that they should make a triple wedding along with Ralph and Josephine and the now-seaman Corcoran and Buttercup. After the wedding, it will be farewell to the sisters and the cousin and the aunts, for Hebe will brook no rivals.

THE HOBBIT: Or, There and Back Again

Author: J. R. R. Tolkien (1892-1973)
First published: 1937
Genre: Novel

Locale: Middle-earth
Time: A mythical past
Plot: Fantasy

Bilbo Baggins, a hobbit, the protagonist. Fifty years old when the story begins, Bilbo is respectable, unadventurous, and predictable. Forced into an unwanted role as burglar with Thorin's expedition, Bilbo encounters a series of monsters and learns with growing self-reliance to use his luck and his wits, becoming the leader of the expedition. By discovering Smaug's weak spot, Bilbo helps slay the dragon, though no one remembers his contribution. One year after setting out, Bilbo returns from his adventure a changed hobbit: No longer respectably predictable, he is a hero, with a true sense of his small but vital place in a wide world.

Gandalf, a wizard, almost a comic character, whose powers remain largely unrevealed. Gandalf chooses Bilbo to accompany the dwarves and travels with them in the early stages of their journey, rescuing them from the trolls, helping the dwarves escape the goblin tunnels, and introducing them to Elrond and Beorn. Gandalf leaves the company in Bilbo's care before they enter Mirkwood, thus letting the hobbit grow into his role as self-reliant hero. The wizard reappears at the end of the quest, helping in the Battle of the Five Armies, and later accompanies Bilbo back to Hobbiton.

Thorin Oakenshield, a dwarf, rightful heir to his grandfather Thror, last King under the Mountain, whose kingdom Smaug destroyed. Thorin is both proud and brave. He proposed the daring quest, but he is also stubborn and prone to greed: He refuses to share the dragon treasure and becomes estranged from Bilbo. In the Battle of the Five Armies, Thorin makes a valiant last stand with his kinfolk, but the great dwarf falls, badly wounded. Lifted from the fray by Beorn, Thorin dies after praising Bilbo and is buried with honor.

Smaug, a greedy, strong dragon. Long ago, Smaug destroyed the town of Dale and the kingdom under the Lonely Mountain. He has accumulated a mountain of treasure, which he uses for a bed. Smaug seems invincible, but Bilbo discovers a soft spot on his left breast; this information enables Bard to slay Smaug during the dragon's attack on Esgaroth.

Beorn, a skin-changer, sometimes a huge man and sometimes a great bear. Beorn, though suspicious, shelters Thorin and company after their escape from the goblins and Wargs. After confirming their story, Beorn offers the dwarves any help within his power. He appears as a bear in the Battle of the Five Armies and routs the goblins just when defeat seems certain.

Bard, a man of Esgaroth, grim of voice and face, the slayer of Smaug. Bard is descended from Girion, last Lord of Dale. After Smaug's death, Bard helps the Elvenking besiege Thorin but joins with elves and dwarves in the Battle of the Five Armies. Later, Bard rebuilds a merry and prosperous Dale.

The old thrush, a bird whose forebears were friendly to the dwarves and to the men of Dale. The old thrush helps slay Smaug, carrying news of the dragon's weak spot to Bard.

Elrond, the lord of Rivendell, where Thorin and company rest before crossing the Misty Mountains. Elrond is half-elven and is noble, wise, venerable, and kind. He finds the moon-letters on Thorin's map, revealing information crucial to Thorin's quest.

Gollum, a small, dark monster (named **Sméagol** and identified as a ruined hobbit in other books). Gollum is fond of fish and goblin meat, and his willingness to try hobbit gives Bilbo his first real trial. In the goblin tunnels where Gollum lives, Bilbo finds a ring, long possessed by Gollum, that makes its wearer invisible. Gollum engages Bilbo in a riddle contest, which the hobbit, by luck and not quite fairly, wins. Learning of the ring's power from Gollum's mutterings, Bilbo follows the monster to the goblins' back door. Choosing fairness over prudence, he does not kill Gollum, but leaps over him to freedom.

The Elvenking, lord of the wood-elves. He imprisons the dwarves in his dungeon, whence they escape with Bilbo's help. Thorin afterward bears a grudge against the Elvenking. After Smaug's death, the Elvenking, who has a weakness for treasure, marches with an army toward the Lonely Mountain, turning aside to help the people of ruined Esgaroth. With Bard, he besieges Thorin but joins dwarves and men in the Battle of the Five Armies.

Dain son of Nain, Thorin's cousin. Dain leads an army of dwarves from the Iron Hills to aid Thorin against the Elvenking and Bard but joins elves and men in the Battle of the Five Armies. Dain, a generous dwarf, becomes King under the Mountain after Thorin's death.

— Jonathan A. Glenn

HOLY GHOSTS

Author: Romulus Linney (1930-   )
First published: 1977
Genre: Drama

Locale: The rural South
Time: An evening in early summer in the 1970's
Plot: Psychological realism

Nancy Shedman, a young, naïve, backwoods Southern woman. She has been married less than a year to an abusive man, Coleman Shedman. After being assaulted by him, Nancy encounters a snake-handling religious cult run by Obediah Senior. Having nowhere to turn and swept away by the church's fanaticism, she decides to leave her husband, take half of the property, and marry the preacher. Nancy begins to waver after learning that she would become the man's seventh wife. Weakening, she is almost ready to return to Coleman until, in an outburst of rage, he strikes her. During the hysteria of the snake-handling ceremony, Nancy remains aloof. She decides that the lifestyle is not right for her at this time and decides to attend a business school in town.

Coleman Hannibal Shedman, Junior, Nancy's jealous, coarse, and abusive young husband. He is the owner/manager of Shedman's Fish Farm, which he inherited from his father. Accompanied by a divorce attorney, he caustically accuses Nancy of infidelity and theft. Coleman is anti-Christian and is appalled that his wife has been sucked in by religious charlatans. During the church service, he curses and attacks the minister and flaunts his sexual knowledge of Nancy. He pleads with Nancy to come back to him, but during his pledge to change, he loses his temper and strikes her. In an attempt to blaspheme the religion, he defiantly partakes in the snake-handling ceremony, only to become a full-fledged convert.

Rogers Canfield, an elderly lawyer with a heart condition. He is a widower living with his unwed daughter. He emerges from retirement to handle Coleman's divorce suit. He is an unshaven, unkempt diplomat who immediately warms up to Nancy. While at the church service, Canfield becomes enamored of Bonnie, causing him to make a fervent commitment to the cult and to resign from Coleman's case.

Reverend Obediah Buckhorn, Senior (oh-beh-DI-uh), an old, authoritative, sometimes dramatic, sometimes genteel religious cult leader. His Church of Pentecostal Snakeholders has claimed numerous lives and is outlawed by the state. Pushed to the limit by Coleman's verbal assaults, Obediah Senior lashes back with a violent outburst, which is followed by a dramatic show of repentance. Obediah's plan to marry Nancy after her divorce goes awry when the news leaks that he has had six former wives, five of whom died from overwork and a sixth who ran off. He is saddened by his loss of Nancy and takes Coleman's conversion in stride.

Obediah Buckhorn, Junior, the preacher's young, handsome, cheerful, and self-confident son. Although a muscle-bound man, he is childlike and still lives with his father. He has recently procured a job as a manager of a bowling alley, somehow rationalizing that bowling and Jesus go together. Obediah Junior meets Nancy following the attack on her by Coleman and introduces her to his father and their religion.

Virgil Tides, a young boy who reads the Scripture. He becomes enraptured by the church service and begins speaking in tongues. Virgil is the first devotee to handle the dangerous rattlers.

Orin Hart, a brawny, simple-minded oaf. Once aggressive and pugnacious, he was transformed into a loving homosexual after entering the cult. He is involved with his longtime friend, Howard.

Howard Rudd, Orin's partner. He is also tough, but not as massive as Orin. He had tried to cut his throat when his wife left him, but Orin saved him.

Bonnie Bridge, a practical, efficient nymphomaniac with traces of youthful beauty. At the church, her duties include making announcements and introducing newcomers. Her religious history consists of sexually submitting to any Christian man who would have her. After running out of men, she would move on to a new church. Once wed to a plumber, she was deserted. Always jealous of her sister, she enticed her into the cult, where the woman died of a snakebite. Bonnie's latest sexual target is Rogers Canfield.

Lorena Cosburg, a meek, drab, middle-aged woman. She never disobeyed or displeased her husband until she started attending this church. She is overcome on her first visit and ecstatically partakes in the handling of the snakes.

Mrs. Wall, the church pianist who befriends Nancy. She is a large, impressive woman who gives a stirring religious testimony.

Billy Boggs, the young church guitarist. Angry, discontented, and guilt-ridden, he confesses to Coleman that he had to get married. After admitting to hating his wife, he sounds more suicidal than enraptured when grabbing hold of the snakes.

Murial Boggs, Billy's young wife. She brings her newborn to the service and asks Cancer Man to be the baby's godfather.

Cancer Man, a middle-aged man fearlessly succumbing to cancer. He is overjoyed by his acceptance into the church and is thrilled to be the godfather of the Boggses' baby.

Carl Spector, a crazy man haunted by the death of his dog. Since entering the cult, he has had comforting visions of his deceased pet.

— *Steven C. Kowall*

HOLY PLACE
(Zona sagrada)

Author: Carlos Fuentes (1928-)
First published: 1967
Genre: Novel

Locale: Mexico City, Mexico, and Madonna dei Monte, Italy
Time: Early to mid-1960's
Plot: Mythic

Guillermo "Mito" Nervo (gee-YEHR-moh MEE-toh NEHR-voh), the narrator, the son of Claudia Nervo, a famous Mexican film star. He is a lanky young man with black eyes, olive skin, and blond hair whose descent into madness is centered on his obsession with his mother and his incestuous desire for her. Kidnapped by Claudia while living with his father and grandmother, he spent his adolescence in boarding schools. Although loved by his mother, he is alternately pushed away from and pulled toward her, based on her whims. While attending a boarding school in Switzerland, he meets Giancarlo, a young man he greatly admires and who tries to seduce him. Guillermo, or "Mito," a diminutive used by Claudia, is a parasite whose physical, mental, and financial existence is dependent on his mother. Guillermo takes Bela as a lover to make Claudia jealous and as a substitute to satisfy his sexual desire for his mother. When Claudia takes Giancarlo as her lover, Guillermo's sanity completely unravels. He enters a sanatorium in Rome. After being released, he returns to Mexico. At the end, Guillermo has been transformed into an abused dog and watches his servants destroy his apartment, one of his "holy places," while fantasizing about tearing Claudia and Giancarlo apart.

Claudia Nervo, a famous Mexican actress and mother of Guillermo. A beautiful and sensual women, she exhibits a keen business sense and a penchant for order and organization. She sees herself as the national idol of the time and likens her role in Mexico to that of Pancho Villa. She keeps Mito on edge, first showering him with attention and presents and then, by stopping payment on his monthly check, forcing him to beg her forgiveness for a slight. She clings to the glamour of her public life and uses her young lover Giancarlo to reaffirm the power of her beauty and fame. Her preoccupation with her career and her entourage leaves her blind to her son's disintegration. Guillermo's obsession with her both irritates and stimulates her.

Giancarlo D'Aquila (gee-ahn-KAHR-loh dah-KEE-lah), a film actor, Claudia's costar and lover. A contemporary of Guillermo, he is young, daring, narcissistic, and carelessly elegant in dress. Guillermo admits that Giancarlo is the masculine counterpart of Claudia. As a young man in Switzerland, Giancarlo attempted to seduce Guillermo. Later, when he becomes Claudia's lover, his youth and his relationship with Claudia and Guillermo are the final blows sending Guillermo into madness.

Bela (BEH-lah), Guillermo's seductive Italian girlfriend and one of Claudia's satellites. When Guillermo meets her, she is made up to look like a diminutive and lesser version of Claudia. Although she becomes Guillermo's lover, their relationship never goes beyond a tentative physical union. Even that is frustrated by Guillermo's obsession with Claudia.

Gudelia (gew-DEH-lee-ah), Guillermo's cook and maid. In the final chapter, assisted by her lover, she destroys Guillermo's apartment as he looks on as a dog.

Jesus (heh-SEWS), Gudelia's lover. He is a strong, handsome man admired by Guillermo for his strength. After Guillermo is transformed into a dog, Jesus beats and kicks him.

— *Geraldine L. Hutchins*

THE HOLY SINNER
(Der Erwählte)

Author: Thomas Mann (1875-1955)
First published: 1951
Genre: Novel
Locale: Lands that became Belgium and France, the North Sea, and Rome
Time: The sixth century
Plot: Romance

Brother Clemens, the narrator, an Irish monk from the cloister of Clonmacnoise who sets about telling the story of the children of Duke Grimald. Clemens tells the story with great sympathy and poetry, believing his tale to be instructional as well as entertaining. Living in Rome, Clemens (his Irish name is Morhold) believes that his tale of a saint has a universal message: The sinner may be the chosen one (the German title translates as "The Chosen One").

Duke Grimald and

Baduhenna, the grandparents of "the Holy Sinner." Grimald is the duke of Flanders and Artois and lives in the Castle Beaurepaire with his wife, Baduhenna. They become the parents of Wiligis and Sibylla, two handsome children who are loved by their father; Baduhenna dies giving birth to the pair. The duke dies seventeen years after his wife, leaving the children in the hands of their guardian, Sieur Eisengrein.

Wiligis and

Sibylla, the two comely children of Duke Grimald and his lady, Baduhenna. After Duke Grimald dies, Wiligis becomes a duke and Sibylla a duchess. The two then commit incest. They confess their sin to Sieur Eisengrein, who sends Wiligis off to join the Crusades and orders Sibylla to Eisengrein's own castle, where she is to have her baby. Wiligis dies on the way to the port of embarkation. Sibylla remains for the time a single woman, repenting of her sin and rejecting all the suitors who come to her.

Grigorss, later **Gregorius**, the so-called **Holy Sinner**. He is the child of Wiligis and Sibylla. Cast adrift in a barrel at the order of Sieur Eisengrein, who believes that God will protect the babe if he approves of his survival, the child is found by the fisher folk of the abbey of Saint Dunstan on the North Sea coast. The child is adopted by the abbot of the abbey, Gregorius, who gives the baby his name and has him reared by a fisher family. At the age of six, the child moves into the monastery. Educated by the monks, Gregorius nevertheless dreams of knightly adventures. He learns that he is of noble blood at the age of seventeen and leaves the abbey to find his parents. His knightly ambitions lead him to succor his mother (unknown to him), save her from a brutal suitor, and marry her. When he discovers his sin, he dons the clothes of a beggar and does penance by living on a bare rock in the middle of a lake for seventeen years. He is chosen by a miracle to become the pope of Rome. He becomes a pious leader of the church.

— *Philip Brantingham*

HOME TO HARLEM

Author: Claude McKay (1889-1948)
First published: 1928
Genre: Novel
Locale: Harlem, New York, and Pittsburgh, Pennsylvania
Time: Immediately after World War I
Plot: Social realism

Jake Brown, a black man from Petersburg, Virginia, who went absent without leave from the Army because he was assigned menial noncombat duties in Europe. He lived with a white woman in London before returning to New York as a stoker and has established a social hierarchy of whites, blacks, and Arabs. He finds Harlem amenable; there he is "happy as a kid" and makes love for love's sake, steering away from the hate, violence, sadism, and commercialism associated with sex in the Black Belt. His love is warm and generous. His first affair, with Felice, pleases both, and he searches for her in earnest after she declines to keep his money. He is honest and versatile, neat and orderly, loyal, streetwise, and principled. He refuses to be a strikebreaker even though he is out of work. He seeks swift satisfactions, but although he is a "free, coarse thing," he avoids drugs, gambling, and exploitation of women. He is stable, moderate, of strong pro-American feelings, and always able to cope. His short time with Congo Rose (for whom he felt no desire) was an act of compassion toward her and her need for a man. His continuing need is for Felice, and eventually he finds her and leaves with her for Chicago, optimistic about a new life there.

Felice, "a burning little brownskin" prostitute who likes Jake and declines to keep his fifty dollars. She is "too nice to be mean" and is honest about her professional activities. As frisky as a kitten, she is the embodiment of natural happiness and joy. Her attachment to Jake appears to be sincere and permanent.

Congo Rose, an entertainer at the nightspot of that name. She takes Jake as a lover when he is broke. When Jake slaps her on the face, she is delighted, but Jake is revolted at her masochism.

Ray, a bookish, serious, deliberate, pessimistic, and cynical Haitian who has been made "impotent by thought." He has attended Howard University but derides its curriculum as deficient in teaching black racial self-consciousness. He is semipuritanical and advocates only responsible sexual relations, though he can be outgoing and emotional. He takes cocaine experimentally with Jake when on a railroad layover in Pittsburgh. He tends to be didactic and antimaterialistic. His pessimism is seen in his dictum, "Civilization is rotten," derived from his extensive reading in race relations, history, and economics, as well as world literature. He needs a serious attachment to a woman and sees Agatha as the one, yet he cannot make a permanent commitment and therefore leaves her. He does not want to be "a contented hog in the pigpen of Harlem." He ships off to Europe as a mess boy.

Agatha, a beauty parlor assistant who is eager to marry Ray, who would meet her physical and intellectual needs. She has been in Harlem for two years, having come from Baltimore. She is "a rich brown girl with soft, amorous eyes," a straight, beautiful girl full of "simple self-assurance and charm." Although neither elegant nor formally educated, she radiates integrity, sincerity, and genuine attachment. Sent by Ray to visit Jake during his sickness, she impresses him with her seriousness, refinement, and honesty. In many ways, she is a Harlem paragon.

Zeddy Plummer, a compulsive gambler who vindictively reports Jake to the authorities for having deserted the Army. As a gambler, informer, strikebreaker, and social parasite who is always broke, he deserves little respect. This "bad-acting, razor-flashing" black man, who had watched over Felice during Jake's two years overseas, is saved by Jake in a fight with an unpaid loan shark. His fleshy lips and salacious laugh are noteworthy.

Susy, a possessive, compulsive prostitute who keeps Zeddy. He describes her as loving and a good cook—compensations for her poor figure and looks. Jake describes her as "fat and ugly as a turkey." She is broad and aggressive. She believes in free love, but not for the man she possesses and supports. She is the matriarch of Myrtle Avenue, and when she learns of Zeddy's visit to another woman, she packs his clothes (minus her gifts to him) and throws them out.

Billy Biasse, a friend of Jake who operates a longshoremen's gambling apartment. A realist, he advises Jake that life in Harlem is dangerous and gives him a gun, which he uses to save himself. He deplores those who gamble beyond their means.

— *Marian B. McLeod*

HOMEBASE

Author: Shawn Wong (1949-　　)
First published: 1979
Genre: Novel

Locale: Primarily Berkeley, San Francisco, and surrounding areas of California; and Guam
Time: The 1950's and 1960's
Plot: Domestic

Rainsford Chan, a fourth-generation Chinese American, named for the town in California where his great-grandfather settled during the Gold Rush. It is through his eyes exclusively that the novel is told. The evocative, elusive narrative consists of interwoven flashbacks recalled by Rainsford as an adult. For most of the novel, he is having a difficult adolescence, marked by the death of his father and, eight years later, that of his mother. These losses are complicated with issues of racial identity: Although he was born in Wyoming and lived in Berkeley, people keep asking him where he is from "originally," expecting "Hong Kong" for an answer because of his Asian features. At one point in the novel, Rainsford shamefully compares being a Chinese American to being a mutant. As a seven-year-old on Guam, Rainsford often goes to outdoor movies with his parents and keeps company with the many sailors on the island. His father gives him a Charlie McCarthy puppet that Rainsford calls "Freddy." With it, Rainsford and his mother practice English and Chinese words. As the only Chinese student in an all-white high school, he letters five times in sports and is voted the most valuable player. His daydreams about committing heroic acts help him develop self-esteem and counteract the racial slurs he often experiences. His habit of dreaming helps him to claim a place in life.

"The Body," the image that stands for all of America to Rainsford. He calls this illusory, blond-haired, whining character his "dream bride," "the shadow," and "the white ghost of all my love life." Because much of the language in the book is highly poetic and many episodes have a dreamlike, illusory quality, it often is difficult to distinguish what really happened from what Rainsford only imagined. This is particularly important to bear in mind in passages that refer to this female entity. Rainsford identifies her as a "pilot" who lands his plane perfectly as he gives instructions from the ground, and as a lover to whom he gives his car, spurning her when she tells him to "go home." These are examples of incidents that make more sense if they are perceived symbolically rather than literally.

Father, an adventurer who once tried to climb Mt. Shasta. Rainsford calls him a "man of journeys"; he covers a lot of territory by himself and in family trips. Rainsford feels the spirit of his father in all the journeys he himself takes, particularly in a canyon near Gold Run.

Mother, who owned a floral shop. She taught Rainsford how to construct exotic floral arrangements. The jade bracelet that she wears becomes an identifying and an endearing symbol to him. Her death when Rainsford is fifteen years old fills him with pity and loneliness. Being orphaned at that age affects him deeply.

Grandfather, who was born in San Francisco but sent to China for safety while his father worked on building a railroad in the Sierras. Eventually, he returned to Angel Island, where he almost died. At one point in the novel, the images of great-grandfather, grandfather, father, and Rainsford himself blur and merge so that they all seem to be the same man. Rainsford's visit to Angel Island at the end of the novel gives him a greater awareness of the violence and survival that his grandfather experienced. By association, he acquires a greater awareness of himself.

Uncle, the husband of Rainsford's mother's sister, a physician and absentminded driver. Rainsford, after his mother's death, moves to Uncle's home in a small town in California, near the ocean.

Aunt, Rainsford's mother's oldest sister. She is enthusiastic about Rainsford's future and wants to do the best for him. Rainsford worked in her children's shop, sweeping floors and doing odd jobs.

— *Jill B. Gidmark*

THE HOMECOMING

Author: Harold Pinter (1930-   )
First published: 1965
Genre: Drama

Locale: North London
Time: Mid-1960's
Plot: Psychological realism

Ruth, a former photographer's model in her early thirties, now married to Teddy and the mother of their sons. On the occasion of her and Teddy's visit to his family home in London, she is a force in the lives of Teddy's father, uncle, and two brothers. As an outsider, she disrupts the comfortable routine of their lives. At the end, she does not leave for the United States with her husband; she admonishes him, at his departure, not to become a stranger. At first, experiencing the family's hostility toward her, she slowly and subtly engages each of the men in a battle of the sexes, in which she emerges as the victor. Her control over Max is emotional; over Lenny, psychological; and over Joey, sexual. Her life with Teddy is sterile. Her psychological mobility is the secret of her eventual dominance over the immobility of the males.

Max, the father of Teddy, Lenny, and Joey, and the domineering, seventy-year-old patriarch of the family. His sons and his brother, Sam, live with him in a shabby ancestral home in London. He constantly threatens his sons and brother, and even Ruth when she arrives. Underneath the animal imagery of his virile language lie the buried uncertainties of his past. These emerge in the course of the play and involve possible violations of his now-deceased wife, Jessie, in the back of Max's taxicab. His conflicts are with his sons as well, even as he insists on a "cuddle" with one of them. His boasts about his secure family life prove to be idealistic. Illusions about his wife and family are shattered as the realities of his past emerge in fragmentary pieces. His emotional tensions find release at the end; crawling over to Ruth and repeating that he is not an old man, he asks her to kiss him.

Lenny, the first of the family to meet Ruth. He is in his early thirties, and his character suggests homosexuality. In his meeting with Ruth, a superiority battle develops in which Ruth is the victor. Lenny, however, proposes that Ruth stay with the family and have an apartment in London in which she will earn money for them by means of prostitution. He plans to make all the necessary arrangements, even to the furnishing of her apartment. In a final ironic gesture, he suggests that Teddy could provide her with names of his American colleagues on their visits to England. In his battle with Ruth, he indulges in monologues of fantasy about women who have attempted to have sex with him and failed. Despite his boasting, he is, finally, at the mercy of Ruth, who moves with the flux of things, using her enigmatic, nonverbalized life force to counter the rigidities and dominance of the men in her life.

Teddy, who is in his middle thirties, a philosophy professor at an American university and Ruth's husband. He is the intellectual of the family. Professionally and domestically, his life adds up to a sterile realization of the American Dream. America is the alien force in the play, and Ruth, like her biblical predecessor, is amid alien corn. She does not accompany him when he leaves for America.

Sam, Max's sixty-three-year-old brother, a taxicab driver who boasts of the rich people he has driven to the airport. He constantly suffers verbal attacks by Max, and at one point his verbal victimization by Max takes physical form as he is struck to the floor by his brother.

Joey, a boxer in his early twenties. Of the three brothers, he is the most physical. In his sexual encounter with Ruth, even he cannot claim victory; he complains that she is only a tease who refused to go "the whole hog" with him.

— *Susan Rusinko*

THE HOME-MAKER

Author: Dorothy Canfield Fisher (1879-1958)
First published: 1924
Genre: Novel

Locale: A small town in New England
Time: Early 1920's
Plot: Domestic realism

Evangeline (Eva) Knapp, a housewife. An intense, dark-haired woman in her early thirties, during thirteen years of marriage she has lost her former beauty and now looks worn and unhappy. Because she hates housework but has nothing else to throw herself into, she is impatient with her husband and children, constantly monitoring their behavior, alternately scolding and taking refuge in a polite but oppressive martyrdom. When she takes a job in Willing's Department Store, she has an outlet for her artistic talent as well as her genius at organization and merchandising. No longer needing to put her passion into housekeeping, she relaxes with her husband and children and becomes as successful at being a mother as she is in her new business career.

Lester Knapp, Eva's husband, a billing clerk at Willing's Department Store. A thin, sallow-faced man in his early thirties, he is miserable at his job. Although he loves his wife, he is aware of the fact that he abandoned his other love, literature, when he left college to marry her. When a new owner takes over the store, Lester is first passed over for promotion and then fired. Helping a neighbor whose house is on fire, he falls from the roof and is crippled. Out of necessity, he begins to take care of the house and children while his wife works. In the process, he discovers that he is as good at being a homemaker as his wife is in business. When, in a domestic crisis, he realizes that he could walk again, he decides to continue his present status rather than break up the happy home situation.

Helen Knapp, the oldest child of Lester and Eva. Between ten and twelve years in age, she is bright and sensitive, but because of the emotional tension at home, she always has been delicate. When her father becomes the homemaker, she enjoys her closeness to him and the intellectual stimulation that he provides for her.

Henry Knapp, the older boy in the Knapp family. Three years younger than Helen, he has inherited his father's thin frame and his weak stomach. The atmosphere under Eva's rule sends him into fits of nausea and vomiting, which clear up when his father takes over the home. After his mother ceases worrying about hairs in her spotless house, Henry is permitted to have the dog he has always wanted.

Stephen Knapp, the youngest child in the Knapp family. An energetic five-year-old, he reacts with anger and defiance to the pressure at home, resorting to his dirty teddy bear for consolation. When his father remains home with him, Stephen has someone to cling to, as well as someone who will channel his passion into proper outlets.

Mattie Farnham, a middle-aged friend of Eva. Although she is devoted to her family, she knows that homemaking is more than just making a perfect home-cooked meal. When Lester is injured, she is willing to be helpful, but she soon finds that sympathy is not needed, because everyone is happier under the new system.

Jerome Willing, the new owner of Willing's Department Store. A dynamic young man, he has an understandable contempt for employees who have no flair for the business, and he is perfectly willing to fire them, as he fires Lester. His own success is based on hard work and on imagination. With the example of his wife's good business mind before him, he rejects the sex-role assumptions so common in business, assesses Eva's talents correctly, and puts her on the ladder to management.

Nell Willing, Jerome's wife. A slender, intelligent woman who loves business as much as her husband does, she functions as his partner and counselor while she creates a pleasant home atmosphere with the help of her maid. From the first, she sees in Eva someone much like herself and urges her husband to hire her.

— *Rosemary M. Canfield Reisman*

THE HOMEWOOD TRILOGY

Author: John Edgar Wideman (1941-   )
First published: 1985
Genre: Novels

Locale: The Homewood section of Pittsburgh, Pennsylvania
Time: Mid-nineteenth century to the 1970's
Plot: Social realism

Damballah, 1981

John Lawson, who sometimes appears in the stories in the persona of **Doot Lawson**. Lawson is the grandson of John French and brother of Tommy Lawson. He returns to Homewood after teaching in Wyoming and learns many of its stories. Losing his individuation as he connects past with present and turns sadness into song, John is the "blues mind" who posits Homewood within a collectivity of ancestry and tradition. Finding a voice to tell his brother's tale, John begins *Damballah* as an alien from his culture. Through stories and memory, he acquires the role of witness from Sybela Owens, the escaped slave at the root of the Lawson family tree, and Aunt May. He learns to listen and discovers himself occupying the place of griot.

John French, the capricious grandfather of the narrator. French is a big, loud, gambling man who loves his family and friends. With Lionel Strayhorn and Albert Wilkes, French engages in rough camaraderie that gives him an undeviating moral sense of ritual that belies his poverty. He scavenges a large RCA Victrola and collects blues records. His records are destroyed by Carl French (his son), Lucy Tate, and their junkie friends during a drug frenzy. After his death, his family members scatter.

Hiding Place, 1981

Bess Simpkins, the granddaughter of Sybela Owens and Charlie Bell. She lives as a hermit in the remains of the family home on top of Bruston Hill, in a figurative and literal past. Having lost an only son in World War II, Mother Bess sustains a self-indulgent presence by not listening to the accidents of the past. Tommy's dream summons familial transcendence, and Mother Bess flees Bruston Hill to tell the truth about Lizabeth's boy.

Tommy Lawson, the narrator's fugitive brother and the great-great-nephew of Mother Bess. Even though he dwells in the selfish center of himself, Tommy has a gift for talk and song. He flees the police, who seek to arrest him for a murder he did not commit. Hiding out at Mother Bess's house, Tommy is intent on denying the significance of the past. With Mother Bess as chronicler, he learns that his existence depended on May saving his mother's life. Born dead, Lizabeth (Tommy's mother) was brought to life when she was plunged into a snowbank. After dreaming about walking on a beach with his son when life was good, Tommy learns the meaning of listening and how the present is contingent on the past.

Clement, a slow-witted orphan who runs errands at Big Bob's barbershop and who makes deliveries at Bruston Hill. Like Mother Bess and Tommy, Clement is alienated, frustrated, and separated from the center of family and community. He becomes involved with Mother Bess and Tommy and watches their connection strengthen.

Sent for You Yesterday, 1983

John Lawson, who learns how to listen. John and Brother Tate are linked by stories and music. He dances to Jimmy Rushing's "Sent for You Yesterday, and Here You Come Today" in the imagined presence of his artistic forebears, Brother Tate and Albert Wilkes. In the dance are all the voices that Lucy earlier heard in Wilkes's playing. The narrator affirms truth by learning to dance.

Albert Wilkes, who returns to Homewood seven years after becoming a fugitive from charges of murder after killing a white policeman. Despite John French's cautions, Wilkes walks around Homewood undisguised. Refusing to conceive of himself as a victim, Wilkes returns to piano playing and to the white woman with whom he had an affair; she was the policeman's wife. Lucy and Brother Tate are listening to his music when the police break down the door and kill him at the piano.

Brother Tate, a silent, scat-singing, African American albino susceptible to Wilkes's piano playing. After informing on Wilkes, Brother Tate is present when the police kill the piano player. Seven years later, Brother has a complicated dream in which he is Wilkes, returning to Homewood. Brother plays the piano for only five years. He stops both playing and talking after the death of his albino son, Junebug. As a historic continuance, Brother becomes a sort of remote maternal presence for the narrator and a substitute for Junebug. Brother Tate, Carl French (the narrator's uncle), and Lucy turn to drugs after claiming that "being a junkie was better than being nothing."

Lucy Tate, the common-law wife of Carl. She is a witness to Wilkes's "brilliant music" and his murder. Like the unnamed boy in *Damballah*, Lucy is able to testify to Wilkes's music, a music that expresses the inexpressible. She tells Doot many of the Homewood stories he learns.

— Bettye J. Williams

HOMO FABER: A Report
(Homo Faber: Ein Bericht)

Author: Max Frisch (1911-1991)
First published: 1957
Genre: Novel
Locale: New York, Central America, and Europe
Time: April-July, 1957
Plot: Psychological realism

Walter Faber, a Swiss engineer working for the United Nations Educational, Scientific, and Cultural Organization (UNESCO). He is a fifty-year-old man who sees life only in terms of human rationality and technology and what is predictable by the laws of logical deduction. He discounts fate and chance as well as the imaginative and artistic sides of the personality. Faber has had lifelong difficulties in committing himself to emotional relationships with women. The novel is narrated by him in retrospect as he lies in the hospital, about to undergo an operation for a serious stomach ailment, perhaps cancer. His stomach problems grow worse throughout his chronicle, and the prognosis for the success of his operation at the novel's conclusion is not good.

Ivy, Faber's twenty-six-year-old lover in New York. As her name suggests, she is "clinging" and desires a more permanent commitment from the engineer; however, he seeks to break off their relationship.

Hanna Piper, a Swiss archaeologist whom Faber abandoned twenty years earlier. He got her pregnant and, fearing any attachment, urged her to get an abortion. Without his knowledge, she gave birth to the child and married Faber's friend. The child, Faber's daughter, is the young woman he falls in love with on the ocean voyage. Hanna's confrontation with Faber at the end of the novel becomes a revelation of his personal failures in life.

Elisabeth (Sabeth), a twenty-year-old student and Faber's lover as well as his illegitimate daughter. She is a very impulsive and artistic individual. In her love affair with Faber, she brings out the emotional and intuitive sides of his personality.

Joachim Hencke, the Swiss owner of a plantation in Guatemala. He is Faber's former friend who married the pregnant Hanna when Faber abandoned her twenty years earlier. He commits suicide, and Faber finds his body near the beginning of the novel.

Herbert Hencke, a fellow airplane passenger with Faber at the beginning of the novel; he turns out to be Joachim's brother. He persuades Faber to travel to the Guatemalan jungle in search of Joachim.

— Thomas F. Barry

THE HONEST WHORE

Authors: Thomas Dekker (c. 1572-1632), with Thomas Middleton (1580-1627) for part I
First published: 1604, 1630
Genre: Drama

Locale: Milan, Italy
Time: Late sixteenth century
Plot: Social satire

Part I, 1604

Bellafront (BEHL-eh-fruhnt), a beautiful prostitute who yearns from the start to find one man to whom she can be true. She falls in love with Hippolito and woos him, but he is an unattainable nobleman. He does, however, prevent her from committing suicide and persuades her to reform. Having renounced her trade, she marries Matheo. In the course of the play, Bellafront becomes a symbol of marital constancy and chastity, able to maintain her resolve even in the face of poverty and other temptations.

Count Hippolito (ee-POH-lee-toh), who is in mourning over the apparent death of his devoted Infelice, whose father simply had given her a sleeping potion to forestall the marriage. Nobly born Hippolito is held in high esteem by his putative father-in-law but is unsuitable because he belongs to a rival family. A malcontented Hippolito announces eternal devotion to his late fiancée and vows to renounce forever the company of women. His tirade against prostitution convinces Bellafront to renounce her trade and initiates the reconciliation with her estranged father.

Gasparo Trebazi (GAHS-pah-roh treh-BAH-tsee), the duke of Milan, who is led by a feud to oppose a marriage between his daughter Infelice and Hippolito. The duke tells Infelice that Hippolito has died, sends her into exile, and plots to poison the suitor, despite his high regard for him. After the doctor falsely reports Hippolito's death, the duke is beset by conflicting emotions, rues his decision, and banishes the doctor. The young couple outwits him, however, and ultimately the duke must accept Hippolito as his son-in-law.

Candido (KAHN-dee-doh), a patient and honest shopkeeper whose refusal to become angry even when provoked makes him the object of cheating and tricks that lead to his incarceration in Bedlam, the London insane asylum. Despite his obsessive good nature, he is a highly regarded businessman and a dedicated member of Milan's senate. Ultimately, he prevails over his wife and tormentors in a subplot that lightens the atmosphere of the play.

Viola (vee-OH-lah), Candido's ill-tempered but loving wife, whose yearning to see him lose his temper causes her to engage with roisterers in a plot against her husband. She later repents these ill-advised actions and seeks his release from Bedlam.

Matheo (mah-tay-oh), a disreputable man about town, friend of Hippolito, and first seducer of Bellafront. He agrees to wed her only when the duke offers him the choice of death or marriage.

Anselmo, a friar at Bethlem Monastery who marries Infelice and Hippolito despite his fear of retribution from the duke. When the ruler's men arrive at the monastery, Anselmo shrewdly disarms them, so that when the newlyweds appear, the duke is powerless to act. Kneeling, Anselmo begs the ruler's pardon and persuades him to bless the match.

Part II, 1630

Count Hippolito, who no longer is a model of virtue but rather is an amoral and selfish hypocrite. He has become a wayward husband to Infelice and the would-be seducer of Bellafront. He again uses rhetoric to achieve his purpose, but this time he fails, even after bribing her with gold. All that can be said in his favor is that he encourages Bellafront's reconciliation with her estranged father.

Bellafront, now wholly reformed and honest in every way but beset by her unscrupulous husband Matheo, to whom she remains loyal, and a turncoat Hippolito, whose advances she resists. She is, as Candido was in the first part of the play, the personification of patience.

Orlando Friscobaldo (ohr-LAHN-doh FREES-koh-bahl-doh), Bellafront's estranged father, whose gruff exterior masks an inner warmth. When Hippolito tells him that Bellafront is poor and her husband is in prison, Friscobaldo says that seventeen years have passed since he last saw her and that all feeling is gone. He then immediately dons a disguise, goes to Matheo as a servant to be near his daughter, and gives Matheo money that he mistakenly thinks will benefit Bellafront.

Matheo, a wild gambler and thief who sells the clothes off the back of his wife, Bellafront. She intervenes to save him from Bridewell prison, but he remains shameless and unrepentant even when threatened with the gallows. The duke pardons him as a favor to Bellafront and Friscobaldo.

Infelice (een-fay-LEE-chay), the duke's daughter and Hippolito's wife, who learns from the servant Pacheco (actually Friscobaldo) about her husband's waywardness and demonstrates a previously unseen strength and shrewdness. Falsely confessing unfaithfulness to Hippolito, she submits to his self-righteous denunciation but then confronts him with evidence of his own transgressions. He is only angered and not at all chastened.

Candido, now a widower and released from Bedlam, but no longer a heroically patient man. He remarries, again to a "shrew," whom he succeeds in taming.

— *Gerald Strauss*

HONEY IN THE HORN

Author: H. L. Davis (1894-1960)
First published: 1935
Genre: Novel

Locale: Oregon
Time: 1906-1908
Plot: Regional

Wade Shiveley, suspected of robbery and murder, though he declares himself innocent. He is hated by his father because he has previously killed his own brother in a fight over an Indian woman. Later he is framed by his relative, Clay Calvert, and hanged by a posse for another murder he did not commit. After his death, he is proved innocent of the murder and robbery for which he was originally jailed.

Uncle Press Shiveley, Wade's father. He sends his son, whom he hates and has vowed to kill, a gun loaded with blank cartridges; he hopes Wade will be killed while trying to break out of jail.

Clay Calvert, who is either Wade's son or Wade's brother's son; nobody ever knows which. He hates Wade but believes him innocent. Sought by the authorities as an accomplice in Wade's escape from jail, he becomes a migratory worker and takes up with a horse trader's daughter. He drifts about Oregon, always seeking and never finding a place where he and his woman can make a real home.

The Horse Trader, a wanderer who ekes out a living trading horses and having his family pick hops in season. He is a weak man who loses most of the family's money by gambling. He dies of natural causes. He is suspected by Clay of having committed the crimes for which Wade is blamed.

Luce, the horse trader's daughter. She takes up with Clay and lives with him. She claims to have shot the man whose murder is blamed on Wade, but her lover believes she is only trying to shield her father, even after his death. She never completely trusts Clay because she is afraid that he may leave her.

Clark Burdon, leader of a band of settlers in eastern Oregon. He befriends Clay.

THE HONORARY CONSUL

Author: Graham Greene (1904-1991)
First published: 1973
Genre: Novel

Locale: Argentina
Time: Early 1970's
Plot: Psychological realism

Doctor Eduardo Plarr, a physician. This lonely, cynical, unhappy man in his mid-thirties is the product of a turbulent childhood. His father was born in England; his mother is South American of Spanish descent. Plarr fled Paraguay with his mother as a child because of political unrest. After completing medical school in Buenos Aires, he chose to establish a practice in a far northern province of Argentina, because this was as close as he could get to his father, who has been languishing in a Paraguayan prison for more than twenty years. Plarr has maintained contact with Paraguayan revolutionaries in hopes that they can help his father escape. They involve him in the kidnapping of Charley Fortnum, with whose wife the doctor has been carrying on an illicit affair.

Charley Fortnum, an English-born maté planter and an honorary consul (an extremely insignificant official of the British government in Argentina). This sixty-year-old alcoholic embarrassed his superiors by marrying a prostitute. Fortnum provides the focus of this black comedy by getting kidnapped by Plarr's revolutionary acquaintances, who mistake him for the American ambassador. Fortnum symbolizes the decline of British prestige vis-à-vis the United States in the postwar world. When he is wounded attempting to escape, his captors are forced to call in Dr. Plarr, who thereby becomes hopelessly entangled in the terrorist plot.

Clara Fortnum, a former prostitute, now Charley Fortnum's wife and Plarr's mistress. This pretty nineteen-year-old of pure Indian extraction is like an innocent child. She is amused by baubles and passively allows herself to be used by both Fortnum and Plarr. Her elderly husband dotes on her and looks forward to the birth of the child he believes to be his. Plarr, who is the real father, has taken Clara as his secret mistress for complex reasons: He envies Fortnum's happiness and is trying to share in the genuine love Fortnum is experiencing. It is because of Clara and their unborn child that Plarr eventually sacrifices his life to save her husband.

Father León Rivas (leh-OHN RREE-vahs), a Catholic priest turned revolutionary. A friend and boyhood schoolmate of Dr. Plarr, he became disillusioned with religion as a means of helping the oppressed people of South America. He is in charge of the bungling band of Paraguayans who kidnap Fortnum. Rivas represents the modern concerned intellectual, particularly the Catholic intellectual, torn between religious precepts and radical socialism. At the climax of the novel, he is emotionally racked when it comes time to carry out his ultimatum that he will kill the honorary consul unless his demands for the release of Paraguayan political prisoners are met.

Aquino (ah-KEE-noh), a poet and terrorist. He also became a friend of Plarr at school in Paraguay. He was arrested after publishing an article critical of American machinations in Paraguay. He is now a follower of Father Rivas and writes only short poems, because he finds it difficult to write longer works after having had three fingers cut off by torturers. He represents another type of South American intellectual who is driven into the Marxist camp by the inflexibility of the feudal establishment and heavy-handed American interference in internal affairs.

Colonel Perez (PEH-rehs), the chief of police. He is shrewd, relentless, and cruel but affects the formal good manners of the upper class. He represents the oligarchical police-state mentality that is widespread in South America. It is Perez who tracks down the kidnappers and orders Plarr, Rivas, and Aquino shot.

Doctor Jorge Julio Saavedra (HOHR-heh HEW-lee-oh sah-VEH-drah), an elderly, rather old-fashioned writer of romantic novels emphasizing fatalistic courage. This sincere but comically pathetic man not only represents the South American mentality of the past but also serves as an antithesis to the author's thesis that life essentially is absurd because only God can see the truth, and that humans therefore should be humble and love one another.

— Bill Delaney

THE HONOURABLE SCHOOLBOY

Author: John le Carré (David John Moore Cornwell, 1931-)
First published: 1977
Genre: Novel
Locale: Hong Kong and Cambodia
Time: The 1970's
Plot: Spy

George Smiley, a veteran of the British intelligence services who is assigned to rebuilding spy networks after the exposure of Bill Haydon, a "mole" working for the Russians. Haydon has compromised British agents all over the world, and Smiley's job is to unravel Haydon's treachery and rebuild the confidence not only of his government but also of the Americans—or, as the British call them, "the cousins"—who are reluctant to share information with the unreliable Brits and who are prone to taking over areas of the world where British intelligence has been dominant. Smiley's problem is not only Karla—his arch Soviet adversary—but also the perceptions of his colleagues, some of whom think he is aging and losing his grip. Smiley's low-key manner and elaborate politeness make him seem weak and vulnerable, whereas in fact he has a better grasp of strategy and of how to expose Karla's agents than anyone else in England or America.

Peter Guillam, Smiley's right-hand man. Although he is fiercely protective of his mentor's power and fends off members of the intelligence service who are angling to replace Smiley, Guillam fears that Smiley's critics may be right: Perhaps he is too old and too dispirited to break Karla's spy network.

Connie Sachs, one of Smiley's ardent supporters. She is a crack researcher who is able to anticipate most of Smiley's moves and to understand that he is well ahead of his colleagues in figuring out Karla's plots. She often articulates Smiley's rationale, when Smiley himself is unable or unwilling to divulge it. Although she is an alcoholic, Smiley has the utmost confidence in her judgment.

Gerald Westerby, known as a "field man" in British intelligence parlance. He takes all the risks, exposing himself mercilessly in an extremely dangerous mission in war-ravaged Cambodia. Westerby has the utmost faith in Smiley's game plan, even though he cannot always fathom it. He works as a journalist (a cover for his spy work) and is assigned by his editor, Bill Craw (another agent), to penetrate the Soviet network established in Hong Kong and Cambodia. Westerby's weakness is women: He cannot seem to sleep at night without them. His work for Smiley is vastly complicated when he falls in love with Elizabeth Worthington, a beautiful woman who is implicated in the network that Westerby is assigned to expose. Westerby's chivalric code and his almost medieval quest to earn the favor of the damsel in distress are part of what makes him the novel's "honorable schoolboy."

Bill Craw, the newspaper editor/British intelligence agent who delivers Smiley's orders to Westerby. Craw is an old hand in the intelligence agency who speaks like a nobleman in her majesty's service, addressing his underlings as "your graces." His employment of such grand language provides an ironic commentary on the grandiose designs of British intelligence, which does not want to concede Britain's rapidly crumbling power and America's ascendancy, especially in Asia.

Elizabeth Worthington, the enigmatic woman who is the key to Westerby's effort to carry out Smiley's plan to rehabilitate the reputation of British intelligence. Westerby wonders whether she is a pawn or a queen in the Soviet scheme of things. He falls in love with her, romanticizing her problems and jeopardizing Smiley's plans by rescuing her and trying to make his own deal with Karla's agents.

Martello, Smiley's equivalent in American intelligence. Although he treats Smiley with oily deference, Martello is conniving to take over Smiley's territory, supplanting British influence in Hong Kong and the rest of Asia with American agents.

— Carl Rollyson

THE HOOSIER SCHOOLMASTER

Author: Edward Eggleston (1837-1902)
First published: 1871
Genre: Novel
Locale: Indiana
Time: c. 1850
Plot: Regional

Ralph Hartsook, the schoolmaster at Flat Creek, Indiana. He makes a place for himself in the community until his enemies accuse him of being a thief. He escapes a mob and gives himself up to the authorities. He is tried and found innocent. Being a friendly and democratic man, he tries to help everyone. He falls in love with Hannah, a hired girl, and marries her.

Hannah Thomson, the "bound girl" at the Means home. She defeats the schoolmaster in a spelling bee. He falls in love with her and marries her.

Bud Means, one of the older pupils in Ralph's school. He becomes the schoolmaster's friend. Chagrined when he is ignored by Martha Hawkins, he falls in with evil companions, but he saves himself and tries to help the schoolmaster.

Martha Hawkins, daughter of the local squire. She is in love with bashful Bud.

Dr. Small, a thief. He is Ralph's enemy and tries to lay his crime upon the schoolmaster's head. At Ralph's trial, he incriminates himself and is later hanged for his misdeeds.

Pete Jones, Dr. Small's accomplice. He tries to lay the blame for the robbery on Mr. Pearson, an honest man. He and his brother are sent to prison as punishment for their part in the robbery.

Walter Johnson, another of Dr. Small's accomplices. He is Ralph's cousin. He turns out to be a religious man who cannot keep his crime hidden. He turns state's evidence and goes unpunished.

Shocky Thomson, Hannah's young brother.

Bill Means, Bud's brother, one of Ralph's pupils.

Granny Sander, a gossipy woman who spreads evil rumors about Ralph.

Mirandy Means, sister of Bud and Bill. Infatuated with the schoolmaster, she tries to come between Ralph and Hannah.

Mrs. Means, mother of Mirandy, Bud, and Bill. She testifies against Ralph at the robbery trial to spite him for spurning Mirandy.

Mr. Pearson, a basketmaker who took in Shocky when his blind mother went to the poorhouse. He is an honest man wrongly accused of the theft.

Mrs. Matilda White, Ralph Hartsook's aunt. She refuses to take in the unfortunate Mrs. Thomson.

Miss Nancy Sawyer, Ralph's hometown friend, who takes in Shocky to prevent his being found out.

Mrs. Thomson, Hannah and Shocky's mother, a poor but honest widow who is blind and who is finally forced to go to the poorhouse. Later, she is able to make a home for Shocky again through the kindness of Nancy Sawyer.

HOPSCOTCH
(Rayuela)

Author: Julio Cortázar (1914-1984)
First published: 1963
Genre: Novel

Locale: Paris and Buenos Aires
Time: The 1950's
Plot: Parable

Horacio Oliveira (oh-RAH-see-oh oh-lee-BA-rah), an Argentine bohemian living in Paris. An intellectual in his forties who distrusts rationality and the intellect, he is engaged in a never-ending search for self-authenticity, a unity in life that he calls the "kibbutz of desire." Lacking purpose and motivation, his principal occupation is as philosopher-in-residence to the Serpent Club, a group dedicated to drinking, American jazz, and endless discussions of art and literature. Aloof and seemingly unable to give of himself, Horacio is condemned to a lonely physical and metaphysical wandering. He abandons the two women in his life, Pola and La Maga, when they need him most. On his return to Argentina, he moves in with a third for comfort's sake. In Argentina, he is employed first in a circus and then in an insane asylum whose atmosphere serves to deepen his despair and growing paranoia. At the end of the novel, his fate is uncertain. He may have committed suicide; he may have survived to become another patient in the asylum.

Morelli (moh-REH-yee), an old avant-garde novelist whose writings have long been debated and admired by the Serpent Club. He is struck down by a car in the streets of Paris and is taken to a hospital. Horacio witnesses the accident but is unaware of the victim's identity. When he visits the victim out of curiosity, Horacio is astonished to discover that this old man is Morelli, a famous author (at least to the Serpent Club) whose every word has been heatedly challenged or supported. Convinced of his imminent death, Morelli gives the key to his apartment to Horacio and asks him and his friends to arrange the material in his notebooks for publication in any way they see fit. These notes and commentaries form the basis of the second theme of the novel, the writing of the novel itself. Morelli's goal has been the creation of the new novel—or, rather, antinovel—fit for the age in which he lives, stripped of all literary conventions, even character and plot development.

La Maga (MAH-gah), Horacio's mistress in Paris, a single parent in her twenties from a typical Uruguayan middle-class background. After being deserted by her lover, she suddenly decides to change her life in one bold stroke. She moves to Paris, ostensibly to study singing, and she changes her name from Lucía to La Maga and that of her son from Carlos Francisco to Rocamandour. She sends her baby to live in the country so that she can concentrate on absorbing the intellectual atmosphere of the city. A member of the Club, she strives to win its members' acceptance but is ridiculed by the others, who laugh at her lack of education and pretensions. La Maga possesses an intuition, a sense of integration with her environment that they admire and that draws Horacio to her in his quest for identity. After the sudden death of her son in her presence, La Maga disappears. Her fate, like that of Horacio, is uncertain. Horacio is convinced that she has drowned herself in the Seine but imagines that he catches a glimpse of her in unexpected moments.

Traveler, Horacio's longtime friend and supposed double. Before Horacio's return to Argentina, Traveler had led a relatively comfortable and placid existence. Content with his unstrenuous job at the circus and secure and happy in his marriage to Talita, whom he loves deeply, Traveler's only quarrel with life seems to be the absurdity of his name: He has never traveled anywhere. His friend's presence, however, brings to the surface long-submerged feelings of anxiety and incompleteness. He also worries about Horacio's growing attachment to Talita. Although he is painfully aware of his friend's mental disintegration, he is still stunned when he realizes that Horacio believes that he, Traveler, will murder Horacio to rid himself of his "twin."

Talita (tah-LEE-tah), Traveler's wife. About the same age as La Maga, but better educated, Talita is disturbed by Horacio's confused identification of her with the Uruguayan woman. She also realizes that somehow she has become a pawn in some obscure game silently being played by Horacio and her husband. Secure in the sense of her own identity, she refuses to let Horacio involve her in his fantasies and elects to remain in her husband's world.

Ossip Gregorovius (AH-sihp greh-gohr-OH-vee-ews), a member of the Serpent Club. Supported by a maiden aunt, Ossip does not have to work and devotes himself to his chief amusement of role-playing. He pretends to be a Russian émigré but is probably from a lower-class British family. He covers up his true origins by inventing incredible stories about his three mothers. Both attracted to and jealous of Horacio, he is in love with La Maga, and Horacio believes he is having an affair with her. He moves into her apartment after La Maga disappears.

Etienne (eh-TYEHN), a French member of the Serpent Club. A painter, Etienne is probably the only member of the group who could be called Horacio's friend. He accompanies Horacio in his visit to Morelli, and it is to him that Horacio entrusts the treasured key to the writer's apartment.

Ronald, an American member of the Serpent Club. A fanatical jazz fan devoted to his wife, Babs, Ronald cheerfully drowns thoughts of advancing age and utter lack of purpose in life in his music and in alcohol.

Babs, Ronald's wife. Equally devoted to her husband and equally drowning in liquor, Babs, in a drunken rage, is the first member of the Club to turn on Horacio after his abandonment of La Maga.

Pola, Horacio's lover in Paris. He does not try to hide their affair from La Maga. He deserts her even though he knows she is dying of breast cancer.

Wong, a Chinese member of the Serpent Club. His main interests are Oriental mysticism and his pornographic collection of torture scenes. He is deported by the French government.

Berthe Trepát (BEHR-teh treh-PAH), an aging pianist. Horacio, one of a handful of people to attend her recital, is struck by the audacity and atrociousness of her playing. He walks her home after the concert, and she mistakes his solicitude for amorous intentions.

Getkrepten, Horacio's former girlfriend in Argentina. He moves in with her to live closer to Traveler and Talita.

Guy Monod (gee moh-NOH), a French member of the Serpent Club who tries to commit suicide and fails, his failure becoming a topic of conversation.

— Charlene E. Suscavage

HORACE

Author: Pierre Corneille (1606-1684)
First published: 1641
Genre: Drama
Locale: Rome
Time: Antiquity
Plot: Tragedy

Horace (oh-RAHS), a Roman warrior. The cities of Rome and Alba are at war, with the battle to be decided by armed combat between three heroes from each side. Horace and his two brothers, the Roman combatants, are victorious over their prospective Alban brother-in-law, Curiace, and his two brothers. All for honor and country, Horace taunts his sister Camille with the glory of Rome. He kills her when she declares that his deed is not patriotism but murder. He defends this act as one of justice, but he is aware that his glory is dimmed because of it, and he wishes to die. The king decrees that Horace's fate shall rest with the gods.

Sabine (sah-BEEN), Horace's Alban wife and the sister of the Alban brothers killed by Horace in combat. Torn between her loyalty to the city of her birth and to the city of her husband, she pleads in vain the cause of home and family against that of honor and patriotism. In despair over her husband's killing of her brothers and the murder of his sister, she wishes only to die.

Camille (ka-MEE-y), Horace's sister and the prospective wife of Curiace. She is killed by Horace when she reviles Rome in her grief over the death of Curiace.

Curiace (kew-RYAHS), Sabine's brother and the prospective husband of Camille. He is killed in combat with Horace.

Old Horace, Horace's father, an ardent patriot and a former warrior.

Julie (zhew-LEE), the confidant of Sabine and Camille.

Valère (vah-LEHR), a Roman warrior.

Tulle (tewl), the ruler of Rome.

HORACKER

Author: Wilhelm Raabe (1831-1910)
First published: 1876
Genre: Novel
Locale: Two German villages
Time: July 25, 1867
Plot: Social realism

Dr. Werner Eckerbusch (VEHR-nehr EH-kehr-bewsh), the vice principal of the local school. Werner is a cheerful, intelligent, and imaginative man, well past middle age, who has been the principal and a teacher in a small village for most of his life. He has not traveled much, having left the village and surrounding area of his birth only during the years in which he was a university student. Werner has a well-developed sense of humor, a serene character, and a great love for the telling of stories and anecdotes. During the mere ten hours in which the events narrated in the novel occur, Werner, along with his colleague and friend Victor Windwebel, hikes across the mountain to visit his longtime friend Christian Winckler, pastor of the neighboring village of Gansewinckel; participates in the recovery of the purported robber and murderer Horacker; and engages in much entertaining conversation. When it is suggested by the inhabitants of Gansewinckel that the captured Horacker should be placed in detention, Werner's oratorical skill allows him to shame the villagers into recognizing some of their own failings and letting Billa, the pastor's wife, care for the hungry and exhausted Horacker. Werner and his wife Ida, along with Christian and Billa Winckler, are magnanimous, open-minded, and unusual. Of the four, Werner is the most playful; he does not mind being the center of attention and succeeds in dazzling everyone with his ability to spin a good tale.

Ida Eckerbusch (EE-dah), his wife. Ida appears to be her husband's equal, if not in style, then at least in content. Much of her married life consists of good-natured verbal sparring with her husband in which, in spite of the fact that she inaccurately quotes the Latin citations she hears from him, she perseveres. Ida's self-confidence is particularly apparent during a coach ride to Gansewinckel. She insists that Neubauer accompany her and Hedwig Windwebel. She completely unnerves the somewhat snooty Neubauer with her irreverence and no-nonsense attitude. Not beyond staging intrigues herself, she insists on sneaking up on the unsuspecting Werner and company in the Gansewinckel parsonage and thus contributes to the good-natured atmosphere in which the case of Horacker is settled.

Victor Windwebel (VIHND-veh-behl), the drawing master. Victor is a youngish drawing teacher and colleague and friend of Werner. He has traveled widely but now has found employment in the small provincial school where Werner feels so much at home. Victor regards Horacker as a romantic and fascinating subject for his drawing board but is his primary pursuer after he and Werner discover the young man in the forest. As a good friend of Werner, Victor promises to benefit from the former's attitude toward life.

Hedwig Windwebel (HEHD-vihg), Victor's wife. Hedwig is quite young and is expecting a child. She is pleasant but emotional and prey to the stories and rumors circulating in the villages, such as the rumor that Horacker has slain Werner and her husband. Ida regards her as a good friend and looks after her.

Neubauer (NOY-bow-ehr), the assistant master at the school. Neubauer is a young man who feels superior to his older colleagues and the villagers. He considers himself to be a poet and regards his assignment to the provincial school beneath his dignity. He can be charming, if he wishes, and occasionally appreciates village life.

Christian Winckler (VIHNK-lehr), the pastor of Gansewinckel. Christian has common sense and understands the foibles of his parishioners. His favorite pastime is reading the eighteenth century German author Christian Fürchtegott Gellert, whose moralistic and pleasant tales give him consolation.

Billa Winckler, Christian's wife. As the wife of the village pastor, the resolute and down-to-earth Billa is an excellent helpmate for her husband. She and Christian are childless and rear the orphaned and impoverished Lottchen Achterhang.

Cord Horacker (HOH-rak-uhr), a young man who escaped from reform school. Horacker is nineteen years old and was sent to reform school because of a number of youthful pranks, the worst of which was stealing a pot of lard. He escapes when he is told erroneously that Lottchen Achterhang no longer loves him, and rumor transforms him into a cunning thief and ruthless murderer. In reality, he is hungry, tattered, and frightened, only too willing to be helped when Werner and Victor find him.

Lottchen Achterhang (LOT-khehn AHKH-tehr-hang), Horacker's girlfriend. Lottchen leaves her place of employment many miles away from Gansewinckel and returns there on foot when she is told that Horacker has run away from the reform school. She arrives at the parsonage dirty and exhausted but revives after being helped by Billa, particularly after Horacker is found.

— Helga Stipa Madland

THE HORSEMAN ON THE ROOF
(Le Hussard sur le toit)

Author: Jean Giono (1895-1970)
First published: 1951
Genre: Novel

Locale: Provence
Time: 1838
Plot: Symbolic realism

Angélo Pardi (pahr-DEE), a twenty-five-year-old hussar colonel making his way home from France to Piedmont, where he had been involved in the Risorgimento (Italian revolution) and from which he had fled after killing an Austrian spy in a duel. As the horseman of the title, Angélo has a "rooftop" view of life, suggested by his flight across the rooftops of Manosque (the author's native village) from angry and panicked villagers who think he has poisoned the town well. As he travels down the cholera-ridden Rhone Valley, he has the habit of questioning his own actions and motivations in the middle of the epidemic. This habit, his fearlessness, and his tendency to describe the epidemic in military terms are complemented by his complete sincerity, selflessness, and idealism. He has an innate sense of justice and believes in the primacy of individual conscience. After descending from the rooftops of Manosque, Angélo continues his journey, successfully meeting challenge after challenge in this heroic tale of self-discovery, which pits him against angry mobs, French militia, a variety of strange individuals, and, ultimately, nature, embodied mainly by the cholera epidemic.

Pauline de Théus (tay-YEWS), the young wife of the elderly Marquis de Théus, who does not appear in the novel. She is the perfect complement to Angélo. It is she who helps him escape from Manosque. Described only as having a face like a fer-de-lance (a venomous tropical American snake or a spearhead), she is his equal in their shared journey, whether scaling walls, handling heavy military pistols, crawling on all fours, or examining her conscience. Like Angélo, she feels compelled to involve herself in the challenges of life under the cholera by confronting them directly. Whereas Angélo experiences elation in doing so, however, Pauline experiences fear. There is a suggestion that it may be her fear that makes her vulnerable to the cholera toward the end of the story, but she survives to continue in life with Angélo. Her survival coincides with the end of the cholera epidemic.

Giuseppe, Angélo's foster brother and fellow revolutionary. He is opportunistic, in contrast to Angélo's idealism. Ironically, it is he who spreads the rumor about the well of Manosque being poisoned, thus causing the townspeople to suspect Angélo and chase him onto the rooftops when they see him near the well.

The Doctor/Goldsmith, something of an alchemist living in a secluded and deserted mountain village. He is nameless and is the last character encountered, but he is the most important after Pauline and Angélo. He serves both as a spokesman for the author's moral point of view and as a kind of mirror for Angélo, explaining the cholera's relationship to humans in metaphorical terms. Meeting him marks the final stage in Angélo's journey of self-discovery. Their discussion of the cholera includes the roles of selfishness and selflessness in one's vulnerability to the disease. He specifically responds to Angélo's queries regarding the behavior of other characters.

The little Frenchman, a young doctor who is never named. He inspires Angélo with his apparently selfless and untiring efforts to save victims of the cholera, only to succumb to the cholera himself. His own egotism is revealed, however, when he says that not a single one of the victims will give him the pleasure of saving them.

The nun, a cigar-smoking, no-nonsense sister who is devoted as much to helping cholera victims "pass over" as to helping them survive. She inspires Angélo with her lack of fear and the strength of her faith.

The solo clarinetist of the Marseilles Opera, a man encountered in the countryside by Pauline and Angélo. He is also in the process of self-discovery in the wilderness of Provence and makes interesting comments about the cholera as some sort of just retribution for humans being out of harmony with nature.

The cloth merchant, the only inhabitant left in a village abandoned because of the cholera. He is a reflective man whose role is like that of the little Frenchman or the nun; that is, he gives Angélo food for thought about the moral meaning of the cholera, suggesting that it is the consequence of people failing to be aware of the earth.

— *Philip H. Lutes*

THE HORSE'S MOUTH

Author: Joyce Cary (1888-1957)
First published: 1944
Genre: Novel
Locale: London
Time: The 1930's
Plot: Picaresque

Gulley Jimson, an aging unconventional artist, ex-jailbird, and occasional thief who has sudden grandiose inspirations for big paintings on such subjects as the Fall and the Creation but who, dogged by ill luck, cannot manage to finish them. His only paintings anyone wants are nudes of Sara Monday, which he did years ago and which he cannot get from her or from Hickson, who obtained most of them. After Gulley accidentally kills Sara, he returns home and paints furiously, trying to finish the Creation before his arrest. In a fall from his scaffold, he suffers a stroke from which he awakes in an ambulance taking him to jail.

Sara Monday, Gulley's onetime model and former mistress, now a fat, frowzy old woman. Visited by Gulley and Coker, she signs a statement that she let Hickson have the paintings she stole from Gulley, and she tries vainly to reawaken Gulley's old interest in her. She refuses to give up a few of the nudes which she kept and which she likes to look at, wistfully remembering her former beauty. The last time Gulley attempts to get a painting from her, he angrily pushes her down the cellar stairs and breaks her back.

Coker, a barmaid, a short, stout, homely woman to whom Gulley owes money and who makes repeated efforts to get it by buying paints for his pictures and urging him to get some of Sara's pictures from Hickson. When she becomes pregnant and loses her job, she moves into Gulley's shed with her mother.

Nosy, a young aspiring artist, green-eyed, hay-haired, and flat-nosed; a stammerer. He worships art and Gulley, and he helps Gulley with his painting of the Creation.

Mr. Hickson, an elderly art collector who obtained from Sara a number of beautiful nudes, which she had stolen when she and Gulley broke up. Though he obtained them legitimately, he is willing to pay Gulley a small sum when Gulley visits him about them. On Hickson's death, the Sara nudes are given to the nation, and Gulley becomes famous.

Professor Alabaster, a critic who plans a biography of Gulley.

Sir William Beeder, Gulley's benefactor, a wealthy art collector whose London apartment (during Sir William's absence) Gulley appropriates and ransacks for pawnable items in order to buy canvas and paints.

HORSE-SHOE ROBINSON

Author: John Pendleton Kennedy (1795-1870)
First published: 1835
Genre: Novel
Locale: The Carolinas
Time: 1780
Plot: Historical

Sergeant Galbraith (Horseshoe) Robinson, a shrewd, rustic, good-natured colonial patriot. Tall, broad, brawny, and erect, he is brave, scornful of the British and their Tory supporters, and ingenious in aiding Butler and others among the patriots. A somewhat idealized version of the pioneer, he may be compared with such historical ones as Daniel Boone and David Crockett and with a fictional one like Leatherstocking.

Major Arthur Butler, his handsome, gentlemanly friend, who is captured along with Horseshoe by Tories, escapes with the aid of John Ramsay and Mary Musgrove, is captured again by British troops, and is rescued this time by Horseshoe. With the end of the Tory ascendancy in South Carolina, Butler and his wife Mildred are free to live a long and happy life together.

Philip Lindsay, a Loyalist because of financial interests in England but sympathetic with Mildred over her distress at Butler's capture. He is fatally wounded while accompanying Tyrrel in a search for Mildred, who had gone to seek clemency for Butler from Cornwallis. Before dying, Lindsay forgives Mildred and Henry for their support of the patriot cause.

Mildred, Lindsay's daughter, secretly married to Butler for a year but forbidden by her father to see him because of his colonial army connections. In her determination to save Butler from harm, she is reminiscent of James Fenimore Cooper's intrepid heroines—even to her fainting when she greets her dear rescued husband.

Henry, Lindsay's son, sympathetic to the American cause. He fights at King's Mountain and discovers Tyrrel's body after the battle.

Wat Adair, a Tory woodman and deceitful former friend of Butler, who thinks him a patriot. He is captured at King's Mountain and punished for his treachery.

Tyrrel, a disguised English officer who visits the Lindsay home supposedly to enlist aid for the Loyalists but actually to court Mildred, who despises him. He is killed at King's Mountain.

Mary Musgrove, a patriot, Wat Adair's pretty relative who warns Butler of Wat's treachery and who later informs the captured Butler of rescue plans for him.

John Ramsay, Mary's sweetheart, a trooper who aids in Butler's first escape but is killed shortly afterward.

James Curry, a rascally Tory spy masquerading as Tyrrel's servant. At King's Mountain, he is captured by rebel forces.

General Gates, commander of the patriot forces.

Lord Cornwallis, gentlemanly commander of the British forces.

Allen Musgrove, Mary's elderly father.

Stephen Foster, a woodman and lieutenant of mounted patriot riflemen.

Michael Lynch, a friend of the Adairs. An opportunist willing to support either side, he submits to Wat's conviction that Tory support is more profitable because the Tories will win.

Hugh Habershaw, captain of a gang of ruffians, including Curry, who capture Butler and Horseshoe.

THE HOSTAGE

Author: Brendan Behan (1923-1964)
First published: 1958
Genre: Drama

Locale: Dublin, Ireland
Time: 1960
Plot: Protest

Patrick, a hero for the Irish Republican Army (IRA) in the 1920's, now the caretaker of a lodging house that is a thinly disguised brothel. Pat has a tendency to exaggerate his service during the 1920's, during which he lost a leg and was imprisoned by the British. Scornful of the current IRA (and most aspects of contemporary life), he uses his leg as an excuse for drinking as much and doing as little work as possible. He retains, however, a genuine affection and respect for Monsewer, who was his leader in the earlier independence movement. His cynical detachment lets him recognize and regret the danger the hostage is in without compelling him to do much to avert that danger. He believes in enjoying whatever pleasures are available, as a way of merely getting through life.

Leslie A. Williams, a nineteen-year-old private in the British army, stationed in Armagh, Northern Ireland. He is the hostage of the title. Too young to vote, innocent of politics and history, and an orphan who does not even have a girlfriend, he is coming out of a pub when the IRA "captures" him, imprisons him in Pat's boardinghouse, and threatens to kill him if the British execute a convicted IRA terrorist they are holding.

Teresa, a country girl serving as skivvy in Pat's boardinghouse. Also nineteen years old, innocent of politics and history, and an orphan, she instinctively realizes that although she is Catholic and Leslie is Protestant, they have more in common with each other than either has with anyone else. The love with which they attempt to bridge the gap between factions is doomed by the selfishness and false pride of partisans on both sides of the issues.

Meg Dillon, Pat's consort, the real managing power behind the boardinghouse. Foul-mouthed and irreverent, she makes few moral judgments as long as the boarders pay the rent.

Monsewer (Monseigneur), the owner of the house and Pat's former IRA commander. British by birth, he adopted his Irish mother's nationality, learned Gaelic at university, and fought for Irish independence. Now comically senile, he is unaware of the real nature of the boardinghouse and imagines that it is a safe house for current IRA fugitives, whom he does not distinguish from freedom fighters of the 1920's.

Miss Gilchrist, a social worker full of pious platitudes. She has a tendency to confuse physical attraction with desire to save men's souls.

IRA Officer, a schoolteacher who serves part-time in the IRA. He is a fanatical patriot full of ridiculous posturing who takes himself and the movement very seriously.

— *Helen Lojek*

THE HOT L BALTIMORE

Author: Lanford Wilson (1937-   )
First published: 1973
Genre: Drama

Locale: Baltimore, Maryland
Time: The 1970's
Plot: Comedy

The Girl, a call girl who resides at the hotel. Blonde, youthful, and attractive despite her professional and other past experiences, she has traveled through all fifty states and is particularly attached to railroads, whose demise she laments greatly. She is extremely talkative and curious, making everybody's business her affair. Energetic and positive, she believes in conviction. She announces that she will not vacate the hotel even though it is scheduled for demolition.

Bill Lewis, the night clerk at the hotel. He is thirty years old and handsome in an ordinary way. Outwardly friendly but quiet, he has a rather clumsy manner with people. He has strong feelings for the Girl that he is unable to communicate. Although he is present through much of the play, his role in the action is minimal.

Millie, a retired waitress. She is an elegant sixty-year-old who maintains a sense of dignity and refinement. Quiet and gentle, she is detached from the present world and seems to experience a rather odd spirituality, believing in ghosts and clinging to her memories of a more satisfactory world.

April Green, a prostitute. No longer young but still attractive in a fleshy way, April views much of life with raucous good humor. She is aggressive, strong, and frequently vulgar. Much of the overt comedy in the play is found in her caustic and witty comments on the situations and characters around her. At the end of the play, it is April who coaxes Jamie to dance with her and gives some sense that things will continue to progress.

Mr. Morse, a retired gentleman. Seventy years old and constantly plagued by both real and imaginary ailments, Mr. Morse is a complainer who manages to give meaning to life only through conflict.

Mr. Katz, the hotel manager. Only thirty-five years old, he distances himself from his surroundings with a gruff and no-nonsense attitude that makes him seem older. He deals with problems in a direct and forceful manner but only when it is absolutely necessary.

Jackie, a young thief. Although she is a pretty, twenty-four-year-old woman, she hides under a masculine appearance and dress. Tough on the exterior, she is blunt, aggressive, and ambitious. She has dreams of establishing a home for herself and her younger brother, and she will go to any ends to fulfill that dream. Her loss of her dream at the end of the play and her abandonment of her brother are forceful elements in establishing the melancholy mood of the piece.

Jamie, her younger brother. He is nineteen years old, small, and physically weak. Passive and withdrawn, he is submissive to his sister. Although not mentally quick, he is alert to the activity that surrounds him. His final moments dancing with April lend a sense of hope that perhaps he will find himself.

Suzy, a prostitute. Flashy and hard, she is thirty years old and well-dressed for her profession. She is outgoing and talkative and refuses to give in to despair, desperately clinging to her belief that things will be better in the future. Rather than mourning the hotel's closing, she brings champagne to celebrate her new future, even though her prospects are far from glowing.

Paul Granger, a student. He is an outsider at the hotel, as is clear from his twenty-year-old, blond, tanned good looks. He is intense and somewhat gruff. He comes to the hotel in search of his long-lost grandfather. His entrance provides a stimulus for action, particularly on the part of the Girl, who immediately adopts his cause as her own.

Mrs. Oxenham, the day desk clerk. Forty-five years old, she is all business and wants nothing to interrupt her orderly day.

Mrs. Bellotti, the mother of a former tenant. A wheedler and a whiner, she has come to persuade Mr. Katz to let her son move back into the hotel. She is the victim of countless catastrophes, which she does not hesitate to describe.

— *John C. Watson*

HOTEL DU LAC

Author: Anita Brookner (1928-)
First published: 1984
Genre: Novel
Locale: Primarily Lake Geneva, Switzerland
Time: Late September in the early 1980's
Plot: Psychological

Edith Hope, a successful writer of popular romantic fiction under a pseudonym. The book opens as Edith arrives at a hotel in a small town in Switzerland. Her friends coerced into taking this undesired holiday at the end of the season because they thought that she needed to get away to recover her normal good sense after an unfortunate incident in London, her home. A serious, hardworking woman in her late thirties, Edith makes no effort to enhance her natural attractiveness with stylish clothes or makeup. She keeps her thoughts and feelings to herself. No one knows about her secret life (her long-standing affair with a married man), nor does she reveal to anyone her decision about her wedding until the ceremony is about to take place. She does write long and wryly humorous letters to her lover, describing her fellow guests and the small events in their lives. She does not mail the letters.

Monica, also called **Lady X**, a young woman who also has been forced to spend some time at this dreary but highly reputable establishment, which serves as a kind of sanctuary for those needing such a place of temporary retirement. Monica's husband, a titled Englishman, has sent her here in the hope that she will recover her health and give him an heir, but Monica is interested only in chocolates and her badly behaved lapdog. Out of loneliness, she and Edith develop a casual friendship.

Iris Pusey, a wealthy widow who is staying beyond the season with her daughter under mysterious circumstances that are never revealed. Mme Pusey is expensively dressed and uses cosmetics and perfume lavishly. She and her daughter have an intensely loving relationship, conversing at length and with animation about clothes and about their extravagant and glamorous former life, when M. Pusey was still living.

Jennifer Pusey, Mme Pusey's daughter. Jennifer dresses and behaves like a young girl but is later revealed to be in her forties, at least. Mme Pusey's true age is disclosed when there is a celebration to honor her seventy-ninth birthday. The mother and daughter seem to be inseparable, spending most of their time shopping, with occasional sightseeing. Jennifer has a secret life that is revealed at the end of the novel.

Madame de Bonneuil (deh-bon-OY), an elderly countess whose stay at the hotel is also a kind of exile. She is forced by her son to live at the hotel until the season ends and then at a convent for the remainder of the year. The countess is lame and completely deaf. Edith pities the old lady, and a gentle act of courtesy is rewarded by the countess's dignified gratitude and momentary pleasure.

Geoffrey Long, a prosperous businessman who has been a devoted son until the recent death of his mother. He is a kind, proper, and mouselike man. Edith accepts his proposal of marriage, but, at the last moment, as the taxi is approaching the registry office where they are to be married, she sees him for what he is and tells the driver to take her home. It is for this incident that Edith's friends have temporarily banished her to the Hotel du Lac.

Philip Neville, the owner of an electronics factory, recently left by his wife and staying at the hotel for a few days. Philip is attentive to Edith, takes her on excursions, and proposes marriage. Edith accepts, knowing that love is not to be part of the arrangement. Edith realizes that her lover will never leave his wife and children and that this may be her last chance at marriage, a state that she does not particularly desire but that her friends are constantly enjoining her to enter. She sees clearly the role that she is to play in Philip's life as an attractive, accomplished hostess and congenial companion in return for a beautiful home, elegant clothes, and as much freedom as she wishes to conduct her private life, provided that she does so discreetly. Philip admits that he plans to stray outside their marriage. Early in the morning of the day they are to leave the hotel, Edith happens to see Philip going out of Jennifer Pusey's room and recalls that she has often heard a door closing near her own room at odd hours of the night. As she did with Geoffrey Long, Edith suddenly perceives the true nature of the man she has agreed to marry.

David Simmonds, an auctioneer at a prestigious London auction house. David has been Edith's lover for many years but has never been able to spend much time with her because of his business and family obligations. At the end of the novel, Edith writes a letter to him, telling him of her decision to marry Philip. Like her other letters to David, this one is not mailed. Shortly after writing it, she sees Philip outside Jennifer Pusey's room. Instead of mailing the letter, she sends David a telegram saying simply that she is returning.

— Natalie Harper

THE HOTEL NEW HAMPSHIRE

Author: John Irving (1942-)
First published: 1981
Genre: Novel
Locale: Maine; Dairy, New Hampshire; Vienna; and New York City
Time: The 1940's to the late 1970's
Plot: Psychological realism

John Berry, the third child of Mary Bates Berry and Winslow Berry. He chronicles the family's life, first from his parents' accounts and later as a sympathetic and reflective eyewitness. His incestuous love for his sister Frannie is cured drastically by the loving Frannie herself. His daily weight lifting and running provide the strength for him to squeeze to death one of the men plotting to blow up the Vienna Opera House and take the Berry family as hostages. John takes good care of his blinded father both in New York and in the old Hotel Arbuthnot-by-the-Sea, which becomes a rape crisis center when John marries Susie.

Winslow (Win) Berry, a dreamer who is always out of touch with reality. His passion for owning and running a hotel propels the family from a small town in Maine, where they owned the Hotel New Hampshire, to a cheap hotel in Vienna run jointly with Freud, and eventually back to the Hotel Arbuthnot-by-the-Sea, where he had met both his future wife and Freud, the bear trainer. When he tries to help Freud blow up a car that contains a bomb before that bomb can activate a larger one in the Vienna Opera House, flying glass blinds him. Later, when he is moved from a New York hotel to Arbuthnot-by-the-Sea, to be cared for by John and a succession of Seeing Eye dogs, he does not realize that there are no guests.

Mary Berry, a woman who had the courage to marry the penniless Winslow and bring up their three children practically single-handedly while he was touring with a performing bear named State O'Maine and later when he was in the Army and then at Harvard. She had two more children and ruled her riotous household gently but firmly, always deferring to her husband even to the extent of selling her family home to buy the first Hotel New Hampshire. She dies in an airplane crash en route to Vienna.

Frannie Berry, a beautiful, oversexed, vulgar woman possessing an outrageous vocabulary of obscenity. She is a loyal and loving family member. After being gang raped in Maine and having a lesbian affair in Vienna with Susie-the-Bear, she becomes a film star. She and her black husband offer to have a baby, then give it to John.

Lilly Berry, the second youngest child, who is diagnosed as a dwarf. She is world-weary at the age of eleven, and she somehow deems herself responsible for the deaths of her mother and young brother. In a futile attempt to exorcise her personal demons, she writes a novel about her family's life. It is sold by her brother Frank to an American publisher and later made into a film in which Frannie has the leading role. When her second book, a serious attempt to portray a philosophy of life, gets mixed reviews, she jumps from her sixteenth-story hotel window.

Frank Berry, the oldest of the family, an honest but discreet homosexual who develops from an awkward boy into a scholar. As an economist and talent agent, he manages the family money effectively. After his mother's death, he becomes an atheist and fatalist.

Freud, a Viennese Jew who sells the bear to Win Berry and years later induces him to become joint owner of a sleazy hotel in Vienna. He sacrifices his life to save the Vienna Opera House and to protect the Berry family.

Susie, a woman so convinced of her ugliness that she hides herself in a bear costume. She helps the blind Freud to run his hotel in Vienna, helps Frannie to recover from having been raped, and goes to New York with the Berry family. She runs various crisis and child care centers. She eventually marries John and turns the Hotel Arbuthnot-by-the-Sea into a clinic for rape victims.

Egg Berry, so called because of the explanation of his prenatal life given to his siblings. He is a lovable small boy who adores the family dog, Sorrow. To assuage his grief after the dog's death, Frank twice performs feats of taxidermy to produce an acceptable pose of Sorrow. Egg dies in the airplane crash with his mother, Mary. Sorrow floats to the surface of the Atlantic, allowing searchers to spot the site of the disaster and recover the bodies.

Chipper Dove, one of Frannie's rapists. Years later, in New York, Frannie and Susie engineer a spectacular act of revenge on him.

— *Dorothy B. Aspinwall*

THE HOUND OF THE BASKERVILLES

Author: Sir Arthur Conan Doyle (1859-1930)
First published: 1902
Genre: Novel
Locale: London and Devon, England
Time: Late nineteenth century
Plot: Detective and mystery

Sherlock Holmes, the greatest living detective and therefore the logical person for Dr. Mortimer to approach in the case of Sir Charles Baskerville's death and the possible danger to his heir. As usual, Holmes dazzles Watson and his visitor with his ability to deduce personal history from observable clues, and he is quick to test the possibility that Mortimer and Sir Henry are being followed. Despite this apparent interest in the case, he pleads prior commitment and sends Watson to Devon in his place. This, it turns out, is a ruse that allows Holmes to spend the next days camped in a neolithic ruin on the moor, where he can observe everyone and everything, while receiving Watson's reports and initiating investigations into Stapleton's background. When he finally enters Baskerville Hall and sees the family portrait of Sir Hugo, he realizes instantly from the resemblance that Stapleton is a throwback to the evil Hugo, whose death through a demoniac hound occurred while he was trying to rape the daughter of a neighbor. Holmes arranges that Sir Henry's visit to the Stapletons will be the occasion to flush out and capture Stapleton.

Dr. John Watson, Holmes's friend, colleague in detection, and chronicler of his adventures. He reports to Holmes by letter from Baskerville Hall, helps to solve the mystery of Barrymore's odd behavior, observes the odd behavior of Stapleton and his "sister," and tracks down Holmes in his hiding place without realizing who he is. He also supplies the information that Stapleton arranged Sir Charles's presence outside his home on the night that he was frightened to death by the hound.

Sir Henry Baskerville, a Canadian, next in line of succession to Sir Charles. He is concerned enough to welcome Holmes's help and advice, but he insists on going onto the moor alone to meet Mrs. Stapleton, with whom he is falling in love. In the end, he is the bait Holmes uses to spring his trap on the hound and Stapleton.

Mr. Stapleton, actually a rival heir who arranged the death of Sir Charles and plans the death of Sir Henry. He is a passionate entomologist and a fearless explorer of the Grimpen Mire, where he keeps the great hound. When he prepares to loose it on a victim, he coats it with phosphorous, which makes the animal glow and appear to breathe fire. In order better to entice Sir Henry, he insists that his wife pretend to be his sister. He dies in the Mire, fleeing from Holmes, Watson, and Inspector Lestrade.

Dr. Mortimer, a friend of Sir Charles who is concerned that the family curse has overtaken him and will overtake his heir. He brings Holmes the old account of the first appearance of the hound and the death of Sir Hugo.

Mrs. Stapleton, who finds her husband's scheme so distasteful that she tries twice to warn Sir Henry against staying in Baskerville Hall. She is found beaten and bound by Stapleton because she could no longer bear his schemes.

Barrymore and

Mrs. Barrymore, Baskerville family servants of long standing. Their odd behavior leads to the discovery that they are supplying food and other necessities to Mrs. Barrymore's younger brother, Selden, who has escaped from Princetown prison.

Selden, the Notting Hill Murderer and Mrs. Barrymore's brother. His escape from prison and his presence on the moor terrify local inhabitants.

— *James L. Hodge*

THE HOUR OF THE STAR
(A Hora da estrela)

Author: Clarice Lispector (1925-1977)
First published: 1977
Genre: Novella
Locale: Rio de Janeiro, Brazil
Time: The 1970's
Plot: Social realism

Rodrigo S. M., the intensely self-conscious narrator who struggles to write the story of Macabéa. He describes himself as an outsider who is essentially classless, as he is considered strange by the upper class, viewed with suspicion by the bourgeoisie, and avoided by the lower class. His financial situation is such that he does not have to worry about where his next meal is coming from. After having caught a glimpse of a girl from the Northeast, he becomes obsessed with creating a life for her. His obsessive self-reflection and marginality suggest to the reader his antecedents in the narrators of Edgar Allan Poe's stories and in Fyodor Dostoevski's Underground Man. He declares that his writing of the narrative is accompanied by a nagging toothache resulting from an exposed nerve and by the music of a street-corner violinist.

Macabéa, a nineteen-year-old orphan from the northeastern Brazilian province of Alagoas. Her parents died when she was an infant, and she was reared by an unloving and abusive aunt. Barely literate, her only education beyond three years of primary schooling was a short typing course. She has migrated to Rio de Janeiro, where she works in an office. Macabéa, born under an unlucky star, covers her blotchy face with a layer of white powder and suffers from a chronic dripping nose and a hacking cough; she emits an unpleasant body odor, for she rarely washes, and she exists on hot dogs, coffee, and soft drinks. Although she affirms her identity by asserting, "I am a typist and a virgin, and I like coca-cola," she is hardly aware of her own existence. What awareness she does have comes strictly through her senses.

Olímpico de Jesus Moreira Chaves, Macabéa's boyfriend, who has also emigrated from the Northeast. In many respects, he is a self-made character, starting with his name, adopted to mask the fact that his true surname, Jesus, marked him as illegitimate. He works in a metal factory transferring metal rods from one area to another, but he insists on calling himself a metallurgist. By murdering a rival and by becoming adept at petty theft, he has confirmed his manhood to himself. A curious artistic sensibility reveals itself in his carvings of effigies of saints, which he refuses to sell because he finds them so attractive. He has a morbid fascination for funerals, which terrify him but which he attends at least twice a week. Although being a bullfighter is his dream (he is fascinated by blood and knives), his goal is to become a politician.

Glória, Macabéa's much more competent officemate, a voluptuous and self-confident young woman. Although both the narrator and Macabéa describe her as ugly, she is well aware of her charms. The daughter of a butcher, she is well fed and lives on a street named after a general. Her animal magnetism and the attraction of her father's profession prove to be irresistible to Olímpico.

Madame Carlota, a talkative fortune-teller Madama Carlota is as interested in relating her own history to Macabéa as she is in revealing what the cards can tell about her client's destiny. She credits Jesus with her rise from prostitute to brothel owner to fortune-teller.

THE HOUSE BEHIND THE CEDARS

Author: Charles Waddell Chesnutt (1858-1932)
First published: 1900
Genre: Novel
Locale: North and South Carolina
Time: Late 1860's
Plot: Social realism

Rowena (Rena) Walden, the beautiful, young heroine of mixed race, whose skin is sufficiently light for her to pass as white. Reared as a black child in the small town of Patesville, Rena resigns herself to the limitations of her existence until the unexpected reappearance of her brother John. At his invitation, Rena joins him in South Carolina, where she passes for white, attends a white finishing school, is accepted into Charleston society, and falls in love with George Tryon, a chivalrous young white man. Idealistic and intelligent, Rena enjoys the freedom of her new situation but is troubled by the deception that she must practice to hide her background. Torn between her past and the bright promise of her future with Tryon, Rena risks discovery by rushing to her mother's sickbed in Patesville. When her secret is revealed and Tryon abandons her, Rena accepts a position as a teacher at a rural black school, but the lecherous advances of Jefferson Wain make her short stay there unbearable. The strain increases when Rena realizes that the school is located near Tryon's estate. In the end, the pressure breaks Rena. Deathly ill, she is returned to her mother's home by the faithful Frank Fowler and dies just before Tryon returns to attempt a reunion.

George Tryon, Rena's fiancé, an aristocratic white Southerner from North Carolina. Handsome, athletic, wealthy, and intelligent, Tryon takes pride in his independence, congratulating himself for being a tolerant and "liberal" man. A romantic, Tryon falls in love with Rena the moment he sees her and swears that he has no interest in her family background. His liberality fails him, however, when he is confronted with Rena's black heritage. Although Tryon abandons Rena and resumes his courtship of Blanche Leary, he is unable to bury his feelings for Rena. At the novel's end, he rushes to Patesville, apparently ready to stand up to societal prejudices, but discovers that Rena has died.

John Warwick, Rena's brother and Tryon's attorney, reared as **John Walden** in Patesville. Warwick, as light-skinned as his sister, moves to South Carolina as a young man and successfully passes as white. Assisted by the disruptions of the war and considerable good fortune, Warwick marries a plantation owner's daughter, becomes a successful lawyer, and inherits the property after his wife's death. Less sentimental than his sister and less tied to the past, Warwick accepts the necessity of cutting himself off from his mother, placing a high priority on his personal freedom and comfort.

Molly Walden, Rena's mother, a free black woman during the era of slavery whose relationship with a prominent planter produced Rena and John. Molly, who is almost as light-skinned as her children, enjoyed privileges as the mistress of a wealthy white man. Long after his death, she continues to feel superior to darker-skinned blacks, but she grudgingly accepts the personal sacrifice she must make to permit her children to advance in the world.

Jefferson Wain, the hypocritical and violent superintendent of black schools in Sampson County. Wain offers Rena a teaching position at a rural black school. It soon becomes evident that his intentions toward Rena are dishonorable. Rena is able to thwart his advances, but the strain of her situation contributes to her physical collapse.

Frank Fowler, an honest black laborer who loves Rena for herself. Fowler saved Rena's life when she was a girl, and he has loved her ever since despite realizing the hopelessness of his obsession. He finds her near death and returns her to her mother's home. Frank's unswerving devotion underscores the inherent values of black manhood, but it is only in her dying moments that Rena recognizes the value of Fowler's affection.

Judge Archibald Straight, an aging Patesville lawyer who encouraged John's early interest in the law and helped facilitate his escape from the town. Judge Straight is a tolerant and kindly man who is able to see beyond the prejudices of his class and time, but his efforts to assist Rena fail to avert tragedy.

Dr. Ed Green, a Patesville doctor who treats Rena and her mother. His racist theories regarding the genetic dangers of miscegenation inflame Tryon's outrage at Rena's deception. Green's proclamations also make Tryon afraid of the social ostracism that would result from public knowledge of his love for Rena.

Peter Fowler, Frank's father. Peter resents the affectations of the lighter-skinned blacks in Patesville and believes that his son is foolish to love Rena when his love is so obviously unrequited.

Blanche Leary, Tryon's blonde girlfriend, his mother's favorite. Beautiful and compliant, Blanche represents the stereotypical ideal of Southern womanhood, but Tryon finds her attractions somehow vacant next to Rena's.

— *Carl Brucker*

THE HOUSE BY THE CHURCHYARD

Author: Joseph Sheridan Le Fanu (1814-1873)
First published: 1863
Genre: Novel
Locale: Chapelizod, a suburb of Dublin
Time: Late eighteenth century
Plot: Horror

Mr. Mervyn, the son of Lord Dunoran, who was an Irish nobleman wrongly convicted and executed for the murder of a man named Beauclerc and whose estates and title were taken from his family because of his conviction. Mervyn takes a house in Chapelizod, a Dublin suburb, in order to find the real murderer and clear his father's name. With the help of Zekiel Irons, he aids in proving Paul Dangerfield guilty of Beauclerc's murder, and thus his father's innocence. He regains his family's good name, and by official action the title and estates are returned to him as his father's heir. As the new Lord Dunoran, he marries the daughter of the commanding general of the Royal Irish Artillery.

Paul Dangerfield (Charles Archer), a stranger who comes to Chapelizod about the same time as Mr. Mervyn. He is rich and liberal, qualities that quickly make him popular. He is really Charles Archer, the murderer of Beauclerc. He beats Dr. Sturk and later arranges for an operation for the doctor, hoping he will die, as the doctor was a witness to the murder of Beauclerc. Dangerfield's good works make it difficult for the authorities to believe he is really Charles Archer and a murderer. His guilt is ascertained; however, he cheats the gallows by dying in jail while awaiting trial.

Zekiel Irons, Archer's accomplice in the murder of Beauclerc. He lives in Chapelizod and becomes alarmed when Archer appears as Paul Dangerfield. Irons goes to Mervyn and gives him information about the murder of Beauclerc and a later murder committed by Archer.

Dr. Barnaby Sturk, a surgeon at the local garrison and a witness to Beauclerc's murder. He threatens Dangerfield, who then beats him terribly. Dr. Sturk regains consciousness long enough to give depositions revealing Archer-Dangerfield as his own assailant and the murderer of Beauclerc.

Charles Nutter, a man suspected of being Dr. Sturk's assailant. He finally proves that he is innocent.

Mrs. Sturk, the doctor's wife.

THE HOUSE BY THE MEDLAR TREE
(I Malavoglia)

Author: Giovanni Verga (1840-1922)
First published: 1881
Genre: Novel
Locale: Sicily
Time: Mid-nineteenth century
Plot: Impressionistic realism

Padron 'Ntoni Malavoglia (N-toh-nee mah-lah-VOHL-yee-ah), head of the once-prosperous family that lives by the medlar tree.

Bastianazzo (bah-stee-ahn-NAHZ-zoh), his son. His ambition to take black beans to Riposto to sell at a huge profit ruins the family when his boat, the *Provvidenza*, is wrecked.

La Longa, Bastianazzo's wife, who distrusts Uncle Crucifix, the moneylender, but signs over to his assignee her rights to the house when he repeatedly demands payment for his loan on the lost beans. She dies of cholera.

'Ntoni, their oldest son, who returns from military service and becomes a smuggler. Caught, he is sentenced to the galleys for five years.

Luca (LEW-kah), their second son, who is conscripted and killed in battle.

Alessio (ah-LEHS-see-oh), their youngest son, who earns the money to regain his house by the medlar tree.

Mena (MEH-nah), their oldest daughter.

Lia (LEE-ah), their youngest daughter, loved by Don Michele.

Uncle Crucifix Dumbbell, a local usurer who takes over the house after his loan to buy beans is not repaid.

Goosefoot, his assistant. Uncle Crucifix pretends to assign his loan to Goosefoot, hoping collection will thus be easier.

Don Michele, commander of the coast guard, who is stabbed by 'Ntoni.

Alfio Mosca (ahl-FEE-oh MOHS-kah), a carter who loves Mena.

A HOUSE FOR MR. BISWAS

Author: V. S. Naipaul (1932-)
First published: 1961
Genre: Novel
Locale: Trinidad
Time: The first half of the twentieth century
Plot: Comic realism

Mohun Biswas, a journalist. When he is born backward, equipped with a sixth finger, he is marked for bad luck. A small, thin boy, he is dreamy and naïve. After growing up in poverty, he has a succession of jobs. During a stint as a sign painter, he is tricked into marrying a member of the possessive Tulsi family. During the rest of his life, he tries to wean his wife from her family and to live in his own home without the Tulsis. When he is forty-two years old, he realizes both dreams, but four years later, he dies of heart disease.

Shama Tulsi Biswas, Mohun's wife. When he meets her, she is sixteen years old, pretty, and slim, with fine features and a nice smile. Unfortunately, after she marries Mohun, she remains a Tulsi and does not fall completely into the role of wife. When he lives with the Tulsis, she treats him with disrespect; when she lives elsewhere with him, she seizes every excuse to return home, often for months. When he takes her and their family to the house he has bought, she finally learns to love and respect him.

Raghu Biswas, Mohun's father. A man obsessed with saving money, he hides his horde so well that his family can never find it. Thinking that Mohun has fallen into a pond, he dives for him and drowns, leaving his wife penniless, with four children to support.

Bipti Biswas, Mohun's mother. A shy woman, she becomes broken and helpless after the death of her husband leaves her in poverty.

Tara, Bipti's older sister. She shows her wealth by adorning herself lavishly with gold and silver jewelry. A decent but domineering woman, she takes responsibility for her widowed sister, taking in her oldest niece and supporting, as well as managing, the rest of the family. It is she who pulls Mohun out of school for his unsuccessful apprenticeship to a pundit.

Mai Tulsi, Shama's mother. A dignified, thin-lipped woman who speaks very proper English, she has trained her large family to reflect her opinions on every matter and to obey her commands without thinking. She is Mohun's antagonist in the battle for his wife and his children.

Govind, the husband of one of Shama's sisters. Unlike Mohun, he endures the dominion of the Tulsis, joins them in mocking Mohun, and beats him, driving him out of the household. When Govind finally beats his own disobedient wife, he acquires her respect, as well as that of the rest of the family.

Savi Biswas, the oldest child of Mohun and Shama. Born at the Tulsi home, she is named by the Tulsis and reared largely by them. When she sings publicly, however, she discovers that the Tulsis can be spitefully jealous of anyone who surpasses the cousins. After Mohun's death, Savi returns from school abroad to support her mother. Ironically, she finds a job paying more than Mohun ever made.

Anand Biswas, Mohun and Shama's son, three years younger than Savi. Despite the fact that he spends much of his childhood with the Tulsis, he identifies with his father, adopting Mohun's contemptuous attitude toward the Tulsi family. Sensing his father's loneliness, at one point Anand chooses to stay with him. Rebellious laborers burn them out, and Anand never recovers from the terror of that experience and from his resulting anger at his father. When Mohun is dying, Anand promises to come home, but he does not come.

— *Rosemary M. Canfield Reisman*

THE HOUSE IN PARIS

Author: Elizabeth Bowen (1899-1973)
First published: 1935
Genre: Novel
Locale: France and England
Time: After World War I
Plot: Psychological realism

Miss Naomi Fisher, Karen Michaelis' friend. She helps Karen when the latter becomes pregnant and has a child by Max Ebhart, Naomi's fiancé. Her home is the setting for the story.

Leopold Moody, a nine-year-old boy. He has come to Naomi's house to see the mother he has never met, Karen Michaelis. When he learns she will not come, he tries to be indifferent, but his stoic attitude dissolves into tears. Only Mme Fisher can console him. He seems pleased when his mother's husband, Ray Forrestier, encourages him to go to his mother.

Henrietta Mountjoy, a sympathetic eleven-year-old girl, who tries to console Leopold that day at Naomi's house.

Mme Fisher, Naomi's invalid mother. She helps young Leopold accept, even if he cannot understand, the world in which he finds himself.

Karen Michaelis, Leopold's mother. After her child's birth, she gives up the child and her fiancé, who is not the boy's father. She finally marries her fiancé, Ray Forrestier, and allows him to overrule her resolve not to have her son in their home.

Max Ebhart, once Naomi's fiancé, he is the father of Leopold, the result of a one-night love affair with Karen. Brilliant and sensitive, he is driven by his predicament into suicide. He kills himself by slashing his wrists.

Ray Forrestier, Karen's fiancé at the time of her brief affair with Max. He eventually marries Karen, and it is he who insists that Leopold join the family, despite Karen's doubts.

HOUSE MADE OF DAWN

Author: N. Scott Momaday (1934-   )
First published: 1968
Genre: Novel
Locale: New Mexico and Los Angeles, California
Time: July 20-August 2, 1945, and January 26-February 28, 1952
Plot: Psychological realism

Abel (ah-BEHL), a World War II veteran who returns to Wolatowa, his native pueblo, in 1945. Thick-chested and stocky, but also agile and athletic, he was orphaned at the age of five, when his mother died, and has been reared by his grandfather, Francisco. Reserved and stoic in his dealings with others, he is out of harmony with the rich traditional life of Wolatowa, in part because of painful memories of childhood but also because of his traumatic war experiences. Sentenced to prison for killing an albino from his village whom he thought was a witch, he is paroled and "relocated" in Los Angeles, where he leads a rootless, alcoholic life.

Francisco, Abel's maternal grandfather. In his late seventies when Abel returns from the war, he was one of the great runners in Wolatowa's ceremonial races when he was younger but is now crippled by disease and a lifetime of hard work. He possesses great personal dignity and is devoted to the rich ceremonial traditions of Wolatowa, which are to him a harmonious mixture of Christian and pagan elements. His death in 1952 begins Abel's reaffirmation of the cultural values of his native place.

Father Olguin (ohl-GEEN), the priest at Wolatowa. Born in Mexico, he is small and swarthy. Because he is weary, is prematurely gray, and has one blind eye, he seems older than his years. He is extremely devout, but he is able to respect the non-Christian traditions of his people.

Fray Nicolás (nee-koh-LAHS), one of Father Olguin's predecessors at Wolatowa, known to Father Olguin only through his journal. Extremely devout, he could not understand his parishioners' religion of combined Christian and pagan elements and assumed that the latter were evidence of devil worship. Francisco was his altar boy.

Angela St. John, the wife of a Los Angeles physician, living temporarily near Wolatowa in 1945. Pale and dark-haired, she is beautiful but, perhaps because she is pregnant, she is disgusted with her own body. Her employment of Abel to cut wood leads to a brief love affair. She visits him seven years later in a Los Angeles hospital.

The albino, who humiliates Abel in the rooster-pull contest. His almost inhuman paleness is eerily combined with powerful physical strength. His apparently unmotivated malice causes Abel to assume that he is a witch and to kill him.

John Big Bluff Tosamah (toh-SAH-mah), who calls himself the Priest of the Sun and presides over religious ceremonies that include visions induced by peyote. Physically graceful, witty, and humorous, he is also loudmouthed and arrogant, and he frequently ridicules others. He is fairly sophisticated in matters of theology, however, and is deeply conscious of his own Kiowa traditions.

Milly, a Los Angeles social worker who becomes Abel's lover. She is a strong-figured, somewhat plain blonde who is graced with the ability to love in spite of a painful past that includes early poverty, abandonment by her husband, and the death of a four-year-old daughter.

Ben Benally (beh-NAHL-lee), a Navajo who is Abel's coworker and friend in Los Angeles. Unlike Abel, he is burdened with no painful memories of the reservation and intends eventually to return to it. Because he is at peace with himself, he is able to adjust to his "relocation" in Los Angeles. Sweet-natured and absolutely decent, he gives Abel his only coat when Abel leaves Los Angeles to return to Wolatowa.

Martinez (mahr-TEE-nehs), a corrupt Los Angeles policeman who extorts money from American Indians. His savage beating of Abel leads to Abel's return to Wolatowa.

— *Robert L. Berner*

HOUSE OF ALL NATIONS

Author: Christina Stead (1902-1983)
First published: 1938
Genre: Novel
Locale: Paris and its suburbs, London, and Amsterdam
Time: 1931
Plot: Social satire

Michel Alphendéry (mee-SHEHL ahl-fehn-day-REE), the technical economics expert at the Bertillon bank, considered by all who know him to be a brilliant man. He is a Marxist and is thought by the banking people to be an idealist and a utopian. Even more surprising to them, Alphendery is honest: He has a limited power of attorney for the bank, allowing him to buy and sell, sign checks, and make decisions, but he never steals or cheats. Although he dislikes the chicanery of the financiers, Alphendery continues working for Jules Bertillon out of loyalty, affection, and inertia, and because he needs money to support his mother and his estranged wife, Estelle, who is unfaithful to him. Alphendery's father was a lawyer and a small banker, and the son has been in finance since he was a small boy. Alphendery would like to make his fortune and get out of banking, but his big chance, in a grain deal with Leon and Jules, is ruined when Jules tries to manage the deal his way and bungles it.

Jules Bertillon (zhewlz behr-tee-YOH[N]), the real owner and policymaker of the Banque Mercure, a private bank in Paris. A fragile-looking, tall, elegantly dressed young man, Jules has the instincts of a gambler, and he makes fortunes for himself at Deauville (by betting on the horses) and on the stock exchange. Speculative and daring, Jules thinks that he can always make money. Jules is cynical, saying that a bank is a confidence trick. Alphendery says that Jules is a financial genius, bound to live and die rich. Most of the bank's clients are rich because Jules does not want to bother with the small fry or listen to them cry about losses. In an atmosphere of world depression, Jules wants to make money, betting on disaster. At one point, Jules says that William, Alphendery, and he should take the clients' 160 million francs and abscond, but Alphendery talks him out of the idea. Jules supports his wife, Claire-Josephe, his children, and most of his idle brothers.

William Bertillon, Jules's older brother, a tall, blond, plump, and staid man. He looks as if he is never troubled by a thought and he pretends to take no notice of the clients in the bank, but he listens to gather information. He nags Jules, but he has a single-minded affection for his brother. He will not hear a word against Jules from anyone else, and he will stand by his brother in the face of trouble. William has formed the Five Brothers Simla Company as a nest egg for the family, although it is a secret from Jules. When Jules is away, leading the life of the idle rich, William manages the banking routine. William holds Alphendery in true affection because of the employee's loyalty to Jules.

Henri Leon (ah[n]-REE lay-OH[N]), who sometimes does business with the Bertillons. He is one of the most brilliant grain traders and option placers on the Continent. Leon has clear brown eyes and long black hair brushed over his mostly bald skull. Short, with a gorilla's chest and dressed in flashy suits, Leon nevertheless gives off the image of power, wealth, and the ability to make money. He is proud of the number of women with whom he has slept and is obsessed with money-making. He falls in love with Margaret Weyman, a calculating American, and sets her up in an apartment. Uncharacteristically, he puts money in a trust for her, and he gives her a generous allowance for living expenses. Leon respects Alphendery's financial sense and his way with words, so Leon always asks Alphendery to compose letters for him, trying to get French and British state honors. In his early days, Julius Kratz was Leon's crony, but they later became bitter enemies.

Aristide Raccamond (ah-rihs-TEED rah-kah-MOH[N]), a Paris stock exchange runner who is always trying to worm his way into the inner circle of the Banque Mercure and to profit from its dealings. Ambitious, energetic, and envious, Raccamond has a sensually rounded body and a solemn, melancholy face. He used to be the office manager and secretary for Leon. Jules considers him unlucky and a bother. Raccamond is pushed to achieve by his plain wife, Marianne, who says that there is nothing in life except money.

Jacques Carriere (zhahk kahr-YEHR), a conceited and impudent young society bachelor, an acquaintance of Jules who frequents the bank. Alphendery says that Carriere is completely rotten, with no sound spot. Challenging Jules, Carriere bets him that England will not go off the sterling silver standard; if Jules loses, he will guarantee payments to Carriere for approximately three years. Jules agrees to pay 122 francs to the British pound, to the sum of 25,000 pounds every four months, a ruinous agreement. Carriere's lawyer makes the agreement even more unfair through substitute wording. The rumor in England is that Carriere will bleed Jules to death. Carriere's motivation is that he is jealous of Jules, whom he sees as fertile, while he sees himself as formless and unable to conceive properly.

Adam Constant (ah-DAHM koh[n]-STAH[N]), one of the bank's tellers, a Marxist and Alphendery's friend. At twenty-four years of age, convinced that his life will be short, he wants to go to China to join the Red Army. Instead, Jules sends him to England to set up an English branch of Bertillon's, the Leadenhall Securities Guarantee Corporation.

Jean Frere (zhah[n] frehr), another of Alphendery's Marxist friends, one who writes articles and book reviews for the *Workers' Almanac*. Frere lives in the country, where he has a garden. To some extent, Frere acts as Alphendery's socialist conscience. Alphendery does not want to embezzle money with Jules partly because of what Frere will think. Alphendery says that when Frere gives him some advice, after about a month Alphendery finds himself taking it.

Richard Plowman, the former head, now retired, of the Timor and Arafura Banking Corporation. He is the closest friend of Jules Bertillon. Richard has a sweet and obliging nature and frequently does favors for friends. The perfect Englishman, he has a long oval face, gray hair, and kind blue eyes. In and out of the bank at all hours, he was one of Jules's first believers.

Daniel Cambo, a wealthy man with a fortune of half a million guilders. He explains to the bankers that he is going into the bazaar business, selling unwanted goods. He will make money from other people's mistakes, from their bankruptcies and bad business judgments. He will deal in human dreck, not in dreck goods.

Davigdor Schicklgruber (DAH-veeg-dohr SHIH-kehl-grew-behr), a Rhineland Jew who resembles the ideal Aryan: blond, blue-eyed, tall, and well-muscled. He seems to be a fool, interested only in chasing women, but he works for Lord Zinovraud, a Scottish peer and multimillionaire. Like many others, Davigdor is a friend of Alphendery, partly because Alphendery gave him a good financial tip that helped Davigdor impress Lord Zinovraud. Davigdor is loyal to the Scottish peer because he expects to be remembered in his will.

— *Kate M. Begnal*

THE HOUSE OF BLUE LEAVES

Author: John Guare (1938-)
First published: 1971
Genre: Drama

Locale: Sunnyside, Queens, New York City
Time: October 4, 1965
Plot: Absurdist

Artie Shaughnessy, a zookeeper and would-be songwriter. Obsessed by a need to be famous, forty-five-year-old Artie fears that it may be too late for him. He looks to Bunny for the support Bananas is too sick to give, but he still has a soft spot for his wife. The play focuses on his attempts to find success, first by having his music blessed by the pope, then by kowtowing to Hollywood celebrities Corrinna Stroller and Billy Einhorn.

Bananas Shaughnessy, Artie's wife, once a fun-loving woman. She has since suffered a nervous breakdown. She is forty-four years old and appears in the play in a nightgown she has worn for the past six months; her eyes are red from crying. Frightened of Artie's threats to send her to a rest home, she does her best to prove that she is still competent and that Artie is wrong to leave her.

Ronnie Shaughnessy, the eighteen-year-old son of Artie and Bananas. He wears a brushcut and large glasses. At the time of the play, Ronnie is absent without leave from the Army. Another victim of Artie's thirst for fame, Ronnie once acted like an idiot in front of Hollywood director Billy Einhorn, who was looking for a boy Ronnie's age to play Huck Finn. Although he sneaks into Artie's apartment in the opening scene, he disappears and does not say anything or enter into the plot until he appears with a bomb intended to kill the pope. When he is discovered by nuns, he is wearing his old altar boy robes.

Bunny Flingus, the Shaughnessys' neighbor and Artie's mistress. Bunny, a plump thirty-nine-year-old gold digger, wants to ride Artie's coattails to fame. It is her idea to have Artie's music blessed by the pope and to "audition" for Corrinna Stroller. Bunny is a wonderful cook but refuses to cook for Artie until they are married. When it is clear that Artie will not succeed as a songwriter, Bunny leaves him for successful filmmaker Billy Einhorn.

Billy Einhorn, a famous Hollywood director. A lifelong friend exactly Artie's age (forty-five), Billy represents all the fame and fortune Artie wants. Although he does not appear in the first act, he is the main topic of conversation, and the high point of the act is Artie's phone call to Billy's home in California. Billy arrives in response to Corrinna's death. Billy's maudlin sentimentalizing is clearly bogus, and his grief over Corrinna disappears as soon as he sees Bunny and steals her from Artie.

Corrinna Stroller, a twenty-two-year-old movie starlet. She starred in Billy's film *Warmonger* but lost her hearing when a prop mine exploded during the filming. Artie sees her as his ticket to fame and plays his songs for her, but she does not hear them. Ronnie's bomb, intended for the pope, kills Corrinna.

— *John R. Holmes*

A HOUSE OF GENTLEFOLK
(Dvoryanskoye gnezdo)

Author: Ivan Turgenev (1818-1883)
First published: 1859
Genre: Novel
Locale: Russia
Time: The nineteenth century
Plot: Psychological realism

Marya Dmitrievna Kalitin (MAH-ryuh DMIHT-ree-ehv-nuh kah-LIH-tihn), a well-to-do widow, about fifty, fadingly pretty, sentimental, self-indulgent, tearful when crossed but sweet otherwise. She is easily taken in by Panshin's blandishments, and she succumbs also to Varvara's sly hypocrisy.

Fedor Ivanitch Lavretsky (FYOH-dohr ih-VAH-nihch lahv-REHT-skihy), called **Fedya** (FEH-dyuh), her cousin, rosy-cheeked, thick-nosed, curly-haired, well-built. As a boy, he was reared according to a Rousseauistic system rigorously applied by his father. After his father's death he attempted to get a university education to supplement his eccentric, secluded, narrow training. Following his marriage to Varvara, he gave up his formal schooling but continued to educate himself through private study. Naïvely trusting his wife to seek her own social entertainment, he was shocked to learn of her infidelity, and he immediately left her. Although he still broods bitterly on Varvara at times, he finds himself falling in love with Lisa. Having learned of Varvara's rumored death, he longs to marry Lisa despite the age difference between them, but his happiness over Lisa's acceptance of his suit is destroyed by Varvara's reappearance. For Lisa's sake and at Marya's insistence, he agrees to live with Varvara but only on a formal basis. He stays with her only briefly. He is finally left with memories of the happy time when he thought Lisa could be his, the only happy moments in his whole life. Lavretsky symbolizes the liberal Russian of Turgenev's day. He has attained a Westernized culture; he loves his country; and he wishes to apply democratic ideas in his relationship with the peasants who till his land according to the agricultural principles he has learned abroad. In appearance, character, and ideas, he resembles Solomin, the hero of *Virgin Soil*, who feels toward the factory workers as Lavretsky does toward the peasants.

Elisaveta Mihailovna Kalitin (eh-lih-zah-VEH-tuh mih-HAH-lov-nuh), called **Lisa**, Marya's slender, dark-haired daughter. Thoughtful and deeply religious, she is troubled because Lavretsky had left Varvara and has never seen their daughter. Despite Varvara's adultery, Lisa believes she should be forgiven and taken back. When it appears that Varvara has died, Lisa at first gently rejects Lavretsky's attentions. Later, recognizing his goodness and deep sincerity, and feeling a spiritual kinship with him despite his indifference to religion, she accepts him. Their happiness is destroyed by Varvara's return. Lisa says goodbye not only to Lavretsky but also to her family and the world, and she becomes a nun. As Lavretsky symbolizes one kind of Russian, Lisa represents another. Her education is limited; she has the standard learning and attainments of a girl of her class; she is traditionalist and conservative in her views. Religion, her comfort and stay from childhood on, offers a retreat in her sorrow.

Varvara Pavlovna (vahr-VAH-ruh PAHV-lov-nuh), Lavretsky's wife, a lovely, intelligent, charming, and gregarious woman who deceived her husband with a young French lover while giving Lavretsky the impression of being a devoted wife. Taking advantage of the rumor of her death, she leaves Paris and comes with her daughter to Vassilyevskoe to seek a reconciliation. Her attempts to win Lavretsky's pity fail, but he agrees to let her stay at Lavriky, where he had taken her as a bride. Because of Lisa and Marya, he lives with her briefly. When he leaves, Panshin becomes Varvara's lover. She soon moves to St. Petersburg and later to Paris, where she resumes her former life, somewhat subdued by age.

Vladimir Nikolaitch Panshin (vlah-DIH-mihr nih-koh-LAH-ihch PAHN-shihn), a government official, a handsome, self-confident, socially accomplished, multilingual, dissipated, cold, and false dilettante. Marya thinks him an eligible prospective son-in-law, but Marfa sees through him, as do Lemm and Lavretsky. After Lisa rejects his offer of marriage, he begins an affair with Varvara, who is later succeeded by a number of other women. He remains a bachelor.

Marfa Timofyevna Pestov (MAHR-fuh tih-moh-FYEHV-nuh pehs-TOHF), the eccentric, independent, bluntly truthful, and sharply critical sister of Marya's father.

Sergei Petrovitch Gedeonovsky (sehr-GAY peht-ROH-vihch geh-deh-on-OF-skih), a bachelor, a councilor, and an inveterate gossip and liar.

Christophor Fedoritch Lemm (krihs-toh-FOHR FYOH-do-rihch lehm), an old German music teacher who detests Russia but is too poor to leave it. He idolizes Lisa and becomes a sympathetic friend of Lavretsky.

Ivan Petrovitch (ih-VAHN), Lavretsky's father. Irresponsible when young and even after his marriage, he returns to Russia from France after his father's death with plans to bring some order and system into Russian life, starting with his own estate and his son. A combination of Anglomaniac, French liberal, and domestic despot, he dominates Fedya, even after his health breaks and he goes blind, until the son is freed by his father's death when Fedya is twenty-three. Turgenev uses Ivan to satirize the foolish efforts of some eighteenth and early nineteenth century Russian liberals to Westernize Russia hurriedly and by force.

Malanya Sergyevna (mah-LAH-nyuh sehr-GEHY-ehv-nuh), a former servant, Lavretsky's mother. Uneducated, submissive, timid, ailing, she dies when Fedya is a child.

Pavel Petrovitch Korobyin (PAH-vehl peht-ROH-vihch koh-ROH-bihn), Varvara's vain, greedy father, a retired general who left the army after an embezzlement scandal. He becomes the overseer of Lavretsky's estate until he is dismissed following Lavretsky's separation from Varvara.

Mihalevitch (mih-hah-LEH-vihch), Lavretsky's university friend who introduced him to Varvara. During a brief visit at Vasilyevskoe, he is noisy, brusque, agrumentative, and critical of what he calls Lavretsky's loafing, which he considers a primary Russian fault.

Glafira Petrovna (glah-FIH-ruh peht-ROHV-nuh), Ivan's harsh-voiced, haughty, dictatorial sister.

Elena Mihalovna (eh-LEH-nuh mih-HAH-lov-nuh), called **Lenotchka** (leh-NOHT-chkuh), Marya's younger daughter.

Nastasya Karpovna Ogarkov (nahs-TAH-syuh kahr-POHV-nuh oh-GAHR-kof), an elderly, childless widow, the cheerful, devoted companion of Marfa Timofyevna.

Agafya Vlasyevna (ah-GAH-fyuh VLAH-sehv-nuh), Lisa's nurse, a peasant who was formerly the mistress of Lisa's maternal grandfather. She is responsible for Lisa's early interest in religion.

Shurotchka (shew-ROHT-chkuh), a young orphan girl given to Marfa Timofyevna by the child's drunken, brutal uncle.

HOUSE OF INCEST

Author: Anaïs Nin (1903-1977)
First published: 1936
Genre: Novella
Locale: Indeterminate
Time: Indeterminate
Plot: Psychological realism

The narrator, easily taken for Anaïs Nin herself. The narrator identifies herself in a poetic and mysterious fashion before introducing the novella's other characters and, ultimately, the House of Incest. She is much more than a bystander throughout the work; for example, she describes her highly erotic relationship with Sabina.

Sabina, the narrator's lover, though the physical consummation of their love is not made explicit. Sabina is portrayed as the complementary missing half of the narrator, capable of all the passions except love, whereas the narrator is capable only of love. Sabina is also a liar; she lies even to herself. She is still essentially innocent and needs the illusions she spins in order to survive psychologically.

Jeanne, a simultaneously imperious and crippled figure fascinated by her image in the mirror and tortured by the fact that she is in love with her brother.

The paralytic, a writer unable to record a single word because of the inherent failure of language to record accurately the full complexity of his inner life.

The modern Christ, an empath so sensitive to other people that he has been essentially flayed alive, "crucified by his own nerves for all our neurotic sins."

The dancer, the novella's concluding figure. The dancer once lost her arms for clutching too firmly at everything she loved. Her arms are returned to her, and she dances toward an escape route from the House of Incest, seeking forms of love in which people do not merely love themselves in another.

— *Ira Smolensky and Marjorie Smolensky*

THE HOUSE OF MIRTH

Author: Edith Wharton (1862-1937)
First published: 1905
Genre: Novel
Locale: New York
Time: Early twentieth century
Plot: Naturalism

Lily Bart, a fascinating, beautiful young woman sacrificed to the false ideals of New York social life, the belief that a "good" marriage is preferable to a happy one and that appearances must be maintained, regardless of the expense. Through the machinations of a jealous wife whose husband has fallen in love with Lily, the hapless woman is eventually brought to social disgrace, poverty, and death.

Lawrence Selden, an intellectual young bachelor lawyer in love with Lily. Although he prefers to remain on the outskirts of New York high society, he is popular and invited into many fashionable homes. Always in the background, he tries to steer Lily's life for her, but he is too weak to marry her.

Gertrude Farish, called **Gerty**, Selden's cousin, who lives alone in a modest apartment and is much taken up with philanthropy. In desperation, Lily goes to her for help, but Gertrude can offer her little solace.

Mr. Rosedale, a young Jewish financier who is trying to enter the upper brackets of New York society. At the beginning of the story, when Lily retains her position in society, he wants to marry her. Later, after her conduct has been questioned and she is willing to marry him, he is no longer interested.

Percy Gryce, a shy young man protected from designing women by his strong-minded, possessive mother. He is much taken with Lily Bart because she shows great interest in his collection of Americana. Eventually, he is frightened off because of Lily's popularity with other men, and he ends up marrying Gwen Van Osburgh.

Mrs. Gryce, Percy's mother, a monumental woman with the voice of a public orator and a mind divided between concern for her son and the iniquities of her servants.

George Dorset, a mournful dyspeptic, unhappily married. He falls in love with Lily and thus arouses his wife's jealousy and resentment, bringing about the scandal that contributes to Lily's downfall.

Bertha Dorset, George Dorset's garrulous, pretty wife, who is vicious in her treatment of Lily Bart after she has learned that her husband has grown fond of her. Mrs. Dorset behaves indiscreetly with Ned Silverton, carries on a clandestine correspondence with Lawrence Selden, and has several other affairs, but she cannot tolerate her husband's affection for Lily.

Ned Silverton, a handsome, weak, young "poet of passion." Spoiled by wealthy patronesses, he develops too expensive a taste for bridge and incurs many gambling debts.

Mrs. Carrie Fisher, a striking divorcée. She takes pity on Lily in the midst of that young woman's poverty and tries to establish for her connections that will help her out of her predicament.

Mrs. Peniston, Lily's aunt, the widowed sister of Hudson Bart, who takes charge of her niece after the death of Lily's parents. Mrs. Peniston gives Lily little affection; however, she leaves her ten thousand dollars when she dies, with instructions that Lily is to use the money in payment of her debts.

Charles Augustus Trenor, called **Gus**, an investment broker, and

Judy Trenor, prominent New York society people. Lily is invited to many parties and cruises on their yacht. Mrs. Trenor seems to exist solely as a hostess, while Mr. Trenor is in Wall Street and deeply interested in his business affairs. He invests for Lily some money she has won at bridge and gets large returns from the small sum. Later, Lily finds out that the returns have been from Trenor's pocket and that she owes him ten thousand dollars. This debt and its implications horrify Lily, and her attempt to repay it precipitates the cause of her breakdown and subsequent death from an overdose of chloral.

Jack Stepney and

Grace Stepney, Lily Bart's cousins. Typical in their conforming attitudes, they obey all the social forms and are shocked by Lily's behavior.

Gwen Van Osburgh, the woman, "reliable as roast mutton," whom Percy Gryce marries. She has a deep affinity with Gryce; they share the same prejudices and ideals and have the same ability to make other standards nonexistent by ignoring them.

Mr. Wetherall and

Mrs. Wetherall, guests at Bellemont, the Dorset estate. They belong to the vast group of people who go through life without neglecting to perform a single one of the gestures executed by the social puppets that surround them.

THE HOUSE OF THE DEAD
(Zapiski iz myortvogo doma)

Author: Fyodor Dostoevski (1821-1881)
First published: 1861-1862
Genre: Novel

Locale: A prison in Siberia
Time: Late 1840's to early 1850's
Plot: Autobiographical

Alexander Petrovich Goryanchikov (peh-TROH-vihch gohr-YAN-chih-kov), the narrator of the main body of the work, a former convict and nobleman. He has a philosopher's curiosity about the characters of people, sometimes speaking in the voice of a social reformer but more often simply awed and fascinated by the human soul itself. His incarceration has changed his life, but he writes a dispassionate memoir. He has found in the prison his ideal observatory, examining there the many strange specimens to be found among the souls of men. Goryanchikov supposedly was put in prison for murdering his young wife out of jealousy, but it soon becomes clear that Goryanchikov is, as the author himself was, a political prisoner. It also becomes clear (as the details of the author's own incarceration reveal) that the narrator is an autobiographical figure.

Sushilov (sew-SHIH-lov), a prisoner who works as Goryanchikov's servant, a literal glutton for punishment. He is pitiable, humble, and even downtrodden, although none of the prisoners has trampled on him. Without being asked, he binds himself to Goryanchikov and takes on every dull and ignoble personal duty that prison life allows. For his efforts, he receives the inconsequential money that Goryanchikov can, intermittently, pay him and the privilege of serving this (only nominally, given his incarceration) superior person. For these privileges, he is painfully, ridiculously grateful. It is known around the prison that Sushilov had "changed places"; that is, he was paid to exchange his identity and lighter sentence for that of another prisoner. This practice was not unheard of in the Russian prison system of the time. Sushilov's exchange is notorious among the prisoners, however, because he exchanged simple banishment for an indefinite period of hard labor in a military prison, for the price of one silver ruble and a red shirt. Sushilov is incorruptible. His is a pure nature, an example of how humble and utterly selfless humans can be.

Aley (AH-lay), a young Tartar prisoner, a youth of inner and outer beauty. Affectionate, warm, and capable of great tenderness of feeling, it is only his strong feeling for duty that has brought him to the prison. His paternalistic elder brothers had, without announcing their purpose, commanded that he join them in a raiding party. Asking no questions (such was his filial devotion), Aley obeyed, ending up, like them, in prison. The narrator is heartened to find a young man of such natural superiority in the prison and is cheered by his straightforward acts of friendship. Aley is also clever, curious, and quick to learn. Goryanchikov is confident that the quality of Aley's character will be proof against corruption in any circumstance. Later, writing his memoirs and remembering Aley, he does not worry about him. He only wonders, wistfully, where he is.

Akim Akimovich (ah-KIHM ah-KIH-moh-vihch), a prisoner who assists Goryanchikov in his first days in the prison. He is naïve, illiterate, extraordinarily moralistic, captious, exacting, and quarrelsome, with a highly Teutonic punctilio. He is phenomenally honest; he will intervene in any injustice, regardless of whether it is a concern of his. He is simple to the last degree; he tries seriously, for example, to argue the prisoners out of their habitual stealing. At the time of his arrest, he had been the commander of a fortress in the Caucasus and had caught a neighboring princeling in an act of treachery. Having brought him to the fortress, Akimovich read him a detailed lecture on how a friendly prince ought to conduct himself in the future and, in conclusion, shot him. Fully aware of the irregularity of his action, he reported it at once to the authorities and was tried, convicted, and sent to prison. Many years later, still considering himself the injured party, he is unable to understand that he did anything he should not have.

Aristov (ah-RIH-stov), the prison's foremost informer. He had been an informer and a blackmailer before his time in prison and had sold the lives of ten men to ensure the immediate gratification of his thirst for the coarsest and vilest pleasures. He had become so addicted to these pleasures that, though an intelligent man, he had taken foolish chances and was sent to prison. The narrator calls him a lump of flesh with teeth and a stomach who, for the smallest gross pleasure, is capable of the most cold-blooded violence; he is an example of the lengths to which the purely physical side of a human can go, unrestrained by any internal standard or discipline.

Orlov, a criminal among criminals. He is an uncommonly evil evildoer, a cold-blooded murderer of old men and children, a man of terrifying strength of will and proudly conscious of that strength. He is contrasted with fleshy and torpid criminals, such as Aristov. In Orlov, one sees only boundless energy, thirst for action, thirst for vengeance, and thirst for the attainment of his goals. He has a strange arrogance, frank and without presumption, as if there were no authority on earth to which he would submit. Orlov has been sentenced to flogging, and this punishment he hurries along, shortening an interim period of recuperation to get on with his plan to escape. Here, however, he overestimates himself, and he dies from his punishment.

— *Fritz Monsma*

THE HOUSE OF THE SEVEN GABLES: A Romance

Author: Nathaniel Hawthorne (1804-1864)
First published: 1851
Genre: Novel

Locale: Salem, Massachusetts
Time: 1850
Plot: Gothic

Colonel Pyncheon, a stern Massachusetts magistrate who, during the famous witchcraft trials of the seventeenth century, sent to his death a man whose property he coveted for himself. Cursed by his innocent victim, the colonel died on the day his big new house, the House of the Seven Gables, built on his victim's land, was officially opened to guests.

Matthew Maule, Colonel Pyncheon's victim, who swore that his unjust accuser should drink blood, as Colonel Pyncheon did when he died.

Thomas Maule, the son of Matthew Maule. As the head carpenter building the House of the Seven Gables, young Maule took an opportunity to build a secret recess in which was hidden the deed by which the Pyncheons hoped to claim a vast domain in Maine.

Jaffrey Pyncheon, one of Colonel Pyncheon's nineteenth century descendants and a man like his ancestor in many ways. A judge, a member of Congress at one time, a member of many boards of directors, and an aspirant to the governorship of his state, he is a rich man who through his own efforts has multiplied the fortune he inherited from his uncle. Although he tries to present himself in a good light, Jaffrey Pyncheon is a hard man and not entirely honest. He destroys one of his uncle's wills that names his cousin Clifford as heir, and he stands by while his cousin is wrongly sent to prison for a murder he did not commit. Convinced that his wronged cousin knows of additional family wealth hidden by their uncle, Jaffrey threatens the broken man with confinement in an insane asylum if the hiding place of the remaining wealth is not revealed. Fortunately for his cousin, Jaffrey dies of natural causes induced by emotion while making his threats.

Clifford Pyncheon, Jaffrey's unfortunate cousin, who serves a thirty-year prison term for allegedly murdering his uncle, who really died of natural causes. A handsome, carefree, beauty-loving man at one time, he emerges from prison three decades later a broken, pale, and emaciated wreck of a human being, content to hide away in the House of the Seven Gables, where he is looked after by his sister Hepzibah and their young cousin Phoebe. Clifford's mind is weakened, and his spirit so broken by misfortune that he actually does strange, if harmless, acts, so that Jaffrey's threat to force Clifford into an asylum could be made good. At Jaffrey's unexpected death, Clifford feels a great release after having been oppressed by his cousin for so long. Clifford, his sister, and Phoebe Pyncheon inherit Jaffrey's fortune and have the promise of a comfortable life in the future.

Hepzibah Pyncheon, Clifford's sister, who lives alone for many years in shabby gentility in the House of the Seven Gables while her brother is in prison. She has few friends, for she seldom leaves the house, and she is so near-sighted that she always wears a frown, making people think she is a cross and angry woman. After the return of her brother from prison, she sets up a little shop in her house to try to provide for herself and Clifford, to whom she is devoted. Opening the shop is very difficult for her, as she dislikes meeting people and believes that entering trade is unladylike for a member of the Pyncheon family.

Phoebe Pyncheon, a young, pretty, and lively girl from the country. She comes to live with Hepzibah when her mother, a widow, remarries. Phoebe takes over the little cent-shop and makes it a profitable venture for Hepzibah. Phoebe also brings new life to the House of the Seven Gables by cheering it with her beauty and song, as well as by tending the neglected flowers and doing other homely tasks. She is highly considerate of her elderly cousins and spends much of her time entertaining Clifford.

Mr. Holgrave, a liberal-minded young daguerreotypist who rents a portion of the House of the Seven Gables from Hepzibah. An eager, energetic young man of twenty-two, he falls in love with Phoebe Pyncheon, and they are engaged to be married. When Phoebe inherits a third of Jaffrey's large fortune, Holgrave decides to become more conservative in his thinking. It is he who reveals the secret recess hiding the now useless deed to the vast tract of land in Maine. He knows the secret because he is a descendant of Thomas Maule. In fact, his name is Maule, but he hides his true identity by assuming for a time the name of Holgrave.

Uncle Venner, an old handyman befriended by the Pyncheons. He is one of the few persons of the town to accept Hepzibah and Clifford as friends when they are in unfortunate circumstances.

THE HOUSE OF THE SLEEPING BEAUTIES
(Nemureru bijo)

Author: Yasunari Kawabata (1899-1972)
First published: 1960-1961
Genre: Novella
Locale: An unnamed hot-spring resort in Japan
Time: 1960
Plot: Psychological realism

Yoshio Eguchi, a sixty-seven-year-old man. A light sleeper with a tendency to have bad dreams, he apparently has had several affairs and remembers the "ugliness" of spending nights with tragic, sad women. Given the opportunity to sleep next to young virgins, heavily drugged and therefore incapable of revealing anything about their lives, he longs for more than the physical touch he is allowed. In the five nights that he spends with six young women, he relives events in his life, all seemingly randomly evoked associations with each woman. Although conscious of the "dreariness" of old age and approaching death, he is indignant about the cavalier attitude to death he finds in the establishment.

Kiga, Eguchi's friend, who introduces him to this special house for older men. Kiga describes the experience of sleeping next to a drugged young woman as "sleeping with a secret Buddha."

The Woman, the unnamed manager of the house, a small woman in her mid-forties with thin lips, a youthful voice, and a calm and steady manner. Polite but firm, she serves Eguchi tea and delivers clear instructions about the strict rules of the house before taking him up to the room with red curtains where he sleeps with a young girl. Her cold efficiency is epitomized by her quick action in removing dead bodies to another establishment and by her ruthless advice to Eguchi to make do with the second girl when one dies during the night.

The First Sleeping Beauty, a short young woman not quite twenty years old, with long hair and wearing no cosmetics. To Eguchi, she gives off the scent of a nursing baby, bringing back several memories, including those of his three daughters as babies and of a young woman with whom he had an affair in his youth.

The Second Sleeping Beauty, described as a "young witch" with deep red lipstick, pink fingernails, and slightly crooked teeth. Her scent brings memories and fantasies associated with peonies and camellias to Eguchi and reminds him primarily of the courtship and marriage of his youngest daughter and a trip they took.

The Third Sleeping Beauty, a small girl with a small face who looks about sixteen years old. Her deathlike sleep reminds Eguchi of his affair only three years earlier with a young married woman in her twenties and provokes phantasms of hyacinths and orchids.

The Fourth Sleeping Beauty, a large, full-bodied, white-skinned young woman who evokes pity in Eguchi and brings a dream of white butterflies.

The Fifth and Sixth Sleeping Beauties, two women Eguchi sees on his last visit. One is rough, wild, dark, and possibly a foreigner; she momentarily rouses a violent passion in Eguchi to strangle her. She dies during the night. The other woman is gentler, more elegant, and fair. Sandwiched between them, Eguchi has a series of erotic nightmares, ending with one associated with red dahlias.

— *Shakuntala Jayaswal*

THE HOUSE OF THE SPIRITS
(La casa de los espíritus)

Author: Isabel Allende (1942-)
First published: 1982
Genre: Novel
Locale: An unnamed South American country much like Chile
Time: The 1920's through the early 1970's
Plot: Magical Realism

Esteban Trueba (ehs-TEH-bahn trew-EH-bah), a landowner and conservative politician. His primary qualities are pride and ambition. After the death of his fiancée, Rosa del Valle, Trueba moves to the long-neglected plantation of Tres Marías and transforms it into a model estate. After marrying Rosa's younger sister Clara, he becomes the father of three legitimate children. In later years, Esteban's political conservatism and his autocratic behavior cause him to be alienated from his family. He wields power unfairly and cruelly. Only after his own granddaughter becomes a victim of the reactionary regime does Esteban come to understand his errors.

Clara del Valle Trueba, his wife. From her atheistic, liberal father and her suffragist mother, Clara inherits her idealism and her independence. Early in her childhood, her family discovers that she can predict the future and commune with spirits. After marrying Esteban, she works to improve the lot of his tenants, but gradually she becomes almost totally involved with the supernatural. After her death, Clara appears to her granddaughter in prison, inspiring her to survive. She challenges Alba to record the life of the family.

Blanca Trueba de Satigny (sa-tihn-yee), their daughter. When she is found to be pregnant by Pedro Tercero García, Blanca is forced by her father to marry a sinister count. Shortly before her daughter Alba is born, she runs away from him and returns home. During the following years, Blanca often sees Pedro secretly, and after the coup she leaves the country with him.

Pedro Tercero García (tehr-SEH-roh gahr-SEE-ah), one of the Tres Marías peasants. A leftist leader, Pedro is also Blanca's lover and the father of her child. When his involvement with Blanca is discovered, Pedro is attacked by Esteban Trueba, but he escapes and moves to the capital. He achieves fame as a radio singer and then becomes a public official in the Socialist government. At the end of the novel, though he is appalled at the fate of his people, Pedro can at least look forward to spending the rest of his life with Blanca.

Alba Trueba (born **Alba de Satigny**), the daughter of Blanca and Pedro and the adored granddaughter of Esteban Trueba. When she joins other students in revolutionary activities, she is arrested and tortured, but she courageously refuses to betray her friends or her lover, Miguel. After her release, she remains with her grandfather, and together they undertake the writing of *The House of the Spirits*.

Esteban García (ehs-TEH-bahn), the evil son of Esteban Trueba's oldest bastard child. He is attracted to Alba, but he hates her for being Trueba's legitimate grandchild. Years later, as Colonel García, one of the most feared men in the police state, he catches Alba in his net and avenges himself by brutalizing her.

Rosa del Valle, Clara's sister. Rosa intended to marry Esteban until her untimely murder by the hands of political antagonists of her wealthy father. Rosa represents otherworldliness, outside this corrupt time and place. She has green hair and a mermaidlike body. Her death shocks Clara into nine years of silence, providing an early lesson into unbelievable realities that Clara will confront throughout her life.

The count, a fortune hunter who marries Blanca. His only function in the text is as a metaphor for the corruption, decadence, and continual encroachment of the Old World on the New. He robs the New World's indigenous inhabitants of their customs, traditions, and soul. His sexual exploitation of the Indian servants reflects his stealing of their histories and their resources. For a minor character, his role in the novel is significant, for it is part of the nonfictional record.

Barrabás (bah-rrah-BAHS), a dog, the closest companion to Clara during her early years. His name is the first word of the novel and one of the last. He shows up at various moments in the text as a unifying symbol that encapsulates time and space and as a creature that crosses reality with fantasy. He is a constant reminder of Clara and what she stands for; he also represents circular time, for he never stays in the past but is continually brought forward in the text. In the conclusion, he is brought up from the basement (the past) and will serve as a rug in Alba's room, which was Clara's room. He will thus be a witness to her writing as he was to Clara's. Barrabás functions ultimately as a bridge through time and memory and, along with Alba, as a signifier of the future.

— *Rosemary M. Canfield Reisman*

THE HOUSE ON MANGO STREET

Author: Sandra Cisneros (1954-)
First published: 1984
Genre: Novel
Locale: A Latino neighborhood in Chicago
Time: Mid-1960's
Plot: Bildungsroman

Esperanza Cordero (ehs-pehr-AHN-sah), a preteenage girl and beginning writer who narrates a chronicle of her Latino neighborhood in Chicago. She describes how some women are victimized by men, and how others resist traditional roles. Briefly, as she begins to develop sexually, she idolizes Sally, a pretty girl whose father beats her for seeing boys. Esperanza is raped when she accompanies Sally to a carnival. To become a writer, she seeks guidance, friendship, and encouragement from Alicia, a struggling student; her friend Minerva; and her Aunt Guadalupe. Her family's "sad" house embarrasses and pains her yet is the catalyst for her imagination and the source of her identity. Esperanza leaves Mango Street but vows to return to her community, her source of inspiration. She often describes a dream house and insists on her need for a house of her own.

Sally, the beautiful older girl whom Esperanza admires and at first tries to emulate. Sally, in makeup and nylons, is attractive to boys. Her strict father equates beauty with trouble, so he confines her inside and beats her for talking to them. The night Esperanza is assaulted at the carnival, Sally has gone off with a boy, abandoning her. Sally escapes her father by marrying a salesman but finds she has traded one imprisonment for another.

Alicia (ah-LEE-see-ah), a struggling university student whose mother has died. As eldest daughter, she must run the house and care for her large family. She gets up with "the tortilla star" to make the day's food. Like Sally, she has a domineering father, but she escapes the house by taking classes. Alicia convinces Esperanza that Mango Street will always be her home, thus instilling in her younger friend a sense of social responsibility and self-determination.

Elenita (eh-lehn-EE-tah), the "witch woman" who reads Esperanza's cards. Elenita reads "a home in the heart" for Esperanza, who leaves disappointed because she wants a real house. Elenita's divination, however, indicates that Esperanza will create a home for herself through her inner life and her writing. Elenita inspires Esperanza with her knowledge of old Mexican folkways and magic.

Guadalupe (gwah-dah-LEW-peh), Esperanza's **Aunt Lupe**, a former swimmer who is now terminally ill and bedridden. Esperanza and her friends ridicule Aunt Lupe in a game. Later, Esperanza feels guilty and sad, so she brings Aunt Lupe books and reads to her. Esperanza shares her poems with Aunt Lupe, who is the first person to encourage her to keep writing.

Minerva (mee-NEHR-vah), a girl slightly older than Esperanza who has two children and an absent husband. They share each other's poems. Minerva's desperation is a fate Esperanza will avoid. Minerva's life is troubled, most of all by her husband. He returns occasionally, talks his way into the house, then inevitably beats her. To escape her troubles, Minerva writes poetry on scraps of paper.

Lucy, Esperanza's new friend from Texas. Lucy is truly a little girl, in contrast to Esperanza's other friends in the barrio who have matured quickly from exposure to the adult world and by social necessity.

Rachel, Lucy's little sister. Rachel is the talker for the two sisters.

Magdalena Cordero (mahg-dah-LEH-nah), called **Nenny**, Esperanza's little sister. Nenny represents the world of childhood innocence Esperanza is about to leave behind.

— *JoAnn Balingit*

THE HOUSE ON THE EMBANKMENT
(Dom na naberezhnoy)

Author: Yuri Trifonov (1925-1981)
First published: 1976
Genre: Novel
Locale: Moscow and Bruskovo
Time: Late 1930's to early 1970's
Plot: Psychological realism

Vadim Alexandrovich Glebov (vah-DIHM ah-lehk-SAN-droh-vihch GLEH-bov), a literary critic whose life has been defined by envy, anger, and caution. He avoids taking firm stands on any issue until the last possible moment, avoids contradicting people, and carefully nurtures his relationships without growing too close, all of which result in his ability to fit in with practically any circle of people without actually committing himself to being a part of any one group exclusively. As a boy, he enjoyed special authority among his friends because his mother worked at a cinema to which he could take his friends without paying. That authority vanished when Lev Shulepnikov moved to the neighborhood because Lev owned a film projector. Glebov eventually enters an institute to study literature, later becoming the lover of Sonya Ganchuk, his adviser's daughter. When an attempt is made to oust his adviser, Glebov does not rise to his defense, which in essence is an act of betrayal. Shortly thereafter, he abandons Sonya. By the end of his career, he is a well-ensconced establishment figure in literary circles, even having the uncommon privilege of being allowed to travel abroad as part of his duties.

Lev Mikhailovich Shulepnikov (mih-KHAH-ih-loh-vihch shew-LEHP-nih-kov), or **Shulepa** (shew-LEH-pah), a childhood friend of Glebov and the chief object of Glebov's childhood envy. Arrogant and bold because of his stepfather's influence, he owns foreign toys, wears good clothing, and is the object of his neighbors' respect and envy. Separated from Glebov during the war, Lev again encounters him at the institute. Eventually, Lev is party to the attempt to oust Professor Ganchuk. When his second stepfather loses his influence, Lev ceases to enjoy his many privileges and ends up poor, haggard, and working in a dead-end job.

Nikolai Vasilievich Ganchuk (nih-koh-LAY gahn-CHEWK), a professor of literature. Although a literary scholar and intellectual, Ganchuk nevertheless idealistically and rather blindly accepts socialist ideology. A participant in the ideological and intellectual literary wars of the 1920's, Ganchuk is fiercely interested in literature and discusses literature and literary criticism with uncommon verve. When Glebov enrolls at the institute, Ganchuk becomes his adviser and champions his cause for graduate student status. When Glebov fails to defend him some years later, Ganchuk forgives him. Within an hour after he is finally removed from the department, he is spotted thoroughly enjoying a pastry in a shop. At the age of eighty-six, after he moves into a much smaller apartment, he is still busy, subscribing to eighteen newspapers and keeping up with popular science and television, and he still longs to hold on to life.

Narrator, a childhood friend of Glebov who remains unidentified in the story. His childhood is consumed with envy of Anton Ovchinnikov, because of the latter's intellectual brilliance, and of Glebov, because of Glebov's ability to get along with anybody. In his old age, the narrator remembers his childhood friends and childhood happiness with scorn and bitterness.

Sonya Ganchuk, Professor Ganchuk's daughter and Glebov's lover during his years at the institute. She is submissive, kind, and sympathetic. Sonya's first response to all people is pity, which sometimes leads to absurdities such as pitying the victimizer almost as much as the victim. She falls in love with Glebov in sixth grade, but he does not think twice about her until he is studying at the institute. Glebov abandons her shortly after her father loses his position. She eventually dies, before her father does.

Boris Lvovich Astrug (LVOH-vihch AH-strewg), a graduate student and member of Ganchuk's clique. He is a poor lecturer, unable to make an impression on people. On that pretext, he is discharged from his position as part of the attack on Ganchuk.

Druzyaev (drew-ZYAH-ehv), the dean of studies at the institute. To discredit Ganchuk, Druzyaev attempts to persuade Glebov to find another adviser on the pretext of avoiding the appearance of nepotism.

Anton Ovchinnikov (ov-CHI-nih-kov), another of Glebov's childhood friends. Modest, musical, and seemingly all-knowing, Anton at an early age senses that his friends are changing and that their carefree childhood has passed irrevocably.

— *Donald E. Livingston, Jr.*

THE HOUSE ON THE HILL
(La casa in collina)

Author: Cesare Pavese (1908-1950)
First published: 1949
Genre: Novel
Locale: Northern Italy
Time: 1943-1945
Plot: Psychological realism

Corrado (kohr-RAH-doh), the narrator, a science teacher in a private school. He is a forty-year-old, self-absorbed bachelor. He is addicted to solitude and agrees with a friend who says that he is bad-tempered, proud, and afraid. He is afraid above all of commitment, either to the people who love him or to the political causes for which his friends and acquaintances are dying, such as Fascism, anti-Fascism, and Communism. The action of the novel is generated as Corrado moves between the city of Turin and the surrounding Piedmont hills, trying to escape the opposing armies and the civil war that begins after Benito Mussolini's fall. Corrado finally escapes to his peasant parents' home, where he ends his narration. Although he finds some feeling of peace in his understanding that he can honor the dead for their sacrifice for their beliefs, Corrado still lives in fear and shame, isolated and alienated.

Cate (KAH-tay), a nurse and anti-Fascist activist. About eight years before the period covered by the novel, Corrado had a love affair with Cate, then an awkward, thin working girl. Her dreams of the future encompassed little more than learning to type and getting a job in a big store. Corrado broke with her in a rather brutal fashion. Eight years later, she is an attractive, courageous, self-possessed woman. She is able to risk her life in anti-Fascist activities, yet is understanding and tolerant of Corrado's weakness. She carefully avoids frightening him by forcing him to commit himself to her or to her son, Dino. She is imprisoned by the Germans, and her fate is unknown as the book ends.

Dino (DEE-noh), Cate's son. He is a playful, imaginative boy who becomes hardened by growing up in the anarchistic turmoil of World War II Italy. Corrado befriends him and finds out that his real name also is Corrado; he realizes that Dino may be his son. Cate, understanding the panic that such a relationship would produce in Corrado, says that he is not the boy's father. Dino grows apart from Corrado and disappears to join the anti-Fascist resistance. His fate is unknown at the end of the book.

Anna Maria, an elegant, rich woman from Corrado's past who appears in the novel only in his memory. She was his lover after he split with Cate. Corrado wanted to marry her, but he came to feel that she was playing with him for her amusement. She took him to the point of suicide, caused him to abandon his planned career as an academic scientist, and embittered him toward women.

Elvira, a forty-year-old unmarried woman who, with her mother, is Corrado's landlady. She loves Corrado, who has contempt for her buttoned-down personality and bony body. She has little interest in public events, only a vague sense of loyalty toward the government in power, but she has the courage to protect Corrado and Dino from the Germans.

Gallo, an old friend of Cate and Corrado. He shared Corrado's youthful dreams of starting a rural school and reforming the countryside. He was killed early in the war.

Fonso, an eighteen-year-old factory worker. He is a cynical, irreverent anti-Fascist who disappears into the hills as a resistance fighter. Fonso, able to commit himself in ways beyond Corrado's ability, becomes Dino's model and hero. Dino leaves Corrado to join Fonso, whose fate is unknown at the end of the book.

— *William E. Pemberton*

THE HOUSE WITH THE GREEN SHUTTERS

Author: George Douglas (George Douglas Brown, 1869-1902)
First published: 1901
Genre: Novel
Locale: Rural Scotland
Time: Late nineteenth century
Plot: Regional

John Gourlay, a Scots merchant. He works hard to become rich and is proud of his house with the green shutters and his other possessions. His pride is insolent; he simply wants more than other people and to be acknowledged as superior. While he works hard, he is also mean, stingy, boastful, and evil. He is ashamed of his weakling son and his slovenly wife. He goes mad and, in his madness, goads his son into murdering him. He dies with no friends and with his wealth all but gone.

Mrs. Gourlay, Gourlay's wife. She was once a pretty woman, but she has become slatternly, having been denied love by her husband. She lavishes all her affection upon her son, who is her only reason for living. She is both a slattern and a bore. After her son's death, she commits suicide, knowing she is consumed by cancer.

Janet Gourlay, their daughter. She also commits suicide after her brother's death.

Young John Gourlay, Gourlay's weak, cowardly, but boastful son. He is unambitious, and only his father's influence keeps him in school. His father wants him to become a minister, but he cannot do the required work at college and is finally expelled for drunkenness and insubordination. Tortured at home by his father, he finally kills him with a poker. After the murder, he commits suicide by taking poison.

James Wilson, a man who returns to Gourlay's village with sufficient money to become the merchant's competitor. By honest, friendly dealing with his customers he expands his business and drives Gourlay into financial ruin.

HOUSEHOLD SAINTS

Author: Francine Prose (1947-   )
First published: 1981
Genre: Novel
Locale: New York City
Time: 1949-late 1960's
Plot: Fable

Joseph Santangelo, a butcher with a thriving business on Mulberry Street. In spite of the fact that he is usually guilty of tipping the scales with his thumb when he is weighing meat, his female customers never complain of being cheated because he gives them total admiration and attention.

Carmela Santangelo, Joseph's mother, who makes sausage from an old and secret recipe. The sausage accounts in large part for the popularity of the market.

Catherine Falconetti, who marries Joseph as a result of her father losing a bet in a pinochle game. Still a virgin and uninitiated in sexual jokes and play, she does not understand what Joseph means when he rubs her hand with his "cheating" thumb, but Joseph understands for the first time the value of maidenhood.

Theresa Santangelo, the daughter of Catherine and Joseph, who at an early age displays many of her grandmother's traits, especially her preoccupation with religion and the saints.

Augie Santangelo, who married Evelyn, sold his share of the butcher shop to his brother Joseph, and with Evelyn moved away to take up a new kind of life, different from that of his immediate family.

Lino Falconetti, Catherine's father, the owner of a radio repair shop across the street from the butcher shop. Whereas the butcher shop is a success, the radio repair shop is not, because radios are no longer in demand.

Nicky Falconetti, the son of Lino and brother of Catherine. He is also unlucky in pinochle and in practically everything else. Nicky's passion is the Saturday afternoon broadcast of the Metropolitan Opera Company.

— *Mary Rohrberger*

THE HOUSEHOLDER

Author: Ruth Prawer Jhabvala (1927-   )
First published: 1960
Genre: Novel
Locale: New Delhi, India
Time: The 1950's
Plot: Fiction of manners

Prem, a newly married young teacher of Hindi at an undistinguished Delhi college. Himself a second-class graduate of a college in the smaller city of Ankhpur, where his father was the principal, Prem is inexperienced in all of his new roles: as teacher, as husband, as father-to-be, and as lonely resident of a big city where he knows few people. During the course of the novel, Prem slowly becomes accustomed to and more competent in his new life, especially in the important role of householder, a concept that includes the assumption of husbandly, parental, and economic responsibilities. Prem's most visible maturing is sexual: As he gradually loses his prudishness and sense of shame, Prem is able to enjoy and appreciate his wife and his role as husband, which leads to his adjustment in the other aspects of his life.

Indu, Prem's young and pregnant wife. Sure and competent in her household and in family matters, Indu is as inexperienced maritally and socially as Prem and is less well educated. At the outset, Indu and Prem each find it difficult to communicate with the other. Indu has a strong sense of her own worth, demonstrated in her returning for a visit to her parents' home when Prem has asked her to stay for his mother's visit. The separation makes each realize a growing fondness for the other, and the marriage really begins on Indu's return.

Sohan Lal, an older professor of mathematics at Khanna College who becomes Prem's friend. Not an especially competent teacher, Sohan Lal is a devoted family man, spiritual and religious in his outlook, resigned to the difficulties and limitations of his life. It is these qualities that attract Prem, despite Prem's knowledge that his father would have advised him to seek a more successful model.

Raj, Prem's college friend from Ankhpur and a minor official in the ministry of food. Raj has been married longer than

Prem and already is a father. For most of the novel, Raj is a reluctant friend who frequently fails to keep engagements with Prem and always allows Prem to finance their meetings. By the end of the novel, however, when Raj and his family visit Prem and Indu, Raj has become a little less uncertain about his new work and therefore less pompous, and Prem has lost his need to dwell on the past in Ankhpur, which used to annoy Raj.

Prem's mother, the widow of a small-town college principal. Prem at first idealizes her care for him. When she comes to visit him in Delhi, she complains about Indu and their household arrangements, and she intrudes on their marital privacy after Indu's return from her family. Prem, in his growing competence and maturity, arranges with one of his sisters to call her home.

Hans Loewe, an intense young German visiting India to explore its spirituality. He takes up with Prem and projects on him the spiritual endowments he is seeking. This situation is comic in effect, because Prem's problems almost entirely center on his material establishment in the world. Despite their mismatch, Hans and Prem do become friends, and, for a time, Hans's friendship is important to Prem's self-confidence.

Swami, a spiritual leader to whom Prem is introduced by Sohan Lal and to whose service Prem enthusiastically declares himself. As Swami anticipates, Prem is not able to carry through; nevertheless, Swami and his followers seem to remain important, if intermittent, elements in Prem's life.

Mr. Chaddha (CHUH-duh), a teacher of history in Khanna College whose classroom Prem shares and whom Prem recognizes as competent and successful. It is Chaddha whom Prem believes should be his model, though Prem dislikes him for his pomposity, his flattery of the principal, and his lack of sensitivity and spirituality.

Mr. Khanna, the principal of the college where Prem teaches. Astute in identifying his college's role, which is to groom well-off but unsuccessful college students to pass their university examinations, he hires second-rate, needy, or inexperienced teachers at low wages, keeping them if they are useful to him and do not give him much trouble. His wife complains that the teachers are a nuisance, though she makes a profit on the poor tea she serves them.

The Seigals, Prem and Indu's comfortably well-to-do and easygoing landlords. Prem would like to approach them for a reduction in his too-high rent but fears to do so.

Romesh Seigal, the Seigals' easygoing and mentally lazy son, a boy about the same age as Prem's students who enjoys nothing but films and on whom Prem seems to be a fairly good influence.

Kitty, a middle-aged Englishwoman, Hans Loewe's landlady. She is kind to Prem and interested in him in an offhanded sort of way.

Sethji, a wealthy, worldly follower of Swami, accepted by Swami but despised by Vishvanathan.

Vishvanathan, an intense, world-renouncing follower of Swami who is sure that his devotion is the only acceptable path.

— Ellen M. Laun

HOUSEKEEPING

Author: Marilynne Robinson (1944-)
First published: 1980
Genre: Novel

Locale: Fingerbone, Idaho
Time: Late 1950's and early 1960's
Plot: Allegory

Ruth Stone, the protagonist and first-person narrator. An awkward adolescent during much of the novel, Ruth is often silent and likes to read. Like the biblical Ruth, she is destined to follow others; first her sister Lucille in a search for acceptance from the town, then her aunt Sylvie in a search for identity. Ruth, though passive and interior, carefully considers the world around her and is a keen observer. She gradually abandons the conventional world of Fingerbone, Idaho, for the lure of a transient lifestyle with Sylvie. As Ruth recollects the events of the novel, she builds her identity.

Lucille Stone, Ruth's younger sister, who is usually the one to lead her older, more shy sister around. Lucille is more interested in being like everyone else than is Ruth. She attempts to participate in the shadowy forms of housekeeping practiced by Sylvie but eventually abandons the hope that her aunt—and eventually, even Ruthie—will ever conform to any recognizable social conventions. Lucille is not content to drift; she is interested in anchoring and some permanence in her life.

Sylvie Foster Fisher, Ruth and Lucille's mysterious aunt. She comes to take care of Ruth and Lucille after Lily and Nona declare themselves unable to do so. Sylvie attempts to overcome her urge to drift and travel without destination in a heroic effort to provide a home for her nieces. Ruth and Lucille know nothing about their aunt when she comes to live with them, and Sylvie volunteers little other than that she is still married to Mr. Fisher and that she left him and has been living a life of satisfied transience. Her pockets are full of odds and ends, and she is generally impervious to the conventions of rearing children. Sylvie does one thing that the other caretakers of Ruth and Lucille have failed to do: She stays until they no longer need her.

Sylvia Foster, Ruth and Lucille's grandmother and Sylvie and Helen's mother. Sylvia's main sense of identification comes from the daily acts of providing a home, first for her three daughters after the surprising death of her husband, Edmund, and later for Ruth and Lucille after the death of their mother, Helen. Sylvia's identity is achieved through her relationships with others—as wife, widow, mother, and grandmother—and her homemaking skills.

Helen Foster Stone, the mother of Ruth and Lucille; Sylvie's sister. Abandoned by her husband with two small daughters in Seattle, Washington, Helen refuses to tell the girls anything about their father. After seven and a half years as a single, working parent, Helen returns to Fingerbone, deposits the girls with Sylvia, and drives a borrowed car into the lake that had earlier claimed her father in a freak train accident.

Lily Foster and

Nona Foster, sisters-in-law to Sylvia Foster who try to care for Ruth and Lucille after Sylvia's death. Unable to deal with the needs of growing girls, the sisters decide to invite Sylvie back to Fingerbone to care for the girls.

Miss Royce, a home economics teacher who eventually takes in Lucille and gives her an opportunity to live a more conventional life than that provided by Sylvie.

— *Virginia Dumont-Poston*

HOW GREEN WAS MY VALLEY

Author: Richard Llewellyn (Richard Dafydd Vivian Llewellyn Lloyd, 1906-1983)
First published: 1939
Genre: Novel
Locale: Wales
Time: The nineteenth or early twentieth century
Plot: Domestic realism

Gwilym Morgan (GWIH-luhm), a Welsh miner. At first sympathetic with union agitators, he is later opposed to strikers and quarrels with his sons over their views. As mine superintendent, he is disliked by many of the workers. He dies in the cave-in of a flooded mine.

Beth Morgan, his wife, whose life is saved by young Huw just before Angharad's birth.

Huw (hew), their son and the narrator, who many years afterward sadly recalls the days of his childhood and young manhood. He remembers the strike troubles that divided the family, his illness from exposure suffered in saving his mother's life, his fights at school and his expulsion for beating the schoolmaster, his joining his brothers in the pits, his leaving to become a carpenter, and finally his entering the mine to find his father and stay with him until he died.

Ivor (EE-vohr), the oldest son, sympathetic with his father's views. He is killed in a mine cave-in.

Davy, another son, the last one to leave the mines. He migrates to New Zealand.

Owen and

Gwilym, two sons who (with Davy) move away from home for a time because of their union views. They later leave the valley for London and then America.

Ianto (YAHN-toh), a son who marries a village girl and leaves the valley. He returns after her death and works in the mines until he leaves for similar work in Germany.

Angharad (AHN-gah-rad), the Morgan daughter who loves Mr. Gruffydd but marries Iestyn.

Bronwen, Ivor's wife, whom Huw loves from the moment he sees her as a child. He goes to stay with her after Ivor is killed.

Marged (MAHR-gehd), Gwilym's wife, who goes mad from love of Owen and burns herself to death.

Iestyn Evans (YEHS-tuhn), son of the mine owner and husband of Angharad.

Mr. Gruffydd (GRIH-fuhth), the new minister who becomes Huw's best friend. He loves Angharad but is too poor to marry her.

Ceinwen Phillips (KEEN-wehn), Huw's sweetheart.

HOW IT IS
(Comment c'est)

Author: Samuel Beckett (1906-1989)
First published: 1961
Genre: Novel
Locale: A wasteland of mud
Time: Indeterminate
Plot: Existentialism

Bom, or **Bem**, the narrator, who is progressing laboriously through mud. He characterizes his breathing as panting; his thoughts are fragments that repeat throughout the narrative. He carries a sack whose position he constantly shifts, with a cord that he periodically loosens as he reaches in the sack for a tin of food. He also scrounges for a can opener. The narrator presents his progress, which he describes as covering long stretches of time, in relation to Pim. There are three parts to the narrative: before Pim, with Pim, and after Pim. In the first part, the narrator broods over fitful, fleeting memories, such as prayer with his mother on a veranda and a pastoral stroll with a girl and a dog in April or May. In the second part, Bom finds and torments Pim. The narrator depicts himself and Pim as two little old men clinging, or glued, together in the mire. It becomes increasingly difficult to distinguish between them. In the third and final part, having been abandoned by Pim, Bom pessimistically speculates that life is a closed system, a circular route involving a tormentor who seeks and finds a victim, who eventually flees to search out a victim of his own while the tormentor endures victimization by some other traveler. The narrator is awaiting his own tormentor, whom he calls Bom.

Pim, the narrator's victim, who may be his alter ego; at times, their identities seem to fuse. The narrator claims that he is taller than Pim, which he attributes to seniority. When he torments Pim, Pim sings a tune to which the narrator cannot make out the words. Pim has a wristwatch that the narrator pulls to his own ear, because the ticking keeps him company. Pim eats nothing, though the narrator offers him food from his sack, and Bom imagines that Pim derives nourishment from the mud by osmosis. The narrator calls Pim a bad student and himself a bad teacher.

Krim, or **Kram**, a scribe who is a witness to the incessant "dance" of victim and tormentor. Krim is aloof, keeping record. He bends over the narrator with a lamp. He may, in fact, be a projection of the narrator, representing his self-conscious awareness.

— *Amy Adelstein*

HOW THE GARCÍA GIRLS LOST THEIR ACCENTS

Author: Julia Alvarez (1950-)
First published: 1991
Genre: Novel
Locale: The Dominican Republic and the United States
Time: The 1950's to the 1980's
Plot: Family

Carlos García, or **Papi**, the overprotective Old World patriarch whose part in a failed coup against dictator Rafael Trujillo sends the family into exile. With the help of an intelligence agent and Dr. Fanning, an American colleague, he is able to set up his medical practice in New York City, providing a good life for his wife (Mami) and his four beloved daughters. The youngest of his father's thirty-five children, he is rooted in the old Hispanic heritage and keeps strong control over his family. He establishes the tradition of celebrating his birthday at his house, with the daughters coming without their men. Even as adults, his daughters play the role of the father's little girls.

Laura García, or **Mami**, the energetic mother of the four girls. She is the most comfortable in the exile life because she had studied in America. Her knowledge of English and lack of a heavy accent, along with her temperament, make her the leader of and mediator for the family in the new land. She is ambitious and takes courses that may lead to a successful career. The girls resent her activities, which keep her away from their needs. She calls them each by the generic pet name "Cuquita." Once settled in the United States, she refuses to go back to the island, where she would be considered to be a house slave, oppressed by a society that expects women to have sons. As a good "Mami," she is always giving advice, constantly telling the girls to guard their virginity and avoid drugs. She rears them in an American style but expects them to live by Hispanic cultural values.

Carla García, the oldest sister, who remembers Christmas in the native country, with decorations, many activities, and toys brought from New York City by the father. She also thinks of Victor Hubbard, the American consul who prepared the upper class for revolution, and the turmoil of the last day on the island, when the secret police stormed into the house looking for Carlos. She resents the celebration of the first year in exile without understanding her parents' ease in sinking roots. She feels homesick and prays to go back. When the family moves from the city to Long Island, she faces discriminatory treatment by a group of boys and confronts a sexual offender. She grows up to become a psychologist and marries one. Always ready to understand others, she is the family therapist.

Sandra García, the second sister, the pretty one. As a child, she exhibits artistic talent and wants to express herself with paintings. In New York City, she hears a woman in her apartment house trying to get the family evicted because of its language, food, and music. At a Spanish restaurant, Sandra sees people paying for the food and music criticized earlier. She wants to be a model as a means of being accepted in the new culture. In order to keep her weight down, she uses drugs that cause addiction and a mental breakdown.

Yolanda (Yoyo) García, the third of the sisters. She learns ghostly tales from Haitian maids as a child, plays with her male cousins, and wanders around restricted places. She remains curious all of her life. Memories of raids by police, violence, and disappearances of uncles stay with her and keep her awake at night. In New York City, she is the only immigrant in her class and is seated apart from the other children as she is tutored in English. Seeking refuge in books and language, she becomes a good student and is chosen in the ninth grade to give a speech. She discovers the power of words and creates poems, eventually becoming a poet and teacher. After suffering from failed relationships and emotional turmoil, she hopes to find her identity in her country of birth, but she is too independent to settle there, in a family compound with guarded walls and a patriarchal society.

Sofia (Fifi) García, the youngest in the family. She competes with the others to be the wildest. When she is sent to the island to reform her American ways, she falls in love with a cousin who dominates her. She leaves college and runs away with another boyfriend, then finally marries a German chemist. Her father forgives her only when she gives him a grandson.

Chucha, the servant of the family in the Dominican Republic. She came to the grandfather's house to escape from a death decreed for all black Haitians by the dictator Rafael Trujillo. She is disliked by other maids because of her race. Devoted to voodoo, she sleeps in a coffin. When the family leaves, she remains to take care of the house. She worries about the Garcías but is certain that they will know how to invent strategies for survival.

HOWARDS END

Author: E. M. Forster (1879-1970)
First published: 1910
Genre: Novel
Locale: England
Time: Early twentieth century
Plot: Domestic realism

Henry Wilcox, a prosperous British businessman who has his fair share of domestic bliss and trouble. He owns Howards End, a country home near London, and it is here that the climactic scenes in the novel take place. At the end of his life, he wills Howards End to his second wife, with the understanding that after her death it is to go to the illegitimate child of his second wife's daughter.

Ruth Wilcox, Wilcox's first wife and Margaret Schlegel's good friend. She becomes ill and dies suddenly after writing a note that leaves Howards End to Margaret. Because the note was not part of the formal will, Wilcox and the rest of the family disregard it.

Helen Schlegel, the sister of Wilcox's second wife, who provides much of the continuity of the novel's narrative line.

She at one time loved Wilcox's younger son. She has a child by a man Wilcox caused to lose his job. It is her baby that Wilcox learns to love just before his death.

Margaret Schlegel, Wilcox's second wife. She is cool, sensible, cautious. She is a good friend to Wilcox's first wife; it was, in fact, to Margaret that Wilcox's first wife willed Howards End just before she died. Margaret is a faithful wife to Wilcox and a good sister to Helen.

Leonard Bast, a poor, reasonably intelligent, rather neurasthenic worker who loses his job by acting on information Wilcox purposefully provides. His life, by accident, becomes woven into the lives of the Wilcox and Schlegel households. Helen has an illegitimate child by him. He dies of a heart attack caused by the shock of unexpectedly seeing Helen and the trauma of a beating administered to him by Wilcox's older son.

Paul Wilcox, Wilcox's younger son, who loved Helen but had been unable to marry her because both families disapproved of the union.

Charles Wilcox, Wilcox's older son, who is sent to prison for beating Leonard Bast. Though Bast dies of a heart attack and not of the injury sustained in the beating, Charles Wilcox is convicted of manslaughter and sent to prison for three years. His son's trial and conviction break Henry Wilcox's health.

Jacky Bast, Leonard's wife, an older woman who tricks Bast into an unpleasant marriage. She has an unsavory reputation caused as much as anything by the fact that she drinks too much.

Theobald Schlegel, Helen and Margaret's brother.

HUDIBRAS

Author: Samuel Butler (1612-1680)
First published: 1663-1678
Genre: Poetry
Locale: England
Time: 1640-1660
Plot: Satire

Sir Hudibras (HEW-dih-bras), a Presbyterian knight and the hero of this poem intended to ridicule the Presbyterians, the religious Independents, and the pretensions of false learning in seventeenth century England. Sir Hudibras is full of learned conversation liberally sprinkled with Latin, Greek, and Hebrew. Riding a skinny nag, he sallies forth with his squire Ralpho, intent on putting to right the sinners of the world. The reforming knight and his squire, obnoxious nuisances both, get the worst of every encounter with sin. In a final humiliation, their ardor is cooled when they are forced to make an undignified exit through the Widow's window and escape on their saddleless horses.

Ralpho, Sir Hudibras' squire. A religious Independent full of high-flown arguments on matters of faith, he accompanies his master on his crusade against sin.

Crowdero, a fiddler captured and put in the stocks by Sir Hudibras and Ralpho.

Trulla, an Amazon who subdues Sir Hudibras and puts him in the stocks in place of Crowdero.

Sidrophel, an astrologer consulted by Sir Hudibras and Ralpho.

Whachum, Sidrophel's apprentice.

The Widow, a wealthy woman who agrees to have Sir Hudibras freed from the stocks if he will consent to a whipping. When he lies to her, she causes his final humiliation and the end of his reforming career.

Orsin, a bear keeper whose escaped bear causes the melee that finally lands Sir Hudibras and Ralpho in the stocks.

Talgol, a butcher.

HUGH WYNNE, FREE QUAKER

Author: Silas Weir Mitchell (1829-1914)
First published: 1897
Genre: Novel
Locale: Colonial America
Time: 1753-1783
Plot: Historical

Hugh Wynne, a young man in Revolutionary War times who is torn between his father's Quakerism and more worldly views. The rigors of his father's religion prove too much, and he leaves the Quakers to become a valiant soldier in the Continental Army fighting for colonial independence. He receives praise from General Washington, wins a captaincy, and after the war marries Darthea Peniston, the girl he loves. A loyal American, he gives up the title to estates in Wales.

John Wynne, Hugh's father, an orthodox Quaker. Bitter when his son leaves his faith, John tries to disinherit Hugh. He fails, however, because his clouded mind causes him to mistake Hugh for Hugh's cousin Arthur. The poor man dies insane.

Gainor Wynne, Hugh's aunt, his father's sister. She is not a Quaker and surrounds herself with worldly friends, including British officers. She wants her nephew to leave the Quaker faith to take part in the patriot cause to free the American colonies. She befriends Hugh when he is cut off by his father.

Jack Warder, Hugh's schoolmate and friend. With Hugh, he becomes a patriot in the American Revolution and serves valiantly in the Continental Army.

Arthur Wynne, Hugh's cousin. He is a deceitful and cruel young man who is a Tory sympathizer and becomes an officer in the British forces during the American Revolution. On one occasion, he leaves his cousin Hugh to die in a filthy prison.

He is Hugh's unsuccessful rival for the hand of Darthea Peniston. A sly villain, he wheedles the family estate in Wales from Hugh's hoodwinked father.

Marie Wynne, Hugh's mother, a loving and understanding woman. She dies while Hugh is still a young man.

Darthea Peniston, a childhood sweetheart of Hugh. She is at one time engaged to Arthur, Hugh's cousin, but she discovers he is a deceitful man and breaks the engagement. Later, she marries Hugh.

THE HUMAN AGE

Author: Wyndham Lewis (1882-1957)
First published: 1955
Genre: Novel
Locale: The waiting area outside Heaven, The Magnetic City, and Matapolis (Hell)
Time: The twentieth century
Plot: Satire

Childermass, 1928

James Pullman, a man who has recently died. He exists in an indistinct dimension in which time and space are flexible. At first, he does not know where he is going or what he is doing. Gradually, he realizes that he is one of many petitioners to a court that will decide if he should be allowed to enter Heaven. He is an intellectual and was a writer of satire in his former life.

Satterthwaite, called **Satters**, a childish individual who was at school with Pullman. The two meet again shortly after they arrive in this mysterious afterworld. Satterthwaite had been unable to cope with his peers and therefore was dependent on Pullman when they were at school; he assumes the same subservient role in this life. Unfortunately, he has many destructive and bullying tendencies. When the two drift into the seventeenth century, he casually destroys Tom Paine.

The Bailiff, the director of the court in the afterworld. In his first appearance, he seems a rather buffoonish figure who presides over the petitioners' requests, dispensing completely arbitrary judgments. He tells all who wait that they have no rights, except the right to petition. He arrives at the court announced by trumpets and borne in a litter carried by Nubian slaves. His personality changes constantly. Although he is a powerful figure, he delights in adopting new and often ridiculous personas.

Hyperides (hi-PEHR-ih-dees), the main challenger to the rule of the Bailiff. At first, he appears as an intellectual, espousing a classical view of life that challenges the Bailiff's arbitrary vulgarity.

Monstre Gai, 1955

James Pullman, no longer a petitioner, having been passed to the next level. He discovers that it is not Heaven but only The Magnetic City, a sort of mad antechamber of Paradise. Soon after he arrives, he becomes aware of a plot by the devil to attack the city and capture its ruler, the Padishah. Pullman gradually becomes enmeshed with the devil's plans, joining the dominating forces in the city, as he becomes heavily involved in the Bailiff's schemes. As their plans collapse, Pullman and the other conspirators are forced to flee to Matapolis, or Hell.

Satterthwaite, a figure even more childish and inept than he appeared at first. In The Magnetic City, it becomes clear that individuals have assumed the roles most typical of their lives. Thus, Satterthwaite will be forever an incontinent schoolboy. He becomes involved with the juvenile gangs who drunkenly roam the streets, causing havoc and destruction.

The Bailiff, whose appearance and identity change yet again in The Magnetic City as he becomes a sinister figure, allied with the devil. Although he appears elegant and statesmanlike, he controls the violent forces that terrorize the city.

Hyperides, who is no longer admirable as a classicist and now is decried as a fascist. He is hated by all except his ardent followers. Even his name is derided as an affectation. In a clash between his forces and those of the Bailiff, he is brutally murdered in a parody of the Crucifixion, stabbed with a nail through the throat, and then dressed in a white pointed cap with "Fool" printed on it. The Bailiff gleefully dances over his corpse.

Father Ryan, a priest. He represents the voice of traditional religious authority in The Magnetic City. When he debates with his opponents, he argues for theocracy and proclaims the glory of the Divine.

Malign Fiesta, 1955

James Pullman, who has become increasingly fascinated by the devil, Lord Sammael. The two enjoy long philosophical conversations, and eventually Pullman becomes the devil's unofficial counselor. In the end, he is rescued from Matapolis, carried away by God's forces, two angels. He turns his thoughts away from the human age to the divine one.

Lord Sammael, the devil, a witty and urbane figure. He is both friendly and charming. His ultimate goal is to remove the distinctions between Heaven and Hell. By eliminating the divine, he can bring about the human age. He requests Pullman's help in drafting the message he plans to send to God discussing various complaints he has held since before Genesis, revealing his plans for the future.

Satterthwaite, who flees with Pullman to Matapolis, where he finds employment as an apprentice gardener, a role he enjoys.

The Bailiff, who in Matapolis continues to be a murderer and a bully.

— Mary E. Mahony

THE HUMAN COMEDY

Author: William Saroyan (1908-1981)
First published: 1943
Genre: Novel
Locale: Ithaca, California
Time: The twentieth century
Plot: Sentimental

Katey Macauley, a widow who is trying to bring up her family alone. She has imaginary talks with her dead husband, in which she discusses family problems with him. She feels that her husband is not dead as long as he lives in the lives of his children. She accepts Tobey into the family after Marcus is killed.

Homer Macauley, Katey's second oldest son, who takes a night job at the telegraph office. He gets up early every day and exercises so that he will be in shape to run the hurdles at the high school. He finds the telegram that Mr. Grogan has typed out telling Katey that Marcus has been killed.

Marcus Macauley, Katey's oldest son, who goes into the Army and makes friends with Tobey George. Tobey has no family of his own, and so Marcus shares stories of his family with Tobey. Marcus wants Tobey to go to his home and marry his sister, Bess, after the war. Marcus is killed in action.

Mary Arena, Marcus' sweetheart.

Tobey George, an orphan whom Marcus befriends in the Army. Tobey is lonely and lives vicariously through Marcus' family. He returns to Marcus' home after the war and, in a sense, takes Marcus' place as a son.

Mr. Grogan, Spangler's assistant in the telegraph office, with whom Homer has long talks concerning the efficacy of war. Mr. Grogan has a weak heart and gets drunk every night. One of Homer's duties is to see that he stays awake. He dies after typing out the message that Marcus has been killed in action.

Thomas Spangler, the manager of the telegraph office.

Bess Macauley and

Ulysses Macauley, Katey's two other children.

Lionel, Ulysses' friend, who takes him to the library and shows him the many books.

THE HUMAN FACTOR

Author: Graham Greene (1904-1991)
First published: 1978
Genre: Novel
Locale: Suburban Berkhamsted and London
Time: Late in the Cold War era
Plot: Spy

Maurice Castle, a sixty-two-year-old agent in British intelligence who is leaking governmental information about South Africa to the Communists. Castle's reason is his gratitude to Carson, a friend who gave Marxism a human face for him by arranging for the escape from prison of Sarah, the black South African Castle later married. Although he is scrupulously careful, Castle suspects that his leaks have been noticed. Nevertheless, Castle conveys to his Russian contact, Boris, information about Uncle Remus, a secret operation of the United States and Britain to protect their shared financial concerns in support of apartheid in South Africa. After Castle's coworker Arthur Davis dies, Castle realizes that the leak had been traced to his office but the wrong man was killed. He dangerously decides to send one more report when he sees in the notes of the South African representative, Cornelius Muller, the words "final solution," a chilling reminder of Nazi horrors. Almost at the same time, Castle uses an emergency telephone signal to arrange his escape from England. With British intelligence now suspecting him, Castle travels in disguise to Moscow on the expectation that the KGB will arrange for Sarah and her young son Sam to follow. The British delay their passage, however. Finally, Castle makes telephone contact with Sarah in England, but shortly into their conversation the line goes dead.

Sarah Castle, Maurice's wife. Sarah worked with Castle when he was a field agent in South Africa. She immediately suspects that the death of Davis was the work of the British. When Castle later tells her that he is what most would consider a traitor, Sarah responds, "Who cares?" She reminds Castle that she and he have their own country and that he has never betrayed that. Talking to Castle in Moscow by telephone from England, she urges him to go on hoping that she will be able to join him.

Arthur Davis, Castle's coworker. Young and incautious in his lunchtime dates with an office worker, Davis is wrongly suspected of being the double agent who is leaking secrets to the Russians. On Dr. Percival's recommendation, the firm kills Davis with a poisonous mold extracted from rancid peanuts. His death confirms to Castle the firm's knowledge of the leak.

Dr. Emmanuel Percival, a member of British intelligence. Percival is summoned by Sir John Hargreaves to deal with the security leak in Castle's office. Percival's inhumanity finds a justifying analogy for killing the double agent in the symmetrical squares of Ben Nicholson's art: the out-of-balance element requires elimination. When later told that the wrong man was murdered, Percival feels no remorse, because for him maintaining security is more important than a correct diagnosis. Percival sees Davis' death, like the firm's prevention of Castle's family from joining him in Moscow, as nothing personal.

Cornelius Muller, a representative of apartheid. Muller opposed Castle seven years earlier in South Africa when Castle broke that country's race laws. Now in England, Muller is smoothly polite in dealing with Castle as a representative of British intelligence. He supplies Castle with particulars about Operation Uncle Remus that Castle conveys to the Communists. Muller also leaves some notes with Castle that include the ominous heading of the "final solution." Muller's knowledge of Castle's earlier friendship with Carson in South Africa makes him suspect Castle, and he tells Hargreaves of his intuition.

Colonel Daintry, the new head of security. Daintry's efforts to bring a measure of humanity to his work are frustrated by Percival's willingness to kill Davis without proof of his guilt. Daintry realizes that his life in the world of secrets has cost him his marriage. He obeys Hargreaves' order to visit Castle and discuss the death of Davis. He relays to his superiors Castle's admission that Davis was not the double agent and then intends to resign his job.

Sir John Hargreaves, Daintry's superior. At his country house one weekend, Hargreaves instructs security officers that they must eliminate the double agent rather than face the embarrassment of a public treason trial. His previous experience in South Africa and his respect for intuition lead him reluctantly to act on Muller's suspicions and send Daintry to question Castle.

Buller, Castle and Sarah's dog. Although an enthusiastic killer of cats, the boxer Buller bestows acceptance and affection indiscriminately on people, and he is the only character in the book to do so. He leaves his spittle "like a bonbon" on the trouser legs of apartheid activist Cornelius Muller as well as on those of the Marxist Halliday. When Castle must leave England, Halliday instructs him to kill Buller so that his unattended barking will not excite the neighbors' suspicions. Castle has difficulty doing so, not because he loves the dog but because he has never before killed anything.

— *Glenn Hopp*

HUMBOLDT'S GIFT

Author: Saul Bellow (1915-)
First published: 1975
Genre: Novel
Locale: Chicago, New York City, Corpus Christi, Houston, Madrid, and Paris
Time: Early 1970's
Plot: Psychological realism

Charles Citrine, a successful and acclaimed American author in his mid-fifties, living in Chicago. He has won the Pulitzer Prize and has been awarded the Legion of Honor, yet his career has become stale and he is reassessing his potential and his human relationships, past and present. He combines a subtle intellect and a strong sense of comic incongruity with a tolerant, mellow personality. Basically good-humored, he is attracted to eccentric and flashy characters, some of whom exist only in his capacious memory. Highly cultured and interested in metaphysics, he explores the philosophy of Rudolph Steiner.

Denise Citrine, Citrine's former wife, the daughter of a federal judge and a graduate of Vassar. She is attractive, upper class, socially ambitious, and at times overbearing. She keeps Citrine's life in turmoil through endless litigation but really desires to have him back because of his fame and culture.

Von Humboldt Fleisher, a deceased avant-garde American poet whose career peaked in the 1930's. He was handsome, large of build, fair, and learned. A fascinating conversationalist, he attracted followers and became Citrine's mentor. A self-diagnosed manic depressive, he became subject to alcoholism and mental illness in his later years and died in poverty and obscurity. He left Citrine an unpublished manuscript.

Kathleen Fleisher Tigler, Humboldt's former wife. She is large, fair-skinned, and attractive. A person of warmth and mature understanding, she helps Citrine secure Humboldt's legacy. Her favorite pastime, reading, indicates her pliant and essentially passive nature.

Rinaldo Cantabile, a minor Chicago mobster who is addicted to marijuana and flamboyant in his lifestyle. He batters Citrine's Mercedes after a disagreement over a gambling debt but afterward assists him in protecting the copyright of his play.

Renata Koffritz, Citrine's mistress, a calm Earth Mother type, large of build, with ample breasts. She possesses a warm personality and a practical nature, contrasting with Citrine's idealism.

Pierre Thaxter, a middle-aged, eccentric editor and intellectual. Outlandishly dressed, he has green eyes and a catlike face. He travels the world pursuing ambitious schemes and exhibits complete incompetence regarding finances. While Citrine awaits publication of an article in Thaxter's projected journal *The Ark*, Thaxter undertakes a new and ambitious project, a series of biographies of demented Third World dictators.

Menasha Klinger, a former punch press operator and electrician, now in his seventies. He knew Citrine as a child and remembers him as the best kid in his part of town in Ypsilanti, Michigan. Despite a broken nose that ruined his voice, he has cherished a lifelong dream of becoming an operatic tenor.

Waldemar Wald, Humboldt's uncle, an aged man living in a nursing home. He recalls with pleasure his life as a racetrack gambler, though his memory is no longer reliable. When Citrine visits him in the nursing home, Waldemar hands over Humboldt's legacy.

Julius "Ulick" Citrine, Citrine's overweight elder brother, aged sixty-five. An aggressive businessman, he lives in Corpus Christi, Texas, with his second wife, Hortense. A wealthy man who lives in luxury, he has a long straight nose, slightly bulging eyes, and a well-trimmed mustache. Despite imminent open-heart surgery, he helps Citrine with his finances.

Anna Dempster "Demmie" Vonghel, Citrine's friend and former mistress, a teacher of Latin at the Washington Irving School in New York City. She died in a South American plane crash. She was highly attractive, with blue eyes, an upturned nose, and shapely legs. Despite her fundamentalist background, she had a record of illegal activities, including petty theft, and was addicted to pills.

George Schwiebel, a successful Chicago contractor, Citrine's friend from his school days. He is a physical fitness enthusiast.

Forrest Tomchek, Citrine's attorney. An aggressive, shrewd, and resourceful negotiator, he leads Citrine's defense of suits brought by his former wife.

Naomi Lutz Wolper, Citrine's childhood sweetheart, now fifty-three years old. Having proven too practical for him, she works as a uniformed guard at a school crossing. In a meeting with him, she demonstrates tolerance and a sense of humor.

— *Stanley Archer*

THE HUNCHBACK OF NOTRE DAME
(Notre-Dame de Paris)

Author: Victor Hugo (1802-1885)
First published: 1831
Genre: Novel
Locale: France
Time: The fifteenth century
Plot: Historical

Quasimodo (kah-zee-MOH-doh), a bellringer abandoned in infancy at Notre Dame Cathedral on Quasimodo Sunday, 1476, and now deaf from the din of the bells he rings. He is also unspeakably ugly, with tusk-like teeth and a wen over one eye, bristling red hair and eyebrows, and a snoutlike nose. Because of his horrible appearance, the Paris crowd selects him King of Fools for the Epiphany celebrations of 1482. During the carnival, he sees Esmeralda, the gypsy who dances before him. When he is later pilloried and beaten, she brings him a drink. From then on, he is her devoted slave and on several occasions saves her from Archdeacon Frollo, his benefactor. When she is hanged through Frollo's scheming, he hurls the priest from the bell tower, then weeps at the death of the only two people he has ever loved. Years later, when the vault of Montfaucon, burial place of criminals, is opened, a skeleton of a woman in white is found in the arms of a misshapen man with a crooked spine. The bones disintegrate into dust when touched.

Esmeralda (ehz-meh-RAHL-dah), a lovely and kindhearted gypsy who possesses an amulet by which she hopes to find her family. She and her goat Djali dance to earn their living. Attracted to Captain Phoebus after he saves her from kidnapping, she agrees to a rendezvous in a house on the Pont St. Michel. There the officer is stabbed by Frollo, but Esmeralda is accused of the crime. Under torture, she confesses to everything and is sentenced to be hanged. With Quasimodo's help, however, she escapes while confessing to Frollo and takes sanctuary in the church. Gringoire deceives her into leaving when the mob attacks Notre Dame. For a time, she hides in the cell of a madwoman, in reality her mother from whom the gypsies had stolen her. Soldiers of Captain Phoebus' company find her there. Clothed in white, she is hanged at dawn.

Pierre Gringoire (pyehr green-GWAHR), a penniless and stupid Parisian poet who falls in love with Esmeralda. He writes a play to entertain the Flemish ambassadors at the Palace of Justice. Captured later by thugs and threatened with hanging, he is freed when Esmeralda promises to marry him, but the marriage is never consummated. At Frollo's bidding, Gringoire tempts the girl from her sanctuary, and she is captured.

Captain Phoebus de Châteaupers (fay-BEWS deh shah-toh-PEHR), loved by Esmeralda. He reveals to Frollo his rendezvous with her and is stabbed by the jealous priest. When Esmeralda is accused of the crime, Phoebus allows her be tried for his murder because he is fearful for his reputation if he appears. Soon he forgets the gypsy and marries his cousin, Fleur-de-Lys.

Claude Frollo (klohd froh-YOH), the archdeacon of Notre Dame, once an upright priest but now a student of alchemy and necromancy as well as a pursuer of women. Determined to possess Esmeralda, he sends Quasimodo in disguise to seize her. Her rescue by Captain Phoebus makes him try to kill the officer. When Esmeralda is accused of the crime, he offers to save her if she will give herself to him. Failing to possess her, he shakes with evil laughter as he looks down from Notre Dame at her hanging in the Place de Gréve. He is found by Quasimodo and hurled to his death on the pavement below.

The Dauphin Charles (doh-FAH[N] shahrl), of France, whose marriage to Margaret of Flanders occasions the celebration at the beginning of the novel.

Charles, cardinal de Bourbon, who provides the dramatic entertainment for the visiting Flemish guests.

Tristan (trees-TAHN), who directs Captain Phoebus' soldiers in search of Esmeralda.

Jacques Charmolue (zhahk shahr-moh-LEW), the king's attorney in the ecclesiastical court that tries Esmeralda for witchcraft.

Philippe Lheulier (fee-LEEP lewl-YAY), the king's advocate extraordinary, who accuses her.

Gudule (gew-DEWL), an ex-prostitute whose daughter Agnes had been stolen by gypsies. She has gone mad and for fifteen years has lived in a cell. She fondles constantly a shoe that her baby had worn. When Esmeralda takes refuge there, she produces its companion, and mother and daughter are briefly reunited.

HUNGER
(Sult)

Author: Knut Hamsun (Knut Pedersen, 1859-1952)
First published: 1890
Genre: Novel
Locale: Norway
Time: Late nineteenth century
Plot: Impressionistic realism

The Narrator, a young man down on his luck who writes articles and plays. He is paid so little for his work, however, that he is desperately hungry most of the time. He tells his story in the feverish state of mind that hunger produces. It is a story of his encounters in the town with girls, beggars, pawnbrokers, old friends, policemen, editors, potential employers. Sick with hunger, he is eventually turned out of his room and, finally and violently, out of the house itself. His story ends when he throws into his landlady's face a crumpled envelope containing a half sovereign and a letter from a woman.

An Old Cripple, a penniless beggar to whom the narrator gives a halfpenny after he has pawned his waistcoat to get the money.

Two Women, who are strolling about the town. They take the narrator for a madman because he tells the younger one that she is losing her book, when the fact of the matter is that she carries no book with her. Later, the younger woman—now The Lady in Black—befriends the narrator because she is an adventuresome girl who is intrigued with the idea of odd experiences, including those madmen might provide for her.

A Company Manager, an employer who refuses to give the narrator a job as a bookkeeper because he had carelessly dated his letter of application several years before he was born.

A Policeman, an officer who sends the narrator to the police barracks as a homeless man.

A Pawnbroker, a merchant who laughs at the narrator when he appears at the pawnshop to sell the buttons from his coat.

An Editor, a kindly gentleman who likes the narrator's work but cannot accept his sketch. He offers the narrator money, certain that the narrator can repay the obligation with his writing, but the narrator refuses the advance.

A Young Clerk, a boy who gives the narrator change for a crown when he has given the boy only a florin with which to buy a candle. The narrator profits by the clerk's mistake by renting a room in a hotel and buying two full meals.

A Landlady, a woman with a family who patiently waits for the narrator to pay his rent. She finally rents his room to a sailor but allows the narrator to sleep in the house. She throws him out of the house, however, when he protests the children's cruel game of sticking straws into the nose of the paralyzed grandfather who lies in a bed before the fire.

A Beautiful Girl, dressed in silk, who appears to the narrator in a dream. She offers him erotic pleasure.

HUON OF BORDEAUX

Author: Unknown
First published: First half of the thirteenth century
Genre: Poetry
Locale: Paris, Jerusalem, Rome, and the fairy kingdom of Mommur
Time: The ninth century
Plot: Epic

Huon de Bordeaux (ew-OH[N] deh bohr-DOH), the older son of the dead duke of Guienne. On his way with his brother Gerard to pay homage to King Charlemagne, he is ambushed by the king's son, Charlot, whom he kills in self-defense. He is then sent, by the angry Charlemagne, on a pilgrimage to Jerusalem. After many adventures, through which he is assisted by Oberon, the fairy king, he returns to court to claim the rights usurped during his absence by his brother.

Gerard (zhay-RAHR), the younger brother of Huon de Bordeaux and the usurper of his rights.

King Charlemagne (shar-leh-MAHN-yeh), who bears little resemblance to the great king of legend. He is pictured as in his dotage, petulant, violent, and unreasonable. Unjustly angry with Huon de Bordeaux, he sends him on a dangerous pilgrimage to Jerusalem.

Charlot (shahr-LOH), King Charlemagne's son, who ambushes Huon de Bordeaux and is killed by him in self-defense.

Oberon (oh-bay-ROH[N]), the dwarf king of the Otherworld, who aids Huon de Bordeaux in his adventures. Granting Huon the right to summon him in the time of danger, Oberon finally brings about the restoration of Huon's rights and promises him the inheritance of his fairy kingdom.

Gawdis (goh-DEE), the amir of Babylon.

Claramond (klah-rah-MOH[N]), Gawdis' lovely daughter, won by Huon de Bordeaux.

Gerames (zhay-RAHM), a hermit and loyal follower of Huon de Bordeaux.

The Abbot of Cluny (klew-NEE), the uncle of Huon de Bordeaux.

Earl Amaury (ah-moh-REE), the evil adviser to Charlot and the cause of his own and Charlot's death at the hand of Huon de Bordeaux.

Duke Naymes (nehm), the wise adviser to King Charlemagne and a well-wisher of Huon de Bordeaux.

HURLYBURLY

Author: David Rabe (1940-   )
First published: 1985
Genre: Drama
Locale: Hollywood, California
Time: The 1980's
Plot: Naturalism

Eddie, a Hollywood casting director. Heavily into drugs and alcohol, upset by the chaos and hypocrisy of the world in which he lives, and unable to maintain relationships with women, he tries to find "clarity" and meaning in his life. Unable to do so, he becomes obsessed with semantics and language, trying to express precisely the swirl of thoughts that go through his mind; this trait drives the other characters to anger and frustration. In spite of being self-centered and foul-mouthed, he demonstrates isolated moments of caring, as in his friendship with Phil. Eddie asserts that Mickey's death saves him from being another Mickey, although it does not provide him with any answers.

Mickey, Eddie's roommate, a casting director. Maintaining a mask of convention and reason, he does not allow himself to respond or react to the provocations and needs of the other characters. Smug, noncommittal, and cynical, he observes their actions with bemused detachment and condescension. His moral passivity and inaction mark him as too carefully controlled to be caring; nevertheless, he is full of resentment and animosity, however veiled, toward Phil, who is taking his place in a friendship with Eddie.

Phil, an out-of-work bit actor. Driven by chaotic and violent inner feelings that he cannot understand, he gradually loses the little self-control that he has. His desperate need for a friendship with Eddie, which causes Mickey to view him as an intruder, brings out the more humane side of his personality. After assaulting Bonnie and kidnapping his child after the most recent separation from his wife, he kills himself in an automobile crash, leaving Eddie to puzzle out the meaning of his death.

Artie, an older Jewish film producer. Constantly making deals that never seem to materialize, he is anxious, obnoxious, and self-deluding. At certain points, he functions like a father figure, trying to give advice. At other times, he attempts to become part of the fraternity of male bonding going on at Eddie's, participating in the use of drugs and women to blunt reality.

Darlene, an attractive photojournalist and Eddie's lover. Tired of Eddie's constant angst and attracted by the relative peace of Mickey's nonseriousness, she, like the other female characters, becomes a source of their arguments. Also like the other female characters, she is viewed as an object to be passed back and forth among them, an attitude that she refuses to accept, asserting that she should have something to say about who she wants to be with.

Bonnie, a divorced mother of one who supports herself as a stripper. Partial to Eddie, she has a reputation as an easy, good-time party girl. After Phil assaults her, she confronts Eddie with her pain, desperation, and anger at his total lack of pity for her.

Donna, a fifteen-year-old runaway. Brought to Eddie's home by Artie, she is willing to exchange sex with any of the men there for a place to stay and food to eat. As dispossessed as Phil, and more abused, she nevertheless has a strong survival instinct.

— *Lori Hall Burghardt*

HURRY HOME

Author: John Edgar Wideman (1941-)
First published: 1970
Genre: Novel
Locale: The United States, Europe, and the ocean off Africa
Time: Mid- and late 1960's
Plot: Psychological realism

Cecil Otis Braithwaite, a black janitor in his thirties. Cecil was only the second black man to receive a law degree from his college. On the night of his graduation, he marries Esther, who supported him through law school. He was a man of dreams, but his hopes have been dashed. After deserting Esther on their wedding night, he spends three years traveling in Europe. He returns to his former life and does not change it but merely sinks further into his depression, caused by the state of his race, his alienation—because of his race—from the type of life he wants to lead, and the miscarriage of his and Esther's child.

Esther Brown Braithwaite, Cecil's wife. Esther has sacrificed her life to Cecil because she believes that he has been chosen by God for greatness. She slaves in the Branbury Arms at Cecil's janitorial job while he is in school, while he is away, and after he returns, hoping to help her husband in some way.

Aunt Fanny, Esther's elderly aunt. She lives with Esther and Cecil and is completely dependent on them. She remembers a time when she was needed by her husband and sons.

Uncle Otis, Cecil's uncle. He is an old man and a fixture in the neighborhood. In Cecil's mind, he literally keeps the lamppost on which he leans from falling over.

Charles Webb, an elderly American writer living in Spain. Webb is the cause of Cecil's travels. Far in Webb's past is an affair with a black woman named Anna, with whom he fathered a son and whom he deserted because of Anna's infidelity. Webb has spent much of his guilty life searching for this son. When he meets Cecil, he wants to believe that his search is over and pays for Cecil's passage to Europe.

Albert, a middle-aged drifter employed by Webb to find Webb and Anna's son. Like Webb, Albert is an expatriate. He briefly becomes Cecil's drinking companion in Spain to dissuade him from continuing his relationship with Webb, thus keeping himself on Webb's payroll.

Anna, a schoolteacher, Webb's former mistress. Before she dies, she writes Webb a letter informing him of the existence of his son, causing Webb to begin his long search.

— *Leigh Woods*

HYDE PARK

Author: James Shirley (1596-1666)
First published: 1637
Genre: Drama
Locale: London, England
Time: Early seventeenth century
Plot: Comedy of manners

Mistress Bonavent, a wife who believes herself a widow. Her husband having been missing for seven years, she considers marriage to her persistent suitor, Lacy. After the marriage, but before its consummation, she learns of her husband's return.

Lacy, her suitor.

Bonavent, a merchant and the husband of Mistress Bonavent. Held captive by Turkish pirates and recently ransomed after seven years' absence, he returns to the sound of his wife's wedding festivities. He makes himself known to her before the second marriage is consummated.

Mistress Carol, Mistress Bonavent's cousin and companion. She flirts with Rider and Venture and plays one against the other; all along, Fairfield is the favored suitor. Turning coquette to test the favorite's affection, she nearly loses him before she is forced to abandon her pride and propose to him. He accepts immediately.

Fairfield, the favored suitor of Mistress Carol. In despair over his lady's off-again, on-again coquettishness, he threatens to become a gelding and free himself from all such concerns. The threat wins her hand on the spot.

Rider and

Venture, Mistress Carol's rejected suitors.

Lord Bonvile, a sporting peer. Under the delusion that Julietta is a lady of easy virtue, he is in hot pursuit of her. When he goes too far in his suit, he receives from the lady a lecture on good breeding, takes it to heart, and finally wins her hand.

Julietta, Fairfield's sister, who is pursued by Lord Bonvile under the mistaken impression that she is a prostitute. She accepts him as a suitor after his thoughts become as lofty as his rank.

Jack Trier, Julietta's betrothed. To test his lady's chastity, the jealous lover leaves her with Lord Bonvile, whom he has told that she is a prostitute. He loses her to Bonvile.

HYPATIA: Or, New Foes with an Old Face

Author: Charles Kingsley (1819-1875)
First published: 1853
Genre: Novel
Locale: Egypt and Italy
Time: Fifth century
Plot: Historical

Philammon (fih-LA-mon), a young monk who leaves the monastic life to see the rich, varied society of Alexandria. Excited by a Christian attack on the city's Jews, he joins the despoilers. Accused of heresy because of his interest in Hypatia, he almost loses his life. After Hypatia's death, he returns to his monastery and later becomes abbot there.

Hypatia (hi-PAY-shee-uh), a beautiful Greek philosopher and teacher, one of the last to champion the Greek gods. She agrees to marry Orestes if he will renounce his Christian faith and aid her in restoring the Greek gods. Her gods, which exist only in her own mind, fail her, and she is torn to pieces by some of Cyril's monks.

Raphael Aben-Ezra (RA-feh-ehl ah-behn-EEZ-rah), a wealthy young Jew. He is Miriam's son, though he does not know it. He becomes Hypatia's pupil but turns from the Greek gods to Christianity.

Miriam (MIH-rih-ehm), an old Jewish crone formerly converted to Christianity until she renounced it and developed a hatred of everyone except Jews. She tells Philammon of his slave status, sends Orestes the false report of Heraclian's victory, and informs Raphael that she is his mother. She dies of wounds received during an attack by the Goths.

Amal (A-muhl), a young Gothic chief who travels up the Nile searching for Asgard, home of the old Gothic gods. In a fight with Philammon, he falls from a tower and dies.

Pelagia (peh-LAY-jee-uh), Amal's mistress and (though he does not at first know it) sister of Philammon; a beautiful courtesan to whose home Philammon flees to avoid being forced to return to his monastery. After Amal's death, she becomes a solitary penitent in the desert. At her death, she is buried with Philammon.

Orestes (oh-REHS-teez), the Roman prefect of Alexandria who envisions a rise in his own fortunes and power if Heraclian succeeds in overthrowing the Goths.

Aufugus (OH-fuh-guhs), a monk who warns Philammon not to go to Alexandria and later attempts to rescue him from Hypatia's influence. Though Philammon does not know it until informed by Miriam, he is Aufugus' slave bought many years earlier.

Cyril (SIH-rihl), the Christian patriarch of Alexandria, who reports to Orestes a Jewish plot to slaughter Alexandria's Christians. By the death of Hypatia, he gains a temporary victory over the Greek religion.

Heraclian (hu-RA-klee-on), a Roman leader who plans to destroy the Gothic conquerors of Rome and make himself emperor. He is defeated.

Victoria, the beautiful blond daughter of Majoricus, saved from two barbarian soldiers by Raphael, who later marries her.

Majoricus (muh-JOH-rih-kuhs), a Roman prefect rescued from a heap of rubble by Raphael and Victoria. He is later killed in battle.

Augustine (oh-GUHS-tihn), the famous philosopher-monk. He persuades Raphael to turn Christian.

THE HYPOCHONDRIAC
(Le Malade imaginaire)

Author: Molière (Jean-Baptiste Poquelin, 1622-1673)
First published: 1674
Genre: Drama
Locale: Paris, France
Time: The seventeenth century
Plot: Comedy

Argan (ahr-GAH[N]), a hypochondriac, though he does not have the melancholia frequently associated with his state. His associates keep things too lively in his house to permit it, and he revels in his poor health. He gauges his health by the number of purges and clysters he has had this month compared to last. If the number is fewer, it is obvious that his condition is worse. He is glad he has only two children; more would leave him with no time for his illnesses. Although he enjoys the attention of two physicians and an apothecary, he is suspicious of their bills and checks them carefully, cutting the amount he intends to pay because "20 sous in the language of an apothecary is as much as to say 10 sous." To have a physician in the family to attend to him at all times is his wish; therefore, he refuses to consider any other as a son-in-law. His temper is revealed in his shouting at his servant when she is not prompt in answering the bell, and he calls her names, including "jade," "carrion," and "impudent." That he is extremely foolish is shown by his worry about orders of the physician to walk in his room: Should it be the long or the broad way? When his brother orders the physician out of the house, Argan is convinced that without his doctor's attention he will die. He is completely taken in by his second wife and her affectionate manner until her true feelings for him are revealed by the maid's trick. This also shows him his daughter's real love, and he permits the marriage to Cléante, provided he will become a physician, or at least an apothecary.

Toinette (twah-NEHT), Argan's servant, a sensible, amusing, and clever young woman. She loves Argan's daughter Angélique, shares her confidences, and aids her love affair. She is also aware of Argan's wife's true feelings toward her hypochondriac husband, and she proposes a test that convinces Argan that his wife is interested only in his money. Toinette gets along with her master very well, though she speaks up against his plan to marry Angélique to a physician and argues with him. She ridicules the young physician Argan has chosen as Angélique's husband, then apes the young man's speeches for those who missed hearing them. In an attempt to cure the hypochondriac of his fear of and respect for physicians, she disguises herself as a physician and ridicules the profession by making absurd diagnoses and diet suggestions. Her final clever plan for Argan to feign death to test the true feelings of his wife and daughter results in a happy close to the play.

Béline (bay-LEEN), Argan's second wife. Her relations with her husband seem calm and affectionate, but her true nature is revealed when she begs Argan not to talk about making his will, though she has the notary at hand to consult with him on this matter. She says she is not interested in his money, then checks on where he has hidden it and on the amount due on notes he has mentioned. She tries to persuade Argan to place both daughters in a convent so that she will get the entire property. Her real nature is revealed by Toinette's trap. On hearing of Argan's supposed death, she states her relief at his demise. She leaves quickly when he is proved to be alive.

Angélique (ahn-zhay-LEEK), Argan's older daughter. Although she is an obedient daughter, she objects to her betrothal to the young physician. When Toinette argues with Argan against his marriage plans for Angélique and the physician, she merely listens. Toinette is her real confidant, especially in questions of her love for Cléante; Toinette says that their conversation for six days was only about him. Part of this conversation is a witty catechism. Despite Angélique's differences with her father, she objects to the trick her uncle plans to play on him, but she agrees when assured it is only a giving in to his fancies and not really a trick on him. When Argan is supposed dead, Angélique's expression of her love and her sense of loss convinces Argan that she should not be forced into an unwelcome marriage.

Cléante (klay-AHNT), the young man in love with Angélique. Because of Argan's objection to him as a suitor, Cléante disguises himself as a music master so that he can see his beloved. He cleverly states the plot of an opera he will sing with her; it is a statement of their own circumstances. Argan sees through the story and calls it an impertinence. Cléante returns at the time of Argan's pretended death, to pay his respects and to try once again for the hypochondriac's good will. After Argan agrees to the marriage if he will become a physician, Cléante promises to become even an apothecary.

Béralde (bay-RAHLD), Argan's brother, who is opposed to physicians because he believes that nature will cure all ills. He recommends Molière's comedies exposing the ridiculousness of physics, if not of physicians. After he forbids the apothecary to administer the clyster ordered by the physician and drives him from the house, he calls his brother a simpleton. He also sees through Béline's plan to have the daughters placed in a convent and warns his brother. Argan, he suggests, should become a physician himself rather than ask Cléante to become one; he could learn all by merely putting on a gown and cap. Finally, he plans an interlude of a doctor's mission in which Argan will play the principal character.

Thomas Diafoirus (toh-MAHS dyah-fwah-REW), the son of Dr. Diafoirus, a stupid young physician favored by Argan as his son-in-law. Although he takes his cues from his father, he forgets parts of his memorized speeches to Angélique and Béline and mistakes one for the other. In medicine, he sticks to the ancients, not believing in any of the experiments of the day. He invites Angélique to witness the dissection of a woman.

Dr. Diafoirus, the father of Thomas, a physician who admits that his son is somewhat of a blockhead. Father and son, after an amusing examination of Argan, tie their diagnosis to Dr. Purgon's, which Argan repeats for them.

Dr. Purgon (pewr-GOH[N]), Argan's regular physician. Angry at the rejection, by Béralde's order, of the clyster he has ordered, he leaves, prophesying Argan's decline in health in four days, from "a bradypepsia to dyspepsia to apepsia to lienteria to dissenteria to dropsy to death."

Bonnefoy (bon-FWAH), a notary. In league with Béline, he tells Argan he cannot will his wife anything because only gifts given now or secretly to friends, for return to his wife later on, are legally permitted.

Fleurant (flew-RAH[N]), an apothecary working with Dr. Purgon. Argan says he is "extremely civil" but believes his charges ought to be more reasonable.

Louison (lwee-ZOH[N]), the younger daughter of Argan. She sides with her sister, though her father does learn from her that Cléante is disguised as the music master. When her father threatens to beat her for not readily volunteering the information, she feigns death.

I

I AM A CAT
(Wagahai wa Neko de aru)

Author: Sōseki Natsume (Kinnosuke Natsume, 1867-1916)
First published: 1905-1906
Genre: Novel
Locale: The house and neighborhood of a schoolteacher in Tokyo
Time: 1905-1906
Plot: Satire

The narrator, a nameless, stray tomcat of obscure origin that has been adopted by the Kushami family of Tokyo. Plain and nondescript in appearance, it is somewhat Persian in type and light grayish yellow in coloring. A creature of feeling and of a sensitive nature, it is highly intelligent, able to read and write the Japanese language. It is curious in its exploration of the world and an acute observer of the lives of human beings, in relation to whom, however, it feels definitely superior. Its principal deficiency is that it is cowardly and unable to catch rats.

Sensei Kushami, the tomcat's owner and a teacher in Tokyo. In his mid-thirties, he is of average build, has a pockmarked face, wears gold-rimmed glasses, sports a handlebar mustache, and suffers from dyspepsia. He wears the Japanese dress of the Meiji period: bowler hat and an *haori* jacket over a kimono. He has a wife, whom he often verbally abuses, and three small daughters, the youngest a baby. A reclusive person, he shuts himself in his study on returning home from school, and he tries to read, invariably falling asleep. He indulges in a variety of cultural enthusiasms: writing haiku and modern poems, painting watercolors, sketching, and playing the violin. He never rises to competence in any of these activities. He also keeps a diary, which is often read by his cat. Kushami is self-centered, self-indulgent, insensitive to the feelings of others, stubborn in his opinions, and contemptuous of businesspeople. His full name in Japanese means "lazy teacher."

Meitei, a friend of Kushami, an aesthetician who is of independent means. He is imaginative, a consummate liar, and a practical joker who consistently takes advantage of Kushami's naïveté. His name in Japanese literally means "puzzling tower."

Kangetsu Mizushima, a former pupil of Kushami who is a doctoral candidate in physics at the Imperial University of Tokyo. His favorite topic of conversation is women, and he likes to insinuate that he has had "adventures" with them. He is missing a front tooth and wears a black cotton *haori* jacket that is too small for him. His personal name, Kangetsu, means "wintry moon."

Mr. Kaneda, a prosperous businessman who lives in expensive housing not far from Kushami's modest dwelling. His name in Japanese means "prosperous rice field."

Hanako Kaneda, his wife. Her personal name, Hanako, means "nose." Because she has a big nose, Kushami and his friends refer to her as Mrs. Nose.

Tomiko Kaneda, the Kanedas' marriageable daughter. Rich and pretty, she is also snobbish, demanding, arrogant, and ill-mannered. Her personal name, Tomiko, means "rich."

Tofu Ochi, a poet. He is a friend of Mizushima, who introduced him to Kushami. He wears an *haori* jacket and a *hakama* divided skirt. His personal name, Tofu, means "east wind."

Tojuro Suzuki, a businessman who is employed by Mr. Kaneda and is an old friend of Kushami. His Western-style suit of English tweed signifies his Western orientation.

The Uncle from Shizuoka, Meitei's elderly uncle, an old-fashioned gentleman who wears the topknot *chommage* hairstyle once worn by gentlemen when they carried two swords. An admirer of the old samurai training and a proponent of Confucian and Zen Buddhist tenets, he carries with him an "iron fan," which is actually a fourteenth-century "helmet splitter."

Yagi Dokusen, a long-faced, bearded friend of Meitei of about forty. He is a poet and a scholar of Zen Buddhist philosophy who tends to monopolize any conversation. His personal name, Yagi, means "billy goat," and his surname, Dokusen, signifies "lonely hermit."

— *Richard P. Benton*

I, CLAUDIUS

Author: Robert Graves (1895-1985)
First published: 1934
Genre: Novel
Locale: Rome
Time: 10 B.C.E.-41 C.E.
Plot: Historical

Tiberius Claudius Drusus Nero Germanicus (ti-BIH-ree-uhs KLOH-dee-uhs DREW-suhs NEE-roh jur-MA-nih-kuhs), emperor of Rome after Caligula; a scholarly author of dull, sententious state histories; lame and a stammerer from childhood. His scholarship and stability bring him into favor with Augustus and Livia, who make him a priest of Mars. Having fainted at a bloody public sword fight, he is barred by Livia from public view. Forced by Livia to marry Urgulanilla, he later divorces her to marry Aelia, whom Tiberius orders him still later to divorce. He is afterward forced by Caligula to marry Messalina, though he loves Calpurnia.

Augustus Caesar (oh-GUHS-tuhs SEE-zur), first emperor of Rome. He suffers stomach disorders and dies, possibly poisoned by Livia.

Livia (LIH-vee-uh), his wife, Claudius' grandmother, a power-mad woman who divorces her boring husband, arranges her marriage to Augustus, and poisons those who interfere with her plans; suspected by Claudius of having poisoned Augustus. She is suspicious of Claudius and Germanicus as plotters against Tiberius, suspected by Claudius of having poisoned Claudius' young son, and set aside by Tiberius, who later refuses to return from Capri for her funeral.

Tiberius, Claudius' uncle, successor to Augustus, son of Livia by an early marriage and husband of Julia. A successful commander against the barbarians but unpopular in Rome, he is responsible for the torture and murder of Postumus, jealous of Germanicus' successes against the Germans, instigator of a reign of terror against Livia's faction, and responsible for the deaths of Sejanus and his children.

Germanicus, Claudius' brother, a successful commander poisoned by Livia and Tiberius because of fear that his popularity would grow too great.

Caligula (kuh-LIHG-yew-luh), successor to Tiberius, Germanicus' depraved son who, with Macro, takes command of the army and smothers the insane Tiberius. Having declared himself both emperor and a god, Caligula is at last murdered because of his excesses.

Julia (JEWL-yuh), daughter of Livia and Augustus and wife of Tiberius. Banished with Tiberius, she is slowly starved to death by Livia.

Urgulanilla (ur-gew-luh-NIH-luh), Claudius' gigantic young first wife forced on him by Livia. Claudius and Urgulanilla detest each other.

Postumus (POS-tew-muhs), son of Augustus. He is banished by his father, restored in Augustus' will, reported killed, then later tortured and actually killed on Tiberius' orders.

Agrippina (AG-rih-pi-nuh), wife of Germanicus.

Sejanus (seh-JAY-nuhs), the friend of Tiberius who arranges Claudius' divorce from Urgulanilla in order for him to marry Aelia. Later, he is killed along with his children on Tiberius' orders.

Aelia (EE-lee-uh), sister of Sejanus by adoption, the second wife of Claudius.

Macro (MAK-roh), commander of the guards, relieved by Caligula and later forced to kill himself.

Messalina (meh-suh-li-nuh), Claudius' third wife, forced on him by Caligula.

Calpurnia (kal-PUR-nee-uh), Claudius' only true friend, a prostitute banished by Caligula.

Urgulania (ur-gew-LAY-nee-uh), the monstrous-looking grandmother of Urgulanilla.

"I DON'T HAVE TO SHOW YOU NO STINKING BADGES!": A New American Play

Author: Luis Miguel Valdez (1940-   )
First published: 1986
Genre: Drama
Locale: Monterey Park, California
Time: Late 1980's
Plot: Satire

Buddy Villa (VEE-yuh), a Hollywood bit-part actor. Buddy is a fifty-seven-year-old Chicano who has risen from the barrio of East Los Angeles to a comfortable middle-class suburban life. Buddy is fiercely proud of having achieved the American Dream of material success, even though it has been bought with an ignoble career playing stereotypical roles such as gardeners or "banditos." Buddy rationalizes his position by pointing to the comfortable life it has given his family and by anointing himself and his wife "The Silent Bit King and Queen of Hollywood." Such bravado compensates for the frustration of never rising to better roles. Buddy's frustration is manifested by his continuous daydreams of new films in which he is the star. Buddy's latent bitterness toward Anglo America is often expressed by his reference to a film in which he played a bandit who dismisses the authorities with the line, "I don't have to show you no stinking badges!"

Connie Villa, Buddy's wife, also a bit-part actress. Connie is a forty-eight-year-old Chicana who only recently joined her husband in film work after a life as a conventional homemaker. Although Connie works professionally only when she can do so in tandem with Buddy, she quietly yearns for better roles and personal independence. When she is offered a speaking role, Buddy refuses her permission to accept the part because he cannot accompany her on location. A clash is avoided only when both are offered parts on a soap opera. Connie is relieved at this turn of events; she usually seems content to defer to Buddy, and she genuinely appreciates the good life Buddy has provided.

Sonny Villa, Buddy and Connie's son, a law school student. Sonny arrives home one day to announce that he is dropping out of Harvard Law School to pursue a new ambition to become a film superstar. Buddy and Connie oppose Sonny's decision because they believe that he is throwing away his opportunity for an autonomous life. Sonny's parents do not see, however, that he is suffering from a classic identity crisis: As the son of immigrants, Sonny is at home neither in the Anglo culture of Harvard nor in the Mexican culture of his ancestors. Sonny's impulsive decision to pursue acting is a self-conscious capitulation to his inability to recover a sense of history in which to root his identity. Sonny ultimately fails in

Hollywood and returns to law school, tacitly accepting his place in a homogenized American culture.

Anita, Sonny's Asian American girlfriend from Boston. Anita is also intent on making it big in Hollywood, which is why she accompanies Sonny home even though she does not return his love for her. Anita's experience in Hollywood acts as a counterpoint to Sonny's, because her healthy self-image and positive outlook are chiefly responsible for her landing a good part in a television series.

— *Mark William Rocha*

I FOR ONE . . .

Author: Frank Sargeson (1903-1982)
First published: 1952
Genre: Novel
Locale: New Zealand
Time: Mid-twentieth century
Plot: Psychological realism

Katherine Sheppard, an unmarried teacher in New Zealand who still lives with her mother. The story is told as a series of diary entries written by this intelligent, idealistic, and somewhat neurotic woman in her thirties who evidently does not realize how strongly she yearns to get out from under her mother's roof and find a permanent love relationship. She has been disappointed by men but keeps hoping to find "Mr. Right," as she describes this imaginary mate in her diary. When she meets Dr. Hubert Nock at a party, she begins to hope that he may turn out to be Mr. Right. Hubert takes an immediate interest in her and quickly leads the eager, impressionable woman to believe that he has serious intentions. Her diary chronicles five months in the life of a fading spinster schoolteacher that are brightened only by occasional meetings with Hubert and daydreams about their future. She is bitterly disappointed when she discovers that Hubert has only been toying with her affections and is in fact already married.

Dr. Hubert Nock, an American psychologist visiting New Zealand in connection with his work. This tall, handsome, middle-aged New Englander appears to be a paragon of male virtues who has stepped out of an illustration in an American magazine advertisement. His behavior toward Katherine, however, proves that he is much more complicated than he appears. Being a professional psychologist, he easily understands her loneliness and longing for affection, and he begins to manipulate her to gratify his vanity. Although he leads Katherine to believe that they will marry, he often disappears for days at a time and then claims that he was ill or involved with work. From her descriptions of him in her journal, it becomes evident that she sees him more as a father figure than as a lover. When he is finally exposed as a cad, Katherine suffers a nervous collapse but then emerges much stronger and more self-reliant.

Katherine's mother, a widow. This aging woman appears to be a drab, conventional, unimaginative homebody until Katherine begins discovering secrets about her past. Katherine learns that her mother loathed her father and, rather than mourning his recent death, is happy to be rid of him. At the end of the novel, Katherine's mother confesses to Katherine that she was wild and rebellious as a young woman and traveled all over New Zealand with Katherine's father while he was still married to another woman. Katherine's new insights about both her parents, whom she has always regarded as models of decorum, help to liberate her from her rigid inhibitions, attributable to her false views of human nature.

Hilda James, Katherine's half sister by her father, an aggressive, affluent, worldly woman in her early fifties. Katherine meets her by accident in a tearoom at the zoo and learns to her horror that her father had been married to and was divorced from Hilda's mother. Hilda provides the first shock to Katherine's puritanical view of the world. Much later, Hilda delivers a final devastating shock to Katherine's house of cards by telling her that Dr. Hubert Nock is her husband.

Helen James, Hilda's teenage daughter. This beautiful, kindhearted girl takes an interest in her new Aunt Katherine and helps nurse her through the nervous collapse that follows Katherine's discovery that Hubert has been deceiving her for the past five months. There are overtones of homosexuality in Katherine's relationship with Helen as well as in Katherine's past relationship with a woman who is a mutual friend of Katherine and Helen. At the end of the novel, it appears that Katherine, having been shocked out of her puritanical stance, is ready to accept her own darker suppressed passions.

— *Bill Delaney*

I GET ON THE BUS

Author: Reginald McKnight (1956-   )
First published: 1990
Genre: Novel
Locale: Senegal
Time: The 1980's
Plot: Psychological realism

Evan Norris, the protagonist and narrator, an alienated African American who has left the United States for two years to teach in Senegal for the Peace Corps. His experiences there generate mental and physical suffering and raise fundamental questions about the nature and viability of his personal and cultural identity.

Wanda Wright, Evan's girlfriend in the United States, with whom he persistently fails to communicate, both during their life together and more literally when he is in Senegal. She is an important point of reference for Evan. Through her, the reader perceives that his troubles are not merely the result of being geographically dislocated.

Aminata Gueye (ah-mee-NAH-tah geh-yay), a student, Evan's Senegalese girlfriend. She is the daughter of a marabout, a Muslim holy man familiar with the occult who gives rise to the various forms of psychological and cultural duress that Evan is forced to undergo. She is a trickster figure, ostensibly attempting to do Evan good but undermining his sense of who he is and what he is doing.

Africa Mamadou Ford, a native of Oakland, California, currently residing in Senegal. His experiences of the country and its culture are models of what Evan has to go through. He tries to help Evan counteract what he perceives to be the effects of culture shock, advising Evan to respond to Senegal in its own terms rather than from an American perspective.

Lamont Samb, Aminata's Senegalese fiancée, a former teacher of French in Wales. Allegedly well versed in phenomena that have caused and that will redress Evan's condition, he is the most menacing and most elusive figure Evan encounters. He provides the culmination of Evan's experiences.

— George O'Brien

I LIKE IT HERE

Author: Kingsley Amis (1922-1995)
First published: 1958
Genre: Novel
Locale: London and Portugal
Time: Mid-1950's
Plot: Social satire

Garnet Bowen, a freelance writer. He is a large man with a well-made frame and an inefficient air. He supports his family with some difficulty on his income from bits of journalism, radio talks, and occasional lectures. He is also a xenophobic Englishman. When an American firm offers him (under the name Garret Owen) a substantial fee to write a travel article, however, he reluctantly decides that he will go abroad. Still another inducement to travel is the opportunity to work for a publishing firm for which he has read an occasional manuscript and with which he hopes to land a permanent position.

Barbara Bowen, Garnet's wife and the mother of his three young children. She is a small, pretty, dark woman who thoroughly approves of her husband's irregular self-employment. She believes that he must be free to do his own work, for he will one day be a fine novelist or dramatist. Unlike her husband, she loves the idea of foreign travel, and her mother is willing to put up much of the money and lend them a car. She wishes especially to visit Portugal.

Bennie Hyman, a principal member of the publishing firm for which Garnet wishes to work. He is a successful young bachelor with an athletic appearance. He has received a manuscript, the first in many years, from a reclusive old novelist living in Portugal. The novelist dealt with only one editor, who has died and left behind no evidence of the relationship. Years before, there were rumors of the novelist's death. The young publisher wants Garnet to take a house in Portugal, meet the recluse, and judge whether he is genuine or an impostor.

Wulfstan Strether, a novelist and recluse who is also known as **Buckmaster**. He is a tall, white-haired, hawk-faced man of sixty. He is the author of a 120,000-word manuscript titled *One Word More*. He is pleased to entertain Garnet, but he is not an easy man to read and is not easily manipulated. His very decent behavior produces feelings of guilt in Garnet, who is also being plagued, as he feared he would be, by an assortment of natives and fellow tourists.

— Patrick Adcock

I NEVER PROMISED YOU A ROSE GARDEN

Author: Hannah Green (Joanne Greenberg, 1932-)
First published: 1964
Genre: Novel
Locale: An American mental hospital
Time: 1948-1951
Plot: Psychological

Deborah F. Blau, an attractive, blonde, sixteen-year-old Jewish teenager who has just been admitted to a mental hospital at the start of the novel. She is diagnosed with schizophrenia. Despite outward signs of privilege, Deborah has retreated into a fantasy world of her own creation, the Kingdom of Yr. Because she is completely dependent on this fantasy world, it is with great reluctance and much genuine fear that she enters into a trusting relationship with her psychiatrist, Dr. Fried. Although very disturbed, Deborah is nevertheless smart and precocious, with a sarcastic, superior manner. Her insults and snide remarks often contain clever wordplay. Her hunger to learn is genuine and divorced from her mental illness: Even when she is most ill, she thirsts for knowledge and cajoles a fellow patient into teaching her Greek and Latin. Her artistic ability also is real, and despite prohibitions against possessing pencils and paper, she manages to find ways to draw. Deborah carries deep within herself the strength and the will to live in the outside world. With Dr. Fried, she eventually learns to recognize and trust that power.

Dr. Clara Fried, thought of as **Furii** by Deborah, a chubby, tiny, gray-haired psychiatrist who has left her war-torn native Germany. She is famous and internationally renowned when she takes Deborah's case. Patient and perceptive, she is careful never to push Deborah past what she can endure. Dr. Fried is admired by her colleagues not only for her intelligence and technique but also for her empathy and touch.

Esther Blau, Deborah's mother. Strong-willed and sophisticated, she tends to keep her true thoughts and emotions hidden from view. With some effort, she is able to face the reality of her daughter's illness. She carries herself with a careful, polished demeanor but is sensitive enough to realize that many of the neighbors see her only as an immigrant's daughter.

Jacob Blau, Deborah's father, an accountant. He is not introspective and has difficulty accepting that Deborah is sick enough to need hospitalization. As a father, he treats Deborah with a mixture of emotions: love for a daughter combined with a guilty, unwanted lust. His overprotectiveness is partly responsible for Deborah's need to create a fantasy world.

Susan (Suzy) Blau, Deborah's sister, who is younger by five years. Although initially "protected" from the truth of Deborah's stay in an institution, she accepts it easily once she is told. Her triumphs and talents often go unnoticed because her parents are caught up in their sorrow for Deborah.

Carla Stoneham, Deborah's friend on Ward D. Before killing herself, her mother killed her brother and tried to kill Carla. Carla and Deborah treat each other with kindnesses that probably would go unnoticed in the outside world.

Miss Coral, a patient on Ward D and Deborah's "tutor." A well-educated mathematician, Miss Coral is a ninety-pound, gray-haired elderly woman capable of amazing feats of violence and long strings of profanity. In between meals and therapy and descents into madness, she teaches Deborah Greek and Latin.

McPherson, a kind attendant on Ward D. A strong and happy man, he looks for similarities between himself and the mental patients.

— Liz Marshall

I, THE SUPREME
(Yo, el Supremo)

Author: Augusto Roa Bastos (1917-   )
First published: 1974
Genre: Novel

Locale: Asunción, Paraguay
Time: 1800-1840
Plot: Historical

José Gaspar Rodríguez de Francia (hoh-SEH GAHS-pahr rrohd-REE-gehs deh FRAHN-see-ah) the supreme dictator of the newly formed Republic of Paraguay. Although he is fundamentally a democratic idealist and believes in the models provided by the United States and France, his experience with the recently liberated population of Paraguay has frustrated his enlightened intentions. Because of his compatriots' lack of education and the imperialist pressures from other emergent republican states such as Argentina and Brazil, he finds himself forced to assume increasingly greater dictatorial powers. Eventually, he succumbs to the seduction of absolute power, assumes the direct control of all areas of government, and withdraws into the secure isolation of his palace. He spends the majority of his time dictating orders to his subordinates and attempting to justify his betrayal of his own ideals. The last few weeks of his life are filled with a sense of decay and disintegration into absolute impotence and fear for his image in posterity.

Policarpo Patiño (poh-lee-KAHR-poh pah-TEEN-yoh), the dictator's constant companion and personal secretary. Essentially a fearful, obsequious, hypocritical mouse of a man, preoccupied more with his creature comforts than with great ideals, Patiño transcribes Francia's dictation and listens to his monologues on a variety of topics. Terrified of the dictator and his tempers, he spends his time contradicting himself in an effort to placate and ingratiate. He is also fond of narrating long tales taken from local superstition and gossip that both interest and enrage his master. He is ignorant and uneducated, and he consistently makes mistakes in the written text of Francia's discourse. At times, his ignorance borders on the comic, as he transposes letters in words to form unconscious plays on words and vulgarities. The dying dictator mockingly sentences him to death and ignominy in one final decree, reducing Patiño to babbling terror.

Juan Parish Robertson, a well-educated English adventurer whose travels bring him and his brother Roberto to Paraguay. The brothers are initially welcomed by the dictator, who befriends them and passes long evenings entertaining them in the palace. They prove to be extremely opportunistic, a characteristic best represented by Juan Robertson's torrid affair with Juana Esquivel, the wealthy octogenarian next-door neighbor of Francia, who showers the young foreigner with gifts and attention. When the dictator requests that they act as intermediaries to sell Paraguayan products to the English Crown, they accept the mission and then betray their benefactor in favor of more lucrative enterprises. Upon their return to civilization, they write two scathing accounts of their adventure, attacking Francia as a monster who maintains his subjects in subhuman conditions and a perpetual reign of terror.

Pilar the Black (pee-LAHR), Francia's trusted personal valet and general servant. Initially portrayed as obedient, he later becomes rebellious. He steals small items from the government to support an Indian woman he loves and their unborn child. One day, he enters the dictator's office and assumes his clothing and identity, becoming virtually indistinguishable from his master. When Francia returns, Pilar goes wild and attacks him, but the guards cannot tell them apart. The dictator is finally obliged to execute him as a traitor but is haunted by guilt afterward.

General Manuel Belgrano (mahn-WEHL behl-GRAH-noh), an Argentine general sent by his government to subdue the Paraguayan provinces. The campaign is not successful; the idealistic Belgrano realizes that the Paraguayan army is prepared to defend the country to the death. He consequently withdraws his forces and later returns as a negotiator to establish a diplomatic alliance. The dictator is touched by the integrity and honor displayed by his former enemy, and they become close friends.

Antonio Manoel Correia da Camara (mah-noh-EHL koh-RRAY-ah dah KAH-mah-rah), a treacherous and deceitful Brazilian envoy sent to negotiate border disputes. He is the diametric opposite of his Argentine counterpart, Belgrano. Where the latter is honest and forthright, Correia is underhanded and secretive.

Bernardo Velazco (beh-LAHS-koh), a loyal royalist governor of Paraguay who becomes a lifelong enemy of Francia, primarily as a result of ideological differences. He attacks the dictator's policies and human nature in a series of letters.

Sultan, Francia's idealistic dog and the dictator's alter ego. He enjoys spending his evenings debating the Robertson brothers on diverse political and mythical topics. At the end, he becomes the primary voice of accusation against the dictator's weaknesses.

I WILL MARRY WHEN I WANT
(Ngaahika Ndeenda)

Authors: Ngugi wa Thiong'o (James Ngugi, 1938-) and Ngugi wa Mirii (1951-)
First published: 1980
Genre: Drama

Locale: Kenya
Time: The 1970's
Plot: Social realism

Kiguunda (kee-gew-EWN-dah), a farm laborer and smallholder of one and one-half acres in postcolonial Kenya. Although his efforts as a Mau Mau guerrilla on behalf of independence have been followed by a life of labor and hardship, he is a proud man. When his employer, Kioi, and others visit him in his one-room, mud-walled home to convert him to Christianity and insist that he "marry" his wife of many years, he takes his sword from the wall and drives them out. Later, believing that their motive was to legitimize a marriage between his daughter Gathoni and their son, he repents, offers to undertake the ceremony, and puts up his smallholding to secure a bank loan that will cover the large expenses of a Christian wedding. After Gathoni is made pregnant and discarded by Kioi's son, Kiguunda again threatens Kioi. Subsequently, he loses his job and his smallholding. He becomes an abusive drunk until his friend and neighbor recalls him to a fervent belief in overthrowing the tyranny of the rich.

Gicaamba (gee-kah-AHM-bah), a factory worker and neighbor and friend of Kiguunda. Gicaamba's proletarian distrust of the native rich, their foreign investors, and the oppressive use both make of Christianity helps at first to keep Kiguunda's own skepticism alive. After Kiguunda is ruined, Gicaamba's militant call to class action revives the broken man's spirit.

Ahab Kioi wa Kanoru (AY-hahb kee-OH-ee wah kah-NOH-rew), a wealthy farmer and entrepreneur with foreign and domestic business contacts. He wishes to convert Kiguunda, who is a natural leader of the farmworkers, to Christianity, as a first step toward using him to keep the other workers productive and docile. When Kiguunda must default on his loan, Kioi acquires his smallholding for a foreign consortium. The land will be used for a factory that will produce toxic and noxious chemicals.

Wangeci (wahn-GAY-see), Kiguunda's wife. She resents their poverty, noting that those who did not wage war against the British have emerged from that period with property and wealth. She also presses Kiguunda to convert for the sake of their daughter's future. She deplores Gathoni's vanity and love of extravagant clothes but does not reject Gathoni when she hears of Gathoni's pregnancy. She quarrels with her husband when he begins drinking but joins him at the end in a song predicting the victory of the workers over their exploiters.

Samuel Ndugire (ihn-dew-GEE-ray), a nouveau riche tea farmer and shopkeeper, as well as a friend of Kioi. He and his wife accompany Kioi and his wife in their attempt to convert Kiguunda to Christianity. He reflects and embellishes Kioi's contemptuous opinions of workers.

Gathoni (gah-DHOH-nee), the daughter of Kiguunda and Wangeci. She is swept off her feet by Kioi's son, who lavishes presents on her. Her pregnancy causes him to jilt her. She becomes a barmaid in a disreputable establishment after Kiguunda throws her out.

Njooki (ihn-joh-OH-kee), Gicaamba's wife. She is nearly as voluble as her husband in her condemnation of the rich, of foreigners, and of Christianity. She tries to warn Kiguunda and Wangeci against Kioi.

Jezebel, Kioi's wife. She is a stern and devout Christian by her own measure; that is, she presumes that God has rewarded her and her family and that those less fortunate have a duty to bear their lot in silence. She, like Kioi, believes that the millions of people who have never heard of Christ will burn forever in hell.

Ikuua wa Nditika (ih-KEW-ew-ah wah ihn-dee-TEE-kah), Kioi's business partner. He is aggressively nonconformist and non-Christian. He shocks Kioi's wife with his predilection for alcoholic drinks and continued practice of polygamy.

— *James L. Hodge*

ICE

Author: Anna Kavan (Helen Woods Edmonds, 1901-1968)
First published: 1967
Genre: Novel

Locale: Probably Northern Europe
Time: The near future
Plot: Surrealism

The narrator, an itinerant soldier and explorer who is ruled by an obsession with a young woman, known only as the girl. He returns home from the tropics, ostensibly to investigate rumors of an impending emergency but actually to pursue this obsession he only dimly understands. The narrator suffers from headaches, insomnia, and horrible dreams, which he has come to enjoy, of the girl's death and destruction. Seeking to protect the girl from her husband and the warden, he actually victimizes her as well. Sadistic and abusive, feeling that only he has the right to inflict pain on her, he loses interest once she is conquered and regains it only when she eludes him once more. He feels a close kinship with the ruthless warden, an identification so strong that he considers them to be identical twins, or even more strongly, "like halves of one being."

The girl, a childlike, vulnerable young woman. Thin and fragile, with pale skin, large dark eyes, and silver-white hair, the girl is timid and highly sensitive. Kept in a permanent state of subjugation, first by her mother and later by the husband, the narrator, and the warden, she is the perfect victim. Although continually in flight from the three men and the ice, she is always recaptured, and she seems as resigned to her fate as victim as she is to the imminent destruction of the world. Only when she finally confronts the narrator about his abusive behavior does she have a chance to break the cycle of victimization.

The warden, a ruthless man possessing great political, military, and personal power. Like the narrator, he pursues and abuses the girl. The warden is a handsome, tall, yellow-haired man with an athletic build and arrestingly bright blue eyes. Arrogant but extremely intelligent, he has a dominant personality. Described as "a born ruler" and "a law unto himself," the warden grows in stature and importance as the world deteriorates, rising from local to national and finally to global prominence. Although charming when it suits his purpose, he has a total disregard for the feelings of others and is selfish, treacherous, and cruel. The strong sense of identity the narrator feels with the warden leads to the almost certain conclusion that the warden and the narrator (and the husband) represent different aspects of the same character.

The husband, an artist who is married to the girl. A massive man, he is moody and sardonic, alternately charming and quarrelsome. He always has an abundance of money but never appears to do any work, leading the narrator to suspect that he is something other than he seems and to the suspicion that the husband and the warden are indeed the same character.

— *Mary Virginia Davis*

THE ICE AGE

Author: Margaret Drabble (1939-   )
First published: 1977
Genre: Novel
Locale: England and the Balkan country of Wallacia
Time: Mid-1970's
Plot: Social

Anthony Keating, an unhappy, once upwardly mobile property developer in his thirties who made rash speculations at the behest of a business associate, Len Wincobank, who later was imprisoned for fraud. Keating, the impassioned lover of Alison Murray, attempts to understand how life went wrong for him. He had worked as a television producer, and in 1968, he interviewed Wincobank. The experience convinced him to go into property development. Now facing imminent bankruptcy, he hopes to be able somehow to keep his spectacular Midlands home and live there with Alison.

Alison Murray, another protagonist. Beautiful, talented, and troubled, she is caught up not only in Keating's plight but also in her own daughters' problems. Daughter Jane has been imprisoned in the mythical country of Wallachia after having run over and killed a Wallachian peasant while on a tourist excursion; she faces a long term of imprisonment. Youngest daughter Molly suffers from the long-term effects of cerebral palsy and demands considerable attention and affection. Alison gave up a promising career as an actress to care for Molly. She is married to a successful but unfaithful actor.

Len Wincobank, a supremely self-confident confidence man who symbolizes the get-rich-quick London go-getter of the 1970's whose greed and vaunting ambition lead to a downfall. Sent to prison for fraudulent dealings, Wincobank not only ruins his own life but also hurts others in the process, primarily Anthony Keating, his disciple. Wincobank, though highly intelligent, clearly lacks a conscience: He shows no remorse over his crimes against society and friends. He speculates that once released from prison, he can go back to his property development schemes.

Jane Murray, the sullen, withdrawn eldest daughter of Alison Murray. She shows little interest in other people, even her own mother. Involved in what clearly should have been seen as involuntary manslaughter, she is treated by Wallachian authorities as a murderer and is therefore given a life sentence. Despite the drabness of prison existence, Jane spurns her mother's offer of comfort and possible release.

— *John D. Raymer*

AN ICELAND FISHERMAN
(Pêcheur d'islande)

Author: Pierre Loti (Julien Viaud, 1850-1923)
First published: 1886
Genre: Novel
Locale: Brittany and at sea
Time: The nineteenth century
Plot: Impressionism

Jean-Marie-Sylvestre Moan (zhah[n]-mah-REE-sihl-VEHS-treh moh-AH[N]), a strongly built, good-looking young Breton with dark beard and gray-blue eyes; innocent and devout. He vainly tries to interest Yann in marrying Gaud. Serving with the French navy in Indochina, he is shot by a Chinese soldier. He dies of his wound while returning to France aboard a transport ship and is buried at Singapore.

Yvonne Moan (ih-VON), his grandmother, toothless but rosy-cheeked, fresh, and pretty despite her age. She is desolated by Sylvestre's death and becomes increasingly enfeebled in mind and body.

Marguerite (Gaud) Mevel (mahr-geh-REET goh meh-VEHL), his charming and wealthy cousin, flaxen-haired, hazel-eyed, with a Grecian profile and a body like a lovely statue; tall, serious, virtuous, quietly poised, and low-voiced. In love with Yann, she longs desperately for him but, ladylike, will not thrust herself upon him. After her father's death, the now poor Gaud becomes a seamstress and goes to live with the bereft Yvonne. Supremely happy when she is finally married to Yann, she bears the grief of his loss with quiet dignity.

Jean (Yann) Gaos (zhah[n] yahn gay-OHS), a fisherman and ex-gunner in the French navy, a giant of a man, clean-shaven, with a curling blond mustache. Kindhearted, he is occasionally rough and almost brutal without intending harm, and now and then given to bursts of temper. Not seriously interested in women, he loves the sea. He is grieved to learn of Sylvestre's death and his burial far from home. Urged by his relatives and Yvonne, he finally proposes to a joyously surprised Gaud, and they are married six days before he leaves again with the fishing fleet. His ship, however, does not return; the sea he loved has married him at last.

Marie Gaos, Sylvestre's fiancée, sister of Yann.

Captain Guermeur (gehr-MEWR), skipper of the *Marie*.

M. Mevel, Gaud's father, a wealthy, semi-piratical speculator who dies after losing his fortune.

Mme Tressoleur (treh-soh-LEWR), a portly, mustached, blunt, coquettish tavern operator.

Guillaume (gee-YOHM), a fisherman on the *Marie*.

THE ICEMAN COMETH

Author: Eugene O'Neill (1888-1953)
First published: 1946
Genre: Drama
Locale: Harry Hope's Saloon in New York City
Time: Summer, 1912
Plot: Tragedy

Harry Hope, the proprietor of a saloon and rooming house on the Lower West Side of New York City. He has been afflicted with agoraphobia since the death of his wife many years earlier. He hated her but cannot admit that he did, even to himself. With pretended reluctance, he gives his roomers free rent and free liquor. Like them, he is an alcoholic.

Ed Mosher, Hope's brother-in-law, a former circus man and a roomer at Harry Hope's.

Pat McGloin, a former police lieutenant and a roomer at Harry Hope's.

Willie Oban, a Harvard Law School alumnus and a roomer at Harry Hope's.

Joe Mott, formerly the proprietor of a gambling house with a black clientele.

Piet Wetjoen, known as **The General**, a former leader of a Boer commando and a roomer at Harry Hope's.

Cecil Lewis, known as **The Captain**, a former captain of British infantry and a roomer at Harry Hope's.

James Cameron, also known as **Jimmy Tomorrow**, a former Boer War correspondent and a roomer at Harry Hope's.

Hugo Kalmar, a former editor of anarchist periodicals. His name suggests Karl Marx.

Larry Slade, a syndicalist-anarchist and a roomer at Harry Hope's. He considers himself to be a withdrawn observer of the others who lacks their pipe dream of someday returning to the real world and a former life. The events of the play finally make him recognize his involvement with the others, especially with a newcomer, Don Parritt, who might conceivably be his son. As a result of Parritt's continual pleading, Larry finally orders him to commit suicide. At the play's end, Larry is the only one unable to return to his pipe dream and therefore will be alone in the saloon until he dies.

Rocky Pioggi, a night bartender.

Don Parritt, a roomer at Harry Hope's. He is a young wanderer seeking Larry and trying to escape from his mother's rejection and from his responsibility for her imprisonment. Realizing the hopelessness of escape, he finally commits suicide by jumping off the fire escape.

Pearl, a roomer at Harry Hope's and a streetwalker.

Margie, a roomer at Harry Hope's and a streetwalker.

Cora, a streetwalker.

Chuck Morello, a day bartender and a roomer at Harry Hope's. He and Pearl have the pipe dream of marrying and buying a farm in New Jersey. Like the others, they come to realize that the dream is false.

Theodore "Hickey" Hickman, a hardware salesman. He periodically goes to the saloon for drinks and is heartily welcomed because he treats all the others and is full of jokes and good cheer. When he shows up for Harry's birthday party, however, his personality has changed, and he tries to force the others to see themselves as they really are, with impossible pipe dreams. He thus ruins the birthday party. The others finally learn that the personality change was caused by his killing his wife. He thinks of the murder as an act of mercy but finally realizes that it was an act of hatred; for this reason, he turns himself over to the police. He psychologically forces almost all of them (except Larry) to go into the real world and to try to fulfill their pipe dreams, in the belief that the realization that they will never fulfill them will make them more content with life as it is. To his dismay, they all return desolated. When Hickey, on realizing that he killed his wife out of hatred, says that he must have been crazy, they accept this eagerly as an explanation of what he has done to them. With the exception of Larry, they can return to their pipe dreams. Hickey's given name ironically means "love of God." His surname suggests that he is a "hick" (from small-town Indiana), and his nickname suggests "blemish."

Moran and

Lieb, the policemen who come to arrest Hickey. Their names suggest, ironically, "death" and "love."

— *Jacob H. Adler*

THE IDES OF MARCH

Author: Thornton Wilder (1897-1975)
First published: 1948
Genre: Novel
Locale: Rome
Time: 45 B.C.
Plot: Historical

Julius Caesar, who expects to be assassinated because many individuals and groups would like to see him dead and his career ended. All he hopes is that his assassins will be true lovers of Rome, not selfish men and women. He believes he has been right in taking over the government of the Roman Empire, for he believes that the masses of people want a strong leader who will make their decisions for them, even though they resent a concurrent loss of freedom. As for himself,

Caesar wonders about life, being unsure of the gods and their influence on human affairs. Though he sometimes feels intuitively there are no gods, he guides himself by the advice of soothsayers and their omens.

Pompeia, Caesar's wife, who is embittered because she is ordered to receive Cleopatra, the queen of Egypt, even though Cleopatra is notorious for her immorality, including an affair with Caesar himself. Pompeia is divorced by Caesar when rumor has it that she gave help to Clodia Pulcher in profaning a religious ceremony devoted to the Good Goddess. Caesar says his wife must be above rumor.

Calpurnia, whom Caesar marries after divorcing Pompeia. When Caesar is about to leave Rome, he entrusts Calpurnia's welfare to Brutus, not knowing Brutus himself will be one of his murderers.

Marcus Brutus, one of Caesar's slayers. Once loyal to Caesar, he is persuaded by his mother, who hates Caesar and is ambitious for her own son, to become an assassin. Brutus is rumored to be an illegitimate son of Caesar.

Clodia Pulcher, a beautiful woman of great wealth and patrician birth. She blames the gods for her immorality. In defiance of law and tradition, she introduces her disguised brother into ceremonies open only to women. Caesar's pardon for her blasphemous action only makes her resentful of him.

Cleopatra, the queen of Egypt, who is making an official visit to Rome. Because of her reputation for intrigue, Caesar believes she may be a conspirator against him.

Catullus, a young poet in love with Clodia Pulcher. For her sake, Catullus writes scurrilous poems and tracts about Caesar. Catullus' death saddens Caesar.

Lady Julia Marcia, Caesar's aunt and a directress of the mysteries of the Good Goddess. She is renowned for her dignity and moral virtue.

THE IDIOT
(Idiot)

Author: Fyodor Dostoevski (1821-1881)
First published: 1868-1869
Genre: Novel
Locale: St. Petersburg, Russia
Time: Mid-nineteenth century
Plot: Psychological realism

Prince Lef Nicolaievitch Myshkin (lehv ni-koh-LI-eh-vihch MEWSH-kihn), a noble man whose behavior at first is only strange and unconventional but who later shows a deterioration of mind. Short, slight, with light hair and moustache, nearly white beard, and searching blue eyes, he arrests the attention of all who see him. His naïve, unblemished goodness, in part the result of his long epilepsy, causes men to doubt him and women to love him. Toward the end of his life, he is wholly compassionate, selfless, and pitying. In his weakened, susceptible condition, he degenerates until he is unable to cope with life, decisions, hatreds, worldliness. Able to see human foibles without malice, to reverence the human condition without judgment, to love without the thought of attainment, he is a Christ figure set in a corrupt society where the facile, dishonest, worldly, and unconscionable prevail in absolute terms of money and position. His deterioration under heavy pressures of murder, disloyalty, vituperation, and vindictiveness is saintly, a martyrdom to unheroic life. A tragic figure, he is destroyed by those whom he loves most, and he is sent to a sanitarium in Switzerland.

Nastasya Filipovna (nahs-TAH-syah fi-lih-POHV-nuh), the tragic figure of despair and vindictiveness with whom the prince identifies himself. Beautiful in a dark, sulky way, Nastasya is the victim of a man's lust. From this degradation, she rises to a sense of power over many men, the power that leads her to her death at the hands of the pathologically jealous Rogozhin. Drawn mysteriously to the benign young invalid, she also helps to determine his fate. A magnificent talker, a kind of actress of many parts, a moody dreamer, a defiant lover, she is a woman of great talents and deep motives.

Madame Lizaveta Prokofyevna Epanchin (lih-zah-VEH-tuh proh-KOH-fyehv-nuh eh-PAHN-chihn), a simple woman of great moodiness, honorable, sensitive, and inherently good. Beneath her outlandish speeches, even insults, she hides hurt feelings and a sensitive nature. Her husband, who loves and honors her, only increases her tensions because of his worldliness and business mind. She understands the goodness of Prince Myshkin, but she finally withdraws her daughter from marriage with him for purely conventional and genetic reasons. She is deeply devoted to her family, proud of her own heritage and position, and very Russian.

General Epanchin, her husband.

Aglaya Ivanovna (ahg-LAH-yuh ih-VAH-nov-nuh), the Epanchins' youngest and most beautiful daughter, betrothed to Prince Myshkin. On her, the family had set a price—the best match to the finest man in all St. Petersburg—and for this reason the pampered beauty is a mass of contradictions with the saving grace of feminine, intuitive insights. She is virginal, capricious, reticent, yet loving, devoted and understanding. Her intense nature will not allow her to think of Nastasya and Myshkin as innocent; her jealousy is sombre and unrelenting, a cause of deep personal tragedy.

Parfen Rogozhin (PAHR-fehn roh-GOH-zhihn), a chance acquaintance of Prince Myshkin. A sensitive but impassioned sensualist who becomes deeply involved in the prince's life, Rogozhin has higher traits than appear in his rough, dark, uncouth, and powerful exterior. His tragic nature, irascible yet contrite, turns him after the violent murder of Nastasya into a blubbering repentant. The world has perverted him through a niggardly father and jealous, vindictive relatives.

Ganya Ardalionovitch (GAH-nyuh ahr-dah-lih-OHN-o-vihch), General Epanchin's secretary. Belying his appearance and manners, he is inwardly a thorough scoundrel. He hopes to marry Aglaya because of her money. He is also involved with Nastasya.

IDYLLS OF THE KING

Author: Alfred, Lord Tennyson (1809-1892)
First published: 1859-1885
Genre: Poetry

Locale: England
Time: The fifth century
Plot: Arthurian romance

King Arthur, of Camelot. His birth is shrouded in great mystery, and he is reared by Merlin the magician. He receives his magic sword Excalibur from the Lady of the Lake and marries Guinevere. With his Round Table knights, he drives out the enemy and unifies his kingdom. He rules wisely and is successful until his Round Table fellowship diminishes in the knights' quest for the Holy Grail. Exposure of Guinevere's infidelity with Lancelot proves thoroughly demoralizing, and in a traitorous revolt, Arthur is mortally wounded. After his last remaining faithful knight returns Excalibur to the Lady of the Lake, three maidens come in a barge to the shore to carry Arthur away as mysteriously as he had come.

Guinevere, Arthur's beloved queen and his inspiration. She falls in love with the courtly, gay Lancelot, whom Arthur had sent to bring her from her father's home. Much later, when her guilty love is exposed, she goes to a nunnery, where she remains until her death.

Lancelot, a knight of the Round Table. His lifelong love for Guinevere is a source of great misery. He is loved by another woman, whom he cannot love in return. At last, the scandal with Guinevere revealed, he leaves Camelot and dies a monk.

Gareth, a knight of the Round Table and a nephew of Arthur, his sister's youngest son. His first quest is on behalf of a lady who is disdainful of her untried knight. Victorious in his quest, he wins her approval and her hand.

Geraint, a knight of the Round Table. Married to Enid, he jealously keeps her away from the court. As a result of his absence from Camelot, his valor is doubted. Enid's reticence on this subject convinces him that she loves another knight, but at last she is able to prove her love. They go to Camelot, where Guinevere welcomes Enid to the court.

Balan, a knight of the Round Table. Returning from a mission for Arthur, he hears mad shrieks and rushes against the knight making them, who is in fact his unrecognized brother.

Balin, Balan's mad brother and a knight of the Round Table. Disillusioned on discovering the intimacy of Guinevere and his idol Lancelot, he leaves hanging on a tree the shield Guinevere had given him. Without the shield, he is unrecognized by his brother. In the struggle between them, Balin kills Balan and is crushed by his own horse.

Gawain, a knight of the Round Table. He falls in love with Elaine of Astolat, who rejects him because she loves Lancelot. Later, he promises to help Pelleas with Ettarre, who has rejected Pelleas' love. At her castle, he tells her he has killed Pelleas, and he becomes intimate with her.

Pelleas, a knight of the Round Table. Suspicious on hearing nothing from Gawain, he steals into Ettarre's castle and finds the lovers in bed together. He places his naked sword across their throats and rushes madly away. After hearing about the scandal of Lancelot and Guinevere, he returns to Camelot, where his rudeness to the queen foreshadows the ruin of the Round Table.

Galahad, the youngest and purest of the knights of the Round Table. The Holy Grail appears to him in all its splendor, but the experience proves fatal to him.

Percivale, the only other knight of the Round Table pure enough, according to Arthur's gloomy prediction, to see the Holy Grail.

Bors, a knight of the Round Table. He reports back to Arthur that he has seen the Holy Grail.

Tristram, a knight of the Round Table. He and Lancelot, equally guilty in loving other men's wives, fight in a tournament that Tristram wins. He then goes to Isolt of Cornwall, whom he loves. Her husband finds the lovers together and kills Tristram.

Modred, the real Judas among the knights of the Round Table. Malevolent and opportunistic, he traps Lancelot and Guinevere. He heads the revolt that ends in Arthur's death.

Bedivere, Arthur's last remaining knight of the Round Table. Reluctant to throw Excalibur into the lake, he falsely reports to Arthur that he has done so but is sent back again. When he finally brings the report that an arm reached from the lake to take the sword, Arthur knows that Bedivere has truly done his bidding.

Merlin, the magician who reared Arthur. Tricked by the wanton Vivien into teaching her his magic powers, he is enchanted by her and left forever a prisoner in a hollow tree.

Kay, a surly knight and Arthur's seneschal.

Lynette, the disdainful lady won by Gareth.

Enid, the faithful wife of Geraint.

Vivien, a vain and coquettish woman of the court. Unsuccessful in her efforts to seduce Arthur, she goes to work on Merlin.

Elaine, the lily maid of Astolat. In love with but rejected by Lancelot, she is loved by Gawain, whom she rejects. She dies of grief and, according to her dying wish, is sent floating in a boat to Camelot, where Arthur and Lancelot find her. She is buried in Camelot.

Ettarre, who is loved by Pelleas, whom she rejects, and by Gawain, to whom she succumbs.

Isolt of the White Hands, Tristram's bride, whom he leaves.

Isolt of Cornwall, the wife of King Mark. She is loved by Tristram.

King Mark of Cornwall, the husband of Isolt of Cornwall and the slayer of Tristram.

Ygerne, the mother of Arthur.

Gorlois, the first husband of Ygerne and possibly Arthur's father.

King Uther, who overcomes Gorlois in battle and immediately forces the widow Ygerne to marry him. Thus, he is possibly Arthur's father.

Bellicent, the daughter of Gorlois and Ygerne and the mother of Gareth.

Morning Star, the first knight overcome by Gareth on Lynette's behalf.

Death, Gareth's fourth opponent in his quest. Death proves to be a mere boy, forced by his brothers to assume a fearful disguise.

Earl Yniol, the impoverished father of Enid.

King Pellam, whose refusal to pay his yearly tribute to Arthur is the occasion for Balan's leaving the court, thus neglecting the care of his mad brother.

Lavaine, the brother of Elaine of Astolat.

IF BEALE STREET COULD TALK

Author: James Baldwin (1924-1987)
First published: 1974
Genre: Novel
Locale: New York City and San Juan, Puerto Rico
Time: The 1950's
Plot: Realism

Clementine "Tish" Rivers, a salesclerk at the perfume counter of a department store, a very slim, nineteen-year-old black woman. Her two foci in life are her fiancé, Fonny, who languishes in jail, and their unborn child. Although not naïve, she is essentially a trusting person, a result of innocence and youth. She draws for her strength on her love for Fonny and the love her family feels for her. Because she has never had any other lover, paramount in her life is getting Fonny, falsely imprisoned for rape, freed so that they can get on with their lives as a family.

Alonzo "Fonny" Hunt, a sculptor of some talent. At the age of twenty-two, he sits powerless in jail, frustrated in his inability to contribute to his legal defense or take care of Tish and his soon-to-be-born child. Unlike Tish, he has not been a part of a close and caring family, so he feels more a member of her family than of his own. The Rivers family trusts him completely with Tish because they recognize his love for her. He knows that he must depend on her and her family to help him win his freedom. He has known Tish since childhood, and they grew up together.

Ernestine Rivers, Tish's twenty-three-year-old sister, who works with children in a settlement house and has connections in the white world. She is more worldly and streetwise than Tish. She takes charge of the family crisis and arranges for a lawyer from her place of employment to take Fonny's case. She can wield a sharp tongue when the need arises, is fiercely loyal, and, because she is clever, has few illusions about how the world works.

Sharon Rivers, the mother of Tish and Sis, forty-three years old. She is the always understanding, sensitive center of the family, providing stability and unstinting love. She even goes to Puerto Rico in an attempt to locate the rape victim and show her that she mistakenly identified Fonny. The mission ultimately proves to be futile, but not because she does not doggedly pursue every possible means of accomplishing her purpose.

Joseph (Joe) Rivers, a longshoreman, the father of Tish and Sis. He remains undefeated by the hard life that he has lived for forty-eight years. A protective, devoted father and husband who sees in Fonny the son that he never had, he will even steal, if necessary, to raise the money required for legal fees and bail.

Frank Hunt, Fonny's father, a garment district worker and former tailor. To a lesser degree, he has followed Fonny into the Rivers family, in which he finds love and solidarity that are absent in his own home. A man defeated by life, he commits suicide when fired from his job as the result of thefts committed to contribute funds to Fonny's defense.

Alice Hunt, Fonny's mother, a zealous Pentecostal church member, self-satisfied in her righteousness. She sees in Tish's pregnancy not her first grandchild but the result of the sin of lust. Proud of her light-brown skin, she looks down on those (such as her husband and son) who are darker. Not surprisingly, she offers her husband little solace when he faces failures in life.

— *J. W. Newcomb*

IF HE HOLLERS LET HIM GO

Author: Chester Himes (1909-1984)
First published: 1945
Genre: Novel
Locale: Los Angeles, California
Time: The 1940's, during World War II
Plot: Social realism

Robert (Bob) Jones, an intelligent and articulate black man. He works as a foreman at the Atlas Shipyard in Los Angeles during World War II. Because the work is defense-related, he has a deferment from the military draft. He recognizes all too pointedly that, despite his obvious ability to perform his job and despite his credentials, including two years of college, he is resented by many, if not most, of the whites at the shipyard. He becomes desperate to have the color of his skin ignored, yet he is too perceptive to have any faith in his becoming anything more than a token black employee. His desperation becomes evident in his angry, reckless driving to and from his job at the shipyard; in his nightmares, which feature chained dogs, crippled blacks, and derisively laughing whites; and in his increasingly strained relations with his fiancée, Alice Harrison.

Alice Harrison, Bob's fiancée. Alice is a social worker and lives at home with her very respectable parents. She admires her father, who is a doctor, and she accepts without question her parents' belief that for black people to succeed, they must adapt themselves to the slow progress toward integration and full equality with whites. She and her social-worker friends have a complacent faith in the value of college education for African Americans. Because she can pass as white, she does not appreciate the immediate bigotry that Bob often experiences because he is clearly black. She seems attracted to Bob because of his intelligence and because his anger represents a challenge to shape his views to her own. When he telephones her after escaping arrest, she is willing to believe that he has raped a white woman. In effect, his arrest is in itself too much of a loss of respectability for her to accept.

Madge Perkins, Bob's colleague. Clearly bigoted in her refusal to work under Bob, she is also perversely bigoted in her attempt to seduce him. She recognizes his latent fear of being found in any sort of compromising position with a white woman. Her accusation of rape is a transparent attempt to keep what little dignity she has in her dreary life.

— *Martin Kich*

IF NOT NOW, WHEN?
(Se non ora, quando?)

Author: Primo Levi (1919-1987)
First published: 1982
Genre: Novel
Locale: Russia, Poland, and Italy
Time: 1943-1945
Plot: Adventure

Menachem Nachmanovich Dajcher, called **Mendel**, a twenty-eight-year-old Jewish watch mender, artilleryman, and partisan. After becoming detached from his Red Army unit, Mendel lives simply and reclusively in the woods, joining first with Leonid and then with various bands of partisan fighters. He is a patient and honest man who broods uncomprehendingly over the brutal murder of his wife and the wholesale destruction of his village. His experiences have made him sensitive to the ubiquitous anti-Semitism of wartime Europe. For his knowledge of Jewish tradition and his wisdom regarding people and war, Mendel is respected by fellow partisans and is consulted on major decisions. He has an innate sense of responsibility for his actions, and he thinks that his intimacy with Line is to blame for Leonid's death.

Leonid, a nineteen-year-old Red Army deserter and escaped prisoner of war. An educated Muscovite Jew who has been a bookkeeper, a thief, and a paratrooper, Leonid is tired of war and longs for peace. He is a moody young man charged with sadness, silent and trustworthy but susceptible to insolence and evasiveness. When a mission excites him, however, he commits himself to it passionately, even rashly. He grows dependent on his love for Line and is consumed with anger and jealousy when she drops him for Mendel. Leonid is killed in a foolishly dangerous move during an attack on a German *Lager* in Poland.

Emmeline, most often called **Line**, a young Jewish woman in the partisan band. Line is small and slight, with dark eyes and surprising strength. She is a serious and intense fighter who holds strong socialist, feminist, and Zionist convictions. Wise and clear-sighted, she is intriguing to others: Leonid becomes her devoted lover, and Mendel is haunted by her power and beauty until he, too, seeks her out. He realizes that he will never fully know her.

Gedaleh Skidler, a twenty-seven-year-old Jewish partisan leader. Gedaleh is a good-humored, vital, and impulsive soldier and tactician who acts freely, according to the exigencies of each new moment. Tall and thin, he is never seen without his violin, which once saved his life by deflecting a bullet and which he plays frequently and with complete joy. Gedaleh knows that the Gedalists' prospects for survival are bleak, but he never loses hope or his ability to make quick, strong decisions in his band's best interests.

Dov Yavor, the chief of the Jewish partisan community whom Mendel and Leonid encounter at Novoselki. Middle-aged and prematurely graying, Dov is a precise and hard-headed leader who has been weathered by war and riddled with lingering injuries. Unlike the other Jewish partisans, who hope someday to begin new lives in Palestine, Dov longs only to return to his native Siberian village, far from the turmoil and threat of war. Once the Gedalists are overcome by the advancing Red Army in Germany, his wish is granted.

Bella, Gedaleh's companion. Bella is close to forty years old, a thin little blond who no longer participates in battle. She is critical, bossy, lazy, and slow-witted, but she brings a much-needed maternal presence to the partisan band, and Gedaleh finds her to be an ideal mate.

Pavel Yurevich Levinski, a proud Russian Jew from the Novoselki community. Pavel has bushy dark hair, a deep voice, and an athletic appearance, and he exhibits a tacit impunity in all he does. A former weight lifter, actor, and radio announcer, he loves telling stories and thrives on attention. His linguistic and theatrical skills help ensure the success of numerous partisan plots and activities.

Piotr Fomich, a deputy in Ulybin's band who leads the Jewish partisans to Ulybin at Turov. Piotr is lighthearted and innocent, and he takes an immediate liking to Mendel. Although not Jewish, he chooses to leave Ulybin and join the Gedalists, and he stays with them, ironically, because of his deep faith in Christ.

Sissl, a woman in the Jewish partisan band. Sissl is sturdy, mature, calm, and trustworthy, but lacking in beauty and mystery. Mendel takes her as a lover, though she in no way thrills him. He eventually leaves her for Line.

Osip Ivanovich Ulybin, the thirty-year-old chief of a band of Russian partisans that will not take on the Novoselki survivors. Ulybin is a dark, muscular man, a stern and coldhearted military tactician whose formidable authority is undermined only by suspicions of his alcoholism.

— *B. P. Mann*

IF ON A WINTER'S NIGHT A TRAVELER
(Se una notte d'inverno un viaggiatore)

Author: Italo Calvino (1923-1985)
First published: 1979
Genre: Novel
Locale: An unnamed city
Time: Late twentieth century
Plot: Antistory

The Narrator, who is unnamed and physically undescribed. The Narrator may be a single person or as many as eleven different writers, each the author of a separate novel, including the encompassing book (supposedly written by Italo Calvino). Each of the novels is told by a person who might plausibly be called the Narrator. The Prime Narrator is the author of the book that enfolds the other ten, and his main theme is the relationship between writers and readers. He is an open and friendly fellow, addressing the Reader (another character) directly, giving hints and directions as to how and why a perceptive reader reads. He points out the novelistic tricks of the other writers, but he himself uses these same devices, displaying and explaining them as the book progresses. In a sense, the Narrator constructs the novel as the reader watches. While he constructs the novel, the Narrator participates in the reactions of his reader. He is amused, baffled, irritated, and intrigued by the devices that the subsidiary authors use. There is an inescapable air of illusion about the entire work, and the Narrator, for all his honest appearance, is a sly and devious character. Within the novel, there are ten more novels and ten more narrators, and it appears that all these narrators are variants of the Narrator. *If on a Winter's Night a Traveler*, the first novel-within-a-novel, has the same title as Calvino's book but is actually a story of espionage. It has become confused in printing with another novel, *Outside the Town of Malbork*, by Polish writer Tazio Bazakbal. It appears that this novel in turn has been mixed with a Cimmerian story, *Leaning from the Steep Slope*, by Ukko Ahti. That appearance is an illusion, for the novel seems to be a Cimbric one, penned by Vorts Jiljandi, with the title *Without Fear of Wind or Vertigo*. At this point, the split Narrator splits again, introducing Ermes Marana, a shadowy translator and literary agent provocateur. Marana seems to be a dark version of the Narrator, practicing plagiarism and deceit to produce the works that next appear: *Looks Down in the Gathering Shadow* (*Regarde en bas dans l'épaisseur des ombres*) by the almost unknown Belgian author Bertrand Vandervelde, and two confusingly titled works by best-selling novelist Silas Flannery, *In a Network of Lines That Enlace* and *In a Network of Lines That Intersect*. Flannery—who is yet another avatar of the Narrator—provides pages from his diary, another kind of book. The Narrator reveals that at least one of the Flannery books is almost certainly a translation by Marana of a Japanese work, *On a Carpet of Leaves Illuminated by the Moon*, by Takakumi Ikoka. Once more, this novel gives way to yet another one: *Around an Empty Grave*, by Latin American writer Calixto Bandera. It in turn fades into the penultimate novel of the entire series, *What Story Down There Awaits Its End?* by Slavic author Anatoly Anatolin. Only then does the Narrator return and bring the enfolding novel to its close. Throughout the novel, the Narrator has been the guide of the Reader; sometimes a wise and avuncular host, sometimes a sly and teasing jester, the Narrator embodies the key aspects of authorship—its talent to entertain and its ability to mystify.

The Reader, a sort of Everyman, a person of indeterminate age, although clearly an adult male, who is unmarried and whose expectations of life seem to have been reduced to a careful minimum. As the story progresses, the Reader learns to raise his standards and his hopes, expecting and finding greater enjoyment both in his reading and in his life. Beyond the obvious attributes given at the start of the book, the Reader is left outwardly a generally shadowy and elusive figure. Calvino is careful not to limit the character by extensive description of his physical appearance or personal history, instead allowing the Reader to develop in a fashion determined by the individual, actual reader. The parallel developments in the book are the Reader's growing fascination with the unfinished novels he confronts, and the Other Reader, or Ludmilla, who joins him on his adventure. This personal relationship develops so that by chapter 7 the two have become lovers, and by the book's end they are married. The Reader becomes a more active and adventurous individual as time goes by, running ever greater risks in pursuit of the elusive books. The journey begins innocently enough in a bookstore and gradually escalates until the Reader is acting as a double agent in the totalitarian nation of Ircania, on a mission from the equally dictatorial state of Ataguitania. As the Narrator becomes, in a sense, the author of each of the succeeding novels, the Reader identifies with the male hero in each of the books, and in the end it is difficult to tell where the original Reader ends and his shadowy selves begin.

The Other Reader, or **Ludmilla**, the Reader's female counterpart, love interest, and, finally, wife. Like the Reader, she is interested in books and in reading; indeed, her love and appreciation of literature are deeper and more instinctive than those of the Reader. She sees both writing and reading as natural acts, and her ideal of an author is one who produces books "as a pumpkin vine produces pumpkins." The physical attributes of the Other Reader are more clearly defined than those of the Reader, in large part because she is described not only by the Narrator but also through the perceptions and desires of the Reader. Both agree that Ludmilla is an extremely attractive and highly intelligent young woman. As first seen (appropriately enough, in a bookstore), she is striking, even beautiful, with large, expressive eyes, flawless skin, and a mane of richly waved hair. Her apartment, which is described in greater detail than the woman herself, reveals her mental and emotional nature: She is practical, yet romantic; her kitchen has a variety of appliances and utensils, but her refrigerator holds only an egg, half a lemon, and a few jars of condiments. On one wall are a number of framed photographs, but some of the frames are empty. The combination of contrary signals and impulses does not create a contradictory character; rather, it establishes Ludmilla as a more believable and realistic person. Ludmilla's main trait is her devotion to reading. Throughout the novel, she remains relatively consistent in her reaction to the succeeding novels that appear, breaking off at their most interesting points. The Reader is exasperated and bewitched by each of the novels in turn; Ludmilla, on the other hand, readily accepts each new work as she finds it, and her interest is less in the plots of characters than in the very presence of the written word. Because of her devotion to the word, Ludmilla appears at times retiring, even shy. She is, however, friendly with a variety of odd and intriguing characters who, like her, are drawn to the life of the mind and the lure of books. In the end, the Reader is the most notable of these characters, and his dominant trait is that he comes closest to matching Ludmilla's passionate devotion.

Lotaria, the antithesis of her sister, Ludmilla. In her own way, she is attractive, but in an odd and not quite appealing way, with a long neck, a bird's face, and a mass of curly hair.

Her voice is harsher and sharper than her sister's and carries an ironic edge to it. Lotaria is intelligent, highly educated, relentless, and humorless. She seeks to reduce reading and literature to a precise, objective science from which the human elements can be completely removed. As in all matters, Lotaria is literal in her quest: Her highest ambition is to perfect a machine that will make it unnecessary for a person actually to read any novel. Instead, mathematical formulas and electronic computations will reduce the meaning of any given book to a set of numbers. Lotaria's approach to literature is purely theoretical. Instead of reacting to a book as either pleasurable or not, or even as good or bad, she must place it within a rigid scheme. In the discussion group that dissects one of the novels, the jargon flows so freely as to obscure all traces of the actual story. This is the approach to literature that Lotaria demands and that is the opposite of the unforced, natural acceptance of her sister.

— Michael Witkoski

IF WINTER COMES

Author: A. S. M. Hutchinson (1879-1971)
First published: 1920
Genre: Novel
Locale: Southern England
Time: 1912-1919
Plot: Social criticism

Mark Sabre, an idealistic man whose love for humanity results in his persecution and betrayal by unsympathetic people. Suspected of fathering the child of a girl he befriends and later of having been responsible for her suicide, he loses his wife, his job, and his reputation. After discovering the identity of the illegitimate child's father, he generously refrains from disclosing it.

Mabel Sabre, his wife, a totally conventional and unsympathetic woman. Never able to understand her husband, she construes his willingness to help an unwed mother as guilt, and she divorces him.

Effie Bright, the daughter of an employee at Sabre's office. Cast off after the birth of her baby by everyone, including her father, Effie appeals for help to Sabre. Later, horrified by the trouble she has caused him, she kills her child and herself.

Lady Nona Tybar, Sabre's former sweetheart and his one understanding friend. She believes in him throughout his troubles and finally marries him.

Mr. Twyning, Sabre's business associate. His misunderstanding and persecution of Sabre are largely responsible for Sabre's ruin.

Harold Twyning, the son of Mr. Twyning. Effie's suicide letter names him as her child's father. Sabre, going to Twyning's office with the letter, finds him grieving over the news that Harold has been killed in battle. Sabre then destroys the letter.

Mr. Fortune, Sabre's employer, concerned that scandal will hurt his business.

Lord Tybar, Nona's charming and unfaithful husband. He is killed in the war.

Mrs. Perch, an old woman whose son wishes to enlist in the army. Sabre's first act of benevolence to Effie, before her troubles begin, is to arrange for her to be Mrs. Perch's companion. The news of young Perch's death kills Mrs. Perch.

Mr. Fargus, Sabre's neighbor and friend.

IGNES DE CASTRO
(A Castro)

Author: António Ferreira (1528-1569)
First published: 1587
Genre: Drama
Locale: Portugal
Time: 1354-1360
Plot: Tragedy

Ignes de Castro (ee-NEHS deh KAH-stroh), the illegitimate daughter of a nobleman. She is beloved by Prince Pedro, the son and heir of King Alfonso. On the death, in childbirth, of Prince Pedro's wife, Ignes de Castro hopes that, now that her lover is provided with a legitimate heir, their love may be made public, their marriage solemnized, and their four children recognized by their grandfather. Before her hopes can be realized, however, she is murdered by the king's advisers.

Prince Pedro (PEH-droh), the heir of Alfonso IV and the lover of Ignes de Castro. Compelled by his father to marry a princess of Castile, he feels free at her death in childbirth to proclaim his love for Ignes de Castro. He pleads with the king for a state wedding and the recognition of their four children. The king refuses, and when Ignes is killed by the royal advisers, Prince Pedro swears vengeance on all involved in the murder, including his father.

Alfonso IV (ahl-FOHN-soh), the king of Portugal and the father of Prince Pedro. In an attempt to put an end to the love of Prince Pedro for the illegitimate Ignes de Castro, he compels his son to marry a princess of Castile, who dies at the birth of a legitimate heir. When his son then begs for a state wedding to Ignes and the recognition of their four children, King Alfonso refuses and permits the murder of Ignes.

Diogo Lopes Pacheco (dee-OH-goh LOH-pehs pah-CHEH-koh),

Pero Coelho (PEH-roh koh-EHL-hoh), and

Gonzalves (gohn-SAHL-vehs), advisers to King Alfonso and the murderers of Ignes de Castro.

THE ILIAD

Author: Homer (c. ninth century B.C.E.)
First transcribed: c. 800 B.C.E.
Genre: Poetry
Locale: Troy
Time: During the Trojan War
Plot: Epic

Achilles (uh-KIH-leez), the son of Peleus and the Nereid Thetis, prince of the Myrmidons, and mightiest of the Achaian warriors at the siege of Troy. At his birth, his mother had dipped him in the Styx, so that all parts of his body are invulnerable to hurt except the heel by which she held him. A young man of great beauty, strength, courage, and skill in battle, he nevertheless possesses two tragic flaws, an imperious will and a strong sense of vanity. Enraged because King Agamemnon orders him to surrender the maid Briseis, whom Achilles had taken as his own prize of war, he quarrels bitterly with the commander of the Greek forces and withdraws from the battlefield. When the Trojan host attacks, driving the Greeks back toward their ships, Achilles remains sulking in his tent. So great is his wrath that he refuses to heed all entreaties that he come to the aid of the hard-pressed Greeks. When the Trojans begin to burn the Greek ships, he allows his friend Patroclus, dressed in the armor of Achilles, to lead the warlike Myrmidons against the attackers. Patroclus is killed by Hector, the Trojan leader, under the walls of the city. Seeing in the death of his friend the enormity of his own inaction, Achilles puts on a new suit of armor made for him by Hephaestus and engages the Trojans in fierce combat. Merciless in his anger and grief, he kills Hector and on successive days drags the body of the vanquished hero behind his chariot while King Priam, Hector's father, looks on from the walls of the city. When the sorrowing king visits the tent of Achilles at night and begs for the body of his son, Achilles relents and permits Priam to conduct funeral rites for Hector for a period of nine days. In a later battle before the walls of Troy, an arrow shot by Paris, King Priam's son, strikes Achilles in the heel and causes his death.

Hector (HEHK-tur), the son of King Priam and Queen Hecuba. As the commander of the Trojan forces, he is the greatest and most human of the heroes, an ideal figure in every respect: a skilled horseman, a brave soldier, an able leader, a man devoted to his family and his city, and the master of his emotions under every circumstance. His courage in battle, his courtesy in conference, his submission to the gods, and his sad fate at the hands of vengeful Achilles provide an admirable contrast to the actions of the blustering, cunning, cruel, and rapacious Greeks.

Andromache (an-DROM-uh-kee), the devoted wife of Hector and the mother of Astyanax. After the fall of Troy, she was taken into captivity by Neoptolemus, the son of Achilles. Still later, according to *The Aeneid*, she married Helenus, the brother of Hector, and ruled with him in Pyrrhus.

Astyanax (as-TI-eh-naks), the young son of Hector and Andromache. During the sack of Troy, Neoptolemus killed the child by hurling him over the city wall.

Agamemnon (ag-eh-MEHM-non), the king of Mycenae and the older brother of King Menelaus, husband of the lovely Helen, whose infidelity brought about the Trojan War. Courageous and cunning but often rash and arrogant, as in his treatment of Achilles, he is the commander of the Greeks in the war. He stands as a symbol of the capable leader, without the heroic qualities of the more dramatic warriors who fight under his command. He is killed by his wife Clytemnestra after his return from Troy.

Menelaus (meh-nuh-LAY-uhs), the king of Sparta and husband of beautiful but faithless Helen, who is seduced and abducted by Paris, the prince of Troy, in fulfillment of a promise made by Aphrodite. He stands more as a symbol than as a man, a victim of the gods and an outraged husband who avenges with brave deeds the wrong done to his honor. At the end of the war, he takes Helen back to Sparta with him. In the *Odyssey*, she is shown presiding over his royal palace.

Helen, the wife of King Menelaus of Sparta and, for nineteen years after her abduction, the consort of Paris. Being confined within the walls of Troy, in the company of doting elders, she plays a minor part in the story. Because she is the victim of Aphrodite's promise to Paris, she does not suffer greatly for her actions. Her attempts at reconciliation unwittingly aid the Greek cause in the capture of Troy.

Paris, the son of King Priam and Queen Hecuba. Called to judge a dispute among Aphrodite, Hera, and Athena, he awarded the prize, the golden apple of discord, to Aphrodite, who in turn promised him the most beautiful woman in the world as his wife. Although his love for Helen, the bride he stole from her husband, has become proud devotion to a principle, Paris nevertheless places himself in jeopardy as a champion of the Trojan cause and offers to meet King Menelaus, the injured husband, in single combat. Aphrodite, fearful for the safety of her favorite, watches over him and saves him from harm. An arrow from his bow strikes Achilles in the heel and kills the Achaian warrior. One story says that Paris was slain by a poisoned arrow from the bow of Philoctetes.

Priam (PRI-am), the king of Troy and the beneficent father of a large family. Although he is not a ruler of Agamemnon's stature, he is a man of shrewdness and quiet strength who suffers much at the hands of fate and the rivalry of the gods. Although he does not condone the abduction of Helen by Paris, he is fair in his judgment of both because he knows that they are victims of Aphrodite's whims. His devotion to his son Hector and his pity for all who suffer in the war elevate him to noble stature.

Hecuba (HEH-kew-buh), the wife of King Priam. Her fate is tragic. She witnesses the death of her sons, the enslavement of her daughter Cassandra, carried into captivity by Agamemnon, and the sacrifice of her daughter Polyxena to appease the shade of Achilles.

Calchas (KAL-kuhs), the seer and prophet of the Greeks. After many animals and men have been slain by the arrows of Apollo, Calchas declares that the destruction is a divine visitation because of Agamemnon's rape of Chryseis, the daughter of Chryses, a priest of Apollo. He counsels that the maid be returned to her father without ransom.

Chryseis (KRIH-see-uhs), a maiden seized by the Greeks during the plundering of Chrysa and given to Agamemnon as a prize of war. Forced by the intervention of Apollo to send the girl back to Chryses, her father, Agamemnon announces that he will in turn take any other maid he desires. His choice is Briseis, the slave of Achilles. Agamemnon's demand leads to a quarrel between the two Greeks.

Briseis (BRI-see-uhs), a captive slave taken by Achilles as a prize of war. Agamemnon's announcement that he intends to take the girl into his own tent leads to a quarrel between the two men. Forced to surrender Briseis, Achilles and his followers retire from the battlefield and refuse to engage in the fierce fighting that follows. Agamemnon returns the girl to Achilles shortly before the sulking warrior undergoes a change of mood and returns to the fighting to avenge the death of his friend Patroclus.

Patroclus (pa-TROH-kluhs), the noble squire and loyal friend of Achilles. His death at the hands of Hector is mercilessly and horribly avenged when Achilles and Hector meet in hand-to-hand combat and the Greek warrior kills his Trojan rival. Reasonable in argument and courageous in the face of great odds, Patroclus distinguishes himself in battle and is sublime in his willingness to die for a cause and a friend.

Odysseus (oh-DIHS-ews), the crafty, middle-aged warrior who, with Diomedes, scouts the Trojan camp, captures a Trojan spy, Dolon, and kills Rhesus, a Thracian ally of the Trojans. Although he is a minor figure in the story, he serves as a foil to haughty Agamemnon and sulking Achilles. He and Nestor are the counselors who interpret rightly the will of the gods.

Diomedes (di-oh-MEE-deez), a valiant Argive warrior who dashes so often and fearlessly between the Greek and Trojan lines that it is difficult to tell on which side he is fighting. He is the companion of Odysseus on a night-scouting expedition in the Trojan camp, and he is the slayer of Pandarus. In hand-to-hand fighting, he attacks Aeneas so fiercely that the gods wrap the Trojan in a veil of mist to protect him from Diomedes' onslaught.

Dolon (DOH-luhn), a Trojan spy captured and put to death by Odysseus and Diomedes.

Nestor (NEHS-tur), the hoary-headed king of Pylos and a wise counselor of the Greeks. Although he is the oldest of the Greek leaders, he survives the ten years of war and returns to his own land, where Telemachus, the son of Odysseus, visits him.

Machaon (meh-KAY-uhn), the son of Asclepius, the famous physician of the ancient world. He is the chief surgeon in the Greek forces. He heals Menelaus after the king of Sparta has been wounded by an arrow from the bow of Pandarus.

Ajax (AY-jaks), the son of Telamon of Salamis and half brother of Teucer. A warrior of great physical size and strength, he uses his mighty spear to hold off the Trojans attempting to burn the Greek ships after breaching the rampart around the vessels. According to a later story, he goes mad when Agamemnon, acting on the advice of Athena, awards the armor of dead Achilles to Odysseus.

Teucer (TEW-sehr), the half brother of Ajax and a mighty bowman. He helps Ajax defend the Greek ships. During one of the Trojan onslaughts, he kills the charioteer of Hector.

Glaucus (GLOH-kuhs), a Lycian ally of the Trojans. Meeting him in battle, Diomedes recognizes the Lycian as a guest-friend by inheritance. To seal a covenant between them, they exchange armor, Glaucus giving up his gold armor, worth a hundred oxen, for the brass armor of Diomedes, worthy only nine oxen.

Sarpedon (sahr-PEE-duhn), the leader of the Lycian allies fighting with the Trojans. He is killed by Patroclus.

Aeneas (ee-NEE-uhs), the son of Anchises and Aphrodite. A warrior descended from a younger branch of the royal house of Troy, he commands the Trojan forces after the death of Hector. Earlier, while trying to protect the fallen body of his friend Pandarus, Aeneas is struck down by Diomedes, who would have slain him if the gods had not hidden the Trojan in a misty cloud. Aeneas' wounds are miraculously healed in the temple of Apollo, and he returns to the battle.

Pandarus (PAN-duh-ruhs), a Lycian ally of the Trojans and a skilled archer. After Paris has been spirited away from his contest with Menelaus, Pandarus aims at the king of Sparta and would have pierced him with an arrow if Athena had not turned the shaft aside. Diomedes kills Pandarus.

Cassandra (ka-SAN-druh), the daughter of King Priam and Queen Hecuba. Gifted with second sight, she is never to have her prophecies believed because she has rejected the advances of Apollo. She becomes Agamemnon's captive after the fall of Troy.

Helenus (HEH-leh-nuhs), the son of King Priam and Queen Hecuba. Like his sister Cassandra, he possesses the gift of second sight. He eventually marries Andromache, the wife of his brother Hector.

Deïphobus (dee-IH-feh-buhs), the son of King Priam and Queen Hecuba. He becomes the husband of Helen after the death of Paris and is killed during the sack of Troy.

Antenor (an-TEE-nor), the Trojan elder who advises that Helen be returned to the Greeks to avoid bloodshed.

Polydamus (po-lih-DA-muhs), a shrewd, clear-headed leader of the Trojans.

Aphrodite (a-froh-DI-tee), the goddess of love. Because Paris had awarded her the fated golden apple and Aeneas is her son, she aids the Trojans during the war.

Apollo (uh-PO-loh), the god of poetry, music, and prophecy, as well as the protector of flocks and the patron of bowmen. He fights on the side of the Trojans.

Athena (uh-THEE-nuh), also called **Pallas Athena**, the goddess of wisdom. She aids the Achaians.

Poseidon (poh-SI-dehn), the god of the sea and earthquakes. The enemy of the Trojans, he aids the Achaians.

Ares (AY-reez), the god of war. Because of Aphrodite, he fights on the side of the Trojans.

Hera (HIHR-uh), the consort of Zeus and the enemy of the Trojans.

Zeus (zews), the supreme deity. He remains neutral, for the most part, during the war.

Thetis (THEE-tihs), a Nereid, the mother of Achilles, whom she aids in his quarrel with Agamemnon.

Hephaestus (hee-FEHS-tuhs), the artificer of the gods. At the request of Thetis, he makes the suit of armor that Achilles is wearing when he slays Hector.

ILL SEEN ILL SAID
(Mal vu mal dit)

Author: Samuel Beckett (1906-1989)
First published: 1981
Genre: Novel
Locale: An unspecified rural location
Time: Indeterminate
Plot: Antistory

"She," an unnamed old woman who lives alone in a stark, unspecified rural area at an indeterminate time. Her body is slowly decaying because of her advancing age, and she is going blind. She spends her days carrying out the most rudimentary of human activities: She does little more than eat, sleep, and stare. Despite or perhaps because of her encroaching blindness, she spends almost all of her time staring. She examines repeatedly the few, rustic items in her small cabin and the slight changes in the harsh, barren landscape surrounding that cabin. She cannot tell whether these changes actually occur or whether they happen because her sight is failing, because they are "ill seen." Like her eyes and body, her mind also seems to be failing. She cannot remember the beginning of a thought when she arrives at its end, and her thoughts seem almost random. She no longer grasps the most basic notions: She has lost her sense of direction, so that the differences between east and west, and north and south, are meaningless to her; time is not continuous for her but seems to move slowly, quickly, or not at all; she cannot find the center of anything, including the "zone of stones" outside her cabin, "at the inexistent centre of a formless place"; and even sky and earth do not always seem distinct for her. These difficulties lead her to wonder what these notions meant for her when she was healthy. She questions the reality of many of the "opposites" humans posit to orient themselves within their world: good and bad, right and wrong, love and hate, reality and illusion, subject and object, self and other, center and periphery, black and white, and pleasure and pain. She suspects that no one has ever understood precisely the meaning of these words, that they may have no meaning at all, and that they have always been "ill said." Because she cannot see properly or think properly, however, she has no way of resolving her suspicions. The suspicions themselves are thus misleading; they are simply a waste of time, whatever time might be. She is isolated and without hope. She can only await death.

— *Matthew K. Davis*

ILLYWHACKER

Author: Peter Carey (1943-   )
First published: 1985
Genre: Novel
Locale: Victoria and New South Wales, Australia
Time: 1886 to the 1980's
Plot: Picaresque

Herbert Badgery, a retired former freelance flier, crack car salesman, entertainer, and confidence man; he is also a convict and a lifetime liar. He claims to have possessed the ability, in his late youth and early manhood, to make himself disappear. In his old age, he is something of a celebrity, claiming to be 139 years old at the time that he tells this tall tale of his life and that of his family, friends, and enemies. He is very bright, having learned to read in his middle age and obtained a college degree by correspondence while in prison; he is intellectually lively despite his age. Severely bandy-legged and only modestly attractive in his prime, he is possessed of brilliant sapphire-blue eyes that do not dim with age, and he has been a passionate lover and loser of women. Interesting in himself, he is well able to spin the tale of his adventures, of trying to make a living through the hard times of the first half of the twentieth century, but his story does not stop there. He has a very peculiar family and is determined to give them full play as they comically and sometimes tragically work out their lives, often hindered by the influence of the rogue parent, Herbert Badgery himself, who has an instinct for putting many feet wrong, an enormous zest for celebrating his errors, and a wicked eye for the follies not only of his own making but also of humankind in general.

Charles Badgery, Herbert's son, the proprietor of the largest pet store in the world, located in Sydney but doing business worldwide. He is physically plain and awkward, as well as deaf in one ear as the result of a parental disciplinary blow from Herbert. Charles leaves home while still in his late teens. He possesses an uncanny gift for capturing and handling wild animals, particularly dangerous snakes. He builds a major business with little capital, only to fall under American financial influence and then under Japanese control. All he wants is his father's approval and his wife's love.

Leah Goldstein, the occasional lover of Herbert. A pretty woman who keeps her physical attractions into middle age, she is the daughter of a Jewish father and a Scottish mother. She starts to study medicine but gets involved with Izzie Kaletsky, the workingman's champion, and marries him, more out of pity than out of love. During the Great Depression of the 1930's, she becomes an exotic dancer, often using snakes, and works for a time in an act with Herbert, living with him and helping him to bring up his children. People constantly call on her for help. She never loses her affection for Herbert, although they are often separated.

Phoebe McGrath, Herbert's wife, but not legally so because he, unknown to Phoebe, was married to another woman at the time of their supposed marriage. Brown-eyed, redheaded, and long-legged, she has an ecstatic sexual beginning to her life with Herbert, but she has literary ambitions, and after bearing two children, she leaves the children and Herbert to try her chances as a poet. Charles supports her financially in her unsuccessful attempts to become a poet of reputation.

Izzie Kaletsky, a Marxist labor writer and agitator, born in Australia of Russian Jewish immigrant parents. He is a small man with dark, curly hair and a pretty face, but he is not physically attractive to Leah, who marries him despite her sexual indifference to him. He proves to be a political orator of surprising power. He loses both of his legs in a railway accident while confronting a company "goon" squad, and for a time Leah takes care of him. She is never able to love him.

Emma Badgery, formerly **Emma Underhill**, a wide-hipped, broad-chested, innocent schoolteacher whom Charles marries. She is so afraid of losing Charles that she spends much of her time in one of the cages in his shop, partially pretending to be as helpless as the animals he cares for. Charles is besotted with her, but her refusal to live a normal life and her forceful determination to avoid psychiatric help make her a constant problem for everyone.

— Charles Pullen

I'M NOT STILLER
(Stiller)

Author: Max Frisch (1911-1991)
First published: 1954
Genre: Novel
Locale: Switzerland, elsewhere in Europe, and the United States
Time: Mid-twentieth century
Plot: Existentialism

Anatol Ludwig Stiller (AN-ah-tohl LEWT-vihg SHTIH-lehr), a sculptor. The novel begins when the protagonist returns to Switzerland after a seven-year disappearance. He claims to be an American, James Larkin White, but is thought to be a missing Zurich artist, Anatol Ludwig Stiller. On the request of his defense counsel, Stiller writes seven notebooks recording his life. As a young man, Stiller fought in the Spanish Civil War, but he believes himself to have acted in a cowardly manner. He wants to be someone he is not and is plagued by an uncertain sense of identity and an inability to accept himself. He is imaginative, insecure, talkative, capricious, and charming. He and his cronies spent countless hours discussing art, but the art he produces is mediocre. His greatest challenge is his marriage to the dancer Julika, a doll-like and aloof woman whose distance and reserve he fails to broach. After a brief affair with Sibylle, he flees to America to begin a new life, but seven years later he returns to Switzerland and reluctantly accepts his old identity. He and Julika move to a farmhouse, where he works as a potter. Two years later, Julika dies, and Stiller lives quietly and alone in the countryside.

Julika Stiller-Tschudy (YEW-lih-kah SHTIH-lehr-TSHEW-dee), a ballet dancer and Stiller's wife. Julika has the lithe and trained body of a dancer, more boyish in its impression than womanly. She is coolly beautiful, with "bluish-green eyes like the edges of colorless window-glass." Her lips are rather thin, and her plucked eyebrows give her a perpetually surprised expression. She has luxurious red hair and an alabaster complexion. She values her dancing, at which she is very successful; she is the primary supporter in the Stiller-Tschudy household. Julika is taciturn, practically unable to express herself verbally and unwilling to reveal anything about her inner life. She keeps her serious illnesses from her husband until the last moment and then withdraws into quiet suffering. Following an apparent cure at Davos, Julika, who appears to be a beautiful object, a work of art rather than a flesh-and-blood woman, succumbs to tuberculosis two years after Stiller's return to Switzerland.

Rolf, Stiller's public prosecutor. As a sensible person who diligently performs his duties, Rolf is Stiller's opposite. During their conversations in Stiller's prison cell, he and Stiller become friends and remain so after Stiller's release. The prosecutor reveals to Stiller that his coolly theoretical view of marriage, that spouses must give each other a great deal of privacy and freedom, collapsed in the light of his wife's confessed infidelity. Ironically, his wife had fallen in love with Stiller, although the prosecutor and Stiller did not meet until after Stiller's reappearance seven years later. In a sense, the prosecutor is both the public accuser and the accusing husband; he is, however, completely nonjudgmental and is more understanding than Stiller's appointed defense counsel. He becomes Stiller's good friend. The prosecutor seems to have acquired a level of equanimity and tolerance that eludes Stiller. In a postscript to Stiller's notebooks, he records the events occurring after Stiller's release from prison.

Sibylle (sih-BIHL-leh), Rolf's wife. The dark-haired Sibylle, in her late twenties, is the mother of a little boy, Hannes. She reluctantly accepts her husband's infidelities, which occur when he is on business trips and are said to have nothing to do with his relationship to her. She retaliates through flirtations at social events. She lacks fulfillment in her marriage, and her interest in Stiller, which began as a provocation to her husband, evolves into a love affair. When she understands that Stiller finally agrees to go to Paris with her only because business is taking him there anyway, she leaves both her husband and Stiller and moves to New York with her son. She supports herself and him by working as a secretary. After several years of separation without a divorce, her husband travels to New York, and Sibylle and Hannes return to Switzerland with him. Sibylle and Rolf have another child and seem to lead a reasonably content married life.

Dr. Bohnenblust (BOH-nehn-blewst), Stiller's defense counsel, appointed by the state. He visits Stiller in his cell and requests that he write down his life story. Bohnenblust is a decent and inoffensive fellow from a good family; he is inhibited but just. Stiller is irritated by his moderation and didacticism. Bohnenblust seems to believe that by trying to talk common sense into Stiller, he can change him.

Knobel (KNOH-behl), Stiller's warden. Knobel is the only one who believes Stiller's claim that he is not Stiller.

— Helga Stipa Madland

AN IMAGINARY LIFE

Author: David Malouf (1934-)
First published: 1978
Genre: Novel

Locale: Tomis, an outpost of the Roman Empire
Time: Approximately A.D. 8-18
Plot: Historical

Ovid (Publius Ovidius Naso), the famous Latin poet. Ovid's character ranges from the self-indulgent frivolity that characterized the real Ovid while he was in exile from Rome in the last decade of his life to the more somber and pensive attitudes that are found in the fictional protagonist. The work is told from the poet's point of view, in the first person. In his place of banishment between the Danube and the Black Sea, the fictional Ovid finds his surroundings cold, bleak, and desolate; however, he reflects that exile is a state of mind. The effects of age and isolation beset him at first. He is fifty years old at the outset, and he wonders whether his writings have been preserved at all in the imperial capital. At times, he muses on earlier memories of Italy. In due course, he finds a sense of closeness to nature, indeed a sense of mystery, in the rude and untamed, but also unspoiled, setting into which he has been cast. Although as an accomplished writer he feels out of place in a locality where his own language is not known, eventually he comes to understand the natives' speech almost as well as Latin. He feels little impulse to indulge in any expressions of disdain for the rather modest level of culture found in those around him. He takes a pronounced and touching interest in the Child's needs, and when he discovers that the boy is in danger, Ovid takes the Child with him into the steppe to the north, where his story ends.

Ryzak, the village headman. He allows Ovid to stay with him and accords Ovid some respect out of deference toward his previous importance in Rome. Ryzak is a taciturn but kindly sort; apparently, his authority is diminished somewhat by his dread of the unknown. He defers to the beliefs in magic propounded by his mother and by the village shaman. When Ryzak receives a bite on his arm, falls into convulsions, and dies, the Child is suspected of exercising malevolent animal powers.

Ryzak's mother, a woman who is nearly eighty years old at the beginning of the novel. She is regarded as possessing a sort of mystical wisdom where spirits and portents are concerned; Ovid believes that she exercises a baleful influence over her son. She seems to suspect that evil, feral powers of some sort are lurking within the Child.

Ryzak's daughter-in-law, who lives with Ryzak and is rearing her son Lullo. When the child Ovid has found becomes ill, she cares for him secretly, in spite of the fear and distrust others in the household feel toward the boy.

The Child, a boy of about eleven whom hunters find in a wild state in a forest. He is tied up like an animal and taken to Ryzak's house. Ovid takes a personal interest in the Child's welfare and is fascinated by the development of his fledgling intellect. When it comes to plain and simple truths about the outside world, the Roman writer believes that he has something to learn from the Child. Eventually, for his own protection, the Child is taken to a remote area some distance from the household.

Lullo, Ryzak's grandson. Although he received lessons in Latin and mathematics from Ovid, he becomes jealous of the Child. Eventually, he wants to have nothing to do with the exiled Roman author.

— *J. R. Broadus*

THE IMMORALIST
(L'Immoraliste)

Author: André Gide (1869-1951)
First published: 1902
Genre: Novel

Locale: Northern Africa, Italy, France, and Switzerland
Time: 1900
Plot: Psychological realism

Michel (mee-SHEHL), the narrator, a twenty-four-year-old archaeologist, brought up in a highly puritanical atmosphere. The product of an exclusively scholastic and bookish education, he marries Marceline only to please his dying father, without really knowing what he is doing. During his honeymoon in North Africa, he contracts tuberculosis. After having this brush with death, he recovers and sets out to mount an all-out war against anything that could threaten his health. He also starts experiencing all kinds of previously unsuspected physical joys and realizes that he carries within himself a precious and occult self that he is determined to free from the constraints of social and moral conformity. His attraction to young boys reveals his unconscious and repressed homosexuality. The harshness of his repression will determine the harshness of his individualism, which will sweep away and destroy anything and everything that stands in its path, including his wife. Marceline's death, however, does not bring him the all-encompassing freedom for which his authentic self had longed. Michel illustrates the dangers and failures of excessive individualism.

Marceline (mahr-seh-LEEN), Michel's wife. During their honeymoon in Africa, she nurses him back to health with a total and loving devotion. She embodies orthodox morality, honesty, and religion, all values that represent a threat to Michel's surging authentic being; hence, he will fiercely reject them. She must therefore disappear. Her miscarriage symbolizes the failure of their union. The ensuing progressive deterioration of her health runs parallel to Michel's recovery. Acting as a sacrificial scapegoat, she falls victim to Michel's harsh theories and dies in the inhuman aridity of the desert, at a time when Michel can no longer restrain the violence of his primitive instincts.

Ménalque (may-NAHLK), a former acquaintance of Michel who spends most of his time traveling in distant lands, engaged in some kind of exploration. An anticonformist, he antagonizes most people with his unconventional and haughty attitude. When Michel meets him again on his return to Paris, their previous reciprocal dislike turns into mutual attraction. Ménalque freely verbalizes Michel's new hidden feelings and brings to light the discrepancy between the latter's alleged "authentic being" and his adopted lifestyle. Rather than being Michel's corrupter, Ménalque personifies Michel's inner voice and puts him face to face with his predicament. He also represents the free individual who, in contrast with Michel, has the courage to live the life corresponding to his innermost tendencies.

Moktir (mohk-TEER), one of the young Arab boys whom Marceline brings to Michel's room in Biskra. He soon becomes Michel's favorite, after Michel catches him stealing a pair of scissors belonging to Marceline. Far from trying to stop him, Michel is fascinated by the act of transgression, which reveals primitive and free instincts and uncovers a nature rich in possibilities.

Charles (shahrl), the son of Michel's caretaker, Bocage. He is a handsome, disciplined seventeen-year-old whose pragmatic intelligence Michel admires. He embodies for Michel the pleasure derived from the deliberate and organized exploitation of one's own resources. He tries to prod Michel into better cultivating his estate, but to no avail.

Bachir (bah-SHEER), a young, handsome Arab boy. Michel interprets his intense physical attraction to Bachir as a love for animal health.

The Heurtevents (ewr-teh-VAH[N]), a family of primitive, immoral farmhands whose incestuous relationships fascinate Michel.

Alcide (ahl-SEED), a young Heurtevent whom Michel joins in poaching on his own estate.

— *Marie-Denise Boros Azzi*

THE IMPORTANCE OF BEING EARNEST: A Trivial Comedy for Serious People

Author: Oscar Wilde (1854-1900)
First published: 1899
Genre: Drama
Locale: London and Hertfordshire
Time: Late nineteenth century
Plot: Comedy of manners

Algernon (Algy) Moncrief, a young man of fashion and considerable worldly charm. He is a confirmed Bunburyist; that is, he uses an imaginary sick friend's name and condition as an excuse to leave London when he finds his aristocratic aunt, Lady Bracknell, too domineering or her dinner parties too dull. He delights in the artificial, the trivial, and the faddish, and he employs them for his own amusement, the only thing about which, as he insists, he is ever serious. Out for a jape, he poses as John Worthing's fictitious brother Ernest to court his friend's ward, Cecily Cardew. Although genuinely in love, he never abandons his pose of reckless pretense or his cynically amusing observations on country and city life, manners, fashions, and relatives.

John (Jack) Worthing, J.P., Algernon Moncrief's friend, who poses as Ernest to win the hand of Algy's cousin, the Honorable Gwendolyn Fairfax, Lady Bracknell's daughter. Also a Bunburyist, he has invented a fictitious brother Ernest, a reprobate who is always getting into scrapes, as an excuse for his frequent visits to London. Jack is serious about most things, especially love. He was a foundling, brought up by a wealthy man who made Jack the guardian of his benefactor's granddaughter, Cecily Cardew. When Jack proposes to Gwendolyn, he arouses Lady Bracknell's displeasure because he cannot trace his family tree. All he knows is that he had been found abandoned in a leather bag left at Victoria Station. Finally, his parentage is traced, and he learns that he is the long-lost son of Lady Bracknell's sister, that Algy is his younger brother, and that his Christian name really is Ernest. This last fact is the most pleasing, for Gwendolyn could not possibly love him under any other name.

Lady Augusta Bracknell, Algernon Moncrief's aunt, a strong-willed woman of fashion who lives only by society's dictates. The hostess at numerous dinner parties to which her nephew is always invited but that he seldom attends, she dominates the lives of all about her in the same compulsive fashion that makes her move only in the best circles. Although Jack Worthing is an eligible young bachelor of means, she rejects his suit of Gwendolyn and advises him to find some acceptable relatives as quickly as possible. Although witty in her pronouncements, she never deviates into good sense about the artificial world she inhabits with other snobs and pretenders. Her sense of social superiority is punctured when she learns that her daughter's rejected suitor is her own nephew.

The Honorable Gwendolyn Fairfax, Lady Bracknell's daughter. She is in love with Jack Worthing, whose name she believes to be Ernest. Although she moves in the same conventional snobbish social world as her mother, her outlook is whimsical and rebellious. Determined to marry the man of her choice, she is pleased to discover that Worthing, once his parentage is revealed, can offer her not only the right name and devotion but also family connections and wealth. She accommodates herself to her good fortune.

Cecily Cardew, an eighteen-year-old given to romantic dreams and a diary of fictitious events. She is the ward of Jack Worthing, who had been adopted by her eccentric grandfather. Lovely, determined, and rusticated, she is seemingly without guile, but she is in reality as poised as her newly discovered friend, Gwendolyn Fairfax. As the dupe of her guardian's story that he has a wicked brother named Ernest in the city, she is charmed and won when that supposed roue, as impersonated by Algy Moncrief, appears in the country. She is also pleased that the man she intends to marry is named Ernest. After learning the truth, she decides that she still loves him, in spite of his having such a name as Algernon.

Miss Letitia Prism, the forgetful authoress of a sentimental three-volume romance, the governess of Cecily Cardew and, earlier, of Jack Worthing. Bent on marriage herself, she contrives to keep her charge's mind on the serious business of learning inconsequentials. In the end, she is revealed as the absent-minded nurse who twenty-eight years earlier had placed the infant Ernest Moncrief in a leather handbag deposited in the cloakroom at Victoria station and the manuscript of her novel in a perambulator.

The Reverend Frederick Chasuble, D.D., an Anglican clergyman who is amenable to performing any rite for anyone at any time, in much the same way that he fits one sermon into many contexts. Delightful in his metaphorical allusions, he meets his match in Miss Prism, whose allusions contain direct revelation of matrimonial intent.

IN A FREE STATE

Author: V. S. Naipaul (1932-   )
First published: 1971
Genre: Short fiction
Locale: Bombay, Washington, D.C., the West Indies, London, and an unnamed African country
Time: 1954-1969
Plot: Social realism

Santosh (SAN-tosh), the protagonist of "One out of Many," an Indian domestic. When his employer, an Indian in government service, is posted to Washington, D.C., the naïve Santosh anticipates a life of freedom in America. His unrealistic view of America is enhanced by his watching television commercials. His lust leads him into an affair with a black maid. Overwhelmed with guilt, he abandons his employer and takes a job as a chef in an Indian restaurant. Lacking a work permit, he is afraid to walk the streets lest he be arrested. Finding himself in a psychological prison, he compromises his earlier dreams and settles for a life of detachment. He marries the black maid, thereby becoming a U.S. citizen, and continues to work as a chef. His final attitude is one of stoic acceptance of his loss of freedom and the recognition that he must merely feed and clothe his body for several years; then life mercifully will be over.

Sahib (SAH-heeb), Santosh's first employer, a benevolent man who works for the Indian government and is sent as its agent to Washington, D.C. He warns Santosh that Washington, D.C., is not like Bombay and that he will not be able to live as comfortably there as he did in India.

Priya (PREE-yah), an Indian restaurateur in Washington, D.C., who lures Santosh away from his first employer. He advises Santosh to forget his wife and children in the hills at home and to marry the black maid and become an American citizen.

The narrator, an unnamed West Indian in "Tell Me Who to Kill," working in London to help his brother, Dayo, get an education. Having known nothing but poverty and hopelessness in his native Trinidad, the narrator devotes all of his energy to helping Dayo to become a success in life. When his brother drops out of school, lies to the narrator, and then finally decides to marry a white woman, the obsessive narrator's crushed dreams turn to savage madness as he seeks to kill someone and to find a scapegoat for his brother's moral and intellectual corruption. Because the enemy is really society itself, he is left only with his madness, frustration, and failure.

Dayo (DAY-oh), the young brother of the narrator of "Tell Me Who to Kill," a Trinidadian living in England and supported by his devoted brother. He attends college for a while, but being essentially lazy, he drops out of school, lies to his brother, and chooses to live his own sort of life rather than the ambitious one shaped for him by his idealistic and self-sacrificing brother.

Bobby, the protagonist of "In a Free State," a white homosexual civil servant who has emigrated from England to an eastern African country, where he serves as an administrative officer in the central government and where he can indulge his sadomasochistic passion with impunity. He relishes the power he holds over the Africans and, at the same time, he desires to be punished by them. Unlike his traveling companion, Linda, he exhibits a sentimental and romantic attitude toward Africa. During a long automobile trip with Linda, Bobby reveals his colonial spirit of arrogance, superiority, and cruelty by knocking an ignorant service station attendant to the ground. Later, Bobby's masochism is revealed when some African military men beat and rob him. When he finally returns to the safety of his white compound, Bobby thinks of leaving Africa, but he quickly displaces that idea with another: He must dismiss his African servant because the man has betrayed his African heritage by drinking and attending a Christian church. Victim and victimizer, Bobby has driven into the heart of darkness and has become an integral part of its corruption.

Linda, a white, middle-aged Englishwoman married to one of the British officials stationed in Africa. She is an acquaintance of Bobby and shares a long automobile trip with him through the African countryside during a period of dangerous political upheaval. Unlike Bobby, she nurses no romantic image of Africa and has always hated the sordid life she has seen there. She is more keenly aware than he is of the menace and brutality that threatens them during their trip. Limited by her colonial prejudices, she nevertheless possesses an instinctive fear of the mysterious, private, and ancient world of the African bush, as well as of the more obvious threat of the ubiquitous African militia.

— Richard Kelly

IN COLD BLOOD

Author: Truman Capote (Truman Streckfus Persons, 1924-1984)
First published: 1966
Genre: Novel
Locale: Kansas
Time: 1959
Plot: Detective and mystery

Perry Edward Smith, a superstitious and sentimental man, an inveterate dreamer with an explosive personality. As a child, Perry was shunted from one orphanage to another, neglected by an alcoholic mother and a father who drifted in search of gold. Perry joined the merchant marine, then the Army, serving a four-year hitch. A motorcycle crash left him with permanently disfigured legs and constant pain. He escapes from a Kansas jail, where he is serving a sentence for burglary, but is recaptured and sent to prison, where he meets Dick Hickock. Dick's plan to rob and kill the Clutters offers Perry a chance to fulfill his dream of treasure hunting in Mexico, a dream that evaporates when the crime nets the pair no money. Convicted along with Dick of the Clutter murders and sentenced to death, Perry spends his time on death row reviewing his life with a degree of self-pity. As he is about to be hanged, he apologizes for his crime but adds that perhaps he could have contributed something worthwhile after all.

Richard Eugene (Dick) Hickock, the twenty-eight-year-old son of poor Kansas farmers. He has been married and divorced twice and has fathered three boys by the time he is sent to prison for writing bad checks. A car accident has given his face an uneven, serpentine look. Intelligent and friendly, he easily talks merchants into cashing checks that later prove worthless. He boasts that, after robbing the Clutters, he will "blast hair all over them walls." Seeing young women as "blond chicken," he secretly plans to rape Nancy Clutter before killing her, but at the last minute Perry prevents him. Dick's wisecracking manner continues through his trial and stint on death row. Only at the foot of the gallows does he turn solemn, politely shaking hands with the four agents who led in his capture and who know that beneath the personable exterior, he is a mean, vicious punk.

Herbert (Herb) Clutter, a wealthy Kansas wheat farmer, the father of four children, a devoted husband, and an active member of the Methodist church. A rumor that he keeps as much as forty thousand dollars in his house with which to pay workers reaches Dick Hickock, who hears it from a cellmate. When Herb is awakened by Dick and Perry, who demand the money, he tries in vain to convince them that it does not exist. He pleads with them not to harm his family and to be especially careful of his wife, Bonnie, whose health is very fragile. His efforts to reason with the two killers end when Perry cuts his throat.

Nancy Clutter, the town favorite. She is sixteen years old, bright, pretty, and outgoing. Her days are active and filled with pie baking, music lessons, rides on her favorite horse, and errands for her mother. In her diary and on the telephone with her close friend, Susan Kidwell, she talks mostly about Bobby Rupp, her boyfriend. Self-possessed enough to chat with Perry as Dick searches the house for money, she is the last of the Clutters to be shot.

Kenyon Clutter, fifteen years old, the youngest Clutter child. He is tall and awkward, and he wears glasses. He busies himself making a hope chest for his sister, Beverly, who is soon to be married, and chasing coyotes in his old truck with a friend. Bound and gagged and laid out on a sofa in the basement, with a pillow placed under his head to make him comfortable, he is the second one to be shot.

Bonnie Clutter, a timid and pious woman in poor health, Herb's wife and the mother of the four Clutter children. She rarely is strong enough to greet the friends who come to the house, staying in her second-story bedroom, where she sleeps alone, too fragile even to share a bed with her husband, who sleeps downstairs. She is the killers' third victim.

Alvin Adams Dewey, a special agent of the Kansas Bureau of Investigation. He heads the team of investigators assigned to the Clutter case. Taciturn and tough, he is a former county sheriff and Federal Bureau of Investigation agent. He knows and respects the Clutter family. He stoically bears the brunt of criticism from the locals who are impatient for the crime to be solved. When the killers are captured in Las Vegas, he and three of his agents return them to Kansas. On the trip back, Alvin elicits from Perry a detailed description of the murders. At the execution, he remembers seeing only Perry's small feet dangling in the air. Later, at the Clutter gravesite, he is reminded of what has been lost and what remains when he encounters Nancy's close friend Susan Kidwell, now studying at the university. She tells him that Bobby Rupp, Nancy's boyfriend, has married "a very nice, beautiful girl," then looks away.

— *Bernard E. Morris*

IN DUBIOUS BATTLE

Author: John Steinbeck (1902-1968)
First published: 1936
Genre: Novel

Locale: California
Time: The 1930's
Plot: Social realism

Mac, a communist labor organizer who organizes a fruit-pickers' strike. After many hardships, in the face of starvation and imminent eviction, the strike seems doomed. Then Mac rallies the strikers with a stirring speech over the body of his friend and co-organizer, Jim Nolan, who is shot when he and Mac are enticed into a trap.

Jim Nolan, the friend and co-organizer, who is finally killed. The son of a workingman whose death was caused by policemen's blows, he has come to communism by way of starvation and early ill-treatment.

London, the leader of the fruit pickers.

Doc Burton, a philosopher and skeptic. He does much to maintain the sanitation of the camp and the strikers' health during the strike. Things worsen after his disappearance. It is in response to a report that he is lying wounded in a field that Jim and Mac rush out into the trap in which Jim is killed.

Al Townsend, the owner of a lunch cart. He gives handouts to the strikers, for whom he feels sympathy. His father permits the strikers to camp on his farm.

Lisa London, the daughter of the camp leader. Mac's influence around the camp greatly increases after he, giving the impression he is a doctor, delivers Lisa of a baby.

Joy, an old and disabled comrade who is killed in an early conflict. Mac's speech on this occasion does much to unify the workers.

Dick, a handsome comrade who uses his charms on women in order to get food for the strikers.

IN SICILY
(Conversazione in Sicilia)

Author: Elio Vittorini (1908-1966)
First published: 1937
Genre: Novel

Locale: Sicily
Time: The 1930's
Plot: Philosophical

Silvestro Ferrauto (fehr-rah-EW-toh), the narrator of the story, who is thirty years old. Disturbed by the turmoil in Italy, he decides to return to his native Sicily, which he left at the age of fifteen. He is especially moved to take the trip after receiving a letter from his father stating that he has left his mother; Silvestro spontaneously decides to visit her in Recalmuto, his birthplace, in part to discover himself. Leaving his job as a Linotype operator in Milan, Silvestro travels by train to Sicily, meeting a number of unique characters who help him to find peace and understanding of the world in which he lives.

Concezione Ferrauto (kohn-chay-ZEE-oh-nay), the narrator's mother, who lives simply in the village and makes a living giving injections to the inhabitants, who are plagued by consumption and malaria. She takes Silvestro on her rounds of giving injections and introduces him to the many different characters in the village. When asked why her husband left her, she pretends that she threw him out. Her simple life impresses Silvestro, especially the stoicism with which she faces the wartime death of Silvestro's brother.

Great Lombard, a nickname given to one of Silvestro's fellow passengers on the train journey across Sicily. He is Sicilian but of Lombard stock; that is, of Germanic background. Silvestro is impressed by his hearty, bold manner, not at all like most of the poor, struggling Sicilians usually encountered. A landowner, he typifies to Silvestro the proud Sicilian spirit, which is not bowed by fate.

The Knife-Grinder, a village character, tattered and poor. He goes through the town offering to grind knives and scissors but finds little to do. Silvestro gives him his pocketknife to grind, and the Knife-Grinder then leads him to Ezechiele, a leatherworker.

Ezechiele (eh-zeh-kee-EHL-ay), a leatherworker and harness maker, a philosopher who takes both the Knife-Grinder and Silvestro to an inn to drink wine. Ezechiele quickly takes on a symbolic nature, calling Silvestro a man who suffers for the "insulted world." He and the Knife-Grinder show pity for Silvestro and his torment over the tumultuous Italy of Benito Mussolini (although no mention is ever made of Mussolini or Fascism). Ezechiele says of Silvestro, "He suffers for the woes of the outraged world."

The Soldier, an unseen voice that Silvestro hears while in the village cemetery and that holds a dialogue with Silvestro. The voice represents Silvestro's younger brother, killed on one of Mussolini's wars of conquest. Silvestro asks him if he suffers, and the voice of the Soldier tells him that he does, especially because of the propaganda and monuments that are raised to the glories of war and soldiery (though the Soldier avoids naming names or giving any specifics).

Mustache and

No Mustache, two Sicilians whom Silvestro meets on the train, men who typify the worst in the Sicilian character for Silvestro. They are callous toward the poor and repressive. "Every starving man is dangerous," states No Mustache. Both characters are symbolic of the Sicilian problem in Silvestro's mind, that of lack of charity and consideration for others.

— *Philip Brantingham*

IN THE BEGINNING

Author: Chaim Potok (1929-   )
First published: 1975
Genre: Novel

Locale: New York City
Time: Primarily the 1920's to the 1940's
Plot: Impressionism

David (Davey) Lurie, the narrator, a Jewish boy growing up in New York City. Davey's childhood is plagued by what he sees as terrifying accidents and is dominated by his illnesses, nose and throat infections made frequent by a deviated septum, the result of falling with his mother the day she brought him home from the hospital as a newborn. His rich imagination is filled with a combination of his father's harsh history, his mother's bittersweet memories, and his cousin Saul's stories from the midrash (commentaries on the Hebrew Scriptures). To the distress of his father and cousin, Davey's brilliant mind eventually leads him to study higher criticism of sacred texts and to question the safely orthodox understandings of Scripture with which he has been reared. After his ordination as a rabbi, Davey leaves home to study for an advanced degree at the University of Chicago. At the end of the novel, in the cemetery at Bergen Belsen, he finds in a vision of his father and his Uncle David courage to "nourish the present" without losing its roots in so tragic a past.

Max Lurie, Davey's father, a real estate agent in New York. Short, thickset, and muscular, Max is known for his strength and his ability to get things done. After serving in the Polish army in World War I, Max returned home to his Polish village, only to find anti-Semitism and pogroms awaiting him. In response, he founded the Am Kedoshim Society to help Jews survive by physical and financial force. During the early parts of the novel, the society is trying to bring its members and their families to America. Max hates the goyim (non-Jews) but is above all a practical man of action. When the stock market crashes, financial and political action become impossible for him, and he suffers an emotional breakdown. Eventually, recognizing that he must rebuild, he learns to repair watches, gradually building a successful business as a jeweler and returning to his involvement in politics.

Ruth Lurie, Davey's mother. A gentle woman reared on a farm in Poland, Ruth has been wounded by the death of her fiancé and by separation from her parents, who remain in Poland. Davey remembers her as constantly writing letters. From Ruth, Davey learns tenderness and joy in the natural world—trees, water, and birds. When all the remaining members of her family in Europe are killed in Bergen Belsen, Ruth is almost destroyed; such realities are part of the burden Davey bears as he leaves the clearly defined boundaries of orthodoxy in search of vital, unowned truth.

Uncle David Lurie, Max Lurie's youngest brother, who was killed in a pogrom in Poland. He was engaged to marry Ruth. An intellectual, David supplied his brother with ideas, which Max then put into action. Uncle David is to Davey Lurie a not-always-welcome role model of intellectual courage and integrity.

Alex Lurie, Davey's younger brother. Practical, athletic, and carefree, Alex is a sharp contrast to his fragile brother. Alex develops a love of fiction and wants to be a teacher and writer of literature.

Saul Lurie, Davey's cousin and friend. When Davey is very young, Saul tells him stories from the midrash and helps him understand his Jewish world. Later, Saul is the model rabbinical student, the model others expect Davey to follow, yet from which he is in reality radically departing.

Shmuel Bader, a successful businessman and operative for various agencies helping European Jews. Bader teaches Davey the Bible and unintentionally starts him on his way to critical study of the Scriptures.

Mrs. Horowitz, a neighbor of the Luries when Davey is very young. A lonely, superstitious woman, Mrs. Horowitz befriends Davey and at her death leaves him several cartons of books, among them works that introduce him to higher critical study of biblical texts.

Rav Tuvya Sharfman, Davey's Talmud teacher after he graduates from college. A lonely and tormented man, tall, thin, and neatly groomed, Rav Sharfman is the greatest living Orthodox Jewish Talmudist. He encourages Davey in his quest for truth and warns him, above all, not to be shallow.

Eddie Kulanski, a Polish boy in Davey's neighborhood, violently anti-Semitic. He and his cousin threaten Davey and one day ambush him, pulling down his shorts and underwear to see his "Jew cock" and badly frightening him.

Larry Grossman, a boy in Davey's class at school. Larry is a large and unintelligent boy who resents Davey's intelligence and reputation. Larry paws Davey when no one is watching and threatens to hurt him. Davey learns from Larry that not all of his enemies are non-Jews.

— *Jonathan A. Glenn*

IN THE CASTLE OF MY SKIN

Author: George Lamming (1927-   )
First published: 1953
Genre: Novel

Locale: Creighton's Village, Barbados
Time: Mid-1930's to mid-1940's
Plot: Bildungsroman

G., a young Barbadian boy who is the narrator and protagonist. He is eight years old at the opening of the novel, which spans the subsequent nine years of his life. He tells the story of his childhood, which was spent in a small village (the fictitious Creighton's Village) in Barbados, where he attends the local school with his friends. Unlike his friends, he wins a scholarship to go to high school. After he has been graduated from high school, he goes to Trinidad to become a teacher in a small school for Venezuelan and other South American students. The novel ends on the eve of his departure to Trinidad. G. is a sensitive and imaginative child whose developing consciousness also records an important part of the history of Creighton's Village and Barbados.

G.'s mother, portrayed by G. as a person who is as capable of laughter as she is of wielding a whip to "roast his tail." She is a capable woman who rears her son single-handedly and works hard to give him his education.

Pa, the father figure of the village. He is the repository of village history and is revered by all the villagers. He apparently earned some money in his youth in Panama, but in the novel he is quite poor. He sells his house after his wife's death and, at the end of the novel, is preparing to move into the Alms House, knowing well that he does not have much longer to live.

Ma, his wife. She is described as balding and wearing a white cloth on her head. She is an intuitive person who is filled with foreboding at the future of Creighton's Village. Significantly, she dies at the end of the riots.

Mr. Creighton, the landlord who owns the village. During the course of the novel, he loses his authority to Mr. Slime. Mr. Creighton figures prominently in the riot scene, when the striking workers from the city come into the village and prepare to attack him. He walks alone through the streets of the village, fully aware of the impending danger; he is saved by the opportune arrival of Mr. Slime, whose mere presence saves Mr. Creighton's life.

Mr. Slime, the village schoolteacher, an entrepreneur, and ultimately the person with the most power in the village. In the beginning, he teaches fifth grade in G.'s school, but he is forced to resign because of his liaison with the wife of the head teacher. He founds the Friendly Society and Penny Bank, which ultimately help him to take control of the economics of the village. He is simultaneously feared and revered by the villagers.

Trumper, one of G.'s childhood friends. He goes to America, discovers the music of Paul Robeson, and is brought to an awareness of his racial identity. He tries to impart this newfound sense of identity to G. when he returns to Barbados.

Boy Blue, another childhood friend of G. He participates in G.'s childhood adventures, along with Trumper and Bob. He eventually joins the police force in the village.

Bob, the fourth member of the quartet of children featured in the novel. He figures prominently in the riot scene when he accidentally strays into the city during the riot and returns to the village with eyewitness reports of the bloodshed in the city. He also grows up to be a policeman.

The shoemaker, a significant villager. His shop is the center for intellectual debates on politics. He has the unique distinction of having read a book, a novel by J. B. Priestley that he uses as his political gospel when trying to interpret important historical events such as World War II.

Mr. Foster, another important villager. He figures prominently in various important sections of the novel. He refuses to leave his house during the flood and is carried down to the river on its roof; he has to be fished out of the water by a rescue party. During the feared riots, he assumes charge of the situation in the village. At the end of the novel, he voices his protest against the takeover of the land by Mr. Slime.

The overseer, the middleman who negotiates between the landlord and the villagers. He is despised by the villagers for his assumption of authority and for rejecting his origins among the villagers. He later is promoted to supervisor of roads, and his pride at this event does not endear him any further to the villagers.

— *Nalini Iyer*

IN THE DITCH

Author: Buchi Emecheta (1944-)
First published: 1972
Genre: Novel
Locale: The slums of northern London
Time: Late 1960's
Plot: Bildungsroman

Adah (AH-duh), the protagonist. A young Nigerian sociology student, she is a mother with middle-class aspirations who is separated from her husband and must rear her five small children, the oldest of whom is eight years old. A talented, qualified young woman, Adah is caught in the machinery of the British welfare state and is inexorably pauperized and humiliated.

The landlord, a mean-spirited and hostile man. Like Adah, he and his wife are Nigerians, but of the Yoruba tribe. A council tenant himself, he illegally sublets a squalid room in his council flat to Adah and her five children, informing the council that Adah is a relative and only a guest. He exploits Adah by charging her double rent because he wants to make money from his flat to pay for his studies. He also terrorizes her and her children with his daily "juju" escapades.

Mrs. Devlin, a kindly Irish woman who lives above the landlord's flat. A mother of two sons, she looks out for Adah and speaks out against the landlord's and the council's exploitation of Adah's desperation.

Whoopey, a mama's girl of feckless optimism. The lonely, dependent single mother of two children has lived with her mother, Mrs. Cox, and sister at the Pussy Cat Mansions all her life. Despite her dependence and her love of alcohol and bars, Whoopey and Mrs. Cox become Adah's most constant companions and friends, providing cushioning comfort and easing her into the society of "ditch dwellers," those living on welfare. A classic example of the characteristic dependency in the welfare system, Whoopey falls deeper in the ditch, still lacking prospects and initiative at the end of the novel.

Mrs. Cook, a Jamaican ditch-dweller and mother of five children. Hers is one of the Mansions' very few so-called problem families with an active father present. With dignity, she extricates her family from the cycle of dependency by choosing to do without welfare assistance, going back to work, and moving her family of seven from council housing into a two-room flat to save five pounds a week.

The Smalls, a quarrelsome family consisting of Mr. Small, his wife, and his mother, Granny. They are characterized by their small-built and angry mien. Mr. Small is the council's resident plumber for the Pussy Cat Mansions. One of the original clans of the Mansions, the Smalls tout themselves as members of the "Establishment" on account of Granny's thirty-year residency at the Mansions. The Smalls, who are nosy and enjoy informing authorities of infractions, rudely initiate Adah into the protocol of the Mansions.

Carol, the "family adviser." She is a lonely, overweight, patronizing officer employed by the welfare council to "police" the "problem families" of the welfare state. As a privileged member of the "Establishment," she masterminds plans to keep the ditch dwellers at her mercy for her own fulfillment. Her manipulative, maternalistic relationship with the Mansions' women—her "cases"—allows her to play the role of a deity who is dispensing charity.

Mr. Persial, a patronizing, middle-class council clerk in charge of emergency housing reallocation. He lectures Adah about the trend away from large families in most civilized societies.

— *Pamela J. Olubunmi Smith*

IN THE HEART OF THE SEAS: A Story of a Journey to the Land of Israel
(Bi-levav yamim: Sippur agadah)

Author: Shmuel Yosef Agnon (Shmuel Yosef Czaczkes, 1888-1970)
First published: 1935
Genre: Novel
Locale: Eastern Galicia and Palestine
Time: Late nineteenth and early twentieth centuries
Plot: Folklore

Hananiah (hah-nah-NI-yah), a holy man who endures hardships and captivity as he drifts on whatever path the Lord sets his feet. He longs for nothing so much as to go to The Land of Israel. His hands are blessed; he can, without instruction or training, perform the skills of all trades. His opportunity to go to Israel arises when nine rabbis and their wives, who are about to embark, welcome him to join them, for he makes the quorum of ten men necessary for the group to pray as a congregation. True to the goodness of his heart, however, he misses the boat's departure while helping a woman try to locate her lost husband. The Lord instructs him to lay his kerchief on the sea, and miraculously he sails to Israel sitting on it. He becomes the subject of legend, and it is said that at the age of one hundred he was like a youth of twenty.

Rabbi Shmuel Yosef (shmew-EHL), the storyteller of the group. At times of danger and hardship during their journey, he cheers the group with tales of salvation and comfort.

Rabbi Yosef Meir (mah-YEHR), whose longing for Israel causes him to divorce his wife because she does not want to accompany him. At the end of the story, she joins him, and they remarry in Israel. They are one of the two families who remain to make their home in The Land.

Rabbi Alter, the teacher, who spends his days studying and teaching the Torah until he realizes that a man is not whole if he resides outside of the holy land of Israel. The most fearful of the group, he is inclined to see evil omens in many events.

Rabbi Alter, the slaughterer, who relinquishes his business to his son-in-law so that he can live in The Land. Like all but two families of the original group, he does not find a way to make a living in Israel and returns to the Exile.

Rabbi Yehudal Mendel, who grieves over the death of his spiritual teacher, the Rabbi Uriel, until God puts it into his heart to go to The Land of Israel.

Rabbi Pesah, the warden of the House of Study. Childless, he and his wife, Tzirel, hope that the soil of Israel will make them fertile. They are blessed with sons and daughters and are one of only two families of the original group who remain in The Land.

Leibush (LAY-behsh), the butcher. He is the only one who is dissatisfied with Israel. He returns to Buczaca, his hometown, at the earliest opportunity.

Rabbi Moshe (MOY-sheh), whose yearning to go to The Land of Israel is so great that he leaves behind his only two daughters.

Rabbi Shelomo (SHLOH-moh), the eldest of the group, a wealthy merchant who gives up the goods of this world to better serve the Lord in The Land of Israel. His faith remains firm throughout the hardships of the first year and the death of his daughter. Unable to earn a living in Israel, he must return to the Exile.

— *Lolette Kuby*

IN THE HEART OF THE VALLEY OF LOVE

Author: Cynthia Kadohata (1956-)
First published: 1992
Genre: Novel

Locale: Los Angeles and elsewhere in Southern California
Time: 2052
Plot: Science fiction

Francie, whose name is short for Francesca, the nineteen-year-old narrator. She quietly enjoys the weirdness of a life lived among people discarded by a future society. The daughter of a Japanese mother and a Chinese/black father, Francesca lives in a futuristic Los Angeles beset by riots, fires, mass unemployment, and gasoline and water shortages. The rich live in armed and gated communities. Like many others, Francie suffers from a new chronic skin disease, but she refuses to be bothered by it. Francie, who was orphaned at the age of fourteen, moves out of her aunt's home after a car accident nearly severs her right arm. She joins the staff of her college's newspaper, where she meets Mark, who becomes her boyfriend. Francie views sex with Mark with the same kind of benevolent distance with which she considers the rest of her topsy-turvy, terminally run-down world full of angry men, freeways ending in mid-air, desert tattoo parlors, and abusive relationships among her friends. After a series of professional setbacks and fights with her increasingly sullen boyfriend, Francie visits a secret spot in the Pasadena Arroyo with him. She digs up a box buried by her friend Jewel's grandfather and deposits in it the two little rocks that she has treated as symbols of her dead parents for five years. With this act, she finally lets go of her hurtful past and readies herself for new adventures.

Mark Trang, Francie's boyfriend, also nineteen years old. He is a reporter for their college newspaper. Francie admires his strong build, pronounced cheekbones, and sensitive hands. His lovemaking with Francie can be wild and passionate, but sometimes he sinks into long silences. He was beaten by his father as a child and is a compulsive thief of restaurant mints. Mark constantly tries to help all of his friends. He even warns an administrator that he is being investigated. When the man is caught in a homosexual liaison with a student athlete and commits suicide, Mark becomes disillusioned with his job, loses weight, and cuts his hair short. At the Pasadena Arroyo, Mark seems to accept that some people are beyond his ability to help them.

Jewel, the managing editor of the student newspaper. In her late thirties, her body bears the scars of her relationship with her abusive boyfriend Teddy. She is outspoken and fond of tight but old-fashioned dresses. Jewel quickly becomes Francie's friend, and Francie is fascinated by her. Jewel finally leaves Teddy and flies to the East Coast. Francie and Mark discover that she took the two gold rings that her grandfather had buried in his box in the Pasadena Arroyo and left behind a slip with her name.

Auntie Annie, Francie's huge aunt. Francie lives with Annie before Annie's life falls apart following the secret arrest and subsequent disappearance of her boyfriend, Rohn. After her niece moves out, Annie rents out her dilapidated bungalow, but she moves back in later, as there is new hope for Rohn's impending release at the novel's end.

Rohn Jefferson, Auntie Annie's equally huge lover, a mellow and good-natured man. Francie believes that their love is genuine, even though they do not look very romantic. Rohn is last seen as he tries to buy some water from Max. It is likely that he was arrested and detained without notice to anybody, as is common in Francie's world.

Max the Magician, a shady desert dweller and black marketeer, the last person to see Rohn before his disappearance.

Emmy and

Hank, Jewel's parents. A former singer and a former nightclub owner, they appear to be locked in a solid love-hate relationship; Francie thinks they are together because they share the same fears. Jewel almost fails to show up at Hank's birthday party, and Mark and Francie muse about their family relations.

Teddy, Jewel's abusive boyfriend, who works in real estate. A short, pushy man, he is a bully but can be charming when in trouble. Mark hates him. He has a second girlfriend but still calls on Jewel and beats her as long as she lives in Los Angeles.

Carl, a fiftyish tattoo artist. He eventually opens a studio in the desert. Tall and smart, he resembles a wild animal. Carl tattoos Francie and Mark and promises to inquire about Rohn.

Madeline Burroughs, a mother of two sons. Matt is a murderer free on appeal, and Pyle is a retarded thirty-four-year-old. Francie befriends Madeline at her bead shop and stays there the night Madeline dies. After her death, Matt skips bail and Pyle is moved to an institution.

Steven and

Nadine, Francie's cousins and childhood friends in Chicago. She remembers their times together with fondness but lost all touch with them after they moved away.

— R. C. Lutz

IN THE LABYRINTH
(Dans le labyrinthe)

Author: Alain Robbe-Grillet (1922-   )
First published: 1959
Genre: Novel
Locale: A French city
Time: During World War II
Plot: New Novel

A lone soldier, a figure who arrives late at night in a snowy northern French city, just ahead of invading enemy troops. He has no name, and no physical description is provided. He spends one night in a barracks, or aid station, where he exchanges his wet uniform for a dry one. The number on the new uniform, now his only identifying mark, is 12,345. He also is treated for fever by an army medic. He is carrying the effects of a dead comrade and is to give them to a man about fifty years old who may or may not be the dead soldier's father. He sees a man of approximately the right age but is fearful of speaking to him. He spends much of his time either looking for a street whose name he cannot remember or in a café. Hanging on the wall of the café is a graphic representation of a café scene. The soldier is able to pass with ease from one to the other. It is in the café that he sees two people who will be part of his story: the boy and the woman.

The woman, a figure who has dark hair and lives in an apartment building into which the soldier stumbles while looking for directions for how to find the street where he is supposed to meet his dead comrade's father. She is also a barmaid, or waitress, in the café and the mother of the boy. She takes pity on the soldier and gives him bread and wine. In the same apartment lives a lame man. In the original French, the woman and the lame man use the formal *vous* when speaking to each other, instead of the more informal, and normal, *tu*. The lame man addresses the soldier as *tu*.

The lame man, a man old enough to be in active service, particularly so because it is wartime. He probably is feigning lameness to avoid military service. He cannot help the soldier find the street he is seeking but tells him about the barracks, or aid station, where he can spend the night. He offers the boy's services as a guide.

The boy, a youth approximately ten to twelve years old. He wears a beret and a cape. He already has met the soldier and is willing to guide him, even against his mother's wishes. He questions the soldier about everything but receives no answers.

The doctor, a man in his fifties who could be the dead comrade's father. He is bald and carries a combination cane and umbrella. He saw the soldier during the soldier's wanderings but never spoke to him. His only actual contact with the soldier, other than simple recognition by sight, is when he gives medical aid to the soldier after the latter is shot by an enemy patrol.

The narrator, who is impossible to identify textually. The narrator speaks in the first person only at the very beginning and the very end of the novel.

— Robert R. Brock

IN THE SHADOW OF THE GLEN

Author: John Millington Synge (1871-1909)
First published: 1904
Genre: Drama
Locale: County Wicklow, in western Ireland
Time: c. 1900
Plot: Comedy

Dan Burke, a white-haired farmer and herder of cows and sheep. He feigns his death and thereby exposes his wife's lack of affection for him. Lying "in state" in the kitchen of their cottage, he eavesdrops on her conversation with the tramp and the young man whom she welcomes into their home. Dan's thirst for whiskey compels him to reveal himself to the tramp when his wife briefly leaves the cottage. When she returns and flirts with Micheal Dara, the young man whom she had gone to meet, he triumphantly decries her and throws Nora and the tramp out of the house. Although he is initially angry with Micheal, he invites him to stay for a drink.

A tramp, who hopes to rest for a night and mend his clothing at the Burke home. He is the first to learn of Dan's trickery. He also encountered Micheal driving mountain ewes earlier in the day. Although he initially seems to comply with Dan's ruse, he defends Nora after her husband tries to oust her from the cottage. Having lost Dan as an ally, he offers to care for Nora when it is clear that both must leave the cottage.

Nora Burke, Dan's wife, who lives in his isolated cottage at the head of a long glen in County Wickham. Having married for her husband's possessions, the lonely younger woman longs for fulfillment in other respects and feels little sadness on the supposed passing of her cold husband. She warmly welcomes the tramp and Micheal when they arrive at the cottage. At the play's conclusion, she leaves the cottage with the tramp.

Micheal Dara, a young herder, a tall, innocent man who proposes to Nora soon after she invites him into the cottage and shows him her possessions. After Nora and the tramp leave, he shares a drink with Dan and toasts his health.

— *David Marc Fischer*

IN THE SHADOW OF THE WIND
(Les Fous de Bassan)

Author: Anne Hébert (1916-)
First published: 1982
Genre: Novel
Locale: Fictional Griffin Creek, between Québec City and the Atlantic Ocean; and Montreal
Time: Summer and autumn of 1936, and autumn of 1982
Plot: Psychological

Stevens Brown, who returns home at the age of twenty, five years after a battle with his father. His letters to a friend in Florida sketch isolated Griffin Creek, settled in 1782 by Royalist exiles from the American Revolution. Their descendants have intermarried for generations. He is the most intense of the violent family men, scarred by his father's brutality and his mother's rejection. He is obsessed with two cousins who have matured into women during his absence. On August 31, 1936, driven by a storm of emotion, he strangles his cousins and sinks their bodies in the sea. In 1982, he surfaces in Montreal, having escaped from a veterans' hospital where he had lived, insane, since fighting in World War II. His last letter and suicide note close the novel.

Olivia Atkins, the housemaid and prisoner of her father and older brothers. She hopes for Stevens' love but fears his latent violence. At the age of seventeen, she is perfect in physical beauty and dutiful domesticity. After death, she is transmuted into the lyric narrative voice "Olivia of the High Seas," in communion with the spirits of her female ancestors. She reflects on the memories of her cousin Stevens and her physical life and family, but she is drawn toward dissolution in the ocean, which is "Mère" (mother) as well as "Mer" (sea).

Nora Atkins, the double cousin of Olivia, fifteen years old in the summer of 1936. She is caught in passion for Stevens. Red-haired like her uncle, Nicholas Jones, and a child of the sun, she revels in her developing body. Her narrative voice celebrates summer and youth. Olivia is outwardly cool, identified with the sea; Nora is earthy and provocative. Her taunts and reproaches to Stevens catalyze his rage. She is the first of the cousins to die. Her body washes ashore, to be buried in Griffin Creek, whereas Olivia's body drifts out to sea.

Nicholas Jones, an Anglican clergyman, the uncle of Stevens and his victims. He is the opening narrator. In 1982, he plans a memorial to the moribund Griffin Creek, painting portraits of male ancestors, modeled on himself. He remembers the power of his beautiful youthful voice, how he used his position to rule Griffin Creek and try to win love from his mother, and how lust for his adolescent nieces awoke the storm of passion that scattered his congregation. A domestic tyrant, he embodies the patriarchal systems of church and government.

Percival Brown, Stevens' brother, who is fifteen years old in 1936. He is the only person who loves and is loved by Stevens. He is the family "idiot," a giant with a cherub's face who often screams instead of talking. He broods on the physical transformation of his maturing cousins but cannot compete for them. He observes the other characters and reports on the disappearance of his cousins and the recovery of relics from the sea. Percival's inner voice is poetic. His sentences are spare and broken, but he sees beyond individuals to their symbolic roles. Percival recognizes his grandmother Felicity as a dolphin, an incarnation of the sea. Percival alerts Irene Jones to her husband's lust for Olivia and Nora.

Felicity Jones, the matriarch of Griffin Creek. Wounded by her husband's chronic infidelity, she loves only her daughters and granddaughters. She rises daily to swim before dawn, taking Nora and Olivia with her. She finds her true nature in the sea.

Irene Jones, the parson's wife. She is silent, cold, and barren. She seems passionless and is the only person who will not dance at the barn dance. After her husband's attempted molestation of Nora, she efficiently hangs herself.

Pam Brown and

Pat Brown, identical twins, sisters of Stevens and Percival. They are innocent observers of the summer drama. Servants to Nicholas Jones, they survive as "old little girls" in 1982. Their portraits of Irene, Nora, and Olivia force Nicholas Jones to remember.

Maureen Macdonald, the widowed kinswoman of the Brown and Atkins families who welcomes Stevens into her home and bed when he returns to Griffin Creek. She pays for her brief summer of renewed sexuality with the pain of Stevens' rejection at summer's end and the horror of guessing his role in the disappearance of Nora and Olivia.

John Erwin McKenna, an Anglophone detective from Montreal who investigates the disappearance of the Atkins girls. Detested by Percival, he is described as obese and greasy. He alternately cajoles and bullies Stevens into a confession that later is disallowed in court.

— *Anne W. Sienkewicz*

IN THE TIME OF GREENBLOOM

Author: Gabriel Fielding (Alan Gabriel Barnsley, 1916-1986)
First published: 1956
Genre: Novel

Locale: Predominantly England, also Ireland and Wales
Time: Late 1930's
Plot: Psychological realism

John Blaydon, a sensitive and thoughtful student, the son of an Anglican minister. Almost thirteen at the opening of the novel, he is thin, pale, and tall; he is preparing to enter the university when the book ends. At a tennis party, he meets and falls deeply in love with Victoria Blount. She becomes his ideal image of love and beauty and seems like a part of his own being; when she is murdered, his life becomes and remains emotionally and spiritually disrupted. Burdened with an obscure sense of guilt and of purposelessness, by early manhood he is even contemplating suicide. Meeting Dymphna Uprichard, a girl much like Victoria, restores his faith in himself and his interest in life and helps confirm his discovery that he has a mission as a writer, though he will train as a physician to gratify his parents.

Victoria Blount, John's platonic love, approximately thirteen years old when he first meets her. She impresses him with her whiteness (metaphorically, her purity). She has fine, long black hair but very pale skin and is dressed all in white for the tennis party. Her large gray eyes shine out of a narrow white face. She has an attractively old-fashioned quality about her that sets her apart from the other children and suggests an ideal of purity and goodness. An innocent, she proposes, when they have wandered away from the party, that she and John go swimming even though they have no bathing suits. He commits himself to protecting her when he saves her from drowning. High-spirited, friendly, and too trusting, over John's protests she accepts a ride from a stranger after she and John have been picnicking in a cave. That stranger takes her back to the cave and strangles her. She lives on in John's mind as a symbol of love and a source of guilt for his not having saved her from harm.

Horab Greenbloom, who is first a student at Balliol College, Oxford, and later a private book publisher. He is an eccentric and very wealthy Jew and the second great influence on John's life. He has an almost Egyptian face, with pitch-black hair and eyes like those depicted on royal tombs; his cheekbones are high, his lips thick, and his nostrils exquisitely curved. He has a wooden leg and a taste for the exciting and bizarre. Generous, intellectually alert (when first met he is writing a book to clarify philosopher Ludwig Wittgenstein's theories), and emotionally perceptive, he is the only adult who really helps John. He comprehends John's sense of guilt and offers him a new perspective on life through the life of the mind, deflecting him from the wish for death.

Dymphna Uprichard, an Irish schoolgirl and a guest at the home of the Bodorgans, neighbors of John in Wales. John's age, she is tall, pale, and delicate, with short curly hair, and she is generous and friendly like the lost Victoria. Although she has almost been the prey of a man who may have been Victoria's killer, she has survived, and her friendship helps to restore John's zest for life.

Kitty Blaydon, John's mother, a strong-minded woman with intense family feelings. She upsets John by implying sexual misconduct with Victoria after the swimming incident but believes his protestations of innocence.

Enid Blount, Victoria's mother, a divorcée who has Victoria's lively manner but in less appealing adult form. To John's disillusionment, she is in bed with her lover when Victoria disappears.

George Harkness, a country landholder, Enid's lover, and a crude, boorish man who also disillusions John about adults, especially by insisting that John lie about his and Enid's whereabouts on the night of the murder.

Gilbert Victor, the headmaster at Rooker's Close, the school to which John is sent after publicity about the murder forces him from his original boarding school, Beowulf's. An Anglican convert, Gilbert insists that an unwilling John attend confession, a disillusioning experience that drives John from his Anglican faith.

Michael Blaydon, John's next older brother, an Oxford student with a greater taste for drinking than for studies. Michael introduces John to Greenbloom.

Melanie Blaydon, John's red-haired younger sister, not yet twelve years old when the novel opens. After they reach puberty, to his chagrin she begins to withdraw from their comradeship into a more feminine world, so that he is immediately receptive to Victoria's friendliness.

Marston, a classmate of young John at boarding school who attempts homosexual relations, contributing to John's fall from innocence and arousing his anger.

— *Harriet Blodgett*

IN THE WILDERNESS
(Olav Audunssøn i Hestviken *and* Olav Audunssøn og hans børn)

Author: Sigrid Undset (1882-1949)
First published: 1925-1927
Genre: Novel

Locale: Norway
Time: Early fourteenth century
Plot: Historical

Olav Audunssøn, the master of Hestviken. When his wife dies, he goes to England. There he is tempted by the pleasures of the flesh and of violence—part of his redemption, he believes, for his unconfessed crime of murder. He returns to Hestviken, where there is conflict between him and his supposed son Eirik. Wounded while fighting the invading Swedes, Olav recovers but feels that he has become an old man.

Eirik, the son of Olav's late wife Ingunn and falsely claimed by Olav. After much conflict, he leaves Hestviken and is reported to be among the men-at-arms at Oslo. Olav goes there to provide Eirik with money and a squire's gear, and the two part amiably.

Cecilia Olavsdatter, the daughter of Olav and Ingunn. A healthy, spirited girl, on one occasion she slashes a man who, after a drinking party, tries to seize her. Olav feels that she should be the boy of the house.

Asger Magnusson, an old friend of Olav. Dying, he asks Olav to foster his daughter.

Bothild Asgersdatter, who, after her father's death, goes to Hestviken, where she and Cecilia live as sisters.

Maerta Birgersdatter, the mother-in-law of Asger. She comes with her granddaughter Bothild to Hestviken. Grim, gaunt, but capable, she runs the house well but does not get along with Eirik.

Torhild Björnsdatter, the mother of a child by Olav; she lives at Rundmyr, the farm he gave her and carries on for her. After she marries, Olav asks her to send their son to live with him, but she refuses.

Ketil, a young man on the farm. Torhild marries him.

Björn, the son of Torhild and Olav.

Liv, a slatternly serving-woman at Hestviken. Returning from England, Olav marries her to his housecarl and sends the pair to live at Rundmyr, so that she will not corrupt his daughter.

Arnketil, Olav's housecarl, married to Liv. After their move, Rundmyr gets a bad name as a place of gaming and wenching and as a thieves' den.

Sira Hallbjorn, a priest who loves falconry and hunting. Olav is often in his company. Sira is killed fighting the invading Swedes.

Sir Ragnvald Torvaldsson, a skillful and courtly knight whom Eirik serves in Oslo.

Duke Eirik, the leader of the invading Swedish troops.

King Haakon, Duke Eirik's father-in-law, against whom the duke is directing his troops.

IN THE WINE TIME

Author: Ed Bullins (1935-   )
First published: 1969
Genre: Drama
Locale: An industrial city in the northern United States
Time: Early 1950's
Plot: Naturalism

Cliff Dawson, an unemployed former Navy man who spent much of his Navy career in the brig. Cliff loves his wife and cares deeply for his nephew; unfortunately, he has few other admirable qualities. Though only in his twenties, Cliff largely has resigned himself to an unpromising life made tolerable through the numbing effects of alcohol. Boastful of his sexual prowess, he is a philanderer who physically abuses his wife and taunts her with his vulgar language. He has been unable to complete his collegiate studies, which were intended to improve his position, or to hold a job for longer than six months. Feeling unable to change the course of his own life, Cliff becomes preoccupied with the future of his nephew, who he believes has a chance of escaping the bleak fate of the inner city by joining the Navy.

Lou Dawson, Cliff's wife, who is in an early stage of pregnancy. She is a twenty-two-year-old black woman who spends her evenings under the influence of alcohol. Although admired by Cliff as a woman of integrity, she lacks concern for her own well-being. She criticizes her husband's abhorrent behavior, yet she realizes that he will not change his ways, and her love for Cliff will not allow any thought of leaving him. Her nephew also receives much of her attention and affection; he has been her ward since his mother (Lou's sister) died of alcohol-related causes. She adamantly opposes her husband's urging the youth to join the armed forces.

Ray, Cliff and Lou's nephew. An amiable youth, he readily gives assistance to those who need him. For him as for his guardians, drinking wine represents a primary form of recreation. Thoughtful, considerate, and usually slow to anger, Ray possesses a sensitivity to life not apparent in the other characters. He expresses love for his girlfriend and an attraction to a mysterious woman with whom he simply exchanges a smile each day. Nearing his sixteenth birthday, he strives toward manhood, appreciative of the affections of his aunt but finding himself drawn more under the influence of Cliff's advice and criticisms.

Red, a black youth in his late teens, Ray's antagonist. Like Cliff, he habitually drinks wine, uses profane language, brags about his sexual skills, and physically abuses women. Audacious and disrespectful, he seems to enjoy inciting hostility in others. Ray has become a special target of his contempt for people because Red sees the younger boy as a weaker opponent unable to answer his provocations effectively.

Bunny Gillette, Ray's attractive black girlfriend. Although well aware of Red's antagonistic relationship with Ray, she does little to discourage both the amorous and the abusive attentions of Red.

Bama, a black youth and Red's companion; he shares his friend's animosity toward Ray.

Doris, Lou's sister. She is a bold black woman in her twenties who carries a knife. Like Cliff and Lou, she has a concern for Ray's welfare.

Tiny, a small and attractive black teenager having an affair with Cliff, though she supposedly is Bama's girlfriend.

Silly Willy Clark, a large black man in his early thirties. He is Cliff's drinking buddy and is prone to pulling pranks.

Minny Garrison, a fat and middle-aged neighbor of the Dawsons. A busybody who detests Cliff's behavior, she once circulated a petition to have the Dawsons evicted from the neighborhood.

— *Addell Austin*

IN WATERMELON SUGAR

Author: Richard Brautigan (1935-1984)
First published: 1968
Genre: Novel
Locale: Indeterminate
Time: Timeless
Plot: Surrealism

The narrator, who has no conventional name; he tells the reader that his name might be anything that the reader happens to think of or any experience that the reader may remember. He seems to be in his late twenties or thirties and lives in the gentle fantasy community iDEATH, where the main activities are making things out of watermelon sugar, enjoying the company of the other citizens of the town, and walking about enjoying the sights, which include many statues of vegetables; many rivers, some of which are only a few inches wide; and the tombs of the dead, which are lighted with foxfire and which lie at the bottoms of the larger rivers. The narrator is writing one of the first books to be written in iDEATH in many years. He is unusual because he enjoys walking at night, an activity in which no one else in the town engages except a girl whom the narrator occasionally sees walking at night with a lantern. When he was a child, his parents were eaten by tigers, but the last tiger was killed some time ago, and the trout hatchery was built on the ashes of the animal's remains. The narrator once had a girlfriend named Margaret; his new girlfriend is named Pauline.

Margaret, the narrator's previous girlfriend, also in her late twenties or early thirties. She has a habit of stepping on the one board of the bridge leading to the narrator's house that makes a noise when it is stepped on. No one else seems to step on this board. Margaret and the narrator got along fine until Margaret began to visit the Forgotten Works, a sort of junkyard outside town where inBOIL and his unpleasant friends liked to drink and make trouble. The narrator wishes that Margaret would leave him alone. After inBOIL and his friends kill themselves, Margaret is the only person who seems to care very much. The narrator sees her hang herself while he is looking at the statue of mirrors. Margaret is buried in the river along with the other citizens of iDEATH.

Pauline, who also is in her twenties or thirties. She often cooks for the citizens of iDEATH at the place where they gather to eat. The narrator meets her there, and they walk around together and spend nights making love. She thinks that inBOIL and his friends are terrible people, and she cleans up the trout hatchery after the members of inBOIL's gang kill themselves there. The narrator later discovers that she is the girl with the lantern whom he has seen on his walks at night.

Charley, the unofficial leader of iDEATH, slightly older than the others. When there is trouble or a question to be answered, everyone naturally turns to him.

inBOIL, Charley's brother, a person who upsets the peace and order of iDEATH by spending time with his friends in the Forgotten Works, making whiskey from the things they find there and getting drunk. One day, they announce that they are going to show the citizens of iDEATH what iDEATH is really about. They gather them all in the trout hatchery and begin to cut off their own noses, fingers, toes, and ears until they bleed to death. This is their idea of what iDEATH really ought to be. The remaining citizens of iDEATH think that this activity is ridiculous and set about cleaning up the mess.

— *James Baird*

INADMISSIBLE EVIDENCE

Author: John Osborne (1929-1994)
First published: 1965
Genre: Drama
Locale: London, England
Time: The 1960's
Plot: Psychological realism

Bill Maitland, a thirty-nine-year-old solicitor who runs his own legal practice in London. He is married to Anna, with whom he has two children. Maitland is facing a midlife crisis that forces him to confront his personal inadequacies, his fear of old age, and his own mortality. In an unhappy marriage, Maitland survives through his dependence on alcohol, pills, and an unusually high amount of sexual activity. Maitland has affairs with all of his female secretaries, in addition to having a permanent mistress, who also supports him emotionally. Maitland relies on everyone around him, but as he gradually is deserted by both staff and clients, he becomes an isolated and lonely figure. The play essentially is Maitland's monologue tracing his psychological and moral disintegration. A dreamlike reality pervades his world, and Maitland continually lapses into a narrative describing his almost unconscious state. For Maitland, the world seems in a state of impermanence. As his self-destruction continues, he lashes out at everything and everyone around him, attacking their values and sense of security.

Hudson, Maitland's managing clerk. Hudson, a comfortable and confident man, is good at his job and demonstrates a strong sense of personal integrity and morality. Although he is sympathetic to Maitland's personal and professional crises, Hudson resists Maitland's suggestion of going into partnership together and leaves him for a rival firm.

Shirley, Maitland's secretary. Shirley is one of Maitland's former mistresses and, from the beginning of the play, is abrupt and hot-tempered. Refusing Maitland's attempts to retain her, Shirley resigns on the pretext of marriage and pregnancy. Shirley is bitter at the treatment that she has received from Maitland, and her final gesture of leaving the firm comes as an act of defiance against Maitland's use of her.

Joy, Maitland's secretary. The complete opposite of Shirley in temperament, Joy likes the attention that Maitland gives her. A self-confessed nymphomaniac, Joy becomes Maitland's mistress. She, too, deserts him by the end of the play.

Liz, Maitland's mistress. Despite the fact that Maitland is married, Liz genuinely cares for Maitland. Feeling unable to help him by the end of the play, however, she can do little more than leave Maitland alone in his office with the assurance that he can always call her.

Jones, a junior clerk, an efficient employee of the company. Reasonably intelligent and interested in his work, Jones probably feels more at ease in the office than in the courtroom. Maitland dislikes him because of his complacent attitude and because he has "all the makings of a good, happy, democratic underdog." Jones, described as puny and arrogant, lacks drive and ambition. Consequently, he is exploited by Maitland for his efficient but colorless labor.

Maples, a homosexual client to be played by the same actor as Jones. Maples shares Jones's physical unattractiveness but none of his other characteristics; he is described as quick-witted and courageous. Maples' gradual understanding of his own sexuality ensures that, like Maitland, he is driven into isolation.

Mrs. Garnsey,

Mrs. Anderson, and

Mrs. Tonks, three characters played by one actress. They provide distorted reflections of Maitland and demonstrate his inability to regain contact with the "real" world.

— *Ian Stuart*

INCIDENT AT VICHY

Author: Arthur Miller (1915-)
First published: 1965
Genre: Drama
Locale: Vichy, France
Time: 1942
Plot: Social realism

Leduc (leh-DEWK), a psychiatrist and former French artillery officer. He protests that Germans have no authority to make arrests in Unoccupied France when he and several others are separately taken into detention on suspicion of being Jews. He tries to organize an escape but is frustrated by the others' apathy and by the German major's show of force. Trained to doubt human rationality, he is persuaded that everyone looks for scapegoats to explain their flaws and pay for their weaknesses. Even Jews, he says, have their "Jews," mistrusting anyone different from themselves. Leduc counsels each person to be honest with himself or herself, one's true identity being more important than a life of safety based on deception. He accuses Von Berg of being relieved that someone else, not himself, will die, yet he accepts the prince's pass to safety when it is offered.

Wilhelm Johann Von Berg (VIHL-hehlm YOH-hahn fon behrk), an Austrian prince. He first questions if the other detainees are Jews, because, as a Catholic, he would be safe. Once he hid three musicians who were suspected, though he could not protect them long from the Nazis. Despite the fact that, as an aristocrat, he has been denouncing the Nazis for their vulgarity, gradually he admits that he knew that his cousin, a baron, was a Nazi. His forgetfulness has been an attempt to absolve himself from complicity. Goaded by Leduc's appeal not to his guilt but to his sense of responsible action, he sacrifices himself by handing his pass to Leduc.

Major, a wounded regular German army officer, twenty-eight years old. As a combat professional, he finds his current assignment demeaning. He has turned cynical in a war that strikes him as absurd. Putting intelligence and decency aside, he now routinely follows Professor Hoffman's orders.

Professor Hoffman, an anthropologist who is an expert on the Racial Laws. He is in charge of measurements and determinations. He tries to prevent Leduc's escape.

Lebeau (leh-BOH), a bearded, unkempt, twenty-five-year-old painter energized by fear. In 1939, he had already packed to leave for America, but his mother refused to leave their furniture behind. His premonitions make him among the most nervous in the group but also one of the most anxious to believe that the Nazis are only searching for spies or for workers in the coal mines.

Monceau (moh[n]-SOH), an actor dressed in frayed elegance. He suggests that they try not to look like victims but that each should create his own reality, just as roles are assumed in the theater. He refuses to believe that the Nazis have extermination ovens.

Bayard (bay-YAHR), a twenty-five-year-old socialist. He argues for solidarity now that these several strangers to one another have been detained together. He advises each to get a screwdriver to be used in opening boxcars from the inside if they are sent to Auschwitz.

Marchand (mahr-SHAH[N]), an impatient, well-dressed merchant. His nonchalance and his quick release confuse the others, because they are convinced that he also is a Jew.

Ferrand (feh-RAH[N]), a café proprietor who brings a repast to the authorities. He has tried before to warn the waiter to leave Vichy.

Waiter,

Gypsy,

Old Jew in his seventies, and

Boy age fifteen, who all are aware that they are considered inferior types by the Nazis and therefore are expendable.

— *Leonard Casper*

THE INCREASED DIFFICULTY OF CONCENTRATION
(Ztížená možnost soustředění)

Author: Václav Havel (1936-)
First published: 1968
Genre: Drama
Locale: A flat in Czechoslovakia
Time: Mid-twentieth century
Plot: Comedy

Dr. Eduard Huml, a social scientist in his mid-forties working on a book about the nature of human happiness. At the same time, he is maintaining a reasonably successful marriage, keeping a mistress, unsuccessfully fighting a physical attraction to his secretary, and submitting to an exhaustive set of examinations from a team of investigative social scientists who have invaded his house and are using him as a model of individuality, measured against computerized norms.

Vlasta Huml, his wife, domestic and supportive, a good cook, and eager to please her husband. She is trying to persuade Huml to end his long-standing affair and reveals that she craves the same attentions that he is showing his mistress, Renata.

Renata, Huml's mistress, roughly thirty years old and "full of fun and games." She is jealous of Huml's wife and spends most of her time trying to persuade Huml to get a divorce.

Blanka, Huml's young and attractive secretary. She takes dictation with blinding speed. She is not altogether innocent but is managing, so far, to fend off Huml's advances.

Dr. Anna Balcar, a beautiful and intelligent social scientist, an interrogator for the team of social scientists invading Huml's house. After maintaining a professional bearing for most of the play, she breaks down and cries, succumbing to Huml's charms when he points out to her that her whole project is a pointless mistake.

Karel Krieble, a technician on the investigating team, in charge of operating and maintaining the proper temperature and atmospheric conditions for Puzuk, a computerlike machine that interprets Huml's answers in the light of statistical social norms.

Emil Machal, the surveyor for the investigating team, charged with gauging floors and doorways, measuring the moisture in the walls, and weighing the bedclothes. Slightly sinister and combative, he is a dangerous force on the team.

Mr. Beck, the titular head of the team, older than the others. His total participation consists of pacing back and forth, gruffly refusing all offers of refreshment, and vowing to go fishing "tomorrow."

— *Thomas J. Taylor*

INDEPENDENT PEOPLE
(Sjálfstœttfólk)

Author: Halldór Laxness (Halldór Kiljan Guðjónsson, 1902-   )
First published: 1934-1935
Genre: Novel

Locale: Iceland
Time: The twentieth century
Plot: Social

Gudbjartur Jonsson (Bjartur), a stubborn, roughly poetic, often cruel, fiercely independent crofter. He loses two wives, one quickly, the other after years of his harshness. He rears Asta, knowing of her illegitimacy. He loses several children in their infancy, Helgi as a child, and Nonni to a home in America. Only Gvendur remains after the ejection of the pregnant Asta, but even Gvendur longs to join Nonni in America and, later, to join the political radicals opposed to the Icelandic government. At last, reunited with Asta after the loss of his big, unfinished home by foreclosure, Bjartur takes her and her children to live with him and Hallbera in the old woman's sod home. Bjartur appears to be a symbol not only of the Icelandic peasant but perhaps of land-loving, independent farmers the world over.

Rosa, Bjartur's first wife, a small, sturdy woman with a cast in one eye; she is pregnant with Asta when she marries Bjartur. A believer in tradition and folk superstition, she opposes Bjartur's scorn of these things. She dies when Asta is born.

Finna, Bjartur's second wife, a pauper sent by Madam Myri to care for Asta. She dies after several years of poor diet, rapid childbearing, and unfeeling scorn and neglect, climaxed by Bjartur's slaughter of her beloved cow.

Asta Sollilja (Sola), Rosa's romantic, imaginative daughter, doomed to unhappiness. Pale-faced and dark-haired, she has, like her mother, a cast in one eye. Pregnant by a drunken, tubercular tutor, she is thrown out by Bjartur, has another child by another father, and is carrying a third when Bjartur comes for her. Independent like Bjartur, she has rejected the offer of Ingolfur, her father, to help her. Consumptive when she is reunited with Bjartur, she has only a short time to live but finds joy in the anticipation of being again with the first man she ever loved. It is ironic that, having lost all his own children, Bjartur should seek out the daughter he had scorned as having none of his blood in her. Symbolically, the two strong independents are drawn to each other.

Gvendur, Bjartur's son who plans to join Nonni in America but who decides to remain at home after falling in love with Ingolfur's only daughter, who later shuns him as an inferior.

Jon (Nonni), Bjartur's younger son, who goes to America to join an uncle just before World War I.

Ingolfur Arnarson Jonsson, Asta's father, manager of a cooperative society.

Helgi, Bjartur and Finna's first son, lost on the moor.

Bailiff Jon of Myri, Bjartur's employer for eighteen years. Slovenly, like a tramp in appearance, he is nevertheless more forceful and complex than the men over whom he exerts authority. Bjartur dislikes him.

Madam Myri, poet wife of Bailiff Jon and mother of Ingolfur Arnarson. She has an aristocratic consciousness of her superiority to people like Bjartur and Rosa.

Thorthur of Nitherkot, Rosa's father, a serenely stoical old man.

Pastor Gudmundur, the parish minister, who is also an able farmer and breeder of fine sheep. Blunt and gruff in speech, he combines superficial Christian views with his apparent unconcern for unfortunate people whom he regards as contemptible sinners.

Hallbera, aged mother of Rosa.

Audur Jonsdottir, ladylike daughter of Bailiff Jon. When she leaves for Reykjavik, Bjartur suspects it is because she is pregnant by a man who camped on his land some time earlier.

Fritha, a talkative, complaining old woman who works one summer for Bjartur.

INDIAN AFFAIRS

Author: Larry Woiwode (1941-   )
First published: 1992
Genre: Novel

Locale: Upper Michigan
Time: The 1970's
Plot: Psychological

Christopher (Chris) Van Eenam, a Lakota Indian on his mother's side. He has gone with his wife, Ellen, to upper Michigan to complete his dissertation. They are staying in the lakeside cabin owned by his wife's grandparents where they had spent their honeymoon seven years ago. Chris had worked at a brokerage house in New York before he decided to go back to school to obtain a Ph.D. in literature. He has just turned thirty and is at a critical juncture in his life. His relationship with Ellen is strained because she is still grieving the loss of their son and has not been able to conceive again. As Chris examines his past, he realizes that all his life he has tried to deny his heritage and tried to pass as a white man. He befriends a group of young Native Americans with an intent to educate them and occasionally buys beer for them. When two of them, in a drunken state, beat an old patriarch on the reservation, Chris feels guilty and refuses to oblige them any more, thus earning their animosity. Through his old friend Beau, Chris meets an activist group planning a protest against development of Indian land. His own past catches up with him as one of his female acquaintances attempts to draw Ellen away from him by involving her in a feminist group. When Ellen is endangered, first by the prowling neighboring youths and then by Gaylin, who sets their cottage on fire, Chris realizes how deeply he cares for her. It also becomes obvious to him that Ellen still loves him. Clear of his doubts and ambiguities, he is able to concentrate on his writing. He is ready to return to New York, this time certain of his own identity and ability to assume responsibilities.

Ellen, who was brought up by her grandparents after her parents' death in an accident. She feels consumed by the tragedies in her young life. Her grandmother had disapproved of Ellen's father, and Ellen suspects that her parents' car accident was a suicide pact. Grandmother Strohe, an ardent Christian Scientist, does not like Ellen's choice of Chris either. Having lost her baby and unable to have another, Ellen feels a tremendous sense of failure. As Chris works on his dissertation, she writes her own book based on the journal she had kept while grieving for her dead son. As she and Chris spend two months in the secluded cottage away from the comforts and conveniences of city life, she has time to reexamine her feelings. A sensitive, intelligent woman, Ellen sees how her grandmother has warped her personality and poisoned her relationship with Chris. She does not approve of Chris's involvement with the young Native Americans but is perceptive enough to realize his need to sort out his own mixed feelings about his identity. Her discovery that she is pregnant again helps her to redirect her life. Armed with her love for Chris and the unborn baby, she is ready to confront her tyrannical grandmother and take control of her own life.

Beau, a young, educated Native American. He never earned a degree but is well read and is able to provide Chris with stimulating intellectual companionship. He lives alone outside the reservation and makes a living by cutting wood for fire. He is disenchanted with the establishment and desires to live a simple life, as his people did. He is, however, more like his hippie contemporaries than he is willing to admit.

Gaylin, a fifteen-year-old Native American brought up by his grandfather. He yearns for the mother that he never had, and his anger and sense of betrayal turn him into a pyromaniac. He has set several fires in the community, one of which ended in the death of an elderly man. He elopes with the young woman who was living with Beau. Fortunately, Chris, Ellen, and Beau escape unhurt when Gaylin sets fire to their cabins.

Art, the owner of the general store. He represents mainstream condescending and patronizing attitudes toward Native Americans. Unaware of the fact that Chris is one of them, he often gives him unsolicited advice on how to behave with the residents of "Pocahontastown"—his name for the reservation.

— *Leela Kapai*

THE INDIAN LAWYER

Author: James Welch (1940-   )
First published: 1990
Genre: Novel

Locale: Helena, Montana, and surrounding areas
Time: 1988
Plot: Moral

Sylvester Yellow Calf, a Blackfeet Indian who is a model of achievement. Formerly a college basketball star, he went on to study law at Stanford and then to become a well-regarded lawyer in a firm in Helena, Montana. Far more materially successful than the childhood friends he has left behind, but not entirely comfortable in upper-middle-class white society, he feels caught between two cultures. As the novel begins, he is being courted by national political organizers as a possible congressional candidate. He also serves on the state parole board, as one member of a group that decides which inmates will be paroled. Vaguely dissatisfied with his relationship with his girlfriend, he is easily seduced by Patti Ann Harwood, an attractive young woman trying to help her husband, a convict who has just been denied parole. As the resulting love affair becomes the focus of a blackmail plot, Sylvester realizes for the first time how easy it is to make a disastrous, life-changing mistake. He discovers that the distance between himself and the convicts he evaluates is smaller than he thought. Fearing that his relationship with Patti Ann will haunt his political career, he withdraws from the congressional race. Disappointed because he thinks he has let down the Indian peoples of Montana, he realizes that he can still serve them. As a lawyer for Indian causes, he will combat the problems of poverty, racism, and alcoholism.

Jack Harwood, a convict in his mid-thirties who was sent to Montana State Prison for two armed robberies. No one in the prison system can understand why he is there. Smart, educated, and married to a lovely, loving woman, he seems to have no reason to commit crimes. Paranoid and fearful, he develops a hatred of Indians after he is stabbed by a tough Indian inmate. His belief that he must leave prison immediately or be killed drives him to concoct a blackmail scheme. He convinces his wife, Patti Ann, to sleep with Sylvester Yellow Calf, who is the only Indian on the parole board. Despite his outward callousness, Jack was once capable of great tenderness toward his wife. He ruined his chances of an early release from prison by escaping to be with her when she needed surgery.

Patti Ann Harwood, Jack's wife of nine years. Married to Jack for one and one-half years before he went to prison, she has remained faithful to him despite many opportunities to stray. She feels guilty for enjoying her affair with Sylvester. The happiness it brings her contrasts sharply with her sad personal history. Her four pregnancies ended in near-fatal miscarriages; ultimately, she required a hysterectomy, which was paid for with the money from one of Jack's robberies. Her relationship with Sylvester eventually offers the promise of a deep friendship.

Shelley Hatton Bowers, a financial analyst and single mother. She is a prominent senator's daughter and Sylvester Yellow Calf's girlfriend. Her relationship with Sylvester has been growing distant for some time. She is not entirely sure how she feels about the difference in their races and is further troubled because Sylvester will not or cannot be open and frank with her. She is cool and collected when Sylvester tells her of his unfaithfulness, her emotions betrayed only by her wet eyes. Their relationship remains in question at the end of the novel.

Lena Old Horn, Sylvester's high school guidance counselor, who first encouraged him to become a lawyer, the new kind of Indian warrior. Their relationship was more intimate than is usual for students and counselors, although they were never lovers. Sylvester seeks her counsel again as he considers running for Congress.

Buster Harrington, Sylvester's boss and political mentor. As the cap to his long career, Harrington hopes to convince his protégé to run for office. Deeply pragmatic, when he hears of Sylvester's entanglement with the Harwoods, he is not angry. Instead, he is merely disappointed that Sylvester did not come to him right away, so that he could have used his considerable power to end the scheme before it snowballed.

Woody Peters, a paroled convict who is Jack Harwood's eyes and ears outside the prison. A key actor in Jack's blackmail plot, he decides to drop Harwood's scheme in favor of one of his own, and he attempts to blackmail Sylvester himself.

Bobby Fitzgerald, another paroled convict, a partner of Woody Peters in the blackmail plot. Although equally as unscrupulous as Woody, Bobby is the less threatening of the two because he is less intelligent.

— Kelly Fuller

INDIAN SUMMER

Author: William Dean Howells (1837-1920)
First published: 1886
Genre: Novel
Locale: Florence, Italy
Time: Shortly after the American Civil War
Plot: Domestic realism

Theodore Colville, a middle-aged American architect who leaves Italy for the United States when a young woman rejects his suit. In the United States, he runs a newspaper for a time and then enters Indiana politics. Defeated at the polls, he returns to Italy to resume his study of architecture. He learns to love two American women, one a middle-aged widow, the other a woman half his age. He almost marries the younger woman, but complications and misunderstandings prevent him from doing so. Finally, he marries the widow.

Imogene Graham, a young woman who falls in love with Colville, though he is old enough to be her father. She finally understands, chiefly through the influence of her mother and the appearance of a young minister, that her love is actually infatuation. She returns to the United States from Italy and marries the minister, who is now established in a prosperous church near Buffalo.

Lina Bowen, a widow who has known Colville for some time. She acts as Imogene's chaperon while Imogene and Colville see each other. She tries to act properly toward the Colville-Imogene affair and not allow her personal bias to enter her discussions with Imogene about the problems that marriage with Colville might produce. When Imogene at last rejects Colville, Lina accepts Colville's suit.

Effie Bowen, Lina's thirteen-year-old daughter, who is very fond of Colville. It is largely through Effie's efforts that Colville and Lina finally decide to marry.

Mr. Morton, a young minister who loves Imogene and goes to Italy to court her. Both return to the United States, and the Colvilles suspect that they will marry.

Mrs. Graham, Imogene's mother, who goes to Italy when she learns that her daughter is thinking seriously of marrying Colville. Her influence on her daughter is instrumental in causing Imogene to see that her love for Colville is only infatuation.

INDIAN SUMMER
(Der Nachsommer)

Author: Adalbert Stifter (1805-1868)
First published: 1857
Genre: Novel
Locale: Vienna, the Austrian Alps, and the subalpine countryside
Time: The 1820's
Plot: Bildungsroman

Heinrich Drendorf (HIN-rihkh DRAYN-dohrf), the narrator, a young man who has been reared in an ideal home, with kindly, wise, and loving parents and a devoted sister, Klotilde. A few years previously, Heinrich and Klotilde had each inherited a substantial sum of money. Now that he is an adult, Heinrich can, by being frugal, live off the income from his inheritance and devote himself to the study of his chosen field, science, without needing to work and support himself. While on one of his scientific journeys, Heinrich meets Risach, whose house, estate, and very existence radiate a profound sense of unity and harmony. He is already quite mature and discerning, but with Risach's guidance, Heinrich gradually acquires a deeper knowledge and understanding of nature, literature, art, and, especially, humanity. Through Risach, Heinrich meets Natalie. Her beauty and his steadily deepening love for her inspire him further in his development, especially in his appreciation of art.

Baron Gustav von Risach (fon REE-zakh), an elderly gentleman farmer and former statesman, a self-made man of humble origins. He becomes Heinrich's mentor. Still very vigorous, mentally and physically, Risach radiates a sense of stability, unity, harmony, serenity, and wisdom, uplifting all around him. Many years ago, while working as a private tutor, he fell in love with one of his students, Mathilde. He dutifully talked to her parents about marriage, but they requested, considering their daughter's youth, that the wedding be postponed. Risach felt obliged to respect the wishes of her parents, but Mathilde viewed his acquiescence to the voice of reason over the heart as a betrayal, not only of their love but also of his own inner self, and angrily broke off their relationship. Somewhat later, when Risach was successful and could marry her, she refused, asserting that she despised him. After many years, Mathilde, like Risach widowed after an unfulfilling marriage, resumed the relationship, retracting her earlier harsh judgment of him. They now live close to each other and, although not married, enjoy a contented "Indian Summer" relationship as close friends.

Natalie Torona (nah-TAHL-yeh), Mathilde's daughter, who falls in love with and marries Heinrich. Her infinite physical beauty is a reflection of the inner, spiritual refinement of her soul. Unlike the way in which her mother had acted as a young woman in love, Natalie shows restraint in her relationship with Heinrich and does not utter a word of complaint when he decides that he must put off their wedding to take an extended trip so that he can bring his level of education up to hers. The love of both young people, Heinrich and Natalie, is patient, restrained, and submissive to their elders.

Mathilde Torona (mah-TIHL-deh), Risach's former beloved, now his closest friend. Mathilde is still beautiful in her mature years and now radiates grace, calm, harmony, and resignation. As with her daughter, her physical beauty reflects the inner beauty of her soul. Like Risach, she positively affects those around her. Mathilde has a touch of regret about their lost past, as when she remarks to Risach that their happiness, just like the roses, has faded. Risach quickly replies, however, that their happiness has not faded, that it merely has taken another form.

Mr. Drendorf, Heinrich's father, a successful merchant and, like Risach, a self-made man. He is an enlightened, kindly employer, a highly cultured man with a deep love of knowledge and art, and an ideal father. In his house reigns a rigorous, almost pedantic orderliness. He strongly supports and promotes his children's efforts to improve themselves.

Mrs. Drendorf, Heinrich's mother. Like her husband, Mrs. Drendorf is an ideal parent—kind, loving, friendly, and self-sacrificing. These noble qualities help her to provide a secure and warm home for her husband and children.

Klotilde Drendorf (kloh-TIHL-deh), Heinrich's sister, two years younger than he is. They share close ties of affection that are unaffected by Heinrich's new relationship with Natalie.

Gustav Torona, Mathilde's son, a few years younger than Heinrich, who is being tutored by Risach. He is handsome, disciplined, quiet, and sensible.

— H. J. Weatherford

INDIANA

Author: George Sand (Amandine-Aurore-Lucile Dupin, Baronne Dudevant, 1804-1876)
First published: 1832
Genre: Novel
Locale: France
Time: Early nineteenth century
Plot: Sentimental

Indiana Delmare (a[n]-dee-ah-NAH dehl-MAHR), a young woman who lives a bored and frustrated existence. She is faithful to her husband but is very friendly with her cousin, Sir Ralph Brown. When Raymon de Ramière begins paying her attentions, she reciprocates, but when she decides to leave her husband to go to de Ramière, she finds, much to her dismay, that he has married someone else. She finally retires to a life of seclusion with Sir Ralph.

Monsieur Delmare, Indiana's husband. He is very suspicious and jealous but never hears of his wife's affairs with de

Ramière. He is a businessman, financially ruined, who retires to the Isle of Bourbon. It is at this point that Indiana leaves him.

Rodolphe Brown (roh-DOHLF), called **Sir Ralph**, Indiana's faithful admirer and cousin. He is a frequent guest in the Delmare house and a trusted friend, and he is very fond of Indiana. After Indiana runs away from her husband and finds that de Ramière is married, she meets Sir Ralph and they decide on a suicide pact. They change their minds, however, and go away to live together as recluses.

Raymon de Ramière (ray-MOH[N] deh rahm-YEHR), Indiana's lover. He is a scoundrel who is found climbing over the Delmare's wall one night. He has actually come to visit Indiana's maid; but once he has met Indiana, he tires of the maid and begins to pursue her mistress. He is fickle, and when Indiana leaves with her husband for the Isle of Bourbon, he marries someone else.

Noun (new[n]), Indiana's maid. She has been de Ramière's mistress for some time before he meets Indiana. She finds that she is pregnant, and she commits suicide because de Ramière refuses to marry her.

INDIANS

Author: Arthur Kopit (1937-)
First published: 1969
Genre: Drama
Locale: The Wild West and Washington, D.C.
Time: Late nineteenth century
Plot: Protest

Buffalo Bill Cody, a boasting Wild West hero and performer in florid buckskin clothes. At times presenting himself as the friend of the American Indians and at other times proudly telling about his killing of Indians and of buffalo, he is an unstable character. Buffalo Bill fails both to bring the Ol' Time President to Sitting Bull's Indian reservation and to enhance mutual understanding between Sitting Bull and the senators. He experiences feelings of guilt for having shot so many buffalo and for having deprived the Indians of their traditional way of life. After unsuccessfully speaking out for the Indians in negotiations with the senators, he ends up justifying the government's Indian policy.

Sitting Bull, a disillusioned but still proud, powerful, and cunning Indian chief who formerly appeared in Buffalo Bill's Wild West show. Sitting Bull considers himself a friend of Buffalo Bill, whom he does not blame for the injustice done to the Indians. He formerly killed General Custer and now lives on a reservation. He asks to see the president, the Great Father, to demand that the whites fulfill their side of the Indian treaties. In the negotiations with the senators, he asks that Indians get all the comforts and wealth enjoyed by whites and insults the president's representatives, an act for which he is killed, by order of the government, in the massacre by Colonel Forsyth's army. After his death, Sitting Bull briefly reappears, reaffirming his pride and his friendship for Buffalo Bill.

John Grass, an Indian in Sitting Bull's reservation who has been educated in a white school. In the negotiations with the senators, he calmly demands that the whites give the Indians what was agreed on in treaties, explains that what the Indians have so far received from the whites is inadequate, and affirms that the Indians were forced into signing these treaties.

Wild Bill Hickok, Buffalo Bill's longtime friend and fellow performer in the Wild West show. Initially, Hickok, out of self-respect, refuses to impersonate himself in Ned Buntline's simplistic Wild West melodrama, *Scouts of the Plains*, but in the end, the prospect of financial gain makes him suggest to Buffalo Bill that a Wild West show be performed simultaneously in different places by numerous Buffalo Bill replicas.

Ned Buntline, a sensationalist journalist and photographer, author of *Scouts of the Plains*. He strives to make Buffalo Bill famous through newspaper articles and Wild West shows and is killed by Wild Bill Hickok, who is dissatisfied with the misrepresentations in Buntline's show.

Ol' Time President, the Great Father and childish president of the United States. Although he and the first lady enjoy the Wild West show performed in the White House, he is not willing to follow Buffalo Bill's request of negotiating personally with the Indians. He thinks that little can be done for the Indians, and he does not see in such negotiations an opportunity for increasing his fame.

Senator Logan, a reasonable politician sent by the president as one of his representatives to negotiate with Sitting Bull. He respects the justified demands of the Indians but does not fulfill them.

Senator Dawes, a condescending politician sent by the president to negotiate with Sitting Bull. He blames the Indians themselves for their predicament.

Senator Morgan, a politician sent by the president to negotiate with Sitting Bull. He treats the Indians as the White Father's children who must be protected from themselves.

Spotted Tail, a disillusioned Indian of mixed tribal ancestry and a friend of Buffalo Bill. He accuses Buffalo Bill of killing buffalo that he will not eat, and he is later shot by the Grand Duke Alexis, who mistakes him for a Comanche.

Chief Joseph, an old Indian chief whom Buffalo Bill had released from prison in exchange for Chief Joseph's agreement to deliver, in Buffalo Bill's Wild West show, the surrender speech that he originally had given in the battle with General Howard.

Colonel Forsyth, a proud colonel of the U.S. Army. He justifies his army's massacre of Indians, in which Sitting Bull is killed.

Grand Duke Alexis, an insensible and thoughtless Russian duke who is visiting America. After meeting with and listening to Buffalo Bill, he wants to hire Buffalo Bill as his bodyguard to protect him from his many enemies. He gives Buffalo Bill a medal for shooting one hundred buffalo with one hundred shots and kills Spotted Tail out of a desire to be like Buffalo Bill.

— Josef Raab

INFANTE'S INFERNO
(La Habana para un infante difunto)

Author: Guillermo Cabrera Infante (1929-)
First published: 1979
Genre: Novel

Locale: Havana, Cuba
Time: The 1940's
Plot: Autobiographical

The narrator, a self-proclaimed Don Juan and a lover of the cinema, serving as both the camera's eye and its operator in the novel, recording his coming of age in Havana. He selects and reports memories from the past and gives a "continuous showing" of Havana viewed in its physical setting. Streets, buildings, parks, and neighborhoods are named and located in terms of their proximity to some thirty-five motion-picture theaters of the city and its surrounding area. The plot progresses from descriptions and fantasies to platonic love, rites of passage, and sexual relationships. The narrator passes through many levels of erotic involvement with women in his quest for happiness.

Zoila (soh-EE-lah), the narrator's mother, described as a "beautiful Communist." Besides instilling in her son a love for the cinema, she also instills a fear of sexuality, particularly of sexually transmitted diseases. She is the matriarch of the household and has a powerful influence over her son's responses to life and to sexuality. As her son reaches adolescence, he must break this close attachment to forge his own identity.

Margarita del Campo (mahr-gah-REE-tah), also known as **Violeta del Valle** (vee-oh-LEH-tah dehl VAH-yeh), an actress, a one-breasted, green-eyed beauty who entraps the narrator in a consuming passion. This is the woman with whom the narrator believes he is truly in love for the first time. More mature than the other women whom he has known, she has been married and is successful in her career. The love relationship between Margarita and the narrator is the most passionate and intimate of all those in the novel. Pervading their interactions, however, are animal instincts and possessiveness. Margarita's possessiveness finds expression in violent acts; she enjoys wreaking vengeance on men by watching them suffer and die.

Juliet Estévez (hew-lee-EHT ehs-TEH-vehs), a liberated married woman who initiates the narrator into sex. In her description, the narrator stresses her euphemistic and pseudoliterary language, language that he finds both annoying and intriguing. Juliet employs romantic language to describe her erotic involvements, but she also recognizes the banal reality that accompanies her sexual encounters.

Etelvina (eht-ehl-VEE-nah), a beautiful young prostitute living in the same building as the narrator's family when he was quite young. The narrator's mother gave him the task of waking Etelvina every morning. His mother also instilled a fear of coming into contact with the prostitute or any other woman who might have a venereal disease.

Lolita (loh-LEE-tah), a maid and one of the narrator's many sexual conquests in the novel. Through her, the narrator parodies a language and a view of romance that finds their origins in the radio soap opera that Lolita avidly follows. She imitates the exaggerated, sentimental language of her soap-opera heroes in the hope that she, too, will become the ideal romantic lover. Her true personality comically emerges when she abandons the affected language of the soap opera in exchange for a flood of obscenities while she is in the height of passion.

— *Genevieve Slomski*

INFANTS OF THE SPRING

Author: Wallace Thurman (1902-1934)
First published: 1932
Genre: Novel

Locale: Harlem, New York
Time: The mid-1920's
Plot: Satire

Raymond Taylor, the protagonist, a young black writer striving to create his first novel and make a major contribution to the "Negro Renaissance." He is sensitive and a bit unsure of both his abilities as a writer and his sexual orientation. He is equally frustrated by his and others' inability to create anything of greatness. For most of his stay at "Niggeratti Manor," the Harlem brownstone where many would-be artists live, he drinks and carouses with friends—some talented, others not—so that he rarely writes.

Paul Arbian, a writer and painter. He is one of the most daring characters in the novel. He openly acknowledges his bisexuality and his distaste for what the older generation of leaders of the "Negro Renaissance" expect the younger artists to produce. Like Raymond, he wants to be an artist in the most free and forward-looking definition of the term.

Stephen Jorgenson, for a short while a resident of the Manor and roommate to Raymond. He is first fascinated with Harlem's black people and then, later, appalled by them. Originally from Copenhagen, Denmark, he is in New York to pursue a Ph.D. at Columbia University, not because he has any real interest in scholarship but because his family will support him only if he is in school.

Samuel Carter, another white character, a liberal missionary type. He is not accepted by any of the many groups he joins, including communists and socialists, because to these groups he is a nonentity. When he "discovers" black people and concludes that he will be their savior, he begins to have meaning in his life. He does not understand, however, that most of the black residents of the Manor think he is an idiot.

Eustace Savoy, a would-be classical singer. He disavows all interest in spirituals, denouncing them as being peasant and folk music unworthy of his artistic talent. Unfortunately, white patrons, who provide the financial rewards for black creative production, are interested only in spirituals.

Pelham Gaylord (George Jones), a would-be portrait artist who functions at the Manor as host, server, and housekeeper. No one thinks he has any talent; he is a copier of the works of European artists. He finds acceptance with a teenage girl.

Euphoria Blake, the owner of the Manor and designer of it as a place for artists to live and mingle. She has a past that is as colorful as her residents. She has been a member of the Communist Party, practiced free love, had a white lover, been jailed, and learned that money is the one thing that equalizes the races.

Lucille, Raymond's confidant and sometimes girlfriend, a secretary who manages to attend many of the parties and discussions at the Manor. She and Raymond have a platonic relationship that becomes increasingly frustrating as she realizes it can never be more than that.

— *Charles P. Toombs*

THE INFERNAL MACHINE
(La Machine infernale)

Author: Jean Cocteau (1889-1963)
First published: 1934
Genre: Drama
Locale: Ancient Thebes
Time: Mythological ancient Greece
Plot: Allegory

Oedipus (EH-deh-puhs), the son of Jocasta and Laius, sovereigns of Thebes. A ruthless, smug, conceited, headstrong, and ambitious young man, he was found on the mountain when still an infant, taken to Polybus and Merope, sovereigns of Corinth, and adopted by them. To escape the dire prediction of the oracle of Delphi, he leaves home and sets out to kill the Sphynx so that he can marry Queen Jocasta and become king of Thebes. Although he was given the answer to the riddle by the Sphynx, he believes himself to be a hero in defeating her and revels in his illusory triumph. After seventeen years of false happiness, the infernal machine crushes its victim by unfolding the dreadful truth. The old man whom he had killed on his way to the Sphynx was his real father, and the woman whom he married was his real mother. Frantic with despair, he blinds himself with Jocasta's pin. The Oedipus of this play is very different from Sophocles' character. He is devoid of any heroic qualities. He is deliberately blind, ignores all the signs that should warn him of his imminent downfall, and lies to himself and to others. Far from being a hero, he is a derisory puppet manipulated by fate.

Jocasta (joh-KAS-tuh), the queen of Thebes, Laius' widow and Oedipus' mother. An eccentric, vain, sensual, capricious, and lonely woman with a strong foreign accent, she shows an irresistible physical attraction to young men. Thus predisposed to incest, she is unable to hear the desperate warnings of her husband's ghost or to interpret the many signs that warn of her impending fate. When she finally learns the truth, she hangs herself with her scarf. Only then does the down-to-earth, ordinary woman regain heroic grandeur. Like Oedipus, she is a ludicrous instrument of fate.

The Sphynx, the goddess of vengeance, an ambiguous creature, half human and half god, who slaughters the young men of Thebes after asking them a riddle, killing those who cannot solve it. Although she is endowed with supernatural powers, she also demonstrates human weaknesses. She first appears as a young girl, weary of killing for the god Anubis. She dreams of sacrificing herself in helping a mortal she could love to triumph over destiny. She tries to make herself attractive to Oedipus and reveals the secret of the riddle to him, thereby allowing him to slay her. She becomes furious after his speedy and triumphant departure. As it turns out, her sacrifice is but another trap set by a higher force, intent on ensnaring her as well as her victim.

Anubis (eh-NEW-bihs), the jackal-headed Egyptian god of the dead. At the Sphynx's side, he constantly reminds her of her role in the infernal machine set up by fate.

Tiresias (ti-REE-see-uhs), the high priest, an aged and blind seer watching over the queen, who calls him **Zizi**. He tries in vain to admonish Jocasta and Oedipus against their imminent marriage. Gazing into his blind eyes, Oedipus starts to see the unfolding of his destiny, but at the crucial moment, he becomes momentarily blind himself. Tiresias' ailing eyes contain the horrendous truth, but Oedipus has not quite deciphered it. Tiresias embodies the last obstacle to Oedipus and Jocasta's wedding.

The ghost of King Laius (LAY-uhs), a pitiful, tormented ghost who scares no one and who does not seem to be able to appear and disappear at will or to convey his message to the living. He desperately tries, but in vain, to prevent the union of the mother and the son. He contributes to the supernatural and tense atmosphere of the play.

The old shepherd, who was ordered by Jocasta to abandon Oedipus in the wilderness so that he could avoid the oracle. Filled with pity for the infant, however, he took Oedipus to Polybus and Merope, sovereigns of Corinth, who adopted him. Summoned now by Oedipus, he tells his story, giving proof that the old man whom Oedipus killed was his father and that Jocasta is his mother.

The Voice, which serves as a prologue. It tells in advance the whole story of the myth, urging the audience to watch out for the slow uncoiling of the infernal machine designed by the gods to annihilate a mortal man.

— *Marie-Denise Boros Azzi*

INFERNO

Author: August Strindberg (1849-1912)
First published: 1897
Genre: Novel
Locale: Paris, France; Germany; and Sweden
Time: 1894-1897
Plot: Expressionism

The narrator, the author's alter ego, who leaves his wife and child to pursue knowledge of chemistry and alchemy. His scientific experiments leave him incapacitated, his hands bleeding. He enters a hospital, where he is surrounded by decay, disease, and death. A brilliant and high-principled man, he is tormented in his soul and body by a number of hidden and diabolical assailants. He sees himself attacked by worldly enemies and, increasingly, otherworldly ones, demons and satanic forces. His soul writhes in fear of shadowy assailants, planning unknown mischief against him. He is disgusted by the stenches, horrid noises, and rude, base people that beset him, and he is in torment as electrical emanations, foul air, and other poisons destroy his health and worry his sanity. He offers this narrative as an account of his trip through nothing less than a literal hell. Throughout the novel, there is no shred of irony, no hint of self-conception, not even the thought that others may find his torments ridiculous. He is utterly self-absorbed. He travels from one location to another to escape his torments, finally settling in Sweden, where he embraces Roman Catholicism and mysticism.

Christine, the narrator's daughter, on whom he attempts to cast a spell. He later visits her, finding temporary consolation. She directs him on the path to a higher love.

Popoffsky, a former compatriot of the narrator who now wants to murder him. He is one of the narrator's many tormentors.

— *Fritz Monsma*

THE INFORMER

Author: Liam O'Flaherty (1896-1984)
First published: 1925
Genre: Novel
Locale: Dublin
Time: The 1920's
Plot: Psychological realism

Francis Joseph McPhillip, an Irish revolutionary. Having killed a man, he is disavowed by the rebel organization and is a lonely fugitive. In his great loneliness, he tries to see his family. Because he is betrayed, the police find him at his parents' home, and he commits suicide.

Gypo Nolan, the informer, a stupid man and an Irish revolutionary. Because he is penniless, he tells the police where to find Francis. He does not really know what he is doing or why. Later, he goes to the McPhillip home and gives Mrs. McPhillip part of his blood money. The rebel organization condemns him for his act, and he is shot as he flees his executioners. He runs into a church to die. There, Mrs. McPhillip forgives his treachery to her son.

Katie Fox, a prostitute who occasionally befriends Gypo out of pity. When he seeks refuge from his organization after having turned informer, Katie discloses his whereabouts, hoping by this act in some way to expiate her own sins.

Bartly, a revolutionary sent to shadow Gypo.

Dan Gallagher, an intelligent revolutionary leader, though he tends to be terrified in an emergency. He loves Mary McPhillip, Francis' sister, and takes action against the man who informed against her brother.

Mr. McPhillip, Francis' father.

Mrs. McPhillip, Francis' mother, who forgives Gypo for informing the police of her son's whereabouts as he lies dying at her feet in church.

Mary McPhillip, Francis' sister, loved by Dan.

Rat Mulligan, a man falsely accused by Gypo of having betrayed Francis.

Maggie, a prostitute patronized by Gypo.

THE INHERITORS

Author: William Golding (1911-1993)
First published: 1955
Genre: Novel
Locale: A mountainous, wooded countryside not far from the sea
Time: The Paleolithic period
Plot: Allegory

Lok, the consciousness through which most of the book is mediated. It is his perceptions of the "new people" that dictate readers' responses to them, and it is through his thoughts and actions that readers come to understand how Neanderthal people could have constructed their reality. By default, he becomes the people's leader after the deaths of Mal and Ha, but it is not a role that sits easily on him. By nature, he is a joker and clown. His decisions are not always the best. Fa's instincts are sounder, and he finds himself deferring to the power of her intuitive intelligence. He understands far less about the new people than she does, not being able to conceive of evil at all. He is gentle, and in the end he wills himself to die.

Fa, Lok's consort. Family relationships do not seem formalized among the people, but she and Lok regard themselves as Liku's parents, even though it is never stated that she is their daughter. Fa has lost one baby but hopes to bear others; this is why she urges Lok to walk away from the catastrophe and start again. She has a priestess role; her pilgrimage to Oa as ice goddess is described. Only females are allowed access to the sacred: This is a main feature of the people's gender roles. Informally, she provides emotional sustenance for Lok, and she hides from him the knowledge of Liku's terrible death.

The old woman, who is never named. She is Mal's consort and retains the tribal memory. She is also the fire carrier, the one who tends and guards it, another gender role. She is perceived as having a religious force within her as a representative of Oa, and the rest of the people treat her with loving awe.

Mal, the people's leader. There is a natural deference to him, even when he appears too old to make new decisions. He is the only one to die naturally, of old age.

Liku, a young girl but old enough to go hunting with Lok and Fa. She is kidnapped by the new people but tries to make friends with Tanakil. She seems to be adjusting easily to the new people's society when she is killed, probably as a human sacrifice or as part of a hunting ritual.

Tuami, who takes over from Lok in the final chapter as the narrative consciousness. He is confused by the conflict and panic over the Neanderthals, whom he now regards as devils. His previous confidence is shattered. He becomes ambivalent about his plans to assassinate Marlan and assume leadership.

Vivani, the *femme fatale* of the novel. She is aware of her femininity as providing both sexual attractiveness and power, as well as in her felt need for a baby to suckle after the earlier accidental death of her own. She is both fulfilled and ashamed in having a Neanderthal baby, whom the others regard as evil.

Tanakil, a girl probably about Liku's age, though much bigger. In the new people's fear, she is left as an exchange for the baby. The experience causes her to go out of her mind. All she can repeat is the word "Liku."

Marlan, an old man and leader of his group, which appears to be a breakaway one, created by his taking Vivani. Because he drives his people rather than leading them, he is accorded only grudging respect, unlike the deference given to Mal.

— David Barratt

THE INIMITABLE JEEVES

Author: P. G. Wodehouse (1881-1975)
First published: 1923
Genre: Novel
Locale: England, France, and New York City
Time: Early 1920's
Plot: Farce

Bertram (Bertie) Wooster, a gentleman, an already confirmed bachelor in his mid-twenties, the epitome of the idle—and vacant—rich. Although Jeeves describes Bertie as "By no means intelligent," he also acknowledges Bertie to be "an exceedingly pleasant and amiable young gentleman." Good-natured Bertie narrates the events of this series of linked stories in a tone that is sprightly though at times faintly defensive when his role as stooge for family and friends and as the object of Jeeves's contempt becomes obvious even to him. Despite his deplorably bad taste in clothes (a source of frequent conflict with Jeeves) and his unabashed love of his idle, luxurious, and socially unredeeming life, Bertie comes across as an innocuous young man of unflagging goodwill.

Jeeves, Bertie's valet, a few years older than Bertie and certainly wiser. Although superbly competent in his duties as a gentleman's gentleman, Jeeves is much more; his master also regards him, with gratitude and some awe, as "a bird of the ripest intellect" and "a sort of guide, philosopher, and friend." Jeeves often extricates Bertie, his friends, and members of his family from unpleasant personal messes; while discreetly dispensing advice and help, Jeeves himself always manages to benefit, financially and romantically. Although Jeeves's overt manner toward his young master is one of dignified loyalty and self-effacing respect, his own superior intelligence, worldliness, and good taste are abundantly evident.

Agatha Gregson, Bertie's aunt. Described by her nephew as "pretty formidable," she is a tall, commanding, gray-haired woman, sharp-nosed and gimlet-eyed. Bertie fears her and her unfailing ability to "snooter" him. On several occasions, she routs Bertie from his life of comfortable sloth and entangles him in unpleasant situations as part of her mission to have him make something useful of himself and fulfill family expectations. She harasses him both at home and abroad; it finally takes the full force of Jeeves's ingenuity to placate her.

Richard "Bingo" Little, a slim, dapper young man-about-town, an old school friend of Bertie. As dim as Bertie, Bingo leads an equally idle life, distinguished only by his penchant for repeatedly falling desperately in love. The women that he desires are either of enough intelligence and breeding to regard his attentions with amused contempt or unsuitably lower class. Tumbling into one scrape after another, Bingo always manipulates Bertie (and, therefore, Jeeves) into extricating him, appealing to Bertie's "old school tie" loyalty. An accomplished parasite, Bingo finally marries the popular novelist Rosie M. Banks, a woman much better, brighter, and wealthier than he deserves.

Mortimer "Old" Little, created **Lord Bittlesham**, the wealthy owner of Little's Liniments. Now retired, his chief interest is food: its preparation and, particularly, its consumption in large quantities. Obese and troubled by gout, Old Little has an explosive temper, especially when he discerns a betrayal of his nephew Bingo's duty to him. Bingo's romantic encounter with radical socialism, especially in the person of the formidable, gold-toothed Charlotte Corday Rowbotham, leads Old Little to cut off Bingo's allowance, giving rise to Bingo's disastrous forays into gambling.

Rosie M. Banks, the author of popular novels extolling the triumph of love over class distinctions. While working as a waitress at a gentleman's club as a means of researching the background for a new novel, she becomes the last in the long series of Bingo's passionate attachments, the woman who finally brings Bingo to matrimony and also placates Old Little. Bertie had earlier assumed Rosie's name and fame to restore Bingo to Old Little's favor; regrettably, the arrival of the real Rosie leaves Old Little to presume thereafter that Bertie is completely mad.

Claude and

Eustace, Bertie's cousins, inseparable twins about twenty years old. Expelled from Oxford for unsuitable behavior, these wastrels become the scourge of Bertie's life. They are so gleefully irresponsible, devoted to pleasure, and adept at sponging that they tax even Jeeves's ingenuity in devising a plan that finally removes them from the Wooster family's sphere and relegates them to the colonies.

Honoria Glossop, the strapping, hearty, horsey daughter of Sir Roderick Glossop. She is briefly an object of Bingo's affections and, for a short while, the horrified Bertie's fiancée, thanks to Aunt Agatha's plans for his future. Another of Jeeves's masterful plots rescues Bertie from matrimony.

— Jill Rollins

THE INNOCENT

Author: Richard E. Kim (1932-   )
First published: 1968
Genre: Novel

Locale: South Korea
Time: Mid-1950's
Plot: War

Major Lee, the narrator, one of a group of Korean army officers involved in a coup d'état. Lee struggles with a moral dilemma: In their effort to rescue the country from a corrupt regime and replace it with moral leaders, the coup members risk becoming as evil as those they seek to overthrow. Lee opposes any plan to shed blood, but other members, especially Colonel Min, see bloodshed as necessary—and therefore justifiable—if their coup is to succeed. When General Ham is killed by the conspirators, Lee realizes that his ideal of an honorable coup is doomed. Finally, he acknowledges the need for people like Min, having learned that tragedy and absurdity result from the collision of good and evil. He embarks for America, saddened by the turmoil his country is suffering and nostalgic for his lost innocence.

Colonel Min, the leader of the conspirators and friend of Lee. Although he respects Lee's intelligence and idealism, Min regards Lee as a sentimental intellectual out of touch with the real world and ineffectual against evil men. Lee's idealism helps Min maintain a clear view of goodness and justice, ideals for which the conspirators are fighting, and to save himself from falling victim to the illusion of omnipotence, as have the evil generals and politicians. Once the coup has succeeded, however, Min no longer needs Lee as moral ballast, and in the very act of sending his idealistic friend off to America, Min is killed by opposition soldiers. The man who sought to achieve a peaceful end by violent means himself falls victim to violence, though he has sacrificed his life for a just cause.

General Ham, the chief opponent of the coup. He attempts to save himself and his fortunes by negotiating with Min. Wily, self-serving, cruel, and unscrupulous, he epitomizes the corruption among the country's leaders. Ham's pride makes him contemptuous of the coup members. In a final act of misjudgment, he challenges Min to stop him from returning to his command headquarters. Min orders his troops to fire on the general's plane, killing the general and all of his men. The act marks Min as a murderer in the eyes of Lee.

Brigadier General Ahn, the chief of the Special Projects section of the South Korean army, a decorated hero and brutally efficient officer. He is found to be a Communist agent whose past is mired in murder, deceit, and cruelty; he is a prime target of the coup members, who want to execute him outright. Lee, however, wants to give Ahn a fair trial to show the world the humanity and high principles of the coup members. Ironically, it is Lee who shoots Ahn as the general attempts to escape after killing Major General Mah. Ahn, who is only wounded, is taken prisoner by the Command Group.

Major General Mah, who controls the Secret Police, Presidential Brigade, and Metropolitan Police. Considered a criminal by members of the coup, he is marked for punishment. Although Lee would have him tried and court-martialed, other members of the coup want him simply killed. The question becomes moot when Ahn, desperate to keep Mah from exposing him, kills Mah.

Lieutenant Cho, an aide to Colonel Min and the son of Min's close friend. He provides Lee with information regarding Min's background, his serving in the Japanese army, his farming in remote Pyungyang, and his killing of the Communist guerrillas who murdered Cho's family. He is among the victorious members of the coup at the end.

Chaplain Koh, who has recruited several generals in support of the coup. He is the spiritual adviser to Major Lee and his moral confidant, counseling the major in the end to temper his idealism with an understanding that humans are imperfect, that events go awry, and that in the best circumstances, good people suffer and die. Koh voices the dilemma created by humanity's struggle to achieve goodness in an imperfect world. In the end, he confesses to Lee that heaven's ways are inscrutable and that men like Min are necessary in the struggle between good and evil.

Colonel McKay, an American intelligence officer in contact with the members of the coup, whom he supports. He maintains the interests of the United States government and monitors events in Korea before and after the coup. McKay admires Lee's brilliant tactical skills in organizing the coup and is sympathetic to Lee's moral dilemma, but he believes that Min's ruthless tactics are necessary in times like these. McKay accompanies Lee out of Korea, serving as Lee's protector and executor of Min's last wish, to send Lee to America.

— Bernard E. Morris

THE INQUISITORY
(L'Inquisitoire)

Author: Robert Pinget (1919-1997)
First published: 1962
Genre: Novel

Locale: In and near Sirancy, France
Time: c. 1960
Plot: New Novel

The interrogator, a criminal investigator of indeterminate age and sex. The interrogator is patient; thorough; obsessed with the details of the possible crime to whose investigation he or she has been assigned; quick-minded, able to remember the smallest details of the affidavit being recorded by a secretary nearby; particularly attentive to information of a perverse or sexual nature; and terse in the wording of questions, possibly simply because they must be written down (the subject of the "grilling" is deaf). The interrogator is professional but indifferent to the discomfort caused by the prolonged questioning and orchestrates the pace of the narrative with two commands: "Go on" and "Cut it short."

The interrogee, an old family retainer or general factotum. He is deaf (but not from birth) and in service to two or possibly three "gentlemen" on a French country estate. His crystal-clear account of the incidents surrounding the disappearance of the secretary to his employers, along with his detailed descriptions of the countryside, the towns, the rooms of every estate, and the personalities and foibles of the inhabitants of his world, make up the text of the novel. Sometimes loquacious, sometimes hesitant, and sometimes angry at the interrogator, but always articulate (his speeches lack punctuation except for occasional commas), he relates what he knows, or what he remembers or thinks he remembers, or what he invents to satisfy the unsatisfiable interrogator. Besides describing the complex social and personal relationships of the area with his remarkable ability to remember details, he reveals the tragic loss of his wife and son, his reluctance to involve himself with the intrigues of the household, and his growing fatigue at answering "the wrong questions" from the interrogator. Although his recollections ring true to the reader, he eventually begins to evade the questions, contradict previous testimony, and possibly admit to the invention of much of his unstructured story; its veracity is often called into question, but its essential reality constitutes the substance of the novel. Like the protagonist in so many postmodern novels, he can be seen as the author himself, struggling with the body of the text, partly invented, partly imperfectly remembered, and partly writing itself, always fictive and always true.

The people in and around Sirancy, France, whose lives are described in the weave of the narrative. Sometimes unimportant storekeepers, servants, or passersby, but at other times rich friends and secret intimates of the "gentlemen," involved in implicitly immoral or illegal liaisons of every kind, these characters move in and out of the interrogee's statement, apparently at random or by a series of concatenative associations explainable only to himself. Many of the characters (townspeople, peasants, hired hands, sophisticated idlers, and hangers-on) come together at an all-night party at the "gentlemen's" estate just prior to the secretary's disappearance. The "gentlemen" employers themselves are never described, except by inference from the events surrounding them.

— *Thomas J. Taylor*

AN INSPECTOR CALLS

Author: J. B. Priestley (1894-1984)
First published: 1947
Genre: Drama
Locale: England
Time: 1912
Plot: Detective and mystery

Inspector Goole, a mysterious figure for social justice who claims to represent the police. A massive, solid, purposeful man of approximately fifty, he calls on the Birling family as Arthur and Sybil Birling celebrate their daughter Sheila's engagement to Gerald Croft. Goole says that he is investigating the reasons for the suicide of a woman variously known as Eva Smith, Daisy Renton, and Mrs. Birling, who has died in agony after drinking disinfectant. Goole relentlessly reveals the role that each Birling (and Croft) has played through social or sexual irresponsibility. After Goole leaves, Arthur calls the chief constable and learns that no such inspector is on the force, but, as the final curtain falls, the telephone rings and Arthur hears that a woman has just died after drinking disinfectant and that an inspector is on his way to ask some questions.

Arthur Birling, a self-satisfied industrialist of about fifty. Heavyset, easy-mannered, and provincial in speech, Arthur, as the play opens, shrugs off the importance of labor unrest and the rumors of a coming war to forecast a rosy future for those of his class. He boasts of progress, of airplanes, of automobiles, and even of such unsinkable ships as the *Titanic*, slated to sail the next week. He confides to Gerald that he expects a knighthood, and he lectures his family members on their duties to themselves, not to the larger community. Shortly after this speech, Goole arrives and reveals that the dead woman was started on her road to death when she was dismissed by Birling for being the ringleader of a group who struck for minimally higher wages. Birling maintains that his attitude was correct, disclaims responsibility, threatens Goole with the wrath of the chief constable, and berates him for upsetting the family.

Sheila Birling, Arthur's daughter, a pretty woman in her twenties. Although engaged to Gerald, she wonders why he ignored her the previous spring and summer. Shown a picture of Eva by Goole, she is horrified to realize that she herself had Eva fired from a sales position that Eva obtained after being dismissed by Arthur. In a bad mood, envious of Eva's looks, she had threatened to close the family account at the shop unless Eva was dismissed. Unlike her parents, Sheila is lastingly changed by Goole's revelations of the social injustices perpetrated by her family.

Gerald Croft, a well-bred man-about-town, approximately thirty years old. The son of a titled rival of Birling, Gerald is happy to unite the firms' futures; the previous year, ignoring Sheila, he was living with Eva, whom he knew as Daisy Renton. He met her at a favorite haunt of prostitutes. Daisy was young, kind, lonely, destitute, and grateful to live for a time as Gerald's mistress. She uncomplainingly accepted the end of the affair. Gerald gave her money to last out the year and thought no more of her future until shown a picture by Goole.

Sybil Birling, the fiftyish wife of Arthur and the mother of Sheila and Eric. Cold, haughty, and conscious of her social superiority to her husband, Sybil regards interest in Eva's problems as a symptom of morbidity. She denies concern and responsibility, even when Goole tells her that, as chairwoman of a charitable organization, she herself had denied one of Eva's final appeals for aid. Eva, who had become pregnant, assumed the name Birling; Sybil was offended by that and by the woman's attitude. Rather than grant help, Sybil insisted that Eva should make an example of the baby's father, who should be forced to confess in public. Eva would not accept help from the man, claiming that he was young, foolish, and a heavy drinker who, unknown to her, had helped Eva by stealing money. Now Sybil learns, and denies, that the young man is her son Eric.

Eric Birling, an immature, heavy-drinking young man in his early twenties. While drunk, Eric picked up Eva, herself hungry, a bit drunk, and down on her luck. He stole money from his father's office to help her until Eva learned of the theft and refused any further aid of that sort. He did not confide in his parents because, with good reason, he doubted that they would understand. Like Sheila, he is profoundly affected by Inspector Goole's revelations of the shared responsibility for Eva's death.

— *Betty Richardson*

THE INSPECTOR GENERAL
(Revizor)

Author: Nikolai V. Gogol (1809-1852)
First performed: 1836
Genre: Drama
Locale: Russia
Time: Early nineteenth century
Plot: Satire

Anton Antonovich Skvoznik-Dmokhanovsky (ahn-TOHN ahn-TOH-nuh-vihch SKVOHZ-nihk-dmew-hahn-OHF-skih), the prefect of a small provincial town in early nineteenth century Russia. He has received a warning letter from a friend that an inspector general is coming, traveling incognito, to visit the district in an attempt to find evidence of bribery and injudicious acts. The prefect calls a meeting of the citizens and orders them to mend their ways. He does not take kindly to their criticism that he has been taking bribes and recently had the wife of a noncommissioned officer beaten.

Ivan Alexandrovich Hlestakov (ih-VAHN ah-lehk-SAHN-druh-vihch hlehs-tah-KOHF), a smartly dressed traveler who, taking lodgings at the local inn, is mistaken for the inspector. A shrewd opportunist, he accepts money and gifts, goes to stay at the prefect's house, and accepts an invitation to an official dinner at the hospital. He gets drunk and goes to sleep. When he awakes, he makes love to the prefect's daughter and asks to marry her. He then requests five hundred rubles from complaining shopkeepers, borrows a coach, and, after writing to a friend an account of his hoax, rides off with promises to return the next day.

Osip (OH-sihp) or **Yosif** (YOH-sihf), Ivan Alexandrovich's elderly and philosophical servant, who considers all gentlefolk peculiar. He is shrewd enough to capitalize on his master's mistaken identity and adds to the hoax by allowing himself to be bribed into revealing all sorts of imaginary details of Ivan Alexandrovich's high place in society. He then advises his master to leave town.

Anna Andreyevna (AHN-nuh ahn-DRAY-ehv-nuh), the prefect's wife, given to arguing about clothes. She enjoys having Ivan Alexandrovich ogle her and delightedly agrees to his proposal of marriage to her daughter.

Marya Antonovna (MAH-ryuh ahn-TOH-nuhv-nuh), the prefect's daughter.

Mishka (MIHSH-kuh), a servant of the mayor.

Piotr Ivanovich Bobchinsky (PYOH-tr ih-VAH-nuh-vihch bohb-CHIHN-skihy) and

Piotr Ivanovich Dobchinsky (dohb-CHIHN-skihy), two squireens of the town who discover a mysterious stranger at the inn and declare him to be the expected inspector general.

Artemy Filippovitch Zemlyanika (ahr-TEH-mihy fih-LIHP-peh-vihch zehm-lyah-NIH-kuh), the manager of the hospital. He believes that if a patient is going to die, he will die. To prepare for the arrival of the inspector general, he provides clean nightcaps for his patients and puts over each bed a Latin sign stating the patient's illness.

Ammos Fyodorovitch Lyapkin-Tyapkin (AHM-muhs FYOH-duh-ruh-vihch LYAHP-kihn-TYAHP-kihn), the local judge, a dedicated huntsman who keeps his guns and his whip in the courtroom.

Stepan Ilyitch Uhovyortov (steh-PAHN ih-lyihch ew-hohv-yohr-TOHF), the police inspector.

Luka Lukich Hlopov (LEW-kuh LEW-kihch hloh-POHF), the head of the local school. He is ordered to curb the unprofessional actions of some of his teachers, such as those of the history teacher who leaps on his desk to describe the Macedonian Wars and the fat one who grimaces and pulls his beard under his necktie.

Shpyokin (SHPYOH-kihn), the postmaster, who reads all the mail. Told to be on the lookout for details about the visit of the inspector general, he opens Ivan Alexandrovich's letter and reads the rogue's description of the muddle-headed town officials and the hoax played on them.

The inspector general, who, at the end of the play, arrives at the inn and sends a policeman to summon the town officials to wait on him immediately.

AN INSULAR POSSESSION

Author: Timothy Mo (1950-   )
First published: 1986
Genre: Novel
Locale: Canton, the Macao Peninsula, Lin Tin Island, and Hong Kong
Time: The 1830's and 1840's
Plot: Historical

Gideon Chase, a young man who, at the age of seventeen, is a junior clerk in the Canton offices of a large American trading firm, the Meridian Company. He is industrious, diligent, quick-witted, and curious. The youngest character and an orphan, he spends much of the first half of the novel watching (and learning from) the others, particularly on their escapades to the "flower boats" and forays into the city proper, as well as to the haven of Macao. Later, he is revealed as the main protagonist, acting on his own initiative, though to higher purpose than his friends; his rites of passage become a main focus of the book. Gideon is at first easily led by his mentor and father figure, Walter Eastman. Gideon absorbs many of Eastman's attitudes, particularly a distaste for the opium trade promoted by the British empire in China. The younger man soon surpasses the elder, in several ways. When Eastman is ignominiously discharged from his position at Meridian, Gideon resigns in support of his friend; moreover, his is the inspiration to begin the newspaper the two publish, *The Lin Tin Bulletin and River Bee*, and his is the more mature and reasonable rhetoric. Gideon also departs from Eastman in his ability (and his willingness) to see the Chinese as people and as individuals, not merely as an abstract value. This attribute is enhanced, if not fostered by, his study of the Chinese language, which, although against the law, allows him to enter the realm of the native. During his excursions through the war, from which struggles Canton emerges as Hong Kong, Gideon learns to see not only the humanity of the oppressed but also the brutality (and sometimes depravity) of the conquerer. Finally, Gideon becomes a more mature, a more discerning, and a more completely developed person than Eastman through his perception of the reality below the gaudy and often deceptive surface.

Walter Eastman, a twenty-four-year-old senior clerk with the Meridian Company in Canton. He is outspoken in his condemnation of the British opium trade, through which the empire financed its Indian ventures and realized a substantial profit for the greedy Crown. Eastman has no compunctions about enjoying the luxurious and often frivolous lifestyle of the foreigners in China, while the natives suffer untold deprivations under the tyrannical yoke of colonization. When dismissed from his position at Meridian for engaging in a love affair with a partner's niece, he uses the opportunity to attack the opium trade through the newspaper that he and Gideon establish, though he dared not leave his job on his own to espouse that same cause. He seems to take more pleasure in baiting his rival editor than in fighting the British imperialists. Eastman is a multifaceted person, though his talents are those of a dilettante; he is perhaps a man who could succeed at anything that he was motivated to do, but he lacks the ambition to apply himself wholeheartedly to any one goal.

Harry O'Rourke, an elderly Briton who is in Canton to escape family responsibilities and debtors. A fairly successful painter, skillful at impressionistic landscapes, he is reduced to attempting to maintain a drunken existence on the fees from selling amateurish portraits. He provides a counterpoint to the two younger men; though rather cynical, instead of discouraging them, he not only provides an impetus but also often offers practical suggestions to their idealistic endeavors. He helps to finance *The Lin Tin Bulletin and River Bee* as well as giving editorial advice, and he encourages Gideon in his study of Chinese. Still, he is not an admirable figure, and it is not difficult to imagine Walter Eastman evolving into just such a creature in the future, though Gideon surely will not.

Father Joaquim Ribeiro (hwah-KEEM rree-BA-roh), a Jesuit priest dedicated to improving the human condition, another mentor to Gideon and a confidant as well. Sympathetic to Gideon's efforts against personal inertia, he first begins to teach Chinese to Gideon, then finds a onetime mandarin, the venerable Ow, to further Gideon's study of the language, though it is at peril of all of their lives. He later discovers an ancient abandoned printing press for Gideon and Eastman to use in publishing their newspaper.

Pedro Remedios (PEH-droh rreh-MEH-dee-ohs), a pirate who is executed for continuing after the uneasy peace the acts that the British praised during the Opium War. He helps Gideon in his search for knowledge and understanding by guiding the younger man on his investigations for the newspaper during the war. He assists in distributing the paper to its readers.

Alice Remington, a niece of the Canton/Macao-based senior partner of the Meridian Company. She is admired by both Gideon Chase and Walter Eastman. When her secret engagement to Eastman is discovered by her uncle, Eastman is dismissed from his job and forbidden to see her again. She exemplifies the intolerant and glib attitude of the British colonists by her letters home: She describes, at great length, dinner parties, the play produced by Eastman and performed by the small group of Occidentals deemed suitable, and other social affairs, including the clothing, appearance, and demeanor of the guests. The outbreak of war is of slight notice to her, deserving only a postscript.

— *Mary Johnson*

THE INSULTED AND THE INJURED
(Unizhennye i oskorblyonnye)

Author: Fyodor Dostoevski (1821-1881)
First published: 1861
Genre: Novel

Locale: St. Petersburg
Time: Mid-nineteenth century
Plot: Social realism

Ivan Petrovitch (ee-VAHN peh-TROH-vihch), the narrator, a young author. He has a selfless devotion to his friends; at a time when his own literary career is at a crux and he might be forgiven for indulging his own concerns, he immerses himself in the troubles of everyone around him. He becomes the universal confidant, and his is the common shoulder on which they cry. An orphan, he was taken in by the Ichmenyevs; he and Natasha had been reared together and fallen in love. Shortly before the main action of the novel, he had made a great success with his first novel and had become engaged to Natasha. The main action covers the period of Natasha's love affair with Alyosha. Ivan never reproaches Natasha for her breach of affection and is only solicitous of her happiness. This novel apparently is his final work, a memoir he is writing from his sickbed, where, undone by the strains of all that happens, he is convinced that he will die.

Natalia "Natasha" Nikolaevna Ichmenyev (nih-koh-LAH-ehv-nah ihch-MEH-nyehv), Nikolai Sergeyitch's daughter, who is in love with Alyosha. She is a beautiful young woman, strong in her character, able to keep a calm understanding of herself and her situation, even when under the compulsions of her sometimes violent passions. Once engaged to Ivan, she has now fallen in love with the sincere but haphazard and weak Alyosha. Her love comes, perhaps, from her own excess of strength. She goes to live with him, thus making her social position forfeit and breaking her from her family, although she has no realistic hope of keeping his affections for long. It is only through the actions of the ever-generous Ivan that, having lost Alyosha, she is peacefully reunited with her family. Although she has this much of a happy ending, it is clear that she will live with her thwarted passion for a long time.

Alexei "Alyosha" Pyotrovitch Valkovsky (pyoh-TROH-vihch vahl-KOV-skee), Prince Valkovsky's son. He is torn between the choice of two women: Natasha, who loves him selflessly, and Katya, who is good-hearted and (more important to Alyosha's conspiring father) immensely rich. He is a charming youth, a handsome, delicate young man with a feminine nervousness; he is merry and kindhearted, with an open soul capable of the noblest feelings and a loving heart. He is candid, grateful, and completely childish. All of his impulses and inclinations are the fruit of excessive nervous impressionability, a warm heart, and an irresponsibility that, at times, almost approaches incoherence. He has an extreme susceptibility to every kind of external influence and a complete absence of will. Although he loves Natasha, in his fashion, he is, in the end, too weak to deny his father.

Prince Pyotr Alexandrovitch Valkovsky (pyohtr ah-lehk-SAN-droh vihch), Alyosha's father, an aristocrat and figure in St. Petersburg society. He is the monster of the story: Through his unchecked rapacity, all the other characters come to grief. He was born of an ancient but financially ruined family, took a government post, married for money, and by means of one intrigue or another, using his rare talent for duplicity, took himself to the pinnacle of society. He is spiteful, cunning, and intensely egotistic. In his connection to Natasha's family, he wants not only to keep his son to his own purposes but also to ruin Nikolai Sergeyitch, to insult Natasha as he spoils her romance, and to show himself to Ivan in his full moral ugliness. He ends the novel triumphant and unreconstructed, having disturbed the moral equilibrium, and, as often as not, the physical constitutions, of the other figures in the novel.

Nikolai Sergeyitch Ichmenyev (sehr-GEH-ihch), Natasha's father, formerly the manager of Prince Valkovsky's estates, now involved in a lawsuit against him. He is a simple-hearted, straightforward, disinterested, and generous man, reserved in his affection. He is delicate about showing his tenderness but is quick to form the bonds of love. Prince Valkovsky has accused him of embezzlement and of conspiring to use Natasha to snare Alyosha and make an advantageous match. It is while the suit is being heard that Natasha goes to live with Alyosha. He is lost, torn by his violent pride and his lavish affection. When the worst has happened with his suit and Natasha's betrothal, his heart, prompted by Ivan and Nellie, melts. He is able to reconstruct his life as he reconstructs his family.

Elena "Nellie" Smith, an orphan taken in by Ivan and, later, by the Ichmenyevs. She is a high-strung girl of thirteen or so, epileptic, with an unstable nervous disposition. She is willful and energetic, at times capricious and gleefully contrary, at times generous and patiently loving. She is the child of a truly broken home: Her mother and grandfather kept an ancient quarrel alive until their deaths, and the identity of her father is the book's dark mystery. Their divisions live on in Nellie. Ivan asks her help in reconciling Natasha to her father: He asks that she tell her own, parallel, story simply and straightforwardly, in the hope of softening Nikolai Sergeyitch's heart. She succeeds, but the strain of recollecting her story unsettles her. She falls into physical disorder and dies at the close of the novel.

— *Fritz Monsma*

INTENSIVE CARE

Author: Janet Frame (Janet Paterson Frame Clutha, 1924-)
First published: 1970
Genre: Novel
Locale: New Zealand; London, England; and Melbourne, Australia
Time: Early 1900's to the 1960's and the future
Plot: Science fiction

Tom Livingstone, a retired New Zealand worker in his seventies. An ordinary old man outwardly, Tom faces the end of his life in disappointment as he realizes that he has fulfilled few of his ambitions and has found little happiness through either his job or his family. It is the novel's intent that the memories, dreams, and fantasies constituting his inner life assume greater importance in character development than do the prosaic events of his daily existence, as he complains of physical ailments, conducts a desultory flirtation with the town's loose woman, and finally dies alone.

Peggy Warren, Tom's girlfriend after his wife's death. Approaching middle age, Peggy works as a nurse in a home for the elderly. She is a brassy, bold, and unrefined sort, considered a bit of a tart by the townspeople. Through her relationship with Tom, she searches for security, which eludes her at his death.

Leonard Livingstone, Tom's drunken, dirty, and disorderly brother, who shares the main character's disappointment with what life offers but finds solace in the bottle, not in dreams.

Pearl Torrance, Tom's daughter, who is enormously obese and overbearing. Her illusions about life faded long ago, leaving her with no sympathy, not even for the battered children whom she serves.

Naomi Whyborn, Tom's daughter, who is dying of cancer. Not appearing within the main narrative, she is introduced through disjointed letters that she writes, but never sends, to her father.

Colin Torrance, Pearl Torrance's son and Tom's grandson, somewhere between thirty and forty years of age. Ordinary in appearance and feckless in behavior, he commits but one significant act: the murder of his lover.

Lorna Kimberly, Colin's girlfriend, young, sensual, unattractive, and stupid. Colin murders her.

Milly Galbraith, a twenty-six-year-old retarded woman whose memoir records most of the futuristic action. Describing herself as fully developed physically, she emerges as one of the novel's most sympathetic characters, for her insight greatly surpasses that possessed by the so-called normal people who inhabit both the realistic and futuristic worlds. Galbraith's only connection to the Livingstone family lies in her love for the pear tree still standing on their former property.

Colin Monk, a mathematics professor and colorless bureaucrat in his forties who blindly helps to administer the "Human Delineation Act" that destroys the retarded Milly Galbraith and may ultimately obliterate him.

— *Robert L. Ross*

INTER ICE AGE 4
(Daiyon kampyōki)

Author: Kōbō Abe (1924-1993)
First published: 1958-1959
Genre: Novel
Locale: Tokyo, Japan
Time: Near future
Plot: Science fiction

Professor Katsumi, the narrator, a computer scientist. Committed to rational explanations, Katsumi comes to see that his own future is not easily controllable. When he builds a computer that will predict the future, he becomes involved in the murder of the man whose future he is predicting. Eventually, Katsumi discovers that the victim had learned of a bizarre project to develop aquans, a race of fishlike humans who could survive the predicted flooding of Earth. Katsumi discovers that his own staff, guided by his computer, are participants in the project. He confronts the computer, and it explains that, as his second self, with an insight into the future that he refuses to accept, it is in control, not him. Because of his objections, Katsumi must be killed.

Tanomogi, Katsumi's assistant. Although the mysterious Tanomogi seems to be helping Katsumi, he has been manipulating his boss. Tanomogi is the murderer that he and Katsumi have been seeking. He feeds Katsumi information about the aquans, but he never specifies his motives for joining the project.

Wada Katsuko, a young female assistant. At times strangely attractive to Katsumi, Wada is the link between the aquan project and the computer laboratory. She also arranges to procure Katsumi's aborted son for the project so that Katsumi can have a part in the future society. Later, she tries to convince Katsumi that he is responsible for the consequences of his actions.

Professor Yamamoto, the head of the aquan breeding facilities. A large, businesslike scientist, Yamamoto dispassionately explains the project and its aims to Katsumi shortly before Katsumi is to be killed.

— *Steven L. Hale*

THE INTERPRETERS

Author: Wole Soyinka (1934-   )
First published: 1965
Genre: Novel
Locale: Lagos and Ibadan, Nigeria
Time: Early 1960's, soon after Nigerian independence
Plot: Social realism

Bandele (bahn-DAY-lay), a professor of history at the University of Nigeria at Ibadan. He smooths social situations of the group, especially when Egbo becomes physical and upsets the group. When Sagoe physically disrupts some events, Bandele calmly states his insights or is a sage presence. At the Oguazors' party, Bandele brings calm to Sagoe's caustic remarks about artificiality in the host and hostess as well as in the decorations. He passes judgment on Dr. Oguazor, the hypocritical medical professor, regarding the pregnant coed. At the unveiling of Kola's pantheon at Joe Golder's concert, Bandele most closely resembles the cerebral tranquillity of Orisa-nla, the principal Yoruba deity.

Egbo, a clerk in the Foreign Office. Heir to a village chiefdom, Egbo most closely represents Ogun in Kola's painting. The myth is that the god Ogun makes the greatest amount of actions of body and of words, so that he is the most successful bridger of the abyss of transition between the visible and invisible worlds. Egbo is the catalyst of the group of friends, for he starts a fight at the nightclub where the superb dancer stimulates him to pursue Simi, who is desired by most men. His sexual initiation fuses with his memories of canoeing back to his village. The coed he takes to Ogumo rock becomes part of Egbo's physical action of a sacrificial nature. After Sekoni's death, Egbo leads the group to the albino Lazarus' church. His response to Joe Golder is physical disgust, even when he disrupts Joe's concert by leaving midway. Egbo does not seem morally responsible but, like Ogun, is a mover.

Biodun Sagoe (bee-OH-dewn sah-GOH-ay), a newspaper reporter for the *Independent Viewpoint* in Lagos. Sagoe pursues Dehinwa; awaking from a hangover, he fantasizes that Sir Derinola is coming out of her wardrobe. To expose that corrupt official's bribe-taking, Sagoe, at an interview, expounds from his book about the Philosophy of Voidancy to Matthew, the errand boy. Later, at the hotel lounge, Sagoe arranges witnesses to Sir Derinola's hints for a bribe. Devastated by Sekoni's death, Sagoe attends a party hosted by Dr. Faseli Oguazor, at which he mocks the accents and manners of his English wife and university guests. In Kola's pantheon, Sagoe is portrayed as Esu, a trickster who is unpredictable.

Kola, a painter and a lecturer in art. Kola is inspired by Sekoni's sculpture to paint a huge canvas of the Yoruba pantheon of traditional gods, represented by his friends. Frustrated because he regards Sekoni's art as much better, Kola makes plodding efforts to find suitable models for some gods. Ecstatic when he sees the albino girl, he asks her to be his model. He works in Joe Golder, who presses to be included in the pantheon. The painting is publicly viewed at Joe's concert. Kola brings the group of friends together again after Sekoni's death.

Sekoni (say-KOH-nee), an engineer, later a sculptor. Sekoni became mentally ill after the dam project on which he was working upcountry was canceled. Corrupt politicians hire an expatriate expert to write a damning report. Sekoni is devastated that local villages will not have electric power. Because Sekoni has explosive moments, he is like Sango, the god of lightning. Nicknamed "Sheikh" for his Muslim heritage, Sekoni embodies both traditional myth and contemporary electrical technology as an engineer. His death devastates his father, who never recovered from the shock of his son marrying a non-Muslim. Sekoni is the initial inspiration for Kola to paint the canvas of the pantheon.

Komolola Dehinwa (koh-moh-LOH-lah day-HEE-nwah), Sagoe's fiancée. Dehinwa, a clerk in the civil service, drove Sagoe home after a party. Caught between traditional female roles and an urban lifestyle, Dehinwa sometimes has to choose women's ways, such as sitting on the side with the women in Lazarus' church. An urban Earth Mother to the group, she demonstrates the dilemma of a modern career woman still expected to adhere to traditional behavior.

Joe Golder, a homosexual quadroon American singer and a lecturer in African history at the University of Nigeria at Ibadan. Joe is represented in Kola's pantheon painting by an animal spirit. Like Erinle, he hunts; his quarry is Noah, the thief. Representing abnormality because he lost touch with his African roots, Joe is most creative when he is singing.

— Greta McCormick Coger

THE INTRUDER
(L'Intruse)

Author: Maurice Maeterlinck (1862-1949)
First published: 1890
Genre: Drama
Locale: A dark room in an old château
Time: Early twentieth century
Plot: Tragedy

The Grandfather, who, like the prophets in the works of Homer and Sophocles, is blind but sees the truth more clearly than the younger people around him. He says exactly what he discerns. His persistent questions about who is in the garden and the sitting room or why the lamp burns less brightly and his accusations that his family is keeping important information from him show him to be, despite his frailty from living nearly eighty years, a seeker of truth on all levels—rational, emotional, and intuitive. The Father remembers that before he became blind he was as reasonable as the others and "never said anything extraordinary." The Father blames Ursula, the eldest daughter, for encouraging The Grandfather too much by answering all of his questions.

The Father, who only once is called Paul by The Grandfather. He is worried about his sickly wife and wishes that his eldest sister, a nun who never arrives, would appear and end his anxious waiting. He is worn out from his wife's childbirth and subsequent illness. At one point, he even blames the child for her difficulties, although his ever reasonable brother points out that it is not the little boy's fault. He becomes irritated by his father-in-law's questions and anxieties, sometimes suggesting to The Uncle that The Grandfather is insane. The Father represents the patriarchal voice of reason that has little time for emotions and intuitions. The fulfillment of The Grandfather's premonitions reflects how limited The Father's viewpoint really is.

The Uncle, who only once is called Oliver by The Grandfather. He appears to be an urban man, a bit uneasy in the rural environment and in the stressful circumstances caused by a very ill sister-in-law and her newborn baby, who never cries. He tries to continue the insipid conversation of the evening, but he probably would rather be somewhere other than this gloomy setting. He criticizes The Grandfather for always worrying too much and for not listening to reason, although he understands that the old man's age permits him to be a little strange. He prefers to believe the doctors and other voices of reason, perceiving that the blind old man has too much time to reflect. He shows how harsh reasonableness can be when he remarks that it is time for his brother to get rid of the stout, ailing Maid-Servant, for soon she will be a burden. In a play that provides speeches generally of one line, The Uncle occasionally speaks more than a single line, although never as many as The Grandfather. Maurice Maeterlinck believed that intuition must always be combined with reason, and The Uncle's reasonableness interacts with The Grandfather's intuitiveness.

The Three Daughters, **Gertrude**, **Geneviève**, and **Ursula**, who often act as a unit. For example, all go to check on the silent infant. The Daughters appear to be young and obedient to the men of the household. Their acute sensitivity cannot, at times, keep them from showing their anxiety through paleness and trembling. Ursula receives the most orders—to open and close windows, describe the weather, and tell the truth to The Grandfather when he is convinced that all the others lie to him.

The Sister of Charity, who serves offstage in the ailing mother's room. She is a silent presence whose caretaking permits the rest of the family to sit discussing together both their fears and mundane topics while they await the doctor. The Sister of Charity makes her only appearance at the end of the play, when her gestures announce that the mother has died. Her silence does not communicate to The Grandfather, who is abandoned in confusion while the others enter the dead woman's chamber.

The Maid-Servant, a feisty woman who insists that she did not leave open the door to the house, tramp too loudly on the steps, or try to barge into the sitting room. She refuses to accept blame for the sounds the nervous men hear, and she does not hesitate to defend herself before The Father. Her outspokenness suggests that the noises were made by The Intruder, because no rational explanation for them is provided by The Maid-Servant.

— *Carole J. Lambert*

INTRUDER IN THE DUST

Author: William Faulkner (1897-1962)
First published: 1948
Genre: Novel
Locale: Jefferson, Mississippi
Time: Early 1930's
Plot: Detective and mystery

Charles (Chick) Mallison, a sixteen-year-old boy. While hunting with two companions, he falls through the ice and is taken home by an old black man, Lucas Beauchamp, to dry out and have some food. All offers of payment are refused by Lucas, leaving Chick with an unpaid obligation on his conscience. When Lucas is accused of murder, Chick goes to the old man's assistance and helps to prove his innocence. He feels himself free of his debt until Lucas appears and insists on paying for services rendered.

Lucas Beauchamp, an old black man. When he takes Chick Mallison home after an accident, he proudly refuses payment for his hospitality and puts the boy in his debt. Later, when Lucas is falsely accused of murder, he is assisted by Chick, who believes he has evened the score until the old man comes to pay for services rendered. When Lucas' two dollars are accepted for "expenses," he demands a receipt.

Gavin Stevens, Chick Mallison's uncle and the lawyer for Lucas Beauchamp.

Aleck Sander, Chick Mallison's young black friend and companion in his efforts to prove Lucas Beauchamp's innocence.

Miss Habersham, an old woman of good family who assists Chick Mallison and Aleck Sander in their efforts on behalf of Lucas Beauchamp.

Hope Hampton, the sheriff.

Crawford Gowrie, the murderer, the proof of whose guilt saves the falsely accused Lucas Beauchamp from the violence of a mob.

THE INVENTION OF MOREL
(La invención de Morel)

Author: Adolfo Bioy Casares (1914-)
First published: 1940
Genre: Novel
Locale: An unidentified island
Time: The twentieth century
Plot: Science fiction

The narrator, an insecure, paranoid fugitive from Caracas, Venezuela. He is the only real character in the novel, which is his quasi-philosophical diary, written on an island that he believes to be part of the Ellice, or Lagoon, Islands in the Central Pacific. He does not mention his crime(s) but does admit to having been condemned to life imprisonment, a sentence that he repeatedly characterizes as unjust. He believed the island to be deserted until the day he began the diary, when a group of approximately a dozen people appeared in what appeared to be abandoned buildings. He is afraid that they will discover him or, worse, that they have come in search of him, but he quickly realizes that they have no interest in him; in fact, he seems to be invisible to them. He becomes infatuated with one of the intruders, a French woman named Faustine. Eventually, he falls in love with her, despite the fact that he has never spoken to her and that she has no consciousness of his existence. He discovers that the intruders are the projections of a machine invented by Morel, the leader of the group. The machine is able to record a period of time in the lives of this group and then project it *ad infinitum*. The only drawback is that the individuals die after the period recorded by the machine. The narrator's quest is to discover how to insert himself into the eternally recurring two-week period in which his beloved dwells. He discovers how to turn on the machines, and, after memorizing the sequence of events of the previously recorded two-week period, he records himself in various situations with Faustine. In these situations, he makes completely appropriate responses to conversations and events, despite the fact that no one knows he is there. His diary ends in ambiguity between feelings of good fortune and bleak anguish over the fact that he will never enter into the consciousness of Faustine.

Morel, a scientist and technologist, tall, bearded, dark-eyed, and slightly effeminate. He is the inventor of the machines that record and project in space and time, and that are capable of capturing feelings and emotions. He brings a group of people to the island to record a two-week period surreptitiously and achieve with them a kind of immortality in both body and soul. Morel loves Faustine and is rejected by her, a situation that is a source of hope for the narrator.

Faustine, a dark-haired, tanned Frenchwoman given to watching sunsets. She is the object of the narrator's quest and is also pursued by Morel. She remains aloof, in disdain of Morel and completely unaware of the narrator. All that is known about Faustine is found in the comments of the narrator's diary. The irony is that Faustine, the object of so much concern on the part of the narrator, never emerges from his obsessive observations to attain independence as a character.

The editor, who supplies footnotes to the text of the diary. The notes cast doubt or pass judgment on certain affirmations of the narrator, such as the possibly mistaken assertion that the island is part of the Ellice Islands. The editor also claims to have removed certain extraneous or impertinent material from the diary as published.

Dalmacio Ombrellieri (dahl-MAH-syoh ohm-bray-LYAY-ree), an Italian rug seller in Calcutta who told the narrator of the island and described it as a perfect refuge despite its reputation for being the center of a mysterious, fatal illness. Ombrellieri helps the narrator get to the island.

Alec,
Dora,
Irene,
Haynes, and
Stoever, some of the people who make up Morel's group. Bits of information are attributed to them by the narrator.

— *Thomas D. Spaccarelli*

THE INVESTIGATION
(Śledztwo)

Author: Stanisław Lem (1921-)
First published: 1959
Genre: Novel

Locale: London, England, and its environs
Time: The 1960's
Plot: Detective and mystery

Gregory, a Scotland Yard lieutenant detective. Tall and lean, with a broad face, square jaw, and dark complexion, he lives in a mysterious rooming house, where barely audible noises at night disturb his sleep. The first case of his career involves finding the perpetrator of a series of apparently related crimes: Several corpses have been removed from mortuaries and strangely mutilated. A well-trained detective, Gregory must find a human cause for these events, but his odd methods of investigation and his passion for truth gradually convince him that these are "natural" reanimations of corpses rather than crimes. He then faces a paradox: Although he believes that there has been no crime, he must still act as if there has been. He cooperates with Chief Inspector Sheppard in fabricating an explanation in which there is a human criminal agent.

Sheppard, a Scotland Yard chief inspector. An older man with rheumatism, he is an eccentric, keeping pictures of executed criminals on the walls of his study. Sheppard directs the strange case, reluctantly giving it to the inexperienced Gregory. He follows Gregory closely, evaluating his work and sometimes criticizing his methods, especially when Gregory makes Sciss his main suspect. He offers a number of hypothetical explanations in which rational agents of various kinds figure. Finally, he provides a workable but fictional solution for the "crimes" that Gregory is willing to support.

Harvey Sciss, a statistical genius. He is thin and dark, with gray eyes, puffy cheeks, and a receding chin. He seems interested in perverted sex and has a heart condition that threatens him with an early death. He develops the theory that the mysterious reanimations are a statistical anomaly with a probable natural cause. They only appear miraculous because they are so rare and because there are elements of a pattern in their occurrence. He repeatedly points out to the police that mass statistics, though they reveal large-scale phenomena, do not explain them.

Armour Black, a best-selling novelist. He is fifty years old, large, dark, and athletic. In an extended conversation with Gregory, Black explains necessary fictions. For the policeman's world to make sense, there must be crimes and criminals; Scotland Yard, he says, has no choice but to interpret these mysterious events as crimes to fit them into this perspective. He predicts that the police will be forced to create a story that explains these events as crimes if they do not discover actual criminal causes.

Dr. McCatt, an associate of Sciss. Like Sciss and Black, McCatt believes that the world is less thoroughly understood than most people believe. He shows Gregory an arcade game to illustrate the necessity of using the human mind to solve problems. Each game, including the detective game, has principles that determine how it is to be played, principles that make the world appear more comprehensible than it really is.

Williams, a suburban London constable. The only eyewitness to one of the events, he reports that he saw a corpse come to life and move about on its own. Because he panicked and ran into the path of a car and is near death when he gives his testimony, Gregory and Sheppard choose not to believe him.

— *Terry Heller*

THE INVINCIBLE
(Niezwyciężony i inne opowiadania)

Author: Stanisław Lem (1921-)
First published: 1964
Genre: Novel

Locale: The planet Regis III in the Lyre Constellation
Time: The distant future
Plot: Science fiction

Rohan, the navigator of the spaceship *Invincible*, which has been sent to explore the planet Regis III. Some time before, another spaceship, the *Condor*, landed on Regis III. Less than two days after arrival, the *Condor* sent a garbled message and then ceased transmitting. The *Invincible* has been sent to learn what happened. Rohan, the protagonist of the novel and the only substantially developed character, is an Everyman who rises to heroic stature. Like his fellow crew members, he is horrified by the discovery of the *Condor*, whose crew—all dead—apparently went mad. Like his comrades, he comes to fear and loathe the force that opposes them on Regis III: swarms of tiny crystalline forms that swoop and scatter like insects and form enormous pulsing clouds with great electromagnetic power. Rohan's triumph comes not in the victory-by-force of the conventional hero but in the recognition—even appreciation—of this "black rain" as an independent form of existence, however alien to humanity.

Horpach, the astrogator (commander) of the *Invincible*. A gray-haired veteran, tall and broad-shouldered, decisive, and seemingly unflappable—a virtual caricature of the steely military leader—Horpach is revealed to be human and vulnerable in a crucial meeting with Rohan.

Lauda, the chief biologist of the *Invincible*. Like Horpach, Lauda is a veteran, unusually old for spaceflight. It is he who first proposes that their enemy on Regis III is the product of eons of inorganic or "machine" evolution, a hypothesis that is confirmed by subsequent events.

— John Wilson

INVISIBLE CITIES
(Le città invisibili)

Author: Italo Calvino (1923-1985)
First published: 1972
Genre: Novel
Locale: Kublai Khan's palace and empire
Time: The thirteenth through the twentieth centuries
Plot: Magical Realism

Marco Polo, a Venetian traveler, now resident in the court of Kublai Khan. Marco is one of many emissaries reporting to Kublai, serving him by helping him to understand the subjects of his vast empire. At first, not knowing the Tartar language, Marco communicates with Kublai by means of gestures and pantomime, sometimes resorting to displaying objects to suggest narratives and descriptions. Once he has learned Tartar, Marco speaks, but, accustomed to the early emblematic communications, Kublai prefers to mix speech with pantomime. A sort of "mute commentary" is created when the two of them sit silently immobile, in private meditation, each imagining what the other is asking or saying. Regardless of idiom, Marco insists that all the cities he describes exist only as he has perceived them and that all communication is an act of creation. The emphasis placed on the perceiver applies equally to Kublai's act of listening. As Marco explains, "It is not the voice that commands the story: it is the ear." Marco's insistence on this theory has the effect of arousing suspicion in Kublai and creates the principal dramatic tension of the story.

Kublai Khan, the Tartar emperor. As a listener to Marco's fantastic descriptions, Kublai is impatient and becomes progressively more domineering. Kublai's interest in the stories is motivated by his determination to possess his empire one day, which he believes he cannot do without knowing and understanding it. He thus hopes for patterns in Marco's descriptions, so that, without knowing every city, he can comprehend the empire. At Marco's claim that none of this is possible, Kublai shows his impatience with varying degrees of intensity: by demanding that Marco describe the cities simply and directly; by physically attacking Marco and accusing him of representing only dreams and moods; and, in occasional desperate attempts, by himself describing cities and asking Marco whether they exist. When Kublai decides to have Marco cease traveling to play chess with him, to deduce cities from configurations of the chessboard, Marco overwhelms Kublai by pointing out the infinite possibilities and suggestions in the very woods of which the board is made. Such exchanges depict Kublai as desperate in his desire for unambiguous realities and as ultimately defeated by Marco's persistent uncertainties.

— Dennis C. Chowenhill

INVISIBLE MAN

Author: Ralph Ellison (1914-1994)
First published: 1952
Genre: Novel
Locale: The Deep South and New York City
Time: The 1940's and early 1950's
Plot: Social

The narrator, the canny, unnamed voice of the story. The narrator looks back on a life begun in the Deep South and brought north to the United States' premier African American city-within-a-city. In language full of richly oblique double meanings and nuances, he speaks of writing "confession," of ending his "residence underground," and of implying in his own specific case history that of an altogether wider, historic black America.

Dr. A. Herbert Bledsoe, the president of the college that the narrator attends. In one guise, Bledsoe plays the perfect Uncle Tom, fawning and grateful, who dances to the tune of Norton, a white philanthropist. In another, he acts as a despot, the college's presiding tyrant known to students as "Old Bucket-head." He expels the narrator in the name of maintaining the image of "Negro" behavior that Bledsoe believes expedient to put before white America.

Mr. Norton, a New England financier and college benefactor. As his name implies, Norton equates with "Northern." He is a figure of would-be liberal patronage who sees his destiny as helping African American students to become dutiful mechanics and agricultural workers. An encounter with the incestuous Truebloods, however, awakens his own dark longings for his dead daughter.

Brother Jack, the leader of the Brotherhood, a revolutionary group. The white, one-eyed leader of the group's central committee, he takes up the narrator as "the new Booker T. Washington." His is the language of "scientific terminology," "materialism," and other quasi-Marxist argot. He leads a witch-hunt against the narrator, only to have his glass eye pop out, showing him as truly a half-seeing, one-eyed Jack.

Tod Clifton, a Harlem activist. Initially, Clifton operates as a Brotherhood loyalist, a youth organizer pledged to fight

African American joblessness, the color line, and Black Nationalists. Fascinated by the Black Nationalist Ras's Caribbean "Africanness," however, he drops out. Tod is shot by a white police officer, and his death sparks a long-brewing Harlem riot.

Ras, the Destroyer, a militant, West Indian Rastafarian. Ras advocates, in the style of Marcus Garvey, a back-to-Africa nationalism. He derides the Brotherhood as a white-run fraud serviced by deluded black lackeys.

—*A. Robert Lee*

THE INVISIBLE MAN: A Grotesque Romance

Author: H. G. Wells (1866-1946)
First published: 1897
Genre: Novel
Locale: England
Time: Late nineteenth century
Plot: Science fiction

Griffin, the Invisible Man. He arrives at a village inn and takes a room. Wearing dark glasses and bushy side whiskers, and having a completely bandaged head, he causes much curiosity in the village. Later, it develops that these are a disguise for his invisibility. Getting into trouble over an unpaid bill, he escapes and begins to terrify the people with his mysterious thefts. Wounded, he flees to a former acquaintance's rooms. He reveals that, to get money for his experiments in invisibility, he robbed his father of money belonging to someone else; as a result his father committed suicide. Going thoroughly mad, he sends his former friend a note announcing that he plans to kill a man each day; his friend is to be the first victim. After a grotesque struggle, the Invisible Man is held by two men and struck with a spade by another man. As he is dying, his body slowly becomes visible.

Dr. Kemp, a physician. Griffin knew him when both were university students. To Kemp, Griffin reveals his story. Later, he says that he plans to use Kemp's rooms as a base for his reign of terror, and he threatens Kemp's life. Kemp goes to the police, with whose aid he finally succeeds in destroying Griffin.

Mr. Hall, the landlord of the Coach and Horses Inn, where Griffin takes a room.

Mrs. Hall, his wife. The Halls are the first to be puzzled by unexplainable activities on the part of their guest. Unintimidated, however, Mr. Hall swears out a warrant for Griffin's arrest after the lodger becomes abusive because of ill feeling over an unpaid bill. After a struggle, Griffin at last unmasks and escapes in the ensuing horror and confusion.

Colonel Ayde, chief of the Burdock police. Kemp goes to him with his information about Griffin. Ayde is wounded by his own revolver, which Griffin has snatched from his pocket.

Marvel, a tramp whom Griffin frightens into aiding him. Griffin's turning on Marvel is the occasion for some eerie scenes of pursuit.

Mr. Wicksteed, who is found murdered. A weird manhunt for Griffin follows.

INVITATION TO A BEHEADING
(Priglashenie na kazn')

Author: Vladimir Nabokov (1899-1977)
First published: 1935-1936
Genre: Novel
Locale: The capital of a fictional European country
Time: The future
Plot: Dystopian

Cincinnatus C., a prisoner awaiting execution. This thirty-year-old schoolteacher is a frail, hypersensitive intellectual who lives in an unspecified land resembling Bolshevik Russia where conformity is unquestionable. His "crime" is only vaguely described as "gnostical turpitude": He is out of step with society; he thinks forbidden thoughts. His main peculiarity is that he can see how the fact of death makes existence pointless. He sees everyone around him enjoying sensual pleasures, like animals, unaware that they are being fattened for slaughter. The novel is mainly the thoughts, fantasies, emotions, and recollections of a man awaiting execution. He both dreads and looks forward to his death. He believes that the soul is immortal and that life is like a bad dream, but he is afraid of awakening from it.

Pierre, the executioner. This fat, jolly, vigorous man is the same age as Cincinnatus and in many respects like a horrible alter ego. Like death itself, he is implacable and inescapable. He forces his friendship on the condemned man and drives him to distraction with his inane conversation and vulgar pranks. At first with the collusion of the jailers, he pretends to be a fellow prisoner so that he can insinuate himself into Cincinnatus' good graces. He is a living embodiment of the protagonist's idea that death is a silly, harmless affair and may actually be a pleasant experience. Eventually, Pierre performs the beheading, but it is described in such a way that it is left ambiguous whether it actually occurred or was only something like waking from a bad dream.

Rodion (ROH-dih-on), a turnkey, a fat, comical figure who, like Pierre, affects a great concern for the condemned man's comfort and peace of mind. He cannot comprehend the horror and loathing that Cincinnatus is experiencing, and he continually admonishes his prisoner to behave better toward others and to enjoy the comforts being provided.

Rodrig Ivanovich (ROD-rihg ee-VAH-noh-vihch), the director of the prison. He is a pompous functionary who wears a toupee and a frock coat. He is very proud of his authority and is concerned about the good name of his institution. Like the others, he thinks that the prisoner should be enjoying his experience.

Emmie, the director's daughter, a cute, frolicsome twelve-year-old nymphet, a prototype of the author's famous Lolita. She is continually slipping into Cincinnatus' cell to flirt with him. She promises to help him escape if he will marry her, but eventually she proves to be part of the conspiracy to play heartless psychological jokes on him.

Marthe, Cincinnatus' faithless wife. She is young, sensual, and phenomenally promiscuous. In fact, she has sexual intercourse with both Rodion and Rodrig on visiting days, as if to torment her husband and show him how indifferent she is to his situation. Her visits make him feel more destitute than ever.

Cecilia C., a middle-aged midwife who claims to be the prisoner's mother. Cincinnatus was reared in an orphanage; he does not know who his father was and is barely acquainted with his mother. He has been so deceived and frustrated by his captors that he no longer trusts anyone. Cecilia, like all the others, is concerned only with her own affairs and has little empathy with her son. She visits him merely out of a sense of duty and because she enjoys playing the role of bereaved mother. She is another aspect of the swinish humanity Cincinnatus hopes to escape through his death.

Roman Vissarionovich (vih-sah-rih-OH-noh-vihch), the condemned man's attorney. A lean, sepulchral individual with a harelip, he is continually visiting the prisoner but is of no assistance whatsoever. He is merely one more of the insensitive functionaries pressing Cincinnatus toward his inevitable execution and imploring him to behave as if their insane world were the epitome of sanity and good order.

— Bill Delaney

IOLA LEROY: Or, Shadows Uplifted

Author: Frances Ellen Watkins Harper (1825-1911)
First published: 1892
Genre: Novel
Locale: North Carolina, Mississippi, Georgia, and several northern states
Time: The last months of the Civil War through Reconstruction
Plot: Social morality

Iola Leroy, a mulatto who refuses to pass into white society. She chooses instead to devote her life to "racial uplift" (advancement of black people) along with her black family members. Iola's father is Eugene Leroy, a white Creole and owner of an estate on the Mississippi River. Her mother is Marie Leroy, a former slave of Eugene whom he sends north to be educated, marries, and brings back to his home as mistress of the plantation. When Iola returns from a northern school, she discovers that her father has died suddenly of yellow fever, that her sister Gracie is near death, and that she and her mother have been reduced to the status of slaves. Only her brother, Harry, who also was sent north, escapes this fate. Near the close of the Civil War, Iola is rescued from slavery by Union soldiers and becomes a nurse at a field hospital. After the war, Iola and her uncle, Robert Johnson, search for lost family members. Through a series of coincidences, they are all reunited—Harry, Iola, Marie, Robert, and Mrs. Johnson (Robert and Marie's mother). With the exception of Harry, they all move north. Iola's experiences with discrimination in the North heighten her awareness of the race problem. After marrying Frank Latimer, a black doctor from the South, Iola returns to North Carolina to continue the struggle for racial uplift.

Robert Johnson, Iola's uncle and male counterpart in the novel. Robert emerges as a leader in the opening chapter, when, as one of the few literate slaves on the plantation, he provides information about the progress of the war. Robert joins the Union army and becomes a lieutenant in a "colored" company; he refused to enlist as a white man. After the war, Robert finds his mother and takes her and the rest of his family north. Serving throughout the novel as the family patriarch, Robert later sells his property, returns to North Carolina, and purchases a large plantation, which he converts into a community of homesteads for freed slaves.

Dr. Gresham, a white New England physician for the Union army. His admiration for Iola's energy and devotion as a nurse turns to love, and he proposes marriage with the condition that she not reveal her race. Iola rejects the proposal. When he encounters her again after the war, he accepts Iola's final rejection of him lovingly and with respect for her fortitude.

Dr. Frank Latimer, a black doctor from the South who meets Iola and her family in the North. Dr. Latimer, like Iola, is offered a life of ease; his paternal grandmother offers him a comfortable position if he will consent to pass for white. He refuses, giving many of the same reasons Iola gives to Dr. Gresham when she rejects his proposal. Thus, Frank Latimer proves to be the perfect match for Iola because they share similar convictions. They marry and work together for racial uplift in the South.

Tom Anderson, a heroic former slave. Tom is among the first liberated slaves to join the Union army. He appeals to the post commander for Iola's release. Although he is not literate, as Robert is, he is well aware of the events unfolding around him and is eager to serve the cause of freedom. Tom dies as honorably as he lived, saving a boat filled with Union soldiers from a Confederate attack by exposing himself to enemy fire.

Aunt Linda, at first a cook on the Johnson plantation, then, after the war, a matriarchal leader of the black community. She furthers the idea of community among the newly freed, chastising those who sell their votes and drink to excess. Her entrepreneurship allows her to purchase property. As a successful woman, she introduces feminist ideals among her acquaintances.

— Shirley W. Logan

IOLANTHE: Or, The Peer and the Peri

Author: W. S. Gilbert (1836-1911)
First published: 1882
Genre: Drama

Locale: England
Time: The nineteenth century
Plot: Satire

The Lord Chancellor, the husband of the supposedly dead Iolanthe. Highly susceptible to feminine charm, he hates to give away his lovely wards in Chancery in marriage. He is sometimes jocular, sometimes severe, and quite jealous of Strephon, who he does not know is his son. The return of Iolanthe keeps him from marrying Phyllis.

Iolanthe (i-oh-LAN-thee), a loving, gentle-hearted fairy, condemned to banishment instead of death by the kindness of the Queen of the Fairies. She has violated the fairy law by marrying a mortal. After her release by the Queen, she risks death a second time to save the happiness of her son.

Strephon (STREH-fon), an Arcadian shepherd, the son of the Chancellor and Iolanthe. He is a fairy down to the waist but human and material in the legs; therefore, he can accomplish none of the fairy tricks such as going through a keyhole or becoming completely invisible. He loves Phyllis, but in his anger at her jealousy, he takes revenge by going into Parliament and thwarting the will of the lords.

Phyllis, a beautiful shepherdess loved by the House of Peers to a man, as well as by the Lord Chancellor and Strephon. Finding Strephon kissing a beautiful girl who apparently is seventeen years old (Iolanthe), she refuses to believe the girl is his mother. Finally, she becomes convinced that he is truthful, and she consents to marry him.

The Queen of the Fairies, a noble-hearted monarch in whom severity and mercy struggle for mastery. She forgives Iolanthe, but angered at the Peers, she sends Strephon into Parliament to destroy their privileges. When Iolanthe reveals herself to the Chancellor, the Queen sentences her to death, but she again relents on finding that all the other fairies have fallen in love with mortals. She is captivated by the manly charms of Private Willis but controls her passion until the fairy constitution is changed to make it a mortal crime not to marry a mortal.

Private Willis, a philosophical sentry who is willing to inconvenience himself to save a female in distress.

The Earl of Mountararat (mount-AY-ruh-rat) and
Earl Tolloler, suitors of Phyllis.

ION
(Iōn)

Author: Euripides (c. 485-406 B.C.E.)
First performed: c. 411 B.C.E.
Genre: Drama

Locale: The temple of Apollo at Delphi
Time: Antiquity
Plot: Tragicomedy

Ion (I-on), the son of Apollo and Creusa, a princess of Athens. At his birth he was, by Apollo's command, hidden in a cave. Unknown to Creusa, Hermes carried the infant from the cave to Delphi. There, he was nurtured in the temple. As keeper of the temple, he leads a happy life, marred only by his ignorance of his origin. At the beginning of the play, Creusa and Xuthus, to whom she has been given in marriage because of his military aid to Athens, come to the temple to seek Apollo's aid because they are childless. Ion and Creusa meet outside the temple, and an immediate sympathy is born between them: Creusa is childless and Ion lacks knowledge of his background. Creusa tells him her own story, alleging it to be that of another woman on whose behalf she wants to question Apollo. Ion, in his sheltered innocence, is shocked that Apollo could have behaved as he did to Creusa and tries to make excuses for him. This is the first contact of Ion's cloistered virtue with worldliness; it is continued through the play, and he quickly acquires self-confidence and strength of will. Apollo gives Ion to Xuthus as his own son and the two, as father and son, leave to celebrate this gift of the god. Creusa, thinking that an alien will come to rule Athens, plots to kill Ion. He learns of her attempts and leads the Delphians to stone her, but she takes refuge at the altar of Apollo. A priestess of Apollo appears with the cradle in which she found Ion, and Creusa recognizes it. Ion suspects a trick to save her life but, after she describes certain tokens left in the cradle, he acknowledges that she is his mother. Athena appears to assure Ion that Apollo is his father (though the fact is to be kept from Xuthus), that he will rule Athens, and that his four sons will sire the tribes that will dwell on the coasts and on the isles of the Aegean Sea.

Creusa (kree-EW-suh), the daughter of Erechtheus, king of Athens. Seduced by Apollo and forced to abandon her child to die, as she believes, she is introduced as a tragic character. In her first interview with Ion, she is able for the most part to keep her sorrow and feeling of rebellion without bounds, but she ends by criticizing Apollo for compelling her to abandon his child. She also reveals that she has not married Xuthus by choice, so that when Ion is revealed as his son, she, out of fear that foreigners will rule Athens, plans to kill Ion. The dynastic theme is important in this play, and Creusa's national loyalty is the major aspect of it. Her belief that Apollo has given Xuthus a son while she will have no other makes the loss of her own son and the treachery of Apollo seemingly more intolerable and emphasizes her role as a tragic figure. When the true facts are revealed, she accepts her triumph, her house is saved, and the stigma of childlessness is removed without any of the moral questionings about the actions of the gods that bother Ion.

Xuthus (ZEW-thuhs), Creusa's husband. He consults the oracle and is told that the first man he meets on leaving the temple will be his son. Meeting Ion, he is so overjoyed that he does not worry over the identity of the mother or the problems of accepting a foreigner as heir to the throne of Athens.

The Chorus of Creusa's Attendants, who mirror the point of view of Creusa entirely. It is their function to amplify her feeling and lend support to what she represents in the play.

An old man, an aged slave to Creusa. He represents the pride of the house he has served; he is devoted but foolish and irresponsible. His questioning of Creusa leads to her account of her relations with Apollo. He suggests and attempts to carry out the poisoning of Ion.

The priestess of Apollo, who reveals, at the god's direction, the cradle she has kept hidden.

Athena (uh-THEE-nuh), the goddess of wisdom. She appears as *dea ex machina* sent by Apollo to assure Ion that the god is his father.

Hermes (HUR-meez), the messenger of the gods, who speaks the prologue. He is not directly concerned in the action, except that he had taken Ion to the shrine at Delphi at Apollo's request. His tone is not emotional or dramatic.

IPHIGENIA IN AULIS
(Iphigeneia ē en Aulidi)

Author: Euripides (c. 485-406 B.C.E.)
First performed: c. 405 B.C.E.
Genre: Drama
Locale: Aulis, on the western coast of Euboea
Time: The beginning of the Trojan War
Plot: Tragedy

Iphigenia (IHF-uh-jih-NI-uh), the older daughter of King Agamemnon. The Greek prophet Calchas has revealed that Iphigenia must be sacrificed to the goddess Artemis to secure a favorable wind for the Greek ships becalmed on their way to conquer Troy. Agamemnon has summoned his daughter to Aulis, where the ships have been delayed, under pretext that she is to be married to Achilles. She appears as a very young and delicate girl, completely devoted to her father. She greets him with affection and gaiety, but the scene is pathetic and filled with tragic irony. When she reappears, she has learned that she is to be sacrificed, and she pleads with her father for her life. Her appeal is entirely in terms of pity and love, for at this point she sees the sacrifice as entirely a matter between her and her father. Agamemnon replies that he does not serve his personal desires but Greece and that Iphigenia must be sacrificed for the good of the Greek cause. He leaves and Achilles enters. Unaware at first of the use of his name to bring Iphigenia to Aulis, he has since learned of the truth and he has promised Clytemnestra, Iphigenia's mother, to defend the girl; he appears to keep the promise. Iphigenia intervenes, however, for she has resolved to die. She is now the arbiter of the fate of Greece, and she will give her life to obey the will of the gods and to punish the barbarians who took Helen away. With a plea to her mother not to hate Agamemnon or to mourn her death, she leaves to go willingly to her sacrifice. She is the only person in the play who is blind to the weakness of Agamemnon; to her he is a great man, sacrificing her for the sake of Greece.

Agamemnon (a-guh-MEHM-non), the commander in chief of the Greek army. He is an ambitious politician but unsure of his own motives and in some respects a coward. At the beginning of the play, he writes a second letter to Iphigenia telling her not to come to Aulis, but his message is intercepted by Menelaus, the husband of Helen and brother of Agamemnon. In the interview between the two brothers, Agamemnon's true character is revealed: He is ambitious to control the Greek forces and, though he sincerely loves his daughter, he agrees to sacrifice her of his own free will. It is clear that he will do so, for a refusal now may mean opposing the whole army. He lies to Iphigenia and Clytemnestra when they appear. After they have learned the truth, he argues that the sacrifice is necessary for the good of Greece.

Clytemnestra (kli-tuhm-NEHS-truh), a commanding and efficient woman who treats her weak husband Agamemnon with scant respect. Refusing to return home, as he suggests, she discovers through a servant his true intention of sacrificing his daughter. By appealing to Achilles' injured pride, she elicits his promise to defend Iphigenia, but she agrees first to appeal to Agamemnon herself. Her speech to her husband is a strong one containing reproach for his past and threats for the future. To Iphigenia's last request that she should not hate her husband, Clytemnestra replies that he acted by guile and in a manner unworthy of a son of Atreus and that for his deeds "he must needs run a fearful course."

Achilles (uh-KIH-leez), the noble Greek warrior whose name is used, without his knowledge, to bring Iphigenia, who expects to become his bride, to Aulis. He comes to speak with Agamemnon and is greeted warmly by Clytemnestra. His amazement causes them to realize the deceit that has been practiced upon them. He is angry at the indignity such usage brings to his name and he promises Clytemnestra, who plays on the insult to his pride, that he will protect Iphigenia. He is self-centered, for he reveals that had his permission been sought he would not have refused it for the sake of Greece. After the appeal to Agamemnon has failed, he reappears; the army is clamoring for the sacrifice and his opposition to it has almost cost him his life. He is true to his promise. Even after Iphigenia's decision to accept her sacrifice, he offers to wait at the altar to defend her if she should change her mind.

Menelaus (meh-neh-LAY-uhs), the husband of ravished Helen and brother of Agamemnon. Eager for the sacrifice of Iphigenia, he intercepts Agamemnon's second letter. Although his interpretation of Agamemnon's motives is prejudiced, it corrects and completes Agamemnon's own. When he is sure that Agamemnon will carry out the sacrifice, he insincerely protests affection and pity; he says he has changed his mind and will not demand the sacrifice.

An old man, a servant of Agamemnon. He sets out with the second message for Iphigenia but is intercepted. Later, he reveals Agamemnon's plan to Clytemnestra and Achilles.

The Chorus of women of Chalcis, who have come to Aulis to see the Greek ships and warriors. Their description of the Greek fleet and army emphasizes the importance of the war to follow.

IPHIGENIA IN TAURIS
(Iphigeneia ē en Taurois)

Author: Euripides (c. 485-406 B.C.E.)
First performed: c. 414 B.C.E.
Genre: Drama

Locale: Tauris, in the present-day Crimea
Time: Several years after the Trojan War
Plot: Melodrama

Iphigenia (IHF-uh-jih-NI-uh), the daughter of King Agamemnon, sister of Orestes and Electra, and a priestess of Artemis in Tauris. According to her opening monologue, Artemis took pity on her just as she was about to be sacrificed at Aulis, snatched her away from the priest's knife, and left a deer in her place. Transported to the land of the barbarian Taurians, she became the priestess of Artemis; it is her duty to preside over the sacrificial murder of all strangers captured by the Taurians. She dislikes both her duties and the country, and her longing for Greece is one of the major themes of the play. After she has spoken the opening monologue, a herdsman brings news that two Greeks have been captured and that Iphigenia must make preparations for their sacrifice. They are Orestes, the brother Iphigenia believes dead, and his friend Pylades. After much questioning in which each is careful not to reveal his identity, brother and sister recognize each other. Orestes, seeking release from the Furies for the murder of his mother, has been ordered to bring the statue of Artemis and Tauris to Attica. Iphigenia devises a plan for escape and Thoas, the king of Tauris, accepts it: She will take Orestes, unfit for sacrifice because of his crime of matricide, and the statue, defiled by his presence, to be cleansed in the sea. The plan succeeds until a storm prevents the Greek ship from leaving the harbor. Just as Thoas is about to send soldiers to kill the Greeks, the goddess Athena appears, orders Thoas to desist from his pursuit, and instructs Iphigenia to establish a new temple to Artemis in Attica. Iphigenia will be its priestess. The characterization of Iphigenia is effective but does not reach great depths; her bitterness against those who would have sacrificed her at Aulis is easily overcome by her longing for Greece and her dislike of the barbarian sacrifices.

Orestes (oh-REHS-teez), the brother of Iphigenia. He arrives at Tauris to steal the statue of Artemis and thus gain release from the pursuit of the Furies. Their pursuit drives him to fits of temporary madness, and during one of these he is captured by the Taurians. When Iphigenia offers, before the recognition scene, to save one of the men if he will deliver a letter to Argos for her, Orestes insists that Pylades be saved. After the recognition, he follows Iphigenia's plan of escape and Athena promises that he will be released from the Furies.

Pylades (PIHL-uh-deez), the faithful friend of Orestes and husband of Electra, sister of Iphigenia and Orestes. He is the apostle of common sense, in sharp contrast to Orestes' restlessness. He saves Orestes from despair over the difficulty of his task when they arrive at Tauris, and he fights to defend his companion when they are attacked by the Taurians. He offers to die with Orestes rather than save himself by delivering Iphigenia's letter; he still has hope that Apollo will save them.

Thoas (THOH-uhs), the king of Tauris. A foil to Greek cleverness, he is the simple-minded barbarian. Iphigenia has no difficulty in deceiving him, for he is convinced that Iphigenia hates all things Greek. He is consistently courteous and kind, and rather too gentle and pious to be the ruler of a people whose barbarity is so strongly emphasized.

Athena (uh-THEE-nuh), the goddess of wisdom. At the end of the play, she orders Thoas to give up his pursuit of the Greeks and to send the Chorus home. She has already asked Poseidon to still the waves. She also instructs Iphigenia in the construction of a new temple to Artemis.

The Chorus of temple maidens, exiles from Greece who long to return home. They agree to aid in Iphigenia's escape by not revealing the plan to deceive Thoas. Athena instructs Thoas to send them back to Greece.

A herdsman, who brings news of the capture of Orestes and Pylades and tells the story of Orestes' madness.

IRONWEED

Author: William Kennedy (1928-   )
First published: 1983
Genre: Novel

Locale: Albany, New York
Time: October and November, 1938
Plot: Regional

Francis Phelan, a baseball player during the 1900's, a part-time gravedigger, and a longtime vagrant as the story begins. Francis is fifty-eight years old, almost toothless, and dressed in tatters when he returns to Albany in 1938. Albany is his birthplace, and he has been in self-imposed exile for twenty-two years, after accidentally dropping and killing his infant son, Gerald. While in Albany, Francis is visited by ghosts from his past as he exorcises his guilt for his wasted years.

Helen Archer, Francis' constant companion on this pilgrimage. Helen is a proud woman who relishes her past as she accompanies Francis on this journey. Nostalgically recalling her Vassar education and singing extempore at the Gilded Cage saloon, Helen remains a devout Catholic and a loyal soulmate to Francis as he relives his past. With a tumor growing within her stomach, Helen yearns for the torch-singing career she abandoned and a normal life with Francis.

Rudy the Kraut, Francis' fellow bum and drinking companion. He is described as slightly crazy and perhaps is, convinced as he is that he has cancer. A harmless, simple man, he becomes a victim of a brick clenched in the hand of a marauding legionnaire.

Old Rosskam, a ragman. Rosskam is seventy-one years old and is proud of his sexual prowess. It is on Rosskam's swing through Francis' old neighborhood that Francis recalls his earlier years with his parents and with Katrina Daugherty.

Oscar Reo, a bartender at the Gilded Cage. Oscar is an old drinking friend of Francis and a former singer on the radio. He is a compassionate part of Francis' past and encourages Helen to sing at the lounge and relive her earlier glories as a torch singer.

The Reverend Chester, a Methodist clergyman who operates the Albany mission. A massive man with wild white hair and an aversion to alcohol of any kind, he provides a warm haven for Francis, Little Red, and Helen at the mission, supplying Francis with new socks and the job with Rosskam.

Pee Wee Packer, the manager of the mission for the Reverend Chester. Pee Wee is a bald, fat man who has found contentment running the mission. After his wife left him penniless and poisoned his dog, he became a bum. He now gives free haircuts at the mission. There is a sanctimonious air about him, especially when he drives Little Red away from the mission for appearing drunk.

Sandra, a victim of the cold and the streets. She appears momentarily in the story as a lifeless figure sprawled on the street. In need of alcohol, she remains battered by the weather until Francis, Helen, and Rudy attempt to bring her into the mission before she freezes. She is later found dead, her body partly mutilated by dogs.

Anne Phelan, Francis' wife. She was abandoned in 1916 by Francis after he accidentally dropped their infant son, Gerald. She has aged in the twenty-two years since Francis left, but she harbors no animosity toward Francis and welcomes him for the turkey dinner he has provided. Along with Francis' children, Billy and Margaret (Meg), and grandchild, Danny Quinn, Anne thankfully invites Francis to retake his place within the Phelan family.

Jack, a friend of Helen and Francis. Jack owns an apartment where Helen and Francis stay for part of Halloween evening. Jack provides Helen and Francis with wine and helps Francis freshen up before he has them leave.

Clara, Jack's companion. She is a contrary woman, besieged by diarrhea when Francis and Helen visit and thus more antagonistic. Although she appreciates Francis' attention, she apparently develops hostility toward Helen because she could be a source of distraction for Jack.

Kathryn Phelan,
Michael Phelan, and
Gerald Phelan, Francis' mother, father, and infant son, respectively. All three appear not as people but as either Francis' direct remembrances or as presences aware of Francis when he visits them at the graveyard.

Katrina Daugherty, Francis' first love, who appears as a ghost. She was the Phelans' neighbor when Francis was growing up. At the age of seventeen, Francis rescued her from scandal when he carried her naked, catatonic form back into the house one July morning in 1897. From that initial encounter, they formed a bond that lasted until she was killed in a fire in 1912. She returns in 1938 to remind Francis of his loss.

Aldo Campione, a horse thief who also appears as a ghost. Francis unsuccessfully attempted to save him from police bullets as he fled from Albany in 1901.

Howard Allen, another ghost, a scab trolley conductor killed by Francis in 1901. Twenty-nine years old, Allen took a strikebreaking job as a trolley conductor, and Francis' killing of him engendered Francis' earlier flight from Albany.

— *Hardin Aasand*

THE ISLAND OF CRIMEA
(Ostrov Krym)

Author: Vassily Aksyonov (1932-)
First published: 1981
Genre: Novel
Locale: The Crimea, Moscow and surrounding countryside, and Paris
Time: Late 1970's
Plot: Alternative history

Andrei Arsenievich Luchnikov (ahr-seh-NIH-yeh-vihch LEWCH-nih-kov), the handsome, Oxford-educated, red-mustached, forty-five-year-old editor of the Russian-language publication *Courier*. He supports Crimea's unification with the Soviet Union. After exploring Russia alone, he returns to Crimea, lives with Tanya, and wins the Crimea Rally. His victory propels his political cause, so that Crimea requests unification with Russia.

Arseny Nicholaevich Luchnikov (ahr-SEH-nee nih-koh-LA-yeh-vihch), Andrei's father, nearly eighty years old, a tall, thin scholar who wears jeans and a leather jacket. A former colonel in the White Army during the civil war, he is killed surrendering to occupying Soviet forces.

Anton Andreevich Luchnikov (ahn-DREH-yeh-vihch), Andrei's tall, blond, nineteen-year-old, politically opposed son. He escapes Crimea with his wife and child during the Soviet occupation.

Marlen "Marlusha" Mikhailovich Kuzenkov (mih-KHA-ih-loh-vihch KEW-zehn-kov), Andrei's friend, the head of the Soviet Foreign Division of the Central Committee and an expert on Crimea. He commits suicide after he realizes that the election will produce reunification.

Dmitri (DMIH-tree), or **Dim Shebeko** (dihm sheh-BEH-koh), Kuzenkov's twenty-five-year-old son, a saxophonist with a jazz-rock band who helps Andrei go underground in Russia.

Tatyana (Tanya) Lunina (tah-TYAH-nah LEW-nih-nah), a thirty-eight-year-old Soviet athlete and KGB agent who is Andrei's mistress. She disappears with Fred Baxter after the Crimea Rally.

Gleb, also called **Hub** and **Champ**, Tanya's husband of fifteen years. A former Soviet decathlon champion, he joins the Soviet Olympic team when Tanya joins the KGB.

Colonel Sergeev (sehr-GEH-yehv), a KGB official in the Foreign Division. He pursues Crimean leaders for arrest and execution during the Soviet occupation.

Colonel Vadim Vostokov (vah-DIHM voh-STOH-kov), a member of the Crimean security forces; he fails to arrest Andrei and friends during the Soviet occupation.

Vitaly Semyonovich Gangut (vih-TAH-lee sehm-YOH-noh-vihch GANG-gewt), a friend of Andrei. He is a famous

Soviet film director who, Andrei believes, stages the Soviet occupation of Crimea for a motion picture.

Oleg Stepanov (OH-lehg steh-PAH-nov), a brutal, anti-Semitic, ambitious Communist who secures the release of Andrei and Gangut from Moscow police.

Krystyna (Christie) Sage, a young, brown-haired American connected with Amnesty International. After the Crimea Rally, she lives with Andrei until the Russian occupation of Crimea, when she is burned to death.

Pamela, a young American with luxurious, sun-bleached hair who marries Anton and bears his son, just before their escape with Ben-Ivan during the Soviet occupation.

Petya Sabashnikov (sah-BAH-shnih-kov), Andrei's blond, balding school classmate, now the Crimean representative to UNESCO. He meets Andrei in Paris.

Volodya (voh-LOH-dyah), **Count Novosiltsev** (noh-voh-SIHL-tsehv), also called **Kamchatka** and **Novo-Sila**, Andrei's forty-six-year-old school classmate, killed driving in the Crimea Rally.

Temosha Meshkov (teh-MOH-shah meh-SHKOV), Andrei's school classmate, now the owner of Arabat Oil Company. He encourages Volodya to enter the auto rally.

"Colonel" Sasha Chernok (CHEHR-nok), Andrei's school classmate, now the commander of Crimea's North Buffer Zone. He is killed when his helicopter is destroyed during the Soviet occupation.

Yury Ignatyev-Ignatyev (YEW-ree ih-GNAH-tyehv-ih-GNAH-tyehv), a Crimean school friend of Andrei who violently opposes Andrei's politics and wants to assassinate him despite a homosexual love for him.

Fyodor Borisovich Buturlin (FYOH-dohr boh-RIH-soh-vihch bew-TEWR-lihn), sometimes called Freddy or Fedya, the fifty-year-old Oxford-educated deputy minister of information in Crimea. He urges Andrei to modify his pro-Soviet stand.

J. P. "Jack" Halloway, sometimes called **Octopus**, a big American associated with Paramount Pictures. He proposes a blockbuster motion picture about the reunification of Russia and Crimea, for which, Andrei thinks, the Russian occupation is staged.

Vitold Yakovlevich (VIH-tohld yah-KOHV-leh-vihch), **General von Witte**, a Crimean general in exile in Paris who tells Andrei Stalin's attitude toward Crimea's reunification with Russia.

Benjamin (Ben-Ivan) Ivanov (ee-VAH-nov), born in 1952, a member of Dim Shebeko's underground jazz group. He helps Anton, Pamela, and their child escape from Crimea to Turkey.

Fred Baxter, a New York banker friend who proposes to Arseny that he lead Crimea into a pro-American policy. He is enraptured by Tanya, who he thinks is a prostitute in Crimea.

Billy Hunt, a South African professional driver in the Crimea Rally.

Conde Portago (KOHN-deh pohr-TAH-goh), the lean and haughty, aloof, thirty-six-year-old Spanish driver in the Crimea Rally.

Mustafa or **Masta Fa**, a young, Crimean-born Tatar racing driver, an associate of Anton and a member of the Yaki party. He participates in the Crimea Rally.

Hua, Arseny's Taiwanese majordomo for forty years.

Vladko Mercator, the owner of a shop in Simferopol, Crimea. He is befriended by Kuzenkov, who wonders why the man should want Soviet unification.

Lidochka Nesselrode (LIH-doch-kah), a young Crimean beauty set on marrying Andrei; she finds herself snubbed.

Sasha Brook, an associate editor of the *Courier*.

Father Leonid, Andrei's priest, who buries Krystyna.

— *Richard D. McGhee*

ISLANDS IN THE STREAM

Author: Ernest Hemingway (1899-1961)
First published: 1970
Genre: Novel
Locale: Bimini, Cuba
Time: Late 1930's and early 1940's
Plot: Adventure

Thomas Hudson, a successful American painter living in Bimini, a big man, well proportioned and tanned, with hair faded and streaked by the sun. He is twice divorced and still in love with his first wife. Generally a casual person, Hudson is intense and private in his love for his sons, yet he allows them space to be themselves and to grow. Some might see him as a permissive parent, allowing this as the normal behavior of a divorced parent who sees his children sporadically throughout a year, but Hudson appears to grant these same measures to all whom he encounters. His is a quiet strength, almost passive; he lives by remembering rather than by pursuing. Long ago, he ceased to worry about things in general, replacing guilt with work. In fact, his work has replaced almost everything but his three sons. Although he cares little for success, he has been successful in almost every way except marriage. Women are welcomed in his life, but he is always glad to see them go, and most important, he has learned how not to get married. He is resolved to be selfish only for his painting and ruthless only for his work; once sorely lacking discipline, he now enjoys life within the limits of a self-imposed discipline and hard work.

Tom, the only child of Hudson's first marriage. He has attended an expensive school and has good, "expensive" manners; he is free and easy, quiet and polite. Long and dark, he has his father's neck and shoulders, as well as long swimmer's legs and big feet. His is a rather Indian face that looks almost tragic when in deep thought or simple repose yet light and full of life at other times. He remembers when he and his parents lived in Paris and often recounts certain episodes to his brothers, who urge him to do so. He is thoughtful, serious, and dutiful; he lives long enough to die in action during World War II.

Tom's mother, a beautiful woman, a film actress, and the first and only woman that Hudson admits to having "really" loved. He still loves her and she him. She visits him in Cuba during the war.

David, the middle son, the older child of Hudson's second marriage. His hair has both the color and the texture of an otter's fur, and he is tanned to a dark gold. Not the athletic type, he has a solid but slight build. To his father, David resembles "the sort of animal that has a sound and humorous life by itself." He is smart and affectionate, has a good sense of justice, and is generally good company. A "Cartesian doubter," David is a zealous arguer. He takes teasing well but sometimes teases roughly, yet he is not mean. Like his brothers, he is well mannered and respectful with adults.

Andrew (Andy), the youngest of Hudson's sons, also born in the second marriage; he is fair and "built like a pocket battleship." Of the three, he is the one most like his father, physically a copy of Hudson, reduced in scale and widened and shortened. Although he is a quiet child, he has a dark side and is "mean" by certain standards. Andy is a precocious child and an excellent, determined athlete with a cold, mature professionalism. His "wickedness" transmuted into a teasing gaiety, Andy displays a sense of a badness growing inside him. Hudson knows, understands, and respects this dark side of his youngest son.

Roger Davis, a writer, Hudson's friend, also living on the island. He is casual and solid in appearance. Though prone to bouts of depression, Roger is not opposed to the "pleasure" of a good fight. Hudson determines that Roger "runs with a pretty seedy lot." Roger's poor luck with women rivals Hudson's. He enjoys the three boys, and they him. With advice and moral support from Hudson, Roger embarks on a renaissance in his writing career.

Honest Lil, a Havana prostitute, an aging, fading beauty. Her dark face is still lovely; she has a beautiful smile and wonderful dark eyes, but a gross fatness has overtaken her body and her lovely dark hair is maintained with dye purchased with money from Hudson. She has been around a while, and all the men have been in love with her at one time or another. She urges Hudson to tell happy stories while they sit and reminisce. As he relates episodes about Paris when Tom was an infant and about an event in Hong Kong, she comments and complains about unhappiness and lack of love. Her observations and questions are insightful and sensitive and allow a view of Hudson that considers and, to some extent, evaluates his past. Hudson is talking to her when his first former wife enters the bar in Havana.

Henry Wood, one of the crew on Hudson's boat, a big, handsome man with good manners. Henry is as delicate on the boat as he is rough with a machine gun.

Willie, another of the crew on Hudson's boat, a dark boy with short, clipped, curly black hair and an artificial left eye with a slightly droopy lid. He is mature and sensitive. On land, he watches after Henry; on the boat, Hudson. Dependable, strong, and constant, Willie takes command when Hudson is wounded but reports to him in such a way as to seem always under the direction of the dying man.

— *Cynthia Jane Whitney*

ISRAEL POTTER: His Fifty Years of Exile

Author: Herman Melville (1819-1891)
First published: 1855
Genre: Novel
Locale: Vermont, Massachusetts, England, France, and the Atlantic Ocean
Time: 1774-1826
Plot: Historical

Israel Potter, a wanderer. Brought up in the rugged New England hills and immersed in their austere virtues, he quarrels with his father and leaves home. He wanders about, the innocent American, for fifty years, and in the course of his many adventures, he becomes the spokesman through whom the author satirizes various ideas and institutions, among them war, patriotism, and so-called civilized behavior.

King George III, whom Israel Potter meets in London. The mad king, realizing that Israel is an American, is ineffectually kind to him after the many snubs Israel has received because of his nationality.

Squire Woodcock, a secret friend of America who befriends Israel Potter and sends him on a mission to Benjamin Franklin.

Benjamin Franklin, who gives Israel Potter lessons in proper behavior based on maxims from *Poor Richard's Almanack*. The lessons, carefully learned, are quickly forgotten.

John Paul Jones, with whom Israel Potter engages in piracy and in the sea fight between the *Bon Homme Richard* and the *Serapis*.

The earl of Selkirk, whose home is plundered by the pirate companions of Israel Potter and John Paul Jones. After receiving a large sum of money from another exploit, the two captains buy back and return the earl's possessions.

Ethan Allen, whom Israel Potter tries unsuccessfully to help escape from England.

THE ISSA VALLEY
(Dolina Issy)

Author: Czesław Miłosz (1911-   )
First published: 1955
Genre: Novel
Locale: Poland
Time: 1904-1918
Plot: Bildungsroman

Thomas Dilbin, the shy, young narrator of his boyhood in a remote corner of Lithuania. An only child left by his parents to live with his grandparents, Thomas is lonely and consoles himself with the wonders of sky, river, and forest that surround him. His environment is a wondrous one in which pagan traditions still hold prominence under a Catholic surface. He soon realizes, however, that his heritage as a member of a Polish landowning family has set him apart from his own countrymen, zealous for the liberation of Lithuania and increasingly hostile to those whom they consider their oppressors.

Casimir Surkont, Thomas' grandfather. Although a member of the Polish gentry, he eschews the traditional occupations of hunting and riding to concentrate on his garden. A lover of peace, he is criticized frequently for his tolerance of and sympathies toward the Lithuanians.

Baltazar, a forester on lands belonging to the Surkonts. Tortured by his senseless killing of a soldier and driven by a black, incoherent dissatisfaction that is destroying his life, Baltazar turns to drink. His manic outbursts and sporadic violence cause others to believe that he is possessed by a devil. In a final act of demonic rage, he destroys all that he has worked for and forces his neighbors to hunt him down.

Romuald Bukowski (ROHM-wahld bew-KOW-skee), Thomas' idol and initiator into the world of the forest. Thomas tries to imitate him in all ways, and his failure to duplicate the hunter's prowess is the first great tragedy of his young life. At first, Romuald is flattered by the attention paid to him by Thomas' Aunt Helen, but he eventually marries his peasant housekeeper, Barbarka, against the wishes of his mother, who is horrified at this affront to the family name and position.

Magdalena, the housekeeper and mistress of the parish priest. After the priest banishes her to a faraway village, she commits suicide. Her body is returned home for burial. Convinced that her spirit is haunting the rectory and its surroundings, the villagers try to exorcise her ghost. When that fails, they resort to a horrible pagan ritual. Magdalena's life and fate haunt Thomas' youthful dreams.

Grandmother Dilbin, Thomas' paternal grandmother. Forced to take shelter with the Surkonts, she dies far from home, blaming her weaknesses for the faults of her sons. Her happy and secure childhood in Riga left her ill-prepared for the harsh realities of life.

Grandmother Misia Surkont, Thomas' maternal grandmother. The exact opposite of Grandmother Dilbin, she cares little for the problems of others. Although her surname is Lithuanian and her family has lived in the region for generations, she delights in patronizing those who are not Polish.

Joseph, Thomas' tutor. A fervent Lithuanian nationalist, he is obliged to teach Thomas to read and write in Polish.

Dominic Malinowski (mah-lih-NOWS-kee), a peasant boy who was Thomas' first hero. A life of subjugation as a tenant on the estates of others has marked him with bitterness and humiliation. To overcome his feelings of inferiority, he tries to dominate others.

Father Monkiewicz (MAHN-keh-vihch), a high-strung parish priest. The son of peasants, he is the spiritual leader of both the landless and the gentry. Although convinced of the reality of the restlessness of Magdalena's spirit, he refuses to grant permission to desecrate her body.

Father Peiksva (PAYKS-vah), another parish priest and Magdalena's lover, known for his golden oratory. He allows her body to be buried in sacred ground and later quietly leaves the parish.

Barbarka, Romuald's beautiful, peasant housekeeper. Her one goal is to become the true mistress of his home, and she succeeds.

Aunt Helen, Thomas' aunt and beekeeper of the estate. She constantly schemes to better her financial situation. She is enamored of Romuald until driven away by Barbarka.

Tekla Dilbin, Thomas' mother. Long absent from her family home, she is only a beautiful legend to Thomas. Although he is overcome by gratitude at her unexpected return, he still harbors feelings of resentment at her abandonment of him.

Masuilis (mah-sew-IH-lihs), the wizard of the village, whose incantations and spells are equal, in the villagers' eyes, to any medicine or spiritual advice.

Lucas, Helen's ludicrous husband.

— Charlene E. Suscavage

THE ITALIAN: Or, The Confessional of the Black Penitents

Author: Ann Radcliffe (1764-1823)
First published: 1797
Genre: Novel

Locale: Italy
Time: 1758
Plot: Gothic

Vincentio di Vivaldi (veen-chehn-TEE-oh dee vee-VAHL-dee), a young nobleman of Naples. Impressed by the grace and voice of the veiled Ellena di Rosalba, he is warned by a ghostly stranger not to seek her identity. Disregarding the warning, he succeeds in learning the young woman's name, falls in love with her, and determines to marry her in spite of his parents' strenuous objections because of her apparent lowly station. His mother's plottings to prevent the alliance set up a train of sinister events through which the young man passes before he is finally united with his beloved.

Ellena di Rosalba (roh-SAHL-bah), a young woman of supposed humble origin who is loved by Vincentio di Vivaldi. Before her wedding, she is abducted and carried off to a strange religious establishment, the first of a series of violent and sinister adventures that end in the revelation of her identity as the daughter of Sister Olivia and the dead Count di Bruno, and at last in her marriage to Vincentio.

The marchesa di Vivaldi, the haughty and vindictive mother of Vincentio di Vivaldi. She plots, with the monk Schedoni, to do away with Ellena di Rosalba in order to prevent her marriage to her son.

The marchese di Vivaldi, Vincentio di Vivaldi's father.

Schedoni (shay-DOH-nee), the marchesa di Vivaldi's confessor and her chief ally in the plot to murder Ellena di Rosalba. He is finally revealed as the second count di Bruno, murderer of the first count, his brother, and as a fugitive in the disguise of a monk.

Sister Olivia, a nun who befriends Ellena di Rosalba and is finally revealed as the former countess di Bruno, Ellena's mother.

Signora Bianchi (bee-AHN-kee), Ellena di Rosalba's aunt and guardian, later revealed as the sister of Sister Olivia.

Paulo Mendrico (pah-EW-loh mehn-DREE-koh), Vincentio di Vivaldi's faithful servant.

Bonorma, Vincentio di Vivaldi's friend.

Beatrice, the servant of Signora Bianchi and Ellena di Rosalba.

Ansaldo di Rovalli, the grand penitentiary.

Brother Jeronimo, a monk.

Spalatro (spah-LAH-troh), an assassin in the pay of Schedoni.

Father Nicola (nee-KOH-lah), a monk who turns against the sinister Schedoni and gathers evidence against him for the Inquisition.

THE ITCHING PARROT
(El periquillo sarniento)

Author: José Joaquín Fernández de Lizardi (1776-1827)
First published: 1816
Genre: Novel

Locale: Mexico
Time: The 1770's to the 1820's
Plot: Picaresque

Pedro Sarmiento (sahr-mee-EHN-toh), nicknamed **Periquillo** (peh-ree-KEE-yoh), meaning "The Itching Parrot," the young rogue protagonist of Spanish America's first novel. As the son of upper middle-class people of Mexico City, he seeks the easiest way of earning a living. A monk's life is too exhausting. He tries other professions: barber, physician, apothecary, beggar, and finally secretary to a colonel in Manila. Finally, a schoolmate, now a priest, turns him to a prosperous, honest life, resulting in Pedro's marriage and respectability.

Señor Sarmiento, Pedro's father, who wants Pedro to become a tradesman.

Señora Sarmiento, who, wanting her son to be a priest, dies of grief at his many vices.

Januario (hahn-eew-AHR-ree-oh), a schoolmate who makes a fool of Pedro for his attentions to Januario's cousin, with whom Januario himself is infatuated.

Don Antonio, a good man, unjustly jailed, who helps Pedro. Later, Pedro finds him destitute and aids him.

The Daughter of Don Antonio, who becomes the wife of the reformed Pedro.

A Scrivener, who arranges Pedro's release from jail so that he may serve as the scrivener's secretary.

IVANHOE

Author: Sir Walter Scott (1771-1832)
First published: 1819
Genre: Novel

Locale: England
Time: 1194
Plot: Romance

Cedric the Saxon, the rude, warlike master of Rotherwood, a small landholder during the reign of Richard I. Obstinately hoping for Saxon independence, he wishes his ward, Lady Rowena, to marry Athelstane of Coningsburgh, a descendant of the ancient Saxon kings, and he disinherits his son, Wilfred of Ivanhoe, for learning Norman customs. When Ivanhoe returns from the Crusades and falls wounded after winning the tournament at Ashby-de-la-Zouche, Cedric allows him to be cared for by strangers. Captured by Normans, Cedric is taken to Torquilstone Castle, but he escapes and helps the besiegers take the castle. In the end he becomes somewhat reconciled to the marriage of Ivanhoe and Rowena and with Norman rule under King Richard I.

Wilfred of Ivanhoe, the chivalrous, disowned hero, a Crusader. Returning home disguised as a pilgrim, he befriends a Jew, Isaac of York, and his daughter Rebecca on the way to the tournament at Ashby. After defeating his opponents in the tourney, he reveals his true identity and faints from loss of blood while accepting the prize from Rowena. Captured with the Jew, along with Cedric and his party, he is cared for by Rebecca at Torquilstone and is rescued by the disguised King Richard. He repays Rebecca's kindness by defending her when she is accused of witchcraft. After Athelstane relinquishes his claim to Rowena, Ivanhoe marries her and enjoys prosperity under Richard's rule.

Lady Rowena, Cedric's beautiful ward. At Rotherwood, she inquires of Ivanhoe's exploits from the disguised knight himself, becomes the tournament queen at his request, and learns his identity after he is declared victor. Seized by Norman knights, she is saved from the advances of a captor and the Torquilstone fire by the timely intervention of Richard, Cedric, and Robin Hood. Happy when Athelstane disclaims her, she weds Ivanhoe.

Isaac of York, an avaricious but kindly Jew. He supplies Ivanhoe with a horse and armor for the tournament and takes him off to be cared for after the knight has been wounded. Isaac is taken prisoner and about to be tortured for his gold when rescuers lay siege to the castle. He is set free but forced to pay a ransom. Learning of his daughter's abduction at the hands of haughty Sir Brian de Bois-Guilbert, he sends for Ivanhoe to rescue her. Sick of England, he and his daughter move to Spain.

Rebecca, the generous, lovely daughter of Isaac of York who returns Ivanhoe's payment for the horse and armor and nurses his wound. She is carried off by an enamoured Templar during the siege. Accused of witchcraft at Templar headquarters, she is rescued from burning by the exhausted Ivanhoe's defense.

Sir Brian de Bois-Guilbert (bree-AH[N] deh BWAH-gheel-BEHR), the fierce and passionate Templar who kidnaps Rebecca, deserts her because of Templar politics, and fights a fatal battle against her defender, Ivanhoe.

Richard the Lion-Hearted, an audacious, hardy king. Secretly returning to England, he saves Ivanhoe's life at the tournament and leads the siege of Torquilstone. After thwarting an ambush, he throws off his disguise of the "Black Sluggard" and claims his rightful throne.

Robin Hood (Locksley), the famed outlaw. He wins an archery contest, supports Richard during the siege of Torquilstone, and becomes a loyal subject of the restored king.

Athelstane of Coningsburgh, the sluggish Saxon knight who half-heartedly woos Rowena and loses fights with Richard and Bois-Guilbert.

Maurice de Bracy (moh-REES deh brah-SEE), an ambitious Norman who captures Rowena; however, he possesses too much honor to pursue his designs on her.

Reginald Front de Boeuf (ray-zhee-NAHL froh[n] deh behf), the savage Norman who seizes Isaac for his gold. He dies of a wound inflicted by Richard amid the flames of Torquilstone.

Prince John, Richard's haughty, unscrupulous brother, who has tried to usurp the throne with the aid of the Norman nobles.

Lucas de Beaumanoir (lew-KAH deh boh-mah-NWAHR), the bigoted, ascetic head of the Templars who presides over Rebecca's trial on a charge of witchcraft. His order is disbanded by Richard because of treasonous activities and plotting against the king and the realm.

Philip Malvoisin (fee-LEEP mal-vwah-ZAH[N]) and

Albert Malvoisin, Templars executed by King Richard for treason.

Waldemar Fitzurse (VAHL-deh-mahr FIHT-tsur-seh), Prince John's wily, aspiring follower, who is banished by Richard.

Aymer (AY-mehr), the comfort-loving prior of Jorvaulx, who is captured by Robin Hood and forced to pay a ransom.

Ulrica (ewl-REE-kah), the Saxon hag who burns Torquilstone in order to be revenged on the Normans.

Gurth (gewrt), Cedric's swineherd and Ivanhoe's loyal servant, who is given his freedom.

Wamba (VAHM-bah), Cedric's quick-witted jester; he helps Cedric escape Torquilstone by dressing him in a priest's robe.

Friar Tuck, Robin Hood's hefty, hearty follower, a hedge priest who treats Richard to a meal.

IVONA, PRINCESS OF BURGUNDIA
(Iwona, księżniczka Burgunda)

Author: Witold Gombrowicz (1904-1969)
First published: 1938
Genre: Drama
Locale: Burgundia
Time: Indeterminate
Plot: Absurdist

Ivona Hopit, an ugly and poor Burgundian peasant girl. Ivona is an insolently silent young woman who seldom responds to the words or actions of others. She refuses to bow to the court or to obey any of their commands. Her sluggishness and enigmatic simplicity elicit the interest of Prince Philip and inspire him to propose marriage. Her eyes are expressive, and on the rare occasions when she speaks, her words are few and often mystical. She is at various times arrogant, vulnerable, angry, or sad, and the prince and the royal court take pains to provoke or interpret her. Ultimately, they all feel threatened in some way and plot her murder. Ivona dies choking on a fish bone at a betrothal banquet in her honor.

Philip, the prince of Burgundia, a troubled and sensitive young man who is restless in his position as heir to the throne and reluctant to accept a conventional, political marriage. Ivona's simplicity attracts his interest: He believes that his richness entitles him to take on her misery, and he decides to make her his princess. He generally speaks honestly and guilelessly but is subject to sharp mood changes. He initially sees Ivona as a heroic challenge who will help him to realize his princely potential, but then he is amazed and intimidated when she grows to love him. He at first delights in the scandal his betrothal precipitates but later becomes touchy and paranoid about the laughter and gossip of the court ladies. He uses his power and the eerie power of Ivona's weakness and silence to taunt and manipulate his parents and the court. Prince Philip is capable of extremes of both vulnerability and cruelty, and at last he seduces Isobel and takes her as his fiancée, heartlessly abandoning Ivona and plotting to cut her throat.

Ignatius, the king of Burgundia, a hearty and good-humored man. He lacks patience and can erupt in sudden rage. Although he is furious at Prince Philip's determination to marry Ivona, the girl subtly reminds him of Queen Margaret and of a mysterious drowning in his guilty past. The reminiscence convinces him that he does not really know his wife. He determines to put Ivona at her ease with a casual chat but finally despairs at her unresponsiveness and flies into a rage that frightens her horribly. This fury leads to his successful plot to murder her at the betrothal banquet.

Margaret, the queen of Burgundia, a poetic soul who loves peace and nature and avoids conflict or scandal at any cost. In her disingenuous manner, she develops a maternal and nurturing attitude toward Ivona. Deep down, she is insecure and untrusting of everyone, including her lady-in-waiting, Isobel. Queen Margaret becomes convinced that the king has discovered her secret notebooks of original poetry. In desperation, she resolves to kill Ivona.

The Lord Chamberlain, King Ignatius' servant and confidant. The Lord Chamberlain is an obsequious and politically astute functionary with a furtive manner and an arrogant attitude. It is his inspiration that results in Ivona's murder by choking.

Isobel, Queen Margaret's lady-in-waiting. Isobel is a straightforward and dutiful servant in whom a proper deference is mixed with a realistic skepticism, especially during

Prince Philip's more juvenile moments. Isobel feels an immediate and singular pity for Ivona but later easily accepts the opportunity to replace her in the prince's affections.

Simon, a friend of Prince Philip. Simon is a rambunctious troublemaker who uncharitably speculates about Ivona's situation and makes rash judgments about her. He later serves as Prince Philip's adviser and henchman in plotting Ivona's murder.

Innocent, a poor young man who is in love with Ivona. Innocent is a fragile and wise, even tragic, figure who speaks honestly and simply. He knows his love for Ivona to be less than heroic: He sees her as a consolation prize for one who deserves no better. Innocent feels a true tenderness for Ivona, however, and pleads with Prince Philip on her behalf.

— *B. P. Mann*

THE IVORY SWING

Author: Janette Turner Hospital (1942-)
First published: 1982
Genre: Novel
Locale: Southern India; Ontario, Canada; and Boston
Time: The 1970's, with flashbacks to the 1960's
Plot: Social realism

Juliet, a housewife and mother. Young, bright, and attractive, she is filled with a zest for life at the same time that she is afraid to embrace it. Torn between the exciting memories of a carefree relationship in Boston with her former lover and the oppressive drudgery of life in India with her husband, Juliet doubts her own identity. She has a spirit of fire and verbally challenges the patriarchy of Trivandrum in Kerala State, but she appears incapable of acting on the values she claims. Even her academic work demonstrates that lack of fulfillment: She has abandoned a doctoral thesis and occasionally alludes to a book that someday she hopes to write.

David, a professor. Restrained but intense, he is introduced as a combination of Auguste Rodin's *The Thinker* and Saint John in the wilderness. His two main passions are for Juliet, his wife, and for Indian culture, so when she agrees to move to India with him for a year's sabbatical, he is ecstatic. When Yashoda, an Indian widow, approaches him for help, he is shocked by his physical attraction to her. Because he is absorbed in analyzing his own emotions, he fails to respond to her needs and later blames himself for her death.

Yashoda, a rich widow. Passionate and sensual, the young woman yearns for excitement, but the Indian caste system of which she is a member enforces that all widows remain private and withdrawn. In fact, though she resides on her wealthy kinsman's estate, she is sentenced to live alone in a forested area. That isolation, however, only serves to encourage her desire for adventure, because the lack of supervision allows her to violate caste laws: She wears flashy jewelry, entertains visitors, and swims in the nude. She possesses a mysterious beauty that overwhelms every man she meets, but fear of that beauty causes her female relatives to shave her head and the townsmen to murder her.

Annie, a free spirit. Motivated by whim and love affairs, she drops out of law school and travels around Asia. As Juliet's younger sister, Annie admires Juliet's stable marriage and her responsibility to her children; ironically, Juliet envies Annie's freedom and lack of restraint. When Annie arrives in India, her carefree lifestyle enchants Yashoda and encourages the young widow to pursue her own desires.

Prabhakaran (prahb-HAHK-ah-rahn), a peon. Only about twelve years old, he is a full-time laborer and bonded servant of Shivaraman Nair. He loves to fish and to play the flute. After he is hired as Juliet's houseboy, he and she develop a parent-child relationship, and Juliet grieves for him when he is murdered.

Shivaraman Nair (shee-vah-rah-MAHN NAH-eer), a wealthy landowner. As a male member of the upper caste, he enjoys numerous privileges that are denied to the majority of Indians. Because he is David and Juliet's landlord, he comes into frequent contact with them, and all three continually challenge Eastern against Western values.

Matthew Thomas, a Christian Indian. A wealthy, elderly man, he helps Juliet avoid a riot and also cares for her family after they are involved in a bus accident. A lonely widower, he turns to Yashoda for companionship, and they become lovers.

Prem, a student. Disturbed by the poverty among the majority of Indians, including his own large family, he seriously advocates Marxist beliefs. After hearing about Yashoda's death, however, he realizes that rich individuals also suffer injustices. One of Annie's numerous conquests, he is stunned when she leaves him to return to a man in Toronto.

— *Coleen Maddy*

J

J. B.: A Play in Verse

Author: Archibald MacLeish (1892-1982)
First published: 1958
Genre: Drama
Locale: A large American city
Time: Mid-twentieth century
Plot: Symbolism

J. B., the protagonist, a successful businessman who is, like Job in the Bible, "an upright man, one that feareth God and escheweth evil." Early in the play, at a Thanksgiving dinner with his loving wife and happy children, he gives thanks to God for their many blessings and says that he has never doubted that God is on his side. Disasters soon befall him: His eldest son, David, is killed by mistake while on Army maneuvers; a daughter, Mary, and another son, Jonathan, are struck down by a drunken driver; his youngest daughter, Rebecca, is raped and murdered; his only remaining child, Ruth, is killed in a bombing raid that levels the town and reduces J. B.'s vast fortune to nothing; his wife leaves him; and he is afflicted with painful sores. All the while, J. B. maintains that God is just, never punishing a person without reason. He takes no comfort from three visitors who offer Marxist, Freudian, and Christian consolations. Asserting to them his essential innocence and integrity, J. B. can find in his own soul nothing deserving of such suffering, yet he refuses to blame God, acknowledges divine omnipotence, and repents. He is visited by Nickles, who prophesies that all will be restored to him in time: wife, family, wealth, and health. Immediately, he notices that his sores have healed. His wife returns, and they make a new beginning in love.

Mr. Zuss, a large, florid, deep-voiced circus vendor with a bunch of balloons tied to his belt. He opens the play when he and his colleague Nickles happen on a sideshow stage under an enormous circus tent. Finding a pair of stage masks for God and Satan, they decide to stage the Job story then and there, looking down on the stage from an aerial platform. Zuss takes the mask of God and is somewhat startled at the biblical grandeur of the words that he utters through it.

Nickles, an elderly, gaunt, and sardonic circus vendor who wears a popcorn tray strapped to his shoulders. He takes the mask of Satan and bets Mr. Zuss that J. B. would lose faith and curse his God if his wealth and happiness were taken from him.

Zophar, a fat, red-raced, cigar-chomping priest who comes with Bildad and Eliphaz to comfort J. B. in his misery. He believes that all people are guilty and that the ability to feel guilt distinguishes people from animals. He cannot help J. B. find in himself a wickedness equal to the enormity of his suffering. Instead, he tells J. B. that his sin was being born human, for the heart of humanity is evil. J. B. calls his the cruelest comfort of all, because it makes God a party to the crimes that he punishes.

Eliphaz, a lean, dark, pipe-smoking man who wears an intern's jacket. He offers J. B. a Freudian analysis of his predicament. Disagreeing with Zophar, he considers guilt a psychophenomenal illusion and the soul an empty, tiny bladder washed this way or that by wind or wave.

Bildad, a squat, thick man who offers J. B. a Marxist explanation of his condition. He considers guilt an accident of sociology, like being born in the wrong century or the wrong class. History operates without regard for one insignificant individual, so a person must expect fortune and misfortune to cancel each other out, he thinks.

Sarah, J. B.'s wife, whose faith in God and love for her husband are weakened by adversity. Blaming God for the deaths of their children, she loses patience with J. B. and leaves him at his lowest point. She cannot stay away, however, and eventually comes back to make a new life with him.

Two messengers, who bear the bad tidings. Dressed as soldiers, they tell J. B. of David's death in the Army. Dressed as reporters, they bring the news of that fatal automobile accident. Dressed as policemen, they describe the rape and murder of Rebecca. Dressed as civil defense officers, they report the bombing in which J. B.'s vast wealth and only remaining child are lost.

— John L. McLean

JACK OF NEWBERY

Author: Thomas Deloney (1543?-1600)
First published: 1597
Genre: Novel
Locale: England
Time: The reign of Henry VIII (1509-1547)
Plot: Picaresque

Jack Winchcomb, known as **Jack of Newbery**, a young weaver. Wild as a young man, he settles down, marries his master's widow, and becomes a solid businessman. He patriotically raises a company of men to fight for Henry VIII against the Scots. He is offered knighthood by that sovereign but declines, saying that he knows his place in the world.

Jack's master's widow, who trusts the young man, putting her business and then herself in his hands. She dies, leaving Jack all of her business and wealth.

Jack's second wife, a younger woman. She is a foolish gossip who makes difficulties for her husband.

Henry VIII, the king of England. Pleased with Jack for being a witty and loyal subject, he offers the weaver knighthood.

Queen Catherine, Henry VIII's queen. She thanks Jack for bringing a company of men to help fight against the Scots.

Cardinal Wolsey, Henry VIII's chancellor. He has Jack and other weavers thrown into prison when they attempt to petition the king.

The Duke of Somerset, who intervenes on Jack's behalf when he is in prison and convinces Cardinal Wolsey that the weavers mean no harm.

Benedick, an Italian merchant. He has an amorous adventure in Newbery and is punished by being put to bed with a pig.

Joan, a pretty girl employed by Jack. She disdains Benedick when he makes advances to her.

Sir George Rigley, a knight who seduces one of Jack's female employees. He is tricked by Jack into marrying the girl. Angry at first, he comes to see the justice of Jack's action and becomes the weaver's friend.

JACK SHEPPARD

Author: William Harrison Ainsworth (1805-1882)
First published: 1839
Genre: Novel
Locale: London, England, and its environs
Time: 1702-1724
Plot: Picaresque

Jack Sheppard, a housebreaker and popular jailbreaker. After many crimes and several escapes, he is seized at his mother's funeral and executed at Tyburn.

Joan Sheppard, his mother, widow of Tom Sheppard (executed for theft). Insane from worry over Jack's dissolute, criminal life, she is put in Bedlam hospital; recovering her senses, she is released. Jonathan Wild reveals that she is Sir Rowland's long-lost sister Constance, stolen in childhood by a gypsy. She kills herself rather than marry Wild after his brutal murder of Sir Rowland.

Owen Wood, a London carpenter who becomes wealthy.

Mrs. Wood, his wife, murdered by Blueskin.

Winifred, their daughter, who marries Thames Darrell.

Sir Rowland Trenchard, an aristocrat plotting to inherit his sister Alvira's estates. He is arrested for treason on Wild's accusation; after his release from prison, he is murdered by Wild.

Thames Darrell, Sir Rowland's nephew and foster son of Owen Wood. He is rescued from drowning as a baby. In youth, he is arrested as a thief and sent to sea after escaping prison with Sheppard. Thrown overboard, he is rescued and taken to France, where he serves under Philip of Orleans. Returning to England to visit the Woods, he learns through letters that he is of noble birth, and he inherits the Trenchard estates.

Darrell, a fugitive drowned while being pursued by a mob led by Sir Rowland; in reality, he is the French marquis de Chatillon and father of Thames Darrell.

Lady Alvira, mother of Thames and widow of Chatillon; later wed by force to her cousin, Sir Cecil Trafford.

Jonathan Wild, a thief-taker. Pretending to aid Sir Rowland's plot, he counterplots to get the Trenchard fortune for himself. Eventually found out, he dies on the same gallows to which he had sent Tom and Jack Sheppard.

Blueskin, the devoted henchman of Jack Sheppard.

Van Galgebrok, a Dutch seaman and conjurer who attempts to drown Thames.

Sir Montacute Trenchard, grandfather of Thames.

JACOB'S ROOM

Author: Virginia Woolf (1882-1941)
First published: 1922
Genre: Novel
Locale: Primarily England
Time: The 1890's through World War I
Plot: Impressionism

Jacob Flanders, the main character, educated at the University of Cambridge to a position of privilege, from which he pronounces stereotypical observations on the classics, women, and the world. After he becomes a casualty of the war, his mother must sort out his belongings in his room at the end of the novel.

Captain Barfoot, whose decorous evening calls on Mrs. Flanders over the years are marked by the local Scarborough gossips as proprietary.

Betty Flanders, Jacob's mother, who helplessly tries to imagine and participate in the independent life of her son (mainly through letters) while remaining tied by economic necessity to Scarborough. At the end, she confronts Jacob's room, to which he will never return.

Dick Bonamy, Jacob's friend, a fellow inheritor of male privilege. Bonamy attends Mrs. Flanders as she faces her deceased son's room and his effects at the end of the novel.

Timmy Durrant, a school friend of Jacob with whom he

sails for a holiday around the Scilly Isles.

Clara Durrant, Timmy's sister, who is in love with Jacob but must remain expectantly silent in deference to custom.

Sandra Wentworth Williams, a beautiful married woman whom Jacob meets while touring Greece. He falls in love with her, half-encouraged by her.

Florinda, a woman with whom Jacob has his first affair, which he breaks off when he sees her in the street on someone else's arm.

Fanny Elmer, an artist's model who reads *Tom Jones* for Jacob's sake. Her heart is broken by Jacob's indifference.

— W. A. Johnsen

JACQUES THE FATALIST AND HIS MASTER
(Jacques le fataliste et son maître)

Author: Denis Diderot (1713-1784)
First published: 1796
Genre: Novel
Locale: Rural France
Time: Mid-eighteenth century
Plot: Picaresque

The narrator, who presents the conversations that compose the book. No description of him is provided. He frequently interrupts his characters to interject comments about the relationship between fiction and reality. He emphasizes the "made-up" character of his work, often changing from one story to another before the first has been completed. He combines authentic references to contemporary events with unexplained and bizarre jumps in chronology. He sometimes mentions other novelists, including Miguel de Cervantes and Samuel Richardson.

Jacques, a valet. He is the hero of the book, and his adventures are its chief subject. His exact age is not given, but he often discusses his military service, which took place twenty years before his dialogues with the Master; therefore, he is probably in his forties. He walks with a limp because one of his knees was shattered while he was in the army. He is attractive to women, as his many adventures indicate. A nonstop talker, he is subject to frequent distractions in his storytelling. He often repeats fatalistic slogans but arrives at no fixed conclusion about the effect on one's actions of accepting fatalism. Fatalism does, however, influence his attitude, which is one of resigned cheerfulness. His tales usually have as their theme the near escapes from disaster occasioned by his frequent romances.

The Master, the principal conversation partner of Jacques. He is not described physically, but, like Jacques, he has seen military service. He is probably somewhat older than his valet. His principal role is to prod Jacques to untangle his stories. Without much success, he endeavors to get Jacques to complete one story before beginning another. He is generally in a good mood but is occasionally grumpy. He is heavily dependent on Jacques.

The innkeeper's wife, the teller of one of the main stories in the book. She is no longer "in the first flush of youth" but is still attractive. She is tall and full-figured, with beautiful hands. Like Jacques, she is a nonstop talker. Beneath a sometimes gruff exterior, she is unusually kindhearted. Her story is about the complicated relations, mixing love and jealousy, between the Marquis des Arcis and Madame de la Pommeraye. She recounts her story with considerable polish. How someone in her circumstances has come to possess intimate knowledge of the nobility is not explained.

— Bill Delaney

JAILBIRD

Author: Kurt Vonnegut, Jr. (1922-   )
First published: 1979
Genre: Novel
Locale: Cleveland, Ohio; Massachusetts; New York City; and rural Georgia
Time: 1977
Plot: Antistory

Walter F. Starbuck, born **Walter Stankiewicz**, a RAMJAC corporation executive and convict. The life of this sixty-four-year-old, "jockey-sized" man has been marked by unwitting mishaps. The son of poor immigrants, he is educated at Harvard by tycoon Alexander Hamilton McCone. He becomes a minor government official, marries Ruth, whom he meets in World War II, and has a son who hates him. In hearings before a committee headed by Richard Nixon, he innocently names his friend Leland Clewes as a Communist, sending him to jail. He is reviled by friends, and Ruth dies. Nixon, now president, invites him to take a White House job, and he is later jailed as a Watergate conspirator. After he is released, he meets Mary Kathleen O'Looney and becomes an officer of the RAMJAC Corporation. He hides the news of her death and suppresses her will, for which he is again jailed. Throughout, he appears as a bumbling innocent who suffers while schemers prosper.

Mary Kathleen O'Looney, a sixty-four-year-old bag lady who is actually **Mrs. Jack Graham** and owner of the conglomerate RAMJAC Corporation. She is tiny and thin, and she wears layers of filthy clothes and enormous purple tennis shoes in which she stores her most vital belongings. She hides her identity to escape those who would cut off her hands for the fingerprints that confirm her orders. While Walter was at Harvard, she was his lover, and they shared leftist political views. She plans to return wealth to the people by leaving her RAMJAC conglomerate to the nation.

Leland Clewes, a salesman for advertising matchbooks and calendars and a former diplomat. Once a tall and handsome Yale man, in his sixties he has lost his hair and wears shabby clothes but remains patiently philosophical. Clewes married Sarah Wyatt, Starbuck's first love, and was a successful diplomat until named as a Communist by Starbuck and sent to jail. After that, he struggles until made a RAMJAC vice president by Starbuck. He harbors no grudges against Starbuck, and his suffering has cemented his marriage.

Sarah Wyatt, Starbuck's first love and Clewes' wife. Also sixty-four years old, she is tall, slender, and sophisticated, with an indefatigable sense of humor. She first dates Starbuck when they are eighteen, and their conversations consist mainly of jokes. She becomes a part-time nurse after Clewes is sent to jail. She and Starbuck briefly resume their joking when he comes out of jail. Her loving marriage to Clewes contrasts with Starbuck's lonely widowhood.

Ruth Starbuck, Walter's wife, an interior decorator and former concentration camp inmate and translator. An Austrian, she is six years younger than Walter and five feet tall. When they meet after the war, she is diminutive, but she grows to 165 pounds before her death in 1974.

Alexander Hamilton McCone, a steel company heir, art collector, and philanthropist. A Harvard graduate, he becomes a shy, stammering recluse. He adopts Walter as his protégé and sends him to Harvard. McCone abandons Walter after discovering his leftist politics.

Dr. Robert Fender, a veterinarian, convict, and science-fiction writer. Tall and big-boned, resembling Charles Lindbergh, he was a farm boy of Scandinavian descent. As a lieutenant in the Army, he becomes the only American in the Korean War convicted of treason. As a life-term convict, he writes science-fiction stories that provide commentary on the plot under the pen names Kilgore Trout and Francis X. Barlow.

— Peter J. Reed

THE JAILING OF CECELIA CAPTURE

Author: Janet Campbell Hale (1947-)
First published: 1985
Genre: Novel
Locale: Tacoma, Washington; San Francisco, California; and a reservation in Idaho
Time: Latter half of the twentieth century
Plot: Bildungsroman

Cecelia Capture, the protagonist, through whose point of view the story is told. Born into a dysfunctional family on a reservation in Idaho, Cecelia early demonstrates academic talent but becomes a high-school dropout and an unmarried teenage mother on welfare. At the age of twenty-one, she enters the City College of San Francisco, where she meets Nathan Welles, whom she later marries. While subsequently attending law school, she is arrested on a charge of driving while intoxicated and is also held for welfare fraud, an old charge. During her weekend incarceration, she reminisces about her past; after her trial, she is freed. A meeting with her husband results in a decision to divorce, thereby freeing her to start a new life.

Nathan Welles, Cecelia's husband, a graduate student and eventually an English professor at a community college in Spokane. Emotionally detached, socially conscious, and extremely rigid, he proves to be an ineffective parent for Corey, Cecelia's son by Bud Donahue, and Nicole, his and Cecelia's daughter.

Will Capture, Cecelia's father, a talented athlete and scholar who wins a football scholarship to Notre Dame. He hurts his knee and flunks out. After serving in World War II, he becomes a prizefighter, then spends a year in prison for almost killing a bigoted white man. His alcoholism and domestic problems lead him to sell part of his land.

Mary Theresa Capture, Cecelia's mother, a bitter woman of Native American and Irish ancestry. She undermines Cecelia's self-confidence by criticizing her daughter's Native American ancestors and perceives herself as a prisoner in her marriage. She leaves Will at one point but returns when he sells his land to buy the family a house.

Bud Donahue, the father of Cecelia's son. He dies in Vietnam and represents, for Cecelia, an ideal against which she measures other men. Only after she visits his grave and bids him good-bye at the end of the novel is she free of her past.

Jim, a former merchant marine from Georgia and one of Cecelia's lovers. When she refuses his offer of marriage, despite the security it would provide, he resentfully resorts to racist remarks to salvage his ego.

Thomas Running Horse, a Sioux whom Cecelia meets at a bar in Roseberg, Oregon, after she has left her family in Spokane to attend law school in San Francisco. Although he represents, for her, the epitome of the Native American male and understands and shares her past, he fails to fulfill her needs because of his sexism, illustrated in a denigrating remark about "educated squaws."

Miss Wade, a welfare caseworker who embodies the failure of institutions to serve their clients. When Cecelia proposes to take academic courses at the City College of San Francisco, Miss Wade ridicules her plans, disparages her intelligence, and suggests that she take vocational courses more appropriate for welfare recipients.

— Thomas L. Erskine

JAKE'S THING

Author: Kingsley Amis (1922-1995)
First published: 1978
Genre: Novel
Locale: London and Oxford, England
Time: Mid-1970's
Plot: Comic realism

Jake Richardson, a reader in early Mediterranean history and a fellow of Comyns College, Oxford. He is fifty-nine years old, thickset, and round-faced; he wears glasses and has a history of being attractive to women. In the past, he had a reputation for being inclined to take advantage of his attractiveness. He is very intelligent, somewhat conservative in his ways, and very quick to react, if usually only in his mind, to the silliness of modern life. He has been ill and seemingly as a result has lost his desire for sex, causing some problems with his wife. He reluctantly takes medical advice, first from his family doctor, then from a psychologist specializing in sexual difficulties, and eventually from a sexual therapist working in group encounters. Too clever, too skeptical, and too impatient to fall in with the chic jargon of contemporary sexual theories, Jake, possessed of a scathing capacity to know fools when he sees them, finally tells off everyone. In the process, his wife leaves him, realizing, as he does, that his problem is not medical or even psychological, but simply a matter of no longer caring to try to please women for the pleasures of sex, which have no hold over him anymore.

Brenda Richardson, Jake's third wife, only forty-seven years old but running somewhat to fat, which they both suspect may have something to do with Jake's disinterest in sex. Still a handsome woman, with lovely green eyes, Brenda is willing to help Jake. She goes on a diet, takes instruction with Jake, and attends therapy with him. Sex is, however, not their only problem, and Brenda, who is a sensible, caring woman, finally recognizes that Jake really does not care all that much for or about her anymore, and she is capable of doing something about it.

Alcestis Mabbott, a middle-aged, fat friend of Brenda, whom Jake despises. A social worker, she is something of a constant adversary of Jake, on most occasions. Brenda calls her "Allie," but Jake's nickname is consistent with his feelings about her: He calls her "Smudger." She proves in the end to be not quite as silly as he thinks.

Geoffrey Mabbott, Alcestis' third husband, a buyer for a chutney firm, although he despises all things Indian. Jake finds him a constant joke; he is a bad dresser and often patently stupid. He attends Jake's therapy group, supposedly to do something about his lack of self-esteem, but admits that he has no hope because he has no interest in anything.

Dr. Proinsias Rosenberg, a Harley Street psychologist, a tiny man with a thick Dublin accent, the son of a German father and an Irish mother. He is short-haired, clean-shaven, brown-eyed, and quite incapable of convincing Jake that he has any chance of solving Jake's problem.

Ed, the "facilitator," an American sex therapist in his late thirties. Heavyset and with a Latin complexion, he is inclined to bring out the worst in Jake with his flashy, seemingly uncaring handling of his patients and his offhanded indifference to their feelings.

Kelly Gambeson, a patient in the therapy group, an attractive young woman with red hair and a good figure, just the type that would have attracted Jake in former times. She is attracted to Jake and tries to seduce him. Not sure of whether she has mental difficulties (she claims not) or is instead fooling, he is shy of her, to a point that is almost disastrous.

Eve Greenstreet, a college secretary, now married but formerly an occasional lover of Jake. Handsome, with a gift for mocking foolish people, she seems to be interested in helping Jake but proves to be more interested in displaying her own cleverness.

Damon Lancewood, an English don at the college. In his sixties, he is white-haired, with a military bearing and a long-time homosexual connection with a local businessman. A sensible confidant for Jake, he listens well and gives Jake some sense of perspective.

— *Charles Pullen*

JALNA

Author: Mazo de la Roche (1879-1961)
First published: 1927
Genre: Novel
Locale: Canada
Time: The 1920's
Plot: Domestic realism

Grandma Whiteoak, the ninety-nine-year-old matriarch of the family. She tyrannizes her grandchildren, giving them physical blows to enforce her whims.

Renny Whiteoak, eldest of Grandma's grandchildren. A bachelor, he holds the family together and supervises their farms. While he has power and position, he does not delight in them. He falls in love with his sister-in-law, Alayne, Eden's wife.

Meg Whiteoak, Renny's sister. She is unmarried because she broke her engagement to Maurice Vaughan after he had fathered an illegitimate child. Many years later, she forgives and marries him.

Maurice Vaughan, Renny's friend and former fiancé of Meg. He is the father of the girl known as Pheasant. He eventually marries Meg.

Eden Whiteoak, Renny and Meg's half brother. He is a dreamer and poet. He marries Alayne Archer, a publisher's reader from New York. He accuses her of nagging when she tries to encourage his writing. He falls in love with Pheasant and deserts Alayne.

Alayne Archer, Eden's wife. She is a gentle, helpful woman. She falls in love with Renny but returns to New York to prevent scandal and divorce.

Piers Whiteoak, half brother to Renny and Meg. He is a plodding man who marries Pheasant. He resents Alayne because the family accepts her more readily than they do his wife.

Finch Whiteoak, half brother to Renny and Meg. He is an unambitious young man who finally is encouraged to be a musician by Alayne.

Wakefield Whiteoak, half brother to Renny and Meg. He is a badly spoiled eight-year-old.

Pheasant Vaughan, the illegitimate daughter of Maurice, and Piers' wife. She makes a play for Eden's attentions.

JANE EYRE

Author: Charlotte Brontë (1816-1855)
First published: 1847
Genre: Novel
Locale: Northern England
Time: 1800
Plot: Domestic realism

Jane Eyre, a plain child with a vivid imagination, intelligence, and great talent in art and music. Left an orphan in childhood, she is forced to live with her Aunt Reed, who was the sister-in-law of her father. At the Reed home, she is mistreated and spurned, and she is finally sent to a charity home for girls. Her education completed, she teaches at the school for several years and then takes a position as a private governess to the ward of Mr. Rochester. After a strange, tempestuous courtship, she and Mr. Rochester are to be married, but the revelation that his insane first wife still lives prevents the wedding. After each has suffered many hardships, Jane and Mr. Rochester are eventually married.

Edward Fairfax Rochester, a gentleman of thirty-five, the proud, sardonic, moody master of Thornfield. Before Jane Eyre's arrival to become a governess in his household, he visits Thornfield only occasionally. After he falls in love with Jane, much of his moroseness disappears. When they are separated because the presence of his insane wife becomes known, Mr. Rochester remains at Thornfield. His wife sets fire to the house, and Mr. Rochester loses his eyesight and the use of an arm during the conflagration, in which his wife dies. Summoned, she believes, by his call, Jane Eyre returns a short time later, and the two are married.

Adele Varens, the illegitimate daughter of Mr. Rochester and a French opera singer, his ward upon her mother's death. She is pale, small-featured, extremely feminine, and not especially talented.

Mrs. Fairfax, the elderly housekeeper at Thornfield. She is extremely kind to Jane and is delighted that she and Mr. Rochester are to be married.

Grace Poole, a stern woman with a hard, plain face, supposedly a seamstress at Thornfield but actually the keeper of mad Mrs. Rochester. Occasionally, she tipples too much and neglects her post.

Bertha Mason Rochester, Mr. Rochester's insane wife, kept in secret on an upper floor at Thornfield. She had lied and her family had lied when Mr. Rochester met her in Jamaica while traveling, for she was even then demented. During Jane's stay at Thornfield, Mrs. Rochester tries to burn her husband in bed. Finally, she burns the whole house and herself, and seriously injures her husband.

Mrs. Reed, an exact, clever, managing woman, the guardian of Jane Eyre. She hates her charge, however, misuses her, and locks her in dark rooms for punishment. At her death, she repents of her actions. Her children turn out badly.

Eliza Reed, her older daughter, a penurious, serious girl who eventually becomes a nun.

John Reed, the son, a wicked child who torments Jane Eyre and then blames her for his own bad deeds. He ends up as a drunk in London and dies in disgrace.

Georgiana Reed, the younger daughter, a pretty, spoiled child who later becomes very fat. She makes a poor marriage.

Bessie Leaven, Mrs. Reed's governess, pretty, capricious, hasty-tempered. Before Jane Eyre leaves the Reed house, Bessie has become fond of her.

Robert Leaven, Bessie's husband and Mrs. Reed's coachman.

Abbot, the Reed's bad-tempered maid.

Mr. Lloyd, an apothecary called in when Jane Eyre becomes sick and feverish after having been locked in a dark room. He suggests that she be sent off to school.

Mr. Brocklehurst, a strict clergyman and the master of Lowood School. He forces the girls to wear short, uncurled hair and plain wrappers, and he feeds them on a starvation diet.

Maria Temple, the supervisor of Lowood School, a pretty, kind woman who tries against tremendous odds to make her pupils' lot as easy and pleasant as possible. She is interested in Jane Eyre's talents and is responsible for her getting a teaching position later at Lowood.

Miss Smith,

Miss Scratcherd, and

Miss Miller, teachers at Lowood School.

Helen Burns, a clever thirteen-year-old pupil at Lowood School, constantly ridiculed and punished by her teachers because she is not neat and prompt. She dies during a fever epidemic.

Miss Gryce, a fat teacher at Lowood School and Jane Eyre's roommate when they both teach there.

Mary Ann Wilson, one of Jane Eyre's fellow students, a witty and original girl.

John and

Leah, the house servants at Thornfield Hall.

Sophie, the French maid.

Mrs. Eshton, a guest at a house party given by Mr. Rochester. Once a handsome woman, she still has a well-preserved style.

Mr. Eshton, her husband, a magistrate of the district.

Amy Eshton, their older daughter, rather small, naïve, and childlike in manner.

Louisa Eshton, the younger daughter, a taller and more elegant young woman.

Lady Lynn, another woman whose family is invited to the Thornfield house party; she is large, stout, haughty-looking, and richly dressed.

Mrs. Dent, another guest, less showy than the others, with a slight figure and a pale, gentle face.

Colonel Dent, her husband, a soldierly gentleman.

The Dowager Lady Ingram, another guest, a proud, handsome woman with hard, fierce eyes.

Blanche Ingram, her daughter, a young woman with an elegant manner and a loud, satirical laugh, to whom Mr. Rochester is reported engaged.

Mary Ingram, her sister.

Henry Lynn and

Frederick Lynn, gentlemen at the party, two dashing sparks.

Lord Ingram, Blanche's brother, a tall, handsome young man of listless appearance and manner.

Mr. Mason, Mr. Rochester's brother-in-law. During a visit to see his sister, she wounds him severely. He halts the marriage of Jane Eyre and Mr. Rochester.

Diana Rivers and

Mary Rivers, daughters of the family with which Jane Eyre takes refuge after running away from Thornfield. They turn out to be her cousins, their mother having been Jane's aunt. At first they do not know that Jane is a relative because she calls herself Jane Eliot.

St. John Rivers, their brother, a complex religious-minded man who wishes to marry Jane but plans to live with her in platonic fashion while they devote their lives to missionary work in India.

Hannah, the Rivers' housekeeper, a suspicious but kind woman.

Rosamund Oliver, a beautiful, kind heiress, the sponsor of the school in which St. John Rivers finds Jane a post. Miss Oliver is coquettish and vain, but she holds real affection for Rivers.

Mr. Oliver, her father, a tall, massive-featured man.

Alice Wood, an orphan, one of Jane's pupils in the school where she teaches after leaving Thornfield.

JAPANESE BY SPRING

Author: Ishmael Reed (1938-   )
First published: 1993
Genre: Novel

Locale: Oakland, California
Time: Early 1990's
Plot: Social satire

Benjamin "Chappie" Puttbutt III, named for two of the most celebrated African American soldiers in the history of the United States by his father, who is a high-ranking career Army man. He is approaching middle age as an untenured faculty member at a large public college. To advance his career, he has chosen a neoconservative academic position and a pacifist approach to conflict; both stances are at odds with his inner nature and upbringing. By rejecting the black consciousness of the 1960's and by choosing to study Japanese to be in touch with the latest trends in global power flows, Puttbutt has denied so much of what he instinctively feels that he has essentially lost any true center of being. He recognizes that he is a loner, sees himself as a survivor, and is pleased that he is capable of resisting his impulses to retaliate with justification when he is insulted, belittled, betrayed, or scorned. His endless rationalizations are an indication that all of his posturing has failed to satisfy some fundamental human needs. Although he is often the focus of the author's satire, with his shifting and calculating, he has an instinctive decency, a very able mind, a solid grasp of his discipline, and a reflective temperament that make him a sympathetic character as well. He stands for the African American man who is forced to adjust to the social realities of late twentieth century America and the weight of American history while attempting to maintain some sense of integrity and self-respect.

Ishmael Reed, who is described as a "modest merchant" who provides "quality literature and videodramas" for society. He is a middle-aged African American writer, community activist, and social critic resembling the author of the novel in many ways. He lives in Oakland, where Puttbutt works at Jack London College, and functions as an observer of the action and occasional narrator in the early stages of the novel. He gradually becomes more involved in conversations with Puttbutt and then is engaged actively in the narrative as an experienced, sardonic commentator providing another perspective for the omniscient "author" who shares his sensibility. As the novel moves toward a kind of resolution, Puttbutt leaves the foreground of the narrative action and Reed's spiritual quest replaces Puttbutt's frantic calculations as the central motif. He stands for a genuine multicultural experience as opposed to the narrow, self-serving, exploitative agendas of many of the characters.

George Eliott Puttbutt, a two star general, Chappie's father. This tough-minded warrior sees life as a constant battle and thrives on combative confrontations with racists. His affection for his son is mixed with disdain for Chappie's choices.

Dr. Yamato, Puttbutt's tutor in the Japanese language. He is an arch conservative in Japanese politics working for the restoration of the Tokogawa regime. He becomes the president of Jack London College temporarily.

Charles Obi, the chair of the black studies program at Jack London College, a candid careerist and realist who understands the vicissitudes of life for an African American professional. He struggles to suppress his justifiable anger while attempting to keep the black studies program viable in a hostile setting and protect his own interests from various adversaries.

Jack Milch, the chair of the "humanity" department at Jack London College. He seems committed to many worthwhile social causes but actually is a complete hypocrite whose interest in African Americans is merely a strategy for self-advancement and whose commitment to "humanity" in the abstract is belied by his imprisonment of his wife and child in a cellar.

Robert Hurt, the dean of humanity at Jack London College, an idealist and aging hippie with a mind-set constructed from liberal 1960's slogans. He believes, to some extent, what he is professing but is also ruled by an agenda of self-advancement.

Jingo Miller, the Japanese-born wife of one of Puttbutt's professors at the Air Force Academy. She is the true love of Puttbutt's life, a woman of wit, culture, and beauty whose brief relationship with him is the source of his decision to choose pacifism as a philosophy of existence.

Professor Crabtree, a classical Eurocentric scholar patterned slightly after writer Saul Bellow. His serious study of traditional literary scholarship does not prevent him from applying himself to the Yoruba language and demonstrating his genuine will to learn by achieving a mastery of its intricate tonal patterns.

— *Leon Lewis*

JASMINE

Author: Bharati Mukherjee (1940-)
First published: 1989
Genre: Novel
Locale: Hasnapur, India; New York City; and Baden, Iowa
Time: 1965-1989
Plot: Social realism

Jasmine Vijh, later called **Jane Ripplemeyer**, the narrator. She was born in Hasnapur, India, and given the name Jyoti. She is the fifth daughter of her parents and the seventh of nine children; as such, she is somewhat unwanted. An astrologer predicts that she is doomed to widowhood and exile. Jasmine is determined to chart the course of her own life. She marries Prakash Vijh at the age of fourteen, and he renames her Jasmine as a means of breaking her from her past. After he is murdered by a Muslim fanatic, Jasmine fulfills Prakash's wish and goes to the United States, entering illegally. She first works as a caregiver for Taylor Hayes, a college professor in New York City. She then flees from Sukhwinder, the man who killed her husband, and moves to Baden, Iowa, where she falls in love with Bud Ripplemeyer and becomes his common-law wife, living as Jane Ripplemeyer. Taylor eventually finds Jasmine, and the two decide to move to California. Jasmine has several identities; she is a different person to different people. To Prakash, she is Jasmine; to Half-Face, the man who raped her, she is the goddess Kali; to Lillian Gordon, who helped her find a job in New York City, she is Jazzy; to Taylor, she is Jase; to Bud, she is Jane. Her various identities finally make Jasmine realize that she is who she wants to make herself. At the end of the book, she is ready to take control of her own destiny.

Prakash Vijh, Jasmine's husband in India. Prakash is an aspiring engineer. He has graduated from a technical college in India and has worked at two jobs, one as a repairman and bookkeeper and the other as a math tutor. Prakash's ambition is to go to the United States and finish his college education. He instills hopes in Jasmine by describing what he has learned about the United States and plays a crucial role in helping reshape her identity.

Taylor Hayes, a college professor. Jasmine works for Taylor for two years as a caregiver. Theirs is a mutually respectful relationship. Both of them share the love for Taylor's adopted child, Duff. In fact, one of the reasons Jasmine decides to move to Iowa is to find out about Duff's origins. After Taylor's wife, Wylie, is divorced from him to be with another man, Taylor expresses his affection for Jasmine. Seeing Sukhwinder in a park, however, precipitates Jasmine's decision to run away from New York City. Eventually, Taylor finds Jasmine and talks her into moving with him to California.

Bud Ripplemeyer, a banker. After Jasmine moves to Baden, Bud's mother finds her a job at the bank where Bud works. Bud falls in love with Jasmine. After his wife divorces Bud, Jasmine moves in with him. Harlan Kroener, a disgruntled farmer who believes that the bank is exploiting him, shoots Bud, paralyzing him. Jasmine takes the responsibility of taking care of him and their adopted son, Du Thien. Bud asks Jasmine to marry him several times, but Jasmine hesitates, for various reasons including the facts that Karin, Bud's divorced wife, still loves him and that she still wishes to escape the astrologer's prediction of widowhood. Finally, Jasmine decides to leave Bud for new opportunities in California.

Du Thien, Jasmine and Bud's adopted son, a Vietnamese refugee. Jasmine's affection for Du results in part from her empathy for him. She can empathize with Du's origin, with the discrimination and mistreatment he receives in school, and with his ambition to prove to the world that he is just as American as everyone else. One of the main reasons why Jasmine decides to move to California with Taylor is to find Du, who has moved to Los Angeles to be with his sister.

Lillian Gordon, a social worker. Lillian is a self-appointed social worker who has dedicated her life to help undocumented immigrants. She saves Jasmine from the street and helps her find her first job in the United States.

Mrs. Ripplemeyer, Bud's mother. She and Jasmine understand each other and share affection.

Half-Face, a trawler captain. After Half-Face smuggles Jasmine into the United States, he rapes her.

Harlan Kroener, a farmer. Harlan's prejudice eventually leads him into shooting Bud.

Darrel Lutz, a struggling farmer, Jasmine and Bud's friend. He has a college degree and is thinking about selling his farm to move to New Mexico. He is in love with Jasmine and eventually commits suicide.

— *Qun Wang*

JASON AND THE GOLDEN FLEECE

Author: Unknown
First published: Unknown
Genre: Novel
Locale: Greece
Time: Antiquity
Plot: Folklore

Jason, a Greek prince whose father has been driven from his throne. Jason is commanded to regain the throne, but to do so he must bring back the Golden Fleece for the usurper, his uncle Pelias. Jason bravely sets out and brings back the Golden Fleece. Although Pelias refuses to keep his promise, he dies that same night, leaving the throne to Jason.

Pelias (PEE-lee-uhs), Jason's cruel uncle, who usurps his brother's throne and plots to kill Jason. When Jason brings back the Golden Fleece to Iolcus, Pelias does not want to fulfill his bargain and give up the throne, but death takes him the same night.

Chiron (KI-ron), a centaur. He is Jason's foster father and tutor.

Herakles (HEHR-uh-kleez) and

Orpheus (OHR-fee-uhs), Jason's companions on the quest for the Golden Fleece.

Argus (AHR-guhs), another of Jason's companions on the quest for the Golden Fleece. He builds the ship *Argo* for Jason.

Zetes (ZEE-teez) and

Calais (KA-lay-uhs), sons of the North Wind, companions of Jason.

Phineus (FIH-nee-uhs), the blind king of Salmydessa, saved from the Harpies by Jason.

Æetes, the king of Colchis, who agrees to give up the Golden Fleece if Jason can accomplish deeds beyond mortal skill and strength.

Medea (mih-dee-uh), a princess of Colchis. She falls in love with Jason, aids him in gaining the Golden Fleece, and returns with him to become his queen in Iolcus.

JAVA HEAD

Author: Joseph Hergesheimer (1880-1954)
First published: 1919
Genre: Novel

Locale: Salem, Massachusetts
Time: The 1840's
Plot: Local color

Gerrit Ammidon, a Yankee sea captain, his father's favorite son; a romantic man with an arresting, blue-eyed gaze. He is critical of the hypocrisy, the pious pretense, and the scandalmongering of his home town. Conscious of having done Nettie an injustice in dropping her because of anger at her grandfather, he confesses his love for her; after Taou Yuen's death, he marries her and takes her with him away from Salem.

Taou Yuen, Gerrit's Chinese bride, a Manchu noblewoman who seems completely out of place in Salem. Gerrit thinks of her as the perfection of aristocratic beauty, charm, and refinement; but she represents the Orient, not America. To save herself from Edward, she commits suicide.

Nettie Vollar, the illegitimate daughter of Kate Dunsack and a seaman who drowned; Gerrit's black-haired, dimpled, pert-nosed former sweetheart and later his wife.

Edward Dunsack, Nettie's weak-willed, drug-addicted uncle, who is resentful of Gerrit's possessing Taou Yuen. Failing to seduce her, he gives her a distorted account of the love affair of Nettie and Gerrit. Drug-crazed, he threatens to strangle Taou Yuen and causes her to commit suicide with opium pills. Edward goes mad.

Captain Jeremy Ammidon, Gerrit's father, senior partner in the firm of Ammidon, Ammidon, and Saltonstone. He dies of a heart attack upon discovering that two of the firm's schooners are transporting opium.

William Ammidon, Gerrit's handsome brother, a money-minded tradesman who disagrees with his father on many trade and shipping matters and who sees no objection to trading in opium if it brings in money. He is sharply critical of Gerrit's marriage. He symbolizes nineteenth century New England commercialism and business ethics.

Rhoda Ammidon, William's cheerful and sensible wife, a large, handsome woman.

Barzil Dunsack, father of Edward and Kate; once a friend but afterward an enemy of Jeremy.

Kate Dunsack Vollar, Nettie's mother.

James Saltonstone, partner of the Ammidons.

Laurel Ammidon, William and Rhoda's young daughter.

JAZZ

Author: Toni Morrison (1931-   )
First published: 1992
Genre: Novel

Locale: Harlem, New York, and Virginia
Time: 1926, with flashbacks to before the Civil War
Plot: Psychological realism

The narrator, never identified by name. Her voice and vision are always unmistakable. Like the neighborhood gossip, she sees, hears, and knows everything. What she does not know, she imagines, chastising herself when she is not as accurate or as reliable as she should be. She is the storyteller who must get the whole story right.

Violet Trace, born in rural Virginia, the third of five children whose insane mother drowned herself in a well. Her father visited his family occasionally as he worked underground for a political party "that favored nigger voting." His absence led to his family's dispossession. She is reared for eleven years by her grandmother, whose Baltimore stories of the beloved blond-haired son of her mistress and a local African American boy corrupt Violet's image of herself and her race. She marries Joe Trace and works the fields with him until they migrate north to Harlem. Twenty years later, she loses control over her actions and words, retreating into silence until a second Violet emerges to strike out at her husband's dead girlfriend. By "killing" that Violet and befriending the dead girl's best friend, Felice, Violet restores herself.

Joe Trace, an orphan and a survivor. He says he remade himself eight times during his life, the last being one time too many. Joe is described as a handsome fifty-year-old, a nice, neighborly man who straightens the children's toys in front of the apartment building, whom people let into their homes to sell them his Cleopatra cosmetics, who walks women home from the trolley, and who is safe. He kills his lover, Dorcas Manfred, when she leaves him for the young "roosters" her own age. His action garners him more sympathy than condemnation, as neighbors understand that he was caught up in a love more powerful than he could control.

Dorcas Manfred, who is reared by her strict aunt, Alice, after her parents are murdered in the East St. Louis riots of 1917. Music, parties, and her own body make her restricted life unbearable. Dorcas is rejected by several young men. She shares evenings with Joe in a rented room, as Joe lavishes gifts and unqualified acceptance upon her. After three months, Joe is not enough. Dorcas needs a young man, young blood, dancing, and jazz. Joe finds her and shoots her.

Alice Manfred, a widowed woman in her fifties who had been frightened for a long time in Illinois, Massachusetts, and New York, until she moved to Harlem, where there were no white people. She rears her niece with strictness to control the fear. Only when she takes Dorcas to the parade commemorating the two hundred people killed in the 1917 riots, drawn in by the drums and the cold black faces, does she feel connected to other African Americans. The drums provide fortitude, but the jazz music young men play from rooftops is dangerous, sexual, and angry. After Violet cuts Dorcas' dead face, Alice lets Violet into her living room, treats her rudely, and lends her Dorcas' photograph. Having lost her own husband years ago, first to another woman and then to death, Alice helps Violet hold onto hers, even though he is her niece's murderer.

Felice, Dorcas' best friend, who becomes part of a "scandalizing threesome on Lenox Avenue" with Joe and Violet three months after Dorcas' death. Reared by a grandmother while both of her parents worked for white people at Tuxedo Junction, she saw them only thirty-two days a year (she has counted). She is Dorcas' alibi the night her friend is killed and the last person Dorcas speaks to. Her first meeting with Joe and Violet Trace is to inquire about the opal ring she loaned Dorcas that last night. She returns because she likes them, and she becomes the catalyst for repair of the Traces' marriage.

— Laura Weiss Zlogar

JEALOUSY
(La Jalousie)

Author: Alain Robbe-Grillet (1922-)
First published: 1957
Genre: Novel
Locale: Indeterminate
Time: After World War II
Plot: Antistory

The narrator, a person unidentified as to age or sex. The narrator of this unusual novel never refers to himself in the first person and in fact is never specifically identified as a person at all. The narrator is probably, however, the owner of the plantation and A . . . 's husband. The repetition of the scenes he describes is evidence that the narrator is obsessed with them. The scenes at the dinner table, for example, suggest that the narrator lives at the plantation, because these descriptions always specify the number of places set, and invariably there is one extra place, which can only be for the narrator. It is possible that the narrator believes that his wife is having an affair with their neighbor, Franck. In French, the title of the novel not only means "jealousy" but is also a pun on *jalousies*, or Venetian blinds, the shutters through which the narrator frequently views scenes, a suggestion that he is spying on his wife and neighbor but also an indication of the narrowness and limitation of the point of view he presents.

A . . ., a beautiful, dark-haired woman who lives in a house on an isolated banana plantation. She is characterized by a few simple repeated actions and by descriptions of certain of her possessions. She reads a book and discusses it with Franck, makes drinks for Franck (and perhaps for her husband—there is always a third glass set out), sits down to dinner, and goes shopping with Franck. On one shopping trip, she and Franck spend the night away at a hotel, ostensibly because his car broke down. The empty and repetitive nature of this existence suggests in itself a reason for her possible infidelity. The only evidence that she commits adultery seems to be circumstantial.

Franck, the owner of the neighboring banana plantation. His wife, Christiane, no longer accompanies him on his visits to the other plantation, providing another cause for the narrator's suspicions. He explains the overnight stay after the shopping trip by admitting that he is a poor mechanic, which may suggest symbolically his inadequacy as a lover, offering an explanation for the return of A . . . and also for the end of the narrator's jealousy (and therefore the end of the narrative).

Christiane, Franck's wife. She never appears at the plantation that provides the setting for all the incidents of the novel. This restriction of setting may imply that the narrator lives there. She acts as a catalyst in the plot through her absences—caused by her susceptibility to the hot and humid climate—that help throw Franck and A . . . together more often and more intimately.

— William Nelles

JEAN-CHRISTOPHE

Author: Romain Rolland (1866-1944)
First published: 1913
Genre: Novels
Locale: Germany, France, and Switzerland
Time: Late nineteenth and early twentieth centuries
Plot: Social

Jean-Christophe Krafft (zhah[n]-krees-TOHF krahft), a musical genius who is uneducated in most phases of life. He has temporary love affairs and gets involved in the syndicalist political movement. He dies alone in Paris, recognized as the world's greatest composer of modern music.

Melchior Krafft (mehl-CHOHR), his virtuoso father.

Louisa (lwee-ZAH), his lower-class mother.

Jean Michel (zhah[n] mee-SHEHL), a famous orchestra conductor and Jean-Christophe's grandfather.

Ada (ah-DAH), a vulgar shop girl who becomes Jean-Christophe's first mistress.

Lorchen (lohr-SHAH[N]), a young farm girl in whose defense Jean-Christophe kills a soldier and has to leave Germany.

Colette Stevens (koh-LEHT stay-VAH[N]), a coquette to whom Jean-Christophe gives music lessons.

Grazia (grah-TSYAH), Colette's cousin, who secretly helps build Jean-Christophe's reputation. After her husband's death, she encourages Jean-Christophe in Switzerland.

Antoinette (ahn-twah-NEHT), who dies of consumption while educating her brother Olivier.

Olivier (oh-lee-VYAY), a writer who admires Jean-Christophe's work. He is killed while with Jean-Christophe in a May Day political riot.

Jacqueline (zhahk-LEEN), a shallow girl, Olivier's wife.

Anna (ah-NAH), a married woman with whom Jean-Christophe has an affair during his Swiss exile.

JENNIE GERHARDT

Author: Theodore Dreiser (1871-1945)
First published: 1911
Genre: Novel
Locale: Chicago, Columbus, Cleveland, and Cincinnati
Time: Late nineteenth century
Plot: Naturalism

Genevieve Gerhardt (Jennie), the oldest of six children of a poor, hardworking glass blower in Columbus, Ohio. Both beautiful and innocent, Jennie is forced to work at a local hotel when her father becomes ill; there, she attracts Senator Brander, who stays at the hotel. When Brander helps her family and keeps her brother out of jail for stealing coal from the railroad, Jennie, in gratitude, sleeps with him. At his sudden death, she is left pregnant. She later moves to Cleveland, where she meets Lester Kane. With her family in need again, she goes on a trip to New York with him in return for his help. Lester finds out about Jennie's daughter and agrees to allow the child to live with them. Jennie realizes that his family's disapproval of their relationship is harming Lester both financially and socially, and she influences him to leave her. He later marries an old childhood sweetheart. Jennie's daughter dies, and she adopts two orphan children. Some years later, while his wife is in Europe, Lester has a heart attack and sends for Jennie, who nurses him until his death.

Lester Kane, the son of a wealthy carriage manufacturer. A weak man, Lester is torn between his desire for social and financial affluence and his feeling for Jennie. He neither marries her nor leaves her, until his father's will demands that he act within three years. Pursued by Mrs. Gerald, a widow, he finally follows his family's wishes and leaves Jennie with a generous settlement.

William Gerhardt, Jennie's father, a poor glass blower. After his wife dies and his children grow up, he lives with Jennie, the daughter of whom he disapproved but who is ultimately kindest to him. He dies in Chicago.

George Sylvester Brander, a senator from Ohio. A bachelor, he intends to marry Jennie but dies of a heart attack.

Wilhelmina Vesta, Jennie's daughter by Senator Brander; she dies of typhoid fever at the age of fourteen.

Mrs. Letty Pace Gerald, a wealthy widow and childhood sweetheart of Lester Kane. Lester finally marries her but is not happy.

Mrs. Gerhardt, Jennie's mother, hardworking and sympathetic. She dies in Cleveland before Jennie moves to Chicago.

Robert Kane, Lester's older brother, vice president of the carriage company. A ruthless financier interested only in power, he influences his father to make the will that cripples Lester.

Archibald Kane, Lester's father. According to his will, Lester must abandon Jennie to get his share in the business. If he marries Jennie, he is to receive ten thousand dollars a year for life; if he continues to live with her without marriage, he gets nothing after three years.

Sebastian Gerhardt (Bass), Jennie's oldest brother and the closest to her.

George Gerhardt, another brother.

Martha Gerhardt, a sister; she becomes a teacher.

William Gerhardt, Jr., a brother who becomes an electrical engineer.

Veronica Gerhardt, a sister who marries a wholesale druggist in Cleveland.

Louise Kane, Lester's youngest sister, a cold woman who discovers that Lester is living with Jennie in a Chicago hotel.

Amy Kane and

Imogene Kane, other sisters.

Mrs. Kane, Lester's mother.

Mrs. Henry Bracebridge, Jennie's Cleveland employer at whose home she meets Lester Kane.

Mr. O'Brien, a lawyer, the executor of Archibald Kane's estate; he suggests that Jennie influence Lester to leave her.

Rose Perpetua and

Henry Stover, orphans adopted by Jennie.

Samuel E. Ross, a real-estate promoter through whom Lester loses money.

JERUSALEM DELIVERED
(Gerusalemme liberata)

Author: Torquato Tasso (1544-1595)
First published: 1581
Genre: Poetry
Locale: The Holy Land
Time: The Middle Ages
Plot: Epic

God, who is on the side of the Christians.

The archangel Gabriel, sent by God in the seventh year of the Crusade to encourage the Crusaders in beginning their march on Jerusalem.

The archangel Michael, sent by God to inspire the Christians during the final stages of the capture of the city.

Satan, who is on the side of the Pagans.

Godfrey de Bouillon, the leader of the Crusaders, victorious after many setbacks.

King Aladine, the pagan king from whom the Crusaders finally take Jerusalem.

Clorinda, a beautiful pagan warrior who scorns female dress. She is instrumental in preventing pagan tyrannies as well as in holding off the Christians for a time. She is killed in combat.

Tancred, a mighty Christian noble in love with Clorinda. He wounds her mortally in combat, then realizes who she is. He has time to ask her pardon and to baptize her before her death.

Erminia of Antioch, who is in love with Tancred. She goes in Clorinda's armor to Tancred's camp when he is wounded, but she is frightened at the last minute and takes refuge with a shepherd.

Argantes, who is sent by the king of Egypt to parley with Godfrey, who haughtily rejects his overtures. He and his army aid Jerusalem, and Argantes is killed in single combat by Tancred.

Rinaldo, an Italian Crusader and the most valorous of all. Banished temporarily after a jousting duel, he is later summoned back and is with the Crusaders when Jerusalem is taken.

Armida, an enchantress in Satan's employ. She treacherously lures fifty Christians to her castle and changes them into fishes; later, she imprisons Tancred. All are liberated by Rinaldo, who then dallies with Armida until summoned back to duty. At last, the pagans defeated, she surrenders herself to Rinaldo.

Hugh, the former commander of the French forces. He appears to Godfrey in a vision and orders him to recall Rinaldo.

Otho, Tancred's companion, who is defeated by Argantes and taken prisoner.

Gernando, a rival of Rinaldo for a certain post. They quarrel, and in the resultant joust, Gernando is killed.

Peter the Hermit, who adds his exhortations to Godfrey's in reminding the Crusaders of their vows to take Jerusalem.

Ismeno, a sorcerer. He advises King Aladine to steal a statue of the Virgin Mary, which later disappears.

Sophronia, a beautiful Christian subject of King Aladine. To save the rest of the Christians from massacre, she confesses to the theft of the statue and is condemned to be burned.

Olindo, who is in love with Sophronia. He hopes to save her by confessing to the theft but is only condemned as well. Clorinda rescues both.

Sweno, the prince of Denmark. He is killed with his followers during his occupation of Palestine. The Crusaders are spurred on by thoughts of vengeance for this deed.

THE JEW OF MALTA

Author: Christopher Marlowe (1564-1593)
First published: 1633
Genre: Drama
Locale: Malta
Time: The fifteenth century
Plot: Tragedy

Barabas (bah-RAB-uhs), the wealthy, miserly Jew of Malta who guides his actions by Machiavellian policy that transcends all human ties of affection and loyalty. With considerable reason, he resents the Christian rulers of Malta, who arbitrarily deprive him of his fortune, and he chooses a particularly cruel form of revenge, setting the young man his daughter loves against the governor's son in a duel fatal to both combatants. Rejected by the two people for whom he has any feeling, his daughter and his servant Ithamore, he contrives the murder of each and finally betrays Malta to its Turkish enemies. He is caught in the trap that he lays for Selim Calymath and dies cursing humankind.

Abigail, his daughter. She lies and professes her conversion to Christianity as a means to retrieve her father's hidden treasure, but the death of Mathias so disillusions her that she enters a nunnery to escape Barabas' evil.

Ithamore (eeth-uh-MOH-ree), Barabas' slave, who is as ruthless as his master. He carries out the murder of Abigail, the friars, and the nuns, and he delivers the fraudulent challenges to Mathias and Lodowick as the Jew wishes. He readily betrays his master, however, to Bellamira, hoping to make her his mistress with his own eloquence and Barabas' money.

Ferneze (fehr-NAY-zay), the governor of Malta. He considers the need of his state to meet the demands of the Turks ample justification for his confiscation of the wealth of the Jewish merchants. He grieves deeply for the death of his son and vows vengeance on those who caused his slaying. It is his craftiness that finally brings Barabas to destruction.

Don Mathias (ma-TEE-uhs), a good young man who wins Abigail's love and tries to gain her father's favor. He is, in a sense, the innocent victim of Barabas' vendetta against Malta, although he is too ready to be jealous of Lodowick's attentions to Abigail.

Lodowick (LOD-oh-wihk), Ferneze's son. Knowing of his friend Mathias' love for Abigail, he visits Barabas' house to catch a glimpse of her and is himself captivated by her beauty. His jealousy also is aroused by Barabas' carefully planted suggestions of Mathias' claims on his daughter, and he is ready to accept the false challenge.

Selim Calymath (SEE-lihm KAL-ih-math), the leader of the Turkish embassy that demands ten years' tribute from Ferneze. He takes Malta through Barabas' treachery, but he finds himself betrayed by his accomplice and is held as hostage by Ferneze after Barabas' death.

Bellamira (BEHL-uh-mee-ruh), an ambitious courtesan who uses Ithamore's susceptibility to her charms as a means to acquire some of Barabas' money.

Pilia-Borsa (PEEL-ee-uh-BOHR-sah), her accomplice, a greedy, resourceful rascal.

Katherine, Mathias' devoted mother. She joins Ferneze in his vow to take vengeance on those who set their sons against each other.

Barnardine (bahr-NAHR-deen) and

Jacomo (yah-KOH-moh), lecherous, avaricious friars who are murdered after they try to blackmail Barabas with information revealed by Abigail in her dying confession.

Martin Del Bosco (mahr-TEEN dehl BOS-koh), the vice admiral of the king of Spain. He promises to help Malta resist the Turks.

THE JEWESS OF TOLEDO
(Die Jüdin von Toledo)

Author: Franz Grillparzer (1791-1872)
First published: 1873
Genre: Drama
Locale: Toledo and its vicinity
Time: c. 1195
Plot: Tragedy

Alfonso VIII (ahl-FOHN-soh), the king of Castile. Made ruler of Castile as a child after the deposition of his tyrant predecessor, Alfonso has been a wise and just ruler of his people. Attracted to Rachel, a beautiful and vain young Jew, he lets his passion cause him to neglect his obligations in the face of an imminent war. He finally realizes and acknowledges his weakness, forgives those who have plotted Rachel's destruction, and reaffirms his duty to the people.

Rachel (rah-CHEHL), a Jewish woman of Toledo. Walking in the royal garden where Jews are forbidden during the king's outing, she is pursued by guards and runs to Alfonso for protection. Attracting the monarch, she arouses in him a passion for her that leads to his shame and remorse and to her death.

Isaac (ee-SAHK), Rachel's mercenary father, who is more concerned about his profits than his daughter's death.

Esther (ehs-tehr), Rachel's gentle sister. Ashamed of her sister's wantonness and her father's greed, she blames them equally with Alfonso for Rachel's tragic death.

Eleanor of England, the queen of Castile. Realizing that Alfonso's infatuation for Rachel is causing him to neglect his responsibilities, she plots the death of Rachel, for which she is forgiven when the king finally acknowledges the foolishness of his passion.

Manrique (mahn-REE-kay), the count of Lara and the ally of Queen Eleanor.

Don Garceran (gahr-THAY-rahn), Manrique's son, who is loyal to Alfonso.

Doña Clara (KLAH-rah), a lady in waiting to Eleanor and the betrothed of Don Garceran.

JILL

Author: Philip Larkin (1922-1985)
First published: 1946
Genre: Novel
Locale: Oxford, England
Time: The Michaelmas term at the University of Oxford, 1940
Plot: Bildungsroman

John Kemp, an undersized eighteen-year-old student at the University of Oxford. Kemp is physically undistinguished except for his silky hair. Kemp begins his career as an undergraduate reading English but is self-conscious and shy. Pressured into testing early for a scholarship, he is frightened and insecure about leaving his working-class home of Huddlesford in northern England. His isolation is intensified when he meets his roommate, Christopher Warner, a crass and worldly public school graduate. Afraid of having no companions, Kemp attempts to imitate students from a higher social class, but his repeated social failures prompt Kemp to become a fantasizer. He creates Jill, an imaginary sister, and embellishes a fantasy life for her until he meets a young woman who appears to be the actual Jill. His pursuit of the real girl ends in disaster when he drunkenly attempts to kiss her and is dunked in a school fountain. Kemp ends the semester in the college infirmary, sick with pneumonia and accepting the death of his love for Jill.

Christopher Warner, Kemp's brash rugby-playing roommate. Taller and stronger than Kemp, Warner is a drinker and a womanizer who manipulates his friends and borrows their possessions. He selfishly breaks open a case of Kemp's tea china before Kemp arrives and in a later episode asks Kemp to leave the room so that he can seduce Elizabeth Dowling.

Elizabeth Dowling, Warner's broad-shouldered girlfriend. Her hair is brushed up from the sides of her head and resembles a helmet. Hypocritical and condescending to Kemp, she falsely flatters him when he sports an unattractive blue bow tie with white dots.

Whitbread, another northern scholar like Kemp. Physically repulsive, Whitbread has a pale, stubbly head and wears steel-rimmed spectacles. Imbued with a feeling of superiority to Warner and his crowd, Whitbread has been scorned by his two older brothers (both electrical engineers) for trying to rise above his class. Kemp, too, comes to dislike Whitbread's snobbishness. He steals Whitbread's cake to serve to Gillian and puts tea and sugar in Whitbread's pockets.

Joseph Crouch, an English master at Huddlesford Grammar School. Not good looking, Crouch is short, with yellowish skin, and wears thick eyeglasses. A dull but dedicated teacher, Crouch makes Kemp his special project for a scholarship. Crouch eventually marries and turns his back on learning. When his school is bombed, he plans to join the Royal Air Force.

Jill, an imaginary girl invented by Kemp. Because her creation was an impromptu one to enable Kemp to capture Warner's attention, he first refers to Jill as his sister, then as a friend, and changes her last name to Bradley. He imagines her to be a clever fifteen-year-old student at Willow Gables School and keeps a diary for her. Kemp even sends her letters and writes a short story in her name.

Gillian, Elizabeth's cousin, who embodies the characteristics of Jill: innocent, with high cheekbones, honey-colored hair, small bony hands, and a serious face. Kemp first sees her in a bookstore and becomes obsessed with meeting her. Although Gillian accepts Kemp's invitation to come to his room for tea, she is not eager for Kemp's friendship because she is staying with her aunt Charlotte while her mother recuperates from an illness. She sends Elizabeth to cancel the appointment.

Mrs. Warner, Christopher Warner's mother. Fond of bridge and golf, she is a former actress who drives a sports car. A stylish, fashionable dresser, she possesses the same broad forehead and jaw as does Christopher and wears her dark hair drawn down to her neck. Kemp finds her quite attractive.

Semple, a student who spends much of his time trying to get others to join the Oxford Union. When Warner topples Semple's cabinet in an attempt to steal food from him, the two struggle. Warner hits him in the eye and is fined three pounds. In retaliation, Warner's friends crucify Semple on the university lawn by pinning him down with croquet hoops over his wrists, ankles, and neck.

Eddy Makepeace, one of Warner's rowdy friends. Eddy was Warner's classmate at Lamprey School, and his father was an official in India.

Joe Kemp, John's father. A retired policeman, he works as a carpenter. He has an enormous body and small head. He goes to visit John in the infirmary in repayment for his son's trip to Huddlesford after it is bombed.

Jack, the scout. Jack's job is to clean the dormitory rooms.

Herbert, a porter at Oxford. A fierce, small man with ginger whiskers, Herbert continues to wear his regimental tie.

— *Jerry W. Bradley*

JOANNA GODDEN

Author: Sheila Kaye-Smith (1887-1956)
First published: 1921
Genre: Novel
Locale: Rural England
Time: Early twentieth century
Plot: Domestic realism

Joanna Godden, a strong woman who upon the death of her father takes firm control of the family farm, Little Ansdore, and her sister Ellen. Her neighbors consider her a foolish, stubborn woman, but she thinks she can operate a farm better than anyone else, and she proves she can; yet her life seems empty of a man after the man she loves, Martin Trevor, dies. After some years, she takes a casual lover and becomes pregnant. She decides to sell the farm and start life anew with her child, though she will not marry the father because she does not really love him.

Martin Trevor, the man who makes Joanna feel for the first time that she is a woman before she is a farmer. He falls ill, however, and dies before he and Joanna can be married.

Squire Trevor, Martin's father. Ellen Godden becomes infatuated with him after her marriage and follows him to Dover.

Albert Hill, a man thirteen years younger than Joanna, whom she meets on a trip. Though he fathers her child, she will not marry him.

Arthur Alce, who loves Joanna deeply. He loves her so much that at her request he marries her sister. His wife thinks, however, that she has stolen the man from Joanna. When Ellen follows Squire Trevor to Dover, Arthur Alce moves away but refuses to give his wife a divorce. He dies accidentally, leaving his farm not to his wife but to Joanna.

Ellen Godden, Joanna's young sister, dominated by Joanna. She marries Arthur thinking she has taken him from Joanna. Later, she becomes infatuated with Squire Trevor. After following him to Dover she returns to live with her sister.

JOB: The Story of a Simple Man
(Hiob: Roman eines einfachen Mannes)

Author: Joseph Roth (1894-1939)
First published: 1930
Genre: Novel
Locale: Zuchnow, the Ukraine, and New York City
Time: c. 1885-1920
Plot: Parable

Mendel Singer, a children's teacher of Hebrew and the Bible. Thirty years old at the beginning of the novel, he is "pious, God-fearing, and ordinary, an entirely commonplace Jew." When he learns that his fourth child, Menuchim, is physically and mentally retarded, he accepts this as the will of God. When he later finds his daughter Miriam with a Cossack, he fears shame to the family and immigrates with her and his wife to America. Years later, he still dreams longingly of Menuchim, left behind in Russia. Already aged and bent in his early sixties, he loses his remaining family to death and mental illness, and in his anguish he blasphemes God for His cruelty. The appearance of Menuchim, who was long believed dead, restores his faith and gives him hope for his last years.

Deborah, Mendel's wife. She is unhappy with her husband's lowly status, his meager earnings, and the hardships of her life with four children. More resolute than he, she believes that God helps those who help themselves. She therefore enables her son Shemariah to escape conscription by having him smuggled across the border. In New York, she is embittered by her pinched circumstances, and she misses Menuchim. After learning that Shemariah has fallen as an American soldier in World War I, she dies of grief.

Jonas, the eldest son. Robust and earthy, he behaves more like a peasant youth than an orthodox Jew. He loves horses and drinking, and he sleeps with the village girls. Wishing to be a soldier, he joins the czar's army, thus placing himself beyond the bounds of Jewish religious law and practice. Later, the news that he is missing in the war compounds his father's grief.

Shemariah (sheh-MAHR-ee-ah), the middle son. Slight but quick-witted, in America he assimilates, casting off his Old World Jewish garb and renaming himself Sam. With his friend Mac, he runs a small department store and speculates in real estate. He provides the steamship tickets for the family's immigration, but his material success as an American brings no joy to his father.

Miriam, the daughter. Lovely and self-willed, she indulges her strong sexual urgings with soldiers of the nearby garrison. She resents her father's traditional ways and longs for the freedom of America. There she works in her brother's store and keeps company with Mac, but she is overcome by psychosis and is confined in an asylum.

Menuchim (meh-NEW-kihm), the youngest son. When, after the war, he finds his father in New York, he is in his early thirties, is married with two children, and is a famous musician in Europe. As a rabbi in Russia had foretold, the once severely retarded boy has grown wise, good, and strong. At the end of the novel, he awakens hope in Mendel for Miriam's recovery and for a reunion with Jonas, who was reported to be alive.

Sameshkin (sah-MAYSH-kihn), a Russian carter in the Singers' village of Zuchnow. He drinks and behaves coarsely but is good-natured. Driving Mendel home from the emigration authorities in Dubno, he comforts the sorrowful Jew.

Kapturak (kahp-TOO-rahk), a hardened, solitary man of indeterminate age. He earns his living by writing letters, appeals, and postal checks for illiterate peasants and Jews and by smuggling conscripts and deserters, Shemariah among them, out of Russia.

Mac, Shemariah's business partner in New York and his messenger to the family in Zuchnow. He is large, good-humored, and loud, radiating American exuberance.

— *Sidney Rosenfeld*

JOE TURNER'S COME AND GONE

Author: August Wilson (1945-)
First published: 1988
Genre: Drama

Locale: A boardinghouse in Pittsburgh, Pennsylvania
Time: August, 1911
Plot: Social

Seth Holly, the owner of a Pittsburgh boardinghouse, in his early fifties. A skilled craftsman born to northern free parents, he supplements income from his boarders with money made from making pots and pans, and he hopes to start his own business soon. On Sunday nights, he plays host to a Juba, a call-and-response dance reminiscent of the ring shouts of African slaves.

Bertha Holly, Seth's wife for twenty-seven years, five years younger than he is. A kind, warm-spirited woman who cares for her boarders, she professes a faith in the healing powers of love and laughter.

Herald Loomis, a thirty-two-year-old searching for his long-lost wife, Martha. He comes to live at the boardinghouse. Dressed in a hat and a long wool coat, he has been roaming the countryside for four years with his daughter, hoping that contact with Martha will somehow bring him peace. A former deacon at the Abundant Life Church in Memphis, he was abducted and forced to work on a chain gang controlled by Joe Turner, the brother of the Tennessee governor, in 1901. His servitude, which lasted seven years, left him deeply anguished. Having worried Seth with his moodiness, Herald is told to leave the boardinghouse after he has a fit during a Juba. When he finally is reunited with Martha, he delivers their child to her, becoming increasingly agitated and bitterly expressing his lack of faith in Christianity. Slashing himself in the chest frees him from the trauma of his years of bondage and solitude and enables him to leave the boardinghouse a healthier man.

Martha Loomis Pentecost, Herald's twenty-eight-year-old wife. Five years after Herald was captured by Joe Turner and she was forced to leave their home, Martha gave up on him and traveled with her Evangelist church group to the North, leaving their child with her mother. She lived in Pittsburgh for three years before moving to Rankin with her church. Glad to be reunited with her daughter but alarmed by Herald's behavior, she tries to persuade him to renew his faith in Jesus Christ.

Bynum Walker, a short, round man in his early sixties. He is a root worker or conjurer who performs pigeon-slaying rituals and supplies boardinghouse tenants with advice and charms. Exuding an air of wisdom and peacefulness, he consoles others with his insights into human nature. Confident that his "binding song" can bring people together, he himself seeks a mysterious "shiny man . . . One Who Goes Before and Shows the Way" whom he once encountered during his wanderings. Able to divine that Herald once labored for Joe Turner, Bynum notes that Herald himself is shining as he leaves the boardinghouse.

Mattie Campbell, a twenty-six-year-old engaged in an honest search for love and companionship. Abandoned by Jack Carper after their two babies die, she hopes that he will someday return to her. Born in Georgia and reared in Texas, she moves in with Jeremy Furlow. After his departure, she seems attracted to Herald and pursues him after he leaves the boardinghouse.

Jeremy Furlow, a boardinghouse resident. He is twenty-five years old, confident, and carefree. He is forced to leave his job as a road builder when he refuses to pay off a white extortionist. A proficient guitarist from North Carolina, he also earns money in local music competitions. After inviting Mattie Campbell to live with him, he becomes attracted to Molly Cunningham and leaves with her to see the world.

Molly Cunningham, about twenty-six years old, a tough and independent resident who does not love or trust others easily. She first appears wearing a fashionably colorful dress and carrying a small cardboard suitcase.

Rutherford Selig, a peddler. He sells wares made by Seth to mill town residents. Roughly as old as Seth, the thin, white-skinned man is also called the People Finder because his customer lists enable him to locate individuals who have traveled from one town to another; apparently, Selig also has a hand in transporting many of them away. Bynum hires him to find the "shiny man," Mattie hires him to find Jack Carper, and Herald hires him to find Martha. Once married to a woman in Kentucky, Selig mentions that his grandfather shipped blacks from Africa and that his father helped capture runaway slaves.

Zonia Loomis, Herald and Martha's eleven-year-old daughter, who befriends Reuben Scott.

Reuben Scott, a boy who lives next door and sells pigeons to Bynum.

— David Marc Fischer

JOHN BROWN'S BODY

Author: Stephen Vincent Benét (1898-1943)
First published: 1928
Genre: Poetry
Locale: United States
Time: 1859-1865
Plot: Epic

Jack Ellyat, a Connecticut boy symbolic of the Northern soldier during the American Civil War. He is an ambitious young man whose favorite dream role is that of Phaeton driving his chariot across the sky, proudly displaying the trophy-sun. Jack, a member of an abolitionist family, is troubled by signs of approaching war. He joins the Connecticut volunteers, is mustered out after the Northern defeat at Bull Run, later joins the Illinois volunteers in Chicago, and acquires the opprobrious nickname of "Bull Run Jack." He is captured after running away at Pittsburg Landing, escapes, finds refuge at John Vilas' farm, and falls in love with John's daughter Melora. Melora gets pregnant, and he is reunited with her at the end of the war. Like most soldiers, Jack bears as best he can the buffeting of fate.

Clay Wingate, Jack Ellyat's opposite in the South. He is the son of a plantation owner and lives at white-pillared Wingate Hall. Clay feels himself become a man as war approaches. He and Sally Dupré are drawn to each other before Clay joins the Black Horse Troop and rides away to the battle of Bull Run. When he returns to his Georgia home on leave, he falls in love with Lucy Weatherby, a Virginia girl, but at the end of the war, when he returns to an accidentally burned and ruined Wingate Hall, the weary and wounded soldier finds Sally Dupré waiting for him. Although used to a soft-living, fox-hunting life, Clay hardens himself into a fierce, efficient soldier.

Luke Breckinridge, a gangling mountain boy who joins up to fight the Yankees simply because the Kelceys, an enemy family, have shown they are not afraid to fight. Luke becomes infatuated with Sophy, a chambermaid at Pollet's Hotel in Richmond. He is delighted when his patrol catches and searches Shippy, a Union spy in the guise of a peddler and Luke's chief rival for Sophy's affections. The patrol finds incriminating evidence in Shippy's boots.

Melora Vilas, the girl who shelters Jack Ellyat and falls in love with him. She is straight and slim, with grave, brown eyes. After the war, with her father and Jack's son, born in Tennessee, she searches for the father of her baby. As she drives her cart up a hill in Connecticut, Jack, who was wounded at Gettysburg, is standing under some elms, waiting.

Lucy Weatherby, a fickle Virginia beauty who is more concerned with the men in her life than with the outcome of the war. Although she has an interlude with Clay Wingate in Pollet's Hotel in Richmond, Lucy seems deeply in love not with Clay or any other suitor but with herself.

Sally Dupré, the daughter of "French" Dupré, a dancing master. Although she is temporarily displaced by Lucy in Clay's affections, she is a faithful lover who waits for her man to come back.

Spade, a slave on the Zachary plantation, near Wingate Hall. He escapes, makes his way to freedom in the "promised land" of the North, and is immediately forced into a labor gang. He later joins the Union army and is wounded in the crater at Petersburg. After the war, Jake Diefer hires him as a field hand on his Pennsylvania farm.

Sophy, the hotel maid whom Luke Breckinridge takes with him when he decides to "leave" the war. Hungry and scared, she willingly goes with him back to his mountains when he announces his intention of putting in a crop and butchering a hog—because there were always hogs in the mountains.

Jake Diefer, a "barrel-chested Pennsylvanian" who volunteers for the Union forces but does not really get his fighting dander up until he discovers that the Johnnie Rebs are fighting on his farm at Gettysburg.

Shippy, the sharp peddler-spy for the Union who is to bring Sophy some perfume from the North but who is caught by a Confederate patrol and accused by jealous Luke Breckinridge. He is hanged after papers proving him to be a spy are found sewed into his boots.

John Vilas, Melora's father. He is a lover of the classics and a lonely, restless man who has made his life a Faustian search for the wilderness stone. During the war, having little sympathy for either side, he hides in the woods to protect his son Bent from recruiters. Later, he accompanies Melora and her child on her search for Jack Ellyat.

JOHN BULL'S OTHER ISLAND

Author: George Bernard Shaw (1856-1950)
First published: 1907
Genre: Drama
Locale: London, England, and Rosscullen, Ireland
Time: Summer, 1904
Plot: Naturalism

Tom Broadbent, an English civil engineer. Large, healthy, and hearty, Broadbent is the "John Bull" (the traditional Englishman) of this comedy of national character. An unconscious hypocrite in the service of the Land Development Syndicate, for which he hopes to develop an estate (including tourist attractions) in Rosscullen, Doyle's birthplace, he is nevertheless full of ingenuous hope that his English efficiency can lay balm to the wounds of the suffering and incompetent Irish. Irish Home Rule, he believes, will work wonders under English guidance, and he is ludicrously unaware of the contradiction. Having arrived in Rosscullen in act 2, he diverts the locals with his speechifying and his antics (he gives Matt Haffigan's pig a ride in his motorcar, with predictably disastrous results), but he also wins nomination as their next candidate for Parliament. He also engages in a half-comic, whirlwind courtship of Nora, in whom he sees all the Irish graces he sentimentally wants to protect and indulge.

Laurence Doyle, Broadbent's partner and housemate, an expatriate Irishman. Doyle is both typical and atypical. His Irish character was bred in the misty climate, which he says is the birthplace of grandiose and hopeless dreams that end in futile laughter and squalor. From this perception comes his fear of returning to Ireland and his people, though his friendship for Broadbent pushes him to do so. All of his adult life has been spent in England: Perhaps, like the expatriate outsider playwright himself, Doyle believes that England has made a man of him, a citizen of the world, capable of action. He voices the playwright's internationalist and socialist political views and also speaks for his optimistic quasi-religious creed of "Creative Evolution."

"Father" Keegan, a defrocked "mad" priest. Mysterious and spiritual, he displays more than a touch of the genius and the saint. He is still revered by the parish, particularly Nora, his favorite, though he has been officially displaced by plump Father Dempsey, a smooth politician. He is prey to the sin of despair, and his insight into the sufferings of a world that he sees as a living hell cannot be assimilated into the comic economy of the play. His oracular pronouncement, "every jest is an earnest in the womb of Time," closes it.

Nora Reilly, Rosscullen's "heiress," with an income of forty pounds sterling per year. Graceful, fastidious, and proud, Nora has the innate delicacy of a born lady without the income. She has waited eighteen years for the return of Doyle, the only man she has met who is fit for her hand, and her charms are beginning to fade. After Doyle disabuses her of this romantic dream, she accepts a useful role in the world as Broadbent's wife: Ireland thus "marries" England.

Tim Haffigan, a fake Irishman, in reality a seedy Glasgow con man with incipient delirium tremens. Haffigan's rollicking stage brogue and "Irish" conviviality fool Broadbent, who wants to employ him to break the ice for him among his "countrymen" in Rosscullen. Broadbent gives Haffigan half a pint of whiskey and a five-pound note before Doyle unmasks and disposes of the impostor.

Barney Doran, the miller. Stout and redheaded, Doran takes the Irish love of a joke to extremes, finding brutal pleasure in cruel fun. He regales the company in Doyle's father's house with the story of Broadbent and the motoring pig.

Matt Haffigan, a peasant farmer. Haffigan has been brutalized and his wits extinguished by years of degrading toil on an unyielding scrap of land. Although his tale of woe touches Broadbent, he is an unpleasant specimen.

— *Joss Lutz Marsh*

JOHN HALIFAX, GENTLEMAN

Author: Dinah Maria Mulock (Mrs. George Craik, 1826-1887)
First published: 1856
Genre: Novel
Locale: Rural England
Time: 1795-1834
Plot: Domestic realism

John Halifax, an orphan who has an honest face and wants only to be given a chance to prove himself. He is given a chance by Abel Fletcher and proceeds to rise in the world by his efforts, honest dealings, and gentlemanly behavior. He wins the hand of a wealthy heiress and becomes a behind-the-scenes political power and a wealthy manufacturer. He is a good husband and father, rearing a fine family before he dies peacefully in his sleep.

Abel Fletcher, a wealthy Quaker, owner of a tannery and mill. He gives John Halifax a chance to prove himself and for many years is the young man's benefactor.

Phineas Fletcher, invalid son of John's benefactor. He and John become fast friends. He sees John's good qualities before anyone else does so.

Ursula March, who becomes John's wife. She loves him even though he is from a lower class and marries him despite opposition from her family and friends. Her love for her husband is so great that when he dies she dies too, as if she cannot bear to be separated from him.

Guy Halifax, the Halifaxes' eldest son and his mother's favorite child. He leaves home after a quarrel with his brother. Later, he almost kills a man in France and flees to America, where he does well. He returns eventually to be reunited joyfully with his family.

Maud Halifax, the Halifaxes' youngest daughter and her father's favorite child. Because she loves a man of whom her father disapproves, she remains unwed many years. Her patience and love are rewarded when the man, Lord Ravenel, proves his worth and is able to marry her.

Lord Ravenel (William), a worldly and wild young man. He wants to marry Maud, but her father refuses to permit the marriage. Ravenel goes to America, proves his worth, returns to England with Guy, and marries Maud with her father's blessing.

JOHN INGLESANT

Author: Joseph Henry Shorthouse (1834-1903)
First published: 1880
Genre: Novel
Locale: England and Italy
Time: The seventeenth century
Plot: Historical

John Inglesant, the hero. The younger of twin sons, he is educated in philosophy and the classics. After a series of adventures in the service of Charles I of England, and later in Italy, he is sent back to England, where he leads a life of contemplation.

Eustace Inglesant. A few minutes older than his brother John, he is given a worldly education. He is murdered by an Italian enemy. Years later, John finds the murderer, who is now a blind monk, and spares his life.

Father St. Clare, a Jesuit and John's tutor. His dream is to return England to the domination of Rome; with this in mind he aids the crown against the Puritans.

Charles I, king of England. Guided by Father St. Clare, John is employed on secret missions by the king. Imprisoned, John refuses to give evidence against the king. After Charles' execution, Father St. Clare arranges John's release.

Lord Glamorgan, an Irish lord attempting to raise an army on Charles' behalf. He sends John to the besieged royal garrison at Chester, with promises of aid.

Lord Biron, commander of the garrison at Chester. After weeks of waiting, he finds that the king has denied plans for the Irish invasion because of a popular outcry. The garrison is lost to the Puritans.

Lauretta Capece, with whom John falls in love in Florence. He marries her and lives with her for several years in Umbria until, returning from a personal mission, he finds the family wiped out by the plague.

Cardinal Chigi, later elected pope. He is John's Italian patron.

The Duke of Umbria, to whom John is sent on a successful mission by the Jesuits.

THE JOKE
(Žert)

Author: Milan Kundera (1929-)
First published: 1967
Genre: Novel
Locale: Czechoslovakia
Time: 1947-1966
Plot: Comic realism

Ludvik Jahn, a student in Communist Czechoslovakia. Ludvik is a cheerful and fun-loving man who learns the hard way how to appraise people and political behavior. At the university in Prague, he develops a crush on a dour fellow student, Marketa, and to shock and amuse her, he sends her a postcard reading, "Optimism is the opium of the people! A healthy atmosphere stinks of stupidity! Long live Trotsky!" This joke is taken seriously; already suspected of individualistic tendencies, Ludvik is expelled from the university and Party and sent to an army penal battalion. Hard work in the mines and social isolation embitter him, and his thwarted love for an eccentric local girl, Lucie, stifles his romantic ideals. Years later, Ludvik encounters Helena, the wife of Pavel, the man responsible for his expulsion. A skilled womanizer, he arranges a tryst with her in his Moravian hometown, where she is reporting on the Ride of the Kings. Once there, he encounters Lucie, his old friend Kostka, and Pavel. In seducing Helena, he discovers the illusory and unsatisfying nature of vengeance deferred. Ludvik is a man of many faces and a calculating role-player. He often miscalculates and must accept unforeseen consequences. He maintains his sense of humor, but his alienation and lingering passion for Lucie prevent him from finding true peace. Ironically, it is in Moravian folk culture, on which he once based his communist vision, that he ultimately finds meaning and sanctuary.

Helena Zemanek, Pavel's wife, a radio feature reporter. Helena is an elegant redheaded woman who, though externally devoted to Pavel and their daughter Zdena, is bored with her emotional life and longs for passion. She falls for Ludvik at once, drawn by his sadness, and is excited by their relationship. Tinged with guilt, she questions her beliefs and perceptions and acts purely on emotional impulse. After her tryst with Ludvik, she believes that they will begin a new life together; when he suddenly abandons her, she becomes desperate and suicidal but is saved by the false labeling of her assistant's laxatives.

Kostka, Ludvik's friend, a hospital virologist. Kostka is a faithful Christian who sees everything in terms of Christian morality. He is tall and thin, attractively unattractive, sensitive, and serious. Like Ludvik, he is expelled from the Party and university, events that he accepts passively as fated. Unhappily married, he meets, comforts, and seduces Lucie. He rationalizes his acts as Christian charity but entertains doubts about his own righteousness. Seeing Ludvik again after many years, Kostka is outwardly friendly and obliging but really pities Ludvik's anger and finds his reappearance irksome. Kostka is a man of deceptions, an uneven mix of meditation and frenzy.

Lucie Sebetka, a resigned young woman from Western Bohemia. Gang-raped as a teenager, then married to a philanderer, Lucie flees to Ostrava, where she meets Ludvik at his penal camp. Her childlike simplicity and vulnerability captivate him. She becomes emotionally devoted to him but cannot accommodate him sexually, and when he pressures her, she flees to a Moravian town. There she befriends Kostka, whose tenderness and concern she finds healing, and for a time they are lovers. She ends up a silent and solitary woman, working in a barbershop.

Pavel Zemanek, the Party chairman of natural sciences, later a university lecturer in Marxism. Pavel is an outspoken Communist Party ideologue. He is attractive and well-liked, with a cocksure complacency, and craves attention and applause. He uses Ludvik's expulsion hearing as a platform for high-blown Party rhetoric and metaphor. Later, he is a negligent and unfaithful husband to Helena, though their daughter Zdena exalts him. When he encounters Ludvik at the Ride of the Kings, he has forgotten their past conflicts, and his diffidence renders pointless any vengeance Ludvik may hope to exact.

Jaroslav, Ludvik's hometown friend, a lover of Moravian folklore. Jaroslav is a towering but gentle man who cares deeply for Ludvik. Organizer of the Ride of the Kings, he fantasizes about being a romantic medieval hero and laments the passage of old customs and church rituals. Playing the cimbalom for an unappreciative young audience on the day of the Ride, Jaroslav has a longing and an inability to escape that bring on a nearly fatal coronary attack.

Marketa, Ludvik's university girlfriend. Marketa is a moderately bright woman whose inaccessible beauty sparks Ludvik's romantic sensibilities. Overly serious, to the point of total gullibility, she is befuddled by Ludvik's joke. Although she intends him no malice, she feels powerless to protect him from the Party's judgment.

— *B. P. Mann*

JONAH'S GOURD VINE

Author: Zora Neale Hurston (1891-1960)
First published: 1934
Genre: Novel
Locale: Alabama and Florida
Time: The post-Civil War period through the early twentieth century
Plot: Historical realism

John Pearson, a black minister and carpenter. He grows up on a Southern sharecropper's farm with his mother, his stepfather, and his two younger brothers. Increasing difficulties with his stepfather force John to leave the farm when he is sixteen years old. On the advice of his mother, he goes to Judge Pearson, who employs him and gives him clothes, along with changing John's last name from Crittenden to Pearson. John is tall and light-skinned, with gray eyes and curly hair. He is powerfully built and handsome. Soon he discovers that he is unable to control his sexual appetite. He has designs on Lucy Potts, the daughter of a well-to-do family. After they are married, John's philandering does not cease. One night when he is out, Lucy's brother, Bud, comes to collect a debt. Finding no money, he takes the bed that Judge Pearson gave the couple as a wedding present. When John returns, he whips Bud severely and must flee to escape prosecution and possible lynching. He goes to Sanford, Florida, and soon sends for his wife and children. He becomes a successful carpenter and later feels the call to preach. As pastor of Sanford's Zion Hope Baptist Church, John becomes a powerful figure in the community and the state. His philandering nevertheless continues. Soon after Lucy dies, John marries Hattie Tyson, who ruins his life, sues him for divorce, and is the catalyst for his leaving the ministry. John then goes to Plant City, Florida, where he meets and marries well-to-do widow Sally Lovelace and becomes the pastor of Pilgrim Rest Baptist Church. John lives in relative bliss and prosperity until he visits Sanford at Sally's urging. While he is in Sanford, John's sexual weakness leads him to give in to a young woman's advances. Disgusted with himself, John flees with his guilt back to Sally but is struck and killed by a train before he gets there. John's death is mourned by people from all over Florida.

Lucy Potts Pearson, John's first wife. Lucy is a petite but outspoken young girl when John first meets her. She is the smartest girl in her school, the lead singer in the Macedonia Baptist Church Choir, and the daughter of the well-to-do Potts family. Lucy encourages and supports John in his efforts, and she orchestrates his rise to prominence in the ministry. Although Lucy is aware of John's many extramarital affairs, she loves and supports him until her death.

Judge Alf Pearson, a wealthy white landowner suspected of being John's father. John's mother sends him to Judge Pearson to find work when he is still a young man. Judge Pearson takes John on as his driver and confidant; gives him clothes, responsibility, and a surname; and encourages him to go to school. In addition, he bails John out of trouble on several occasions and often counsels him about his various escapades with women. Finally, Judge Pearson engineers John's escape from prosecution by giving him money and the sound advice that distance is the only cure for certain diseases.

Amy Crittenden, John's mother. Amy had belonged to Judge Pearson before emancipation, and her eldest son is suspected to be Pearson's son. Amy is a champion of the worth of such unions between slave and master and a tenacious fighter when her husband attacks her for her defense of the light-skinned John.

Ned Crittenden, John's stepfather. Ned is a violent and lazy man. These characteristics are aggravated by alcohol and the false perception that his wife favors her mulatto son over him and their darker-skinned sons. His increasing violence toward his wife forces John to whip him soundly, which in turn results in John's leaving home.

Hattie Tyson Pearson, John Pearson's second wife. John had been in an affair with Hattie prior to Lucy's death, and he marries her three months after Lucy dies. The self-centered Hattie has the effect of dismantling all the good things that Lucy and John had built up.

Sally Lovelace Pearson, John's third wife. Sally is a wealthy widow in Plant City, Florida, where John goes following his departure from Sanford and the Zion Hope Baptist Church. With her love, money, and influence, Sally helps John put his life back together. Sally grieves hard when John is killed but is thankful that she found happiness with him, even though it was short-lived.

— *Warren J. Carson*